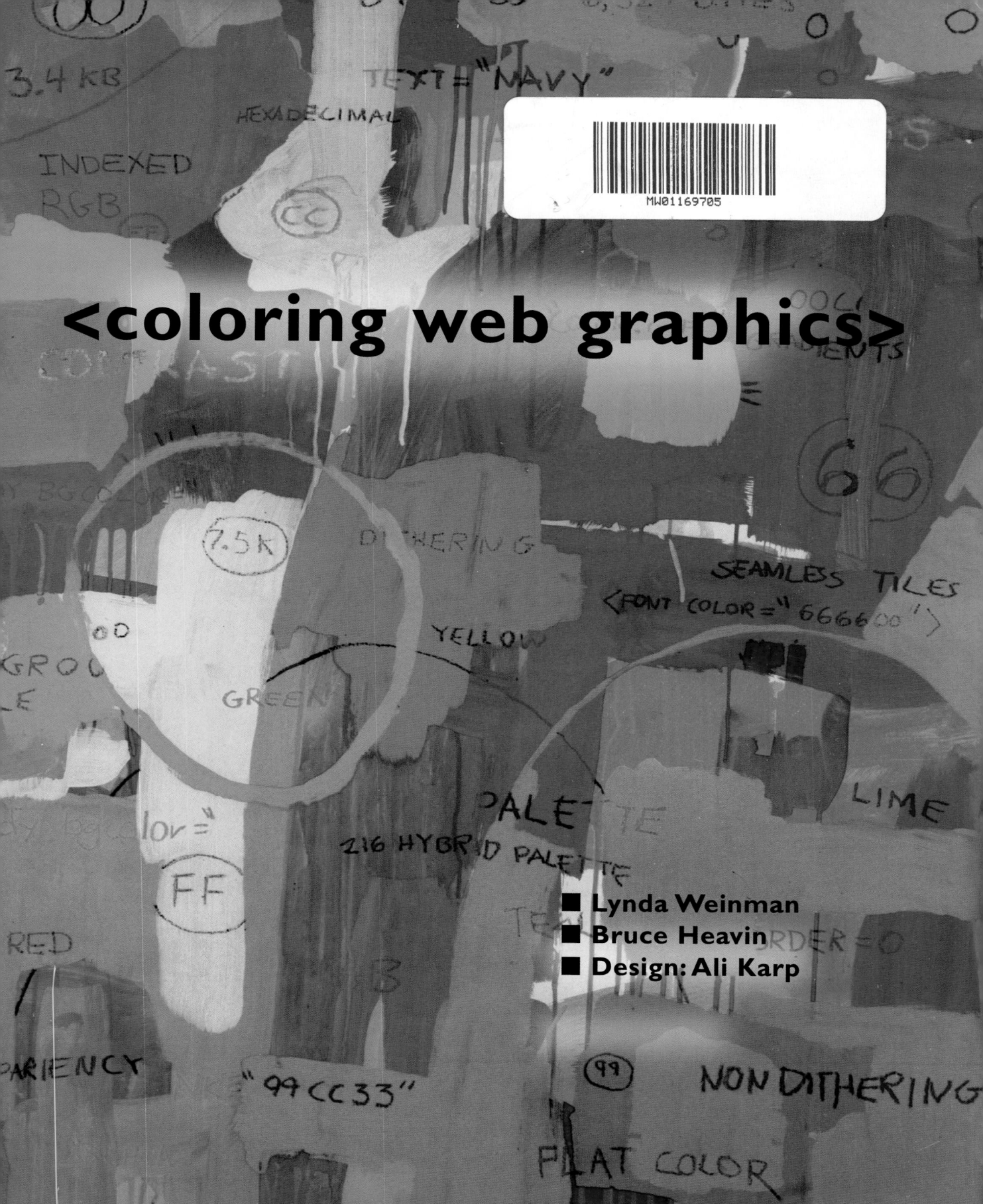

<coloring web graphics>

■ Lynda Weinman
■ Bruce Heavin
■ Design: Ali Karp

MW01169705

Coloring Web Graphics

By Lynda Weinman & Bruce Heavin

Published by: New Riders Publishing
201 West 103rd Street
Indianapolis, IN 46290 USA

Printed in the United States of America 1234567890
ISBN:1-56205-669-7

Warning and Disclaimer

Every effort has been made to make this book as complete and as accurate as possible, but no warranty or fitness is implied. The information is provided on an "as is" basis. The author(s) and New Riders Publishing shall have neither liability nor responsibility to any person or entity with respect to any loss or damages arising from the information contained in this book or from the use of the disks or programs that may accompany it.

Trademark Acknowledgments

All terms mentioned in this book that are known to be trademarks or service marks have been appropriately capitalized. New Riders Publishing cannot attest to the accuracy of this information. Use of a term in this book should not be regarded as affecting the validity of any trademark or service mark.

Publisher: Don Fowley
Publishing Manager: David Dwyer
Marketing Manager: Mary Foote
Managing Editor: Carla Hall

Coloring Web Graphics Credits

Product Development Specialist
John Kane

Software Specialist
Steve Flatt

Project Editor
Jennifer Eberhardt

Acquisitions Coordinator
Stacey Beheler

Administrative Coordinator
Karen Opal

Cover Artwork, Spread Illustrations, and Photography
Bruce Heavin

Cover Production
Aren Howell

Book Designer
Ali Karp

Production Manager
Kelly Dobbs

Production Team Supervisor
Laurie Casey

Production Analysts
Jason Hand
Erich Richter

Production Team
Barbara Borri
Joe Millay
Gwen Stramler
Megan Wade
Steven Weinman

Indexer
Sharon Hilgenberg

■ Lynda Weinman and Bruce Heavin. (photos: Tom Delmundo)

■ Lynda Weinman

Lynda Weinman writes full-time for a living now, but in the past has been a designer, animator, magazine contributor, computer consultant, instructor, moderator, and lecturer. She lives in California with her seven-year-old daughter, 2 cats, 1 snake, and 5 computers. She has taught Web Design, Interactive Media Design, Motion Graphics, and Digital Imaging classes at Art Center College of Design in Pasadena, California (though she is currently taking a break from teaching). Lynda contributes regularly to *The Net*, *MacUser*, *Step-by-Step Graphics*, *New Media*, and *Full Motion* magazines. She likes the Web so much, she even has a domain for her name:

■ http://www.lynda.com

■ Bruce Heavin

Bruce Heavin is an acclaimed painter and illustrator whose mastery of color is evident in all of his work. His clients include Adobe, E! Entertainment Television, *Outside*, *Computer Life*, *MacUser*, and *Keyboard* magazines. He is responsible for the distinctive covers of all of Lynda's Web design books, which were created using acryllic paints and crayons. Bruce's work combines computer techniques and traditional painting techniques. He has designed graphics for numerous Web sites and CD-ROMs, including pieces for DreamWorks SKG Interactive Web site. He's almost always available for illustration assignments (hint hint), and works out of his home on a Mac PPC 8500. A portfolio of Bruce's images are on-line at his Web site.

■ http://www.stink.com

■ Lynda with her daughter Jamie in a serious moment (photo: Bruce Heavin)

■ This book is dedicated to Jamie Cat

■ Book Designer Ali—a rare moment away from her Mac

Lynda's Acknowledgements

To **Bruce** who is the coolest, funniest, most talented, most supportive person I've ever met. I love you!

To **Jamie** who is the coolest, funniest, most talented, most cherished daughter I've ever met. I love you!

To **Ali Karp** who never slept, rested, or dated during this entire project. Her dedication, skill, and perfectionism never ceased to amaze me. You rule. ■ alink@earthlink.net

To **Ali's Mom** who went way beyond the call of motherly duty.

To **John Kane** who is a peach of a fellow. Thanks for listening to everything, always being there, and being so darned good at your new job!

To **David Dwyer** for all the opportunities he has given me. Thank you for believing in this project, David!

To **Crystal Waters** for her friendship, humor, love, and support.

To **Joy Silverman** for inspiring me and being my role model.

To Homegurrrl's Web Design Mailing listmember **Amy Rosenthal** for her generosity with the FreeHand and Painter CLUTs she painstakingly made and shared in this book's CD. Not to mention talking to me late at night about palettes and CLUTs and other geeky stuff.

To **Mary Thorpe** for being her incredible, helpful self.

To my **friends** and **family** for their patience, understanding, love, and support.

To **Ivan Hoffman** for being so thorough and caring.

To **Helene Atkin** for NPR!

Very special thanks to **PhotoDisc** ■ http://www.photodisc.com for the use of their incredible stock footage collection to demonstrate image compression in this book!

Bruce's Acknowledgements

To **Lynda**. You bring out the best in me. You are the most beautiful person. I love you.

Joe Maller for the late night support and his never-ending ability to push me way too far on any given project. I think those efforts resulted in this book going way beyond what I had originally intended.
■ http://www.joemaller.com

Don Barnett for his incredible insight into ideas for media and animation. Perhaps one of the greatest multimedia designers ever! You're the person who can do what nobody else can. Keep proving them wrong!
■ http://www.cris.com/~nekton/barnett.html

Kathy Tafel for putting up with my antics while working at *The Net* magazine; figuring out how to work with color images on the Web and compressing them down beyond belief. And yes, I can still make the smallest GIFs, hands down!

Crystal Waters for the occasional words of help. I'll never call on Fridays at 9-10 pm again.
■ http://www.typo.com

To **family and friends** for their support.

In memory of **Dwight Harmon** who unknown to the world, changed the face of art forever. Your encouragement and wisdom continues on.

■ Bruce Heavin, back when he was a Pilgrim

■ Illustration for
Los Angeles Times Magazine

■ Illustration for
Outside magazine

■ Illustration for
The Net magazine

■ contents at a glance

Introduction

3 Web File Formats 36

4 Color Principles 60

5 Imaging Techniques   74

6   Color Groupings/Swatches/Directory   110

7 Color-Related HTML Tags   266

Introduction

Why Buy an Entire Book about Web Color?

If you're going to create Web pages, you're going to need to work with color. The truth is, anyone who creates a Web page is forced into the role of visual designer, whether they consider themselves qualified or not. What many Web designers do not realize is that color is handled differently by different browsers, by different computer platforms, and by different operating systems. Because of this, one has to contend with an assortment of new and foreign concepts such as hexadecimal code, color cubes, dithering, and palette shifting.

Most of us don't think of color as abstract mathematical numbers or strange new terms; we choose color using our emotions and intuition. Color is a science, but color is also an art form. Keeping this in mind, *Coloring Web Graphics* puts the art back into the decision-making process, while respecting the sciences involved.

As Web designers, it should be our goal to make creative design decisions with the full understanding of the possibilities and limitations of the Web as its own medium. Because the Web has numerous limitations and constraints, creative thinking is required to solve its problems. Blaming technology or software tools doesn't solve visual problems; rather, we must put our creativity to the test in order to find workarounds within the Web's strange new rules.

Control Freaks

Most designers want one thing when it comes to images, alignment, and overall composition: C-O-N-T-R-O-L! It drives us nuts to accept that there isn't a method to achieve this. We have no possible way to dictate the computer platform with which our Web pages are viewed. We have no control over the bit-depth and the amount of colors on the screen of the user. We have no way to adjust viewers' monitors (brightness/contrast). We have no way to force others to use desired plug-ins.

You can ask your users to make their screen soooo wide. You can ask your users to turn off underlining for links. You can ask users to choose certain fonts for their browsers. You can request others to use certain browsers. You can ask users to do practically anything so that your site looks as you intended, but the reality is that many won't bother. This book takes a different approach, one that advocates learning how to make our visuals—be it the color of our text, images, movies, or animated buttons—flexible enough to hold up under a multitude of situations.

This book teaches you all about color on the Web. It describes all kinds of color-related Web concepts such as bit-depth and color cubes, dithering and palettes, and hexadecimal colors. Though these subjects might not seem appealing at first, understanding them will put you in control of how your pages are viewed by others. The only way to harness that precious control everyone wants is through knowledge and understanding of how the Web handles color.

This Book's Goals

Our goal with this book is to present this material in as non-intimidating and useful manner possible. Bruce and I are artists, and we've made a conscious effort to make our information oriented to other artists (and non-artists who find themselves suddenly in the role of the artist).

For example, we know that the browser-safe colors are in a 6x6x6 color cube. Knowing that doesn't help anyone understand how to work with those colors artistically or make images with them. We consider our role to be translators of technical information, to make Web color accessible to people who want to use these colors. It's not so important to know where a certain color of blue is on an abstract cube; it's much more important to see it with the other blues, or understand what other blue colors might work, or how to make an image read with the specific blue, or how to make sure the same blue is viewed across multiple computer platforms.

■ note

A CMYK Warning!

Alas, this book has created a cruel twist of information delivery! It's all about computer color, computer screen delivery, and RGB colors, and yet it's printed on paper using inks and CMYK color! Well, we don't think paper is dead, or that books are a lost cause in this age of digital domination. Books do certain things better than computers, and computers do certain things better than books. Besides, nothing beats having an easily transportable, batteryless information source with no RAM requirements or technical expertise required to use it!

In all seriousness, this book was written with the intent to be a useful guide to Web designers. We can't help that two very different technologies abound—one for printed color and one for computer screen-based color. The problem is inherent in the two opposing mediums—the colors in the book will not perfectly match the digital files' colors on your computer screen. Our advice? Use the book as a reference, and use the digital files from the *Coloring Web Graphics* CD-ROM as your true guides.

Foreword from Bruce Heavin

I first started to design for the Web when I was asked to create imagery for *The Net* magazine's site in 1995. I had no prior experience with the medium as I searched the Web for examples using my America Online browser on my Macintosh 640AV. I was just an illustrator with ideas, and a new medium to call my toy.

Things began to disturb me as it became more and more apparent that the images I made were not the same as what I saw over AOL's browser. Later I got another service and used Netscape and things looked a lot better, but problems still existed and some colors tended to dither miserably while a select few didn't. Color perplexed and plagued me. GIF image file sizes fluctuated wildly all over the board as I loved to play with different bit-depths, image-editing programs, and types of images to see how to get the files as small as possible. My greatest success in GIF file compression was a single GIF experiment that was 64k in size but would expand to be 128 megs when opened in Photoshop!

Lynda Weinman had just started on a book, *Designing Web Graphics*. I worked with her to find colors that wouldn't dither across multiple platforms. We eventually found these colors and named them the "browser-safe" color palette. We covered lots of ground in her first book, but have since discovered that designers need a lot more information relating specifically to color. Thus *Coloring Web Graphics* was born. Until now, most people saw the possibilities of color on the Web as limited to a 6X6X6 cube that isn't friendly to designers or artists. Within the book we will present the colors in ways that make sense to the point that you won't have to think about a 6X6X6 palette.

One of the main objectives I set out with in making this book was that I wanted to get the choices of color away from looking like an unusable, mysterious color cube and into a usable spectrum of color, values, and saturation.

Computer graphics should not only belong to the computer programmer and the engineer, but should be usable for the artist as well. The tools we use for making Web sites shouldn't puzzle us, but empower us to do exactly what we set out to do. Web design can become intimidating and useless when the available tools are more difficult to deal with than that of our content, concepts, and designs. It is important to understand how to set up your computer with all the right tools and have the knowledge to use them. The biggest challenge for creating graphics on the Web should be our ideas, concepts, and compositions. It is my hope to leave you all with just that after you finish this book.

Foreword from Lynda Weinman

I have always found the subject of color more than a little baffling. I've never studied formal color theory, and have learned how to work with color intuitively using my gut instincts. As a result, I've never had the confidence that I used color "properly," or was in full control over communicating ideas with color.

I am certain that I am not alone in my color insecurities. I have watched many newcomers begin Web pages and make color choices that were not optimum, or worse—make colors that were subject to change depending from which platform and browser they were viewed. My guess is that anyone who has to use color and make color decisions would welcome a little guidance from a master.

As an instructor at Art Center, many extraordinary students crossed my path, and often influenced me as much as I influenced them. One of these students was Bruce Heavin who, in addition to having a wonderful and original painting style, had some of the best mastery of color I had ever seen.

Bruce graduated several years ago, and we stayed in touch. When it came time to decide on a cover for my first book, *Designing Web Graphics*, New Riders Publishing acted on my suggestion to commission Bruce to paint it. While working on the book, Bruce took a heightened interest in the book's content after he was asked to design his first Web site.

Certain that the browsers were using a fixed palette that no one had published or distributed, Bruce came over to my house and went to work between Mac and PC trying to identify which colors were being used by Netscape in 256-color environments. We identified the browser-safe color palette by trial and error—and later discovered that it was a mathematical cube that was used in many browsers and across many platforms.

Long story short—Bruce has an amazing wealth of knowledge about color; specifically, color on the computer. I figured if we combined his knowledge with my background in teaching digital design techniques we could come up with a pretty useful resource for Web designers. Fortunately our publisher, New Riders, agreed, and you're holding the results in your hand.

How This Book Works

This book was written so that it doesn't have to be read in a linear order. Feel free to flip around, pick up ideas here and there, and leave the rest for some other time.

The CD-ROM

Note that the software on the CD-ROM is not freeware. By purchasing this book, you have purchased the software on the CD-ROM. This software is not intended for distribution to anyone other than the owner of this book. You may use the clip art, with the hope that you will respect the third-party folders that request shareware fees. If you use shareware art on your site, be a champ and pay up! The files located in the SWATCH folder may not be posted to your Web or FTP site, published electronically or in print, or distributed in any manner without the express permission of Lynda Weinman and and Bruce Heavin.

What You'll Find on the CD-ROM

The *Coloring Web Graphics* CD-ROM has three main directories: CLUTS, SWATCHES, and CLIPART. The organizational structure is printed at the beginning of Chapter 6, "Color Groupings/Swatches/ Directory." Some of the things you'll find are

- Browser-Safe Color Lookup Tables (CLUTs) to load into Photoshop, Painter, FreeHand, Photo-Paint, and Paint Shop Pro.
- Swatches that include suggested color themes for your Web pages.
- Browser-safe clip art for use on your Web pages.

■ What the Chapters Cover

Chapter 1: Computer Color Overview

Understand how computers display color, and the differences between color in print and on the Web. This chapter examines dithering, screen bit-depth, gamma, and monitor settings.

Chapter 2: Browser-Safe Color

This chapter describes what browser-safe color is, why it's useful, and when (and when not) to use it.

Chapter 3: Web File Formats

This chapter covers how to make small, fast, and high-quality Web graphics. A thorough review of GIF and JPEG compression, with lots of visual charts to help you understand how to optimize your own images.

Chapter 4: Color Principles

This chapter covers the essential parts of color theory that relate specifically to Web design. Learn how hue, saturation, value, contrast, brightness, and texture affect your Web-bound artwork.

Chapter 5: Imaging Techniques

This chapter has step-by-step tutorials to teach you how to use browser-safe colors in Photoshop, Paint Shop Pro, Photo-Paint, FreeHand, GifBuilder, GIF Construction Set, Director, and Illustrator.

Chapter 6: Color Groupings/Swatches/Directory

Here's where you'll find the guide to the *Coloring Web Graphics* CD-ROM. Use this print-based directory to find the file on the CD that you or your clients want to use.

Chapter 7: Color-Related HTML Tags

This chapter addresses how to add color-related tags to HTML pages, within WYSIWYG or text-based editors.

Glossary

Can't remember what a certain Web color-related term means? You've come to the right place.

web graphics >

The Coloring Web Graphics Web Site

Every good book deserves a good Web site. Especially books about the Web. There is no better medium with which to update information, correct mistakes, or notify readers about new, cool (or not-so-cool) stuff.

Check out our site at ■ http://www.lynda.com/coloringbook/, or go to the front page of www.lynda.com where you'll find links to this book and other Web design-related books.

Feel free to visit Bruce's personal site too. His work can be found at ■ http://www.stink.com.

And, we both love e-mail (though we can't promise to answer everyone!), so feel free to write us about *Coloring Web Graphics*.
Bruce Heavin: bruce@stink.com
Lynda Weinman: lynda@lynda.com

■ New Riders Publishing

The staff of New Riders Publishing is committed to bringing you the very best in computer reference material. Each New Riders book is the result of months of work by authors and staff who research and refine the information contained within its covers.

As part of this commitment to you, the NRP reader, New Riders invites your input. Please let us know if you enjoy this book, if you have trouble with the information and examples presented, or if you have a suggestion for the next edition.

Please note though: New Riders staff cannot serve as a technical resource for Web graphics or for questions about software or hardware-related problems. Please refer to the documentation that accompanies your software or to the applications' Help systems.

If you have a question or comment about any New Riders book, there are several ways to contact New Riders Publishing. We will respond to as many readers as we can. Your name, address, or phone number will never become part of a mailing list or be used for any purpose other than to help us continue to bring you the best books possible.

You can write us at the following address:

New Riders Publishing
Attn: Publisher
201 W. 103rd Street
Indianapolis, IN 46290

If you prefer, you can fax New Riders Publishing at:

(317) 817-7448.

You can also send electronic mail to New Riders
at the following Internet address:

jkane@newriders.mcp.com

NRP is an imprint of Macmillan Computer Publishing.
To obtain a catalog or information, or to purchase any
Macmillan Computer Publishing book, call (800) 428-5331
or visit our Web site at ■ http://www.mcp.com.

Thank you for selecting *Coloring Web Graphics*!

Computer Color Overview

Computer Color

Creating color artwork for the Web is very different than other color delivery mediums because you're publishing your work to people's screens instead of printed pages. Computer screen-based color is composed of projected light and pixels instead of ink pigments, dot patterns, and screen percentages.

In many ways, working with screen-based color can be more fun than working with printed inks. No waiting for color proofs, or working with CMYK values that are much less vibrant than RGB. No high-resolution files. No dot screens to deal with.

Yes, working on the computer for computer delivery is a lot easier in some ways, but don't be fooled into thinking that what you see on your screen is what other people will see on theirs. Just like its print-based counterpart, computer screen-based color has its own set of nasties and gremlins.

Working with computer screen-based color introduces a whole new vocabulary of terms, such as additive light, bit-depth, gamma, calibration, dithering, and banding. Working with computer screen-based color for the Web introduces even more involved concepts, such as cross-platform compatibility, video cards, and different operating systems.

Let's start at the beginning and define some terms before we get too far into this stuff. In this chapter, we'll take you through a short tour of some of the core issues related to computer and Web-based color. It's our goal throughout this book to stay away from ultra-technical information and communicate the essence of what you need to know in order to produce colors on Web pages that appear true to how you intended them.

Web Color

Everything that is wonderful about the Web—global accessibility, cross-platform compatibility, networked distribution, and ever-improving technology—has a trade-off somewhere down the color graphics creation road. On a printed page, everyone sees the same colors (with the exception of those who are visually impaired). A printed page has fixed dimensions. A printed page is designed once and forever stays the same. A printed page cannot be changed once it is finished.

The Web differs from the printed page in more ways than you might imagine. It is not enough to approach Web authoring with good ideas and great artwork. Understanding the medium is necessary in order to ensure that others view your designs and colors as you intended.

Here's a short list of the things that are different about the Web as a publishing medium, as it pertains to color:

- People view your artwork with monitors that have a wide variety of bit-depth settings.
- Various computer monitors have differing color calibration and gamma default settings.
- Different operating systems affect the way colors are displayed.
- Different Web browsers affect the way color is displayed.
- People judge your site not only by its artistic content, but by its speed. Color can affect speed, believe it or not!

Creating color images and screens for the Web can be done without understanding the medium's limitations, but the results may not be what you were hoping for. The focus of this chapter is to describe the Web and computer color environment, and to clue you in on known pitfalls and solutions that will offer you maximum control over how your artwork is ultimately seen.

RGB Versus CMYK

So how does color make it to your computer screen? Your monitor displays light in the form of pixels. Pixel colors are created from red, green, and blue lights that mix together optically to form other colors. Once combined, these three colors create a color space called RGB. Another common color space is called CMYK, which is formed from cyan, magenta, yellow, and black. CMYK color space on a computer was invented to simulate printing inks, and is used commonly by print designers. Web designers are screen-based, hence we use RGB color space only.

CMYK colors are subtractive, meaning that mixing multiple colors creates black. This color space was created for computer graphics that will be printed on paper.

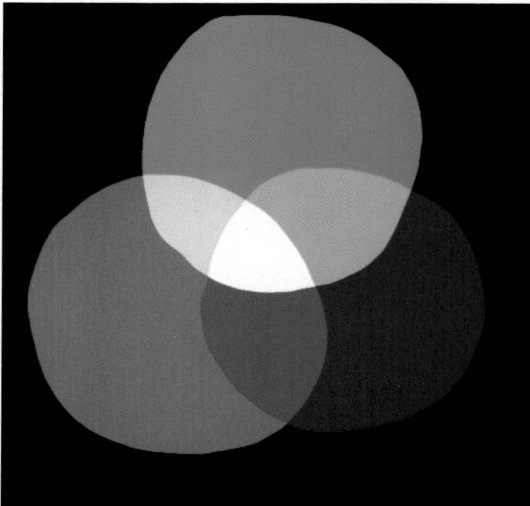

RGB color is additive, meaning that mixing multiple colors creates white. This color space was created for computer graphics that will be viewed on the computer screen.

An understanding of RGB versus CMYK can be summarized:

- ■ CMYK color is used to simulate printing inks.
- ■ CMYK is used by print designers.
- ■ Web designers are screen-based.
- ■ RGB color space is used by all computer screens.

Therefore, Web designers always use RGB and never CMYK! Note: Photoshop and Paint Shop Pro use RGB color space as their default. Instructions on how to change an image from CMYK to RGB in Photoshop follow in Chapter 5, "Imaging Techniques."

Calibration and Gamma

If you've ever owned two television sets, you know the color from set to set can vary wildly. Anyone who works for a company with more than one computer knows that the colors shift between systems—even between identical operating systems and identical hardware.

Some attempt to regulate color screens through *calibration*, or adjusting a monitor's color, brightness, and contrast settings. One of the problems with color on computer screens is that very few monitors are calibrated accurately to one another. Shades of a color often vary wildly from computer to computer, and from platform to platform.

Across different computer platforms, the calibration problem is amplified by gamma differences. Gamma dictates the brightness and contrast of the computer's display. Macs, for example, are typically much brighter than PCs because of the differences in Macintosh's native gamma settings. Both calibration and gamma pose variables that are impossible to control in Web design.

■ note

More Facts About Gamma

If you're interested in learning more about gamma, check out the following URLs:

- http://www.inforamp.net/~poynton/
- http://www.w3.org/pub/WWW/TR/PR-png 960701.html#GammaAppendix
- ftp://ftp.inforamp.net/pub/users/poynton/doc/ Mac/Mac_gamma.pdf
- http://www.boutell.com/boutell/png/PNG-GammaAppendix.html

Here is the same Web page, photographed on 4 different platforms and monitors:

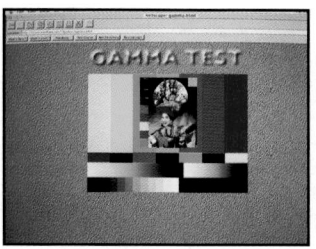

mac

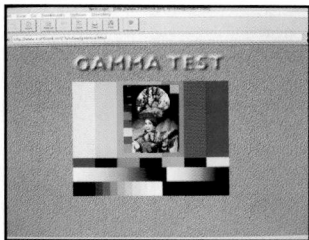

pc

sgi

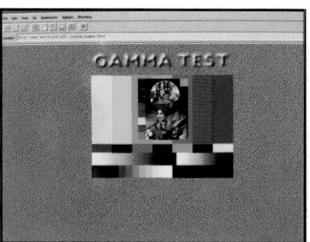

sun

Though these numbers vary widely from different sources, it is generally reported that Mac and SGI monitors are close to the same but PCs are much darker.

Here are some average factory settings:

- SGI monitors=1.7 gamma
- Mac monitors=1.8 gamma
- PC monitors=2.5 gamma

High Resolution Versus Low Resolution

Since your delivery medium is a computer screen, and not a printed page, high-resolution files are not part of Web design life. High resolution is defined as anything that can't be displayed at its intended size at a 1:1 magnification on a computer screen. Average computer screens display 72 pixels per inch, so anything prepared at 72 ppi (pixels per inch) or dpi (dots per inch) is defined as a low-resolution file, and anything above is considered high resolution.

For those of you who have worked with high-resolution graphics files before, you might remember that in order to view them 1:1, you generally have to use the magnifying glass tool many times, resulting in a huge cropped image on your computer screen. The reason for this is that a computer screen can't physically display a high-resolution file. High-resolution graphics are intended to be printed on high-resolution printers, not displayed on standard computer monitors. If you put a high-resolution file on the Web it can only display at 1:1 magnification, meaning it will appear much bigger than you intended.

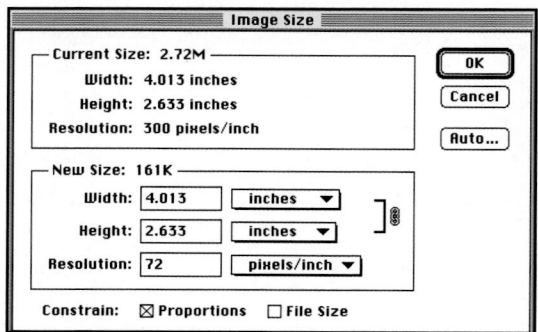

Here's a graphic measuring approximately 4 x 2 inches at 72 dots per inch.

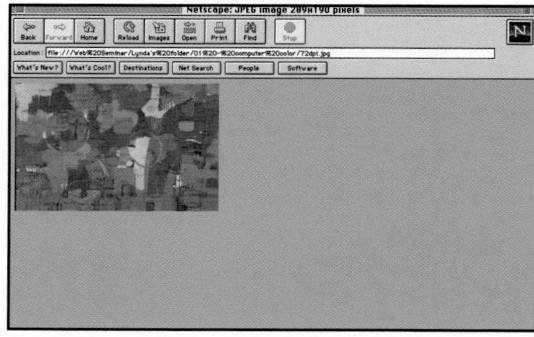

The 72 dpi image is true to its correct size in inches when posted to a Web page.

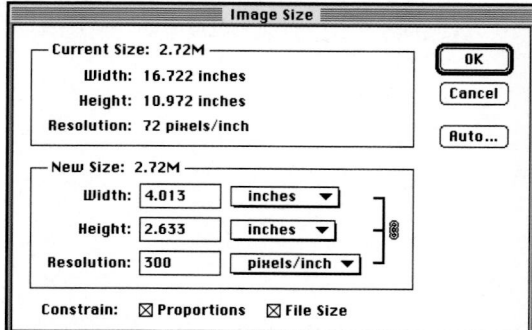

Here's an example of setting up a high-resolution image. It measures approximately 4 x 2 inches at 300 dots per inch.

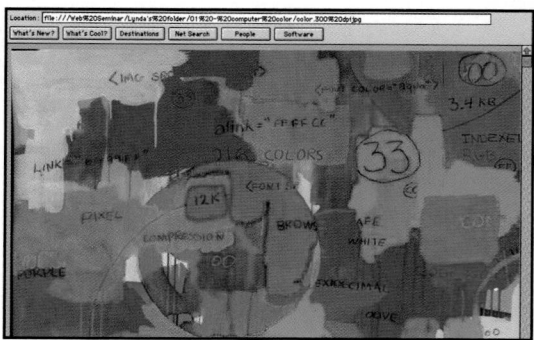

It's quite a bit larger than 4 x 2 inches on the Web. What happened? The browser converted the graphic to 72 dpi, so it is more than three times bigger than intended.

Most likely, your goal for working at high resolution would be to ensure the highest possible quality for your image, though in actuality you would defeat that purpose.

You should always work at "screen resolution" when authoring images for the Web (or any other screen-based medium, such as television or interactive multimedia). The accepted measurement of screen resolution is 72 dpi—or 72 dots per inch.

Whenever working on images for the Web, set your graphics to be measured in pixels, not inches. Inches are needed when creating artwork that will be printed on paper, and pixels are the standard unit of measurement for screen-bound images.

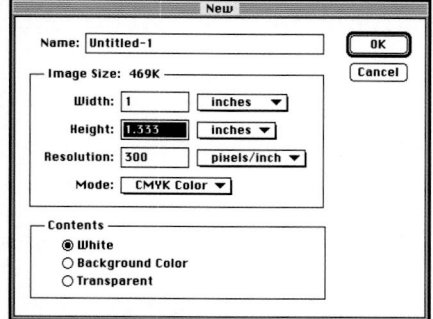

In Photoshop, most print designers are used to working in CMYK, at high resolutions.

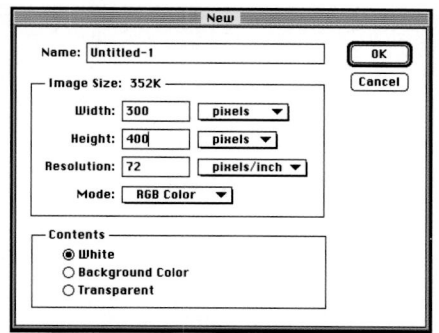

Web designers using Photoshop should always set the color space to RGB, and the dpi to 72.

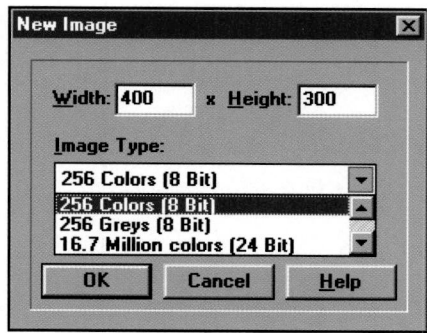

Paint Shop Pro defaults to RGB at 72 dpi, so you don't have to worry about changing settings for Web graphics.

web graphics >

Bit-Depth

Uh oh, the dreaded bit-depth topic! For those math-phobic people, this will most likely be an intimidating-sounding subject. Bear with us. Bit-depth is very important in understanding Web graphics. Bit-depth refers to how many colors reside in an image. The number of colors in an image can have a HUGE impact on file size. Here's how bit-depth is calculated:

32-bit	16.7+ million colors plus an 8-bit (256-level) grayscale mask
24-bit	16.7+ million colors
16-bit	65.5 thousand colors
15-bit	32.8 thousand colors
8-bit	256 colors
7-bit	128 colors
6-bit	64 colors
5-bit	32 colors
4-bit	16 colors
3-bit	8 colors
2-bit	4 colors
1-bit	2 colors

Here's a visual guide to bit-depth settings:

8-bit 256 colors

7-bit 128 colors

6-bit 64 colors

5-bit 32 colors

4-bit 16 colors

3-bit 8 colors

2-bit 4 colors (includes b&w and 2 colors)

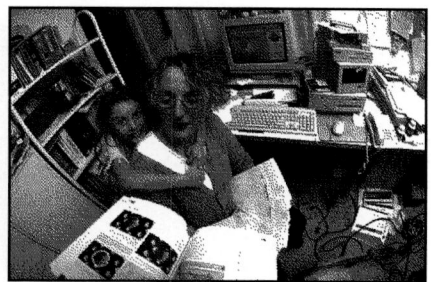

1-bit 2 colors (b&w only)

web graphics >

Dithering and Banding

When an image with millions of colors is converted to an image with 256 colors or less, image quality is lost. Basically, when colors are removed from the image, some sacrifices have to be made. This can take place in two forms: dithering or banding. Here are some definitions to remember:

- Dithering is the positioning of different colored pixels within an image that uses a 256-color palette to simulate a color that does not exist in the palette. A dithered image often looks noisy, or composed of scattered pixels.

- An Adaptive Palette is used to convert an image to 256 colors based on existing colors within the image. Generally, adaptive-based dithering looks the best of all dithering methods.

- Screen Dithering is what happens when a 24-bit or 16-bit image is viewed on a computer with a 256-color card. The image's color is reduced to 256 colors, and the "dither" looks uniform, as if a pattern was used.

- Banding is a process of reducing colors to 256 or less without dithering. It produces areas of solid color, and generates a posterized effect.

Understanding the terminology of dithering and banding is important in Web design, as these are often effects that are undesirable. Bringing down the quality of images is necessary at times for speed considerations, but riding the line between low file size and good enough quality means that you will often encounter unwanted results. These new terms help define the problems you'll encounter when creating Web graphics, and will be used throughout the rest of the book.

Screen dithering takes the form of a repeated pattern and creates a moiré appearance.

The dots within a "screen dithered" image look uniform, based on a generalized screen pattern.

This is an example of "image dithering" using an adaptive palette. It will typically look a lot better than "screen dithering" because the dither pattern is based on the content of the image, not a preset screen.

Even though the image is composed of pixellated dots, they are less obvious and objectionable because there's no obvious pattern or screen.

The banding in this image is obvious. It looks like a posterization effect.

Here's a close-up of the banding. Instead of the dots you'll find in dithering methods, the computer takes the image and breaks it into regions of solid color.

Monitor's Bit-Depth

So far, we defined bit-depth as it relates to images. There are actually two instances where understanding bit-depth is important. The first is to understand the bit-depth of an image, and the second is to understand the bit-depth of your end viewer's monitor. This time we're discussing the monitor's bit-depth, not the bit-depth of images.

Most professional digital artists have 24-bit monitors (that can display up to 16.7 million colors). The average computer user (hence the average member of your Web-viewing audience) has an 8-bit (256 color) monitor. This makes sense if you think about it, because the majority of computer monitors are owned by average people, who bought the least expensive version of their computer system, not professional graphics artists who might have greatly enhanced systems.

Herein lies a huge problem. The majority of people who create artwork for Web sites are viewing the artwork under better conditions than the average end user. This makes for a communication gap; one that this book hopes to bridge rather than to skim over, or worse—ignore.

If a computer system only has an 8-bit color card, it cannot physically view more than 256 colors at once. When people with 256-color systems view your Web screens, they cannot see images in 24-bit, even if they want to.

Here's an example of a 24-bit image that has not been converted to 256 colors, when viewed on a 256-color system. This demonstrates an example of screen dithering.

■ step-by-step

How to Change Your Monitor's Bit-Depth

We recommend that you always run a bit-depth preview test on your Web pages before you send them out for the world to see. Change your monitor settings to 256 colors, and you'll see how your artwork translates under those conditions.

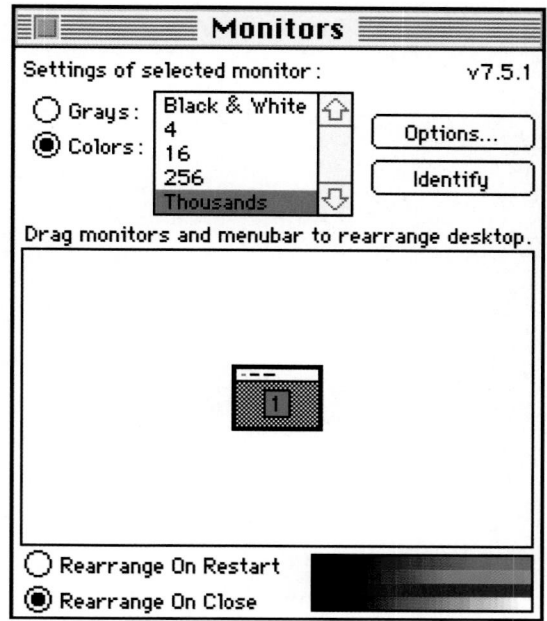

Macintosh: Open the control panel called "Monitors" or "Sights and Sound." (Control panel items are located in your System Folder.)

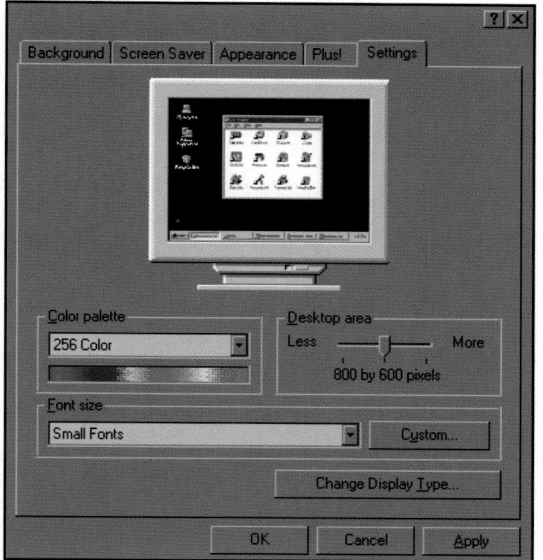

Windows 95: Access your display properties by using your right mouse button and selecting Display properties.

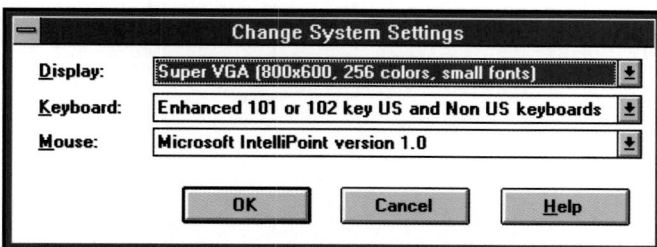

Windows 3.1: From Program Manager, display the Change System Settings dialog box by double-clicking on the Windows Setup icon (generally found in the Main program group) and Choosing Change System Settings from the Options menu.

Hexadecimal Color?

Before the Web came along, few people other than pro-grammers, math students, and mathematicians had any need to work with hexadecimal numbers. Just think, before the Web came along there were all kinds of things you'd never done before! You can now add converting RGB values to hexadecimal values to your list.

Hexadecimal numbers in Web design are used to convert RGB values so HTML can understand which colors you've chosen. To describe the color R:255 G:00 B:51, the hexa-decimal code would look like: FF0033. Here's the most minimal sample code for an HTML page that has the fol-lowing color scheme:

```
<html>
<body bgcolor="003333" text="33CCCC" link="336699"
vlink="006666" alink="00CC99"
</body>
</html>
```

These swatches demonstrate the RGB-to-hex conversion process.

text	link	vlink	alink	bgcolor
33CCCC	336699	006666	00CC99	003333
R:51	R:51	R:0	R:0	R:0
G:204	G:102	G:102	G:204	G:51
B:204	B:153	B:102	B:153	B:51

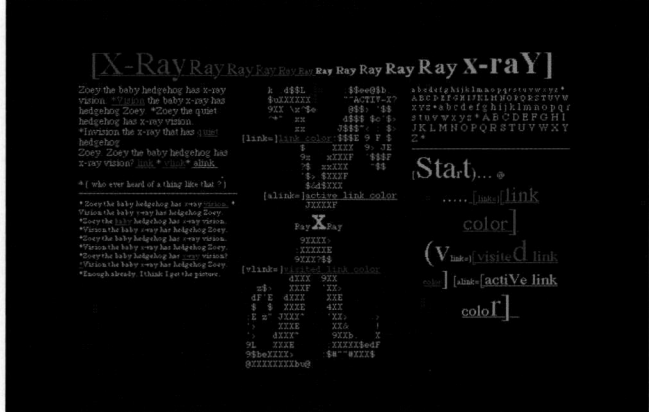

Here are the results of the hexadecimal HTML code to create back-ground, text, link, visited link, and active link colors.

00=00	01=01	02=02	03=03	04=04	05=05	06=06	07=07	08=08
09=09	10=0A	11=0B	12=0C	13=0D	14=0E	15=0F	16=10	17=11
18=12	19=13	20=14	21=15	22=16	23=17	24=18	25=19	26=1A
27=1B	28=1C	29=1D	30=1E	31=1F	32=20	33=21	34=22	35=23
36=24	37=25	38=26	39=27	40=28	41=29	42=2A	43=2B	44=2C
45=2D	46=2E	47=2F	48=30	49=31	50=32	51=33	52=34	53=35
54=36	55=37	56=38	57=39	58=3A	59=3B	60=3C	61=3D	62=3E
63=3F	64=40	65=41	66=42	67=43	68=44	69=45	70=46	71=47
72=48	73=49	74=4A	75=4B	76=4C	77=4D	78=4E	79=4F	80=50
81=51	82=52	83=53	84=54	85=55	86=56	87=57	88=58	89=59
90=5A	91=5B	92=5C	93=5D	94=5E	95=5F	96=60	97=61	98=62
99=63	100=64	101=65	102=66	103=67	104=68	105=69	106=6A	107=6B
108=6C	109=6D	110=6E	111=6F	112=70	113=71	114=72	115=73	116=74
117=75	118=76	119=77	120=78	121=79	122=7A	123=7B	124=7C	125=7D
126=7E	127=7F	128=80	129=81	130=82	131=83	132=84	133=85	134=86
135=87	136=88	137=89	138=8A	139=8B	140=8C	141=8D	142=8E	143=8F
144=90	145=91	146=92	147=93	148=94	149=95	150=96	151=97	152=98
153=99	154=9A	155=9B	156=9C	157=9D	158=9E	159=9F	160=A0	161=A1
162=A2	163=A3	164=A4	165=A5	166=A6	167=A7	168=A8	168=A9	170=AA
171=AB	172=AC	173=AD	17=AE	175=AF	176=B0	177=B1	178=B2	179=B3
180=B4	181=B5	182=B6	183=B7	184=B8	185=B9	186=BA	187=BB	188=BC
189=BD	190=BE	191=BF	192=C0	193=C1	194=C2	195=C3	196=C4	197=C5
198=C6	199=C7	200=C8	201=C9	202=CA	203=CB	204=CC	205=CD	206=CE
207=CF	208=D0	209=D1	210=D2	211=D3	212=D4	213=D5	214=D6	215=D7
216=D8	217=D9	218=DA	219=DB	220=DC	221=DD	222=DE	223=DF	224=E0
225=E1	226=E2	227=E3	228=E4	229=E5	230=E6	231=E7	232=E8	233=E9
234=EA	235=EB	236=EC	237=ED	238=EE	239=EF	240=F0	241=F1	242=F2
243=F3	244=F4	245=F5	246=F6	247=F7	248=F8	249=F9	250=FA	251=FB
252=FC	253=FD	254=FE	255=FF					

Here is a handy chart to use when dealing with RGB number conversions (0-255) to hex. The browser-safe colors are highlighted.

%	RGB	HEX
100%	255	FF
80%	204	CC
60%	153	99
40%	102	66
20%	51	33
0%	0	0

Some programs request RGB percentages, instead of specific RGB values. Refer to this chart for conversions.

Browser - Safe Color

Introduction to Browser-Safe Specs

What is all this fuss over browser-safe colors, anyway? Let's look at what the function of a browser is, first. Browser software is your window into the Web. You can't see Web pages without the browser, so the browser plays a huge role in how your images are displayed; especially when viewed on 256-color systems.

Fortunately, the most popular browsers—Netscape, Mosaic, and Internet Explorer—all share the same palette-management process. They work with the system palettes of each respective platform: Mac, Windows, and Win95. This means that any artwork you create will be forced into a variety of different palettes, depending on which operating system it is viewed from.

Thankfully, there are common colors found within the 256-system palettes—216 common colors, in fact. Each operating system reserves 40 colors out of the possible 256 for its own use. This means that if you stick to the 216 common colors, they will be universally honored between browsers, operating systems, and computer platforms.

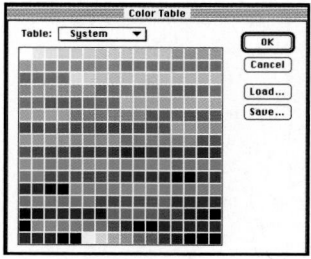 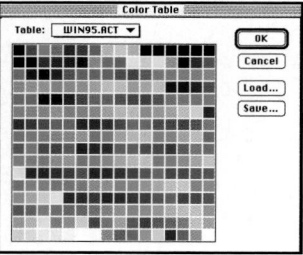 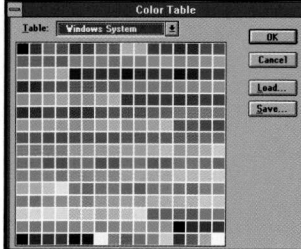

Mac System Palette   Win95 Palette   Windows Palette

Even though these three palettes look entirely different, they share 216 common colors. If you use the shared colors, referred to in this book as "browser-safe" colors, you will eliminate a lot of cross-platform inconsistencies of color artwork published over the Web.

Why Work Within a Limited Palette?

Although it is wonderful and nice to design using a large monitor and a 16 million+ color range, most people who view your work will only have computers capable of seeing images in 256 colors on a monitor that can't go beyond 640X480 in size. When we work with colors other than that of the 216 browser-safe colors, the browsers will convert the colors anyway. This will have an adverse effect on your artwork, as the following examples demonstrate.

Hexadecimal-Based Artwork

Web-page color schemes generally are chosen using hexadecimal values, which can lead to the following problem. If you choose a hexadecimal value for a one-color background based on the color that appears on your millions-of-colors monitor, you may well have chosen a value that is not browser safe. If that's the case, and the end user views the image on a 256-color monitor, the browser will convert it to one of the 216 safe colors—it will shift the color you've chosen to its own palette.

The site pictured here uses the hexadecimal code:

```
<BODY BGCOLOR="090301" TEXT="436E58"
LINK="CF7B42" VLINK="323172" ALINK="ffffff".
```

You should be able to tell, just by looking, that these colors are not browser safe! That's because browser-safe hex combinations are always formed from variations of 00, 33, 66, 99, CC, and FF.

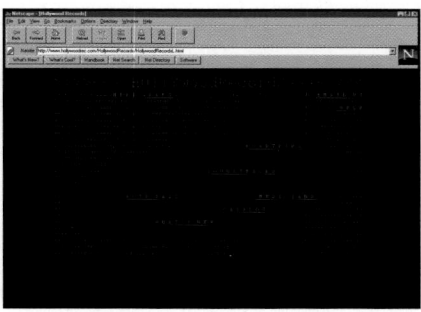

PC 8-bit display   Mac 8-bit display

This comparison demonstrates the kind of color shifting that occurs with hexadecimal-based artwork on 8-bit systems if the colors used are not browser safe.

Illustration-Based Artwork

With illustration-based artwork, if you created logos, cartoons, or drawings in colors outside of the 216, you guessed it—the browser converts them anyway! Instead of shifting the color, which is what will happen with hexadecimal-based color, the browser will dither the artwork. Ugh!

On a millions-of-colors display, you might not notice any differences between these two different colored versions of Lynda's Homegurrl Page logo.

On an 8-bit display, look at what happens to the top version: it is filled with unwanted dots, caused by dithering. Why? The colors in the bottom logo are browser safe, and the colors in the top are not.

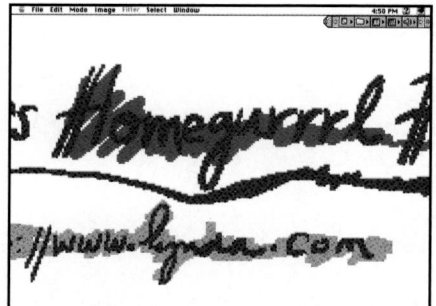

Here's a close-up of the non-browser-safe dithered version on the left, compared to the browser-safe nondithered version on the right.

Photograph-Based Artwork

Photographs are the one type of artwork that really does not benefit from using browser-safe colors. You see, browsers convert photographs to their own fixed palette, but they do a great job of it, unlike the terrible job they do with hexadecimal-based and illustration-based artwork.

Here are some comparisons that support this case:

Viewed in 24-bit **Viewed in 8-bit** **Viewed in 24-bit** **Viewed in 8-bit**

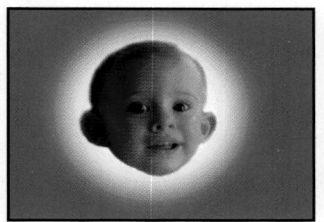 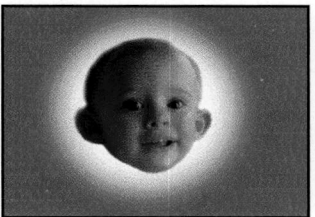  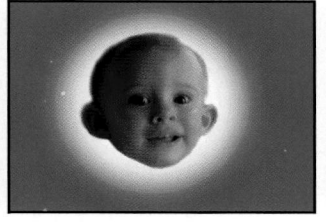 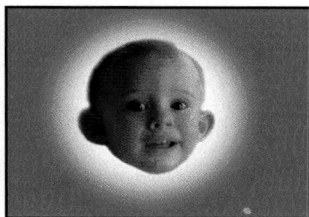

adaptive 8-bit file 35k   JPEG (low quality) 11k

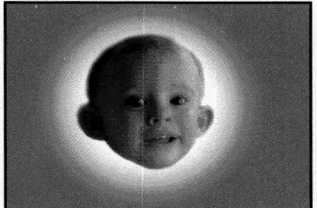 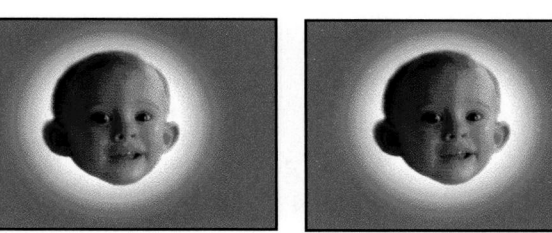

browser-safe palette 50k   system palette 52k

The images on the left of this study were all viewed from a browser in 24-bit. Which ones on the left have the highest quality? The JPEG, which is a 24-bit file; and the adaptive file, which is an 8-bit file based on the colors within the image, not an outside palette as in the case of the images saved with the system or browser-safe palette. The right-side images show how these photographs looked within a browser viewed from a millions+ color system (24-bit). The right-side images all look worse than when viewed in the 24-bit browser, but are there any significant quality benefits from having saved them with different methods? We think not. The results of this study? It is not necessary to convert photograph-based images to the browser-safe palette, or even an 8-bit palette. The browser does its dithering dirty work regardless of how you prepare the image. It's best to leave the image in an adaptive palette or 24-bit file format so that the photographs will have the added advantage of looking better in 24-bit browser environments. JPEGs will always produce the smallest file size for photographs and have the added advantage of being a 24-bit file format, unlike GIF, which cannot save images at higher bit-depths than 8-bit (256 colors).

Browser-Safe Color Summary

So, you may think that all this hubbub over browser-safe colors need not apply to you. If you think your site will only be viewed from millions-of-colors monitors (24-bit), you might be right. It's always important to decide who your audience is before you design a site, and create artwork that is appropriate for your viewers.

Our recommendation is this: If you are going to pick colors for backgrounds, type, text, links, and illustrations, why not choose cross-platform compatible colors? We agree that the notion of working with 216 colors is pretty limited, especially in light of how sophisticated computer graphics systems are today. We've tried to make working browser safe a bit more attractive by creating suggested color families and palettes for you to choose from. It is our hope that the tools this book offers, in terms of organizing these 216 colors in the pages that follow and showing you how to make hybrid variations of them, will make working browser safe more attractive than not.

What Does the Browser-Safe Palette Look Like?

The 216-color palette for the Web has only 6 red values, 6 green values, and 6 blue values that range in contrast. Sometimes this palette is referred to as the 6X6X6 palette, or the 6X6X6 cube. This palette is a predetermined palette that, as of yet, can't be changed. It's the way browsers are pre-programmed, and designers have no HTML controls over the way that browsers handle palette managment.

The RGB values found within the 216-color palette have some predictable similarities: the numbers are all formed from variations of 00, 51, 102, 153, 204, and 255.

The hexadecimal values found within the 216-color palette have some pre-dictable similarities too: they are all formed from variations of 00, 33, 66, 99, CC, and FF.

The Front Side of the Mathematical Cube

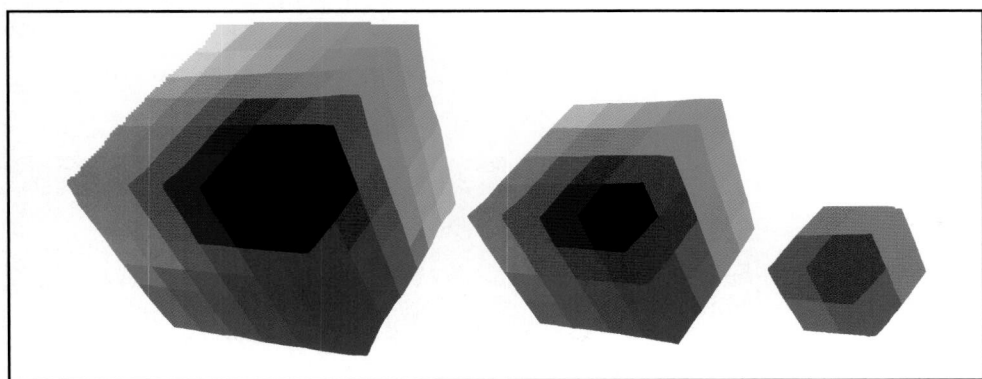

Outer cube: full saturation; Middle cube: middle saturation; Inner cube: low saturation

The Back Side of the Mathematical Cube

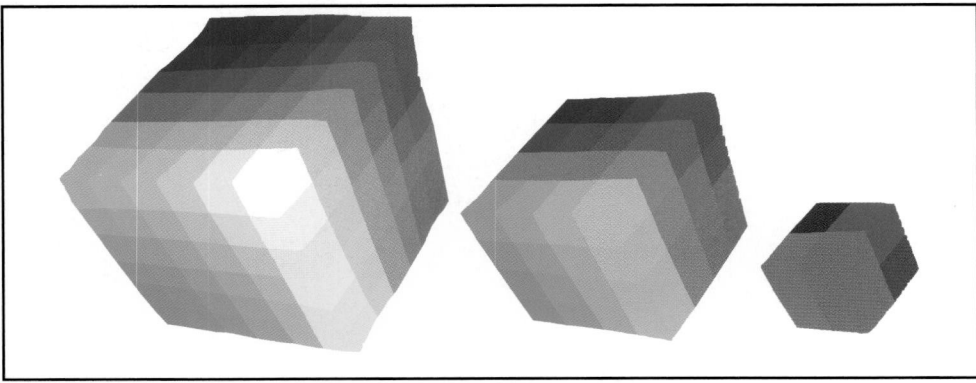

Outer cube: full saturation; Middle cube: middle saturation; Inner cube: low saturation

It should be no surprise that these colors were picked by math, not beauty. Knowing the pattern of the numeric values is useful, because you can easily check your code or image documents to see if they contain these values.

Here's a version of the browser-safe palette, straight out of the computer.

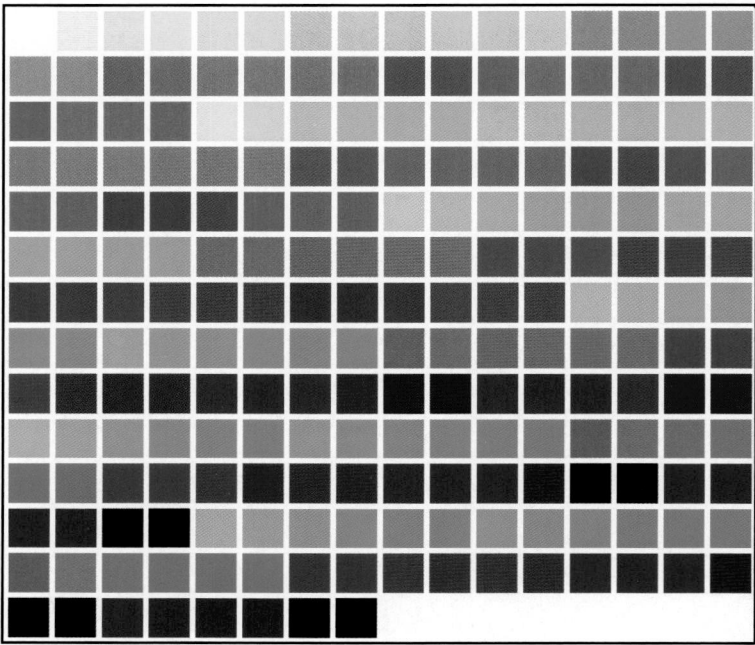

Notice how these colors have no sense of organization? It's that math versus beauty thing again!

The browser-safe palette can be organized many different ways. It's our feeling that by organizing the colors differently—by hue, by value, by saturation, by lights, by darks—that these colors form usable palettes to design with.

These three swatch set examples take the 216 colors and provide color ramps from red to every other color in the browser-safe palette. The swatch set on the left shows a fully saturated palette, while the swatch set on the right shows a desaturated palette. By organizing these colors in a visual manner rather than a mathematical manner, Web designers can work with these colors and make better choices than by picking them out of a disorganized mathematical array.

In the example below, the colors are arranged in a usable palette for Web artists. You can load these palettes (which are inside the SWATCHES/ODDBALL folder on the *Coloring Web Graphics* CD-ROM) into any paint program and use the Eyedropper tool to pick browser-safe colors.

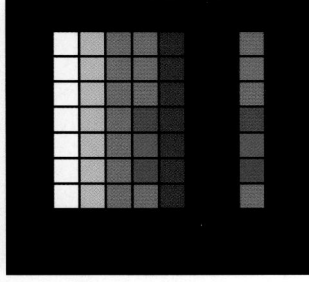

Low saturation (mfd)

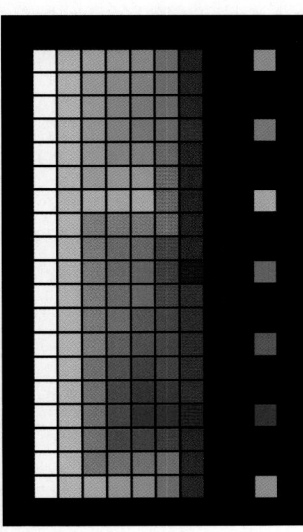

Middle saturation (rmd)

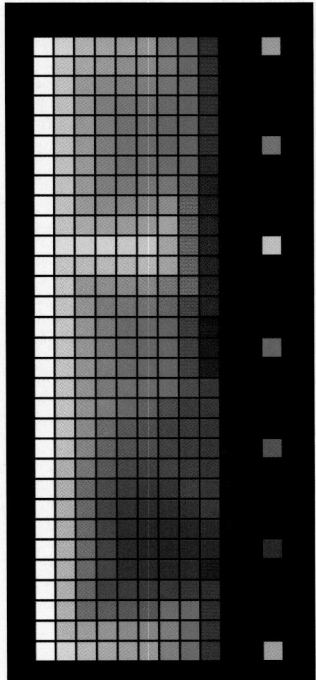

Full saturation (rmfs)

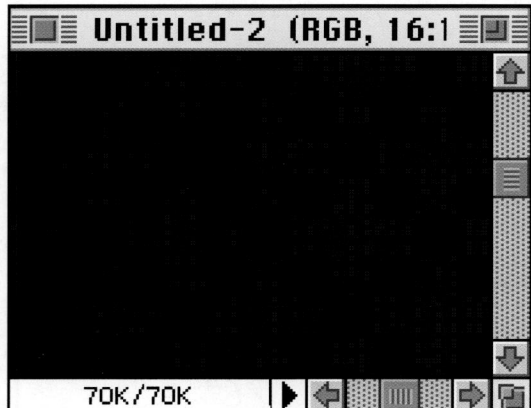

At a magnified view, you can see that Don made a pixel-by-pixel pattern of 3 different browser-safe colors.

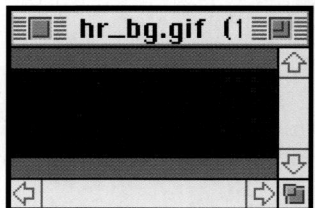

At a 1:1 view, the pattern looks solid, and creates an optical illusion of a color found outside the palette, even though it is still technically browser safe. We call these colors *hybrid colors* within this book.

What Are Hybrid-Safe Colors?

Hybrid-safe colors were originated by Don Barnett and Bruce Heavin when working on a prototype Web site for DreamWorks Interactive SKG ■ http://www.cris.com/~Nekton/sources/net_barn.htm.

Don Barnett wanted to use colors that didn't shift or dither in 256-color environments, but he didn't like any of the 216 colors he had to choose from. He came up with the idea of forming a pre-dithered pattern, on a pixel-by-pixel basis, of multiple browser-safe colors. This created an optical mixture of colors, tricking the eye into thinking it was a new color outside of the 216 limited palette.

This page of hybrid colors was created by Don Barnett for the DreamWorks Interactive SKG site. This file is on the *Coloring Web Graphics* CD-ROM, inside the CLIPART\TILES\DONB folder. Instructions on how to make hybrid colors and insert them into HTML are found in Chapter 5, "Imaging Techniques."

How Do You Work with Browser-Safe and Hybrid Colors?

Ok, you might be thinking; you've convinced me that I might as well use these colors. But, how?

Hybrid color files must be loaded into the <body background> tag of an HTML document.

Here is the basic, most rudimentary HTML you would need in order to load hybrid color files into the background of your Web pages:

```
<html>
<body background="hybrid.gif">
</body><html>
```

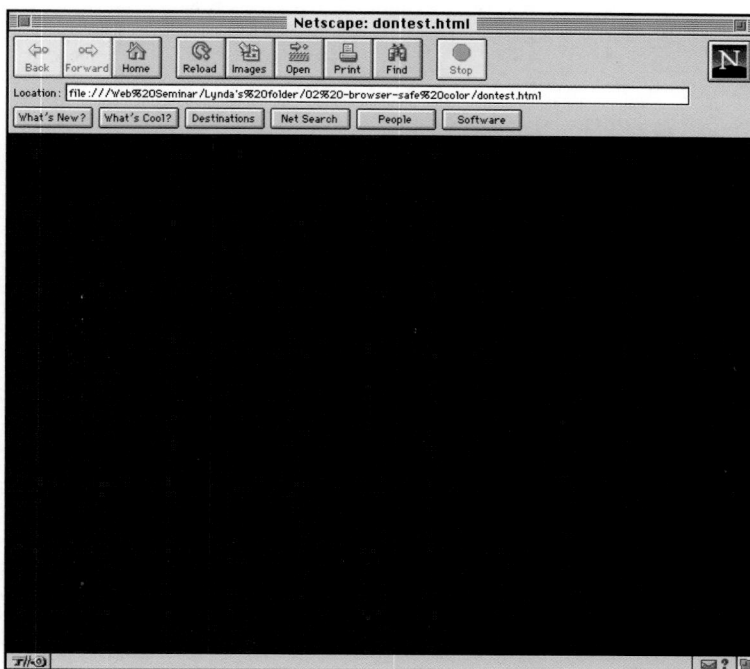

On the left is the source file for the HTML. It is repeated unlimited times, depending on how big the browser window is. To the right of the source file is the final screen in Netscape, filled repeatedly with a browser-safe seamless tile.

■ note

The Book's CD-ROM

Bruce Heavin, with some help from Don Barnett, Joe Maller, and Lynda Weinman, has created zillions of files found on the CD-ROM that pertain to the browser-safe and hybrid 216 palettes. These files are cataloged, and thumbnail views of them are presented in Chapter 6, "Color Groupings/ Swatches/Directory." They come in a few different flavors and categories, and this section of the book explains how to use them. Detailed instructions for palette creation, seamless tile creation, and working with palettes are found in Chapter 5, "Imaging Techniques."

web graphics >

■ step-by-step

Photoshop Swatch Palettes

Photoshop Swatch palettes have the extension .aco at the end of them. To use these files, follow these steps:

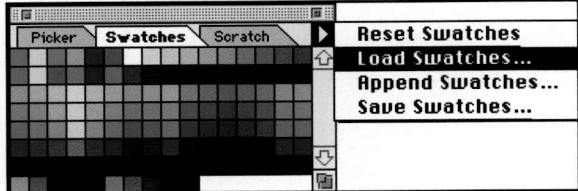

Step 1. Open Photoshop.

Step 2. Choose Palette, Show Swatches to display the Swatch Palette.

Step 3. Click on the right arrow and select Load Swatches.

Now you can open any .aco document found in the SWATCHES/ACO folder on the *Coloring Web Graphics* CD-ROM.

Note: You can load multiple swatch sets into the Photoshop Swatch Palette by choosing Append Swatches instead of Load Swatches.

■ note

Imaging Programs other than Photoshop

All of the Photoshop Swatch palettes have also been saved as .gif files, which can be found in the SWATCHES/GIF folder of the *Coloring Web Graphics* CD-ROM. Most imaging programs, including Paint Shop Pro and Corel Photo-Paint, can open GIF files. Use the eyedropper tool in these programs to select colors from the palettes.

■ step-by-step

Paint Shop Pro .pal file

With Paint Shop Pro, you can make and load custom palettes. Paint Shop Pro does not recognize the Photoshop .aco extension, however. JASC, the company that makes Paint Shop Pro, distributes a browser-safe 216 palette called netscape.pal. It's on our *Coloring Web Graphics* CD-ROM, inside the CLUTS/PSP folder.

To load the netscape.pal palette, follow these steps:

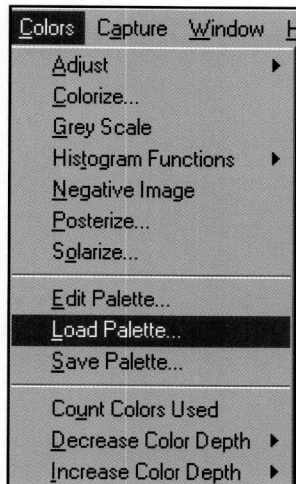

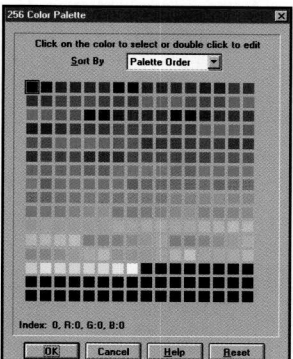
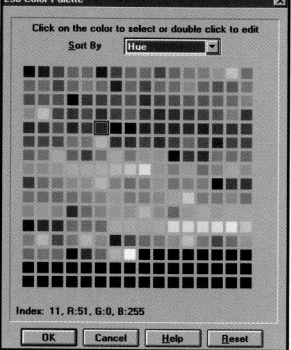
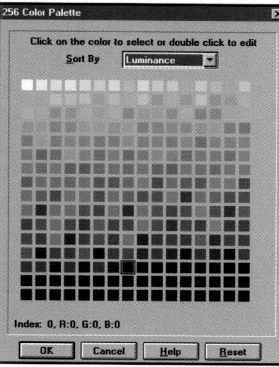

Select Load Palette from the Colors menu, then select the netscape.pal file. When you double-click on the foreground color in the Tools Palette, it brings forward the palette window.

One of the extra-special-nifty things that Paint Shop Pro does is organize any .pal file by palette, hue, or luminance value. We wish Photoshop could do this too!

Browser-Safe Color Charts Organized by Hue

330000 R=051 G=000 B=000	**660000** R=102 G=000 B=000	**990000** R=153 G=000 B=000	**CC0000** R=204 G=000 B=000	**FF0000** R=255 G=000 B=000	**663333** R=102 G=051 B=051	**993333** R=153 G=051 B=051	**CC3333** R=204 G=051 B=051
CC0033 R=204 G=000 B=051	**FF3366** R=255 G=051 B=102	**990033** R=153 G=000 B=051	**CC3366** R=204 G=051 B=102	**FF6699** R=255 G=102 B=153	**FF0066** R=255 G=000 B=102	**660033** R=102 G=000 B=051	**CC0066** R=204 G=000 B=102
CC0099 R=204 G=000 B=153	**FF33CC** R=255 G=51 B=204	**FF00CC** R=255 G=000 B=204	**330033** R=051 G=000 B=051	**660066** R=102 G=000 B=102	**990099** R=153 G=000 B=153	**CC00CC** R=204 G=000 B=204	**FF00FF** R=255 G=000 B=255
FF99FF R=255 G=153 B=255	**FFCCFF** R=255 G=204 B=255	**CC00FF** R=204 G=000 B=255	**9900CC** R=153 G=000 B=204	**CC33FF** R=204 G=051 B=255	**660099** R=102 G=000 B=153	**9933CC** R=153 G=051 B=204	**CC66FF** R=204 G=102 B=255
330099 R=051 G=000 B=153	**6633CC** R=102 G=051 B=204	**9966FF** R=153 G=102 B=255	**3300CC** R=051 G=000 B=204	**6633FF** R=102 G=051 B=255	**3300FF** R=051 G=000 B=255	**000000** R=000 G=000 B=000	**000033** R=000 G=000 B=051
666699 R=102 G=102 B=153	**6666CC** R=102 G=102 B=204	**6666FF** R=102 G=102 B=255	**9999CC** R=153 G=153 B=204	**9999FF** R=153 G=153 B=255	**CCCCFF** R=204 G=204 B=255	**0033FF** R=000 G=051 B=255	**0033CC** R=000 G=051 B=204
3399FF R=051 G=153 B=255	**6699CC** R=102 G=153 B=204	**99CCFF** R=153 G=204 B=255	**0099FF** R=000 G=153 B=255	**006699** R=000 G=102 B=153	**3399CC** R=051 G=153 B=204	**66CCFF** R=102 G=204 B=255	**0099CC** R=000 G=153 B=204
00CCCC R=000 G=204 B=204	**33CCCC** R=051 G=204 B=204	**66CCCC** R=102 G=204 B=204	**99CCCC** R=153 G=204 B=204	**00FFFF** R=000 G=255 B=255	**33FFFF** R=051 G=255 B=255	**66FFFF** R=102 G=255 B=255	**99FFFF** R=153 G=255 B=255
006633 R=000 G=102 B=051	**339966** R=051 G=153 B=102	**00CC66** R=000 G=204 B=102	**66CC99** R=102 G=204 B=153	**33FF99** R=051 G=255 B=153	**99FFCC** R=153 G=255 B=204	**00FF66** R=000 G=255 B=102	**009933** R=000 G=153 B=051
009900 R=000 G=153 B=000	**339933** R=051 G=153 B=051	**669966** R=102 G=153 B=102	**00CC00** R=000 G=204 B=000	**33CC33** R=051 G=204 B=051	**66CC66** R=102 G=204 B=102	**99CC99** R=153 G=204 B=153	**00FF00** R=000 G=255 B=000
66CC33 R=102 G=204 B=051	**99FF66** R=153 G=255 B=102	**66FF00** R=102 G=255 B=000	**336600** R=051 G=102 B=000	**669933** R=102 G=153 B=051	**66CC00** R=102 G=204 B=000	**99CC66** R=153 G=204 B=102	**99FF33** R=153 G=255 B=051
333300 R=051 G=051 B=000	**666600** R=102 G=102 B=000	**666633** R=102 G=102 B=051	**999900** R=153 G=153 B=000	**999933** R=153 G=153 B=051	**999966** R=153 G=153 B=102	**CCCC00** R=204 G=204 B=000	**CCCC33** R=204 G=204 B=051
CC9900 R=204 G=153 B=000	**FFCC33** R=255 G=204 B=051	**996600** R=153 G=102 B=000	**CC9933** R=204 G=153 B=051	**FFCC66** R=255 G=204 B=102	**FF9900** R=255 G=153 B=000	**663300** R=102 G=051 B=000	**996633** R=153 G=102 B=051
CC3300 R=204 G=051 B=000	**FF6633** R=255 G=102 B=051	**FF3300** R=255 G=051 B=000	**333333** R=051 G=051 B=051	**666666** R=102 G=102 B=102	**999999** R=153 G=153 B=153	**CCCCCC** R=204 G=204 B=204	**FFFFFF** R=255 G=255 B=255

FF3333 R=255 G=051 B=051	**996666** R=153 G=102 B=102	**CC6666** R=204 G=102 B=102	**FF6666** R=255 G=102 B=102
993366 R=153 G=051 B=102	**FF3399** R=255 G=051 B=153	**CC6699** R=204 G=102 B=153	**FF99CC** R=255 G=153 B=204
663366 R=102 G=051 B=102	**993399** R=153 G=051 B=153	**CC33CC** R=204 G=051 B=204	**FF33FF** R=255 G=051 B=255
9900FF R=153 G=000 B=255	**330066** R=051 G=000 B=102	**6600CC** R=102 G=000 B=204	**663399** R=102 G=051 B=153
000066 R=000 G=000 B=102	**000099** R=000 G=000 B=153	**0000CC** R=000 G=000 B=204	**0000FF** R=000 G=000 B=255
3366FF R=051 G=102 B=255	**003399** R=000 G=051 B=153	**3366CC** R=051 G=102 B=204	**6699FF** R=102 G=153 B=255
33CCFF R=051 G=204 B=255	**00CCFF** R=000 G=204 B=255	**003333** R=000 G=051 B=051	**006666** R=000 G=102 B=102
CCFFFF R=204 G=255 B=255	**00FFCC** R=000 G=255 B=204	**00CC99** R=000 G=204 B=153	**33FFCC** R=051 G=255 B=204
33CC66 R=051 G=204 B=102	**66FF99** R=102 G=255 B=153	**00CC33** R=000 G=204 B=051	**33FF66** R=051 G=255 B=102
33FF33 R=051 G=255 B=051	**66FF66** R=102 G=255 B=102	**99FF99** R=153 G=255 B=153	**CCFFCC** R=204 G=255 B=204
CCFF99 R=204 G=255 B=153	**99FF00** R=153 G=255 B=000	**669900** R=102 G=153 B=000	**99CC33** R=153 G=204 B=051
CCCC66 R=204 G=204 B=102	**CCCC99** R=204 G=204 B=153	**FFFF00** R=255 G=255 B=000	**FFFF33** R=255 G=255 B=051
CC6600 R=204 G=102 B=000	**CC9966** R=204 G=153 B=102	**FF9933** R=255 G=153 B=051	**FFCC99** R=255 G=204 B=153

CC9999 R=204 G=153 B=153	**FF9999** R=255 G=153 B=153	**FFCCCC** R=255 G=204 B=204	**FF0033** R=255 G=000 B=051
FF0099 R=255 G=000 B=153	**990066** R=153 G=000 B=102	**CC3399** R=204 G=051 B=102	**FF66CC** R=255 G=102 B=204
996699 R=153 G=102 B=153	**CC66CC** R=204 G=102 B=204	**FF66FF** R=255 G=102 B=255	**CC99CC** R=204 G=153 B=204
9933FF R=153 G=051 B=255	**9966CC** R=153 G=102 B=204	**CC99FF** R=204 G=153 B=255	**6600FF** R=102 G=000 B=255
333366 R=051 G=051 B=102	**333399** R=051 G=051 B=153	**3333CC** R=051 G=051 B=204	**3333FF** R=051 G=051 B=255
0066FF R=000 G=102 B=255	**003366** R=000 G=051 B=102	**0066CC** R=000 G=102 B=204	**336699** R=051 G=102 B=153
336666 R=051 G=102 B=102	**009999** R=000 G=153 B=153	**339999** R=051 G=153 B=153	**669999** R=102 G=153 B=153
009966 R=000 G=153 B=102	**33CC99** R=051 G=204 B=153	**66FFCC** R=102 G=255 B=204	**00FF99** R=000 G=255 B=153
00FF33 R=000 G=255 B=051	**003300** R=000 G=051 B=000	**006600** R=000 G=102 B=000	**336633** R=051 G=102 B=051
33FF00 R=051 G=255 B=000	**33CC00** R=051 G=204 B=000	**66FF33** R=102 G=255 B=051	**339900** R=051 G=153 B=000
CCFF66 R=204 G=255 B=102	**99CC00** R=153 G=204 B=000	**CCFF33** R=204 G=255 B=051	**CCFF00** R=204 G=255 B=000
FFFF66 R=255 G=255 B=102	**FFFF99** R=255 G=255 B=153	**FFFFCC** R=255 G=255 B=204	**FFCC00** R=255 G=204 B=000
FF6600 R=255 G=102 B=000	**993300** R=153 G=051 B=000	**CC6633** R=204 G=102 B=051	**FF9966** R=255 G=153 B=102

Browser-Safe Color Charts Organized by Luminance

FFFFFF R=255 G=255 B=255	**FFFFCC** R=255 G=255 B=204	**FFFF99** R=255 G=255 B=153	**CCFFFF** R=204 G=255 B=255	**FFFF66** R=255 G=255 B=102	**CCFFCC** R=204 G=255 B=204	**FFFF33** R=255 G=255 B=051	**CCFF99** R=204 G=255 B=153
99FF99 R=153 G=255 B=153	**CCFF00** R=204 G=255 B=000	**CCCCFF** R=204 G=204 B=255	**66FFFF** R=102 G=255 B=255	**FFCC66** R=255 G=204 B=102	**99FF66** R=153 G=255 B=102	**CCCCCC** R=204 G=204 B=204	**66FFCC** R=102 G=255 B=204
33FFFF R=051 G=255 B=255	**CCCC66** R=204 G=204 B=102	**66FF66** R=102 G=255 B=102	**FF99CC** R=255 G=153 B=204	**99CCCC** R=153 G=204 B=204	**33FFCC** R=051 G=255 B=204	**CCCC33** R=204 G=204 B=051	**66FF33** R=102 G=255 B=051
FF9966 R=255 G=153 B=102	**99CC66** R=153 G=204 B=102	**33FF66** R=051 G=255 B=102	**CC99CC** R=204 G=153 B=204	**66CCCC** R=102 G=204 B=204	**00FFCC** R=000 G=255 B=204	**FF9933** R=255 G=153 B=051	**99CC33** R=153 G=204 B=051
9999FF R=153 G=153 B=255	**33CCFF** R=051 G=204 B=255	**CC9966** R=204 G=153 B=102	**66CC66** R=102 G=204 B=102	**00FF66** R=000 G=255 B=102	**FF66CC** R=255 G=102 B=204	**9999CC** R=153 G=153 B=204	**33CCCC** R=051 G=204 B=204
00FF00 R=000 G=255 B=000	**CC66FF** R=204 G=102 B=255	**6699FF** R=102 G=153 B=255	**00CCFF** R=000 G=204 B=255	**FF6666** R=255 G=102 B=102	**999966** R=153 G=153 B=102	**33CC66** R=051 G=204 B=102	**CC66CC** R=204 G=102 B=204
FF6600 R=255 G=102 B=000	**999900** R=153 G=153 B=000	**33CC00** R=051 G=204 B=000	**FF33FF** R=255 G=051 B=255	**9966FF** R=153 G=102 B=255	**3399FF** R=051 G=153 B=255	**CC6666** R=204 G=102 B=102	**669966** R=102 G=153 B=102
996699 R=153 G=102 B=153	**339999** R=051 G=153 B=153	**CC6600** R=204 G=102 B=000	**669900** R=102 G=153 B=000	**00CC00** R=000 G=204 B=000	**CC33FF** R=204 G=051 B=255	**6666FF** R=102 G=102 B=255	**0099FF** R=000 G=153 B=255
339933 R=051 G=153 B=051	**CC3399** R=204 G=051 B=153	**666699** R=102 G=102 B=153	**009999** R=000 G=153 B=153	**FF3300** R=255 G=051 B=000	**996600** R=153 G=102 B=000	**339900** R=051 G=153 B=000	**FF00FF** R=255 G=000 B=255
CC3333 R=204 G=051 B=051	**666633** R=102 G=102 B=051	**009933** R=000 G=153 B=051	**FF0099** R=255 G=000 B=153	**993399** R=153 G=051 B=153	**336699** R=051 G=102 B=153	**CC3300** R=204 G=051 B=000	**666600** R=102 G=102 B=000
6633CC R=102 G=051 B=204	**0066CC** R=000 G=102 B=204	**FF0033** R=255 G=000 B=051	**993333** R=153 G=051 B=051	**336633** R=051 G=102 B=051	**CC0099** R=204 G=000 B=153	**663399** R=102 G=051 B=153	**006699** R=000 G=102 B=153
9900CC R=153 G=000 B=204	**3333CC** R=051 G=051 B=204	**CC0033** R=204 G=000 B=051	**663333** R=102 G=051 B=051	**006633** R=000 G=102 B=051	**990099** R=153 G=000 B=153	**333399** R=051 G=051 B=153	**CC0000** R=204 G=000 B=000
990033 R=153 G=000 B=051	**333333** R=051 G=051 B=051	**660099** R=102 G=000 B=153	**003399** R=000 G=051 B=153	**990000** R=153 G=000 B=000	**333300** R=051 G=051 B=000	**3300FF** R=051 G=000 B=255	**660066** R=102 G=000 B=102
330066 R=051 G=000 B=102	**0000CC** R=000 G=000 B=204	**330033** R=051 G=000 B=051	**000099** R=000 G=000 B=153	**330000** R=051 G=000 B=000	**000066** R=000 G=000 B=102	**000033** R=000 G=000 B=051	**000000** R=000 G=000 B=000

FFFF00 R=255 G=255 B=000	**FFCCFF** R=255 G=204 B=255	**99FFFF** R=153 G=255 B=255	**CCFF00** R=204 G=255 B=102	**FFCCCC** R=255 G=204 B=204	**99FFCC** R=153 G=255 B=204	**CCFF33** R=204 G=255 B=051	**FFCC99** R=255 G=204 B=153
FFCC33 R=255 G=204 B=051	**99FF33** R=153 G=255 B=051	**CCCC99** R=204 G=204 B=153	**66FF99** R=102 G=255 B=153	**FFCC00** R=255 G=204 B=000	**99FF00** R=153 G=255 B=000	**FF99FF** R=255 G=153 B=255	**99CCFF** R=153 G=204 B=255
FF9999 R=255 G=153 B=153	**99CC99** R=153 G=204 B=153	**33FF99** R=051 G=255 B=153	**CCCC00** R=204 G=204 B=000	**66FF00** R=102 G=255 B=000	**CC99FF** R=204 G=153 B=255	**66CCFF** R=102 G=204 B=255	**00FFFF** R=000 G=255 B=255
33FF33 R=051 G=255 B=051	**CC9999** R=204 G=153 B=153	**66CC99** R=102 G=204 B=153	**00FF99** R=000 G=255 B=153	**FF9900** R=255 G=153 B=000	**99CC00** R=153 G=204 B=000	**33FF00** R=051 G=255 B=000	**FF66FF** R=255 G=102 B=255
CC9933 R=204 G=153 B=051	**66CC33** R=102 G=204 B=051	**00FF33** R=000 G=255 B=051	**FF6699** R=255 G=102 B=153	**999999** R=153 G=153 B=153	**33CC99** R=051 G=204 B=153	**CC9900** R=204 G=153 B=000	**66CC00** R=102 G=204 B=000
6699CC R=102 G=153 B=204	**00CCCC** R=000 G=204 B=204	**FF6633** R=255 G=102 B=051	**999933** R=153 G=153 B=051	**33CC33** R=051 G=204 B=051	**CC6699** R=204 G=102 B=153	**669999** R=102 G=153 B=153	**00CC99** R=000 G=204 B=153
00CC66 R=000 G=204 B=102	**FF33CC** R=255 G=051 B=204	**9966CC** R=153 G=102 B=204	**3399CC** R=051 G=153 B=204	**CC6633** R=204 G=102 B=051	**669933** R=102 G=153 B=051	**00CC33** R=000 G=204 B=051	**FF3399** R=255 G=051 B=153
FF3366 R=255 G=051 B=102	**996666** R=153 G=102 B=102	**339966** R=051 G=153 B=102	**CC33CC** R=204 G=051 B=204	**6666CC** R=102 G=102 B=204	**0099CC** R=000 G=153 B=204	**FF3333** R=255 G=051 B=051	**996633** R=153 G=102 B=051
9933FF R=153 G=051 B=255	**3366FF** R=051 G=102 B=255	**CC3366** R=204 G=051 B=102	**666666** R=102 G=102 B=102	**009966** R=000 G=153 B=102	**FF00CC** R=255 G=000 B=204	**9933CC** R=153 G=051 B=204	**3366CC** R=051 G=102 B=204
009900 R=000 G=153 B=000	**CC00FF** R=204 G=000 B=255	**6633FF** R=102 G=051 B=255	**0066FF** R=000 G=102 B=255	**FF0066** R=255 G=000 B=102	**993366** R=153 G=051 B=102	**336666** R=051 G=102 B=102	**CC00CC** R=204 G=000 B=204
FF0000 R=255 G=000 B=000	**993300** R=153 G=051 B=000	**336600** R=051 G=102 B=000	**9900FF** R=153 G=000 B=255	**3333FF** R=051 G=051 B=255	**CC0066** R=204 G=000 B=102	**663366** R=102 G=051 B=102	**006666** R=000 G=102 B=102
663300 R=102 G=051 B=000	**006600** R=000 G=102 B=000	**6600FF** R=102 G=000 B=255	**0033FF** R=000 G=051 B=255	**990066** R=153 G=000 B=102	**333366** R=051 G=051 B=102	**6600CC** R=102 G=000 B=204	**0033CC** R=000 G=051 B=204
003366 R=000 G=051 B=102	**3300CC** R=051 G=000 B=204	**660033** R=102 G=000 B=051	**003333** R=000 G=051 B=051	**330099** R=051 G=000 B=153	**660000** R=102 G=000 B=000	**003300** R=000 G=051 B=000	**0000FF** R=000 G=000 B=255

web graphics >

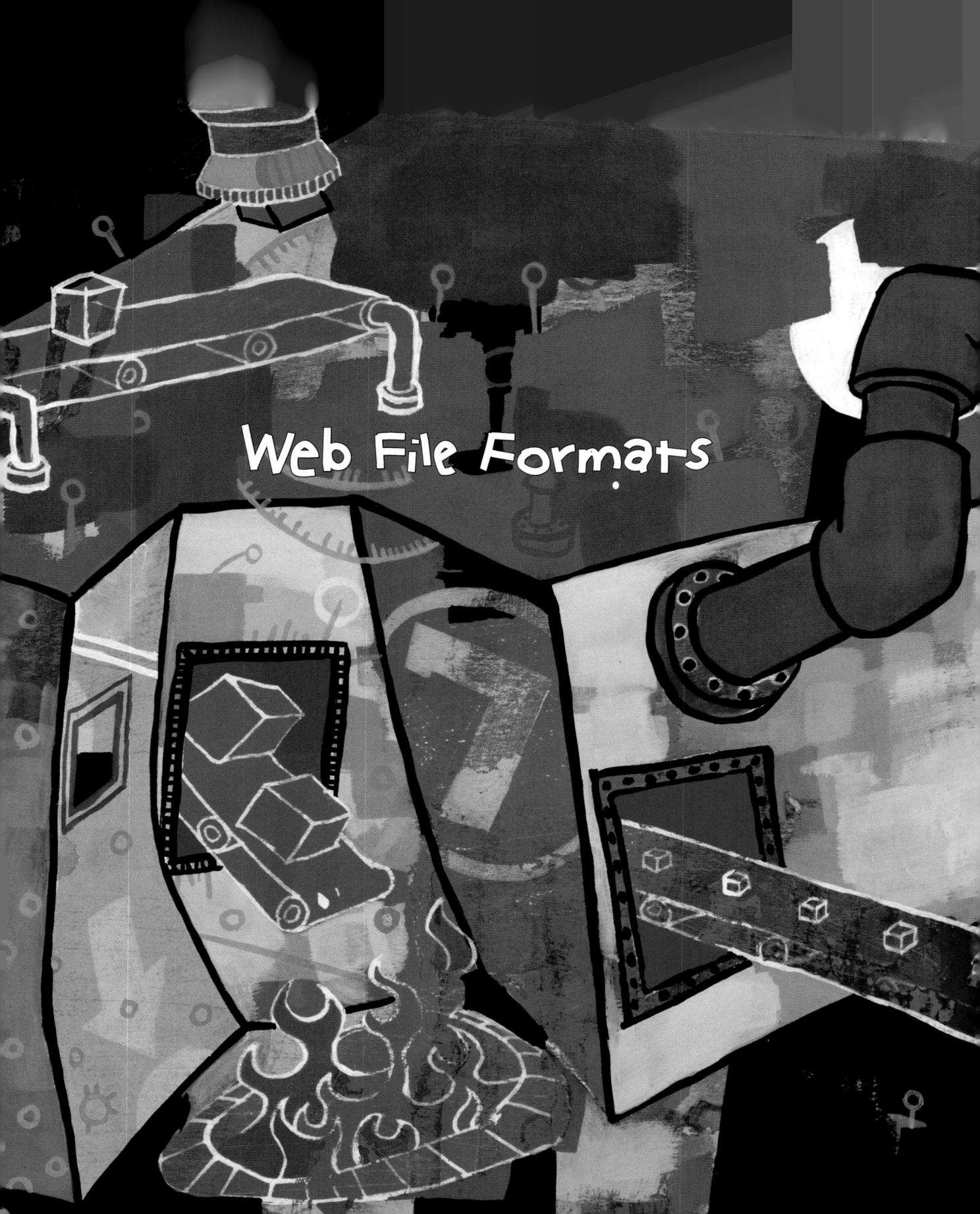

Web File Formats

Color and Web File Formats

What does color have to do with file formats, you may ask? Lots! We will examine file formats for the Web from a few different color-related angles in this book, such as how to make color images small in file size so that they download quickly, and how file formats and color palettes affect the visual integrity of Web-bound artwork.

There are two main file formats for the Web so far: JPEGs and GIFs. Both of these file formats have been widely adopted because they compress images dramatically. On the Web, small files (not just in dimensions, but in file size) result in speedy graphics. It's no longer necessary to only create compelling visuals and information—the speed with which your site is viewed is also subject to critique. As anyone who has ever surfed the Web knows, if a site is too slow, most of us will click onward and elsewhere.

Working with compression methods isn't anything anyone has ever had to think much about before the Web. So, if you're new to Web graphics authoring, and these file formats are unfamiliar to you, don't sweat it. They're new to just about everyone.

JPEG stands for Joint Photographic Experts Group, and GIF stands for Graphic Interchange Format. These names tell you, in each respective acronym, which format is best for which kind of image. JPEGs were designed to compress photographs, and GIFs were designed to compress graphics.

There will be times when you will want to make a photograph into a GIF, such as with transparent GIFs and animated GIFs, and times when you want to make a graphic into a JPEG, such as when a logo or graphic is combined with a photograph. This chapter serves as a valuable reference whenever you question which file format to use and why.

GIF Compression

Unlike most other computer graphic file formats, GIF (Graphic Interchange Format) was designed specifically for online delivery, as it was originally developed for CompuServe in the late 1980s. The file format compresses graphics beautifully, but can also be used for photographic images. Whenever you create graphics, such as logos, illustrations, or cartoons, we recommend the GIF file format.

GIF uses a compression scheme called LZW, which is based on work done by Lempel-Ziv & Welch. The patent for LZW compression is owned by a company called Unisys, which charges developers like Netscape and Photoshop licensing and royalty fees for selling products that use the GIF file format. End users, such as ourselves (Web designers) and our audience (Web visitors), do not have to pay licensing fees or worry about any of this. There is some speculation that the GIF file format may be less prevalent at some point because of the fees, but we hope not. GIFs are accepted by all browsers, GIFs are small, and GIFs do things that many other file formats do not, such as animation, transparency, and interlacing.

The GIF file format, by definition, can only contain 256 colors or less. This is not the case with JPEGs, which by definition contain millions of colors (24-bit). Because GIFs are an indexed-color file format (256 colors or less), it's extremely beneficial to have a thorough understanding of bit-depth settings and palette management when preparing GIF images. We provide such an understanding in this chapter, and we offer specific instructions on how to create images using these file formats in Chapter 5, "Imaging Techniques."

There are two different flavors of GIF: GIF87a and GIF89a. GIF87a supports transparency and interlacing, while GIF89a supports transparency, interlacing, and animation (more information on these features follows). As of this book's printing, the major browsers (Netscape, Microsoft Internet Explorer, and Mosaic) all support both GIF format specifications. You don't really have to refer to the names GIF89a or GIF87a unless you want to sound techie. Most of us simply call these files by the features used, be it a transparent GIF, animated GIF, or plain vanilla GIF.

GIF compression is lossless, meaning that the GIF compression algorithm will not cause any unwanted image degradation. The process of converting a 24-bit image to 256 or fewer colors will cause image degradation on its own, however, so don't get too excited yet!

■ note

"GIF" Pronunciation

First of all, how is GIF pronounced? Some people say it with a soft g as in jiffy, and some with a hard g as in gift. You have our blessing to say it either way. Because no one seems to agree, perhaps it could be said that there is no correct pronunciation?

Making Small GIFs

The GIF file-compression algorithm offers impressive file size reduction, but the degree of file size savings has a lot to do with how you create your GIF images. Understanding how GIFs compress is the first step in this process.

LZW compression looks to patterns of data. Whenever it encounters areas in an image that do not have changes, it can implement much higher compression. This is similar to another type of compression called run-length compression (used in BMP, TIFF, and PCX formats), but LZW writes, stores, and retrieves its code a little differently. Similar to many types of run-length compression, though, GIF compression searches for changes along a horizontal axis, and whenever it finds a new color, it adds to the file size.

  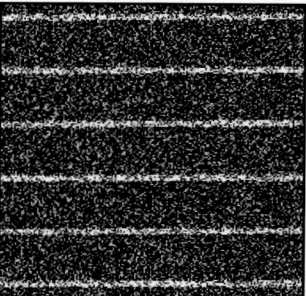

Here's an original image saved as a GIF image that contains horizontal lines. It is 6.7k.

Here's the identical image, only flipped on its side so the lines are vertical. It's a whopping 42% bigger at 11.5k!

Try adding noise to the original? You'll be adding 88% to the file size. This one is 56k!

So what does the line test really teach? That artwork that has horizontal changes compresses better than artwork that doesn't. That anything with noise will more than quadruple your image's file size. That large areas of flat color compress well, and complicated line work or dithering does not.

GIFs for Illustration-Style Imagery

GIFs work much better for graphics than photographs. By graphics, we mean illustrations, cartoons, or logos. Such graphics typically use areas of solid color, and GIFs handle compression of solid color better than the varied colors found in photographs.

With all GIFs, the fewer colors (lower bit-depth), the smaller the resulting file. You should remember this fact when considering whether to improve image quality through anti-aliasing.

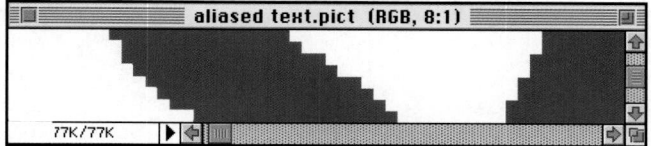

Here's an example of aliased text. It resulted in a file that totaled 3.8k when saved as a GIF.

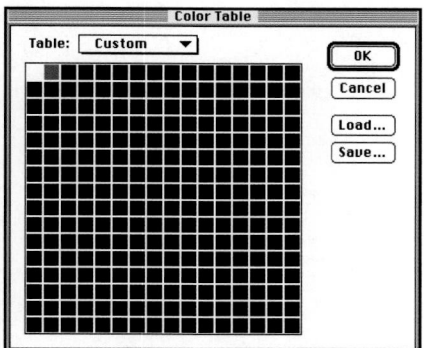

Close-up View: Aliasing does not disguise the jaggy nature of pixel-based artwork.

The aliased artwork used only 4 colors.

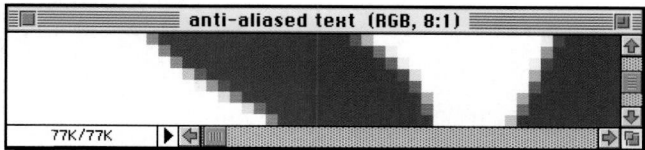

Here's an example of anti-aliased text. It resulted in a file that's 5k when saved as a GIF. The anti-aliasing caused the file to be 24% larger!

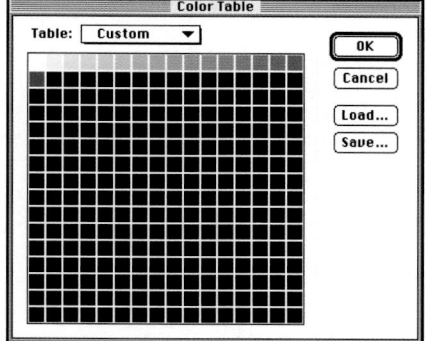

Close-up View: This close-up shows how anti-aliasing creates a blended edge. This blending disguises the square-pixel-based nature of computer-based artwork.

The anti-aliased artwork used 18 colors.

Most computer artists have never considered working with aliased artwork. It's assumed that artwork will always look better if it has anti-aliased edges. This is simply not true! Artists have never had to factor size of files into their design considerations before. Having something load 24% faster is nothing to balk at. In many cases, aliased artwork looks just as good as anti-aliased artwork, and choosing between the two approaches is something that Web designers should consider whenever possible.

As well as considering whether to use aliased or anti-aliased graphics, you should also always work with browser-safe colors when creating illustration-based artwork for the Web. Examples of how browser-safe colors improve the quality of illustrations were shown in Chapter 2, "Browser-Safe Color." You'll find precise instructions for choosing browser-safe colors for creating custom illustrations in Chapter 5, "Imaging Techniques."

Here's an example of a 700 x 1134 pixel GIF file created by Bruce Heavin that totals only 7.1k! Why? Lots of solid color and no anti-aliasing. This image has only 4 colors.

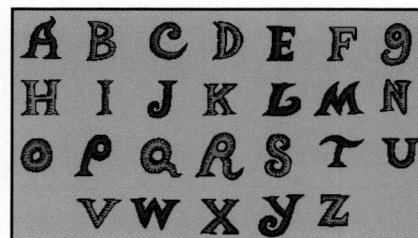

Artwork by Yuryeong Park for the Hot Hot Hot site ■ http://www.hothothot.com. The entire site is done in aliased graphics, and no page exceeds 30k, even though all pages have many images per page.

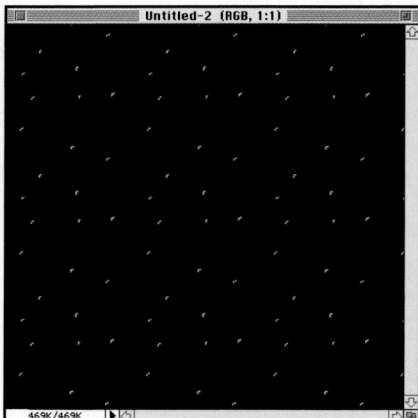

A background tile, previewed in Photoshop, created by Don Barnett. The source tile is only 1.7k. The savings from aliased graphics can really add up!

GIFs for Photographic Imagery

GIFs are definitely designed to handle graphics better than photographs. That doesn't mean that there won't be times when you have to turn photographs into GIFs anyway. You may want to use transparency or animation, which are two features that JPEGs do not offer.

GIFs can be saved at any bit-depth from 8-bit down to 1-bit. The bit-depth refers to how many colors the image contains. Generally, the lower the bit-depth, the smaller the GIF.

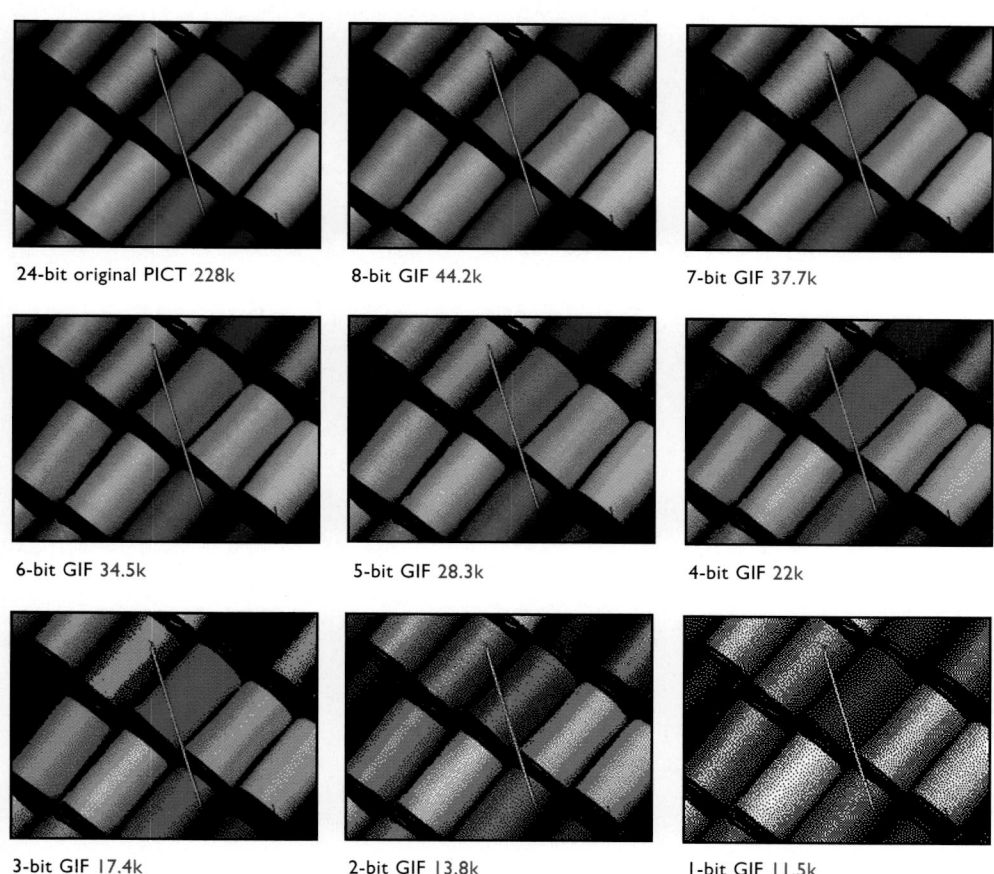

24-bit original PICT 228k   8-bit GIF 44.2k   7-bit GIF 37.7k

6-bit GIF 34.5k   5-bit GIF 28.3k   4-bit GIF 22k

3-bit GIF 17.4k   2-bit GIF 13.8k   1-bit GIF 11.5k

Your job when preparing a GIF is to take it down to its lowest bit-depth level and still maintain acceptable image quality. Depending on how important this image is, acceptable quality falls somewhere between 6-bit and 4-bit, which offers a 22-50% file size reduction over the 8-bit version.

The questions you will have to answer, based on the content of the images you are creating, are how many colors to assign to an image, and which dithering and color mapping method to choose from.

Color mapping refers to the colors that are assigned to a GIF image and can either be taken from the image or a pre-determined palette of colors:

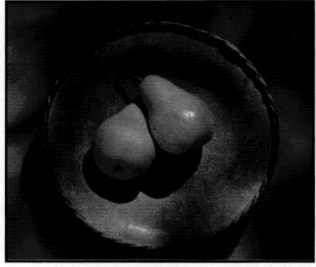 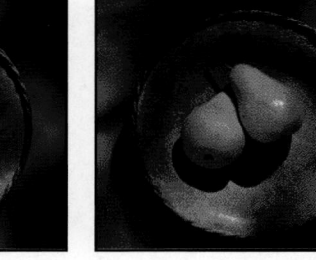 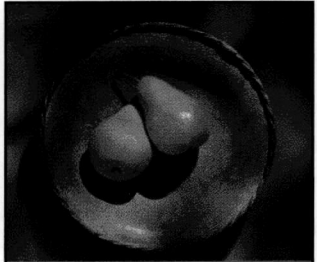

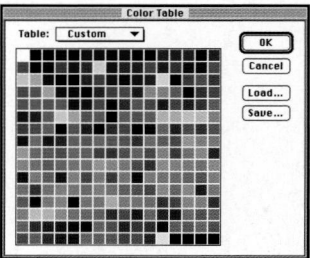

adaptive palette

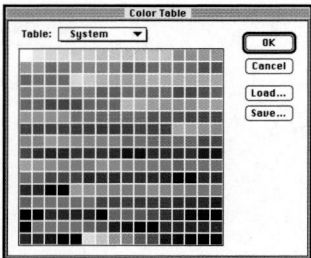

mac system palette

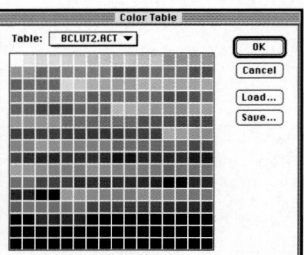

216 browser-safe palette

The adaptive palette looks the best because the colors are based on the content of the image. Paint Shop Pro calls this type of palette a nearest color palette. Photoshop calls it an adaptive palette.

The system palette image looks much worse. Even though it has the same number of colors as the adaptive palette, the colors are unrelated to the image and detract from the quality.

The browser-safe palette looks worst of all. Not only does it use fewer colors, but just like the system palette, the colors are unrelated to the image.

It's clear that an adaptive or nearest color palette gives the best results to the image, but what about when it's seen in a browser? The following color table shows the results:

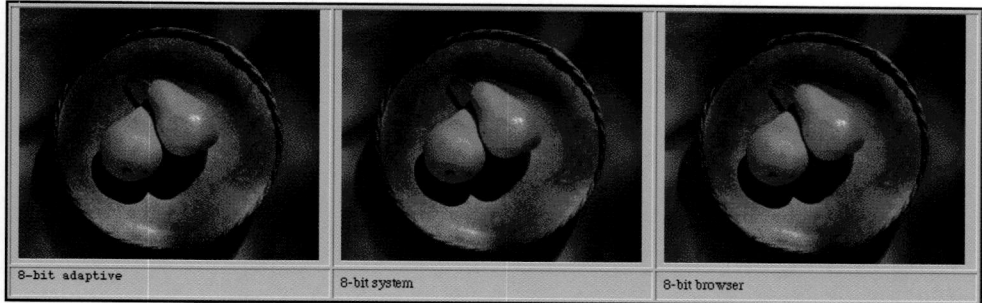

This example demonstrates how the images display in an 8-bit Web browser. See any differences? The differences are minor, if any, aren't they? This is what visitors to your site would see if they had only an 8-bit display.

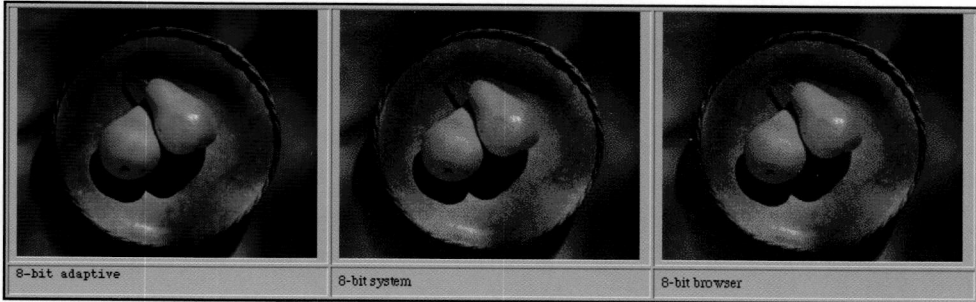

This example demonstrates how the images display in a 24-bit Web browser. The adaptive GIF looks the best, does it not? The moral of the story? Use adaptive palettes for photographs saved as GIFs, and let the 8-bit browsers out there remap your colors on-the-fly for you. This allows your 24-bit viewing audience to see these images at their best, and your 8-bit viewing audience is none the worse off.

Making a choice between dithering methods also plays a huge role in creating smaller GIFs. Any type of "noise" introduces added file size. Unfortunately, whenever you're working with photograph-based GIFs, dithering of one type or another must be employed to reduce the 24-bit color.

GIF saved with dithering 30.1k   GIF without dithering 23.7k

GIF saved with dithering 40.2k

GIF saved in Photoshop's dither none method 38.2k

In this example, the GIF that did not use dithering is an impressive 21% smaller. The only problem is, it looks awful! Sometimes file savings does not warrant loss of quality. Whenever a photograph contains glows, feathered edges, or subtle gradations, you will have to use dithering when converting from 24-bit to 8-bit in order to maintain quality.

There's almost no perceivable difference between these two images, regardless of whether a dithering method is used to convert to 8-bit color or Photoshop's dither none method was chosen. Why? This image has a lot of solid areas of color to begin with. The file savings between 40.2k and 38.2k is not huge either, but the non-dither method will still yield a smaller file size.

Instructions for how to set up dither and no-dither methods for Photoshop and Paint Shop Pro are in Chapter 5, "Imaging Techniques." Both programs offer the capability to set the "dithering" or "no-dithering" method.

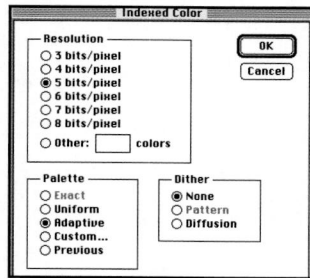

In Photoshop, you could choose from the dither methods of None, Pattern, or Diffusion. None would create the smallest possible GIF files, but that doesn't ensure they'll look good.

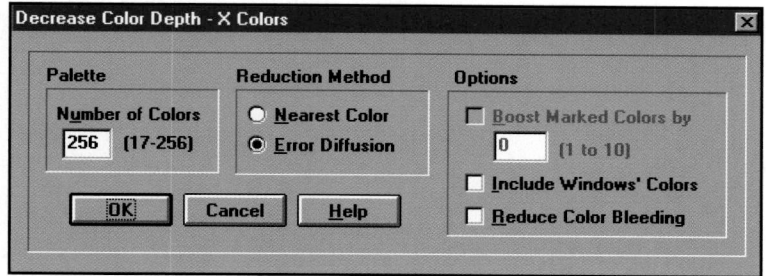

In Paint Shop Pro, you would dither a photograph by choosing Error Diffusion. You would not dither by choosing Nearest Color.

To summarize, in order to make smaller GIFs, you should:

- Try to save the file at the lowest possible bit-depth, while monitoring quality.

- Try to avoid dithering, if the image can withstand it. In Photoshop, within the Index Color window, choose Dithering:None. In Paint Shop Pro, inside the Decrease Colors window, choose Nearest Color.

There is never one pat answer for making the smallest possible GIFs. Choices between bit-depth and dithering methods should always be based on the image's content. In general, images with subtle gradations will need to be dithered. Images with areas of solid color will look fine without dithering.

web graphics >

Interlaced GIFs

If you've surfed the Web much, you've encountered interlaced GIFs. They're those images that start out blocky and appear less and less blocky until they come into full focus.

These examples simulate the effect of interlacing on a browser. The image starts chunky and comes into focus over time. This allows the end viewer to decide whether to wait for your graphic to finish or click onward.

In theory, interlacing is supposed to make it possible for your end viewer to get a rough idea of your visuals, and to make a decision whether to wait or click onward before the image finishes rendering. Again—in theory, this is supposed to save time. Unfortunately, if the end viewer is forced to wait for the entire image to finish coming into focus to read essential information, it is often a frustrating experience. In other words, interlaced images save time if you don't have to wait for them to finish.

Our recommendation is that you do not use interlaced GIFs for important visual information that is critical to viewing your site. An imagemap or navigation icon for example, must be seen in order to fulfill its function. While interlaced GIFs serve their purpose on nonessential graphics, they only frustrate end users when used on essential graphics.

Another problem with interlacing is when it's used with transparency. Interlaced, transparent GIFs will often not finish the final render pass and will look chunky and unprofessional.

Graphics & Multimedia	CAD	Internet	Networking
Macromedia	AutoCad	Webmaster	Windows NT
Web-Design	MicroStation	Java	NetWare
3D Studio MAX	AutoCAD LT	Web-Design	MTBK
		VRML	CNK
		Threexames	Operating System
			Security

Here's a compelling reason to avoid transparent, interlaced GIFs for main navigation artwork. Sometimes the interlacing doesn't finish rendering and then you're left with unreadable artwork.

Transparent GIFs

Transparent GIFs are used to create the illusion of irregularly shaped artwork. All computer-made images end up in rectangular-shaped files; it's the nature of the medium. Certain file formats, such as GIF, can store masked regions, which create the illusion of shapes other than rectangles. This "masked region" appears to be transparent.

For example, you could create a red circle inside a blue square computer document. By instructing the blue background color of the circle to disappear, or be transparent, the red circle appears to be free floating over another image. Transparency works by creating masked regions that are instructed to disappear when combined with other files.

Here's an example of artwork from Lynda's Homegurrrl site that has been defined to be transparent. The gray color was instructed to drop out within transparency software. Precise instructions for creating transparent artwork in popular image-editing programs are found in Chapter 5, "Imaging Techniques."

Transparency comes in two forms: 8-bit transparency and 1-bit transparency. 8-bit transparency is the best, but it isn't supported by GIFs or by Web browsers. 8-bit transparency is what is used by the file formats Photoshop, TGA, and PICT. 8-bit transparency is also called alpha channel-based transparency and can support up to 256 different levels of opacity (which is why it looks so great!). GIFs support 1-bit transparency, which makes it a much more limited type of masking.

This screen shows the transparent artwork in context. Once the GIF transparency is recognized within the browser software, the browser allows the rectangular artwork to appear irregularly shaped.

This image represents the type of compositing you can do in Photoshop with 8-bit transparency, where it can easily display differing levels of transparency, glows, and blurs. GIF transparency is unfortunately much more crude than this.

■ note

PNG

The only type of Web file format that supports 8-bit transparency is PNG, which was not widely implemented at the time this chapter was written. If you are interested in more information about PNG, try ■ http://quest.jpl.nasa.gov/PNG/png.html. GIF is much more common than PNG, and supported by far more browsers, so it is still much more practical to get your GIF-making chops up to speed and make the best of what it offers.

Animated GIFs

Animated GIFs are part of the GIF89a specification. They are formally called multiblock GIFs because multiple images can be stored as separate blocks within a single GIF document. When the GIF document is viewed, the multiple images display, one at a time, and produce streaming animation.

Streaming is a wonderful and appropriate method for displaying animation over the Web. Streaming means that each frame of the animation displays one after the other, so that your end user doesn't have to wait for the whole file to download before seeing anything. Other animation formats in the past required that the entire movie download before a single frame could be viewed.

Animated GIFs function much like automated slide shows. They can include custom palette information and be set to play at different speeds. They can include interlacing and transparency, too! The beauty of animated GIFs is that they require no plug-ins, and the authoring tools to create them are often free and easy to learn. As well, major browsers (Netscape, Internet Explorer, and Mosaic) support them, so you can include them in Web pages without worrying about compatibility or accessibility. Specific instruction on how to create animated GIFs and apply custom palettes is available in Chapter 5, "Imaging Techniques."

Just like other GIF files, the number of colors and amount of noise in the frames affect the overall file size. If you have a 100-frame animation with each frame totaling 5k, your animated GIF will be 500k. It simply multiplies in size according to how many frames you create and the file size of the individual frame of artwork. On the other hand, your end viewer is really only waiting for 5k servings at a time, so it's nothing like the painful waiting that a standard 500k GIF would incur!

■ note

Popular GIF animation authoring tools

GIF Construction Set/bookware (Windows/Win95)
■ http://www.mindworkshipcom/alchemy/alchemy.html

GIFBuilder/freeware (Mac)
■ http://iawww.epfl.ch/Staff/Yves.Piguet/clip2gif-home/GifBuilder.html

Some good animated GIF references

Royal Frazier's awesome site
■ http://member.aol.com/roalef/gifanim.htm

GIFBuilder's FAQ
■ http://iawww.epfl.ch/Staff/Yves.Piguet/clip2gif-home/GifBuilder Doc/GifBuilder-FAQs.html

Here's a 30-frame animation, found on Lynda's Homegurrl site at ■ http://www.lynda.com/anim.html. It's hard to tell the subtle changes from frame to frame when viewed in sequence, but once the frames are played in motion over time, the '50s man appears to be bobbing his head, waving his finger, and has little lines flowing from the side of his head. It totals 64k in size. Why? It's only two colors, with no anti-aliasing.

JPEG

The JPEG (pronounced jay-peg) file format offers a 24-bit alternative to the 8-bit GIF file format. This is especially great for photographic content because 24-bit photographs do not dither!

 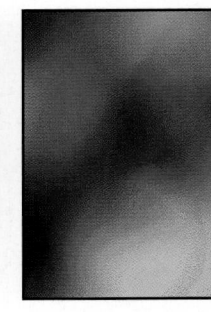

JPEG 7.9k   GIF 22.3k

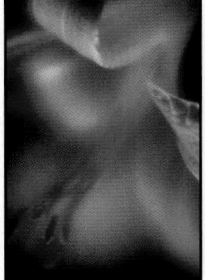 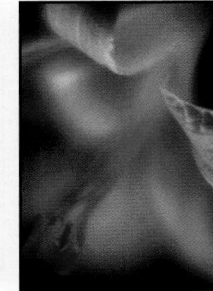

JPEG 13.7k   GIF 46.9k

JPEG 18.6K   GIF 34.4k

JPEG handles images with subtle gradations beautifully. This is in part because the file format allows the image to remain in 24-bit. Compare the 8-bit GIF to the 24-bit JPEG. They will not only be bigger in file size (in these examples anywhere from 47%-70%!), but they look worse, too!

JPEG was developed specifically for photographic-style images. It looks to areas with subtle tonal and color changes and offers the best compression when it encounters that type of imagery. It actually does not compress solid color well at all!

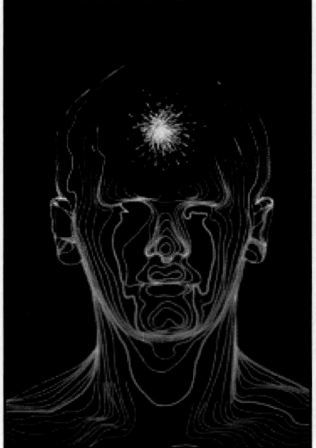

Here's an image with a lot of solid color, saved as a JPEG. It is 49.5k.

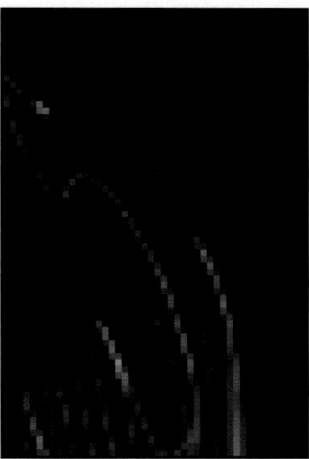

Here's a close-up of JPEG artifacts.

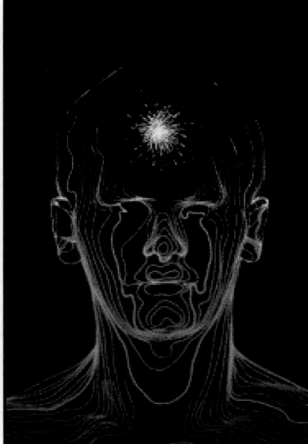

Not only does the GIF look better (no artifacts!), but it is also 39% smaller at 24.2k.

JPEG is a lossy compression algorithm, meaning that it removes information from your image, and therefore causes a loss in quality. JPEG does a great job of doing this, so the difference in information data is often not visible or objectionable. It does introduce artifacts in some instances, especially where it encounters solid colors. This is a byproduct of its lossy compression methods.

Unlike the GIF file format, JPEGs require both compression and decompression. This means that JPEG files need to decompress when they're viewed. Even though a GIF and a JPEG might be identical sizes, or sometimes even when the JPEG is smaller, the JPEG might take longer to download or view from a Web browser because of the added time required to decompress.

Another difference between GIF and JPEG is the fact that you can save JPEGs in a variety of compression levels. This means that more or less compression can be applied to an image, depending on which looks best.

The following examples were taken from Photoshop. Photoshop employs the JPEG compression settings of max, high, medium, and low. In Photoshop, these terms relate to quality, not the amount of compression.

| max | high | med | low |

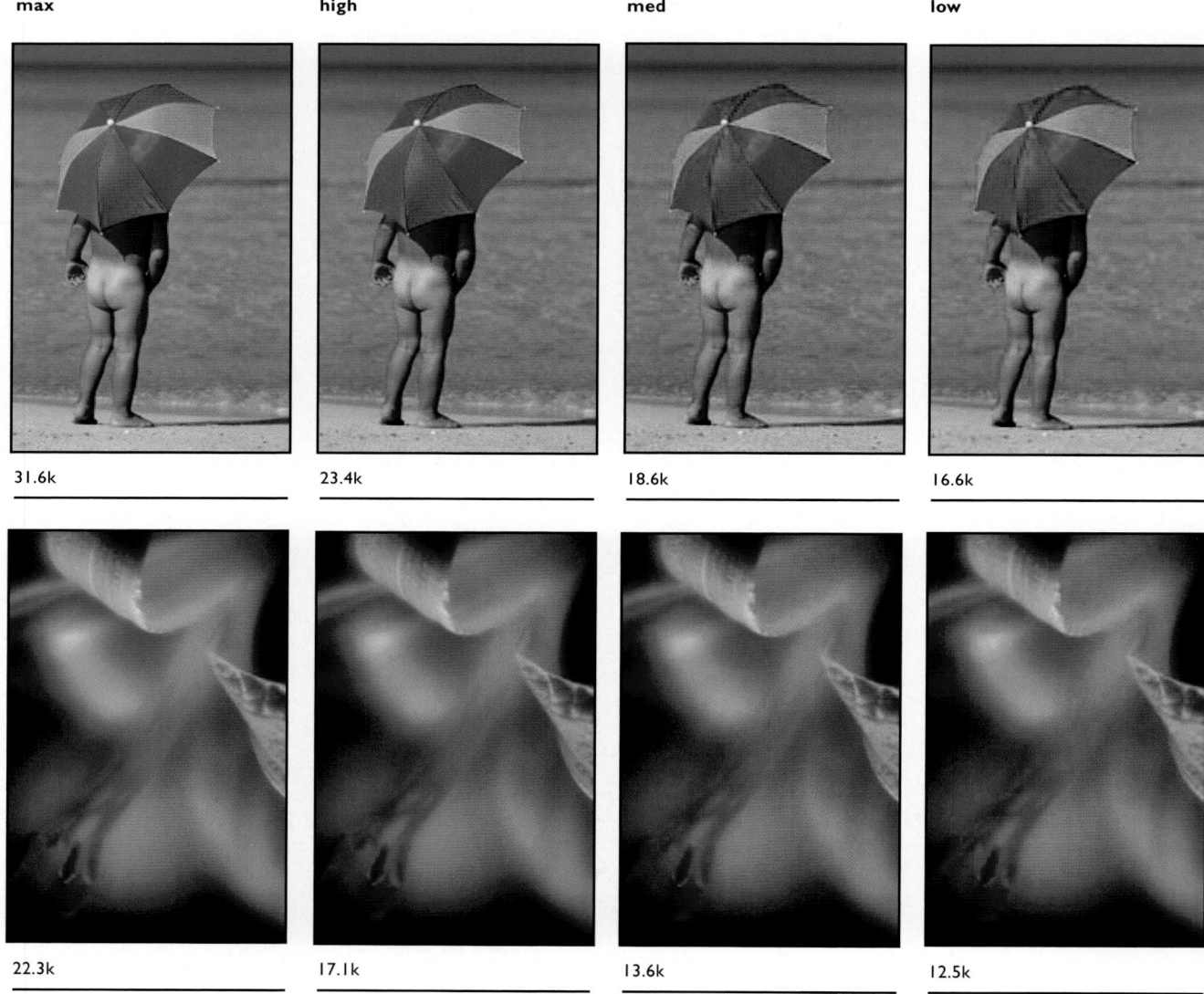

| 31.6k | 23.4k | 18.6k | 16.6k |

| 22.3k | 17.1k | 13.6k | 12.5k |

You can see by this test that there's not a whole lot of difference between low quality and high quality, except with graphics. As we've said, leave graphics for GIF and photographs for JPEGs. Although there are good reasons for saving photographs as GIF (animation, transparency, and interlacing), there are no good reasons for saving graphics as JPEGs, unless the graphics are combined with photographs. With photographic content in general, don't be afraid to try low-quality settings; the file size saving is usually substantial, and the quality penalties are not too steep.

max   **high**   **med**   **low**

42.6k   31.6k   23k   20k

23.9k   20k   17.9k   6.4k

Progressive JPEGs Versus Standard JPEGs

Progressive JPEGs are a new entrée into our Web graphics file format vocabulary. This type of JPEG boasts much higher compression rates than regular JPEG and supports interlacing (where the graphic starts chunky and comes into focus). They were initially introduced by Netscape, and are now additionally supported by MSIE and Mosaic. Progressive-JPEG-making tools for Mac and PCs are listed at: ■ http://www. in-touch.com/pjpeg2.html#software.

Pro-JPEGs boast superior compression to regular JPEGs. They also give you a wider range of quality settings. Instead of Photoshop's standard Max, High, Medium, and Low settings, pro-JPEGs can be set in quality from 0-100. We simulated a comparison here, using the settings of 100, 75, 25, and 0.

 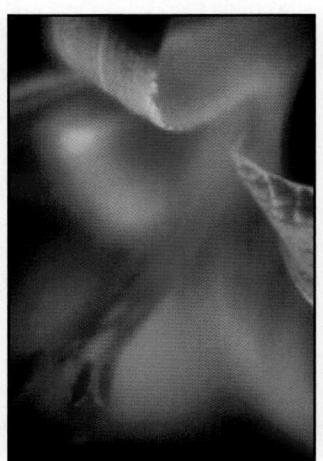 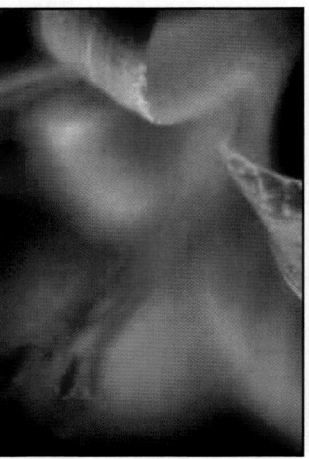 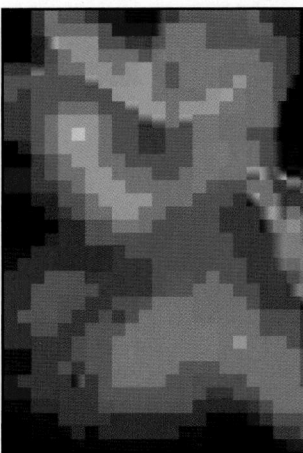

max 28.9k   high 12.4k   med 10.5k   low 8.7k

■ **note**

Progressive JPEGs

There are many tools for creating progressive JPEGs. We used a plug-in to Photoshop called ProJPEG, made by Boxtop Software and available from ■ http://www.aris.com/boxtop/ProJPEG/welcome.html. The great thing about this plug-in is it allows you to preview the results before you commit. Yee haw!

HTML for Embedding Images

Regardless of whether you're using a regular GIF, animated GIF, transparent GIF, interlaced GIF, JPEG, or Progressive JPEG format, the HTML is usually the same.

You must first learn to save the file with the proper extension. Here's a handy list:

GIF	.gif
Interlaced GIF	.gif
Transparent GIF	.gif
Animated GIF	.gif
JPEG	.jpg
Progressive JPEG	.jpg

To insert a graphic into an HTML page, use this tag:
<img src="myimage.gif">

To link an image to another image or HTML page, use this tag
<a href="www.destination_url.com"><img src="myimag.jpg"></a>

To get rid of the border of an image that's been linked, do this:
<a href="www.destination_url.com"><img src="myimag.jpg" border=0></a>

The HTML is the easy part—it's understanding how to optimize graphics, choosing which file format for which type of image, and making the images and content that will be much harder to master!

Girl

dirt

pool

corn

Sky

firetruck

Oranges

Color Principles

GraSS

night

Color Principles

Anyone who has ever seriously studied color theory will most likely report that it is an overwhelmingly technical and deeply complex subject. General color theory is way too involved to cover given the size and purpose of *Coloring Web Graphics*. For this reason, we have chosen to break down color theory concepts into understandable and practical bytes, geared toward helping artists and non-artists understand how to work with color, with a Web-specific focus. The overriding principle of this chapter is that it is not necessary to understand all the technical aspects of color. It is far more important to understand how color works in context and in relationship to other colors, and how to use this information to make well-designed Web pages.

Some people suggest that color has "meaning," such as red means mad or blue means cold. Depending on who you talk to, in different cultures and different countries, and even different age groups, the meanings of specific colors can vary. Some cultures use black for mourning for instance, whereas others use black for weddings. We believe that response to color is personal and subjective, and we see no purpose here in documenting or reporting the underlying meanings behind color.

It's not to say that color doesn't mean very specific things to people. Color is often associated with symbolism. Color definitely evokes emotions. What one person likes another might dislike. Color is subjective, and it is not for us to say what is "good" color and what is "bad" color.

Instead, we want to share principles and observations about color that are helpful when making color decisions with artwork and Web pages. This chapter sheds light on color terminology and contains useful tips and practices related to computer screen-based color.

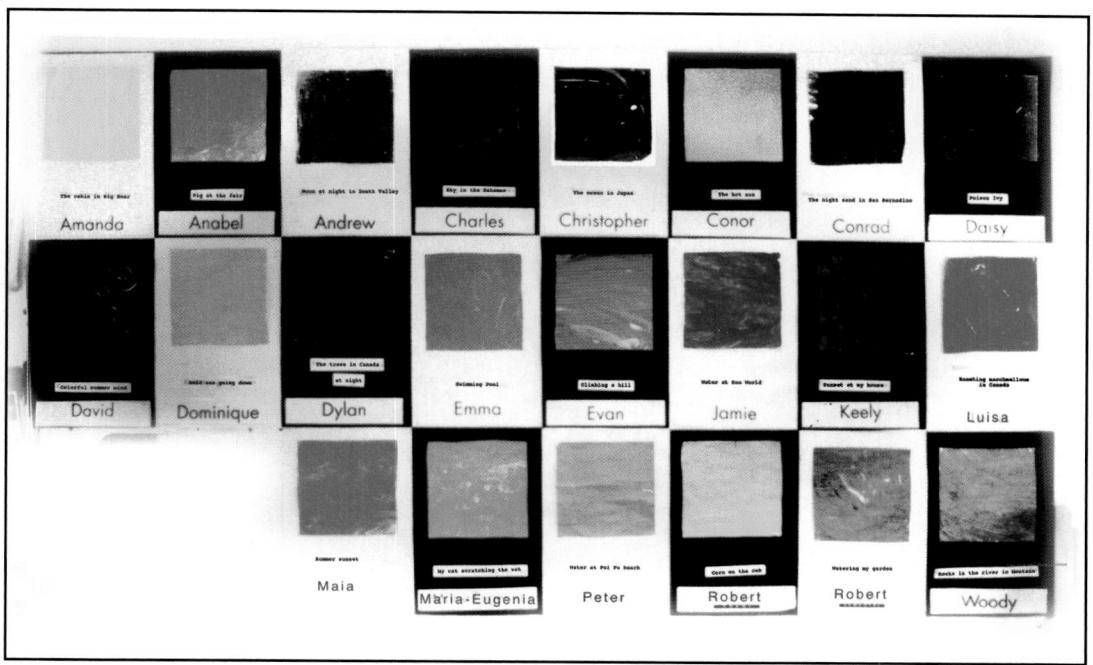

By strange coincidence Jamie, Lynda's daughter, was studying color this term in grade school. Here's an example of 6- and 7- year-olds' renditions of color meanings. From top left to bottom right—some of the children's color definitions: The cabin in big bear, Pig at the fair, Moon at night in Deer Valley, Sky in the Bahamas, The ocean in Japan, The hot sun, The night sand in San Bernadino, Poison Ivy, Colorful summer wind, Gold sun going down, The trees in Canada at night, Swimming pool, Climbing a hill, Water at Sea World, Sunset at my house, Roasting marshmallows in Canada, Summer sunset, My cat scratching the vet, Water at Poi Pu Beach, Corn on the cob, Watering my garden, and Rocks in the river in Montana. Who is to say what a color means to someone? These children's free associations are not only charming; they reveal that defining color is both personal and subjective.

Color Terminology

Like any science, color has specific terminology. Use this visual glossary as a reference for explanations of key terms used when describing color.

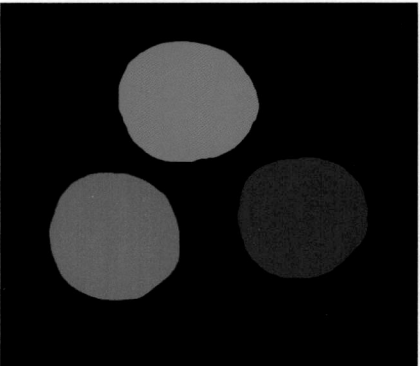

Primary Colors are calculated differently on the computer than with traditional paint and pigment. As a child, you may have learned that primary colors are red, blue, and yellow. From those primary colors, any other color can be mixed. On the computer, however, primary colors are made of projected light. When mixing color with light, the hues red, green, and blue are required as the basis to create all the other colors in the visible RGB color spectrum.

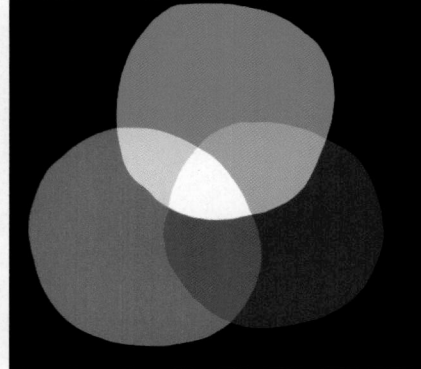

Secondary Colors are the colors in between primary colors. Secondary colors on the computer are created by mixing the primary colors with light. If you mix red and green, you will get yellow; blue and green will create cyan; and red and blue will form magenta.

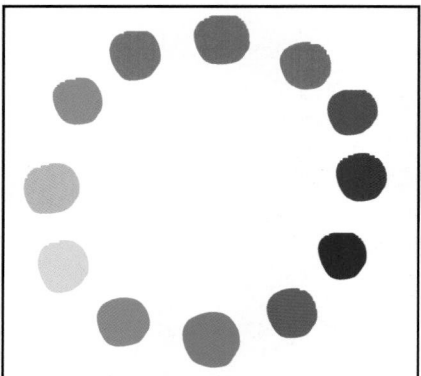

The **Color Wheel** Defines all the Hues in the Visible Spectrum.

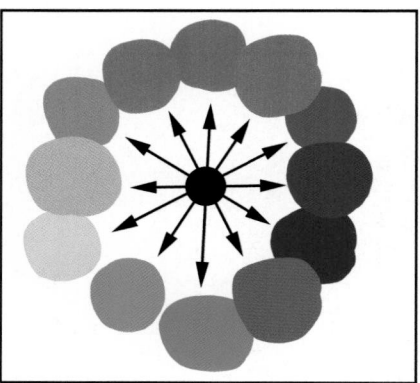

Complementary Colors are created from opposing color hues on the color wheel.

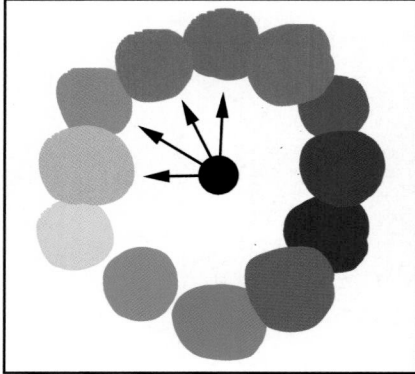

Analogous Color brackets a color hue on either side of the color wheel. If you were to pick red, for example, its analogous neighbors would be orange to one side and purple to the other.

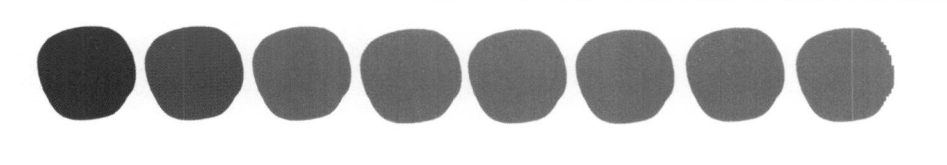

Here's an example of red being pushed in two directions: cool to the left, and warm to the right.

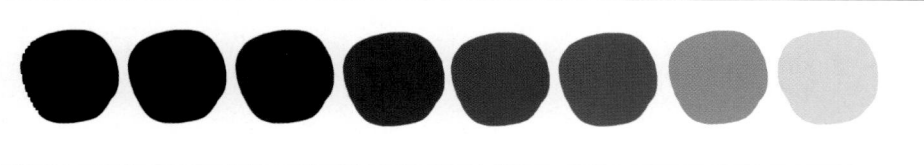

t**Value** is the term used to describe the range from light to dark in your image.

low contrast

normal contrast

high contrast

Contrast is the degree of separation between values.

brightness adjustment

normal adjustment

darkness adjustment

Brightness adds white, or tints your image, whereas the lack of brightness adds black, or tones your image.

Saturation defines the intensity of color.

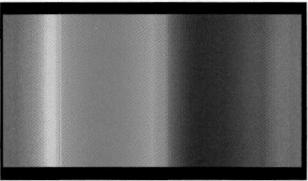

Hue defines a linear spectrum of the color wheel.

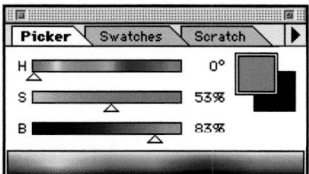

Combining Hue, Value, and **Saturation** can create any color in the RGB color space.

How to Control the "Read" of an Image

The notion of "reading" might evoke associations of textbooks and phonics lessons, but images also have to tell stories, convey information, and provide hierarchy. There are many methods for making images "read," and this section of this chapter concentrates on the role of **value**, **contrast** and **brightness**, **saturation**, and **texture** and **noise** and their affect on the readability of images or Web pages.

The Importance of Value

Value plays the most important role in the overall read of any image, page, or composition. This principle applies to everything from illustrations to photographs to 3D renderings to text.

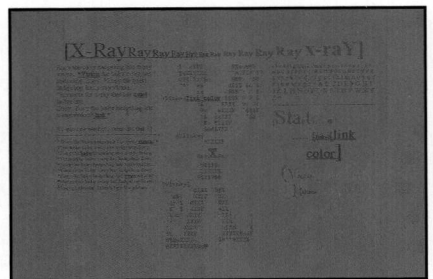

Notice how it's impossible to read the text in this example because the text's value is similar to the value of the background.

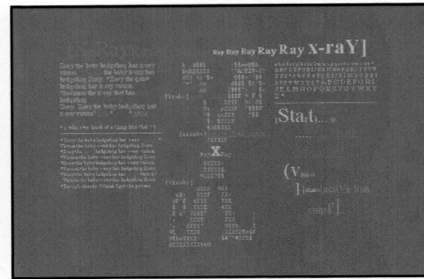

This example shows balanced text color values, which enables the text to be readable.

Value is especially important in context of Web graphics. Differences in computer platforms, gamma settings, or a monitor's calibration can wreak havoc on the readability of images. A dark image created on one machine will come out black, or appear tinted on another. Macintosh computers are generally lighter than Windows-based machines. Web pages can now also be viewed over television screens, which will introduce a whole new set of headaches to deal with, which we will understand better once Web-based television is more prevalent.

So how do we know if we are making an image with values that will display properly on other machines? Well, we don't know, but we can make sure that our image has a good range from black to white. Don't place all the important information in the dark areas, because they might go to black and fade out on someone's PC. And the same goes for light areas. We can't have absolute control over how someone will see our images, so making them as readable as possible in terms of value should be your highest priority. Always view your images on other platforms to see if your images achieve their intended values. A great exercise is to temporarily throw your monitor in grayscale mode and then view your image to see if its values are reading as you expected.

The Importance of Brightness and Contrast

An image with low contrast can be a tough thing to read. Contrast is also important in relation to text legibility. Your background needs to contrast the value of your text so that it will separate from the background in order to be an easy read.

24-bit or 8-bit display

grayscale display

b&w display

Does your Web page stand the brightness and contrast test? Don't count on people viewing your images on color monitors only; there are tons of portable computers that have grayscale and limited 1-bit displays.

Black-and-white monitors on some computers and laptops have the tendency to use an automatic setting of 50% contrast threshold when it comes to displaying type. This will make viewing text that doesn't have the wide degree of separation very difficult. Any portion of the image that is above middle gray will go to black, and any part of the image that is below 50% gray will go to white. Because of this, you may want to consider making your most important information very high in contrast so that it can be read under all monitor conditions.

When you place text upon a background tile with a lot of high contrast noise, the text may become next to invisible, if not unreadable. Here are a few solutions:

- Choose similar values for the colors within the tile, thereby reducing your tile's contrast. The text that goes on a background will read better if it contains a distinct value. If the background is light, make the text dark. If the text is dark, make the background light. If the foreground is about 50% gray in value, you can choose to make your background dark or light.

- Make your text larger so that it reads solid against noise.

- Instead of using HTML-based text, make your text an image. If you have dark text against a dark background, give it a light outline, or glow. If you have light text against a light background, give it a dark outline, or dropshadow.

The Importance of Saturation

Color saturation is the measurement of color intensity. Full saturation represents the purest color attainable without adding any tint or any tone (black or white). Desaturation is the lack of color intensity—the more desaturated a color on the computer in RGB color space, the closer to gray it becomes. On the computer screen, red, green, and blue in their purest forms are fully saturated colors.

Images with too much color and saturation can lead to a visual headache and cause all the colors to scream for equal attention. Toned, tinted, or varied grayed-out colors can provide a visual contrast from fully saturated colors.

Some suggested methods to vary saturation for effective design include:

- Using saturation as a visual compositional device that suggests areas of interest or lack of.
- Bringing attention to some text, button, or element.
- Separating on-screen items by contrasting saturation levels.

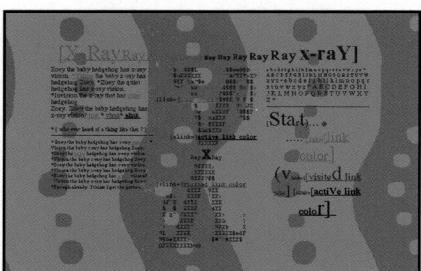

This image has an excessive amount of saturation. The background tile totally overwhelms the text.

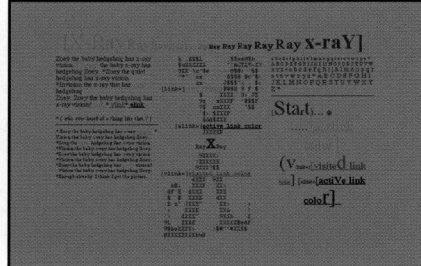

Notice how the saturated links show up, and everything that is desaturated merges into the background.

The Importance of Texture and Noise

Texture, patterns, and noise can help you organize your page in the same way you can organize and design composition with color, value, and saturation. When viewing images with texture, we tend to interpret and group textures and patterns into more general shapes. If our minds can't organize the patterns, we interpret it as visual noise and tend to pass over it for something more identifiable.

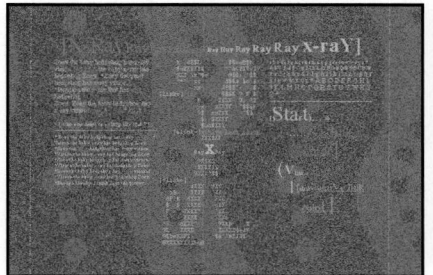

Here's an example of the noisy textured background competing with the readability.

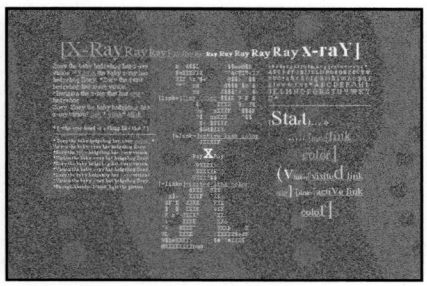

It's improved by increasing the contrast between the text and noisy background.

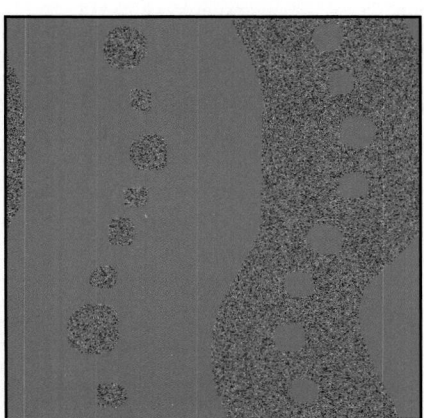

Our eyes distinguish this pattern by its texture, rather than its color differences. Texture, if handled properly, is another device with which to create visual interest and readability.

If you have areas of texture next to a lack of texture, they will contrast and become more visible and obvious with greater degrees of change. The more the value ranges in a texture, the more obvious it will become to the eye. Problems can occur when background textures are too wild in contrast of value, color, and saturation because it fights the text and imagery for attention, thus losing your viewer. If textures have too much and obvious noise and contrast, text at normal sizes tends to get lost.

How to Unify Colors

One solution toward unifying colors is that the colors all need to have something that ties them together: a color, saturation level, or value. Another way to unify colors is by pushing the entire image toward a hue, tint, tone, saturation, or value.

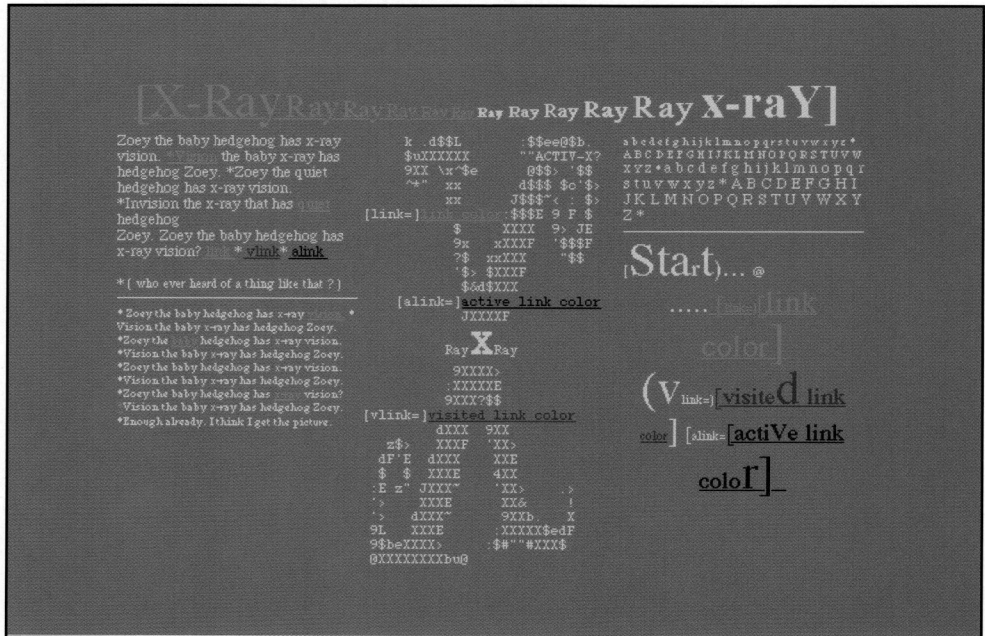

Here's an example of creating "unified color." Bruce created this color example by using one of the analogous color swatch sets, found in Chapter 6, "Color Groupings/Swatches/Directory."

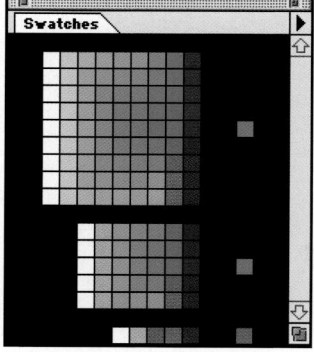

Here's an example of one of the analogous color swatches (file name: ga.aco or ga.gif, located in the SWATCH folder on the *Coloring Web Graphics* CD-ROM) that Bruce used for the unified color example.

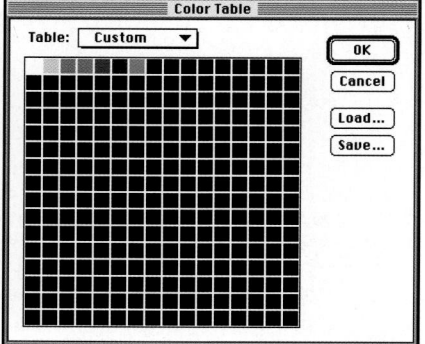

These are the eight colors that Bruce chose from the green analogous color swatch set.

Everything Is Relative

Color is never actual; it is relative to whatever color it's placed next to. A color that seems yellow-green to the eye at first might switch and appear to be yellow when a similar color with more green is placed right next to it. Why is this? We perceive color by its relative relationships to the surrounding colors. The same goes for relationships of value and saturation.

blue-green alone

yellow-green alone

When placed together, the yellow-green looks more yellow and the blue-green looks more blue.

If we show a middle gray by itself we see it for what it is. However, if we place a noticeably lighter gray next to the existing one, the existing one will appear darker. Our minds need reference in relationship to color and value in order to get its bearings.

In actuality, they are two very different shades of colored gray. This demonstrates our minds' tendency to judge color in relationship to other colors.

In this example the grays look identical.

We also tend to view value in relative terms. If an entire image is dark without much contrast, our minds will explore the image and define the lightest areas in the image to be the lights and the darkest areas in the image to be dark, thus completing an entire range. Now this image would look good and register on a dark page. But if you make elements on your page that go lighter than the lightest area on the image, then the image is perceived to be dark.

With a darker element on the screen, such as this black background, the image appears more washed out.

Since this image has pure blacks and pure whites, the black background and white type balance out, without appearing lighter or darker in relationship to anything else.

In this example, black reads as black in this image, but white reads as middle gray.

With white text, the image looks darker than before. Since there is no white in this photograph, the image reads as darker than when the type was gray.

This text color represents the black point of this image on this page.

Black and white points of an image are relative, as the examples above demonstrate.

Here's an example of a grayscale ramp with a solid middle-gray bar in the middle. Notice how the bar looks like it gradates as well. This is an optical illusion caused by our perceptual inclination to judge value in relationship to other values.

When the middle-gray bar is viewed by itself, it doesn't look gradated anymore.

For the most part, our minds always view imagery in relative terms. Texture seems to be stronger when placed next to areas of no or different texture. Green-blue wants to be greener when placed next to a blue. Understanding the balance between these relationships is key to making images that communicate through color and value. Everything is relative to everything else. Understanding this key enables you to create images and Web pages that have balance, readability, and control.

Imaging Techniques

A lot of what has been discussed in this book is useless unless you know how into put it into practice. There are lots of popular imaging programs for Web graphics, so we've included tips and techniques related to color for many software packages in this chapter. Bruce and I both use Photoshop, which is the imaging tool of choice in most professional Web design circles (as well as most other professional design-related circles!). We do understand, however, that not everyone is a professional, nor can everyone afford imaging programs with professional price tags, so we've mixed a healthy dose of Photoshop tutorials alongside tutorials for other imaging programs, such as Paint Shop Pro, Photo-Paint, Painter, FreeHand, Director, GifBuilder, and GIF Construction Set.

The core of this book's purpose is to help you choose colors from a limited color family that look good and work consistently over Web browsers. Chapter 6, "Color Groupings/Swatches/Directory," is a visual directory to guide you through the contents of the *Coloring Web Graphics* CD-ROM. You may choose to work with any of the files on our CD-ROM or to create your own artwork when following along with the tutorials found in this chapter.

How to Load a Browser-Safe Swatch Palette into Photoshop

Custom swatch palettes are one of the key components of our CD-ROM. They enable you to choose from browser-safe colors that are organized by color relationships rather than by mathematics. These swatch palettes load into Photoshop Mac/Win/Win95 versions 2.0-4.0. To load palettes into Photoshop's Swatch Palette, follow these steps:

Step 1: Choose Windows, Palettes, Show Swatches. Using the upper right arrow, choose Load Swatches from the pull-down menu.

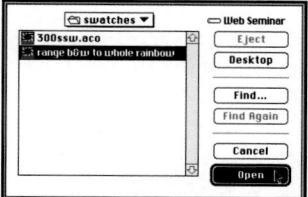
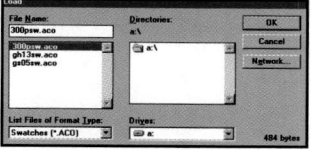

Step 2: Select from any of the files within the SWATCHES\ACO folder on the *Coloring Web Graphics* CD-ROM. The custom swatch set appears as a new set inside Photoshop's Swatch Palette.

How to Append a Swatch Set

Let's say you would like to have more than one swatch set open at a time. You can append as many swatch sets as memory allows.

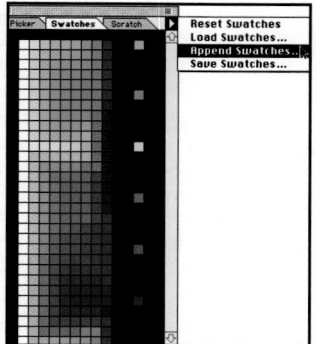

Step 1: Using the upper right arrow, choose Append Swatches.

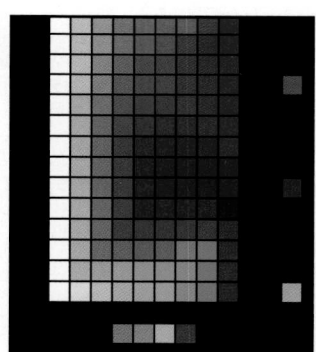

Step 2: The new swatch set will appear below the existing swatch set. If you want to save the appended swatch set, use the upper right arrow and choose Save Swatch. On PCs these files must use an .aco file-name extension.

How to Use the Browser-Safe Swatch Sets

Use browser-safe colors when you are creating custom artwork, illustrations, cartoons, and logos for Web delivery.

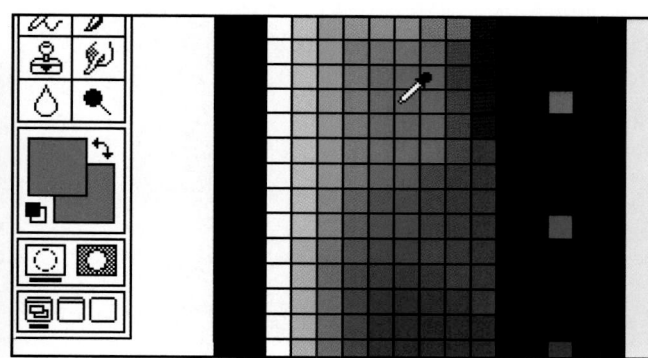

Use the Eyedropper Tool to click on a color within the swatch set. This causes the color to appear in the Foreground Color area of the Photoshop Toolbox. Choose any paint tool, and it will use the color you selected from the swatch set.

How to Add/Replace a Color to a Swatch Set

There may be times when you wish to edit a browser-safe swatch set, such as when you want to make your own limited browser-safe palette for certain favorite colors, or for any other purpose that might arise. This example shows how to add a color to an existing set. The same process would apply if you wished to make a set from scratch using all your own color choices.

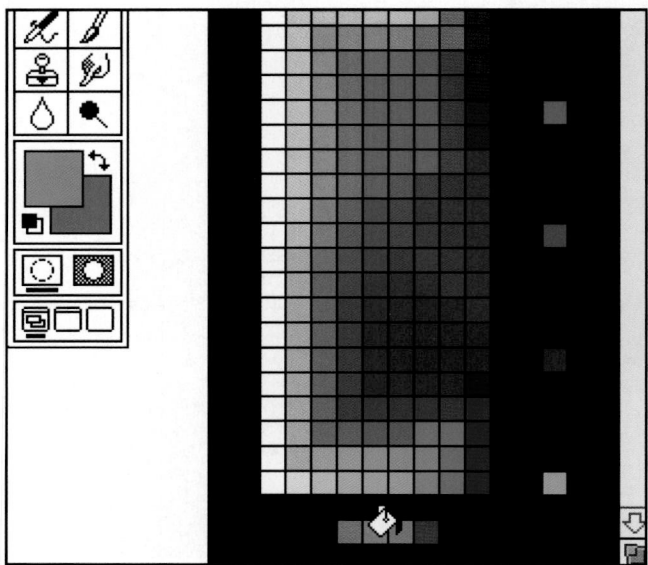

Make sure the new color you wish to add is in the Foreground Color area of the Photoshop Toolbox. Hold down the Shift Key, and your cursor will change to the Paint Bucket Tool. Click to fill one or more color cells. If you want to insert new colors and leave the existing colors in place, use the Shift-Option keys on the Mac, or Shift-Alt keys on the PC. This will cause the existing colors to shift to the right.

How to Subtract Colors from a Browser-Safe Swatch Set

You may also wish to cut certain colors out of the browser-safe color swatch sets if you are making your own favorite browser-safe color set, or for whatever other reason might arise.

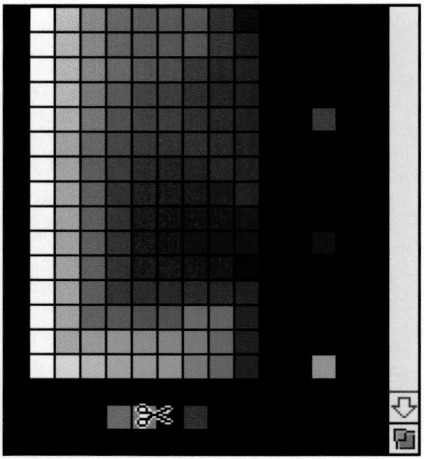

Begin by positioning your cursor over the color you wish to remove. On a Mac, hold down the Command key, and your cursor will change to the Scissor Tool. On a PC, hold down the Ctrl key to display the Scissors Tool. Click to remove the color. The remaining cells of color will move to the left.

How to Save a New Swatch Set

Once you get the hang of making swatch sets, you may want to save your own library.

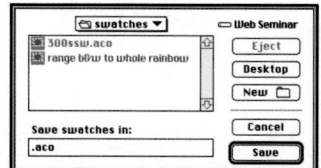
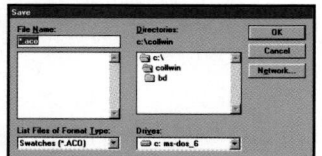

Click on the Swatch Palette arrow to select Save Swatches. It's important to put the .aco extension at the end of your file names. Macs don't require this extension, but if you ever want a PC-based Photoshop user to be able to use the custom set you created, its file name must include this extension.

Swatch Sets for Imaging Programs Other Than Photoshop?

All the Photoshop swatch files on the *Coloring Web Graphics* CD-ROM are also available as GIF files. This means that any imaging program that can read GIF files can view and select from these suggested color families.

The GIF versions of the swatch sets are located inside the SWATCH\GIF folders on the *Coloring Web Graphics* CD-ROM. These files follow the same naming conventions of the Photoshop swatch files shown in Chapter 6, with the exception of the file-name extension: instead of .aco, these files have a .gif extension.

Simply open these files and use the eyedropper tool to select from a browser-safe swatch set in any imaging program that supports this type of color picking.

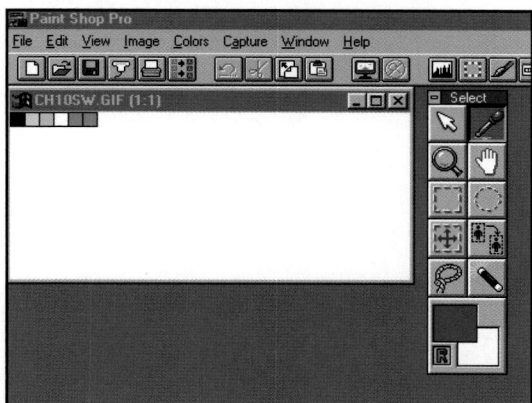

To use the color swatches on the *Coloring Web Graphics* CD-ROM in programs other than Photoshop, open any file within the SWATCHES\GIF folder. You can use the eyedropper tool to select colors from these swatches, just like in Photoshop.

How to Load the Browser-Safe Palette into Paint Shop Pro

We include a browser-safe palette for Paint Shop Pro, called netscape.pal, located in the CLUT folder of the *Coloring Web Graphics* CD-ROM. The following instructions show how to load the palette.

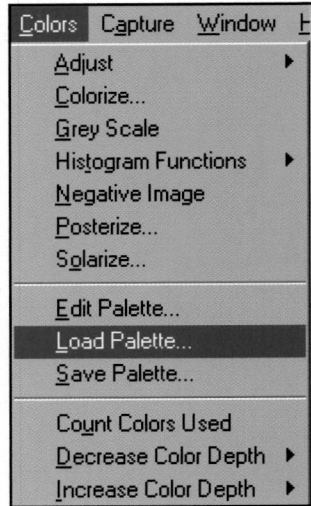

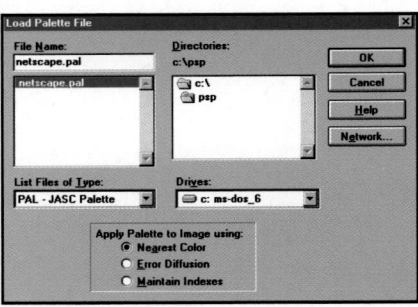

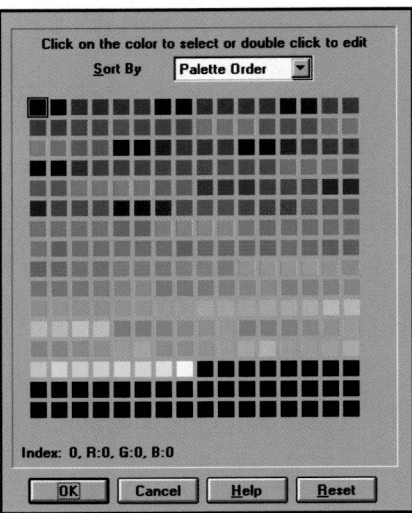

Step 1: Under the Color menu, select Load Palette.

Step 2: Select the file netscape.pal, located in the CLUT folder on the *Coloring Web Graphics* CD-ROM.

Step 3: The palette will appear. It can be sorted by Palette Order, Hue, and Luminance by changing the Sort By setting.

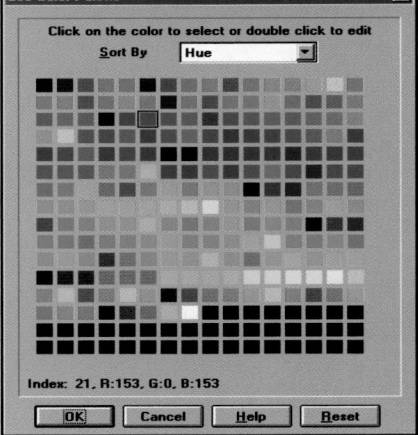

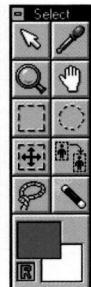

Step 4: Double-click on the foreground color in the Toolbar. In this example, it's a turquoise color.

Step 5: The color palette that you just loaded becomes active. Double-click on a browser-safe color you would like to paint with. Click OK, or press the Return key.

Step 6: The browser-safe color appears in the foreground color picker. Select any painting tool, and it will use this color.

How to Load a Browser-Safe Palette into Photo-Paint

Photo-Paint 6.0 supports the capability to load a custom palette into its color table. We have supplied a file called 216clut.cpl, available inside the CLUT folder on the *Coloring Web Graphics* CD-ROM.

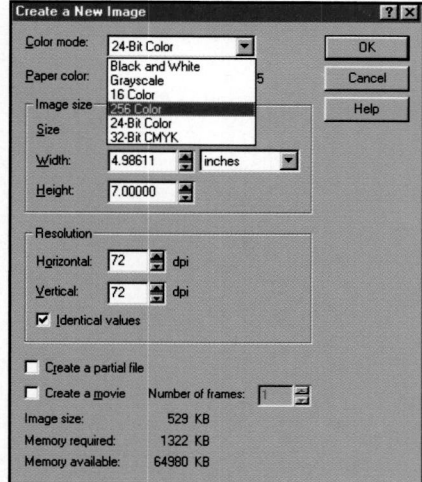

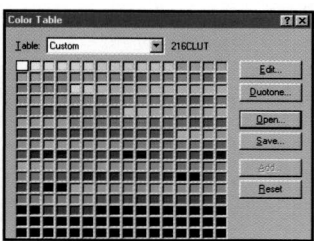
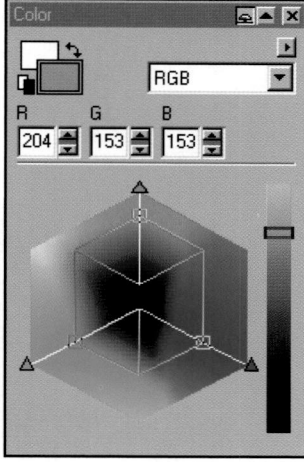

Step 1: Open a 256-color document, or create a new file using 256 colors.

Step 2: Under the Image menu, select Color Table.

Step 3: The Color Table window will open, where you can load and save custom palettes. To load the browser-safe palette, choose it from the CLUT folder on the *Coloring Web Graphics* CD-ROM. The file name is 216clut.cpl. This places the colors in the palette bar at the bottom of the screen and inside the Color window.

Photo-Paint has a really neat interface when you pick a color, showing you the color cube and where your selection is being pulled from.

How to Load a Browser-Safe Palette into Painter

Painter enables you to work with its own version of swatch sets, called Color Sets. You'll find a browser-safe CLUT for Painter located inside the CLUT\PAINTER folder on the *Coloring Web Graphics* CD-ROM. Drag this file into Painter's Color, Weaves, Grads folder on your hard drive before you begin. (Special thanks to Amy Rosenthal for creating and sharing this palette.)

Step 1: Open the Art Materials Palette, highlight Sets, and then click on the Library button.

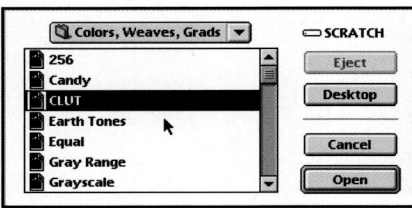

Step 2: Load the CLUT file.

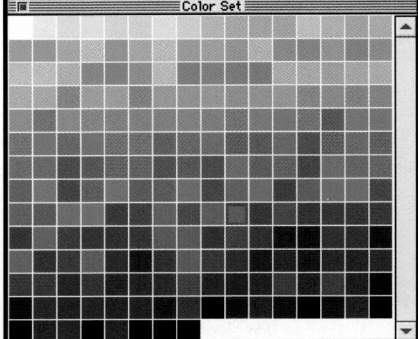

Step 3: A new browser-safe Color Set appears.

What Is a CLUT and What Do You Do with One?

A CLUT is an acronym for Color LookUp Table. A color lookup table is the file that assigns the specific colors to any 8-bit or lower bit-depth computer image. CLUTs can be applied to images two different ways in Photoshop.

Note that any of the Photoshop .aco swatch files on the *Coloring Web Graphics* CD-ROM can be used as CLUT files within the Color Table window.

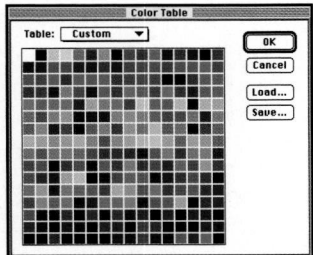

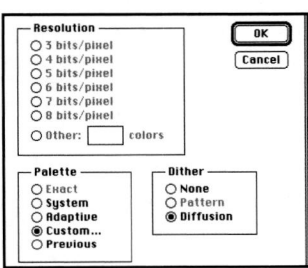

If your image is already in Index mode, go to the Mode menu and choose Color Table, which opens the Color Table dialog box. By clicking the Load or Save button, you can create and apply custom CLUTs to images.

If your image is not in 256 colors yet, choose Index Color under the Mode menu to display the Indexed Color dialog box. Selecting the Custom radio button in the Palette section and clicking on OK opens the Color Table window.

■ warning

Applying Browser-Safe Colors to Existing Artwork

There are times when you might have an image that you wish to convert to browser-safe colors. This can be done by using the technique described above. However, it's very rare for an image to look good when a new CLUT is applied to an existing image. Photoshop determines how to subsitute the new colors, and it might not yield the results you expected. It's always best to create artwork with browser-safe colors first, and not rely on post-processing techniques to fix existing artwork.

Reducing Colors in GIF Files Using Photoshop

Chapter 3, "Web File Formats," described the file-saving advantages of working with limited color palettes whenever using the GIF file format. Here's how to implement procedures that create the smallest possible GIF files.

 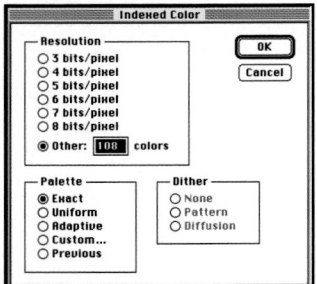

Step 1: An RGB image has to be converted to Indexed Color mode before it can be saved as a GIF. Under the Mode menu, choose Indexed Color.

Step 2: You can type any number into this dialog box. Try to go so low that the image looks bad, and then back off a step. This ensures that you've pushed the limits to how few colors are needed in order to make a small file that still maintains acceptable quality.

Photoshop's Indexed Color Dialog Box

The Indexed Color dialog box has three important functions: setting the resolution, the palette, and the dither. The **resolution** affects the bit-depth of the image. The **palette** sets which colors are used, and the **dither** tells the program which color reduction method to use—dithering, screen, or no dithering.

As Chapter 3, "Web File Formats," describes, the factors of resolution, palette, and dither all play an important role in creating optimized (small in file size) Web images. In order to implement your knowledge about file size savings, it's necessary to understand how to adjust resolution, palette, and dither settings in Photoshop.

Photoshop Resolution Settings

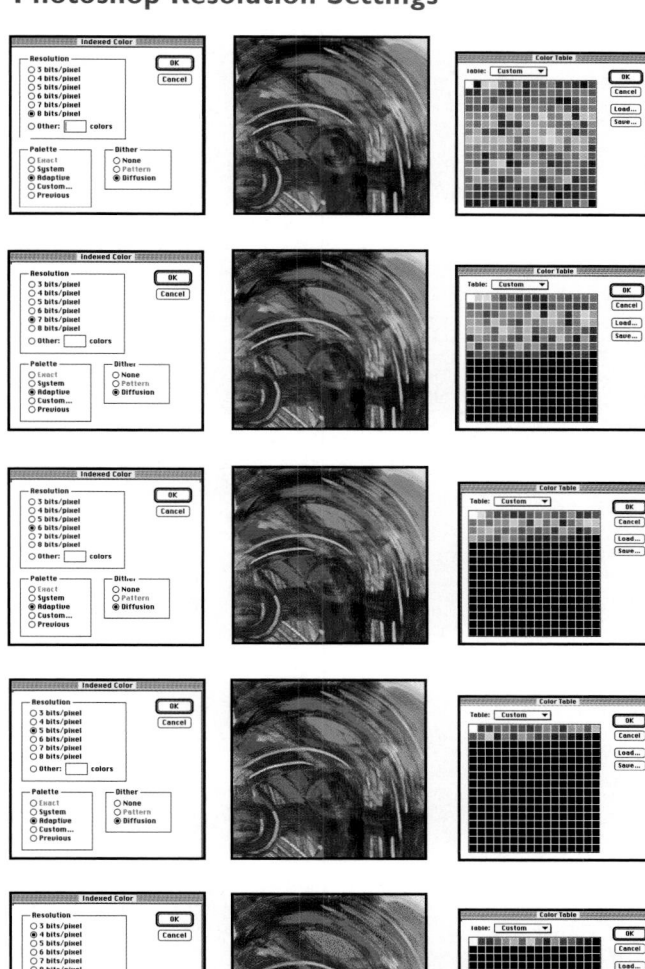

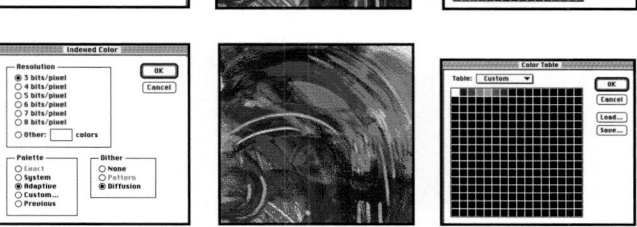

When you convert from RGB to Indexed Color mode, you are presented with the dialog box on the left. The middle row of images shows the results of the respective color depth changes. The Color Table images on the right show the resulting colors contained within each image.

Photoshop Palette Settings

Adaptive

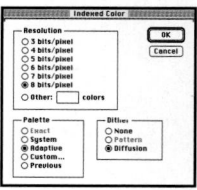  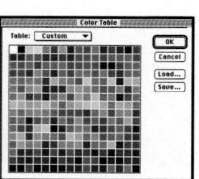

System

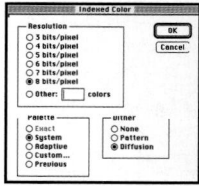  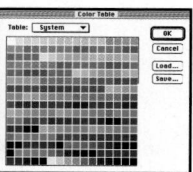

Custom

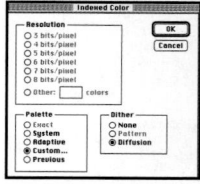  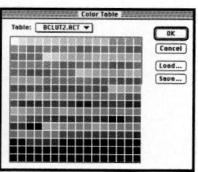

Exact

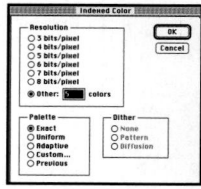  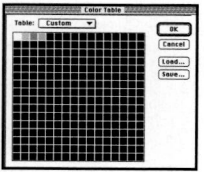

Previous

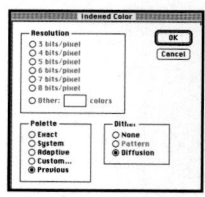  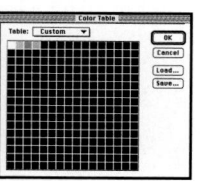

An **Adaptive** palette picks from 256 colors that are most commonly found in the original image. A **System** palette assigns a fixed palette to the original image. A **Custom** palette enables you to assign a custom palette to the image, such as the browser-safe palette. An **Exact** palette allows you to select from the exact colors found within the image. This works only with images that contain less than 256 colors; otherwise Photoshop has to substitute colors based on whatever settings you request. A **Previous** palette applies whatever palette was last used.

Photoshop Dither Settings

None

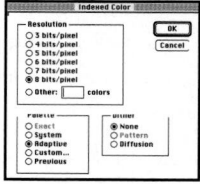 

Diffusion

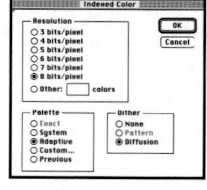 

A **None** dither method uses flat colors to represent colors. In some images, this creates a posterization effect, or banding. When saving GIF files, images without dithering will always be smaller than images with dithering. Sometimes, you need to choose dithering, even though it creates a larger GIF file, because it will improve the quality of the image. A **Diffusion** dither method uses dithering (alternating pixels of different colors to create the illusion of colors not found within the palette). Adding diffusion dither to a GIF image will always increase file size, but sometimes the quality advantages are worth it. **Screen** dither (not shown) produces a uniform pattern dither, increases GIF files sizes, and rarely improves the image's appearance.

Reducing Colors in Photo-Paint

Photo-Paint has an interface similar to Photoshop's Indexed Color dialog box.

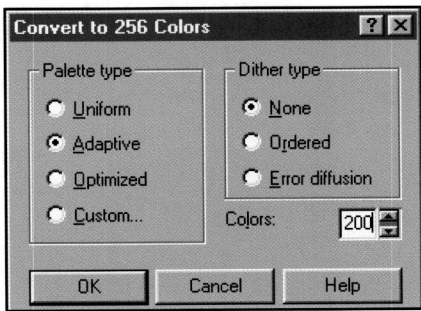

■ A **Uniform** palette type produces the same palette over and over again. This is the appropriate type when you are using Photo-Paint's batch processing feature and want to convert a series of images to the same palette.

■ An **Adaptive** Palette type produces a color palette based on the colors found within the image. It is similar to the Exact setting in Photoshop.

■ An **Optimized** Palette type produces the best 256 colors for re-creating the image. This feature is the same as Photoshop's adpative palette setting.

■ A **Custom** Palette type enables you to assign a specific palette (like the browser-safe 216) to an image.

■ A **None Dither** type produces a banding effect.

■ An **Ordered Dither** type produces a screen dither effect.

■ An **Error diffusion** dither type produces a random dither based on the image itself.

■ **Colors** determines at what bit-depth the image is saved.

Reducing Colors in Paint Shop Pro

Here is Paint Shop Pro's version of decreasing color-depth options.

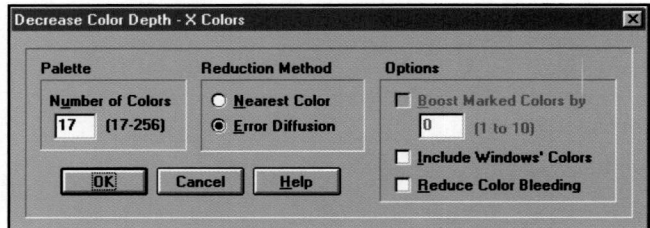

- **Number of Colors** dictates the color depth of the image.

- The **Nearest Color** reduction method is the same as Dither None in Photoshop and Photo-Paint. It will create a banded appearance.

- **Error Diffusion** will create dithering based on the image itself.

- **Boost Masked Colors** allows you to select colors within the document and have the palette weigh toward favoring those colors.

- **Include Windows' Colors** ensures that the 16 colors within Windows are reserved in the image's color table.

- **Reduce Color Bleeding** reduces the left-to-right color bleeding that sometimes occurs with the Error Diffusion Settings.

■ note

The Windows 16 Palette

Sixteen colors are reserved for a native palette assigned to Windows machines. Unfortunately, only the last six colors are browser safe. There are some cases where you might want to use these colors in a Windows-based Intranet, where cross-platform compatibility is not an issue. The win16.clut is located in the CLUT\WIN16 folder on the *Coloring Web Graphics* CD-ROM.

The 16 reserved native colors for Windows systems. Only the last 6 colors are browser safe.

How to Ensure Your Artwork Stays Browser Safe

If you work with browser-safe colors when you create artwork, you still have the important task of ensuring that those colors remain browser safe during the file format conversion process.

Unfortunately, files that are converted to JPEGs do not retain precise color information. The lossy compression method used throws away information, and unfortunately some of that information has to do with color control. Because of this, there is no way to accurately control color using the JPEG file format.

Here's an example of a solid browser-safe color, with the hex readout of 204, 204, 51.

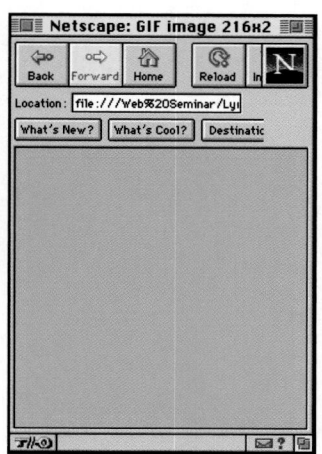

When saved as a GIF file, this color stayed browser safe.

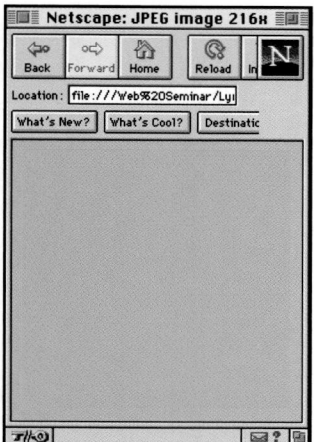

When saved as a JPEG, the color shifted from 204, 204, 51 to 202, 205, 52. It is no longer browser safe, as evidenced by the dither when displayed in Netscape under 8-bit monitor conditions.

We emphasized in Chapter 3, "Web File Formats," that JPEGs are not good for graphics. Not only do they compress graphics poorly, but they introduce artifacts into images, which alters color information.

What this means is that you cannot accurately match foreground GIFs to background JPEGs, foreground JPEGs to background GIFs. Even if you prepare images in browser-safe colors, they will not remain browser safe when converted to JPEG, no matter what you do. We've already established that JPEGs are not good for solid colors in Chapter 3. This is one more reason not to use JPEGs when dealing with flat-style illustration, logos, cartoons, or any other graphical image that would not lend itself to having unwanted dithering.

Next follows an example where an image was created that used a photographic background and browser-safe colors for the type.

Here's a 24-bit image that uses a photographic-style background with flat-style lettering. The letters were created using browser-safe colors.

This is an example of the image saved with an adaptive palette as a GIF.

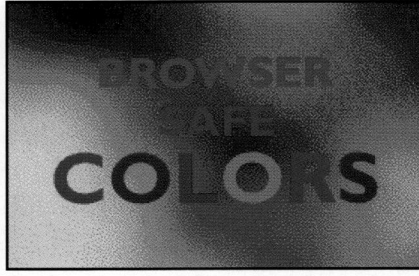

This is an example of the image saved with the browser-safe palette as a GIF.

When viewed from Netscape in 256 colors, the adaptive palette version caused the lettering to dither.

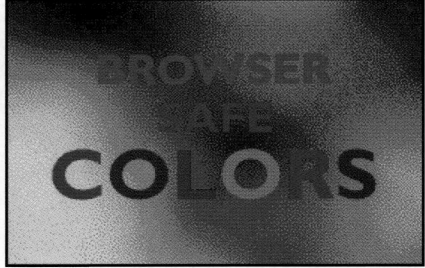

When viewed from Netscape in 256 colors, the browser-safe palette version caused the lettering to look fine.

GIFs, on the other hand, do offer precise color control. If you create an image using browser-safe colors that is less than 256 colors, Photoshop will let you save it with an Exact Palette. The only problem is when you create images that exceed 256 colors. In order to save these types of images as GIFs, some of the colors must be discarded.

This is when it's useful to use a Custom Palette setting in Photoshop and load the bclut2.aco file from the CLUT file on the *Coloring Web Graphics* CD-ROM. You can't trust an adaptive palette to preserve browser-safe colors.

Removing Unwanted Browser-Safe Colors in Photoshop

At times you will apply the browser-safe palette to a file in order to ensure that the colors within honor the 216 color range. The problem is, you might want to reduce the number of colors to less than 216 in order to create smaller GIF files.

The following example shows you how to apply a browser-safe palette and then reduce the color depth.

Bruce created an illustration in colors other than browser safe.

He converted them to browser-safe colors, using the 216 browser-safe CLUT file (called bclut2.aco) located in the CLUT folder on the *Coloring Web Graphics* CD-ROM.

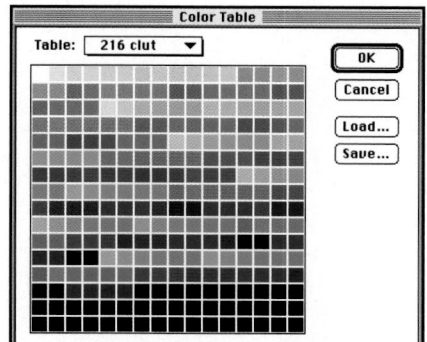

The image is now browser safe, but it is also 216 colors! That's a few too many colors than are necessary for this image. By leaving the image this way it would generate a 16.8k GIF.

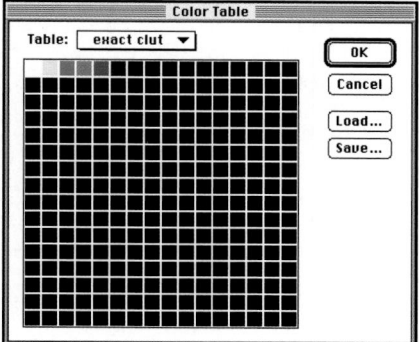

There was no reason for the image to include all 216 colors. By changing the image back to RGB mode and then back to Indexed Color mode, Bruce chose Exact Palette the second time. This image only needs to be assigned 7 colors! When saved as a GIF with only 7 colors, the image is 13k, a 22.6% savings that didn't affect visual image quality in the least.

Common Problems with GIF Transparency

If you've navigated the Web much, you've seen GIF images with fringing, halos, and matte lines around the edges. This is a common problem with transparency because images with soft edges (anti-aliasing, feathers, glows, and drop shadows) pick up parts of the color they were created against.

The principle of the problem is easy to understand. Since the mask is only 1-bit or one color, any artwork that requires blended edges, such as anti-aliased, gradated, feathered, and glowing artwork, will pick up parts of the color they were created against. You will need to take some extra measures to make the masks work.

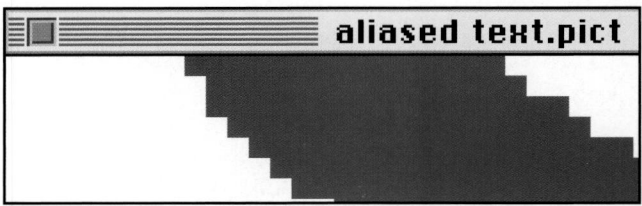

The top image shows a close-up of an anti-aliased edge. Notice how its jaggy edges blend into the white background. The bottom image shows an aliased edge. It doesn't blend to the background color. Because transparency is limited to 1-bit, or one color, it picks up the residual color around the edges of an anti-aliased graphic. This causes unwanted fringing around the edges, and creates a halo or matte line when used on a Web page.

This figure shows four types of edges for artwork: aliased, anti-aliased, with a shadow, and with a glow.

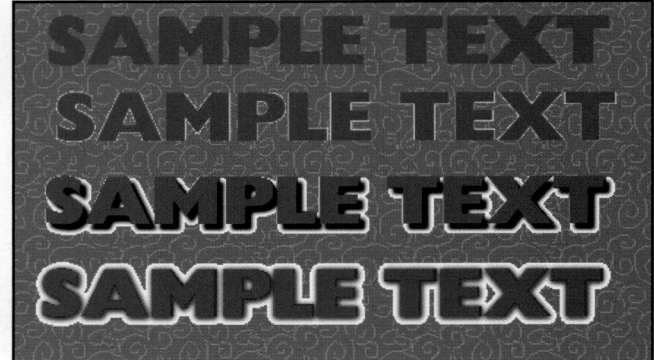

When the different examples of edges are made into transparent GIFs using 1-color transparency, notice how every example except the aliased top version picked up the background color they were made against. That's because the images with soft edges picked up parts of the white color they were created against. This created an unsightly problem, which is commonly called a halo, fringe, or matte line in the industry.

One popular solution is to build artwork against the same color background that it will be seen against in the Web browser. The artwork will look terrible when you make it, but it will look fine once overlayed against the final background in a Web browser.

Here's an example of the identical artwork with anti-aliased, shadowed, and blurry edges against the same color background of the target page.

When the transparency is set, the files look pretty terrible. They won't look good again until they are laid over a green background. If prepared this way, you will correct their predisposition to favor any other color, which will eliminate unwanted fringes, halos, and matte lines.

The end result looks quite acceptable now. Look ma, no matte lines!

There are tons of transparency programs for the Mac and PC. Too many programs to cover in this book, in fact! If you use the technique of creating your anti-aliased images against your target background color and then use any transparency program, you'll fix the problem of bad edges.

■ note

URLs for Transparency Tricks and Tips:

Online Transparent GIF creation:
■ http://www.vrl.com/Imaging/invis.html

Thomas Boutell's WWW FAQ on Transparency:
■ http://sunsite.unc.edu/boutell/faq/tinter.htm

Chipp Walter's Excellent GIF transparency tutorial:
■ http://204.96.160.175/IGOR/photosho.htm

How to Create a Common Palette for Animated GIFs

The GIF89a format spec allows not only for animation, but for custom palette handling as well. It's possible to assign a common palette to all the images within an animation. This is advisable because some of the browsers have been known to cause palette flashing on animated GIFs that don't use a uniform color lookup table. Palette flashing causes your artwork to suddenly switch from having a normal appearance to flashing rainbow/psychedelic colors at whim. It's not a pretty sight, trust us!

Making a common palette for a series of images is sometimes referred to as a super palette. In Photoshop, the idea is that you import a series of images into one single file, convert it to indexed color, and then save the palette from the Color Table dialog box. Once you've saved the palette, you can reapply the palette you saved to each individual image through the Custom or Previous settings in Photoshop. Here's a step-by-step example from Bruce.

Step 1: Here are six individual frames of artwork Bruce designed for his animation sequence.

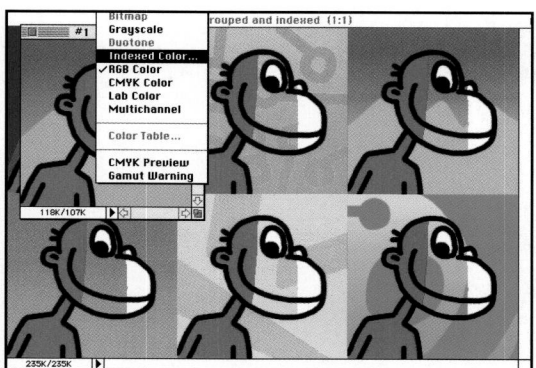

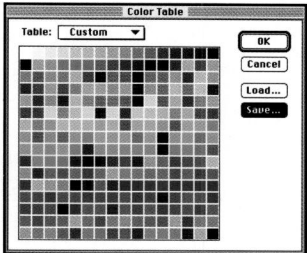

Step 2: Once all the images were in one file, Bruce changed the mode from RGB to Indexed Color.

Step 3: Under the Image menu, Bruce chose Color Table.

Step 4: He saved the custom CLUT by clicking on Save.

Step 5: This is what the CLUT file looks like on the Mac desktop. Windows users must save these files with an .aco extension.

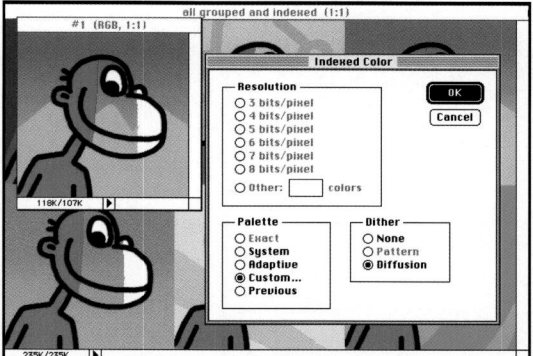

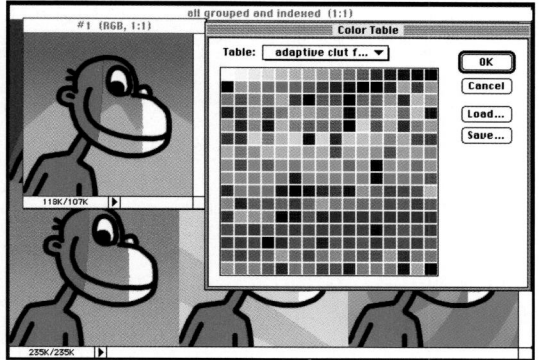

Step 6: Bruce then opened each individual image and applied the Custom Palette.

Step 7: Inside the Color Table dialog box, Bruce chose to load the CLUT he saved.

The end result of this process created six independent images that all share a common palette. The palette is optimized specifically for these images. This technique will ensure the best possible looking color fidelity for animated GIFs.

How to Use a Custom Palette in GifBuilder

GifBuilder ■ http://iawww.epfl.ch/Staff/Yves.Piguet/clip2gif-home/GifBuilder.html is a popular GIF animation tool for the Macintosh. It has lots of great features, including the ability to work with custom palettes.

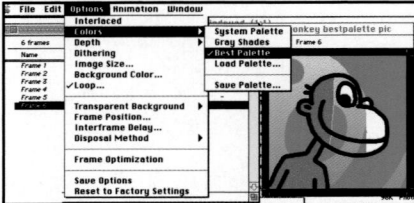

In this example, Bruce chose the Best Palette option in GifBuilder. Notice the dithering inside the red body of the monkey.

Using GifBuilder's Load Palette feature, Bruce applied the Photoshop CLUT he saved from the earlier exercise. It yields superior results.

Loading a Common Palette into GIF Construction Set

GIF Construction Set for Windows ■ http://www.mindworkshop.com/alchemy/alchemy.html doesn't accept Photoshop palettes. It does, however, adopt whatever palette the artwork was set to. If you create artwork that is mapped to a common palette and then import this artwork into GIF Construction Set, you'll get excellent results.

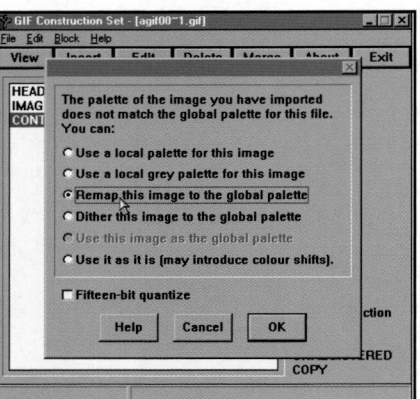

In order for GIF Construction Set to honor the image's common palette, the setting "Remap this image to the global palette" must be chosen.

Making a Super Palette in DeBabelizer

DeBabelizer is renowned as an excellent Mac-based batch image processor. (Windows version coming soon.) The term *batch procecessing* describes the capability to repeat a computer operation, such as "changing a palette," in an automated manner. DeBabelizer does many of the things Photoshop does, but the batching capability lets you apply the results over an entire folder of images at a time.

DeBabelizer has a routine called Super Palette that examines the contents of images contained within a folder of color images, and creates a common CLUT automatically. It then applies the CLUT to each of the individual images that were contained in the folder. This can be a great timesaver, overdoing it on a file-by-file basis in Photoshop. DeBabelizer has a confusing interface, but its functionality is essential to anyone author-ing vast quantities of images for multimedia or Web design.

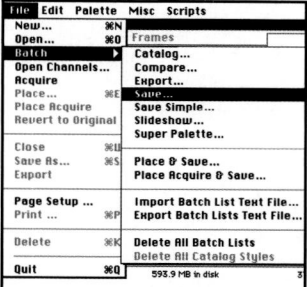

The first step to using DeBabel-izer for a Super Palette is to do a Batch, Save. This saves a path to the contents of a folder, and instructs the program to run whatever script is chosen over a series of images or folders.

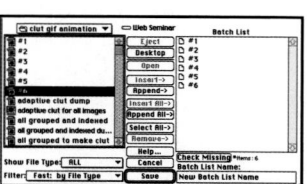

You create your Batch List by click-ing on individual files or folders.

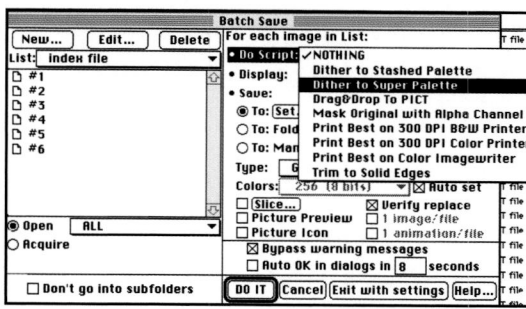

Once you've set up a Batch List, the choice to Dither to a Super Palette is one of the many scripting options avail-able to you. The Super Palette does the same process automatically that Bruce did to each image in the "How to Create a Common Palette for Animated GIFs" section of this chapter.

■ note

Photoshop 4.0

The latest version of Photoshop introduced a new scripting feature that should make the task of creating common palettes a lot easier. It may provide some competition for DeBabelizer's Super Palette feature, but will have to be custom programmed. This feature ships as a default script in DeBabelizer.

Vector-Based Artwork

The two most popular image file formats for the Web—GIF and JPEG—are bitmap-based formats. Bitmap artwork is composed of pixel-based artwork, meaning that every pixel takes up memory and is accounted for in the file format. Vector file formats are based on code that instructs the computer to draw the artwork, and furnishes information like the radius of a circle or the length of a line.

Most vector-based drawing programs enable you to move objects around on the screen and align artwork with grids using precise control and offer much more elaborate type lay-out treatments than their bitmap counterparts. For this reason, many artists work with vector-based software programs to begin with, and later export their artwork into bitmap programs where the images can be saved as GIFs and JPEGs. This section of this chapter evaluates processes for creating browser-safe vector-based artwork in three popular vector-based imaging programs: Adobe Illustrator, Macromedia's FreeHand, and CorelDraw.

For more in-depth information about these three programs, check out the following URLs:

- http://www.adobe.com/prodindex/illustrator/main.html
- http://www.macromedia.com/software/freehand/index.html
- http://www.corel.com/products/graphics&publishing/draw7/index.htm

Working with CorelDraw

At the time of this chapter, the current shipping version of CorelDraw supported the capability to output files in RGB. The only problem was that it didn't allow you to specify the palette. The next version, 7.0, promises to allow custom palette assignments. It's best to create artwork in CorelDraw that is close to the colors you want to use, and then to bring the artwork into Photo-Paint to convert the colors to the browser-safe CLUT. The Photo-Paint 216 palette is called 216clut.cpl. and is available in the CLUT\PP folder on the *Coloring Web Graphics* CD-ROM.

Working with Adobe Illustrator

Adobe Illustrator is an extremely useful program in that it does many things better than Photoshop. Some of the reasons to use Illustrator are its better handling of text, and its capability to position artwork accurately and create object-oriented artwork that is resolution independent.

The only problem using Illustrator for Web graphics is that it works only in CMYK. It's impossible to load the browser-safe color chart or swatch sets into a CMYK environment. Most artists who use Illustrator for browser-safe color artwork create the artwork in black and white in Illustrator and then import the artwork into Photoshop where they use the browser-safe swatches for re-coloring the images.

Note that version 6.0 of Illustrator will let you save GIF files and convert them to a specified palette, including one that contains the 216 browser-safe colors.

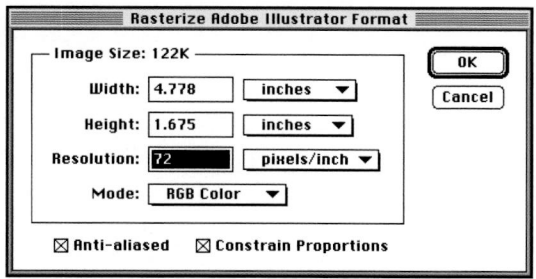

Illustrator is a popular software program because of its superior type handling, accurate positioning features, and resolution-independent drawing tools. Unfortunately it works only in CMYK color, so it's impossible to author Web color images directly. Create artwork in black and white first, and save it as a native Illustrator file.

When you open the file in Illustrator, you'll be prompted to rasterize the artwork. This converts the artwork from the Illustrator vector format to the Photoshop bitmap format.

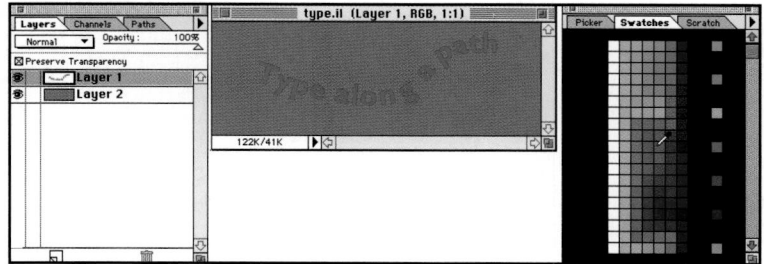

Once the artwork is rasterized in Photoshop, it can be painted with the browser-safe color swatches, just like artwork that originated in Photoshop.

Working with FreeHand

Artists who use FreeHand for its excellent type-handling tools and vector-drawing tools are in luck! FreeHand allows users to work directly in RGB, and will support the 216 palette.

FreeHand works with RGB percentages rather than specific RGB values. It's possible to mix browser-safe colors right in RGB within FreeHand. Just remember these conversions:

%	RGB	HEX
100%	255	FF
80%	204	CC
60%	153	99
40%	102	66
20%	51	33
0%	0	0

Thanks to the generousity of Amy Rosenthal, we have also included the browswer-safe palette that she painstakingly made for FreeHand on the *Coloring Web Graphics* CD-ROM. This file is inside the CLUT\FHAND folder, and it's named clut.bcs. The following steps will enable you to access this palette in FreeHand: values. It's possible to mix browser-safe colors right in RGB within FreeHand.

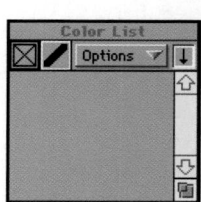

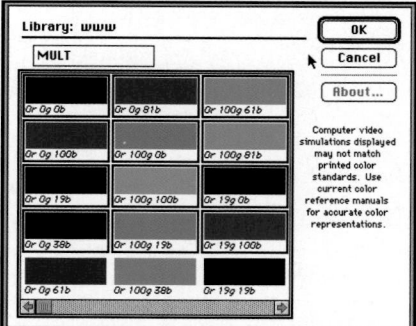

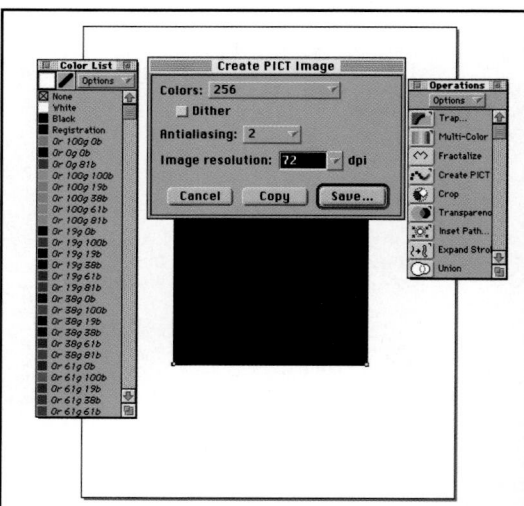

Step 1: Open the Color List Palette. Under Options, choose Import. Locate the clut.bcs file, within the CLUT folder on the *Coloring Web Graphics* CD-ROM.

Step 2: Double-click on the file name clut.bcs and this window will appear. Hold the Shift key down to select all the color chips within the set, and click OK.

Step 3: If you use these colors to paint with, you can save them as a PICT file for conversion to GIF in another program. Highlight the artwork, and select Create PICT in the Operations palette. Make sure that Dither is left unchecked in the Save window. This will ensure that the browser-safe color selection will be preserved.

Working with Color Picker-Based Applications

Certain programs don't let you mix colors by percentages or RGB values. A few such programs include Adobe PageMill, Claris Homepage, and BBEdit, which all rely on the Apple Color Picker to choose custom colors.

Pantone has come to the rescue with a product called ColorWeb ■ http://www.pantone.com. This Internet-safe color picking system includes two components: a printed swatch set and a System Color Picker that displays the 216 safe colors inside the Apple Color Picker dialog box.

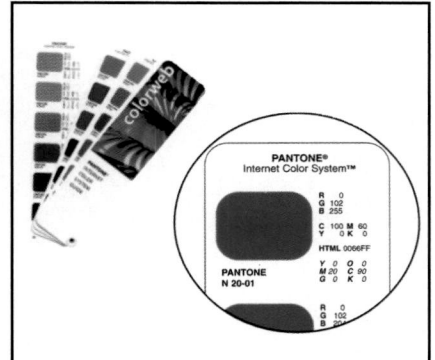

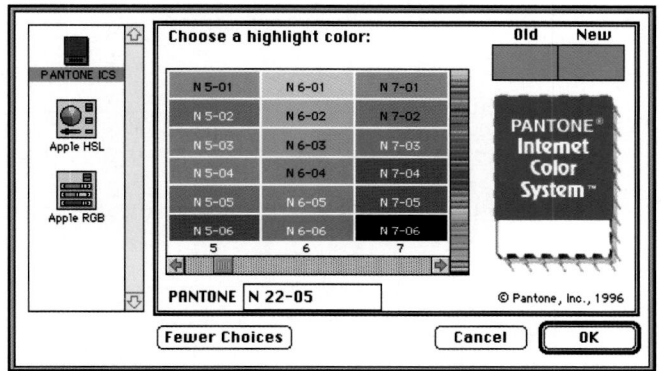

The Pantone Internet Color Guide looks like a typical Pantone color swatch book, only it has a Web-color spin. It presents and organizes the 216 browser-safe colors in chromatic order, and lists the values for RGB, CMYK, Hexadecimal, and Hexachrome (their proprietary color format for picking printing ink colors).

If you install Pantone's ColorWeb software, it will add another entry into the Apple Color Picker choices, called Pantone ICS, that will enable you to pick from the 216 browser-safe colors.

It should be noted that there is no perfectly accurate way to convert CMYK values to RGB. The numbers that the Pantone Internet Color Guide cites for CMYK Internet-safe values are ballpark approximations intended for print only, and do not yield browser-safe colors when converted to RGB. The two color spaces—RGB and CMYK—do not share common colors consistently. Some RGB colors are outside of the CMYK color gamut, and there is nothing anyone can adjust to create a reliable conversion method.

The ColorWeb software is an excellent (Mac-only) tool that offers the capability to pick browser-safe colors in programs that do not support RGB decimal or RGB percentage-based values. Pricing and order information is available at the Pantone Web site.

Custom Palettes for Shockwave Documents

Macromedia Director is an interactive authoring tool that has a huge installed user base. With the announcement of Shockwave, a plug-in that makes Director projects viewable from the Web, Director-based projects are situated to become a common file type on the Web.

It's possible to assign custom palettes to Director documents. Information on this process is available from ■ http://www.macromedia.com/support/technotes/shockwave/developer/shocktechnotes/palettes/colpalette.html. Director 5.0 even ships with a 216-color palette, which is located under the Xtras pull-down menu. The file is called PALETTES on Macintoshes and Palettes.cst on Windows.

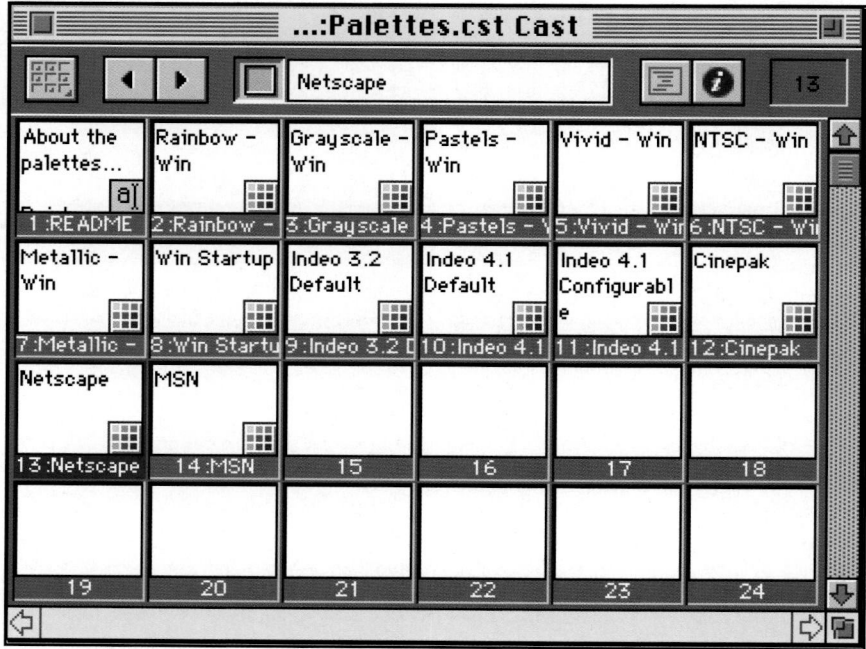

Director 5.0 ships with a series of palettes, including a broswer-safe palette called Netscape.

Hybrid Color Background Tile Creation in Photoshop

You can extend the 216-color limit by creating or using hybrid color tiles, as we described in Chapter 2, "Browser-Safe Color." By checkerboarding or alternating color pixels, you can mix new colors that create the illusion of colors found outside the 216 limit. There are tens of thousands of browser-safe color combinations possible. We show hundreds of examples in the context of suggested color families in Chapter 6, "Color Groupings/Swatches/Directory," and offer those for your use as electronic files on the *Coloring Web Graphics* CD-ROM.

Let's say you want to make your own hybrid color combinations, though. It's possible to make them in any paint program. Unfortunately, with the exception of Photoshop, most paint programs don't let you preview the results until you've created an HTML document and look at the results in a Web browser.

The object is to make a repeating pattern of pixels. There are two types of patterns that work the best: horizontal lines and checkerboards. The reason for this is at a 1:1 ratio, these patterns are the least obvious. We supply templates of these two types of files in black and white on the *Coloring Web Graphics* CD-ROM—they are called ckrbd.gif and lines.gif, and are located in the CLIPART\BRUCEH\TILES folder.

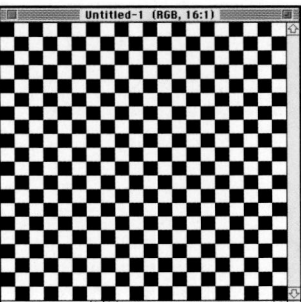
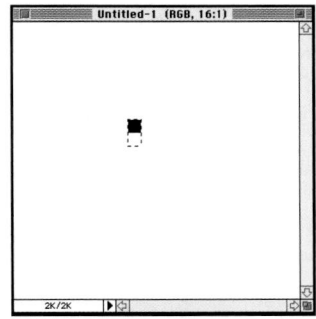
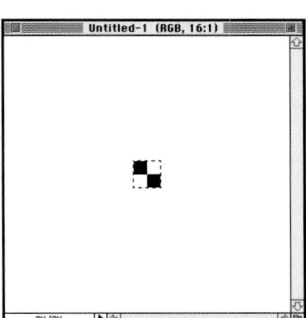

Close-up views of the two types of patterns used for hybrid tile creation.

Creating the pattern for the hybrid tiles can be created with two or four selected pixels, and then defining a pattern based on these selections.

In Photoshop, creating these patterns can be done with a few simple pixels.

Step 1: Using the smallest Pencil Tool, inside a magnified document, create the base art for the pattern tile. Use the Marquee Selection Tool to select either two or four pixels.

Step 2: Under the Edit menu, choose Define Pattern.

Step 3: Create a larger document. Make sure it's an even number of pixels so that the tile will repeat properly in a browser without any erroneous lines or glitches. Under the Edit menu, choose Fill. In the Fill dialog box, select Fill with Pattern.

Tip: You'll get the best looking results if you choose colors that are close in value. This creates the best optical mixture, which tricks the eye into seeing one mixed color as opposed to two distinct mixed colors.

Coloring Hybrid Tiles in Photoshop

Once you have black-and-white color tiles (or any other color combination), you can recolor the tile easily.

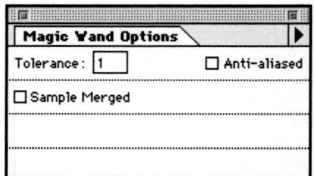

Step 1: Set the Magic Wand Tool to a tolerance of 1. This ensures that it will select only one color. Select a single pixel of either black or white. If the tile is two colors other than black and white, select one of those colors.

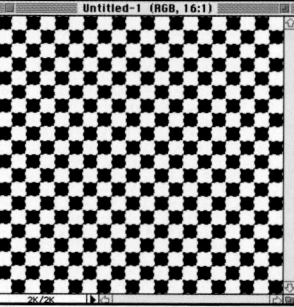

Step 2: Under the Select Menu, choose Select Similar. This selects everything in the image that has the same color you originally chose. It's now easy to fill this selection with any color you want, using the Edit, Fill menu. To fill the opposite color, choose Select, Inverse, which reverses the selection, and then proceed to fill with another color.

■ tip

Photoshop Shortcuts

A shortcut for filling a selection is to select a color so that it appears in your foreground color toolbar. On Macs, Use Option-Delete, and Alt-Delete on PCs.

A shortcut for filling with a pattern is Shift-Delete on the Mac and on the PC.

Coloring Pattern Tiles in Photoshop

The process for coloring pattern tiles is the same for filling hybrid tiles.

To recolor any of the tiles on the CD, make your selection with the Magic Wand Tool set to a Tolerance of 1. Under the Select Menu, choose Select Similar. It's now easy to fill this selection with any color you want, using the Edit, Fill menu. To fill the opposite color, choose Select, Inverse, which reverses the selection, and proceed to fill with another color.

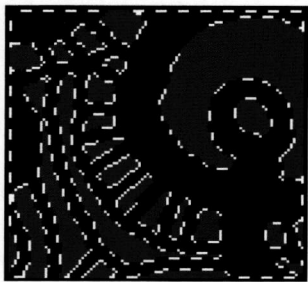

To recolor any of the tiles on the CD, make your selection with the Magic Wand Tool set to a Tolerance of 1. Under the Select Menu, choose Select Similar. It's now easy to fill this selection with any color you want, using the Edit, Fill menu. To fill the opposite color, choose Select, Inverse, which reverses the selection, and proceed to fill with another color.

Previsualizing Tiles in Photoshop

Working with the Fill with Pattern feature in Photoshop, it's possible to previsualize tileable patterns before sending them to the Web browser for the world to see. We'll work with Don Barnett's artwork (shmancy.gif, available inside the folder CLIPART\DONB\TILES) to show how this is done.

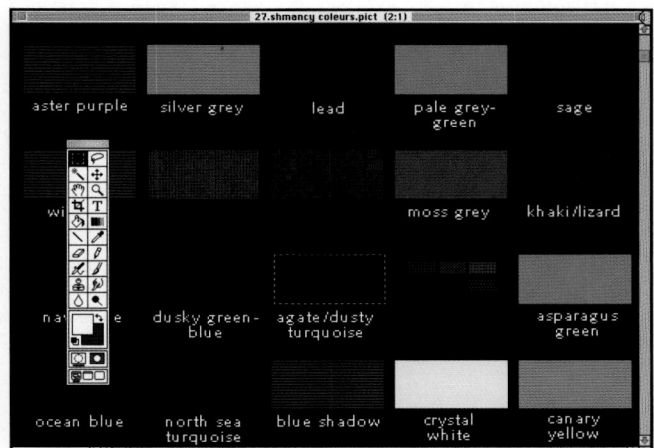

Step 1: Zoom into the file to accurately select the rectangular swatch. Under the File menu, choose Define Pattern.

Step 2: Open a blank Photoshop document that will represent your Web page. Select All and choose Edit, Fill. In the Fill dialog box, choose Fill with Pattern.

How to Create Your Own Seamless Tile in Photoshop

We've shown you how to make your own hybrid and recolor existing tiles from the CD, but how are those seamless tiles created to begin with? The following step-by-step tutorial follows Bruce Heavin's process, using Photoshop, the offset filter, and browser-safe colors.

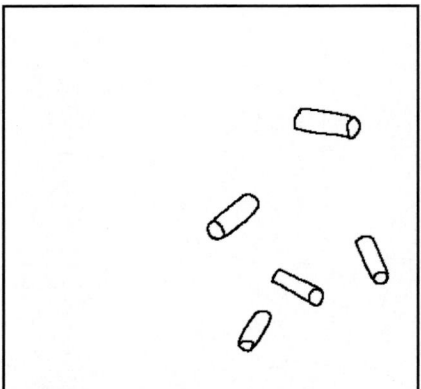

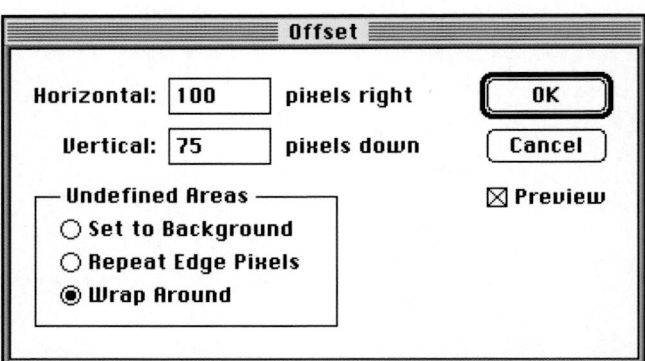

Step 1: Bruce begins drawing intentionally at one side of a 400 x 400 pixel, 72 dpi document. The dimensions of this computer file does not matter, except that its size dictates the number of repeats once the image is tiled in a browser. A small pattern will repeat more times than a large pattern. The size limit in most browsers is 1200 x 1200 pixels, which would almost fill a 21" monitor.

Step 2: Bruce uses the Offset Filter (Filter, Other, Offset) and enters an arbitrary amount of distance. Be sure to check the Wrap Around feature. The offset filter moves the artwork by whatever value you insert into the horizontal and vertical move boxes. When Wrap Around is selected, it moves the artwork and shows the edge mirrored on its opposite side whenever the artwork is moved beyond the edge of the computer file. This helps you see where the seams are and allows you to fix any problems with the image's edges that might cause a repeated pattern's seams to show.

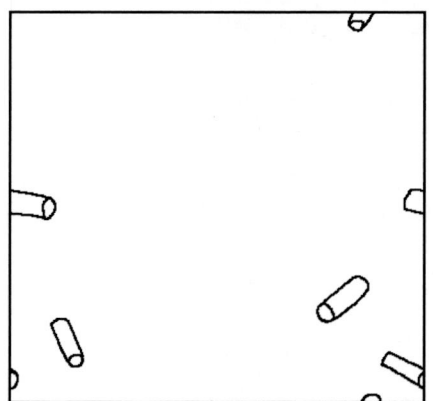

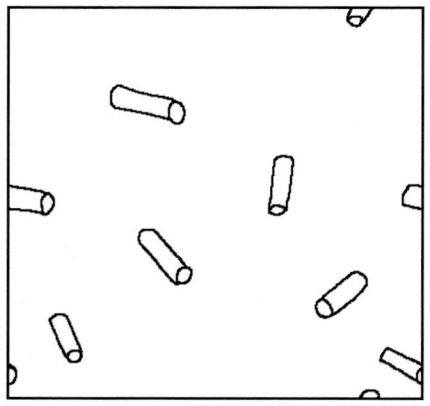

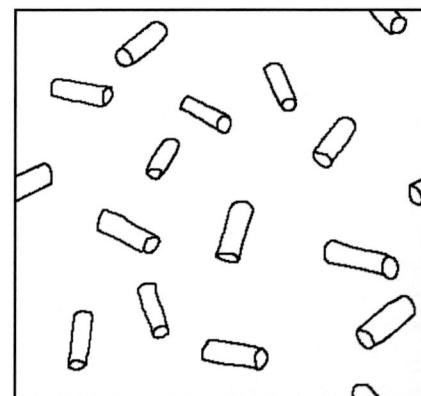

Step 3: Here are the results of the offset. Notice how his artwork has shifted and is mirrored on the opposite sides of the shift. This allows Bruce to work on the edges of this image, making sure that there are no obvious seams in his artwork.

Step 4: Bruce starts to fill in the areas that the Offset Filter show as blank.

Step 5: He repeats the Offset Filter, and continues to add artwork where he sees gaps.

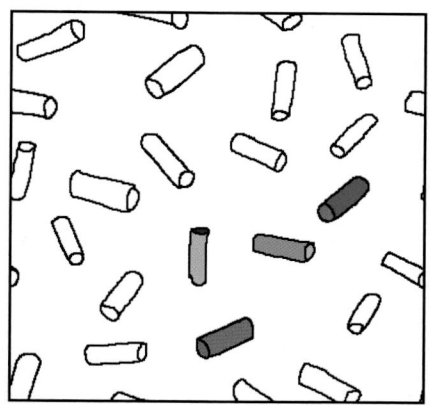

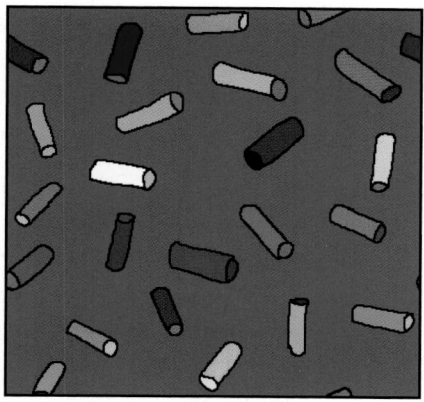

Step 6: He is finished drawing the outlines only after the Offset Filter no longer shows any gaps. He then paints in the outlines, using browser-safe colors (of course!).

Step 7: Here's the finished 400 × 400 tile.

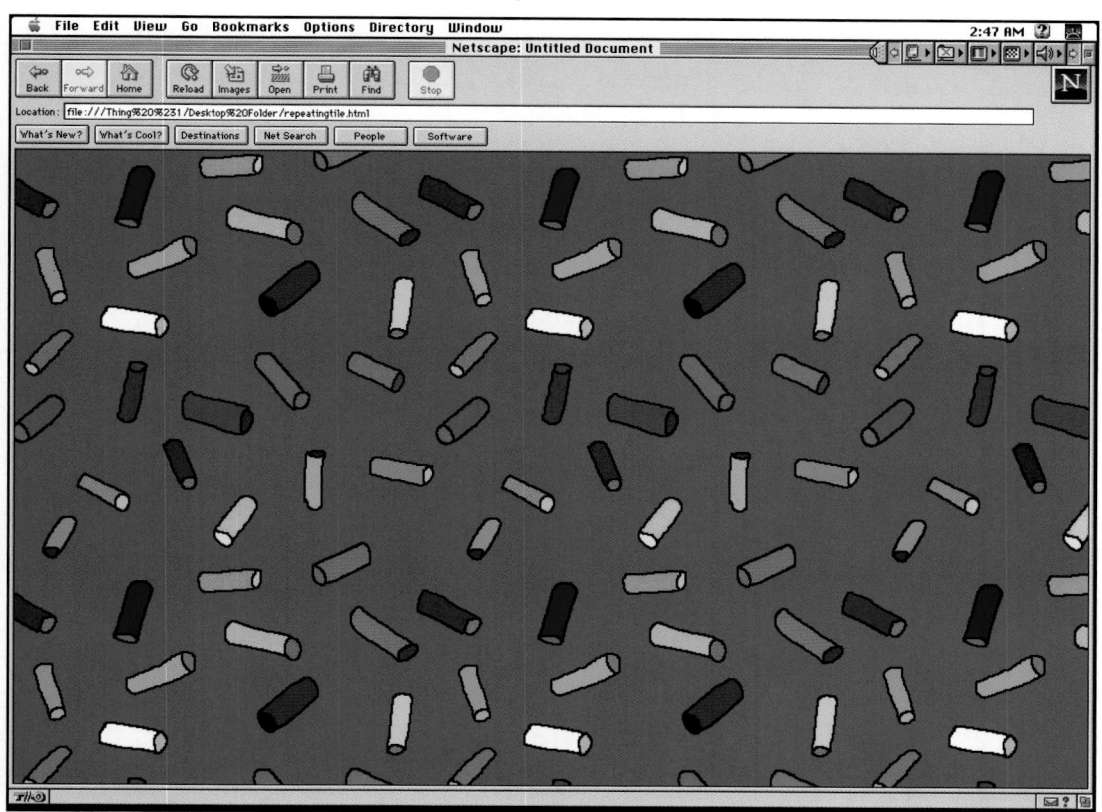

Step 8: Here's an example of the tile in use on a sample Web page. Notice how it's difficult to see any repeats in the artwork? That's the result of creating the artwork using the Offset Filter in Photoshop.

Using a Logo for a Tiled Background

Custom illustrations are great for background tiles, but aren't always appropriate for the job at hand. Many companies like to have their logos repeated as a background image. Here's a simple example of how to use the Photoshop Offset Filter for this task.

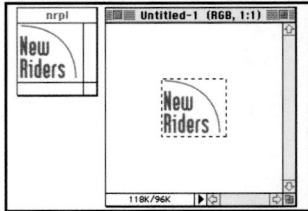

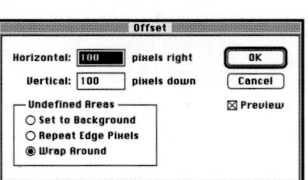

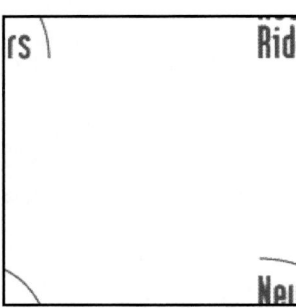

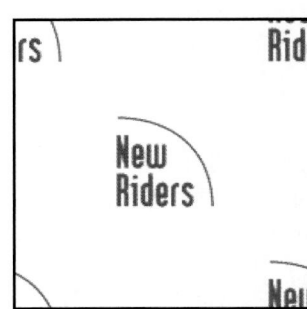

Step 1: In this example, Lynda took the New Riders Publishing logo and copied it into the center of a 200 x 200 pixel, 72 dpi blank Photoshop document.

Step 2: Because she wanted a more uniform alignment than Bruce in his example, she chose to offset the image by half its dimensions (100 x 100).

Step 3: With the Wrap Around feature checked, this offset repositioned the logo into the four corners of the image.

Step 4: She pasted the logo into the center again.

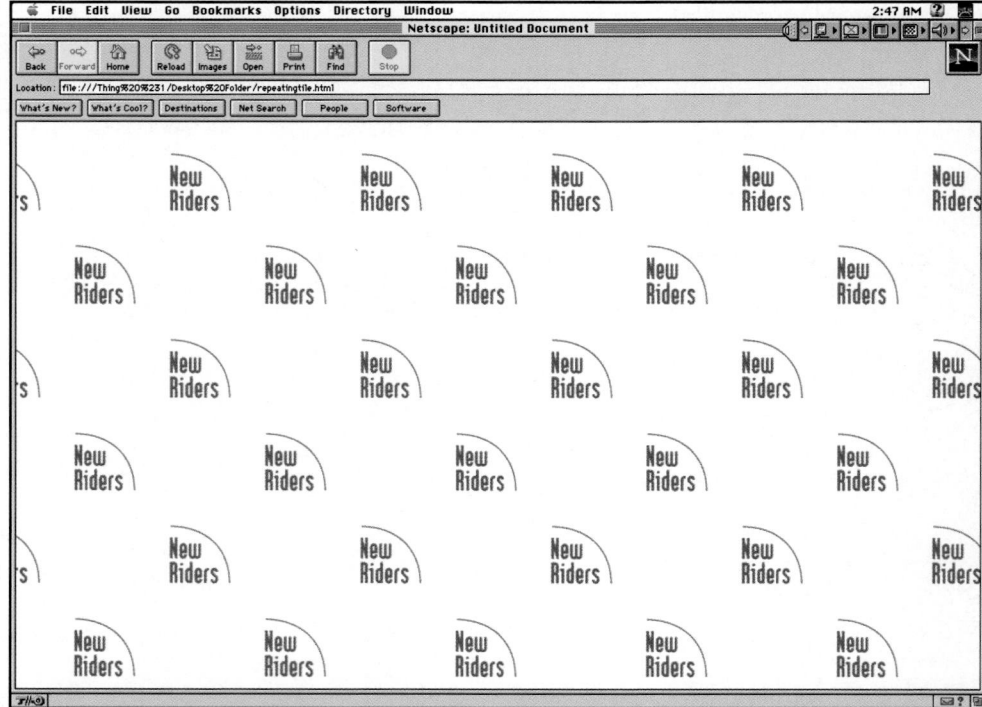

Step 5: Here's the finished example of what this looks like in a browser window.

Previsualizing Web Pages in Photoshop

Most designers would never dream of publishing their work without trying out a few different versions first. We have supplied a template of Don Barnett's Xray.psd file (located in the SWATCH\ODDBALL folder on the *Coloring Web Graphics* CD-ROM) for precisely this purpose. It has the different elements of a Web page separated onto transparent layers that can be filled and changed with ease.

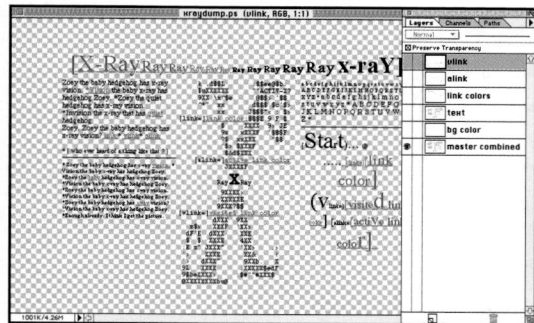

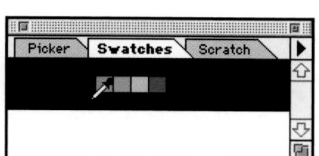

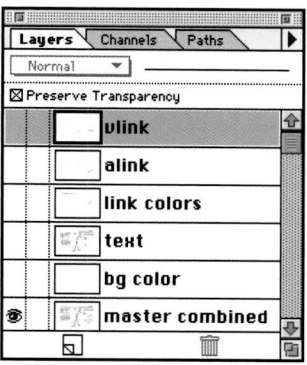

Step 1: Open the Xray.psd file. Try switching different eyes on and off. You'll see how the different elements such as text, links, visited links, active links, and background color are all separated onto distinct layers.

Step 2: Using the Swatches Palette, open a suggested color family file that you like from the CD. Use the Eyedropper and select a color that you wish to fill with.

Step 3: By checking Preserve Transparency, you can fill the parts of the layer that have an image on them, and it masks out the rest. In the case of the vlink layer, it would only fill the text with the color you choose. Without Preserve Transparency checked, you would instead fill the entire image, obliterating your file!

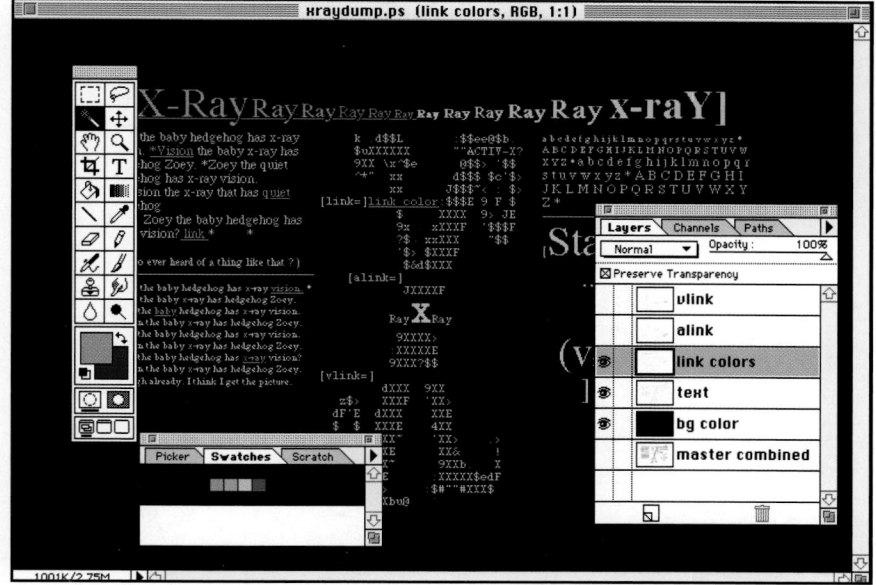

Step 4: You can try out different color combinations to your heart's content. Use Chapter 6, "Color Groupings/Swatches/Directory," or the browser-safe color charts to find the hex conversions to include in your HTML page. Instructions for creating HTML with hex are found in Chapter 2, "Browser-Safe Color."

Color Groupings / Swatches / Directory

How This Chapter Works

This chapter serves as a guide to the electronic files found on the *Coloring Web Graphics* CD-ROM. You (or your clients) can choose colors from the printed charts of suggested color groupings. These suggested groupings can be used exactly as you see them, or as a starting point for your own color explorations. The principle behind this chapter is that the 216 colors can form appealing color schemes when selected from choices that form color relationships.

The cross-platform *Coloring Web Graphics* CD-ROM is organized using three main folders: CLUTS, SWATCHES, and CLIPART. All of the file names on the CD were limited to eight characters or less so that users with older Windows or DOS systems could access the files too.

> REMEMBER: This book was printed in CMYK and the files are all stored electronically in RGB. The two color spaces are very different, and the printed book is not an accurate reference to the colors contained within the electronic files.

You'll find file names printed alongside images in this chapter. You can use the CD-ROM guide on the next pages to locate where files are stored on the CD, or use standard search or find file software to search by the file's name.

THE FOLDER MARKED CLUTS: THE MATERIAL CONTAINED IN THIS FOLDER MAY NOT BE USED IN ANY MANNER WHATSOEVER OTHER THAN TO VIEW THE SAME ON YOUR COMPUTER AND MAY BE USED IN YOUR DESIGN OR OTHER WORK ON YOUR COMPUTER ONLY BUT NOT OTHERWISE. THIS MATERIAL IS SUBJECT TO ALL OF THE RESTRICTION PROVISIONS OF THE ACCOMPANYING SOFTWARE LICENSE. SPECIFICALLY BUT NOT IN LIMITATION OF THESE RESTRICTIONS, YOU MAY NOT DISTRIBUTE OR TRANSFER THIS PART OF THE SOFTWARE DESIGNATED AS "CLUTS" NOR ANY OF YOUR DESIGN OR OTHER WORK CONTAINING ANY OF THE SOFTWARE DESIGNATED AS "CLUTS" NOR ANY OF YOUR DESIGN OR OTHER WORK CONTAINING ANY SUCH "CLUTS," ALL AS MORE PARTICULARLY RESTRICTED IN THE ACCOMPANYING SOFTWARE LICENSE.

THE FOLDER MARKED CLIPART\LICENSOR: THE MATERIAL CONTAINED IN THIS FOLDER MAY BE USED ONLY ON YOUR PERSONAL, NON-COMMERCIAL WEB SITE BUT NOT OTHERWISE. YOU MAY NOT OTHERWISE DISTRIBUTE OR TRANSFER IT.

THE FOLDER MARKED SWATCHES: THE MATERIAL CONTAINED IN THIS FOLDER MAY NOT BE USED IN ANY MANNER WHATSOEVER OTHER THAN TO VIEW THE SAME ON YOUR COMPUTER AND MAY BE USED IN YOUR DESIGN OR OTHER WORK ON YOUR COMPUTER ONLY BUT NOT OTHERWISE. THIS MATERIAL IS SUBJECT TO ALL OF THE RESTRICTION PROVISIONS OF THE ACCOMPANYING SOFTWARE LICENSE. SPECIFICALLY BUT NOT IN LIMITATION OF THESE RESTRICTIONS, YOU MAY NOT DISTRIBUTE OR TRANSFER THIS PART OF THE SOFTWARE DESIGNATED AS "SWATCHES" NOR ANY OF YOUR DESIGN OR OTHER WORK CONTAINING ANY OF THE SOFTWARE DESIGNATED AS "SWATCHES" NOR ANY OF YOUR DESIGN OR OTHER WORK CONTAINING ANY SUCH "SWATCHES," ALL AS MORE PARTICULARLY RESTRICTED IN THE ACCOMPANYING SOFTWARE LICENSE.

THE FOLDER MARKED CLIPART\3RDPARTY: THE MATERIAL CONTAINED IN THIS FOLDER MAY BE USED ONLY IN ACCORDANCE WITH ALL OF THE PROVISIONS OF ANY THIRD PARTY LICENSES CONTAINED IN THIS SOFTWARE AND FOLDER. READ ALL FILES PROVIDED, INCLUDING BUT NOT LIMITED TO "READ ME" FILES FOR SUCH RESTRICTIONS. NOTHING CONTAINED IN THIS LICENSE AGREEMENT SHALL BE DEEMED TO GRANT TO YOU ANY PERMISSION OR RIGHTS OF ANY NATURE WHATSOEVER WITH REGARD TO SUCH MATERIALS CONTROLLED BY THIRD PARTIES.

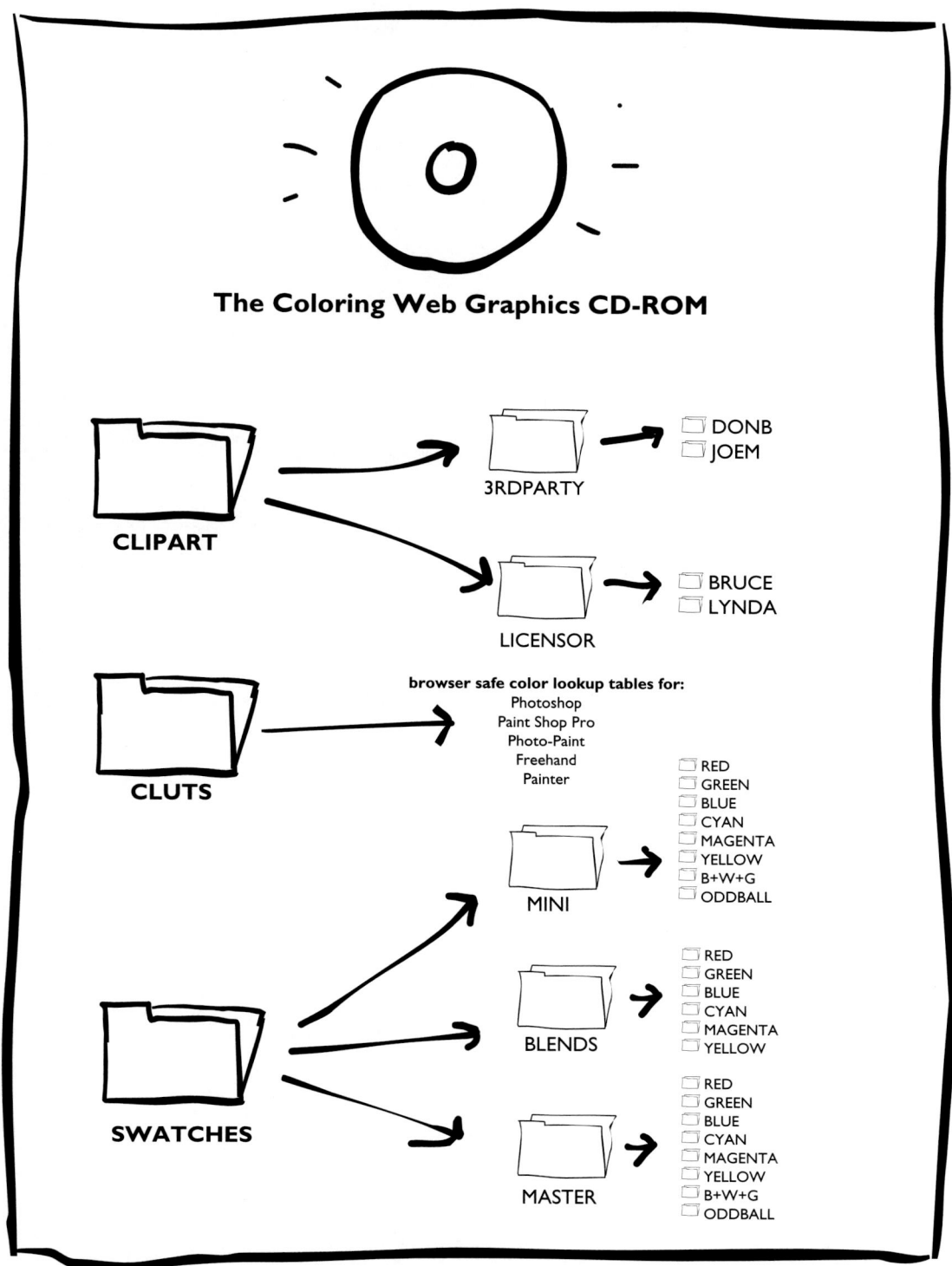

The Coloring Web Graphics CD-ROM

CLIPART

3RDPARTY → DONB / JOEM

LICENSOR → BRUCE / LYNDA

CLUTS → browser safe color lookup tables for:
Photoshop
Paint Shop Pro
Photo-Paint
Freehand
Painter

SWATCHES

MINI → RED / GREEN / BLUE / CYAN / MAGENTA / YELLOW / B+W+G / ODDBALL

BLENDS → RED / GREEN / BLUE / CYAN / MAGENTA / YELLOW

MASTER → RED / GREEN / BLUE / CYAN / MAGENTA / YELLOW / B+W+G / ODDBALL

File Organization

In this chapter, you'll find a directory to the thousands of images contained on the cross-platform compatible *Coloring Web Graphics* CD-ROM. This introduction outlines how the files are organized, and the meanings behind some of the legends and naming conventions.

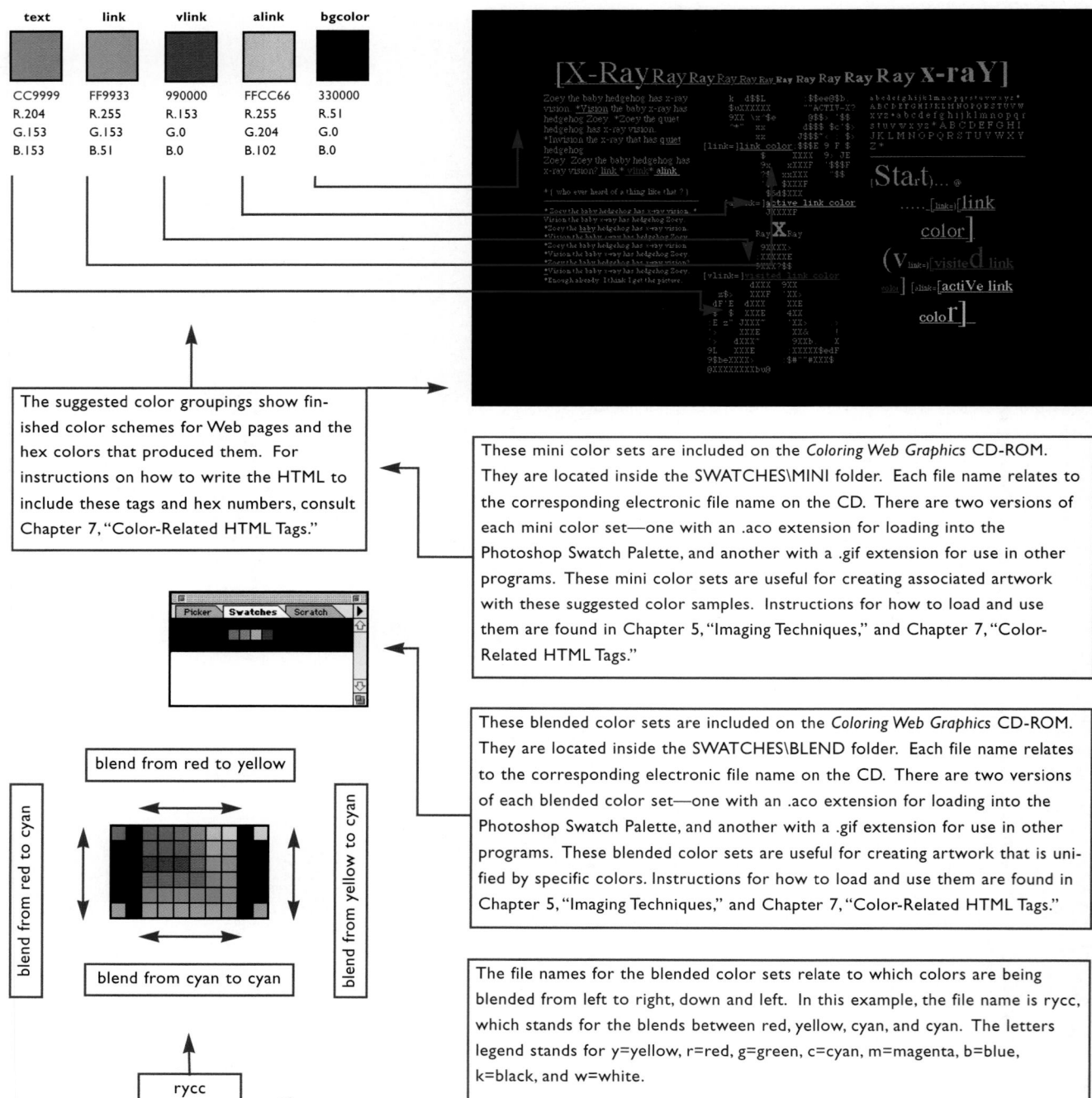

text	link	vlink	alink	bgcolor
CC9999	FF9933	990000	FFCC66	330000
R.204	R.255	R.153	R.255	R.51
G.153	G.153	G.0	G.204	G.0
B.153	B.51	B.0	B.102	B.0

The suggested color groupings show finished color schemes for Web pages and the hex colors that produced them. For instructions on how to write the HTML to include these tags and hex numbers, consult Chapter 7, "Color-Related HTML Tags."

These mini color sets are included on the *Coloring Web Graphics* CD-ROM. They are located inside the SWATCHES\MINI folder. Each file name relates to the corresponding electronic file name on the CD. There are two versions of each mini color set—one with an .aco extension for loading into the Photoshop Swatch Palette, and another with a .gif extension for use in other programs. These mini color sets are useful for creating associated artwork with these suggested color samples. Instructions for how to load and use them are found in Chapter 5, "Imaging Techniques," and Chapter 7, "Color-Related HTML Tags."

These blended color sets are included on the *Coloring Web Graphics* CD-ROM. They are located inside the SWATCHES\BLEND folder. Each file name relates to the corresponding electronic file name on the CD. There are two versions of each blended color set—one with an .aco extension for loading into the Photoshop Swatch Palette, and another with a .gif extension for use in other programs. These blended color sets are useful for creating artwork that is unified by specific colors. Instructions for how to load and use them are found in Chapter 5, "Imaging Techniques," and Chapter 7, "Color-Related HTML Tags."

blend from red to yellow

blend from red to cyan

blend from yellow to cyan

blend from cyan to cyan

rycc

The file names for the blended color sets relate to which colors are being blended from left to right, down and left. In this example, the file name is rycc, which stands for the blends between red, yellow, cyan, and cyan. The letters legend stands for y=yellow, r=red, g=green, c=cyan, m=magenta, b=blue, k=black, and w=white.

The Master Color Palettes are located inside the SWATCHES\MASTER folder on the *Coloring Web Graphics* CD-ROM. Each file name relates to the corresponding electronic file name on the CD. There are two versions of each master color set—one with an .aco extension for loading into the Photoshop Swatch Palette, and another with a .gif extension for use in other programs. These master color palettes are useful for working with colors organized by all the possible variations of a master color in relationship to the other colors. Instructions for how to load and use these swatch-based color families are found in Chapter 5, "Imaging Techniques," and Chapter 7, "Color-Related HTML Tags."

At the front of each of the sections in this chapter, you'll find master color palettes for each color. This example is the master palette for the color red. You can tell the palette's master color by the nine squares in the upper left corner.

bruce10.gif

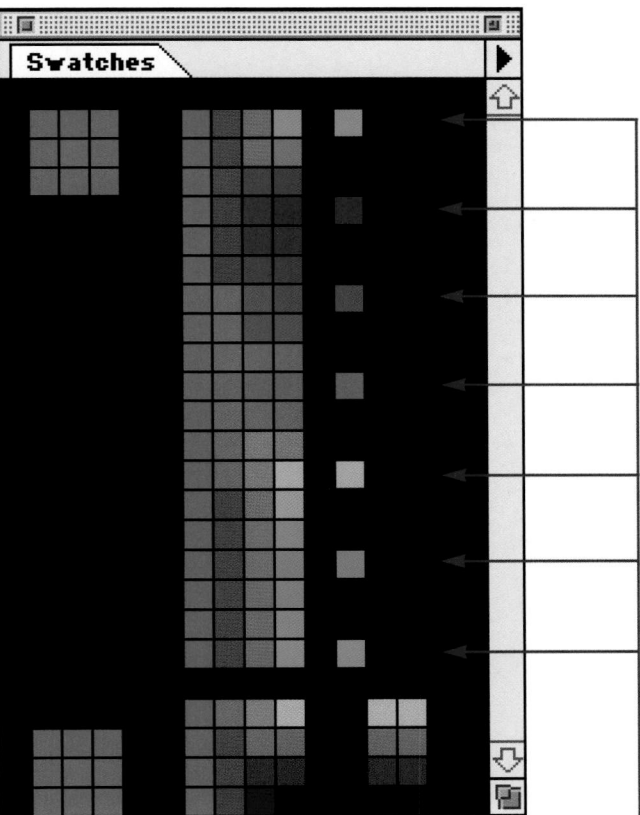

The CLIPART section of the CD-ROM contains artwork organized by artist. This file, for example would be found inside the CLIPART\LICENSOR\BRUCE folder.

The color square at the ends represents the key primary and secondary colors of the 216-color spectrum, which are: cyan, blue, magenta, red, yellow, and green. The master color palette shows all the blended steps from its color (in this example, red) to all the other colors. This can offer an extremely useful organization for artwork that is custom-tailored for the color red.

RED

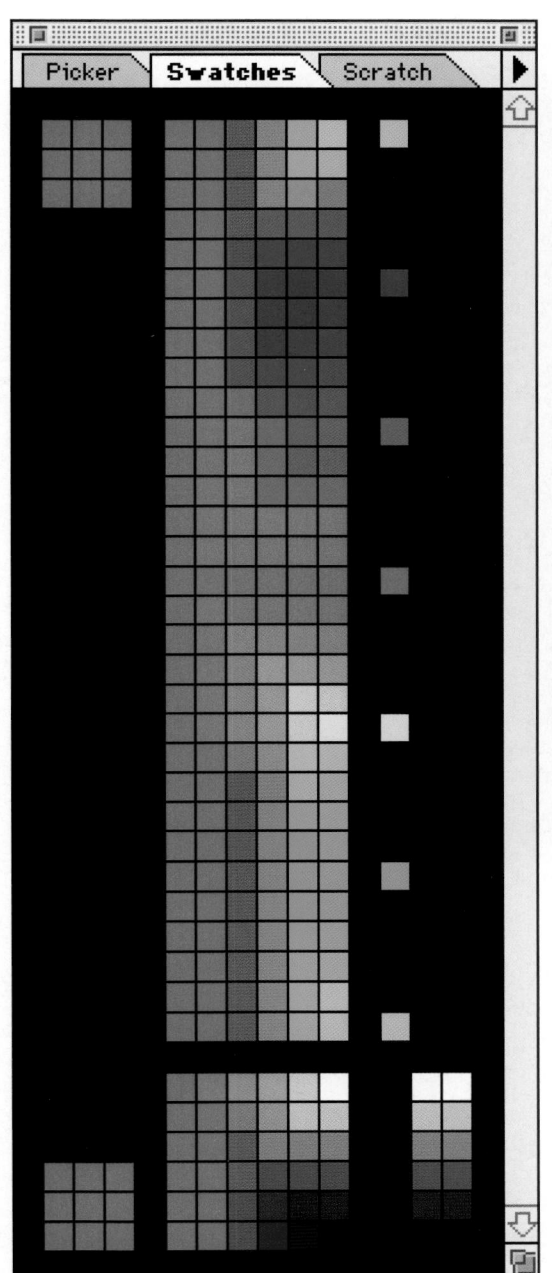

mrs

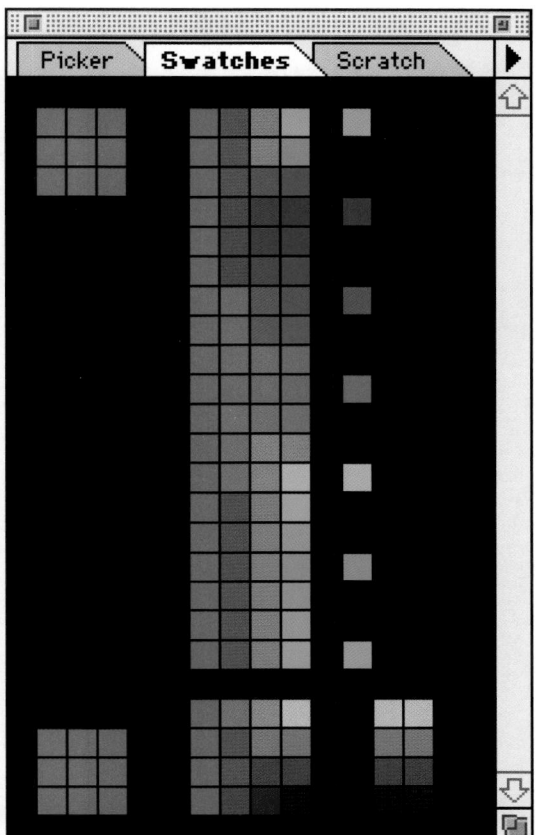

mrd

text
660033
R. 10
G. 0
B. 51

link
FF0066
R. 255
G. 0
B. 102

vlink
CC9999
R. 204
G. 153
B. 153

alink
FF0000
R. 255
G. 0
B. 0

bgcolor
FFCCCC
R. 255
G. 204
B. 204

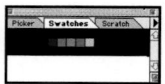

rs01sw

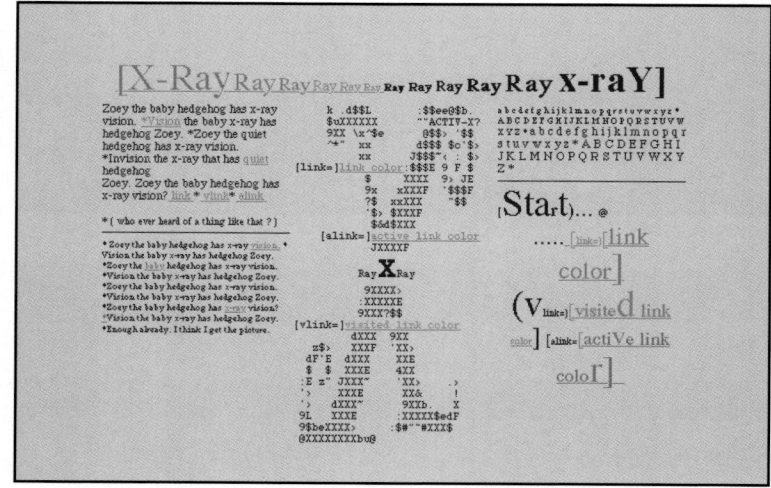

---

text
663300
R. 102
G. 51
B. 0

link
FF0000
R. 255
G. 0
B. 0

vlink
996666
R. 153
G. 102
B. 102

alink
FF9900
R. 255
G. 153
B. 0

tile colors
FFCCCC
R. 255
G. 204
B. 204

FFCC99
R. 255
G. 204
B. 153

rp01sw

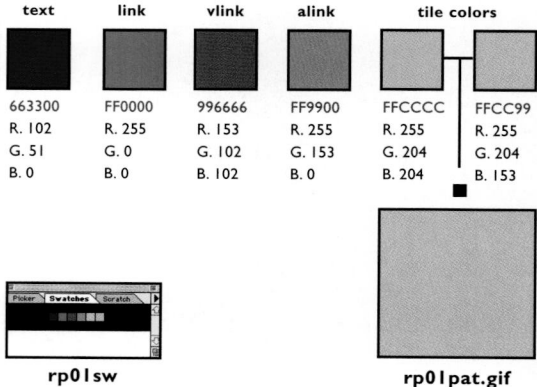

rp01pat.gif

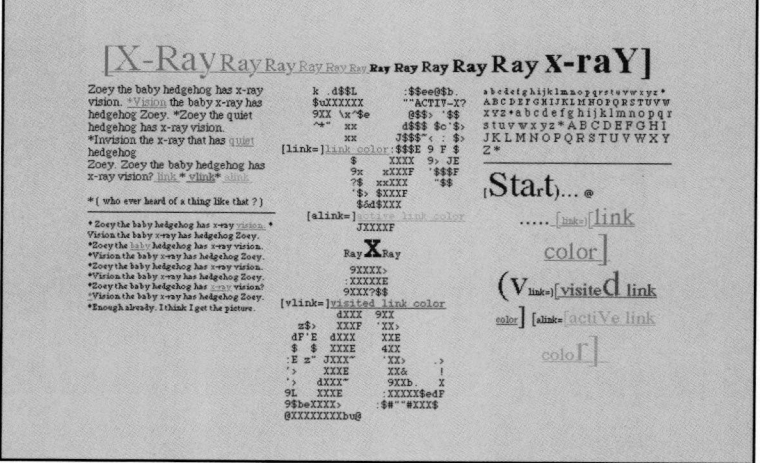

---

text
660000
R. 102
G. 0
B. 0

link
FF3300
R. 255
G. 51
B. 0

vlink
FF6666
R. 255
G. 102
B. 102

alink
FFFFFF
R. 255
G. 255
B. 255

hybrid colors
FFCCCC
R. 255
G. 204
B. 204

FFCC99
R. 255
G. 204
B. 153

rh01sw

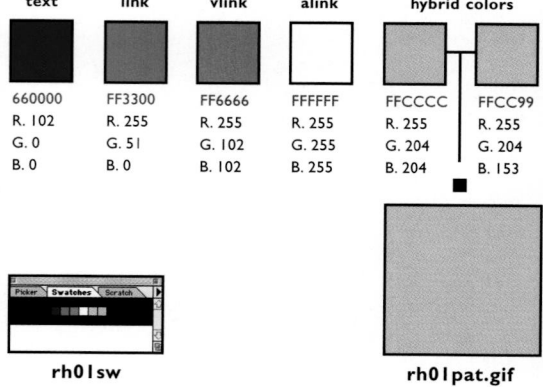

rh01pat.gif

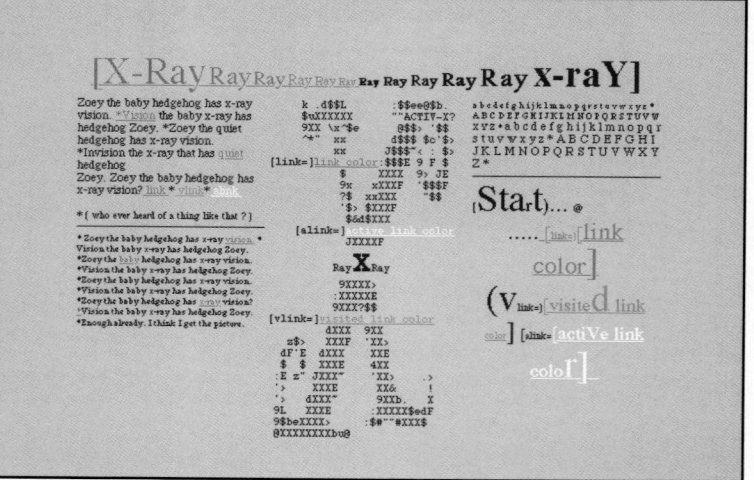

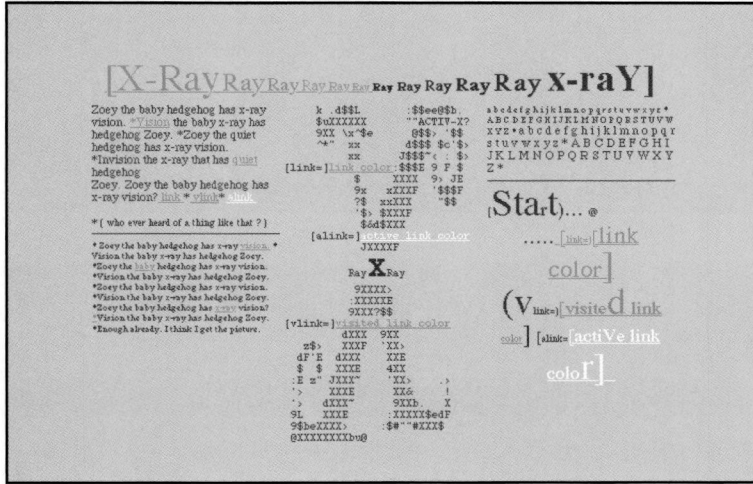
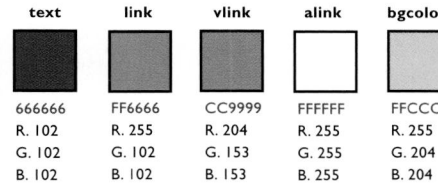
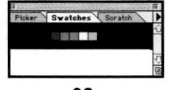

rs02sw

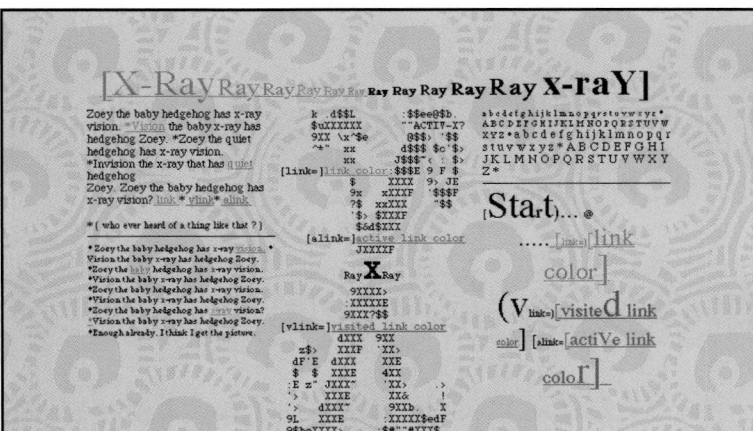
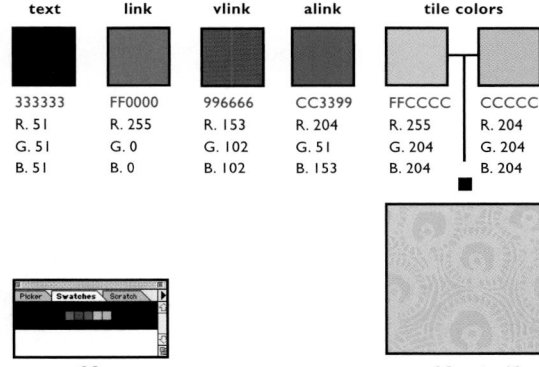

rp02sw

rp02pat.gif

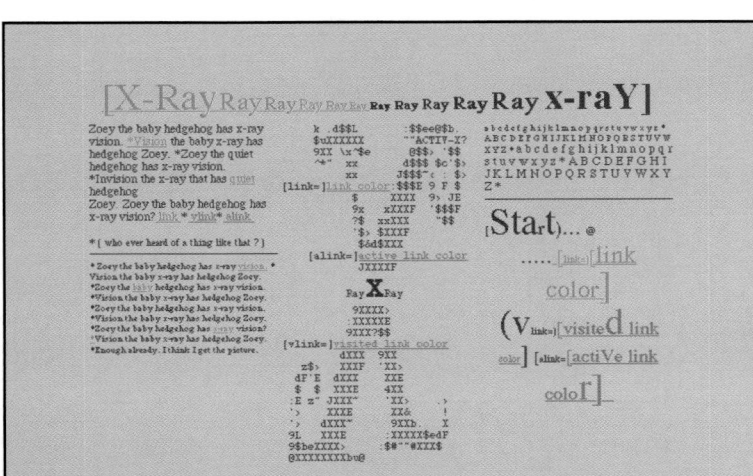
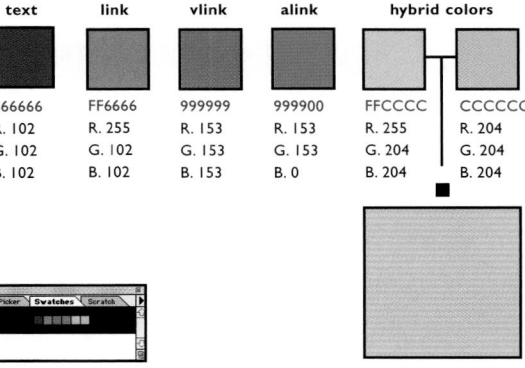

rh02sw

rh02pat.gif

web graphics>

text	link	vlink	alink	bgcolor
330033	CC0033	663366	FF3333	FF6666
R. 51	R. 204	R. 102	R. 255	R. 255
G. 0	G. 0	G. 51	G. 51	G. 102
B. 51	B. 51	B. 102	B. 51	B. 102

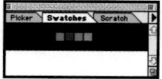

rs03sw

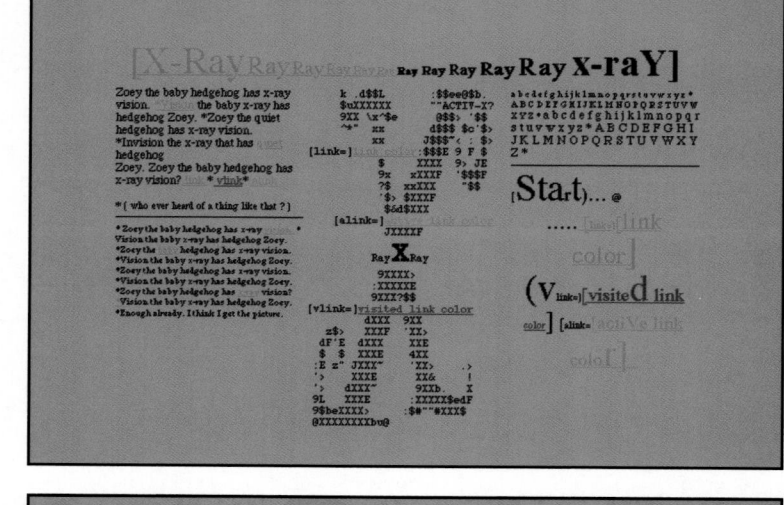

text	link	vlink	alink	tile colors	
330000	CC0033	FF9966	CCCC33	FF6666	FF6633
R. 51	R. 204	R. 255	R. 204	R. 255	R. 255
G. 0	G. 0	G. 153	G. 204	G. 102	G. 102
B. 0	B. 51	B. 102	B. 51	B. 102	B. 51

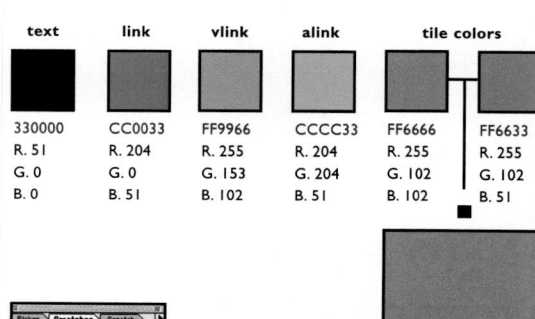

rp03sw

rp03pat.gif

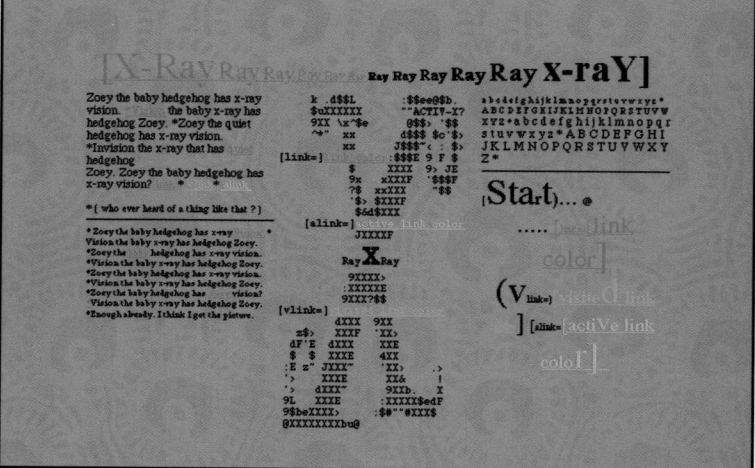

text	link	vlink	alink	hybrid colors	
333333	FF0000	CC9999	FF9900	FF6666	FF6633
R. 51	R. 255	R. 204	R. 255	R. 255	R. 255
G. 51	G. 0	G. 153	G. 153	G. 102	G. 102
B. 51	B. 0	B. 153	B. 0	B. 102	B. 51

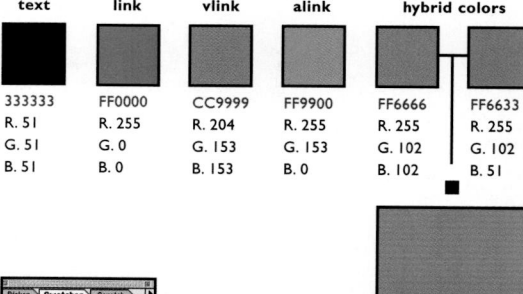

rh03sw

rh03pat.gif

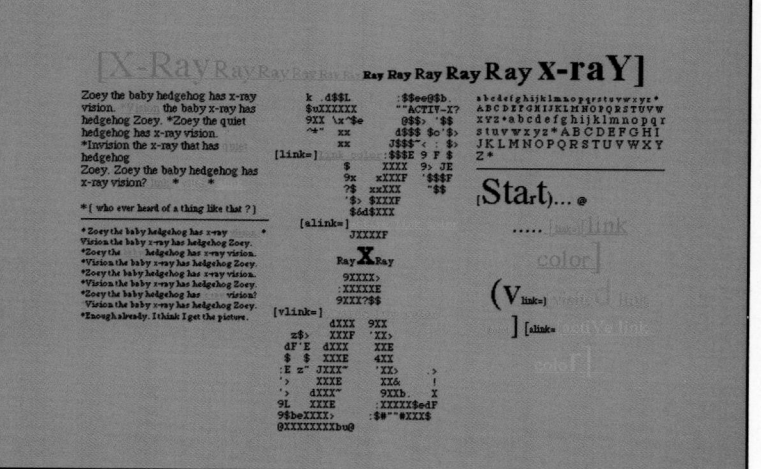

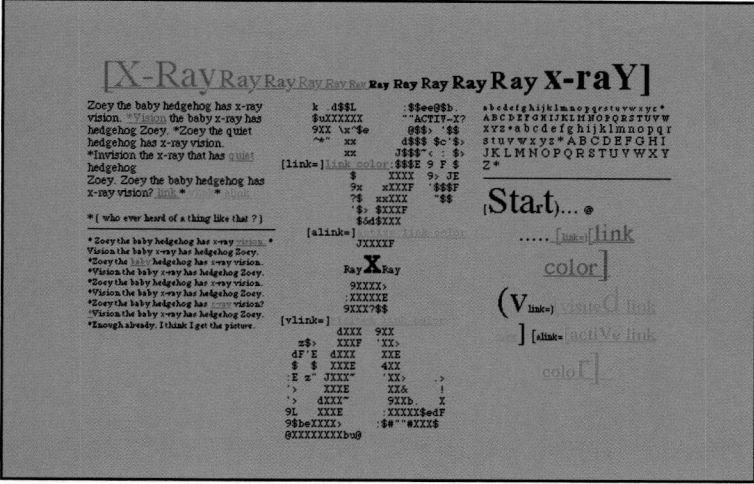

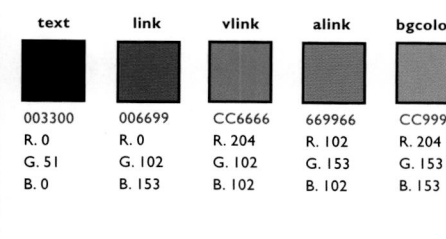

text	link	vlink	alink	bgcolor
003300	006699	CC6666	669966	CC9999
R. 0	R. 0	R. 204	R. 102	R. 204
G. 51	G. 102	G. 102	G. 153	G. 153
B. 0	B. 153	B. 102	B. 102	B. 153

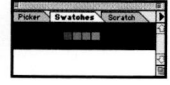

rs04sw

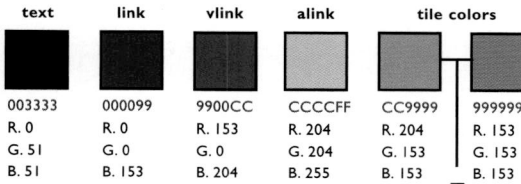

text	link	vlink	alink	tile colors	
003333	000099	9900CC	CCCCFF	CC9999	999999
R. 0	R. 0	R. 153	R. 204	R. 204	R. 153
G. 51	G. 0	G. 0	G. 204	G. 153	G. 153
B. 51	B. 153	B. 204	B. 255	B. 153	B. 153

rp04sw

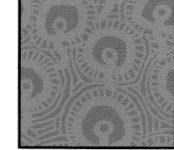

rp04pat.gif

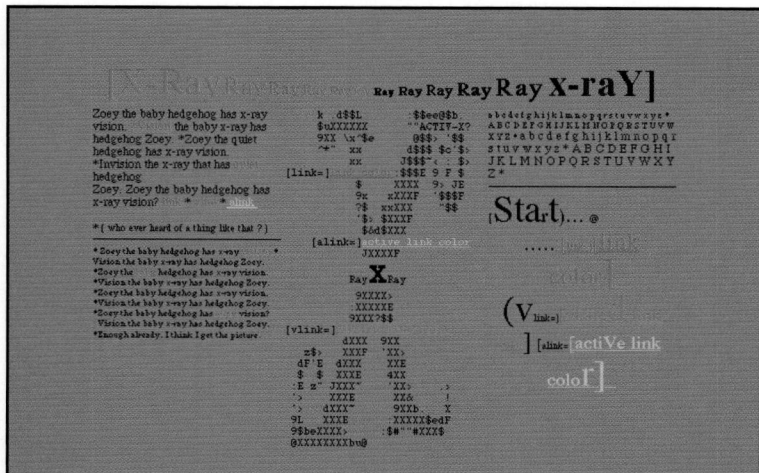

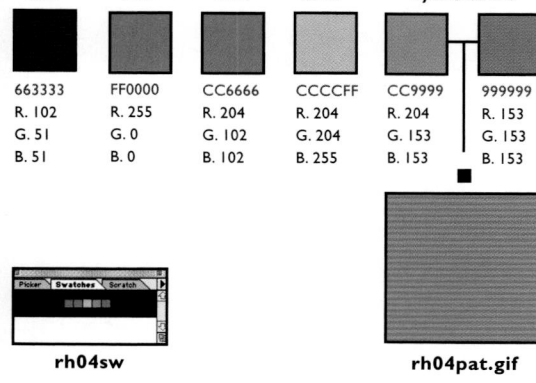

text	link	vlink	alink	hybrid colors	
663333	FF0000	CC6666	CCCCFF	CC9999	999999
R. 102	R. 255	R. 204	R. 204	R. 204	R. 153
G. 51	G. 0	G. 102	G. 204	G. 153	G. 153
B. 51	B. 0	B. 102	B. 255	B. 153	B. 153

rh04sw

rh04pat.gif

text	link	vlink	alink	bgcolor
FFFFCC	66FF66	669966	00FF00	FF3333
R. 255	R. 102	R. 102	R. 0	R. 255
G. 255	G. 255	G. 153	G. 255	G. 51
B. 204	B. 102	B. 102	B. 0	B. 51

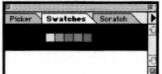

rs05sw

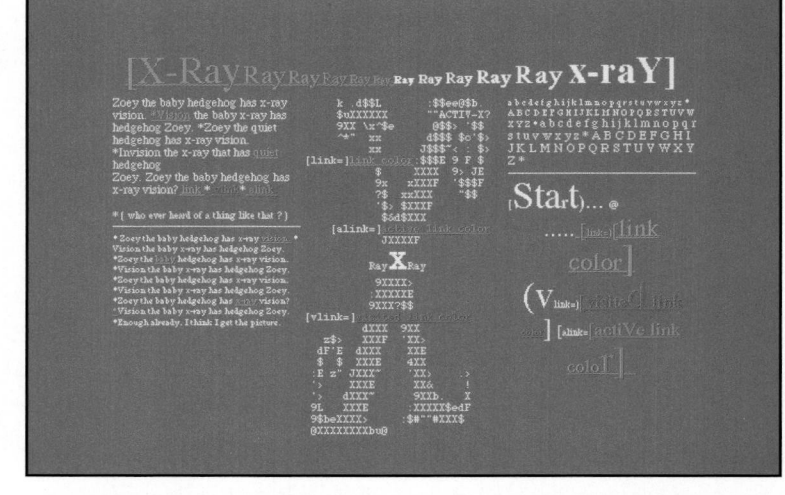

text	link	vlink	alink	tile colors	
FFFFCC	FFFF33	CCCC99	990000	FF3333	CC3333
R. 255	R. 255	R. 204	R. 153	R. 255	R. 204
G. 255	G. 255	G. 204	G. 0	G. 51	G. 51
B. 205	B. 51	B. 153	B. 0	B. 51	B. 51

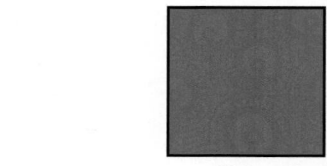

rp05sw

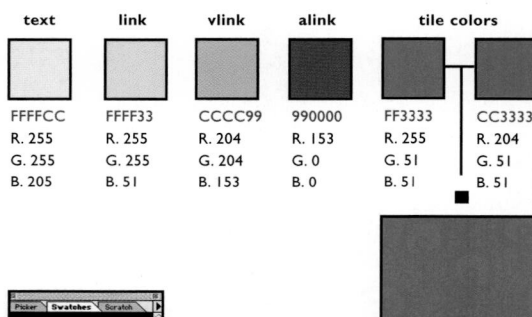

rp05pat.gif

text	link	vlink	alink	hybrid colors	
FFFF99	FFFFFF	CC9999	990000	FF3333	CC3333
R. 255	R. 255	R. 204	R. 153	R. 255	R. 204
G. 255	G. 255	G. 153	G. 0	G. 51	G. 51
B. 153	B. 255	B. 153	B. 0	B. 51	B. 51

rh05sw

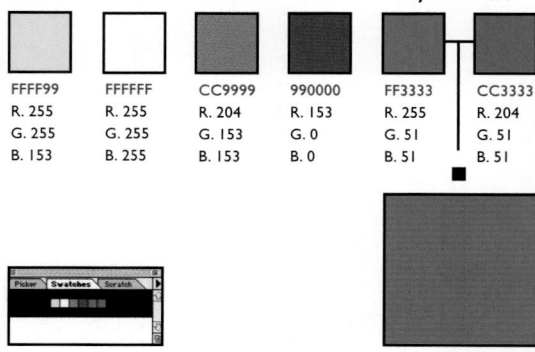

rh05pat.gif

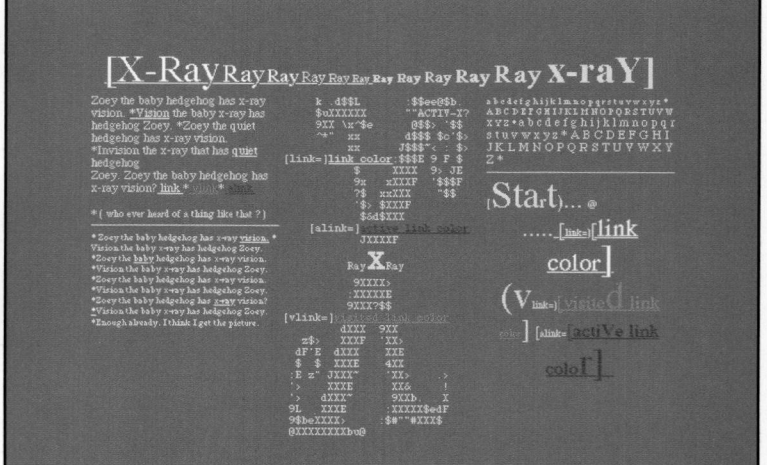

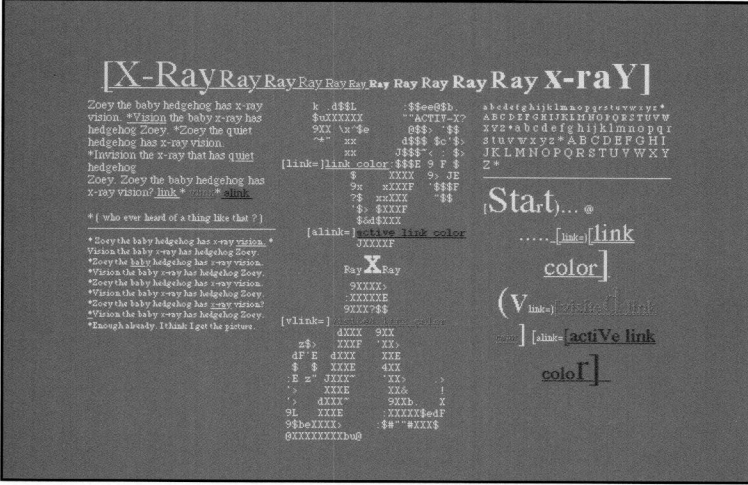

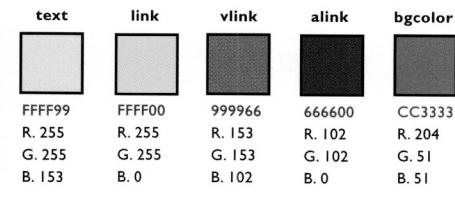

text	link	vlink	alink	bgcolor
FFFF99	FFFF00	999966	666600	CC3333
R. 255	R. 255	R. 153	R. 102	R. 204
G. 255	G. 255	G. 153	G. 102	G. 51
B. 153	B. 0	B. 102	B. 0	B. 51

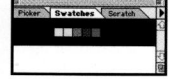

rs06sw

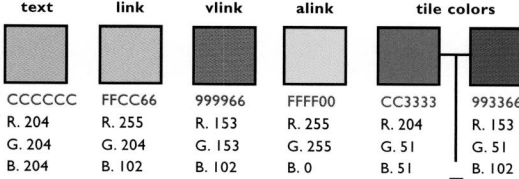

text	link	vlink	alink	tile colors	
CCCCCC	FFCC66	999966	FFFF00	CC3333	993366
R. 204	R. 255	R. 153	R. 255	R. 204	R. 153
G. 204	G. 204	G. 153	G. 255	G. 51	G. 51
B. 204	B. 102	B. 102	B. 0	B. 51	B. 102

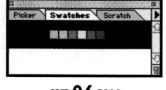

rp06sw

rp06pat.gif

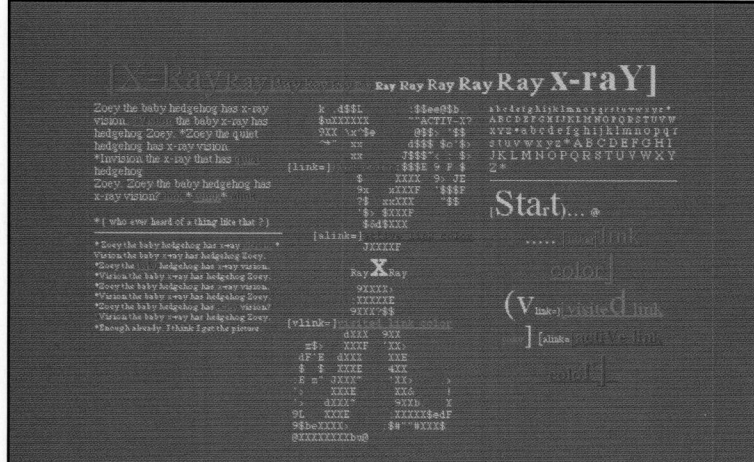

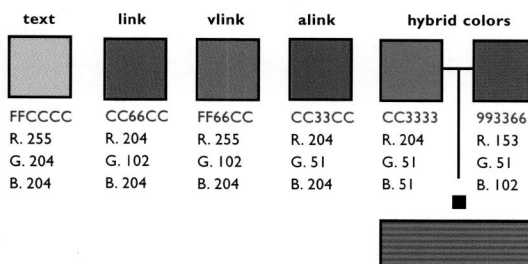

text	link	vlink	alink	hybrid colors	
FFCCCC	CC66CC	FF66CC	CC33CC	CC3333	993366
R. 255	R. 204	R. 255	R. 204	R. 204	R. 153
G. 204	G. 102	G. 102	G. 51	G. 51	G. 51
B. 204	B. 204	B. 204	B. 204	B. 51	B. 102

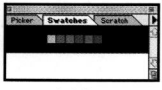

rh06sw

rh06pat.gif

text	link	vlink	alink	bgcolor
FFCCCC	FFFFOO	CCCC33	FFFF99	FF0000
R. 255	R. 255	R. 204	R. 255	R. 255
G. 204	G. 255	G. 204	G. 255	G. 0
B. 204	B. 0	B. 51	B. 153	B. 0

rs07sw

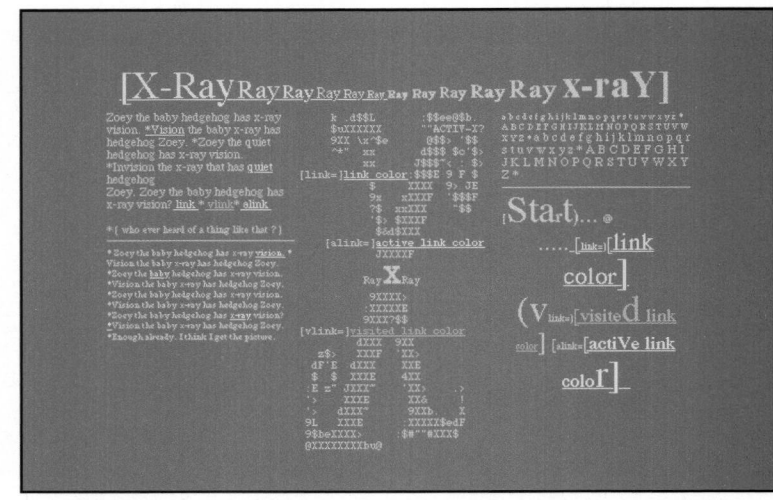

text	link	vlink	alink	tile colors	
CCFF99	00FF00	33CC33	666600	FF0033	CC3333
R. 204	R. 0	R. 51	R. 102	R. 255	R. 255
G. 255	G. 255	G. 255	G. 102	G. 0	G. 51
B. 153	B. 0	B. 512	B. 0	B. 51	B. 51

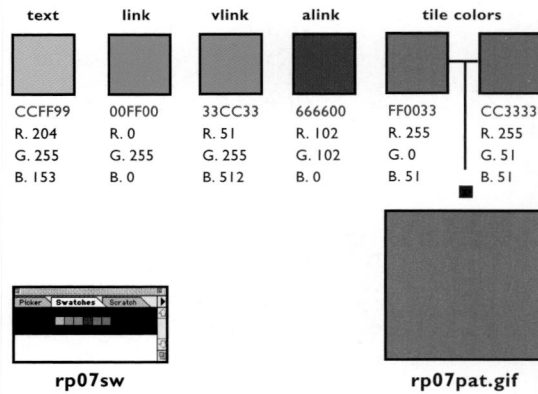

rp07sw   rp07pat.gif

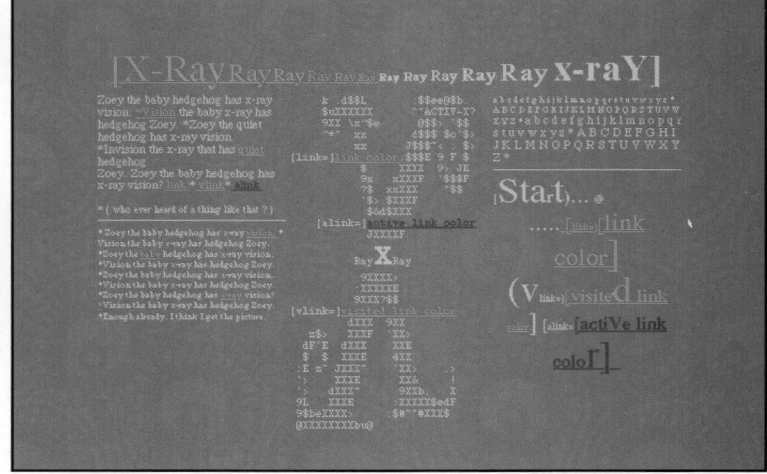

text	link	vlink	alink	hybrid colors	
FFCCCC	FFCC33	CCFFFF	FF9966	FF0000	CC3333
R. 255	R. 255	R. 204	R. 255	R. 255	R. 255
G. 204	G. 204	G. 255	G. 154	G. 0	G. 51
B. 204	B. 51	B. 255	B. 102	B. 0	B. 51

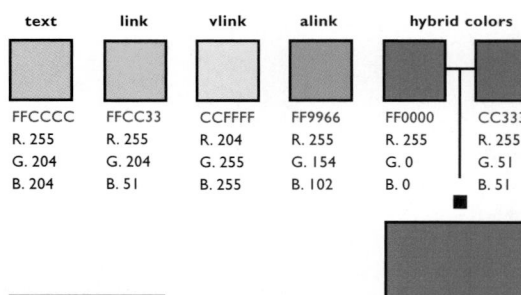

rh07sw   rh07pat.gif

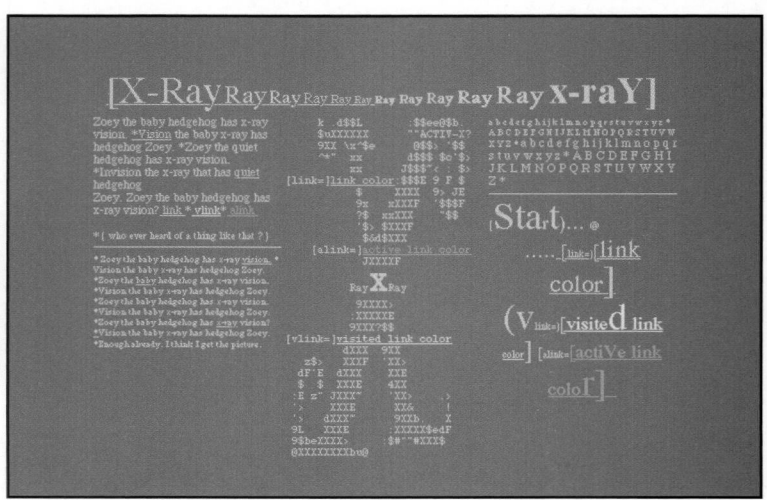

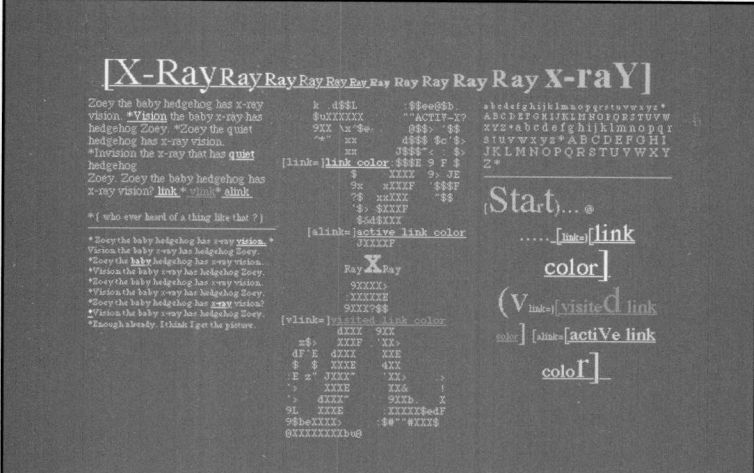
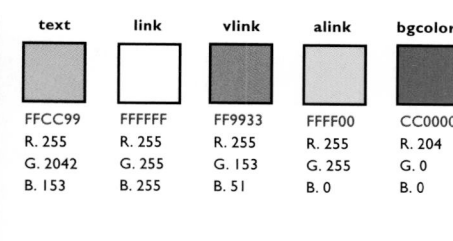
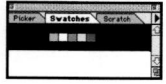

text	link	vlink	alink	bgcolor
FFCC99	FFFFFF	FF9933	FFFF00	CC0000
R. 255	R. 255	R. 255	R. 255	R. 204
G. 2042	G. 255	G. 153	G. 255	G. 0
B. 153	B. 255	B. 51	B. 0	B. 0

rs08sw

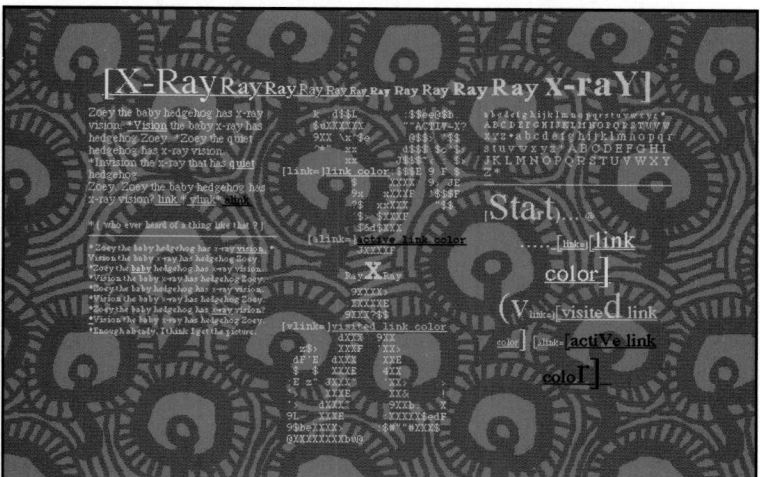
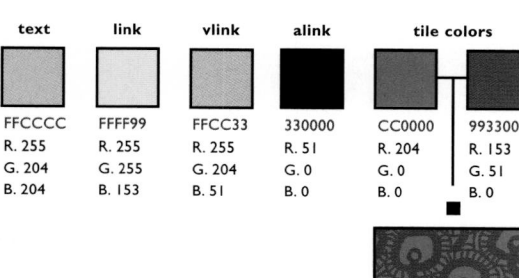

text	link	vlink	alink	tile colors	
FFCCCC	FFFF99	FFCC33	330000	CC0000	993300
R. 255	R. 255	R. 255	R. 51	R. 204	R. 153
G. 204	G. 255	G. 204	G. 0	G. 0	G. 51
B. 204	B. 153	B. 51	B. 0	B. 0	B. 0

rp08sw

rp08pat.gif

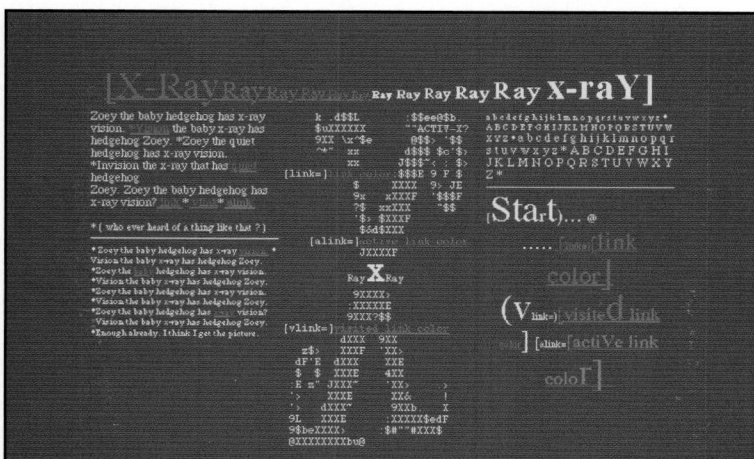
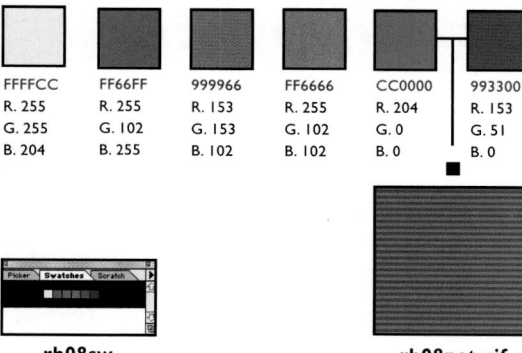

text	link	vlink	alink	hybrid colors	
FFFFCC	FF66FF	999966	FF6666	CC0000	993300
R. 255	R. 255	R. 153	R. 255	R. 204	R. 153
G. 255	G. 102	G. 153	G. 102	G. 0	G. 51
B. 204	B. 255	B. 102	B. 102	B. 0	B. 0

rh08sw

rh08pat.gif

text	link	vlink	alink	bgcolor
FFCCFF	FFFF00	CCCC33	CCCC99	993300
R. 255	R. 255	R. 204	R. 204	R. 153
G. 204	G. 255	G. 204	G. 204	G. 51
B. 255	B. 0	B. 51	B. 153	B. 0

rs09sw

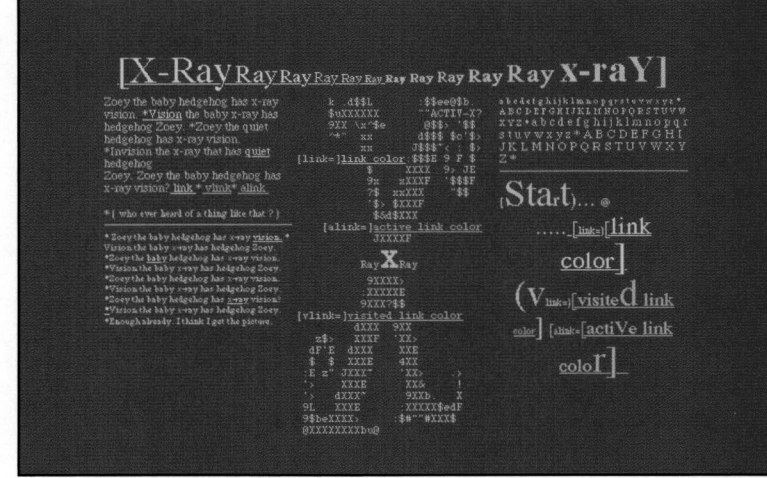

text	link	vlink	alink	tile colors	
CCFFFF	6666FF	9999CC	666666	993300	333333
R. 204	R. 102	R. 153	R. 102	R. 153	R. 51
G. 255	G. 102	G. 153	G. 102	G. 51	G. 51
B. 255	B. 255	B. 204	B. 102	B. 0	B. 51

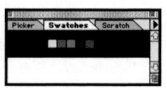

rp09sw

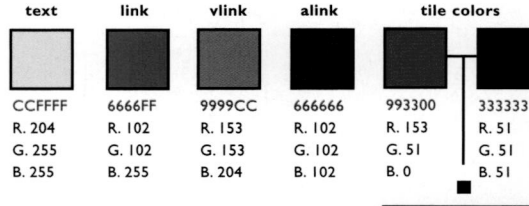

rp09pat.gif

text	link	vlink	alink	hybrid colors	
FFCCFF	CCCC33	CCCC99	999999	993300	333333
R. 255	R. 204	R. 204	R. 153	R. 153	R. 51
G. 204	G. 204	G. 204	G. 153	G. 51	G. 51
B. 255	B. 51	B. 153	B. 153	B. 0	B. 51

rh09sw

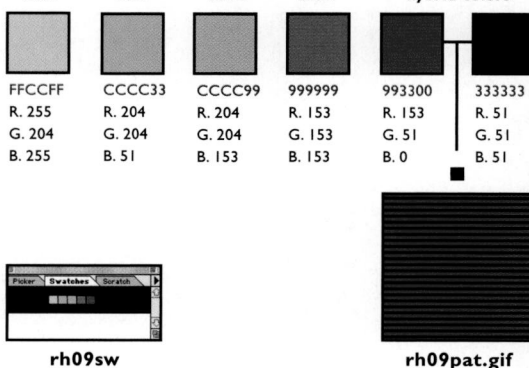

rh09pat.gif

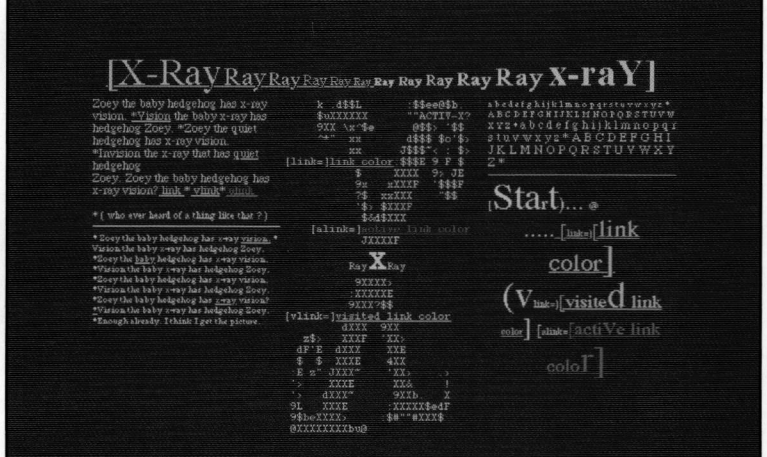

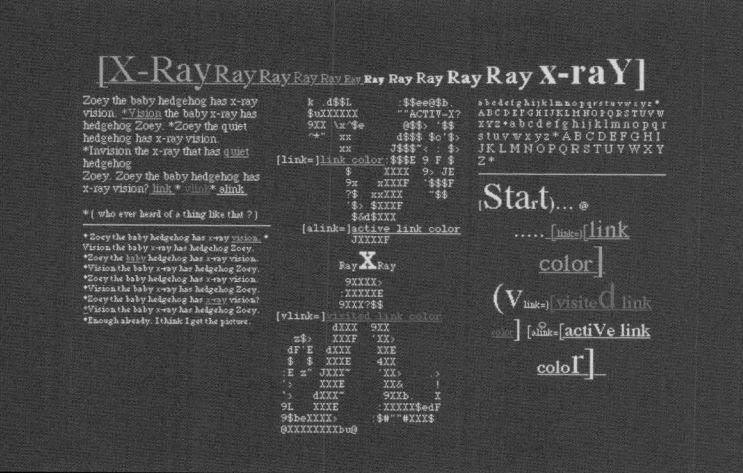

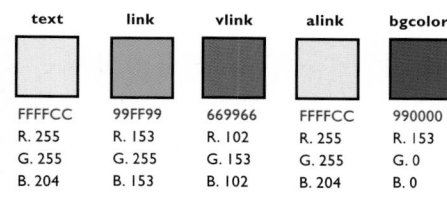

text	link	vlink	alink	bgcolor
FFFFCC	99FF99	669966	FFFFCC	990000
R. 255	R. 153	R. 102	R. 255	R. 153
G. 255	G. 255	G. 153	G. 255	G. 0
B. 204	B. 153	B. 102	B. 204	B. 0

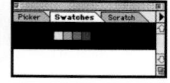

rs10sw

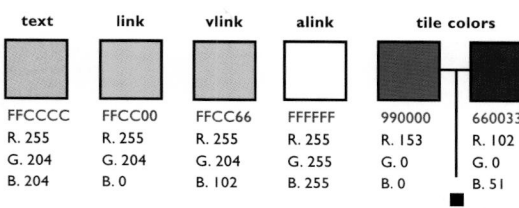

text	link	vlink	alink	tile colors	
FFCCCC	FFCC00	FFCC66	FFFFFF	990000	660033
R. 255	R. 255	R. 255	R. 255	R. 153	R. 102
G. 204	G. 204	G. 204	G. 255	G. 0	G. 0
B. 204	B. 0	B. 102	B. 255	B. 0	B. 51

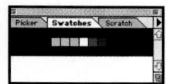

rp10sw

rp10pat.gif

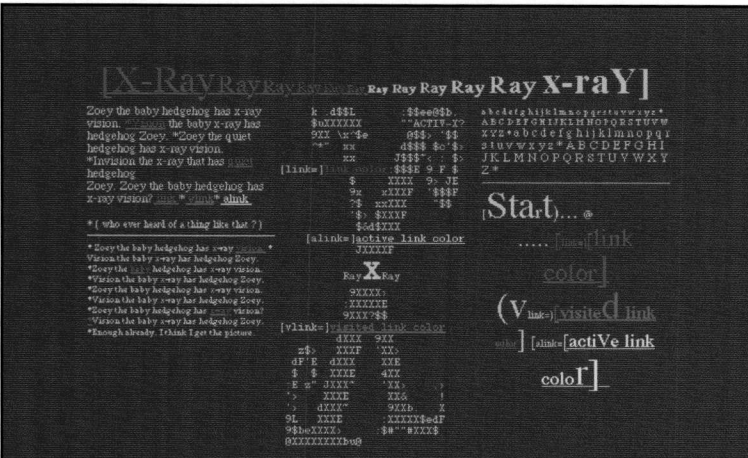

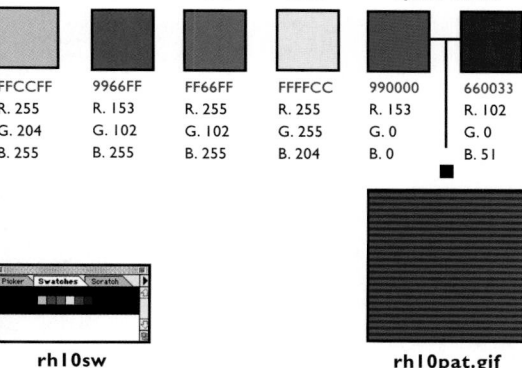

text	link	vlink	alink	hybrid colors	
FFCCFF	9966FF	FF66FF	FFFFCC	990000	660033
R. 255	R. 153	R. 255	R. 255	R. 153	R. 102
G. 204	G. 102	G. 102	G. 255	G. 0	G. 0
B. 255	B. 255	B. 255	B. 204	B. 0	B. 51

rh10sw

rh10pat.gif

text	link	vlink	alink	bgcolor
FFCC99	FF3300	996666	CC6666	660000
R. 255	R. 255	R. 153	R. 204	R. 102
G. 204	G. 51	G. 102	G. 102	G. 0
B. 153	B. 0	B. 102	B. 102	B. 0

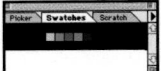

rsl1sw

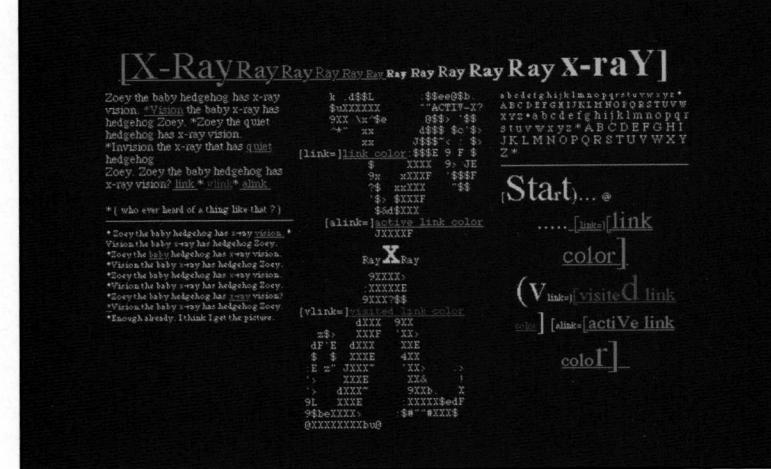

text	link	vlink	alink	tile colors	
CCCC99	66CCFF	CCCC33	CCCCCC	660033	660000
R. 204	R. 102	R. 204	R. 204	R. 102	R. 102
G. 204	G. 204	G. 204	G. 204	G. 0	G. 0
B. 153	B. 255	B. 51	B. 204	B. 51	B. 0

rpl1sw   **rpl1pat.gif**

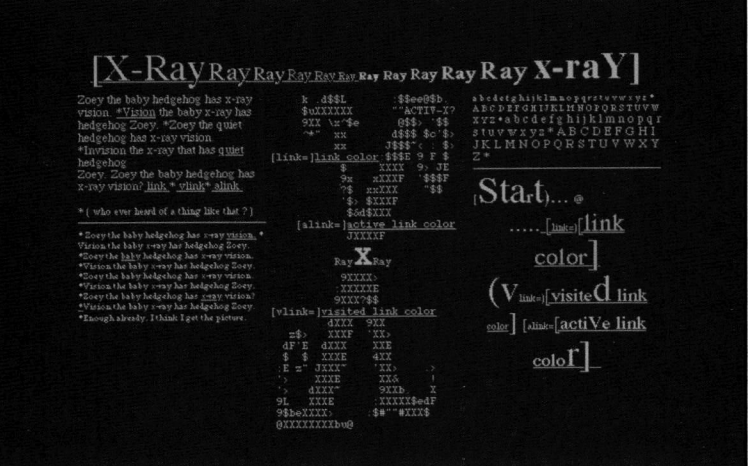

text	link	vlink	alink	hybrid colors	
FF9999	FF3333	996666	CCCCCC	660033	660000
R. 255	R. 255	R. 153	R. 204	R. 102	R. 102
G. 153	G. 51	G. 102	G. 204	G. 0	G. 0
B. 153	B. 51	B. 102	B. 204	B. 51	B. 0

rhl1sw   **rhl1pat.gif**

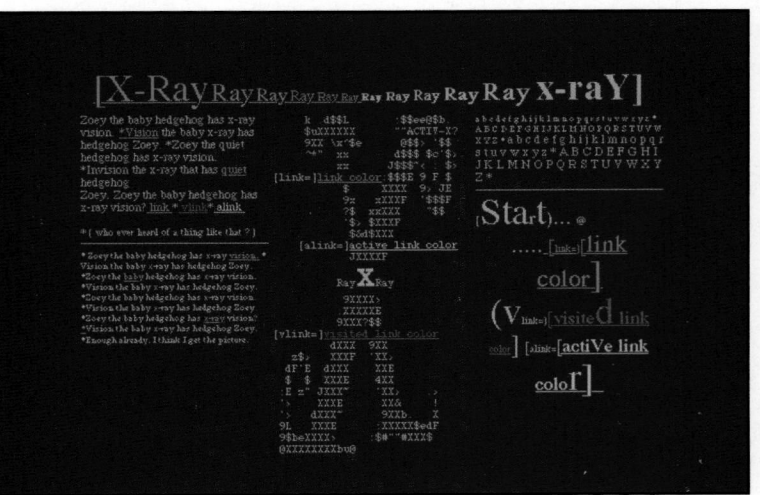

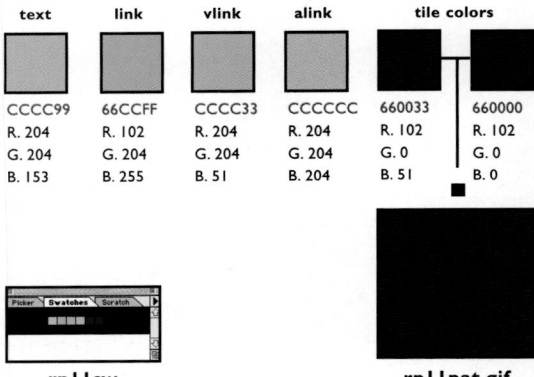

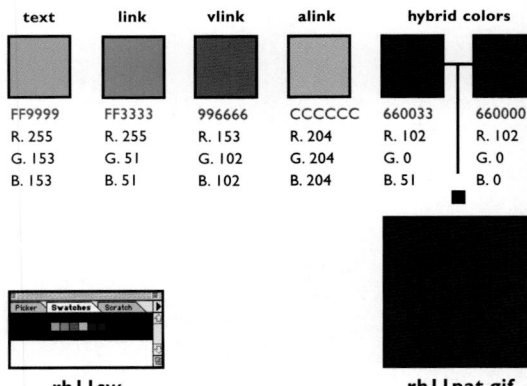

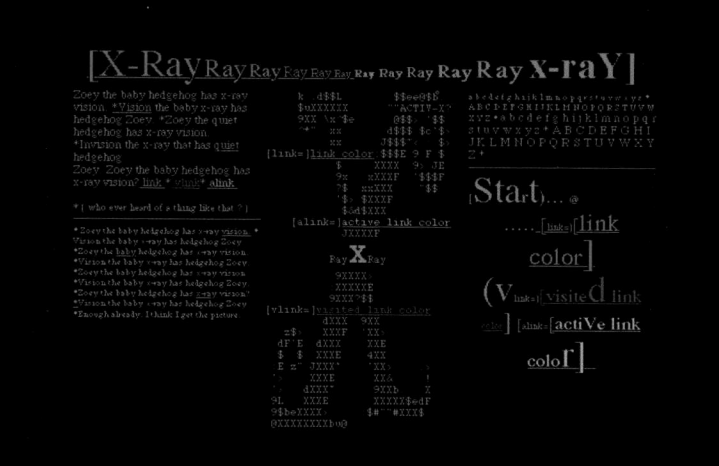

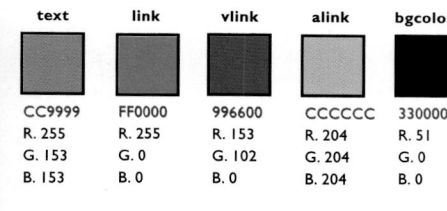

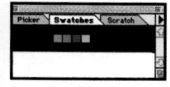

text	link	vlink	alink	bgcolor
CC9999	FF0000	996600	CCCCCC	330000
R. 255	R. 255	R. 153	R. 204	R. 51
G. 153	G. 0	G. 102	G. 204	G. 0
B. 153	B. 0	B. 0	B. 204	B. 0

rs12sw

text	link	vlink	alink	tile colors	
FFCC99	FF9900	CC6633	FF0000	330033	330000
R. 255	R. 255	R. 255	R. 255	R. 102	R. 102
G. 204	G. 153	G. 102	G. 0	G. 0	G. 0
B. 153	B. 0	B. 51	B. 0	B. 102	B. 0

rp12sw

rp12pat.gif

text	link	vlink	alink	hybrid colors	
FFCCCC	FF0000	666633	FF6666	330033	330000
R. 255	R. 255	R. 102	R. 255	R. 51	R. 51
G. 204	G. 0	G. 102	G. 102	G. 0	G. 0
B. 204	B. 0	B. 51	B. 102	B. 51	B. 0

rh02sw

rh02pat.gif

text	link	vlink	alink	bgcolor
FFCCCC	FFFF66	FFCC99	CCCCCC	663333
R. 255	R. 255	R. 255	R. 204	R. 102
G. 204	G. 255	G. 204	G. 204	G. 51
B. 204	B. 102	B. 153	B. 204	B. 51

rs13sw

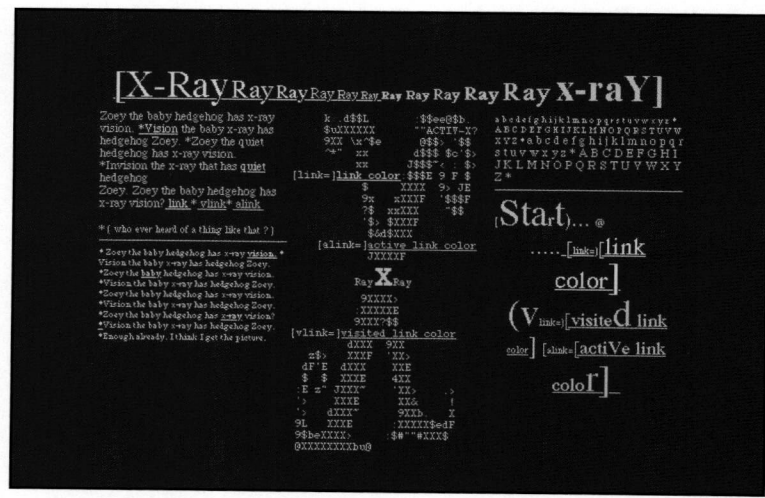

text	link	vlink	alink	tile colors	
FFCC99	FFFF66	999966	FFFF00	333300	663333
R. 255	R. 255	R. 153	R. 255	R. 51	R. 102
G. 204	G. 255	G. 153	G. 255	G. 51	G. 51
B. 153	B. 102	B. 102	B. 0	B. 0	B. 51

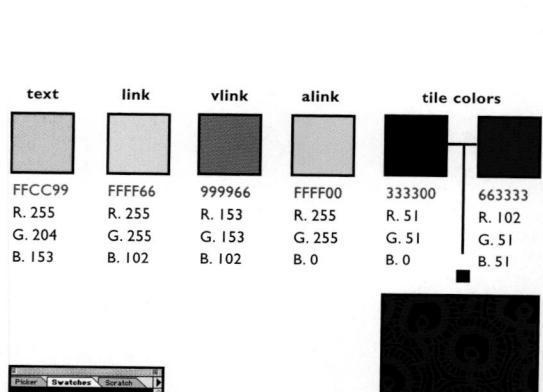

rp13sw

rp13pat.gif

text	link	vlink	alink	hybrid colors	
FFCC99	CCCC33	999966	FFFF99	333300	663333
R. 255	R. 204	R. 153	R. 255	R. 51	R. 102
G. 204	G. 204	G. 153	G. 255	G. 51	G. 51
B. 153	B. 51	B. 102	B. 153	B. 0	B. 51

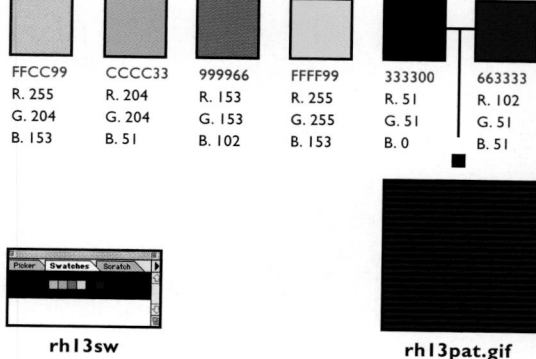

rh13sw

rh13pat.gif

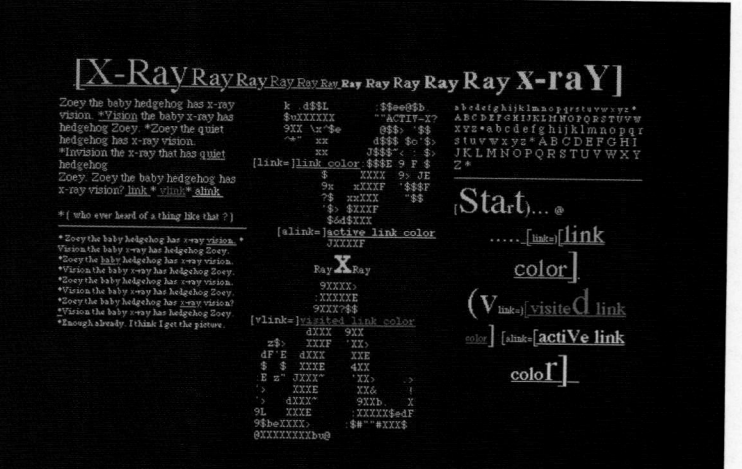

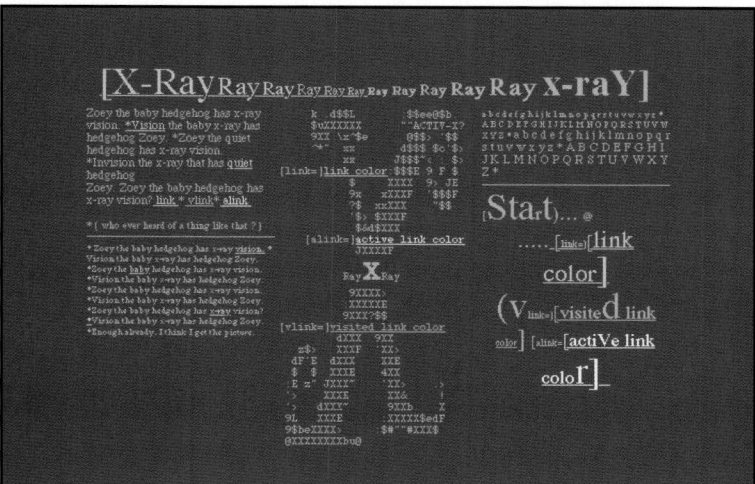

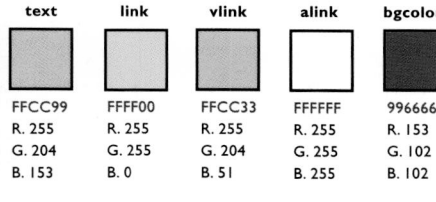

text	link	vlink	alink	bgcolor
FFCC99	FFFF00	FFCC33	FFFFFF	996666
R. 255	R. 255	R. 255	R. 255	R. 153
G. 204	G. 255	G. 204	G. 255	G. 102
B. 153	B. 0	B. 51	B. 255	B. 102

rs14sw

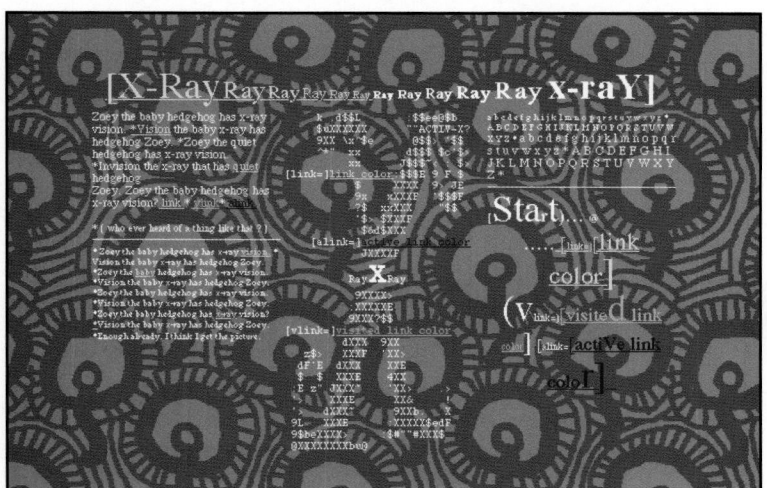

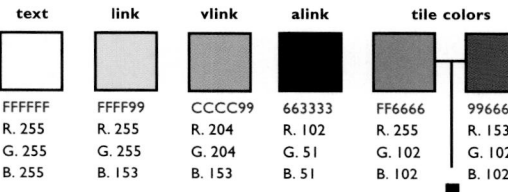

text	link	vlink	alink	tile colors	
FFFFFF	FFFF99	CCCC99	663333	FF6666	996666
R. 255	R. 255	R. 204	R. 102	R. 255	R. 153
G. 255	G. 255	G. 204	G. 51	G. 102	G. 102
B. 255	B. 153	B. 153	B. 51	B. 102	B. 102

rp14sw

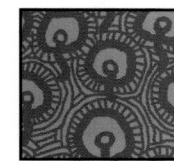

rp14pat.gif

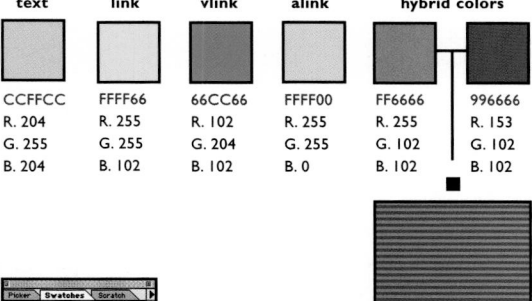

text	link	vlink	alink	hybrid colors	
CCFFCC	FFFF66	66CC66	FFFF00	FF6666	996666
R. 204	R. 255	R. 102	R. 255	R. 255	R. 153
G. 255	G. 255	G. 204	G. 255	G. 102	G. 102
B. 204	B. 102	B. 102	B. 0	B. 102	B. 102

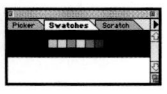

rh14sw

rh14pat.gif

text	link	vlink	alink	bgcolor
660000	FF0000	663333	FF6666	CC9999
R. 102	R. 255	R. 102	R. 255	R. 204
G. 0	G. 0	G. 51	G. 102	G. 153
B. 0	B. 0	B. 51	B. 102	B. 153

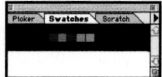

rs15sw

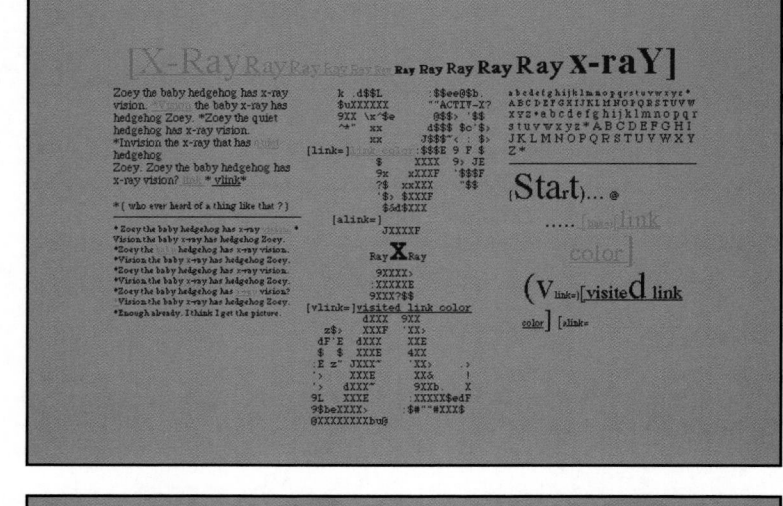

text	link	vlink	alink	tile colors	
663333	993300	666633	333333	CC9999	CC9966
R. 102	R. 153	R. 102	R. 51	R. 204	R. 204
G. 51	G. 51	G. 102	G. 51	G. 153	G. 153
B. 51	B. 0	B. 51	B. 51	B. 153	B. 102

rp15sw

rp15pat.gif

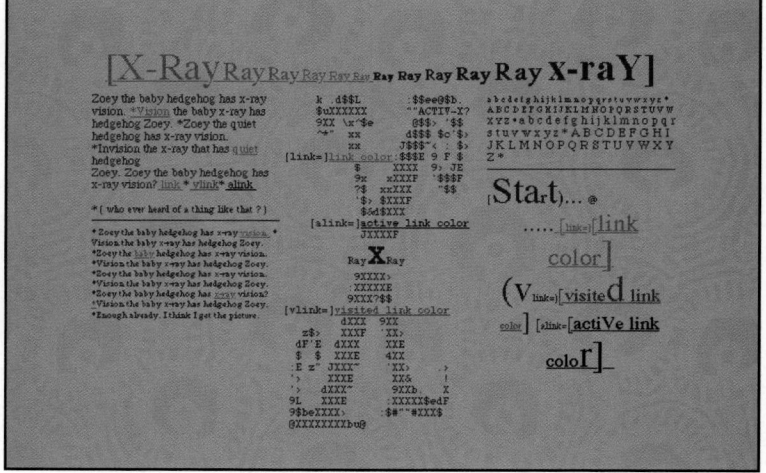

text	link	vlink	alink	hybrid colors	
663333	FFFF99	CCCCCC	FFFF00	CC9999	CC9966
R. 102	R. 255	R. 204	R. 255	R. 204	R. 204
G. 51	G. 255	G. 204	G. 255	G. 153	G. 153
B. 51	B. 153	B. 204	B. 0	B. 153	B. 102

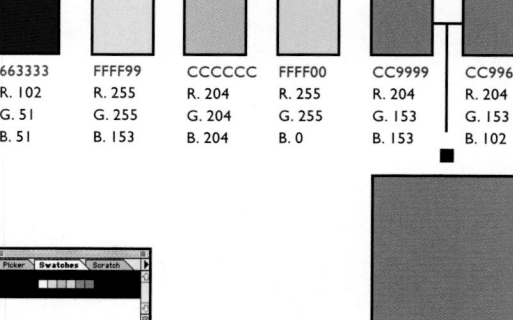

rh15sw

rh15pat.gif

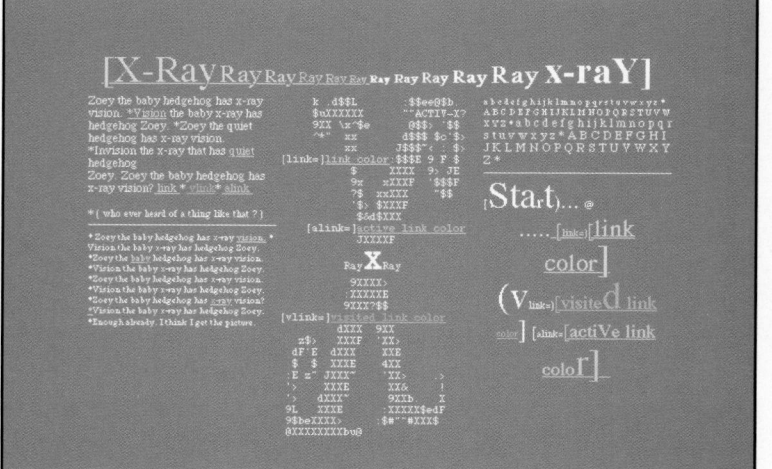

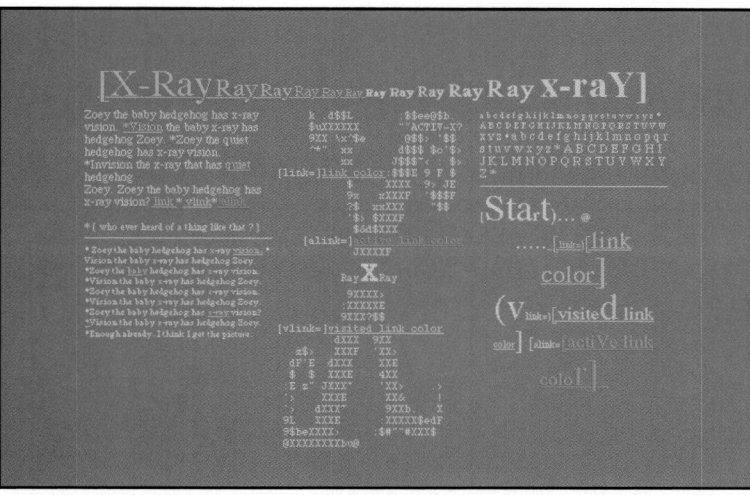
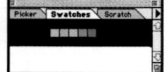

text	link	vlink	alink	bgcolor
FFCC99	99FF99	CCCCCC	00FF00	CC6666
R. 255	R. 153	R. 204	R. 0	R. 204
G. 204	G. 255	G. 204	G. 255	G. 102
B. 153	B. 153	B. 204	B. 0	B. 102

rs16sw

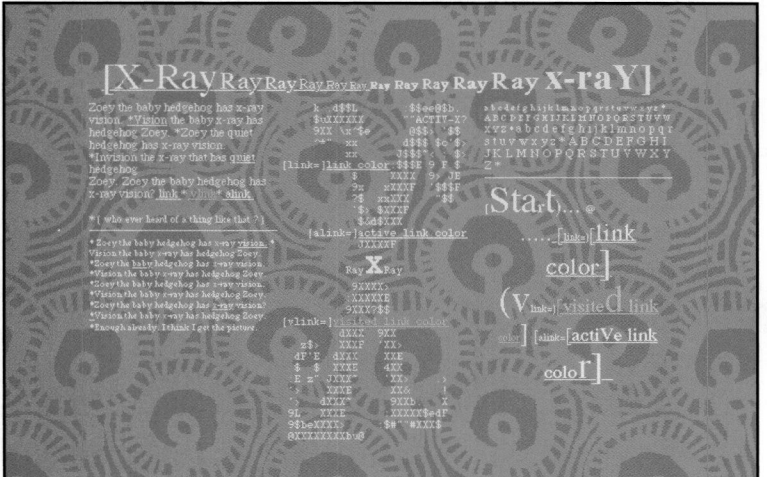
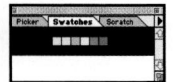

text	link	vlink	alink	tile colors	
FFFF00	FFFF99	CCCC99	FFFFCC	FF6666	CC6666
R. 255	R. 255	R. 204	R. 255	R. 255	R. 204
G. 255	G. 255	G. 204	G. 255	G. 102	G. 102
B. 0	B. 153	B. 153	B. 204	B. 102	B. 102

rp16sw

rp16pat.gif

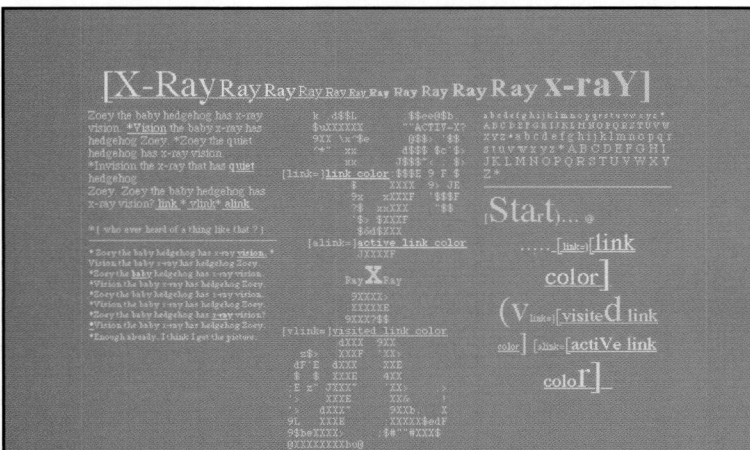
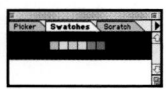

text	link	vlink	alink	hybrid colors	
FFCC33	FFFF99	CCFFCC	FFFF00	FF6666	CC6666
R. 255	R. 255	R. 204	R. 255	R. 255	R. 204
G. 204	G. 255	G. 255	G. 255	G. 102	G. 102
B. 51	B. 153	B. 204	B. 0	B. 102	B. 102

rh16sw

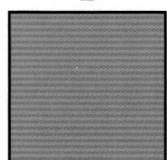

rh16pat.gif

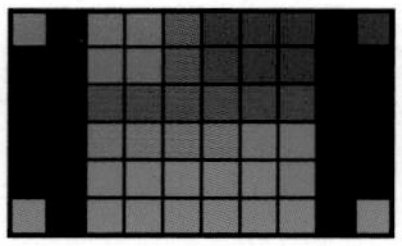

rbgg	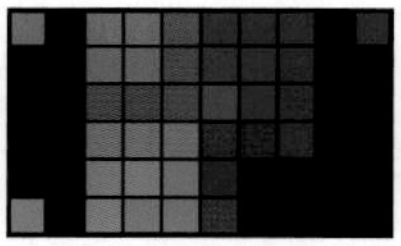 rbgk	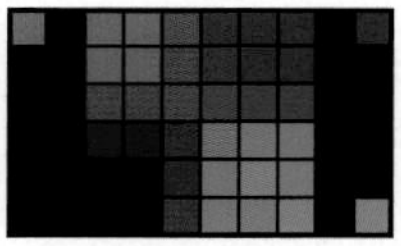 rbkg	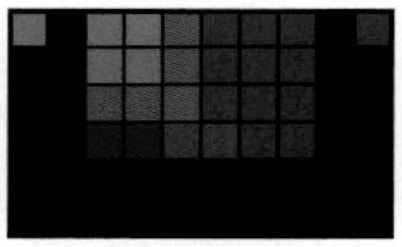 rbkk	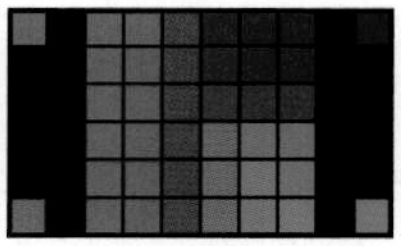 rbrg
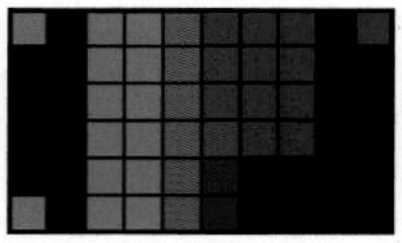 rbrk	 rbry	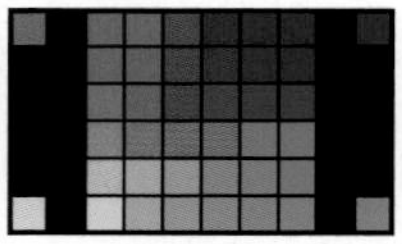 rbyg	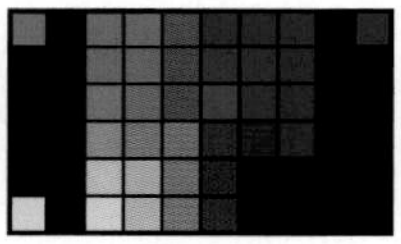 rbyk	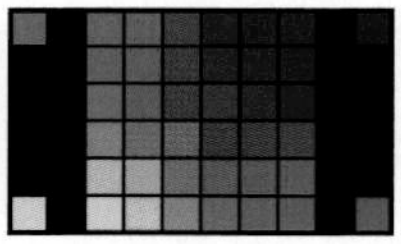 rbyr
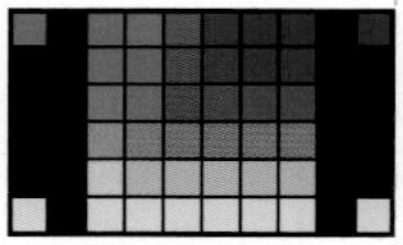 rbyy	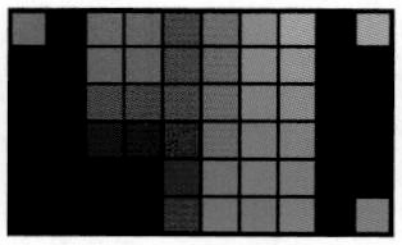 rckg	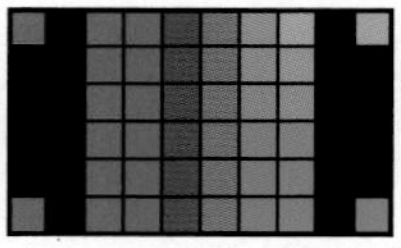 rcrg	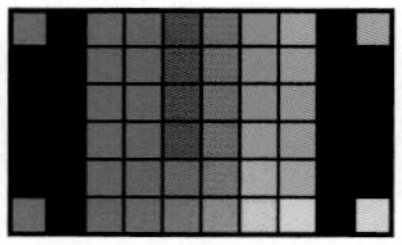 rcry	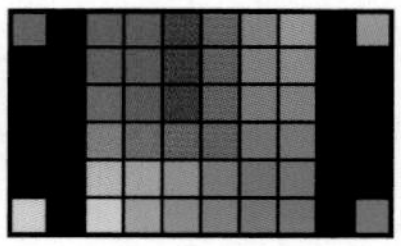 rcyg
 rgbc	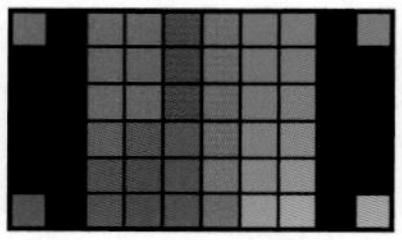 rgmc	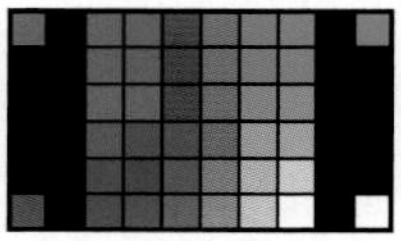 rgmw	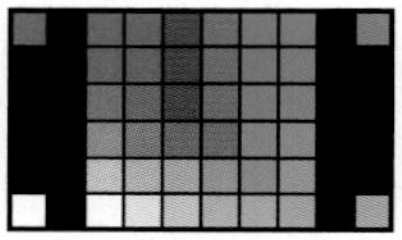 rgwc	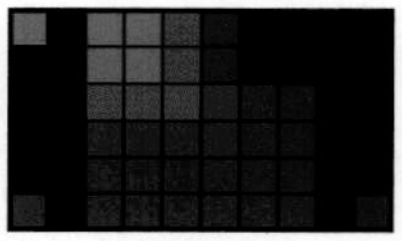 rkbb
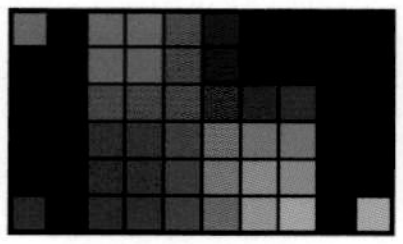 rkbc	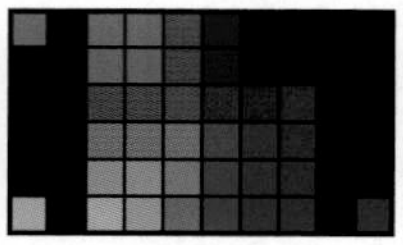 rkcb	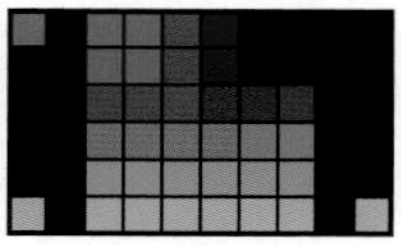 rkcc	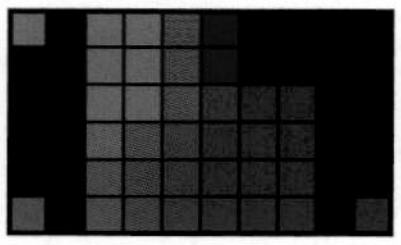 rkmb	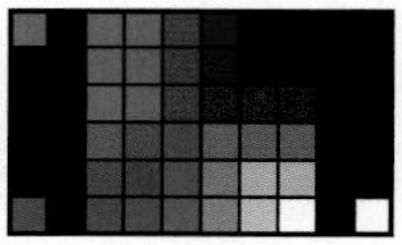 rkmc
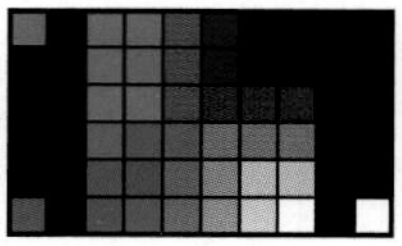 rkmw	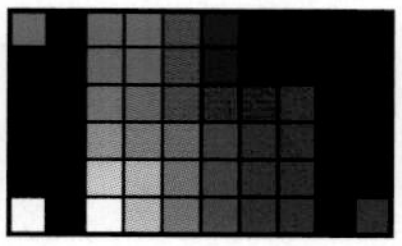 rkwb	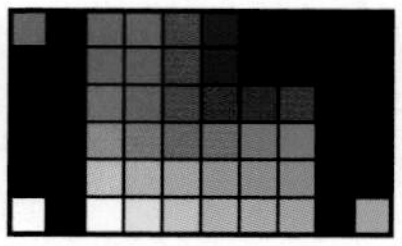 rkwc	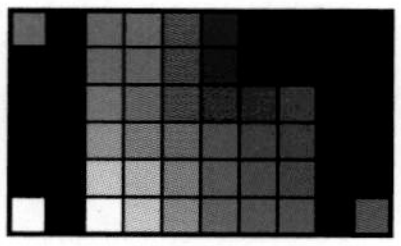 rkwm	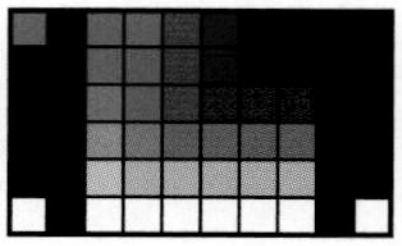 rkww
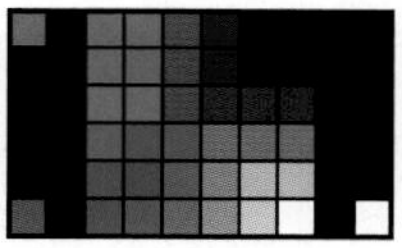 rmgg	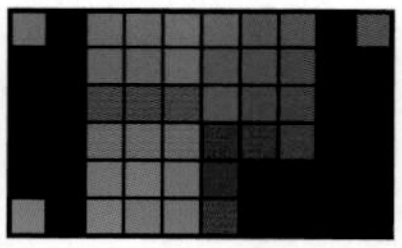 rmgk	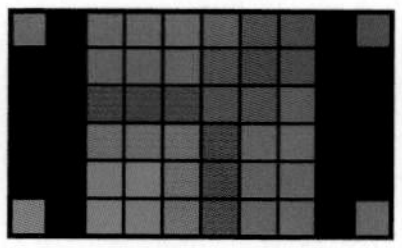 rmgr	 rmgy	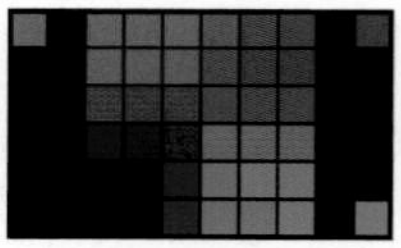 rmkg

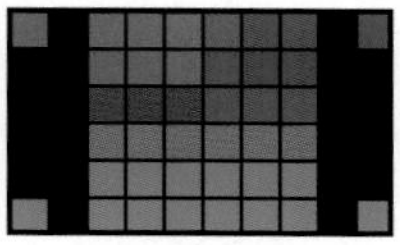

rmgg

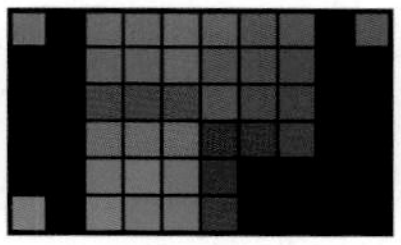

rmgk

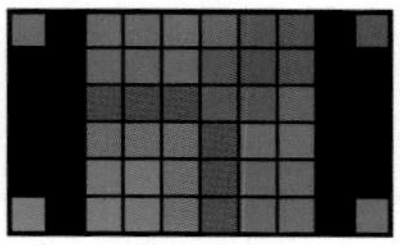

rmgr

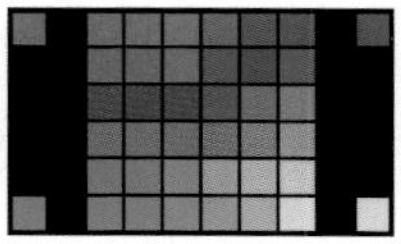

rmgy

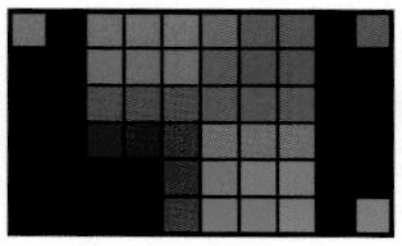

rmkg

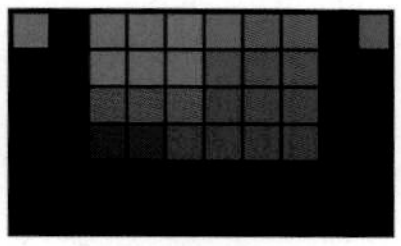

rmkk

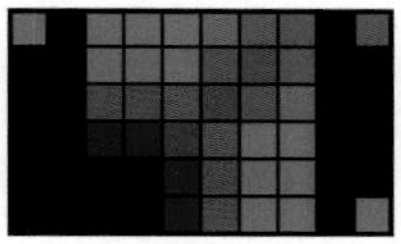

rmkr

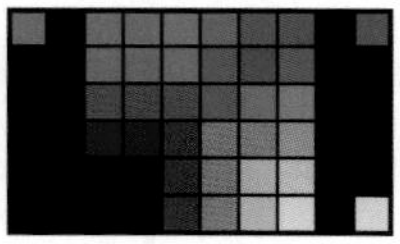

rmky

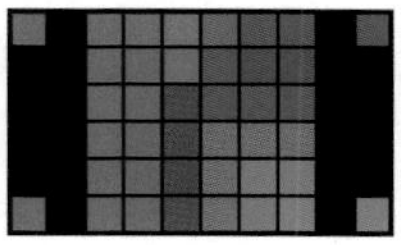

rmrg

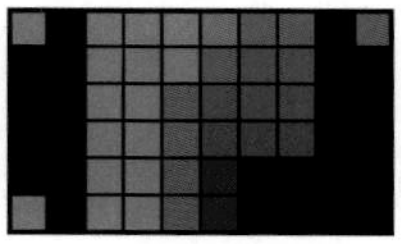

rmrk

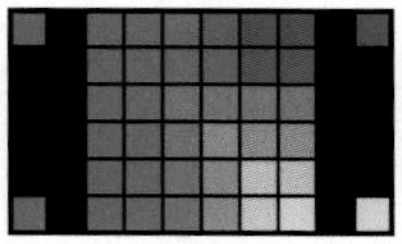

rmry

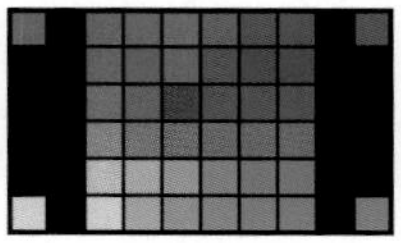

rmyg

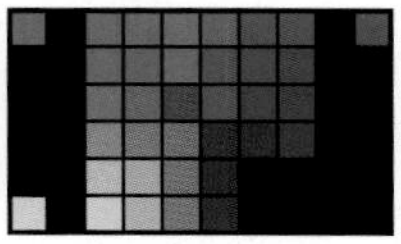

rmyk

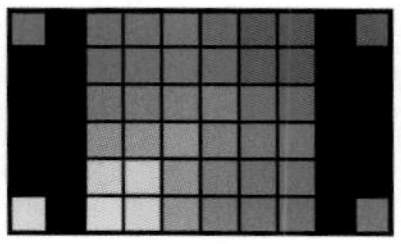

rmyr

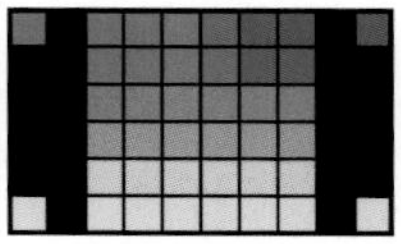

rmyy

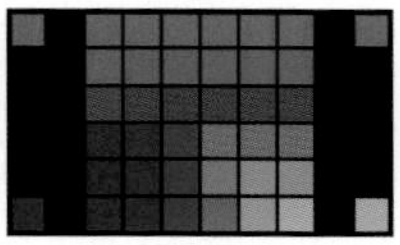

rrbc

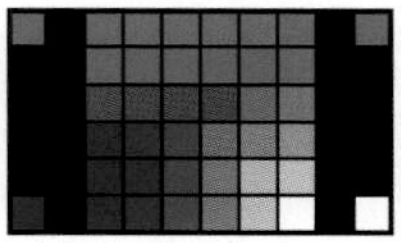

rrbw

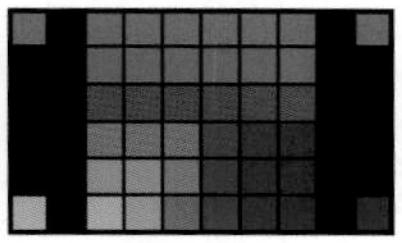

rrcb

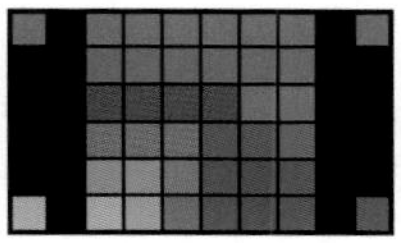

rrcm

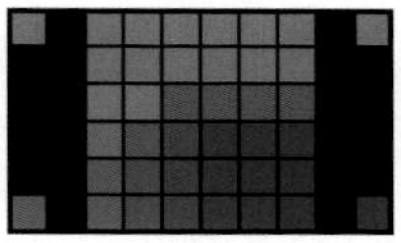

rrmb

rrmc

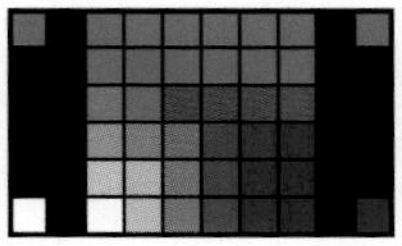

rrwb

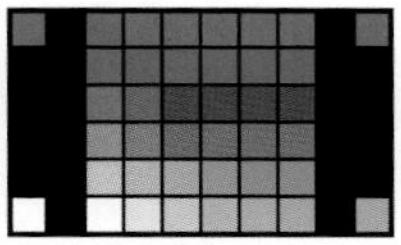

rrwc

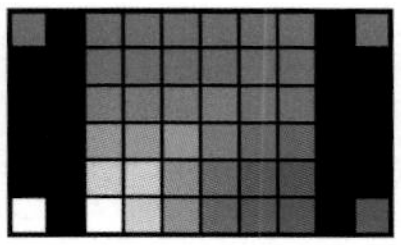

rrwm

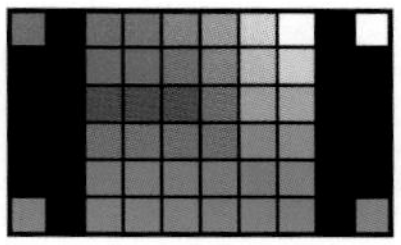

rwgg

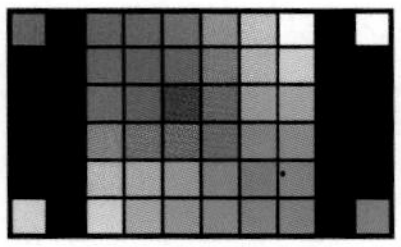

rwy

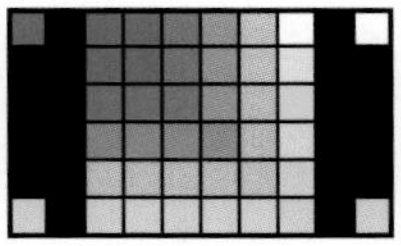

rwyy

rybc

rybw

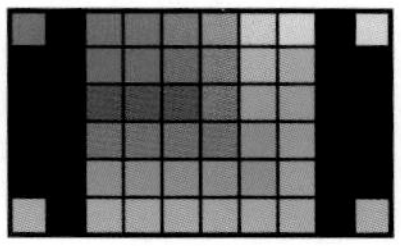

rycc

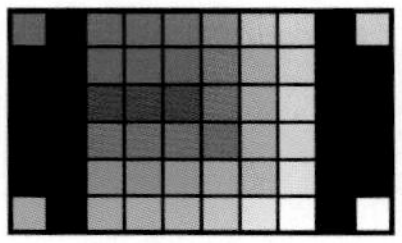

rycw

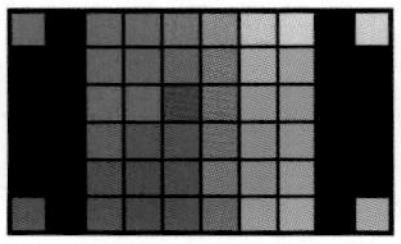

rymc

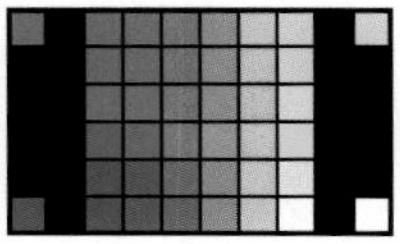

rymw

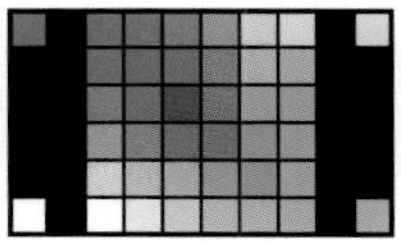

rywc

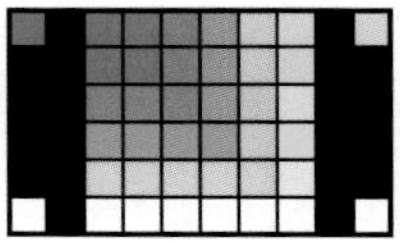

ryww

GREEN

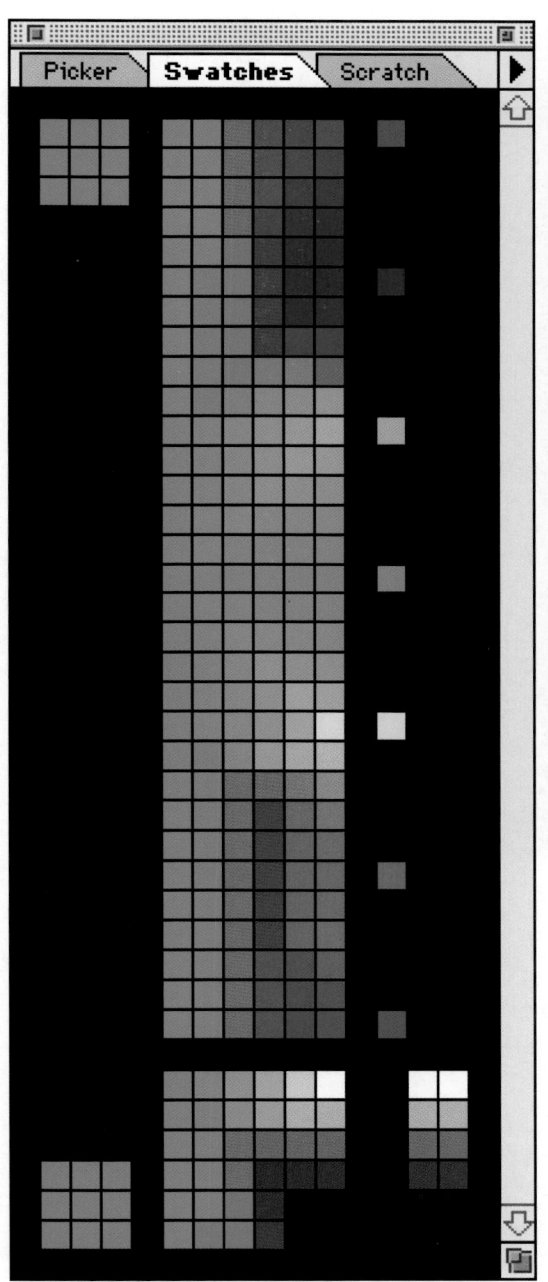

rgsw.aco

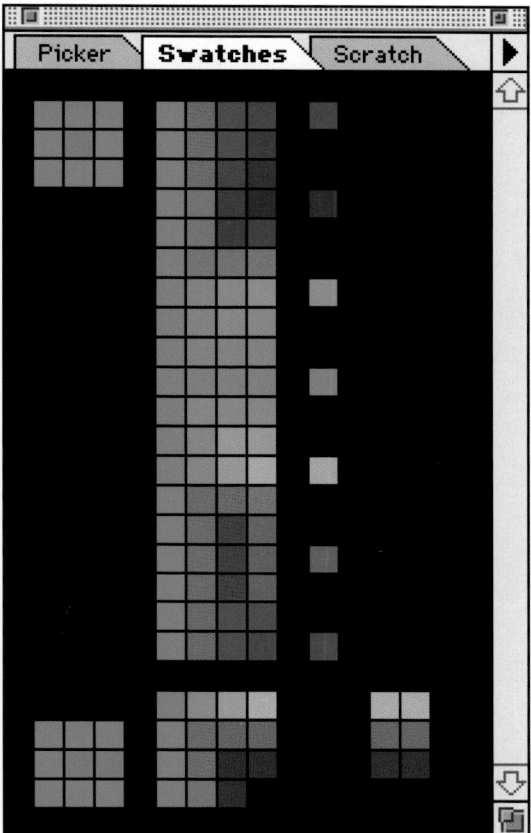

mgd

web graphics >

text	link	vlink	alink	bgcolor
333300	999900	33CC00	006600	CCFFCC
R. 51	R. 153	R. 51	R. 0	R. 204
G. 51	G. 153	G. 204	G. 102	G. 255
B. 0	B. 0	B. 0	B. 0	B. 204

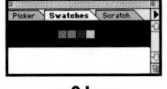

gs01sw

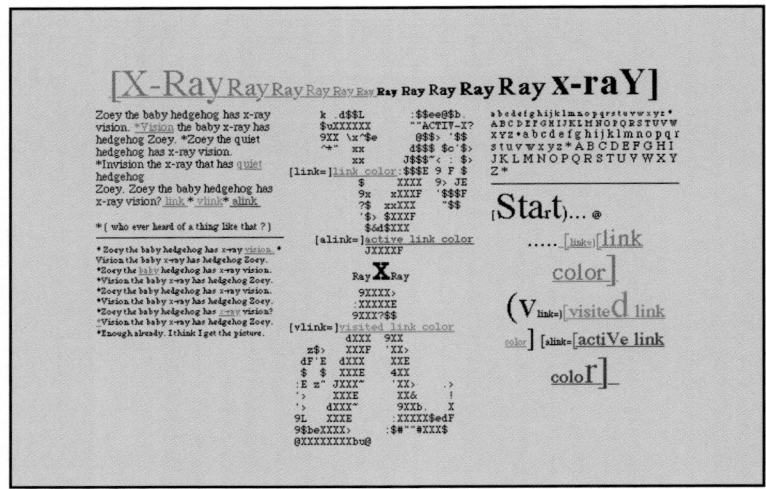

text	link	vlink	alink	tile colors	
336633	0066CC	009999	666600	CCFFCC	FFFFFF
R. 51	R. 0	R. 0	R. 102	R. 204	R. 255
G. 102	G. 102	G. 153	G. 102	G. 255	G. 255
B. 51	B. 204	B. 153	B. 0	B. 204	B. 255

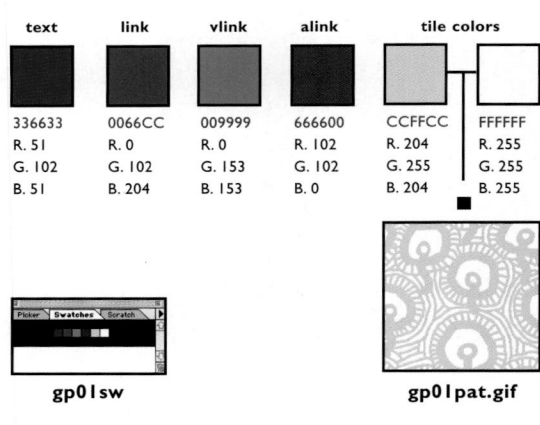

gp01sw **gp01pat.gif**

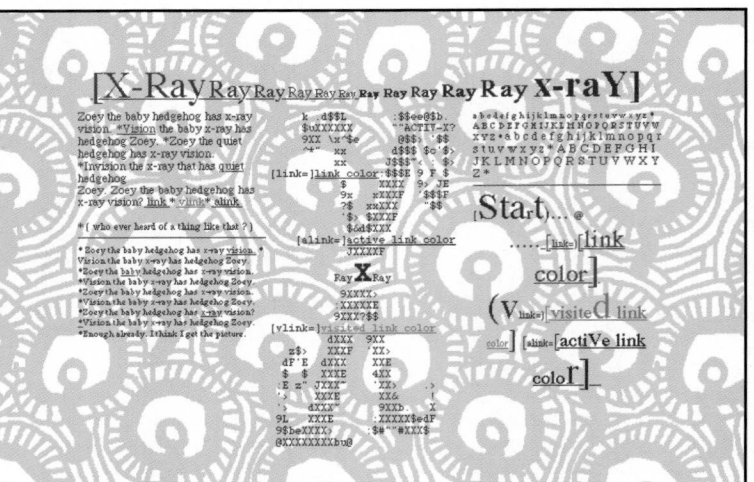

text	link	vlink	alink	hybrid colors	
666600	009900	006600	00FF00	CCFFCC	FFFFFF
R. 102	R. 0	R. 0	R. 0	R. 204	R. 255
G. 102	G. 153	G. 102	G. 255	G. 255	G. 255
B. 0	B. 0	B. 0	B. 0	B. 204	B. 255

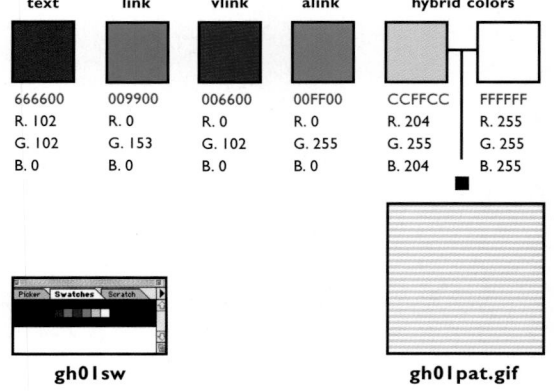

gh01sw **gh01pat.gif**

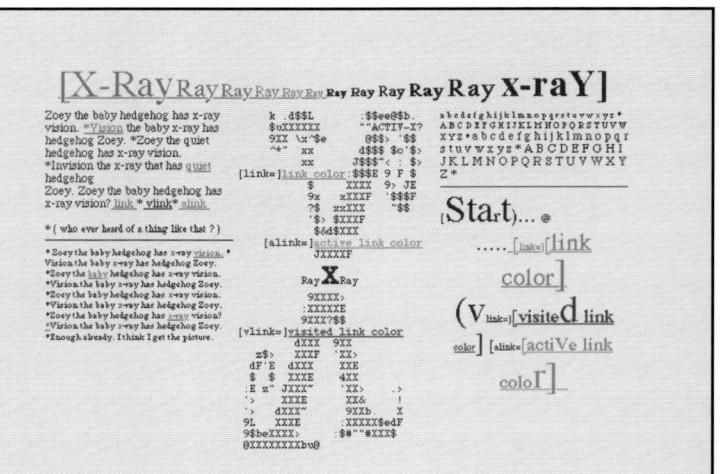

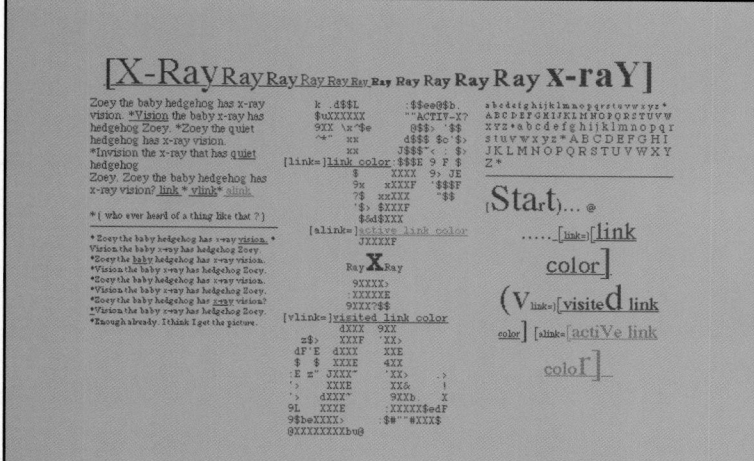

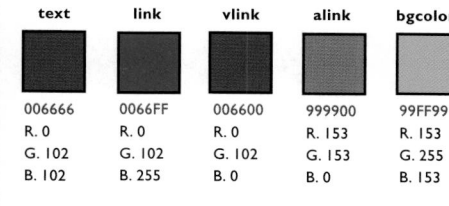

text	link	vlink	alink	bgcolor
006666	0066FF	006600	999900	99FF99
R. 0	R. 0	R. 0	R. 153	R. 153
G. 102	G. 102	G. 102	G. 153	G. 255
B. 102	B. 255	B. 0	B. 0	B. 153

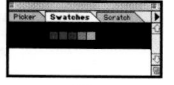

gs02sw

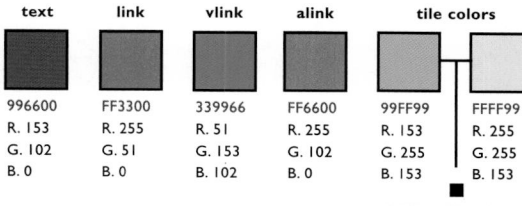

text	link	vlink	alink	tile colors	
996600	FF3300	339966	FF6600	99FF99	FFFF99
R. 153	R. 255	R. 51	R. 255	R. 153	R. 255
G. 102	G. 51	G. 153	G. 102	G. 255	G. 255
B. 0	B. 0	B. 102	B. 0	B. 153	B. 153

gp02sw

gp02pat.gif

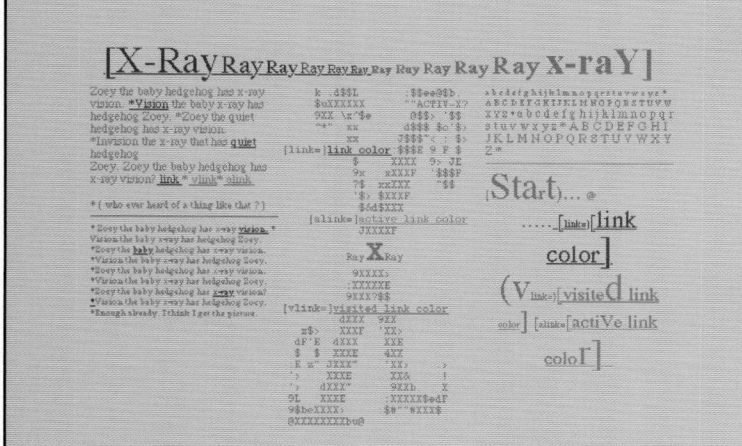

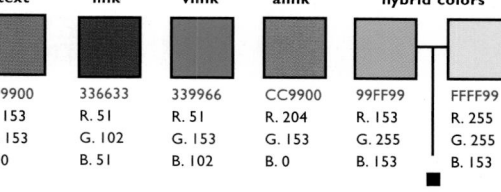

text	link	vlink	alink	hybrid colors	
999900	336633	339966	CC9900	99FF99	FFFF99
R. 153	R. 51	R. 51	R. 204	R. 153	R. 255
G. 153	G. 102	G. 153	G. 153	G. 255	G. 255
B. 0	B. 51	B. 102	B. 0	B. 153	B. 153

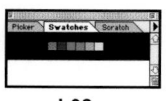

gh02sw

gh02pat.gif

text	link	vlink	alink	bgcolor
336666	999900	339900	009999	CCFF99
R. 51	R. 153	R. 51	R. 0	R. 204
G. 102	G. 153	G. 153	G. 153	G. 255
B. 102	B. 0	B. 0	B. 153	B. 153

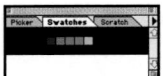

gs03sw

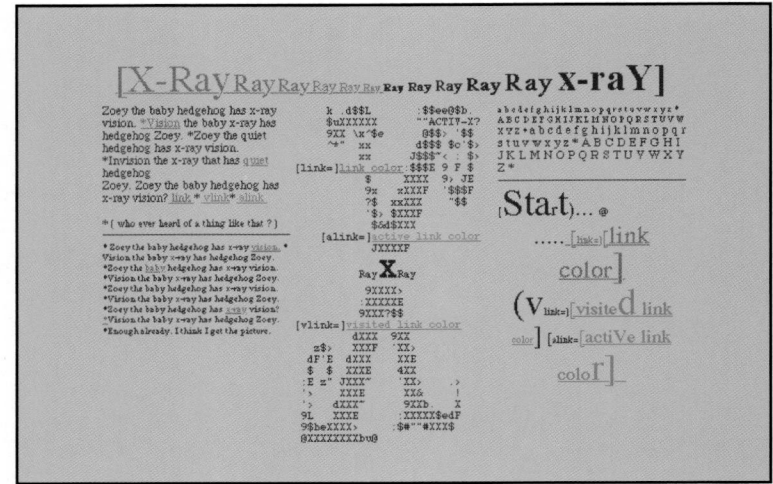

text	link	vlink	alink	tile colors	
333366	3399FF	0000FF	999900	CCFF99	FFFF99
R. 51	R. 51	R. 0	R. 153	R. 204	R. 255
G. 51	G. 153	G. 0	G. 153	G. 255	G. 255
B. 102	B. 255	B. 255	B. 0	B. 153	B. 153

gp03sw

gp03pat.gif

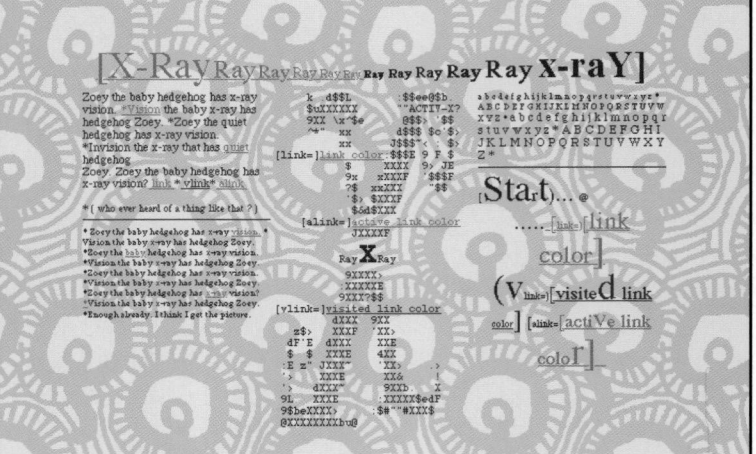

text	link	vlink	alink	hybrid colors	
336633	00CC00	996600	009999	CCFF99	FFFF99
R. 51	R. 0	R. 153	R. 0	R. 204	R. 255
G. 102	G. 204	G. 102	G. 153	G. 255	G. 255
B. 51	B. 0	B. 0	B. 153	B. 153	B. 153

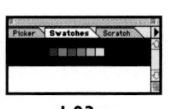

gh03sw

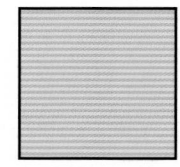

gh03pat.gif

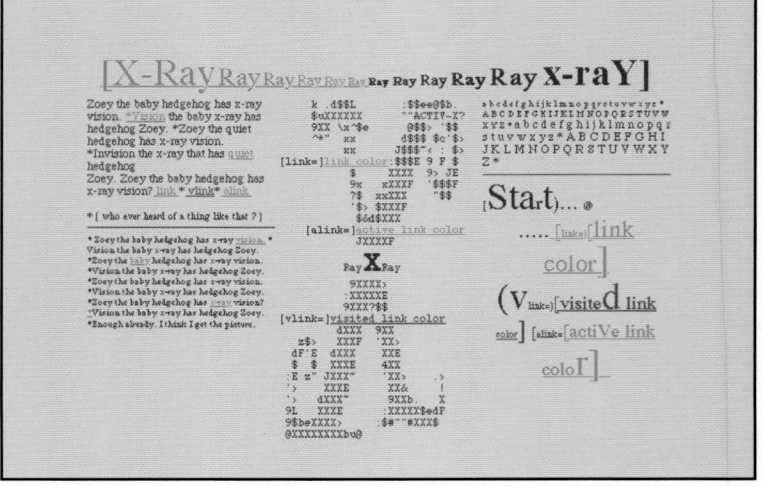

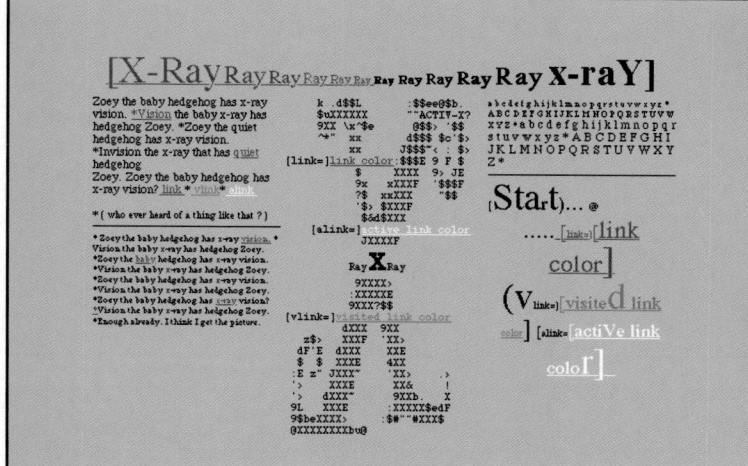

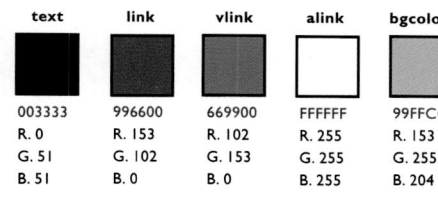

text	link	vlink	alink	bgcolor
003333	996600	669900	FFFFFF	99FFCC
R. 0	R. 153	R. 102	R. 255	R. 153
G. 51	G. 102	G. 153	G. 255	G. 255
B. 51	B. 0	B. 0	B. 255	B. 204

gs04sw

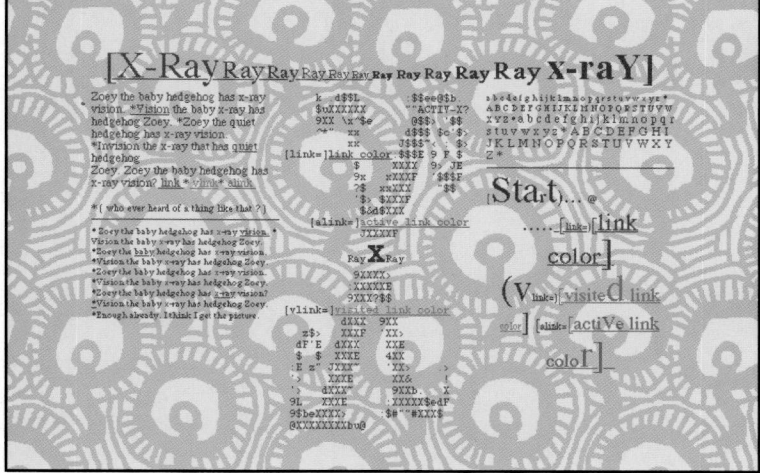

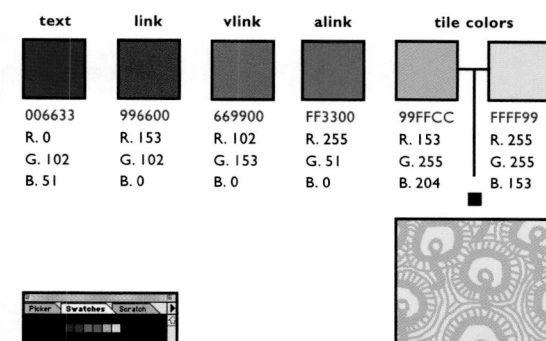

text	link	vlink	alink	tile colors	
006633	996600	669900	FF3300	99FFCC	FFFF99
R. 0	R. 153	R. 102	R. 255	R. 153	R. 255
G. 102	G. 102	G. 153	G. 51	G. 255	G. 255
B. 51	B. 0	B. 0	B. 0	B. 204	B. 153

gp04w

gp04pat.gif

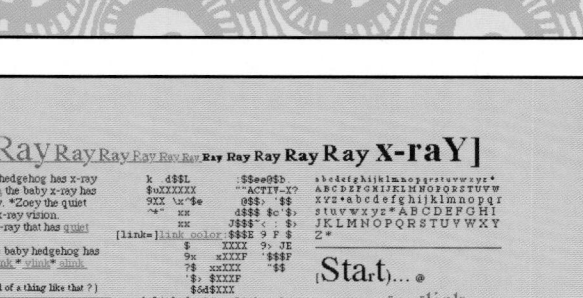

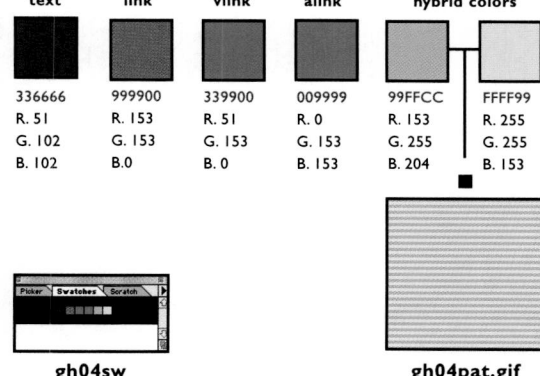

text	link	vlink	alink	hybrid colors	
336666	999900	339900	009999	99FFCC	FFFF99
R. 51	R. 153	R. 51	R. 0	R. 153	R. 255
G. 102	G. 153	G. 153	G. 153	G. 255	G. 255
B. 102	B. 0	B. 0	B. 153	B. 204	B. 153

gh04sw

gh04pat.gif

text	link	vlink	alink	bgcolor
006699	336600	666600	003300	66FF66
R. 0	R. 51	R. 102	R. 0	R. 102
G. 102	G. 102	G. 102	G. 51	G. 255
B. 153	B. 0	B. 0	B. 0	B. 102

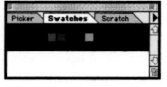

gs05sw

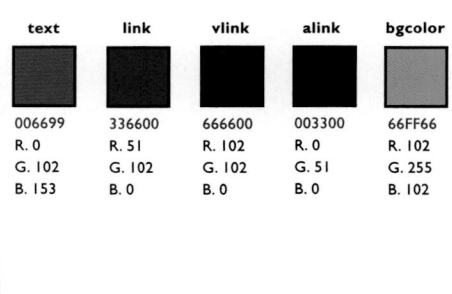

text	link	vlink	alink	tile colors	
336633	0099CC	669900	003366	66FF66	66FFCC
R. 51	R. 0	R. 102	R. 0	R. 102	R. 102
G. 102	G. 153	G. 153	G. 51	G. 255	G. 255
B. 51	B. 204	B. 0	B. 102	B. 102	B. 204

gp05sw

gp05pat.gif

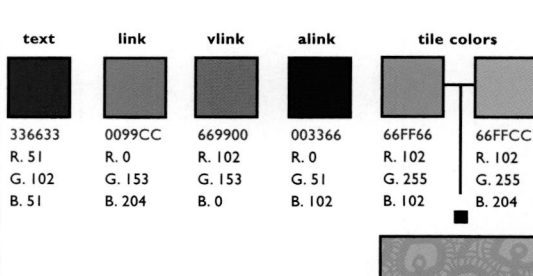

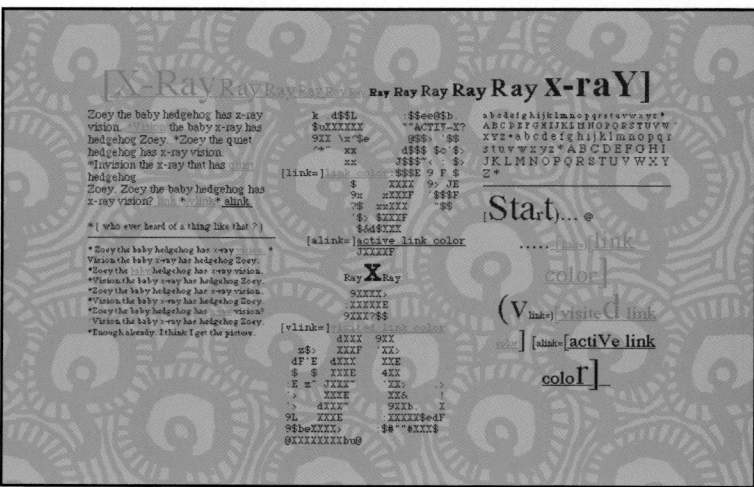

text	link	vlink	alink	hybrid colors	
666633	999900	009966	669900	66FF66	66FFCC
R. 102	R. 153	R. 0	R. 102	R. 102	R. 102
G. 102	G. 153	G. 153	G. 153	G. 255	G. 255
B. 51	B. 0	B. 102	B. 0	B. 102	B. 204

gh05sw

gh05pat.gif

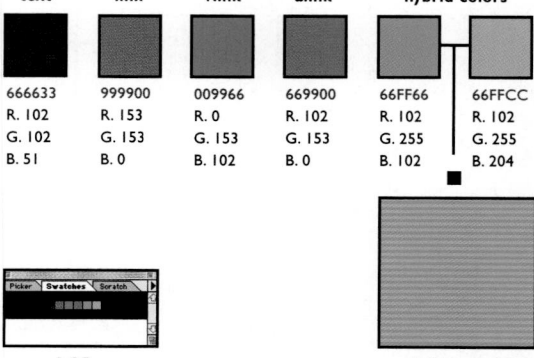

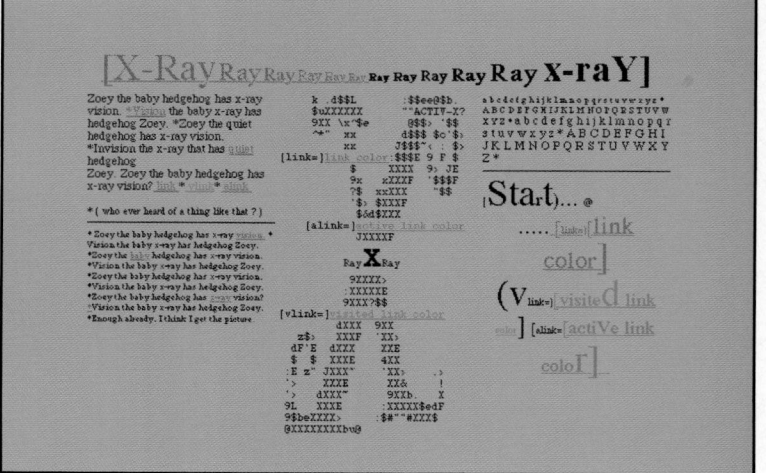

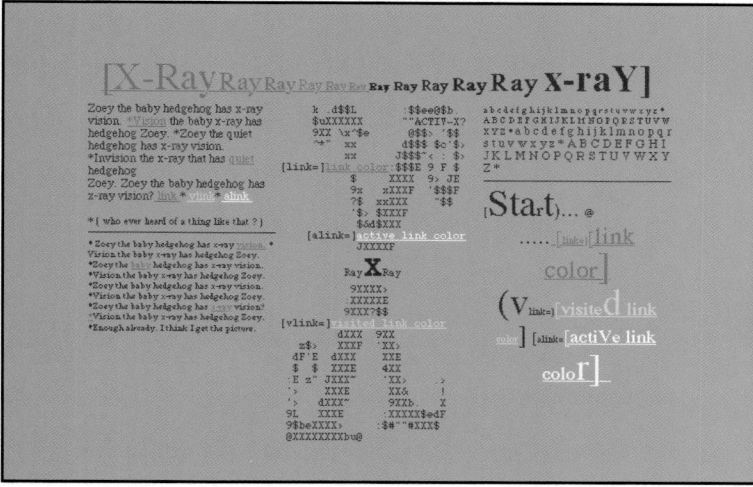

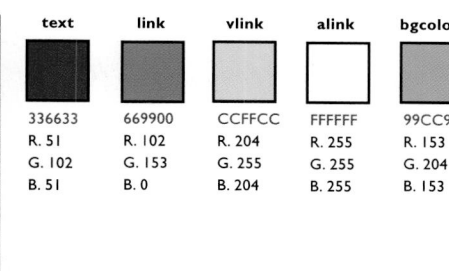

	text	link	vlink	alink	bgcolor
	336633	669900	CCFFCC	FFFFFF	99CC99
	R. 51	R. 102	R. 255	R. 255	R. 153
	G. 102	G. 153	G. 255	G. 255	G. 204
	B. 51	B. 0	B. 204	B. 255	B. 153

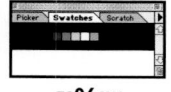

gs06sw

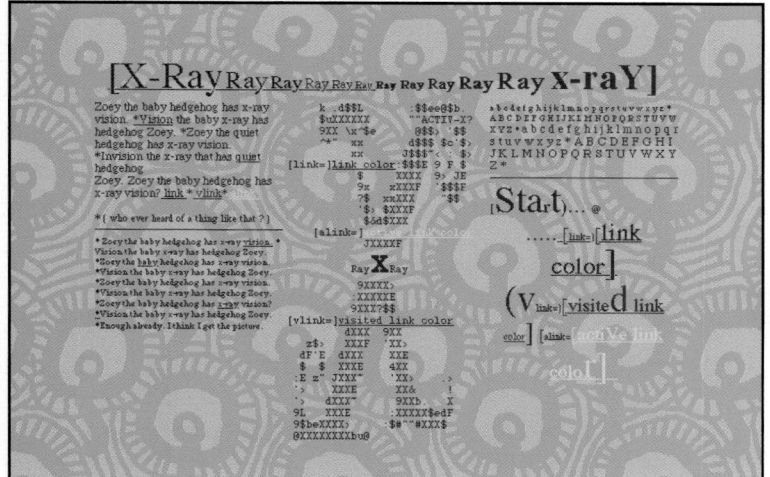

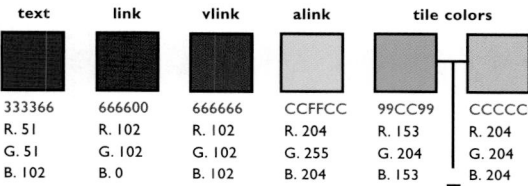

	text	link	vlink	alink	tile colors	
	333366	666600	666666	CCFFCC	99CC99	CCCCCC
	R. 51	R. 102	R. 102	R. 204	R. 153	R. 204
	G. 51	G. 102	G. 102	G. 255	G. 204	G. 204
	B. 102	B. 0	B. 102	B. 204	B. 153	B. 204

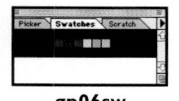

gp06sw

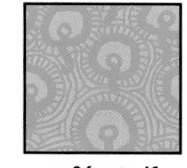

gp06pat.gif

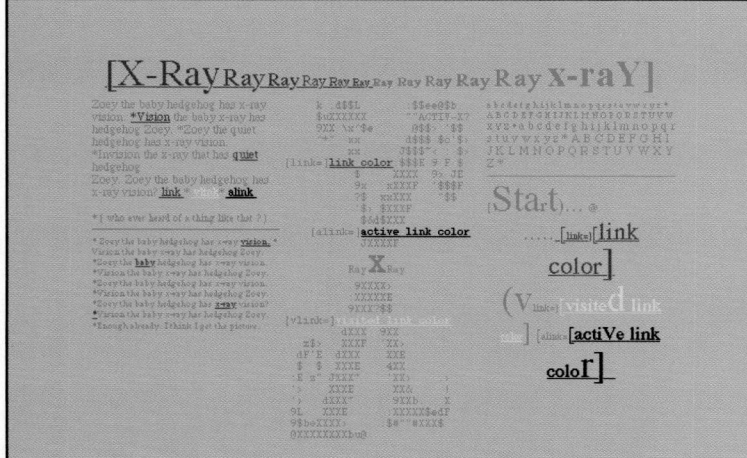

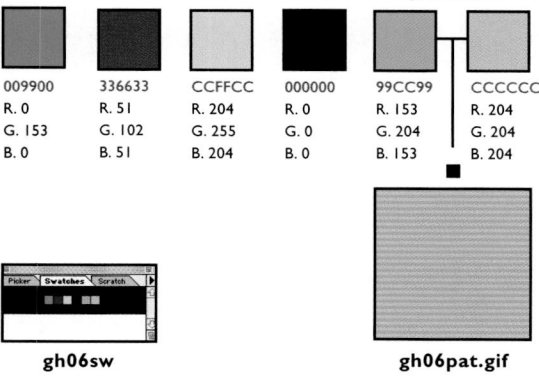

	text	link	vlink	alink	hybrid colors	
	009900	336633	CCFFCC	000000	99CC99	CCCCCC
	R. 0	R. 51	R. 204	R. 0	R. 153	R. 204
	G. 153	G. 102	G. 255	G. 0	G. 204	G. 204
	B. 0	B. 51	B. 204	B. 0	B. 153	B. 204

gh06sw

gh06pat.gif

text	link	vlink	alink	bgcolor
336666	0066CC	669999	CCFFFF	99CC66
R. 51	R. 0	R. 102	R. 204	R. 102
G. 102	G. 102	G. 153	G. 255	G. 204
B. 102	B. 204	B. 153	B. 255	B. 102

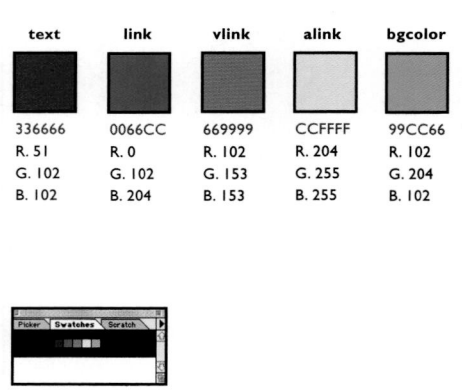

gs07sw

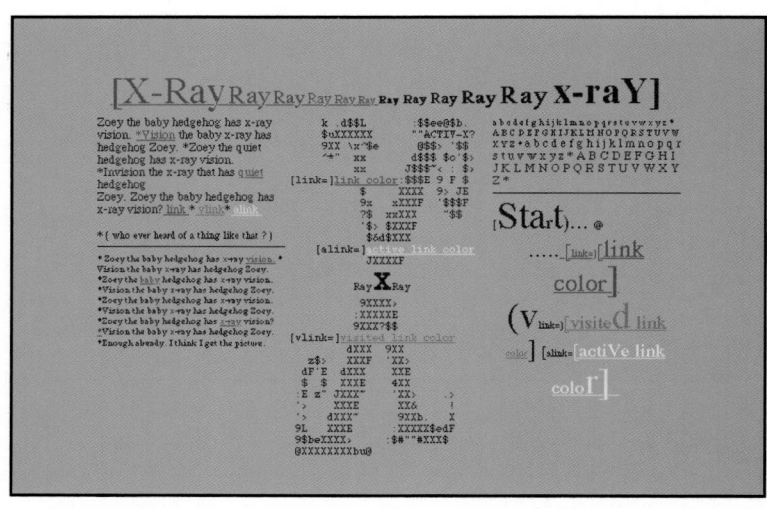

text	link	vlink	alink	tile colors	
003300	CC6600	666600	999900	99CC66	CCCC99
R. 0	R. 204	R. 102	R. 153	R. 153	R. 204
G. 51	G. 102	G. 102	G. 153	G. 204	G. 204
B. 0	B. 0	B. 0	B. 0	B. 102	B. 153

gp07sw

gp07pat.gif

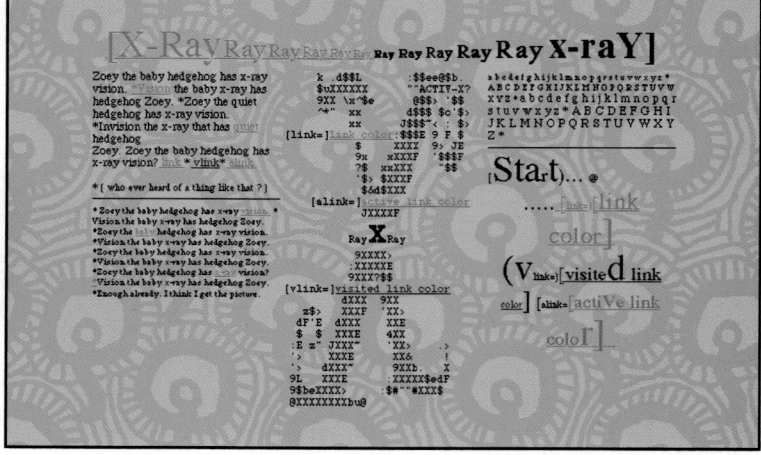

text	link	vlink	alink	hybrid colors	
663333	FFFF00	FF6666	996666	99CC66	CCCC99
R. 102	R. 255	R. 255	R. 153	R. 153	R. 204
G. 51	G. 255	G. 102	G. 102	G. 204	G. 204
B. 51	B. 0	B. 102	B. 102	B. 102	B. 153

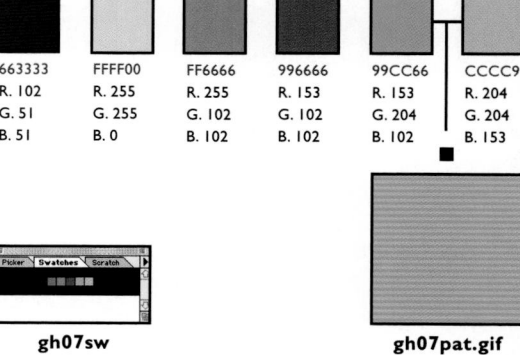

gh07sw

gh07pat.gif

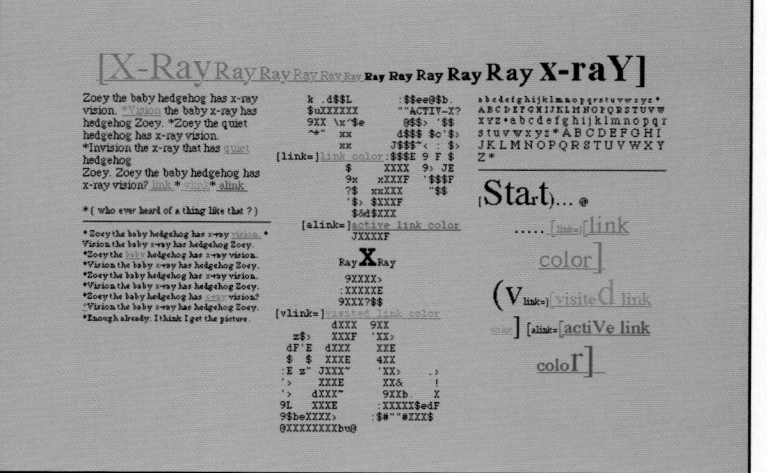

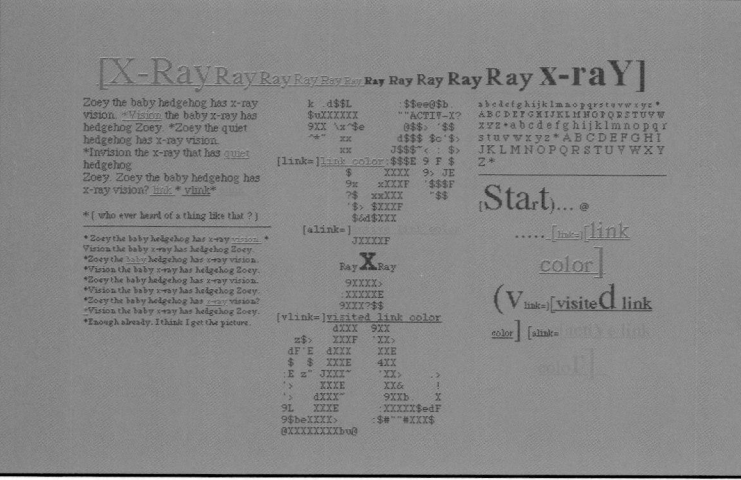

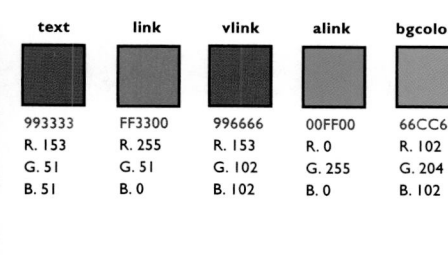

text	link	vlink	alink	bgcolor
993333	FF3300	996666	00FF00	66CC66
R. 153	R. 255	R. 153	R. 0	R. 102
G. 51	G. 51	G. 102	G. 255	G. 204
B. 51	B. 0	B. 102	B. 0	B. 102

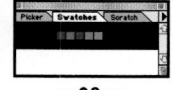

gs08sw

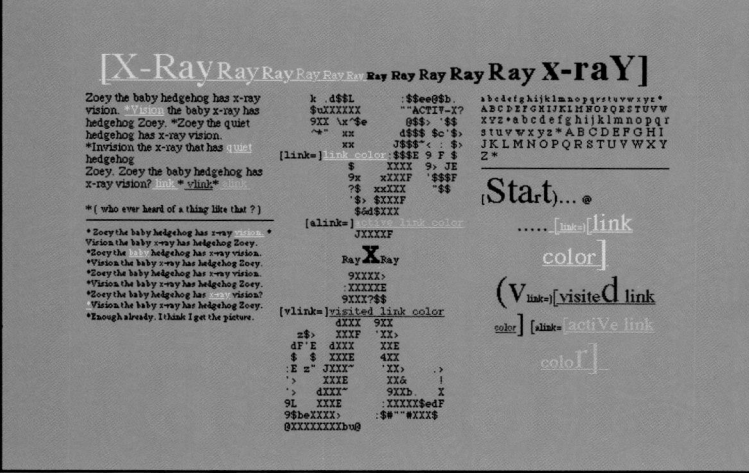

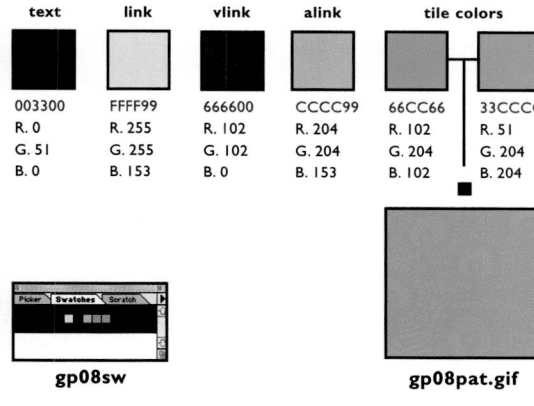

text	link	vlink	alink	tile colors	
003300	FFFF99	666600	CCCC99	66CC66	33CCCC
R. 0	R. 255	R. 102	R. 204	R. 102	R. 51
G. 51	G. 255	G. 102	G. 204	G. 204	G. 204
B. 0	B. 153	B. 0	B. 153	B. 102	B. 204

gp08sw

gp08pat.gif

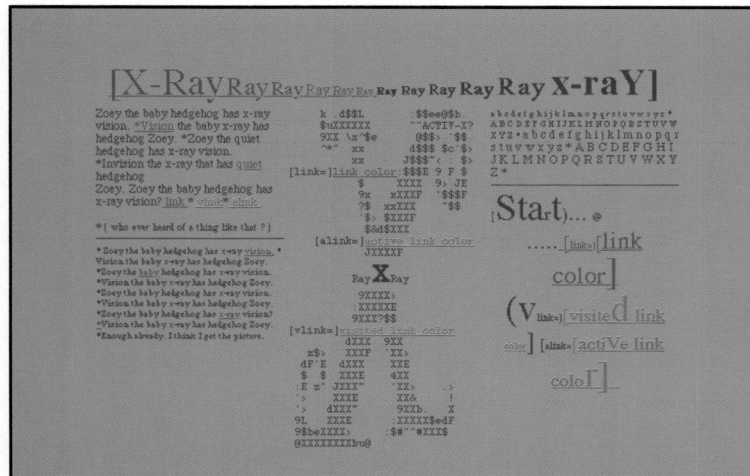

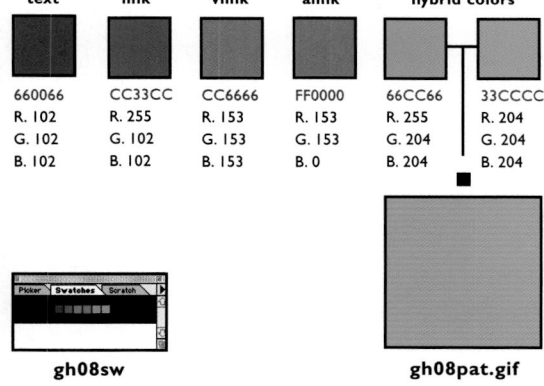

text	link	vlink	alink	hybrid colors	
660066	CC33CC	CC6666	FF0000	66CC66	33CCCC
R. 102	R. 255	R. 153	R. 153	R. 255	R. 204
G. 102	G. 102	G. 153	G. 153	G. 204	G. 204
B. 102	B. 102	B. 153	B. 0	B. 204	B. 204

gh08sw

gh08pat.gif

text	link	vlink	alink	bgcolor
336633	0066FF	6666CC	CCFFFF	33FF00
R. 51	R. 0	R. 102	R. 204	R. 51
G. 102	G. 102	G. 102	G. 255	G. 255
B. 51	B. 255	B. 204	B. 255	B. 0

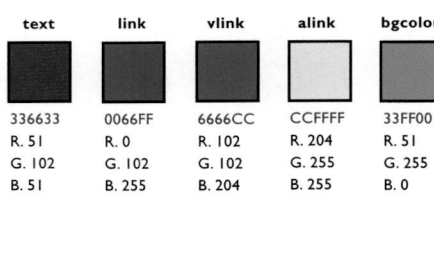

gs09sw

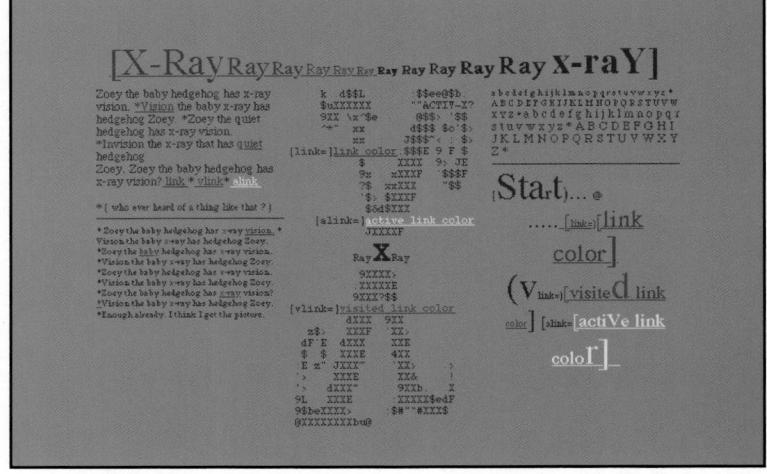

text	link	vlink	alink	tile colors	
666600	FF6600	CC6633	999900	66FF66	33FF00
R. 102	R. 255	R. 204	R. 153	R. 102	R. 51
G. 102	G. 102	G. 102	G. 153	G. 255	G. 255
B. 0	B. 0	B. 51	B. 0	B. 102	B. 0

gp09sw

gp09pat.gif

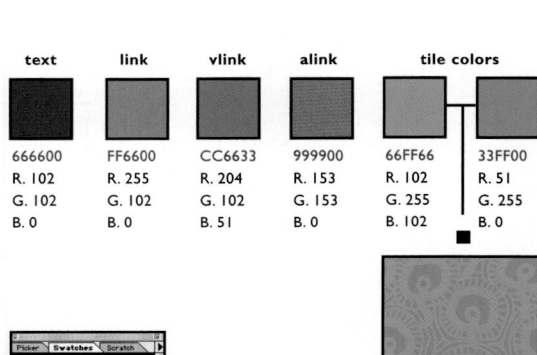

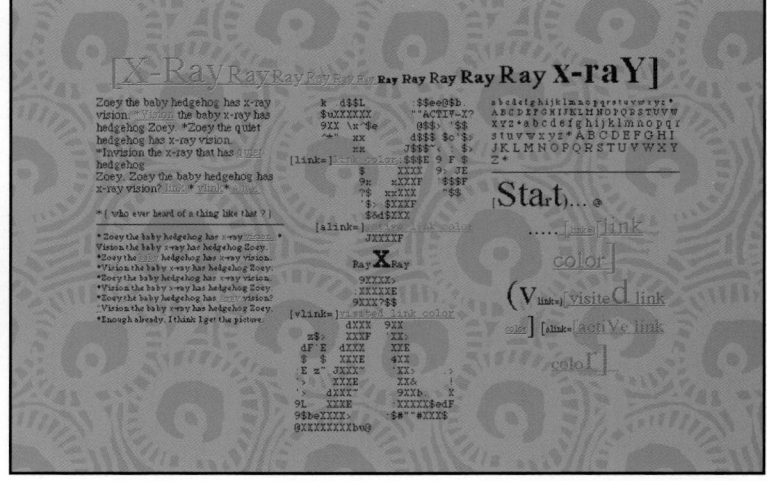

text	link	vlink	alink	hybrid colors	
006633	0066CC	669966	CCFFFF	33FF00	66FF66
R. 0	R. 0	R. 102	R. 204	R. 51	R. 102
G.102	G. 102	G. 153	G. 255	G. 255	G. 255
B. 51	B. 204	B. 102	B. 255	B. 0	B. 102

gh09sw

gh09pat.gif

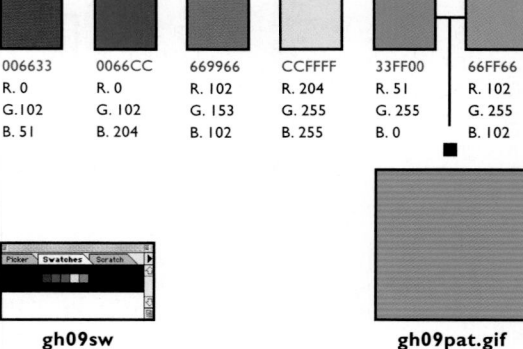

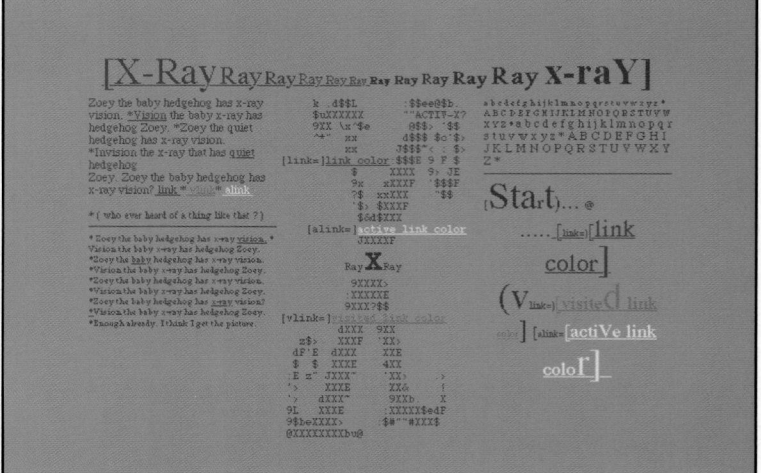

coloring

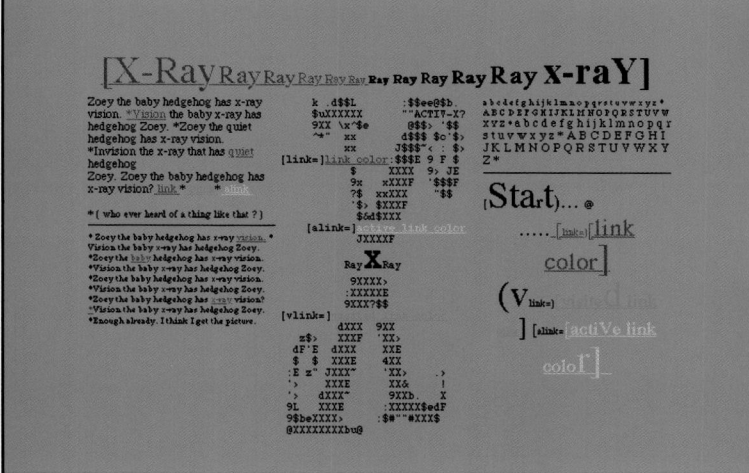

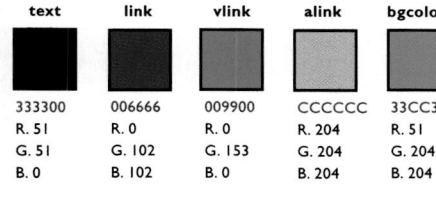

text	link	vlink	alink	bgcolor
333300	006666	009900	CCCCCC	33CC33
R. 51	R. 0	R. 0	R. 204	R. 51
G. 51	G. 102	G. 153	G. 204	G. 204
B. 0	B. 102	B. 0	B. 204	B. 204

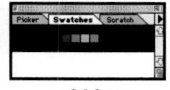

gs010sw

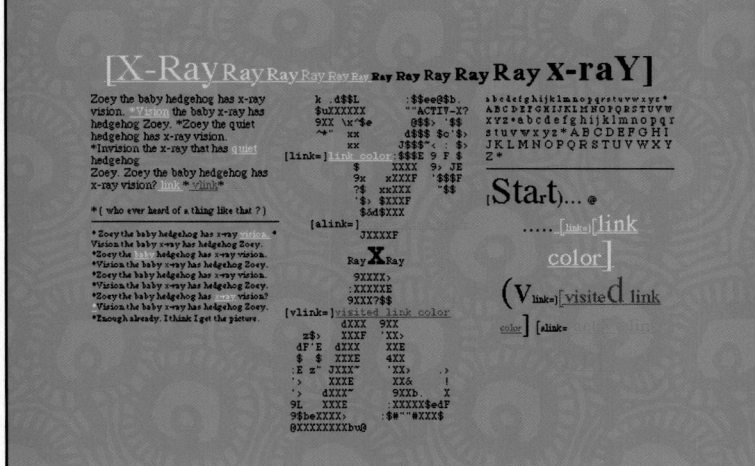

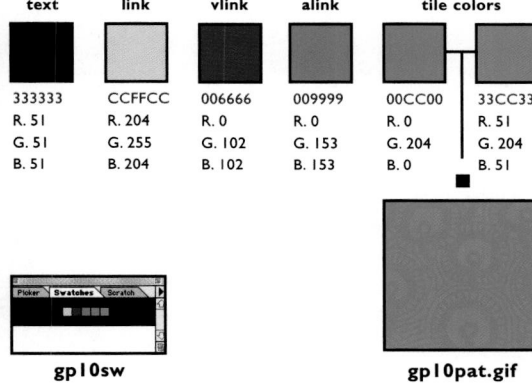

text	link	vlink	alink	tile colors	
333333	CCFFCC	006666	009999	00CC00	33CC33
R. 51	R. 204	R. 0	R. 0	R. 0	R. 51
G. 51	G. 255	G. 102	G. 153	G. 204	G. 204
B. 51	B. 204	B. 102	B. 153	B. 0	B. 51

gp10sw

gp10pat.gif

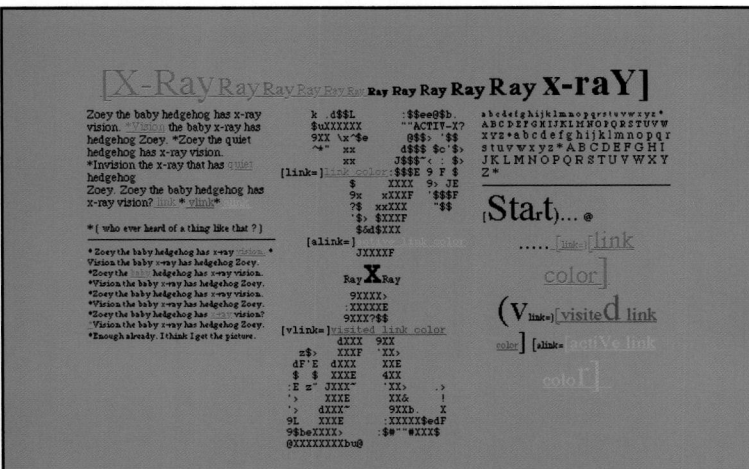

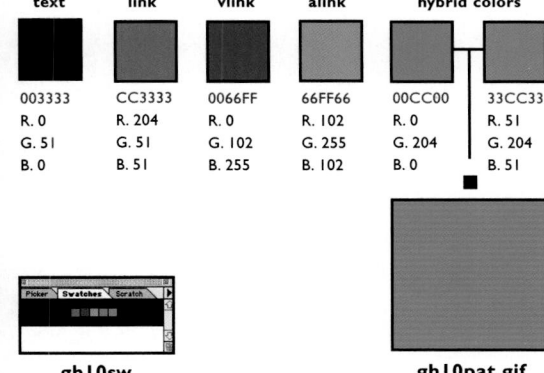

text	link	vlink	alink	hybrid colors	
003333	CC3333	0066FF	66FF66	00CC00	33CC33
R. 0	R. 204	R. 0	R. 102	R. 0	R. 51
G. 51	G. 51	G. 102	G. 255	G. 204	G. 204
B. 0	B. 51	B. 255	B. 102	B. 0	B. 51

gh10sw

gh10pat.gif

text	link	vlink	alink	bgcolor
333300	993333	66CC66	000000	339933
R. 51	R. 153	R. 102	R. 0	R. 51
G. 51	G. 51	G. 204	G. 0	G. 153
B. 0	B. 51	B. 102	B. 0	B. 51

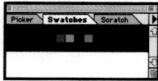

gs11sw

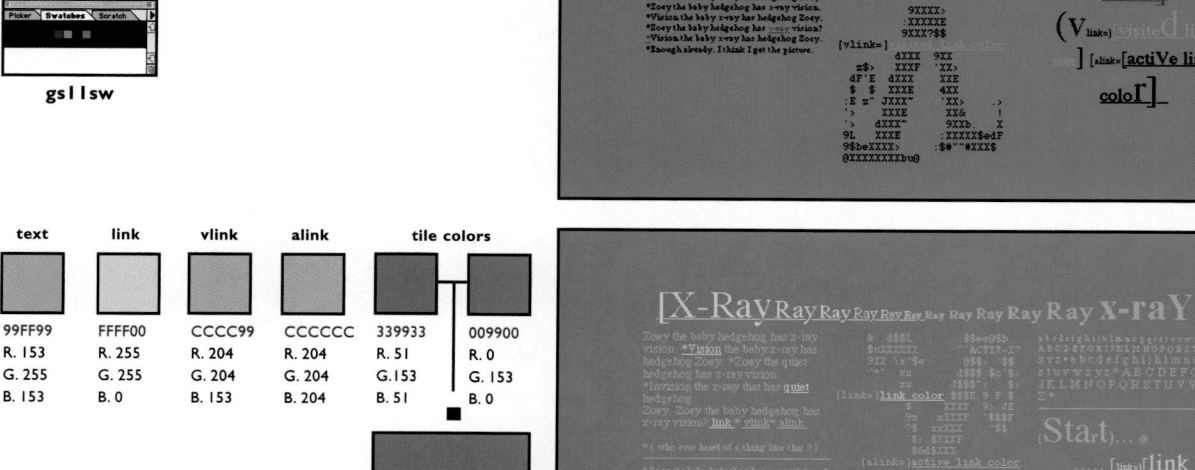

text	link	vlink	alink	tile colors	
99FF99	FFFF00	CCCC99	CCCCCC	339933	009900
R. 153	R. 255	R. 204	R. 204	R. 51	R. 0
G. 255	G. 255	G. 204	G. 204	G.153	G. 153
B. 153	B. 0	B. 153	B. 204	B. 51	B. 0

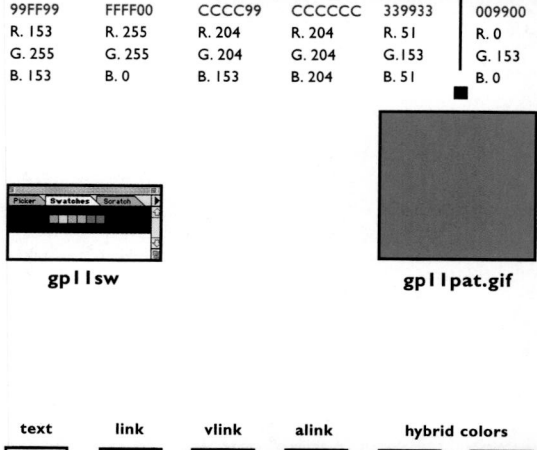

gp11sw

gp11pat.gif

text	link	vlink	alink	hybrid colors	
FFFF99	FFCC00	CCCCCC	336633	009900	339933
R. 255	R. 255	R. 204	R. 51	R. 0	R. 51
G. 255	G. 204	G. 204	G. 102	G. 153	G.153
B. 153	B. 0	B. 204	B. 51	B. 0	B. 51

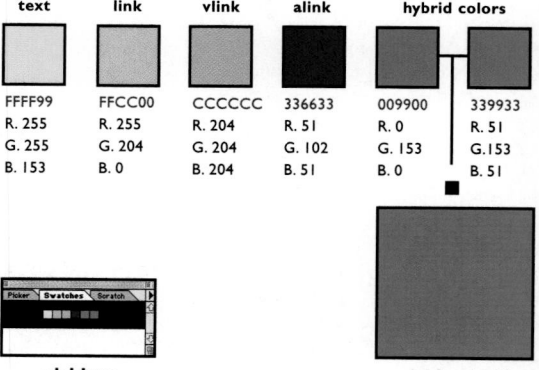

gh11sw

gh11pat.gif

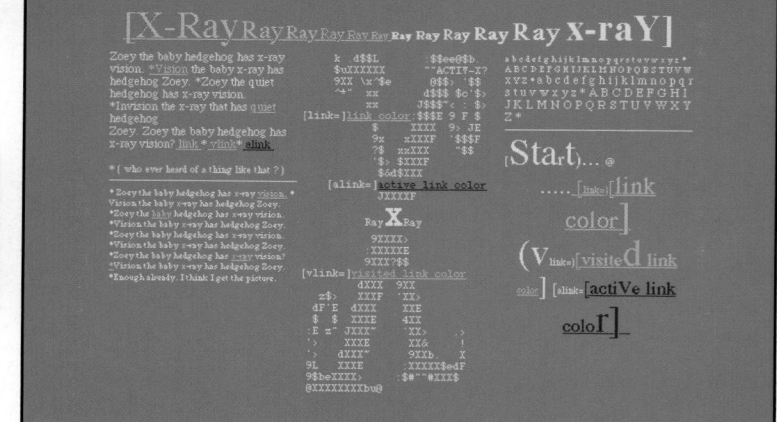

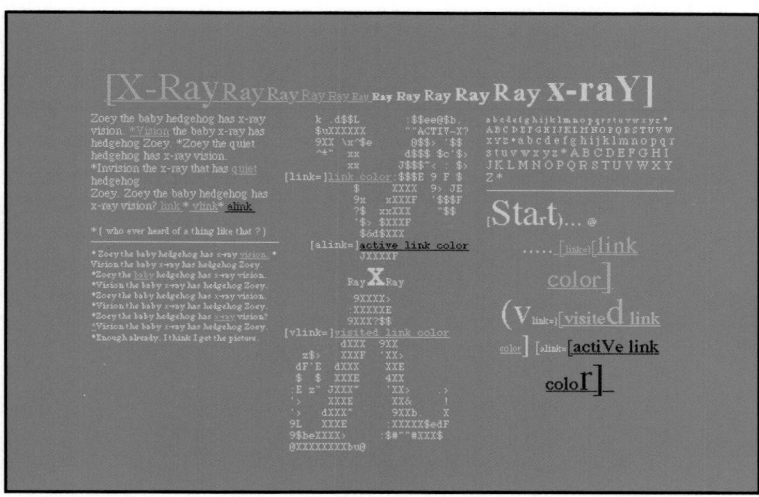

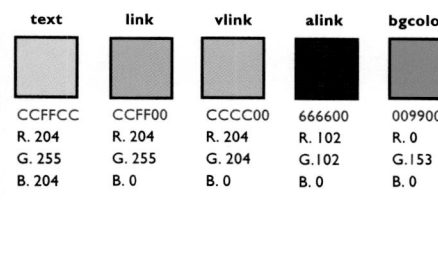

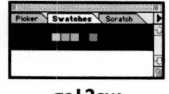

text	link	vlink	alink	bgcolor
CCFFCC	CCFF00	CCCC00	666600	009900
R. 204	R. 204	R. 204	R. 102	R. 0
G. 255	G. 255	G. 204	G.102	G.153
B. 204	B. 0	B. 0	B. 0	B. 0

gs12sw

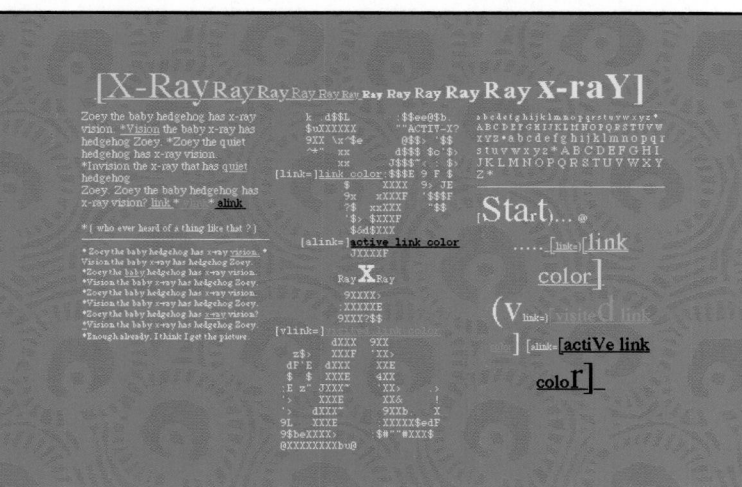

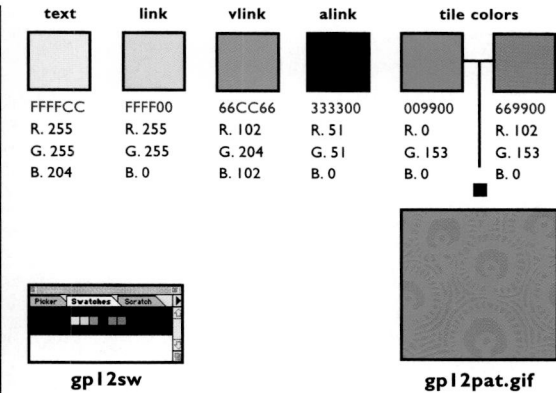

text	link	vlink	alink	tile colors	
FFFFCC	FFFF00	66CC66	333300	009900	669900
R. 255	R. 255	R. 102	R. 51	R. 0	R. 102
G. 255	G. 255	G. 204	G. 51	G. 153	G. 153
B. 204	B. 0	B. 102	B. 0	B. 0	B. 0

gp12sw

gp12pat.gif

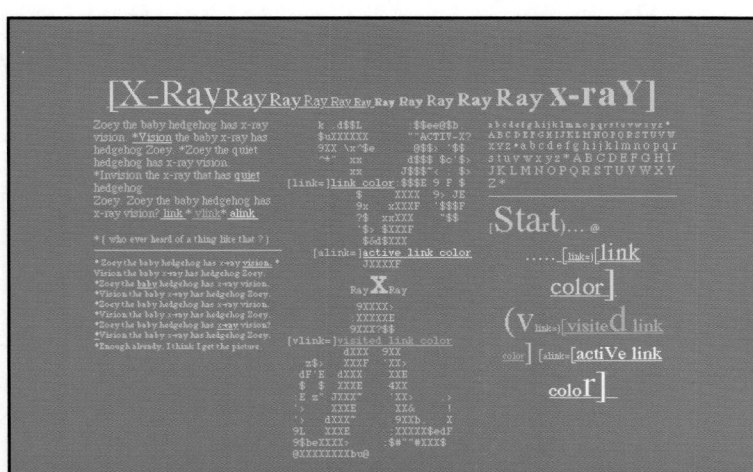

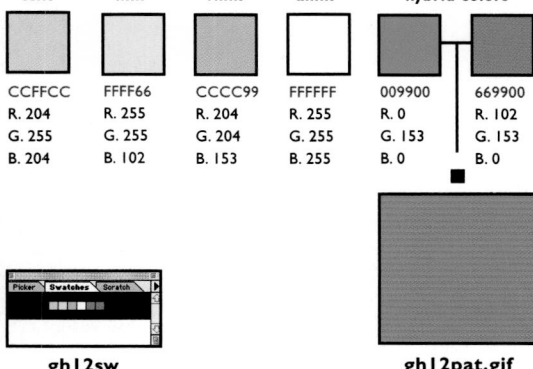

text	link	vlink	alink	hybrid colors	
CCFFCC	FFFF66	CCCC99	FFFFFF	009900	669900
R. 204	R. 255	R. 204	R. 255	R. 0	R. 102
G. 255	G. 255	G. 204	G. 255	G. 153	G. 153
B. 204	B. 102	B. 153	B. 255	B. 0	B. 0

gh12sw

gh12pat.gif

text	link	vlink	alink	bgcolor
CCCC99	99FF99	33CC33	669966	006600
R. 204	R. 153	R. 51	R. 102	R. 0
G. 204	G. 255	G. 204	G.153	G. 102
B.153	B. 153	B. 51	B. 102	B. 0

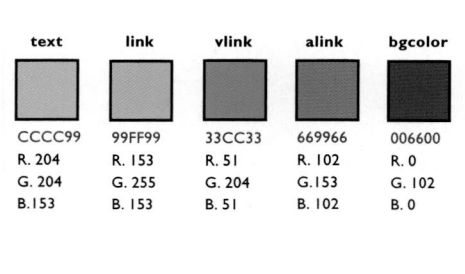

gs13sw

text	link	vlink	alink	tile colors	
CCCC99	6699FF	9999CC	33CCCC	006633	006600
R. 204	R. 102	R. 153	R. 51	R. 0	R. 0
G. 204	G.153	G. 153	G. 204	G. 102	G. 102
B.153	B. 255	B. 204	B. 204	B. 51	B. 0

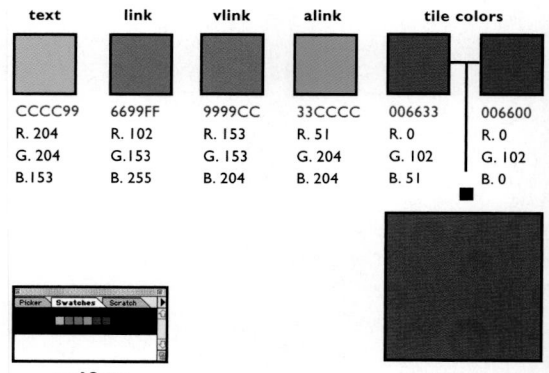

gp13sw

gp13pat.gif

text	link	vlink	alink	hybrid colors	
FFFFCC	FFCC66	CC9999	FF6600	006600	006633
R. 255	R. 255	R. 204	R. 255	R. 0	R. 0
G. 255	G. 204	G. 153	G. 102	G. 102	G. 102
B. 204	B. 102	B. 153	B. 0	B. 0	B. 51

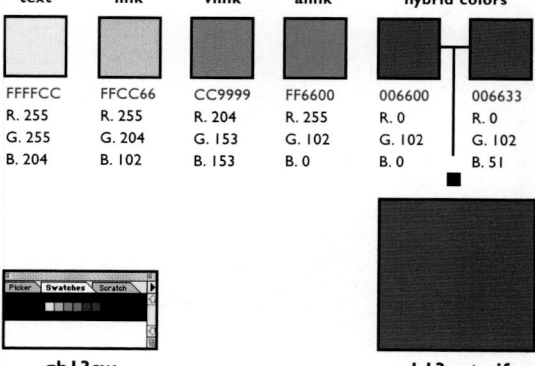

gh13sw

gh13pat.gif

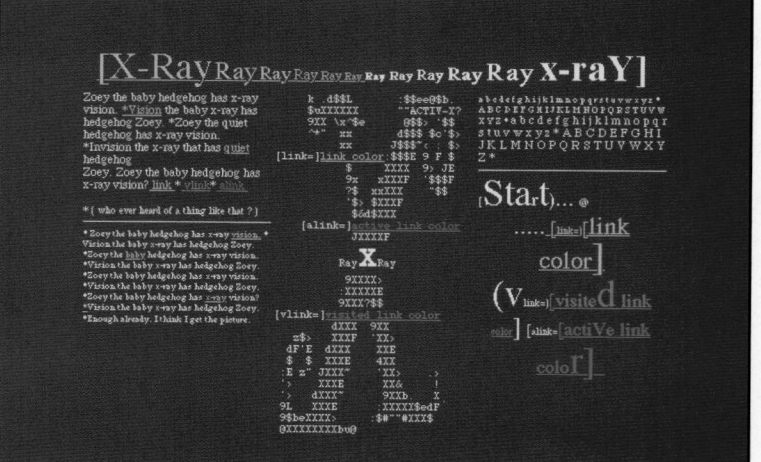

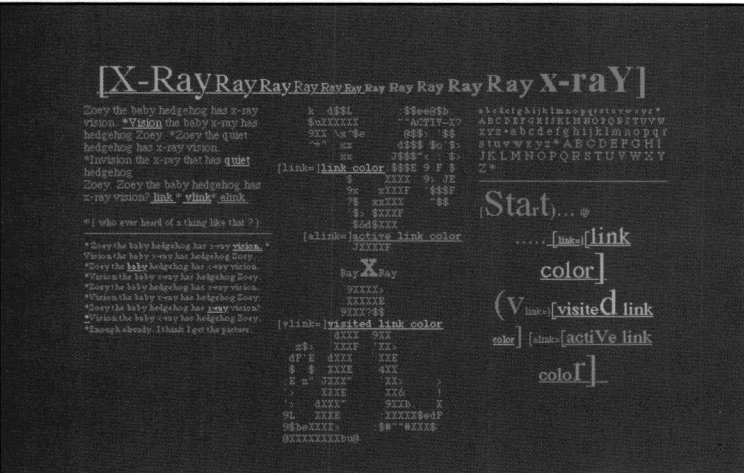

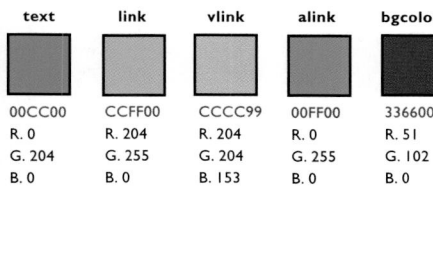

	text	link	vlink	alink	bgcolor
	00CC00	CCFF00	CCCC99	00FF00	336600
	R. 0	R. 204	R. 204	R. 0	R. 51
	G. 204	G. 255	G. 204	G. 255	G. 102
	B. 0	B. 0	B. 153	B. 0	B. 0

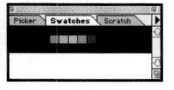

gs14sw

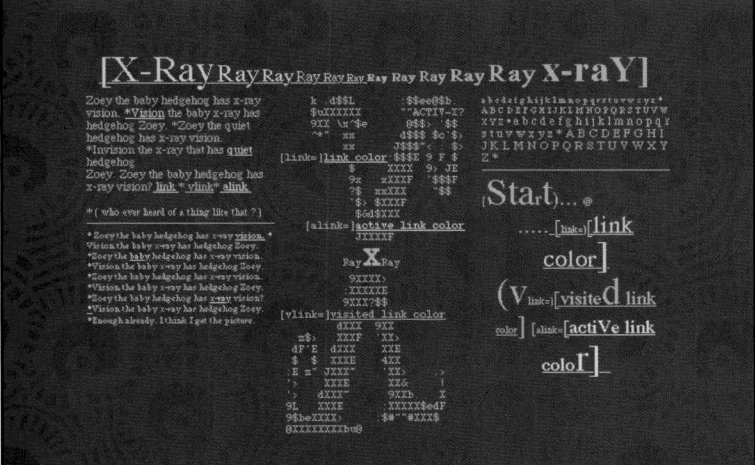

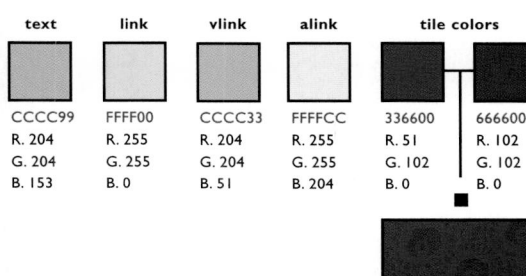

	text	link	vlink	alink	tile colors	
	CCCC99	FFFF00	CCCC33	FFFFCC	336600	666600
	R. 204	R. 255	R. 204	R. 255	R. 51	R. 102
	G. 204	G. 255	G. 204	G. 255	G. 102	G. 102
	B. 153	B. 0	B. 51	B. 204	B. 0	B. 0

gp14sw

gp14pat.gif

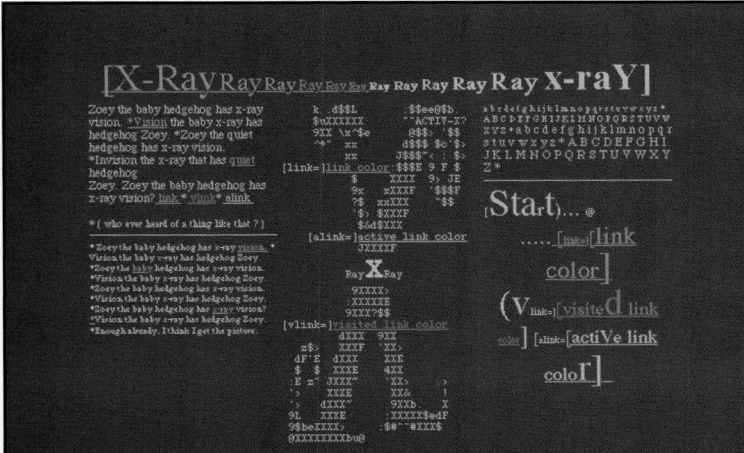

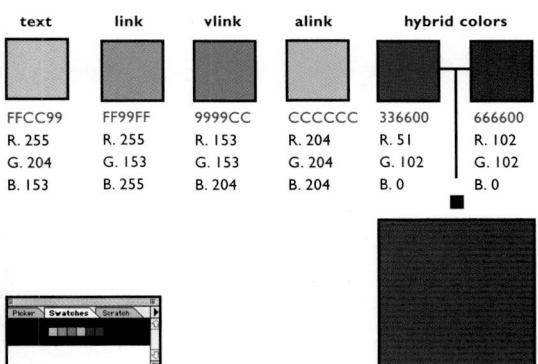

	text	link	vlink	alink	hybrid colors	
	FFCC99	FF99FF	9999CC	CCCCCC	336600	666600
	R. 255	R. 255	R. 153	R. 204	R. 51	R. 102
	G. 204	G. 153	G. 153	G. 204	G. 102	G. 102
	B. 153	B. 255	B. 204	B. 204	B. 0	B. 0

gh14sw

gh14pat.gif

text	link	vlink	alink	bgcolor
999999	CCCC33	996600	FFFFCC	003300
R. 153	R. 204	R. 204	R. 255	R. 0
G. 153	G. 204	G. 102	G. 255	G. 51
B. 153	B. 51	B. 0	B. 204	B. 0

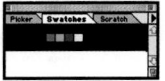

gs15sw

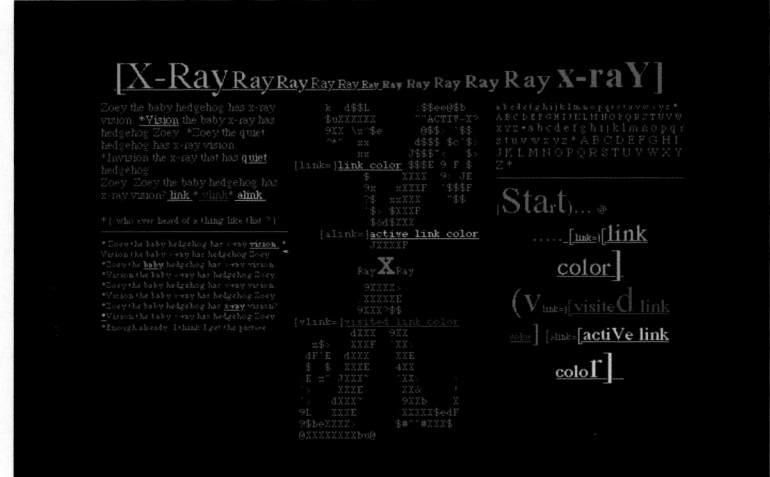

text	link	vlink	alink	tile colors	
33CC99	CCCC33	996600	99CC99	003333	003300
R. 51	R. 204	R. 153	R. 153	R. 0	R. 0
G. 204	G. 204	G. 102	G. 204	G. 51	G. 51
B. 153	B. 51	B. 0	B. 153	B. 51	B. 0

gp15sw

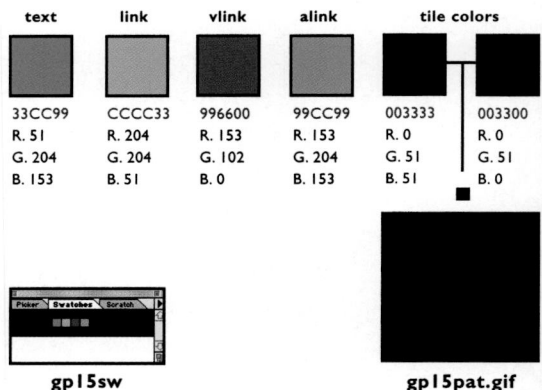

gp15pat.gif

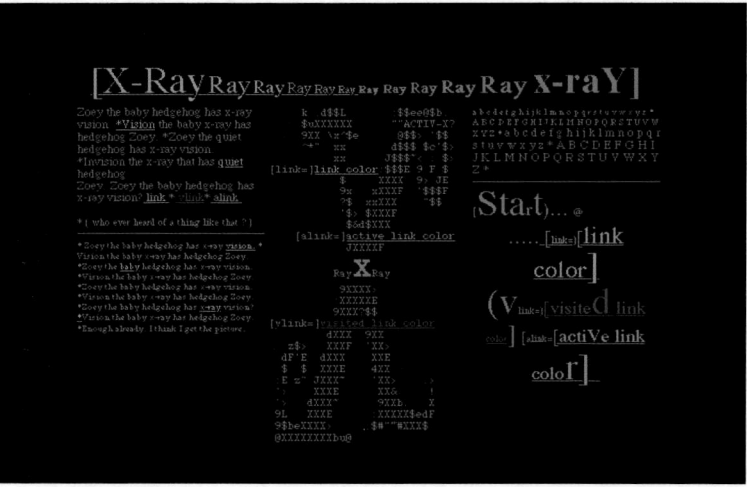

text	link	vlink	alink	hybrid colors	
33CC99	999933	666633	99CC99	003300	003333
R. 51	R. 153	R. 102	R. 153	R. 0	R. 0
G. 204	G. 153	G. 102	G. 204	G. 51	G. 51
B. 153	B. 51	B. 51	B. 153	B. 0	B. 51

gh15sw

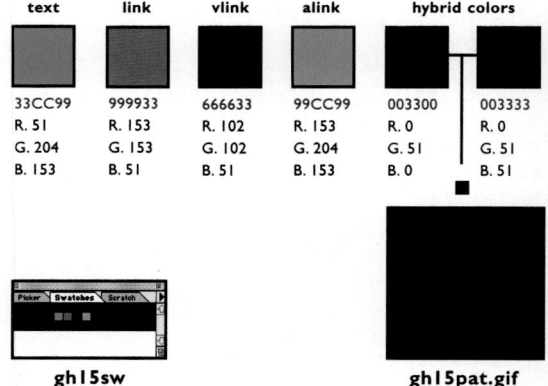

gh15pat.gif

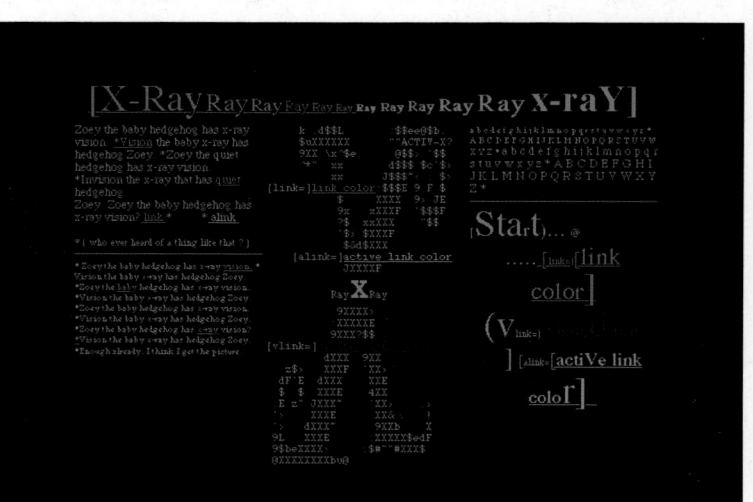

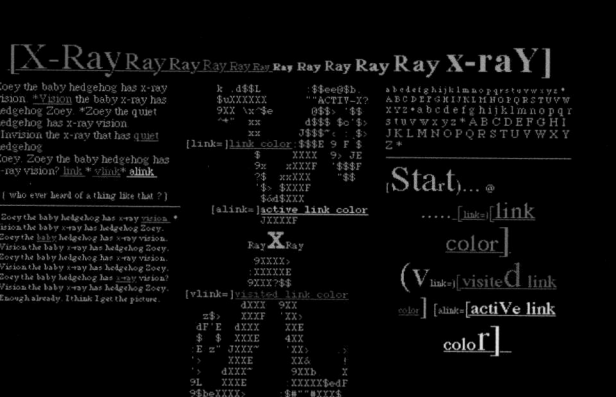

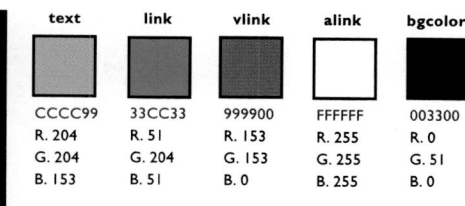

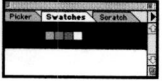

text	link	vlink	alink	bgcolor
CCCC99	33CC33	999900	FFFFFF	003300
R. 204	R. 51	R. 153	R. 255	R. 0
G. 204	G. 204	G. 153	G. 255	G. 51
B. 153	B. 51	B. 0	B. 255	B. 0

gs16sw

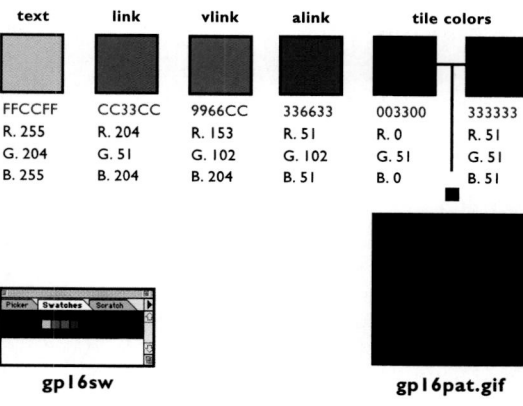

text	link	vlink	alink	tile colors	
FFCCFF	CC33CC	9966CC	336633	003300	333333
R. 255	R. 204	R. 153	R. 51	R. 0	R. 51
G. 204	G. 51	G. 102	G. 102	G. 51	G. 51
B. 255	B. 204	B. 204	B. 51	B. 0	B. 51

gp16sw

gp16pat.gif

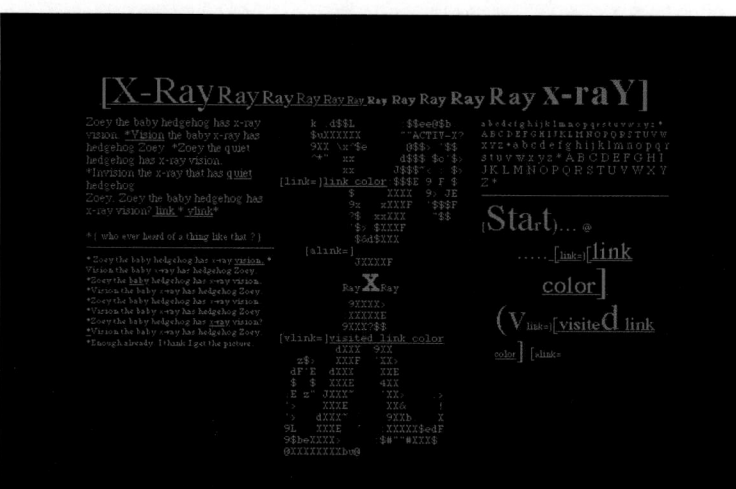

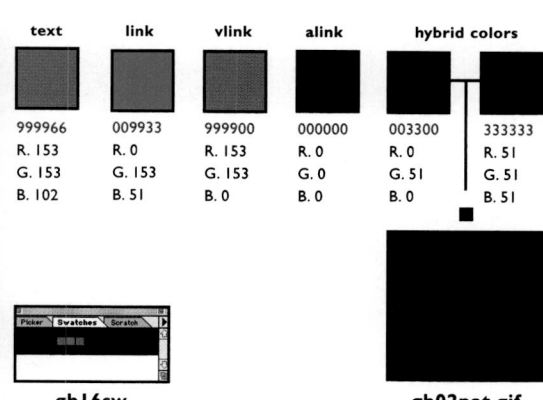

text	link	vlink	alink	hybrid colors	
999966	009933	999900	000000	003300	333333
R. 153	R. 0	R. 153	R. 0	R. 0	R. 51
G. 153	G. 153	G. 153	G. 0	G. 51	G. 51
B. 102	B. 51	B. 0	B. 0	B. 0	B. 51

gh16sw

gh02pat.gif

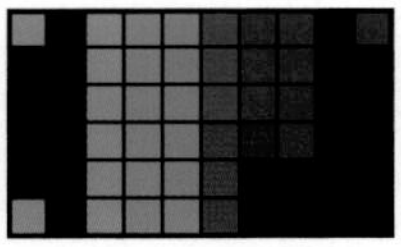

gbgk 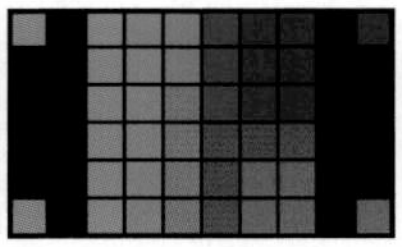 gbgr 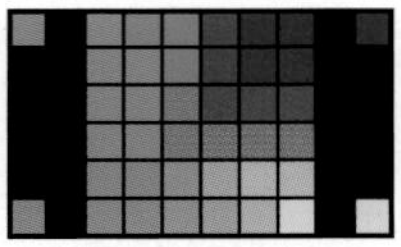 gbgy 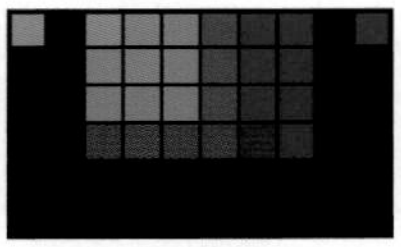 gbkk 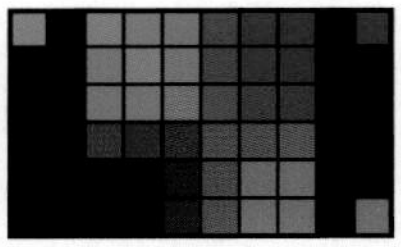 gbkr

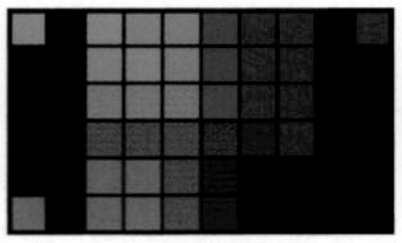

gbrk 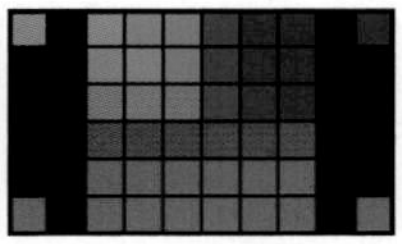 gbrr 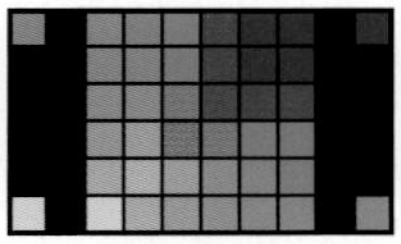 gbyg 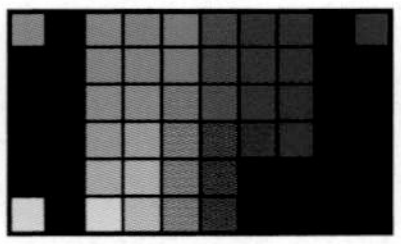 gbyk 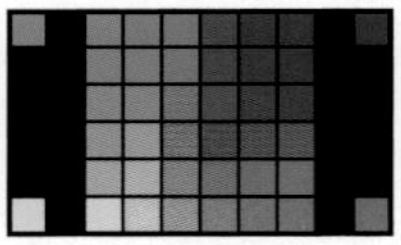 gbyr

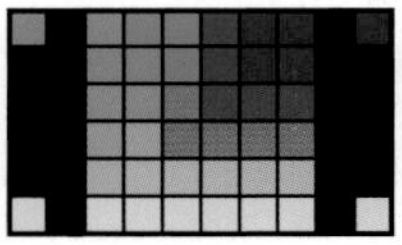

gbyy 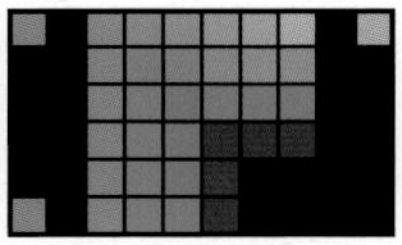 gcgk 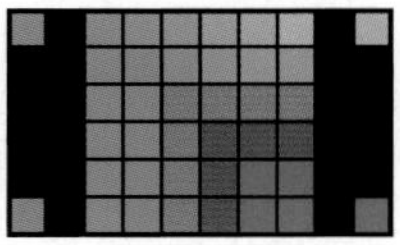 gcgr 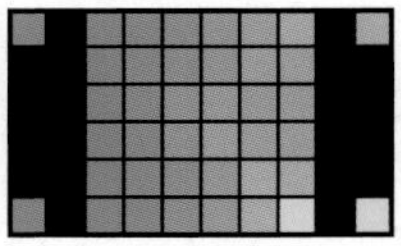 gcgy 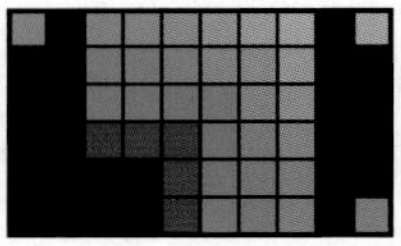 gckg

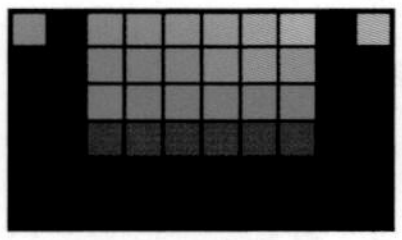

gckk 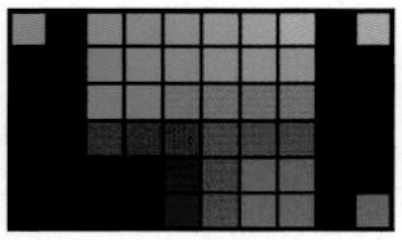 gckr 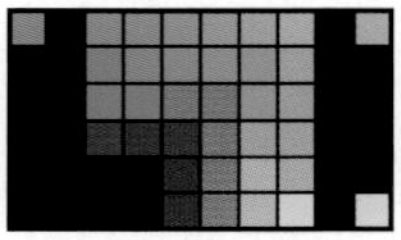 gcky 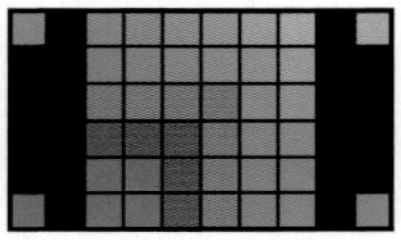 gcrg 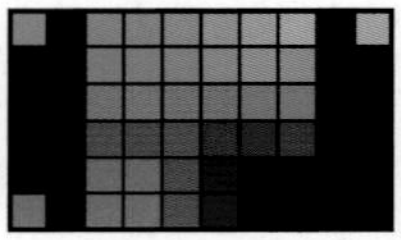 gcrk

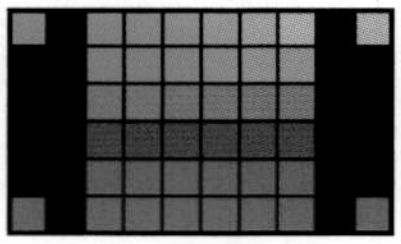

gcrr 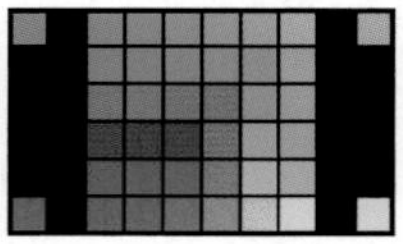 gcry 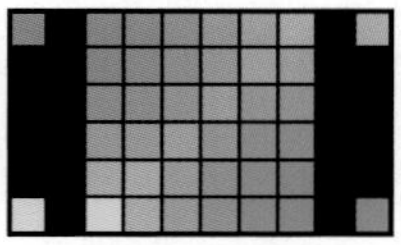 gcyg 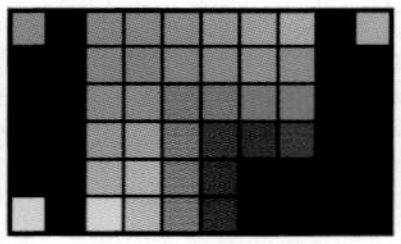 gcyk 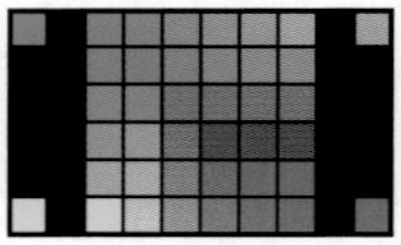 gcyr

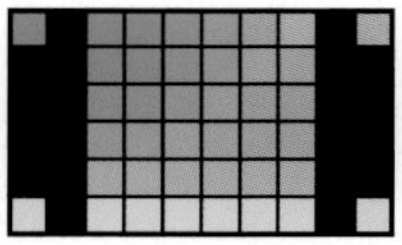

gcyy 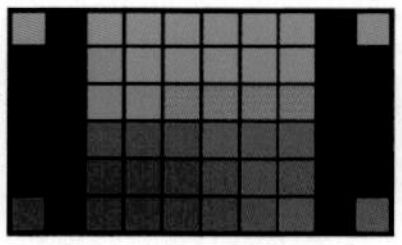 ggbm 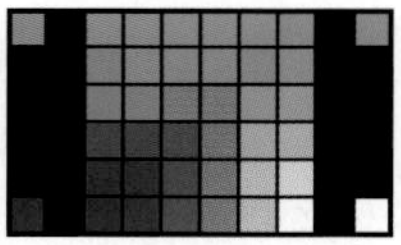 ggbw 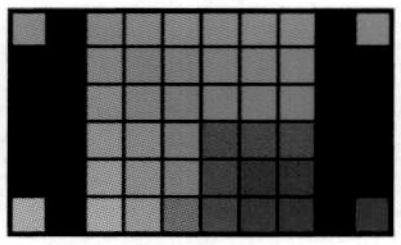 ggcb 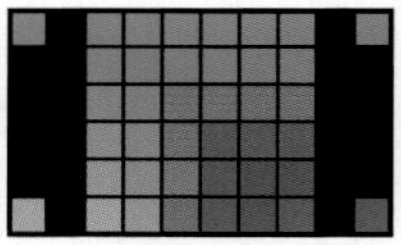 ggcm

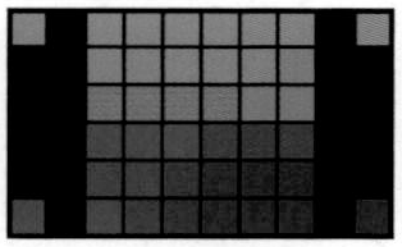

ggmb 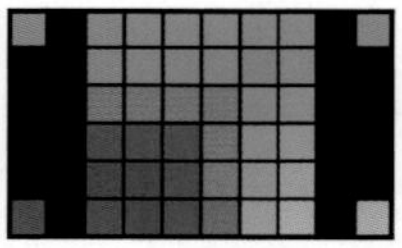 ggmc 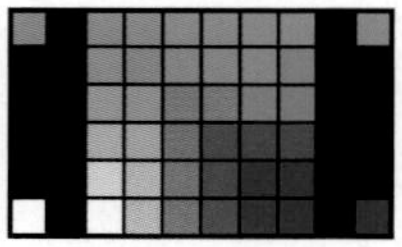 ggwb 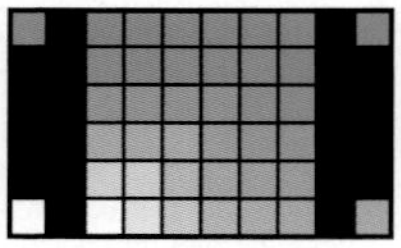 ggwc 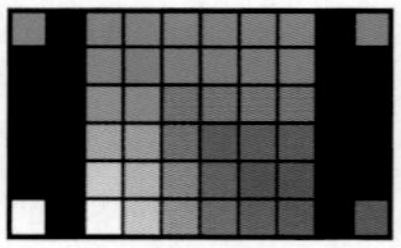 ggwm

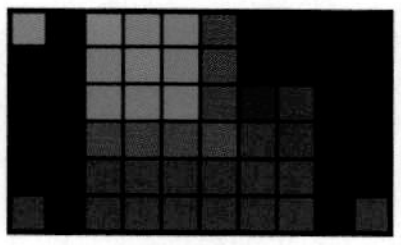

gkbb 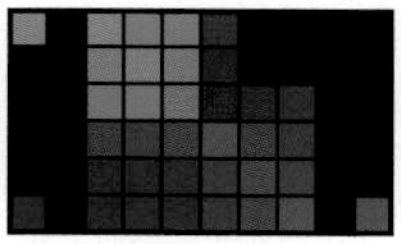   gkbm 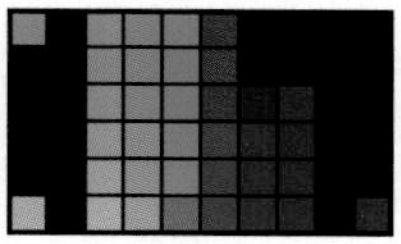   gkcb 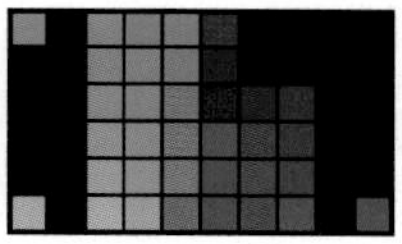   gkcm 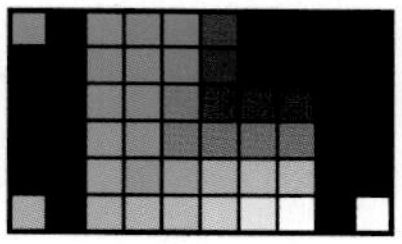   gkcw

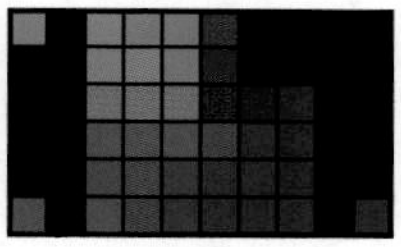

gkmb 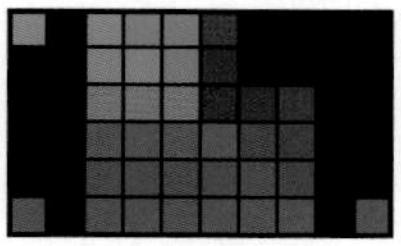   gkmm 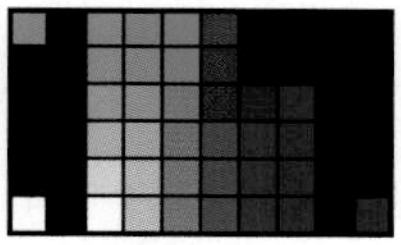   gkwb 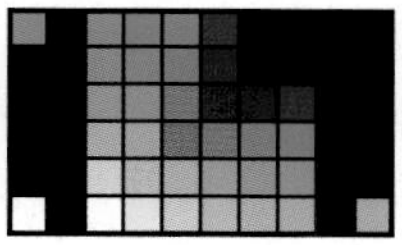   gkwc 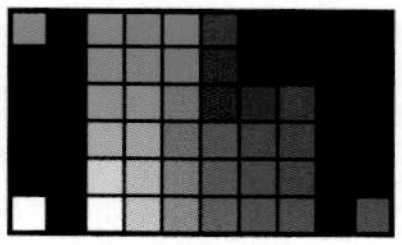   gkwm

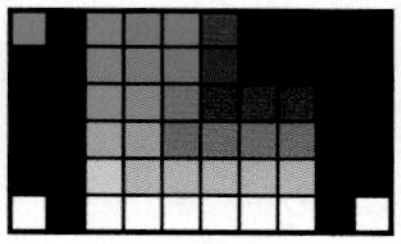

gkww 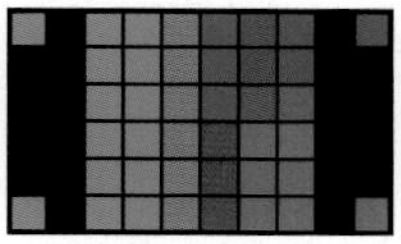   gmgr 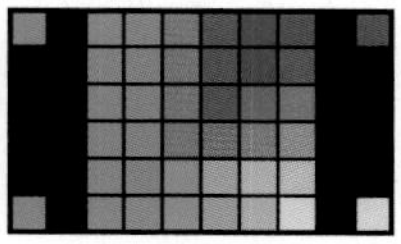   gmgy 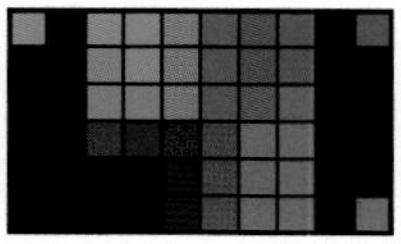   gmkr 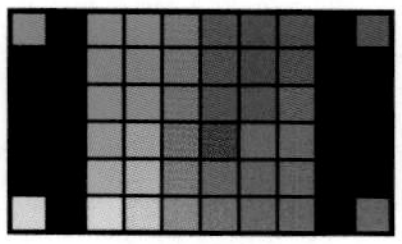   gmyr

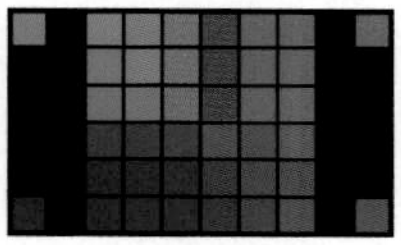

grbm 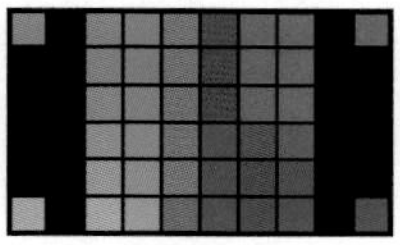   grcm 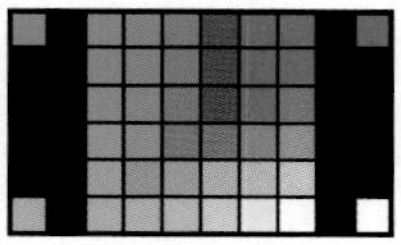   grcw 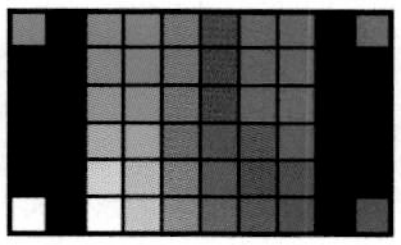   grwm 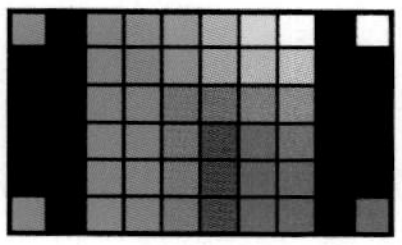   gwgr

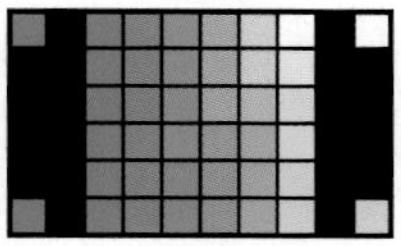

gwgy    gwkr    gwky 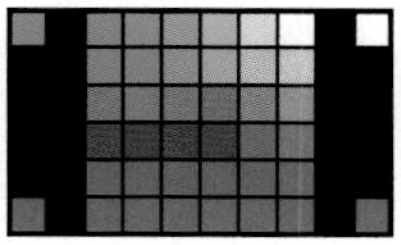   gwrr 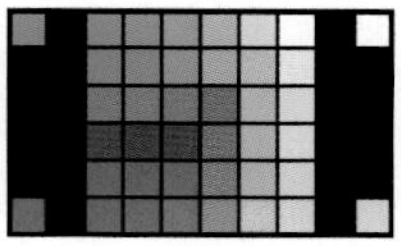   gwry

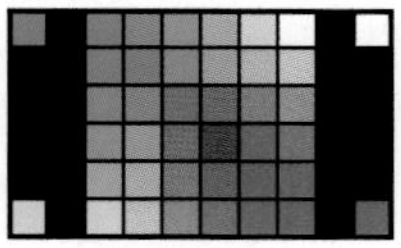

gwyr 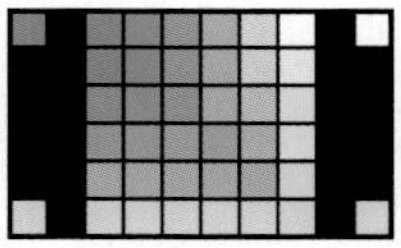   gwyy    gybm 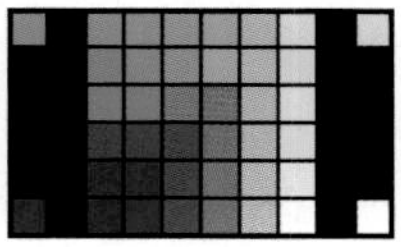   gybw 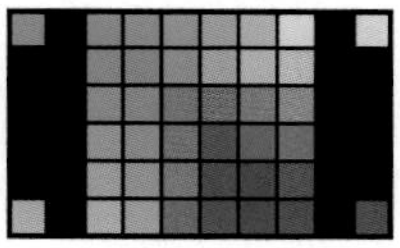   gycm

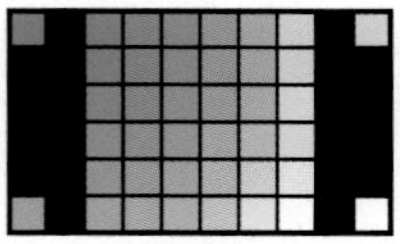

gycw    gymm 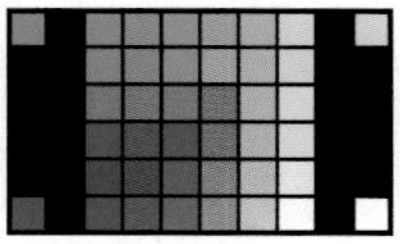   gymw 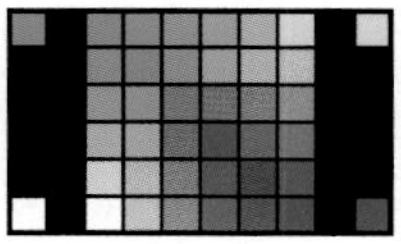   gywm 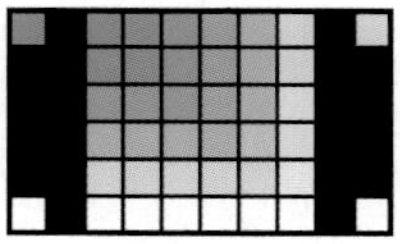   gyww

BLUE

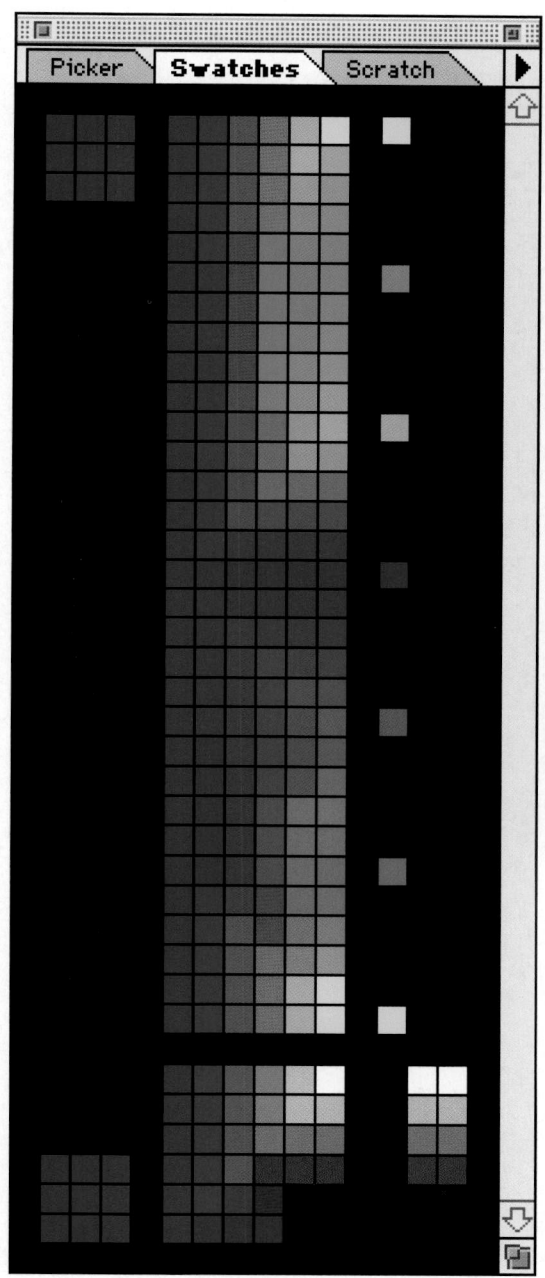

mbs

mbd

text	link	vlink	alink	bgcolor
006666	666633	009933	666699	CCCCFF
R. 0	R. 102	R. 0	R. 102	R. 204
G. 125	G. 102	G. 153	G. 102	G. 204
B. 102	B. 51	B. 51	B. 153	B. 255

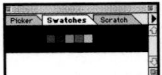

bs01sw

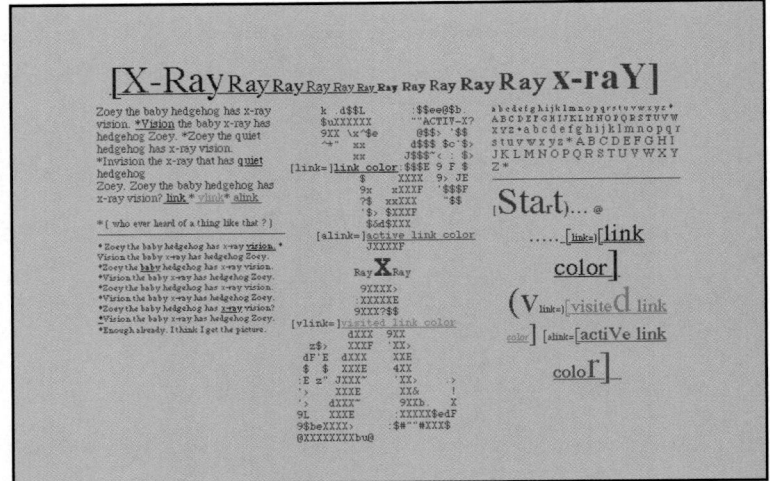

text	link	vlink	alink	tile colors	
333366	3333CC	996600	FFFFFF	CCCCCC	CCCCFF
R. 51	R. 51	R. 153	R. 255	R. 204	R. 204
G. 51	G. 51	G. 102	G. 255	G. 204	G. 204
B. 102	B. 204	B. 0	B. 255	B. 204	B. 255

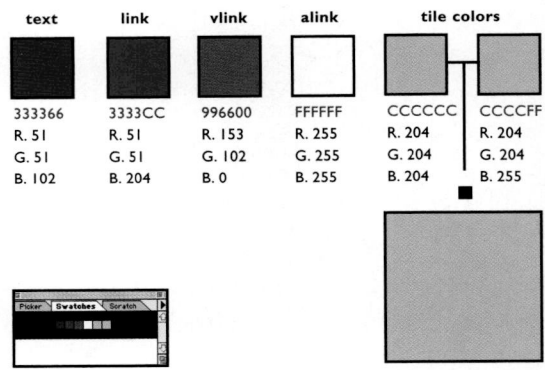

bp01sw   **bp01pat.gif**

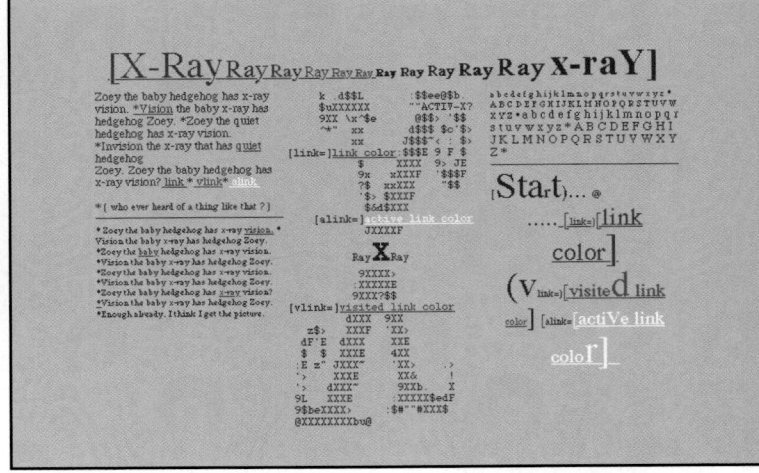

text	link	vlink	alink	hybrid colors	
666699	CC33CC	996699	FF00CC	CCCCCC	CCCCFF
R. 102	R. 204	R. 153	R. 255	R. 204	R. 204
G. 102	G. 51	G. 102	G. 0	G. 204	G. 204
B. 153	B. 204	B. 153	B. 204	B. 204	B. 255

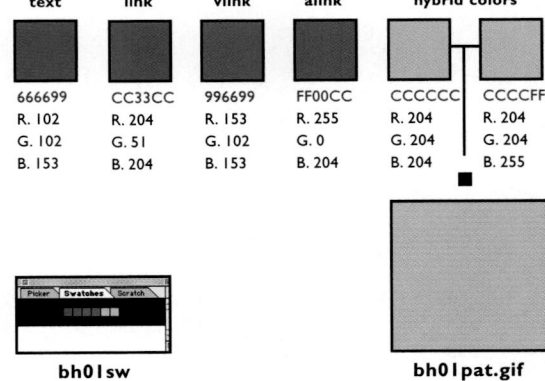

bh01sw   **bh01pat.gif**

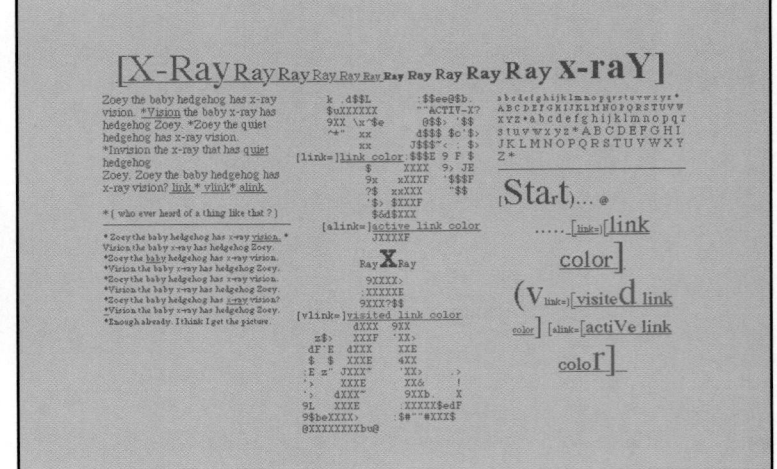

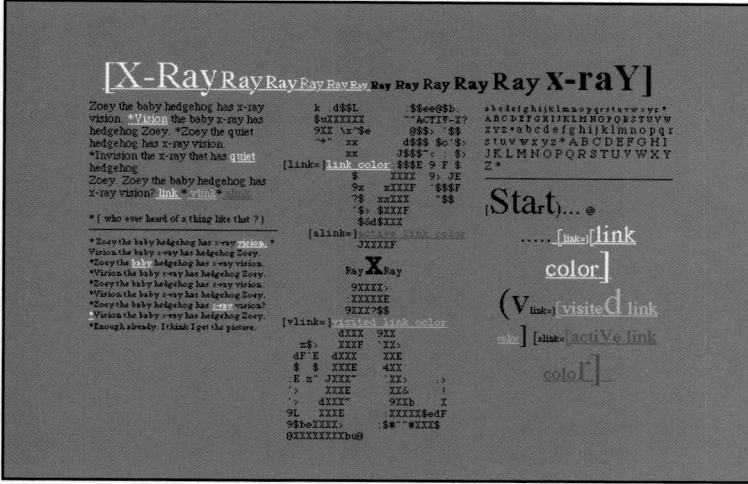

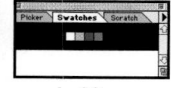

text	link	vlink	alink	bgcolor
333300	FFFFFF	CCFFFF	6666FF	9999FF
R. 51	R. 255	R. 204	R. 102	R. 153
G. 51	G. 255	G. 255	G. 102	G. 153
B. 0	B. 255	B. 255	B. 255	B. 255

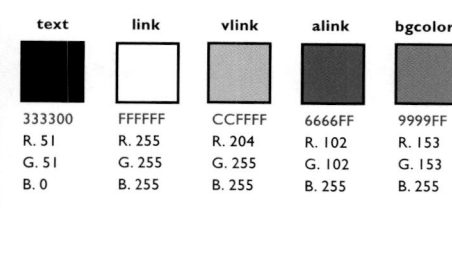

bs02sw

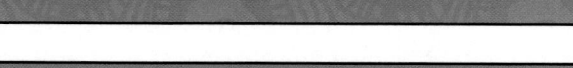

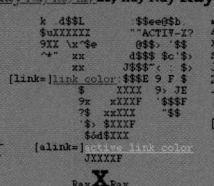

text	link	vlink	alink	tile colors	
333366	0000FF	666666	FF00FF	CC99FF	99FFFF
R. 51	R. 0	R. 102	R. 255	R. 204	R. 153
G. 51	G. 0	G. 102	G. 0	G. 153	G. 255
B. 102	B. 255	B. 102	B. 255	B. 255	B. 255

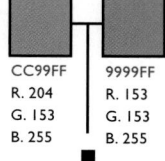

bp02sw

bp02pat.gif

text	link	vlink	alink	hybrid colors	
333300	0000FF	006699	CCCCCC	CC99FF	9999FF
R. 51	R. 0	R. 0	R. 204	R. 204	R. 153
G. 51	G. 0	G. 102	G. 204	G. 153	G. 153
B. 0	B. 255	B. 153	B. 204	B. 255	B. 255

bh02sw

bh02pat.gif

text	link	vlink	alink	bgcolor
333366	CC00CC	9900CC	FF0000	9999CC
R. 51	R. 204	R. 153	R. 255	R. 153
G. 51	G. 0	G. 0	G. 0	G. 153
B. 102	B. 204	B. 204	B. 0	B. 204

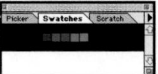

bs03sw

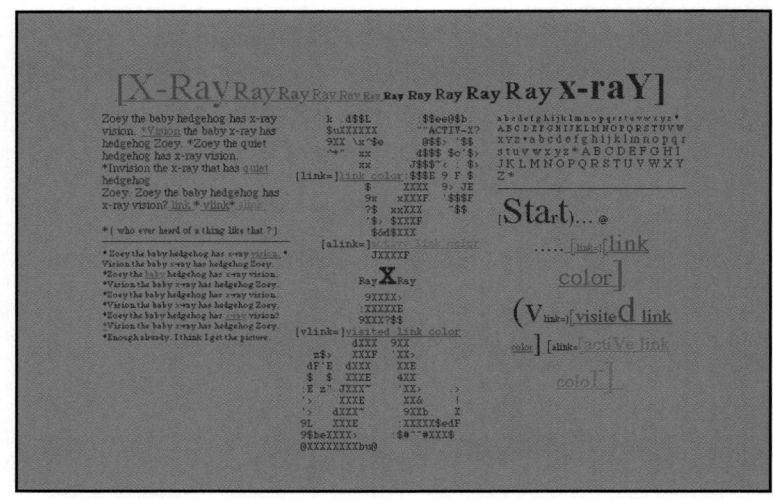

text	link	vlink	alink	tile colors	
663333	FF0000	CC3333	CC6666	CC99FF	9999CC
R. 102	R. 255	R. 204	R. 204	R. 204	R. 153
G. 51	G. 0	G. 51	G. 102	G. 153	G. 153
B. 51	B. 0	B. 51	B. 102	B. 255	B. 204

bp03sw

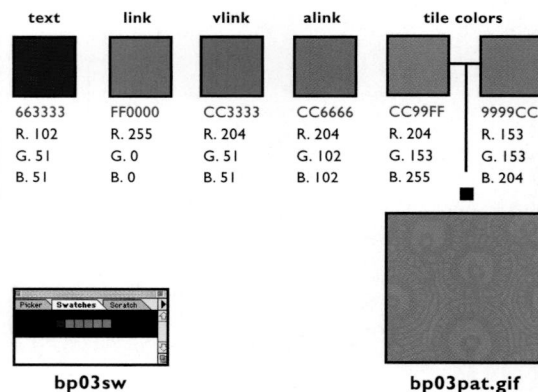

bp03pat.gif

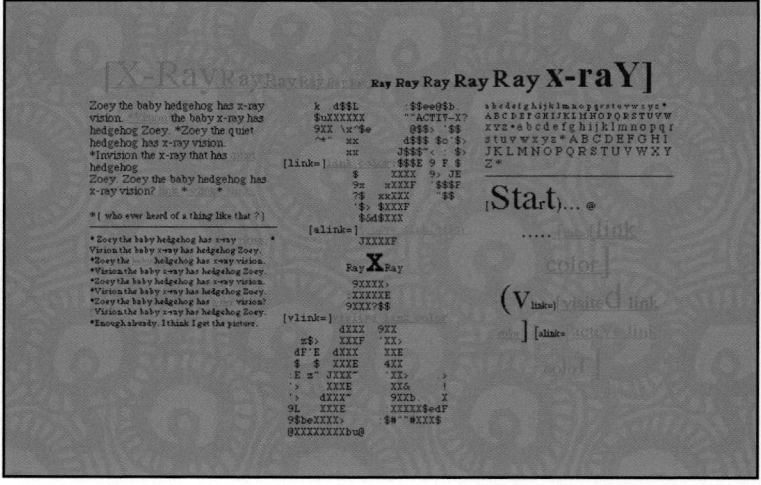

text	link	vlink	alink	hybrid colors	
333333	0033FF	6666CC	CCCCCC	CC99FF	9999CC
R. 51	R. 0	R. 102	R. 204	R. 204	R. 153
G. 51	G. 51	G. 102	G. 204	G. 153	G. 153
B. 51	B. 255	B. 204	B. 204	B. 255	B. 204

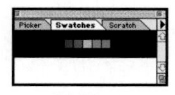

bh03sw

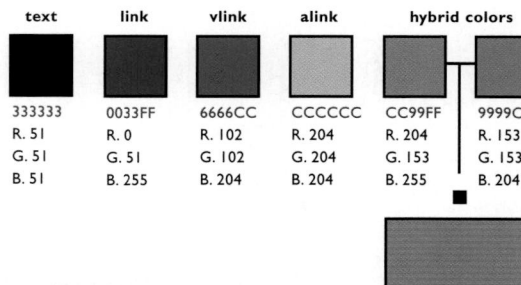

bh03pat.gif

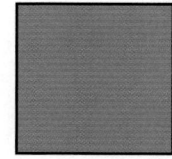

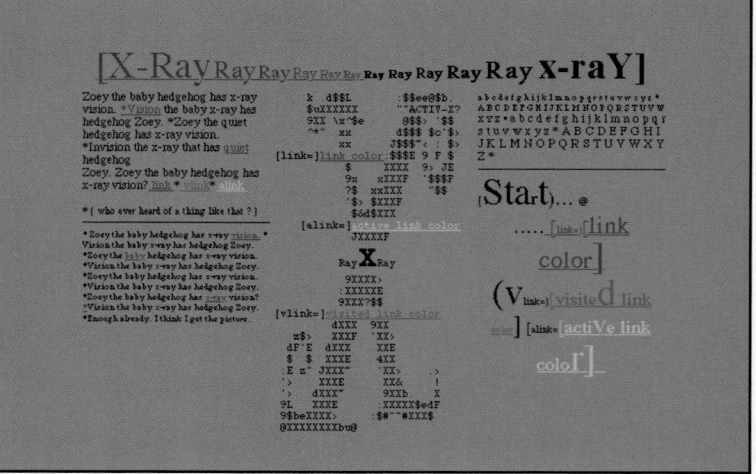

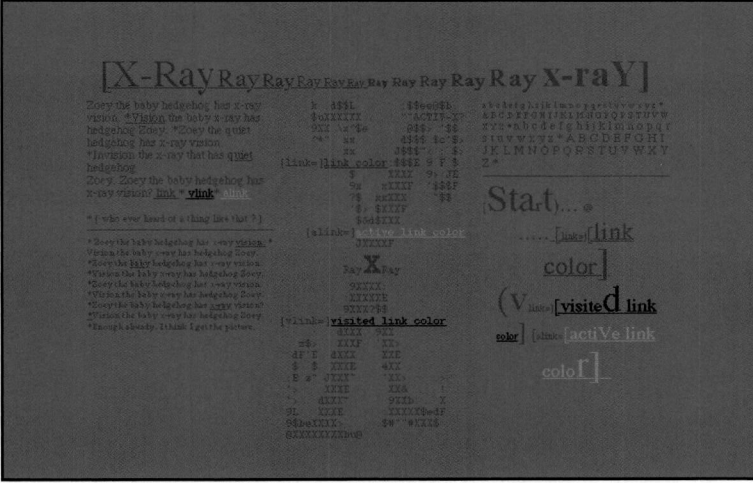

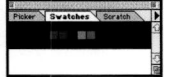

	text	link	vlink	alink	bgcolor
	003399	0000CC	333333	9999FF	6666FF
	R. 0	R. 0	R. 51	R. 153	R. 102
	G. 51	G. 0	G. 51	G. 153	G. 102
	B. 153	B. 204	B. 51	B. 255	B. 255

bs04sw

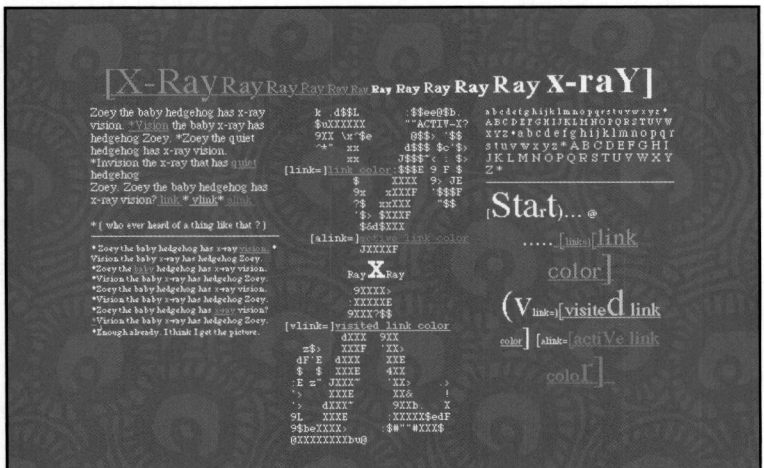

	text	link	vlink	alink	tile colors	
	FFFFFF	99FF33	FFFF00	00CC00	9966FF	6666FF
	R. 255	R. 153	R. 255	R. 0	R. 153	R. 102
	G. 255	G. 255	G. 255	G. 204	G. 102	G. 102
	B. 255	B. 51	B. 0	B. 0	B. 255	B. 255

bp04sw

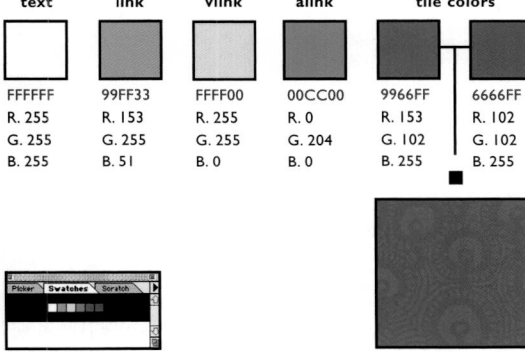

bp04pat.gif

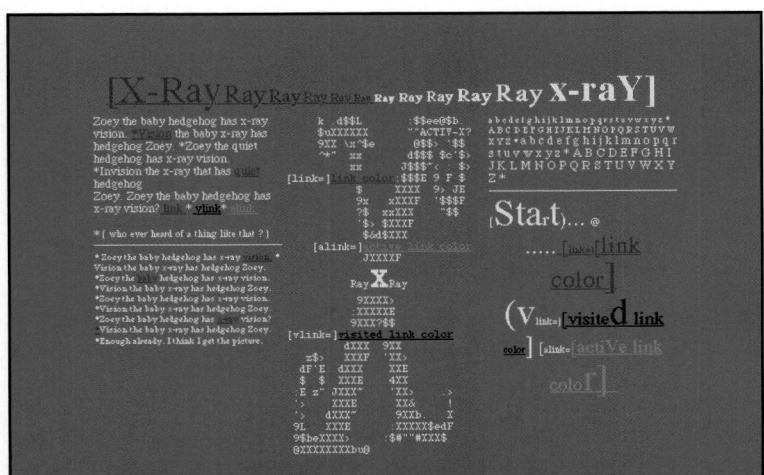

	text	link	vlink	alink	hybrid colors	
	CCFFFF	0000FF	333333	9999FF	9966FF	6666FF
	R. 204	R. 0	R. 51	R. 153	R. 153	R. 102
	G. 255	G. 0	G. 51	G. 153	G. 102	G. 102
	B. 255	B. 255	B. 51	B. 255	B. 255	B. 255

bh04sw

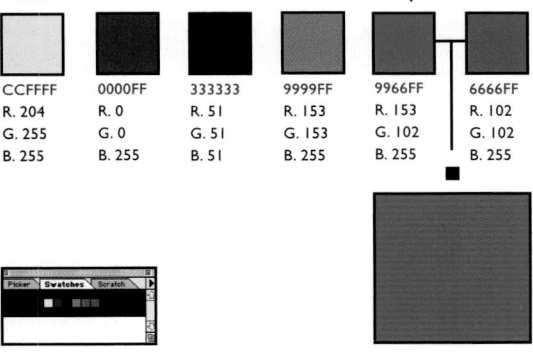

bh04pat.gif

text	link	vlink	alink	bgcolor
99CC99	00FF00	339933	FFFFFF	3333FF
R. 153	R. 0	R. 51	R. 255	R. 51
G. 204	G. 255	G. 153	G. 255	G. 51
B. 153	B. 0	B. 51	B. 255	B. 255

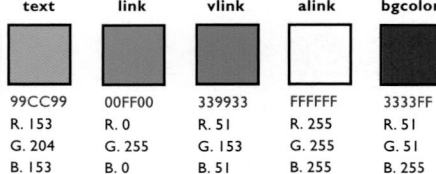

bs05sw

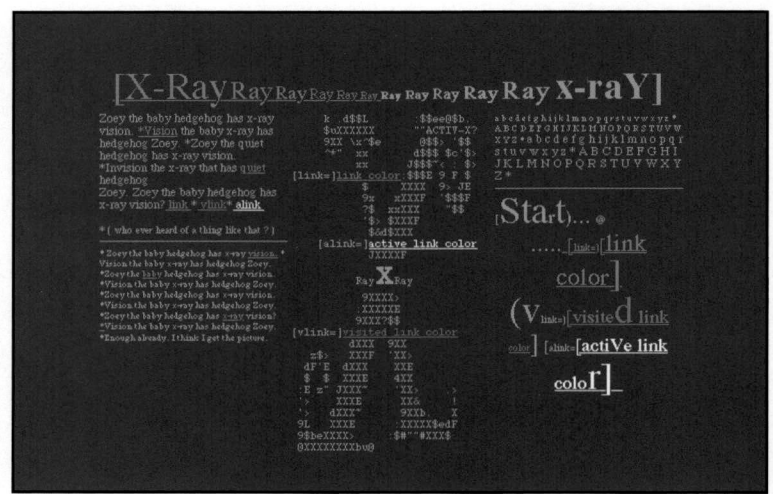

text	link	vlink	alink	tile colors	
CCCCFF	FFCC33	999999	FFFFFF	6633FF	3333FF
R. 204	R. 255	R. 153	R. 255	R. 102	R. 51
G. 204	G. 204	G. 153	G. 255	G. 51	G. 51
B. 204	B. 51	B. 153	B. 255	B. 255	B. 255

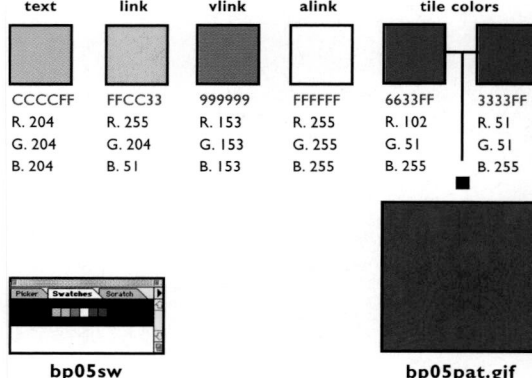

bp05sw

bp05pat.gif

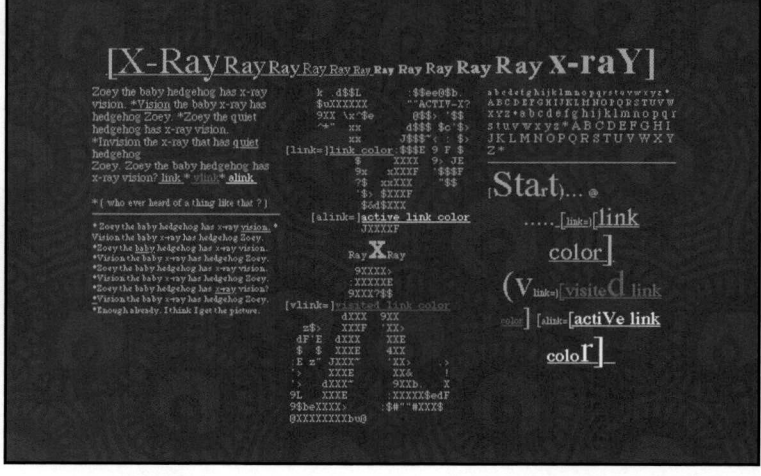

text	link	vlink	alink	hybrid colors	
000033	9999FF	0000FF	666699	6633FF	3333FF
R. 0	R. 153	R. 0	R. 102	R. 102	R. 51
G. 0	G. 153	G. 0	G. 102	G. 51	G. 51
B. 51	B. 255	B. 255	B. 153	B. 255	B. 255

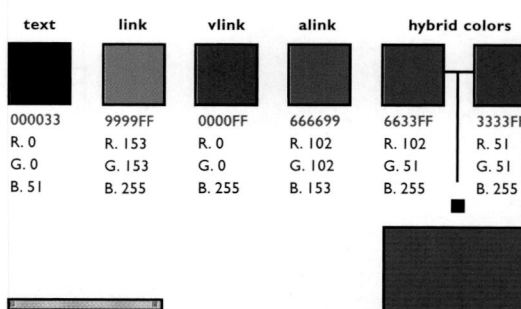

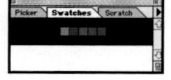

bh05sw

bh05pat.gif

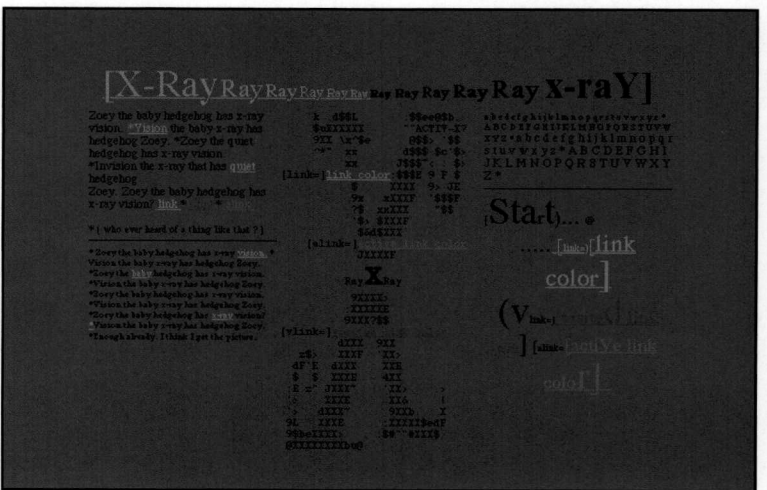

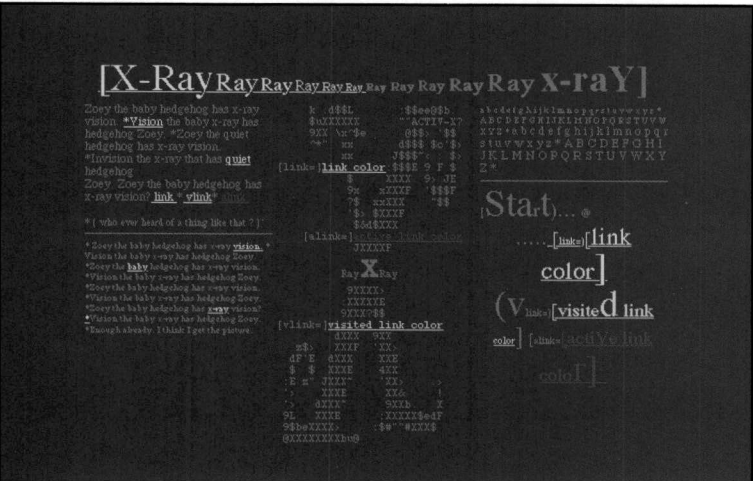

text	link	vlink	alink	bgcolor
9999CC	FFFF99	FFFF00	666699	3300FF
R. 153	R. 255	R. 255	R. 102	R. 51
G. 153	G. 255	G. 255	G. 102	G. 0
B. 204	B. 153	B. 0	B. 153	B. 255

bs06sw

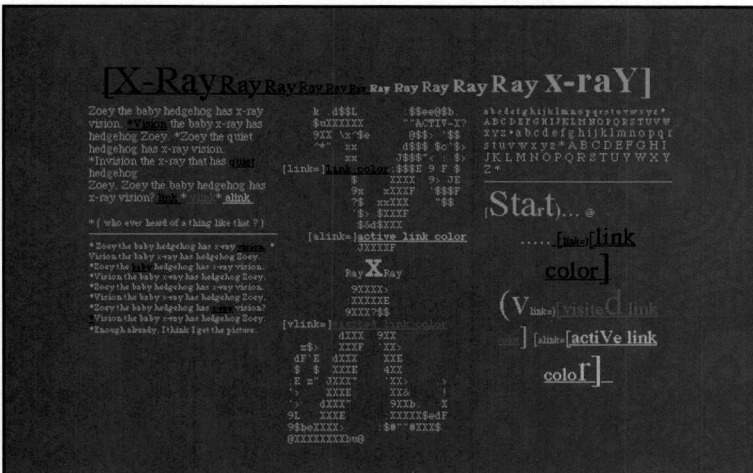

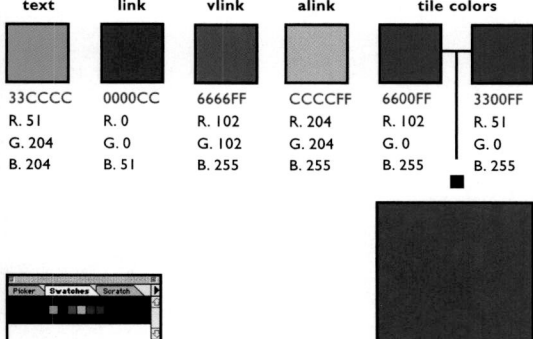

text	link	vlink	alink	tile colors	
33CCCC	0000CC	6666FF	CCCCFF	6600FF	3300FF
R. 51	R. 0	R. 102	R. 204	R. 102	R. 51
G. 204	G. 0	G. 102	G. 204	G. 0	G. 0
B. 204	B. 51	B. 255	B. 255	B. 255	B. 255

bp06sw

bp06pat.gif

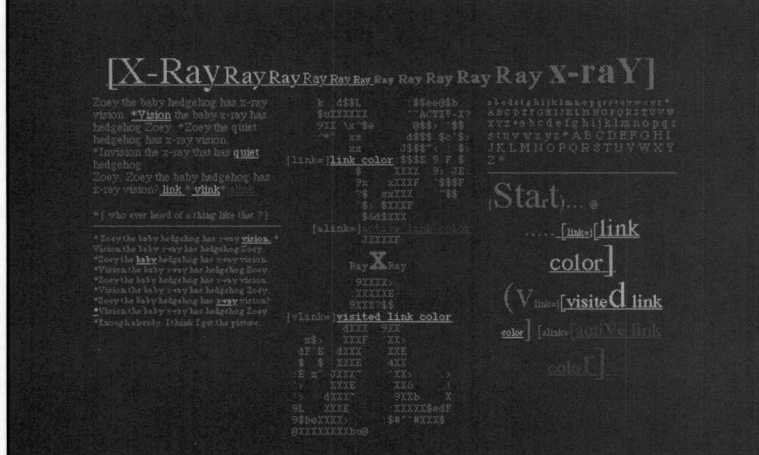

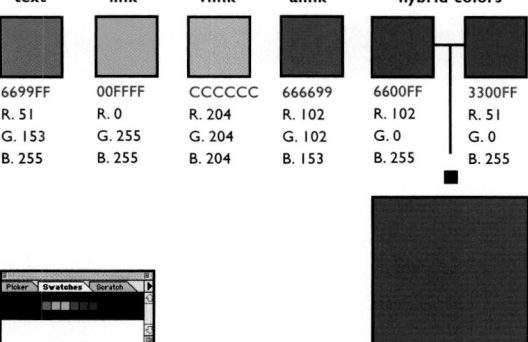

text	link	vlink	alink	hybrid colors	
6699FF	00FFFF	CCCCCC	666699	6600FF	3300FF
R. 51	R. 0	R. 204	R. 102	R. 102	R. 51
G. 153	G. 255	G. 204	G. 102	G. 0	G. 0
B. 255	B. 255	B. 204	B. 153	B. 255	B. 255

bh06sw

bh06pat.gif

text	link	vlink	alink	bgcolor
999999	0066FF	9966FF	333333	333399
R. 153	R. 0	R. 153	R. 51	R. 51
G. 153	G. 102	G. 102	G. 51	G. 51
B. 153	B. 255	B. 255	B. 51	B. 153

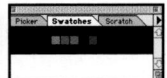

bs07sw

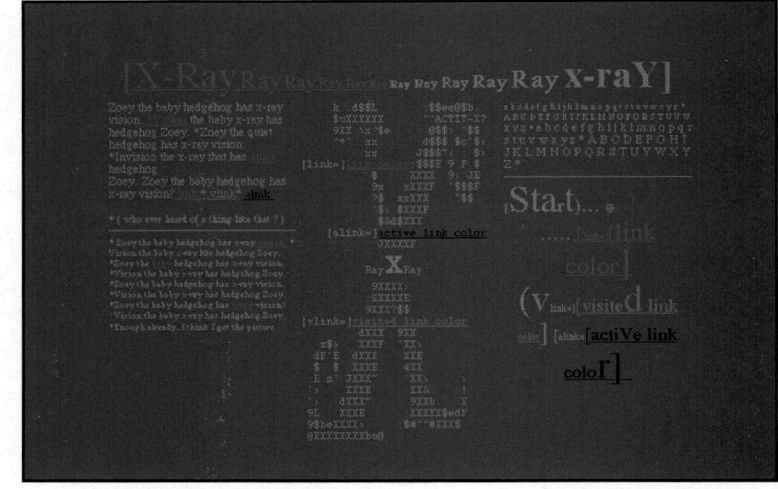

text	link	vlink	alink	tile colors	
CCCC99	CCCC00	CC9933	FFFF00	663399	333399
R. 204	R. 204	R. 204	R. 255	R. 102	R. 51
G. 204	G. 204	G. 153	G. 255	G. 51	G. 51
B. 153	B. 0	B. 51	B. 0	B. 153	B. 153

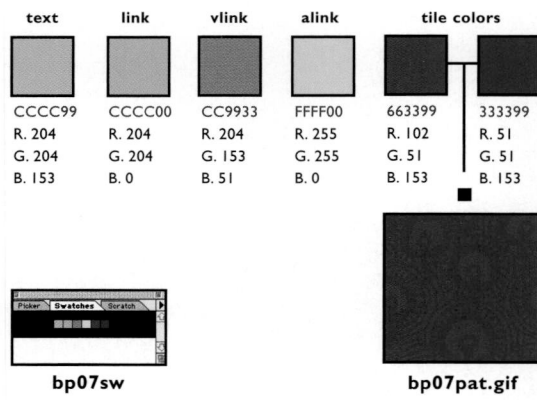

bp07sw　　　　　**bp07pat.gif**

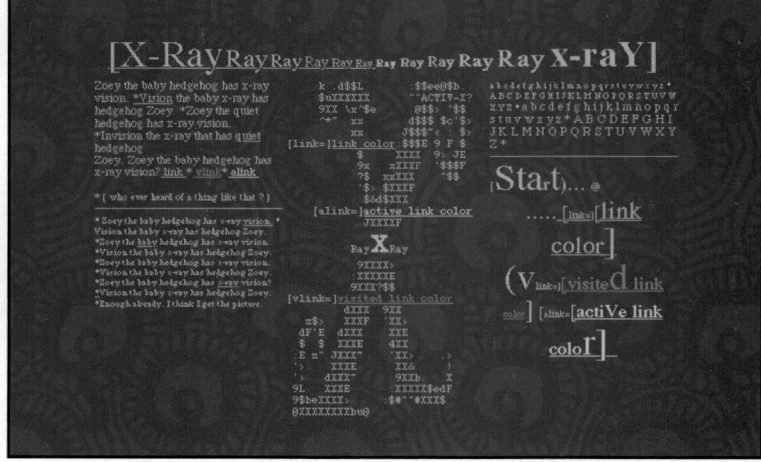

text	link	vlink	alink	hybrid colors	
FFCC66	FFFF00	CC9933	FF6600	663399	333399
R. 255	R. 255	R. 204	R. 255	R. 102	R. 51
G. 204	G. 255	G. 153	G. 102	G. 51	G. 51
B. 102	B. 0	B. 51	B. 0	B. 153	B. 153

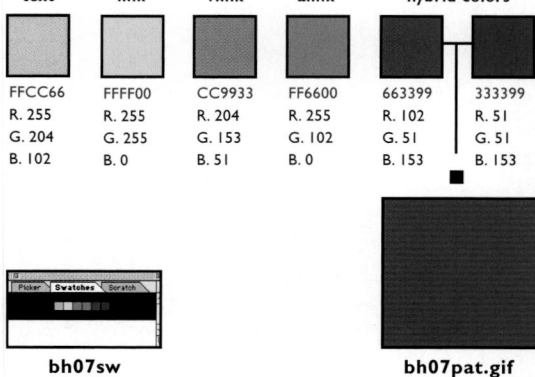

bh07sw　　　　　**bh07pat.gif**

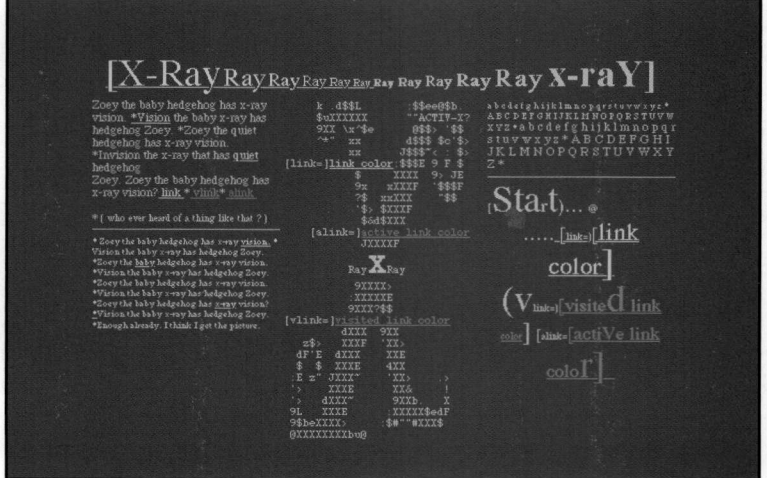

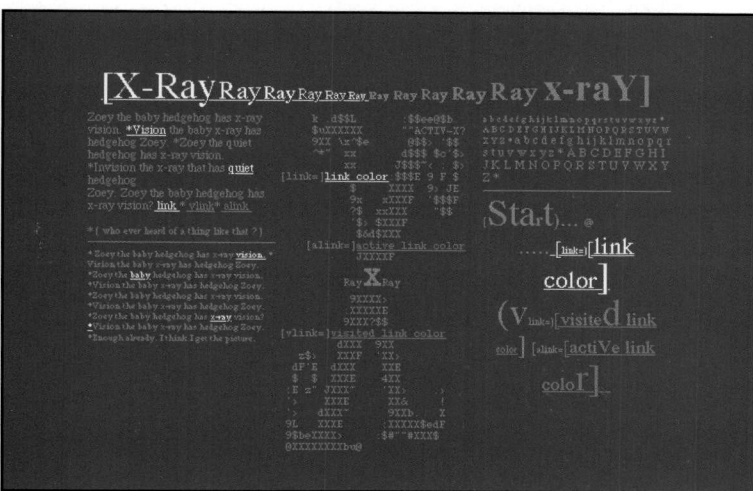

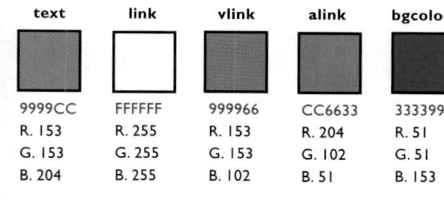

text	link	vlink	alink	bgcolor
9999CC	FFFFFF	999966	CC6633	333399
R. 153	R. 255	R. 153	R. 204	R. 51
G. 153	G. 255	G. 153	G. 102	G. 51
B. 204	B. 255	B. 102	B. 51	B. 153

bs08sw

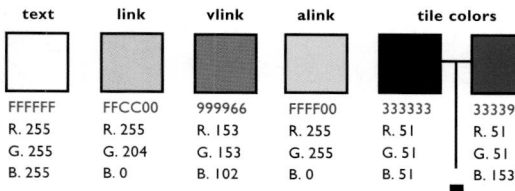

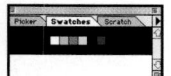

text	link	vlink	alink	tile colors	
FFFFFF	FFCC00	999966	FFFF00	333333	333399
R. 255	R. 255	R. 153	R. 255	R. 51	R. 51
G. 255	G. 204	G. 153	G. 255	G. 51	G. 51
B. 255	B. 0	B. 102	B. 0	B. 51	B. 153

bp08sw

bp08pat.gif

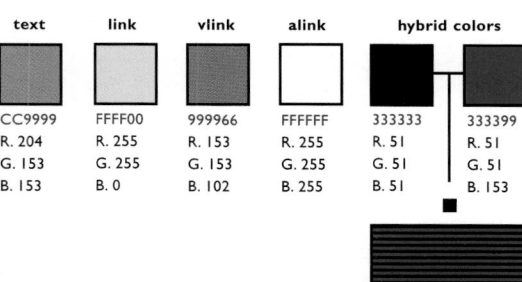

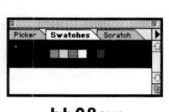

text	link	vlink	alink	hybrid colors	
CC9999	FFFF00	999966	FFFFFF	333333	333399
R. 204	R. 255	R. 153	R. 255	R. 51	R. 51
G. 153	G. 255	G. 153	G. 255	G. 51	G. 51
B. 153	B. 0	B. 102	B. 255	B. 51	B. 153

bh08sw

bh08pat.gif

text	link	vlink	alink	bgcolor
CC99CC	FF33FF	666666	3333CC	333366
R. 204	R. 255	R. 102	R. 51	R. 51
G. 153	G. 51	G. 102	G. 51	G. 51
B. 204	B. 255	B. 102	B. 204	B. 102

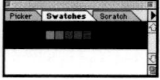

bs09sw

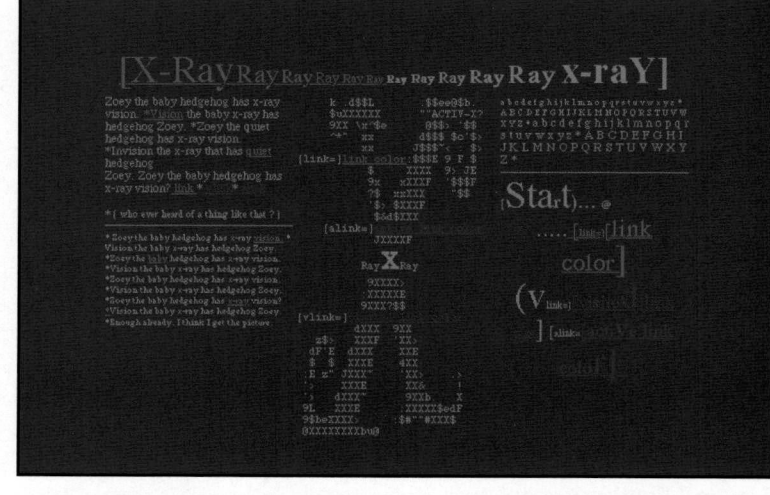

text	link	vlink	alink	tile colors	
FF9999	FF3333	9966FF	CC0000	333333	333366
R. 255	R. 255	R. 153	R. 204	R. 51	R. 51
G. 153	G. 51	G. 102	G. 0	G. 51	G. 51
B. 153	B. 51	B. 255	B. 0	B. 51	B. 102

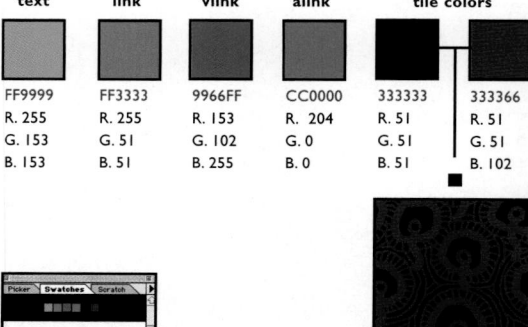

bp09sw   **bp09pat.gif**

text	link	vlink	alink	hybrid colors	
9999CC	6666FF	666666	3333CC	333333	333366
R. 153	R. 102	R. 102	R. 51	R. 51	R. 51
G. 153	G. 102	G. 102	G. 51	G. 51	G. 51
B. 204	B. 255	B. 102	B. 204	B. 51	B. 102

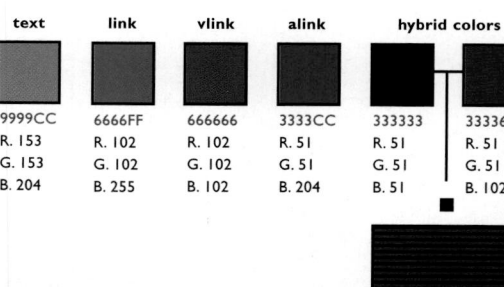

bh09sw   **bh09pat.gif**

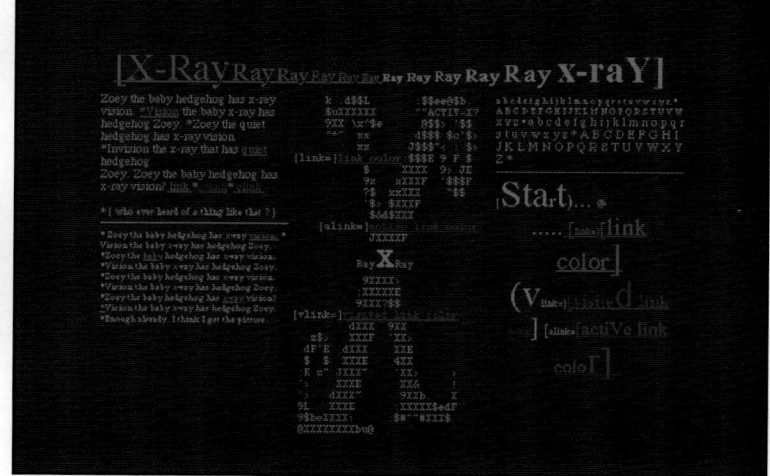

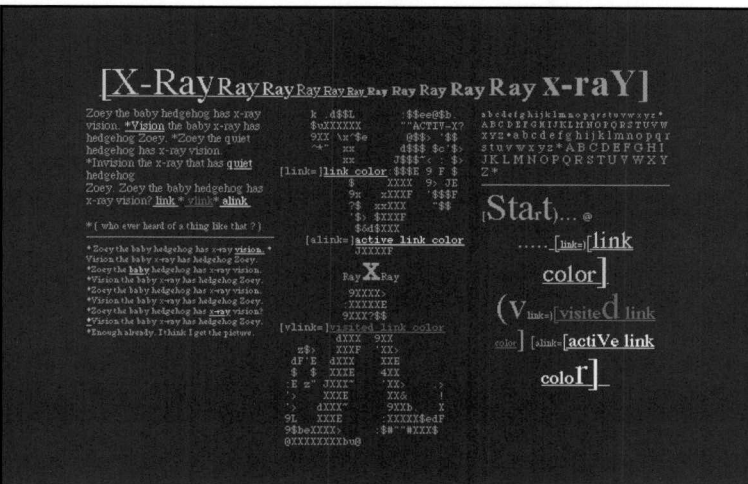

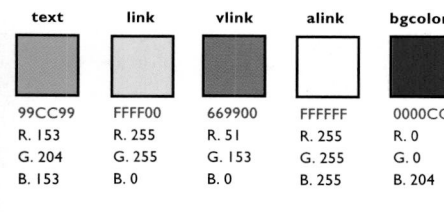

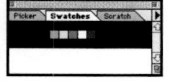

text	link	vlink	alink	bgcolor
99CC99	FFFF00	669900	FFFFFF	0000CC
R. 153	R. 255	R. 51	R. 255	R. 0
G. 204	G. 255	G. 153	G. 255	G. 0
B. 153	B. 0	B. 0	B. 255	B. 204

bs10sw

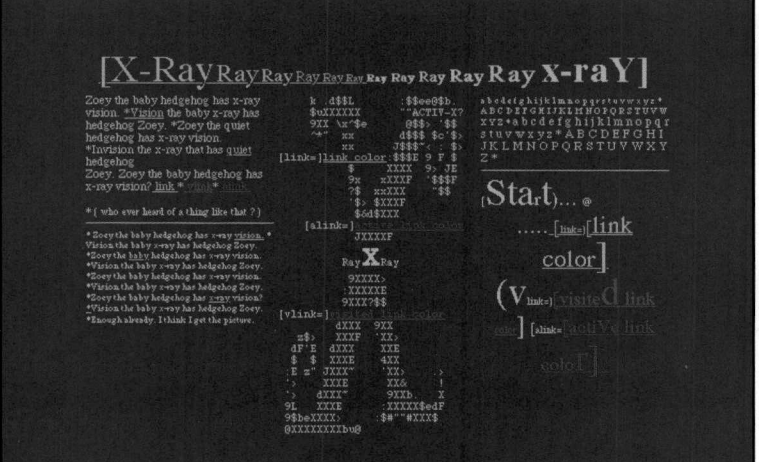

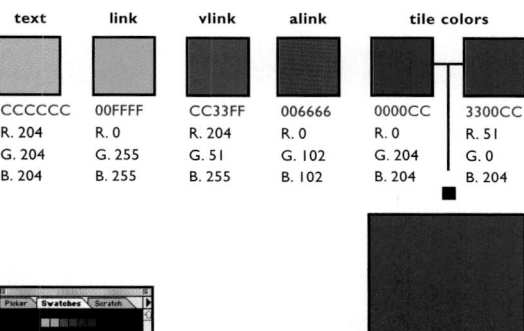

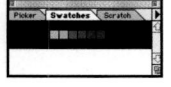

text	link	vlink	alink	tile colors	
CCCCCC	00FFFF	CC33FF	006666	0000CC	3300CC
R. 204	R. 0	R. 204	R. 0	R. 0	R. 51
G. 204	G. 255	G. 51	G. 102	G. 204	G. 0
B. 204	B. 255	B. 255	B. 102	B. 204	B. 204

bp10sw   **bp10pat.gif**

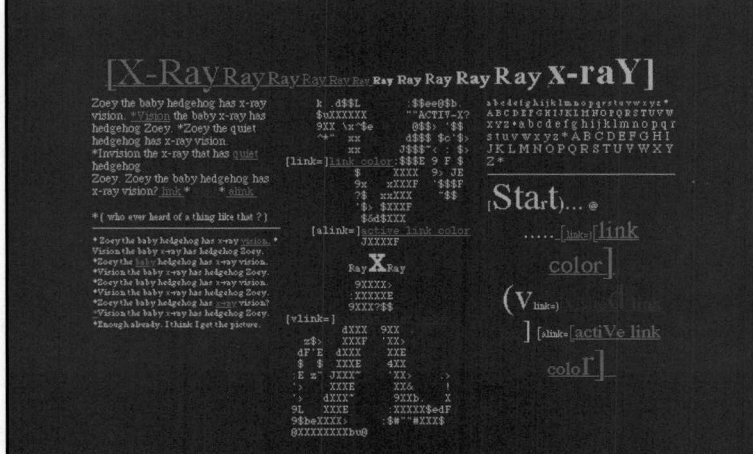

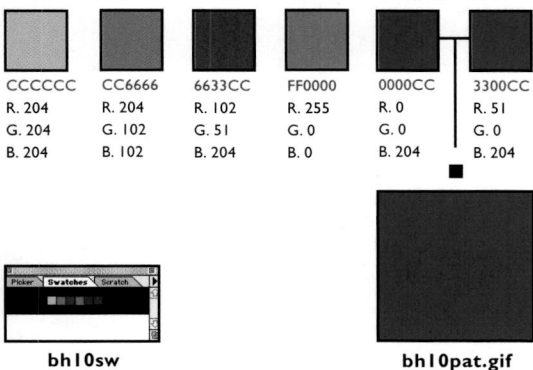

text	link	vlink	alink	hybrid colors	
CCCCCC	CC6666	6633CC	FF0000	0000CC	3300CC
R. 204	R. 204	R. 102	R. 255	R. 0	R. 51
G. 204	G. 102	G. 51	G. 0	G. 0	G. 0
B. 204	B. 102	B. 204	B. 0	B. 204	B. 204

bh10sw   **bh10pat.gif**

text	link	vlink	alink	bgcolor
6666FF	999966	666600	003333	000099
R. 102	R. 153	R. 102	R. 0	R. 0
G. 102	G. 153	G. 102	G. 51	G. 0
B. 255	B. 100	B. 0	B. 51	B. 153

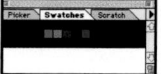

bs11sw

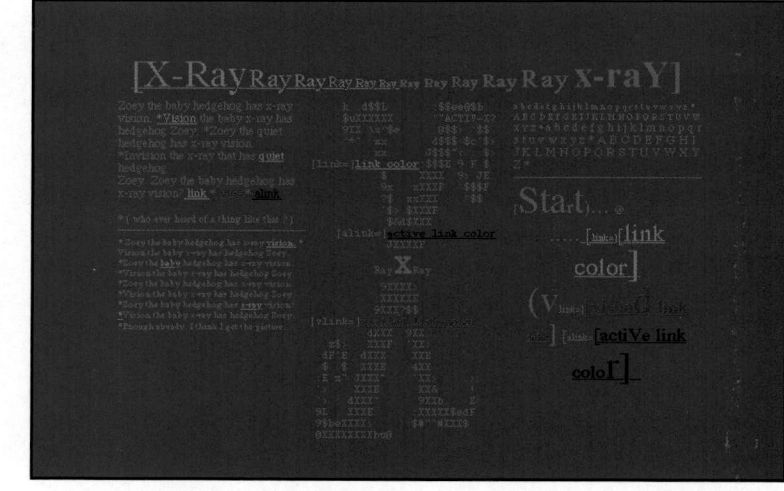

text	link	vlink	alink	tile colors	
9999CC	FFFFFF	009966	3333FF	330099	000099
R. 153	R. 255	R. 0	R. 51	R. 51	R. 0
G. 153	G. 255	G. 153	G. 51	G. 0	G. 0
B. 204	B. 255	B. 102	B. 255	B. 153	B. 153

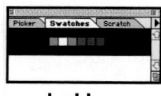

bp11sw

bp11pat.gif

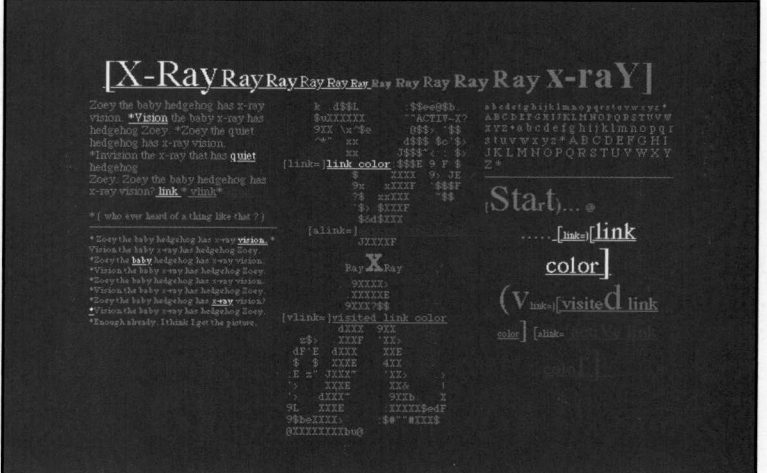

text	link	vlink	alink	hybrid colors	
9999CC	FF6666	009966	669966	330099	000099
R. 153	R. 255	R. 0	R. 102	R. 51	R. 0
G. 153	G. 102	G. 153	G. 153	G. 0	G. 0
B. 204	B. 102	B. 102	B. 102	B. 153	B. 153

bh11sw

bh11pat.gif

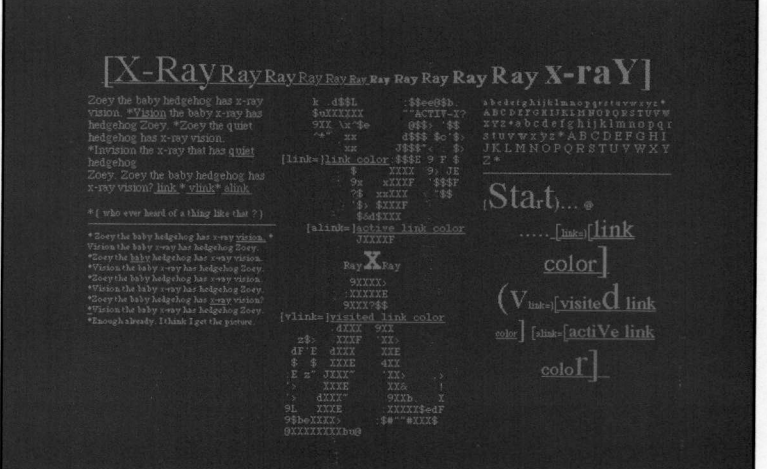

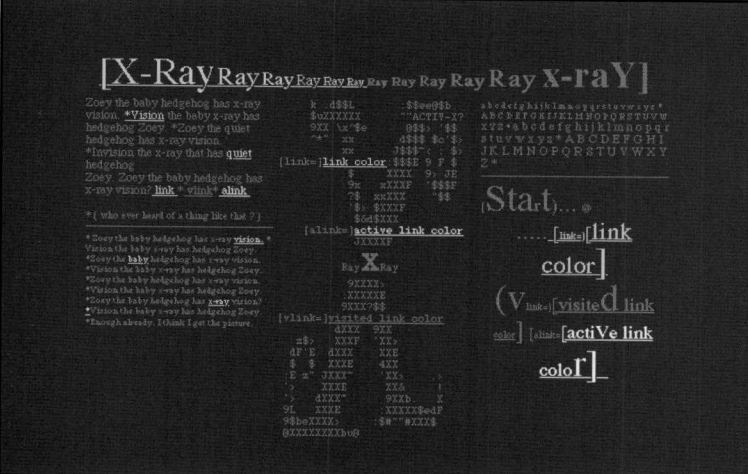

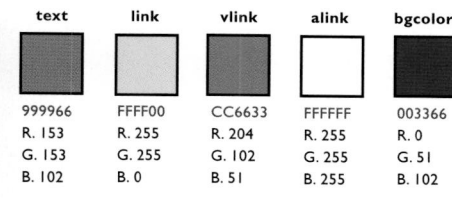

text	link	vlink	alink	bgcolor
999966	FFFF00	CC6633	FFFFFF	003366
R. 153	R. 255	R. 204	R. 255	R. 0
G. 153	G. 255	G. 102	G. 255	G. 51
B. 102	B. 0	B. 51	B. 255	B. 102

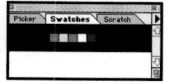

bs12sw

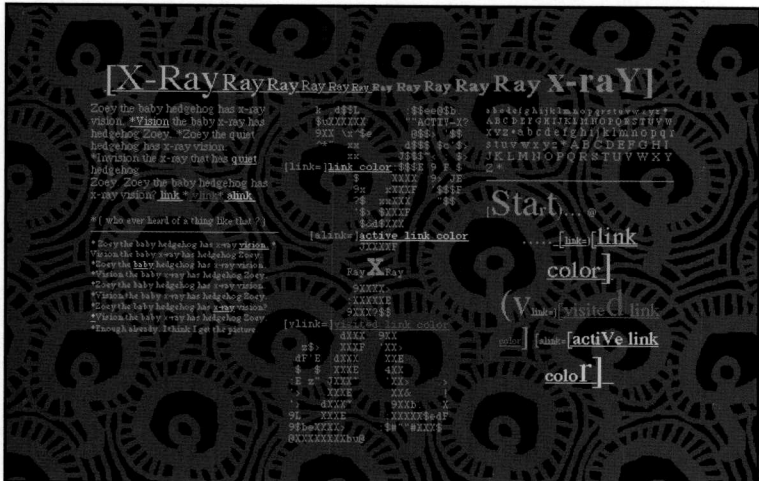

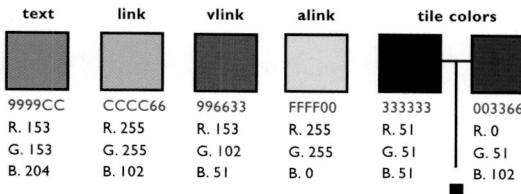

text	link	vlink	alink	tile colors	
9999CC	CCCC66	996633	FFFF00	333333	003366
R. 153	R. 255	R. 153	R. 255	R. 51	R. 0
G. 153	G. 255	G. 102	G. 255	G. 51	G. 51
B. 204	B. 102	B. 51	B. 0	B. 51	B. 102

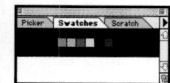

bp12sw

bp12pat.gif

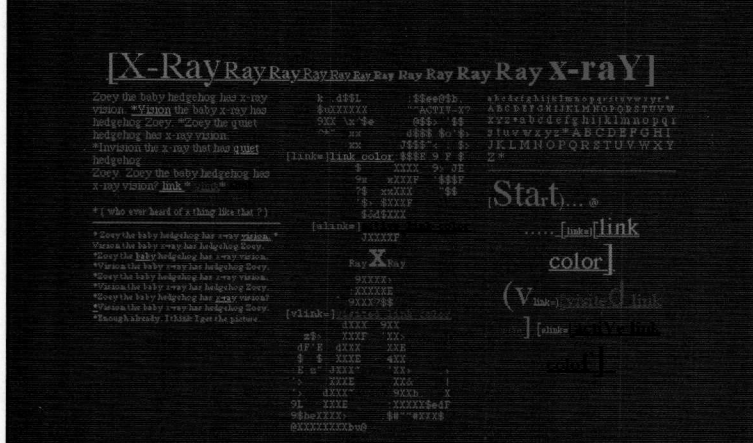

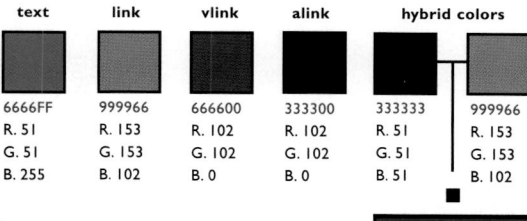

text	link	vlink	alink	hybrid colors	
6666FF	999966	666600	333300	333333	999966
R. 51	R. 153	R. 102	R. 102	R. 51	R. 153
G. 51	G. 153	G. 102	G. 102	G. 51	G. 153
B. 255	B. 102	B. 0	B. 0	B. 51	B. 102

bh12sw

bh12pat.gif

text	link	vlink	alink	bgcolor
999966	33FF33	009900	333333	000066
R. 153	R. 51	R. 0	R. 51	R. 0
G. 153	G. 255	G. 153	G. 51	G. 0
B. 102	B. 51	B. 0	B. 51	B. 102

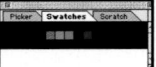

bs13sw

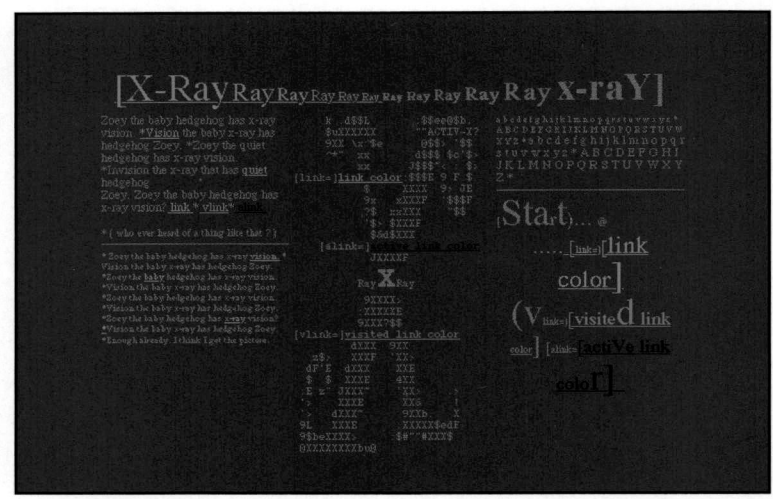

text	link	vlink	alink	tile colors	
9966FF	FF00FF	CC66CC	663366	330066	000066
R. 153	R. 255	R. 204	R. 102	R. 51	R. 0
G. 102	G. 0	G. 102	G. 51	G. 0	G. 0
B. 255	B. 255	B. 204	B. 102	B. 102	B. 102

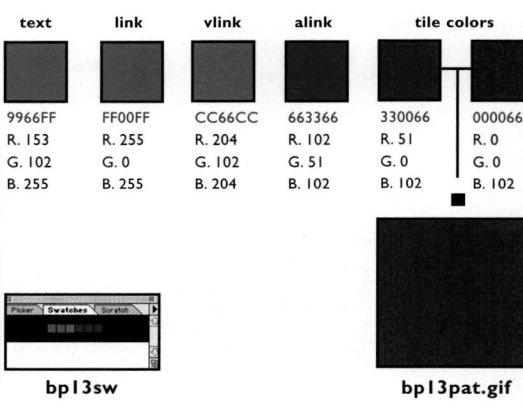

bp13sw

bp13pat.gif

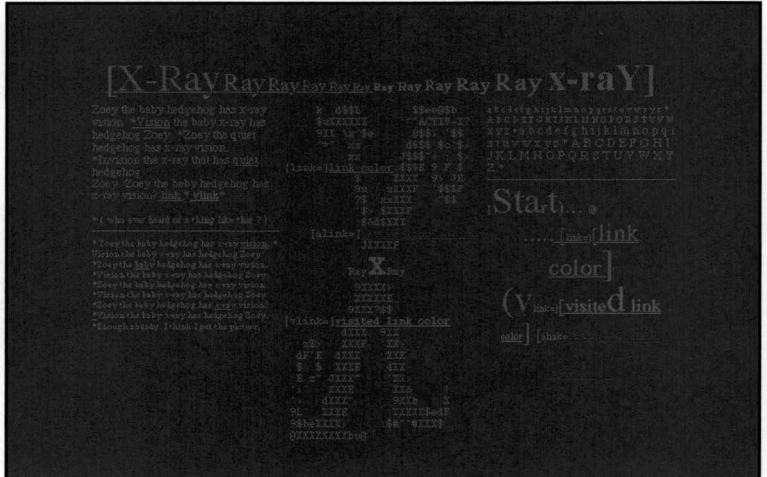

text	link	vlink	alink	hybrid colors	
009999	00CC00	669966	006600	330066	000066
R. 0	R. 0	R. 102	R. 0	R. 51	R. 0
G. 153	G. 204	G. 153	G. 102	G. 0	G. 0
B. 153	B. 0	B. 0	B. 0	B. 102	B. 102

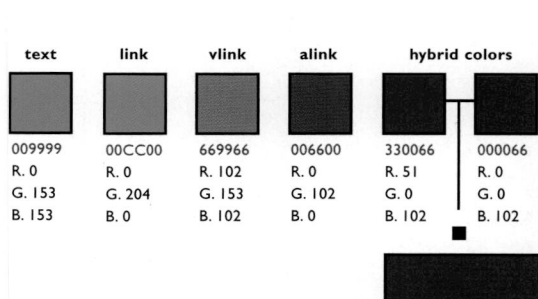

bh13sw

bh13pat.gif

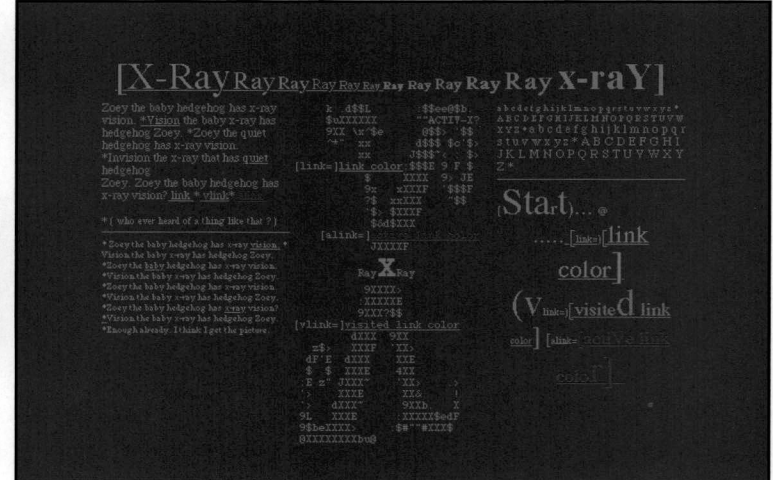

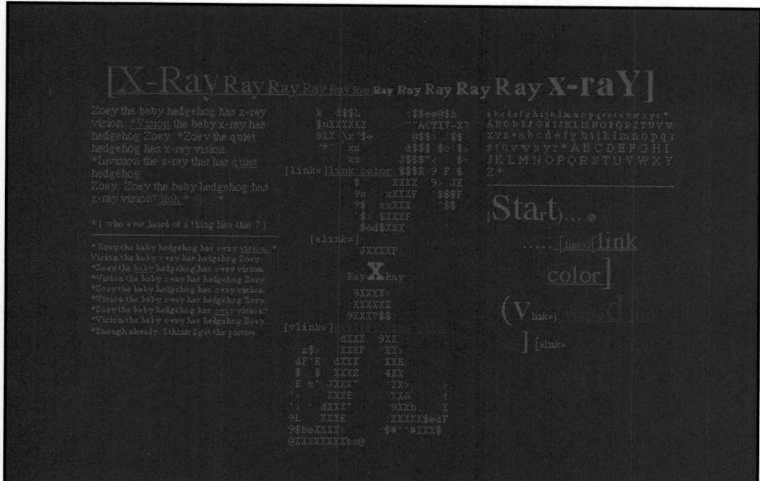

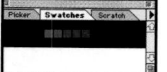

text	link	vlink	alink	bgcolor
996699	6666FF	6600FF	0000FF	000066
R. 153	R. 102	R. 102	R. 0	R. 0
G. 102	G. 102	G. 0	G. 0	G. 0
B. 153	B. 255	B. 255	B. 255	B. 102

bs14sw

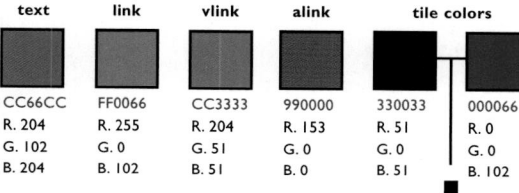

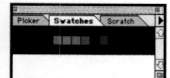

text	link	vlink	alink	tile colors	
CC66CC	FF0066	CC3333	990000	330033	000066
R. 204	R. 255	R. 204	R. 153	R. 51	R. 0
G. 102	G. 0	G. 51	G. 0	G. 0	G. 0
B. 204	B. 102	B. 51	B. 0	B. 51	B. 102

bp14sw

bp14pat.gif

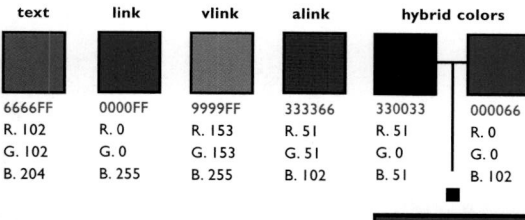

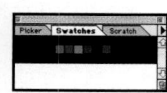

text	link	vlink	alink	hybrid colors	
6666FF	0000FF	9999FF	333366	330033	000066
R. 102	R. 0	R. 153	R. 51	R. 51	R. 0
G. 102	G. 0	G. 153	G. 51	G. 0	G. 0
B. 204	B. 255	B. 255	B. 102	B. 51	B. 102

bh14sw

bh14pat.gif

text	link	vlink	alink	bgcolor
666699	9999FF	999999	3333FF	000033
R. 102	R. 153	R. 153	R. 51	R. 0
G. 102	G. 153	G. 153	G. 51	G. 0
B. 153	B. 255	B. 153	B. 255	B. 51

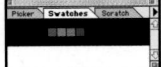

bs15sw

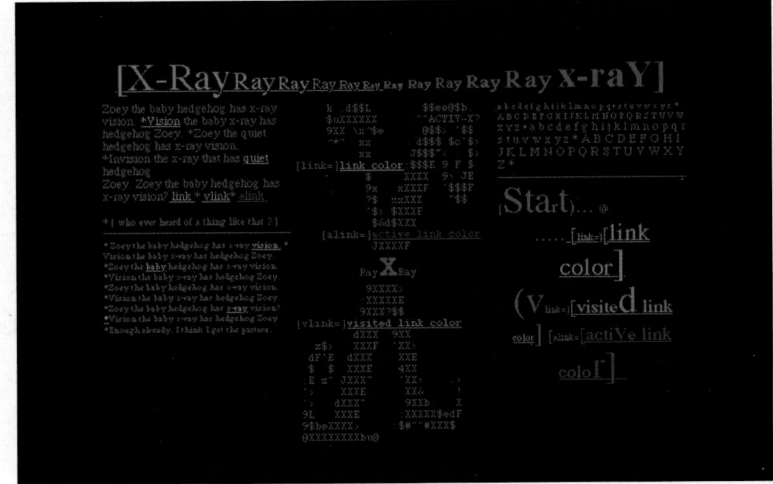

text	link	vlink	alink	tile colors	
9999CC	FFFFFF	666666	CC33CC	330033	000033
R. 153	R. 255	R. 102	R. 204	R. 51	R. 0
G. 153	G. 255	G. 102	G. 51	G. 0	G. 0
B. 204	B. 255	B. 102	B. 204	B. 51	B. 51

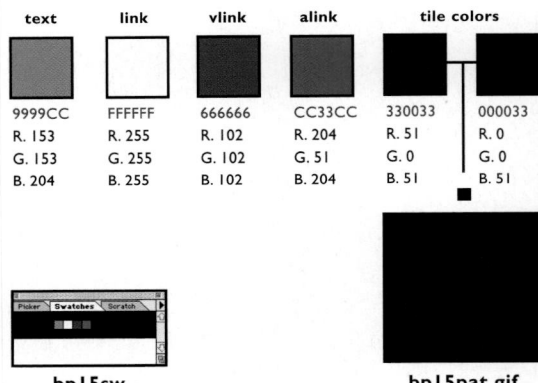

bp15sw   **bp15pat.gif**

text	link	vlink	alink	hybrid colors	
CC66CC	FF99FF	999999	CC33CC	330033	000033
R. 204	R. 255	R. 153	R. 204	R. 51	R. 0
G. 102	G. 153	G. 153	G. 51	G. 0	G. 0
B. 204	B. 255	B. 153	B. 204	B. 51	B. 51

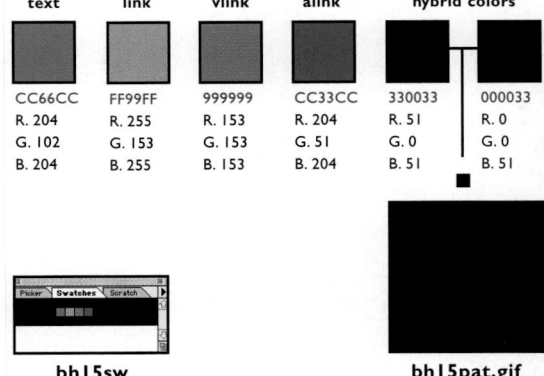

bh15sw   **bh15pat.gif**

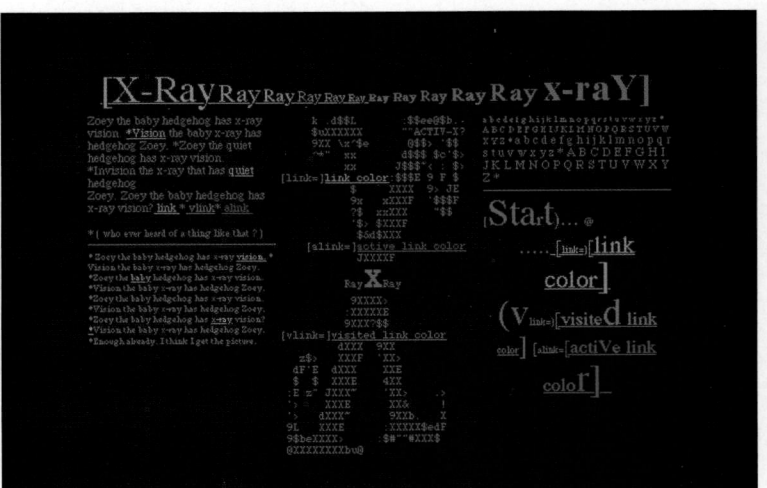

coloring

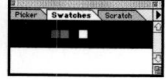

text	link	vlink	alink	bgcolor
996666	FF0000	333333	FFFFFF	000033
R. 153	R. 255	R. 51	R. 255	R. 0
G. 102	G. 0	G. 51	G. 255	G. 0
B. 102	B. 0	B. 51	B. 255	B. 51

bs16sw

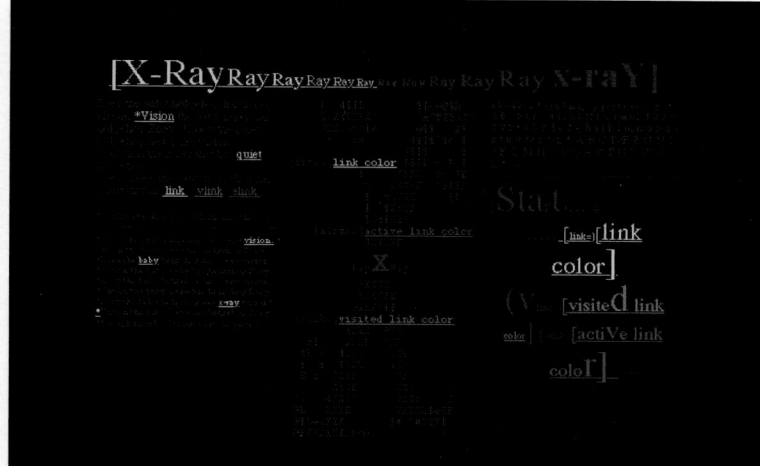

text	link	vlink	alink	tile colors	
666633	FFFF00	999999	996666	000000	000033
R. 102	R. 255	R. 153	R. 153	R. 0	R. 0
G. 102	G. 255	G. 153	G. 102	G. 0	G. 0
B. 51	B. 0	B. 153	B. 102	B. 0	B. 51

bp16sw

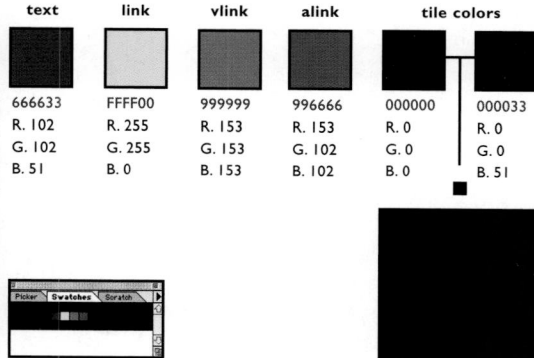

bp16pat.gif

text	link	vlink	alink	hybrid colors	
336666	CCCC99	999999	996666	000000	000033
R. 51	R. 204	R. 153	R. 153	R. 0	R. 0
G. 102	G. 204	G. 153	G. 102	G. 0	G. 0
B. 102	B. 153	B. 153	B. 102	B. 0	B. 51

bh16sw

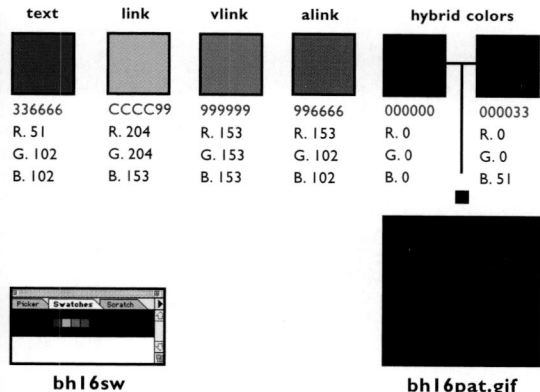

bh16pat.gif

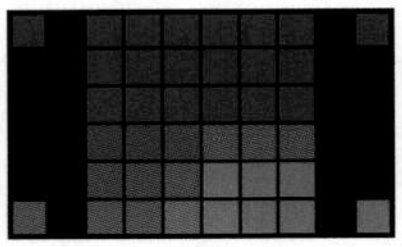

bbmr	 bbmy	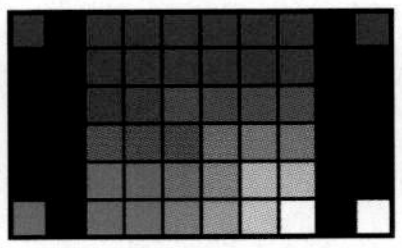 bbrw	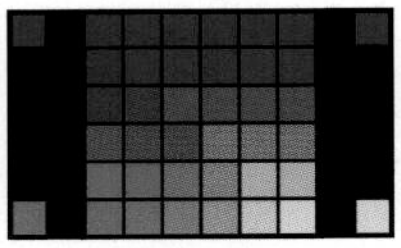 bbry	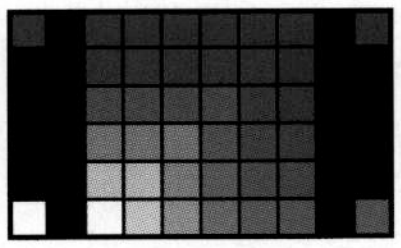 bbwm
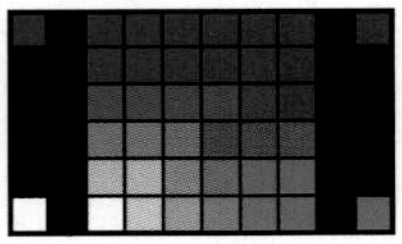 bbwr	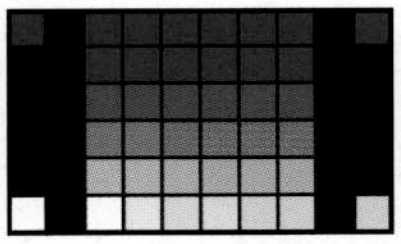 bbwy	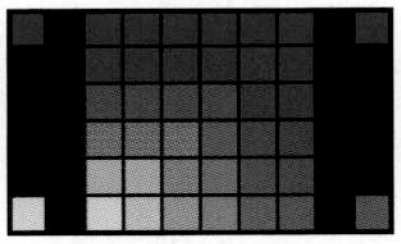 bbym	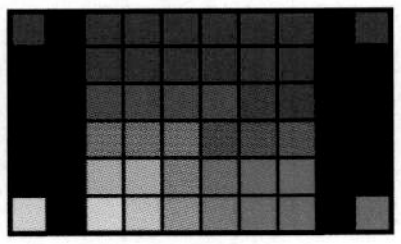 bbyr	 bcmw
 bcmy	 bcrw	 bcry	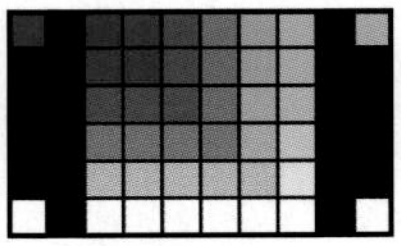 bcww	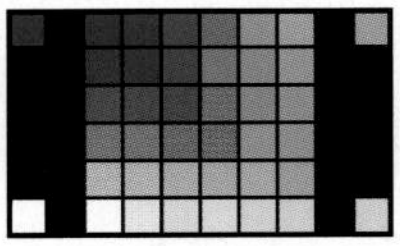 bcwy
 bcyw	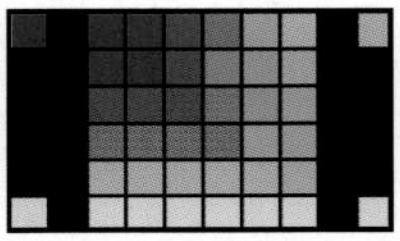 bcyy	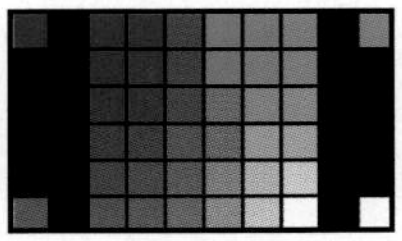 bgmw	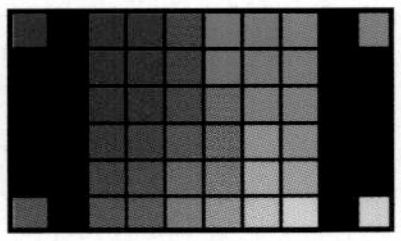 bgmy	 bgry
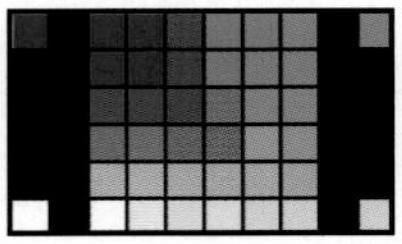 bgwy	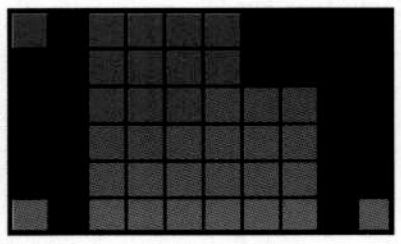 bkmm	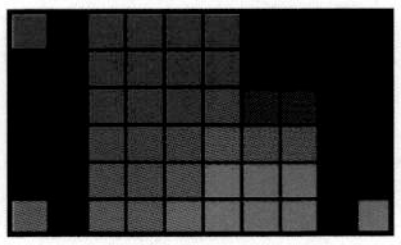 bkmr	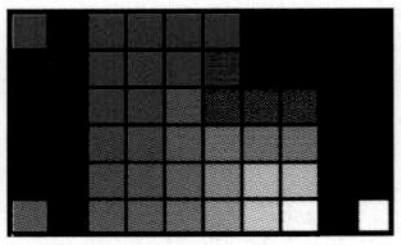 bkmw	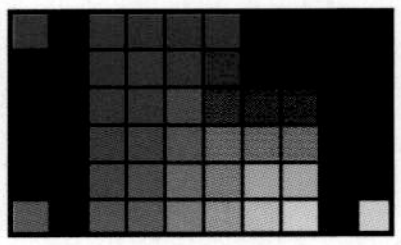 bkmy
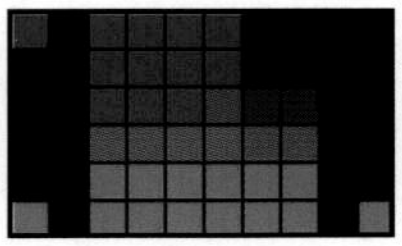 bkrr	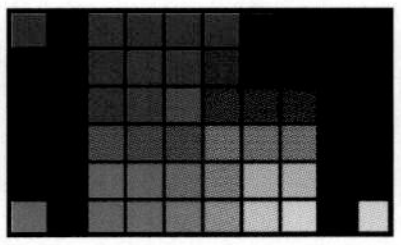 bkry	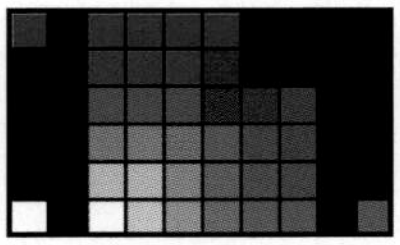 bkwm	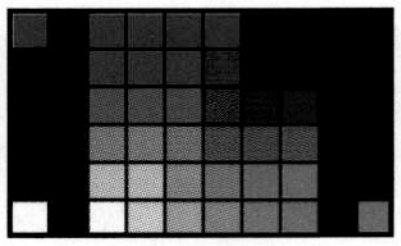 bkwr	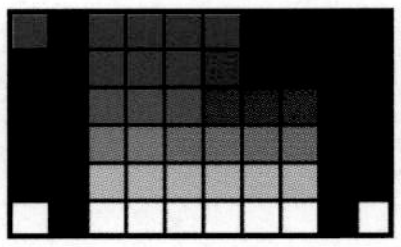 bkww
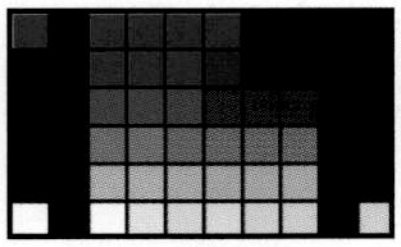 bkwy	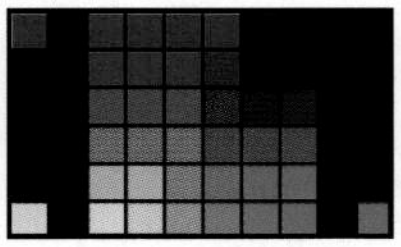 bkyr	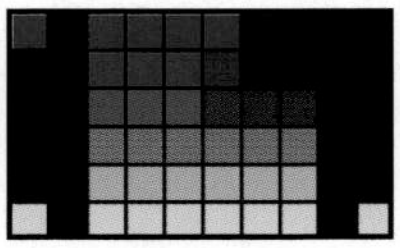 bkyy	 bmbc	 bmbg

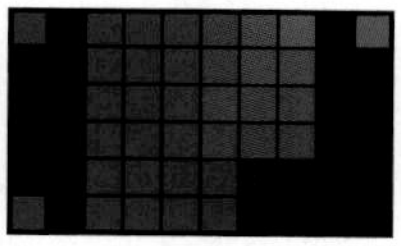

bmbk	 bmcb	 bmcc	 bmcg	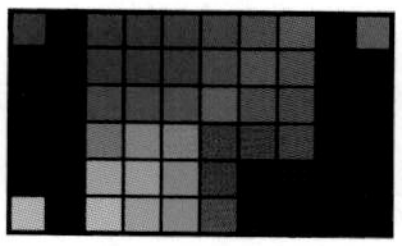 bmck
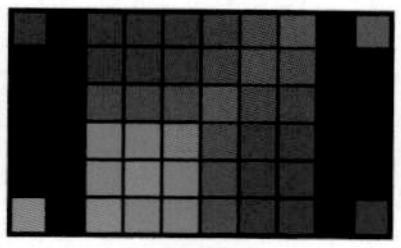 bmgb	 bmgc	 bmgg	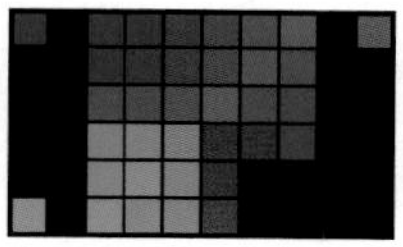 bmgk	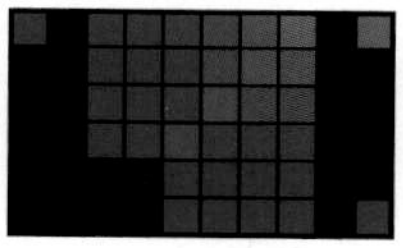 bmkb
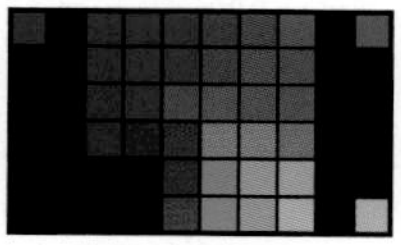 bmkc	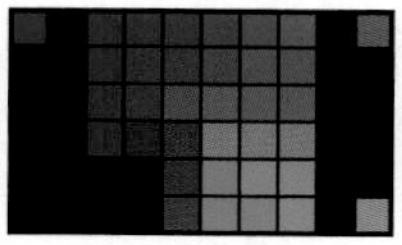 bmkg	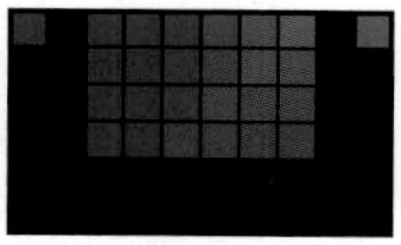 bmkk	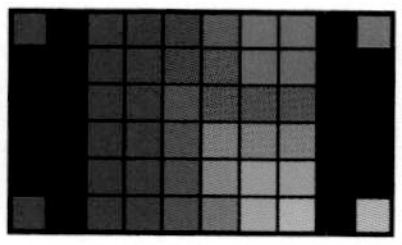 brbc	 brbg
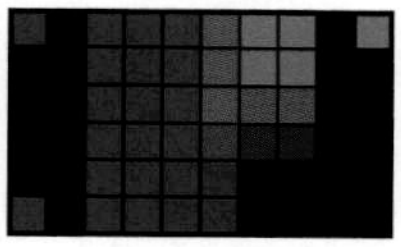 brbk	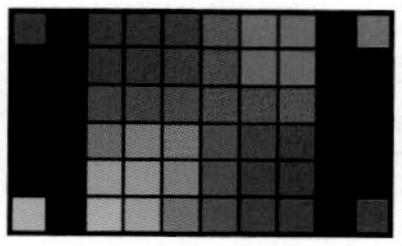 brcb	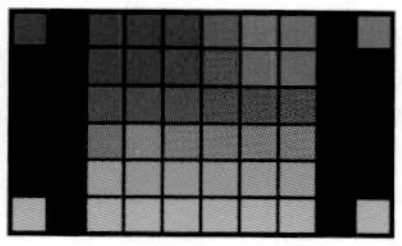 brcc	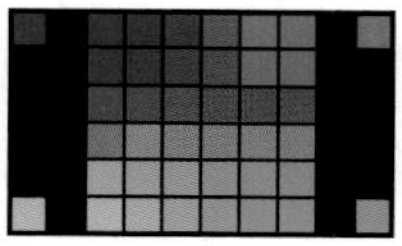 brcg	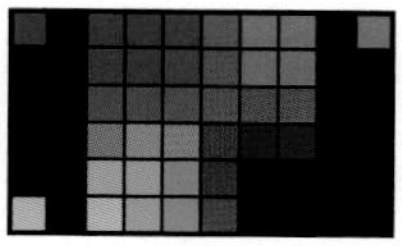 brck
 brgg	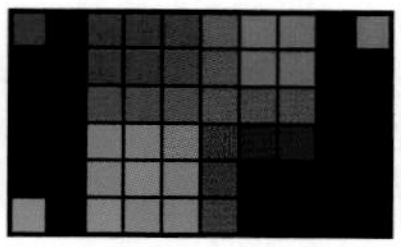 brgk	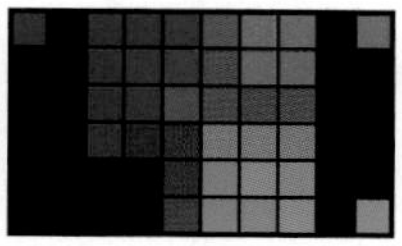 brkg	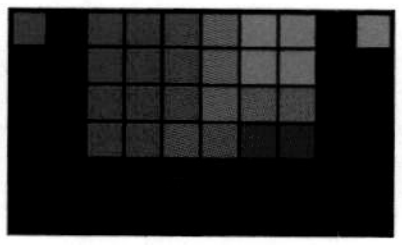 brkk	 bwbc
 bwbg	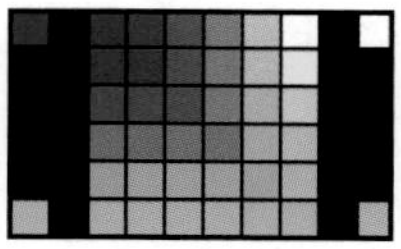 bwcc	 bwcg	 bwgc	 bwgg
 bwkc	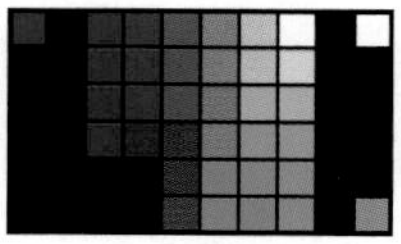 bwkg	 bybc	 bybg	 bycg

CYAN

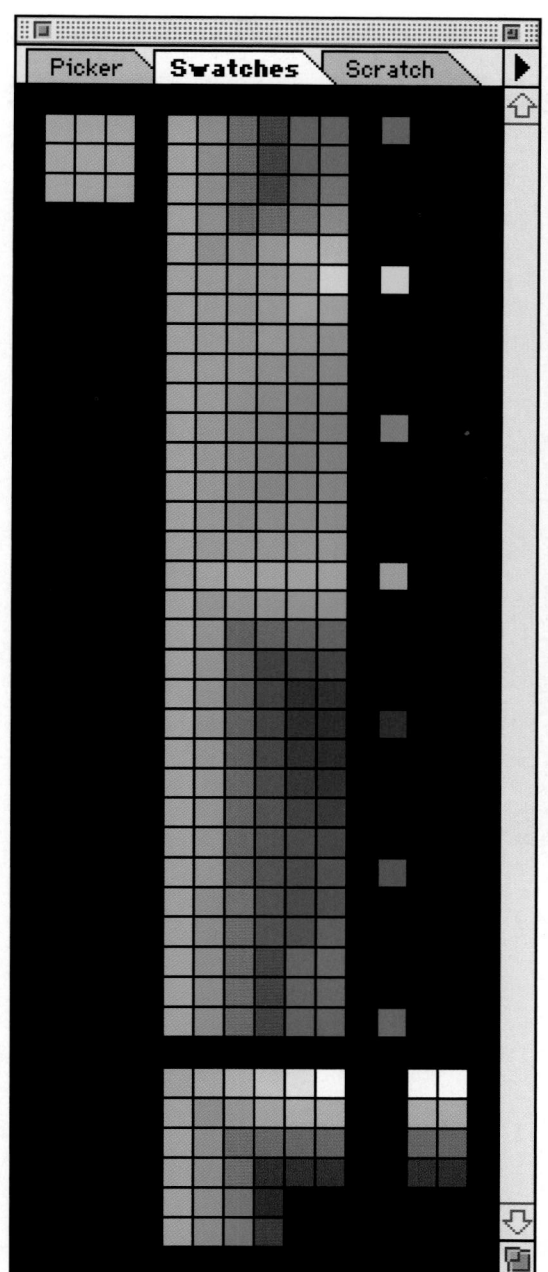

mcs

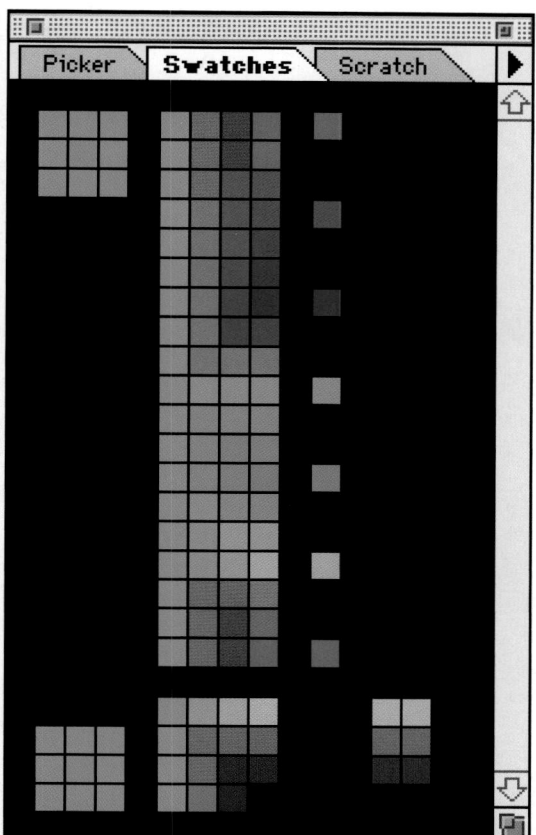

mcd

text	link	vlink	alink	bgcolor
669999	6666CC	336666	0000FF	CCFFFF
R. 102	R. 102	R. 51	R. 0	R. 204
G. 153	G. 102	G. 102	G. 0	G. 255
B. 51	B. 204	B. 102	B. 255	B. 255

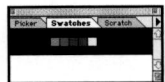

cs01sw

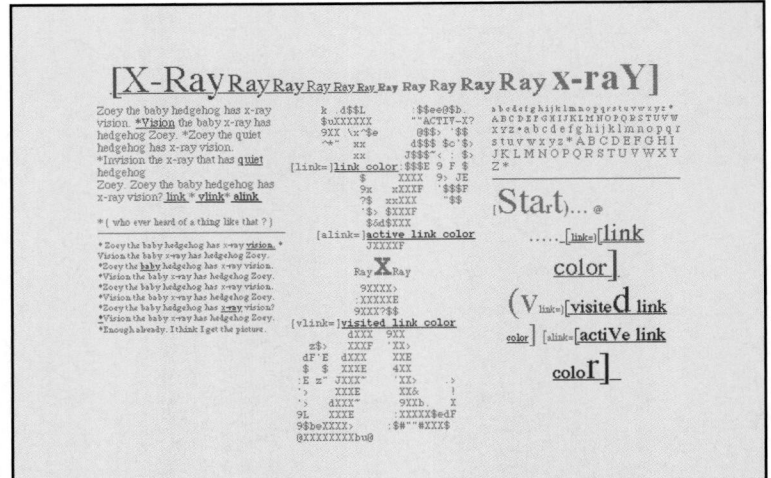

text	link	vlink	alink	tile colors	
666666	999933	CCCC66	CCCCCC	FFFFFF	CCFFFF
R. 102	R. 255	R. 153	R. 255	R. 255	R. 255
G. 51	G. 0	G. 102	G. 153	G. 204	G. 204
B. 0	B. 0	B. 102	B. 0	B. 204	B. 153

cp01sw

cp01pat.gif

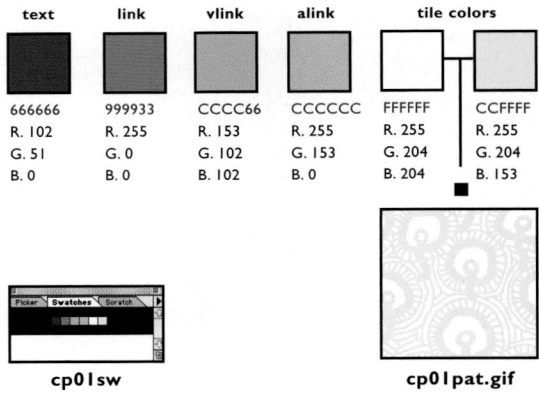

text	link	vlink	alink	hybrid colors	
666699	0000FF	6666CC	CCCCCC	FFFFFF	CCFFFF
R. 102	R. 255	R. 255	R. 255	R. 255	R. 255
G. 0	G. 51	G. 102	G. 255	G. 204	G. 204
B. 0	B. 0	B. 102	B. 255	B. 204	B. 153

ch01sw

ch01pat.gif

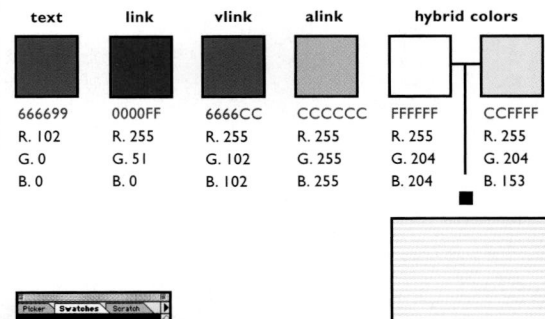

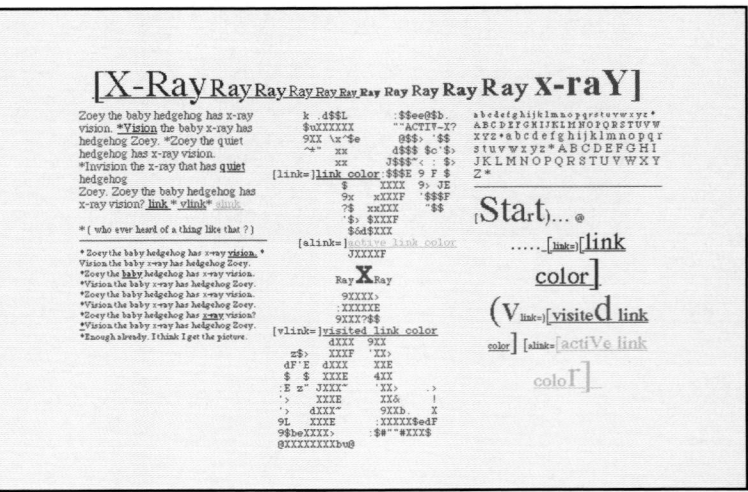

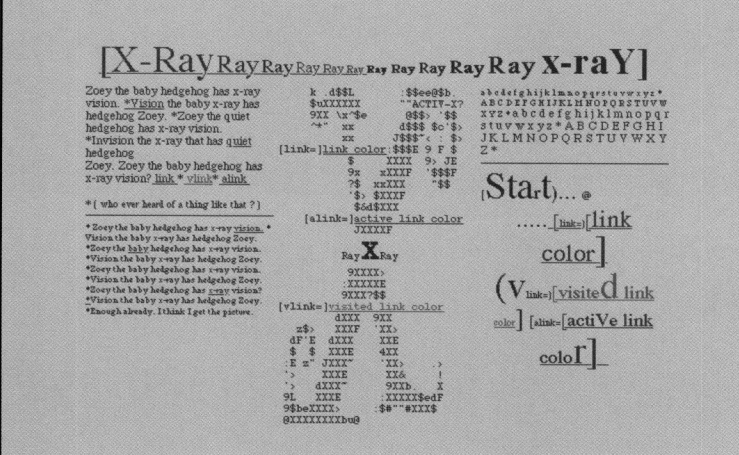

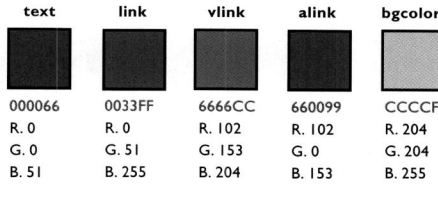

text	link	vlink	alink	bgcolor
000066	0033FF	6666CC	660099	CCCCFF
R. 0	R. 0	R. 102	R. 102	R. 204
G. 0	G. 51	G. 153	G. 0	G. 204
B. 51	B. 255	B. 204	B. 153	B. 255

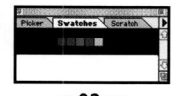

cs02sw

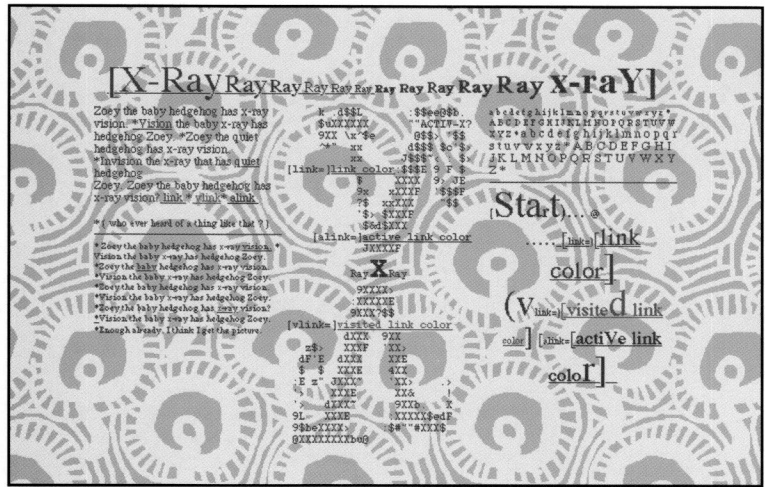

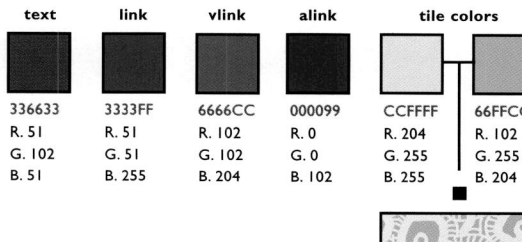

text	link	vlink	alink	tile colors	
336633	3333FF	6666CC	000099	CCFFFF	66FFCC
R. 51	R. 51	R. 102	R. 0	R. 204	R. 102
G. 102	G. 51	G. 102	G. 0	G. 255	G. 255
B. 51	B. 255	B. 204	B. 102	B. 255	B. 204

cp02sw

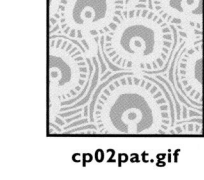

cp02pat.gif

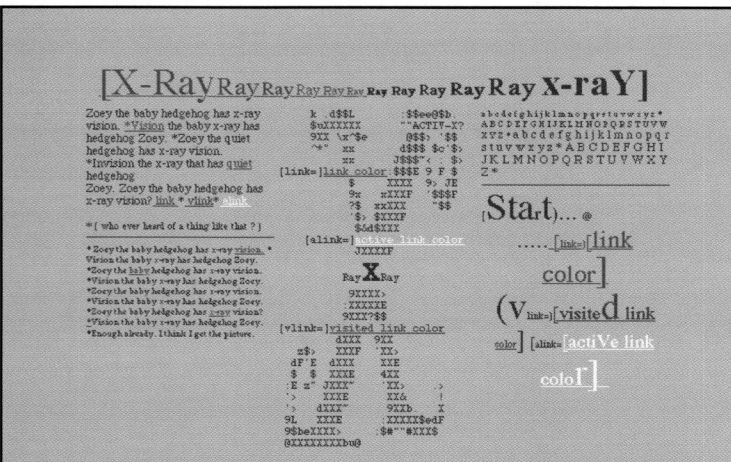

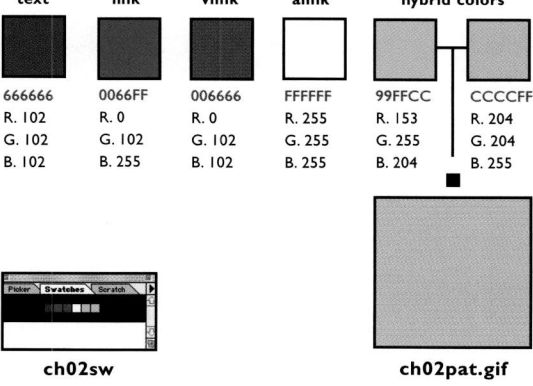

text	link	vlink	alink	hybrid colors	
666666	0066FF	006666	FFFFFF	99FFCC	CCCCFF
R. 102	R. 0	R. 0	R. 255	R. 153	R. 204
G. 102	G. 102	G. 102	G. 255	G. 255	G. 204
B. 102	B. 255	B. 102	B. 255	B. 204	B. 255

ch02sw

ch02pat.gif

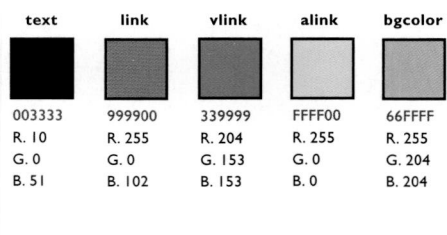

text	link	vlink	alink	bgcolor
003333	999900	339999	FFFF00	66FFFF
R. 10	R. 255	R. 204	R. 255	R. 255
G. 0	G. 0	G. 153	G. 0	G. 204
B. 51	B. 102	B. 153	B. 0	B. 204

cs03sw

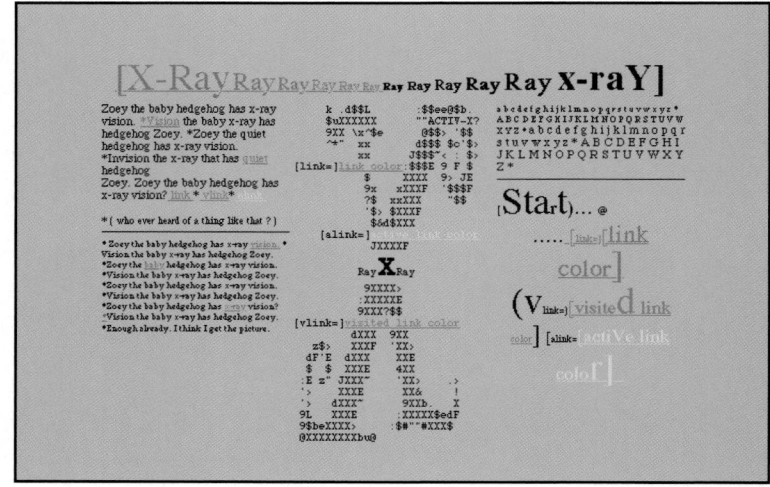

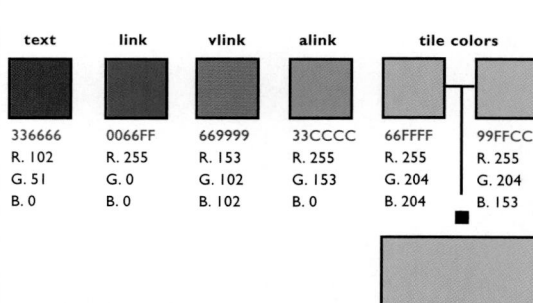

text	link	vlink	alink	tile colors	
336666	0066FF	669999	33CCCC	66FFFF	99FFCC
R. 102	R. 255	R. 153	R. 255	R. 255	R. 255
G. 51	G. 0	G. 102	G. 153	G. 204	G. 204
B. 0	B. 0	B. 102	B. 0	B. 204	B. 153

cp03sw

cp03pat.gif

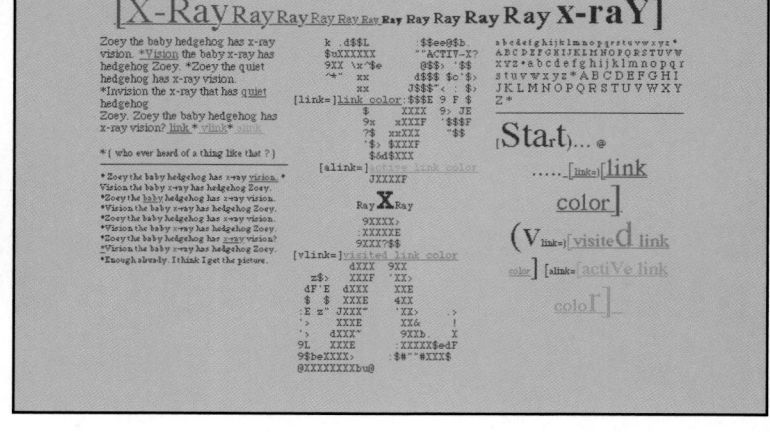

text	link	vlink	alink	hybrid colors	
336633	669900	66CC66	3366CC	66FFFF	99FFCC
R. 51	R. 102	R. 102	R. 51	R. 102	R. 153
G. 102	G. 153	G. 204	G. 102	G. 255	G. 255
B. 51	B. 0	B. 102	B. 204	B. 255	B. 204

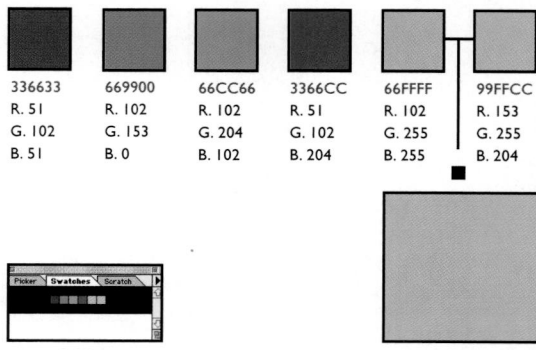

ch03sw

ch03pat.gif

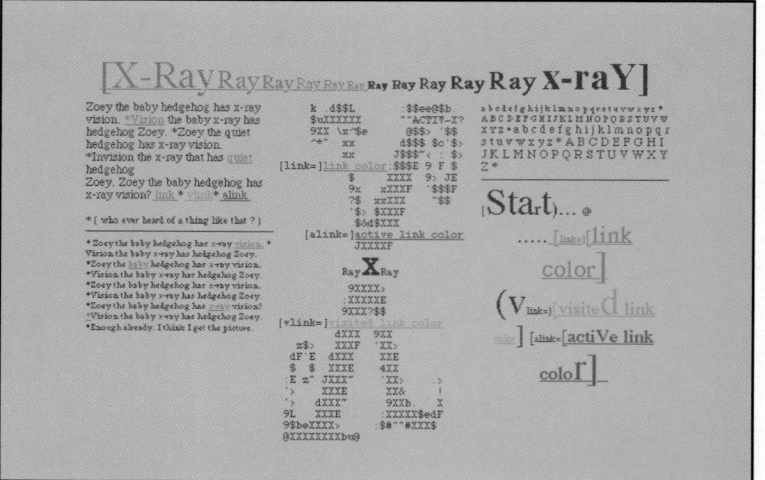

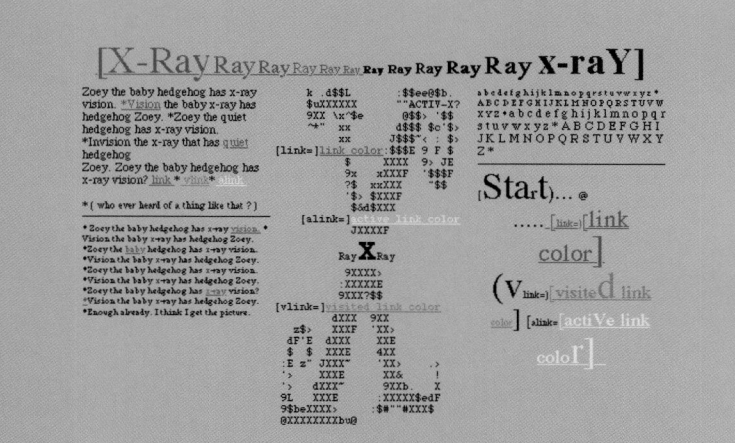

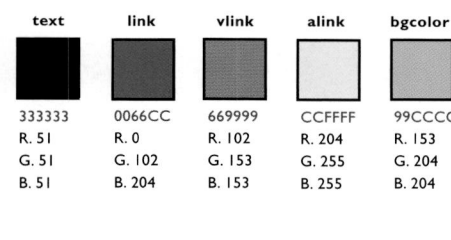

text	link	vlink	alink	bgcolor
333333	0066CC	669999	CCFFFF	99CCCC
R. 51	R. 0	R. 102	R. 204	R. 153
G. 51	G. 102	G. 153	G. 255	G. 204
B. 51	B. 204	B. 153	B. 255	B. 204

cs04sw

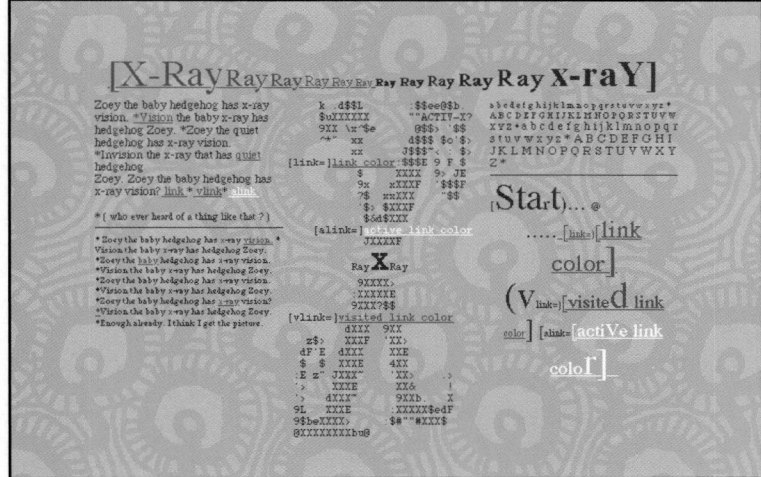

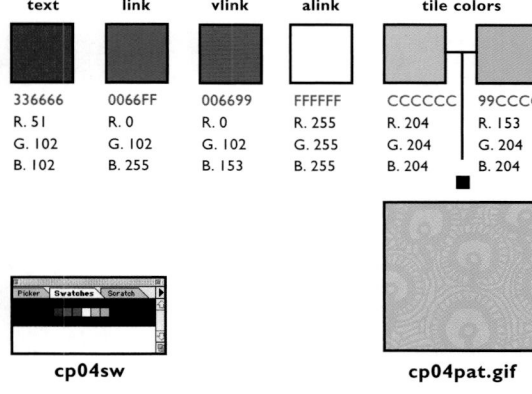

text	link	vlink	alink	tile colors	
336666	0066FF	006699	FFFFFF	CCCCCC	99CCCC
R. 51	R. 0	R. 0	R. 255	R. 204	R. 153
G. 102	G. 102	G. 102	G. 255	G. 204	G. 204
B. 102	B. 255	B. 153	B. 255	B. 204	B. 204

cp04sw

cp04pat.gif

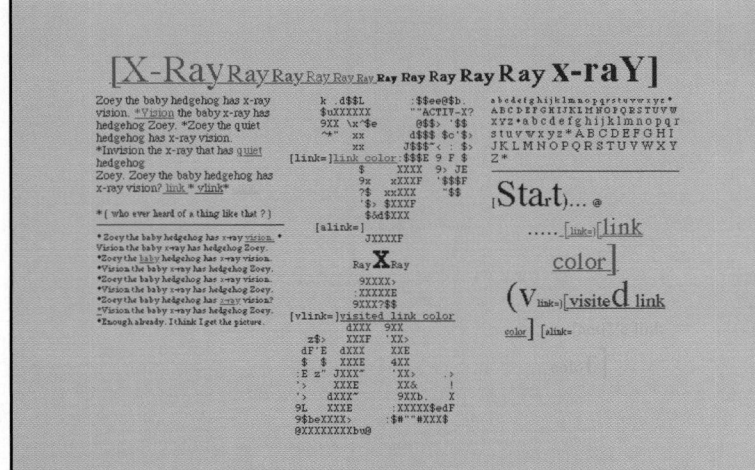

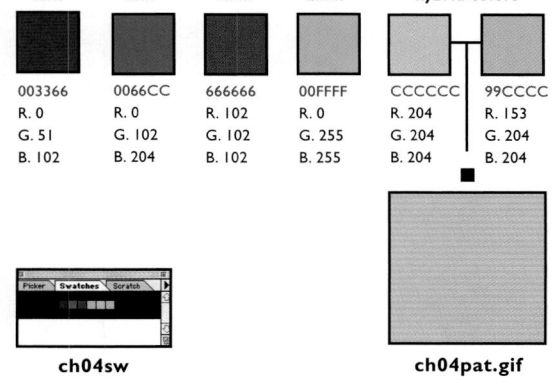

text	link	vlink	alink	hybrid colors	
003366	0066CC	666666	00FFFF	CCCCCC	99CCCC
R. 0	R. 0	R. 102	R. 0	R. 204	R. 153
G. 51	G. 102	G. 102	G. 255	G. 204	G. 204
B. 102	B. 204	B. 102	B. 255	B. 204	B. 204

ch04sw

ch04pat.gif

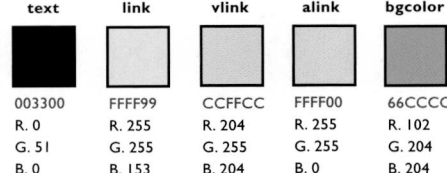

text	link	vlink	alink	bgcolor
003300	FFFF99	CCFFCC	FFFF00	66CCCC
R. 0	R. 255	R. 204	R. 255	R. 102
G. 51	G. 255	G. 255	G. 255	G. 204
B. 0	B. 153	B. 204	B. 204	B. 204

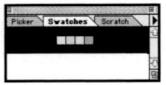

cs05sw

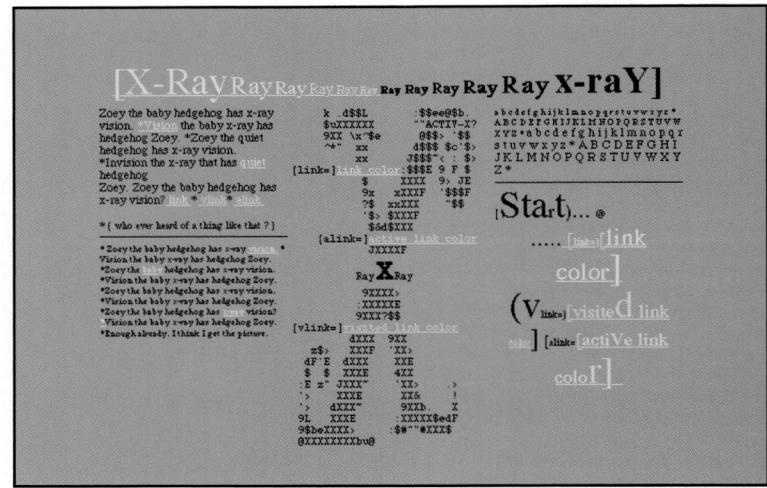

text	link	vlink	alink	tile colors	
663300	FF3300	996666	FF6666	99CCFF	66CCCC
R. 102	R. 255	R. 153	R. 255	R. 153	R. 102
G. 51	G. 51	G. 102	G. 102	G. 204	G. 204
B. 0	B. 0	B. 102	B. 102	B. 255	B. 204

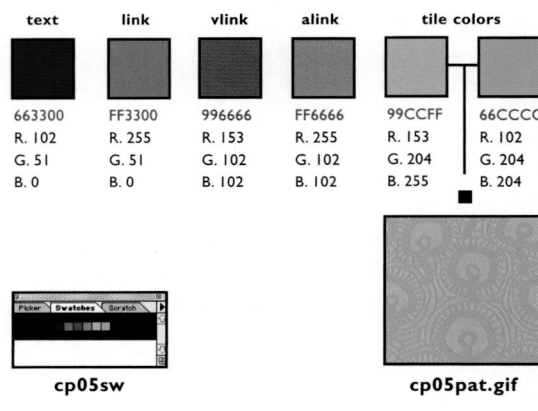

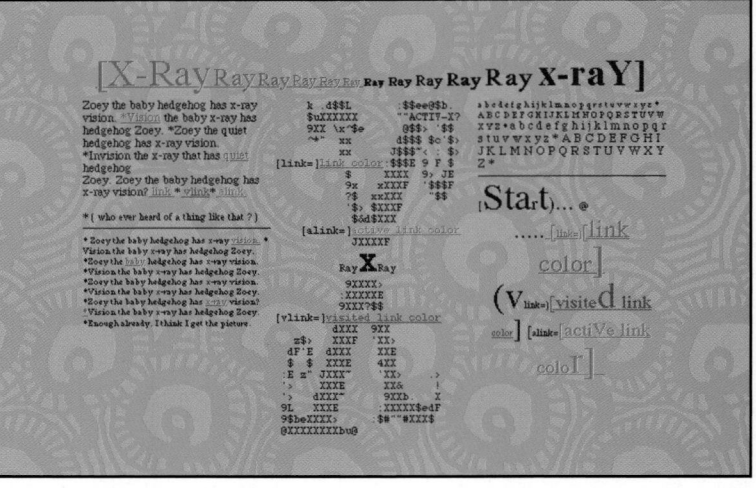

cp05sw

cp05pat.gif

text	link	vlink	alink	hybrid colors	
663300	FF6600	996666	FF0000	99CCFF	66CCCC
R. 102	R. 255	R. 153	R. 255	R. 153	R. 102
G. 51	G. 102	G. 102	G. 0	G. 204	G. 204
B. 0	B. 0	B. 102	B. 0	B. 255	B. 204

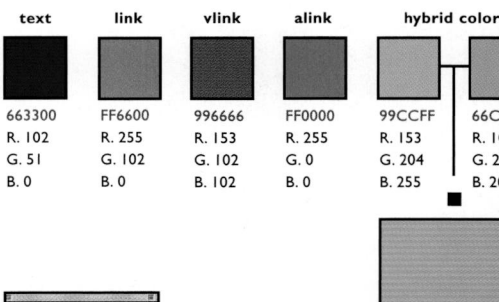

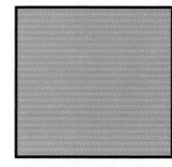

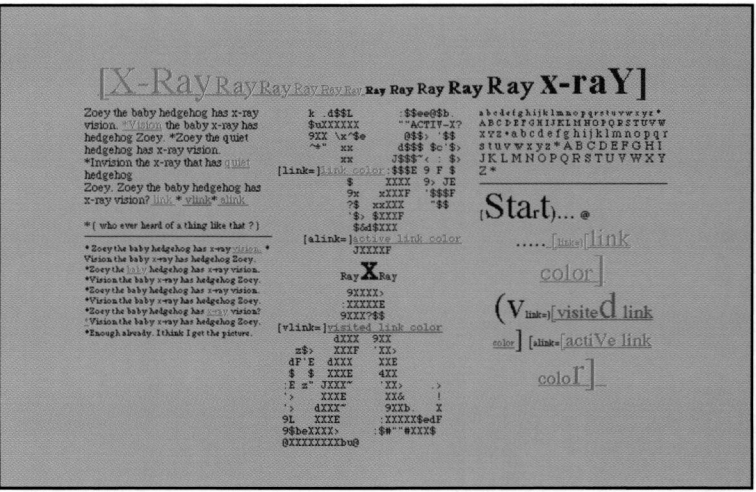

ch05sw

ch05pat.gif

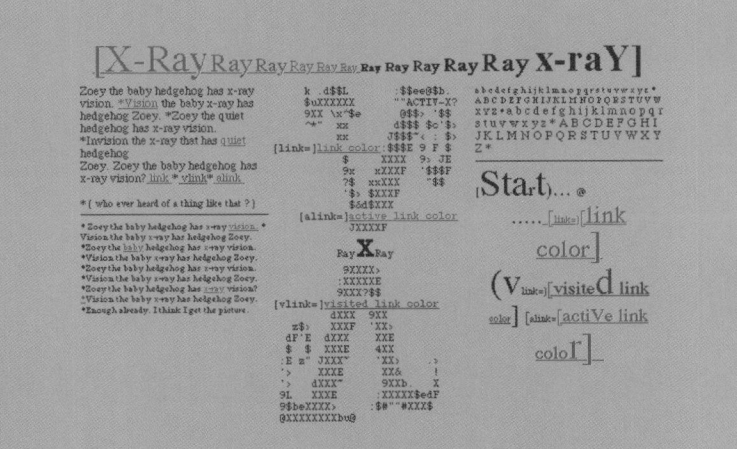

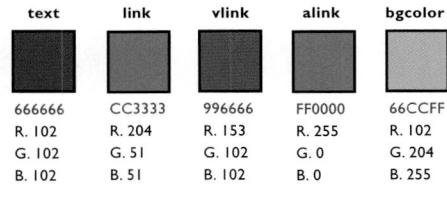

text	link	vlink	alink	bgcolor
666666	CC3333	996666	FF0000	66CCFF
R. 102	R. 204	R. 153	R. 255	R. 102
G. 102	G. 51	G. 102	G. 0	G. 204
B. 102	B. 51	B. 102	B. 0	B. 255

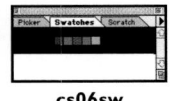

cs06sw

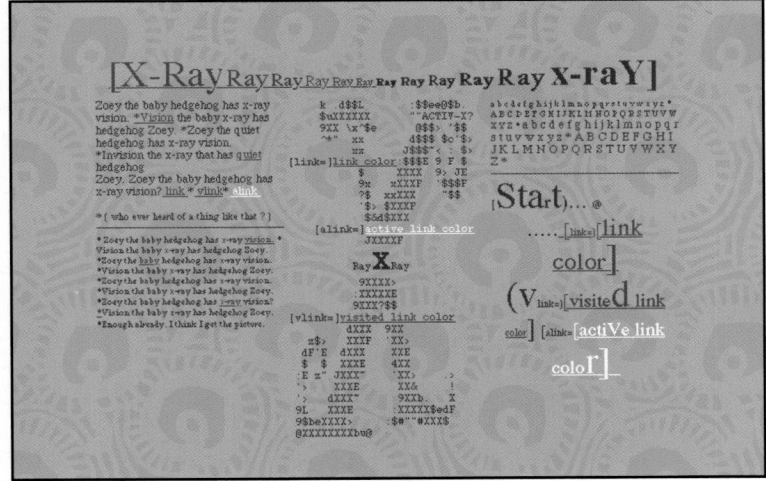

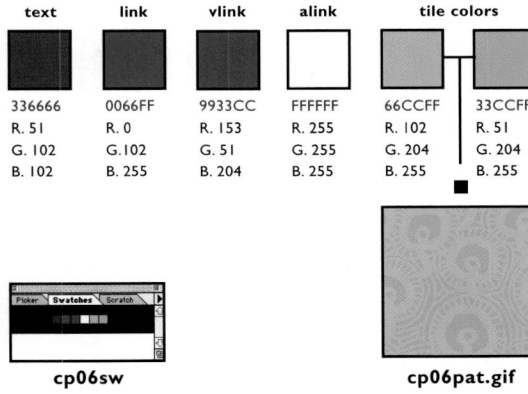

text	link	vlink	alink	tile colors	
336666	0066FF	9933CC	FFFFFF	66CCFF	33CCFF
R. 51	R. 0	R. 153	R. 255	R. 102	R. 51
G. 102	G. 102	G. 51	G. 255	G. 204	G. 204
B. 102	B. 255	B. 204	B. 255	B. 255	B. 255

cp06sw

cp06pat.gif

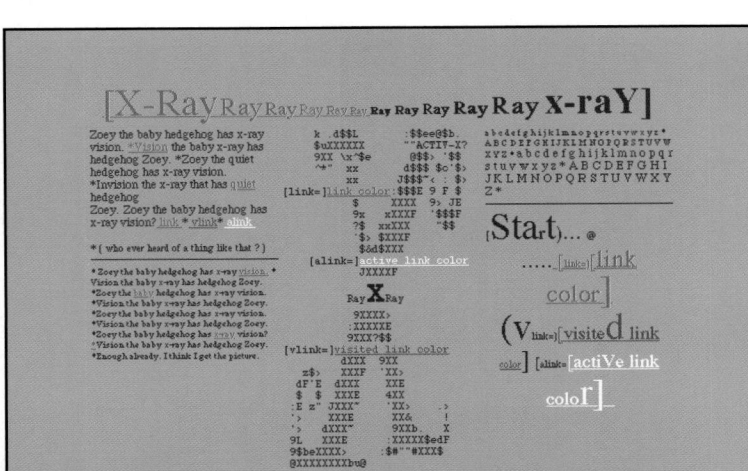

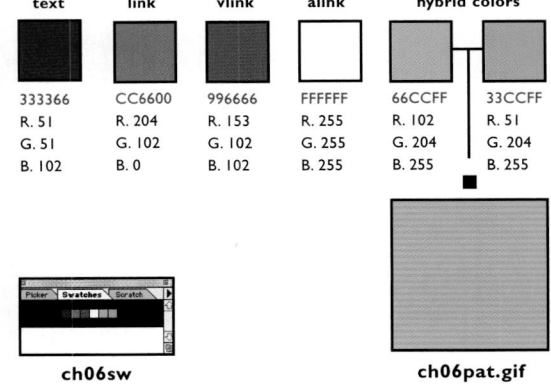

text	link	vlink	alink	hybrid colors	
333366	CC6600	996666	FFFFFF	66CCFF	33CCFF
R. 51	R. 204	R. 153	R. 255	R. 102	R. 51
G. 51	G. 102	G. 102	G. 255	G. 204	G. 204
B. 102	B. 0	B. 102	B. 255	B. 255	B. 255

ch06sw

ch06pat.gif

text	link	vlink	alink	bgcolor
333399	CC00CC	663366	330033	00CCFF
R. 51	R. 204	R. 102	R. 51	R. 0
G. 51	G. 0	G. 51	G. 0	G. 204
B. 153	B. 204	B. 102	B. 51	B. 255

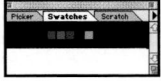

cs07sw

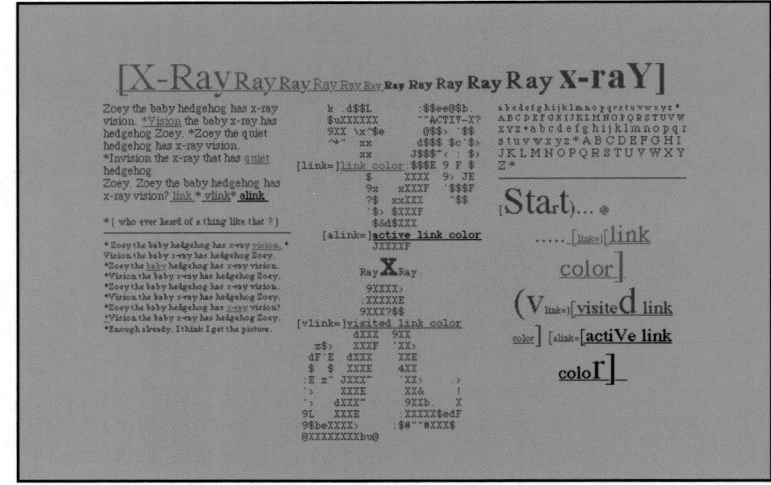

text	link	vlink	alink	tile colors	
003300	FF0000	CC33CC	FF9999	00CCFF	00CC99
R. 0	R. 255	R. 204	R. 255	R. 0	R. 0
G. 51	G. 0	G. 51	G. 153	G. 204	G. 204
B. 0	B. 0	B. 204	B. 153	B. 255	B. 255

cp07sw

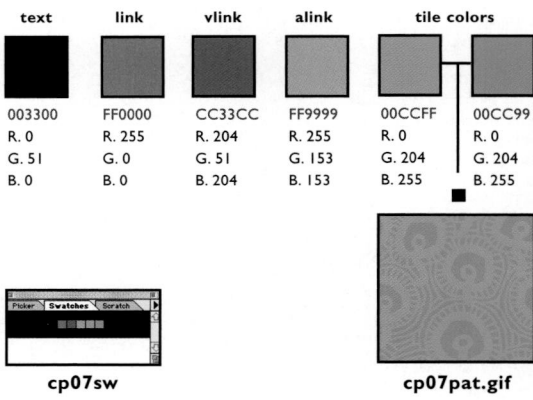

cp07pat.gif

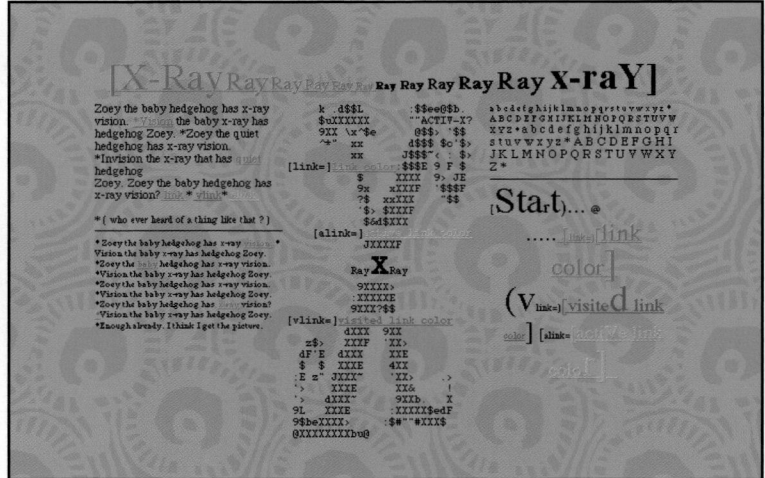

text	link	vlink	alink	hybrid colors	
666666	FFFFFF	FFFF99	FFFF00	00CCFF	00CC99
R. 102	R. 255	R. 255	R. 255	R. 0	R. 0
G. 102	G. 255	G. 255	G. 255	G. 204	G. 204
B. 102	B. 255	B. 153	B. 0	B. 255	B. 153

ch07sw

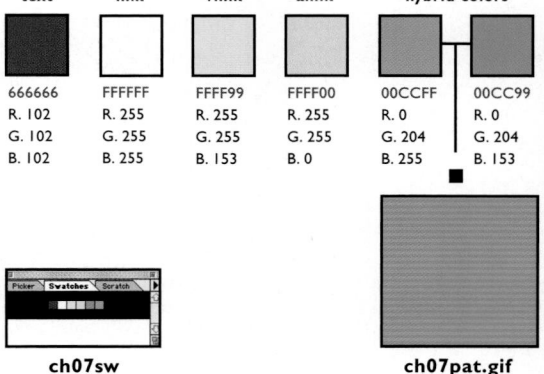

ch07pat.gif

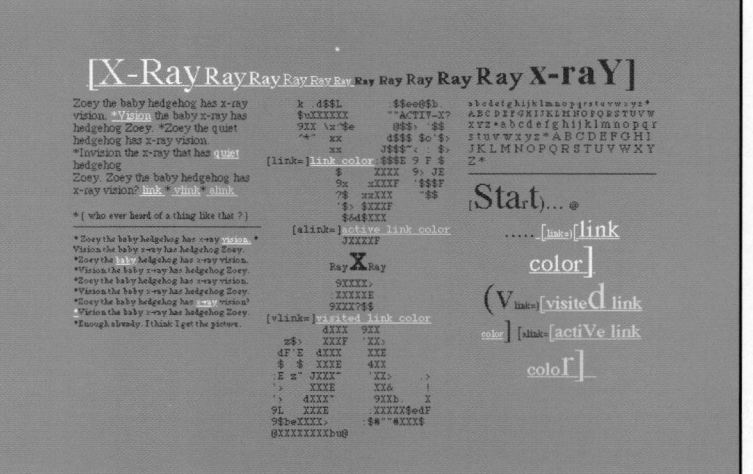

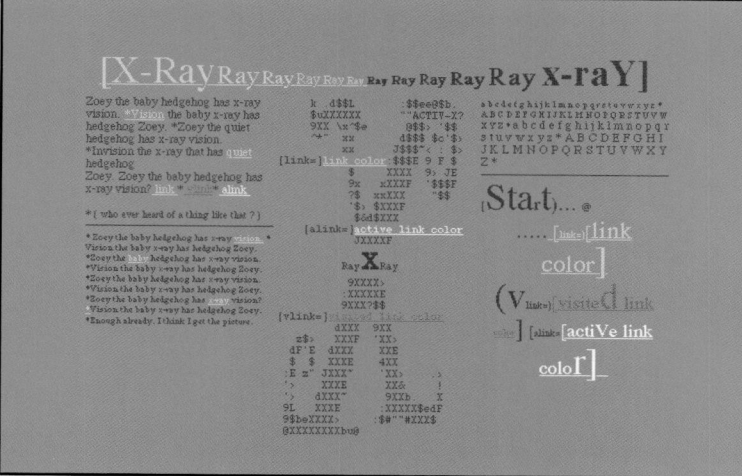

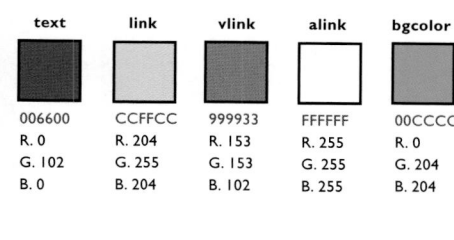

text	link	vlink	alink	bgcolor
006600	CCFFCC	999933	FFFFFF	00CCCC
R. 0	R. 204	R. 153	R. 255	R. 0
G. 102	G. 255	G. 153	G. 255	G. 204
B. 0	B. 204	B. 102	B. 255	B. 204

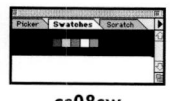

cs08sw

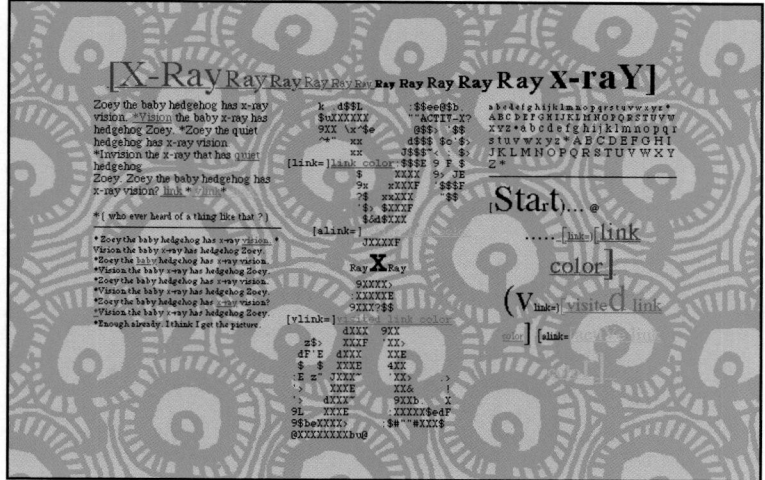

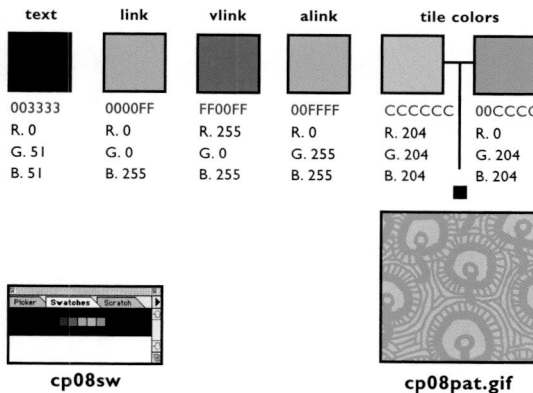

text	link	vlink	alink	tile colors	
003333	0000FF	FF00FF	00FFFF	CCCCCC	00CCCC
R. 0	R. 0	R. 255	R. 0	R. 204	R. 0
G. 51	G. 0	G. 0	G. 255	G. 204	G. 204
B. 51	B. 255	B. 255	B. 255	B. 204	B. 204

cp08sw

cp08pat.gif

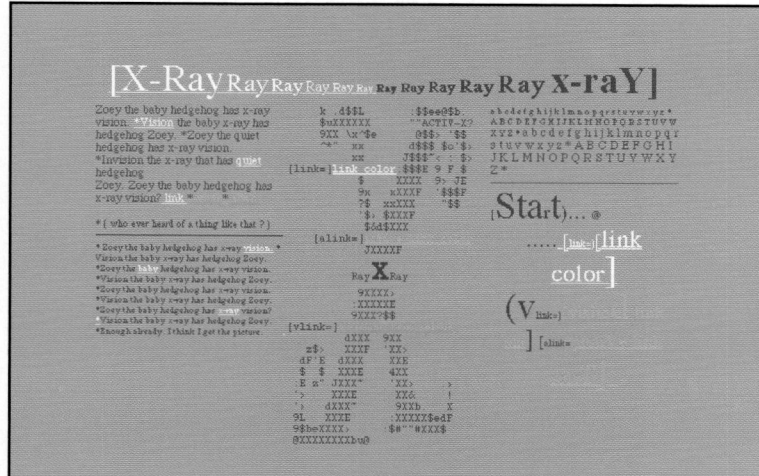

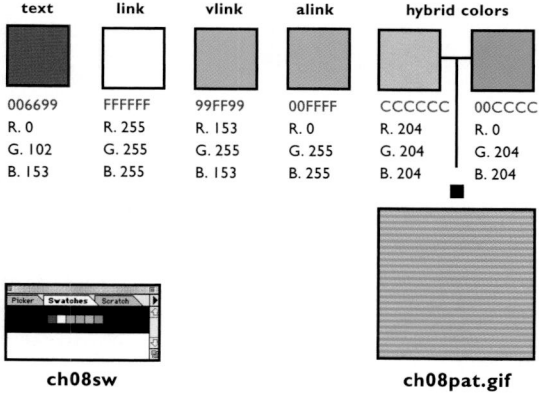

text	link	vlink	alink	hybrid colors	
006699	FFFFFF	99FF99	00FFFF	CCCCCC	00CCCC
R. 0	R. 255	R. 153	R. 0	R. 204	R. 0
G. 102	G. 255	G. 255	G. 255	G. 204	G. 204
B. 153	B. 255	B. 153	B. 255	B. 204	B. 204

ch08sw

ch08pat.gif

text	link	vlink	alink	bgcolor
FFFFFF	FFFF00	CCCCCC	CCCC33	009900
R. 255	R. 255	R. 204	R. 204	R. 0
G. 255	G. 255	G. 204	G. 204	G. 153
B. 255	B. 0	B. 204	B. 51	B. 0

cs09sw

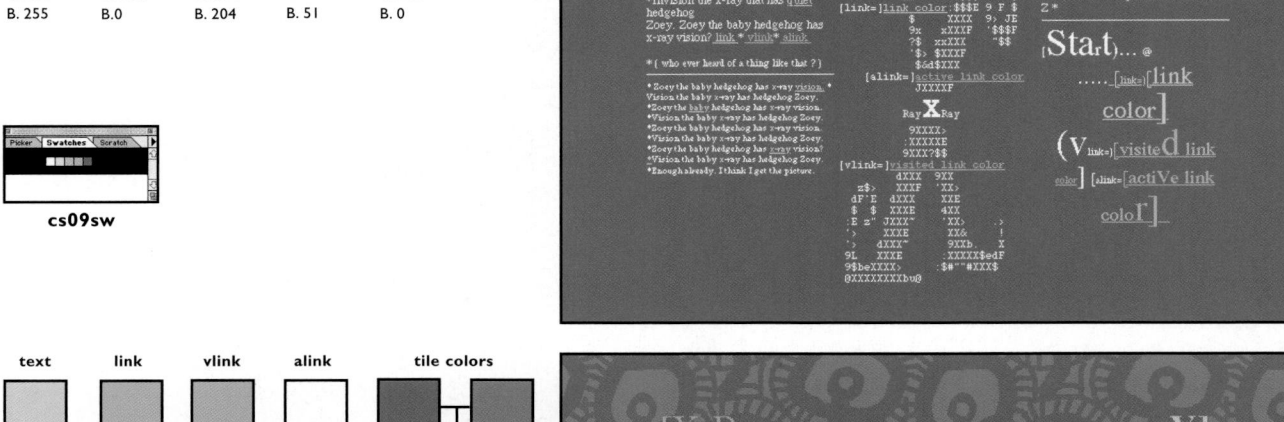

text	link	vlink	alink	tile colors	
99FFFF	00FFFF	99CCCC	FFFFFF	0099FF	3399CC
R. 153	R. 0	R. 153	R. 255	R. 0	R. 51
G. 255	G. 255	G. 204	G. 255	G. 153	G. 153
B. 255	B. 255	B. 204	B. 255	B. 255	B. 204

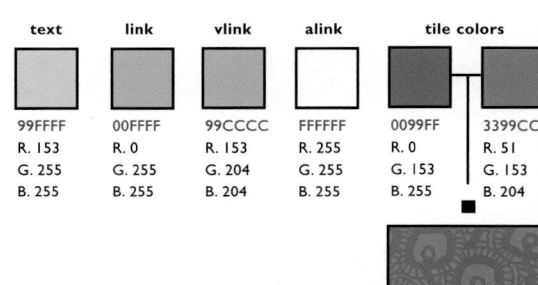

cp09sw   cp09pat.gif

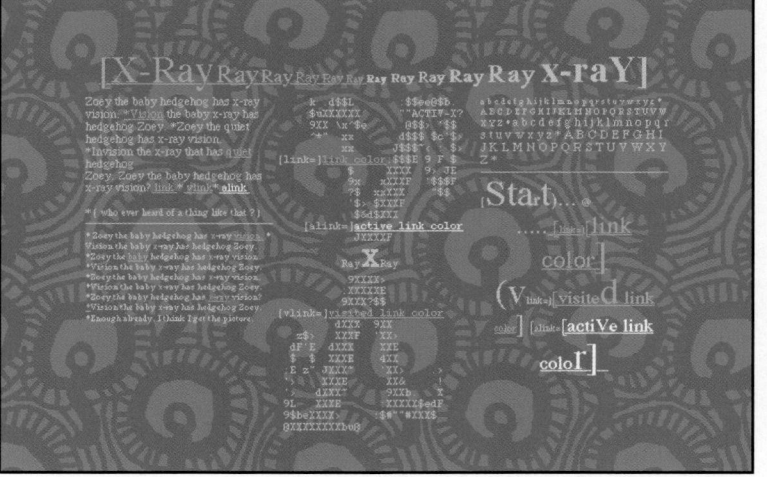

text	link	vlink	alink	hybrid colors	
333333	0000FF	99CCCC	FFFFFF	0099FF	3399CC
R. 0	R. 0	R. 153	R. 255	R. 0	R. 51
G. 51	G. 0	G. 204	G. 255	G. 153	G. 153
B. 51	B. 255	B. 204	B. 255	B. 255	B. 204

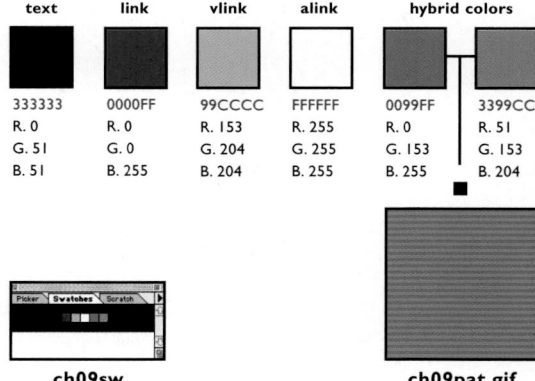

ch09sw   ch09pat.gif

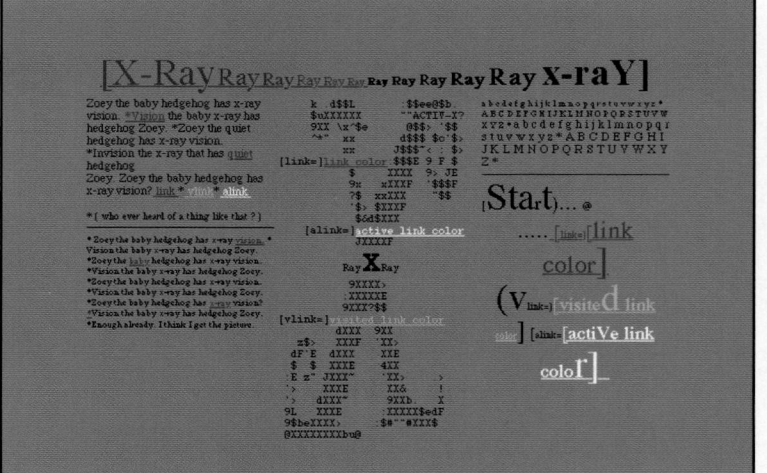

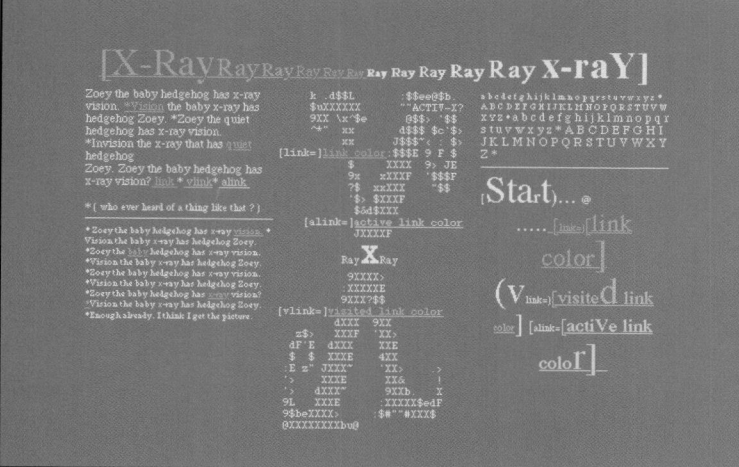

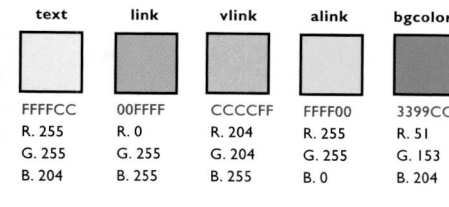

text	link	vlink	alink	bgcolor
FFFFCC	00FFFF	CCCCFF	FFFF00	3399CC
R. 255	R. 0	R. 204	R. 255	R. 51
G. 255	G. 255	G. 204	G. 255	G. 153
B. 204	B. 255	B. 255	B. 0	B. 204

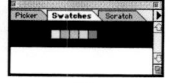

cs10sw

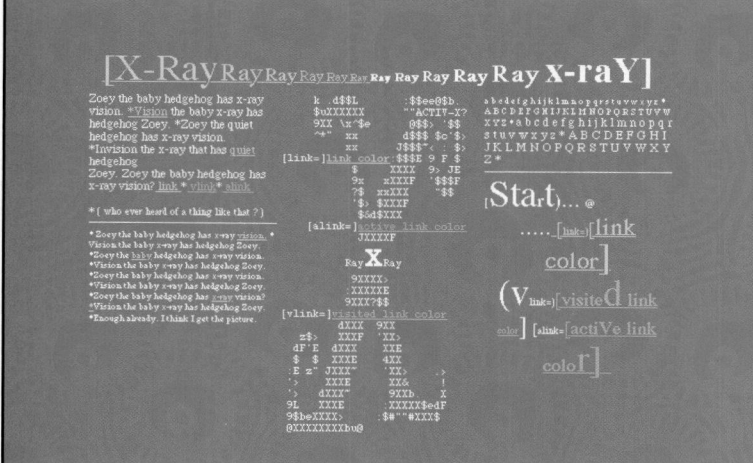

text	link	vlink	alink	tile colors	
FFFFFF	FFFF00	CCCC99	CCCC33	0099CC	009999
R. 255	R. 255	R. 204	R. 204	R. 0	R. 0
G. 255	G. 255	G. 204	G. 204	G. 153	G. 153
B. 255	B. 0	B. 153	B. 51	B. 204	B. 153

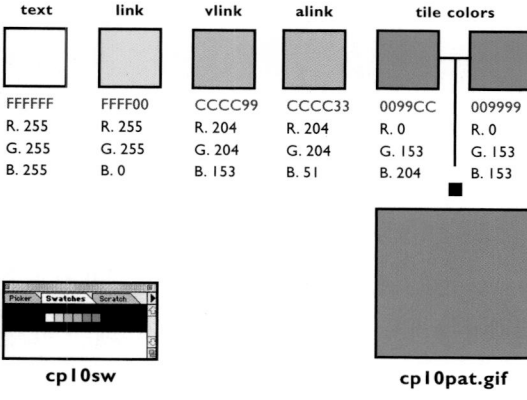

cp10sw

cp10pat.gif

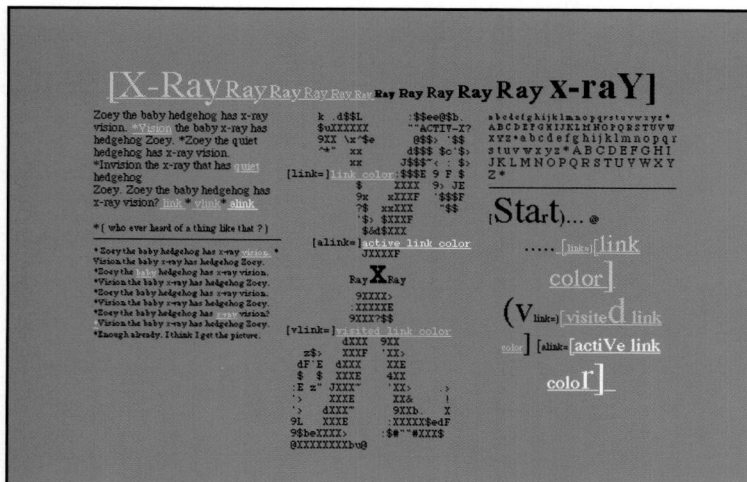

text	link	vlink	alink	hybrid colors	
003333	99FFFF	CCCCCC	FFFFFF	0099CC	009999
R. 0	R. 153	R. 204	R. 255	R. 0	R. 0
G. 51	G. 255	G. 204	G. 255	G. 153	G. 153
B. 51	B. 255	B. 204	B. 255	B. 204	B. 153

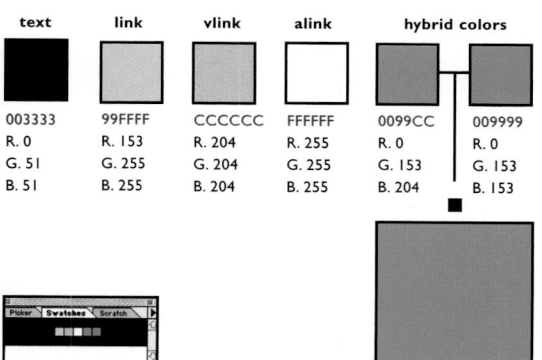

ch10sw

ch10pat.gif

text	link	vlink	alink	bgcolor
99FFFF	33CCFF	CCCCCC	336666	339999
R. 153	R. 51	R. 204	R. 51	R. 51
G. 255	G. 204	G. 204	G. 102	G. 153
B. 255	B. 255	B. 204	B. 102	B. 153

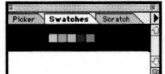

cs11sw

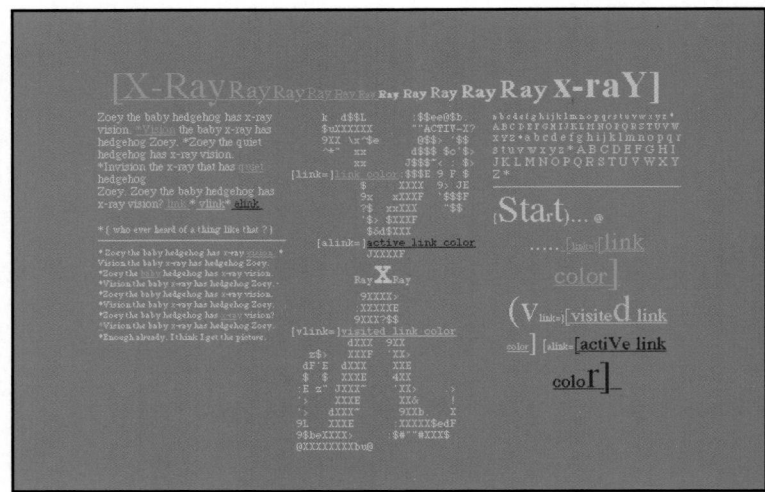

text	link	vlink	alink	tile colors	
FFFFFF	FFFF00	66FF00	666600	999999	339999
R. 255	R. 255	R. 102	R. 102	R. 153	R. 51
G. 255	G. 255	G. 255	G. 102	G. 153	G. 153
B. 255	B. 0	B. 0	B. 0	B. 153	B. 153

cp11sw

cp11pat.gif

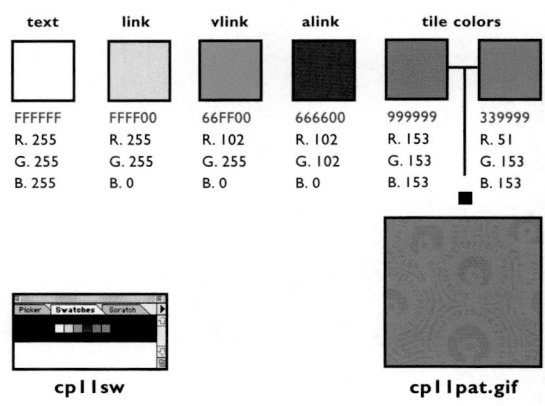

text	link	vlink	alink	hybrid colors	
CCFFCC	66CC66	CCCCCC	CCCC00	999999	339999
R. 204	R. 102	R. 204	R. 204	R. 153	R. 51
G. 255	G. 204	G. 204	G. 204	G. 153	G. 153
B. 204	B. 102	B. 204	B. 0	B. 153	B. 153

ch11sw

ch11pat.gif

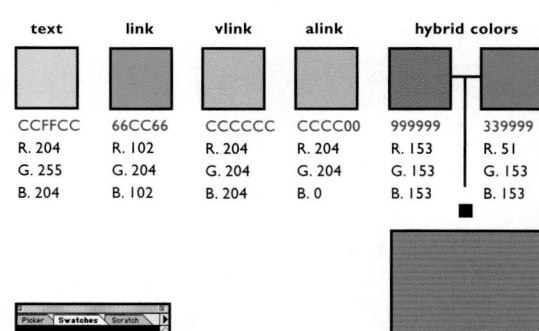

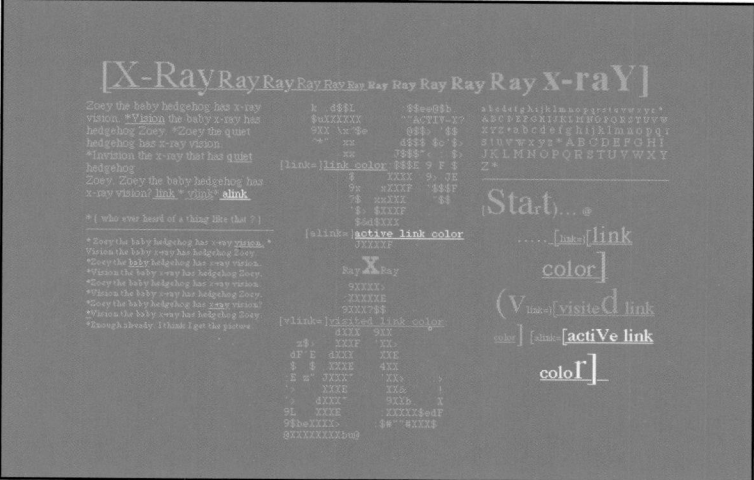

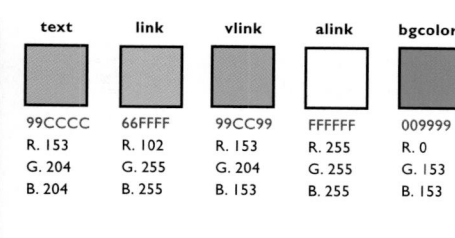

text	link	vlink	alink	bgcolor
99CCCC	66FFFF	99CC99	FFFFFF	009999
R. 153	R. 102	R. 153	R. 255	R. 0
G. 204	G. 255	G. 204	G. 255	G. 153
B. 204	B. 255	B. 153	B. 255	B. 153

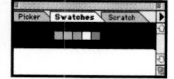

cs12sw

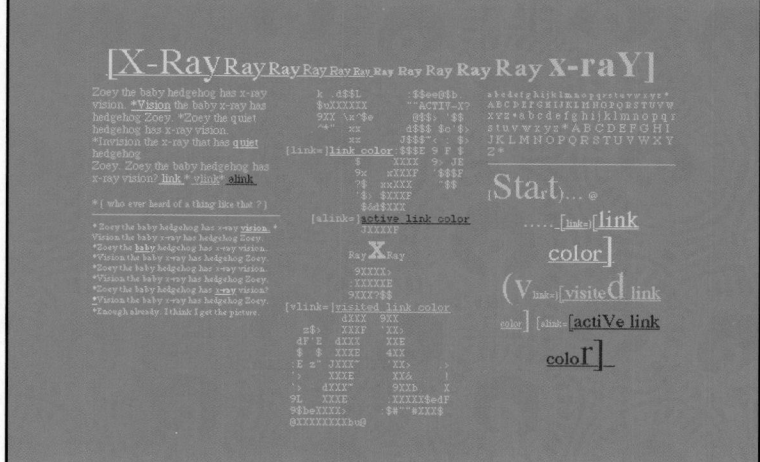

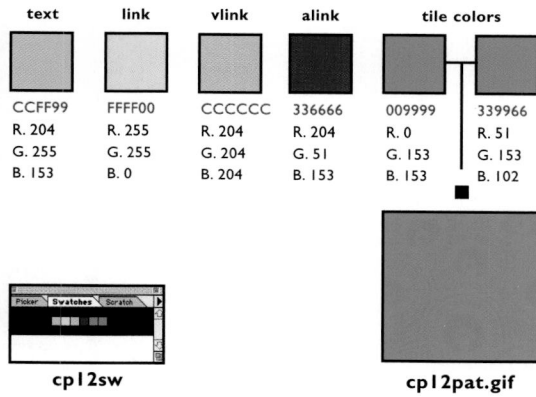

text	link	vlink	alink	tile colors	
CCFF99	FFFF00	CCCCCC	336666	009999	339966
R. 204	R. 255	R. 204	R. 204	R. 0	R. 51
G. 255	G. 255	G. 204	G. 51	G. 153	G. 153
B. 153	B. 0	B. 204	B. 153	B. 153	B. 102

cp12sw

cp12pat.gif

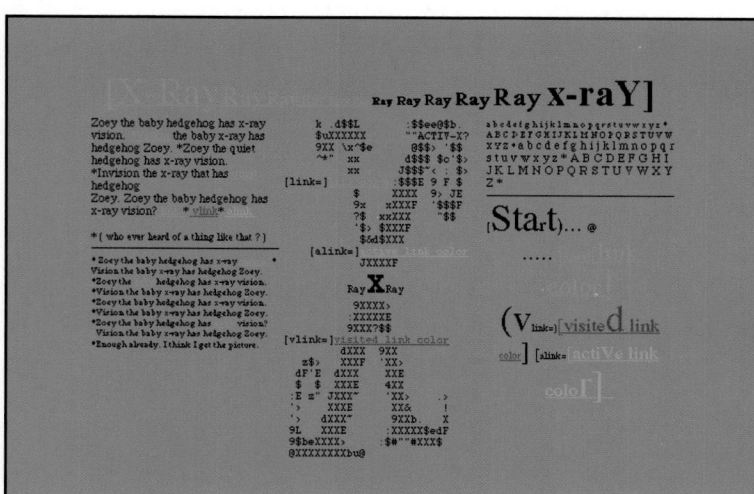

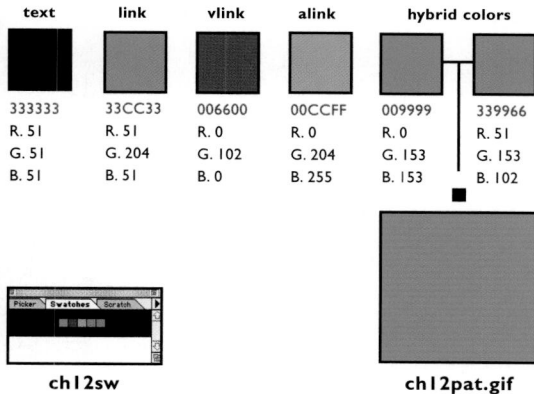

text	link	vlink	alink	hybrid colors	
333333	33CC33	006600	00CCFF	009999	339966
R. 51	R. 51	R. 0	R. 0	R. 0	R. 51
G. 51	G. 204	G. 102	G. 204	G. 153	G. 153
B. 51	B. 51	B. 0	B. 255	B. 153	B. 102

ch12sw

ch12pat.gif

text	link	vlink	alink	bgcolor
99CC99	33CC33	999900	00FF00	336666
R. 153	R. 51	R. 153	R. 0	R. 51
G. 204	G. 204	G. 153	G. 204	G. 102
B. 153	B. 51	B. 0	B. 0	B. 102

cs13sw

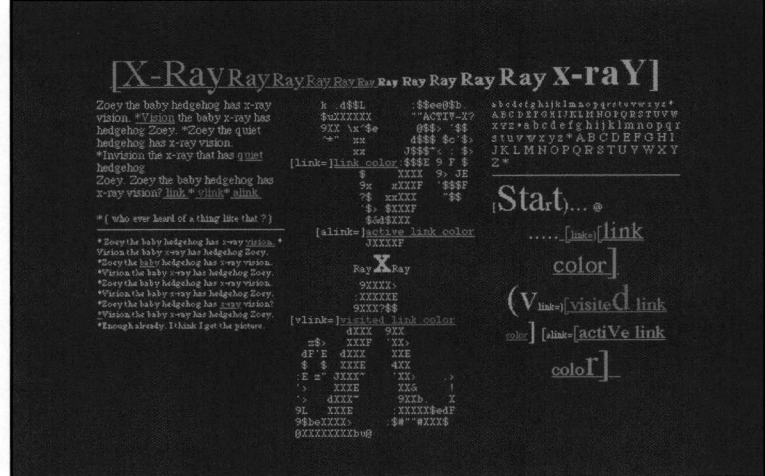

text	link	vlink	alink	tile colors	
CCCCCC	33CCCC	33CC33	99CCCC	666666	336666
R. 204	R. 51	R. 51	R. 153	R. 102	R. 51
G. 204	G. 204	G. 204	G. 204	G. 102	G. 102
B. 204	B. 204	B. 51	B. 204	B. 102	B. 102

cp13sw

cp13pat.gif

text	link	vlink	alink	hybrid colors	
CC9966	FFCC66	999900	FFFF00	666666	336666
R. 204	R. 255	R. 153	R. 255	R. 102	R. 51
G. 153	G. 204	G. 153	G. 255	G. 102	G. 102
B. 102	B. 102	B. 0	B. 102	B. 102	B. 102

ch13sw

ch13pat.gif

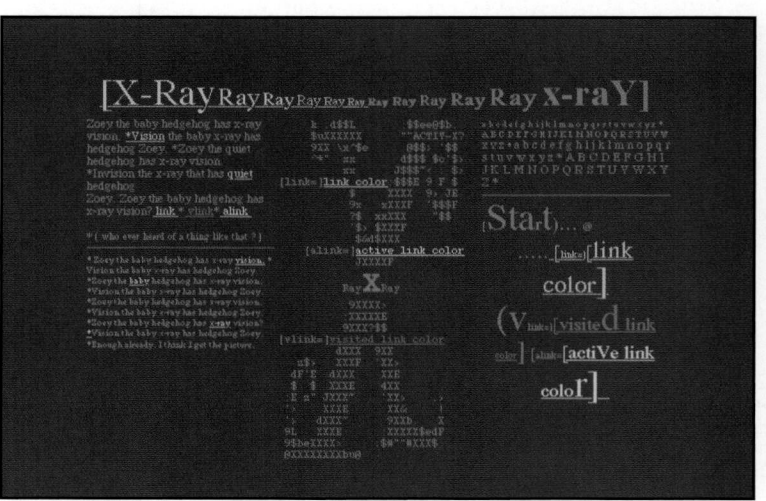

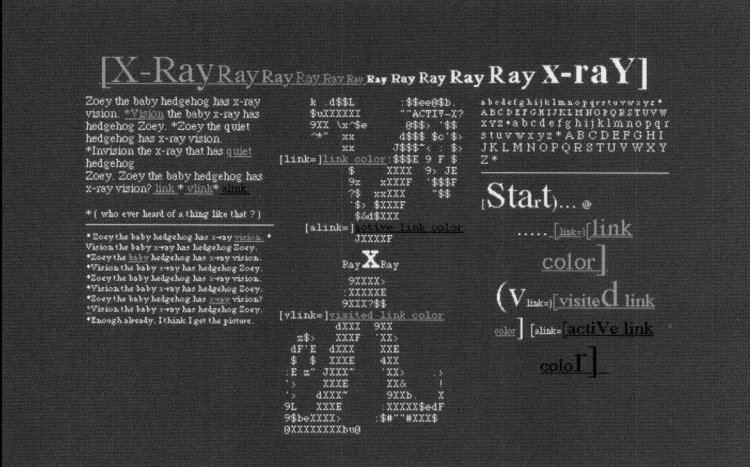

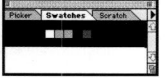

text	link	vlink	alink	bgcolor
FFFFFF	00FFFF	99CCFF	333333	006666
R. 255	R. 0	R. 153	R. 51	R. 0
G. 255	G. 255	G. 204	G. 51	G. 102
B. 255	B. 255	B. 255	B. 51	B. 102

cs14sw

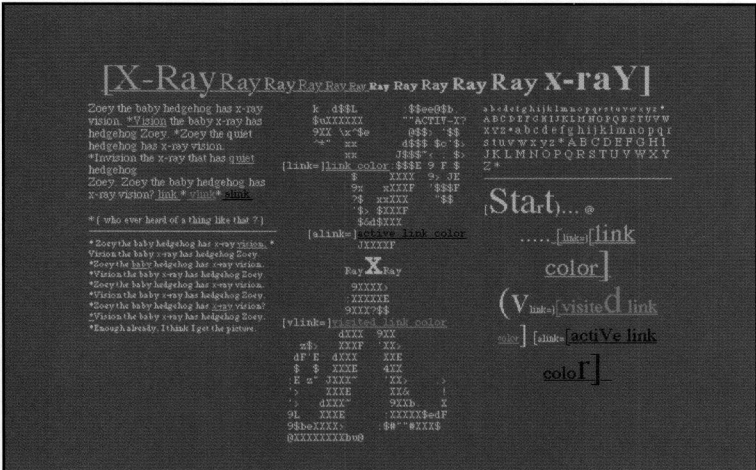

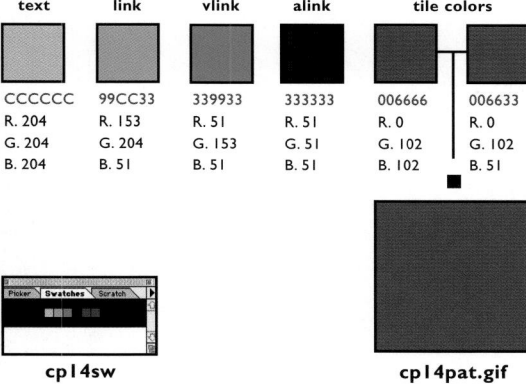

text	link	vlink	alink	tile colors	
CCCCCC	99CC33	339933	333333	006666	006633
R. 204	R. 153	R. 51	R. 51	R. 0	R. 0
G. 204	G. 204	G. 153	G. 51	G. 102	G. 102
B. 204	B. 51	B. 51	B. 51	B. 102	B. 51

cp14sw **cp14pat.gif**

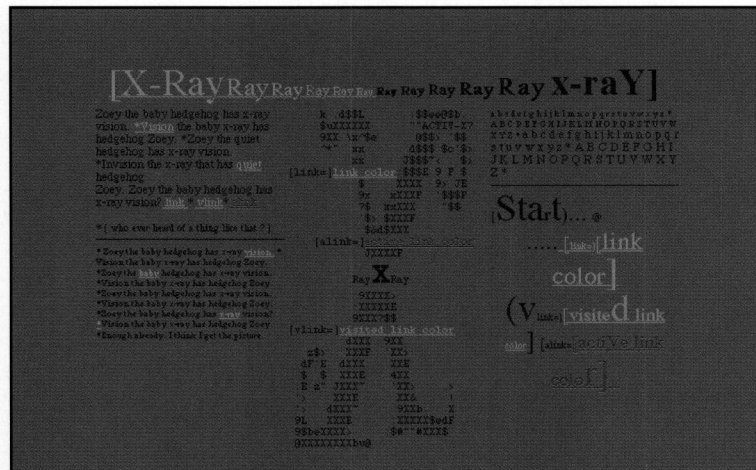

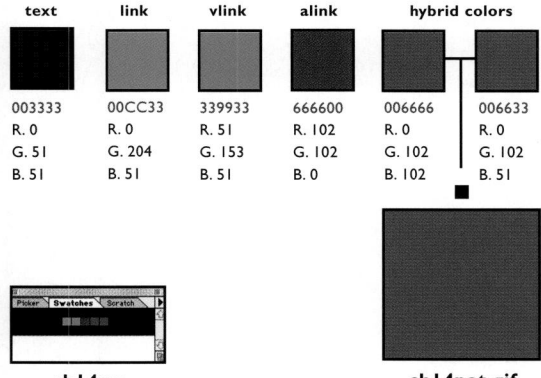

text	link	vlink	alink	hybrid colors	
003333	00CC33	339933	666600	006666	006633
R. 0	R. 0	R. 51	R. 102	R. 0	R. 0
G. 51	G. 204	G. 153	G. 102	G. 102	G. 102
B. 51	B. 51	B. 51	B. 0	B. 102	B. 51

ch14sw **ch14pat.gif**

Color Groupings/Swatches/Directory

(page 192)

text	link	vlink	alink	bgcolor
FF9999	FF3333	FF6633	666699	003366
R. 255	R. 255	R. 255	R. 102	R. 0
G. 153	G. 51	G. 102	G. 102	G. 51
B. 153	B. 51	B. 51	B. 153	B. 102

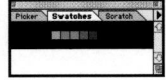

cs15sw

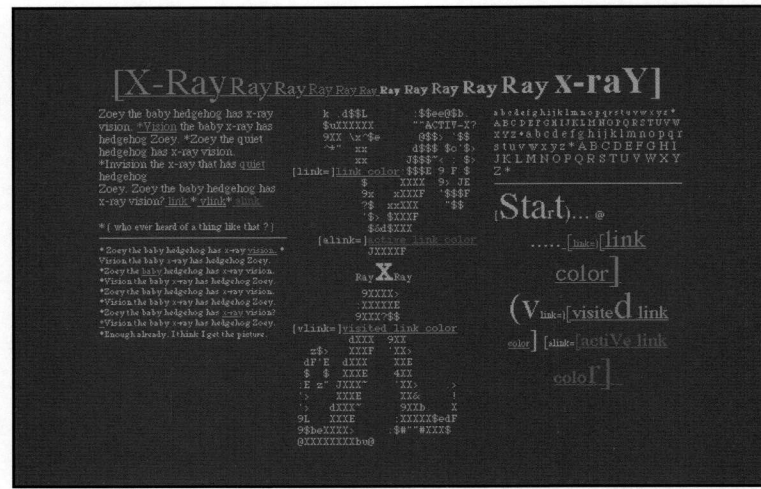

text	link	vlink	alink	tile colors	
6666CC	CC3333	CC6666	000033	003366	003333
R. 102	R. 204	R. 204	R. 0	R. 0	R. 0
G. 102	G. 51	G. 51	G. 0	G. 51	G. 51
B. 204	B. 51	B. 102	B. 51	B. 102	B. 51

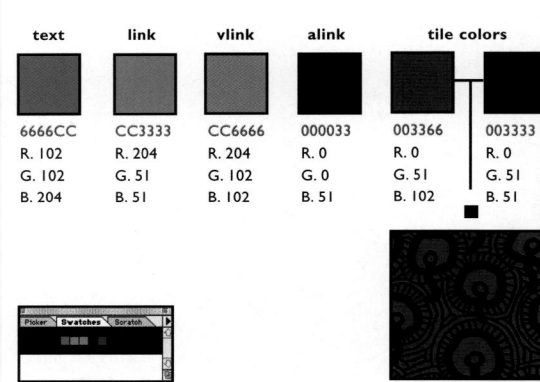

cp15sw

cp15pat.gif

text	link	vlink	alink	hybrid colors	
9999CC	3399CC	6666FF	666666	003366	003333
R. 153	R. 51	R. 102	R. 102	R. 0	R. 0
G. 153	G. 153	G. 102	G. 102	G. 51	G. 51
B. 204	B. 204	B. 255	B. 102	B. 102	B. 51

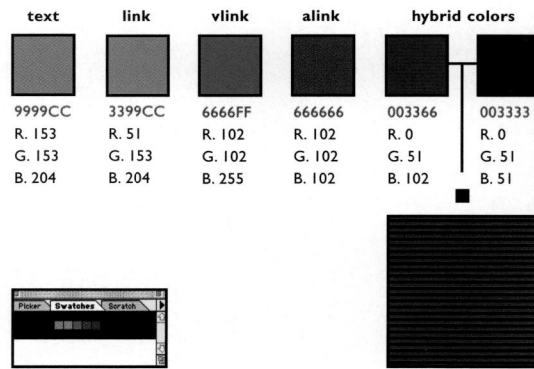

ch15sw

ch15pat.gif

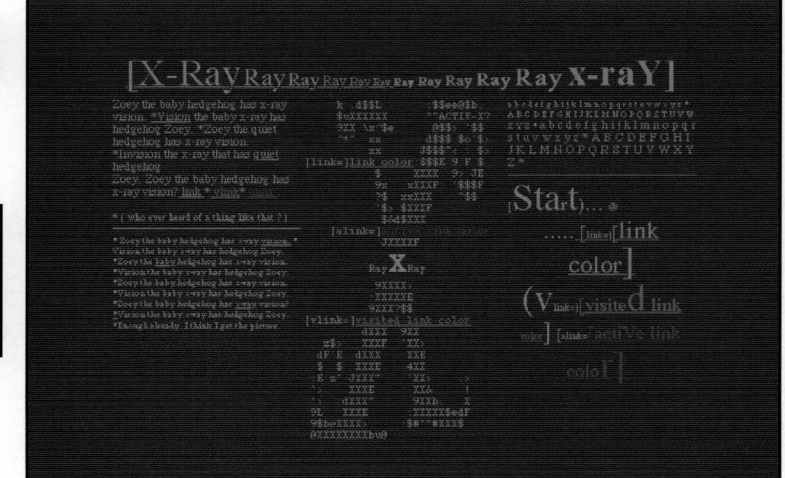

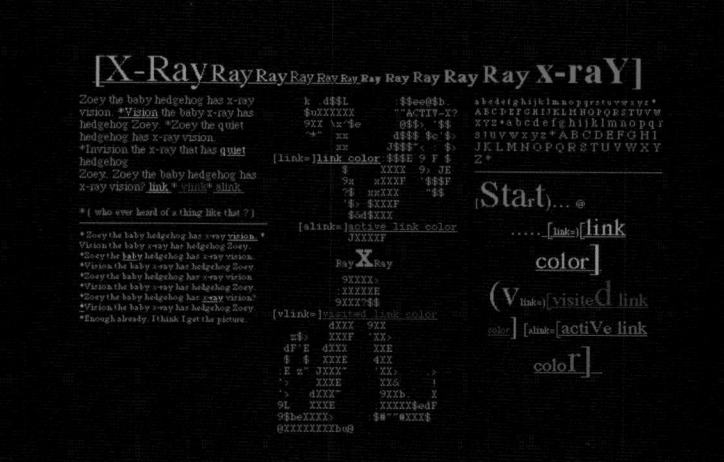
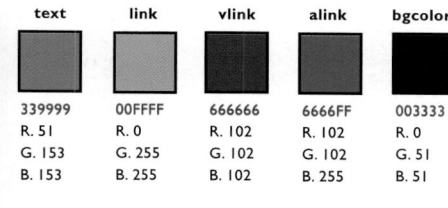
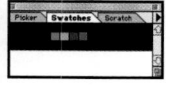

cs16sw

text	link	vlink	alink	bgcolor
339999	00FFFF	666666	6666FF	003333
R. 51	R. 0	R. 102	R. 102	R. 0
G. 153	G. 255	G. 102	G. 102	G. 51
B. 153	B. 255	B. 102	B. 255	B. 51

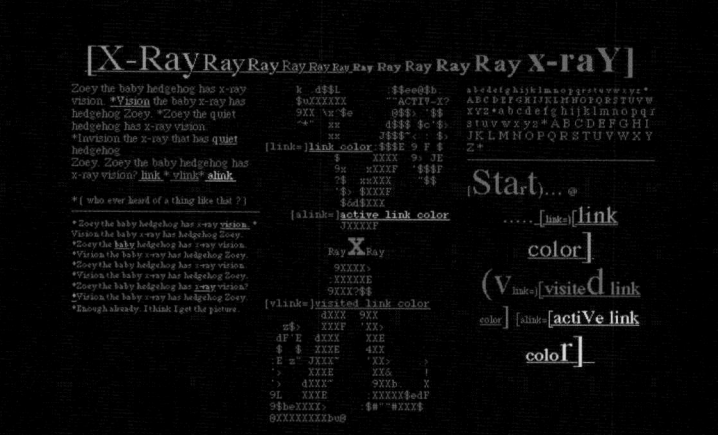
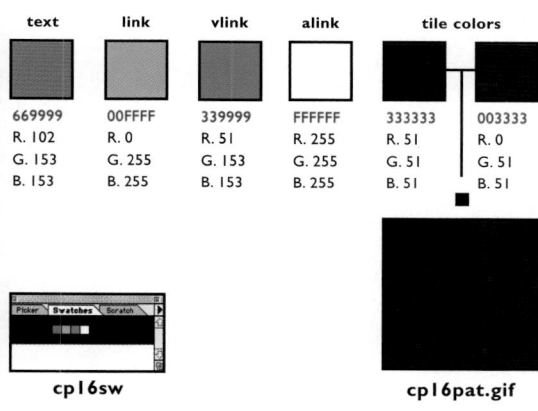

cp16sw   **cp16pat.gif**

text	link	vlink	alink	tile colors	
669999	00FFFF	339999	FFFFFF	333333	003333
R. 102	R. 0	R. 51	R. 255	R. 51	R. 0
G. 153	G. 255	G. 153	G. 255	G. 51	G. 51
B. 153	B. 255	B. 153	B. 255	B. 51	B. 51

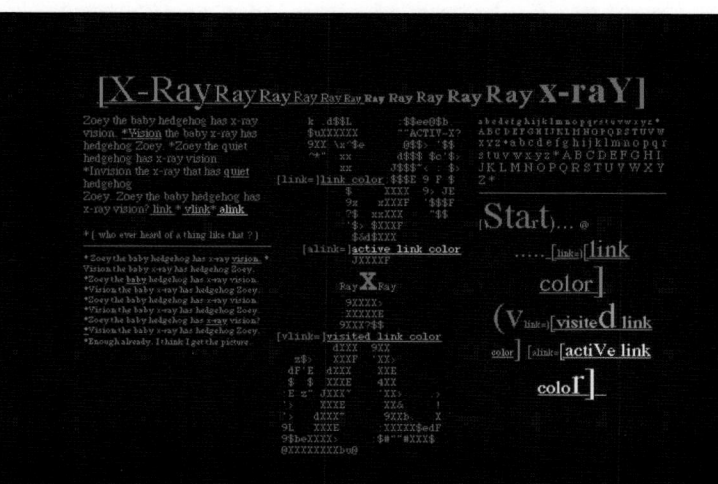
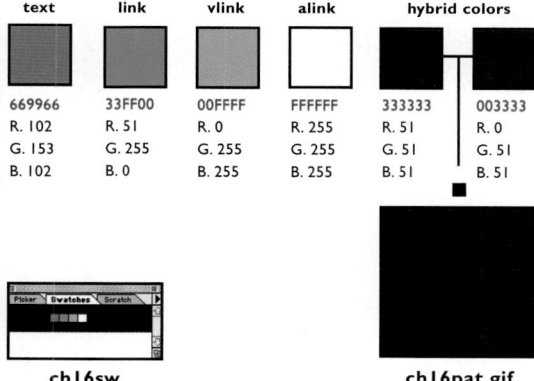

ch16sw   **ch16pat.gif**

text	link	vlink	alink	hybrid colors	
669966	33FF00	00FFFF	FFFFFF	333333	003333
R. 102	R. 51	R. 0	R. 255	R. 51	R. 0
G. 153	G. 255	G. 255	G. 255	G. 51	G. 51
B. 102	B. 0	B. 255	B. 255	B. 51	B. 51

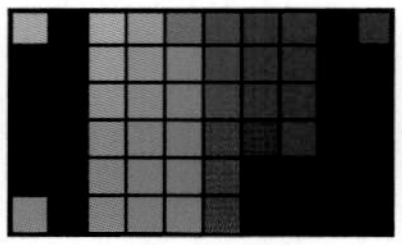

cbgk

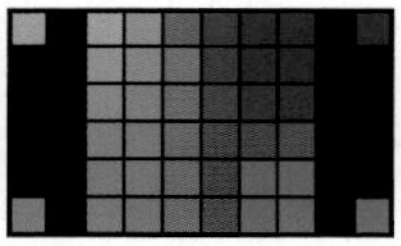

cbgr

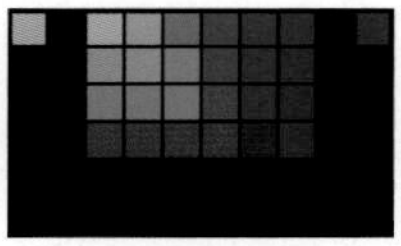

cbkk

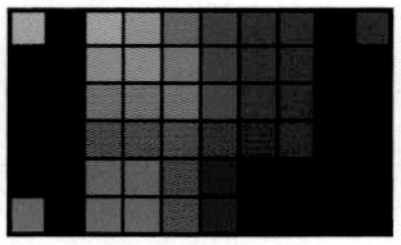

cbkr

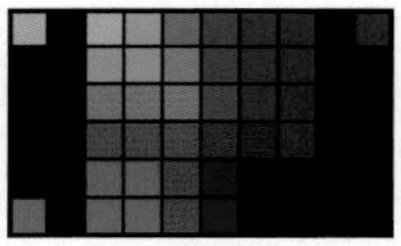

cbrk

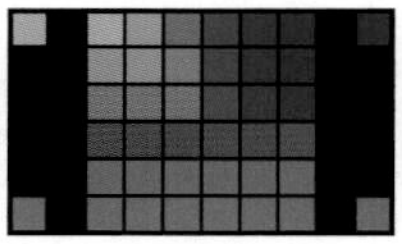

cbrr

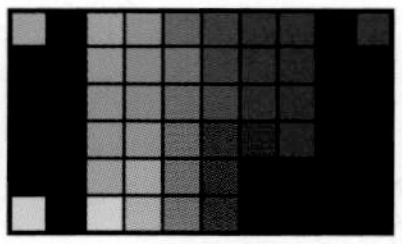

cbyk

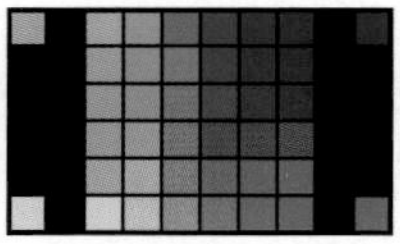

cbyr

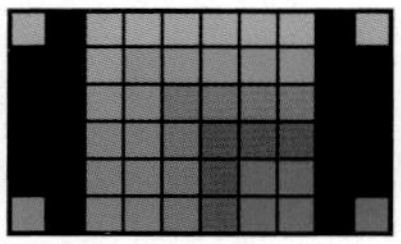

ccgr

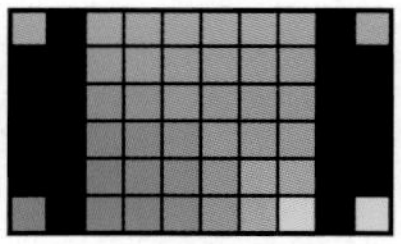

ccgy

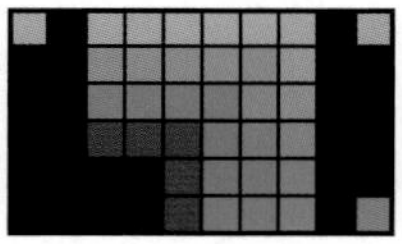

cckg

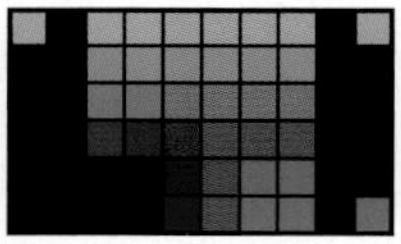

cckr

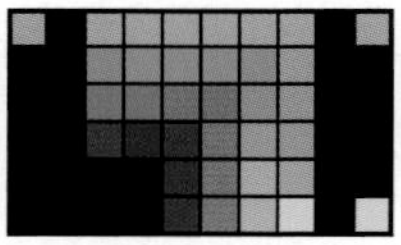

ccky

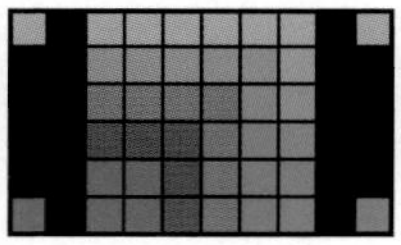

ccrg

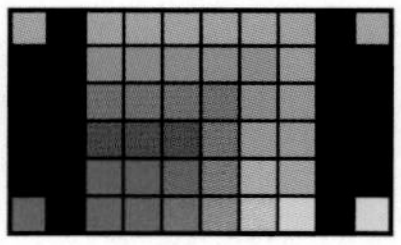

ccry

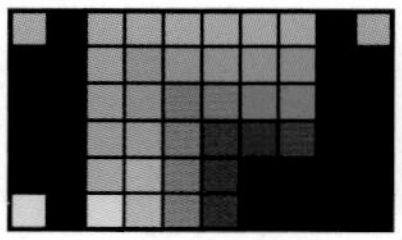

ccyk

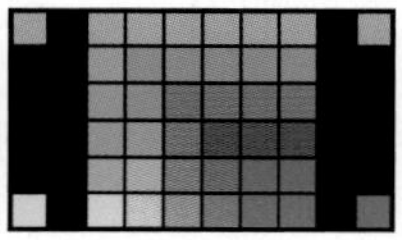

ccyr

cgbb

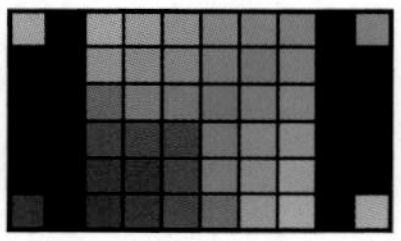

cgbc

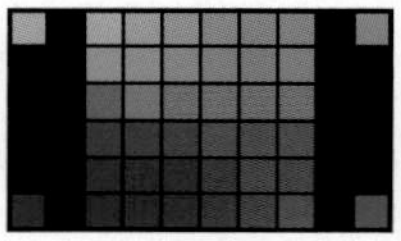

cgbm

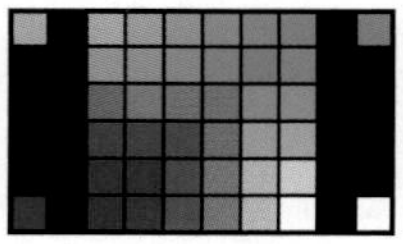

cgbw

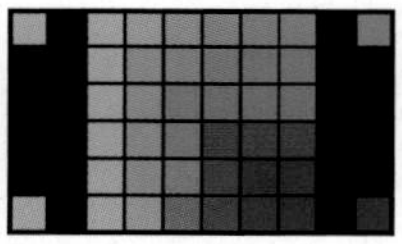

cgcb

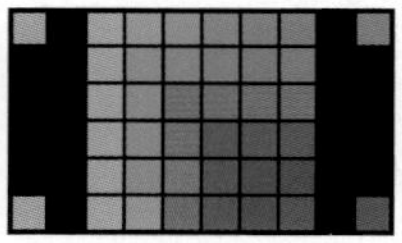

cgcm

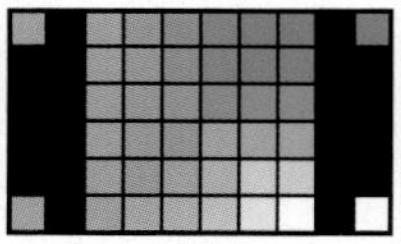

cgcw

cgmb

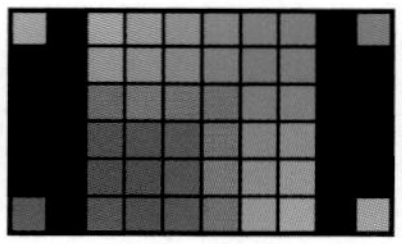

cgmc

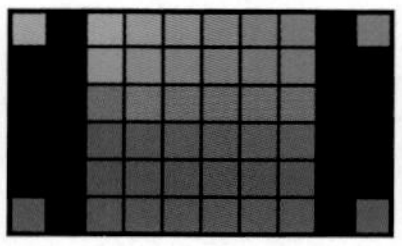

cgmm

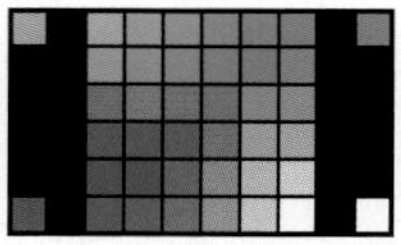

cgmw

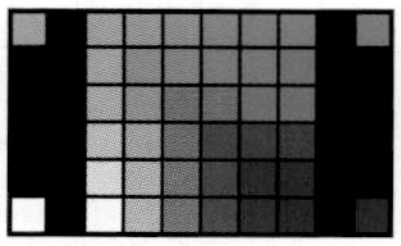

cgwb

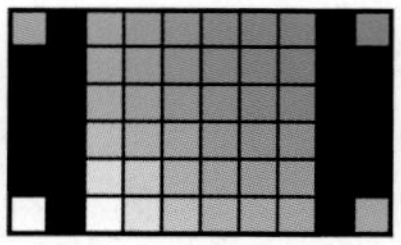

cgwc

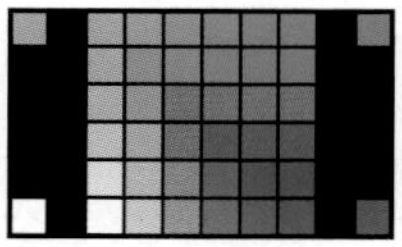

cgwm

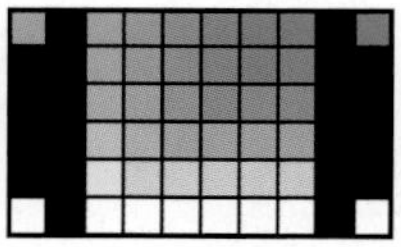

cgww

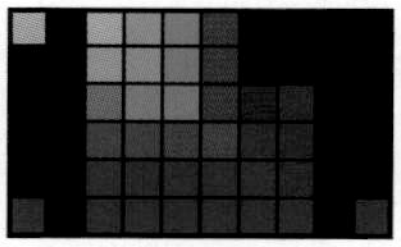

ckbb

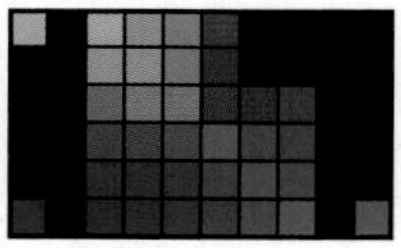

ckbm

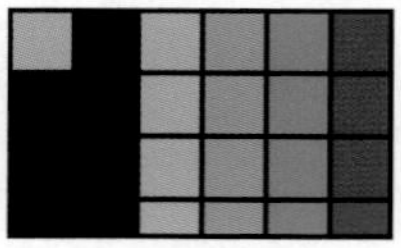

ckcb

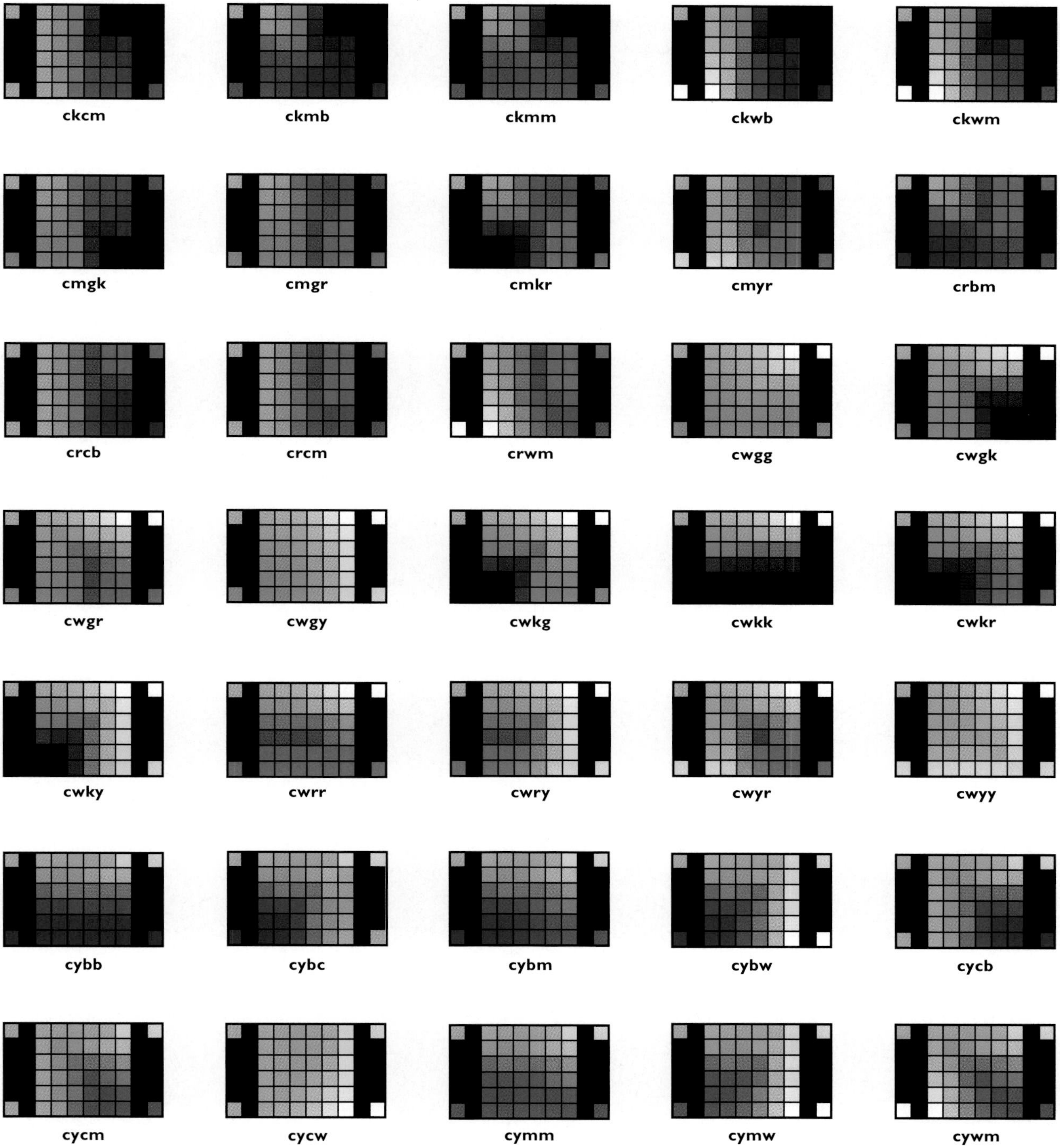

ckcm ckmb ckmm ckwb ckwm

cmgk cmgr cmkr cmyr crbm

crcb crcm crwm cwgg cwgk

cwgr cwgy cwkg cwkk cwkr

cwky cwrr cwry cwyr cwyy

cybb cybc cybm cybw cycb

cycm cycw cymm cymw cywm

MAGENTA

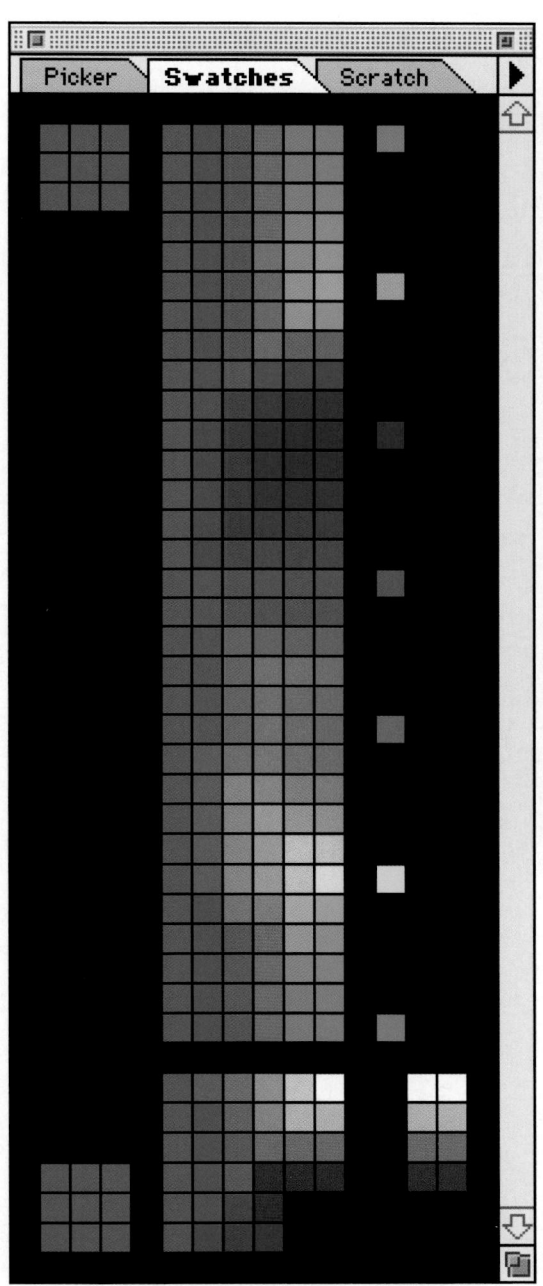

mms

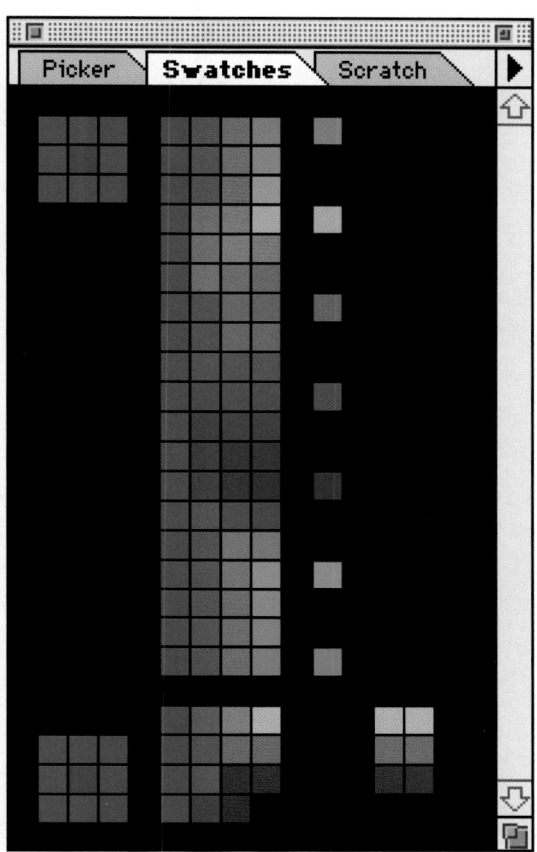

mmd

text	link	vlink	alink	bgcolor
6666CC	0000FF	CC33CC	9999CC	FFCCFF
R. 102	R. 0	R. 204	R. 153	R. 255
G. 102	G. 0	G. 102	G. 153	G. 204
B. 204	B. 255	B. 204	B. 204	B. 255

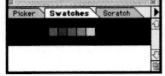

ms01sw

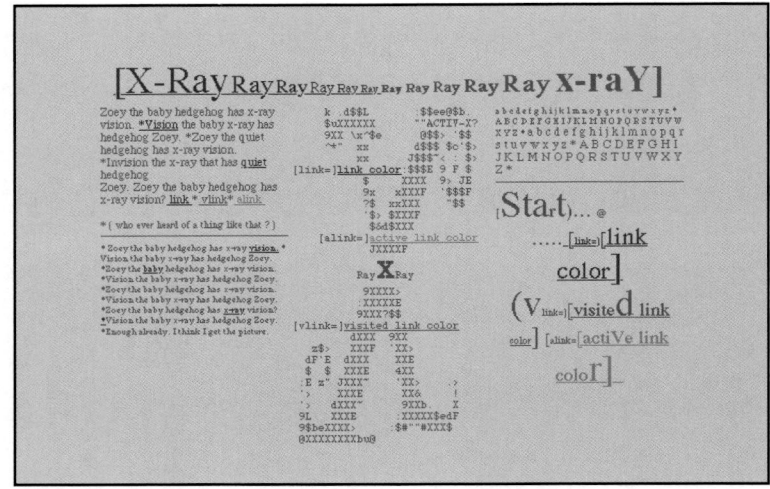

text	link	vlink	alink	tile colors	
666666	FF00000	FF00FF	FF9999	FFCCFF	CCCCFF
R. 102	R. 255	R. 255	R. 255	R. 255	R. 204
G. 102	G. 0	G. 0	G. 153	G. 204	G. 204
B. 102	B. 0	B. 255	B. 153	B. 255	B. 255

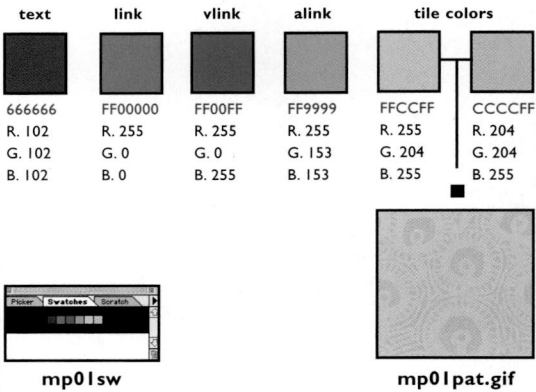

mp01sw   **mp01pat.gif**

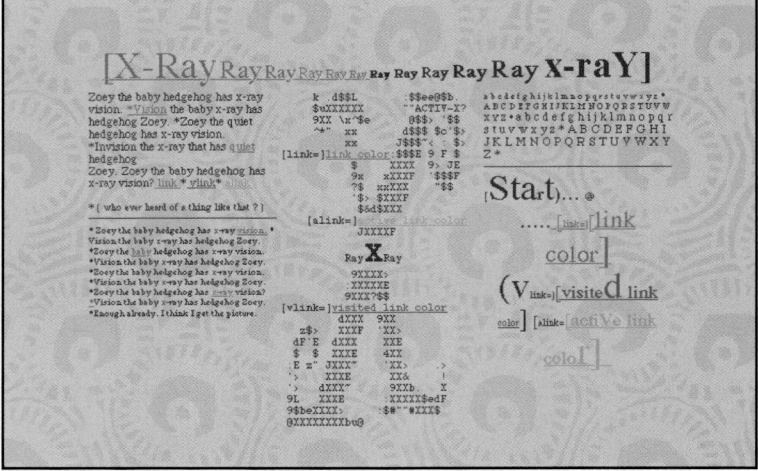

text	link	vlink	alink	hybrid colors	
996699	FF00FF	993399	FFFFFF	CCCCFF	FFCCFF
R. 153	R. 255	R. 153	R. 255	R. 204	R. 255
G. 102	G. 0	G. 51	G. 255	G. 204	G. 204
B. 153	B. 255	B. 153	B. 255	B. 255	B. 255

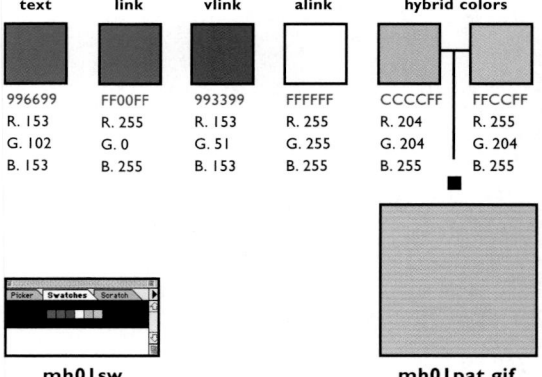

mh01sw   **mh01pat.gif**

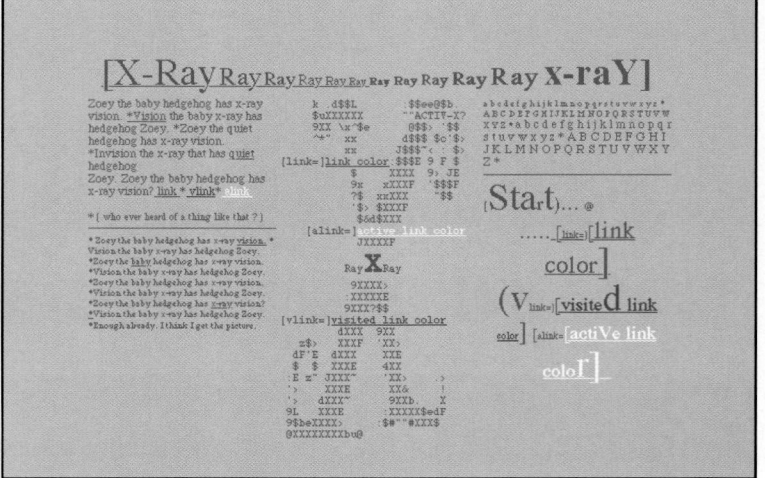

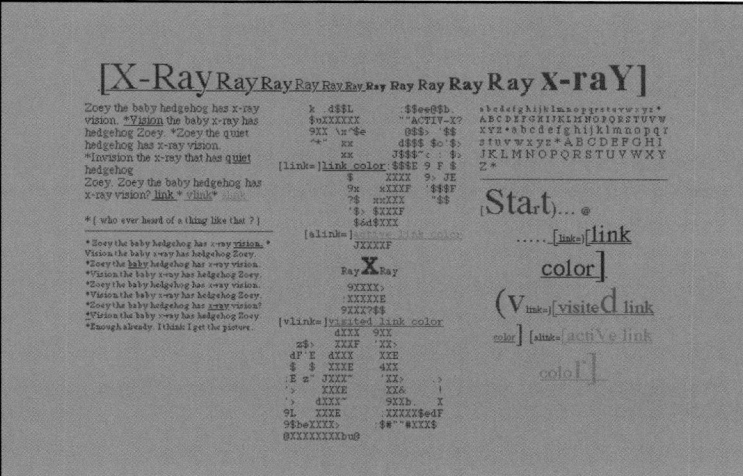

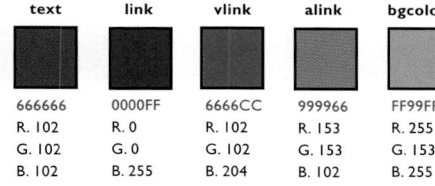

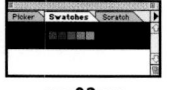

	text	link	vlink	alink	bgcolor
	666666	0000FF	6666CC	999966	FF99FF
	R. 102	R. 0	R. 102	R. 153	R. 255
	G. 102	G. 0	G. 102	G. 153	G. 153
	B. 102	B. 255	B. 204	B. 102	B. 255

ms02sw

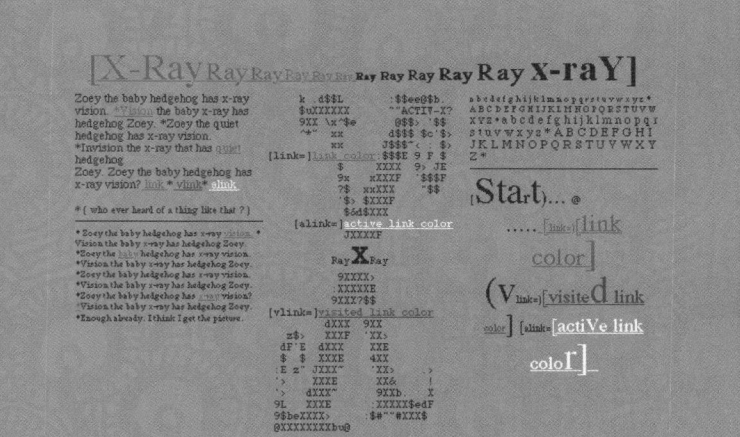

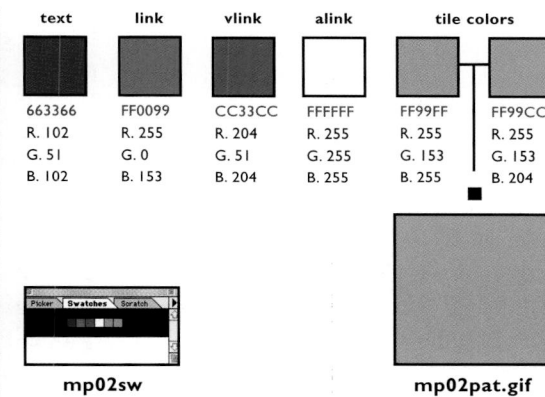

	text	link	vlink	alink	tile colors	
	663366	FF0099	CC33CC	FFFFFF	FF99FF	FF99CC
	R. 102	R. 255	R. 204	R. 255	R. 255	R. 255
	G. 51	G. 0	G. 51	G. 255	G. 153	G. 153
	B. 102	B. 153	B. 204	B. 255	B. 255	B. 204

mp02sw   **mp02pat.gif**

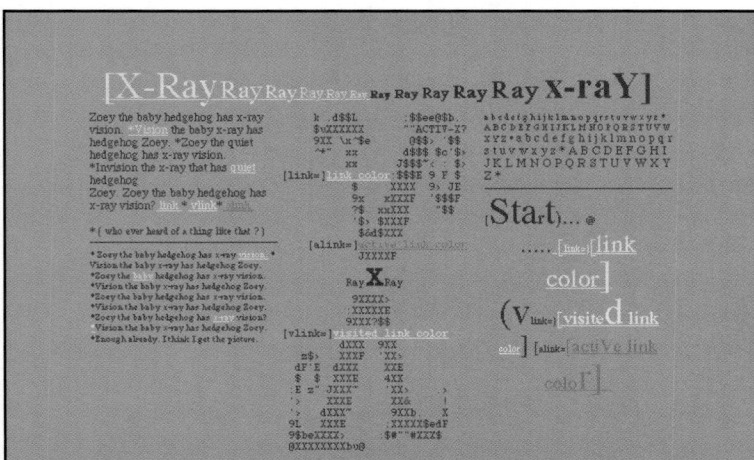

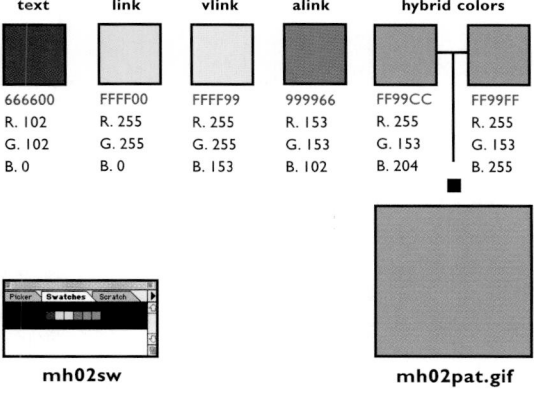

	text	link	vlink	alink	hybrid colors	
	666600	FFFF00	FFFF99	999966	FF99CC	FF99FF
	R. 102	R. 255	R. 255	R. 153	R. 255	R. 255
	G. 102	G. 255	G. 255	G. 153	G. 153	G. 153
	B. 0	B. 0	B. 153	B. 102	B. 204	B. 255

mh02sw   **mh02pat.gif**

text	link	vlink	alink	bgcolor
333399	0033FF	666666	0099FF	CC99FF
R. 51	R. 0	R. 102	R. 0	R. 204
G. 51	G. 51	G. 102	G. 153	G. 153
B. 153	B. 255	B. 102	B. 255	B. 255

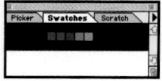

ms03sw

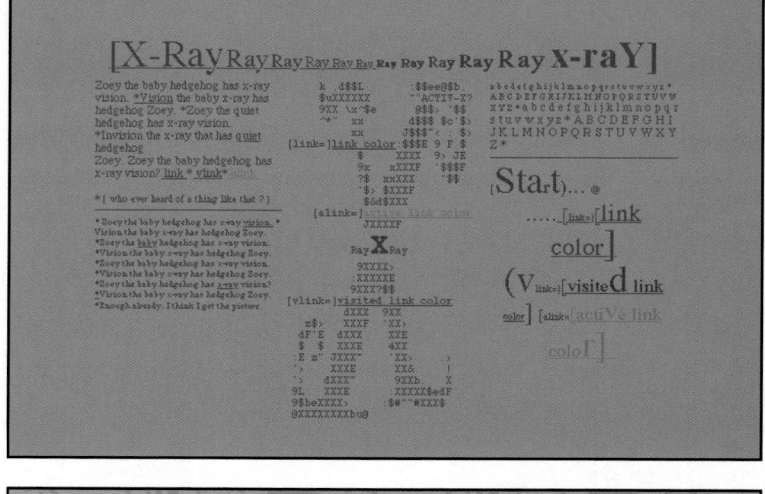

text	link	vlink	alink	tile colors	
993399	FF0000	0000FF	FFCCCC	FF99CC	CC99FF
R. 153	R. 255	R. 0	R. 255	R. 255	R. 204
G. 51	G. 2	G. 0	G. 204	G. 153	G. 153
B. 153	B. 0	B. 255	B. 204	B. 204	B. 255

mp03sw

mp03pat.gif

text	link	vlink	alink	hybrid colors	
663399	CC3333	996666	FF0000	FF99CC	CC99FF
R. 102	R. 204	R. 153	R. 255	R. 255	R. 204
G. 51	G. 51	G. 102	G. 0	G. 153	G. 153
B. 153	B. 51	B. 102	B. 0	B. 204	B. 255

mh03sw

mh03pat.gif

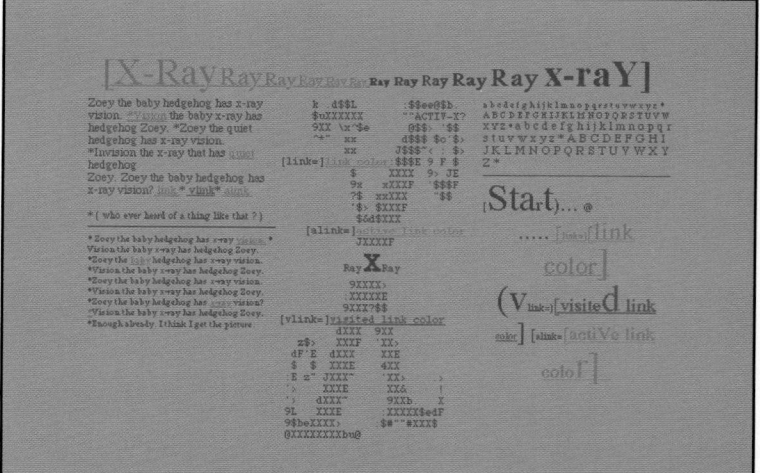

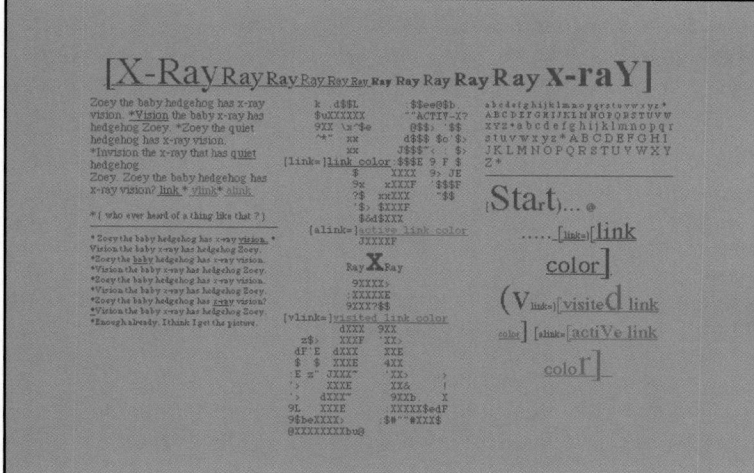

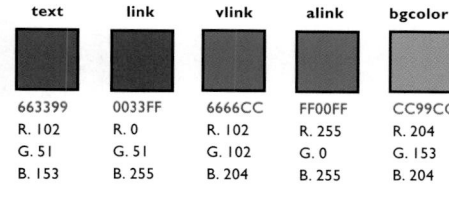

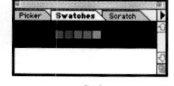

text	link	vlink	alink	bgcolor
663399	0033FF	6666CC	FF00FF	CC99CC
R. 102	R. 0	R. 102	R. 255	R. 204
G. 51	G. 51	G. 102	G. 0	G. 153
B. 153	B. 255	B. 204	B. 255	B. 204

ms04sw

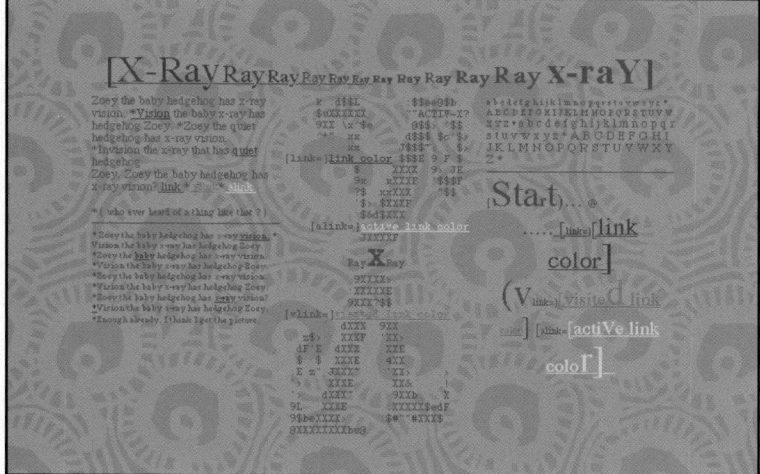

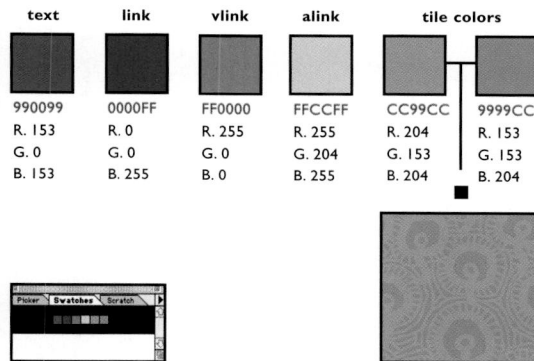

text	link	vlink	alink	tile colors	
990099	0000FF	FF0000	FFCCFF	CC99CC	9999CC
R. 153	R. 0	R. 255	R. 255	R. 204	R. 153
G. 0	G. 0	G. 0	G. 204	G. 153	G. 153
B. 153	B. 255	B. 0	B. 255	B. 204	B. 204

mp04sw

mp04pat.gif

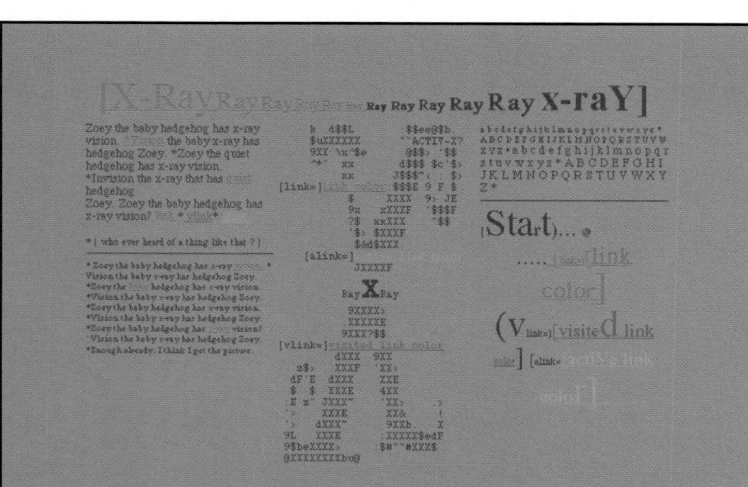

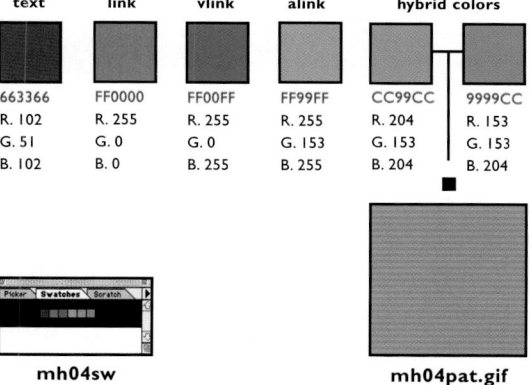

text	link	vlink	alink	hybrid colors	
663366	FF0000	FF00FF	FF99FF	CC99CC	9999CC
R. 102	R. 255	R. 255	R. 255	R. 204	R. 153
G. 51	G. 0	G. 0	G. 153	G. 153	G. 153
B. 102	B. 0	B. 255	B. 255	B. 204	B. 204

mh04sw

mh04pat.gif

text	link	vlink	alink	bgcolor
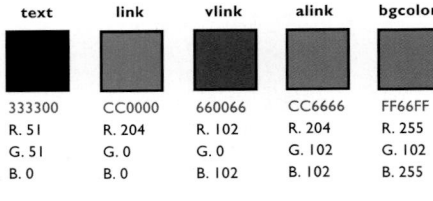				
333300	CC0000	660066	CC6666	FF66FF
R. 51	R. 204	R. 102	R. 204	R. 255
G. 51	G. 0	G. 0	G. 102	G. 102
B. 0	B. 0	B. 102	B. 102	B. 255

ms05sw

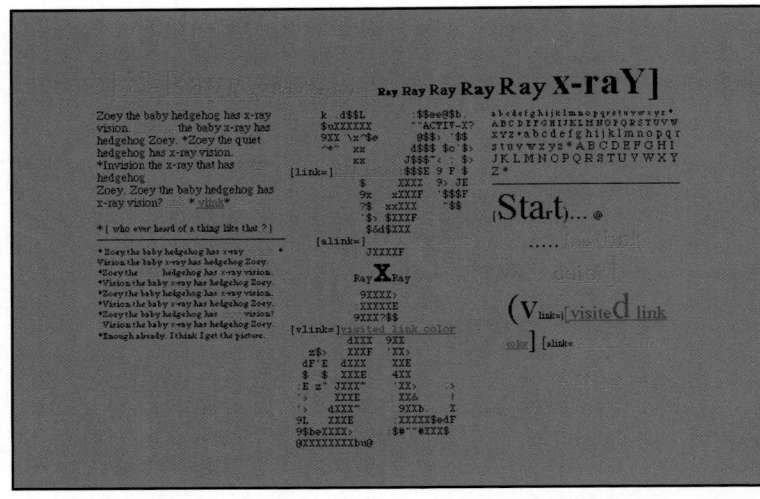

text	link	vlink	alink	tile colors	
990000	FF0000	996633	CCCCCC	FF66FF	CC9999
R. 153	R. 255	R. 153	R. 204	R. 255	R. 204
G. 0	G. 0	G. 102	G. 204	G. 102	G. 153
B. 0	B. 0	B. 51	B. 204	B. 255	B. 153

mp05sw

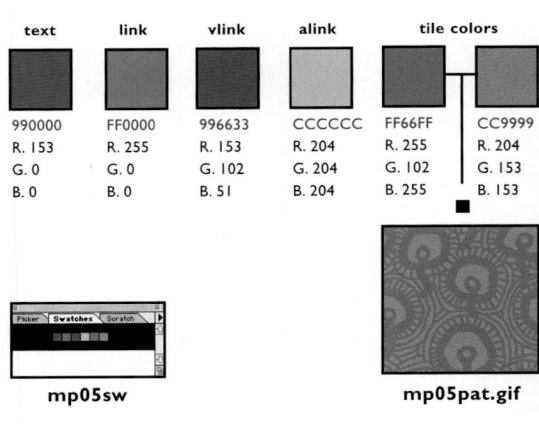

mp05pat.gif

text	link	vlink	alink	hybrid colors	
FFFFFF	FF0000	CC6633	336666	FF66FF	CC9999
R. 255	R. 255	R. 204	R. 51	R. 255	R. 204
G. 255	G. 0	G. 102	G. 102	G. 102	G. 153
B. 255	B. 0	B. 51	B. 102	B. 255	B. 153

mh05sw

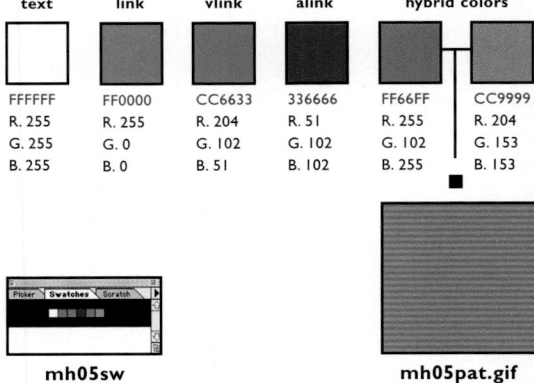

mh05pat.gif

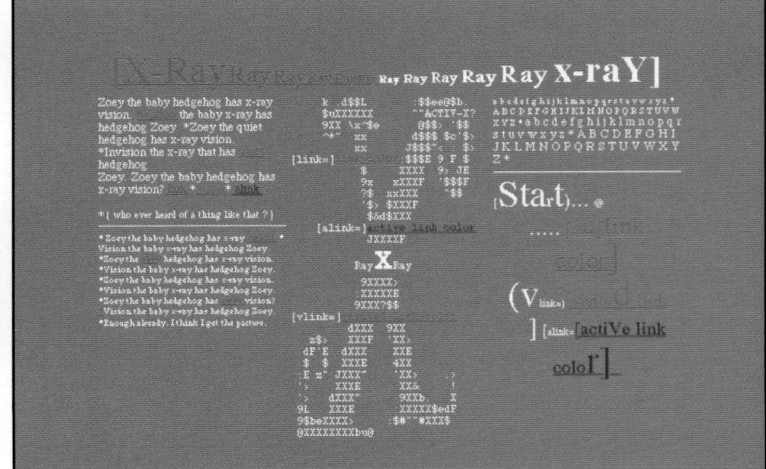

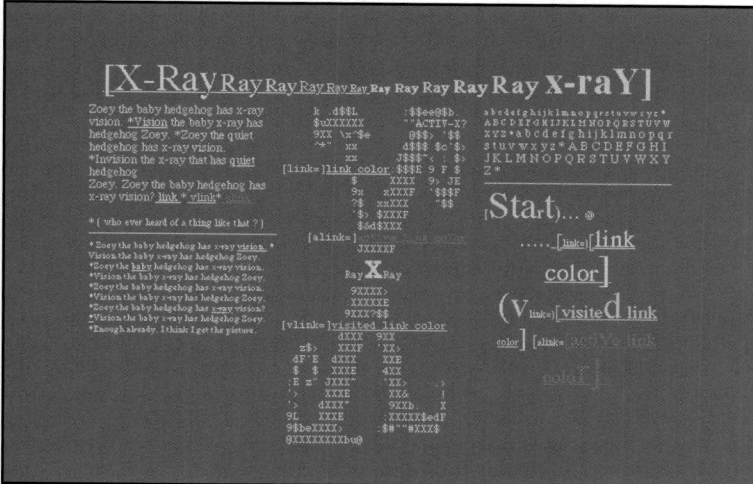

	text	link	vlink	alink	bgcolor
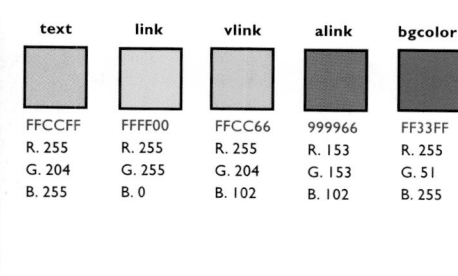	FFCCFF	FFFF00	FFCC66	999966	FF33FF
	R. 255	R. 255	R. 255	R. 153	R. 255
	G. 204	G. 255	G. 204	G. 153	G. 51
	B. 255	B. 0	B. 102	B. 102	B. 255

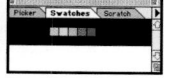

ms06sw

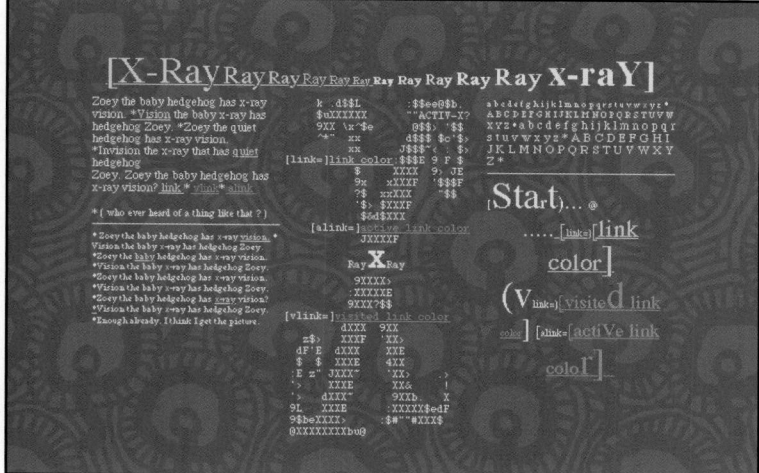

	text	link	vlink	alink	tile colors	
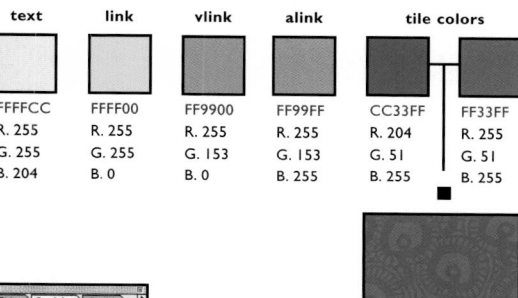	FFFFCC	FFFF00	FF9900	FF99FF	CC33FF	FF33FF
	R. 255	R. 255	R. 255	R. 255	R. 204	R. 255
	G. 255	G. 255	G. 153	G. 153	G. 51	G. 51
	B. 204	B. 0	B. 0	B. 255	B. 255	B. 255

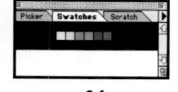

mp06sw

mp06pat.gif

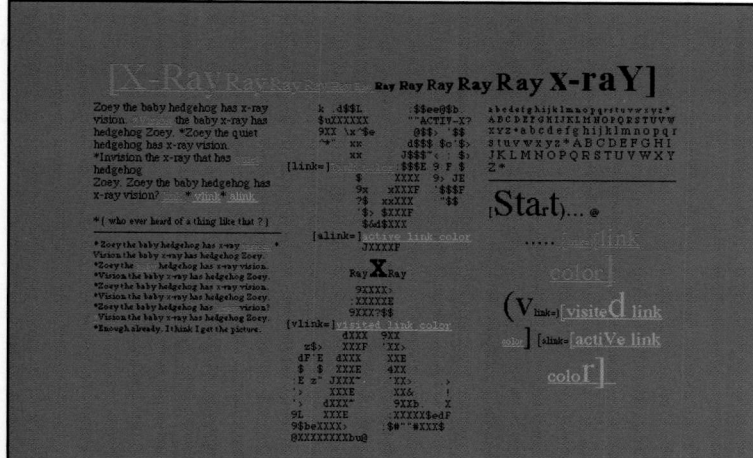

	text	link	vlink	alink	hybrid colors	
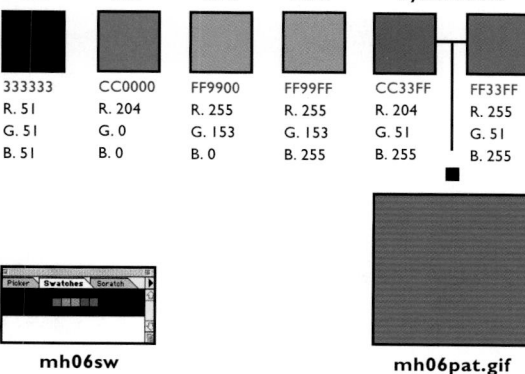	333333	CC0000	FF9900	FF99FF	CC33FF	FF33FF
	R. 51	R. 204	R. 255	R. 255	R. 204	R. 255
	G. 51	G. 0	G. 153	G. 153	G. 51	G. 51
	B. 51	B. 0	B. 0	B. 255	B. 255	B. 255

mh06sw

mh06pat.gif

ms07sw

text	link	vlink	alink	bgcolor
CCCCCC	FFCC66	99CCFF	CCCCCC	CC66CC
R. 204	R. 255	R. 153	R. 204	R. 204
G. 204	G. 204	G. 204	G. 204	G. 102
B. 204	B. 102	B. 255	B. 204	B. 204

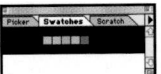

ms07sw

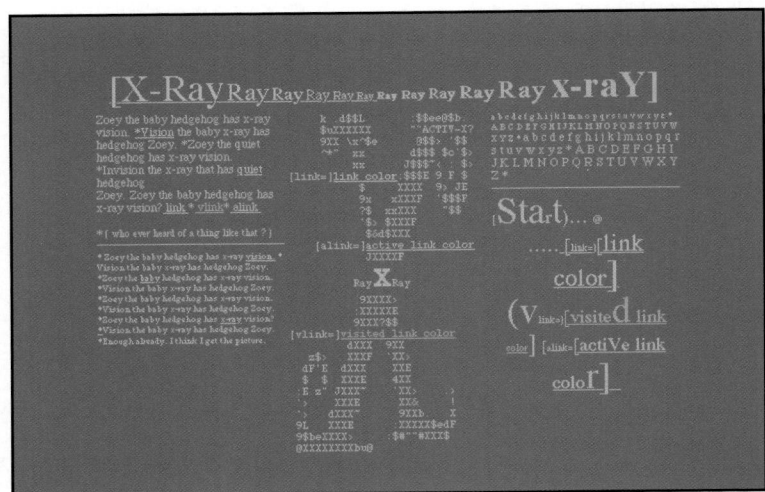

mp07sw

text	link	vlink	alink	tile colors	
FFFFFF	FFFF00	FFCC66	FF00FF	CC66CC	996699
R. 255	R. 255	R. 255	R. 255	R. 204	R. 153
G. 255	G. 255	G. 204	G. 0	G. 102	G. 102
B. 255	B. 0	B. 102	B. 255	B. 204	B. 153

mp07sw

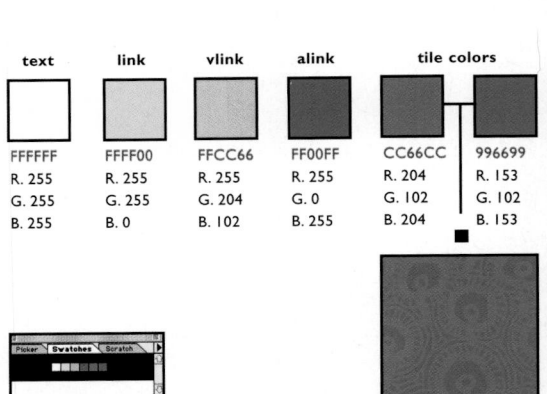

mp07pat.gif

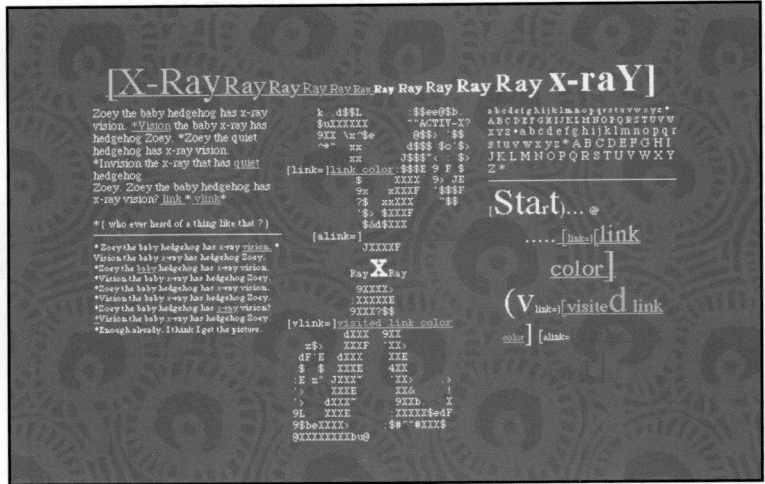

mh07sw

text	link	vlink	alink	hybrid colors	
330066	00FFFF	CCCCFF	CCCCCC	CC66CC	996699
R. 51	R. 0	R. 204	R. 204	R. 204	R. 153
G. 0	G. 255	G. 204	G. 204	G. 102	G. 102
B. 102	B. 255	B. 255	B. 204	B. 204	B. 153

mh07sw

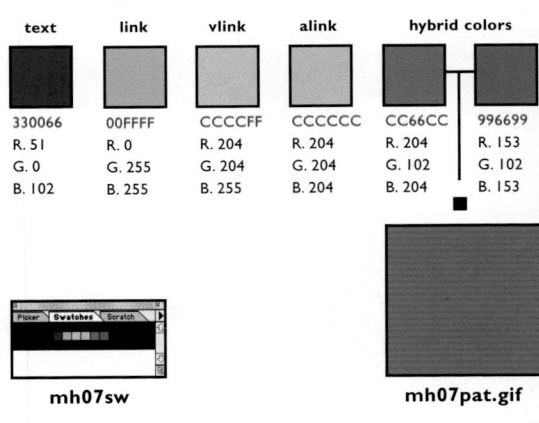

mh07pat.gif

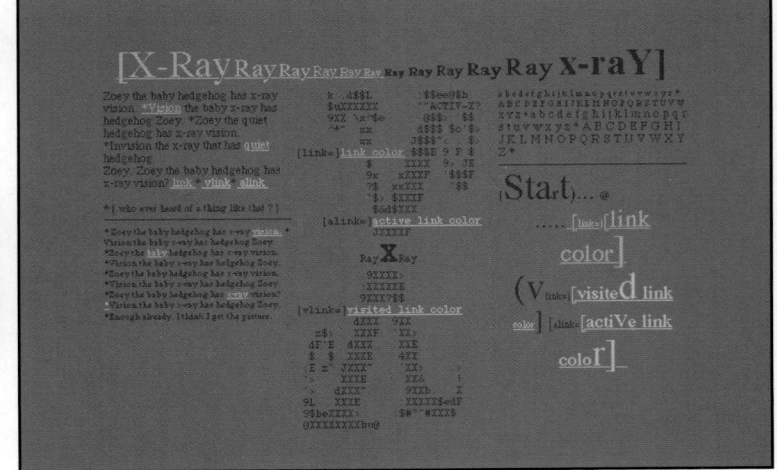

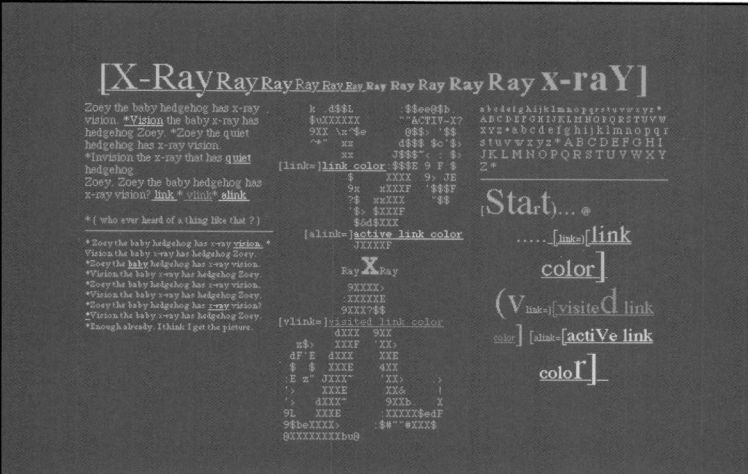

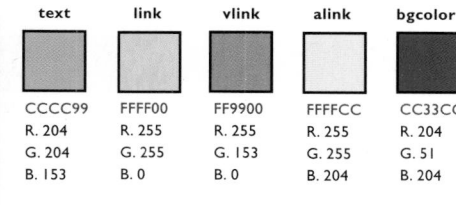

text	link	vlink	alink	bgcolor
CCCC99	FFFF00	FF9900	FFFFCC	CC33CC
R. 204	R. 255	R. 255	R. 255	R. 204
G. 204	G. 255	G. 153	G. 255	G. 51
B. 153	B. 0	B. 0	B. 204	B. 204

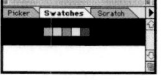

ms08sw

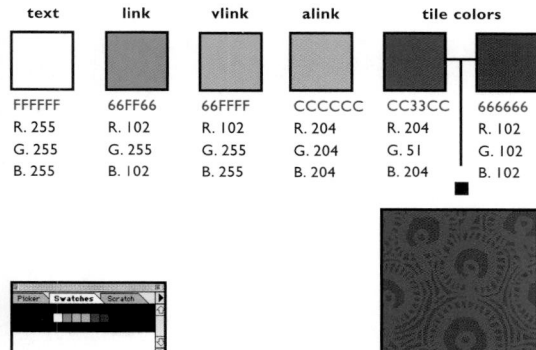

text	link	vlink	alink	tile colors	
FFFFFF	66FF66	66FFFF	CCCCCC	CC33CC	666666
R. 255	R. 102	R. 102	R. 204	R. 204	R. 102
G. 255	G. 255	G. 255	G. 204	G. 51	G. 102
B. 255	B. 102	B. 255	B. 204	B. 204	B. 102

mp08sw

mp08pat.gif

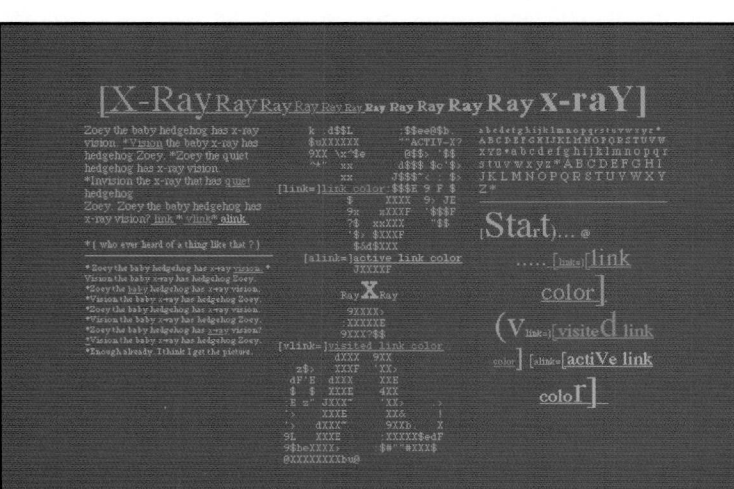

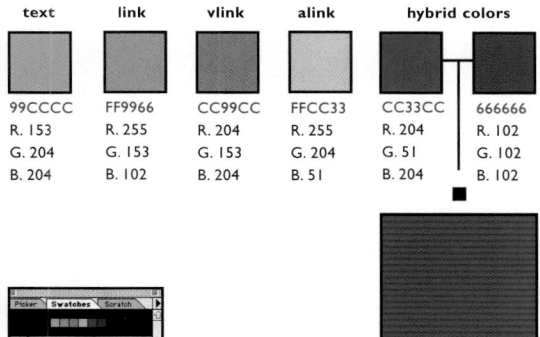

text	link	vlink	alink	hybrid colors	
99CCCC	FF9966	CC99CC	FFCC33	CC33CC	666666
R. 153	R. 255	R. 204	R. 255	R. 204	R. 102
G. 204	G. 153	G. 153	G. 204	G. 51	G. 102
B. 204	B. 102	B. 204	B. 51	B. 204	B. 102

mh08sw

mh08pat.gif

text	link	vlink	alink	bgcolor
CCCCCC	6699CC	9999CC	FFFFFF	9933CC
R. 204	R. 102	R. 153	R. 255	R. 153
G. 204	G. 153	G. 153	G. 255	G. 51
B. 204	B. 204	B. 204	B. 255	B. 204

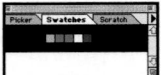

ms09sw

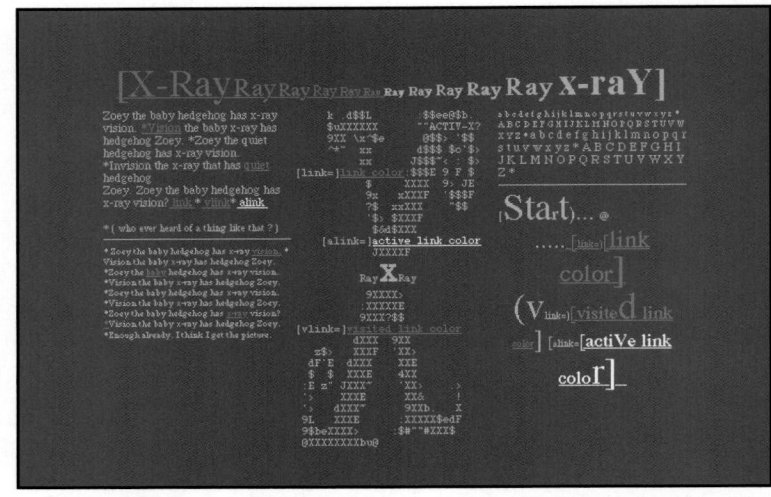

text	link	vlink	alink	tile colors	
CCCCFF	00FFFF	9999FF	CCFFFF	9933CC	CC00FF
R. 204	R. 0	R. 153	R. 204	R. 153	R. 204
G. 204	G. 255	G. 153	G. 255	G. 51	G. 0
B. 255	B. 255	B. 255	B. 255	B. 204	B. 255

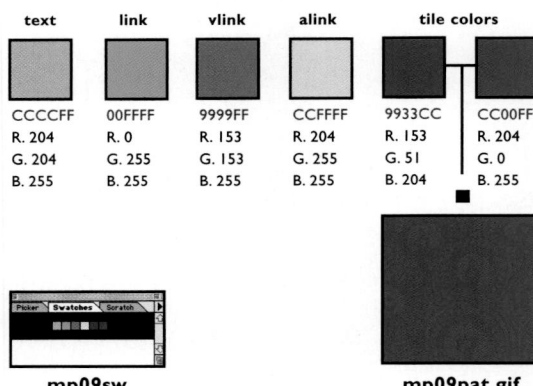

mp09sw   mp09pat.gif

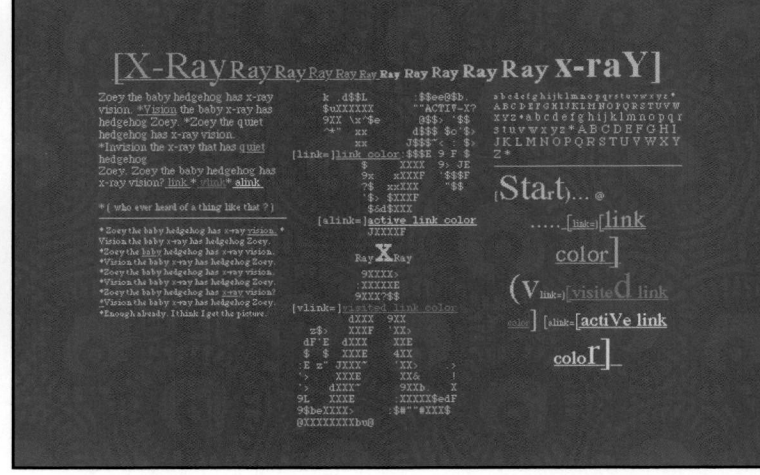

text	link	vlink	alink	hybrid colors	
FFCCCC	FFCC00	CC9900	FF3300	9933CC	CC00FF
R. 255	R. 255	R. 204	R. 255	R. 153	R. 204
G. 204	G. 204	G. 153	G. 51	G. 51	G. 0
B. 204	B. 0	B. 0	B. 0	B. 204	B. 255

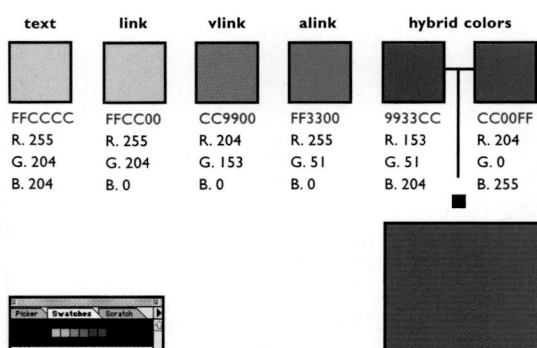

mh09sw   mh09pat.gif

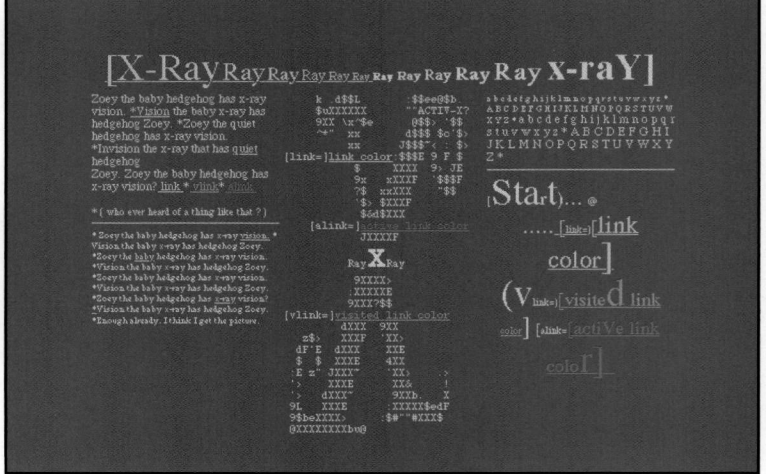

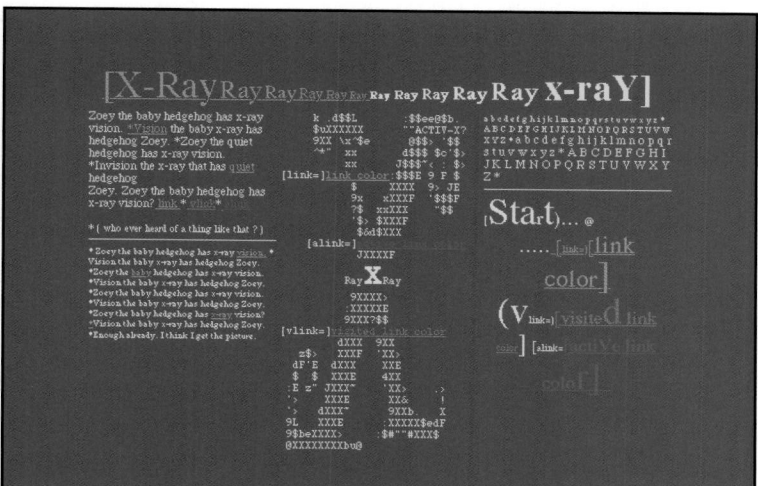

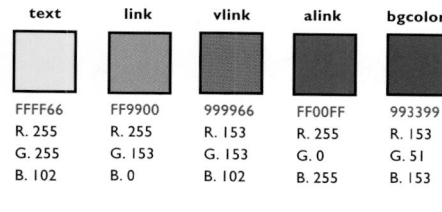

text	link	vlink	alink	bgcolor
FFFF66	FF9900	999966	FF00FF	993399
R. 255	R. 255	R. 153	R. 255	R. 153
G. 255	G. 153	G. 153	G. 0	G. 51
B. 102	B. 0	B. 102	B. 255	B. 153

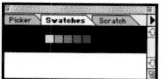

ms10sw

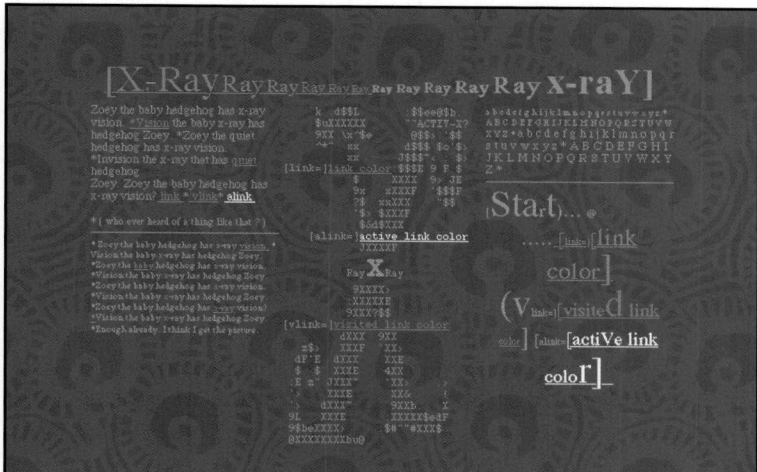

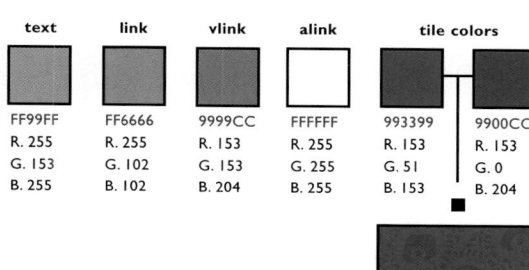

text	link	vlink	alink	tile colors	
FF99FF	FF6666	9999CC	FFFFFF	993399	9900CC
R. 255	R. 255	R. 153	R. 255	R. 153	R. 153
G. 153	G. 102	G. 153	G. 255	G. 51	G. 0
B. 255	B. 102	B. 204	B. 255	B. 153	B. 204

mp10sw

mp10pat.gif

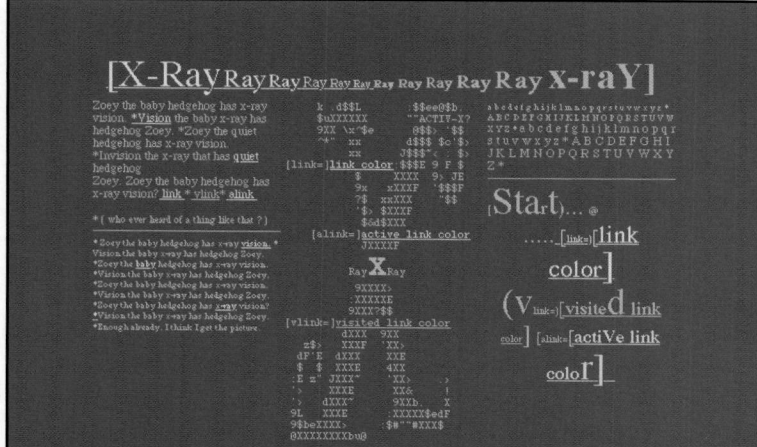

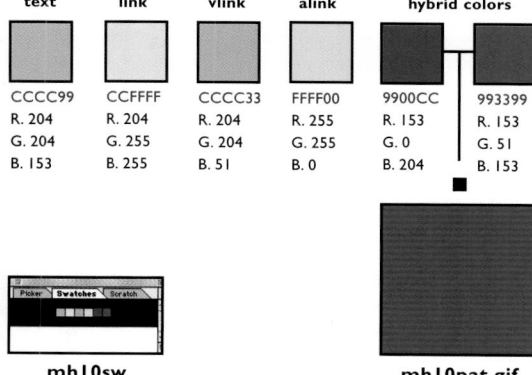

text	link	vlink	alink	hybrid colors	
CCCC99	CCFFFF	CCCC33	FFFF00	9900CC	993399
R. 204	R. 204	R. 204	R. 255	R. 153	R. 153
G. 204	G. 255	G. 204	G. 255	G. 0	G. 51
B. 153	B. 255	B. 51	B. 0	B. 204	B. 153

mh10sw

mh10pat.gif

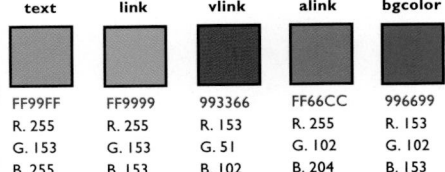

text	link	vlink	alink	bgcolor
FF99FF	FF9999	993366	FF66CC	996699
R. 255	R. 255	R. 153	R. 255	R. 153
G. 153	G. 153	G. 51	G. 102	G. 102
B. 255	B. 153	B. 102	B. 204	B. 153

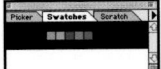

ms11sw

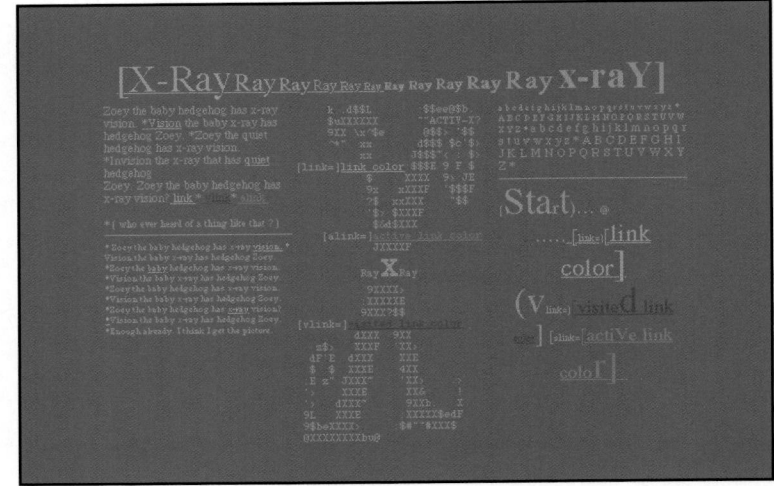

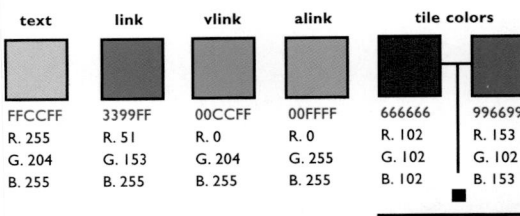

text	link	vlink	alink	tile colors	
FFCCFF	3399FF	00CCFF	00FFFF	666666	996699
R. 255	R. 51	R. 0	R. 0	R. 102	R. 153
G. 204	G. 153	G. 204	G. 255	G. 102	G. 102
B. 255	B. 255	B. 255	B. 255	B. 102	B. 153

mp11sw

mp11pat.gif

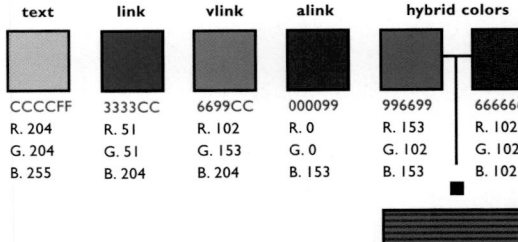

text	link	vlink	alink	hybrid colors	
CCCCFF	3333CC	6699CC	000099	996699	666666
R. 204	R. 51	R. 102	R. 0	R. 153	R. 102
G. 204	G. 51	G. 153	G. 0	G. 102	G. 102
B. 255	B. 204	B. 204	B. 153	B. 153	B. 102

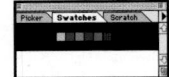

mh11sw

mh11pat.gif

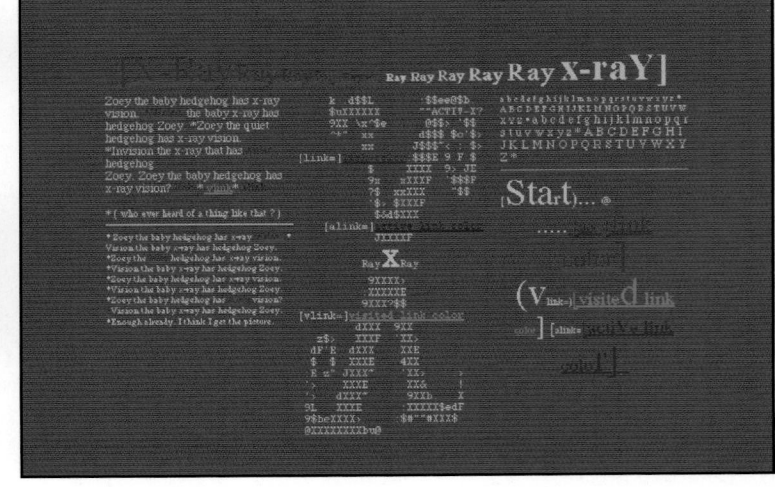

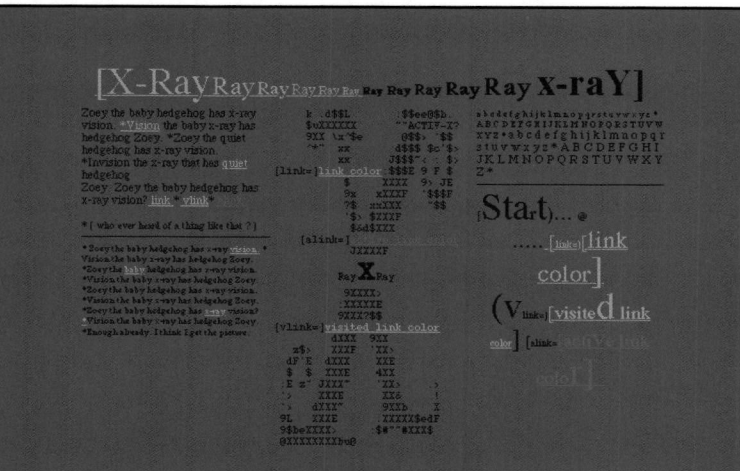
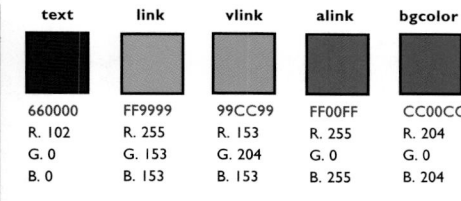
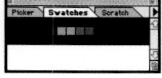

text	link	vlink	alink	bgcolor
660000	FF9999	99CC99	FF00FF	CC00CC
R. 102	R. 255	R. 153	R. 255	R. 204
G. 0	G. 153	G. 204	G. 0	G. 0
B. 0	B. 153	B. 153	B. 255	B. 204

ms12sw

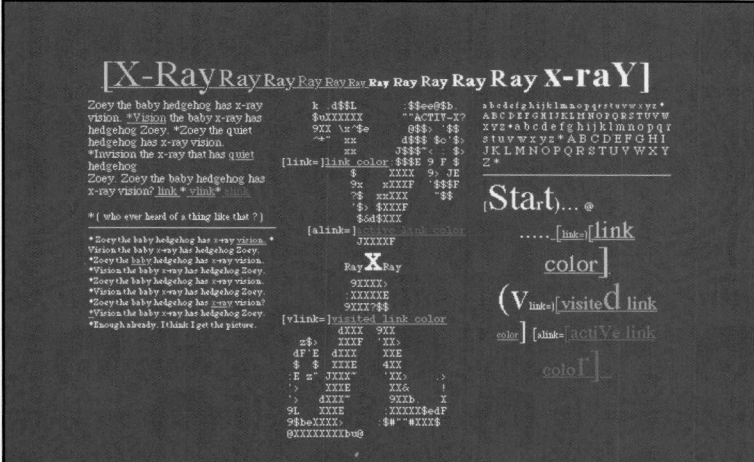
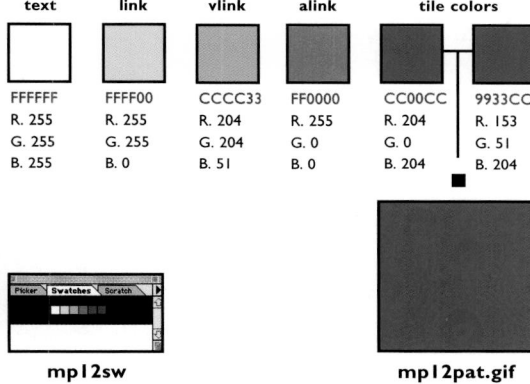

text	link	vlink	alink	tile colors	
FFFFFF	FFFF00	CCCC33	FF0000	CC00CC	9933CC
R. 255	R. 255	R. 204	R. 255	R. 204	R. 153
G. 255	G. 255	G. 204	G. 0	G. 0	G. 51
B. 255	B. 0	B. 51	B. 0	B. 204	B. 204

mp12sw **mp12pat.gif**

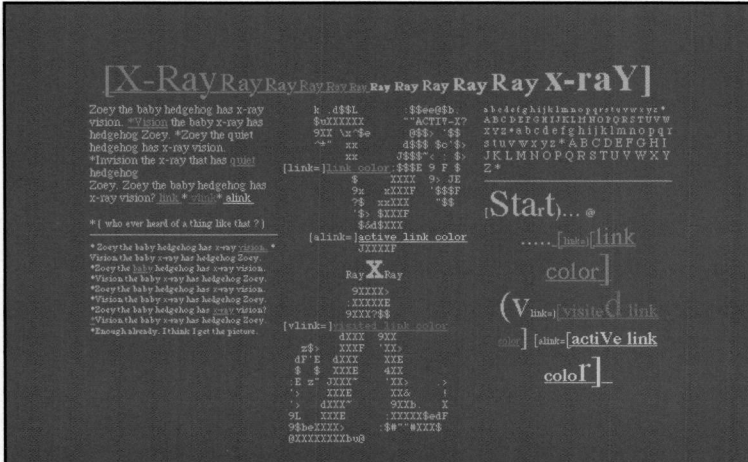
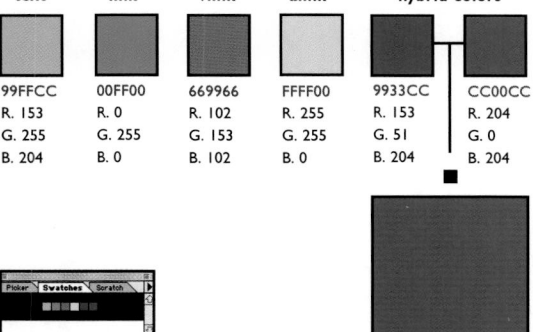

text	link	vlink	alink	hybrid colors	
99FFCC	00FF00	669966	FFFF00	9933CC	CC00CC
R. 153	R. 0	R. 102	R. 255	R. 153	R. 204
G. 255	G. 255	G. 153	G. 255	G. 51	G. 0
B. 204	B. 0	B. 102	B. 0	B. 204	B. 204

mh12sw **mh12pat.gif**

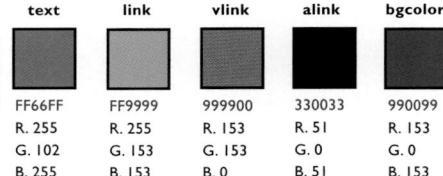

text	link	vlink	alink	bgcolor
FF66FF	FF9999	999900	330033	990099
R. 255	R. 255	R. 153	R. 51	R. 153
G. 102	G. 153	G. 153	G. 0	G. 0
B. 255	B. 153	B. 0	B. 51	B. 153

ms13sw

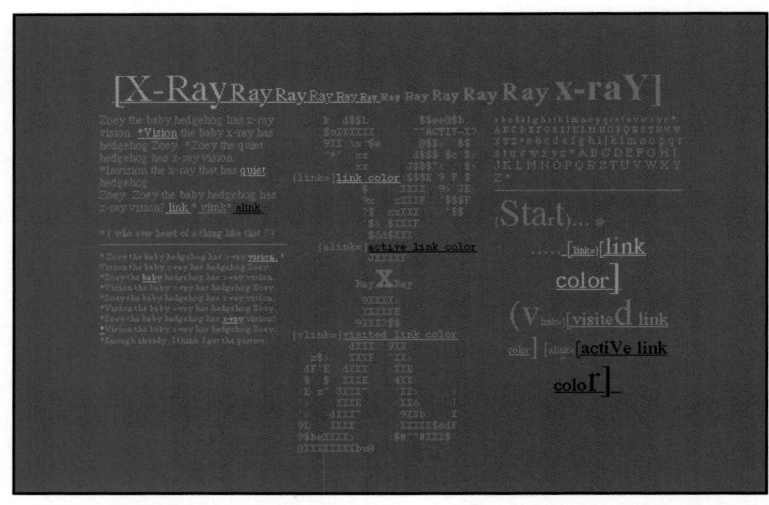

text	link	vlink	alink	tile colors	
9999FF	FFFFFF	FFCC66	FFFF00	990099	660099
R. 153	R. 255	R. 255	R. 255	R. 153	R. 102
G. 153	G. 255	G. 204	G. 255	G. 0	G. 0
B. 255	B. 255	B. 102	B. 0	B. 153	B. 153

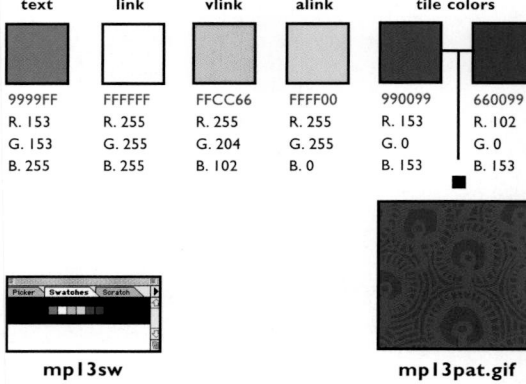

mp13sw   mp13pat.gif

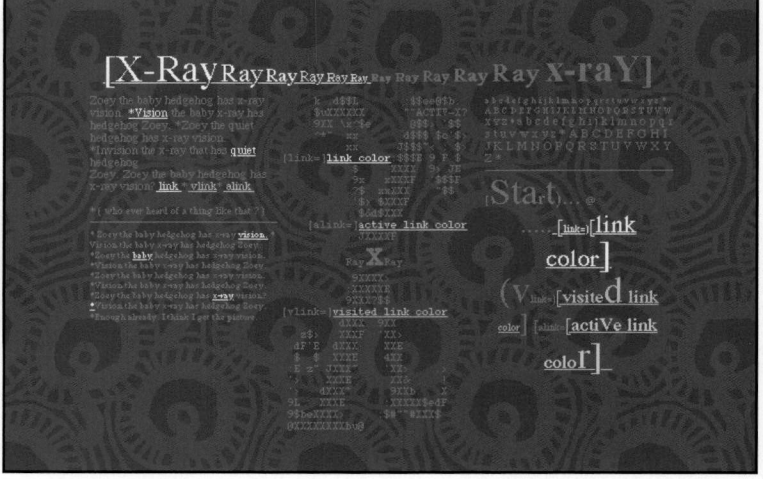

text	link	vlink	alink	hybrid colors	
FFCCCC	FF6666	6666FF	FFFFFF	990099	660099
R. 255	R. 255	R. 102	R. 255	R. 153	R. 102
G. 204	G. 102	G. 102	G. 255	G. 0	G. 0
B. 204	B. 102	B. 255	B. 255	B. 153	B. 153

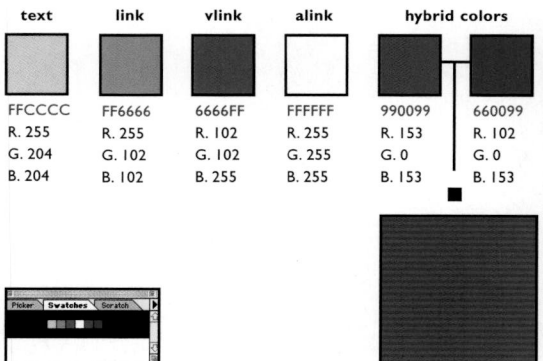

mh13sw   mh13pat.gif

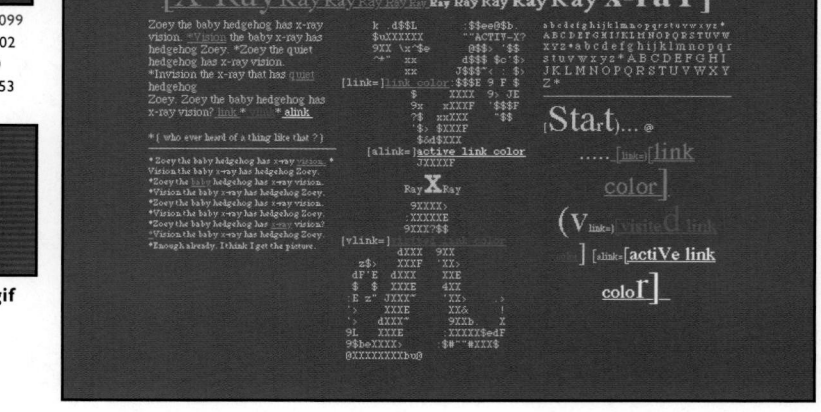

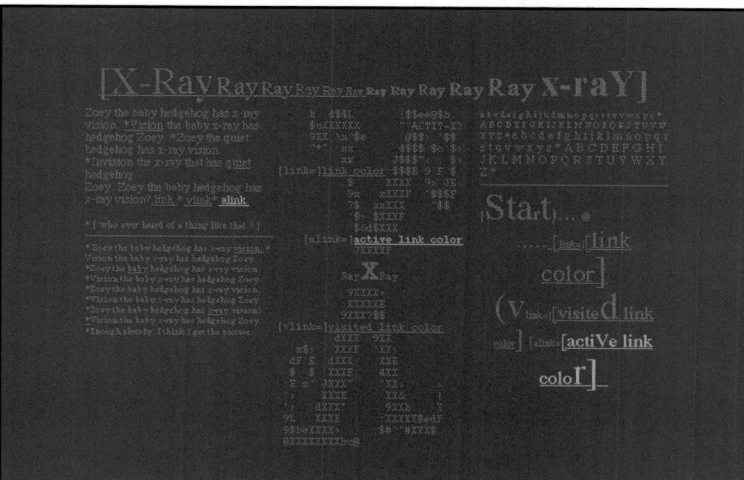

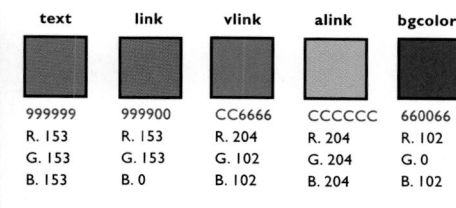

text	link	vlink	alink	bgcolor
999999	999900	CC6666	CCCCCC	660066
R. 153	R. 153	R. 204	R. 204	R. 102
G. 153	G. 153	G. 102	G. 204	G. 0
B. 153	B. 0	B. 102	B. 204	B. 102

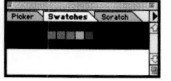

ms14sw

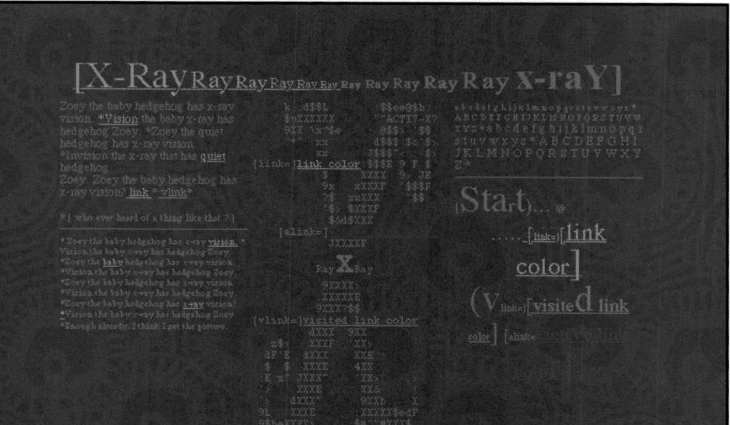

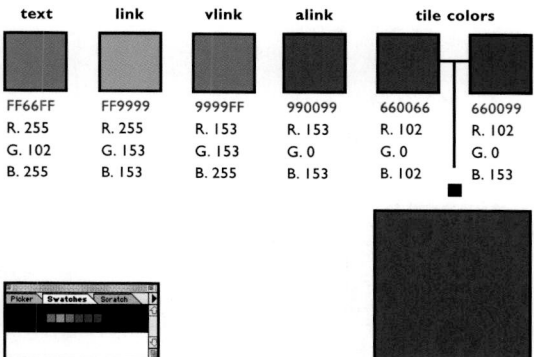

text	link	vlink	alink	tile colors	
FF66FF	FF9999	9999FF	990099	660066	660099
R. 255	R. 255	R. 153	R. 153	R. 102	R. 102
G. 102	G. 153	G. 153	G. 0	G. 0	G. 0
B. 255	B. 153	B. 255	B. 153	B. 102	B. 153

mp14sw

mp14pat.gif

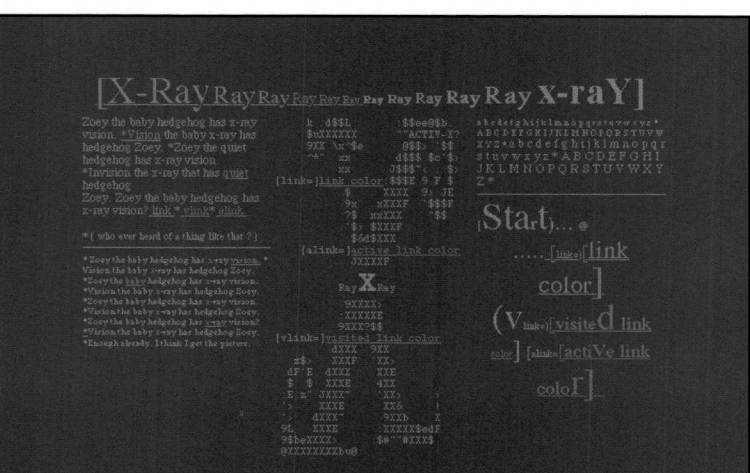

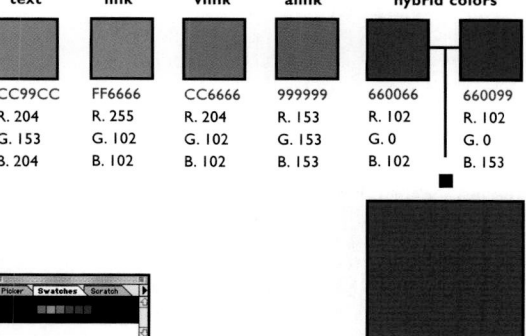

text	link	vlink	alink	hybrid colors	
CC99CC	FF6666	CC6666	999999	660066	660099
R. 204	R. 255	R. 204	R. 153	R. 102	R. 102
G. 153	G. 102	G. 102	G. 153	G. 0	G. 0
B. 204	B. 102	B. 102	B. 153	B. 102	B. 153

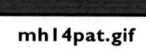

mh14sw

mh14pat.gif

text	link	vlink	alink	bgcolor
9999CC	6666FF	999999	0000FF	663366
R. 153	R. 102	R. 153	R. 0	R. 102
G. 153	G. 102	G. 153	G. 0	G. 51
B. 204	B. 255	B. 153	B. 255	B. 102

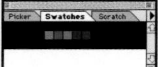

ms15sw

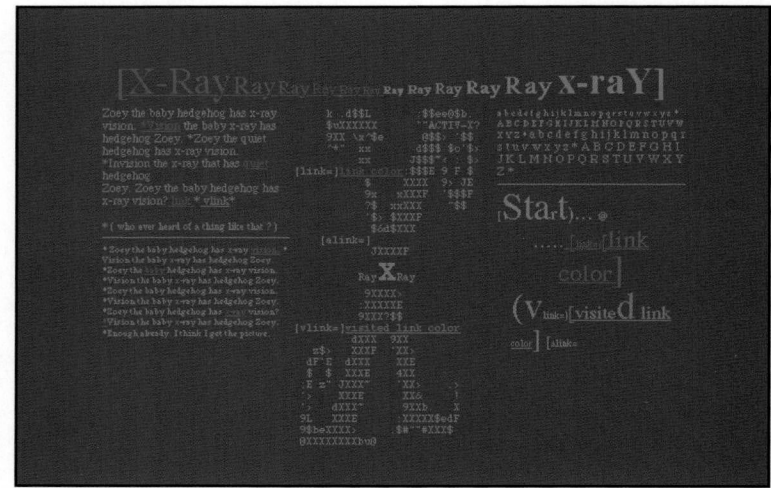

text	link	vlink	alink	tile colors	
CCCCCC	FF66FF	FF6666	FFFFFF	663366	333333
R. 204	R. 255	R. 255	R. 255	R. 102	R. 51
G. 204	G. 102	G. 102	G. 255	G. 51	G. 51
B. 204	B. 255	B. 102	B. 255	B. 102	B. 51

mp15sw

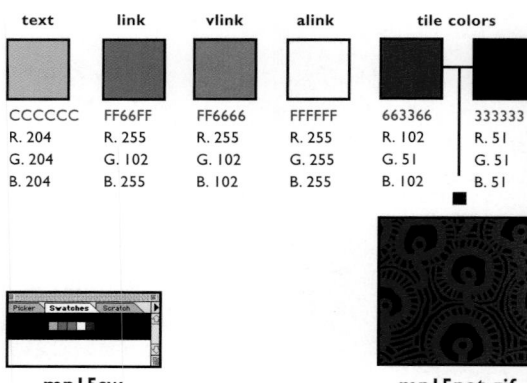

mp15pat.gif

text	link	vlink	alink	hybrid colors	
669999	33CC33	669966	33FF00	663366	333333
R. 102	R. 51	R. 102	R. 51	R. 102	R. 51
G. 153	G. 204	G. 153	G. 255	G. 51	G. 51
B. 153	B. 51	B. 102	B. 0	B. 102	B. 51

mh15sw

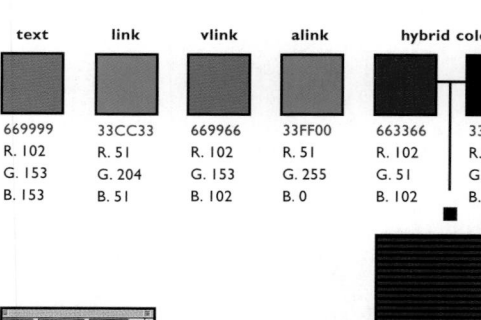

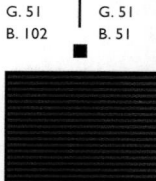

mh15pat.gif

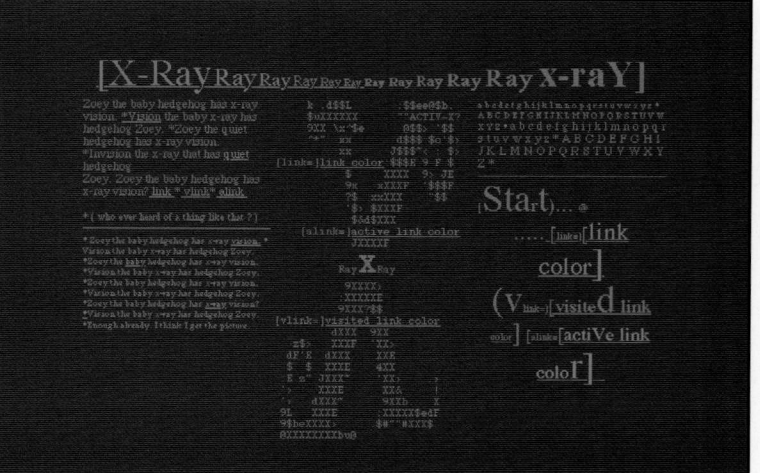

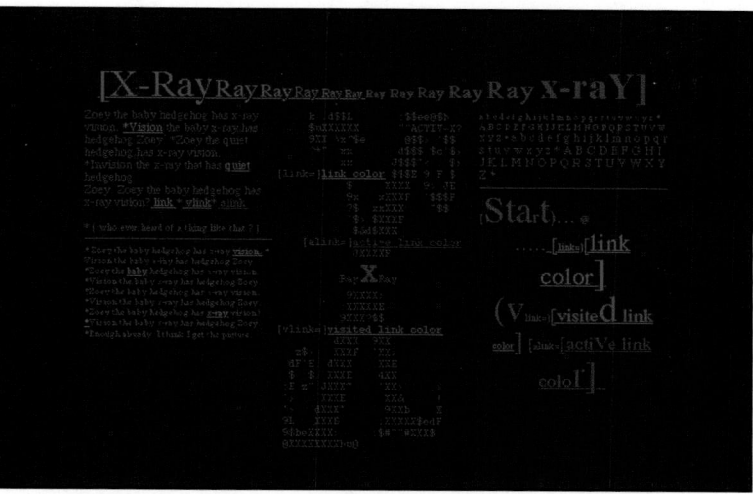

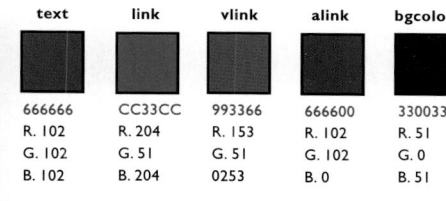

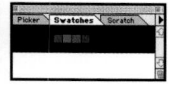

text	link	vlink	alink	bgcolor
666666	CC33CC	993366	666600	330033
R. 102	R. 204	R. 153	R. 102	R. 51
G. 102	G. 51	G. 51	G. 102	G. 0
B. 102	B. 204	0253	B. 0	B. 51

ms16sw

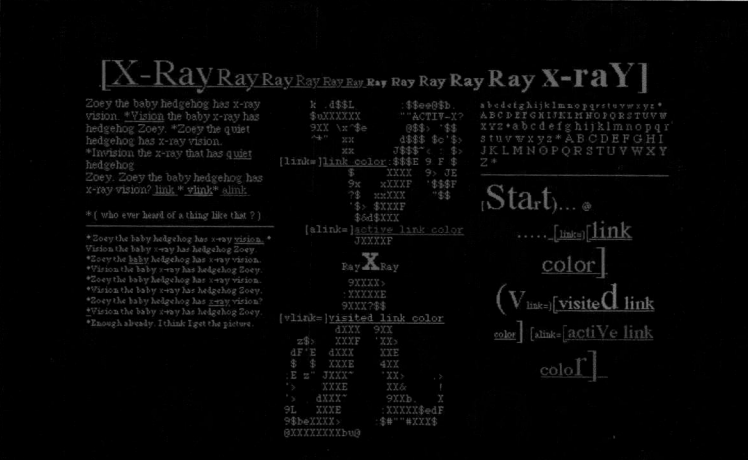

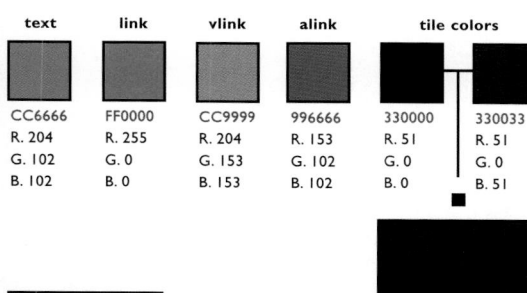

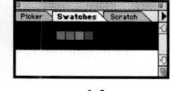

text	link	vlink	alink	tile colors	
CC6666	FF0000	CC9999	996666	330000	330033
R. 204	R. 255	R. 204	R. 153	R. 51	R. 51
G. 102	G. 0	G. 153	G. 102	G. 0	G. 0
B. 102	B. 0	B. 153	B. 102	B. 0	B. 51

mp16sw

mp16pat.gif

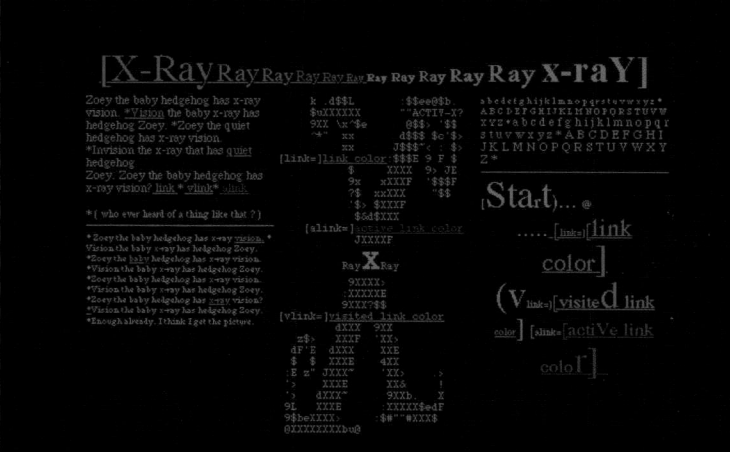

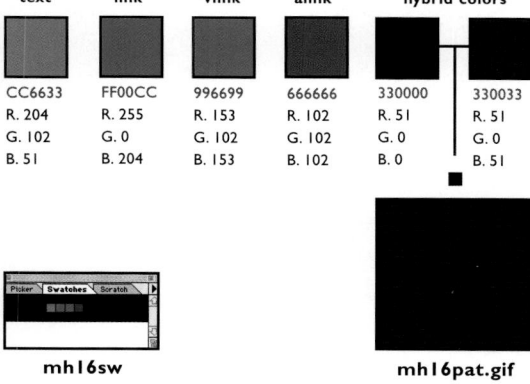

text	link	vlink	alink	hybrid colors	
CC6633	FF00CC	996699	666666	330000	330033
R. 204	R. 255	R. 153	R. 102	R. 51	R. 51
G. 102	G. 0	G. 102	G. 102	G. 0	G. 0
B. 51	B. 204	B. 153	B. 102	B. 0	B. 51

mh16sw

mh16pat.gif

mbgg

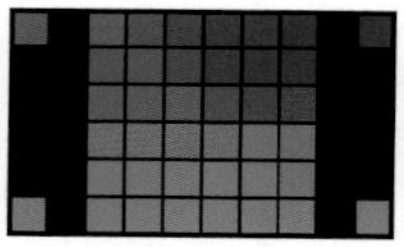

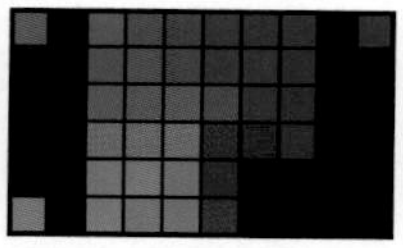

mbgk

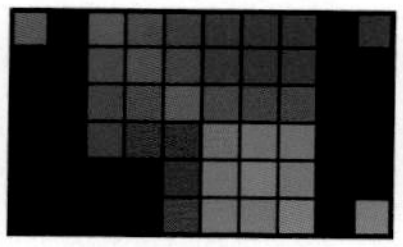

mbkg

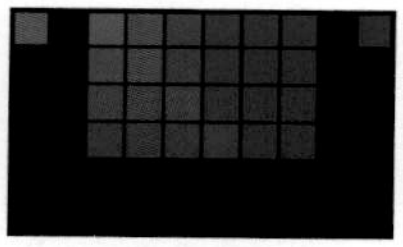

mbkk

mbrg

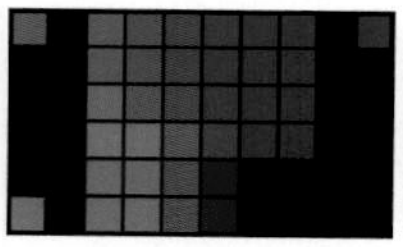

mbrk

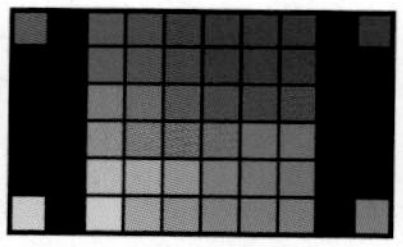

mbyg

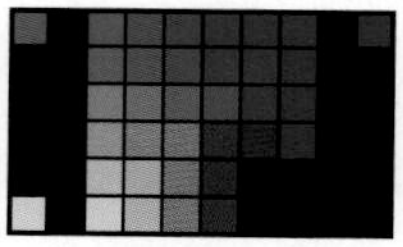

mbyk

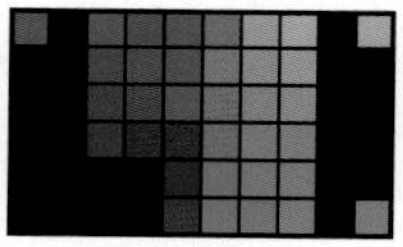

mckg

mcrg

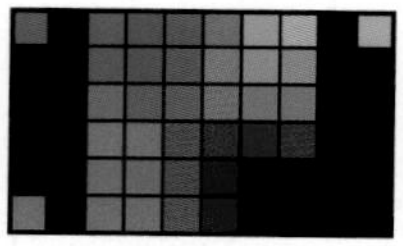

mcrk

mcyg

mgbc

mgmb

mgmc

mgwc

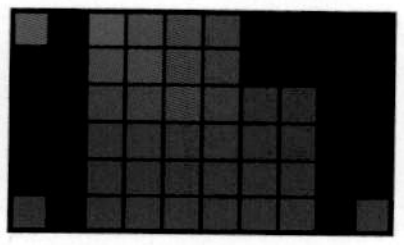

mkbb

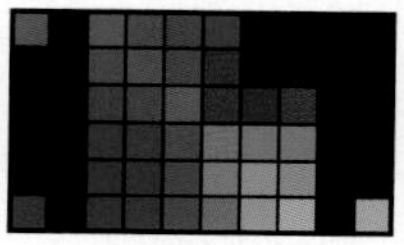

mkbc

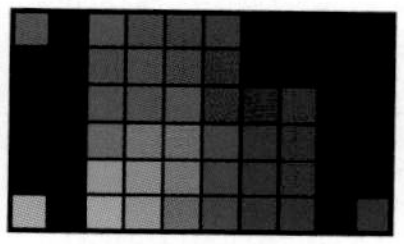

mkcb

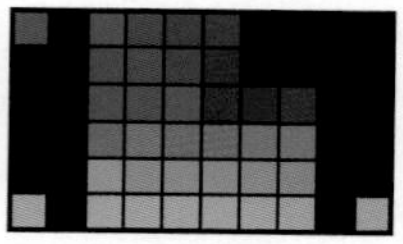

mkcc

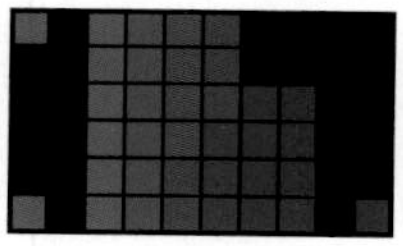

mkmb

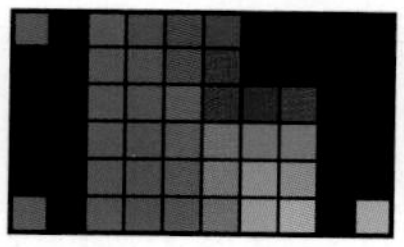

mkmc

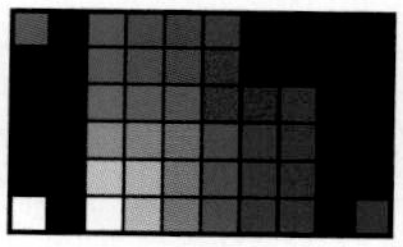

mkwb

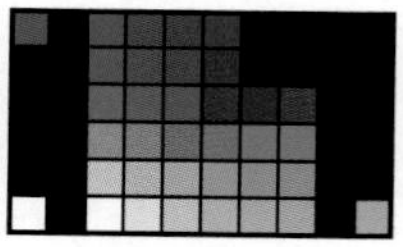

mkwc

mmgr

mmgy

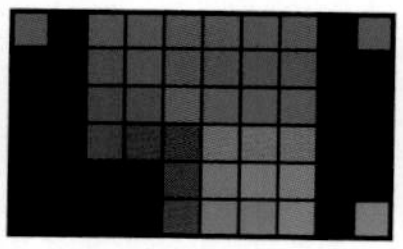

mmkg

mmkr

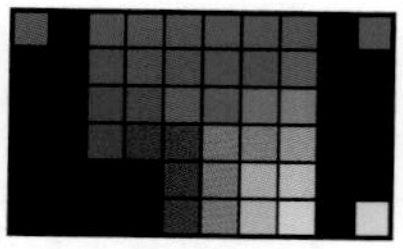

mmky

mmrg

mmry

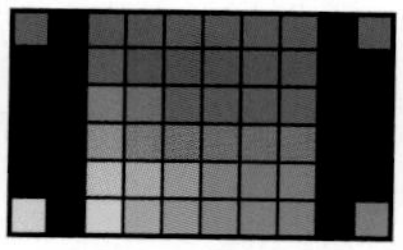

mmyg

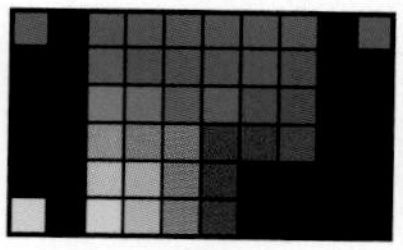

mmyk

mrbb

mrbc

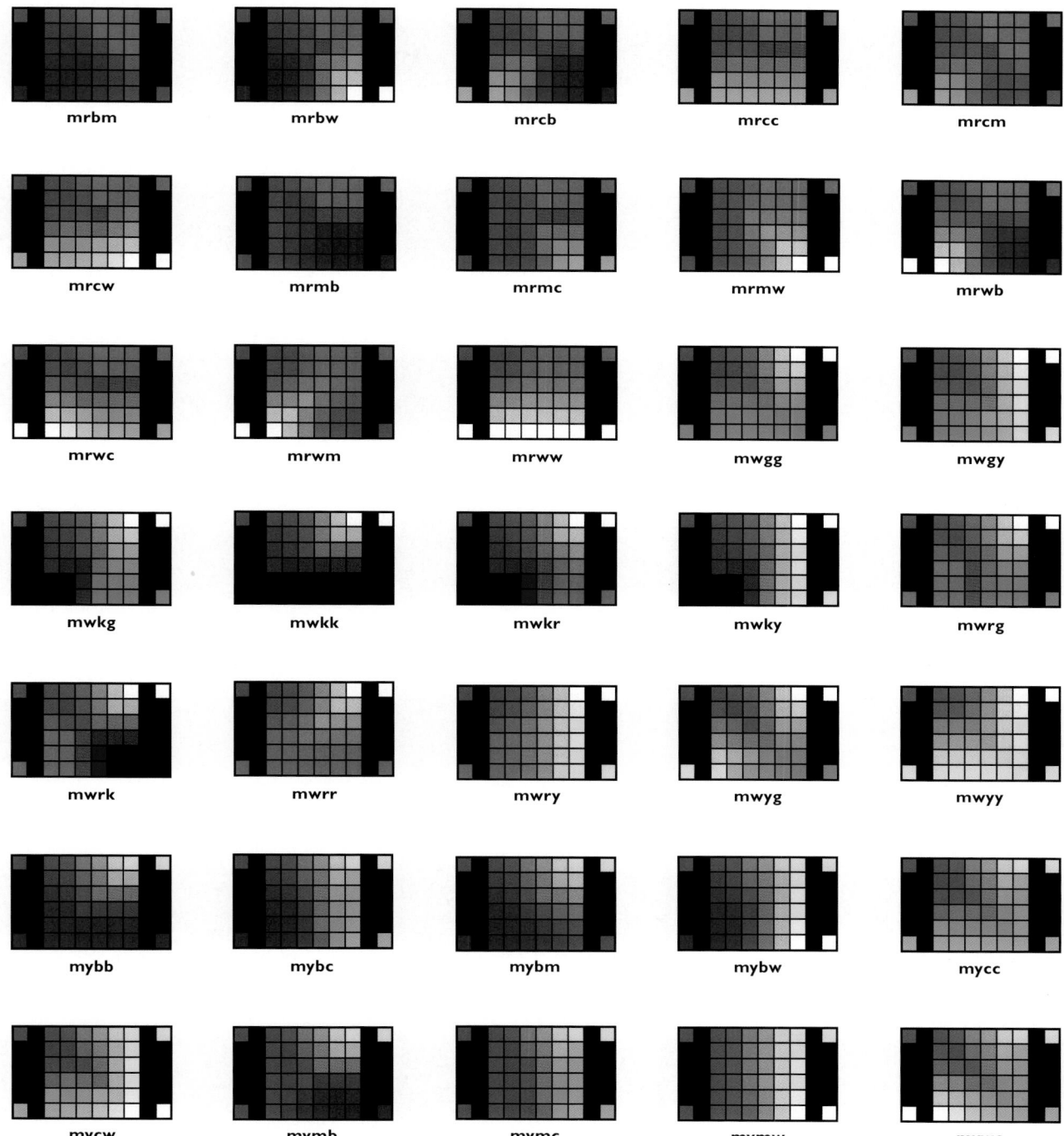

mrbm	mrbw	mrcb	mrcc	mrcm
mrcw	mrmb	mrmc	mrmw	mrwb
mrwc	mrwm	mrww	mwgg	mwgy
mwkg	mwkk	mwkr	mwky	mwrg
mwrk	mwrr	mwry	mwyg	mwyy
mybb	mybc	mybm	mybw	mycc
mycw	mymb	mymc	mymw	mywc

YELLOW

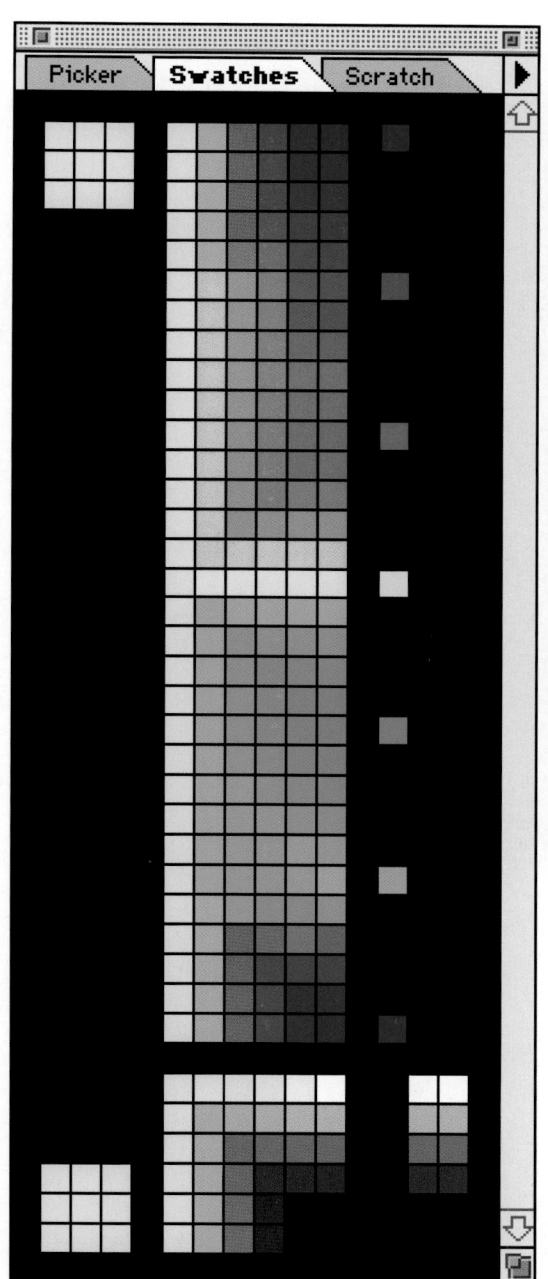

mys

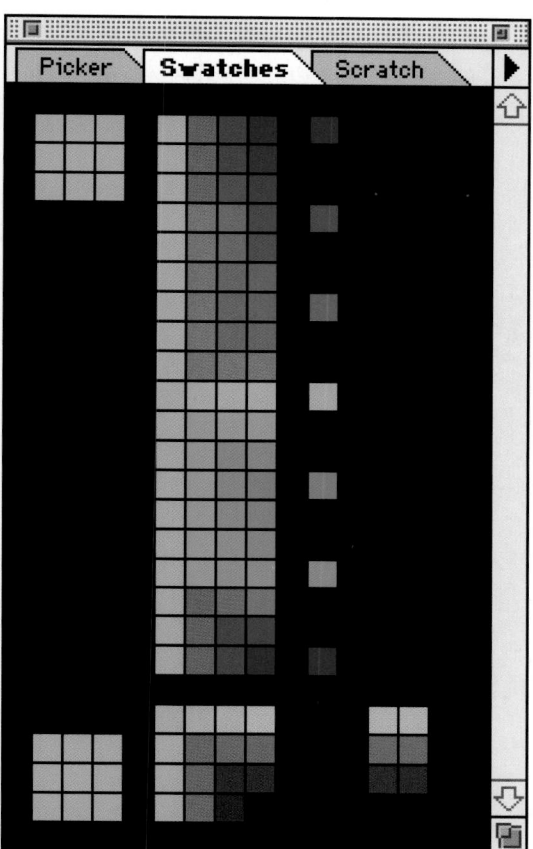

myd

text	link	vlink	alink	bgcolor
000000	FFFFCC	666600	999999	CCCC66
R. 0	R. 204	R. 102	R. 153	R. 204
G. 0	G. 255	G. 102	G. 153	G. 204
B. 0	B. 255	B. 0	B. 153	B. 204

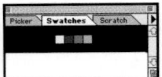

ys01sw

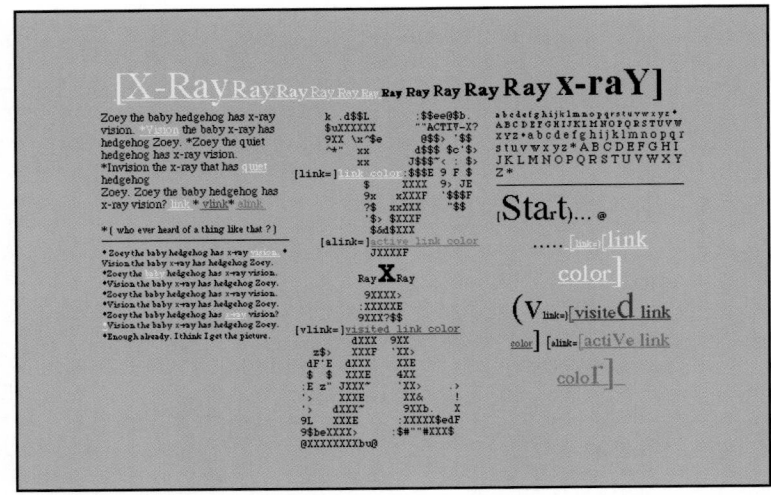

text	link	vlink	alink	tile colors	
000000	FFFF00	999966	666600	CCCCCC	CCCC66
R. 0	R. 255	R. 153	R. 102	R. 204	R. 204
G. 0	G. 255	G. 153	G. 102	G. 204	G. 204
B. 0	B. 0	B. 102	B. 0	B. 204	B. 102

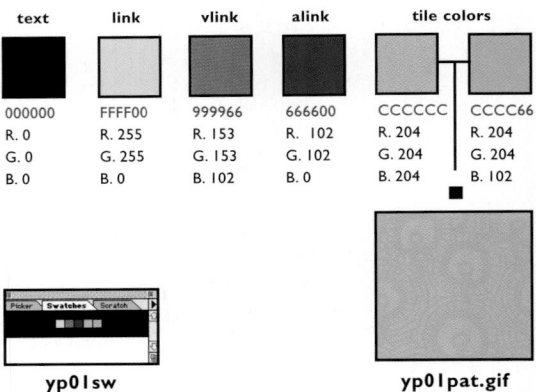

yp01sw

yp01pat.gif

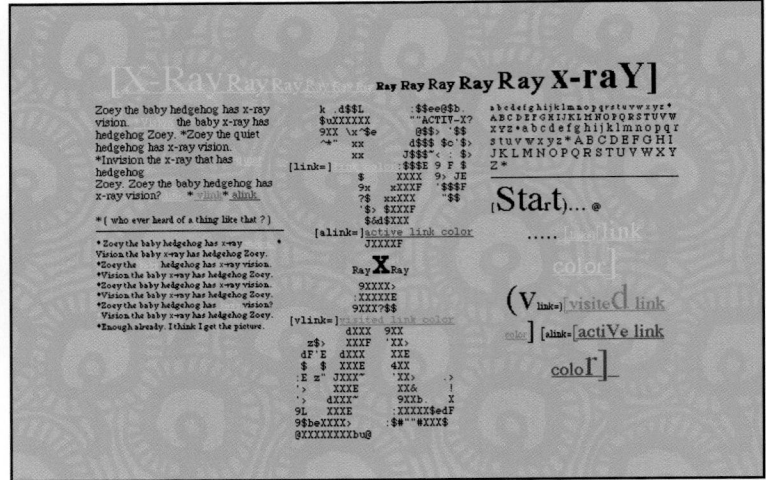

text	link	vlink	alink	hybrid colors	
000000	FFFFCC	999966	666633	CCCC66	CCCCCC
R. 0	R. 255	R. 153	R. 102	R. 204	R. 204
G. 0	G. 255	G. 153	G. 102	G. 204	G. 204
B. 0	B. 204	B. 102	B. 51	B. 102	B. 204

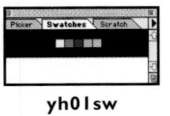

yh01sw

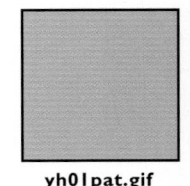

yh01pat.gif

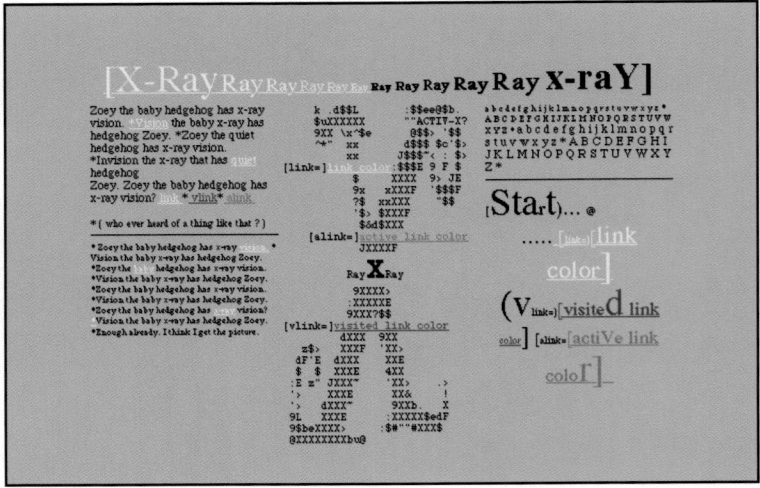

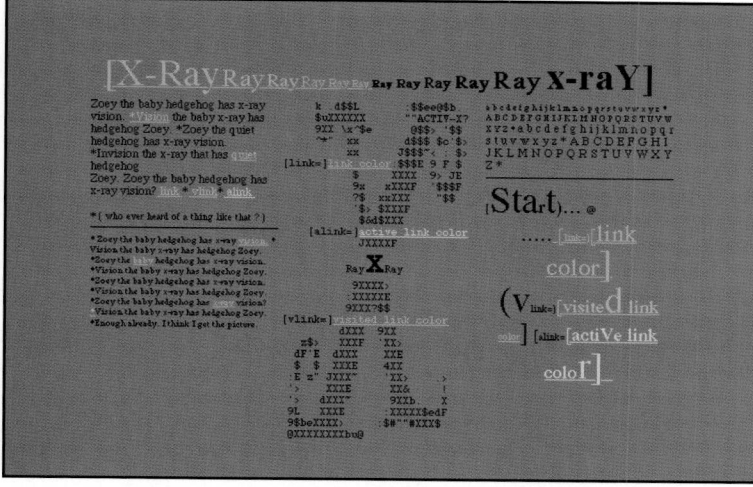

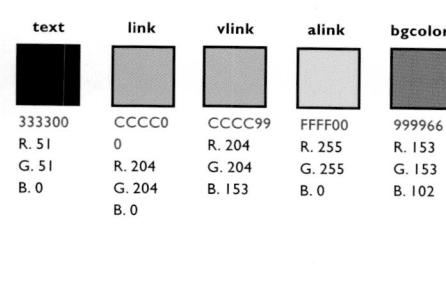

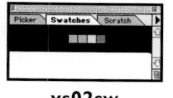

text	link	vlink	alink	bgcolor
333300	CCCC0	CCCC99	FFFF00	999966
R. 51	0	R. 204	R. 255	R. 153
G. 51	R. 204	G. 204	G. 255	G. 153
B. 0	G. 204	B. 153	B. 0	B. 102
	B. 0			

ys02sw

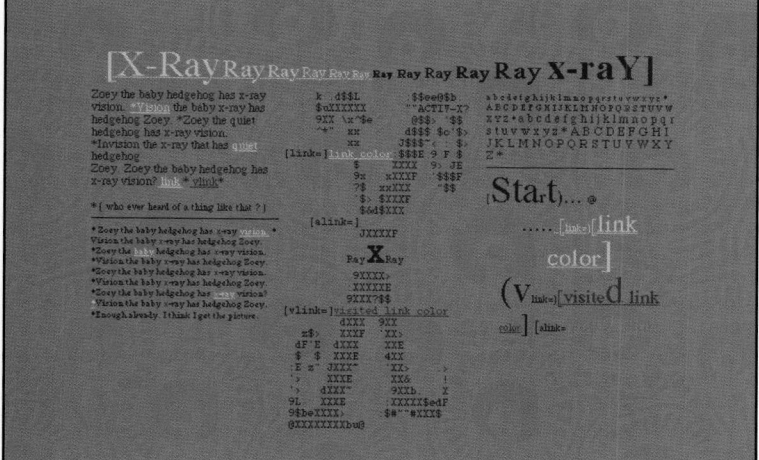

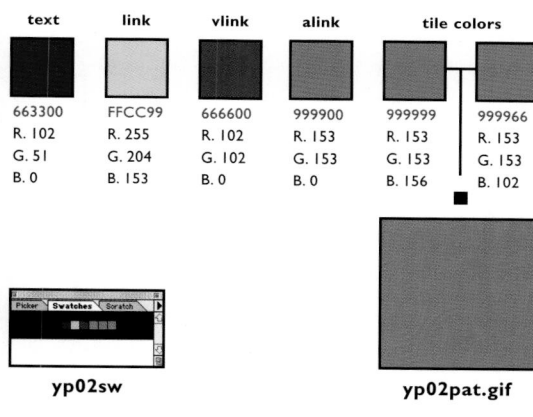

text	link	vlink	alink	tile colors	
663300	FFCC99	666600	999900	999999	999966
R. 102	R. 255	R. 102	R. 153	R. 153	R. 153
G. 51	G. 204	G. 102	G. 153	G. 153	G. 153
B. 0	B. 153	B. 0	B. 0	B. 156	B. 102

yp02sw

yp02pat.gif

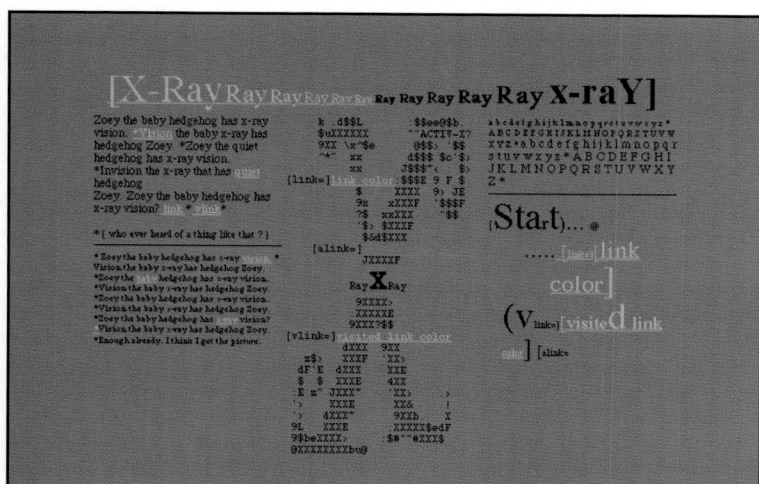

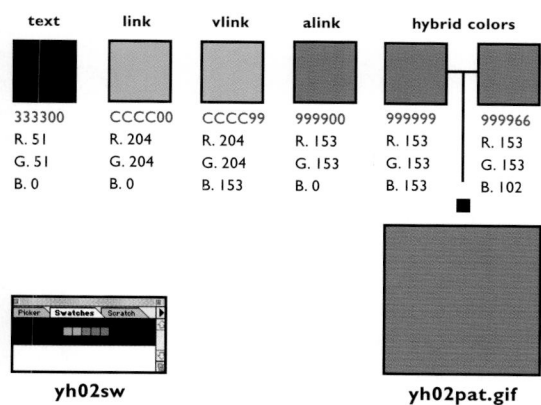

text	link	vlink	alink	hybrid colors	
333300	CCCC00	CCCC99	999900	999999	999966
R. 51	R. 204	R. 204	R. 153	R. 153	R. 153
G. 51	G. 204	G. 204	G. 153	G. 153	G. 153
B. 0	B. 0	B. 153	B. 0	B. 153	B. 102

yh02sw

yh02pat.gif

text	link	vlink	alink	bgcolor
333300	FFFF66	FFFF00	FFFFFF	CCCC33
R. 51	R. 255	R. 255	R. 255	R. 204
G. 51	G. 255	G. 255	G. 255	G. 204
B. 0	B. 102	B. 0	B. 255	B. 51

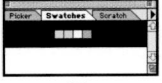

ys03sw

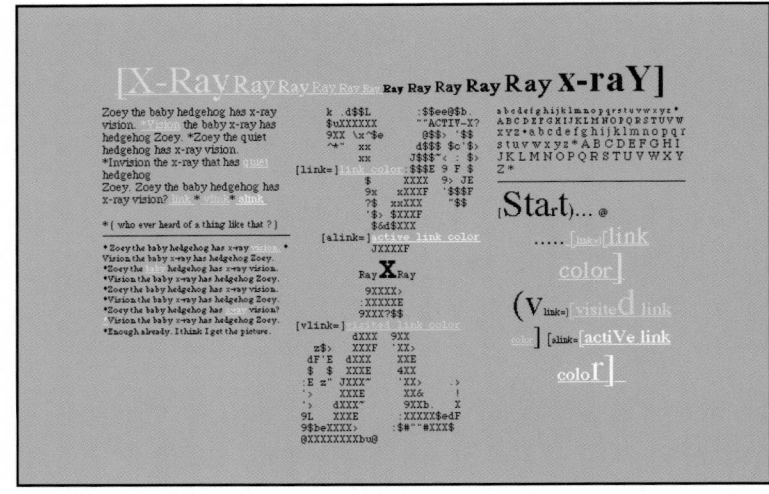

text	link	vlink	alink	tile colors	
333300	FF0000	666633	999966	CCCC33	CCCC66
R. 51	R. 255	R. 102	R. 153	R. 204	R. 204
G. 51	G. 0	G. 102	G. 153	G. 204	G. 204
B. 0	B. 0	B. 51	B. 102	B. 514	B. 102

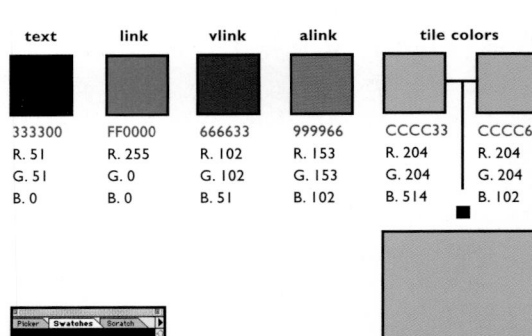

yp03sw

yp03pat.gif

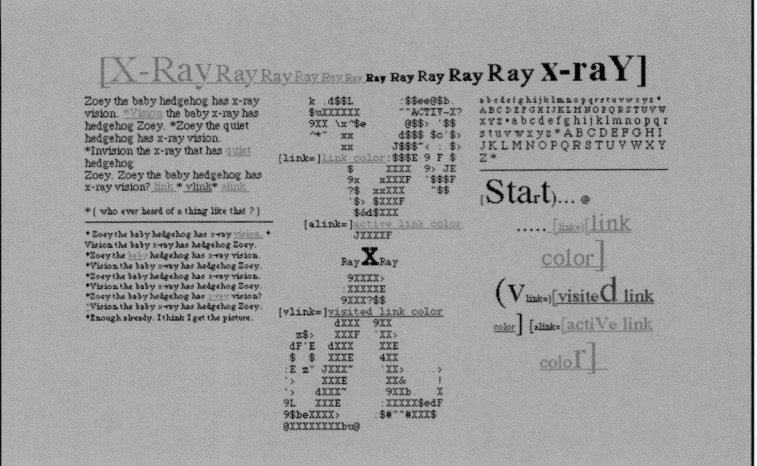

text	link	vlink	alink	hybrid colors	
666633	CC3333	9966CC	996666	CCCC33	CCCC66
R. 102	R. 204	R. 153	R. 153	R. 204	R. 204
G. 102	G. 51	G. 102	G. 102	G. 204	G. 204
B. 0	B. 51	B. 204	B. 102	B. 51	B. 102

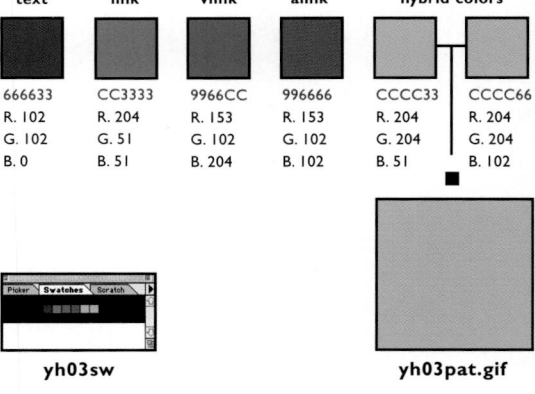

yh03sw

yh03pat.gif

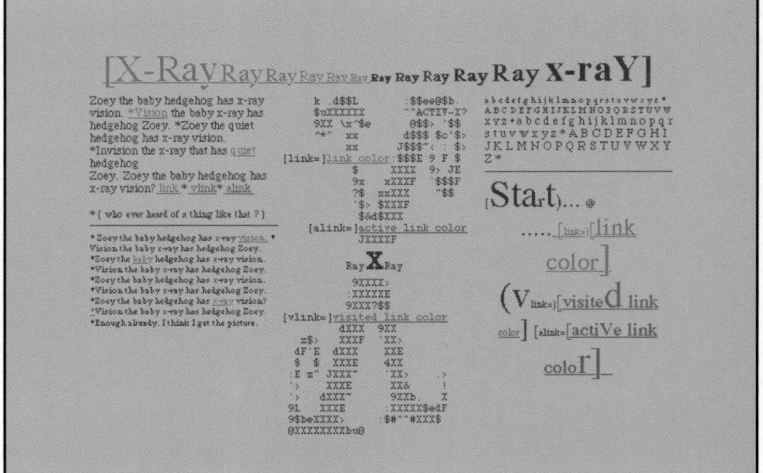

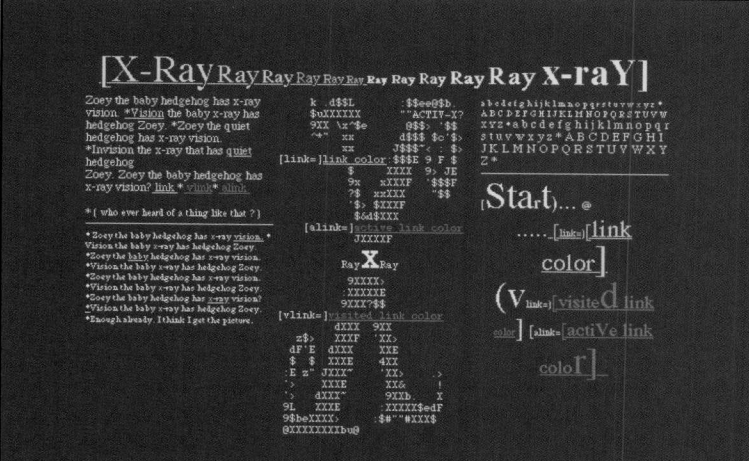
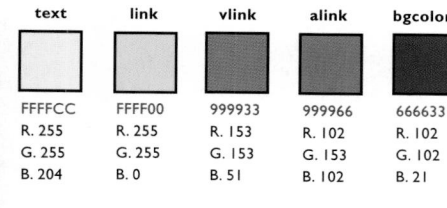

text	link	vlink	alink	bgcolor
FFFFCC	FFFF00	999933	999966	666633
R. 255	R. 255	R. 153	R. 102	R. 102
G. 255	G. 255	G. 153	G. 153	G. 102
B. 204	B. 0	B. 51	B. 102	B. 21

ys04sw

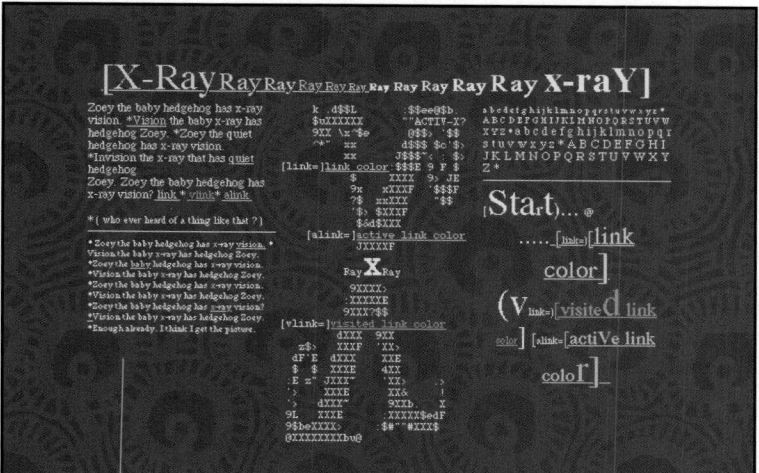
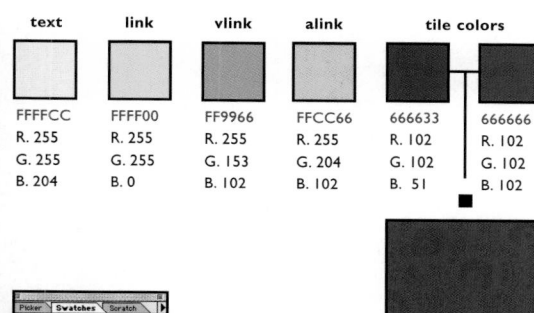
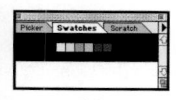

text	link	vlink	alink	tile colors	
FFFFCC	FFFF00	FF9966	FFCC66	666633	666666
R. 255	R. 255	R. 255	R. 255	R. 102	R. 102
G. 255	G. 255	G. 153	G. 204	G. 102	G. 102
B. 204	B. 0	B. 102	B. 102	B. 51	B. 102

yp04sw

yp04pat.gif

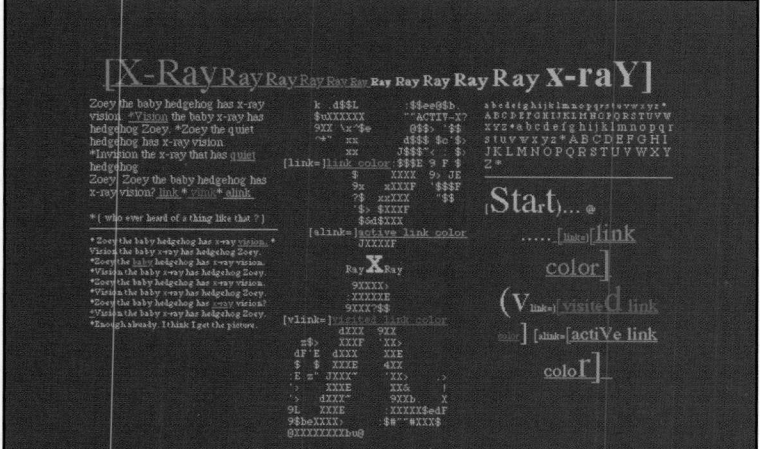
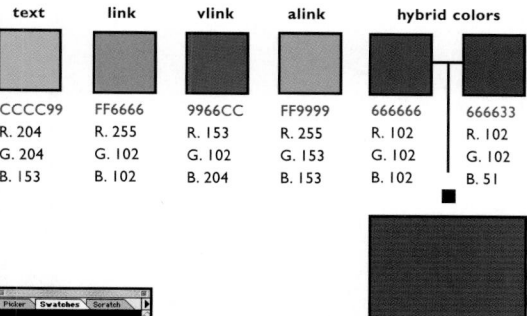

text	link	vlink	alink	hybrid colors	
CCCC99	FF6666	9966CC	FF9999	666666	666633
R. 204	R. 255	R. 153	R. 255	R. 102	R. 102
G. 204	G. 102	G. 102	G. 153	G. 102	G. 102
B. 153	B. 102	B. 204	B. 153	B. 102	B. 51

yh04sw

yh04pat.gif

web graphics >

text	link	vlink	alink	bgcolor
CCCC66	FFFF00	CCCCCC	666600	333300
R. 204	R. 255	R. 204	R. 102	R. 204
G. 204	G. 255	G. 204	G. 102	G. 204
B. 102	B. 0	B. 204	B. 0	B. 204

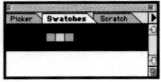

ys05sw

text	link	vlink	alink	tile colors	
FFFFCC	00CCCC	009966	006600	333300	333333
R. 255	R. 0	R. 0	R. 0	R. 51	R. 51
G. 255	G. 204	G. 153	G. 102	G. 51	G. 51
B. 204	B. 204	B. 102	B. 0	B. 51	B. 51

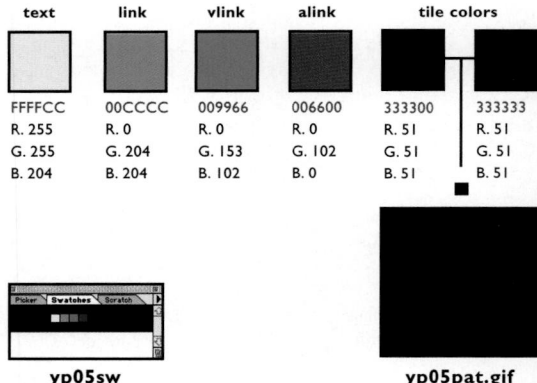

yp05sw

yp05pat.gif

text	link	vlink	alink	hybrid colors	
CCCC99	CCCC00	CC9999	FFFF00	333300	333333
R. 204	R. 204	R. 204	R. 255	R. 51	R. 51
G. 204	G. 204	G. 153	G. 255	G. 51	G. 51
B. 153	B. 0	B. 153	B. 0	B. 0	B. 51

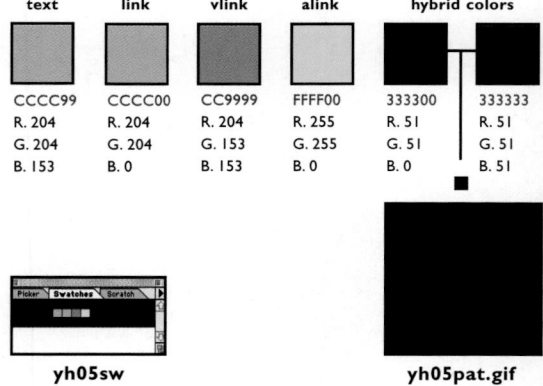

yh05sw

yh05pat.gif

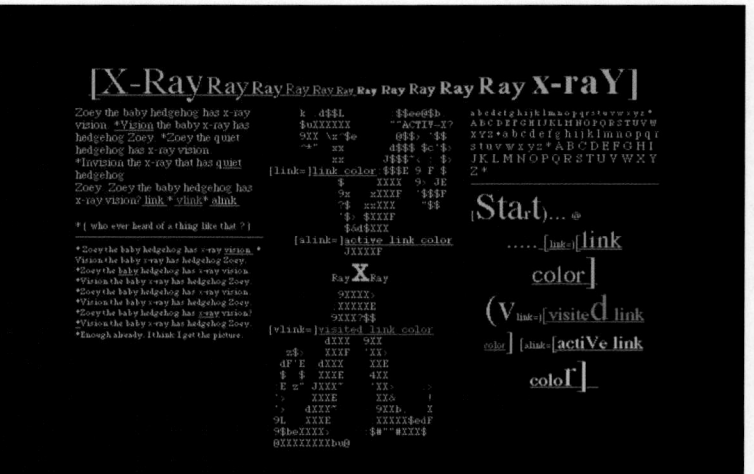

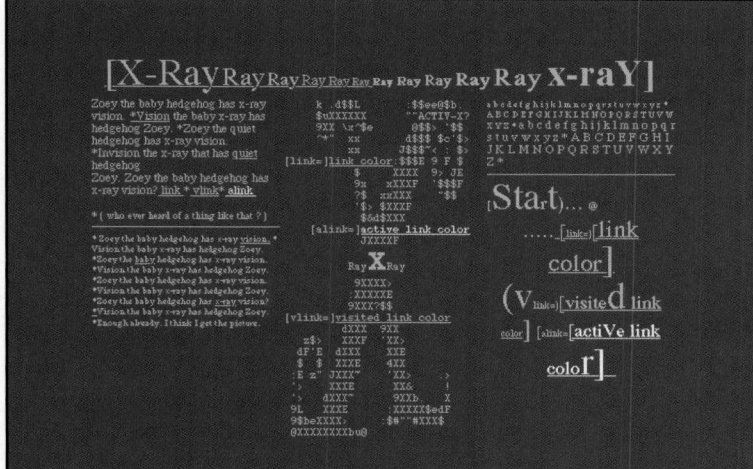

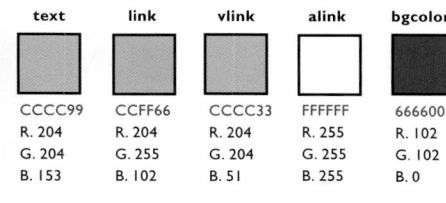

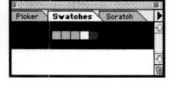

text	link	vlink	alink	bgcolor
CCCC99	CCFF66	CCCC33	FFFFFF	666600
R. 204	R. 204	R. 204	R. 255	R. 102
G. 204	G. 255	G. 204	G. 255	G. 102
B. 153	B. 102	B. 51	B. 255	B. 0

ys06sw

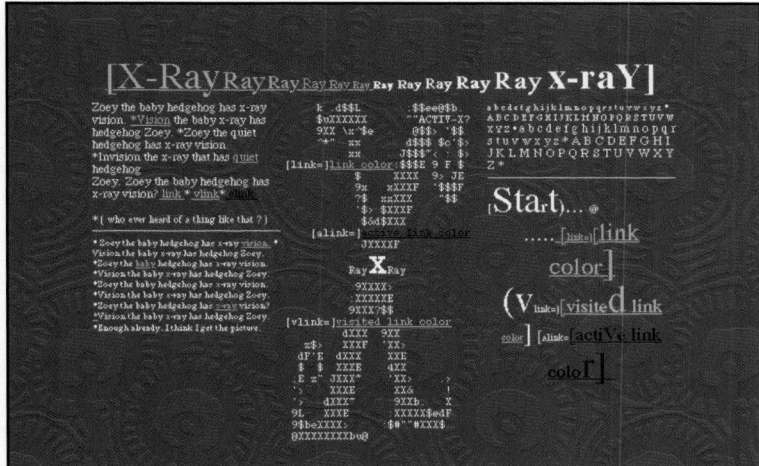

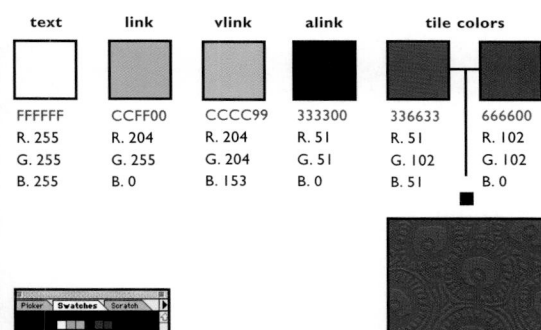

text	link	vlink	alink	tile colors	
FFFFFF	CCFF00	CCCC99	333300	336633	666600
R. 255	R. 204	R. 204	R. 51	R. 51	R. 102
G. 255	G. 255	G. 204	G. 51	G. 102	G. 102
B. 255	B. 0	B. 153	B. 0	B. 51	B. 0

yp06sw **yp06pat.gif**

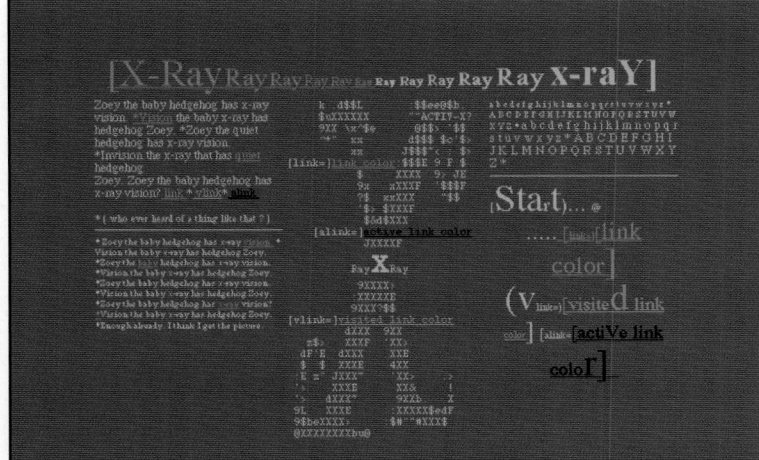

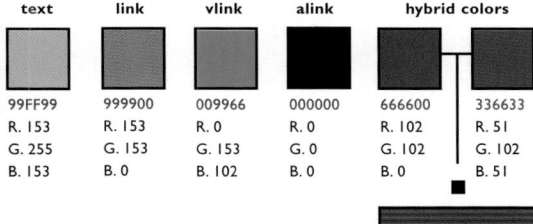

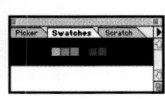

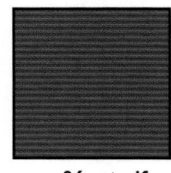

text	link	vlink	alink	hybrid colors	
99FF99	999900	009966	000000	666600	336633
R. 153	R. 153	R. 0	R. 0	R. 102	R. 51
G. 255	G. 153	G. 153	G. 0	G. 102	G. 102
B. 153	B. 0	B. 102	B. 0	B. 0	B. 51

yp06sw **yp06pat.gif**

text	link	vlink	alink	bgcolor
000000	CC0000	666666	0000FF	CCCC00
R. 0	R. 204	R. 102	R. 0	R. 204
G. 0	G. 0	G. 102	G. 0	G. 204
B. 0	B. 255	B. 102	B. 255	B. 0

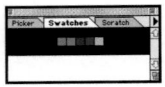

ys07sw

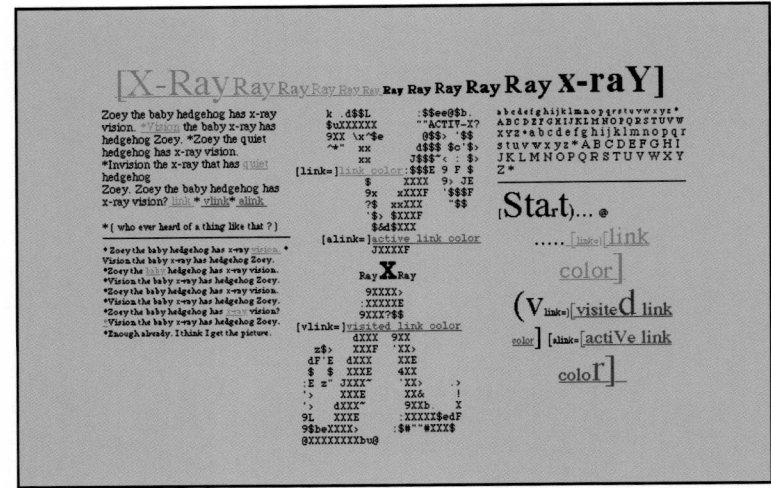

text	link	vlink	alink	tile colors	
333333	FFFFFF	666666	FFFF66	FFCC00	CCCC00
R. 51	R. 255	R. 102	R. 255	R. 2554	R. 204
G. 51	G. 255	G. 102	G. 255	G. 204	G. 204
B. 51	B. 255	B. 102	B. 102	B. 0	B. 0

yp07sw

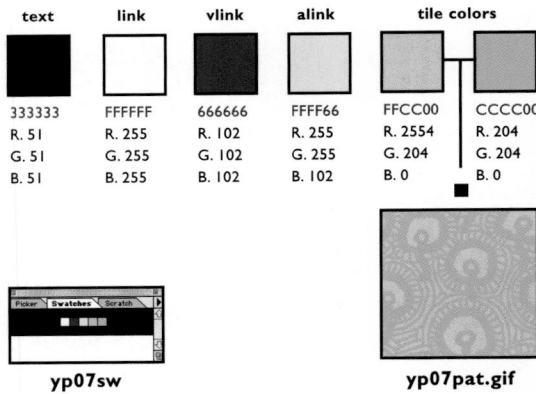

yp07pat.gif

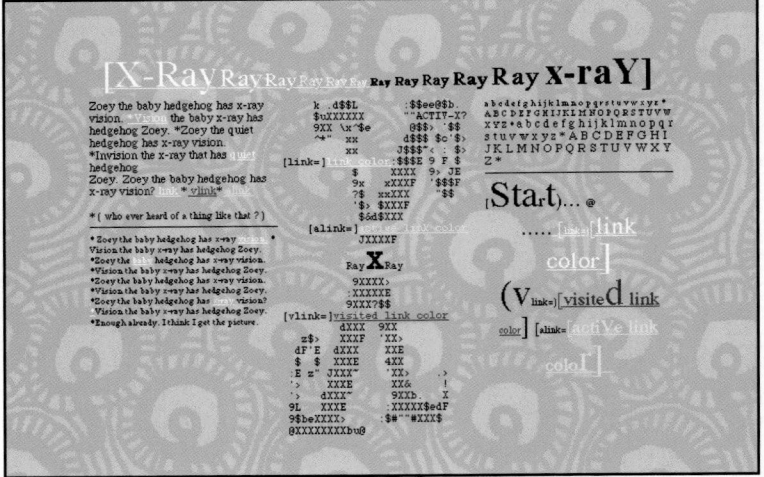

text	link	vlink	alink	hybrid colors	
333333	006633	999900	009999	FFCC00	CCCC00
R. 51	R. 0	R. 153	R. 0	R. 255	R. 204
G. 51	G. 102	G. 153	G. 153	G. 204	G. 204
B. 51	B. 51	B. 0	B. 153	B. 0	B. 0

yh07sw

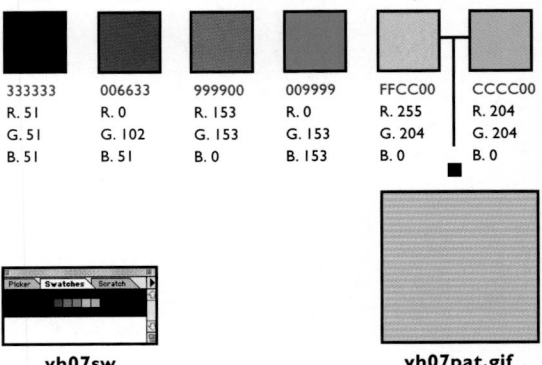

yh07pat.gif

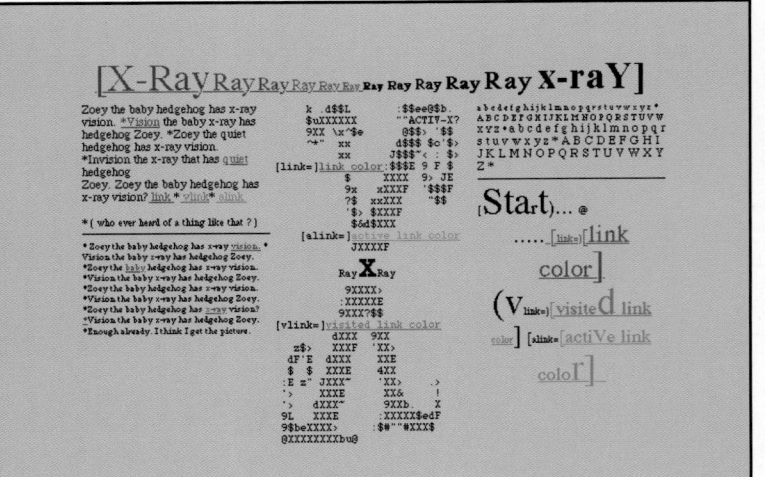

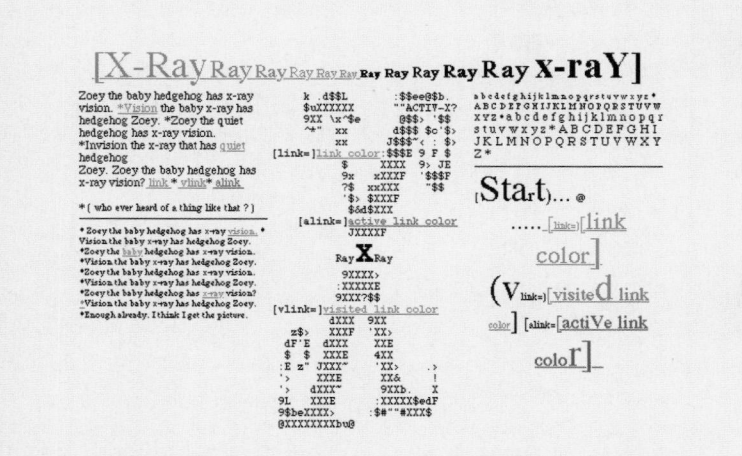

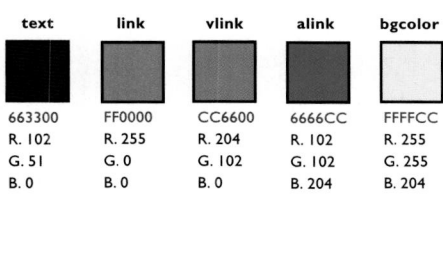

text	link	vlink	alink	bgcolor
663300	FF0000	CC6600	6666CC	FFFFCC
R. 102	R. 255	R. 204	R. 102	R. 255
G. 51	G. 0	G. 102	G. 102	G. 255
B. 0	B. 0	B. 0	B. 204	B. 204

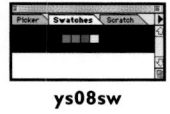

ys08sw

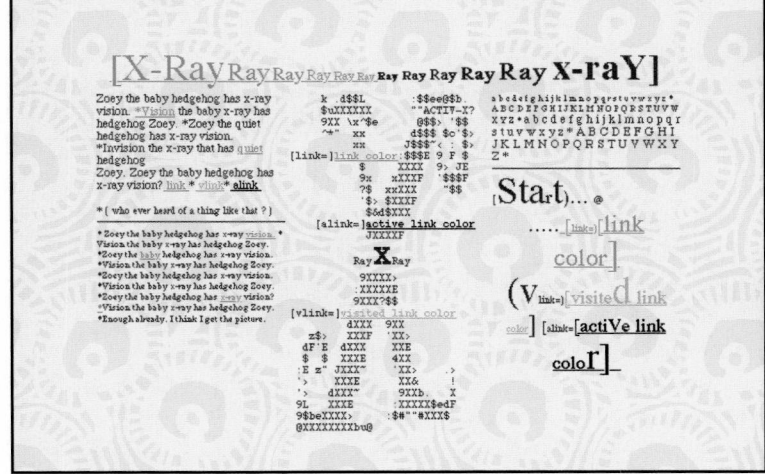

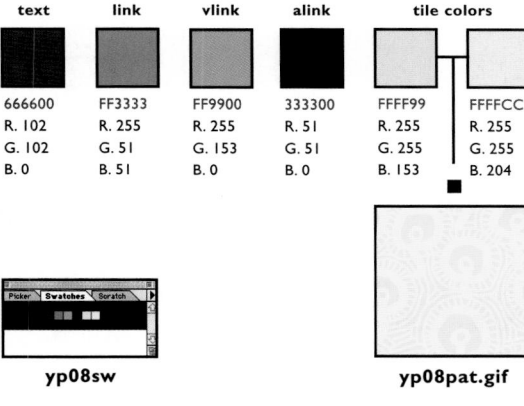

text	link	vlink	alink	tile colors	
666600	FF3333	FF9900	333300	FFFF99	FFFFCC
R. 102	R. 255	R. 255	R. 51	R. 255	R. 255
G. 102	G. 51	G. 153	G. 51	G. 255	G. 255
B. 0	B. 51	B. 0	B. 0	B. 153	B. 204

yp08sw

yp08pat.gif

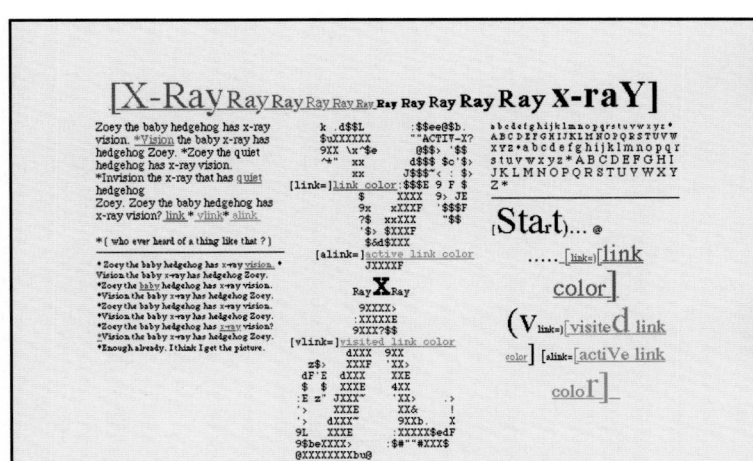

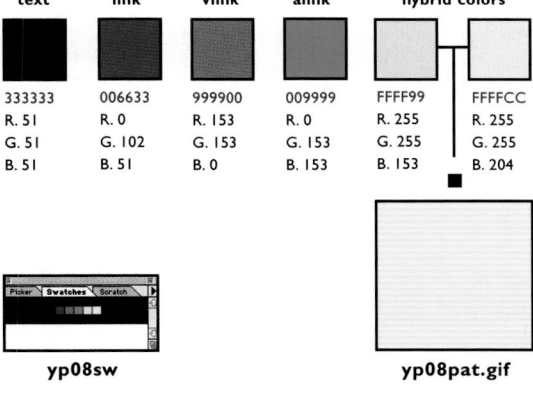

text	link	vlink	alink	hybrid colors	
333333	006633	999900	009999	FFFF99	FFFFCC
R. 51	R. 0	R. 153	R. 0	R. 255	R. 255
G. 51	G. 102	G. 153	G. 153	G. 255	G. 255
B. 51	B. 51	B. 0	B. 153	B. 153	B. 204

yp08sw

yp08pat.gif

text	link	vlink	alink	bgcolor
996600	FF3300	FF6600	FF0000	FFFF99
R. 153	R. 255	R. 255	R. 255	R. 255
G. 102	G. 51	G. 102	G. 102	G. 255
B. 0	B. 0	B. 0	B. 0	B. 153

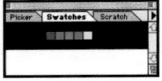

ys09sw

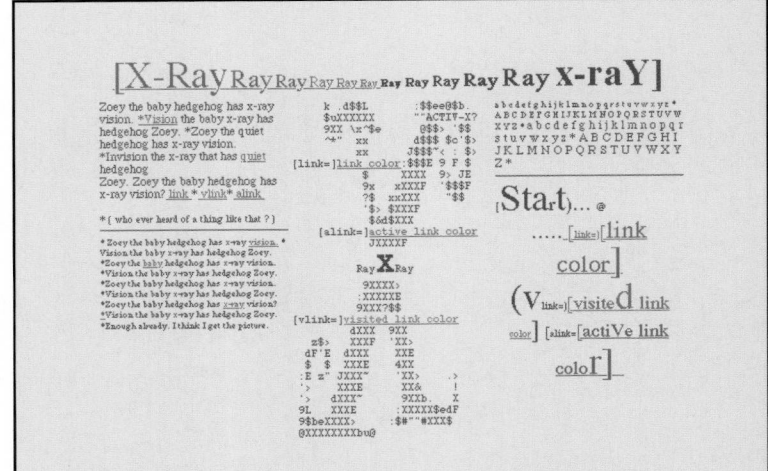

text	link	vlink	alink	tile colors	
660000	FF0000	999900	CC6600	FFFF99	FFFF66
R. 102	R. 255	R. 153	R. 204	R. 255	R. 255
G. 0	G. 0	G. 153	G. 102	G. 255	G. 255
B. 0	B. 0	B. 0	B. 0	B. 153	B. 102

yp09sw

yp09pat.gif

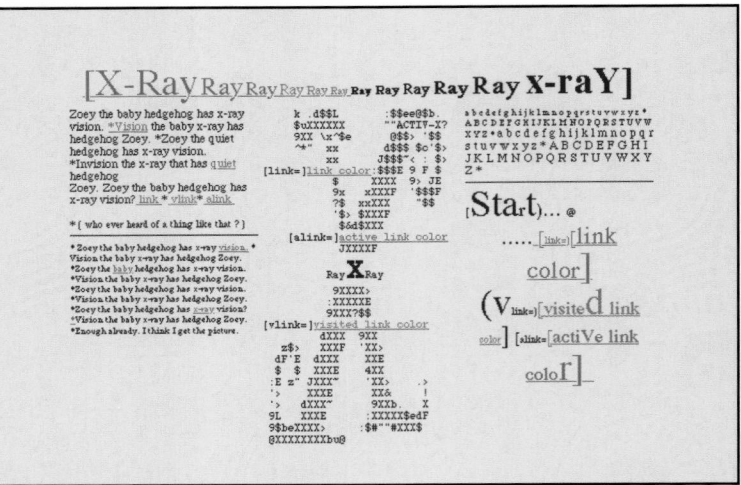

text	link	vlink	alink	hybrid colors	
333300	990000	FF6600	000000	FFFF99	FFFF66
R. 51	R. 153	R. 255	R. 0	R. 2554	R. 255
G. 51	G. 0	G. 102	G. 0	G. 255	G. 255
B. 0	B. 0	B. 02	B. 0	B. 153	B. 102

yh09sw

yh09pat.gif

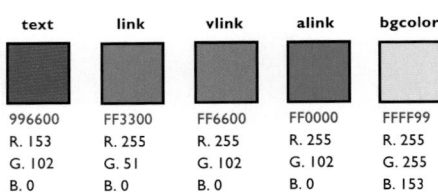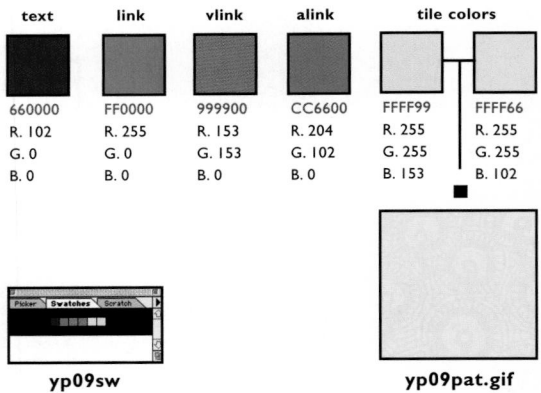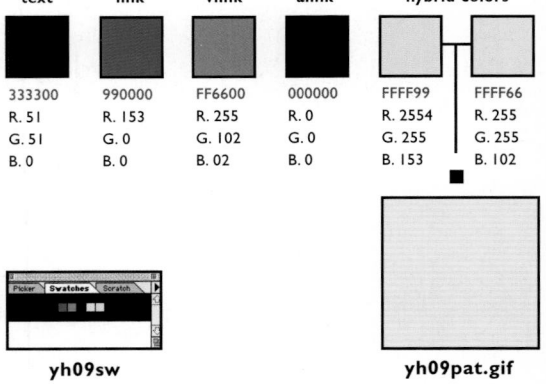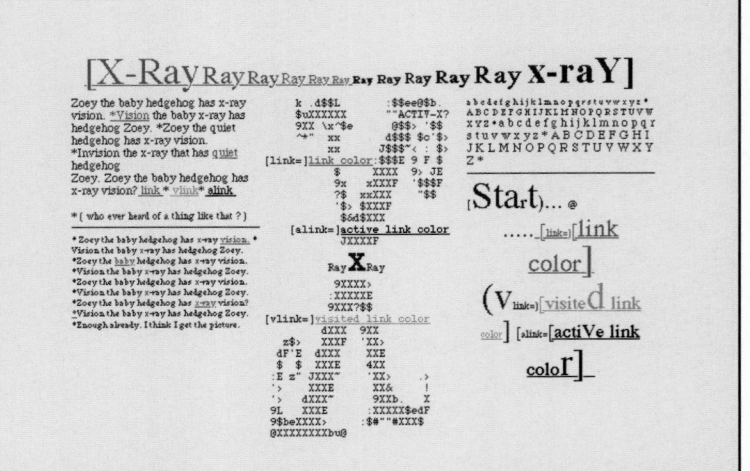

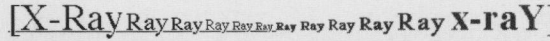

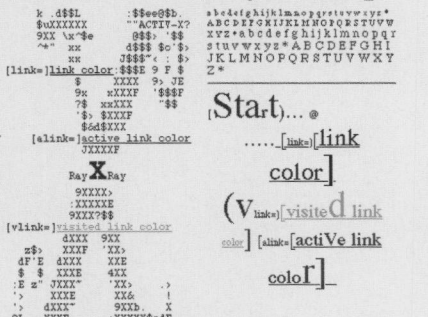

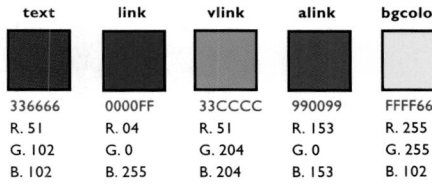

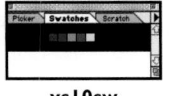

text	link	vlink	alink	bgcolor
336666	0000FF	33CCCC	990099	FFFF66
R. 51	R. 04	R. 51	R. 153	R. 255
G. 102	G. 0	G. 204	G. 0	G. 255
B. 102	B. 255	B. 204	B. 153	B. 102

ys10sw

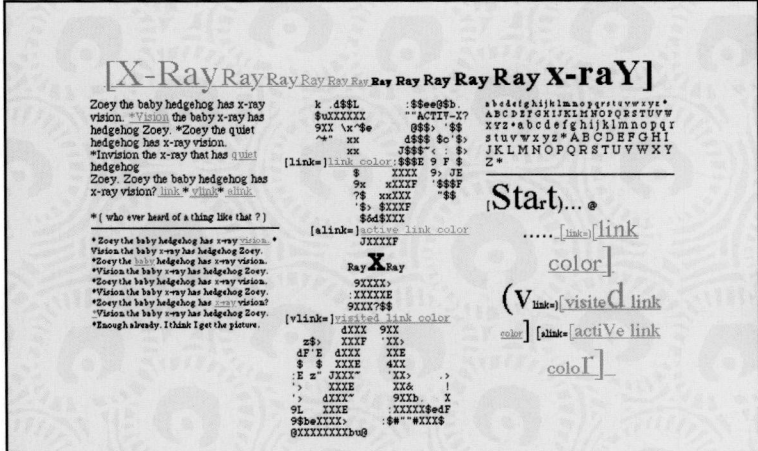

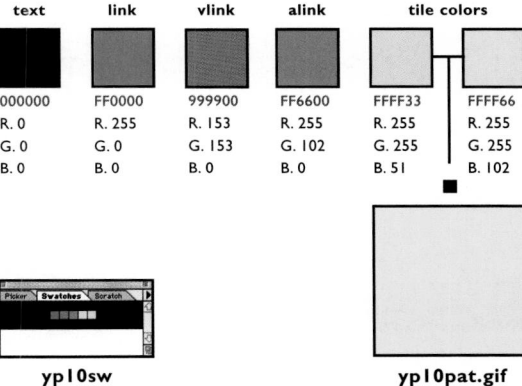

text	link	vlink	alink	tile colors	
000000	FF0000	999900	FF6600	FFFF33	FFFF66
R. 0	R. 255	R. 153	R. 255	R. 255	R. 255
G. 0	G. 0	G. 153	G. 102	G. 255	G. 255
B. 0	B. 0	B. 0	B. 0	B. 51	B. 102

yp10sw **yp10pat.gif**

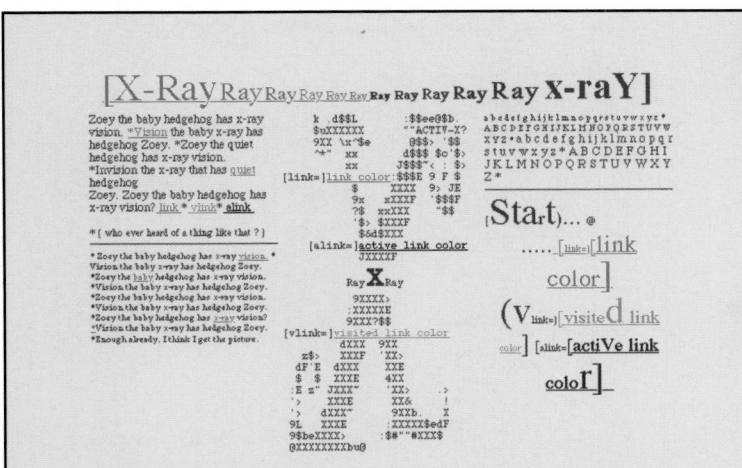

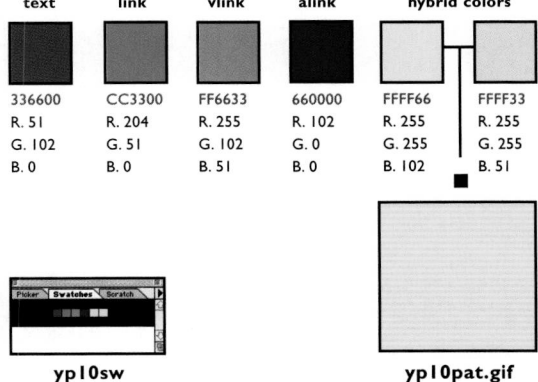

text	link	vlink	alink	hybrid colors	
336600	CC3300	FF6633	660000	FFFF66	FFFF33
R. 51	R. 204	R. 255	R. 102	R. 255	R. 255
G. 102	G. 51	G. 102	G. 0	G. 255	G. 255
B. 0	B. 0	B. 51	B. 0	B. 102	B. 51

yp10sw **yp10pat.gif**

text	link	vlink	alink	bgcolor
333333	FFFF00	FFCC66	666600	FF9900
R. 51	R. 255	R. 255	R. 102	R. 255
G. 51	G. 255	G. 204	G. 102	G. 153
B. 51	B. 0	B. 102	B. 102	B. 0

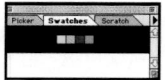

ys11sw

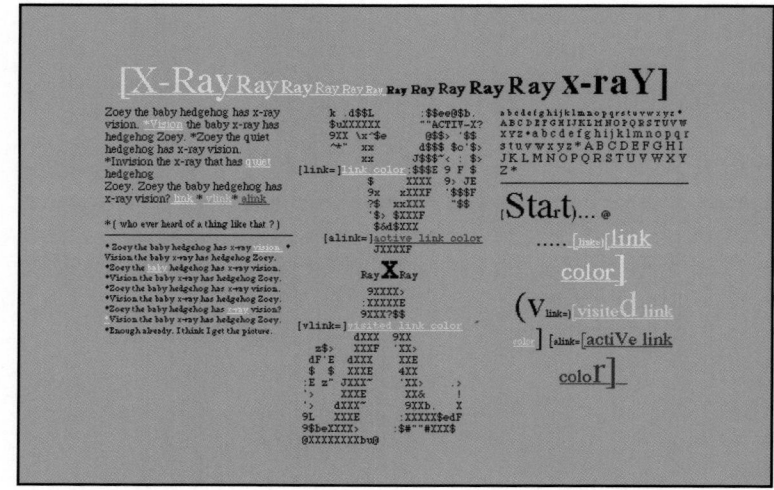

text	link	vlink	alink	tile colors	
003300	006666	336633	FFFF00	FF9900	FF9933
R. 0	R. 0	R. 51	R. 255	R. 255	R. 255
G. 51	G. 102	G. 102	G. 255	G. 153	G. 153
B. 0	B. 102	B. 51	B. 0	B. 0	B. 51

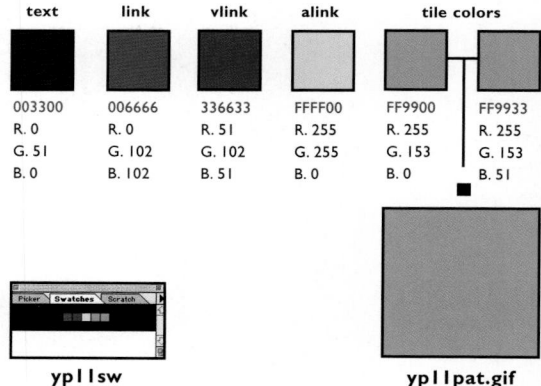

yp11sw

yp11pat.gif

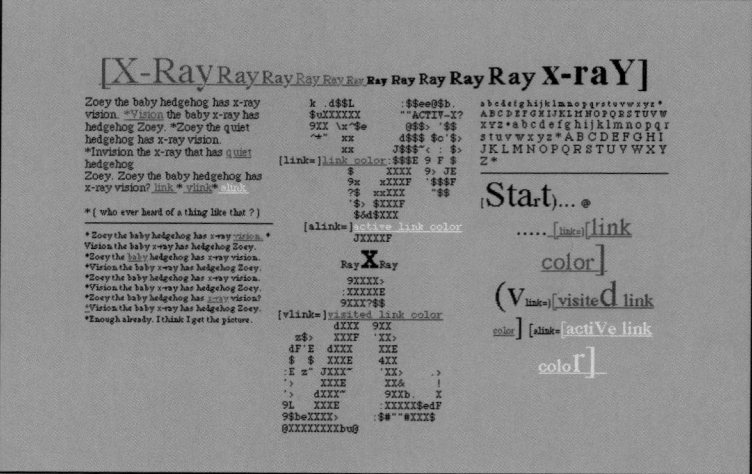

text	link	vlink	alink	hybrid colors	
333333	FFFFCC	CCCCCC	FFFF00	FF9900	FF9933
R. 51	R. 255	R. 204	R. 255	R. 255	R. 255
G. 51	G. 255	G. 204	G. 255	G. 153	G. 153
B. 51	B. 204	B. 204	B. 0	B. 0	B. 51

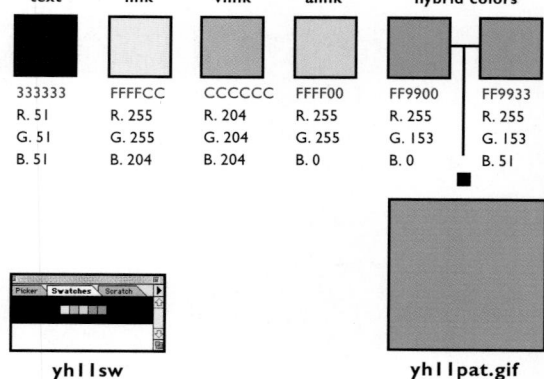

yh11sw

yh11pat.gif

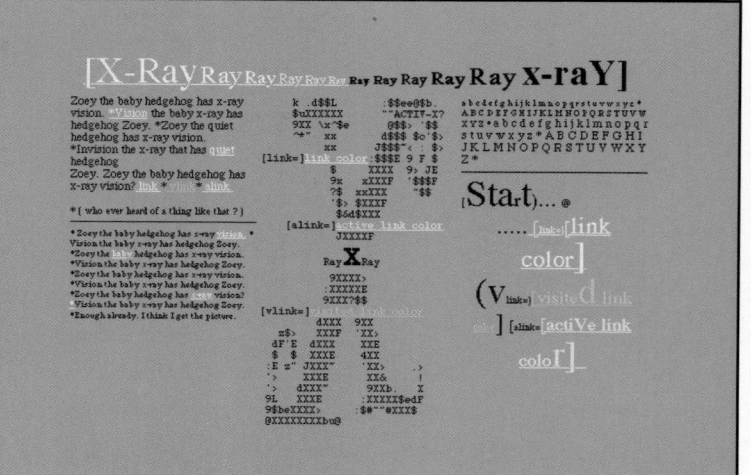

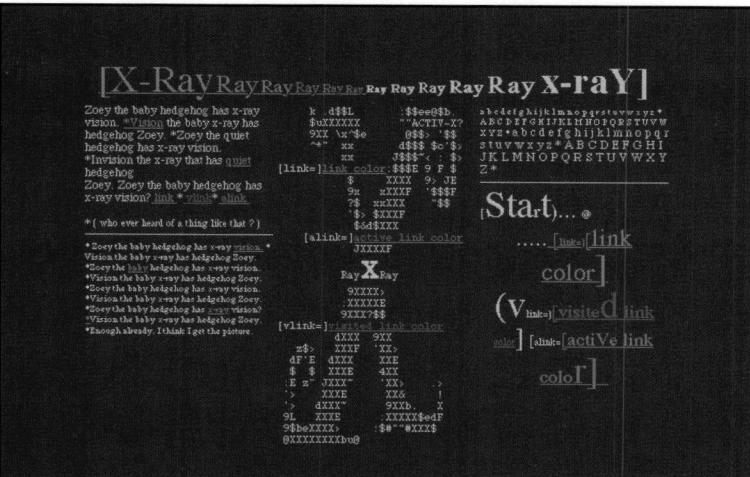

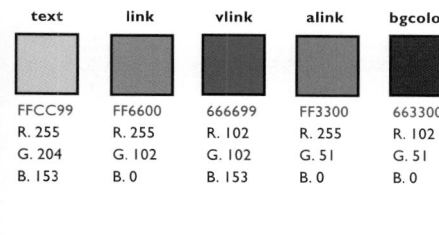

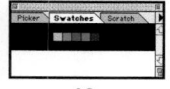

text	link	vlink	alink	bgcolor
FFCC99	FF6600	666699	FF3300	663300
R. 255	R. 255	R. 102	R. 255	R. 102
G. 204	G. 102	G. 102	G. 51	G. 51
B. 153	B. 0	B. 153	B. 0	B. 0

ys12sw

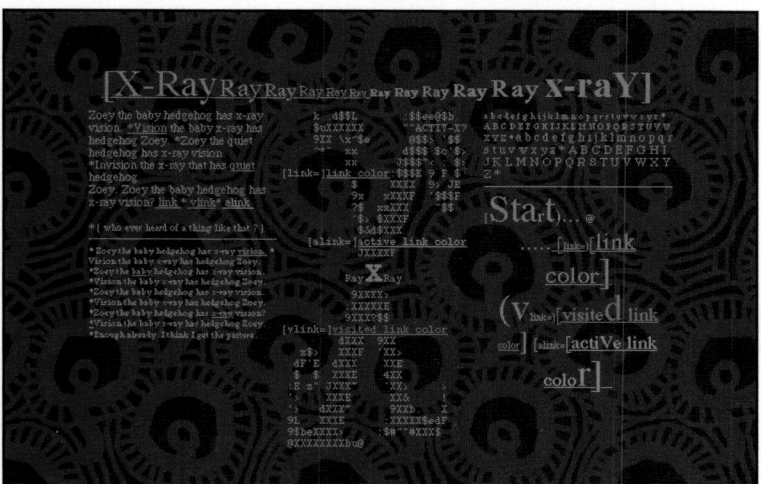

text	link	vlink	alink	tile colors	
9999CC	999900	CC6600	66CC00	333333	663300
R. 153	R. 153	R. 204	R. 102	R. 51	R. 102
G. 153	G. 153	G. 102	G. 204	G. 51	G. 51
B. 214	B. 0	B. 0	B. 0	B. 51	B. 0

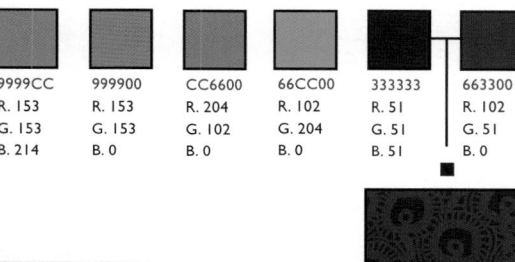

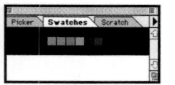

yp12sw

yp12pat.gif

text	link	vlink	alink	hybrid colors	
CCCCFF	6666FF	666666	0000FF	333333	663300
R. 204	R. 102	R. 102	R. 0	R. 51	R. 102
G. 204	G. 102	G. 102	G. 0	G. 51	G. 51
B. 255	B. 255	B. 102	B. 255	B. 51	B. 0

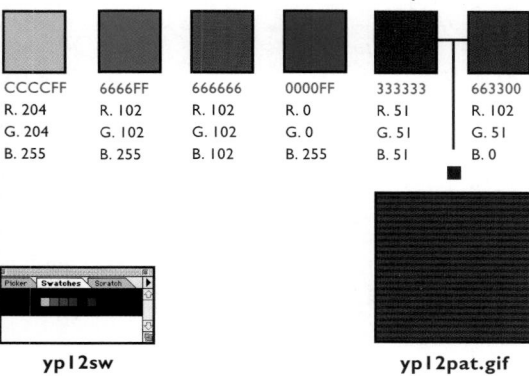

yp12sw

yp12pat.gif

text	link	vlink	alink	bgcolor
333333	006633	999900	009999	FFCC99
R. 51	R. 0	R. 153	R. 0	R. 255
G. 51	G. 102	G. 153	G. 153	G. 204
B. 51	B. 51	B. 0	B. 153	B. 153

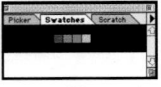

ys13sw

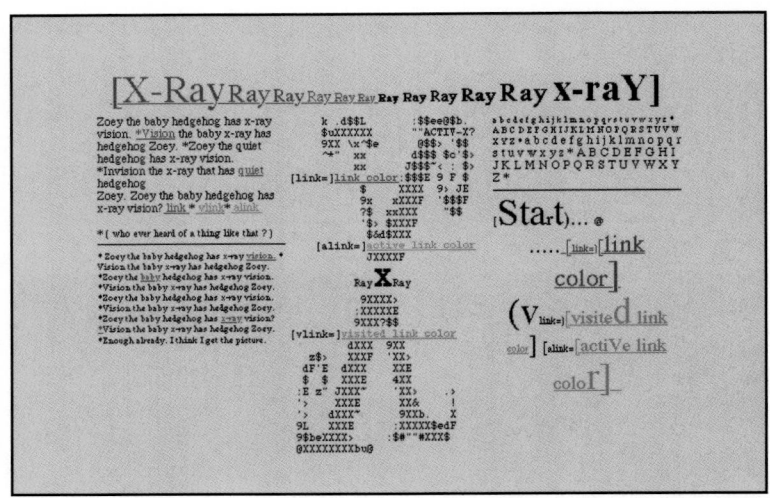

text	link	vlink	alink	tile colors	
663300	CC6600	666666	FF3300	FFCC66	FFCC99
R. 102	R. 204	R. 102	R. 255	R. 255	R. 255
G. 51	G. 102	G. 102	G. 51	G. 204	G. 204
B. 0	B. 0	B. 0	B. 0	B. 102	B. 153

yp13sw

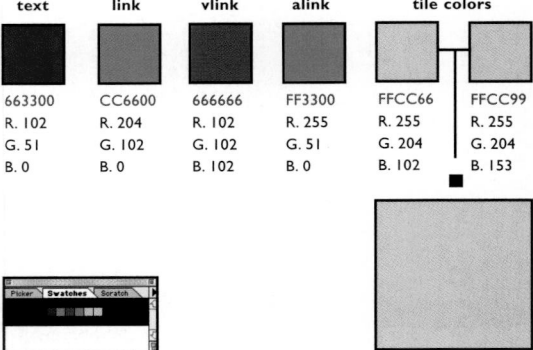

yp13pat.gif

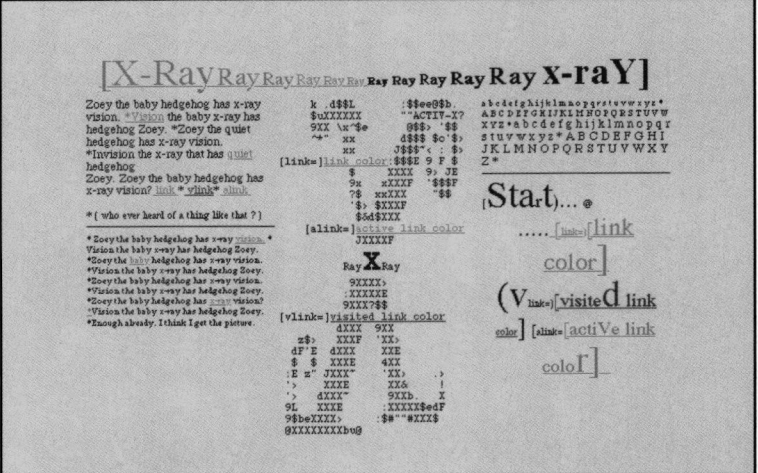

text	link	vlink	alink	hybrid colors	
663300	FF6600	999900	FF3300	FFCC66	FFCC99
R. 102	R. 255	R. 153	R. 255	R. 255	R. 255
G. 51	G. 102	G. 153	G. 51	G. 204	G. 204
B. 0	B. 0	B. 0	B. 0	B. 102	B. 153

yh13sw

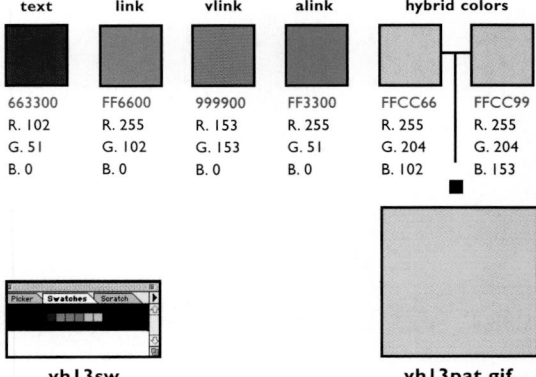

yh13pat.gif

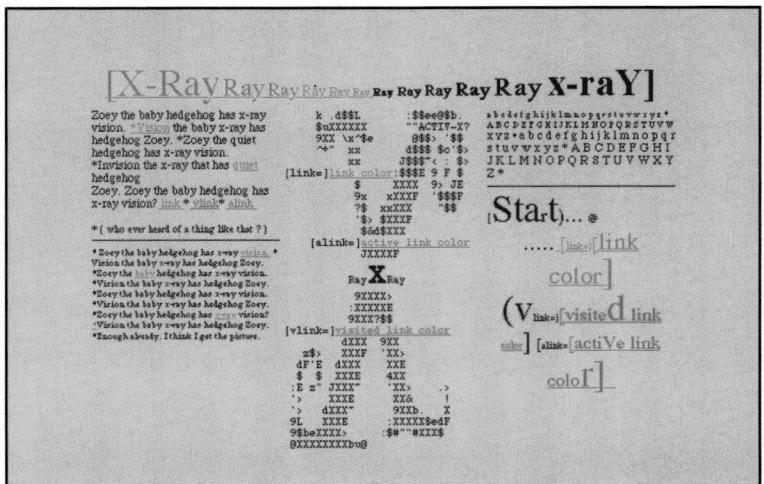

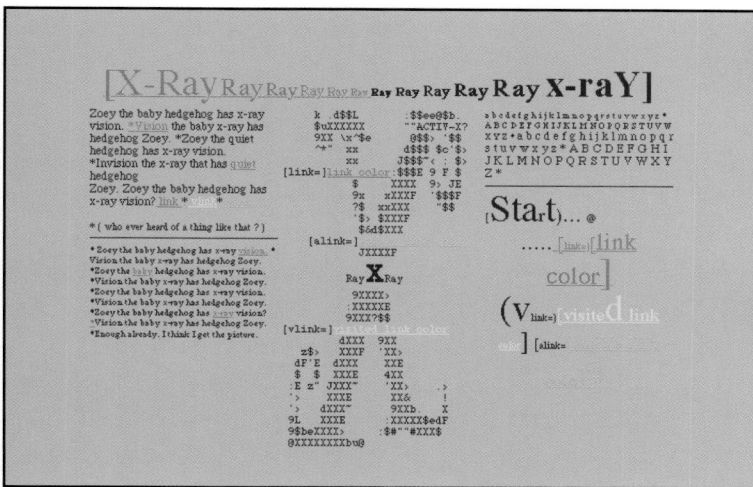

text	link	vlink	alink	bgcolor
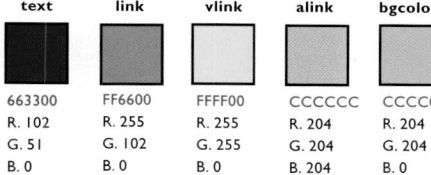				
663300	FF6600	FFFF00	CCCCCC	CCCC00
R. 102	R. 255	R. 255	R. 204	R. 204
G. 51	G. 102	G. 255	G. 204	G. 204
B. 0	B. 0	B. 0	B. 204	B. 0

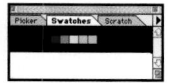

ys14sw

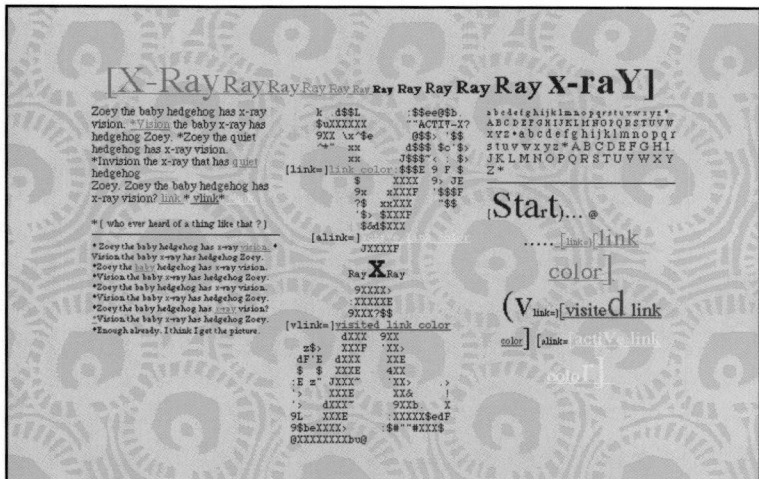

text	link	vlink	alink	tile colors	
663333	FF0000	006600	FFFF00	CCCC00	FFCC66
R. 102	R. 255	R. 0	R. 255	R. 204	R. 255
G. 51	G. 0	G. 102	G. 255	G. 204	G. 204
B. 51	B. 0	B. 0	B. 0	B. 0	B. 102

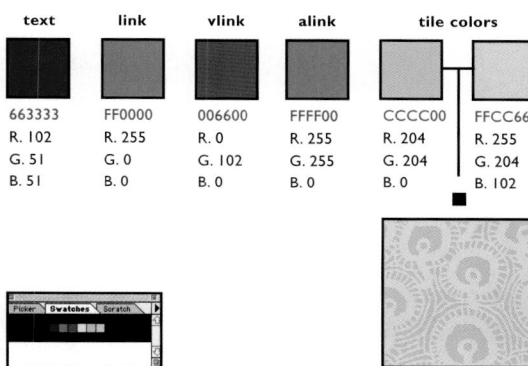

yp14sw   yp14pat.gif

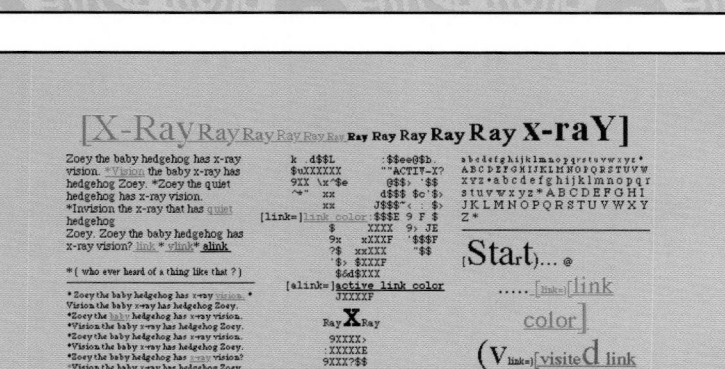

text	link	vlink	alink	hybrid colors	
333300	FF0000	996666	000000	CCCC00	FFCC66
R. 51	R. 255	R. 153	R. 0	R. 204	R. 255
G. 51	G. 0	G. 102	G. 0	G. 204	G. 204
B. 0	B. 0	B. 102	B. 0	B. 0	B. 102

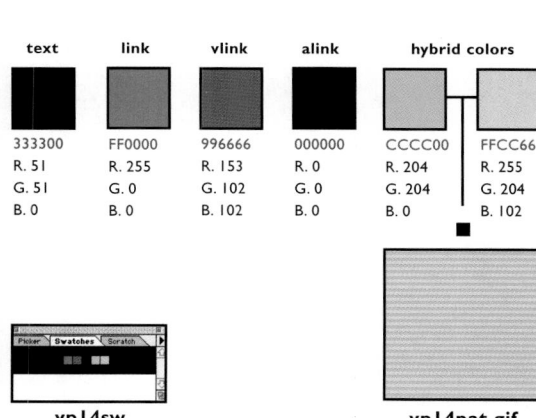

yp14sw   yp14pat.gif

text	link	vlink	alink	bgcolor
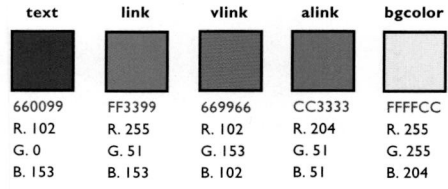				
660099	FF3399	669966	CC3333	FFFFCC
R. 102	R. 255	R. 102	R. 204	R. 255
G. 0	G. 51	G. 153	G. 51	G. 255
B. 153	B. 153	B. 102	B. 51	B. 204

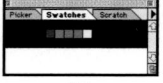

ys15sw

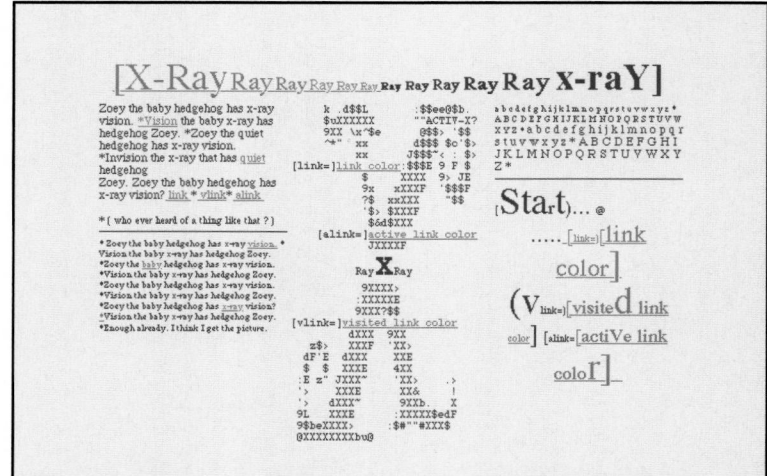

text	link	vlink	alink	tile colors	
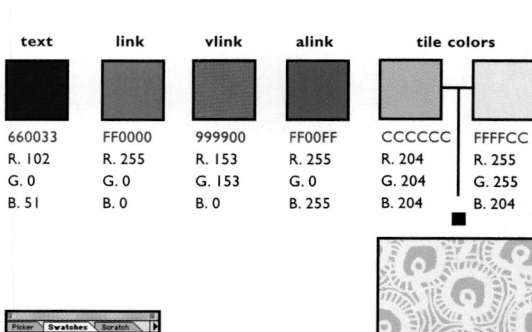					
660033	FF0000	999900	FF00FF	CCCCCC	FFFFCC
R. 102	R. 255	R. 153	R. 255	R. 204	R. 255
G. 0	G. 0	G. 153	G. 0	G. 204	G. 255
B. 51	B. 0	B. 0	B. 255	B. 204	B. 204

yp15sw

yp15pat.gif

text	link	vlink	alink	hybrid colors	
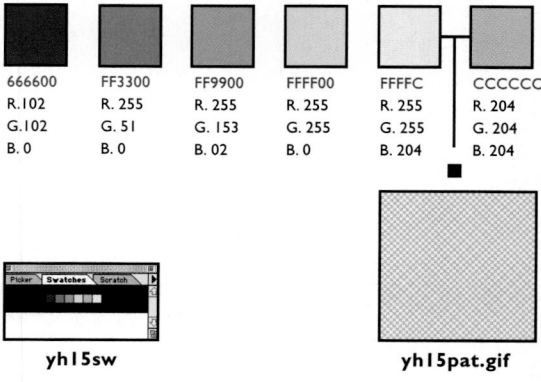					
666600	FF3300	FF9900	FFFF00	FFFFC	CCCCCC
R.102	R. 255	R. 255	R. 255	R. 255	R. 204
G.102	G. 51	G. 153	G. 255	G. 255	G. 204
B. 0	B. 0	B. 02	B. 0	B. 204	B. 204

yh15sw

yh15pat.gif

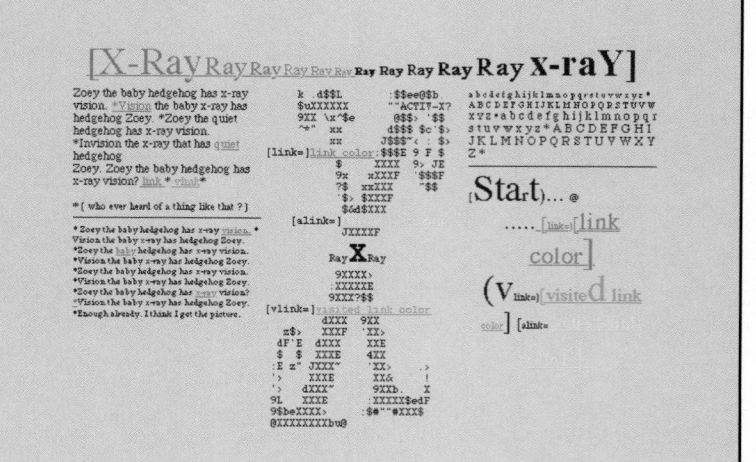

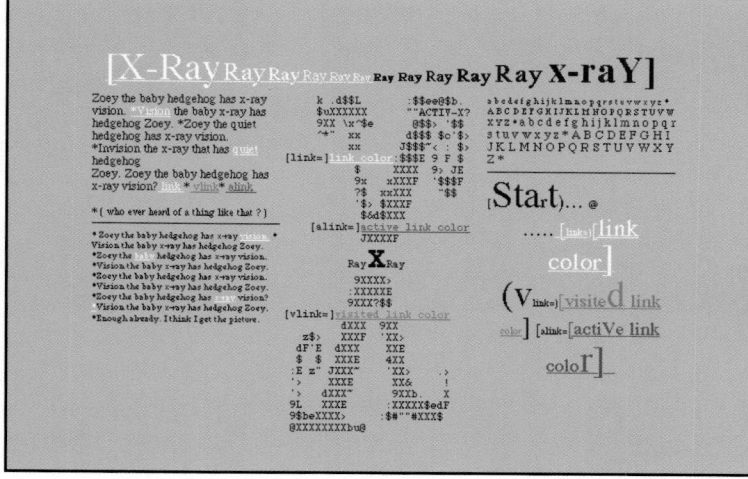
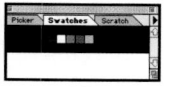

text	link	vlink	alink	bgcolor
663300	FFFFFF	669966	996666	CCCC99
R. 102	R. 255	R. 102	R. 153	R. 204
G. 51	G. 255	G. 153	G. 102	G. 204
B. 0	B. 255	B. 102	B. 102	B. 153

ys16sw

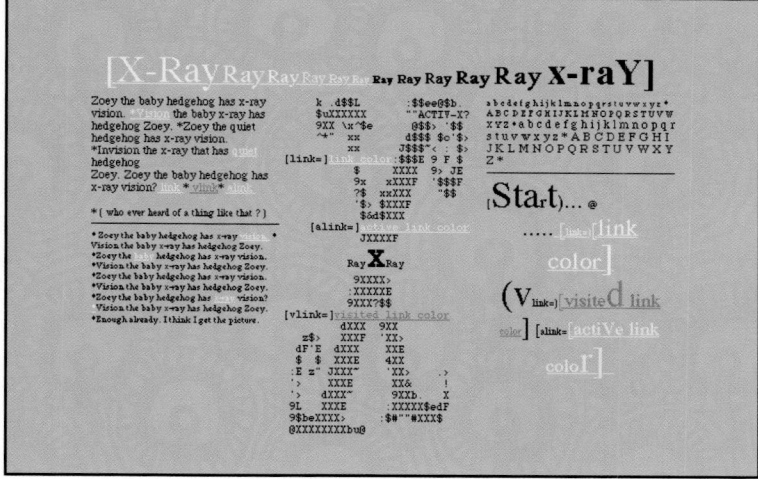
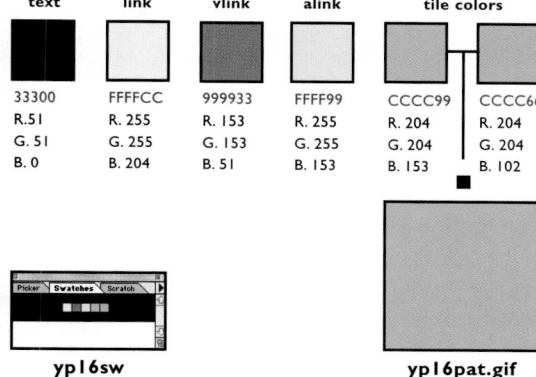

text	link	vlink	alink	tile colors	
33300	FFFFCC	999933	FFFF99	CCCC99	CCCC66
R. 51	R. 255	R. 153	R. 255	R. 204	R. 204
G. 51	G. 255	G. 153	G. 255	G. 204	G. 204
B. 0	B. 204	B. 51	B. 153	B. 153	B. 102

yp16sw

yp16pat.gif

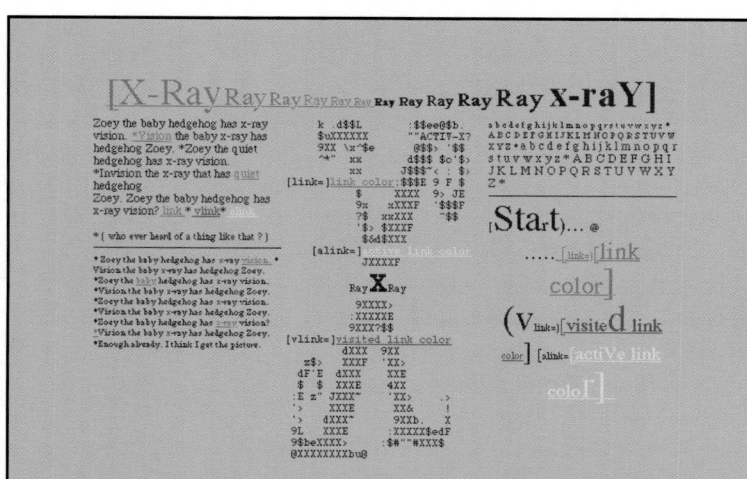
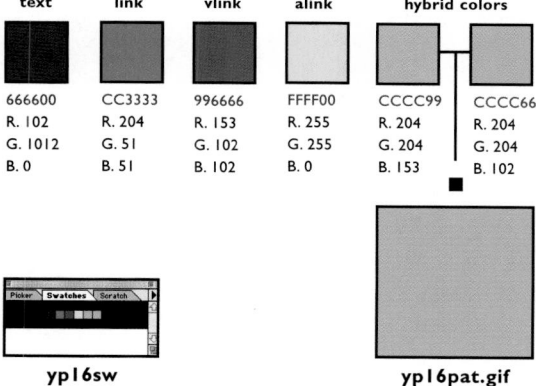

text	link	vlink	alink	hybrid colors	
666600	CC3333	996666	FFFF00	CCCC99	CCCC66
R. 102	R. 204	R. 153	R. 255	R. 204	R. 204
G. 1012	G. 51	G. 102	G. 255	G. 204	G. 204
B. 0	B. 51	B. 102	B. 0	B. 153	B. 102

yp16sw

yp16pat.gif

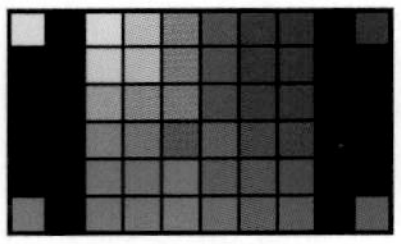

ybrm	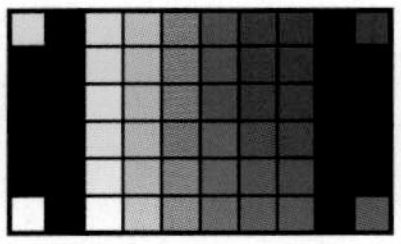 ybwm	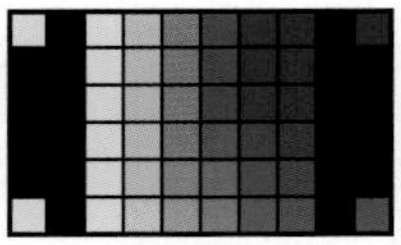 ybym	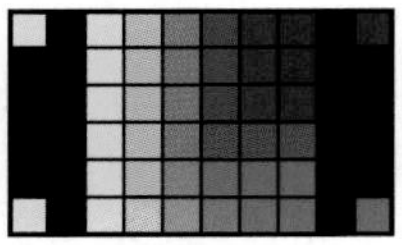 ybyr	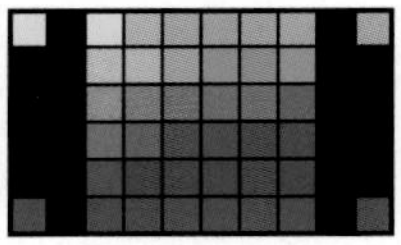 ycmm
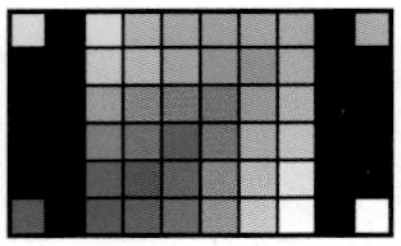 ycmw	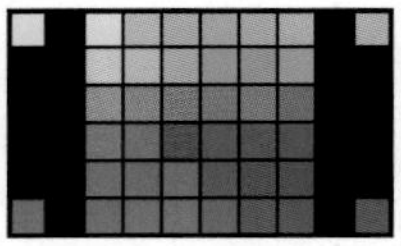 ycrm	 ycrr	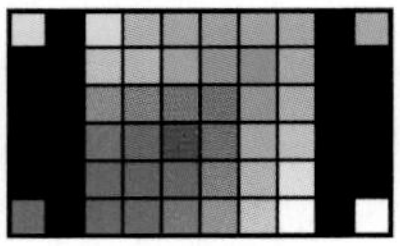 ycrw	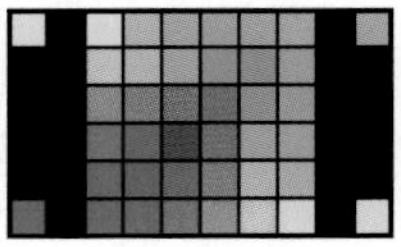 ycry
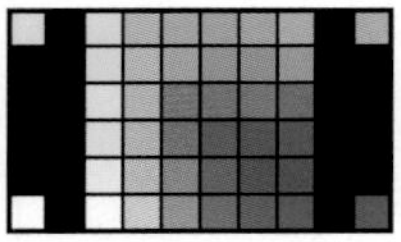 ycwm	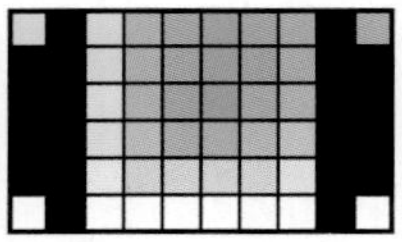 ycww	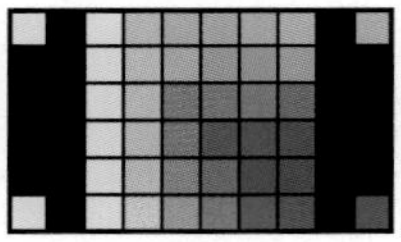 ycym	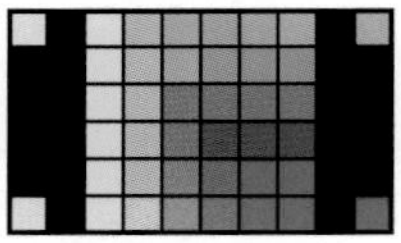 ycyr	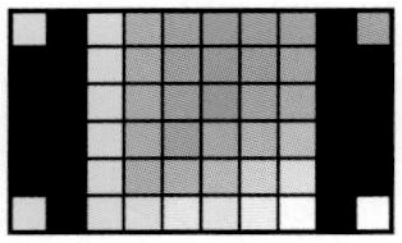 ycyw
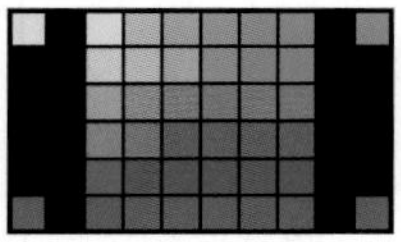 ygmm	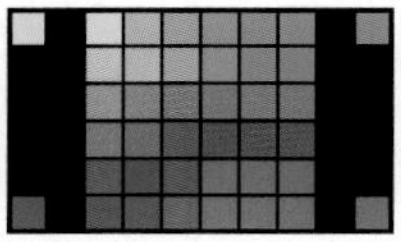 ygmr	 ygmw	 ygmy	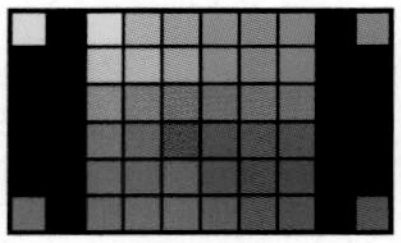 ygrm
 ygrr	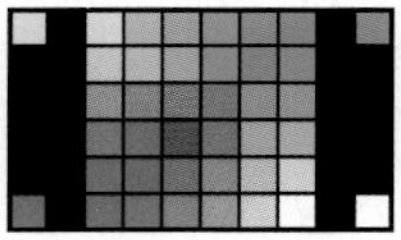 ygrw	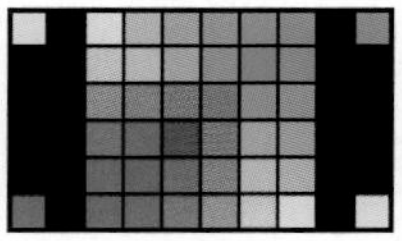 ygry	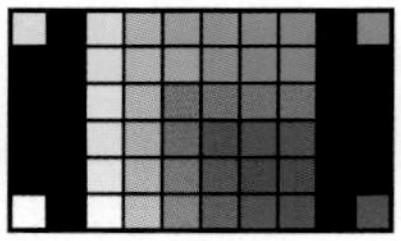 ygwm	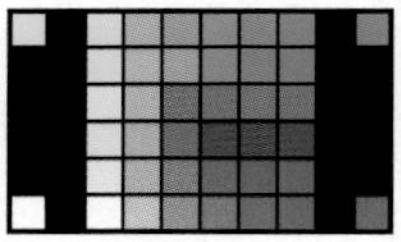 ygwr
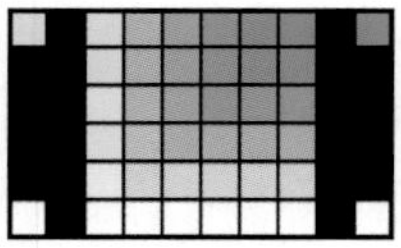 ygww	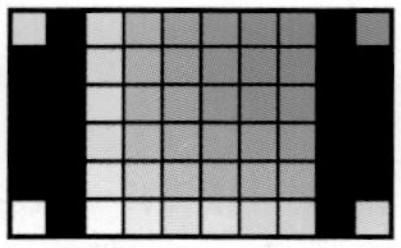 ygwy	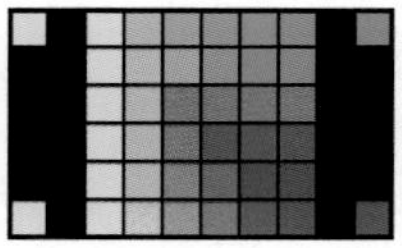 ygym	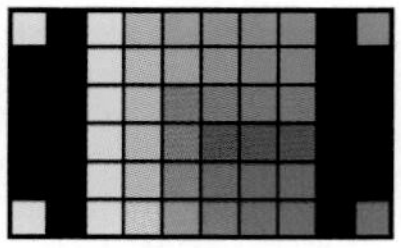 ygyr	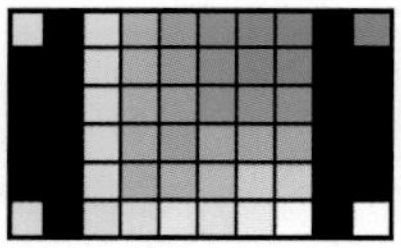 ygyw
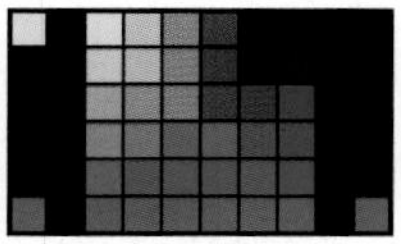 ykmm	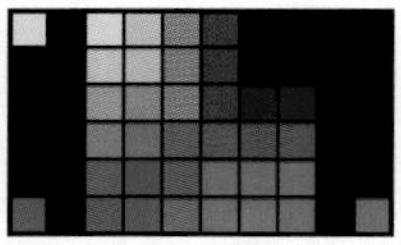 ykmr	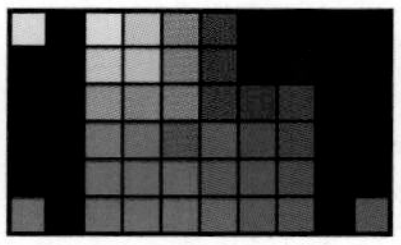 ykrm	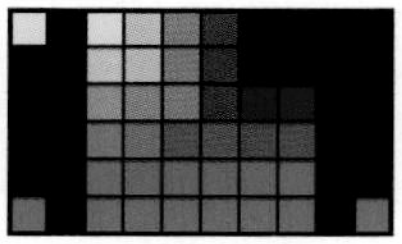 ykrr	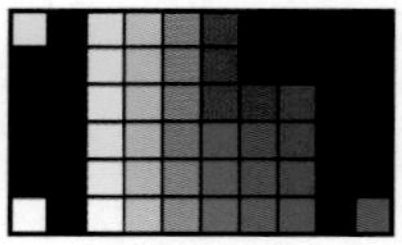 ykwm

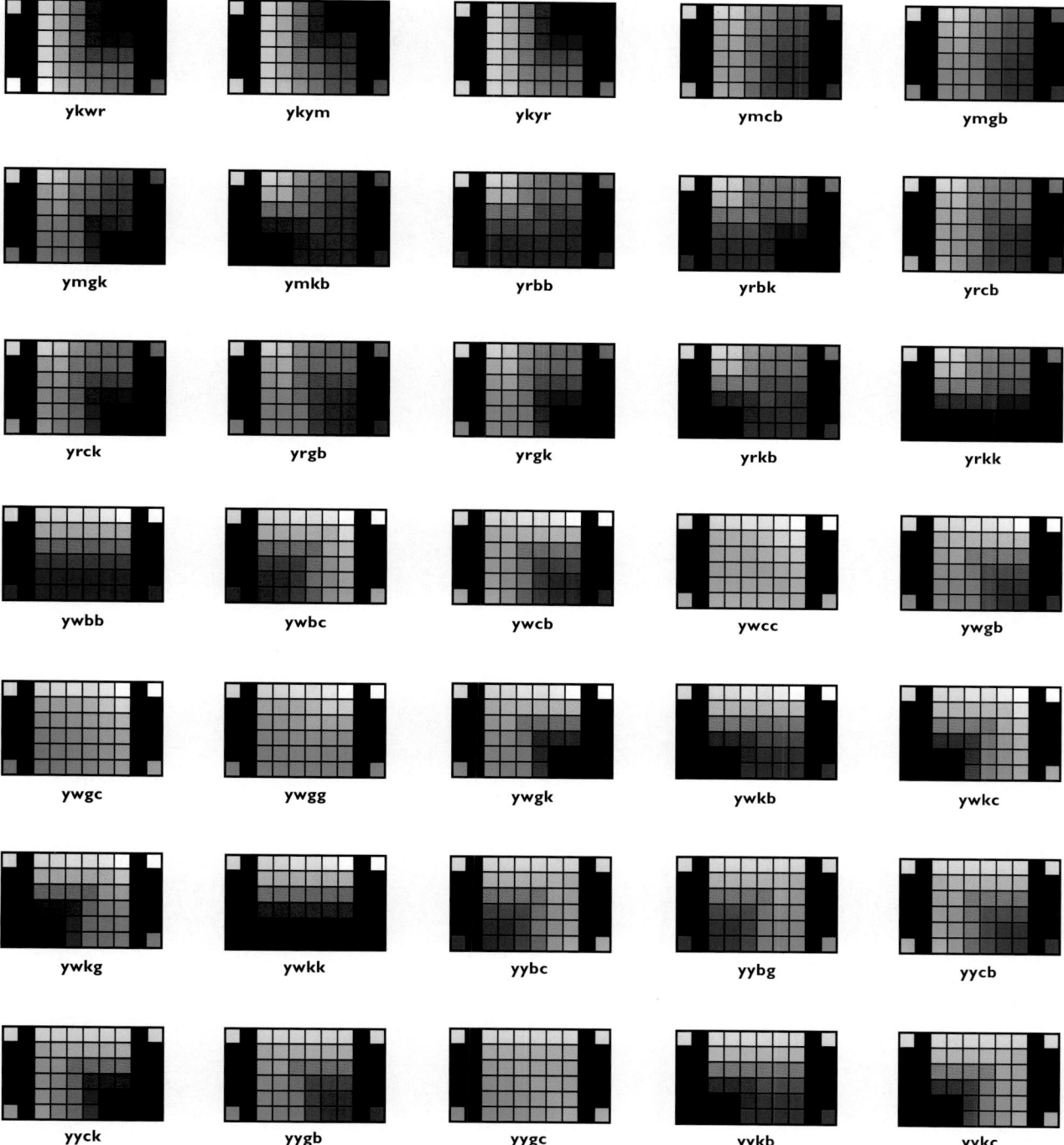

ykwr	ykym	ykyr

ymcb ymgb

ymgk ymkb yrbb yrbk yrcb

yrck yrgb yrgk yrkb yrkk

ywbb ywbc ywcb ywcc ywgb

ywgc ywgg ywgk ywkb ywkc

ywkg ywkk yybc yybg yycb

yyck yygb yygc yykb yykc

MONOCHROMATIC

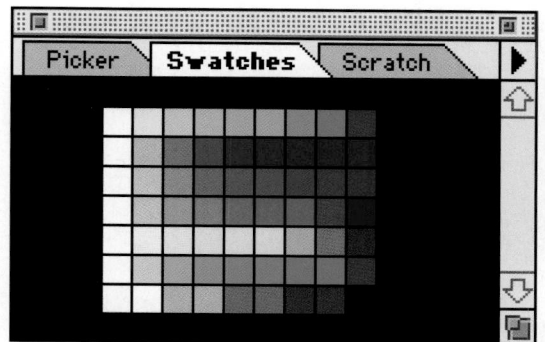

odd06

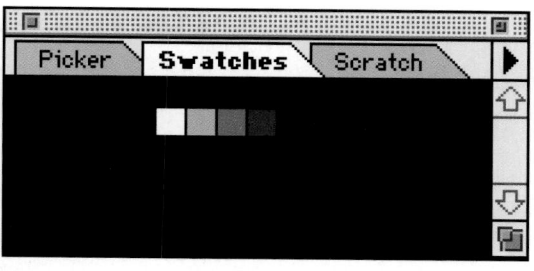

odd04

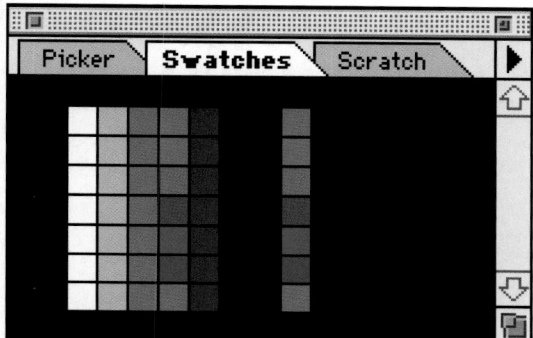

med

text	link	vlink	alink	bgcolor
339933	33FF00	666666	666600	000000
R. 51	R. 51	R. 102	R. 102	R. 0
G. 153	G. 255	G. 102	G. 102	G. 0
B. 51	B. 0	B. 102	B. 0	B. 0

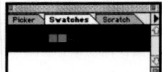

ks01sw

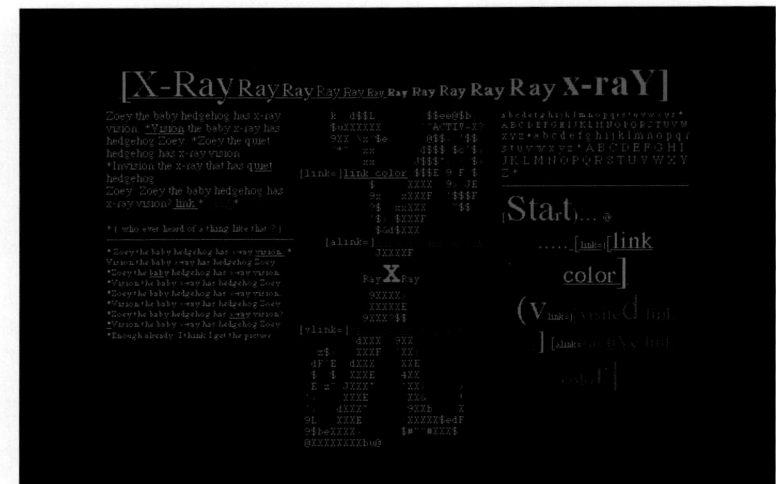

text	link	vlink	alink	bgcolor
CC6666	FF0000	CC3333	990000	000000
R. 204	R. 255	R. 204	R. 153	R. 0
G. 102	G. 0	G. 51	G. 0	G. 0
B. 102	B. 0	B. 51	B. 0	B. 0

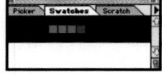

ks02sw

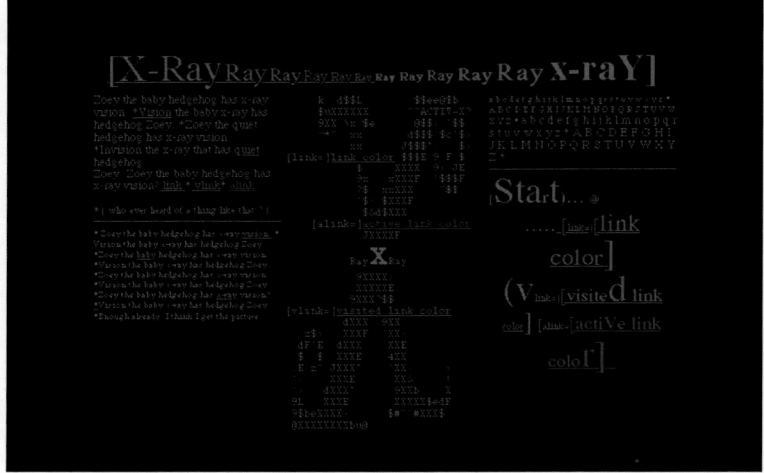

text	link	vlink	alink	bgcolor
999966	FFFF00	999933	FFFF99	000000
R. 153	R. 255	R. 153	R. 255	R. 0
G. 153	G. 255	G. 153	G. 255	G. 0
B. 102	B. 0	B. 51	B. 153	B. 0

ks03sw

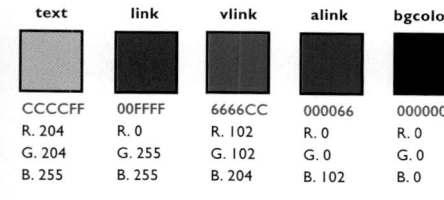
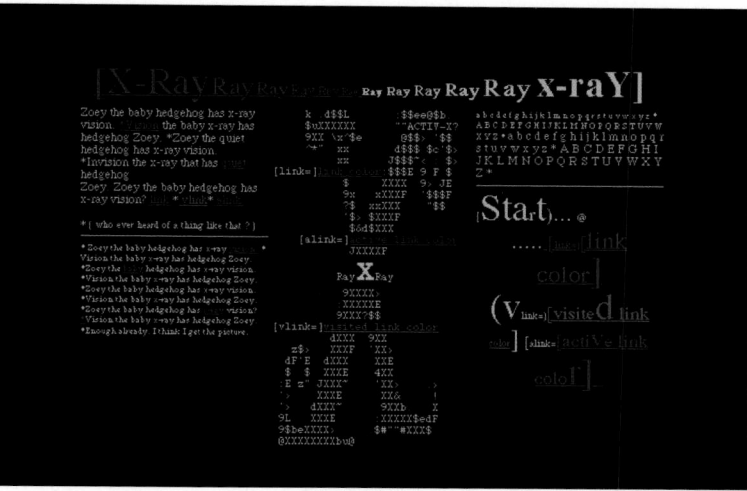
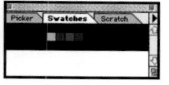

text	link	vlink	alink	bgcolor
CCCCFF	00FFFF	6666CC	000066	000000
R. 204	R. 0	R. 102	R. 0	R. 0
G. 204	G. 255	G. 102	G. 0	G. 0
B. 255	B. 255	B. 204	B. 102	B. 0

ks04sw

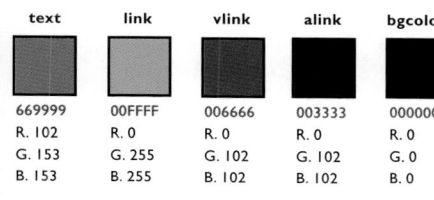
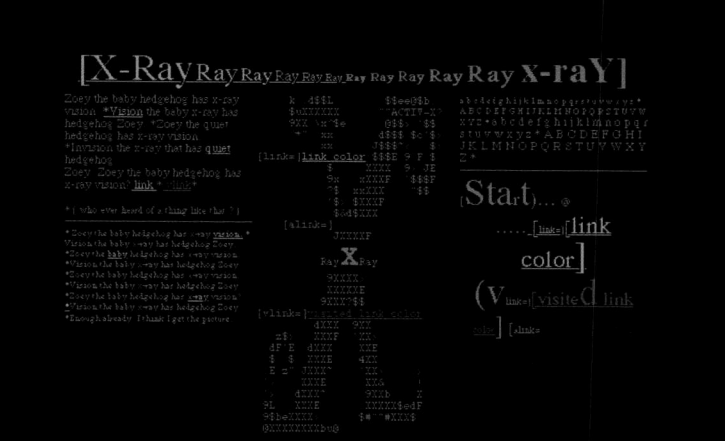
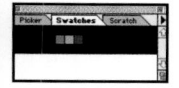

text	link	vlink	alink	bgcolor
669999	00FFFF	006666	003333	000000
R. 102	R. 0	R. 0	R. 0	R. 0
G. 153	G. 255	G. 102	G. 102	G. 0
B. 153	B. 255	B. 102	B. 102	B. 0

ks05w

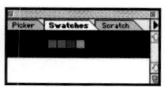

text	link	vlink	alink	bgcolor
996699	FF00FF	663366	FF99FF	000000
R. 153	R. 255	R. 102	R. 255	R. 0
G. 102	G. 0	G. 51	G. 153	G. 0
B. 153	B. 255	B. 102	B. 255	B. 0

ks06sw

text	link	vlink	alink	bgcolor

660000	FF0000	CC6666	996666	CCCCCC
R. 102	R. 255	R. 204	R. 153	R. 204
G. 0	G. 0	G. 102	G. 102	G. 204
B. 0	B. 0	B. 102	B. 102	B. 204

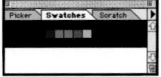

gls01sw

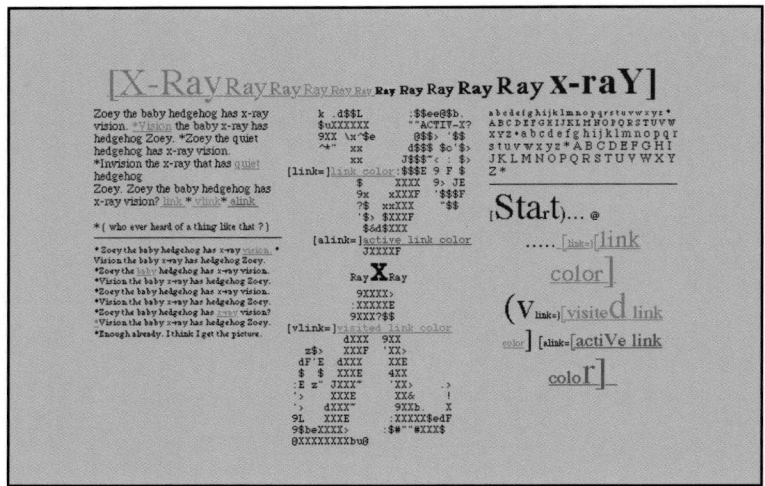

663366	FF00FF	990099	FFFFFF	CCCCCC
R. 153	R. 255	R. 153	R. 255	R. 204
G. 51	G. 0	G. 0	G. 255	G. 204
B. 153	B. 255	B. 153	B. 255	B. 204

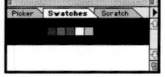

gls02sw

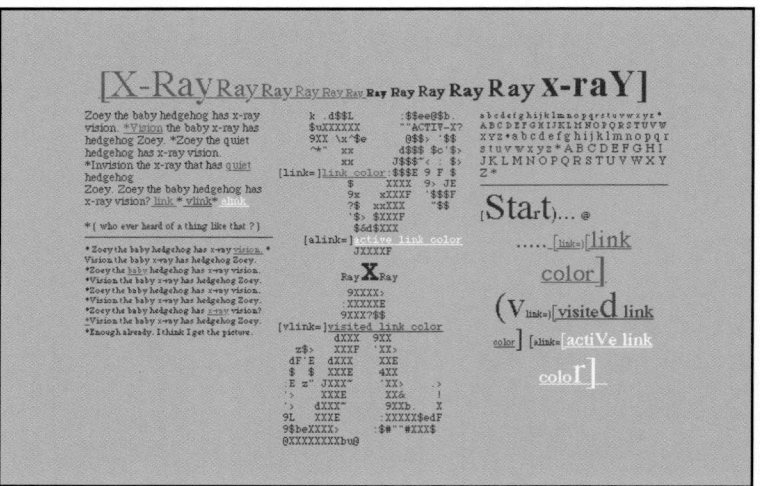

333366	0000FF	6666FF	9999FF	CCCCCC
R. 51	R. 0	R. 153	R.153	R. 204
G. 51	G. 0	G. 153	G. 153	G. 204
B. 102	B. 255	B. 255	B. 255	B. 204

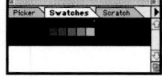

gls03sw

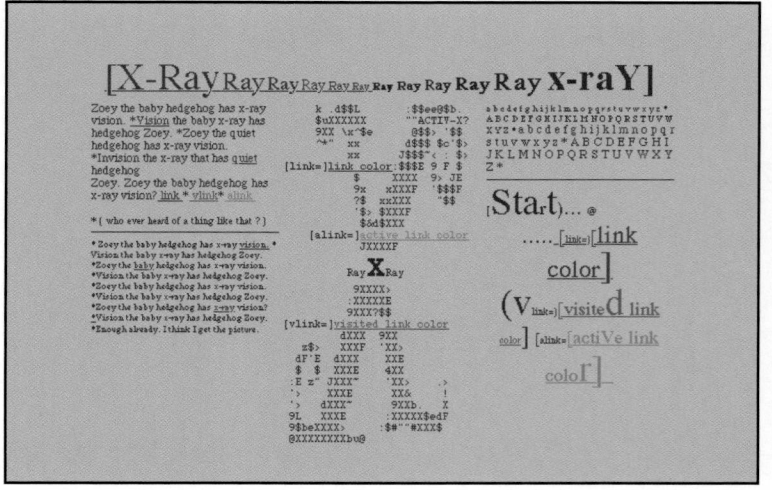

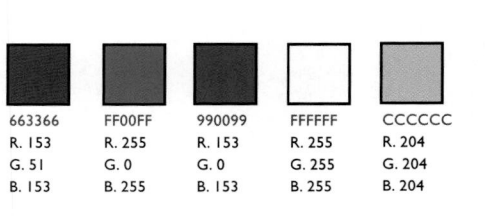
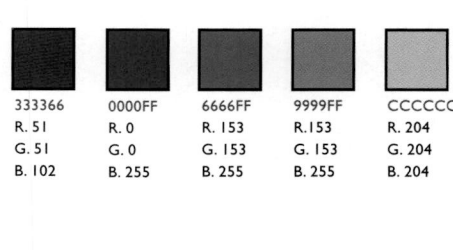

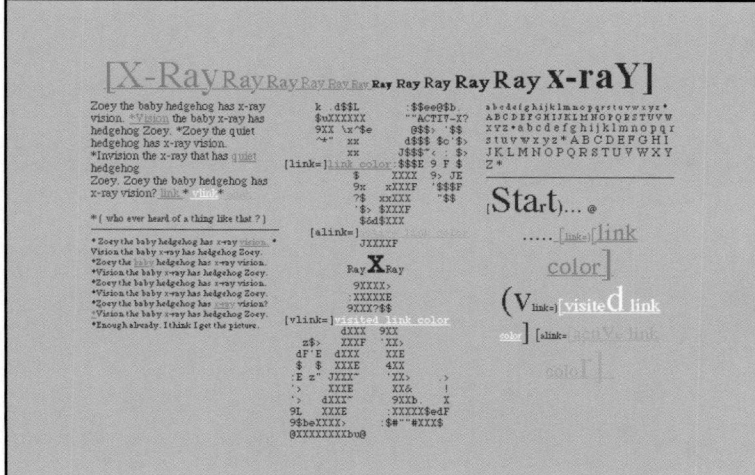

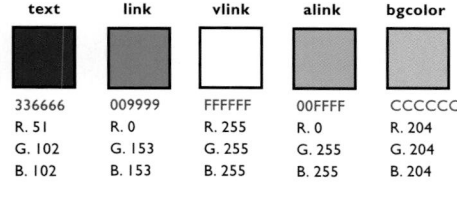

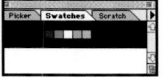

text	link	vlink	alink	bgcolor
336666	009999	FFFFFF	00FFFF	CCCCCC
R. 51	R. 0	R. 255	R. 0	R. 204
G. 102	G. 153	G. 255	G. 255	G. 204
B. 102	B. 153	B. 255	B. 255	B. 204

gls04sw

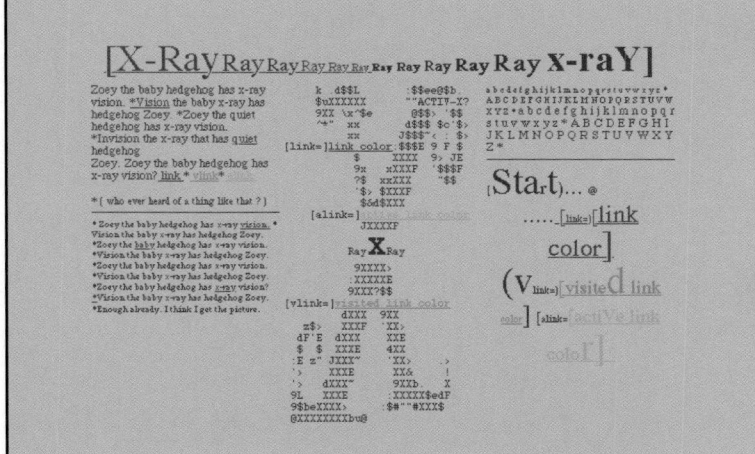

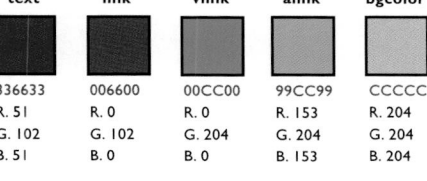

text	link	vlink	alink	bgcolor
336633	006600	00CC00	99CC99	CCCCCC
R. 51	R. 0	R. 0	R. 153	R. 204
G. 102	G. 102	G. 204	G. 204	G. 204
B. 51	B. 0	B. 0	B. 153	B. 204

gls05sw

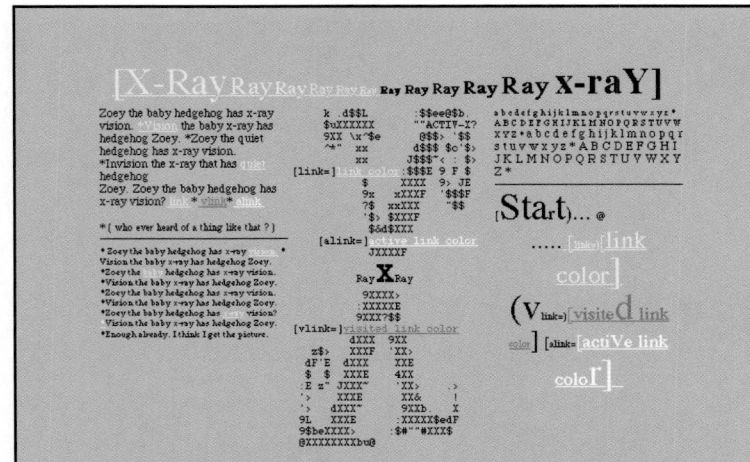

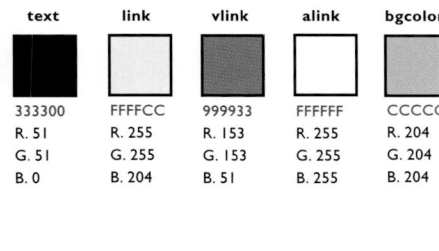

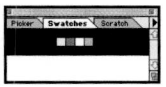

text	link	vlink	alink	bgcolor
333300	FFFFCC	999933	FFFFFF	CCCCCC
R. 51	R. 255	R. 153	R. 255	R. 204
G. 51	G. 255	G. 153	G. 255	G. 204
B. 0	B. 204	B. 51	B. 255	B. 204

gls06sw

text	link	vlink	alink	bgcolor
333300	FFFF00	CCCC33	FFFF99	999999
R. 51	R. 255	R. 204	R. 255	R. 153
G. 51	G. 255	G. 204	G. 255	G. 153
B. 0	B. 0	B. 51	B. 153	B. 153

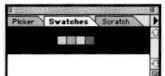

g2s01sw

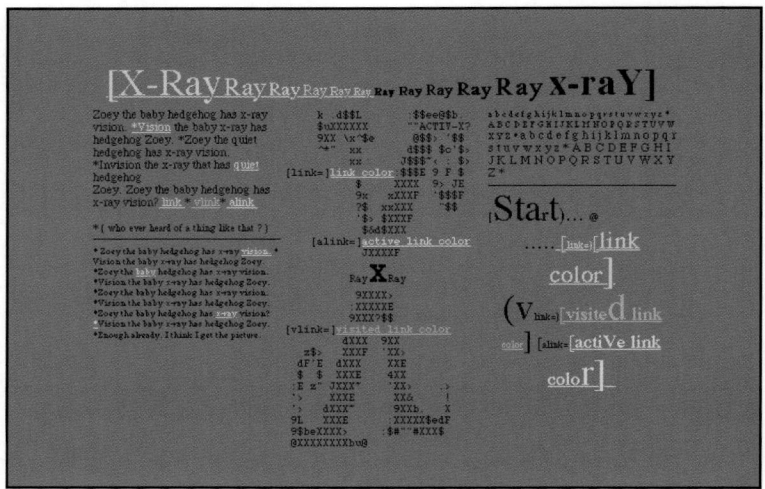

text	link	vlink	alink	bgcolor
FFFFFF	FF00FF	993399	FF66FF	999999
R. 255	R. 255	R. 153	R. 255	R. 153
G. 255	G. 0	G. 51	G.102	G. 153
B. 255	B. 255	B. 153	B. 255	B. 153

g2s02sw

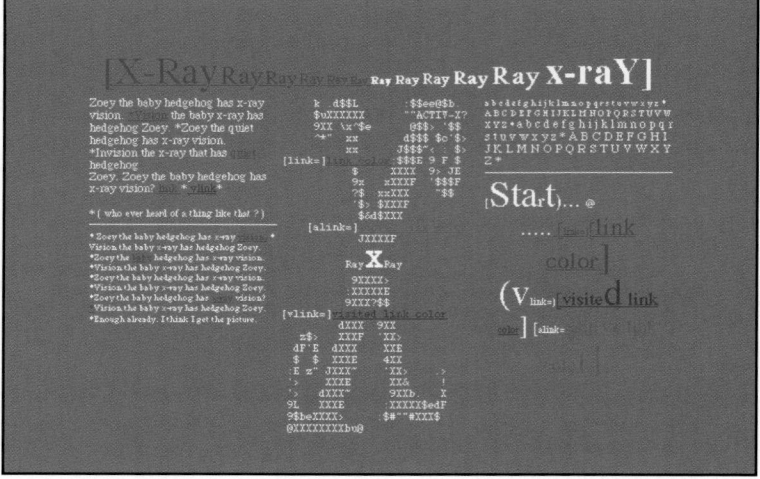

text	link	vlink	alink	bgcolor
663333	FF0000	CC3333	660000	999999
R. 102	R. 255	R. 204	R. 102	R. 153
G. 51	G. 0	G. 51	G. 0	G. 153
B. 51	B. 0	B. 51	B. 0	B. 153

g2s03sw

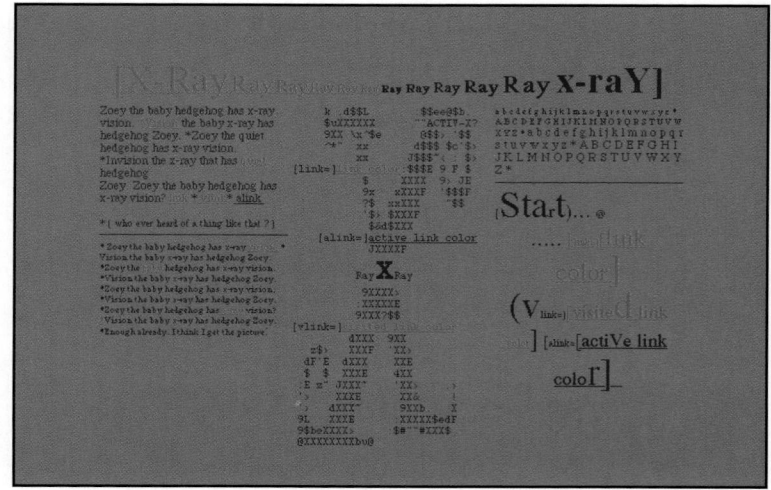

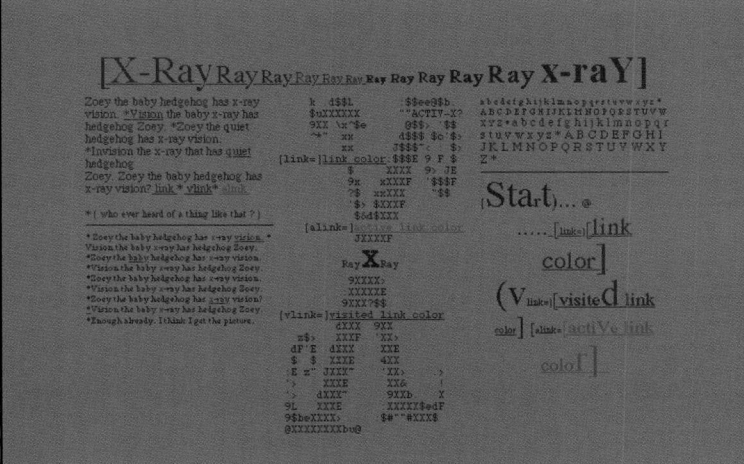

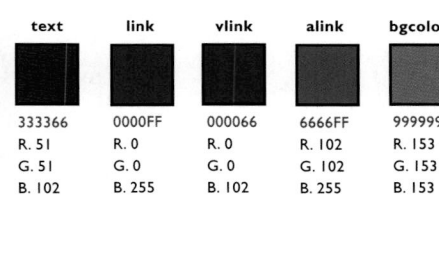

text	link	vlink	alink	bgcolor
333366	0000FF	000066	6666FF	999999
R. 51	R. 0	R. 0	R. 102	R. 153
G. 51	G. 0	G. 0	G. 102	G. 153
B. 102	B. 255	B. 102	B. 255	B. 153

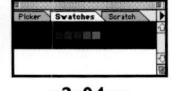

g2s04sw

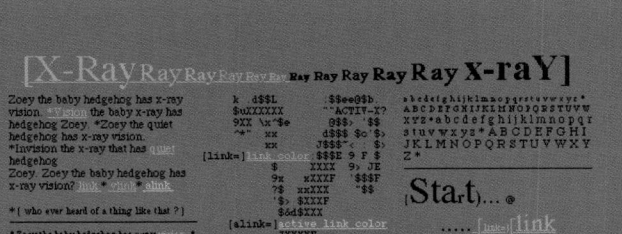

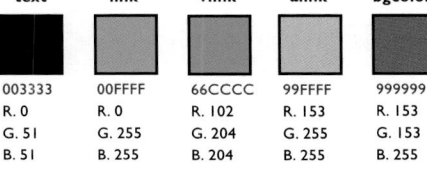

text	link	vlink	alink	bgcolor
003333	00FFFF	66CCCC	99FFFF	999999
R. 0	R. 0	R. 102	R. 153	R. 153
G. 51	G. 255	G. 204	G. 255	G. 153
B. 51	B. 255	B. 204	B. 255	B. 255

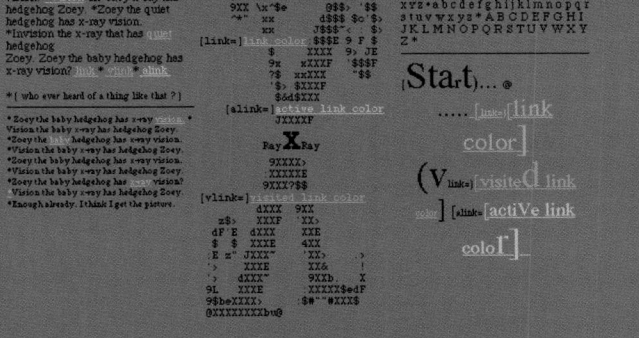

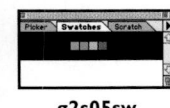

g2s05sw

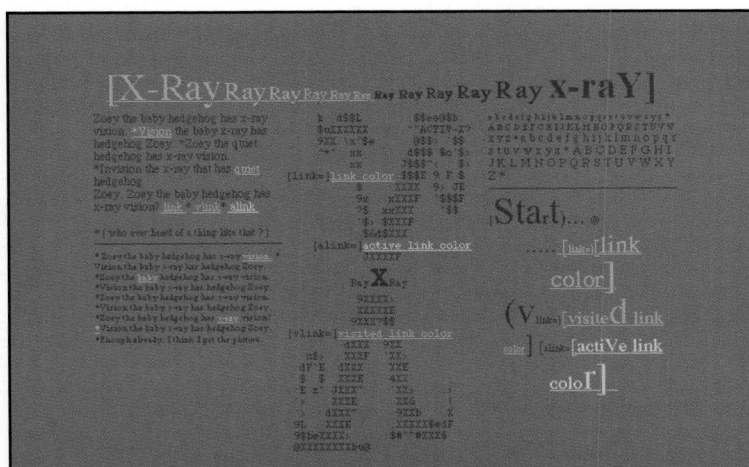

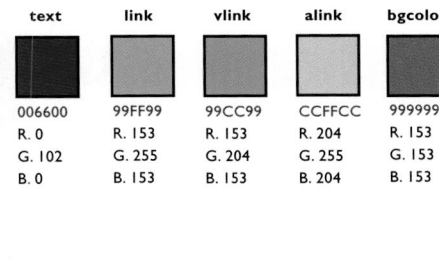

text	link	vlink	alink	bgcolor
006600	99FF99	99CC99	CCFFCC	999999
R. 0	R. 153	R. 153	R. 204	R. 153
G. 102	G. 255	G. 204	G. 255	G. 153
B. 0	B. 153	B. 153	B. 204	B. 153

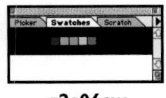

g2s06sw

text	link	vlink	alink	bgcolor
99CCCC	00FFFF	66CCCC	CCFFFF	666666
R. 153	R. 0	R. 102	R. 204	R. 102
G. 204	G. 255	G. 204	G. 255	G. 102
B. 204	B. 255	B. 204	B. 255	B. 102

g3s01sw

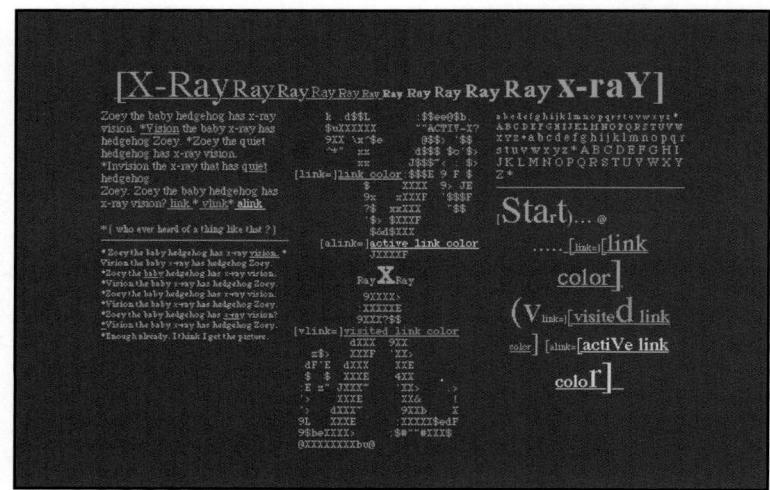

text	link	vlink	alink	bgcolor
99CC99	00FF00	CCFFCC	003300	666666
R. 153	R. 0	R. 204	R. 0	R. 102
G. 204	G. 255	G. 255	G. 51	G. 102
B. 153	B. 0	B. 204	B. 0	B. 102

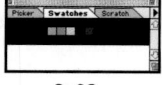

g3s02sw

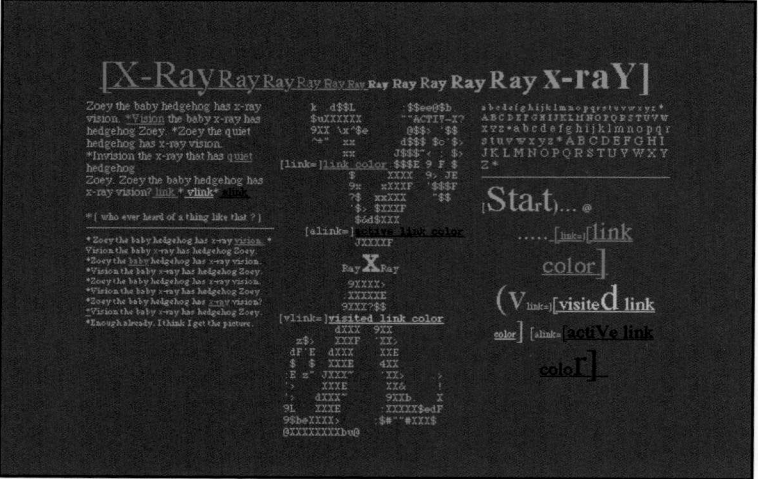

text	link	vlink	alink	bgcolor
CCCC99	FFFF00	FFFF99	999900	666666
R. 204	R. 255	R. 255	R. 153	R. 102
G. 204	G. 255	G. 255	G. 153	G. 102
B. 153	B. 0	B. 153	B. 0	B. 102

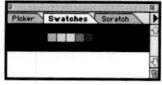

g3s03sw

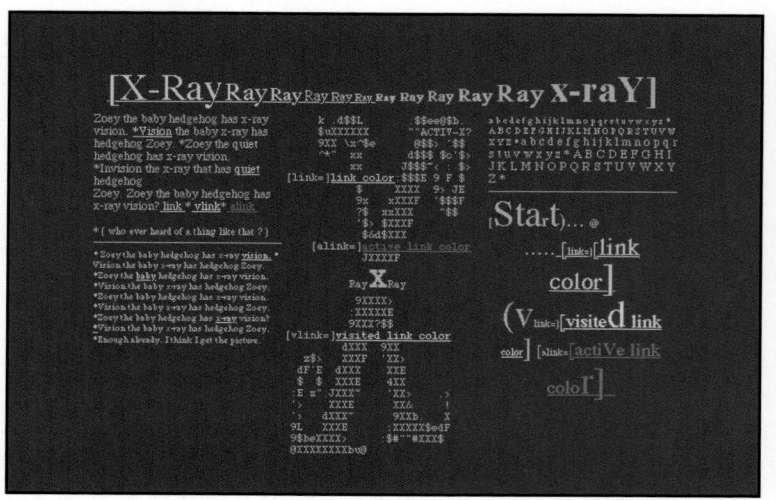

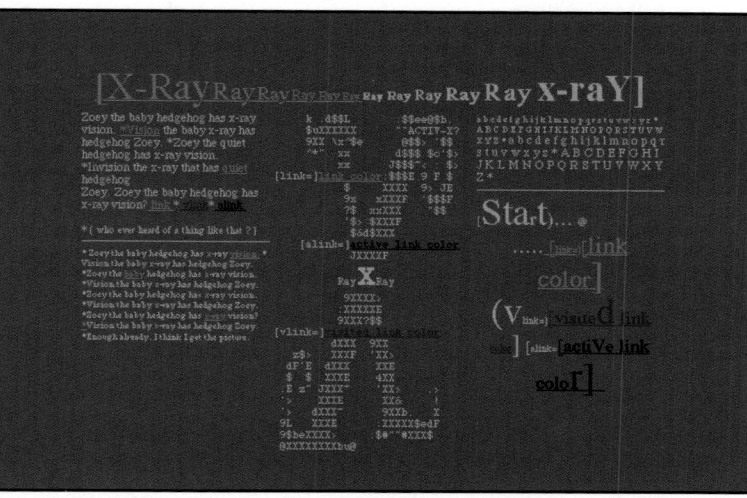

text	link	vlink	alink	bgcolor
FF9999	CC0000	663333	330000	666666
R. 255	R. 204	R. 102	R. 51	R. 102
G. 153	G. 0	G. 51	G. 0	G. 102
B. 153	B. 0	B. 51	B. 0	B. 102

g3s04sw

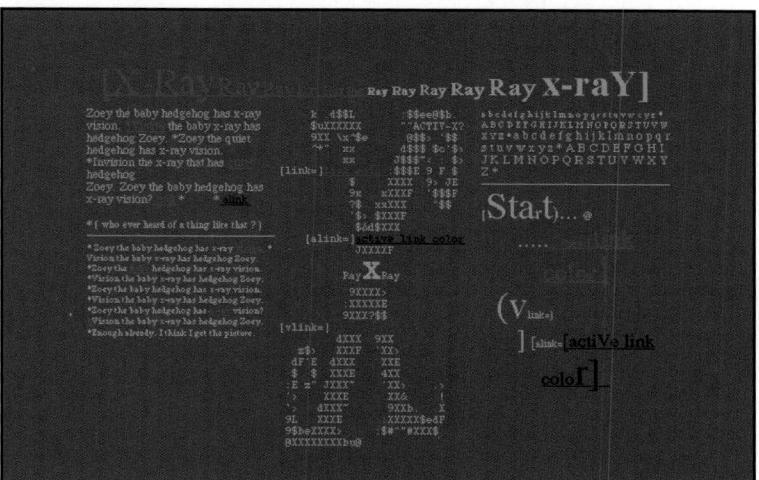
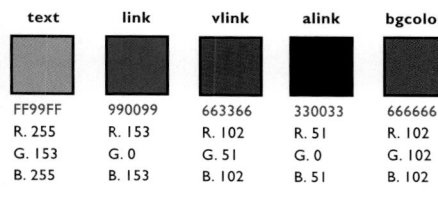
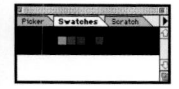
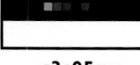

text	link	vlink	alink	bgcolor
FF99FF	990099	663366	330033	666666
R. 255	R. 153	R. 102	R. 51	R. 102
G. 153	G. 0	G. 51	G. 0	G. 102
B. 255	B. 153	B. 102	B. 51	B. 102

g3s05sw

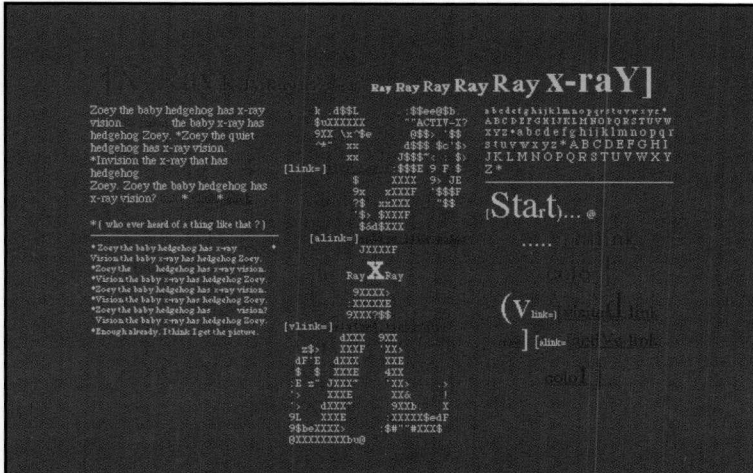
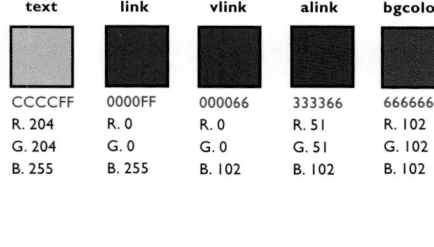
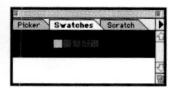

text	link	vlink	alink	bgcolor
CCCCFF	0000FF	000066	333366	666666
R. 204	R. 0	R. 0	R. 51	R. 102
G. 204	G. 0	G. 0	G. 51	G. 102
B. 255	B. 255	B. 102	B. 102	B. 102

g3s06sw

text	link	vlink	alink	bgcolor
669999	00FFFF	66CCCC	CCFFFF	333333
R. 102	R. 0	R. 51	R. 204	R. 51
G. 153	G. 255	G. 204	G. 255	G. 51
B. 153	B. 255	B. 204	B. 255	B. 51

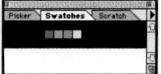

g4s01sw

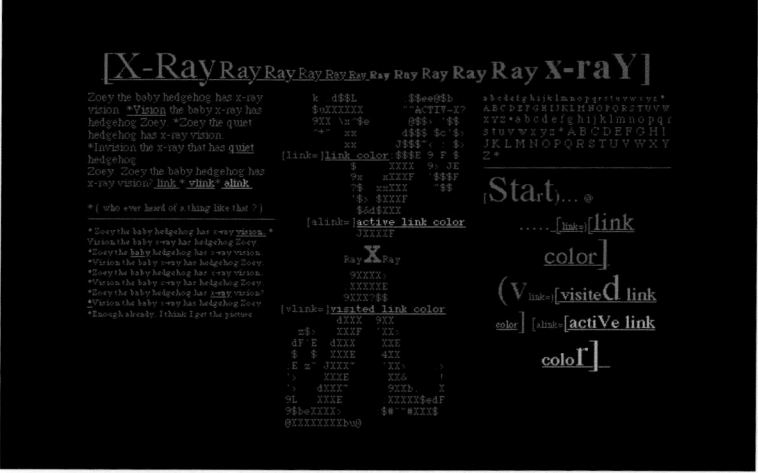

text	link	vlink	alink	bgcolor
669966	33CC33	99CC99	CCFFCC	333333
R. 102	R. 51	R. 153	R. 204	R. 51
G. 153	G. 204	G. 204	G. 255	G. 51
B. 102	B. 51	B. 153	B. 204	B. 51

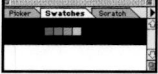

g4s02sw

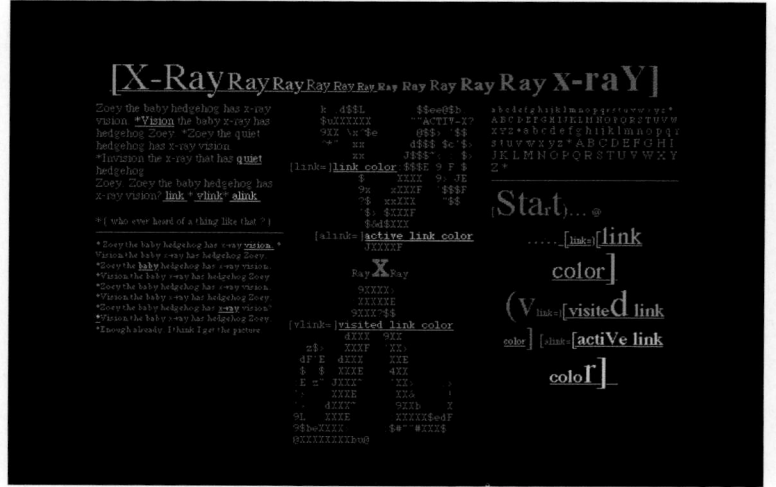

text	link	vlink	alink	bgcolor
999966	CCCC33	CCCC99	FFFFCC	333333
R. 153	R. 204	R. 204	R. 255	R. 51
G. 153	G. 204	G. 204	G. 255	G. 51
B. 102	B. 51	B. 153	B. 204	B. 51

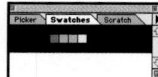

g4s03sw

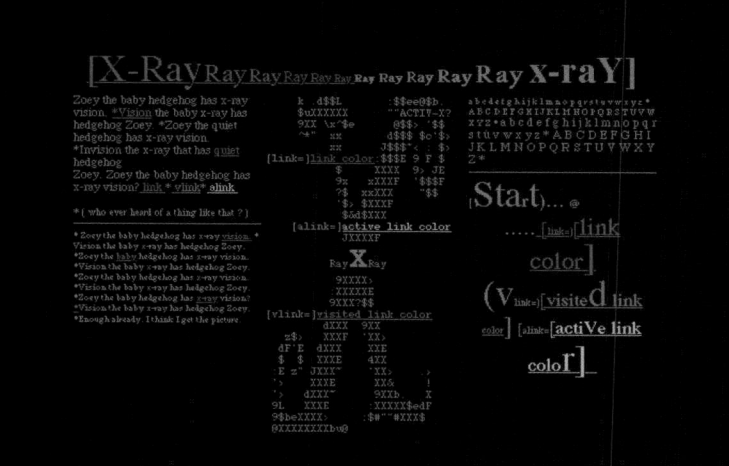

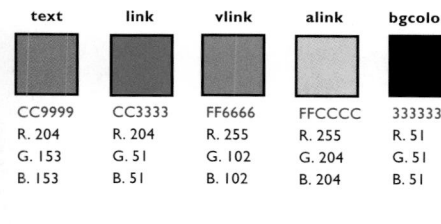

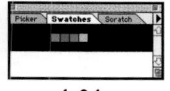

text	link	vlink	alink	bgcolor
CC9999	CC3333	FF6666	FFCCCC	333333
R. 204	R. 204	R. 255	R. 255	R. 51
G. 153	G. 51	G. 102	G. 204	G. 51
B. 153	B. 51	B. 102	B. 204	B. 51

g4s04sw

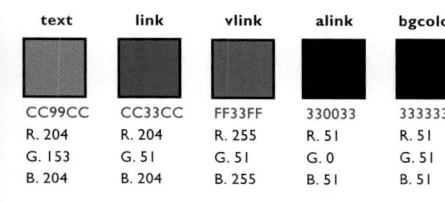

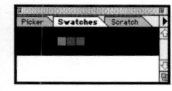

text	link	vlink	alink	bgcolor
CC99CC	CC33CC	FF33FF	330033	333333
R. 204	R. 204	R. 255	R. 51	R. 51
G. 153	G. 51	G. 51	G. 0	G. 51
B. 204	B. 204	B. 255	B. 51	B. 51

g4s05sw

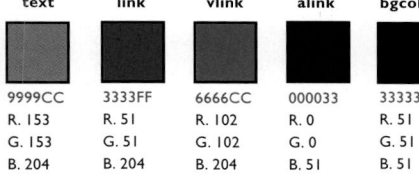

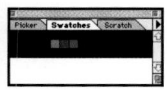

text	link	vlink	alink	bgcolor
9999CC	3333FF	6666CC	000033	333333
R. 153	R. 51	R. 102	R. 0	R. 51
G. 153	G. 51	G. 102	G. 0	G. 51
B. 204	B. 204	B. 204	B. 51	B. 51

g4s06sw

text	link	vlink	alink	bgcolor
333333	000000	999999	FFFFFF	CCCCCC
R. 51	R. 0	R. 153	R. 255	R. 204
G. 51	G. 0	G. 153	G. 255	G. 204
B. 51	B. 0	B. 153	B. 255	B. 204

g1s07sw

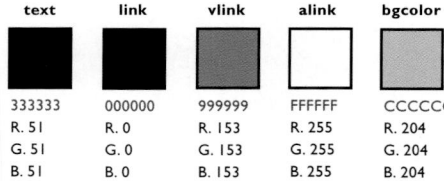

text	link	vlink	alink	bgcolor
333333	000000	666666	FFFFFF	999999
R. 51	R. 0	R. 102	R. 255	R. 153
G. 51	G. 0	G. 102	G. 255	G. 153
B. 51	B. 0	B. 102	B. 255	B. 153

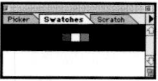

g2s07sw

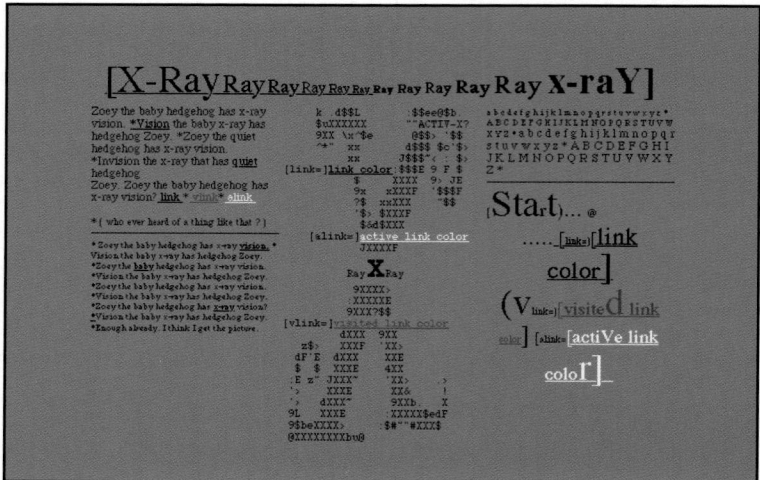

text	link	vlink	alink	bgcolor
FFFFFF	000000	999999	CCCCCC	666666
R. 255	R. 0	R. 153	R. 204	R. 102
G. 255	G. 0	G. 153	G. 204	G. 102
B. 255	B. 0	B. 153	B. 204	B. 102

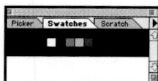

g3s07sw

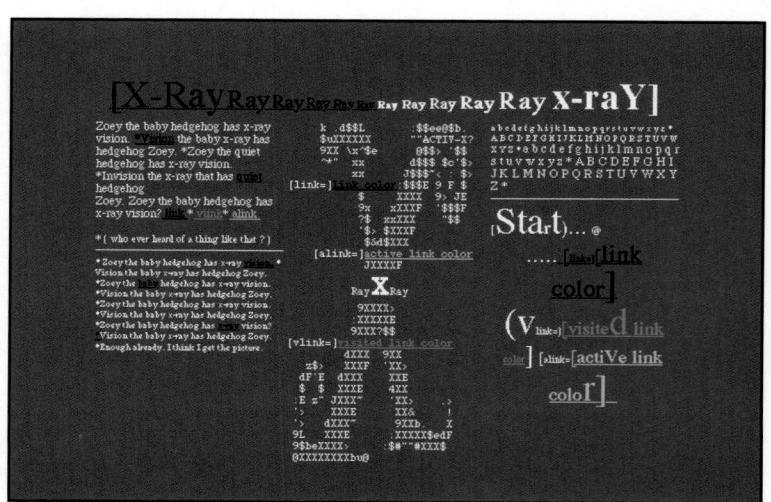

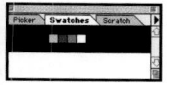

	text	link	vlink	alink	bgcolor

	CCCCCC	666666	999999	FFFFFF	333333
	R. 204	R. 102	R. 153	R. 255	R. 51
	G. 204	G. 102	G. 153	G. 255	G. 51
	B. 204	B. 102	B. 153	B. 255	B. 51

g4s07sw

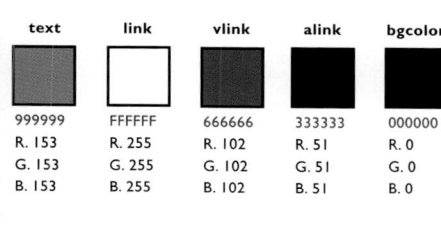

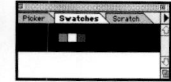

	text	link	vlink	alink	bgcolor
	999999	FFFFFF	666666	333333	000000
	R. 153	R. 255	R. 102	R. 51	R. 0
	G. 153	G. 255	G. 102	G. 51	G. 0
	B. 153	B. 255	B. 102	B. 51	B. 0

ks07sw

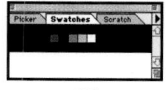

	text	link	vlink	alink	bgcolor
	666666	000000	999999	CCCCCC	FFFFFF
	R. 102	R. 0	R. 153	R. 204	R. 255
	G. 102	G. 0	G. 153	G. 204	G. 255
	B. 102	B. 0	B. 153	B. 204	B. 255

ws07sw

text	link	vlink	alink	bgcolor
996666	FF0000	663333	FF9999	FFFFFF
R. 153	R. 255	R. 102	R. 255	R. 255
G. 102	G. 0	G. 51	G. 153	G. 255
B. 102	B. 0	B. 51	B. 153	B. 255

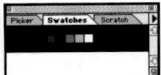

ws01sw

text	link	vlink	alink	bgcolor
996699	990099	663366	FF00FF	FFFFFF
R. 153	R. 153	R. 102	R. 255	R. 255
G. 102	G. 0	G. 51	G. 0	G. 255
B. 153	B. 153	B. 102	B. 255	B. 255

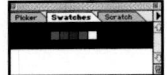

ws02sw

text	link	vlink	alink	bgcolor
666699	3333FF	333366	0000CC	FFFFFF
R. 102	R. 51	R. 51	R. 0	R. 255
G. 102	G. 51	G. 51	G. 0	G. 255
B. 153	B. 255	B. 102	B. 204	B. 255

ws03sw

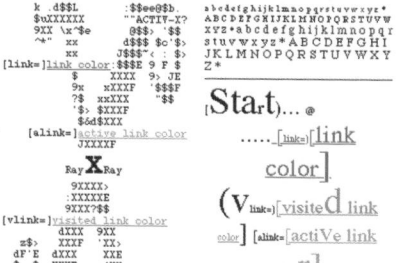

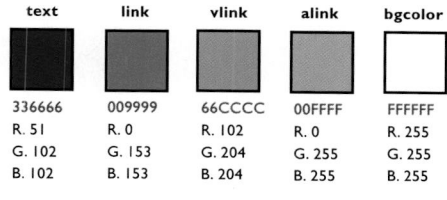

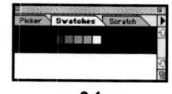

text	link	vlink	alink	bgcolor
336666	009999	66CCCC	00FFFF	FFFFFF
R. 51	R. 0	R. 102	R. 0	R. 255
G. 102	G. 153	G. 204	G. 255	G. 255
B. 102	B. 153	B. 204	B. 255	B. 255

ws04sw

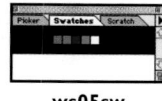

text	link	vlink	alink	bgcolor
669966	009900	336633	00FF00	FFFFFF
R. 102	R. 0	R. 51	R. 0	R. 255
G. 153	G. 153	G. 102	G. 255	G. 255
B. 102	B. 0	B. 51	B. 0	B. 255

ws05sw

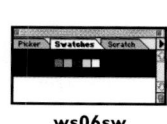

text	link	vlink	alink	bgcolor
999966	CCCC00	666633	FFFF66	FFFFFF
R. 153	R. 204	R. 102	R. 255	R. 255
G. 153	G. 204	G. 102	G. 255	G. 255
B. 102	B. 0	B. 51	B. 102	B. 255

ws06sw

ODDBALL

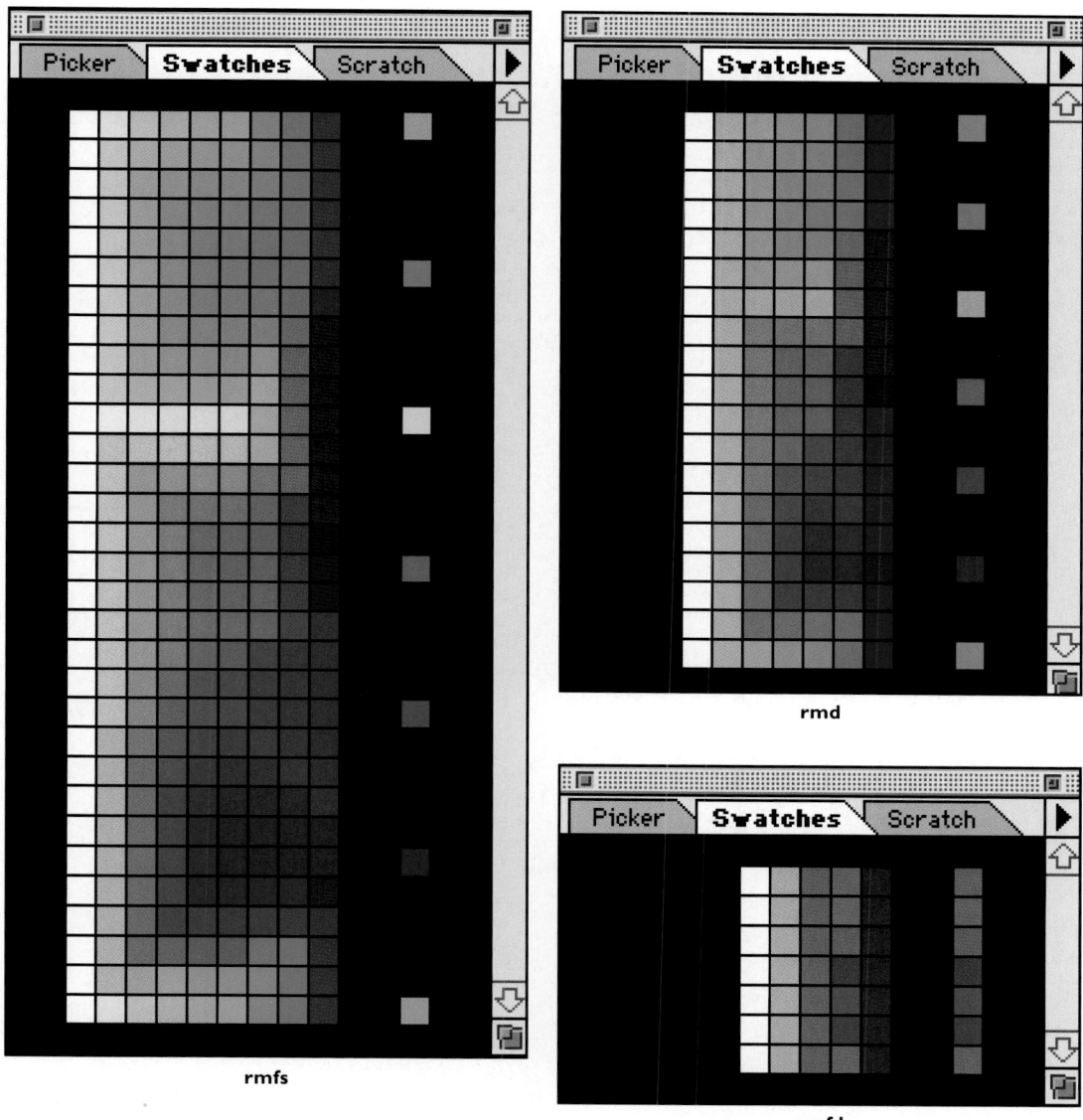

rmfs

rmd

rmfd

The oddball swatches compose all the colors of the cube, organized in different ways. Load these palettes when you don't have an exact color scheme in mind—you'll find they help organize the colors into workable relationships.

web graphics >

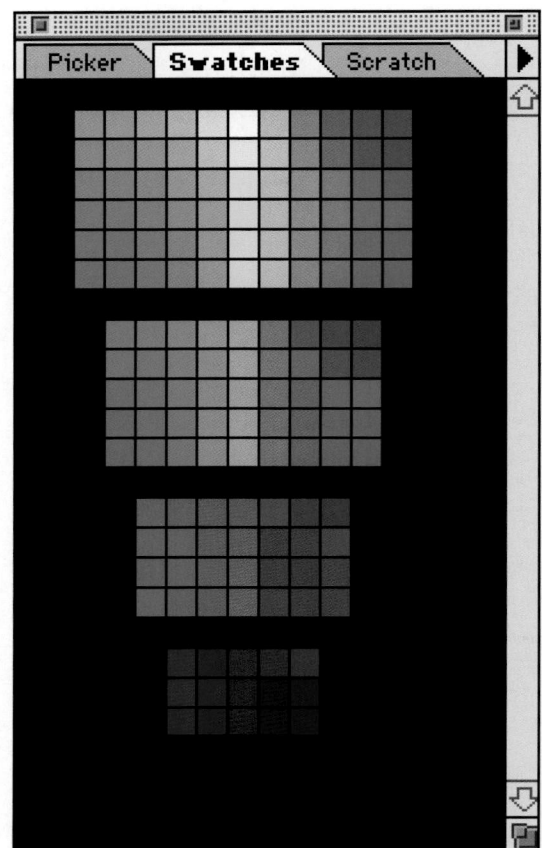

odd22

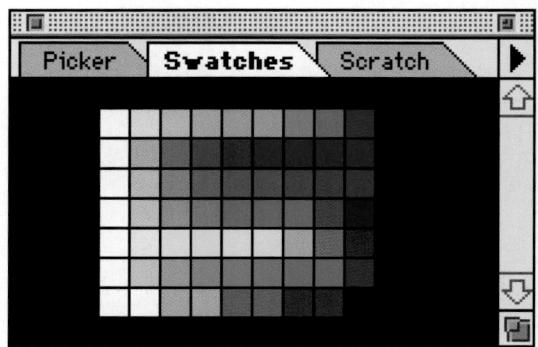

odd06

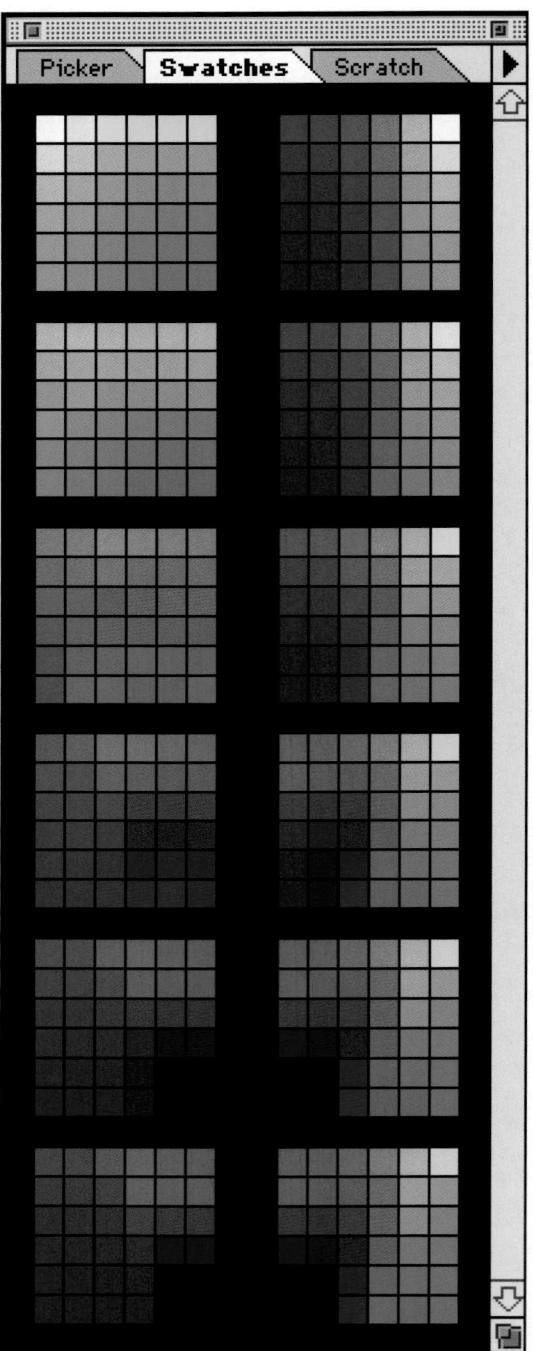

odd05

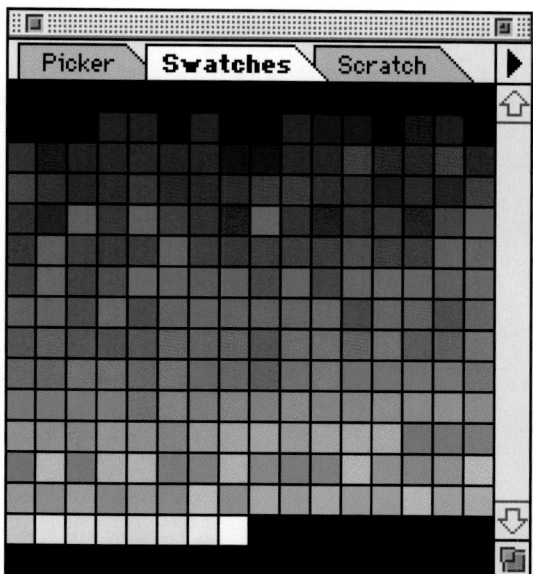

odd01

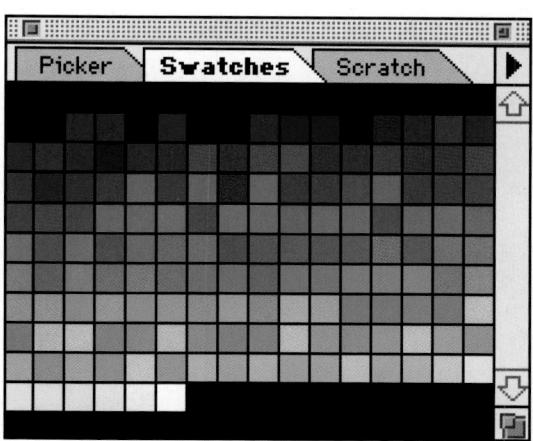

odd03

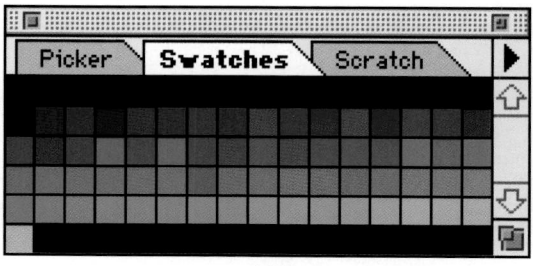

odd02

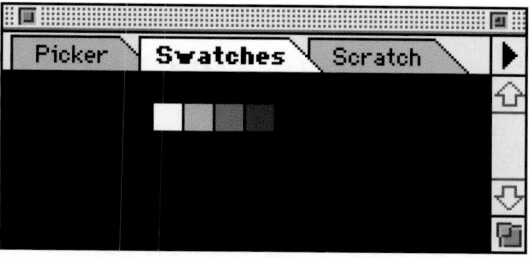

odd04

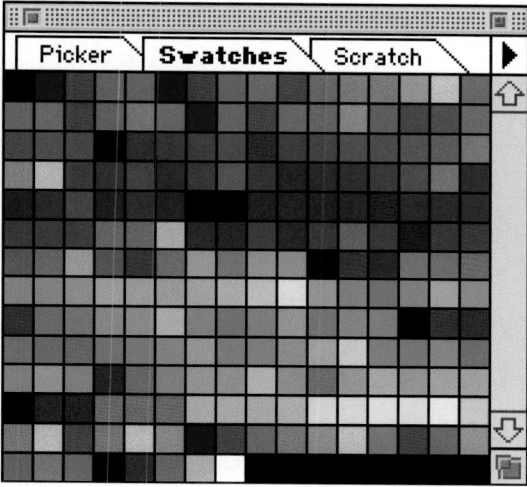

huesw

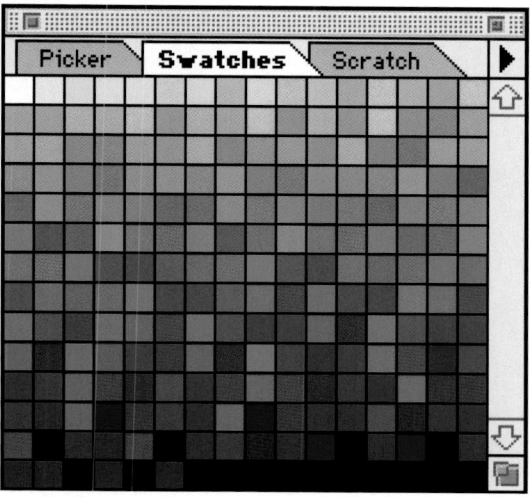

lumsw

The **huesw** and **lumsw** files match the browser-safe color charts at the end of Chapter 3, "Browser-Safe Color."

Analagous

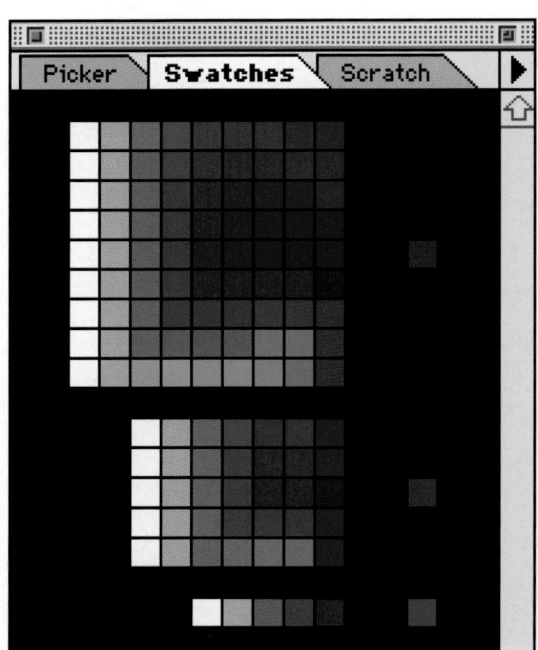
ba

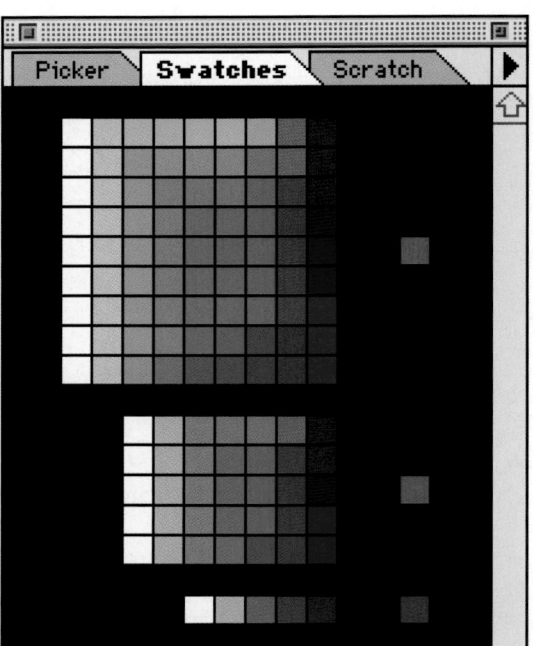
ra

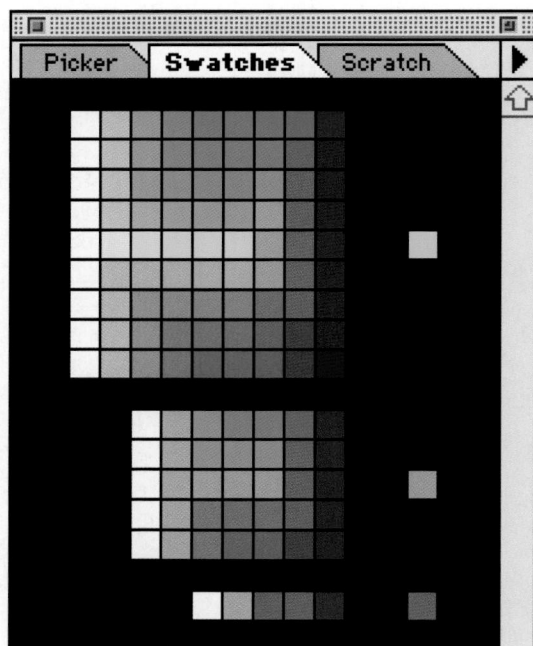
ya

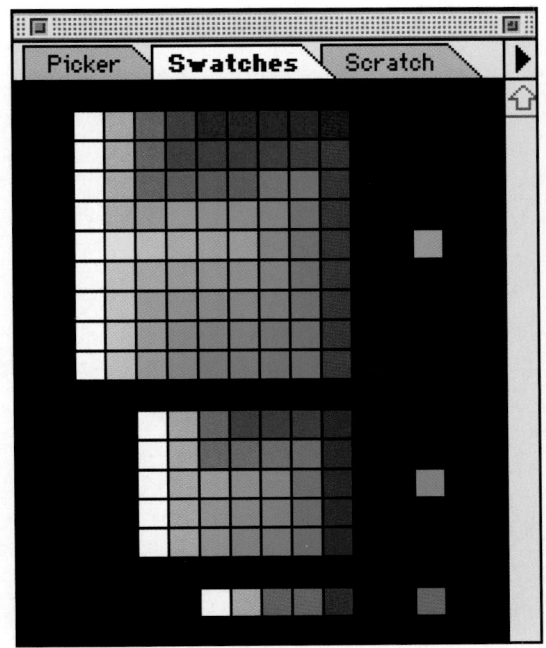

ca

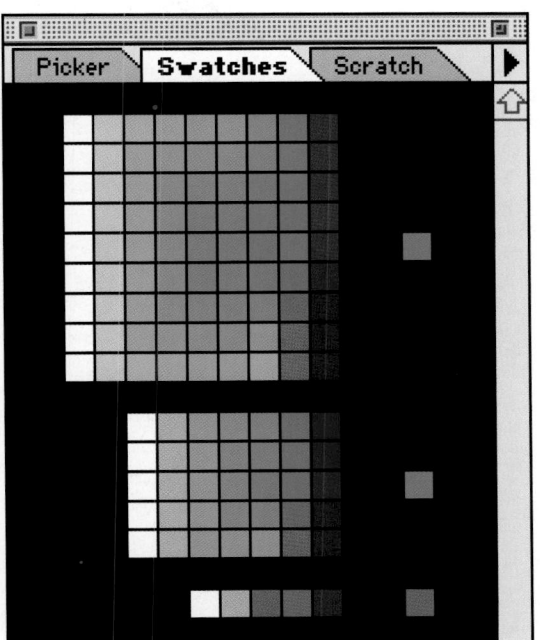

ga

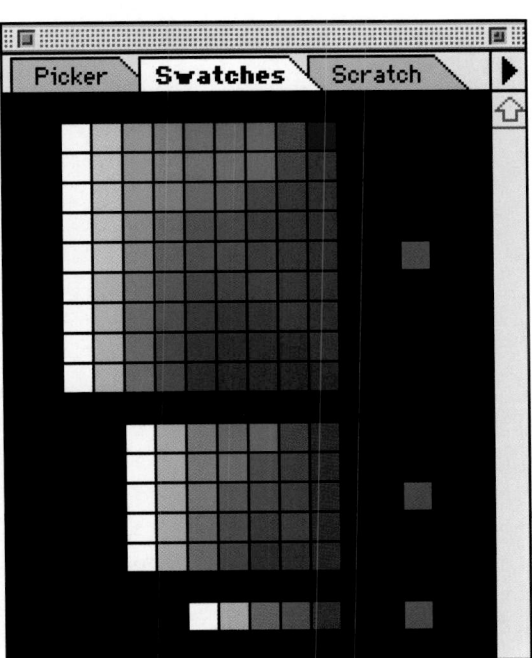

ma

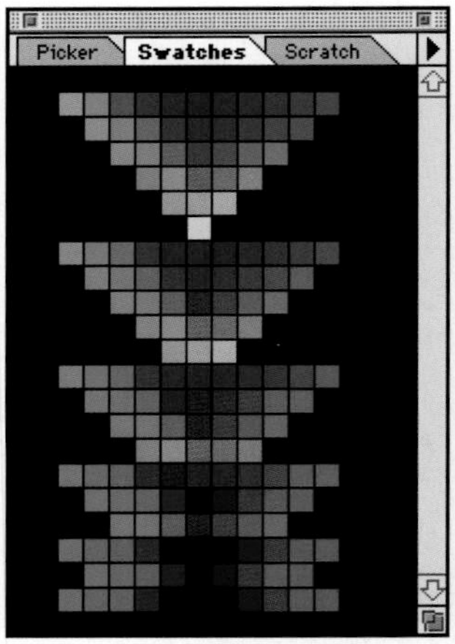

odd09

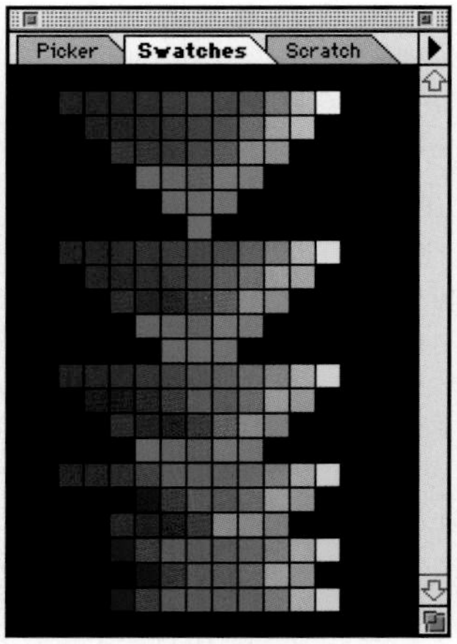

odd15

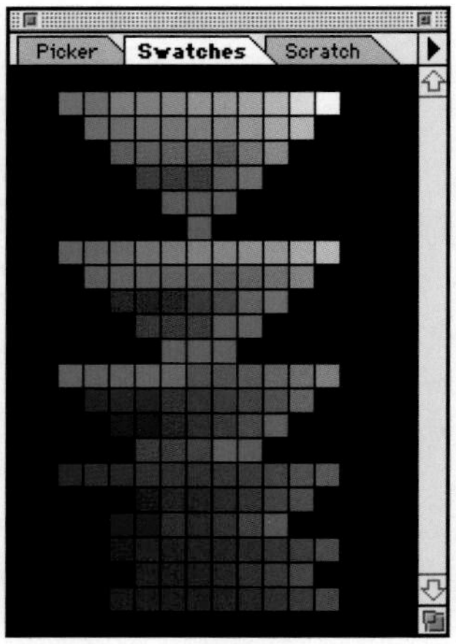

odd11

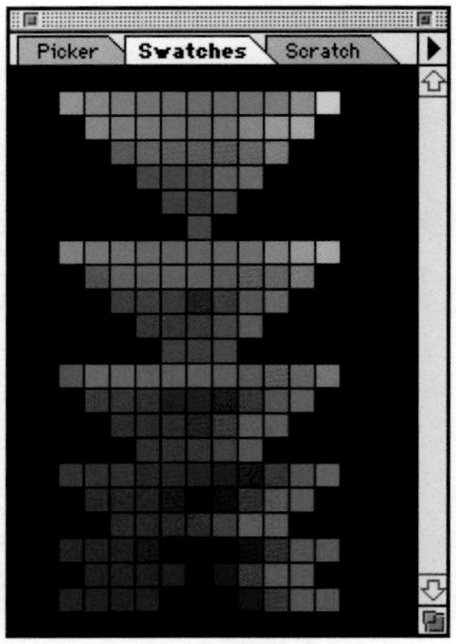

odd09

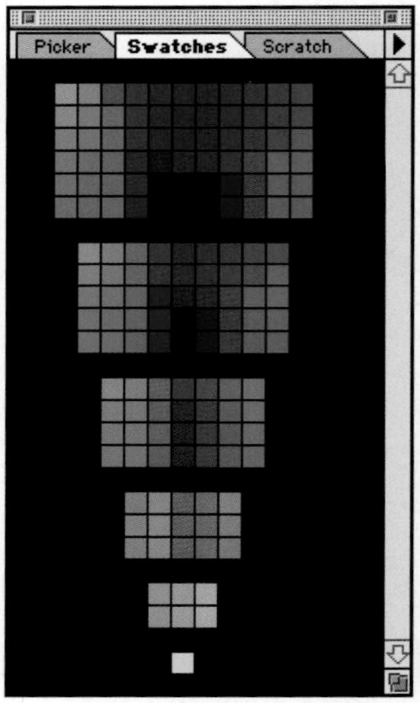

odd18

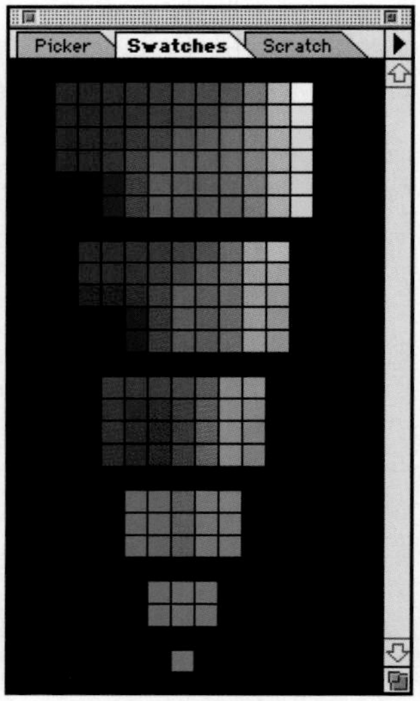

odd16

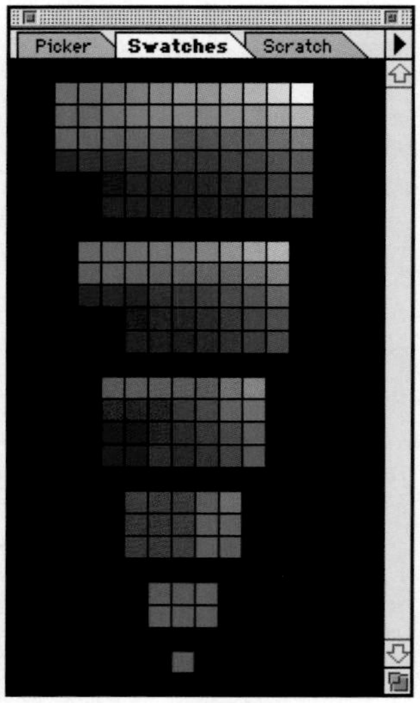

odd12

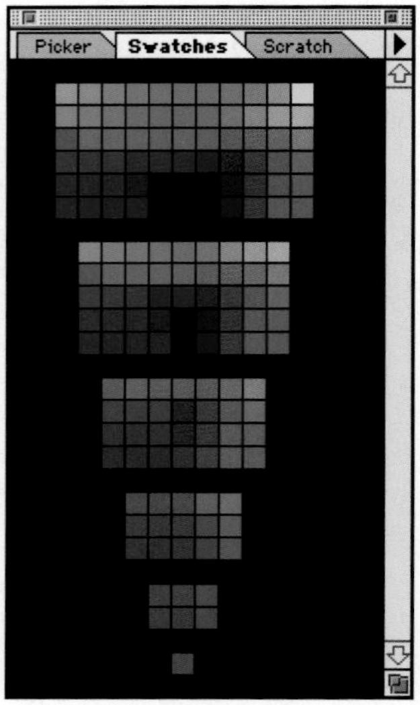

odd10

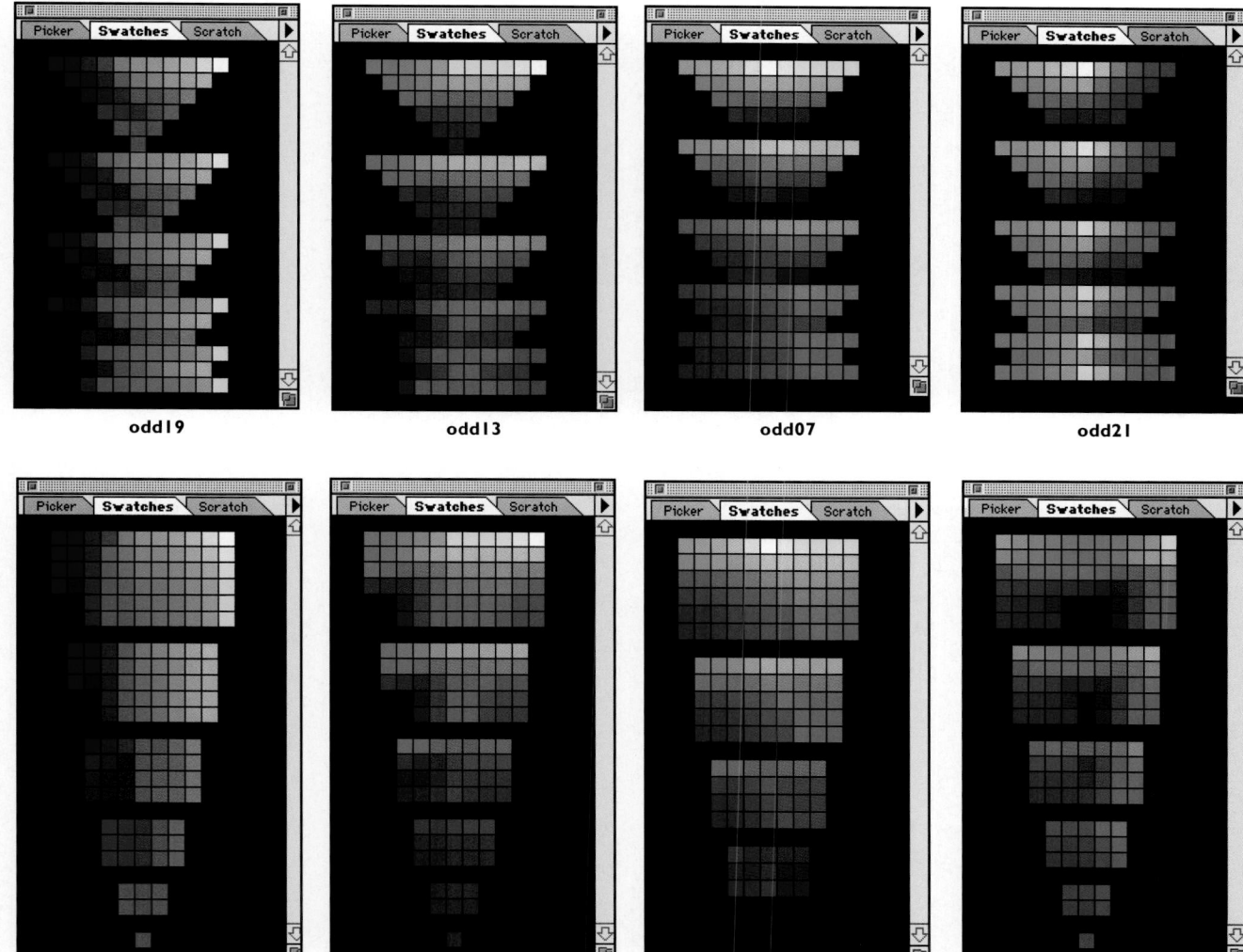

odd19   odd13   odd07   odd21

odd20   odd14   odd08   odd10

Clipart

The browser-safe tiles, buttons, and rules included in this chapter are located on the *Coloring Web Graphics* CD-rom inside the CLIPART folder.

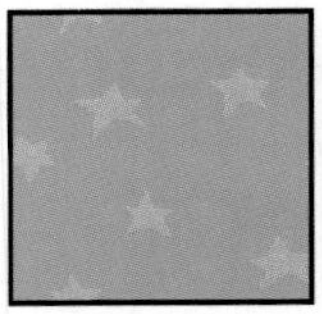

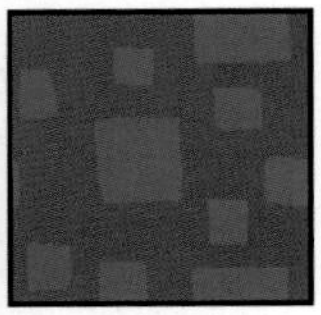

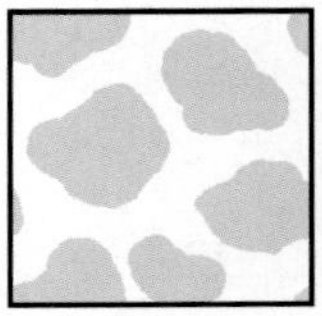

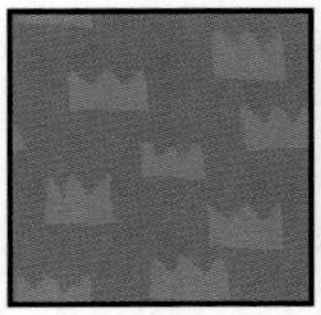

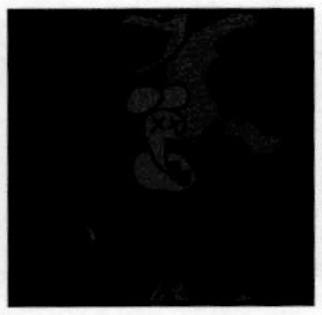

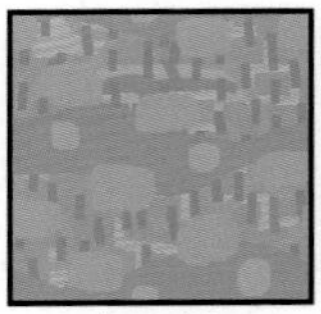

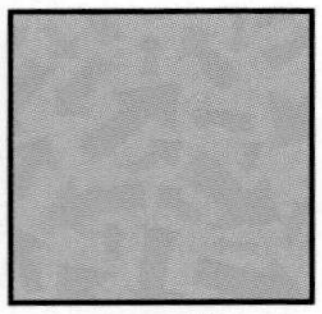

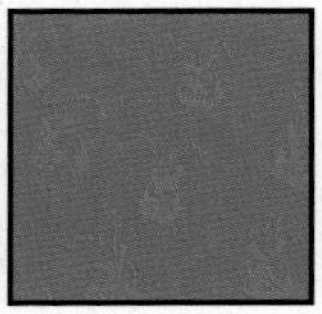

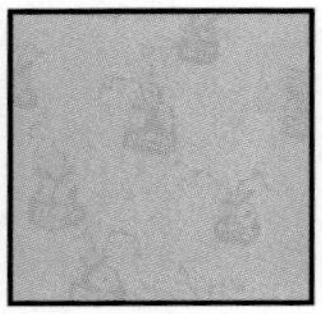

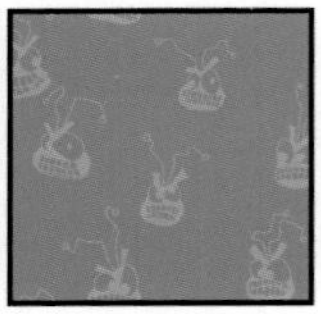

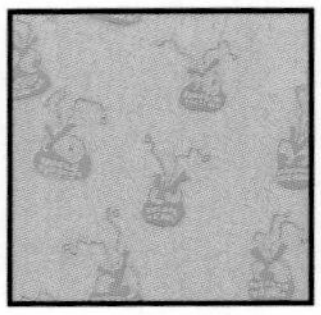

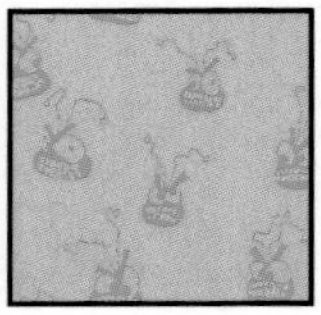

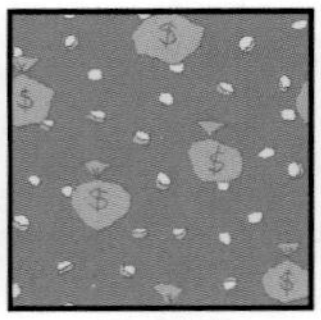

bruce01	bruce02	bruce03	bruce04	bruce05	bruce06	bruce07	bruce08
bruce17	bruce18	bruce19	bruce20	bruce21	bruce22	bruce23	bruce24
 bruce33	bruce34	bruce35	bruce36	bruce37	bruce38	bruce39	bruce40
bruce49	bruce50	bruce51	bruce52	bruce53	bruce54	bruce55	bruce56
 bruce65	bruce66	bruce67	bruce68	bruce69	bruce70	bruce71	bruce72

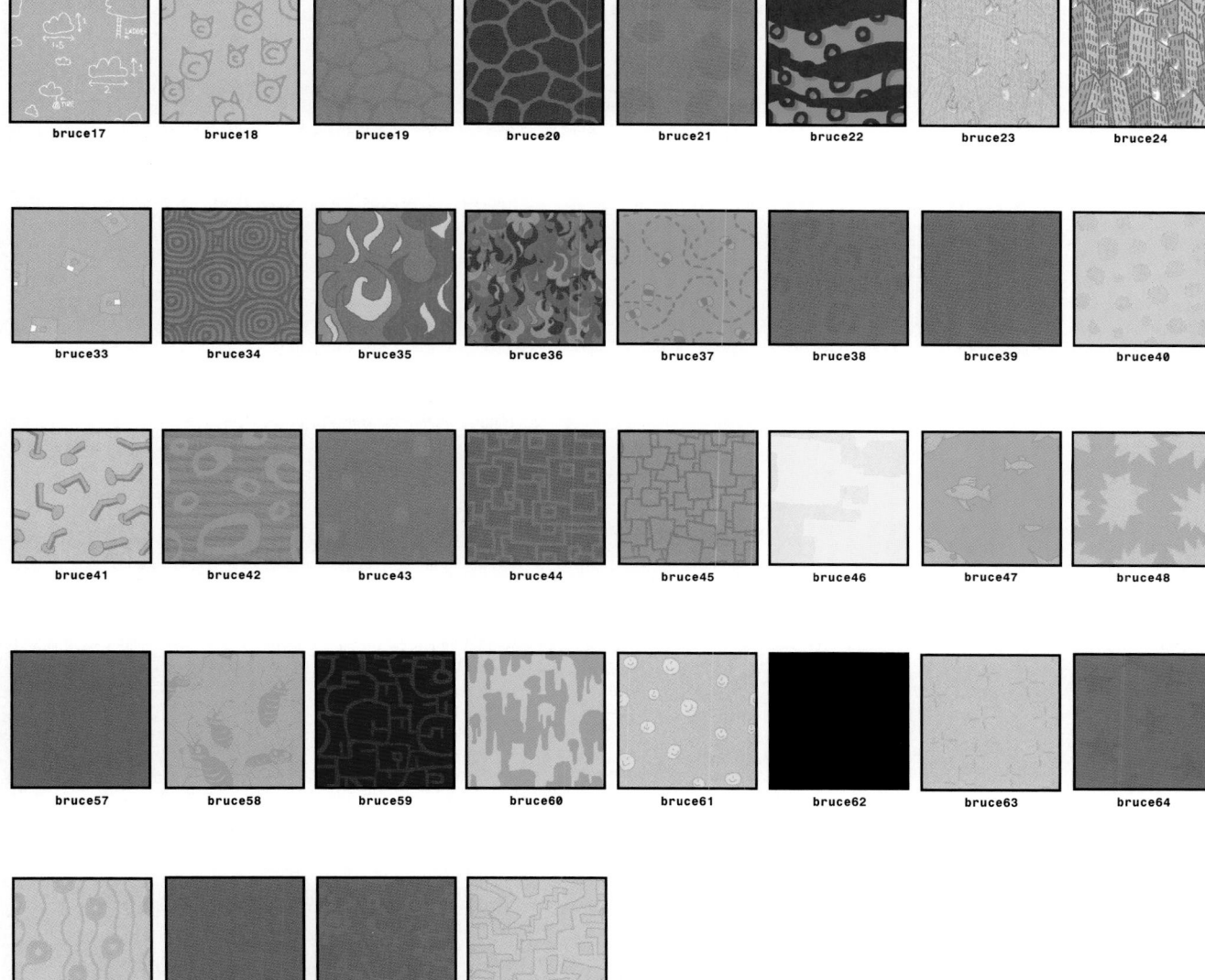

| bruce17 | bruce18 | bruce19 | bruce20 | bruce21 | bruce22 | bruce23 | bruce24 |

| bruce33 | bruce34 | bruce35 | bruce36 | bruce37 | bruce38 | bruce39 | bruce40 |

| bruce41 | bruce42 | bruce43 | bruce44 | bruce45 | bruce46 | bruce47 | bruce48 |

| bruce57 | bruce58 | bruce59 | bruce60 | bruce61 | bruce62 | bruce63 | bruce64 |

| bruce73 | bruce74 | bruce75 | bruce76 |

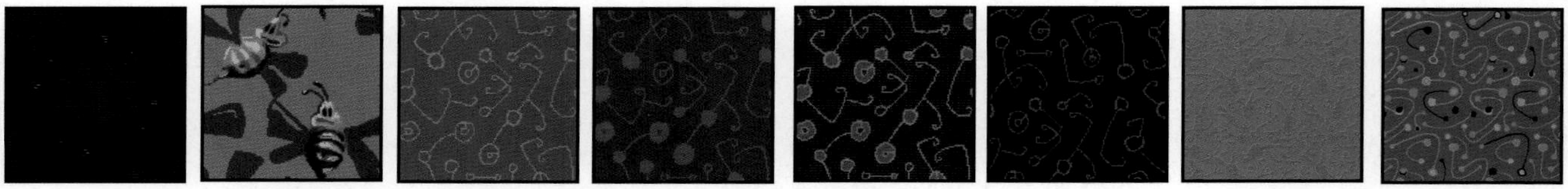

donb01	donb02	donb03	donb04	donb05	donb06	donb07	donb08
donb17	donb18	donb19	donb20	donb21	donb22	donb23	donb24
donb33	donb34	donb35	donb36	donb37	donb38	donb39	donb40
donb49	donb50	donb51	donb52	donb53	donb54	donb55	donb56

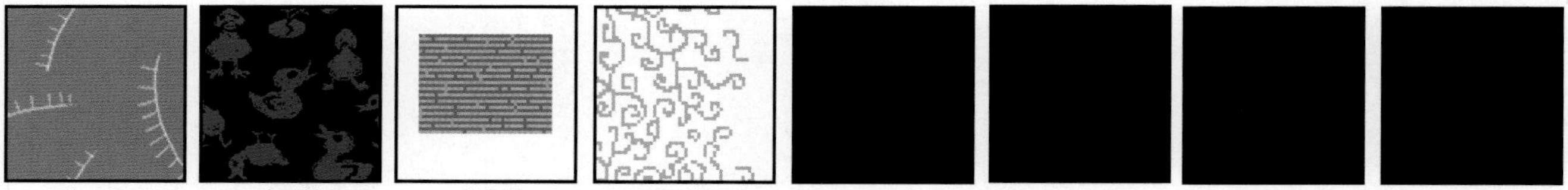

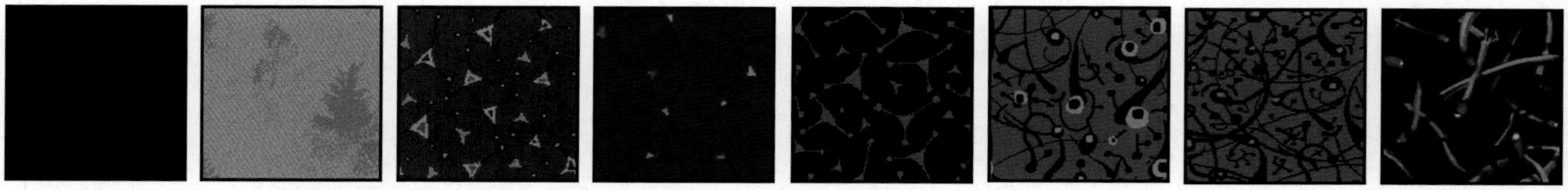

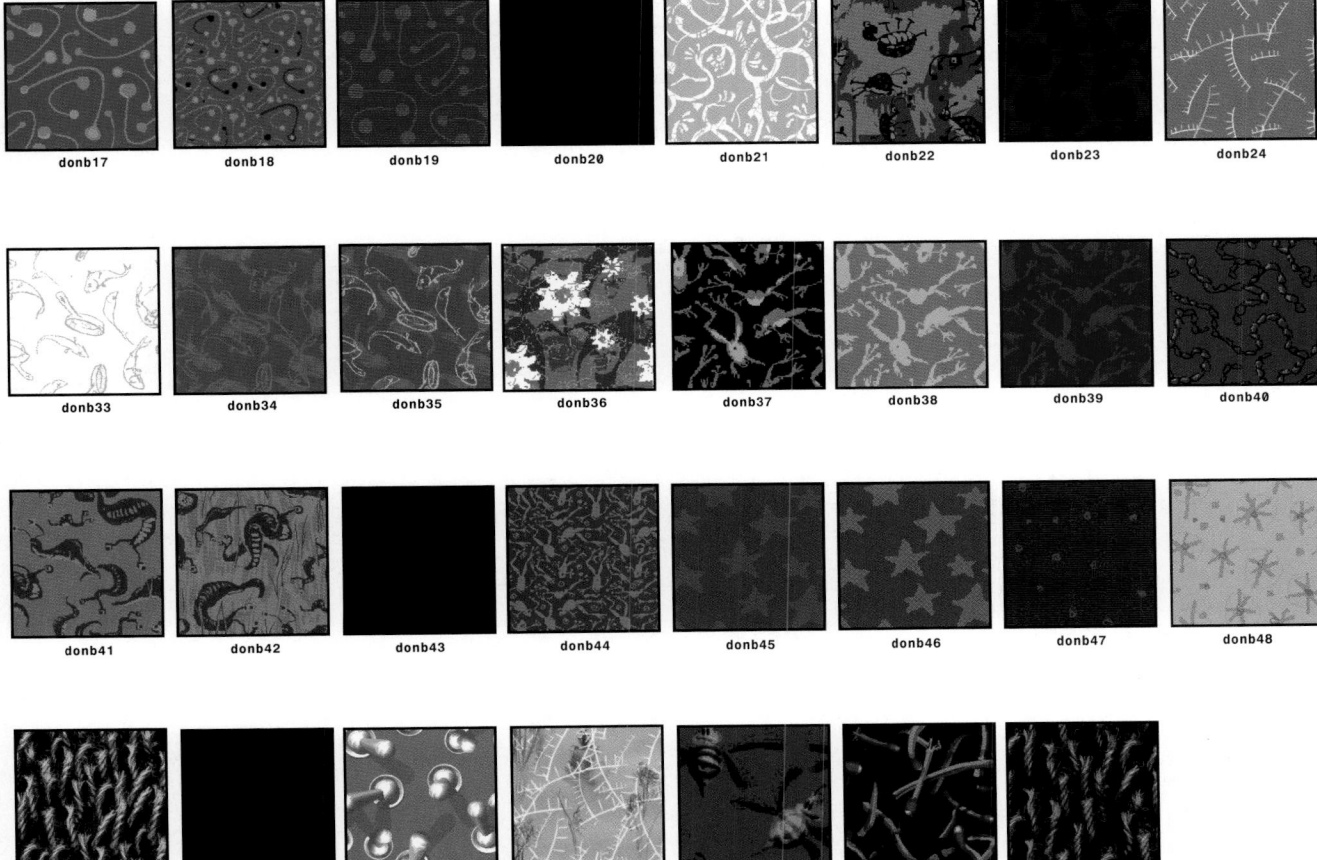

donb17 donb18 donb19 donb20 donb21 donb22 donb23 donb24

donb33 donb34 donb35 donb36 donb37 donb38 donb39 donb40

donb41 donb42 donb43 donb44 donb45 donb46 donb47 donb48

donb57 donb58 donb59 donb60 donb61 donb62 donb63

web graphics

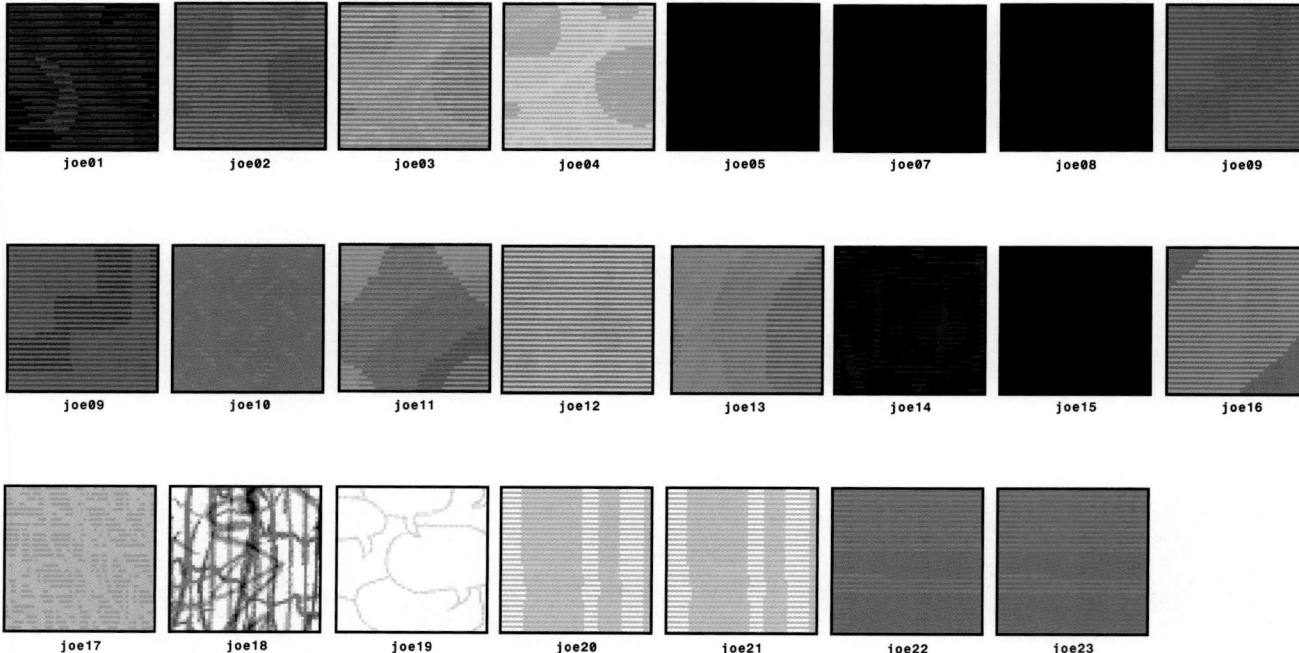

joe01 joe02 joe03 joe04 joe05 joe07 joe08 joe09

joe09 joe10 joe11 joe12 joe13 joe14 joe15 joe16

joe17 joe18 joe19 joe20 joe21 joe22 joe23

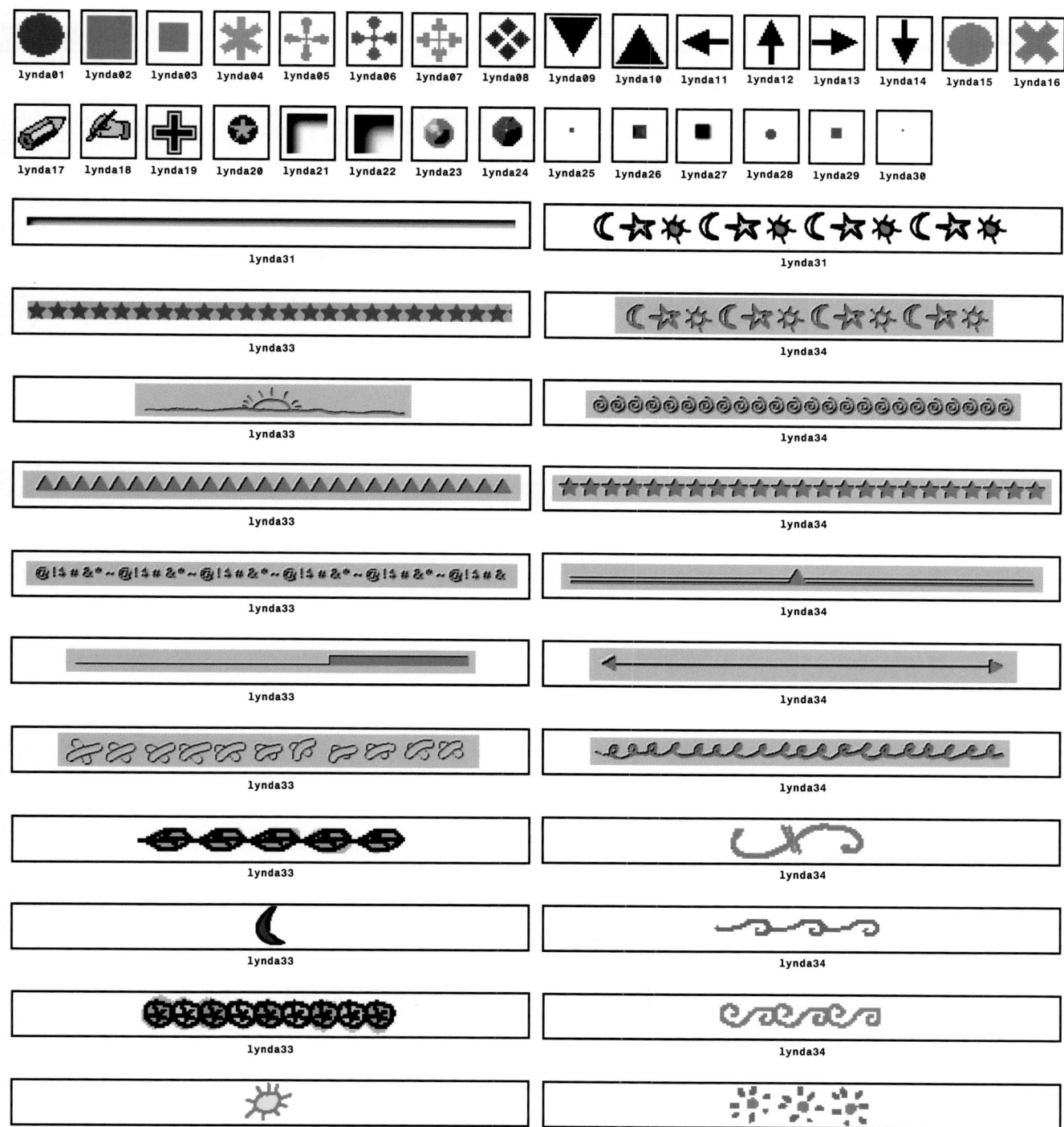

lynda01 lynda02 lynda03 lynda04 lynda05 lynda06 lynda07 lynda08 lynda09 lynda10 lynda11 lynda12 lynda13 lynda14 lynda15 lynda16

lynda17 lynda18 lynda19 lynda20 lynda21 lynda22 lynda23 lynda24 lynda25 lynda26 lynda27 lynda28 lynda29 lynda30

lynda31

lynda31

lynda33

lynda34

lynda33

lynda34

lynda33

lynda34

lynda33

lynda34

lynda33

lynda34

lynda33

lynda34

lynda33

lynda34

lynda33

lynda34

lynda33

lynda34

lynda33

lynda34

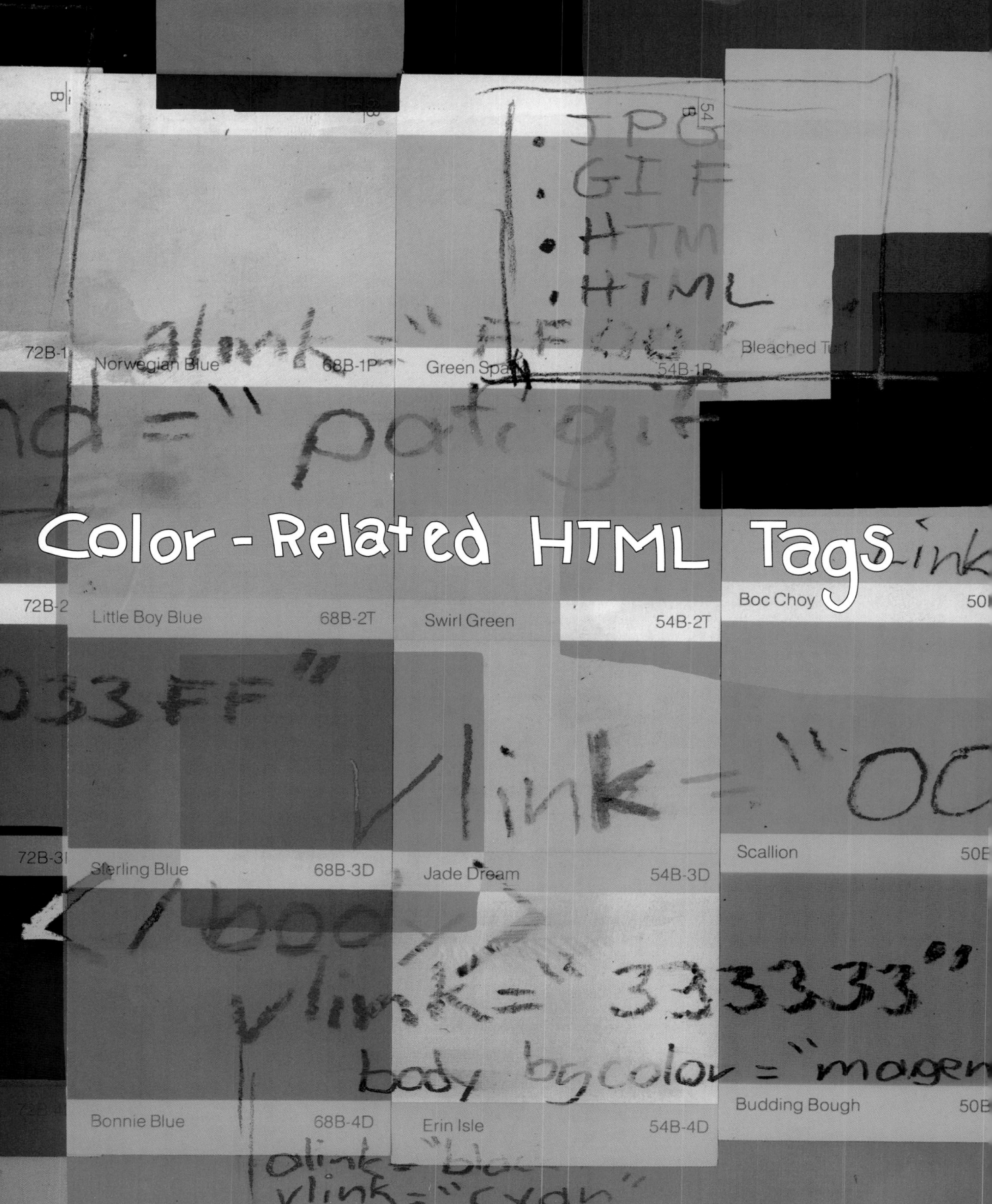

Color-Related HTML Tags

Color-Related HTML Tags

Now for the fun (?) part. How does this all this come together on a Web page? Web pages are written in a low-level programming language called HTML (**H**yper**T**ext **M**arkup **L**anguage). You can write HTML code in a standard text editor, dedicated HTML editor, or WYSIWYG (**W**hat**Y**ou**S**ee**I**s**W**hat**Y**ou**G**et) HTML editor. Some WYSIWYG editors allow you to edit HTML source code directly, and some do not. Because some of the color tags discussed in this chapter may not be supported by WYSIWYG editors, you may have to edit your files later to add the foreign HTML tags. You can always begin a page in a WYSIWYG editor and then later edit the source code in a text editor in order to add additional tags.

The Basic Structure of HTML

HTML code has a basic structure, which dictates where certain markup tags belong. Here is the most basic HTML structure:

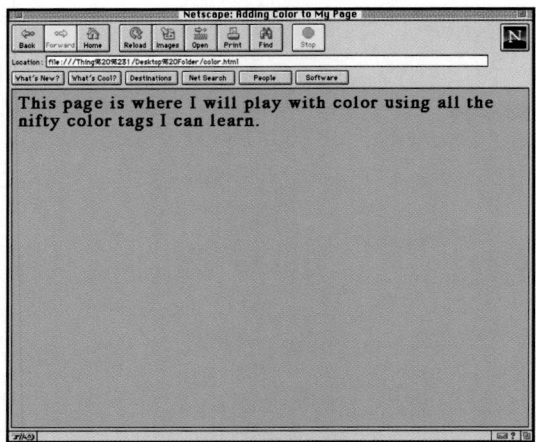

This is a basic Web page with no color added.

1 `<HTML>`
2 `<HEAD>`
3 `<TITLE>Adding Color to My Page</TITLE>`
`</HEAD>`
4 `<BODY>`
5 `<H1>This page is where I will play with color using all the nifty color tags I can learn. </H1>`
`</BODY>`
`</HTML>`

1 `<HMTL>, </HTML>` An HTML document must open and close with this identifying tag.

2 `<HEAD>,</HEAD>` Header information, such as the title of the document, must open and close with this tag.

3 `<TITLE>, </TITLE>` is where you name the title of your HTML document. If you leave this undone, the document will appear as Untitled in Web browsers.

4 `<BODY>,</BODY>` The body of the document, such as text, images, links, and multimedia content, goes in between these opening and closing tags.

5 `<H1>, </H1>` A header tag for first-level headers. In some browsers, this causes the text contained within it to be sized larger than normal text and to be bold.

Adding Color to a Web Page

To add variety within HTML, you include special tags called attributes. Attributes modify the existing material; applying italic to text is an example of using an attribute. When used in HTML, attributes are nested within their parent tags. So, to add color to the body text, you would place the attribute within the <BODY> tag. To add color to the page in our example, you would add the following HTML code:

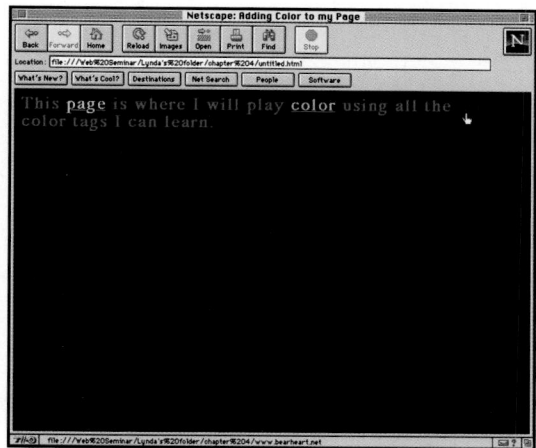

Color was added to this page using hexadecimal RGB values and attributes of BGCOLOR and TEXT placed within the <BODY> tag.

1 BGCOLOR, LINK, VLINK, ALINK, and TEXT are attributes that are nested inside the <BODY> tag. Here's a list of possible attributes that relate to color within the <BODY> tag:

BGCOLOR	Color of the background of the Web page
TEXT	Color of the text
LINK	Color of the link
VLINK	Color of the link after it has been visited
ALINK	Color of the active link while the mouse is depressed on a link

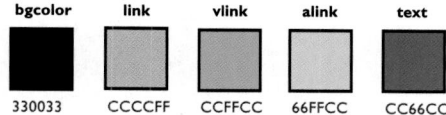

Each of these color chips represents the hexadecimal color used in the example on this page.

```
<HTML>
<HEAD>
<TITLE>Adding Color to my Page</TITLE>
</HEAD>
<BODY BGCOLOR="330033"
LINK="ccccff"
VLINK="ccffcc"
ALINK="66ffcc"
TEXT="cc66cc">
<H1>
This<A
HREF="http://www.lynda.com/">page</A>
is where I will play
<A HREF="http://color.com/">color</A>
using all the
<A HREF="www.bearheart.net">nifty </A>
color tags I can learn.
</H1>
</BODY>
</HTML>
```
1 (marker at `</HEAD>` line)

Using Color Names Instead of Hex

You don't have to use hexadecimal numbers inside the color attribute tags; you can use words, too. Here's a list of color names that will work in Netscape.

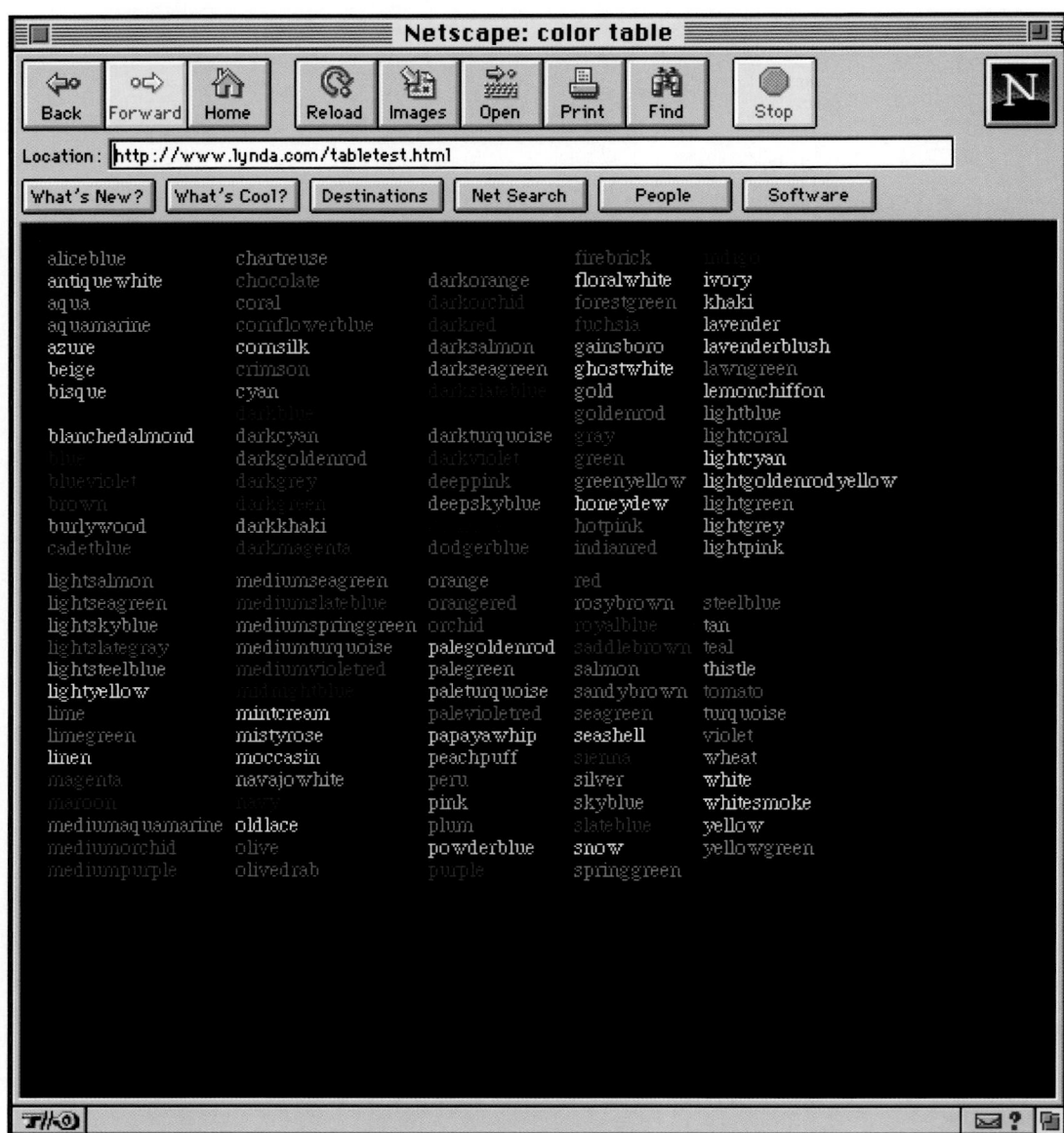

Using any of the names inside the color attribute tags will generate colored text in Netscape.

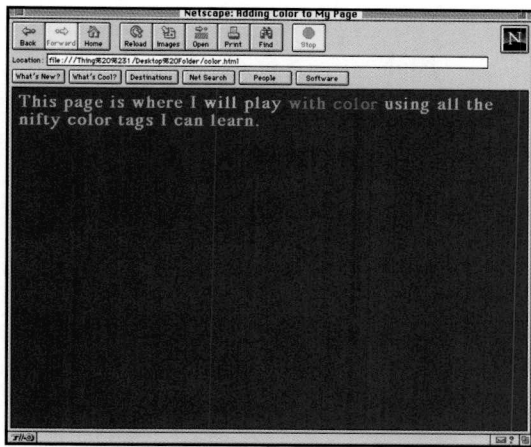

Here's an example of using color names instead of hexadecimal values to define color.

```
<HTML>
<HEAD>
<TITLE>Adding Color to My Page</TITLE>
</HEAD>
<BODY BGCOLOR="lightgreen"
TEXT="darkgreen">
<H1>This page is where I will play
with color using all the nifty color
tags I can learn.
</H1>
</BODY>
</HTML>
```

1 You don't have to use hexadecimal numbers to define color—certain color names work as well. Here's an example of using "lightgreen" and "darkgreen" as color names within the <BODY> tag.

Warning: Color Names Are Rarely Browser Safe

Here are charts showing how the color names translate to hex values. Notice how very few of them are browser safe. Since browsers, when viewed in 256 colors, will convert the color names to their own palettes on the fly, we also show a column of numbers that refers to how the browser-safe colors round up or down in a 256-color environment. In some cases the colors round off differently on Macs and PCs. The few existing browser-safe colors are highlighted as well. Note: for the purpose of this demonstration, we have chosen the abbreviation "B-S" to represent the term browser-safe.

B-S	Color Name	HEX 24-bit Mac/PC	256 MAC	256 PC
	aliceblue	F0F8FF	99CC00	99CC00
	antiquewhite	FAEBD7	FFFFCC	FFFFCC
■	**aqua**	**00FFFF**	**00FFFF**	**00FFFF**
	aquamarine	7FFFD4	66FFCC	66FFCC
	azure	F0FFFF	FFFFFF	FFFFFF
	beige	F5F5DC	FFFFCC	FFFFCC
	bisque	FFE4C4	FFFFCC	FFCCCC
■	**black**	**000000**	**000000**	**000000**
	blanchedalmond	FFEBCD	FFFFCC	FFFFCC
■	**blue**	**0000FF**	**0000FF**	**0000FF**
	blueviolet	8A2BE2	9933FF	9933CC
	brown	A52A2A	993333	993333
	burlywood	DEB887	CCCC99	CCCC99
	cadetblue	5F9EA0	669999	669999
	chartreuse	7FFF00	66FF00	66FF00
	chocolate	D2691E	CC6600	CC6633
	coral	FF7F50	FF6666	FF6666
	cornflowerblue	6495ED	6699FF	6699FF
	cornsilk	FFF8DC	FFFFCC	FFFFCC
	crimson	DC143C	CC0033	CC0033
■	**cyan**	**00FFFF**	**00FFFF**	**00FFFF**
	darkblue	00008B	000099	000099
	darkcyan	008B8B	009999	009999
	darkgoldenrod	B8860B	CC9900	CC9900
	darkgray	A9A9A9	CC00FF	CC00CC
	darkgreen	006400	006600	006600
	darkkhaki	BDB76B	CCCC66	CCCC66
	darkmagenta	8B008B	990099	990099
	darkolivegreen	556B2F	666633	666633
	darkorange	FF8C00	FF9900	FF9900
	darkorchid	9932CC	9933CC	9933CC
	darkred	8B0000	990000	990000
	darksalmon	E9967A	FF9966	FF9966
	darkseagreen	8FBC8F	99CC99	99CC99
	darkslateblue	483D8B	333399	333399
	darkslategray	2F4F4F	333333	336666
	darkturquoise	00CED1	00CCCC	00CCCC

B-S	Color Name	HEX 24-bit Mac/PC	256 MAC	256 PC
	darkviolet	9400D3	9900CC	9900CC
	deeppink	FF1493	FF0099	FF0099
	deepskyblue	00BFFF	00CCFF	00CCFF
	dimgray	696969	666666	666666
	dodgerblue	1E90FF	0099FF	3399FF
	firebrick	B22222	CC3333	993333
	floralwhite	FFFAF0	FFFFFF	FFFFFF
	forestgreen	228B22	339933	339933
■	**fuchsia**	**FF00FF**	**FF00FF**	**FF00FF**
	gainsboro	DCDCDC	CCCCCC	CCCCCC
	ghostwhite	F8F8FF	FFFFFF	FFFFFF
	gold	FFD700	FFCC00	FFCC00
	goldenrod	DAA520	CC9933	CC9933
	gray	808080	999999	999999
	green	008000	009900	009900
	greenyellow	ADFF2F	99FF33	99FF33
	honeydew	F0FFF0	FFFFFF	FFFFFF
	hotpink	FF69B4	FF66CC	FF66CC
	indianred	CD5C5C	CC6666	CC6666
	indigo	4B0082	330099	330099
	ivory	FFFFF0	FFFFFF	FFFFFF
	khaki	F0E68C	FFFF99	FFFF99
	lavender	E6E6FA	FFFFFF	FFFFFF
	lavenderblush	FFF0F5	FFFFFF	FFFFFF
	lawngreen	7CFC00	66FF00	66FF00
	lemonchiffon	FFFACD	FFFFCC	FFFFCC
	lightblue	ADD8E6	99CCFF	99CCFF
	lightcoral	F08080	FF9999	FF9999
	lightcyan	E0FFFF	FFFFFF	CCFFFF
	lightgoldenrodyellow	FAFAD2	FFFFCC	FFFFCC
	lightgreen	90EE90	99FF99	99FF99
	lightgrey	D3D3D3	CCCCCC	CCCCCC
	lightpink	FFB6C1	FFCCCC	FFCCCC
	lightsalmon	FFA07A	FF9966	FF9966
	lightseagreen	20B2AA	33CC99	339999
	lightskyblue	87CEFA	99CCFF	99CCFF
	lightslategray	778899	669999	669999

B-S	Color Name	HEX 24-bit Mac/PC	256 MAC	256 PC
	lightsteelblue	B0C4DE	CCCCCC	99CCCC
	lightyellow	FFFFE0	FFFFFF	FFFFFF
■	**lime**	**00FF00**	**00FF00**	**00FF00**
	limegreen	32CD32	33CC33	33CC33
	linen	FAF0E6	FFFFFF	FFFFFF
■	**magenta**	**FF00FF**	**FF00FF**	**FF00FF**
	maroon	800000	990000	990000
	mediumaquamarine	66CDAA	66CC99	66CC99
	mediumblue	0000CD	0000CC	0000CC
	mediumorchid	BA55D3	CC66CC	CC66CC
	mediumpurple	9370DB	9966CC	9966CC
	mediumseagreen	3CB371	33CC66	33CC66
	mediumslateblue	7B68EE	6666FF	6666FF
	mediumspringgreen	00FA9A	00FF99	00FF99
	mediumturquoise	48D1CC	33CCCC	33CCCC
	mediumvioletred	C71585	CC0099	CC0099
	midnightblue	191970	000066	000066
	mintcream	F5FFFA	FFFFFF	FFFFFF
	mistyrose	FFE4E1	FFFFFF	FFFFFF
	moccasin	FFE4B5	FFFFCC	FFFFCC
	navajowhite	FFDEAD	FFCC99	FFCC99
	navy	000080	000099	000099
	oldlace	FDF5E6	FFFFFF	FFFFFF
	olive	808000	999900	999900
	olivedrab	6B8E23	669933	669933
	orange	FFA500	FF9900	FF9900
	orangered	FF4500	FF3300	FF3300
	orchid	DA70D6	CC66CC	CC66CC
	palegoldenrod	EEE8AA	FFFF99	FFFF99
	palegreen	98FB98	99FF99	99FF99
	paleturquoise	AFEEEE	99FFFF	99FFFF
	palevioletred	DB7093	CC6699	CC6699
	papayawhip	FFEFD5	FFFFCC	FFFFCC
	peachpuff	FFDAB9	FFCCCC	FFCCCC
	peru	CD853F	CC9933	CC9933
	pink	FFC0CB	FFCCCC	FFCCCC
	plum	DDA0DD	CC99CC	CC99CC

B-S	Color Name	HEX 24-bit Mac/PC	256 MAC	256 PC
	powderblue	B0E0E6	CCFFFF	99CCFF
	purple	800080	990099	990099
■	**red**	**FF0000**	**FF0000**	**FF0000**
	rosybrown	BC8F8F	CC9999	CC9999
	royalblue	4169E1	3366FF	3366CC
	saddlebrown	8B4513	993300	993300
	salmon	FA8072	FF9966	FF9966
	sandybrown	F4A460	FF9966	FF9966
	seagreen	2E8B57	339966	339966
	seashell	FFF5EE	FFFFFF	FFFFFF
	sienna	A0522D	996633	996633
	silver	C0C0C0	CCCCCC	CCCCCC
	skyblue	87CEEB	99CCFF	99CCFF
	slateblue	6A5ACD	6666CC	6666CC
	slategray	708090	669999	669999
	snow	FFFAFA	FFFFFF	FFFFFF
	springgreen	00FF7F	00FF66	00FF66
	steelblue	4682B4	3399CC	3399CC
	tan	D2B48C	CCCC99	CCCC99
	teal	008080	009999	009999
	thistle	D8BFD8	CCCCCC	CCCCCC
	tomato	FF6347	FF6633	FF6633
	turquoise	40E0D0	33FFCC	33CCCC
	violet	EE82EE	FF99FF	FF99FF
	wheat	F5DEB3	FFCCCC	FFCCCC
■	**white**	**FFFFFF**	**FFFFFF**	**FFFFFF**
	whitesmoke	F5F5F5	FFFFFF	FFFFFF
■	**yellow**	**FFFF00**	**FFFF00**	**FFFF00**
	yellowgreen	9ACD32	99CC33	99CC33

web graphics >

Coloring Individual Lines of Text

You can also assign specific colors to individual lines of text by using the <FONT> tag. Here's some sample code:

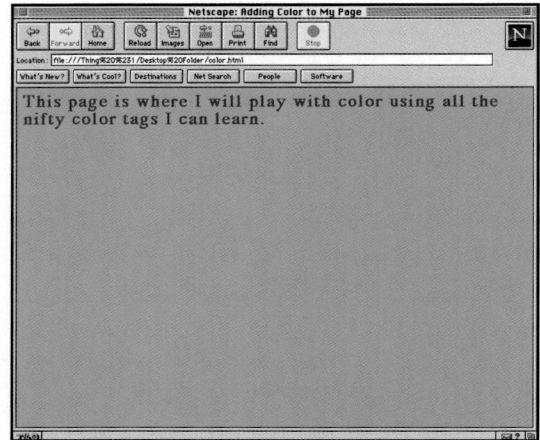

Here's an example of using the <FONT> tag to insert color attributes so that individual words or letters can be colored.

```
<HTML>
<HEAD>
<TITLE>Adding Color to My Page</TITLE>
</HEAD>
<BODY BGCOLOR="660099"
TEXT="CCCCFF">
<H1>This page is where I
```
1 `<FONT COLOR="99FFFF">will </FONT>`
```
<FONT COLOR="CCFF99">play </FONT>
<FONT COLOR="CC99CC">with</FONT>
<FONT COLOR="CC0000">color </FONT>
using all the nifty color tags I can
learn.
</H1>
</BODY>
</HTML>
```

1 The <FONT> tag can contain a color attribute, which can be specified using color names or hex numbers. It must be closed with a </FONT> tag each time you want the specific colored text attribute to end.

Coloring Links

Link color can affect the border color around linked images or the color of linked text. Here's an example of how to set this up in an HTML document.

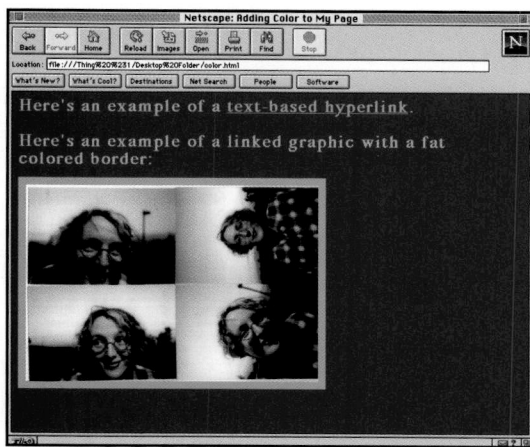

Here's an example of creating colored links. The border around the graphic was made wider with the BORDER attribute.

1 The LINK attribute within the <BODY> tag establishes the color for the linked text or graphic. The <A HREF></A> tag is producing linked text.

2 The IMG SRC tag inserts an image, and the BORDER attribute enables you to set a width for the border, measured in pixels. Note: If you don't want a border, you can set this to BORDER=0.

```
<HTML>
<HEAD>
<TITLE>Adding Color to My Page</TITLE>
</HEAD>
<BODY
BGCOLOR="660099"
TEXT="CCCCFF"
LINK="CCFF00">
<H1>Here's an example of a <a
href="http://www.stinkabod.com">text-based
hyperlink</a>
<p>
Here's an example of a linked graphic with
a fat, colored border: </H1>
<p>
<a href="http://www.stinkabod.com"><img
src="fourlynda.gif" border=10></a>
</BODY>
</HTML>
```

1 marks `TEXT="CCCCFF"` line.

2 marks `<a href="http://www.stinkabod.com"><img` line.

Inserting a Background Image

Chapter 2, "Browser-Safe Color," shows how to insert a hybrid-safe tile into a page. That same technique will work for a solid color background tile or a pattern tile. Here's how to set up this technique:

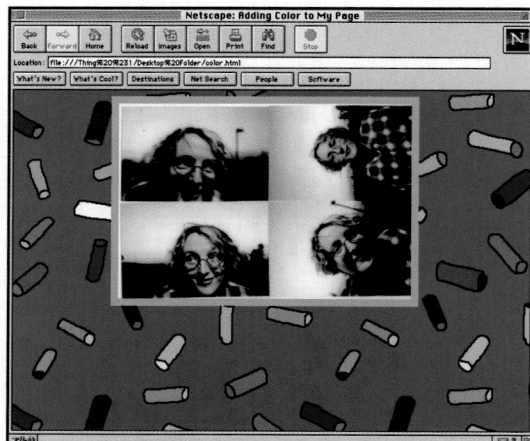

Here's an example of inserting a background image. You can insert a solid color image, a hybrid color image, a repeating tile image, or a seamless tile image. It's the same code, just a different graphic file!

```
<HTML>
<HEAD>
<TITLE>Adding Color to My Page</TITLE>
</HEAD>
<BODY
BACKGROUND="tile.gif"
TEXT="CCCCFF"
LINK="CCFF00">
<center>
<a href="http://www.stinkabod.com"><img
src="fourlynda.gif" border=10></a>
<center>
</BODY>
</HTML>
```

1 The BACKGROUND attribute within the <BODY> tag enables you to insert an image into the background of the Web page. This image can be any kind of image (.jpeg or .gif), and could be a solid color, a hybrid color, a seamless tile image, or a repeating tile image.

Adding Color to Tables

The BGCOLOR attribute works in table cells as well as the body of the HTML document. Here's some sample code that demonstrates this technique:

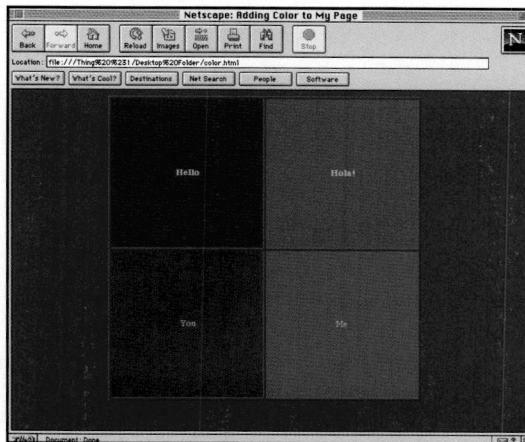

Here's an example of coloring cells within a table, using the BGCOLOR attribute within the <TABLE> tag.

```
<HTML>
<HEAD>
<TITLE>Adding Color to My Page</TITLE>
</HEAD>
<BODY BGCOLOR="660099"
TEXT="CCCCFF">
<center>
<table border >
<tr><th bgcolor="003366" height=200
width=200>Hello</th>
<th bgcolor="990033" height=200
width=200>Hola!</th>
<tr ><td bgcolor="666600" height=200
width=200 align=middle>You</td><td
bgcolor="996666" height=200width=200
align=middle>Me</td>
</table>
</center>
</BODY>
</HTML>
```

1 The <CENTER> tag instructs the table to be centered in the page.

2 The <TABLE> tag establishes the beginning of the table command. The BORDER attribute assigns an embossed border to the table.

3 <TR> initiates a table row. TH stands for table header. Everything within the <TH> tag will automatically be bold and centered. The BGCOLOR attribute allows a color to be established within the table cell, and can be specified using hexadecimal color or color names. The HEIGHT and WIDTH tags assign dimensions to the table cells, using pixel-based measurements. The ALIGN=middle attribute centers the text within the table cells.

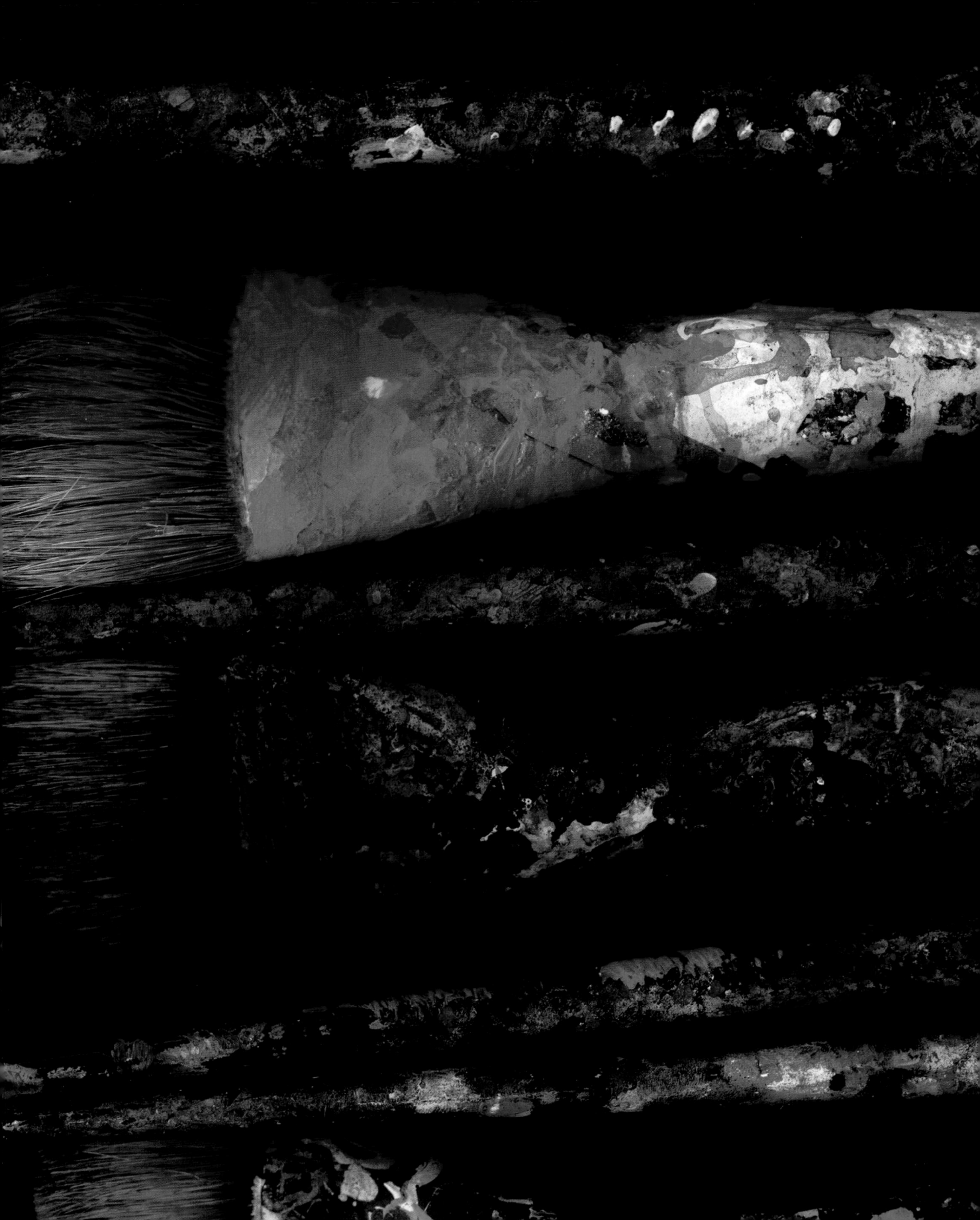

Glossary

Glossary

8-bit graphics: A color or grayscale graphic or movie that has 256 colors or less.

16-bit graphics: A color image or movie that has 65,500 colors.

24-bit graphics: A color image or movie that has 16.7 million colors.

32-bit graphics: A color image or movie that has 16.7 million colors, plus an 8-bit masking channel.

adaptive dithering: A form of dithering in which the program looks to the image to determine the best set of colors when creating an 8-bit or smaller palette. See dithering.

additive color: The term for RGB color space that uses projected light to mix color.

aliasing: In bitmapped graphics, the jagged boundary along the edges of different-colored shapes within an image. See anti-aliasing.

analagous colors: Brackets a color hue on either side of the color wheel.

anti-aliasing: A technique for reducing the jagged appearance of aliased bitmapped images, usually by inserting pixels that blend at the boundaries between adjacent colors.

artifacts: Image imperfections caused by compression.

bit-depth: The number of bits used to represent the color of each pixel in a given movie or still image. Specifically: Bit-depth of 2=black-and-white pixels. Bit-depth of 4=16 colors or grays. Bit-depth of 8=256 colors or grays. Bit-depth of 16=65,536 colors. Bit-depth of 24=(approximately) 16 million colors.

bitmapped graphics: Graphics that are pixel-based, as opposed to object-oriented. Bitmapped graphics are what the computer can display, because it's a pixel-based medium, whereas object-oriented graphics can be viewed in high resolution once they are sent to a printer. Graphics on the Web are bitmapped because they are viewed from a computer screen-based delivery system.

brightness: Adds white or tints an image, whereas lack of brightness adds black or tones an image.

browser: An application that enables you to access World Wide Web pages. Most browsers provide the capability to view Web pages, copy and print material from Web pages, download files over the Web, and navigate throughout the Web.

browser-safe colors: The 216 colors that do not shift between platforms, operating systems, or most Web browsers.

CLUT: Color LookUp Table. An 8-bit or lower image file uses a CLUT to define its palette.

color mapping: A color map refers to the color palette of an image. Color mapping means assigning colors to an image.

complementary colors: Created from opposing color hues on the color wheel.

compression: Reduction of the amount of data required to re-create an original file, graphic, or movie. Compression is used to reduce the transmission time of media and application files across the Web.

contrast: The degree of separation between values.

dithering: The positioning of different-colored pixels within an image that uses a 256-color palette to simulate a color that does not exist in the palette. A dithered image often looks noisy, or composed of scattered pixels. See adaptive dithering.

dpi: Dots Per Inch is a term used mostly by print graphics-based programs and professionals, and is a common measurement related to the resoluton of an image. See screen resolution.

extension: Abbreviated code at the end of a file that tells the browser what kind of file it's looking at. Example: a JPEG file would have the extension .jpg.

fixed palette: An established palette that is fixed. When a fixed palette Web browser views images, it will convert images to its colors and not use the colors from the original.

gamma: Gamma measures the contrast that affects the midtones of an image. Adjusting the gamma lets you change the brightness values of the middle range of gray tones without dramatically altering the shadows and highlights.

gamut: A viewable or printable color range.

GIF: A bitmapped color graphics file format. GIF is commonly used on the Web because it employs an efficient compression method. See JPEG.

GIF89a: A type of GIF file that supports transparency and multi-blocks. Multi-blocks create the illusion of animation. GIF89a files are sometimes referred to as "transparent GIFs" or "animated GIFs."

hexadecimal: A base 16 mathematics calculation, often used in scripts and code. Hexadecimal code is required by HTML to describe RGB values of color for the Web.

HTML: HyperText Markup Language. The common language for interchange of hypertext between the World Wide Web client and server. Web pages must be written using HTML. See hypertext.

hue: Defines a linear spectrum of the color wheel.

hypertext: Text formatted with links that enable the reader to jump among related topics. See HTML.

interlaced GIFs: The GIF file format allows for "interlacing," which causes the GIF to load quickly at low or chunky resolution and then come into full or crisp resolution.

JPEG: Acronym for Joint Photographic Experts Group, but commonly used to refer to a lossy compression technique that can reduce the size of a graphics file by as much as 96 percent. See GIF.

links: Emphasized words in a hypertext document that act as pointers to more information on that specific subject. Links are generally underlined and may appear in a different color. When you click on a link, you can be transported to a different Web site that contains information about the word or phrase used as the link. See hypertext.

lossless compression: A data compression technique that reduces the size of a file without sacrificing any of the original data. In lossless compression, the expanded or restored file is an exact replica of the original file before it was compressed. See compression.

lossy compression: A data compression technique in which some data is deliberately discarded in order to achieve massive reductions in the size of the compressed file.

mask: The process of blocking out areas in a computer graphic.

moiré: A pattern that results when dots overlap.

Postscript: A sophisticated page description language used for printing high-quality text and graphics on laser printers and other high-resolution printing devices.

primary colors: The theory behind primary colors is that these colors are the starting point from which any other colors can be mixed. On the computer, the primary colors are red, green, and blue because color mixing is additive (created with light). With pigment the primary colors are red, blue, and yellow because color mixing is subtractive.

progressive JPEG: A type of JPEG that produces an interlaced effect as it loads, and that can be 30 percent smaller than standard JPEGs. It is not currently supported by many Web browsers.

saturation: Defines the intensity of color.

screen resolution: Screen resolution generally refers to the resolution of common computer monitors. 72 dpi is an agreed upon average, though you will also hear of 96 dpi being the resolution of larger displays.

secondary colors: The colors in between primary colors.

tables: Tables create rows and columns, like in a spreadsheet, and can be used to align data and images.

tag: ASCII text indicators with which you surround text and images to designate certain formats or styles.

transparent GIFs: A subset of the original GIF file format that adds header information to the GIF file, which signifies that a defined color will be masked out.

true color: The quality of color provided by 24-bit color depth. 24-bit color depth results in 16.7 million colors, which is usually more than adequate for the human eye.

value: The range from light to dark in an image.

WYSIWYG: Pronounced wizzy-wig. A design philosophy in which formatting commands directly affects the text displayed on-screen, so that the screen shows the appearance of the printed text.

■ colophon

The preliminary art direction for *Coloring Web Graphics* was sketched on paper. This book was then designed and produced using QuarkXPress, Adobe Photoshop, and Microsoft Word on a Power Macintosh 7100/80. All of the text was set in the Adobe Gill Sans family except for the HTML/CODE, which was set in Macmillan's MCPDigital, and the red square Zapf Dingbats. *Coloring Web Graphics* was printed on 80lb. Influence Soft Gloss paper and was produced digitally using Adobe software. Prepress consisted of Postscript computer-to-plate technology (filmless process) printed by Shepard Poorman, Indianapolis, Indiana. The cover illustration was painted with acrylics and crayons and then drum scanned. *Coloring Web Graphics* was first printed in an edition of twenty thousand copies.

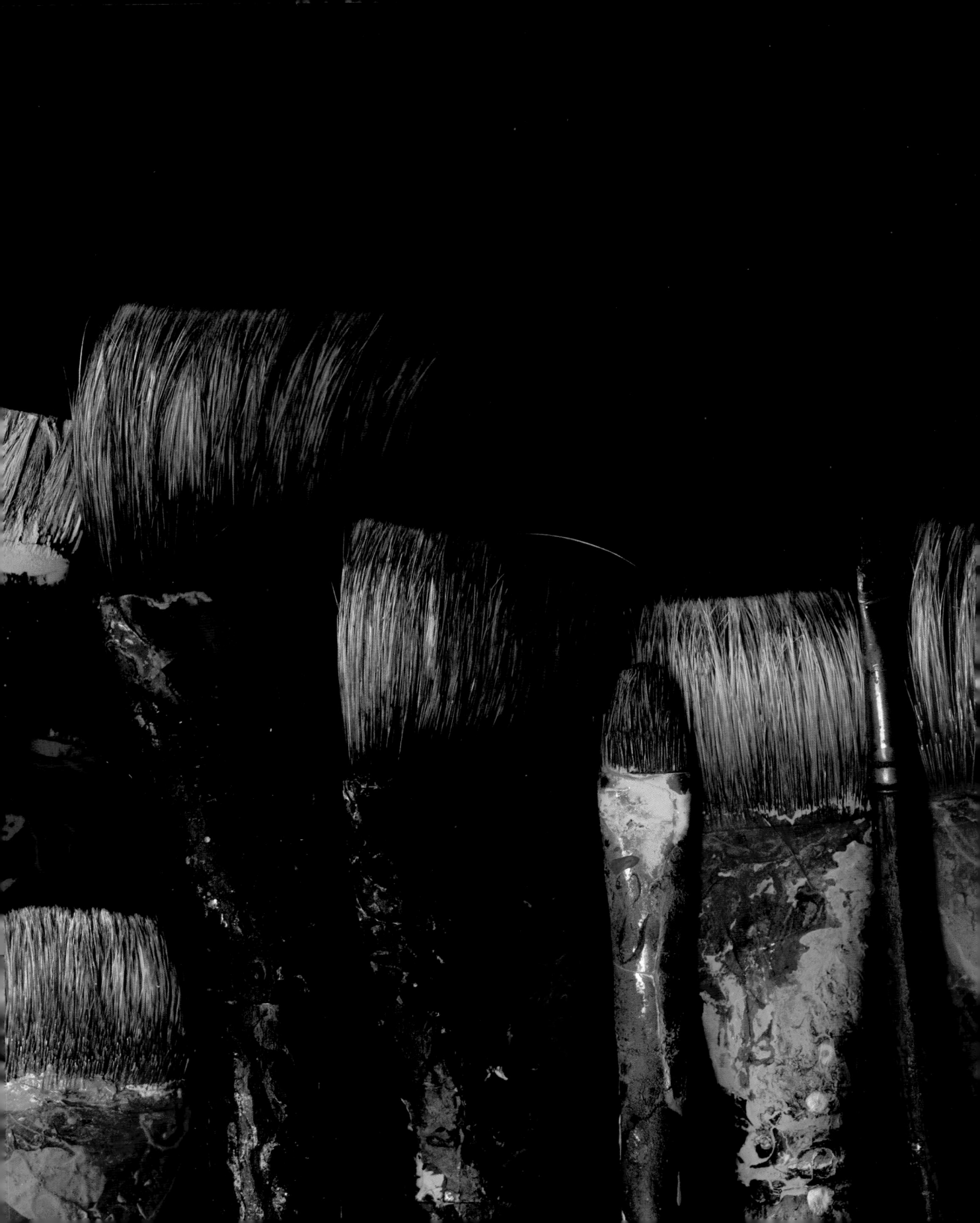

Index

color names
  hexadecimal equivalents of, 272-273
  HTML (HyperText Markup Language) and,
    270-271
color picker-based applications, 101
color principles
  children's view of, 63
  meaning of color, 62
color swatches, analogous, 70
Color Wheel, 64
color-related HTML tags, 268-277
color-safe palettes in Macromedia Director, 102
Coloring Web Graphics CD-ROM
  216clut.cpl file, 98
  .aco swatch files, 83
  bclut2.aco file, 90-91
  blended color sets, 114
  browser-safe color files, 29
  browser-safe color palettes, 27
  ckrbd.gif file, 103
  CLIPART folder, 112-113, 115
  CLIPART\BRUCE\TILES folder, 103
  CLIPART\DON\TILES folder, 105
  CLIPART\LICENSOR\BRUCE folder, 115
  CLUT folder, 80, 112-113
  clut.bcs file, 100
  CLUT\PAINTER folder, 82
  CLUT\WIN16 folder, 88
  file organization, 114-115
  ga.aco and ga.gif files, 70
  GIF folder, 30
  hybrid-safe color files, 29
  lines.gif file, 103
  master color palettes, 115
  mini color sets, 114
  PSP folder, 31
  shmancy.gif file, 105
  SWATCH/GIF folder, 79
  Swatches folder, 30, 112-113
  SWATCHES\ACO folder, 77

  SWATCHES\BLEND folder, 114
  SWATCHES\MASTER folder, 115
  SWATCHES\MINI folder, 114
  SWATCH\ODDBALL folder, 109
  Xray.psd file, 109
ColorWeb, 101
common palette, 94-95
complementary colors, 64, 280
compression, 281
  loseless, 39
  lossy, 55, 89
  LZW (Lempel-Ziv & Welch) compression
    scheme, 39-40
  run-length, 40
computers
  color, 4
  primary colors, 64
contrast, 65, 67, 281
Corel Draw, 98
custom palettes, 86
  Shockwave, 102

D

DeBabelizer, 97
desaturation, 68
dithering, 12-13, 22, 281
  photographs, 46
  screen, 12-13
dpi (dots per inch), 8, 281
DreamWorks Interactive SKG site, 28

E

embedding images and HTML (HyperText Markup
  Language), 59
Exact palette, 86
Excellent GIF transparency tutorial site, 93
extension, 281

W

X

Here's What People Are Saying About Designing Web Graphics, also by Lynda Weinman:

"No Digital Fluff! Do you need to know it all and know it fast? Then *Designing Web Graphics* is the answer."
-Russell Brown, Sr. Creative Director, Adobe Systems, Inc.

"Your book has been incredibly useful for answering questions and providing inspiration. One of my team members made this comment: 'There are a lot of books out there that supposedly will answer all your questions about how to do things for the Web, but Lynda's book actually does!' I just love the logical and concise organization, and thorough discussion of each topic. And the 'Browser CLUT Palette' —that's worth 50 bucks all by itself!"
-Dave Roh, Simon & Schuster Elementary Group

"I just picked up your book *Designing Web Graphics*. Although I was already aware of about 75 percent of what your book covers, I still found it VERY, VERY helpful. It is well written and seems to keep in mind the fact that designers will be reading it. So in short, I'd like to thank you for providing me with a tool I can both learn from and hand off to others to help teach them the ins and outs of online design."
-Dom Moreci, Monnens-Addis Design

"I just want to let you know that I am sooo glad someone has finally assembled such a complete and useful reference on the subject. As a graphic designer who is increasingly finding himself asked to design graphics for Web sites, I have been feeling my way around in the dark on matters such as color palettes and cross-platform issues. Your book pulls everything together in one place and I will not hesitate to recommend it to colleagues in the same situation as myself."
-Mark Fitzgerald

"Your book is excellent!! It rocks!! It was a total lifesaver on my redesign project. Thank you, thank you, thank you!! It was so refreshing to read a book that isn't written by a 'tech-head' who is only interested in technology—you did a wonderful job of giving me not only the details, but also how they fit into the bigger picture and why they matter. I really appreciate writing that puts things in perspective. Your book does an excellent job. Your sense of humor definitely made it a fun read—I can't think of any better title for cross-platform issues than 'Platform Hell!'"
-Dana Giles

"I am a designer in the Philadelphia area—new to designing Web stuff—I just bought your book and WOW it is very good! Wish I had had a teacher like you in art school. Anyway, just wanted to say I am enjoying your book and home page—you have a refreshing style (open and fun)."
-Victoria Land

"You opened doors to so many problems I was encountering and had nowhere to go for the answers. Your book CLEARLY defines and illustrates every detail. I just can't thank you enough for taking the time for this project."
-Joan Smith

"Love the book! You made it easy and gave excellent samples that are easy to learn and expand on."
-Julie A. Kreiner, JAK Graphic Solutions, Chicago, IL

■ **Coming January 1997:**
<designing web graphics.2>

Designing Web Graphics.2
Lynda Weinman
$50.00 USA
350 pages
ISBN:1-56205-715-4

New Riders Publishing
201 West 103rd Street
Indianapolis, IN 46290
1-800-428-5331
■ http://www. mcp.com/newriders

(Products and names mentioned in this document are trademarks of their respective companies.)

Fold Here

REGISTRATION CARD

Coloring Web Graphics

Name _____ Title _____

Company _____ Type of business _____

Address _____

City/State/ZIP _____

E-mail/Internet _____ Phone _____

Would you like to be placed on our preferred mailing list?   ❑ yes   ❑ no

Have you used/purchased New Riders books before?   ❑ yes   ❑ no

Where did you purchase this book? Check one.
❑ Bookstore chain   ❑ Independent bookstore ❑ Computer store
❑ Wholesale club   ❑ College bookstore   ❑ Other _____

What influenced your decision to purchase this title? _____
_____

Which of the following operating systems do you use? Check all that apply.
❑ Windows 3.x   ❑ Windows 95   ❑ Windows NT
❑ Macintosh   ❑ SGI   ❑ Other _____

What are the names of the software programs you use currently? _____
_____
_____

Which of the following best describes your work environment? Check one.
❑ Self-employed   ❑ Small business   ❑ Large business

Which of the following do you create/develop for? Check all that apply.
❑ Games   ❑ Motion pictures   ❑ Web sites
❑ Print   ❑ Other

What online services and Web sites do you visit on a regular basis? _____
_____
_____

What trade shows do you attend? _____

What computer book titles do you consider your most valuable sources of information?
_____

What applications/technologies would you like to see us publish in the future?
_____

8. LIMITATION AND DISCLAIMER OF WARRANTIES.

a) THE SOFTWARE AND RELATED WRITTEN MATERIALS, INCLUDING ANY INSTRUCTIONS FOR USE, ARE PROVIDED ON AN "AS IS" BASIS, WITHOUT WARRANTY OF ANY KIND, EXPRESS OR IMPLIED. THIS DISCLAIMER OF WARRANTY EXPRESSLY INCLUDES, BUT IS NOT LIMITED TO, ANY IMPLIED WARRANTIES OF MERCHANTABILITY AND/OR OF FITNESS FOR A PARTICULAR PURPOSE. NO WARRANTY OF ANY KIND IS MADE AS TO WHETHER OR NOT THIS SOFTWARE INFRINGES UPON ANY RIGHTS OF ANY OTHER THIRD PARTIES. NO ORAL OR WRITTEN INFORMATION GIVEN BY LICENSOR, ITS SUPPLIERS, DISTRIBUTORS, DEALERS, EMPLOYEES, OR AGENTS, SHALL CREATE OR OTHERWISE ENLARGE THE SCOPE OF ANY WARRANTY HEREUNDER. LICENSEE ASSUMES THE ENTIRE RISK AS TO THE QUALITY AND THE PERFORMANCE OF SUCH SOFTWARE. SHOULD THE SOFTWARE PROVE DEFECTIVE, YOU, AS LICENSEE (AND NOT LICENSOR, ITS SUPPLIERS, DISTRIBUTORS, DEALERS, OR AGENTS), ASSUME THE ENTIRE COST OF ALL NECESSARY CORRECTION, SERVICING, OR REPAIR.

b) LICENSOR warrants the disk(s) on which this copy of the Software is recorded or fixed to be free from defects in materials and workman- ship, under normal use and service, for a period of ninety (90) days from the date of delivery as evidenced by a copy of the applicable receipt. LICENSOR hereby limits the duration of any implied warranties with respect to the disk(s) to the duration of the express warranty. This limited warranty shall not apply if the disk(s) have been damaged by unreasonable use, accident, negligence, or by any other causes unrelated to defective materials or workmanship.

c) LICENSOR does not warrant that the functions contained in the Software will be uninterrupted or error free and Licensee is encouraged to test the Software for Licensee's intended use prior to placing any reliance thereon. All risk of the use of the Software will be on you, as Licensee.

d) THE LIMITED WARRANTY SET FORTH ABOVE GIVES YOU SPECIFIC LEGAL RIGHTS AND YOU MAY ALSO HAVE OTHER RIGHTS WHICH VARY FROM STATE TO STATE. SOME STATES DO NOT ALLOW THE LIMITATION OR EXCLUSION OF IMPLIED WARRANTIES OR OF INCIDENTAL OR CONSEQUENTIAL DAMAGES, SO THE LIMITATIONS AND EXCLUSIONS CONCERNING THE SOFTWARE AND RELATED WRITTEN MATERIALS SET FORTH ABOVE MAY NOT APPLY TO YOU.

9. LIMITATION OF REMEDIES. LICENSOR's entire liability and Licensee's exclusive remedy shall be the replacement of any disk(s) not meeting the limited warranty set forth in Section 8 above which is returned to LICENSOR with a copy of the applicable receipt within the war- ranty period. Any replacement disk(s) will be warranted for the remainder of the original warranty period or thirty (30) days, whichever is longer.

10. LIMITATION OF LIABILITY. IN NO EVENT WILL LICENSOR, OR ANYONE ELSE INVOLVED IN THE CREATION, PRODUCTION, AND/OR DELIVERY OF THIS SOFTWARE PRODUCT BE LIABLE TO LICENSEE OR ANY OTHER PERSON OR ENTITY FOR ANY DIRECT OR OTHER DAMAGES, INCLUDING, WITHOUT LIMITATION, ANY INTERRUPTION OF SERVICES, LOST PROFITS, LOST SAV- INGS, LOSS OF DATA, OR ANY OTHER CONSEQUENTIAL, INCIDENTAL, SPECIAL, OR PUNITIVE DAMAGES, ARISING OUT OF THE PURCHASE, USE, INABILITY TO USE, OR OPERATION OF THE SOFTWARE, EVEN IF LICENSOR OR ANY AUTHORIZED LICENSOR DEALER HAS BEEN ADVISED OF THE POSSIBILITY OF SUCH DAMAGES. BY YOUR USE OF THE SOFTWARE, YOU ACKNOWLEDGE THAT THE LIMITATION OF LIABILITY SET FORTH IN THIS LICENSE WAS THE BASIS UPON WHICH THE SOFTWARE WAS OFFERED BY LICENSOR AND YOU ACKNOWLEDGE THAT THE PRICE OF THE SOFTWARE LICENSE WOULD BE HIGHER IN THE ABSENCE OF SUCH LIMITATION. SOME STATES DO NOT ALLOW THE LIMITATION OR EXCLUSION OF LIABILITY FOR INCIDENTAL OR CONSE- QUENTIAL DAMAGES SO THE ABOVE LIMITATIONS AND EXCLUSIONS MAY NOT APPLY TO YOU.

11. UPDATES. LICENSOR, at its sole discretion, may periodically issue updates of the Software which you may receive upon request and payment of the applicable update fee in effect from time to time and in such event, all of the provisions of the within License Agreement shall apply to such updates.

12. EXPORT RESTRICTIONS. Licensee agrees not to export or re-export the Software and accompanying documentation (or any copies thereof) in violation of any applicable U.S. laws or regulations.

13. ENTIRE AGREEMENT. YOU, AS LICENSEE, ACKNOWLEDGE THAT: (i) YOU HAVE READ THIS ENTIRE AGREEMENT AND AGREE TO BE BOUND BY ITS TERMS AND CONDITIONS; (ii) THIS AGREEMENT IS THE COMPLETE AND EXCLUSIVE STATEMENT OF THE UNDERSTANDING BETWEEN THE PARTIES AND SUPERSEDES ANY AND ALL PRIOR ORAL OR WRITTEN COMMUNICATIONS RELATING TO THE SUBJECT MATTER HEREOF; AND (iii) THIS AGREEMENT MAY NOT BE MODIFIED, AMENDED, OR IN ANY WAY ALTERED EXCEPT BY A WRITING SIGNED BY BOTH YOURSELF AND AN OFFICER OR AUTHORIZED REPRESENTATIVE OF LICEN- SOR.

14. SEVERABILITY. In the event that any provision of this License Agreement is held to be illegal or otherwise unenforceable, such provision shall be deemed to have been deleted from this License Agreement while the remaining provisions of this License Agreement shall be unaf- fected and shall continue in full force and effect.

15. GOVERNING LAW. This License Agreement shall be governed by the laws of the State of New York applicable to agreements wholly to be performed therein and of the United States of America, excluding that body of the law related to conflicts of law. This License Agreement shall not be governed by the United Nations Convention on Contracts for the International Sale of Goods, the application of which is expressly excluded. No waiver of any breach of the provisions of this License Agreement shall be deemed a waiver of any other breach of this License Agreement.

16. RESTRICTED RIGHTS LEGEND. Use, duplication, or disclosure by the Government is subject to restrictions as set forth in subparagraph (c)(1)(ii) of the Rights in Technical Data and Computer Software clause at 48 CFR § 252.227-7013 and DFARS § 252.227-7013 or subpara- graphs (c) (1) and (c)(2) of the Commercial Computer Software-Restricted Rights at 48 CFR § 52.227.19, as applicable. Contractor/manufac- turer: LICENSOR: NEW RIDERS PUBLISHING, LYNDA WEINMAN, BRUCE HEAVIN, c/o NEW RIDERS PUBLISHING, 201 West 103rd Street, Indianapolis, In 46290.

LICENSE AGREEMENT

THIS SOFTWARE LICENSE AGREEMENT CONSTITUTES AN AGREEMENT BETWEEN YOU AND NEW RIDERS PUBLISHING, LYNDA WEINMAN, AND BRUCE HEAVIN ("LICENSOR" HEREINAFTER, BOTH JOINTLY AND INDIVIDUALLY). YOU SHOULD CAREFULLY READ THE FOLLOWING TERMS AND CONDITIONS BEFORE OPENING THIS ENVELOPE. COPYING THIS SOFTWARE TO YOUR MACHINE, BREAKING THE SEAL, OR OTHERWISE REMOVING OR USING THE SOFTWARE INDICATES YOUR ACCEPTANCE OF THESE TERMS AND CONDITIONS. IF YOU DO NOT AGREE TO BE BOUND BY THE PROVISIONS OF THIS LICENSE AGREEMENT, YOU SHOULD PROMPTLY DELETE THE SOFTWARE FROM YOUR MACHINE.

TERMS AND CONDITIONS:

1. GRANT OF LICENSE. In consideration of payment of the License Fee, which was a part of the price you paid for this product, LICENSOR grants to you (the "Licensee") a non-exclusive right to use and display this copy of a Software program, along with any updates or upgrade releases of the Software for which you have paid (all parts and elements of the Software as well as the Software as a whole are hereinafter referred to as the "Software") on a single computer only (i.e., with a single CPU) at a single location, all as more particularly set forth and limited below. LICENSOR reserves all rights not expressly granted to you as Licensee in this License Agreement.

2. OWNERSHIP OF SOFTWARE. The license granted herein is not a sale of the original Software or of any copy of the Software. As Licensee, you own only the rights to use the Software as described herein and the magnetic or other physical media on which the Software is originally or subsequently recorded or fixed. LICENSOR retains title and ownership of the Software recorded on the original disk(s), as well as title and ownership of any subsequent copies of the Software irrespective of the form of media on or in which the Software is recorded or fixed. This license does not grant you any intellectual or other proprietary or other rights of any nature whatsoever in the Software.

3. USE RESTRICTIONS. As Licensee, you may use the Software only as expressly authorized in this License Agreement under the terms of paragraph 4. You may physically transfer the Software from one computer to another provided that the Software is used on only a single computer at any one time. You may not: (i) electronically transfer the Software from one computer to another over a network; (ii) make the Software available through a time-sharing service, network of computers, or other multiple user arrangement; (iii) distribute copies of the Software or related written materials to any third party, whether for sale or otherwise; (iv) modify, adapt, translate, reverse engineer, decompile, disassemble, or prepare any derivative work based on the Software or any element thereof; (v) make or distribute, whether for sale or otherwise, any hard copy or printed version of any of the Software nor any portion thereof nor any work of yours containing the Software or any component thereof; (vi) use any of the Software nor any of its components in any other work.

4. THIS IS WHAT YOU CAN AND CANNOT DO WITH THE SOFTWARE. Even though in the preceding paragraph and elsewhere LICENSOR has restricted your use of the Software, the following are the only things you can do with the Software and the various elements of the Software. There are several different kinds of folders in the Software, each containing different materials and different restrictions.

a) THE FOLDER MARKED CLUTS: THE MATERIAL CONTAINED IN THIS FOLDER MAY NOT BE USED IN ANY MANNER WHATSOEVER OTHER THAN TO VIEW THE SAME ON YOUR COMPUTER AND MAY BE USED IN YOUR DESIGN OR OTHER WORK ON YOUR COMPUTER ONLY BUT NOT OTHERWISE. THIS MATERIAL IS SUBJECT TO ALL OF THE RESTRICTION PROVISIONS OF THIS SOFTWARE LICENSE. SPECIFICALLY BUT NOT IN LIMITATION OF THESE RESTRICTIONS, YOU MAY NOT DISTRIBUTE OR TRANSFER THIS PART OF THE SOFTWARE DESIGNATED AS "CLUTS" NOR ANY OF YOUR DESIGN OR OTHER WORK CONTAINING ANY OF THE SOFTWARE DESIGNATED AS "CLUTS" NOR ANY OF YOUR DESIGN OR OTHER WORK CONTAINING ANY SUCH "CLUTS," ALL AS MORE PARTICULARLY RESTRICTED IN THE WITHIN SOFTWARE LICENSE.

b) THE FOLDER MARKED CLIPART\LICENSOR: THE MATERIAL CONTAINED IN THIS FOLDER MAY BE USED ONLY ON YOUR PERSONAL, NON-COMMERCIAL WEB SITE BUT NOT OTHERWISE. YOU MAY NOT OTHERWISE DISTRIBUTE OR TRANSFER IT.

c) THE FOLDER MARKED SWATCHES: THE MATERIAL CONTAINED IN THIS FOLDER MAY NOT BE USED IN ANY MANNER WHATSOEVER OTHER THAN TO VIEW THE SAME ON YOUR COMPUTER AND MAY BE USED IN YOUR DESIGN OR OTHER WORK ON YOUR COMPUTER ONLY BUT NOT OTHERWISE. THIS MATERIAL IS SUBJECT TO ALL OF THE RESTRICTION PROVISIONS OF THIS SOFTWARE LICENSE. SPECIFICALLY BUT NOT IN LIMITATION OF THESE RESTRICTIONS, YOU MAY NOT DISTRIBUTE OR TRANSFER THIS PART OF THE SOFTWARE DESIGNATED AS "SWATCHES" NOR ANY OF YOUR DESIGN OR OTHER WORK CONTAINING ANY OF THE SOFTWARE DESIGNATED AS "SWATCHES" NOR ANY OF YOUR DESIGN OR OTHER WORK CONTAINING ANY SUCH "SWATCHES," ALL AS MORE PARTICULARLY RESTRICTED IN THE WITHIN SOFTWARE LICENSE.

d) THE FOLDER MARKED CLIPART\3rd PARTY: THE MATERIAL CONTAINED IN THIS FOLDER MAY BE USED ONLY IN ACCORDANCE WITH ALL OF THE PROVISIONS OF ANY THIRD PARTY LICENSES CONTAINED IN THE SOFTWARE AND FOLDER. READ ALL FILES PROVIDED, INCLUDING BUT NOT LIMITED TO "READ ME" FILES FOR SUCH RESTRICTIONS. NOTHING CONTAINED IN THIS LICENSE AGREEMENT SHALL BE DEEMED TO GRANT TO YOU ANY PERMISSION OR RIGHTS OF ANY NATURE WHATSOEVER WITH REGARD TO SUCH MATERIALS CONTROLLED BY THIRD PARTIES.

e) OTHER THAN THESE EXCEPTIONS IN 4a) THROUGH d), ALL OF THE RESTRICTIONS CONTAINED IN THIS LICENSE APPLY IN FULL.

5. COPY RESTRICTIONS. The Software and accompanying written materials are protected under United States copyright laws. Unauthorized copying and/or distribution of the Software and/or the related written materials is expressly forbidden. You may be held legally responsible for any copyright infringement that is caused, directly or indirectly, by your failure to abide by the terms of this License Agreement. Subject to the terms of this License Agreement and if the software is not otherwise copy protected, you may make one copy of the Software for backup purposes only. The copyright notice and any other proprietary notices which were included in the original Software must be reproduced and included on any such backup copy.

6. TRANSFER RESTRICTIONS. The licensee herein granted is personal to you, the Licensee. You may not transfer the Software nor any of its components or elements to anyone else, nor may you sell, lease, loan, sublicense, assign, or otherwise dispose of the Software nor any of its components or elements without the express written consent of LICENSOR, which consent may be granted or withheld at LICENSOR's sole discretion.

7. TERMINATION. The license herein granted hereby will remain in effect until terminated. This license will terminate automatically without further notice from LICENSOR in the event of the violation of any of the provisions hereof. As Licensee, you agree that upon such termination you will promptly destroy any and all copies of the Software which remain in your possession and, upon request, will certify to such destruction in writing to LICENSOR.

\<designing web graphics.2\>

■ Words: Lynda Weinman
■ Design: Ali Karp

Designing Web Graphics.2

By Lynda Weinman

Published by: New Riders Publishing
201 West 103rd Street
Indianapolis, IN 46290 USA

Copyright © 1997 by Lynda Weinman
Printed in the United States of America 2 3 4 5 6 7 8 9 0
ISBN:1-56205-715-4
Library of Congress Cataloging-in-Publication
Data available upon request.

Warning and Disclaimer

Every effort has been made to make this book as complete and as accurate as possible, but no warranty or fitness is implied. The information is provided on an "as is" basis. The author(s) and New Riders Publishing shall have neither liability nor responsibility to any person or entity with respect to any loss or damages arising from the information contained in this book or from the use of the disks or programs that may accompany it.

Trademark Acknowledgements

All terms mentioned in this book that are known to be trademarks or service marks have been appropriately capitalized. New Riders Publishing cannot attest to the accuracy of this information. Use of a term in this book should not be regarded as affecting the validity of any trademark or service mark.

Publisher: Don Fowley
Publishing Manager: David Dwyer
Marketing Manager: Mary Foote
Managing Editor: Carla Hall

Designing Web Graphics.2 Credits

Product Development Specialist
John Kane

Software Specialist
Steve Flatt

Senior Editor
Sarah Kearns

Project Editor
Jennifer Eberhardt

Acquisitions Coordinator
Stacey Beheler

Administrative Coordinator
Karen Opal

Cover Artwork, Spread Illustrations, Photography
Bruce Heavin

Cover Production
Aren Howell

Book Designer
Ali Karp
Alink Newmedia
■ alink@earthlink.net

Production Manager
Kelly Dobbs

Production Team Supervisors
Gina Rexrode, Joe Millay

Production Team
Dan Caparo, Megan Wade,
Daniela Raderstorf

Indexer
Sharon Hilgenberg

Lynda's early days exploring color theory issues, obviously in preparation for the web design series she authors today.

■ Lynda Weinman

Lynda Weinman writes full-time for a living now, but in the past has been a designer, animator, magazine contributor, computer consultant, instructor, moderator, and lecturer. She lives in California with her husband, seven-year-old daughter, 2 cats, and 5 computers. She has taught Web Design, Interactive Media Design, Motion Graphics, and Digital Imaging classes at Art Center College of Design in Pasadena, California (although she is currently taking a break from teaching). Lynda contributes regularly to *Web Techniques*, *MacUser*, *Step-by-Step Graphics*, *Web Studio*, and *How* magazines. She likes the web so much, she even has a domain for her name:

■ http://www.lynda.com

Lynda, get a life!

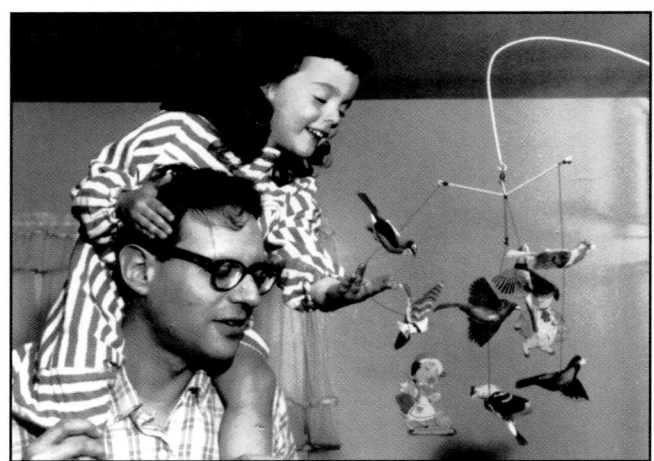

This book is dedicated to my dad, from whom I inherited my height, eyeglass prescription, and computer acumen.

A face is like a work of art.
It deserves a great frame.

Special thanks to Gai, Barbara, and Ruth from L.A. Eyeworks (fierce sister eyewear, yeah!) for featuring me in their ad campaign when the first edition of *Designing Web Graphics* was released. It's the only formal head shot I own of myself, and I actually felt glamorous for the first time in my life! Thanks to Greg Gorman and the L.A. Eyeworkers for letting me reprint it here and use it on the back cover. Photo Credit: Greg Gorman

Lynda's Acknowledgements

My daughter Jamie, who keeps me grounded in the real world, not just the World Wide Web. I love you my sweetheart, and can't wait to have more time with you now that this book is finished!

My brand spankin' new husband Bruce Heavin, without whom I could not have survived the last year of writing four books. Your support, love, and encouragment has made all the difference. And the beautiful covers you painted and incredible images you created didn't exactly suck either! There are no words to describe how much I appreciate and love you.

My book designer, Ali Karp, who cared more about the integrity of this second edition than anyone can measure. Who made sure everything was designed to work correctly with the information and pushed me and herself as hard as humanly possible. You are one awesome friend, collaborator and designer, girlfriend!
■ alink@earthlink.net

My very awesome New Riders team—**John Kane** and **Jennifer Eberhardt**. You were great to work with—let's do it again sometime <g>.

My dear friend **George Maestri** for helping me find the right publisher for the first *Designing Web Graphics*.

David Dwyer for listening to George.

■ In a not-so-glamorous, more true-to-life photo shoot, here I am striking more typical poses. Photo Credit: Bruce Heavin

My dear friend **Crystal Waters** who is always there for me, even when I talk about the web.

My dear friend **Joy Silverman** for her love and supportiveness. Plus when I grow up I want to look like her.

My other close women friends—**Ann Monn**, **Khyal Braun**, **Deborah Caplan**, and **Windy Litvak** who I rarely see, but always carry with me.

My moms—**Carolyn Graysen**, **Ann Weinman**, **Sharyl Heavin**, and **Françoise Kirkland**. Hey, I got lucky and have a lot of moms!

My bro **William Edward Weinman**, who heaped tons of great HTML advice on me and talked to me about my chapters even when he had no time to do so.

My sistah **Pamela** who just graduated from nursing school! Congrats, Pam. You rule!

Steve Weinman for the video, the palette help, and overall supportiveness.

Josh Weinman for the great party.

Mary Thorpe for her beautiful laugh, smile, heart, spirit, and support.

Christopher Schmitt for hanging in there with HTML and graphic help even though I barely had time to explain what I needed.

Web Design List Members **Hung Doan**, **Suzanne Stephens**, and **A. E. Fullerton** for your help. **All the listees** who provided tips, advice, suggestions, and URLs.

Ivan Hoffman for help, warmth, and advice.

Classic PIO Partners (800-370-2746) and **Digital Stock** (■ http://www.digitalstock.com) for use of their great stock photographs.

Erik Holsinger and **Mark Wheaton** for their help with video and sound information in the first edition of *Designing Web Graphics*. A lot of your work appears in the second edition, too. Thank you both again!

A designer's view of laying out the book—from desktop to finished document. We chose to mimic a web aesthetic with our design of *dwg.2*, using underlined text and colored pull quotes. Dashed line boxes were used for tips, notes, and warnings because it reminded us of Bruce's cover artwork. Our goal was to create a playful, inviting, accessible book that was specifically tailored to the information at hand.

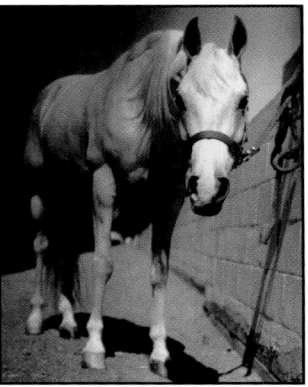

My favorite book designer, Ali, with her best friend/mom at a local horse show. To the right, Ali's horse Smoke—always ready to smile for her camera.

■ contents at a glance

3   Web File Formats   44

4   Low-Bandwidth Graphics   70

7 Transparent Artwork 164

8   Background Tiles   188

9   Rules, Bullets, and Buttons   204

10 Navigation-Based Graphics

222

Web-Based Typography   **250**

14   Animation   330

Introduction

BROWSER

33 FF

OOBB

Width="500"

<STRONG>

Upg

Height="600"

IMAGE OPTIMIZATION

<center>

Imaging techniques

Web file formats

back="FFFFCC"

@link="cyan"

Animation, sound and

LYNDA.COM

<BODY>

33

www Design

Introduction

It's been a year since the first edition of *Designing Web Graphics*, and what a year it's been. My conviction that visual design would play a pivotal role in the advancement of the web has been validated by new and better HTML features, better browsers, better imaging tools, better techniques, and *better sites!* The need to concentrate on design for the web as a separate entity from programming has never been more timely.

If you are a professional visual designer, you are most likely being asked to design web sites or are currently already doing so. If you are a nondesigner making web sites, you are finding yourself in the role of visual designer, whether you feel qualified or not.

My goal is to speak to both the professional designer and the novice nondesigner in this book, and make sure to explain concepts and techniques as clearly as possible, avoiding hype, fluff, and intimidation. Who needs to be overwhelmed by technical writing when the subject at hand is technical enough?

At the same time the web has gotten more friendly toward designers, it's also gotten more complex. The early web a year ago was not only more primitive, it was also easier to learn. As more options and technologies emerge, the learning curve climbs upward as well. I write in a friendly, easy going style because I don't think the information needs to be presented in a complicated way. Whenever I can explain something in plain English and avoid jargon or assumptions, I do.

Web design is in its infancy. Anyone claiming to be an expert has been doing this work for maybe three or four years—at the most. My attitude is that we are all new at this stuff, even those so-called expert folks. I consider myself both a student and a teacher of web design. There's never been a reason to understand file compression, navigational techniques, color palettes, animation, and sound in one visual design discipline. And visual design should not be entirely separated apart from information design and/or programming design. Great sites work on all levels, not just visual design. The web makes it possible and necessary to combine many different disciplines at once, and it's one rare superhuman who can do it all well.

I am just as jazzed as the next person to see web technology advance and improve. All kinds of techniques are described here, from very advanced to very simple. Keep in mind, however, that just because a site throws every new bell and whistle into its mix doesn't make it a great site. In fact, more often the reverse is true!

The web is a publishing medium, and there's room for all types of publishers and all types of sites. I personally hope that the homespun nature of the web never gets edged out by the more advanced sites. At that point, we will have lost the true meaning behind this revolutionary new publishing model.

This web has leveled the playing field to spread across continents, economics, races, genders, and politics. It enables anyone to be a publisher or consumer of information. This is the first time in history that publishing has not been controlled by government, large institutions, the media, and/or big business. It's a mom-and-pop kind of world, where dog and cat home pages might get accessed as often as well-funded corporate sites. The web plays havoc with our sense of hierarchy. You can throw all the money in the world at a site, but basic publishing and design skills that are within reach of anyone are what will make a site stand apart from the crowd.

It's funny how we talk about web sites so differently from other types of visual design mediums. We don't look at a site as we would with printed artwork or text—we go to a site. We talk about web pages as if they are places. We use verbs such as surfing, navigating, browsing, and lurking to describe our actions as we view pages. What's going on? Why are these terms associated with viewing web sites?

The web is an environment. Even though we're looking at a flat screen, often sitting motionless except to move our mouse or type at a keyboard, we are moving. We are moving through information, through geography, through images, and through sounds and video. This is a dynamic medium and one of the most challenging design mediums ever created.

Good design, however, is not just about making beautiful images. There actually are design constraints and limits specific to this medium. It is my goal to bridge those limits and constraints, and to help designers, programmers, and hobbyists understand the medium to make the best use of it.

Good design aids communication; it doesn't exclude its intended audience. If you choose to ignore the limits of the web, you choose to exclude your public. This is not print, this is not TV, and this is not a CD-ROM. The web is its own, very different environment. It has its own quirks and rules and weaknesses, and this book is a place you can turn to learn about what they are.

How Is the Second Edition Different from the First?

The first edition of *Designing Web Graphics* shepherded a lot of other firsts. It was the first book written by a designer for designers on the subject of web design. It was the first book to address low-bandwidth graphics as a subject larger than a few page's mention. It was the first book to describe browser and cross-platform differences in detail. It was the first book to discuss cross-platform palette and color management. It was also the first book I ever wrote, and researching the subject spurred me to create my first web site.

That's not to suggest I'm a stranger to computer graphics. Far from it in fact. I got my first computer in 1982 and have been creating graphics and teaching almost ever since. The web is actually a throwback to more primitive days of computing. Before WYSIWYG editors existed, we used to have to add commands such as bold, italic, and underline in the form of tags. There was no such thing as a millions of color video card for a personal computer until the late 1980s. When I first looked around the web, even though I had never authored a page, I recognized many similarities to the olden days of computer graphics from the decade before.

That's not to say my first experiences were not frustrating. I downloaded an HTML editor, but didn't understand how to use it. I wanted to make images with transparent edges, but didn't understand how. I wanted to know why certain images had blue borders and some didn't. Why some appeared out of focus at first and then sharpened. It was such a strange new landscape, but I wanted so badly to understand it and be in control of it.

At that time, there were no web design books—only a few HTML books. I decided to write the first edition of *Designing Web Graphics* because I couldn't find the book I needed! Today, any respectable computer section in a bookstore has entire shelves devoted to the subject of web development. There are now dozens of books on web design, hundreds on HTML and Java, and probably hundreds more to come. Creating web sites has become the digital gold rush of the '90s.

There was a glaring need for my first book. Now that there all kinds of competing web design titles are out there, why is there a need to write *Designing Web Graphics* all over again? For one thing, readers write to me all the time. I didn't realize that people wrote to authors about their books! I thought people wrote only when they had complaints. I've been amazed by the volume of encouraging and grateful e-mails I've received about *Designing Web Graphics*, and I want to keep servicing the people who seem to appreciate my work. As a teacher, I used to have 18 to 100 students a semester who I might have the privilege of influencing or inspiring. What a rush to have tens of thousands of students all of a sudden! I like this book-writing thing, and as long as you readers spur me on, my guess is I'll keep going at it.

Besides all that, the web design landscape has evolved and changed over this past year. One of the major advancements has been the proliferation of new HTML editors that make web page authoring much more automatic and easy than in the past. The focus now is much less on the programming and much more on the content, speed, interactivity, and appearance of web sites. I'm very excited to produce a new, updated version of *Designing Web Graphics* that will address the many new design and graphics issues of web publishing.

When I proposed doing a second edition of this book, I thought it would be easier to produce than the first. Instead, I have practically rewritten the book from start to finish because there's that much more to write about now. Those of you who already own the first edition will find lots of new information in this second version.

What's New

Here's a brief list of what's new in *DWG.2*:

- Pricing Guidelines
- Copyright Information
- Equipment Suggestions
- HTML Editor Suggestions
- Hybrid-Safe Color Creation
- PNG
- WebTV Specifications
- Digital Watermarks
- PNG Transparency
- Client-Side Imagemaps
- Frames
- New Alignment Tags
- Scanning Tips
- GIF Animation
- Photoshop 4.0 Tips
- Programming Actions Palettes
- Embedded Sound
- Embedded QuickTime
- JavaScript Button Rollovers
- Expanded Typography Section

As you can see, there's a lot that has been added to this second edition of *Designing Web Graphics*. My publisher and I hope to come out with annual updates of this book, as long as the medium warrants it and we receive your encouragement to do so.

How This Book Works

Writing about web design is a tricky thing because there are so many overlapping concepts. For example, tables can be used for layout and alignment, or for cutting apart images to save on file size and downloading time. Teaching about linked graphics and navigation involves both image creation techniques and HTML or CGI. Sometimes, making the decision about which chapter to put with which subject is difficult! For this reason, I have intentionally structured this book so that readers can approach it in a nonlinear manner. Whenever a subject is mentioned in more than one chapter, it is clearly noted.

Those who use the web for information often wonder if they need to buy a book, when so much information is available for free right on the Net. Indeed, the Net is an invaluable resource, and this book is not meant to be a substitute for it but rather an enhancement. Few will dispute the advantages to having all the information you need in a compact, transportable, and easy-to-read form. Books have not lost their importance in the age of networked information, but must work in tandem with electronic resources to be as effective as possible. This book (of course!) has a sister web site at ■ http://www.lynda.com/dwg2/.

Although it might be possible to read or skim this book in a single day, the information inside is far too overwhelming to absorb in a single sitting. It took me many months to write the first *Designing Web Graphics* and many more months to write the second edition. Even with that many months, I could not have possibly understood the task at hand without many more years of experience under my belt as a computer graphics artist and teacher. The task of collecting all this information in one place is enormous and, frankly, never feels finished. The web changes and evolves constantly, but once the ink is dry on this book's pages, it will forever be there.

That's why there are many references to outside information sources in this book. Everything from other URLs, other books, magazines, conferences, newsgroups, mailing lists, and CD-ROMs are offered as support resources whenever a new subject is touched upon. I wrote this book with the full understanding that information will change and evolve, and gave you outside channels to get to that new information. Updates and errata will be posted at my web site as well. Just remember how to spell my name—with a "y"—and you'll be able to e-mail me or check in on my web site at any time. I can't promise to answer everyone, but I do whenever time permits.

lynda@lynda.com
■ http://www.lynda.com

■ what the chapters cover

Which <...ing web graphics> Book Is Right For You?

Now that there are three different books to choose from, I get a lot of e-mail from people saying they want to buy one of my books, but aren't sure which one is right for them.

Designing Web Graphics.2 is appropriate for designers and nondesigners who are planning or already creating web sites. This book is the cornerstone of my series, which is tailored for newcomers to web design. Surprisingly I get just as much e-mail from experienced web designers who've bought the first edition and have learned a lot of new information. *Designing Web Graphics.2* covers web design from A through Z. It is a comprehensive web design book that you'll use as a reference as you develop your own sites. Most people report that their copy of the first edition has become dog-eared, and that of every web book they own, it's the one book they keep by their computer at all times.

Deconstructing Web Graphics approaches learning web design through a different means. Because most of the HTML buffs I know taught themselves through viewing other's source code, I thought it would be great to select from inspirational sites and both view and explain their code for readers. Behind-the-scenes profiles are made of programmers, designers, photographers, and illustrators, and everything from Photoshop layers to Shockwave/Lingo files are analyzed and demystified. This book is great for experienced designers looking for inspiration and improvement, and non-hands-on people who want an overview of issues surrounding web design.

Coloring Web Graphics is half book, half software. The book is a definitive guide to color on the web. Everything from file compression to dithering to browser-safe colors is thoroughly explained. My co-author, Bruce Heavin, assembled hundreds of suggested browser-safe color combinations for web sites. The CD-ROM includes swatches that can be loaded into Photoshop, Paint Shop Pro, Painter, Photo-Paint, and FreeHand. The book offers lots of step-by-step tutorials, and the CD-ROM swatches provide endless ideas for successful and cross-platform compatible color schemes.

A Final Note from the Author

I view the web as a both a revolutionary place and a historical event unfolding before my eyes, in my lifetime. I am drawn to the web as a place of enormous possibility. It's a great honor to have something to contribute to this medium that might help make it a better place. Not just a better looking place, but a more usable and accessible place, too.

Although the web started as a grass-roots movement, it has quickly escalated to big business. Even if you don't own a computer, these days you can't escape noticing web addresses everywhere. URLs are in magazine ads, television commercials, billboards, and junk mail. The web has taken the world by storm, with an unstoppable momentum that has inspired new pressures on the public to participate.

This is both positive and negative. I view the historical time we're in now as a digital revolution. Anything that is digital is somehow supposed to be better than anything that isn't. It's causing a lot of people to lose job security, and there's a lot of anxiety about getting up to speed. I hear so many people complain that they'll never catch up, and they feel defeated. The stakes seem high, and unfortunately they are.

Personally, I enjoy the challenge of computers and the web, and am a participant by choice not pressure. I do, however, completely understand that digital is not for everyone, in the same way no religion or political belief is correct for everyone. It's my goal to write about this stuff in a comforting way, and help those through it who are lost, intimidated, or defeated. Those who catch the wave almost always have a good time once they know how to ride. Information is power. It's far better to understand than to fear.

The World Wide Web has brought people, platforms, and operating systems together that were never intended to necessarily mix. With that comes controversy, greed, very high stakes, and a sense of panic. If I can do anything to alleviate that fear and instead instill my own sense of excitement and fascination, my job will be done.

Thank you for sharing my work with me.

■ New Riders Publishing

The staff of New Riders Publishing is committed to bringing you the very best in computer reference material. Each New Riders book is the result of months of work by authors and staff who research and refine the information contained within its covers.

As part of this commitment to you, the NRP reader, New Riders invites your input. Please let us know if you enjoy this book, if you have trouble with the information and examples presented, or if you have a suggestion for the next edition.

Please note, however: New Riders staff cannot serve as a technical resource for web graphics or for questions about software or hardware-related problems. Please refer to the documentation that accompanies your software or to the applications' Help systems.

If you have a question or comment about any New Riders book, there are several ways to contact New Riders Publishing. We will respond to as many readers as we can. Your name, address, or phone number will never become part of a mailing list or be used for any purpose other than to help us continue to bring you the best books possible.

You can write us at the following address:

> New Riders Publishing
> Attn: Publisher
> 201 W. 103rd Street
> Indianapolis, IN 46290

If you prefer, you can fax New Riders Publishing at:

> (317) 817-7448.

You can also send electronic mail to New Riders
at the following Internet address:

> jkane@newriders.mcp.com

NRP is an imprint of Macmillan Computer Publishing.
To obtain a catalog or information, or to purchase any
Macmillan Computer Publishing book, call (800) 428-5331
or visit our Web site at ■ http://www.mcp.com.

Thank you for selecting *Designing Web Graphics.2*!

Getting Started in Web Design

BROWSER SAFE COLOR

33 FF FF

0033

<STRONG>

Width = "500"

<img src="

IMAGE OPTIMIZATION

Height = "600"

Imaging techniques

Web file Formats

bgcolor = "FFFFCC"

Alink = "cyan"

Animation, sound and

LYNDA.COM

33

<BODY>

www Design

Web Design as a Career Path

Web page design is one of the most sought after careers in digital design today. It's still so new that there are no set rules, standards, or certificates that qualify anyone officially as a web designer. There are lots of people out there with questionable experience who call themselves web designers, and lots of clients who've hired them and been burned.

If you're already a professional designer, you probably already have decent design skills. Whether you learned them in school or are self-taught is not necessarily a measure of how good you are. Good training helps, and having a design degree looks great on paper, but there are also plenty of successful designers who are self-taught.

> ### ■ tip
> Design Resources
> Check out the "Design Resources" section at the back of this book for names of schools, magazines, books, and resources for design and web design.

Although web design schools will probably exist some day, for the moment you get your web design education a few different ways:

- Books, like this one
- By studying and reverse-engineering successfully designed sites
- Reading other web design books and related magazine articles
- Referencing online web design resources
- Joining web design UseNet groups and listservs
- Joining design organizations
- Attending conferences or taking seminars

If you're getting started in design and the web for the first time, and are not a professional, you have a longer path ahead of you because it really helps to be grounded in traditional design first. Here are some suggestions to jump-start your design career:

- Study design books
- Read design magazines
- Attend a design conference or take a seminar
- Attend a design school or certificate program

There's no one secret technique for becoming a designer. Some people have instinctive design sensibilities and excel professionally with no training or effort, whereas others must study their entire careers. It is always possible to improve. Those who think they know it all or don't need to evolve are usually full of it. Keep your mind open to change and new information, and you will excel in this field.

How to Charge for Web Design

Because the field of web design is so new, pricing for web design services is still all over the map. You'll hear of jobs that pay minimum wage on an hourly basis, or jobs that pay over $100k per year. You'll hear about people creating web pages for $50.00 each or designing a single site for $100,000.00. Learning to price your services is an art and a challenge, to put it mildly.

If it helps at all, know that the pricing struggle is shared by everyone who does this type of work. There is no set market value for web design. My guess is this will settle down at some point, and that standards might develop, but for the moment they do not exist. Even for fields in design that have standards, such as magazine illustration work or graphic design, there are still some who charge below market value and those who regularly command much higher rates.

I always recommend that you do not start out in business for yourself if you are a first-time web designer. Work for a web design firm before you start your own. Observe how they do things, and don't think you are any smarter or better than they are until you get at least a few jobs under your belt. There's a lot to web design besides understanding what to do technically. Besides being a desirable designer, negotiation skills, people skills, being on time and on budget, and troubleshooting skills all factor into the picture.

When I ran my freelance business as a motion graphics designer many years ago, I was very good at bidding jobs and rarely, if ever, got burned. Part of my skill was that I truly understood how long something would take me to finish. I had worked with clients who knew what they wanted, and worked with clients who designed everything by committee and changed directives often and without warning. I learned to assess my clients pretty well, and bill accordingly. I knew how much money I wanted to make in a given amount of time and could estimate what I would need to bid in order to accomplish my goals. Even so, it took me years of practice to get good at bidding. Don't expect to walk into this profession and make a financial killing out of the gate.

If you've never created a web site, it's hard to know how long it will take you to finish the job. How does one bill if one has never done something before? And yet, many people find themselves in these very shoes—often without intent, just by happenstance. I recommend being honest. If you fake your way through a job contract, it will take a toll on your nerves, your work, and your reputation.

Make sure you represent yourself clearly when you take on a job and don't lead your client into unrealistic expectations. You need to educate your clients as well as service them. A common misunderstanding about web design is that it has a fixed end. Web pages usually need to be designed, and then *maintained*. Make sure your role is defined clearly and that you get a contract, as well as an advance. It's normal to ask for 1/2 to 1/3 payment up front to cover your expenses.

You might want to compare the prices that other companies charge. Internet service providers (ISPs) often list their pricing strategies. For a list of over 4,000 national ISPs, check out this link:

■ http://thelist.iworld.com/

Many new web designers cannot afford a lawyer, so check out this great book that establishes pricing standards and includes boilerplate contracts for graphic designers:

**Graphic Artists Guild Handbook:
Pricing & Ethical Guidelines**
Publisher: Practical Patchwork
Retail: $24.95 ■ ISBN: 0932102085
■ http://www.gag.org/pegs.html

The 1996 edition did not include anything for web designers, but it still gives a good explanation of pricing and bidding procedures, as well as legal contracts for independent design production.

Don't forget, in addition to your time, to factor in such things as equipment, training, rent, software, insurance, and taxes. Being in business for yourself as a web designer is tempting, but it can have a lot of hidden costs and pitfalls.

Learn to Use Search Engines

Search engines are great ways to find things you need to know about web design (or anything else in the universe, for that matter). If you're looking for advice, tutorials, reviews, or new software or hardware, look to the web first! It's the greatest encyclopedia ever created.

Here are some URLs of my favorite search engines:

- http://www.altavista.digital.com
- http://www.yahoo.com
- http://www.excite.com
- http://www.hotbot.com
- http://www.webworkstudio.com

As well as knowing which search engines to use, it's very important to know how to use a search engine. Most of the search engines have help-based tutorials that can make all the difference. The goal of a search is to come up with the exact matches you want. Most engines fail to find the correct response or correct number of responses because the search is too broad.

Using ■ www.altavista.digital.com, for example, I typed **Lynda Weinman**. The search engine reported 2,487 occurrences of the name Weinman and 20,685 occurrences of the name Lynda. But when I put my name in quotes, as **"Lynda Weinman"**, the search engine knew to report only occurrences of that exact combination of words and yielded the more accurate result of 600.

For a great tutorial on using search engines, try this link:

- http://www.webreference.com/content/search/

How to List Your Site with Search Engines

You can also register your web sites with search engines. This is usually a free but time-consuming process. Here are some URLs to contact:

- http://www.yahoo.com
- http://www.altavista.digital.com
- http://www.excite.com
- http://www.lycos.com
- http://guide.infoseek.com
- http://www.mckinley.com
- http://www.webcrawler.com
- http://www.opentext.com
- http://www.hotbot.com
- http://www.infomarket.ibm.com
- http://www.nln.com
- http://www.shareware.com

Most likely, you'll need to create a summary of your site, using 25 words or less, to describe "keywords" that others might find you by.

Or if you don't want to do the work yourself, try this service, which will submit your site listing to many different search engines:

- http://www.submit-it.com/

Choose Your Tools

Everyone, at some point in their web design life, has to answer some basic questions. What platform should I use? Which software should I get? Which type of HTML editor should I use? How much RAM do I need? What kind of scanner do I need? This chapter walks you through some of these important decisions you'll need to make.

The ideal setup for a web design studio would be to own a Mac, PC, Sun, and SGI; have a full video and sound studio; and own all the imaging, video, sound, and authoring software in the universe. No one will be quite so lucky, but that gives you an idea of how limitless the possibilities are for equipment acquisitions!

So, here are some very general guidelines. Macs and PCs are going to have the widest range of web design tools. Most of your web audience will be on Macs or PCs. So even if you're lucky enough to work on a higher-end Unix platform, you might consider getting one of these lower-end platforms to author web pages. At the very least, it will give you a reality checkpoint.

Which Flavor: Mac or PC?

The web is unusual in that no other type of design has ever required such an understanding of cross-platform differences and compatibility issues. Even multimedia developers have always had the option of creating distinct titles for different computer platforms. As evidence, it's very common in the CD-ROM section of store shelves to see two different aisles for Mac and PCs. And computer stores almost never even have aisles for Unix platforms! With authoring for the web, regardless of which platform you own, you'll be creating material for every platform.

Chances are, you already have a computer. If you don't, and are considering getting one for the purposes of web design, then you have some serious decisions to make. Be forewarned that this is a topic of great passion and controversy. This subject is known to stir up more trouble than a presidential debate!

Macs Versus PCs

There's a great irony in web design: most professional web designers and art directors are on Macs, but most of the audience they design for is on PCs. The Mac was the first mainstream operating system to have a GUI (graphical user interface). Because most visual designers go for that sort of thing (myself included), it should be no surprise that we would end up using Macs. Even now that Win95 emulates a lot of that same interface, there are many die-hard Mac users who vow they will never switch. For the time being, the Mac is still the most popular design platform.

I am not suggesting that you do not use or buy a PC. I am not suggesting that PCs are inferior. I am just stating some facts. It is true that there are many more PCs in circulation than Macs, but it is also true that the Mac is still the most popular platform for visual design folks. Popular doesn't necessarily mean best, it just means the numbers are bigger.

Some Mac advantages: You'll find that the majority of design-based software comes out on the Mac before the PC. You'll find that most service bureaus that deal with desktop publishing are biased toward Macs, not PCs. Most likely, you'll find more support among other artists and designers if you are on a Mac.

Some PC advantages: Most end users are on PCs. Most browser software comes out first for the PC, and often never fully supports the Mac. The PC has a bigger market share than the Mac, so equipment and peripherals are often less expensive.

There is truly no wrong or right platform. Regardless of which platform you buy, you will be able to design web pages. My suggestion is to try out the software and equipment you want to get before you buy it. Ask around. Find sites that you admire and ask what equipment and software their designers recommend. There's no wrong decision here; just make sure your choice fits your budget, needs, and taste.

It's always important to check your site on platforms other than that from which you authored. If you are lucky enough to own two platforms, this can be done in the luxury of your own office, studio, or home. If not, make sure you locate another system where you can preview your site. As future chapters will describe in detail, what you see on one platform ain't necessarily what you see on others. This is a universal problem and will be the case regardless of which platform you decide to own.

System Requirements

Believe it or not, web authoring is not a very taxing activity for a computer system. It's not necessary to have the fastest and newest machine, as is in other disciplines such as desktop publishing, digital video, or 3D rendering. It's possible to get by with much less than the top-of-the-line when it comes to equipment. I recommend instead that you put your investments in RAM or great imaging software, such as Photoshop, than in the latest and greatest computer model.

Let's break down the key components of a computer system—processor speed, RAM, hard disk, video and sound cards, monitor, CD-ROM drive, modem, and scanner—and evaluate their importance for web authoring:

Processor speed: These days, we often hear about fast processor speeds, sometimes even in excess of 500 megahertz. How important a factor is processing speed in terms of web design? Not very. Processing speed helps with 3D graphics rendering and the speed of rendering television or film-sized movies. It really helps when you're working with a huge, high-resolution image that's being prepped for printing. Making images for the web requires that you work in low resolution. Processing speed helps with complex, math-intensive computer operations. Unless you are planning to use your computer for those types of projects in addition to web design, a fast processor is going to buy you very few advantages.

RAM: You can never have too much RAM or hard disk space. Having RAM makes it possible to work with multiple software applications. It lets you keep an HTML editor, an imaging program, and a web browser open at the same time. This will save you more time (and isn't your time worth money, too?) than you may imagine. Never skimp on RAM, if you can possibly avoid it. A minimum requirement would be 16mb, and maximum would be...? Well, as I said, you can never have too much RAM!

Hard disk(s): You can never have too much hard disk space. Just like a job where the amount of work seems to fill however long the deadline lasts, most projects take up all the hard disk space you have. I highly recommend getting a removable storage system in addition to a permanent hard drive. Zip drives are great; Jaz drives are sublime!

Video cards: Most computer systems ship with a video card preinstalled. For this reason, many new computer buyers aren't even aware of their video card's features or capabilities. The video card is what dictates how many colors your monitor can display. Most of the web audience will have 8-bit color (256 color) or less. Images look much better with millions (24-bit) or thousands (16-bit) of color displays. If you have the chance, go for a card with the highest possible bit depth (24-bit). This allows you to design for everyone—those with the lowest and highest common denominator.

Sound cards: If you plan to work with sound, you will need a sound card. Again, many contemporary computers ship with these cards built-in. The web today mostly offers 8-bit sound because those files are smaller and faster to download. Regardless, just like with video cards, it's always best to start with the highest quality and down-scale for your audience later.

Monitors: The majority of your audience will be on standard 640x480 monitors. It's much more fun to design on a larger monitor, however, because you can have more room for all the menus, windows, and palettes that most popular imaging programs sport these days. Almost any kind of monitor will do (make sure it will work with the kind of video card you get), but the bigger the better for ease of use with design.

CD-ROM drive: A lot of software these days ships on CDs. Installing software off a CD is very handy, but if you're using your CD-ROM drive for this purpose only, speed doesn't matter much. If you're going to play games or look at CD-ROM titles, however, you'll want 2X speed at the very least.

Modem: Picking a modem is often based on price versus performance. I suggest you choose one based on the latter, not the former. The faster the better. If you're uploading files to a web site, you will be grateful for transfer at the fastest possible speed. Getting a modem is not something to skimp on if you're planning on doing this kind of work seriously.

Scanner: Because you'll be working with low-resolution imagery, dots per inch and image quality are not your primary considerations when choosing a scanner for web design. Speed is the primary concern; pick a scanner that can scan in color quickly. For the low resolution of web images, speed is the only factor that will make any difference in your production flow.

Software

Software by nature is fluid. It will always change. That is its purpose! If it stayed the same, we would all complain. This fact doesn't make for a very comfortable authoring or learning environment, however. How many other professions or hobbies do you know of where the tools change and evolve constantly? You can bemoan this fact or embrace it. If you plan to make your living doing anything in the digital arts, changing software is a fact of life.

There are two categories of software: that which you must buy and that which is free and downloadable off the web. Most likely, you will have to buy software sooner or later, even though at times it seems that everything anyone would ever want can be found on the web. This section helps you weigh some of the software decisions, makes recommendations, and lists resources.

Imaging Programs

In order to create graphics for the web, you will need some image-making software. This book concentrates primarily on Photoshop, Painter, Paint Shop Pro, and Photo-Paint techniques.

Photoshop is the most popular imaging software among professional designers on any platform for almost any purpose—not just web design. Not surprisingly, it also has the most depth and features over other software packages reviewed in this book. I use Photoshop primarily, and Painter occasionally. Those are definitely my favorites, and this book will be weighed in their favor.

I know, however, that not everyone needs nor can afford professionally priced and feature-based programs such as Photoshop and Painter. For this reason, I've taught myself a couple of other, less-expensive imaging programs: Paint Shop Pro and Photo-Paint. Whenever possible in this book, I'll share imaging techniques in these programs, too.

If you're going to make your living off web design, don't skimp on imaging software—bite the bullet and buy Photoshop. I have rarely heard of anyone who was sorry they did. Becoming literate in Photoshop is the number-one most important skill you can possess. There are wonderful books on Photoshop imaging techniques that beautifully augment this book's content.

■ **tip**

Recommended Reading

The Photoshop WOW! Book
Publisher: Peachpit Press
Authors: Linnea Dayton and Jack Davis
Retail Price: $39.95 ■ ISBN 1-56609-178-0

**Adobe Photoshop for Macintosh Classroom
in a Book, Second Edition**
Publisher: Hayden Books
Author: Adobe Press
Retail Price: $45.00 ■ ISBN: 1-56830-118-9

Imaging Essentials
Publisher: Hayden Books
Author: Luanne Seymour Cohen and Tanya Wendling
Retail Price: $39.95 ■ ISBN: 1-56830-051-4

Designer Photoshop
Publisher: Random House
Author: Rob Day
Retail Price: $30.00 ■ ISBN: 0-679-75326-5

Adobe Photoshop: A Visual Guide for the Mac
Publisher: Addison Wesley
Authors: David Biedney and Bert Monroy
Retail Price: $34.95 ■ ISBN: 0-201-48993-7

Shareware and Freeware Programs

The web is a great distribution medium. I predict that someday we will get all our software and updates via the web, instead of off of retail shelves or out of mail-order catalogues. One of the coolest things about the web is that it allows the small developer a distribution avenue to write niche market software.

Some of my favorite web authoring tools come from the web. There are all kinds of imaging, animation, HTML, and browser-related software choices available. A favorite source for this type of software is at ■ http://www.shareware.com. You can search by software name, company, or type of product.

Learning HTML

This is not a general, all-purpose HTML book, but it includes HTML techniques when they are relevant to visual design. I recommend that you supplement this book with an HTML book if you are serious about learning how to code yourself. These are my favorites:

**Teach Yourself Web Publishing with HTML 3.2
in a Week, Third Edition**
Publisher: Sams.net
Author: Laura Lemay
Retail Price: $29.99 ▪ ISBN: 1-57521-192-0
■ http://slack.lne.com/Web/HTML3.2

HTML Quick Reference
Publisher: Que
Author: Robert Mullen
Retail Price: $19.99 ▪ ISBN: 0-7897-0867-1
■ http://www.mcp.com/390160932287319/que/developer_
expert/htmlqr/

HTML for the World Wide Web: Visual QuickStart Guide
Publisher: Peachpit Press
Author: Elizabeth Castro
Retail Price: $17.95 ▪ ISBN 0-201-88448-8
■ http://www.peachpit.com/peachpit/titles/catalog/88448.html

What Does HTML Look Like?

If you've never seen HTML, here's a sample from my home page of what it looks like. HTML has a basic structure, and this sample illustrates some of the key aspects of HTML. By the way, studying my code or anyone else's is a great way to teach yourself how to write your own. It's a tried and true method that most HTML experts recommend and practice.

The finished web page, viewed from within a browser.

```
1   <HTML>
2   <HEAD>
3   <TITLE>Lynda's Homegurrrlpage</TITLE>
    </HEAD>
4   <BODY BACKGROUND="/ltspiralpat.gif"
5   BGCOLOR="CCCCCC" TEXT="003366" LINK="330066"
    VLINK="663399" ALINK="CC33FF">
6   <CENTER>
    <IMG SRC="newlogo.gif">
    <P>
    <CENTER>
7   <IMG SRC="man.gif">
8   <P>
    </HTML>
```

1 **\<HTML\>**, **\</HTML\>**: All HTML pages begin and end with the open and closed **\<HTML\>** tag.

2 **\<HEAD\>**: The **\<HEAD\>** tag contains header information, such as the title of the page.

3 **\<TITLE\>**: The title of the page goes inside the **\<TITLE\>** tag.

4 **\<BODY\>**, **BACKGROUND**: The **\<BODY\>** tag is where you set up body elements. In this case, the HTML is requesting a **BACKGROUND=/ltspiralpat.gif**. This instructs the browser to take the ltspiral image and repeat it until it fills the screen. The amount of repeats are dictated by the size of the tile and the size of the screen of the end user. For more information on background tiles, check out Chapter 8, "Background Tiles," and Chapter 13, "Layout and Alignment Techniques."

5 **BGCOLOR, TEXT, LINK, VLINK, ALINK:** The **<BODY>** tag is also where you set up web page colors. Below, you'll see my color choices for the background color, text, links, visited links, and active links (the color of the link as you depress the mouse button to click on it). These colors are specified by their hexadecimal equivalents of RGB values. If this sounds Greek to you, check out Chapter 6, "Browser-Safe Color."

bgcolor	text	link	vlink	alink
CCCCCC	003366	330066	663399	CC33FF
R. 204	R. 0	R. 51	R. 102	R. 204
G. 204	G. 51	G.0	G. 51	G. 51
B. 204	B. 102	B. 102	B. 153	B. 255

6 **<CENTER>:** The **<CENTER>** tag centers whatever is included in it. You would close the tag to specify other types of alignments with **</CENTER>**.

7 **<IMG SRC>:** An **<IMG SRC>** tag instructs the browser to display an image.

newlogo.gif

man.gif

These two images were used inside the <IMG SRC> tag on my home page. Both are transparent GIFs, meaning that the background colors (black and grey, respectively) dropped out on the final web page. For more information on transparency, check out Chapter 3, "Web File Formats," and Chapter 7, "Transparent Artwork."

8 **<P>:** The **<P>** tag inserts a paragraph break (single line space) between text or images.

The above example scratches only the surface of HTML. There are lots of references to HTML in this book, with the most extensive information found in Chapter 17, "HTML for Visual Designers."

HTML Software

I had the great pleasure of writing my own magazine column for a while (until I got too busy writing books), and the favorite headline I ever wrote was HTML SUCKS! It felt so good to come right out and say it—in big, bold headline letters no less! No one, except a die-hard programmer (and no offense to you folks at all) would want, by choice, to work with HTML.

For those of you who don't know what it is (is there anyone left?), HTML stands for **H**yper**T**ext **M**arkup **L**anguage. It is the language with which web pages are written, and therefore designed, although most designers would cringe at the thought of calling HTML a design layout language.

And that's precisely the point. HTML was not written to be a design language. It was written to be a display language, with the intent that it might display differently on different machines and operating systems. Ever notice how browser software allows you to change your fonts and their sizes, and whether images and links are turned on or off? HTML was supposed to be a transportable language that could be customized to the end-user machine's liking.

HTML is what made the web possible, but HTML has also become known as a designer's nightmare. There has never been a design medium in the past that allowed its audience to change the content at whim. If you are used to creating artwork for magazines, television, books, or annual reports, you're used to having a sense of comfort that what you see as the final result is what everyone will see. When it's finished, it can never be changed. HTML plays havoc with a designer's quest for control. It is one of the strangest design mediums ever unleashed upon us, and that is because it was never intended to be a design medium in the first place.

Many of the chapters in this book teach you how to trick HTML into obedience, but the starting point is HTML whether we like it or not. HTML is the language of the web. Do you have to know HTML to design web pages? No, but it sure helps. Frankly, some of my all-time favorite sites were designed by artists who never touched the code. They teamed up with an HTML programmer and did what they knew best—design.

My definition of a designer is that we are control freaks. It is in our nature to want to control how our artwork looks; that's why we are good at what we do. Most of us, in fact, are passionate about making our artwork look just exactly to our liking. Web page design is definitely full of intense challenges, and you can decide to take them on or pass the buck to a programmer.

Should You Learn HTML?

I am old in computer design years, having participated to one degree or another in computer graphics since 1980. I remember the days when all the popular word processors required that you add mark-up tags to text. If you wanted something to be bold or italic, for example, you had to key in a cryptic code next to the respective word in order to instruct the software to print the intended result. The software program never previewed the text in a graphical form, and you really didn't know if it would turn out how you expected until you saw hard copy.

Needless to say, HTML gives me a sense of déjà vu. And truthfully, HTML is not a real programming language. A real programming language makes HTML look like a piece of cake. HTML is a mark-up language, and an easy one at that. If motivated, most people are capable of teaching themselves HTML. It's more intimidating than it is difficult.

The real question is—is it really necessary to know HTML? I think it is, but not in all cases. The advantage to knowing and understanding HTML is that you will be in better control of knowing what is possible and what is not. You will not have to hear "No" from someone else who might not care about your design as much as you do. You will know how to bid jobs more easily and how to guide clients through their jobs more easily. If you're a client, you'll know what to ask for and what not to ask for. You'll know if your hired gun is ripping you off or is an unexploited genius. The truth is, if there was a magic HTML pill, you would gladly take it. Everyone prefers to be "in the know" if the price isn't too high.

If you want to learn HTML, there are a few different camps to sub-scribe to: those who learn HTML and understand what the tags do and mean, those who use an HTML editor to help them with auto-mated tags, and those who use a WYSIWYG HTML editor, and don't know why anything works but get finished web pages anyway. Let's examine the options.

How to Learn HTML

I taught myself HTML by using a stripped-down word processor. I wrote every tag by hand because that is how I learn new things the best. I typically learn best by doing, not reading or studying. I viewed the source of pages I liked and often copied what I liked as a starting point. I wanted to understand HTML because that is the kind of person I am. I am not representative of everybody, but this learning method fit my personality.

As an experienced teacher, I can tell you for certain that different people have different learning methods, different aptitudes, and different needs and goals. **There is no one right way to learn HTML.** If you really want to understand what you're doing and why, the method I used works great. It requires patience and persistence and the acceptance that you'll make mistakes and won't get instant results. The payoff is that you'll understand what you're doing and will approach this medium with a greater degree of confidence.

There are great online tutorials for learning HTML. A few of my favorites are:

- http://www.microsoft.com/workshop/design/design-contents1.htm#des
- http://help.netscape.com/links.html
- http://ncdesign.kyushu-id.ac.jp/

Another great way to learn HTML is to study other people's source code. In most popular browsers, you'll find a source view option located under the File menu. Browse the web looking for pages you like; view their source and learn the tricks of the trade. There's no better way.

Text-Based HTML Editors

HTML editors are dedicated word processors that have automated tags built in. Normally, these tags are accessible via menu commands or handy toolbars. If you don't know a word of HTML, these types of editors will baffle you. What good is an automated tag if you don't understand what tags do in the first place?

If you practice the methods of teaching yourself HTML in a standard word processor as described earlier, you will come to want and appreciate a text-based HTML editor. Some of them have spell-checkers, HTML checkers (to validate, or ensure, that you've written correct HTML), search-and-replace functionality, and broken-link checkers.

Most HTML editors are found on the web and can be downloaded for free or for free trial periods. The best way to find HTML editors is on the web itself. Here are some good starting points:

- http://www.shareware.com
- http://www.yahoo.com/Computers_and_Internet/Internet/World_Wide_web/HTML_Editors/Macintosh/
- http://www.yahoo.com/Computers_and_Internet/Internet/World_Wide_web/HTML_Editors/MS_Windows/

Here are some reviews and comparisons of popular HTML editors that can be found online:

- http://www.cnet.com/Content/Reviews/Compare/11htmleds/
- http://www.dsport.com/sjm/resources.html
- http://www.pcmag.com/iu/features/1520/_open.htm

WYSIWYG HTML Editors

WYSIWYG (**W**hat**Y**ou**S**ee**I**s**W**hat**Y**ou**G**et) stands for a new breed of HTML editor that takes the pain out of writing this damn stuff. At least it seems that way. WYSIWYG editors don't require that you know a word of HTML— in fact many of them shield you from it so successfully that you may author pages and never understand or learn a word of code.

There's nothing wrong with that! I mean, how many people write their own word processing software or PostScript commands? People who like and understand how to program live for this stuff, and very few of the rest of us enjoy it much at all.

The problem is that HTML tags change all the time. New file formats and plug-ins and browser features make this a changing landscape unparalleled by typical word processing or PostScript software. Web design and development is an emerging medium, and we're all eager guinea pigs to propel it further!

The only way that WYSIWYG editors could truly keep pace would be if they changed on a weekly basis. This is not to suggest that they aren't useful at all. Au contraire! They are wonderful. Anyone who has ever programmed frames or a complicated nested table will be in ecstasy letting a program do it for them without coding. I use WYSIWYG editors myself—especially when I'm in a hurry. They are fantastic timesavers and help you get your ideas out quickly without being bogged down by programming strange tags and adding opening and closing brackets and slashes everywhere.

The problem is that once you've gotten the web design bug, you'll want to try new things that the WYSIWYG editor won't support. And, if you've relied exclusively on the editor to compose pages, you will not have gotten any of the necessary skills to understand how to extend its capabilities. WYSIWYG editors often throw in their own HTML tags that certain browsers don't recognize. Or you might want to use a new plug-in or file format that they don't support yet. It's an easier, but more limited, architecture.

The perfect world would be to have the browser also be the HTML editor. Every time the browser changes, the HTML editor changes, too. Well, without naming names—even the most popular browser-based WYSIWYG HTML software doesn't fully support its own tags. These editors still have some growing up to do—but I'll be the first in line to endorse them once they're mature.

Understanding the Web Environment

2

LYNDA.COM

www.Design

Welcome to the Weird World of Web Graphics

I don't know about you, but I feel enormous excitement to witness and participate in the emergence of the web as a new communication medium. I never imagined a scenario where everyone could be, depending on personal choice, an author or spectator, a publisher or subscriber, an information source or information retriever.

There's never been a distribution medium like the web. Where else could you reach a potential audience of millions of people without spending a fortune in time, money, and research to mail your work to them? It's platform-independent. The web doesn't care whether you're on a Mac, Windows, Sun, or SGI workstation. There are no geographical boundaries. Someone in Germany can look at my site as easily as someone who lives around the corner.

The web has no hierarchy. By looking at a site, you can't tell whether the author is male, female, black, white, Asian, Hispanic, handicapped, rich, poor, old, or young. If you have a cool site, there's no one stopping more viewers from visiting yours than any number of boring well-funded corporate sites. Is this really an example of where the best designer wins? So far, yes. It represents freedom of expression in its most idealistic, raw form.

Whatever valid criticisms exist of the web as a design medium, visuals play a huge role in the popularity of the World Wide Web. Artists have an opportunity to define the look and feel of the web, and I doubt there's ever been another case in history where individuals, not institutions, have had a chance to influence a medium of this importance and magnitude. This is the world unlike any of us ever dreamed—all connected across geographical and computer platform boundaries, all capable of being interactive spectators or active contributors.

Although the web may be considered by many the latest, most advanced technology in computing, it is a very disconcerting authoring environment for most artists. Graphics are indisputably one of the key components that have made the web so popular and exciting. Even so, the graphic tools and techniques available to create visuals are confusing and limited. Most visual designers and computer artists using today's advanced imaging programs are going to feel lost when first introduced to authoring for the web.

This is partially because the web, like all graphical user interfaces, is easy to view and use, but more difficult to create for. It's one of those ironies life is full of; if it's easy to use, it's generally hard to make. It used to be that you could define yourself as just a writer, an illustrator, a typographer, a layout artist, an animator, a sound designer, a programmer, or an interface designer and that was enough. The web merges all these separate disciplines into one integrated communication medium, and it's enough to make a single individual feel easily overwhelmed. A few superhumans do it all well, but they are the exception, not the rule.

There are many parallels to web design and the early days of desktop publishing. Remember what happened to typography with the invention of the laser printer? Designers were horrified to see page layouts generated with bad spacing, poor font choices, mismanaged type sizes, and an uneducated sense of placement. Things have settled down since then, and with a little maturity the same will be true of the web.

Designing for the Computer Screen, Not the Printed Page

Everything that is wonderful about the web—global accessibility, cross-platform compatibility, networked distribution, and ever-improving-technology—has a tradeoff somewhere down the graphics creation road. On a printed page, everyone sees the same thing (with the exception of those who are visually impaired). A printed page has fixed dimensions. A printed page is designed once and forever stays the same. A printed page cannot be changed once it is finished.

Creating artwork for the web is very different from other visual delivery mediums because you're publishing your work to people's computer screens instead of printed pages. Computer systems vary widely. Some have small screens, some large. Some have color, some do not. Different operating systems deal with color differently. Some people have fast Internet connections, some do not. Different browsers display artwork differently. Different computer platforms have different fonts. It's the biggest design nightmare you could ever dream up—and your one chance of harnessing control over it is to understand the nature of the beast.

You can't possibly design a page that will look the same under all conditions without pandering to the lowest common denominator. That is not the route I advocate in this book. I believe that knowledge gives you power—if you arm yourself with an awareness of what can work and what can go wrong, and take whatever measures within your control to avoid the common pitfalls of this medium, your design can triumph over the obstacles.

This chapter reviews browser differences, monitor settings, and cross-platform compatibility issues, and offers an overview of bit-depth settings and gamma. These issues represent some of the common pitfalls to which web designers can fall prey.

Browser Differences

What is a browser, and what does it do? It's software that reads web pages and displays them for you. Different browsers can interpret the visual content of a web page differently. If you are a designer, this means you have the maddening task of designing a presentation that is subject to change according to which browser it's viewed from.

In the first edition of *Designing Web Graphics*, the introduction chapter to browsers was called "Browser Hell!" Back then, there were dozens of browsers with huge gaps in feature sets. Browsers have improved to the point now where that chapter heading is no longer appropriate because we've emerged from the browser hell era of the past to the present era of the browser wars. Competition has served us web designers well. The major discrepancies between feature sets that existed a year ago have become much less problematic.

Why do browsers interpret the pages differently? Shouldn't there be fixed standards? The browser interprets HTML (**H**yper**T**ext **M**arkup **L**anguage) code, which is the type of programming required to author web pages. HTML uses tags for including links, graphics, and other media on a web page. HTML was created as an attempt to be a universally accepted, cross-platform standard language for displaying information, text, and visuals on the web. Standards usually involve a standards committee, and committees often take a long time to agree on what they will officially support.

Officially sanctioned HTML of the old days allowed for one-color text, text that was left-justified with paragraph breaks, left-justified images, and little else. This understandably created frustration among designers and web browser developers who wanted to see the web evolve faster than the time it took outside committees to make formal decisions.

Entrepreneurial developers (primarily Netscape) took matters into their own hands and made web browsers that supported more options, without the blessings or participation of the HTML standards committee. New HTML code was developed that was supported only on proprietary browser systems, starting with Netscape and followed by others. This created outrage among some, and an outpouring of support from others who created an avalanche of web pages that included these new, unofficial HTML features.

As designers, it is not surprising that we want as many design features for the web as we can get our hands on. HTML today enables us to do a lot more than it used to, and we are grateful for every small morsel of design flexibility newly thrown our way. The downside is that some of these new design options have created a more confusing web design environment.

HTML for Different Browsers

In the first edition of *Designing Web Graphics*, I showed a full-color chart of the same HTML page in 11 different browsers and how you couldn't predictably rely on colored backgrounds, invisible borders, transparent GIFs, or even tables between different browsers. The level of differences today don't warrant that kind of visual chart. Most of the tags this book discusses work in the major three browsers: Netscape, Microsoft Internet Explorer (MSIE), and Mosaic. AOL's browser is the only popular browser that seriously lags behind the rest, but now that AOL will let you use other browsers, this should not be of much concern to web designers.

An invaluable resource for checking on browser discrepancies was put together by Kevin Ready, co-author of the book *Hybrid HTML Design: A Multi-Browser HTML Reference*. You'll find a table that shows all known HTML tags and which browsers support which tags here:

■ http://www.browserbydesign.com/resources/appa/apa1.htm

The book, *Hybrid HTML Design,* details how to design pages that are not only intended for display in all browsers, but perform optimally in each as well.

Hybrid HTML Design: A Multi-Browser HTML Reference
Publisher: New Riders Publishing
Authors: Kevin Ready and Janine Warner
Retail Price: $35.00 ■ ISBN: 1-56205-617-4

You can get the latest updates about browser versions at this marvelous site created by Dave Garaffa:

■ http://www.browserwatch.iworld.com

Here's a chart that was prepared by the Browserwatch site, dated 11/01/96:

Browser Types Visiting BrowserWatch
(Must Have .25% Share Or Better) ▪ printed with permission

Netscape Navigator	64.8%
Microsoft Internet Explorer	20.3%
Cyberdog	3.21%
Ibrowse	2.87%
Lynx	1.19%
IBM WebExplorer	0.92%
QuarterDeck Mosaic	0.83%
SPRY_Mosaic	0.77%
Amiga-AWeb	0.49%
Opera-2.1	0.47%
AOL (For Windows)	0.46%
FFiNet32.DLL	0.27%
AmigaVoyager	0.24%

Cross-Platform Hell!

One of the coolest things about the World Wide Web is that it's cross-platform, and people on Macs, PCs, Suns, and SGIs all get to communicate together in the same location for the first time in history.

If you're curious to know the percentage of systems used to access the web, here's the breakdown according to ■ http://browserwatch.iworld.com/stats/stats.html:

Windows	61.5%
Macintosh	23.2%
Unix	6.92%
Amiga	3.63%
OS/2	2.53%
Unknown	1.98%
VM/CMS	0.05%
NeXT	0.04%
Sega Saturn	0.01%

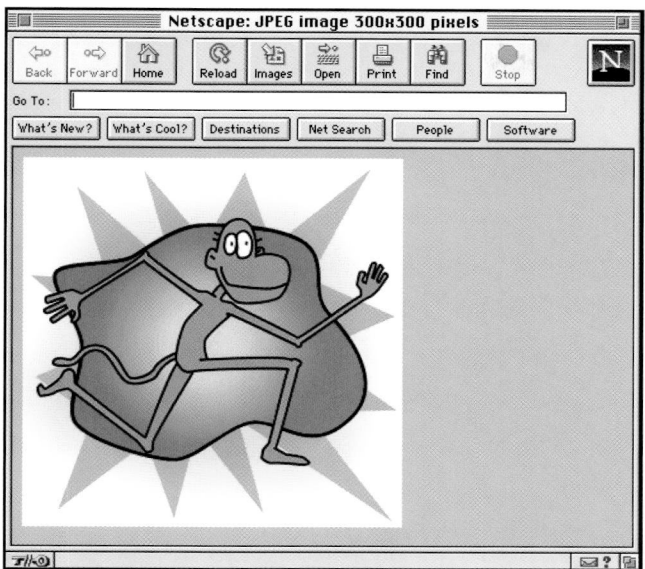

Here is an image viewed in a browser in 24-bit color.

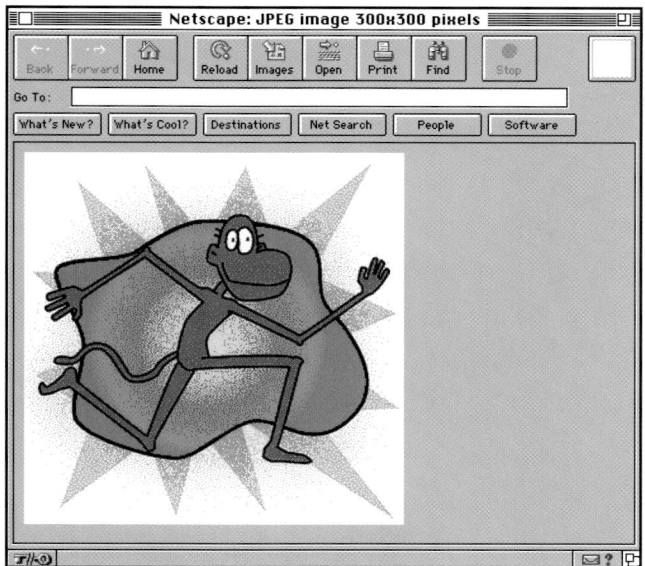

Here's what the same image would look like on a limited color monitor (4-bit or 16-color).

The unfortunate fact about cross-platform authoring is that viewers log on to the web by using different computers with different color spaces, color cards, monitor types, and monitor sizes. If you want to make yourself sad, spend hours creating a beautiful full-color graphic and then view it on someone's portable computer with a 4-bit color display. It's not a pretty sight. This is typical of some of the things that can happen unexpectedly to artwork that you post to your web site.

What can you do about such unplanned cross-platform discrepancies? In the case of viewers looking at your site from black-and-white portables or machines intended for video games, there's not much you can do except accept that the web will never offer full control over how your site is displayed. It's both the beauty of the medium and the curse of it. However, if you decide to make a site that relies on 24-bit color and a 21" monitor, you can see by the chart on the left how much you're probably limiting your potential audience.

Cross-Platform Color Calibration Issues

One of the problems with color on computer screens is that few monitors are calibrated accurately to one another. Shades of a color often vary wildly from computer to computer, and from platform to platform. (If you've ever owned two television sets, you know the color from set to set can vary wildly.) Anyone who works for a company with more than one computer knows that the colors shift between systems—even between identical operating systems and identical hardware.

Color calibration is a distressing problem for web designers who expect the colors they've picked to look the same on everyone's system. Macs, PCs, SGIs, and Suns all have different color cards and monitors, and none of them are calibrated to each other.

Mac

PC

SUN

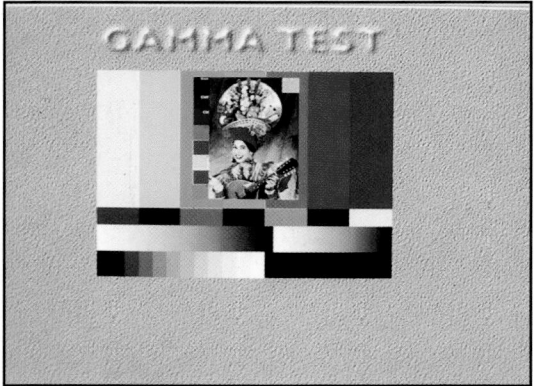

SGI

Because you now see for yourself that you have no control over the calibration of systems that your work will be viewed on, what can you do to make good-looking graphics that look good everywhere? What becomes more important than the colors you pick and what is stressed throughout this book is the contrast and value of a graphic. If you achieve contrast and value balance, the brightness and darkness, or color differences, on various platforms are going to be less objectionable.

Does your page pass the bit-depth test? Here's my home page viewed in **8-bit color**, **grayscale**, and **black and white**.

Across different computer platforms, the calibration problem is amplified by gamma differences. Gamma dictates the brightness and contrast of the computer's display. Macs, for example, are typically much brighter than PCs because of the differences in Macintosh's native gamma settings. Both calibration and gamma pose variables that are impossible to control in web design.

Although these numbers vary widely from different sources, it is generally reported that Mac and SGI monitors are close to the same, but PCs are much darker.

Average factory settings for Mac monitors	1.8 gamma
Average factory settings for SGI monitors	1.7 gamma
Average factory settings for PC monitors	2.5 gamma

Value is especially important in the context of web graphics. Differences in computer platforms, gamma settings, or a monitor's calibration can wreak havoc on the readability of images. A dark image created on one machine may come out black or appear tinted on another. Macintosh computers are generally lighter than Windows-based machines. Web pages can now also be viewed over television screens, which are calibrated differently from computer monitors altogether.

So how do you know if you are creating an image with values that will display properly on other machines? You can start by making sure your images have a good range from black to white. Don't place all the important information in the dark areas because they might go to black and fade out on someone's PC. And the same goes for light areas. There is no absolute control over how someone will see your images, so making them as readable as possible in terms of value should be your highest priority. Always view your images on other platforms to see whether your images achieve their intended values.

A great exercise is to temporarily throw your monitor in grayscale mode and then view your image to see whether its values are reading as you expected. This converts all the color data to blacks, whites, and grays. This change of settings yields much better feedback about brightness and contrast than a color display can.

Colors are notoriously deceptive when judging brightness and darkness because variables, such as a florescent color or subtle hand tinting, are overpowering when judging value.

Here's an example of the original image.

When viewing the image in grayscale, it almost disappears! This is because the values (lights and darks) are close together.

Here is the color-corrected version.

See how the grayscale version looks.

Personally, when working on my Mac, I try to make graphics a little lighter than I normally would, knowing that they'll display darker on PCs. When working on my PC, I do the opposite and make graphics slightly darker. There's no way to make it work perfectly everywhere, but knowing these general differences makes you an "informed" web designer so that you can make educated guesses about overall color brightness. I recommend that you always view your graphics on as many platforms as possible and make necessary changes when needed based on informed feedback.

Cross-platform authoring is possible on the web, but that doesn't necessarily mean it looks good. Take the following items into consideration, and you'll be able to make the best of a difficult design situation:

- ■ Your pages will look different on different computer monitors and platforms.
- ■ Check your pages on other platforms and make informed decisions for changes if necessary.
- ■ Pay attention to the brightness and contrast of a graphic, and it will look best even when viewed under poor monitor conditions.

High Resolution Versus Low Resolution

Because your delivery medium is a computer screen and not a printed page, high-resolution files are not part of web design life. High-resolution graphics are intended to be printed on high-resolution printers, not displayed on standard computer monitors. A typical screen resolution is 72 dpi and a high-resolution image is often 300+ dpi. You should always work at "screen resolution" when authoring images for the web (or any other screen-based medium, such as television or interactive multimedia). The accepted measurement of "screen resolution" is 72 dpi, or 72 dots per inch. This is because most standard computer monitors use 72 pixels for every inch of screen space.

For those of you who have worked with high-resolution files before, you may remember that in order to view them 1:1, you generally have to use the magnifying glass tool many times, resulting in a huge cropped image on your computer screen. The reason for this is that a computer screen can't physically display a high-resolution file. If you put a high-resolution file on the web, it can display only at 1:1 magnification, meaning that it will appear much bigger than you intended. Most likely, your goal for working in high resolution is to ensure the highest possible quality for your image, although in actuality, you would defeat that purpose.

> ■ **tip**
>
> Measurements for the Web Whenever working on images for the web, set your graphics to be measured in pixels, not inches. Inches are needed when creating artwork that will be printed on paper; pixels are the standard unit of measurement for screen-based bound images.

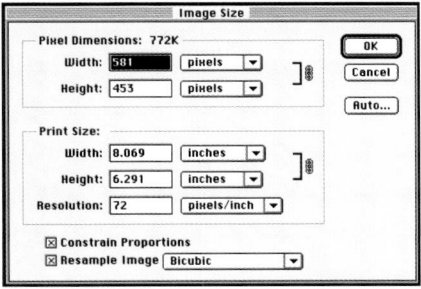

Here's a 72 dpi image in Netscape of my lovely daughter after eating melted chocolate. It appears exactly the way we want it to appear.

Go under the Image menu and select Image Size in Photoshop. This shows what the resolution is—in this case it's 72 dpi.

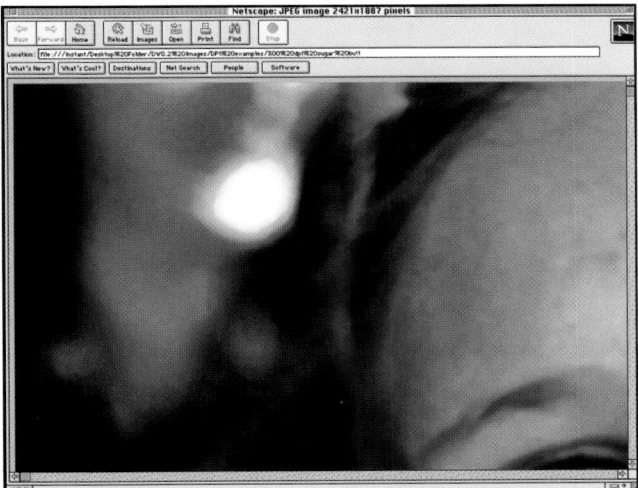

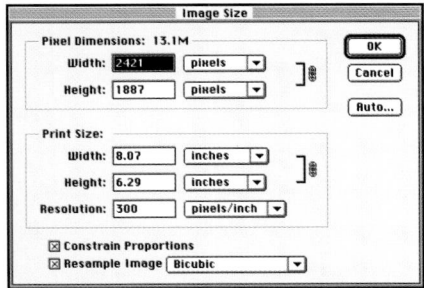

Here's an example of the 300 dpi image displayed in Netscape. Get the picture?

In this second example, the resolution is set to 300 dpi. In print graphics this would improve the appearance of this image significantly. In web graphics it results in an image that is way too big for the screen to display.

Bit Depth

Uh-oh, the dreaded bit-depth subject! For those math-phobic people, this topic will most likely sound intimidating. Bit depth is extremely important in understanding web graphics. Bit depth can refer to the number of colors in an image or the number of colors a computer system is capable of displaying. Bit-depth is "calculated" by figuring that 1-bit equals two colors and then multiplying 2 times 2 to arrive at each higher bit depth. Here's is a handy chart for convenient reference that identifies the different standard bit-depth levels.

32-bit	16.7+ million colors + 8-bit (256 level) grayscale mask
24-bit	16.7+ million colors
16-bit	65.5 thousand colors
15-bit	32.8 thousand colors
8-bit	256 colors
7-bit	128 colors
6-bit	64 colors
5-bit	32 colors
4-bit	16 colors
3-bit	8 colors
2-bit	4 colors
1-bit	2 colors

Here's a visual guide to refer to whenever you need it:

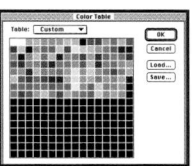

8-bit ▪ 45.3k ▪ 256 colors

7-bit ▪ 38.2k ▪ 128 colors

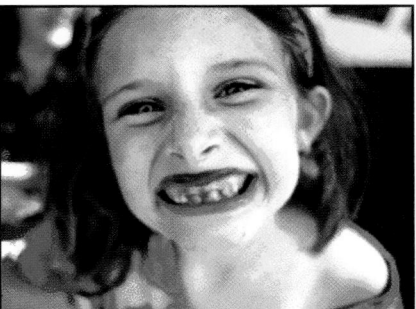
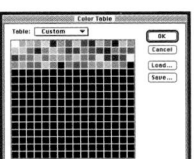
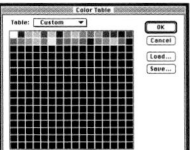

6-bit ▪ 32k ▪ 64 colors

5-bit ▪ 26.7k ▪ 32 colors

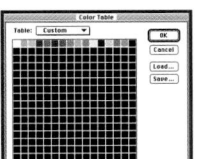
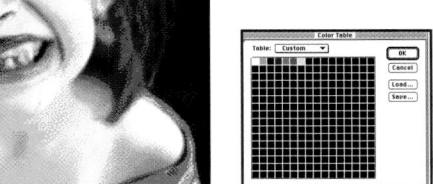

4-bit ▪ 21.4k ▪ 16 colors

3-bit ▪ 15.9k ▪ 8 colors

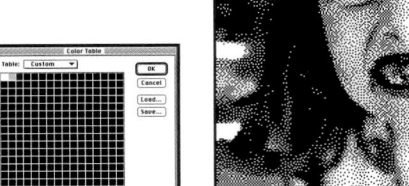
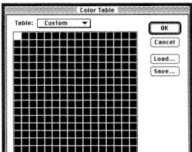

2-bit ▪ 10.7k ▪ 4 colors

1-bit ▪ 7.2k ▪ 2 colors

Notice the lower the bit depth, the lower the quality and the lower the file size becomes? You will find much more information about how to choose which bit depth for your web graphics in Chapter 4, "Low-Bandwidth Graphics."

Monitor's Bit Depth

So far, bit depth has been defined as it relates to images. There are actually two instances where understanding bit depth is important. The first is to understand the bit depth of an image, and the second is to understand the bit depth of your end viewer's monitor. In this section, let's look at the monitor's bit depth, not the bit depth of images.

Most professional digital artists have 24-bit monitors (which can display up to 16.7 million colors). The average computer user—hence the average member of your web-viewing audience—has an 8-bit (256 color) monitor. This makes sense if you think about it because the majority of computer monitors are owned by average people who bought the least expensive version of their computer system, not professional graphic artists who might have greatly enhanced systems.

Herein lies a huge problem. The majority of people who create artwork for web sites are viewing the artwork under better conditions than the average end user. This makes for a communication gap—one this book hopes to bridge rather than skim over, or worse, ignore.

If a computer system has only an 8-bit color card, it cannot physically view more than 256 colors at once. When people with 256 color systems view your web screens, they cannot see images in 24-bit, even if they want to. They can't prevent it, and neither can you. Specific advice for working with 8-bit color and files is provided in Chapter 4, "Low-Bandwidth Graphics" and Chapter 6, "Browser-Safe Color."

■ step-by-step

How to Change Your Monitor's Bit Depth

I recommend that you always run a bit-depth preview test on your web pages before you send them out for the world to see. Change your monitor settings to 256 colors, and you'll see how your artwork translates under those conditions.

Instructions follow to change your computer's monitor to display in 256 colors so that you can preview the bad news before others do.

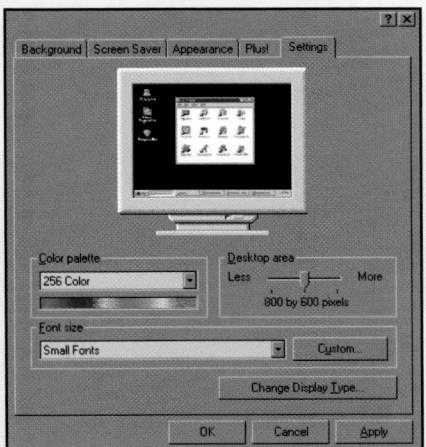

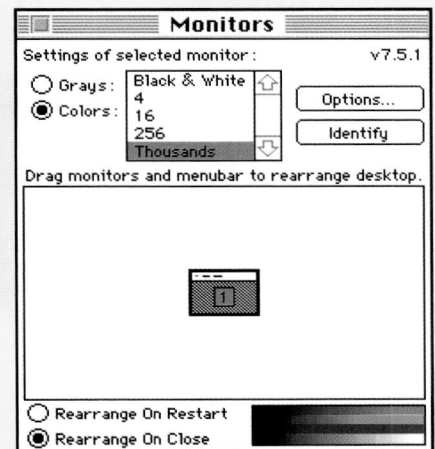

Windows 95: Access your display properties by using your right mouse button and selecting Display properties.

Macintosh: Open the control panel called "Monitors" or "Sights and Sound." (Control panel items are located in your System Folder.)

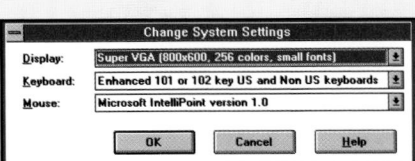

Windows 3.1: From Program Manager, display the Change System Settings dialog box by double-clicking on the Windows Setup icon (generally found in the Main program group) and choosing Change System Settings from the Options menu.

Web File Formats

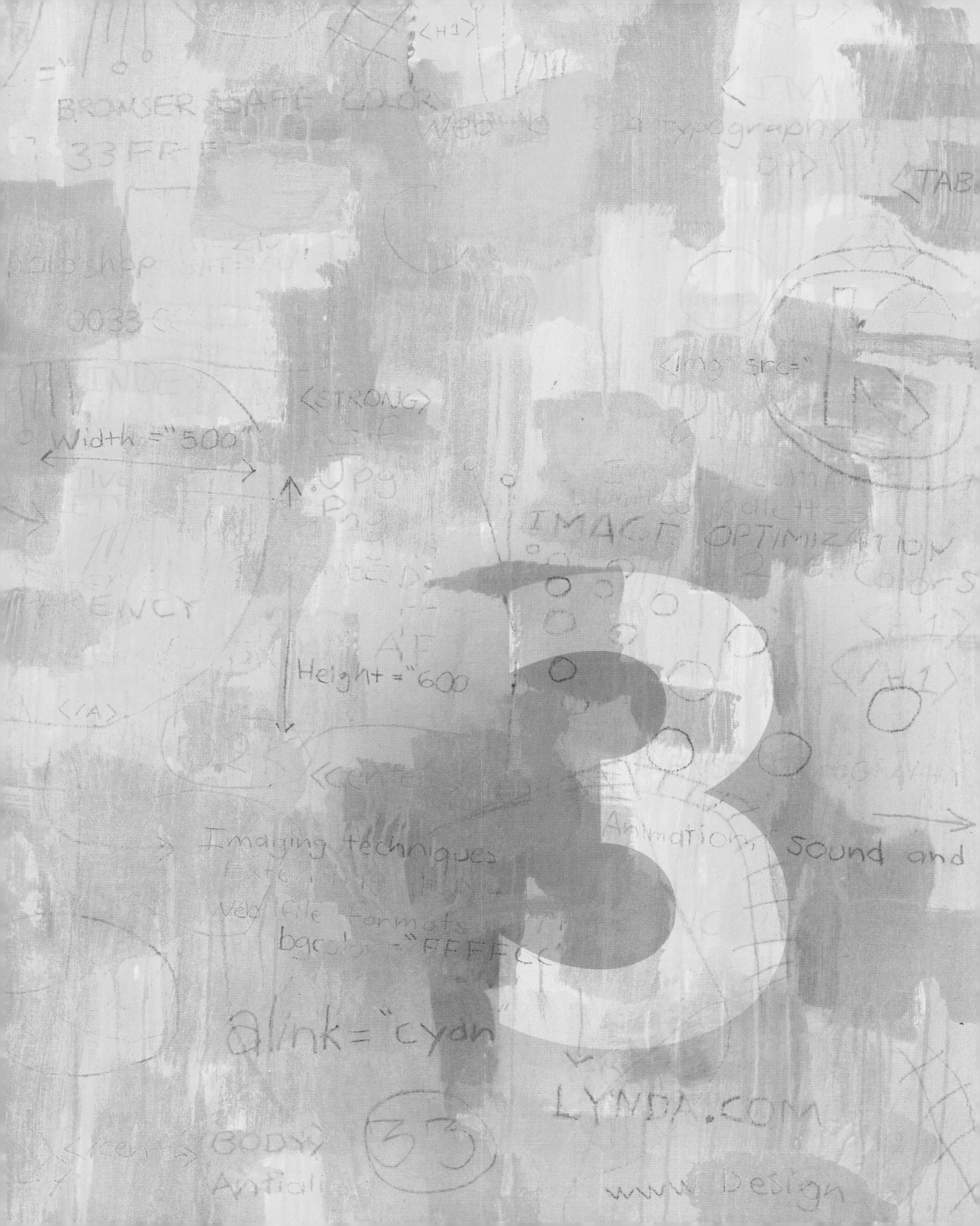

BROWSER SAFE COLOR

33FF

0033CC

<STRONG>

Width ="500"

.JPG
.PNG

IMAGE OPTIMIZATION

Height ="600"

Imaging techniques

bgcolor="FFFECC"

alink="cyan"

Animation, sound and

LYNDA.com

3

33

<center> <BODY>

www Design

Compression File Formats

What do all file formats for the web have in common? Compression. Compression is the key to making small graphics. Compression is not a necessary feature in other computer graphic file format specifications, which is why the file formats you'll find on the web might be new to you. Web-based image file formats have to implement impressive compression schemes in order to transform large images to small file sizes. Unfortunately, at times, with compression comes loss of quality.

Some web file formats use lossy compression techniques, meaning that there will be some loss of quality to the resulting images. Don't let that scare you, though; there is no way these file formats could impose the required amount of compression needed for web delivery and not sacrifice some quality. Remember once again, print quality is not expected on the web.

The two types of image file formats most commonly accepted by graphic web browsers are JPEGs and GIFs. One difference between them is that JPEGs can be 24-bit (include up to 16.7 million colors) and GIFs must be 8-bit or less (256 colors maximum).

JPEG stands for **J**oint **P**hotographic **E**xperts **G**roup, and GIF stands for **G**raphic **I**nterchange **F**ormat. These names tell you, in each respective acronym, which format is best for which kind of image. JPEGs were designed to compress photographs, and GIFs were designed to compress graphics.

There will be times when you will want to make a photograph into a GIF, such as with transparent GIFs and animated GIFs, and times when you want to make a graphic into a JPEG, such as when a logo or graphic is combined with a photograph. This chapter will help you answer which file format to use and why.

It's easy to convert to JPEGs and GIFs from other image file formats, such as PICT, BMP, TGA, TIFF, or EPS, if you have the proper software. Many other imaging programs support JPEGs and GIFs.

This section examines the pros and cons of web-based image file formats and gives you an understanding of how to choose which file format is appropriate for specific styles of artwork. The next chapter, "Low-Bandwidth Graphics," offers instruction and tips on how to make the smallest possible JPEGs and GIFs.

HTML for Embedding Images

Regardless of whether you're using a regular GIF, animated GIF, transparent GIF, interlaced GIF, JPEG, or Progressive JPEG format, the HTML is usually the same.

You must first learn to save the file with the proper extension. Here's a handy list:

To insert a graphic into an HTML page, use this tag:
`<IMG SRC=``"myimage.gif"`**`>`**

GIF	.gif
Interlaced GIF	.gif
Transparent GIF	.gif
Animated GIF	.gif
JPEG	.jpg
Progressive JPEG	.jpg

To link an image to another image or HTML page,
use this tag:
`<A HREF=``"www.destination_url.com"`**`>`**
`<IMG SRC=``"myimag.jpg"`**`></A>`**

To get rid of the border of an image that's been linked,
use this tag:
`<A HREF=``"www.destination_url.com"`**`>`**
`<IMG SRC=``"myimage.jpg"` **`BORDER=0></A>`**

The HTML is the easy part—it's understanding how to optimize graphics, choosing which file format for which type of image, and making the images and content that will be much harder to master!

■ note

Naming Conventions for JPEGs and GIFs

When saving a JPEG or GIF file for a web page, always use the three letter extension of either .jpg or .gif at the end of your file name. Because many servers that store web graphics are Unix-based, it is important to pay close attention to whether your files are named with upper- or lowercase titles. The HTML document must exactly match the upper- or lowercase structure of the file name. For example, if you have something saved as "image.jpg" on your server, and your HTML reads "image.JPG", the file will not load! For more information on storing graphics on servers and file naming conventions, refer to Chapter 17, "HTML for Visual Designers."

GIF File Formats

Unlike most other computer graphic file formats, GIF (**G**raphic **I**nterchange **F**ormat) was designed specifically for online delivery because it was originally developed for CompuServe in the late 1980s. The file format compresses graphics beautifully, but can also be used for photographic images. Whenever you create graphics, such as logos, illustrations, or cartoons, we recommend the GIF file format.

GIF uses a compression scheme called LZW, which is based on work done by Lempel-Ziv & Welch. The patent for LZW compression is owned by a company called Unisys, which charges developers such as Netscape and Photoshop licensing and royalty fees for selling products that use the GIF file format. End users, such as ourselves (web designers) and our audience (web visitors), do not have to pay licensing fees or worry about any of this. There is some speculation that the GIF file format may be less prevalent at some point because of the fees, but we hope not. GIFs are accepted by all browsers, GIFs are small, and GIFs do things that many other file formats do not, such as animation, transparency, and interlacing.

The GIF file format, by definition, can contain only 256 colors or less. This is not the case with JPEGs, which by

definition contain millions of colors (24-bit). Because GIFs are an indexed color file format (256 colors or less), it's extremely beneficial to have a thorough understanding of bit-depth settings and palette management when preparing GIF images.

There are two different flavors of GIF: GIF87a and GIF89a. GIF87a supports transparency and interlacing whereas GIF89a supports transparency, interlacing, and animation (more information on these features follow). As of this book's printing, the major browsers (Netscape, Internet Explorer, and Mosaic) all support both GIF format specifications. You don't really have to refer to the names GIF89a or GIF87a unless you want to sound techie. Most of us simply call these files by the features used, be it a transparent GIF, animated GIF, or plain vanilla GIF.

GIF compression is lossless, meaning that the GIF compression algorithm will not cause any unwanted image degradation. The process of converting a 24-bit image to 256 or fewer colors will cause image degradation on its own, however, so don't get too excited!

GIFs for Illustration-Style Imagery

GIFs work much better for graphics than photographs. By graphics, we mean illustrations, cartoons, or logos. Such graphics typically use areas of solid color, and GIFs handle compression of solid color better than the varied colors found in photographs. Because the GIF file format is lossless, illustrations with limited colors (less than 256) won't lose any quality. Because JPEG is a lossy method, it actually introduces image artifacts into solid color.

■ **note**

GIF Pronunciation

First of all, how is GIF pronounced? Some people say it with a soft g as in jiffy and some with a hard g as in gift. You have our blessing to say it either way. Because no one seems to agree, perhaps it could be said that there is no correct pronunciation?

GIFs for Photographic Imagery

GIFs are definitely designed to handle graphics better than photographs. But that doesn't mean there won't be times where you have to turn photographs into GIFs anyway. You may want to use transparency or animation, which are two features that JPEGs do not offer.

GIFs can be saved at any bit depth from 8 bits down to 1 bit. The bit depth refers to how many colors the image contains. Generally, the lower the bit depth, the smaller the GIF.

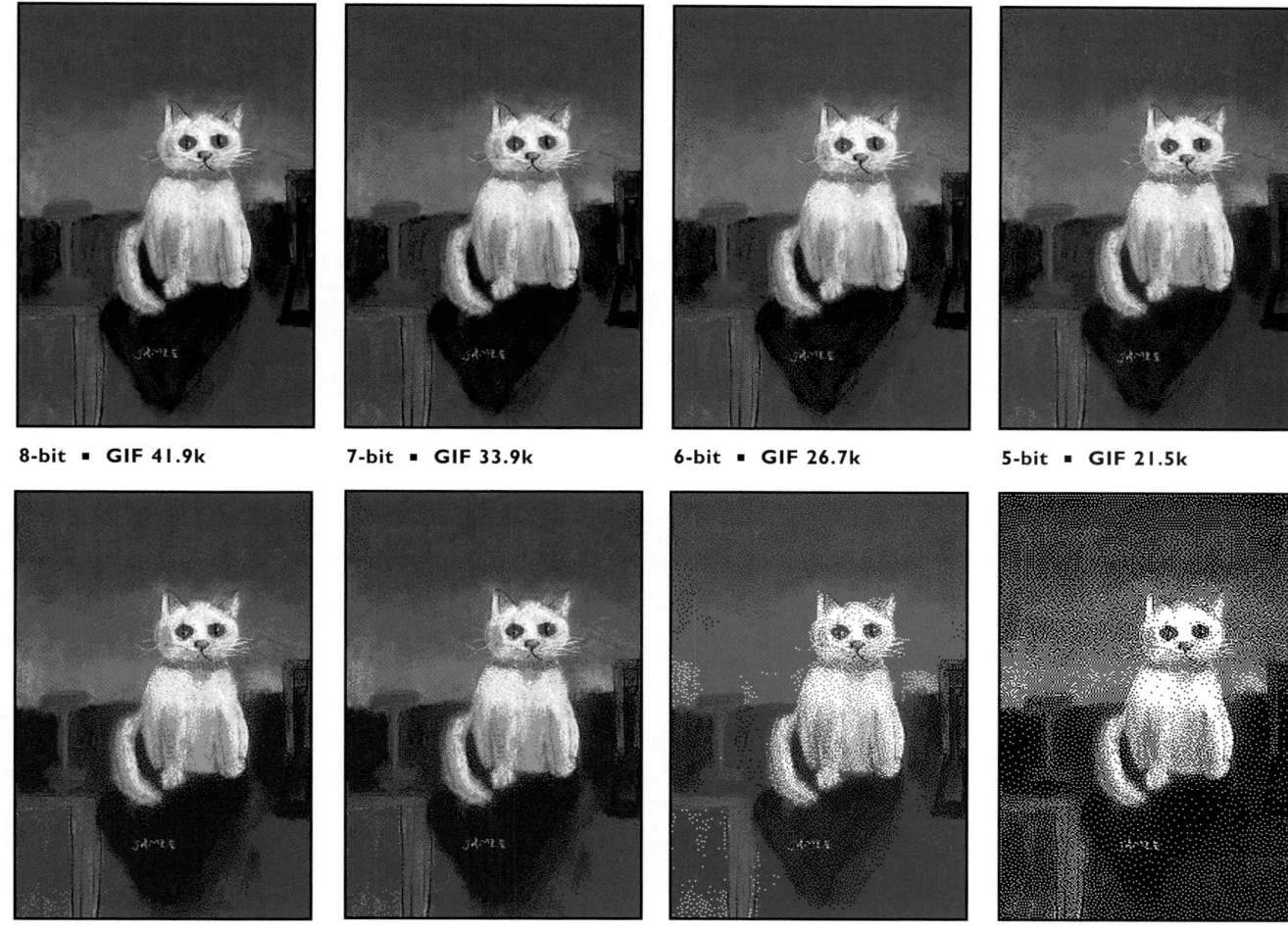

| 8-bit ▪ GIF 41.9k | 7-bit ▪ GIF 33.9k | 6-bit ▪ GIF 26.7k | 5-bit ▪ GIF 21.5k |

| 4-bit ▪ GIF 15.0k | 3-bit ▪ GIF 11.8k | 2-bit ▪ GIF 8.5k | 1-bit ▪ GIF 7.1k |

Your job when preparing a GIF is to take it down to its lowest bit-depth level and still maintain acceptable image quality. Depending on how important this image is, acceptable quality falls at 5-bit, which offers a 49% file size reduction over the 8-bit version.

Controlling Your Color Mapping

Color mapping refers to the colors that are assigned to a GIF image and can be taken from either the image or a predetermined palette of colors. Photoshop calls palettes that are derived from existing colors adaptive palettes. It enables you to apply external palettes (system or browser-safe are two examples) or makes a best-guess palette (adaptive) based on the content of your image. While the numbers of colors in an image (bit depth) affect the size of the graphic, the palette additionally affects the quality of your image. Some images can support fewer colors, while others cannot. If you understand how color affects size and quality, you will create better looking and faster loading web pages. For techniques required to assign color maps to images, check out Chapter 6, "Browser-Safe Color."

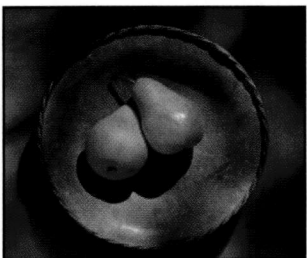 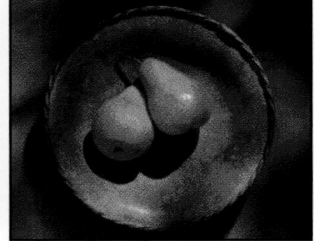 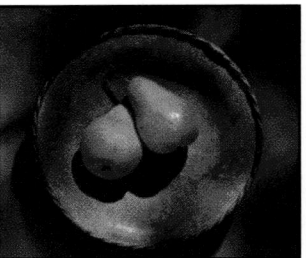

adaptive palette **Mac System palette** **216 browser-safe palette**

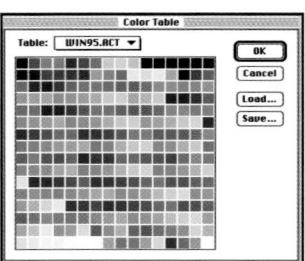 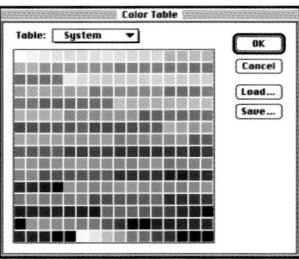 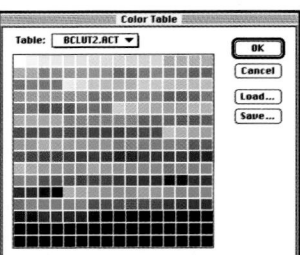

The adaptive palette looks the best because the colors are based on the content of the image. Paint Shop Pro calls this type of palette a Nearest Color palette. Photoshop calls it an adaptive palette.

The system palette image looks much worse. Although it has the same number of colors as the adaptive palette, the colors are unrelated to the image and detract from the quality.

The browser-safe palette looks worst of all. Not only does it use fewer colors, but just like the system palette, the colors are unrelated to the image.

It's clear that an adaptive or nearest color palette gives the best results to the image, but what about when it's seen in a browser? The following shows the results:

This example demonstrates how the images display in an 8-bit web browser. See any differences? The differences are minor, if any, aren't they? This is what visitors to your site would see if they had only an 8-bit display.

This example demonstrates how the images display in a 24-bit web browser. The adaptive GIF looks the best, does it not? The moral of the story? Use adaptive palettes for photographs saved as GIFs, and let the 8-bit browsers out there remap your colors on-the-fly. This enables your 24-bit viewing audience to see these images at their best, and your 8-bit viewing audience is none the worse off.

Interlaced GIFs

If you've toured the web much, you've encountered interlaced GIFs. They're those images that start out blocky, and appear less and less blocky until they come into full focus.

Interlacing doesn't affect the overall size or speed of a GIF. In theory, interlacing is supposed to make it possible for your end viewer to get a rough idea of your visuals and to make a decision whether to wait or click onward before the image finishes rendering. Again—in theory—this is supposed to save time. Unfortunately for the end viewer, being forced to wait for the entire image to finish coming into focus to read essential information is often a frustrating experience. In other words, interlaced images save time if you don't have to wait for them to finish.

Our recommendation is that you do not use interlaced GIFs for important visual information that is critical to viewing your site. An imagemap or navigation icon, for example, must be seen in order to fulfill its function. Although interlaced GIFs serve their purpose on nonessential graphics, they only frustrate end users when used on essential graphics.

These examples simulate the effect of interlacing on a browser. The image starts chunky and comes into focus over time. This allows the end viewer to decide whether to wait for your graphic to finish or click onward.

Transparent GIFs

Transparent GIFs are used to create the illusion of irregularly shaped artwork. All computer-made images end up in rectangular-shaped files; it's the nature of the medium. Certain file formats, such as GIF, can store masked regions, which create the illusion of shapes other than rectangles. This "masked region" appears to be transparent.

Transparency comes in two forms: 8-bit transparency and 1-bit transparency. 8-bit transparency is the best, but it isn't supported by GIFs or by web browsers. 8-bit transparency is what is used by the file formats PSD (Photoshop), TGA, and PICT. 8-bit transparency is also called alpha channel-based transparency and can support up to 256 different levels of opacity (which is why it looks so great!). GIFs support 1-bit transparency, which makes it a much more limited type of masking. For more information on transparent GIFs, turn to Chapter 7, "Transparent Artwork."

Here's an example of artwork from Lynda's Homegurrrl site that has been defined to be transparent. The gray color was instructed to drop out within transparency software.

This shows the transparent artwork in context. Once the GIF transparency is recognized within browser software, the browser enables the rectangular artwork to appear irregularly shaped.

This image represents the type of compositing you can do in Photoshop and 8-bit transparency, where it can easily display differing levels of transparency, glows, and blurs. GIF transparency is unfortunately much more crude than this.

Animated GIFs

Animated GIFs are part of the GIF89a specification. They are formally called multi-block GIFs because multiple images can be stored as separate blocks within one single GIF document. When the GIF document is viewed, the multiple images display, one at a time, and produce a streaming animation.

Streaming is a wonderful and appropriate method for displaying animation over the web. Streaming means that each frame of the animation displays one after the other, so that your end user doesn't have to wait for the whole file to download before seeing anything. Other animation formats in the past required that the entire movie download before a single frame could be viewed.

Animated GIFs function much like automated slide shows. They can include custom palette information and be set to play at different speeds. They can include interlacing and transparency, too! The beauty of animated GIFs is that they require no plug-ins, and the authoring tools to create them are often free and easy to learn. As well, major browsers (Netscape, Internet Explorer, and Mosaic) support them, so you can include them in web pages without worrying about compatibility or accessibility. Specific instruction on how to create animated GIFs and apply custom palettes is available in Chapter 14, "Animation."

Just like other GIF files, the number of colors and amount of noise in the frames affect the overall file size. If you have a 100-frame animation with each frame totaling 5k, your animated GIF will be 500k. It simply multiplies in size according to how many frames you create and the file size of the individual frame of artwork. On the other hand, your end viewer is really waiting for only 5k servings at a time, so it's nothing like the painful waiting that a standard 500k GIF would incur!

■ **note**

Popular GIF animation authoring tools:

GIF Construction Set/bookware (Windows/Win95)
■ http://www.mindworkshipcom/alchemy/alchemy.html

GIFBuilder/freeware (Mac)
■ http://iawww.epfl.ch/Staff/Yves.Piguet/clip2gif-home/GifBuilder.html

Some good animated GIF references:

Royal Frazier's awesome site
■ http://member.aol.com/roalef/gifanim.htm

GIFBuilder's FAQ
■ http://iawww.epfl.ch/Staff/Yves.Piguet/clip2gif-home/GifBuilder Doc/GifBuilder-FAQs.html

---

Here's a 30-frame animation, found on Lynda's Homegurrl site at ■ http://www.lynda.com/anim.html. It's hard to tell the subtle changes from frame to frame when viewed in sequence, but once the frames are played in motion over time the '50s man appears to be bobbing his head and waving his finger, and has little lines flowing from the side of his head. It totals 64k in size. Why? It's only two colors, with no anti-aliasing.

JPEG

The JPEG (pronounced jay-peg) file format offers a 24-bit alternative to the 8-bit GIF file format. This is especially great for photographic content because 24-bit photographs do not dither! One added advantage to dealing with JPEGs is that they don't need you to define the palette for them, unlike GIFs. Whenever an image format includes millions of colors (24-bit), palette and color mapping issues disappear. This is because enough colors are allowed to rely on the original image's color information, and substitute colors are no longer necessary.

| JPEG ▪ 8.2k | GIF ▪ 19.3k | JPEG ▪ 7.1k | GIF ▪ 17.6k |

| JPEG ▪ 9.5k | GIF ▪ 5.2k | JPEG ▪ 2.5k | GIF ▪ 17.3k |

JPEG handles images with subtle gradations beautifully. This is in part because the file format enables the image to remain in 24-bit. Compare the JPEG images to the left to the 8-bit GIF images to the right. The JPEGs compress photographic-style images better than graphic style images and look better too!

JPEG was developed specifically for photographic-style images. It looks to areas with subtle tonal and color changes and offers the best compression when it encounters that type of imagery. It actually does not compress solid color well at all!

Here's an image with a lot of solid color, saved as a low-quality JPEG. It totals 7.6k.

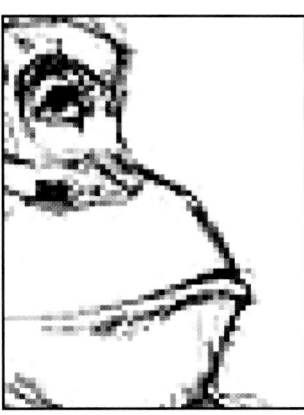

Here is a close-up of the artifacts present in the JPEG.

The GIF looks better (no artifacts!), but it is larger at 17.6k.

JPEG is a lossy compression algorithm, meaning that it removes information from your image and, therefore, causes a loss in quality. JPEG does a great job of doing this so the difference in information data is often not visible or objectionable. It does introduce artifacts in some instances, especially where it encounters solid colors. This is a by-product of its lossy compression methods.

Unlike the GIF file format, JPEGs require both compression and decompression. This means that JPEG files need to decompress when they're viewed. Although a GIF and a JPEG might be identical sizes, or sometimes even when the JPEG is smaller, the JPEG may take longer to download or view from a web browser because of the added time required to decompress.

Another difference between GIF and JPEG is the fact that you can save JPEGs in a variety of compression levels. This means that more or less compression can be applied to an image, depending on which looks best.

The following examples were taken from Photoshop. Photoshop employs the JPEG compression settings of max, high, medium, and low. In Photoshop, these terms relate to quality, not the amount of compression.

| 4.6k | 6.1k | 8.2k | 10.5k | 16.3k |

| 7.1k | 9.0k | 11.1k | 11.8k | 15.1k |

You can see by this test that there's not a whole lot of difference between low quality and high quality, except with graphics. As we've said, leave graphics for GIF and photographs for JPEGs. Although there are good reasons for saving photographs as GIF (animation, transparency, and interlacing), there are no good reasons for saving graphics as JPEGs, unless the graphics are combined with photographs. With photographic content in general, don't be afraid to try low-quality settings; the file size saving is usually substantial, and the quality penalties are not too steep.

Progressive JPEGs Versus Standard JPEGs

Progressive JPEGs are a new entrée into our web graphics file format vocabulary. This type of JPEG boasts much higher compression rates than regular JPEG and supports interlacing (where the graphic starts chunky and comes into focus). They were initially introduced by Netscape, and are now additionally supported by MSIE. Progressive-JPEG-making tools for Mac and PCs are listed at ■ http://www.in-touch.com/pjpeg2.html#software.

Pro-JPEGs boast superior compression to regular JPEGs. They also give you a wider range of quality settings. Instead of Photoshop's standard max, high, medium, and low settings, pro-JPEGs can be set in quality from 0–100. We simulated a comparison here by using the settings of 100, 75, 25, and 0.

  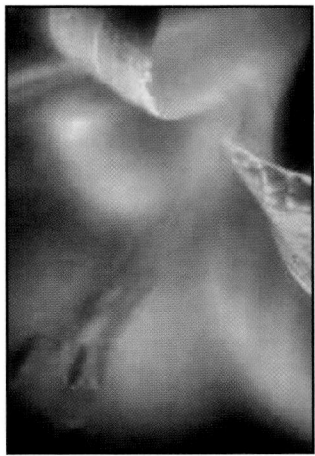 

max 28.9k   high 12.4k   med 10.5k   low 8.7k

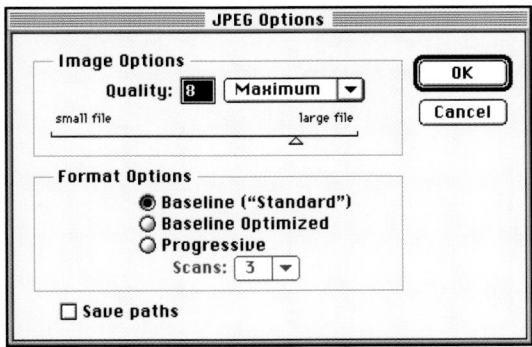

The interface to Photoshop 4.0's JPEG Options.

■ **note**

Photoshop 4.0 Settings

There are lots of tools available to write progressive JPEGs, but here are the settings for Photoshop 4.0's version:

Baseline Standard: Enables you to save up to 10 quality levels.

Baseline Optimized: Enables you to save up to 10 quality levels—a little better file savings than Baseline Standard.

Progressive: Progressive JPEGs are often quite smaller, but are not supported by all browsers.

PNG

PNG (**P**ortable **N**etwork **G**raphics, or more fondly known as PNG Not GIF) holds great promise as a new web file format. The W3C (World Wide Web Consortium at ■ http://www.w3.org/pub/WWW/Press/PNG-PR.en.html) has made a formal endorsement of PNG, which strongly indicates that Netscape and MSIE will support it as an inline file format in the near future.

PNG is a lossless compression method, meaning that no quality loss is incurred when it's applied to images. Unlike GIF or JPEG, PNG can be stored at many different bit depths using different storage methods. GIF, for example, can be stored only in 8-bit or lower bit depths. JPEGs must be stored in 24-bit and no lower. PNG can be stored in either 8-bit or 24-bit or 32-bit. PNG also has a multitude of different filtering methods. This makes optimizing PNG images a daunting task, as you'll see by the PNG image charts in Chapter 4, "Low-Bandwidth Graphics."

PNG was developed by Thomas Boutell (visit his amazing site at ■ http://www. boutell.com, and the W3C spec pages for PNG at ■ http://www.boutell.com/ boutell/png/). Unlike JPEG and GIF, PNG was created to be a cross-platform file format and contains information about the characteristics of the authoring platform so that viewing software can automatically compensate and display the image correctly.

What this means is that Macs and PCs, which each utilize different gamma settings (see Chapter 2, "Understanding the Web Environment" for more information on gamma), can adjust properly for images created in the PNG file format. This is way cool!

For an excellent description of gamma, check out:
■ http://www.cgsd.com/papers/gamma_intro.html

PNG also supports a far superior interlacing scheme than GIF. GIF interlacing gives a preview of the image after 1/8th of the image data has been recognized, whereas PNG gives a preview after only 1/64th of the image has loaded.

With alpha channel support (see Chapter 7, "Transparent Artwork," for a step-by-step example of creating PNG transparency), all the transparency problems of halos, matte lines, and fringing will be history. Alpha channels offer superior masking results, meaning that designers will be able to prepare images with glows, blurs, soft edges, and fades that will display beautifully on web browsers that support PNG.

Unfortunately, when this chapter was written, the major browsers (Netscape, MSIE, and Mosaic) still did not support PNG. There were a couple of plug-ins that enabled you to see PNG files, but neither supported transparency properly. They are:
■ http://iagu.on.net/jsam/png-plugin/
■ http://codelab.siegelgale.com/solutions

Photoshop 4.0 supports creating images in the PNG file format. The Photoshop documentation does not explain what any of the PNG settings do, unfortunately! When in doubt about image formats, I turn to my trusty book:

> **Graphic File Formats**
> Publisher: O'Reilly & Associates
> Authors: James D. Murray and William VanRyper
> Retail: $79.95 ▪ ISBN: 0932102085

Photoshop doesn't include any documentation about the PNG settings, but here's what I've pieced together from my research:

Interlace
- ■ **None:** No interlacing
- ■ **Adam7**: The sequel to the popular television show Adam 12, featuring pre-pubescent cops... No, wait! This function has a funny name, but all it does is interlace the image.

Filter
- ■ **None:** Like the name says, this filter offers no compression whatsoever!
- ■ **Sub:** Compares and averages pixel values next to each other on a horizontal axis.
- ■ **Up:** Compares and averages pixel values next to each other on a vertical axis.
- ■ **Average:** Averages all the pixel values in the document.
- ■ **Paeth:** Uses linear calculations to average and compare the different pixel values.
- ■ **Adaptive:** Best guess.

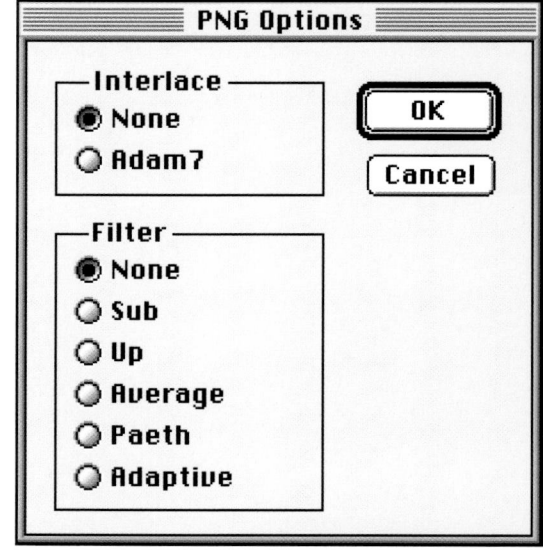

Interlacing is either off or Adam7 (who names these things?). Filtering is applied to the data before it's compressed, and the filtering process is reversed after the image is decompressed, restoring the data to its original values. This is how PNG compression can generate file savings and also be lossless at the same time.

Digital Watermarks

The term watermark is traditionally used to describe special printed paper that guarantees proof of authenticity and ownership. Dollar bills are a good example of watermarked currency that has special information embedded in the paper stock to prevent counterfitting.

Digital watermarks are a new technology that follows a similar principle, only the embedded copyright information is not visible until loaded into a computer that can read it. Watermarking technology can embed copyright notification, ownership, audience (adult or general interest material), and usage information (restricted, or royalty free). The water-mark signature can be read by Digimarc's PictureMarc plug-in.

Digimarc (■ http://digimarc.com/) offers a digital watermarking service that offers watermarking software and a database/retrieval service for professionals. Digimarc's fee structure is listed on its site.

The PictureMarc plug-in for Photoshop is digital watermarking software that enables you to embed watermarks into digital documents for print or web-based submission. When PictureMarc is invoked, you are given the opportunity to obtain your own creator ID, which links your images to up-to-date contact information that is stored on the Digimarc site.

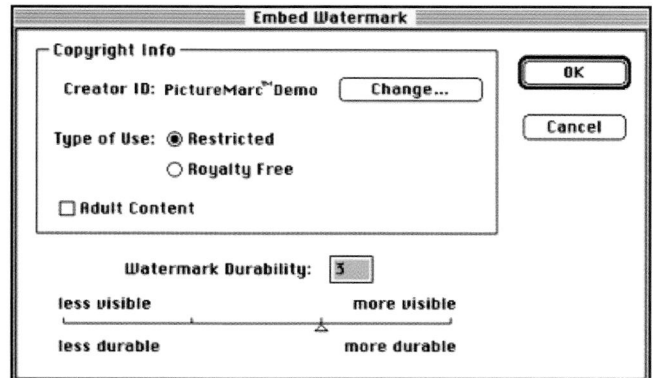

This is the dialog box used by the watermarking Photoshop plug-in PictureMarc, distributed by ■ http://digimarc.com/.

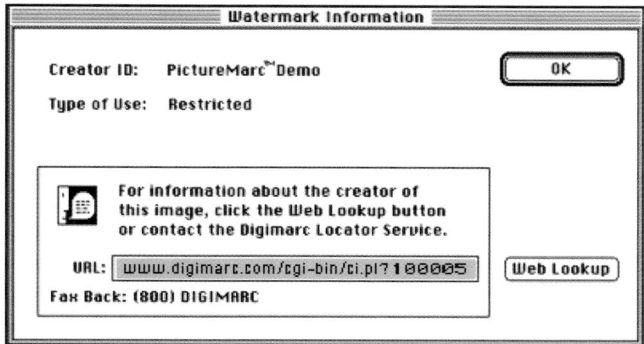

Every time an image is opened or scanned into Photoshop, PictureMarc performs a quick detection and adds a © to the image window's title bar.

By clicking on the © on the title bar, PictureMarc launches your web browser, displays detailed information about the image, and lists whatever contact details you have provided.

This service supports CMYK, RGB, LAB, Grayscale, and Index Color colorspaces and works with any file format type that Photoshop supports on NT, Win95, Win3.1, and Mac (68000 and PPC) platforms. A minimum image size of 256x256 pixels is required, which makes its usefulness for the web limited to larger images, thereby unfortunately excluding navigational graphics, buttons, bullets, and rules.

WebTV

Just when you thought you might have this web graphics thingy licked, along comes another display medium to add to the stack of cross-platform, cross-browser, and cross-operating systems considerations.

WebTV Networks, Inc. has released the first (expect more of these types of systems from other companies, too) set-top box to offer Internet/web connection through standard television sets.

The advent of web delivery via television screens introduces a new audience to our pages, as well as opens a new can of worms for our authoring concerns. WebTV is the subject of controversy among web designers. People have differing opinions about whether WebTV is a good or bad thing, whether you should or should not design for it, and whether it makes pages look ugly or acceptable.

As you can see by the set-up screen on the next page, WebTV allows end viewers to set up their preferences for text size and size adjustments. Here's one more area where you have to relinquish that precious design control most of us crave.

Television is a very different medium than the computer. It has lower resolution: a standard computer monitor displays 640x480 pixels, whereas a standard television monitor displays 544x378. Television uses NTSC color space, which is very sensitive to highly saturated colors, such as pure reds, greens, blues, yellows, cyans, and magentas. Television is interlaced, meaning that it displays two alternating images to create a single image. This can cause single pixel lines to jitter. The WebTV system uses a convolution filtering system to reduce flicker, and it works quite well.

The majority of people who have actually viewed WebTV (go to your local electronics store to check it out) are impressed at how well their pages translate. Expect that the font tags you use (for more information on HTML font tags, check out Chapter 11, "Web-Based Typography") will be altered to a largeish, sans serif typeface as shown on the next page.

> ### ■ note
>
> Designing for WebTV
>
> If you're curious to know how to design for WebTV, check out their developer docs at:
>
> ■ http://webtv.net/devdocs/styleguide/sguide-2.html#MARKER-9-1

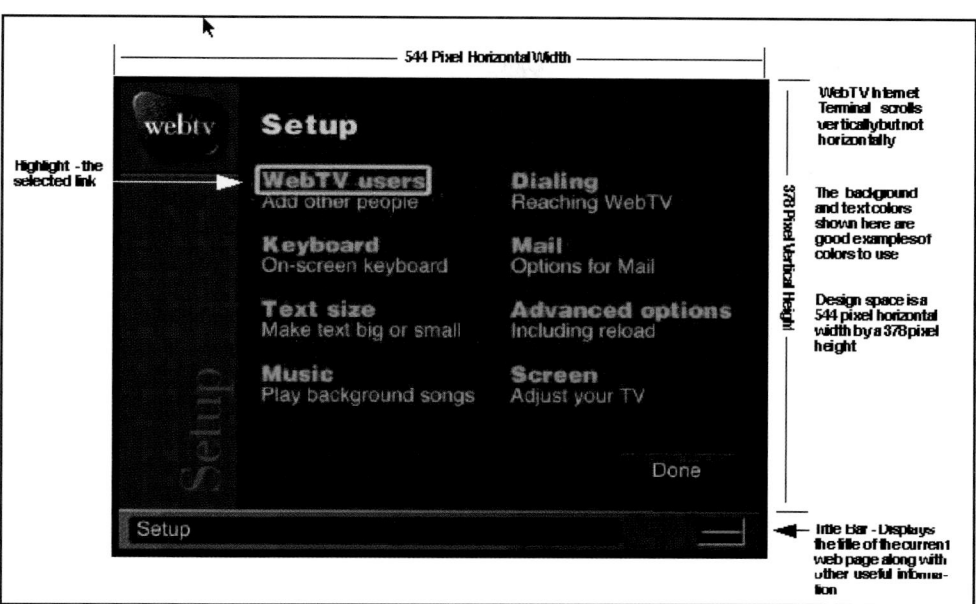

This screen shows the setup options for WebTV viewing.

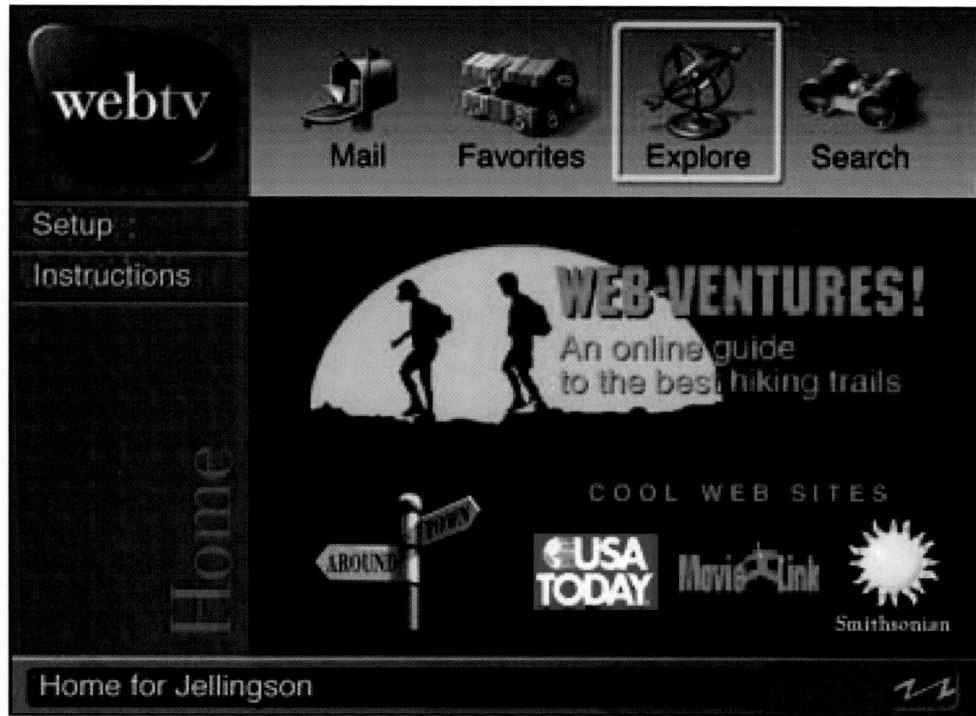

The WebTV home page shows how large the type displays and how the cursor creates a yellow bounding box on top of linked graphics.

WebTV Features

WebTV supports:
Animated GIFs
Tables
Background Color
Colored Text
Background Tiles
Sound (RealAudio v2, AU, WAV, VMF, AIFF, Shockwave audio, GSM, MPEG II audio, and layer 3 MPEG 1)
Inline JPGs, GIF89a

WebTV does not support
VRML plug-ins
JavaScript
QuickTime
Proprietary plug-ins
Java
Frames

WebTV plans to support:
JavaScript
Java
Frames

Unsupported WebTV HTML Tags

HTML Committee
<APPLET>
<a TITLE REL REV URN>
<DFN>
<dl COMPACT>
<form ENCTYPE>
<FRAME>
<FRAMESET>
<img ALT LOWSRC>
<meta NAME>
<NEXTID>
<ol COMPACT>
<PARAM>
<pre WIDTH>
<SCRIPT>
<STYLE>
<table HEIGHT>
<td NOWRAP>
<ul COMPACT>
<textarea WRAP>

Netscape
<BLINK>
<body ALINK>
<EMBED>
<isindex PROMPT>
<li VALUE>
<SERVER PUSH>
<WBR>

Internet Explorer
<font FACE>
<img DYNSRC LOOP>
<PLAINTEXT>

> ■ **note**
>
> The Price of WebTV
> Many of the plug-in-based and streaming movie technologies are too RAM intensive. Remember, WebTV is not a computer, and has a price-point that doesn't support high-end dedicated hardware.

WebTV Design Tips

A list follows that offers design tips if you would like your sites to be WebTV friendly. This was culled from the Design Tips list found on the WebTV site at ■ http://www.webtv.net and includes my comments, annotations, and tips as well.

■ Some designers say not to use full red or full white; both cause screen distortion. Many sites use pure-white backgrounds for their web pages, however, and so far those that I've personally viewed over WebTV have looked acceptable.

■ Use client-side imagemaps instead of server-side imagemaps; it works better with a remote control. See Chapter 10, "Navigation-Based Graphics," for details on programming client-side imagemaps.

■ Avoid small text sizes in HTML and graphics. If you do use small text sizes, WebTV will convert them to a larger font on-the-fly. You don't really have to redesign your pages; it's just that WebTV will go in and change your small typefaces for you.

■ Avoid narrow columns; images are scaled and text will wrap frequently.

■ Try to reduce the number of items on your page because television audiences are used to looking at one focal point.

■ Use light-colored text against dark-colored backgrounds; television audiences find it easier to read.

■ Don't use horizontal single pixel lines because they flicker on television sets.

■ Use images with size hints (the <IMG> WIDTH and HEIGHT attributes) to speed up load time.

■ The best way to ensure your page looks good on WebTV is to view it on a WebTV Internet terminal.

Comparing WebTV to the Net: www.lynda.com

Net: ■ http://www.lynda.com viewed through Netscape.

WebTV: Click on the arrows to scroll up or down an entire screen. The type will be enlarged by the WebTV browser to enhance readiblity on a television monitor.

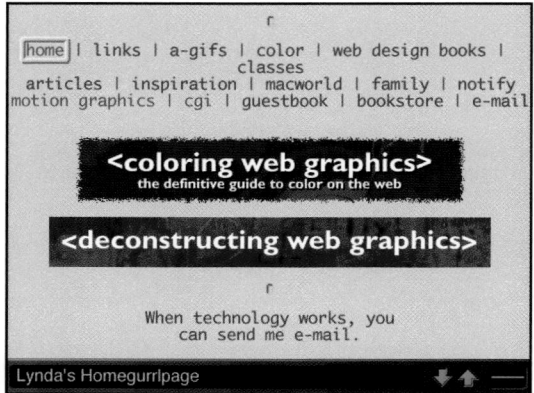

WebTV: The navigation bar at the bottom of my site shows the way WebTV links are highlighted in yellow bounding boxes.

Comparing WebTV to the Net: www.540.com

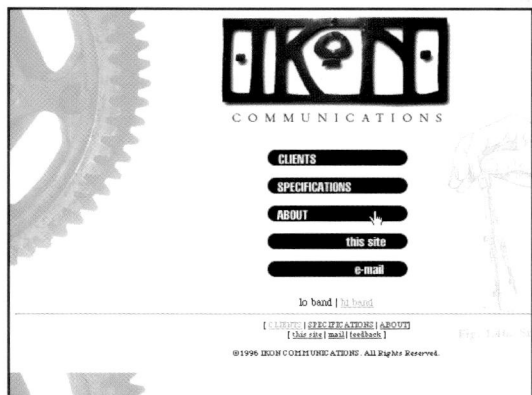

WebTV: Here's a screen from ■ http://www.540.com. It has image-based type, instead of HTML-based type.

WebTV: Image-based type is not altered by the Preferences that are set in WebTV.

WebTV: Ikon's home page includes both imagemaps and HTML-based text.

WebTV: The imagemaps work just fine, and the HTML-based text is enlarged just like on my site. These sites really hold up pretty well, considering!

Low-Bandwidth Graphics

BROWSER SAFE
33FF

0038

<STRONG>

Width = "500"

// FRENCY

Height = "600"

<A>

<center>

Imaging techniques
Web file format
bgcolor = "FFFFCC"

@link = "cyan"

<H1>

<TAB

<Img src="

IMAGE OPTIMIZATION
colors

<H1>

Animation, sound and

33

LYNDA.COM

<BODY>
Antial   www Design

Low-Bandwidth Graphics

There's never been a design medium before where speed was an important judgment factor. No one looks through a magazine and says, "Oh, this image was only 90mb, and look, this one was just 5mb!" On the web, unlike other design mediums, file size makes it impossible to see the artwork if it's too big. The truth with web graphics is that an image can be stunning and communicate critical information, but if it's too big, your audience will never wait around long enough to see it. Making images speedy means learning how to make small file sizes, and that's precisely what this chapter advocates.

So you know images on the web have to be small, but how small is small? If you are a digital print designer, you probably don't blink at large file sizes, and working on images ranging from tens to hundreds of megabytes is a common, everyday fact of life. Even if you aren't working in graphics or print, you've been hearing that web graphics have to be small—but again, how small is small? A handy rule of thumb is to consider that the average person viewing the web is using a 14.4 modem, and you can expect it to take one second per kilobyte for an image to transfer. This means that a 60k file would take one minute to download, and one of your 10mb files could take almost 3 hours!

How do you translate your many-megabyte-sized file down to something small enough to fit on an average floppy disk? The two file formats of the web, GIF and JPEG, both offer impressive compression schemes. Saving in these formats, as long as your images are less than 640x480 pixels, at 72 dpi in RGB, will make fitting them on a floppy disk easy regardless of how complex your graphic is. Even though fitting a large graphic on a floppy may seem like a giant accomplishment if you're used to large files, this file size still won't cut it for the web.

This chapter walks you through the stages of making smaller images, not in dimensions but in file size. You'll learn how to "read" the file size of a graphic, understand what the file format is doing to an image, and know which file formats to use on which types of images. In the end, you should have a much better sense of to how to create the smallest possible images for web delivery.

One thing to keep in mind while designing your graphics is that print quality is not expected on the web, and a big difference exists between what looks good on paper and what looks good on screen. You will always need to work in RGB at 72 dpi for the web. This is because 72 dpi is the resolution of computer screens. You are delivering your end result to computer screens, not high-resolution printers. CMYK and high resolution are reserved for print graphics only. You'll love this change once you get over the shock of it. In print, you never know what you'll get until it's printed; for online graphics, what you see IS what you get. It'll probably be hard to go back to those huge, unwieldy print resolution files once you've experienced the luxury of working small.

How to Know What Size Your File Really Is

Your new web vocabulary will include measuring web images by kilobytes, or k, from now on. For those who are mathematically mindful, a kilobyte is composed of 1024 bytes; a megabyte is composed of 1,048,576 bytes; and a gigabyte has 1,073,741,824 bytes. Files measuring in the megabytes and gigabytes will not be allowed on well-designed web pages—they take too long to view! Because of this, you'll often get the directive from a client to keep page sizes within a certain file size limit. Or you might have an internal goal of not exceeding 30k per page. It's necessary to understand how to read the file size of a document if you're trying to make it fall within a certain target range of acceptability.

How can you tell how many kilobytes an image is? Most Photoshop users think the readout in the lower left corner of a document informs them about the file size. Not true! These numbers relate to the amount of RAM Photoshop is allocating to your image and its scratch disk virtual memory scheme.

584K/733K

The size reading at the bottom left corner of a Photoshop window is deceptive. It refers to how much RAM and disk space the Photoshop 3.0 file takes up, and has no relation to what the file size will be once saved in a web image file format, like GIF or JPEG.

You also might look to your hard drive for the file size. Notice that the file size numbers are all nicely rounded figures: 11k, 33k, and 132k. Your computer rounds up the size of a file to the next largest number depending on how large your hard drive partition is. Have you ever had a file read two different file sizes on a hard drive and a floppy? That's because the computer rounds off the size of the file depending on what size storage media it's on.

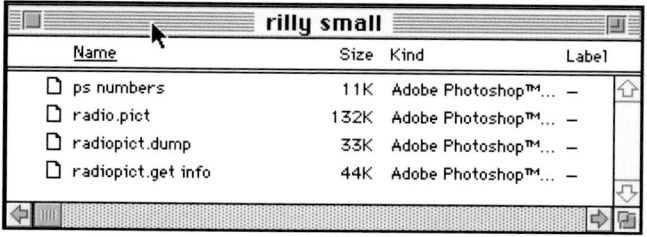

A Mac file menu, showing rounded file sizes. The rounding relates to how the hard drive is partitioned and not the true file size.

On a Mac, the only way to get information about the true byte size of a file is to do a Get Info command. First, highlight the file you want to check in the Finder, go to the File menu, and then choose Get Info.

The Get Info dialog box for the Mac, showing the disk size of 44k and the true file size of 36k.

Using Win95 on the PC, the file size shown in the menu is very close to the actual file size, with rounding to the next lowest number occurring. Under DOS you can get a more accurate reading of the file size, but it is not much different from what you see in Windows.

Making graphics and images that work on the web requires that images have as small a file size as possible. Understanding how compression affects image size and what types of file formats are appropriate for images is key to responsible web design.

■ note

To Icon or Not to Icon

Photoshop typically saves images with an icon. The icon is a small, visual representation of what the image looks like, which the file references. Photoshop icons take up a little extra room on your hard drive. This ultimately won't matter because when you send the files to your server, you'll transmit them as raw data, which will strip off the icon anyway. But if your goal is to get a more accurate reading of the true file size, you should set your preferences in Photoshop to not save an icon.

To set your preferences to not save the icon, choose File, Preferences, General. In the General dialog box, set the Image Previews to Ask When Saving.

The General Preferences dialog, where icons can be turned off.

In Photoshop 4.0, go under File, Preferences, choose File Saving, and this dialog box will enable you to set icons on or off.

Making Small GIFs

The GIF file-compression algorithm offers impressive file size reduction, but the degree of file size savings has a lot to do with how you create your GIF images. Understanding how GIFs compress is the first step in this process.

GIFs use a compression scheme known as LZW compression, which looks to patterns of data. Whenever it encounters areas in an image that do not have changes, it can implement much higher compression. This is similar to another type of compression called run-length compression (used in BMP, TIFF, and PCX formats), but LZW writes, stores, and retrieves its code a little differently. Similar to many types of run-length compression, however, GIF compression searches for changes along a horizontal axis, and whenever it finds a new color, adds to the file size.

Here's an original image saved as a GIF image that contains horizontal lines. It is 6.7k.

Here's the identical image, only flipped on its side so that the lines are vertical. It's 72% bigger at 11.5k!

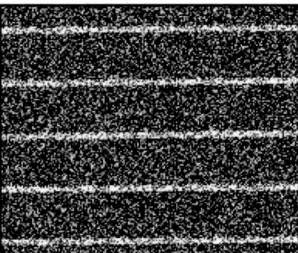

Try adding noise to the original. You'll be expanding the file size by more than eight times to 56k!

So what does the line test really teach? That artwork that has horizontal changes compresses better than artwork that doesn't. That anything with noise will more than quadruple your image's file size. That large areas of flat color compress well, and complicated line work or dithering does not.

Aside from the visual complexity of the image, there are two additional factors that affect file size: bit depth and dithering methods. With all GIFs, the fewer colors (lower bit depth), the smaller the resulting file. You should remember this fact when considering whether to improve image quality through anti-aliasing.

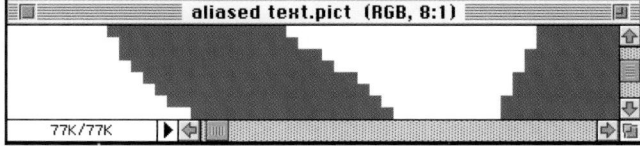

Here's an example of aliased text. It resulted in a file that totaled 3.8k when saved as a GIF.

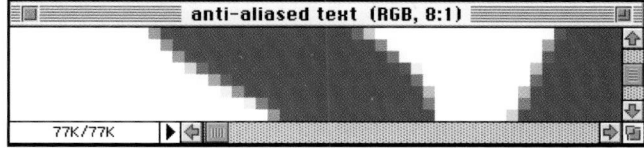

Here's an example of anti-aliased text. It resulted in a file that's 5k when saved as a GIF. The anti-aliasing caused the file to be 32% larger!

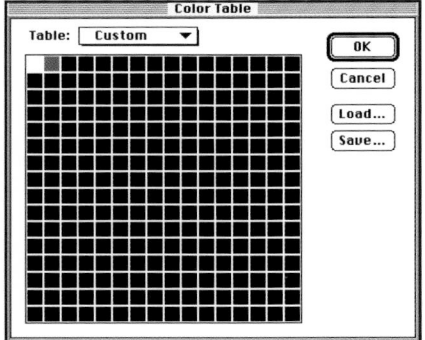

Close-up view: Aliasing doesn't disguise the jaggy nature of pixel-based artwork.

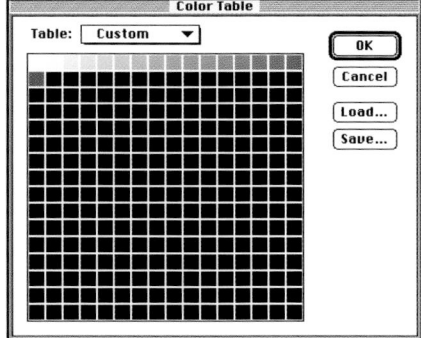

Close-up view: Anti-aliasing creates a blended edge. This blending disguises the square-pixel-based nature of computer-based artwork.

The aliased artwork used only 4 colors.

The anti-aliased artwork used 18 colors.

Aliased Artwork

Most computer artists have never considered working with aliased artwork. It's assumed that artwork will always look better if it has anti-aliased edges. This is simply not true! Artists have never had to factor size of files into their design considerations before. Having something load 32% faster is nothing to balk at. In many cases, aliased artwork looks just as good as anti-aliased artwork, and choosing between the two approaches is something that web designers should consider whenever possible.

As well as considering whether to use aliased or anti-aliased graphics, you should also always work with browser-safe colors when creating illustration-based artwork for the web. Examples of how browser-safe colors improve the quality of illustrations are demonstrated in Chapter 6, "Browser-Safe Color."

Here's an example of a 700x1134 pixel GIF file created by Bruce Heavin that totals only 7.1k! Why? Lots of solid color and no anti-aliasing. This image has only 4 colors.

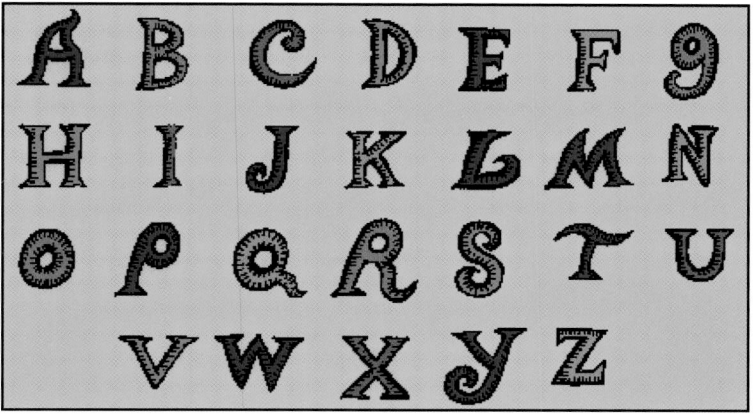

Artwork by Yuryeong Park for the Hot Hot Hot site ■ http://www.hothothot.com. The entire site is done in aliased graphics, and no page exceeds 30k, even though there are several images per page.

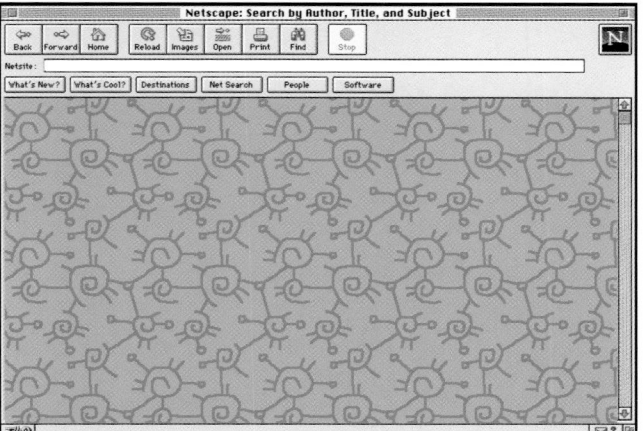

A background tile repeated in Netscape, by Bruce Heavin. The source tile is only 2.23k. The savings from aliased graphics can really add up!

Dithering and Banding

When an image with millions of colors is converted to an image with 256 colors or less, image quality is lost. Basically, when colors are removed from the image, some sacrifices have to be made. This can take place in two forms: dithering or banding. Here are some definitions to remember:

- **Dithering** is the positioning of different colored pixels within an image that uses a 256-color palette to simulate a color that does not exist in the palette. A dithered image often looks noisy, or composed of scattered pixels.

- **Adaptive palettes** are used to convert the image to 256 colors based on existing colors within the image. Generally, adaptive-based dithering looks the best of all dithering methods.

- **Screen dithering** is what happens when a 24-bit or 16-bit image is viewed on a computer with a 256-color card. The image's color is reduced to 256 colors, and the "dither" looks uniform, as if a pattern was used.

- **Banding** is a process of reducing colors to 256 or less without dithering. It produces areas of solid color and generates a posterized effect.

Understanding the terminology of dithering and banding is important in web design because these are often effects that are undesirable. Bringing down the quality of images is necessary at times for speed considerations, but riding the line between low file size and good enough quality means that you will often encounter unwanted results. These new terms help define the problems you'll encounter when creating web graphics and will be used throughout the rest of the book.

Screen dithering takes the form of a repeated pattern, and creates a moiré appearance.

The dots within a "screen dithered" image look uniform, based on a generalized screen pattern.

This is an example of **image dithering** using an adaptive palette. It will typically look a lot better than "screen dithering" because the dither pattern is based on the content of the image, not a preset screen.

Even though the image is composed of pixellated dots, they are less obvious and objectionable because there's no obvious pattern or screen.

The **banding** in this image is obvious. It looks like a posterization effect.

Here's a close-up of the banding. Instead of the dots you'll find in dithering methods, the computer takes the image and breaks it into regions of solid color.

To Dither or Not to Dither?

Dithering methods play a huge role in creating smaller GIFs. Any type of "noise" introduces added file size. Unfortunately, whenever you're working with photograph-based GIFs, dithering of one type or another must be employed to reduce the 24-bit color.

Saved with dithering: 40.2k

Saved without dithering: 38.2k

There's almost no perceivable difference between these two images, regardless of whether a dithering method is used to convert to 8-bit color or Photoshop's dither none method was chosen. Why? This image has a lot of solid areas of color to begin with. The file savings between 40.2k and 38.2k is not huge either, but the non-dither method still yields a smaller file size.

Saved with dithering: 30.1k

Saved without dithering: 23.7k

In this example, the GIF that did not use dithering is an impressive 21% smaller. The only problem is, it looks awful! Sometimes file savings does not warrant loss of quality. Whenever a photograph contains glows, feathered edges, or subtle gradations, you will have to use dithering when converting from 24-bit to 8-bit in order to maintain quality.

Instructions for how to set up dither and no-dither methods for Photoshop, Paint Shop Pro, and Photo-Paint are described later in this chapter. All programs offer the capability to set the "dithering" or "no dithering" method.

To summarize, in order to make smaller GIFs, you should:

- ■ Try to save the file at the lowest possible bit depth, while monitoring quality.

- ■ Try to avoid dithering, if the image can withstand it.

Photoshop Dither Settings

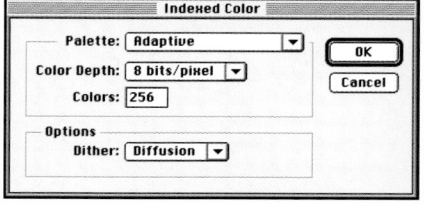

Dither Diffusion establishes a dither in the image.

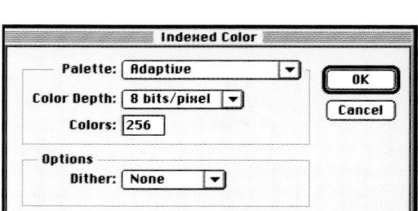

Dither None avoids dithering altogether but sometimes creates unwanted banding.

■ note

GIF Choices

There is never one pat answer for making the smallest possible GIFs. Choices between bit depth and dithering methods should always be based on the image's content. In general, images with subtle gradations will need to be dithered. Images with areas of solid color will look fine without dithering.

Photoshop's Indexed Color Dialog Box

The Indexed Color dialog box has three important functions: setting the resolution, the palette, and the dither. The resolution affects the bit depth of the image. The palette sets which colors are used, and the dither tells the program which color reduction method to use—dithering, screen, or no dithering.

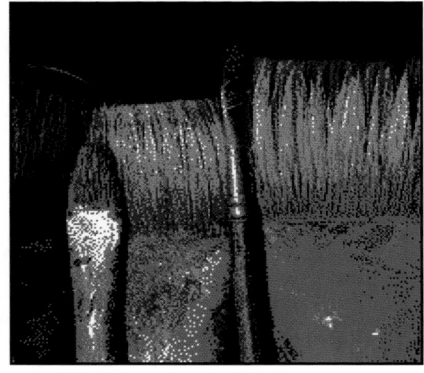

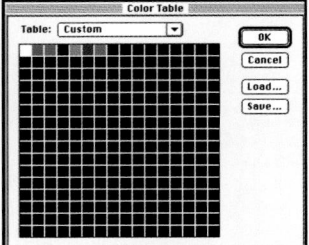

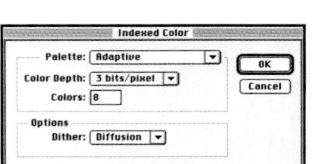

3-bit ▪ 19.8k

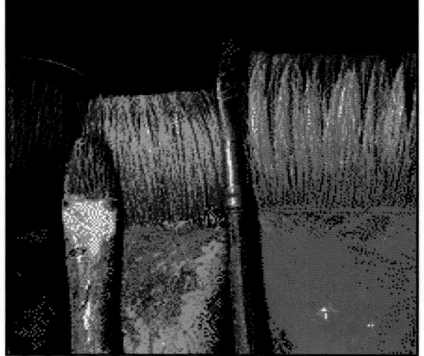

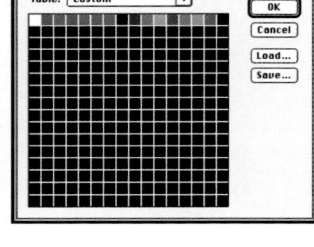

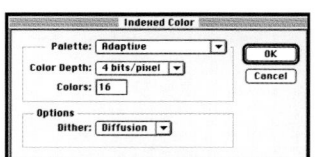

4-bit ▪ 26k

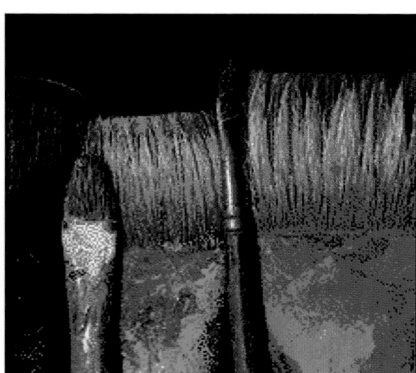

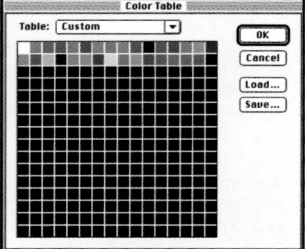

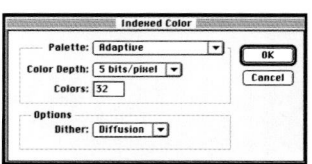

5-bit ▪ 31.2k

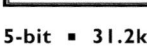

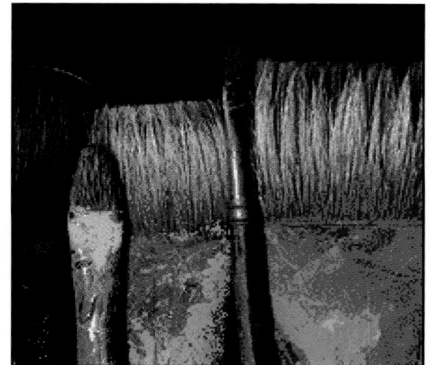

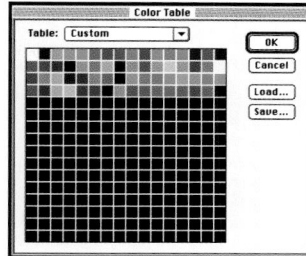

6-bit ▪ 39.7k

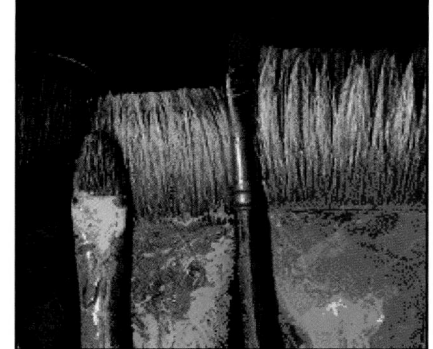

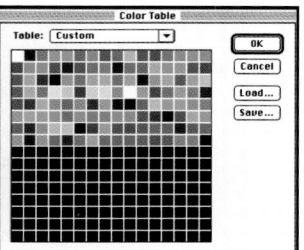

7-bit ▪ 47.5k

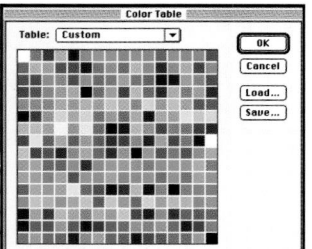

8-bit ▪ 55.4k

When you convert from RGB to Indexed Color mode, you are presented with the dialog box on the left. The middle row of images shows the results of the respective color-depth changes. The Color Table images on the right show the resulting colors contained within each image.

Photoshop Palette Chart

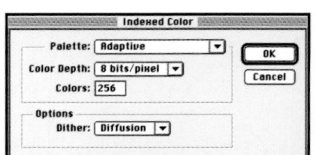  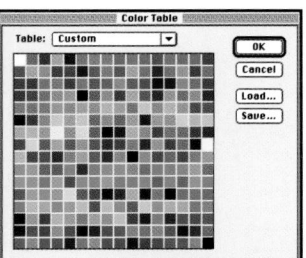

Adaptive: An adaptive palette is created from 256 colors found within the image ▪ 55.4k

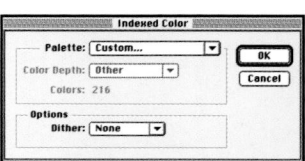  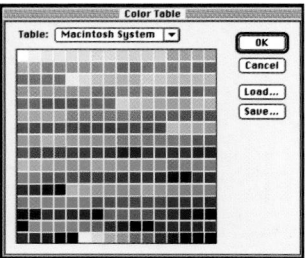

Custom: Custom enables you to load a palette of your choosing ▪ 48.3k

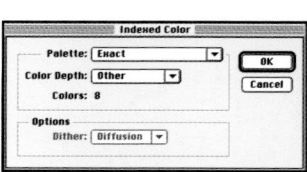 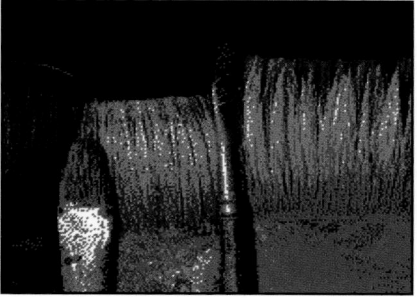 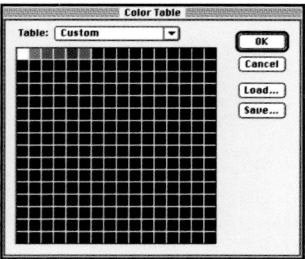

Exact: An exact palette uses the exact colors found within the image

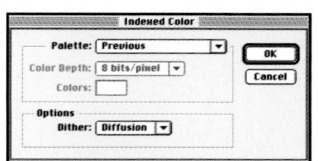 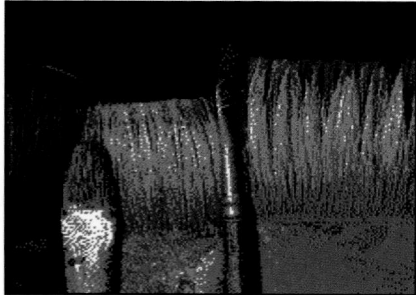 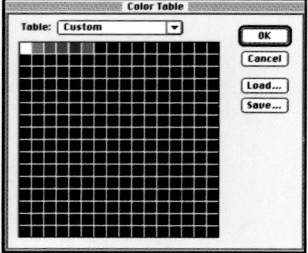

Previous: Uses the palette from the last conversion

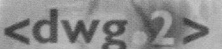

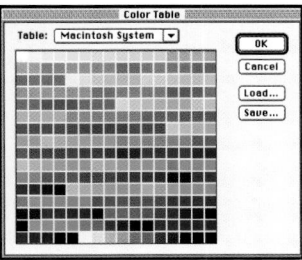
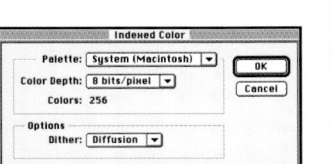

Mac Sytem: Uses the Macintosh system palette ▪ 48.3k

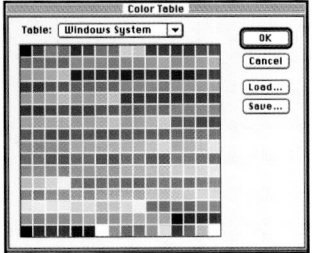
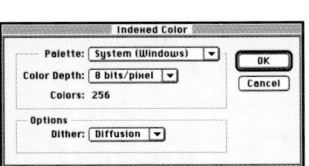

Windows Palette: Uses the Windows system palette ▪ 44.7k

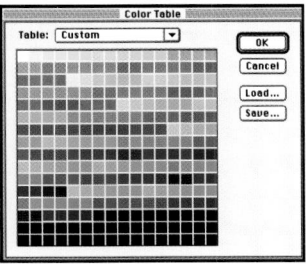
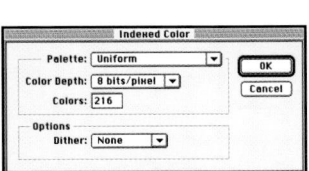

Uniform: Creates a mathematical palette based on RGB pixel values ▪ 44.3k

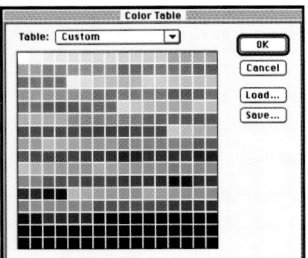
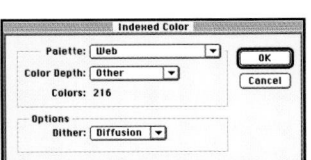

Web: Creates a palette based on the browser-safe 216 color cube ▪ 42k

How to Use the Image Compression Charts

The next time someone asks you, "Which is better, PNG, GIF or JPEG?" you can answer confidently that there is no one compression that is better than another. Different types of compression are meant to work with different specific kinds of images. Creating the absolute smallest image you can requires that you understand the differences between images and the differences between compression methods.

You can use the following pages as guides to compressing your own images. If you have a specific image in mind, compare it to this page to see which type of image catagory it falls under. Turn to those pages and compare the file savings of PNG, GIF, and JPEG compression methods. This should help you find a ballpark compression setting and save you the time of putting each of your images through all these settings!

The four images on the right are put through the following types of compression methods:

PNG	Dithered ▪ 8-bit/below
	Not Dithered ▪ 8-bit/below
GIF	Dithered ▪ 8-bit/below
	Not Dithered ▪ 8-bit/below
JPEG	Low, Med, High, Max

The Image Compression Charts work with these four specific types of images:

Lynda Illustration is a good representative image of a flat-style illustration graphic.

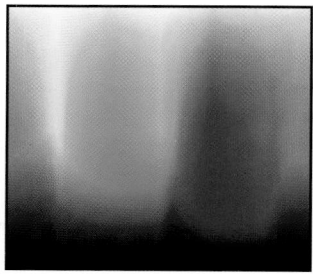

Spectrum represents a good example of a soft focus, gradation, and very colorful image.

Kitty Cats Photoshop is a good example of a gradated background combined with a cartoony illustration.

Sourpuss is a good example of a standard photograph with skin tones.

Image Compression Charts ▪ PNG Dithered

1-bit 2-bit 3-bit 4-bit

5-bit 6-bit 7-bit 8-bit

The 4-bit version of this graphic looks as good as the 8-bit version. Using the sub filter, the PNG file is only 15.4k.

	sub	up	average	paeth	adaptive
1-bit	12.8k	15.1k	14k	14.7k	13.7k
2-bit	13.3k	14.8k	14.3k	14.5k	14.4k
3-bit	11.9k	13.1k	13.2k	13k	12.8k
4-bit	15.4k	17.5k	18.9k	17.2k	17.4k
5-bit	17.4k	20.1k	22.2k	19.8k	20.2k
6-bit	18.1k	20.6k	23k	20.3k	20.8k
7-bit	18.6k	21.2k	23.6k	20.9k	21.1k
8-bit	18.6k	21.2k	23.6k	20.9k	21.3k

Image Compression Charts ▪ PNG Nondithered

1-bit   2-bit   3-bit   4-bit

5-bit   6-bit   7-bit   8-bit

The 4-bit version is still the best choice, but without dithering it's shrunk to 12.4k using the sub filter PNG method. Not bad!

	sub	up	average	paeth	adaptive
1-bit	8k	8.6k	8.3k	8.4k	8.1k
2-bit	10.1k	11k	10.9k	10.7k	10.6k
3-bit	12.9k	12.7k	13k	12.8k	12.7k
4-bit	**12.4k**	14k	14.7k	13.9k	13.8k
5-bit	13.3k	15.2k	16.2k	15.2k	14.9k
6-bit	13.8k	15.6k	16.9k	15.5k	15.2k
7-bit	13.9k	15.8k	17k	15.8k	15.4k
8-bit	14k	15.8k	17k	15.8k	15.5k

Image Compression Charts ▪ GIF Dithered

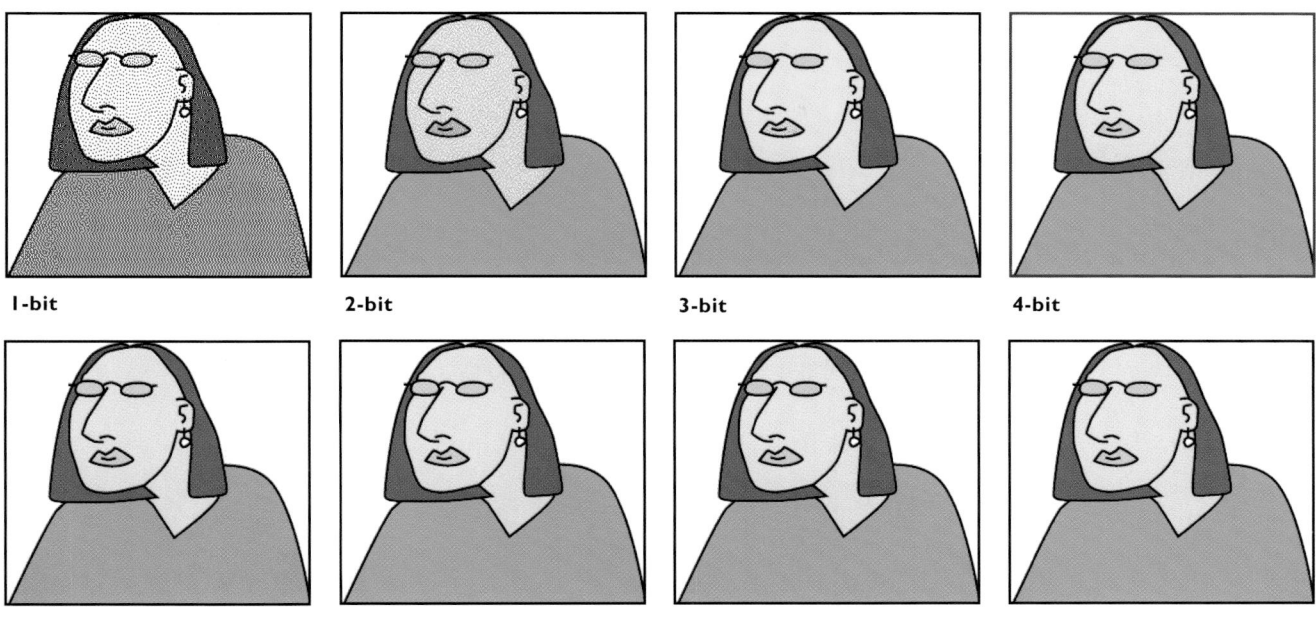

1-bit   2-bit   3-bit   4-bit

5-bit   6-bit   7-bit   8-bit

The 4-bit dithered GIF offers the best quality at the lowest file size price. At 6.3k, it's significantly smaller than its PNG counterpart.

	GIF Dithered
1-bit	5.4k
2-bit	5.2k
3-bit	4.3k
4-bit	**6.3k**
5-bit	9.1k
6-bit	9.8k
7-bit	10.2k
8-bit	10.2k

Image Compression Charts · GIF Nondithered

1-bit 2-bit 3-bit 4-bit

5-bit 6-bit 7-bit 8-bit

The 4-bit nondithered GIF is the best possible choice for this image. It yields the best quality at the lowest file savings. At 4.7k, it beats out dithered GIFs and all the PNG and JPEG examples.

	GIF Nondithered
1-bit	2.1k
2-bit	3.3k
3-bit	4.2k
4-bit	**4.7k**
5-bit	5.4k
6-bit	6.1k
7-bit	6.5k
8-bit	6.5k

Image Compression Charts ▪ JPEG

low

 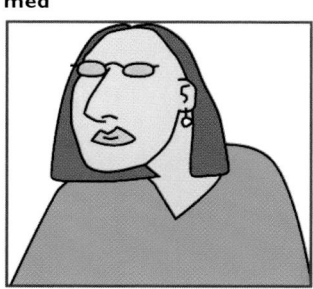  

med   high   max

baseline standard

baseline optimized

progressive

The low JPEG picked up some unwanted compression artifacts, but the medium version looks great. Still at 9.3k, it's much larger than the nondithered GIF.

	standard	optimized	progressive
low	7.7k	8.7k	7.5k
med	9.5k	10.6k	**9.3k**
high	13.3k	14.6k	12.9k
max	30.4k	20.6k	17.9k

Image Compression Charts • PNG Dithered

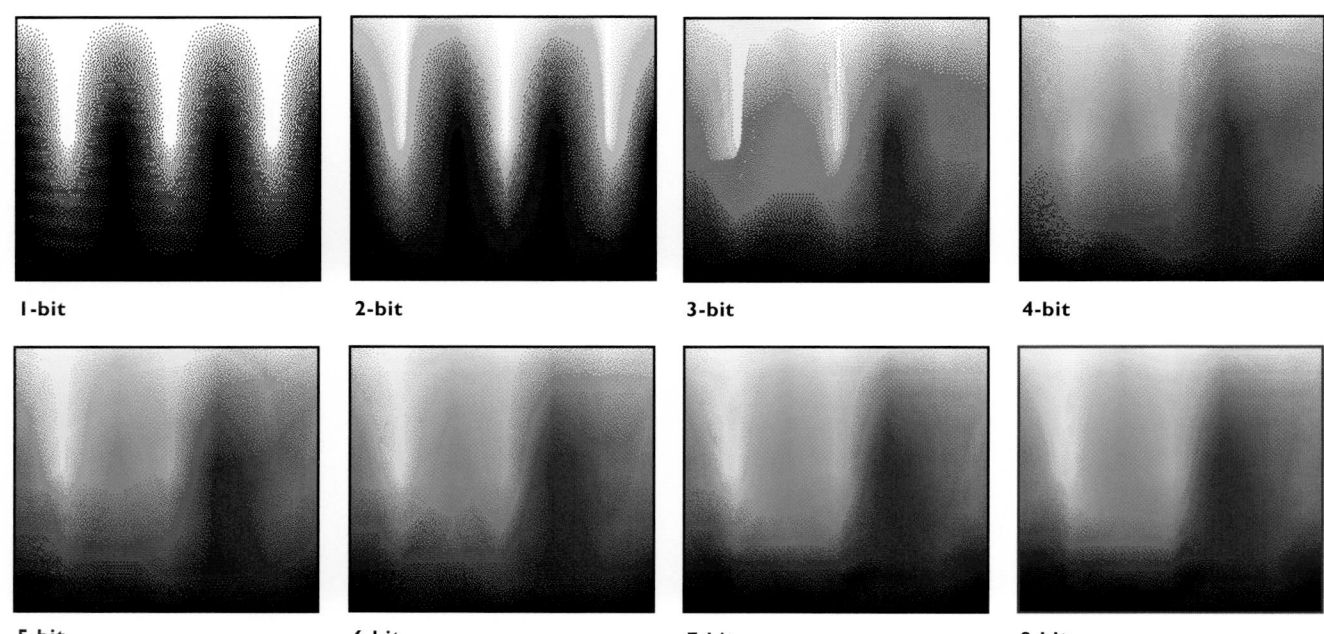

1-bit   2-bit   3-bit   4-bit

5-bit   6-bit   7-bit   8-bit

The spectrum gradient doesn't hold up well in low bit depths. I would pick 8-bit as the only acceptable example here. Once again, the sub filter yields the highest compression results at 30.9k.

	sub	up	average	paeth	adaptive
1-bit	11.2k	14.9k	13.5k	14.2k	13.4k
2-bit	15.7k	29k	18.5k	19.4k	19.4k
3-bit	17.7k	23.9k	24.1k	22.8k	23.7k
4-bit	21.7k	29.6k	30.8k	28.1k	29k
5-bit	23.8k	32.6k	34k	30.8k	32k
6-bit	26.1k	35.2k	38k	33.5k	34.4k
7-bit	28.1k	38.1k	41.8k	36.3k	37.4k
8-bit	30.9k	41k	45.4k	38.9k	37.5k

Image Compression Charts ▪ PNG Nondithered

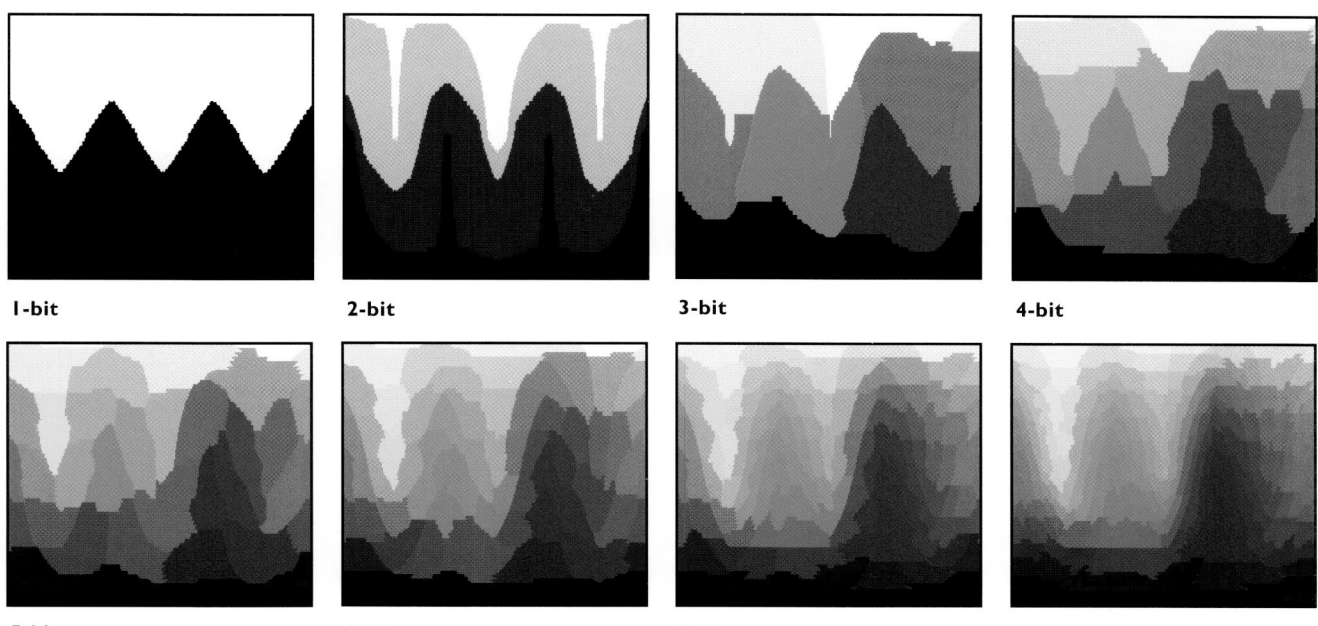

1-bit   2-bit   3-bit   4-bit

5-bit   6-bit   7-bit   8-bit

As you can see, none of these examples are acceptable. The subtle gradient is totally lost without dithering. The files sizes are significantly smaller, but the quality is so poor that it's of no use.

	sub	up	average	paeth	adaptive
1-bit	3.9k	3.9k	4k	3.9k	3.9k
2-bit	5.1k	4.6k	5.2k	4.7k	4.6k
3-bit	5k	4.9k	5.7k	4.9k	4.9k
4-bit	5.5k	5.4k	6.6k	5.4k	5.4k
5-bit	6.4k	6.1k	7.8k	6k	6.2k
6-bit	7.21k	7k	9.5k	7k	7k
7-bit	8.6k	8.4k	11.6k	8.2k	8.3k
8-bit	10k	10.2k	14.4k	10k	9.9k

Image Compression Charts ▪ GIF Dithered

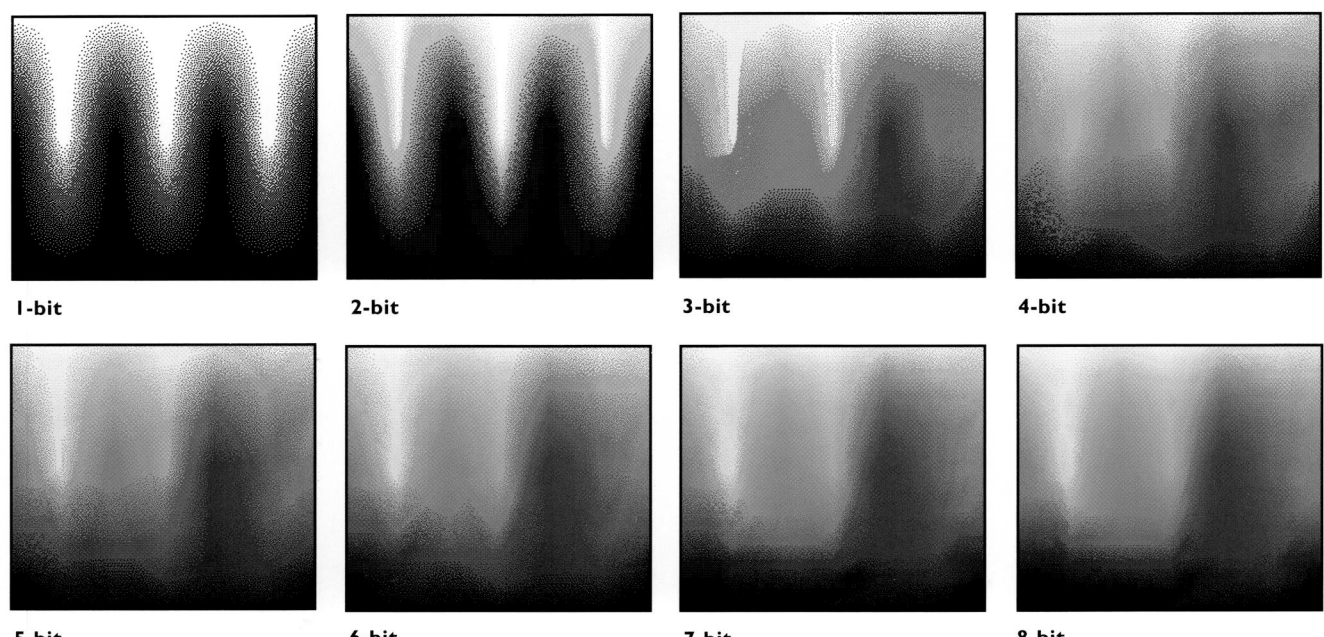

1-bit   **2-bit**   **3-bit**   **4-bit**

5-bit   **6-bit**   **7-bit**   **8-bit**

The 8-bit dithered GIF has the least amount of obvious dithering. At 33k it's large for a web graphic, but within an acceptable range. This graphic fared a little better as a PNG using the sub filter, at 30k.

	GIF Dithered
1-bit	6.7k
2-bit	10.5k
3-bit	13.8k
4-bit	17.9k
5-bit	20.7k
6-bit	24.3k
7-bit	28.2k
8-bit	33k

Image Compression Charts ▪ GIF Nondithered

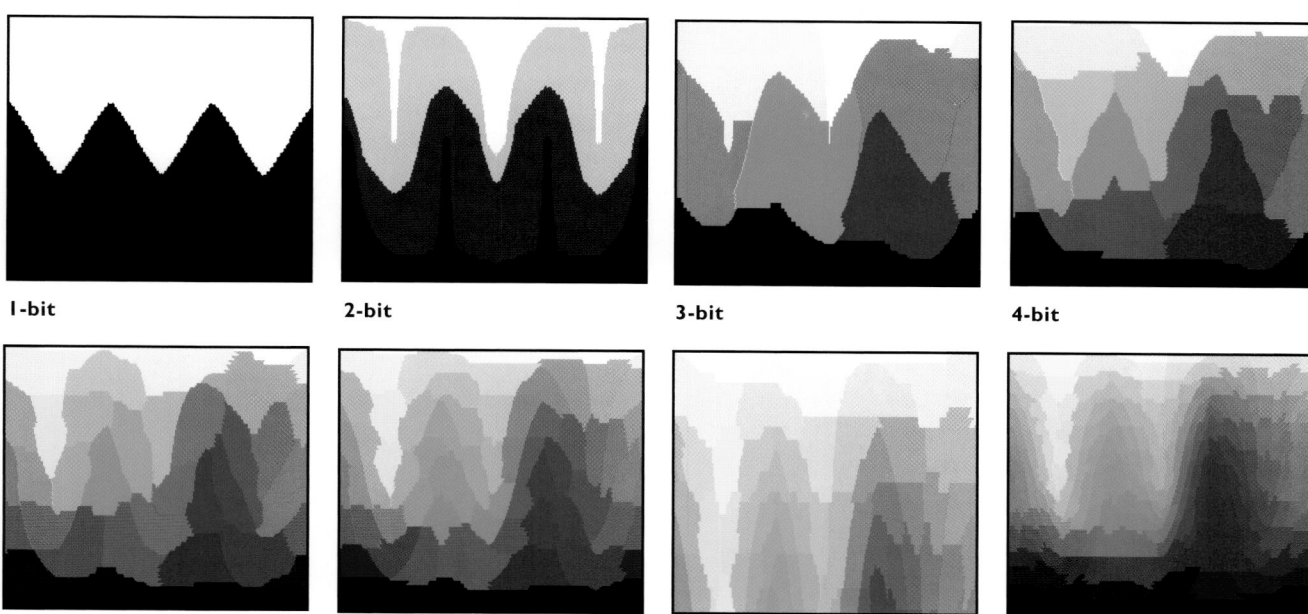

1-bit   2-bit   3-bit   4-bit

5-bit   6-bit   7-bit   8-bit

The nondithered GIF has unusable quality, regardless how much these small file sizes tempt you.

	GIF Nondithered
1-bit	.9k
2-bit	3k
3-bit	2.6k
4-bit	3.4k
5-bit	5k
6-bit	7k
7-bit	10k
8-bit	14.1k

Image Compression Charts ▪ JPEG

low   med   high   max

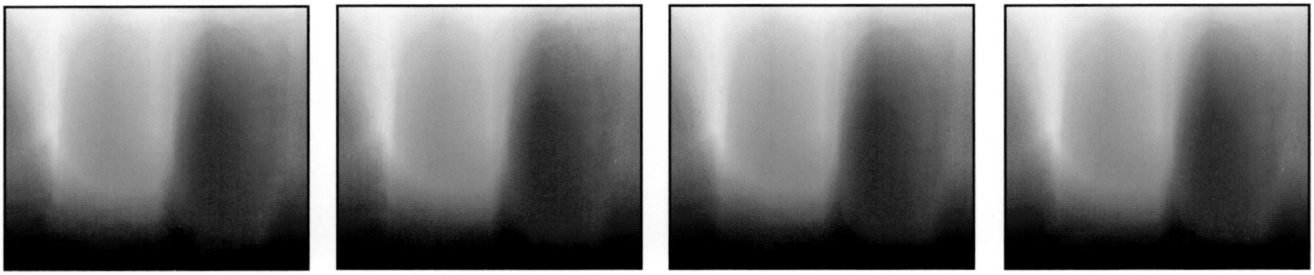

baseline standard

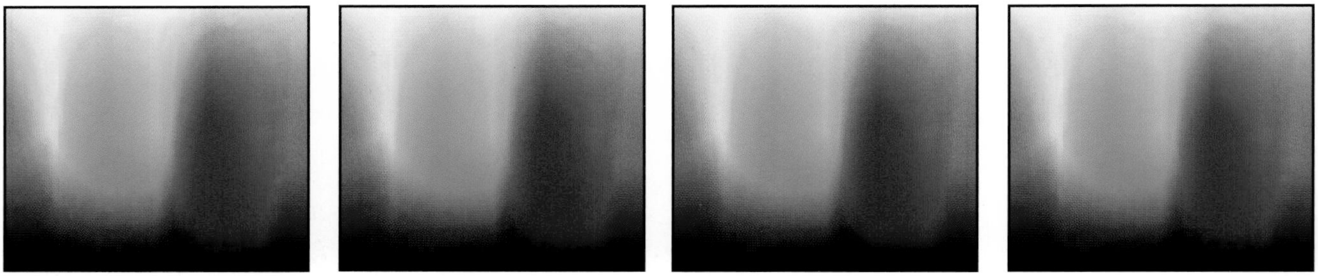

baseline optimized

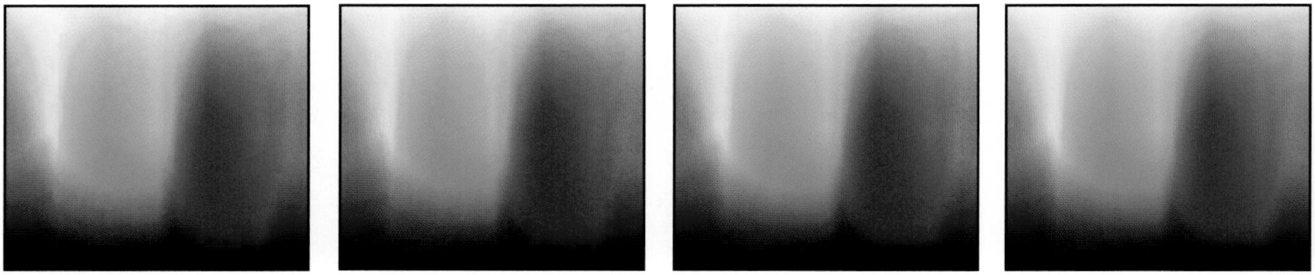

progressive

Once again, the low-quality JPEG setting is perfectly acceptable. It's only 3.8k—less than 1/10th the size of PNG or GIF with better quality to boot. JPEGs will always yield the smallest and best-looking graphics if the image includes gradients or soft focus.

	standard	optimized	progressive
low	4.3k	3.7k	3.8k
med	4.9k	4.4k	4.4k
high	9.5k	8.2k	8.3k
max	13.3k	11.7k	11.4k

Image Compression Charts ▪ PNG Dithered

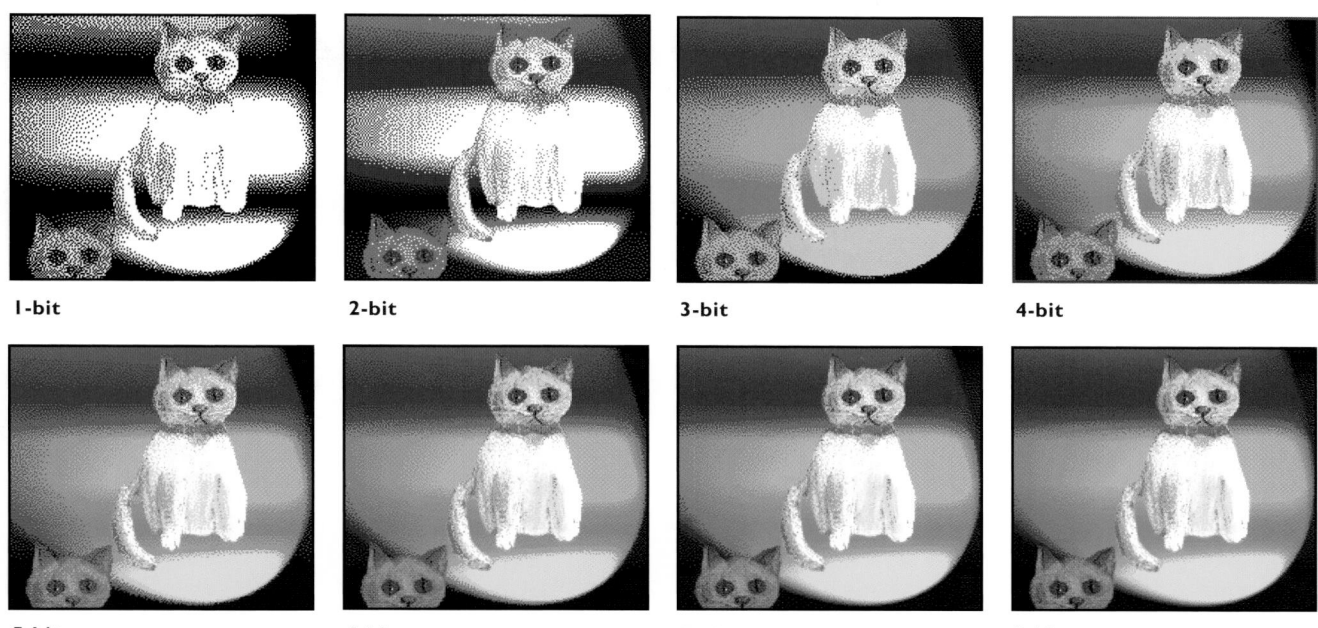

| 1-bit | 2-bit | 3-bit | 4-bit |

| 5-bit | 6-bit | 7-bit | 8-bit |

This image doesn't look great as a PNG, but of all the settings the 4-bit version yields acceptable quality and small enough size. The sub filter yields the smallest file size for this graphic. A 4-bit dithered GIF, however, looks identical and is significantly smaller than the dithered PNG.

	sub	up	average	paeth	adaptive
1-bit	11.4k	14.1k	13k	13.6k	12.2k
2-bit	13.3k	16.1k	16k	15.7k	16k
3-bit	14.2k	16.8k	16.6k	16.3k	16.8k
4-bit	16.4k	19.8k	19.5k	19.2k	19.6k
5-bit	19.7k	23.5k	24.6k	22.8k	23.1k
6-bit	22.1k	26k	27.6k	25.4k	25.6k
7-bit	24.7k	28.8k	30.6k	28.2k	28.8k
8-bit	27.2k	31.7k	33.5k	31.1k	30.6k

Image Compression Charts · PNG Nondithered

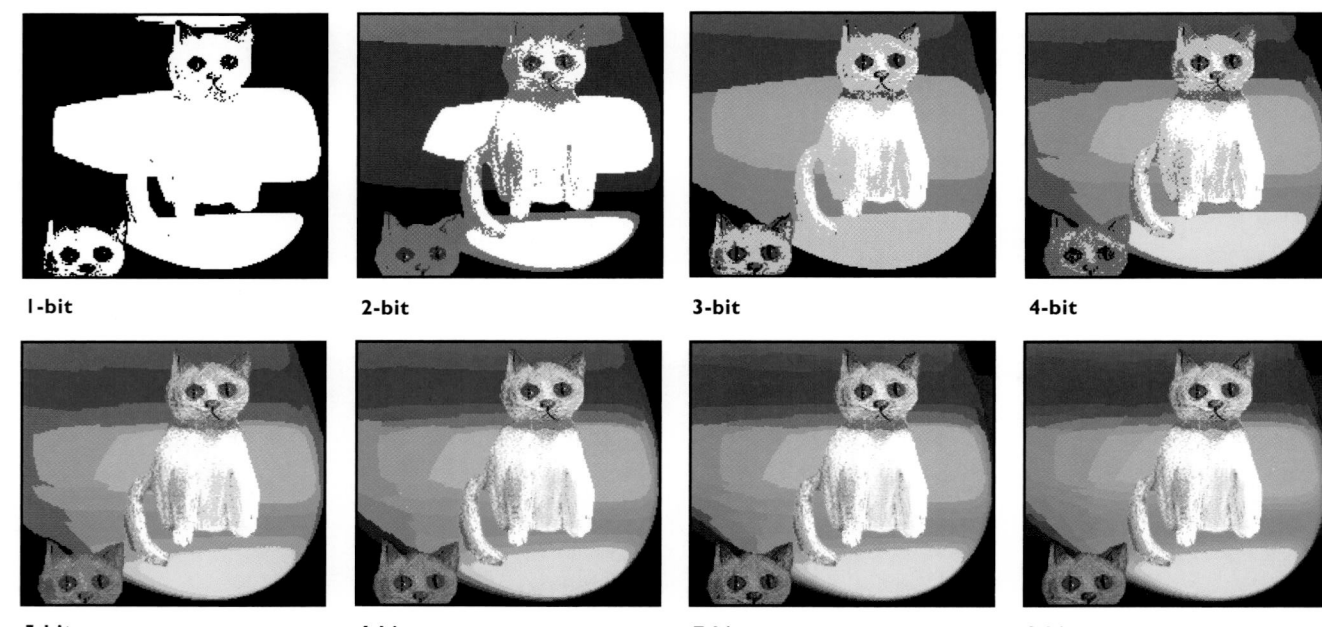

1-bit   2-bit   3-bit   4-bit

5-bit   6-bit   7-bit   8-bit

The gradient background in this image looks terrible as a nondithered graphic. Use dithering, even though the file sizes will be larger.

	sub	up	average	paeth	adaptive
1-bit	4.9k	5k	5k	5k	5k
2-bit	6.5k	6.6k	7.2k	6.7k	6.7k
3-bit	7.8k	7.9k	8.6k	7.9k	7.9k
4-bit	8.6k	8.7k	9.4k	8.7k	8.8k
5-bit	12.3k	13k	14.9k	13k	13.2k
6-bit	14.6k	15.1k	17k	15.2k	15.6k
7-bit	16.6k	17k	19k	17.3k	17.6k
8-bit	18.2k	18.6k	20.5k	19k	18.9k

Image Compression Charts ▪ GIF Dithered

1-bit 2-bit 3-bit 4-bit

5-bit 6-bit 7-bit 8-bit

This image doesn't look great as a GIF, but of all the settings the 4-bit version yields acceptable quality and small enough size. This 4-bit dithered GIF, however, looks identical to the 4-bit dithered PNG, but is significantly smaller.

	GIF Dithered
1-bit	4.3k
2-bit	7.1k
3-bit	7.9k
4-bit	**10.3k**
5-bit	13.1k
6-bit	15.6k
7-bit	19.5k
8-bit	23.5k

Image Compression Charts • GIF Nondithered

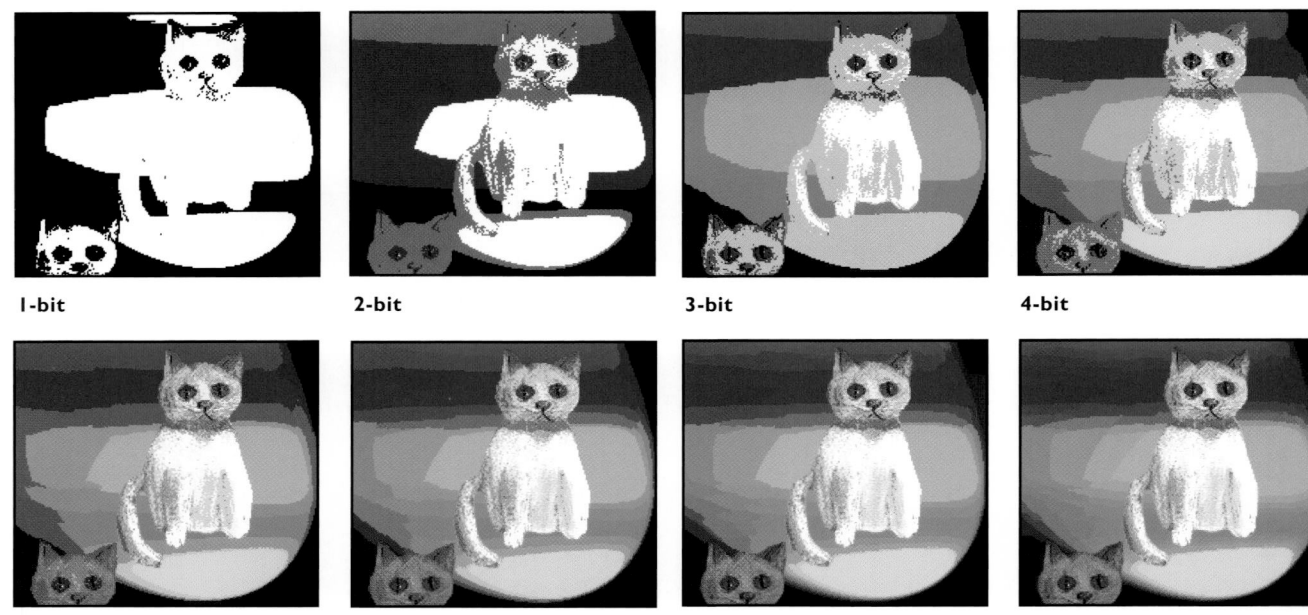

| | 1-bit | 2-bit | 3-bit | 4-bit |

5-bit   6-bit   7-bit   8-bit

The gradient background in this image looks terrible as a nondithered graphic. Use dithering, even though the file sizes will be larger.

	GIF Nondithered
1-bit	1.5k
2-bit	2.9k
3-bit	4k
4-bit	5.2k
5-bit	8k
6-bit	10.4k
7-bit	13.2k
8-bit	15.9k

Image Compression Charts ▪ JPEG

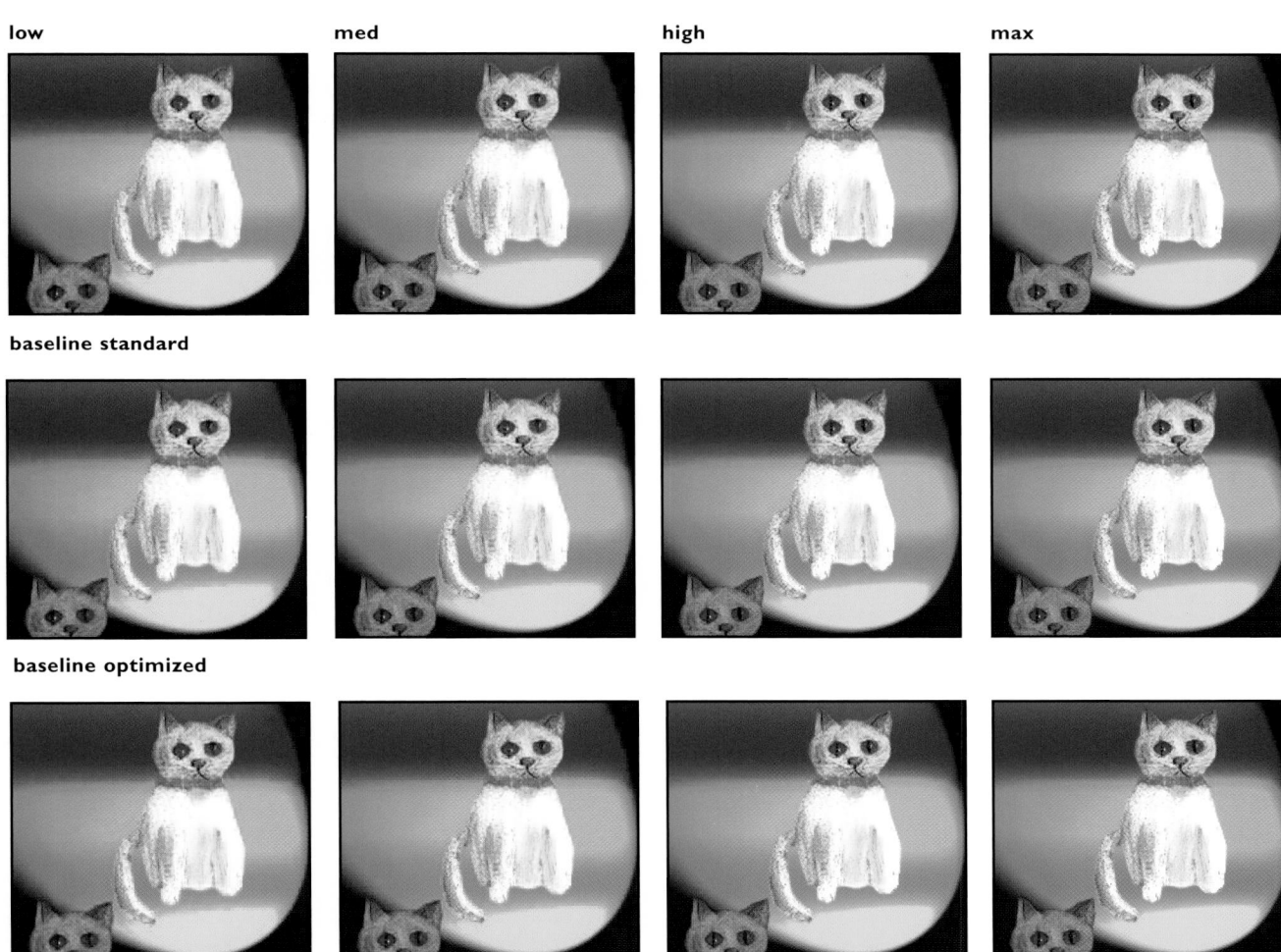

low   med   high   max

baseline standard

baseline optimized

progressive

This image looks great as a low baseline standard JPEG. It is smaller than the GIF or PNG, too! This is because gradients and soft edges always look best as JPEGs.

	standard	optimized	progressive
low	8.4k	8.1k	8.1k
med	12.2k	10.2k	10.2k
high	16.1k	15.6k	15.5k
max	24.7k	23.9k	23.5k

Image Compression Charts ▪ PNG Dithered

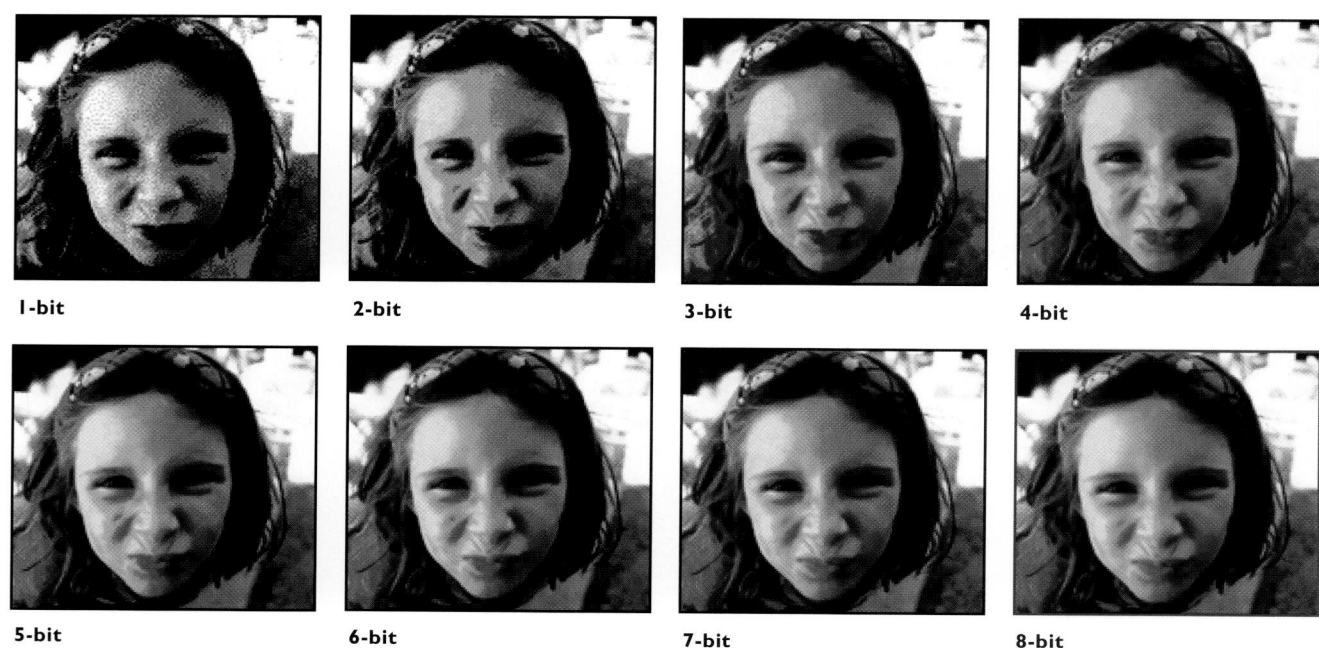

| | 1-bit | 2-bit | 3-bit | 4-bit |
| 5-bit | 6-bit | 7-bit | 8-bit |

This image doesn't hold up well in 8-bit and lower bit depths. Even in 8-bit, little dots appear on Jamie's nose. The sub filter created the lowest file size of all the 8-bit PNG examples, but at 73.5k it's well above an acceptable range for the web.

	sub	up	average	paeth	adaptive
1-bit	17.7k	23.7k	21.8k	22.7k	21.5k
2-bit	22.1k	27.1k	24.7k	26.2k	27.1k
3-bit	30.7k	37.4k	37.5k	35.9k	36.6k
4-bit	37.9k	45.6k	45.6k	44k	42.9k
5-bit	46.2k	54.3k	54.3k	52.8k	54.9k
6-bit	57.1k	66.1k	66.1k	64.65k	66.7k
7-bit	65.6k	75k	75k	73.4k	75k
8-bit	**73.5k**	82.5k	90.5k	80.8k	78.6k

Image Compression Charts ▪ PNG Nondithered

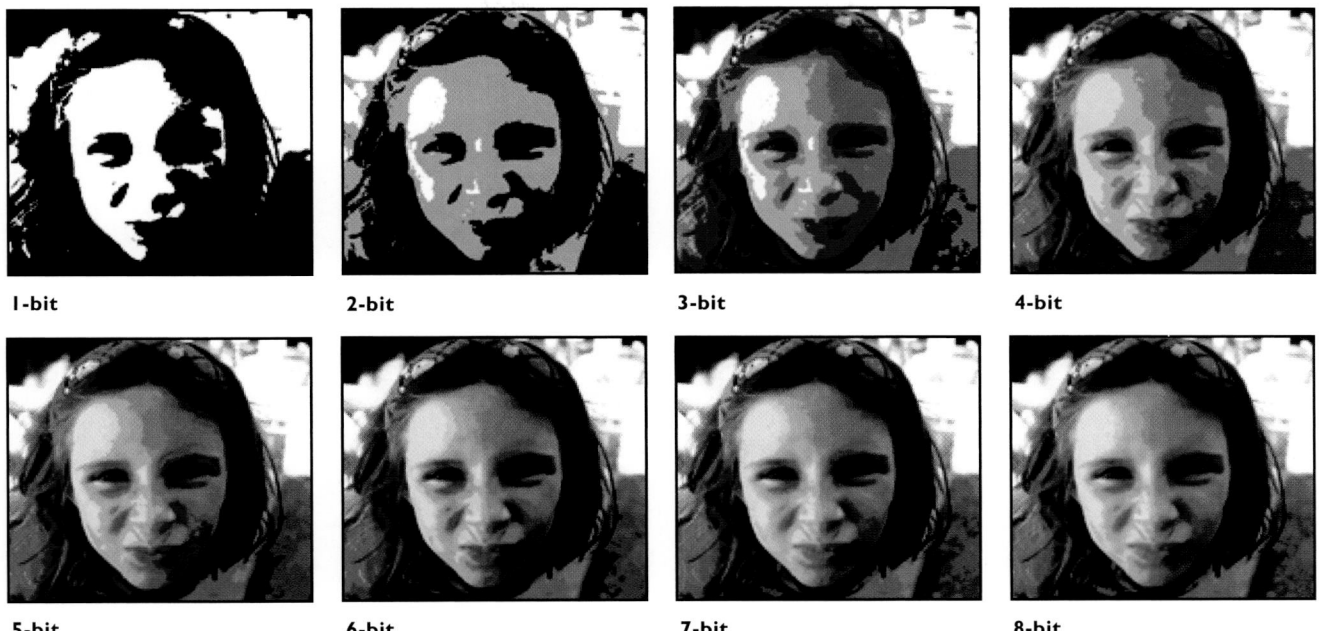

1-bit   2-bit   3-bit   4-bit

5-bit   6-bit   7-bit   8-bit

Unless you're looking for a posterized style, none of these examples are acceptable. The skin tones and subtle tones in Jamie's face make this image a difficult subject for 8-bit and lower nondithered compression types.

	sub	up	average	paeth	adaptive
1-bit	7.2k	7.2k	7.4k	7.2k	7.3k
2-bit	12.9k	12.5k	12.8k	12.5k	12.3k
3-bit	19.9k	19.6k	22.7k	19.6k	19.7k
4-bit	25.6k	26.1k	31.2k	26.1k	26.2k
5-bit	33.4k	34k	40k	34k	34.1k
6-bit	43.2k	45k	53.1k	44.8k	44.4k
7-bit	50.9k	53.1k	63.5k	52.7k	53.3k
8-bit	60k	63.3k	74.8k	62.5k	61.8k

Image Compression Charts ▪ GIF Dithered

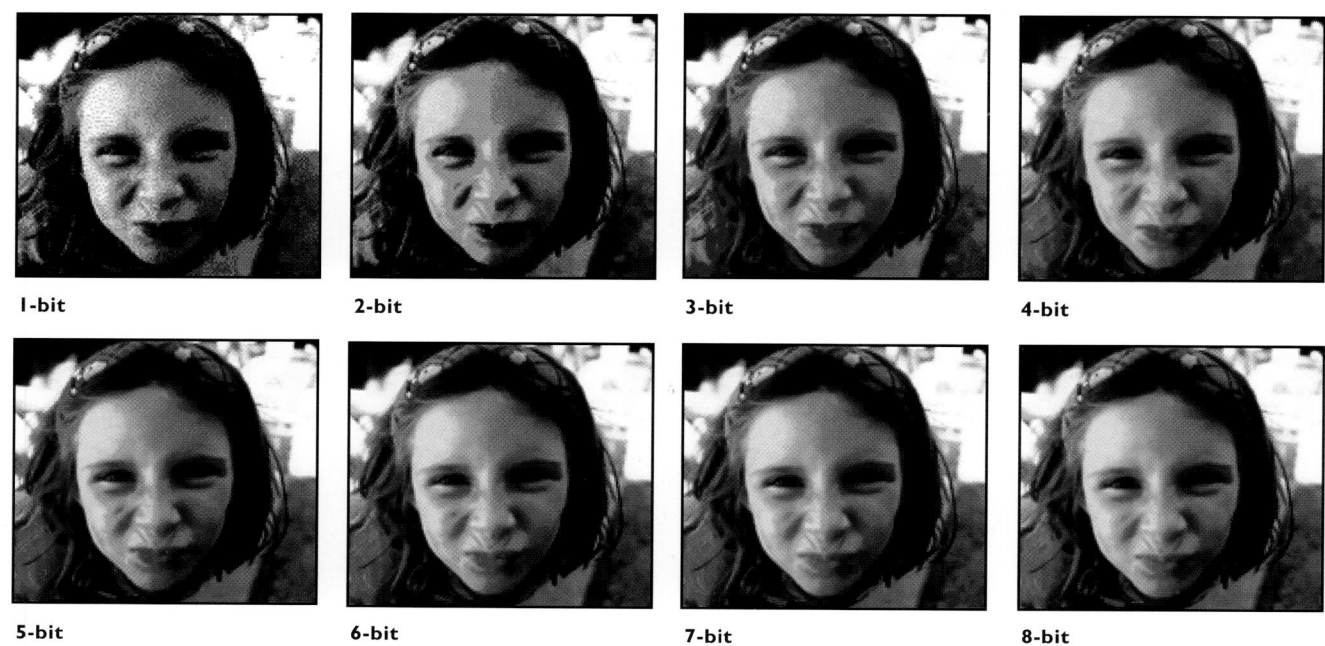

1-bit **2-bit** **3-bit** **4-bit**

5-bit **6-bit** **7-bit** **8-bit**

This image doesn't hold up well in 8-bit and lower bit depths. Even in 8-bit, little dots appear on Jamie's nose. Even though the 8-bit GIF at 65k is smaller than its 8-bit PNG counterpart, it's still well above an acceptable size range for the web.

	GIF Dithered
1-bit	10.8k
2-bit	15k
3-bit	22.8k
4-bit	28.2k
5-bit	36.7k
6-bit	46.2k
7-bit	54.9k
8-bit	65k

Image Compression Charts ▪ GIF Nondithered

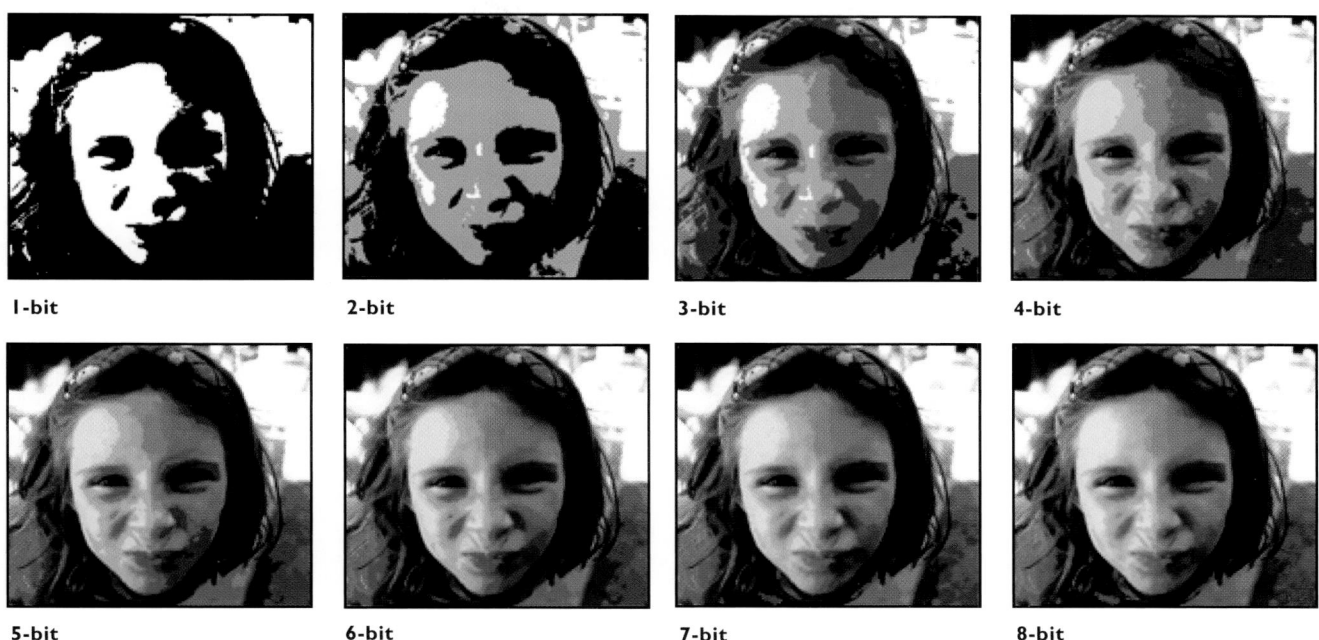

1-bit   2-bit   3-bit   4-bit

5-bit   6-bit   7-bit   8-bit

Unless you're looking to create a posterized style image, none of these settings yield acceptable quality.

	GIF Nondithered
1-bit	4.1k
2-bit	8.6k
3-bit	14.1k
4-bit	19.4k
5-bit	26.4k
6-bit	35.3k
7-bit	43.5k
8-bit	54.2k

Image Compression Charts · JPEG

low   med   high   max

baseline standard

baseline optimized

progressive

The low quality JPEG looks great—all the subtleties in Jamie's skin tone are preserved. And at 12.6k the size is right, too!

	standard	optimized	progressive
low	12.9k	12.5k	12.6k
med	17.6k	17.3k	17.2k
high	29.8k	29.2k	29.3k
max	50.5k	49.3k	48.7k

24-Bit JPEGs Versus 24-Bit PNGs

On the preceding Image Compression Charts, you may have noticed that PNG was compared using only 8-bit and lower bit-depth settings. That is because 24-bit PNG files are quite huge!

This is a 24-bit max quality JPEG. It is 49.3k.

This is a 24-bit PNG using the sub filter. It is 224k!

Applying PNG compression in 24-bit has the advantage over JPEG of being lossless. JPEG uses lossy compression, which means it permanently throws away information in an image. PNG is compressed using any number of filters and is then decompressed when viewed. This enables PNG to retain every original detail and pixel, with no loss of quality or difference between its original noncompressed source.

On low-resolution images for the web, the quality difference between JPEG and PNG is imperceptible. My recommendation is that you always choose JPEG over PNG for photographic style 24-bit images. The only time PNG compression compares favorably is when it is used in 8-bit and lower bit depths. PNG has two advantages over JPEG and GIF: it can store gamma information and will adjust automatically for the gamma of its target platform (gamma is explained in Chapter 2, "Understanding the Web Environment"), and PNG supports 8-bit transparency (otherwise known as alpha channels). You can find examples of PNG transparency in Chapter 7, "Transparent Artwork."

Reducing Colors in GIF Files Using Photoshop

Chapter 3, "Web File Formats," described the file-saving advantages of working with limited color palettes whenever using the GIF file format. Here's how to implement procedures that create the smallest possible GIF files.

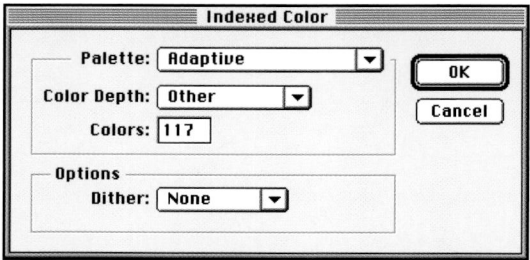

Step 1: An RGB image has to be converted to Indexed Color mode before it can be saved as a GIF. Under the Mode menu, choose Indexed Color.

Step 2: You can type any number into this dialog box. Try to go so low that the image looks bad, and then back off a step. This ensures that you've pushed the limits to how few colors are needed in order to make a small file that still maintains acceptable quality.

Reducing Colors in Photo-Paint

Photo-Paint has an interface similar to Photoshop's Indexed Color dialog box.

■ A **Uniform palette** type produces the same palette over and over again. This is the appropriate type when you are using Photo-Paint's batch processing feature and want to convert a series of images to the same palette.

■ An **Adaptive palette** type produces a color palette based on the colors found within the image. It is similar to the Exact setting in Photoshop.

■ An **Optimized palette** type produces the best 256 colors for re-creating the image. This feature is the same as Photoshop's Adaptive palette setting.

■ A **Custom palette** type allows you to assign a specific palette (such as the browser-safe 216) to an image.

■ A **None Dither** type produces a banding effect. An **Ordered Dither** type produces a **screen dither** effect.

■ An **Error Diffusion Dither** type produces a random dither based on the image itself.

■ **Colors** determines at what bit depth the image is saved.

Reducing Colors in Paint Shop Pro

Here is Paint Shop Pro's version of decreasing color-depth options.

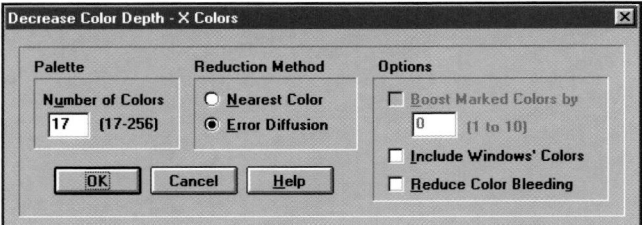

- ■ **Number of Colors** dictates the color depth of the image.

- ■ The **Nearest Color** reduction method is the same as Dither None in Photoshop and Photo-Paint. It creates a banded appearance.

- ■ **Error Diffusion** will create dithering based on the image itself.

- ■ **Boost Masked Colors** allows you to select colors within the document and have the palette weigh toward favoring those colors.

- ■ **Include Windows' Colors** ensures that the 16 colors within Windows are reserved in the image's color table.

- ■ **Reduce Color Bleeding** reduces the left-to-right color bleeding that sometimes occurs with the Error Diffusion Settings.

■ **note**

The Windows 16 Palette

Sixteen colors are reserved for a native palette assigned to Windows machines. Unfortunately, only the last six colors are browser safe. There are some cases where you might want to use these colors in a Windows-based Intranet, where cross-platform compatibility is not an issue. The win16.clut is located at my web site: ■ ftp://luna.bearnet/com/pub/lynda/.

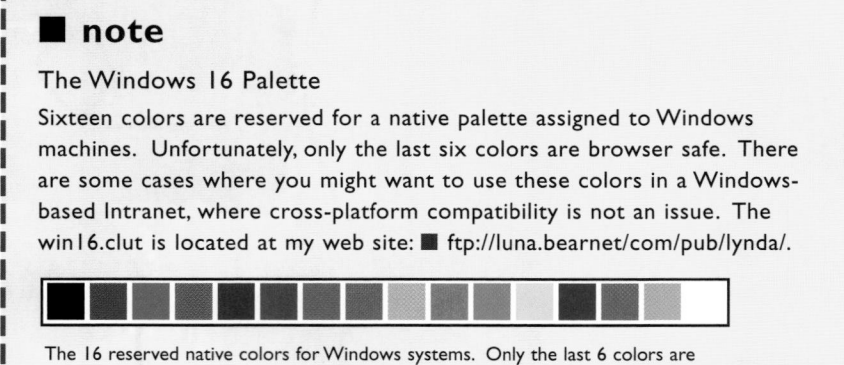

The 16 reserved native colors for Windows systems. Only the last 6 colors are browser safe.

■ note

Other Compression Tools and Resources

GIF/JPEG Smart Saver

Windows 95 and NT file optimization tool that includes previews so you can judge side to side how much compression a GIF or JPEG can withstand. A demo is availabe for downloading at
■ http://www.ulead.com/products/noslip.htm

HVS Color

A Windows or Mac Photoshop and DeBabelizer plug-in that optimizes GIF images with a proprietary algorithm.
■ http://www.digfrontiers.com/

GIF Wizard

An online file reduction service—runs any image through its automatic filter and reduces the file size on-the-fly. Way, way, way cool!
■ http://www.raspberryhill.com/gifwizard.html

PhotoGIF

Mac-only Photoshop plug-in that includes transparency tools and image and palette optimization features, and works with animated GIFs, too!
■ http://www.boxtopsoft.com/PhotoGIF/

ProJPEG

Mac-only Photoshop plug-in that offers baseline or progressive JPEG support and previews the results before you commit.
■ http://enlil.boxtopsoft.com/ProJPEG

The Bandwidth Conservation Society

Cool tutorials and great information about image optimization.
■ http://www.infohiway.com/faster/index.html

■ note

Compression Rules in a Nutshell

■ Avoid noise in GIF images.

■ Whenever possible, don't dither GIFs.

■ Use the least amount of colors in a GIF while maintaining acceptable quality.

■ Always try the lowest amount of JPEG compression while maintaining acceptable quality.

■ PNG compresses better on 8-bit.

Photoshop 4.0 Actions Palette

Photoshop 4.0 has a wonderful new addition called the Actions palette that makes life easier for those of us who regularly perform repetitive Photoshop tasks. The Actions palette enables us to create macros, which automate multiple Photoshop commands with the click of a button.

Macros are created by having Photoshop observe your actions during a recording session, which enables the program to memorize your steps. In addition to repeating multiple commands to a single image, actions can be applied to hundreds of images at a time. This is called batch processing.

Imagine you had 100 images that you wanted to index to a specific palette, shrink down to thumbnails, and save in the GIF file format. It might take you anywhere from 3–5 minutes for each image in order to finish this operation manually. An Action palette could do this task to 100 images in a matter of a few minutes. No one likes doing a repetitive task for hours on end when a computer can do it in minutes!

Step-by-Step Actions Palette Programming

Here's a step-by-step exercise to teach yourself Action palettes for web graphics authoring. This tutorial will teach you to create an action that makes a small thumbnail of a larger image by resizing it to a specific size, indexing the image to an adaptive palette, and then saving the image as a GIF.

Step 1: This demonstration will use this large streaking monkey image, illustrated by Bruce Heavin.

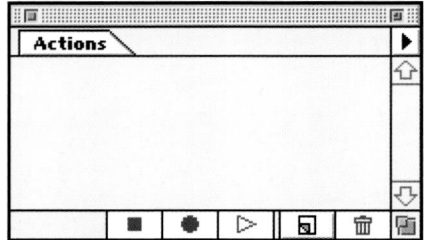

Step 2: Under Window, select Show Actions. Make sure you are not in the Button mode. To turn this off, go to the arrow in the upper right corner of the Actions palette and pull down the menu to toggle the "Button Mode" off. When you are out of Button mode, your Actions palette should look like this.

Step 3: It's always best to work on a copy of the image when programming a macro. This is so you don't damage the original image in the process of creating the action process. That's not to say that you will damage a file; it's simply a recommended precautionary measure. Copies can be made easily in Photoshop by selecting the Duplicate function from the Image menu.

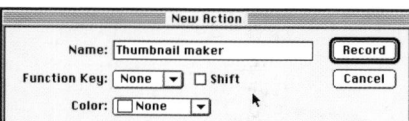

Step 4: Click on the upper arrow of the Actions palette to access the setting New Action or the page icon at the bottom of the screen to initiate the recording session. A dialog box will prompt you to name your action, define a function key, and select a color for the button. Insert the name, "Thumbnail maker", or any other name that is appropriate for what you plan to record. When you're finished, press Record to begin.

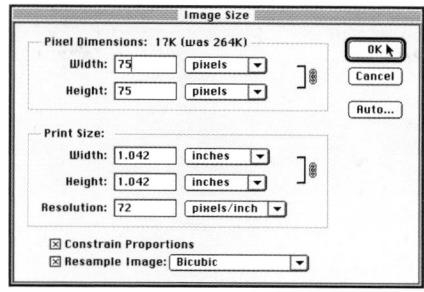

Step 5: The first step in this recording session will be to establish the amount of image size reduction. Under the menu item Image, select Image Size. This example shows changing the settings to 75 pixels high with constrained proportions checked. Once OK is pressed, the monkey image will shrink down to icon size.

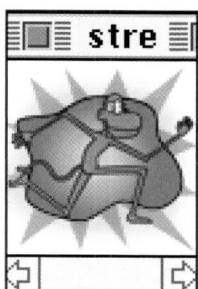

Step 6: The results of the image size scaling should match what you requested.

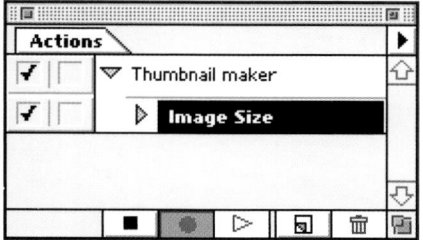

Step 7: The Actions Palette will now show the Thumbnail maker macro. Click on the twirly triangle to see the Image Size command. The Image Size layer can be twirled down as well.

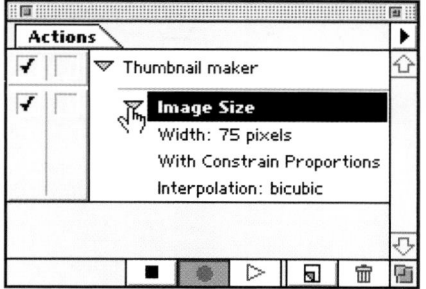

Step 8: If you want to change the settings, you can press Stop (the square at the bottom of the palette). Highlight Image Size and drag it into the little trash can and repeat the process again till you get it right. Press Record to continue the macro so you can add more functions to the actions set.

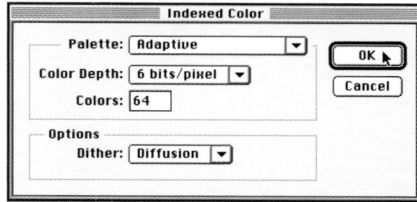

Step 9: Select Image, Mode, Indexed Color. Click OK once you have entered the setting you want.

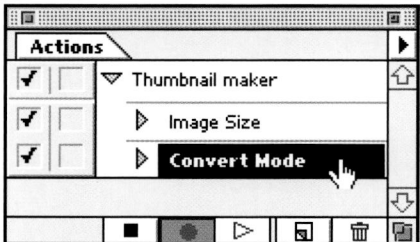

Step 10: Now the Actions palette should include the last operation.

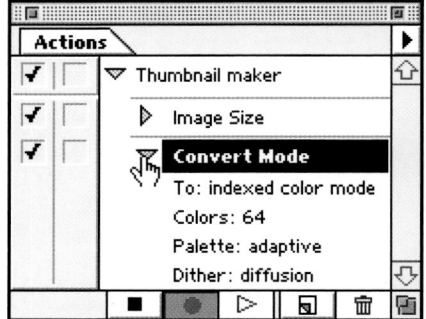

Step 11: The details of the action will be visible by pressing on the little twirly arrow.

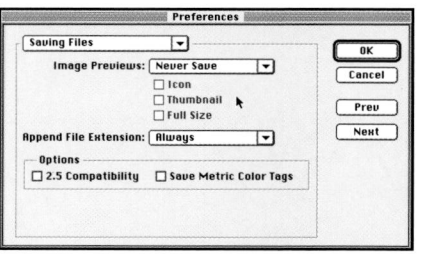

Step 12: The last action remaining to program is the save command. Before doing so, make sure your preferences are set up the way you want. Under File, Preferences, Saving Files, choose Append File Extension to "Always." This is so Photoshop will know to put the .gif extension at the end of the new thumbnail image. Choose Never Save in the Image Preview pull-down menu so that the file will be as small as possible. Icon's and previews make larger files.

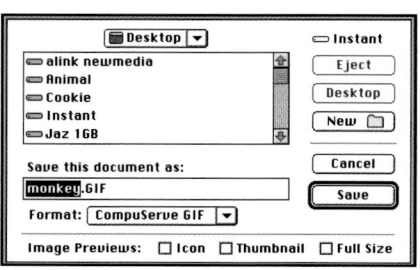

Step 13: Choose File, Save As, and type the name of the file. The GIF extension will be filled in automatically.

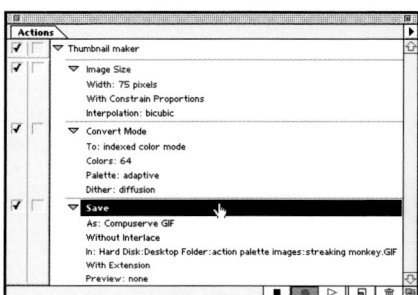

Step 14: Once you're finished programming the macro, press Stop on the recorder so that further actions won't be recorded. The Actions palette should now contain the actions that were recorded and should look something like this.

Batch File Processing

Now that the Actions macro is complete, you can create a batch process to apply the macro to a folder of images. Again, if this is your first time or if you simply want to be cautious, work on a backup of the folder, not the only copy!

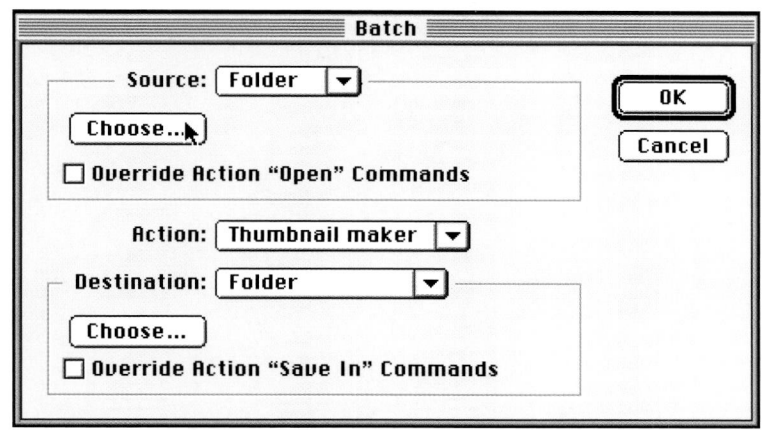

Step 1:. To begin, hold down the upper right arrow to select Batch from the Actions palette options.

Step 2: A dialog box will appear. Click on the Choose button and select the folder that contains the images you wish to process. Next, select from the Actions pull-down to see the list of actions. In this example, the choice Thumbnail maker is selected. In the Destination pull-down, choose Folder. Click the Choose button to tell the computer where your folder is located. When everything is selected to your specifications, press OK and you can go get a cup of coffee for a moment while the computer does its business. If you have nothing else to do, you can watch the computer do its action to each of the images as they go by. Tada! You're a god! Well at least a Photoshop actions god.

■ note

Actions Palette Options

If you want to apply your action only to a single image, you can easily do so. Open the image you wish to apply the action to. Open the Actions palette and press the action you want. If you assigned the Action palette to a function key, you can press that key to activate the button.

There are many more features in the Actions palette that haven't been touched on here. Actions can be created to perform any number of functions needed on an everyday basis for your web images. To get a more in-depth look at Action palettes, consult the manual that came with your copy of Photoshop 4.0.

Hexadecimal Color

BROWSER

33 FF

0033 CC

Width ="500

<STRONG>

Height ="600

IMAGE OPTIMIZATION

5

Imaging techniques

bgcolor="FFFFCC

@link="cyan

<BODY>

LYNDA.COM

www. Design

Hexadecimal Shmexadecimal

I'm happy to say that until the web came along, I lived a long happy life without uttering a word about hexadecimal code to anyone. Now that I'm devoting an entire chapter to the subject, I hope you'll understand that this was not my idea. I think working with hexadecimal math is a nuisance and wish it wasn't a part of web design. Unfortunately, no one asked me!

Hexadecimal math code is often used by software programs and programmers but has always been invisible to casual computer users. Seasoned digital artists are already accustomed to defining color choices through RGB or CMYK values. We are shielded from paying much attention to RGB and CMYK numerics because programs such as Photoshop let us select color by appearance, not by mathematical values.

Working with color on the web is not nearly as intuitive as specifying color in Photoshop and other imaging programs. If you want to use colors—as in colored text, colored links, colored backgrounds, and colored borders—describing them by their hexadecimal values is the only way HTML lets you do it. You can also add colored backgrounds by loading an image into the background of your page (see Chapter 8, "Background Tiles"), but if you want solid colors, using hexadecimal code is the most efficient way because the colors will download faster.

Hexadecimal is derived from base 16 mathematics. Regular numbers are derived from base ten mathematics. Here's a table that shows how base ten math converts to base 16 math.

#	0	1	2	3	4	5	6	7	8	9	10	11	12	13	14	15
HEX	0	1	2	3	4	5	6	7	8	9	A	B	C	D	E	F

In this chart the numbers on the top are base ten and the numbers on the bottom are base 16, otherwise known as hexadecimal.

Hexadecimal numbers in web design are used to convert RGB values so that HTML can interpret which colors you've chosen. RGB colors range from values of 0–255. Here is a helpful chart when dealing with RGB number conversions (0–255) to hex. The browser-safe colors are highlighted. If you don't know what browser-safe colors are yet, you will once you read Chapter 6, "Browser-Safe Color."

00=00	01=01	02=02	03=03	04=04	05=05	06=06	07=07	08=08
09=09	10=0A	11=0B	12=0C	13=0D	14=0E	15=0F	16=10	17=11
18=12	19=13	20=14	21=15	22=16	23=17	24=18	25=19	26=1A
27=1B	28=1C	29=1D	30=1E	31=1F	32=20	33=21	34=22	35=23
36=24	37=25	38=26	39=27	40=28	41=29	42=2A	43=2B	44=2C
45=2D	46=2E	47=2F	48=30	49=31	50=32	**51=33**	52=34	53=35
54=36	55=37	56=38	57=39	58=3A	59=3B	60=3C	61=3D	62=3E
63=3F	64=40	65=41	66=42	67=43	68=44	69=45	70=46	71=47
72=48	73=49	74=4A	75=4B	76=4C	77=4D	78=4E	79=4F	80=50
81=51	82=52	83=53	84=54	85=55	86=56	87=57	88=58	89=59
90=5A	91=5B	92=5C	93=5D	94=5E	95=5F	96=60	97=61	98=62
99=63	100=64	101=65	**102=66**	103=67	104=68	105=69	106=6A	107=6B
108=6C	109=6D	110=6E	111=6F	112=70	113=71	114=72	115=73	116=74
117=75	118=76	119=77	120=78	121=79	122=7A	123=7B	124=7C	125=7D
126=7E	127=7F	128=80	129=81	130=82	131=83	132=84	133=85	134=86
135=87	136=88	137=89	138=8A	139=8B	140=8C	141=8D	142=8E	143=8F
144=90	145=91	146=92	147=93	148=94	149=95	150=96	151=97	152=98
153=99	154=9A	155=9B	156=9C	157=9D	158=9E	159=9F	160=A0	161=A1
162=A2	163=A3	164=A4	165=A5	166=A6	167=A7	168=A8	168=A9	170=AA
171=AB	172=AC	173=AD	17=AE	175=AF	176=B0	177=B1	178=B2	179=B3
180=B4	181=B5	182=B6	183=B7	184=B8	185=B9	186=BA	187=BB	188=BC
189=BD	190=BE	191=BF	192=C0	193=C1	194=C2	195=C3	196=C4	197=C5
198=C6	199=C7	200=C8	201=C9	202=CA	203=CB	**204=CC**	205=CD	206=CE
207=CF	208=D0	209=D1	210=D2	211=D3	212=D4	213=D5	214=D6	215=D7
216=D8	217=D9	218=DA	219=DB	220=DC	221=DD	222=DE	223=DF	224=E0
225=E1	226=E2	227=E3	228=E4	229=E5	230=E6	231=E7	232=E8	233=E9
234=EA	235=EB	236=EC	237=ED	238=EE	239=EF	240=F0	241=F1	242=F2
243=F3	244=F4	245=F5	246=F6	247=F7	248=F8	249=F9	250=FA	251=FB
252=FC	253=FD	254=FE	**255=FF**					

This chart shows how RGB values, which range from 0–255, convert to hexidecimal mathematics.

To describe the RGB color RED:255 GREEN:00 BLUE:51, the hexadecimal code would look like FF0033. Here's the most minimal sample code for an HTML page that has the following color scheme:

```
<HTML>
<BODY BGCOLOR="003333" TEXT="33CCCC"
LINK="336699" VLINK="006666" ALINK="00CC99"
</BODY>
</HTML>
```

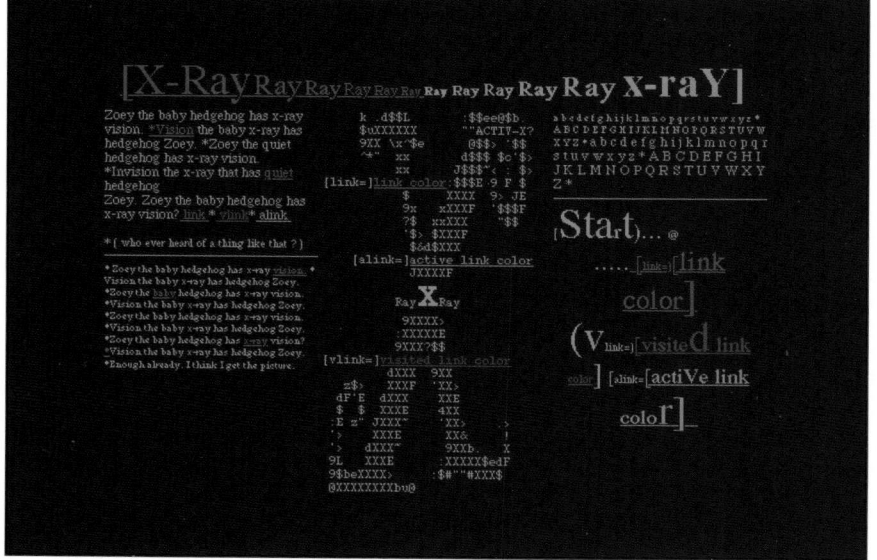

Here are the results of the hexadecimal HTML code to create background, text, link, visited link, and active link colors.

bgcolor	text	link	vlink	alink
003333	33CCCC	336699	006666	00CC99
R:0	R:51	R:51	R:0	R:0
G:51	G:204	G:102	G:102	G:204
B:51	B:204	B:153	B:102	B:153

These swatches demonstrate the RGB-to-hex conversion process.

Hexadecimal Resources

Many resources for converting RGB to a hex number exist on the web. There are two different options: hex converters and hex calculators. Both options are covered in the following sections.

Web Hex Converters

There are a number of sites on the web that let you plug RGB values into them and then generate hex code for your values on-the-fly. This can be convenient when you're working and want a quick visualization of what a certain color scheme will look like. Some sites even go so far as to accept RGB input and then automatically output hex and HTML. Here are my favorites:

> Inquisitor Mediarama's RGB-HEX Converter
> ■ http://www.echonyc.com/~xixax/Mediarama/hex.html
>
> Test your hex color choices on-the-fly
> ■ http://www.hidaho.com/c3/
>
> Click on any color, and hex numbers will appear
> ■ http://www.schnoggo.com/rgb2hex.html

Hex Calculators

Finally, there are hexadecimal calculators that take the RGB values you enter and convert the math automatically. Once you have converted your RGB numbers, you are ready to use the resulting hex in your HTML code.

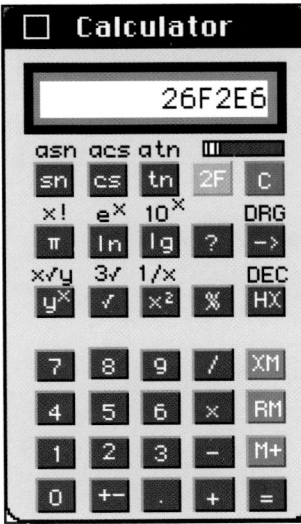

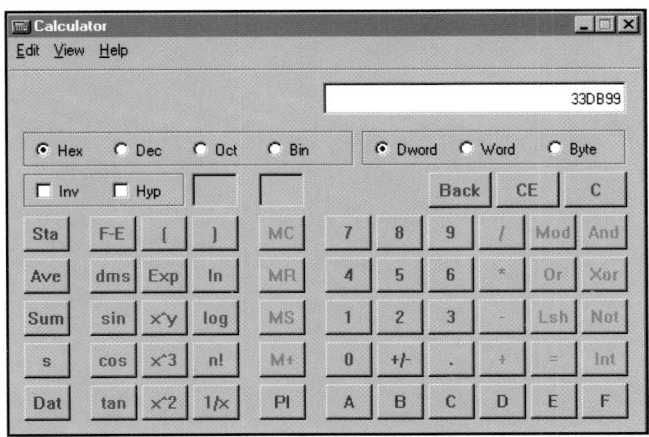

PCs ship with a hex calculator, which is found in the Accessories group. Open the Calculator and then under View, select Scientific. This changes the standard calculator to a scientific calculator. Then, simply select the Hex option to start converting your RGB values.

For **Mac** users, you can download a great hex calculator written by Joseph Cicinelli, called Calculator II, from ■ ftp://ftp.amug.org/pub/mirrors/info-mac/sci/calc/calculator-ii-15.hqx.

Color-Related HTML Tags

Now for the fun (not) part. How does all this come together on a web page? Web pages are written in a low-level programming language called HTML (**H**yper**T**ext **M**arkup **L**anguage). You can write HTML code in a standard text editor, dedicated HTML editor, or WYSIWYG (**W**hat**Y**ou**S**ee**I**s**W**hat**Y**ou**G**et) HTML editor. Some WYSIWYG editors allow you to edit HTML source code directly, and some do not. Because some of the color tags discussed in this chapter may not be supported by WYSIWYG editors, you may have to edit your files later to add the foreign HTML tags. You can always begin a page in a WYSIWYG editor and then later edit the source code in a text editor in order to add additional tags.

Adding Color Using HTML

To add variety within HTML, you include special tags called attributes. Attributes modify the existing material; applying italic to text is an example of using an attribute. When used in HTML, attributes are nested within their parent tags. So to add color to the body text, you would place the attribute within the <BODY> tag. To add color to the page in our example, you would add this HTML code.

```
<HTML>
<HEAD>
<TITLE>Adding Color to My Page</TITLE>
</HEAD>
<BODY BGCOLOR="660099"TEXT="CCCCFF">
<H1>This page is where I will play
with color using all the nifty color
tags I can learn.
</H1>
</BODY>
</HTML>
```

1

1 **BGCOLOR** and **TEXT** are attributes that are nested inside the **<BODY>** tag. The **BGCOLOR** attribute instructs the background of the HTML page to be colored. The **TEXT** attribute instructs the text to be colored. The content of these tags can contain hexadecimal values that represent RGB colors.

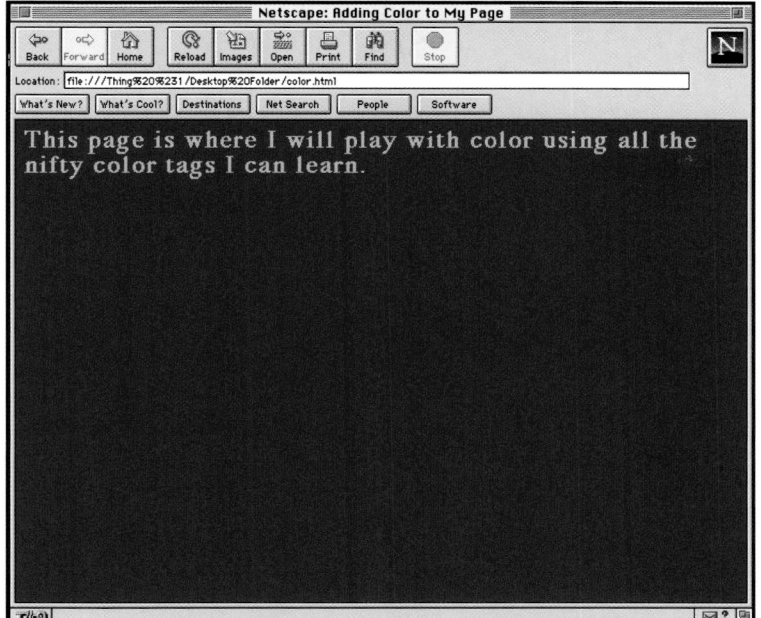

Color was added to this page using hexadecimal RGB values and attributes of **BGCOLOR** and **TEXT** placed within the **<BODY>** tag.

Here's a list of possible attributes that relate to color within the <BODY> tag:

BGCOLOR	Color of the background of the web page
TEXT	Color of the text
LINK	Color of the link
VLINK	Color of the link after it has been visited
ALINK	Color of the active link while the mouse is depressed on a link

Using Color Names Instead of Hex

You don't have to use hexadecimal numbers inside the color attribute tags; you can use words, too. Here's a list of color names that will work in Netscape.

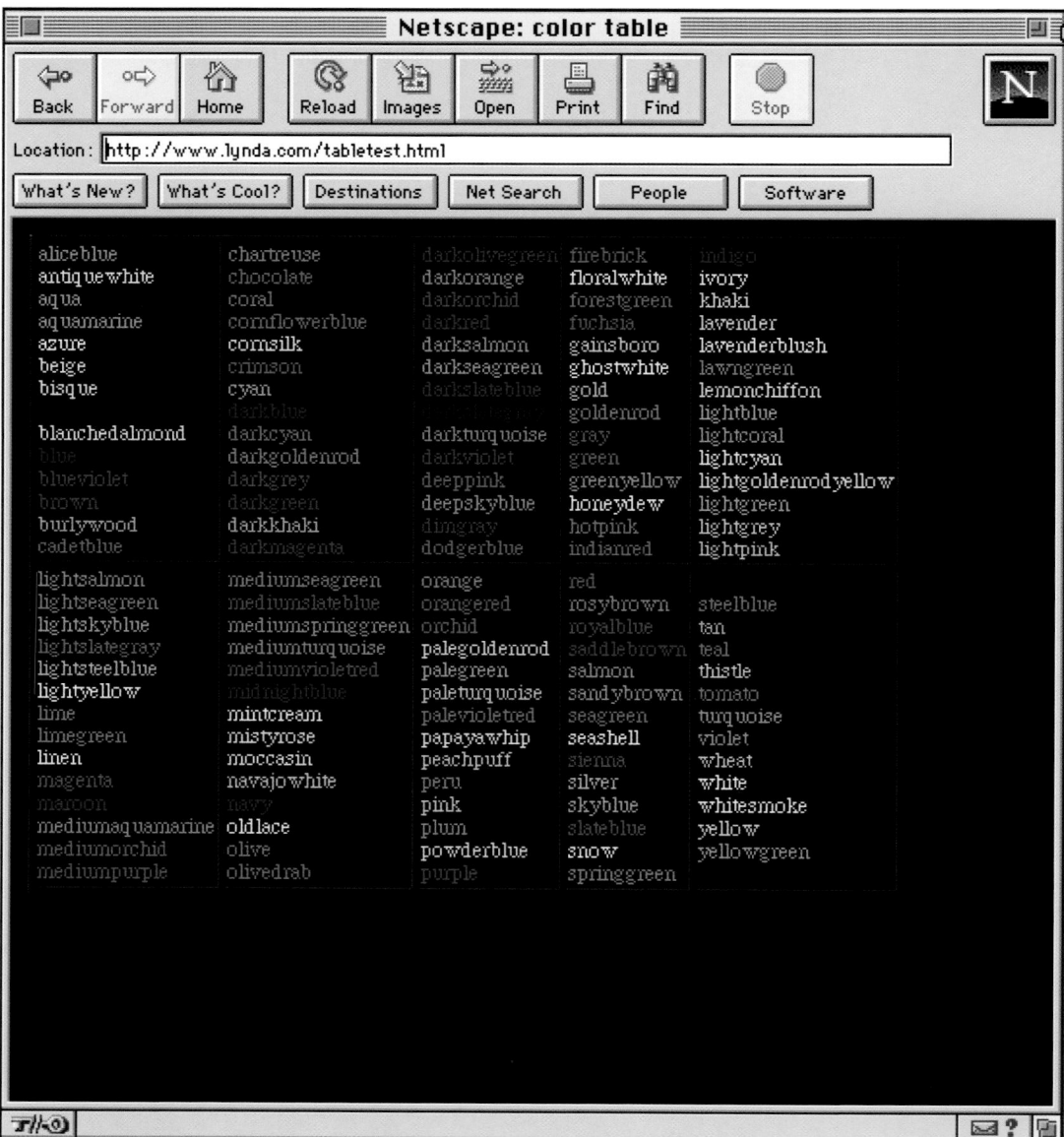

Using any of the names inside the color attribute tags will generate colored text in Netscape.

```
<HTML>
<HEAD>
<TITLE>Adding Color to
My Page</TITLE>
</HEAD>
<BODY BGCOLOR="lightgreen"
TEXT="darkgreen">
<H1>This page is where I will
play with color using all the
nifty color tags I can learn.
</H1>
</BODY>
</HTML>
```

1 You don't have to use hexadecimal numbers to define color—certain color names work as well. Here's an example of using "lightgreen" and "darkgreen" as color names within the **<BODY>** tag.

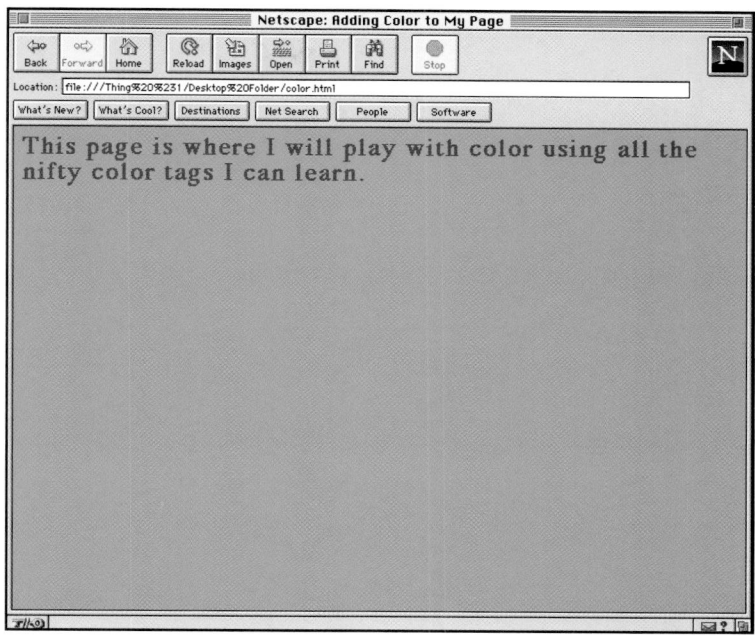

Here's an example of using color names instead of hexadecimal values to define color.

Coloring Individual Lines of Text

You can also assign specific colors to individual lines of text by using the <FONT> tag. Here's some sample code.

```
<HTML>
<HEAD>
<TITLE>Adding Color to
My Page</TITLE>
</HEAD>
<BODY BGCOLOR="660099"
TEXT="CCCCFF">
<H1>This page is where I
<FONT COLOR="99FFFF">will </FONT>
<FONT COLOR="CCFF99">play </FONT>
<FONT COLOR="CC99CC">with </FONT>
<FONT COLOR="CC0000">color </FONT>
using all the nifty color
tags I can learn.
</H1>
</BODY>
</HTML>
```

1 The **<FONT>** tag can contain a color attribute, which can be specified by using color names or hex numbers. It must be closed with a **</FONT>** tag each time you want the specific colored text attribute to end.

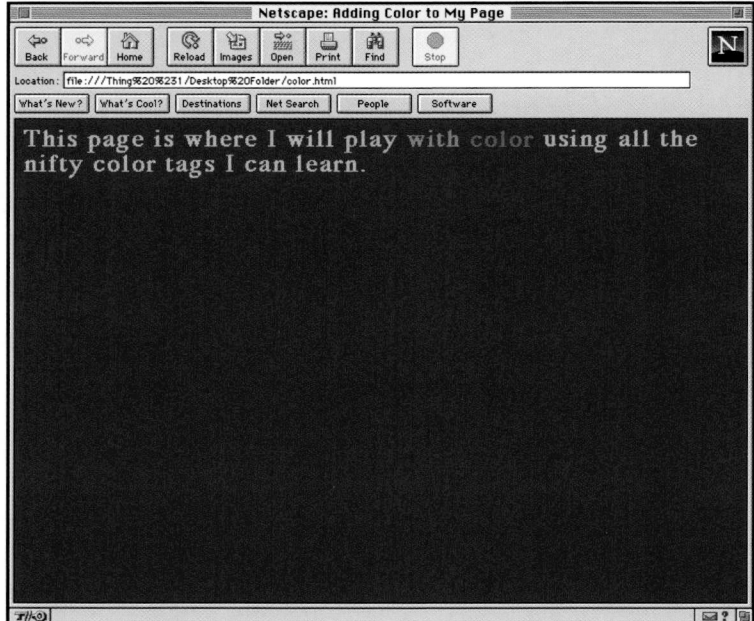

Here's an example of using the **<FONT>** tag to insert color attributes so that individual words or letters can be colored.

Coloring Links

Link color can affect the border color around linked images or the color of linked text. Here's an example of how to set this up in an HTML document.

```
<HTML>
<HEAD>
<TITLE>Adding Color to
My Page</TITLE>
</HEAD>
<BODY BGCOLOR="660099"
TEXT="CCCCFF" LINK="CCFF00">
<H1>Here's an example of a
<A HREF="http://www.stinkabod.com">text-
based hyperlink</A>.
<P>Here's an example of a
linked graphic with a fat,
colored border: </H1>
<P>
<A HREF="http://www.stinkabod.com"> <IMG
SRC="fourlynda.gif" BORDER=10></A>
</BODY>
</HTML>
```

1 The **LINK** attribute within the **<BODY>** tag establishes the color for the linked text or graphic. The **<A HREF></A>** tag produces linked text.

2 The **<IMG SRC>** tag inserts an image, and the **BORDER** attribute enables you to set a width for the border, measured in pixels. Note: If you don't want a border, you can set this to **BORDER=0**.

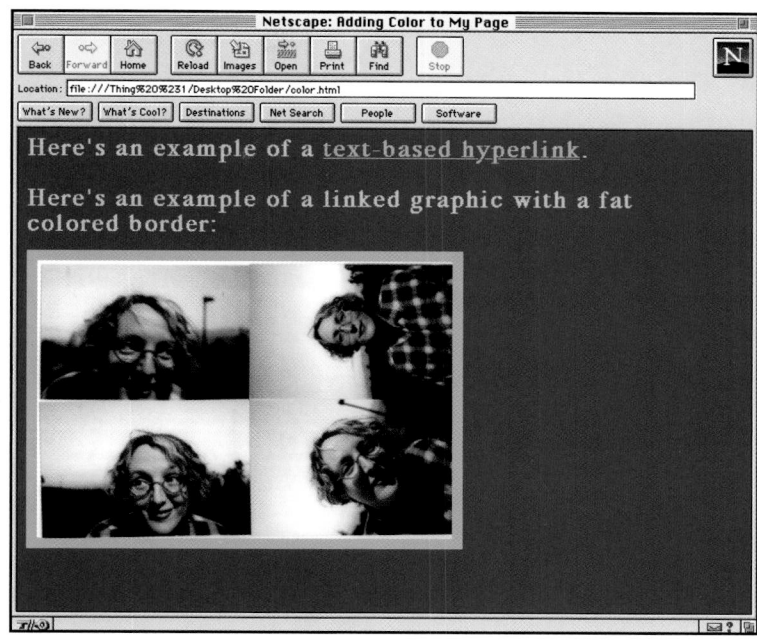

Here's an example of creating colored links. The border around the graphic was made wider with the **BORDER** attribute.

Inserting a Background Image

If you want to use an image in the background of your web page, instead of a hex color, this is how you would structure the HTML.

```
<HTML>
<HEAD>
<TITLE>Adding Color
to My Page</TITLE>
</HEAD>
<BODY
BACKGROUND="tile.gif"
TEXT="CCCCFF" LINK="CCFF00">
<CENTER>
<A HREF="http://www.stinkabod.com"><IMG
SRC="fourlynda.gif"
BORDER=10></A>
<CENTER>
</BODY>
</HTML>
```

1 The **BACKGROUND** attribute within the **<BODY>** tag enables you to insert an image into the background of the web page. This image can be any kind of image (.jpg or .gif), and can be a solid color, a hybrid color, a seamless tile image, or a repeating tile image.

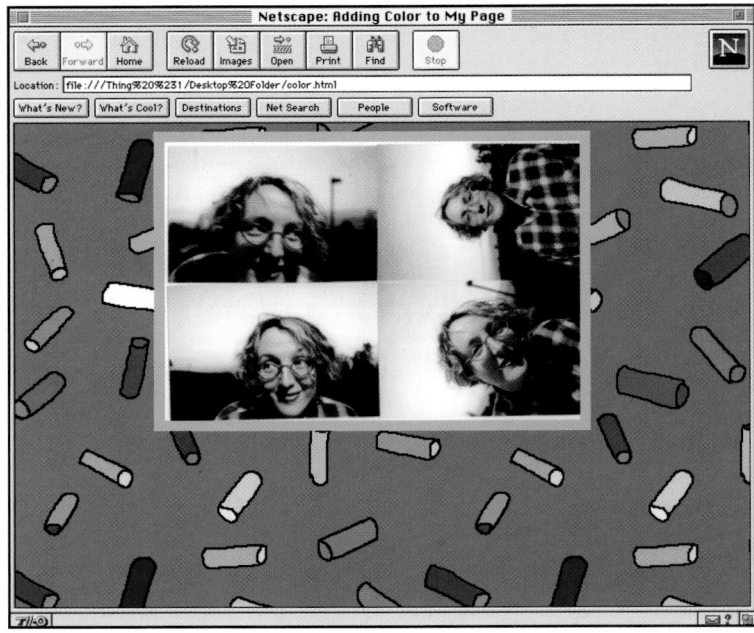

Here's an example of inserting a background image. You can insert a solid color image, a hybrid color image, a seamless tile image, or a repeating tile image. It's the same code, just a different graphic file!

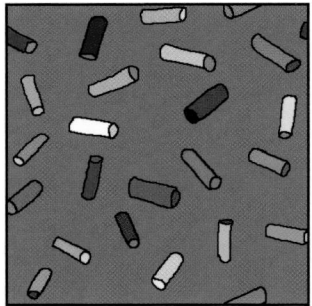

tile.gif

Adding Color to Tables

The BGCOLOR attribute works in table cells as well as the body of the HTML document. Here's some sample code that demonstrates this technique:

```
<HTML>
<HEAD>
<TITLE>Adding Color
to My Page</TITLE>
</HEAD>
<BODY BGCOLOR="660099"
TEXT="CCCCFF">
1 <CENTER>
2 <TABLE BORDER>
3 <TR><TH BGCOLOR="003366" HEIGHT=200
WIDTH=200>Hello</TH>
<TH BGCOLOR="990033" HEIGHT=200
WIDTH=200>Hola!</TH>
<TR><TD BGCOLOR="666600" HEIGHT=200
WIDTH=200
ALIGN=MIDDLE>You</TD><TD BGCOLOR="996666"
HEIGHT=200 WIDTH=200 ALIGN=MIDDLE>Me</TD>
</TABLE>
</CENTER>
</BODY>
</HTML>
```

1 The **<CENTER>** tag instructs the table to be centered in the page.

2 The **<TABLE>** tag establishes the beginning of the table command. The **BORDER** attribute assigns an embossed border to the table.

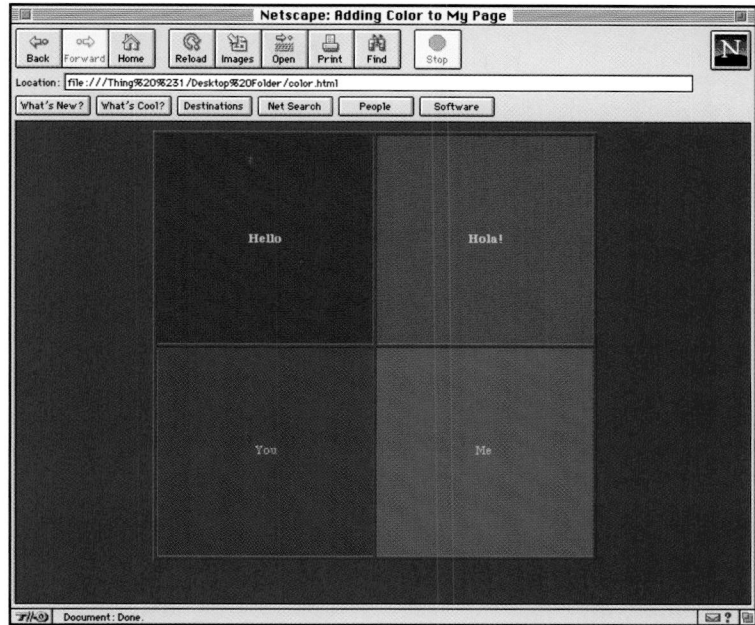

Here's an example of coloring cells within a table by using the **BGCOLOR** attribute within the **<TABLE>** tag.

3 **TR** initiates a table row. **TH** stands for table header. Everything within the **<TH>** tag will automatically be bold and centered. The **BGCOLOR** attribute allows a color to be established within the table cell and can be specified by using hexadecimal color or color names. The **<HEIGHT>** and **<WIDTH>** tags assign dimensions to the table cells by using pixel-based measurements. The **ALIGN= MIDDLE** attribute centers the text within the table cells.

Computer Color

Creating color artwork for the web is very different from other color delivery mediums because you're publishing your work to people's screens instead of printed pages. Computer screen-based color is composed of projected light and pixels instead of ink pigments, dot patterns, and screen percentages.

In many ways, working with screen-based color can be more fun than working with printed inks. No waiting for color proofs or working with CMYK values that are much less vibrant than RGB. No high-resolution files. No dot screens to deal with. Yes, working on the computer for computer delivery is a lot easier in some ways, but don't be fooled into thinking that what you see on your screen is what other people will see on theirs. Just like its print-based counterpart, computer screen-based color has its own set of nasties and gremlins.

The web differs from the printed page in more ways than you might imagine. It is not enough to approach web authoring with good ideas and great artwork. Understanding the medium is necessary in order to ensure that others view your designs and colors as you intended.

Here's a short list of the things that are different about the web as a publishing medium as it pertains to color:

- People view your artwork with monitors that have a wide variety of bit-depth settings.
- Various computer monitors have differing color calibration and gamma default settings.
- Different operating systems affect the way colors are displayed.
- Different web browsers affect the way colors are displayed.
- People judge your site not only by its artistic content, but by its speed. Color can affect speed, believe it or not!

Creating color images and screens for the web can be done without understanding the medium's limitations, but the results may not be what you are hoping for. The focus of this chapter is to describe the web and computer color environment, and to clue you in on known pitfalls and solutions that will offer maximum control over how your artwork is ultimately seen.

RGB Versus CMYK

The color of a pixel is made up of three projected colors of light that mix together optically. The projected lights form the colors red, green, and blue. Once mixed together, these three colors create a color space called RGB. Sometimes you'll also hear about CMYK color space, which is formed from cyan, magenta, yellow, and black. CMYK color space on a computer is used to simulate printing inks and is used commonly by print designers. Web designers are "screen" based, hence we use RGB color space only.

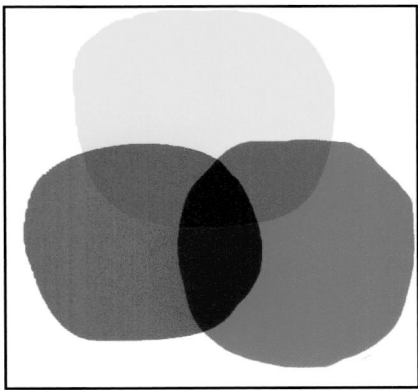

CMYK colors are subtractive, meaning that mixing multiple colors creates black. This color space was created for computer graphics that will be printed on paper.

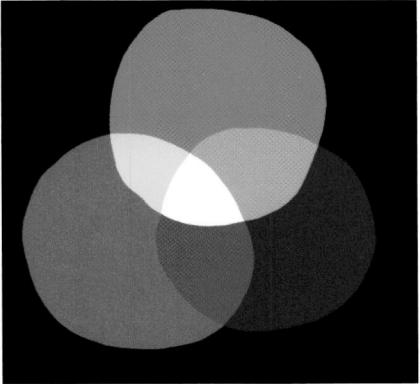

RGB color is additive, meaning that mixing multiple colors creates white. This color space was created for computer graphics that will be viewed on computer screens.

Introduction to Browser-Safe Specs

Browser software is your window into the web. You can't see web pages without the browser, so the browser plays a huge role in how your images are displayed, especially when viewed on 256-color systems.

Fortunately, the most popular browsers (Netscape, Mosaic, and Internet Explorer) all share the same palette management process. They work with the system palettes of each respective platform: Mac, Windows, and Win95. This means that any artwork you create will be forced into a variety of different palettes, depending on which operating system it is viewed from.

Although these three palettes look entirely different, they share 216 common colors. If you use the shared colors, referred to in this book as "browser-safe" colors, you will eliminate a lot of cross-platform inconsistencies with color artwork published over the web.

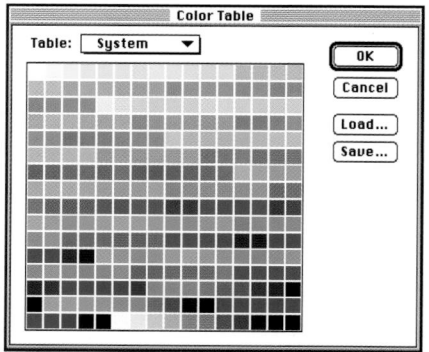

Mac System Palette

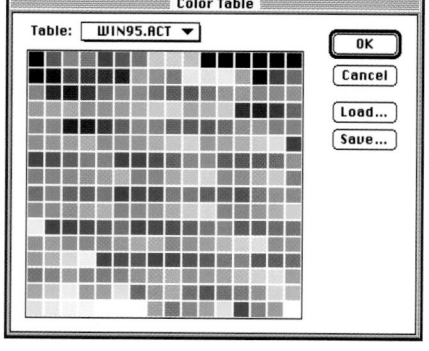

Win95 Palette

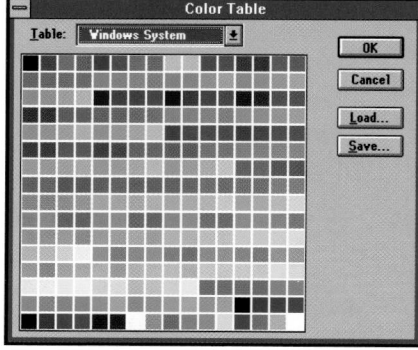

Windows Palette

Thankfully, there are common colors found within the 256 system palettes—216 common colors, in fact. Each operating system reserves 40 colors out of the possible 256 for its own use. This means that if you stick to the 216 common colors, they will be universally honored between browsers, operating systems, and computer platforms.

Why Work Within a Limited Palette?

Although it is wonderful and nice to design using a large monitor and 16 million+ color range, most people who view your work will have computers capable of seeing images in only 256 colors on a monitor that can't go beyond 640x480 in size. When we work with colors other than that of the 216 browser-safe colors, the browsers will convert the colors anyway. This will have an adverse effect on your artwork, as the following examples demonstrate.

Hexadecimal-Based Artwork

Web page color schemes are generally chosen by using hexadecimal values instead of embedded artwork (see more details in Chapter 5, "Hexadecimal Color"). If you choose a one-color background on your millions-of-color monitor and the end user views the image on a 256-color monitor, the browser will convert it to one of the 216 colors anyway. It will shift the colors you've chosen to its own palette.

Hexadecimal code is used instead of RGB values within HTML. If you don't understand what I mean, be sure to read Chapter 5, "Hexadecimal Color."

Here's a site that used the following hexadecimal code:

```
<BODY BGCOLOR="#090301" TEXT="#436E58" LINK="#CF7B42" VLINK="#323172" ALINK="#ffffff"
```

You should be able to tell, just by looking, that these colors are not browser safe! Remember, browser-safe hex combinations are always formed from variations of 00, 33, 66, 99, CC, and FF.

Mac 8-bit display

PC 8-bit display

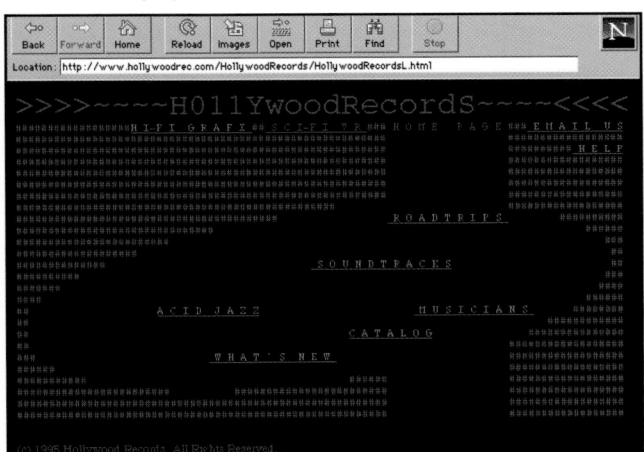 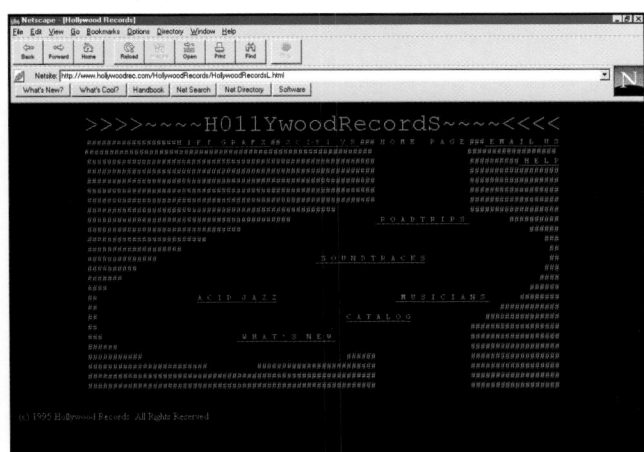

This comparison demonstrates the kind of color shifting that occurs with hexadecimal-based artwork, on 8-bit systems, if the colors used are not browser safe.

Illustration-Based Artwork

With illustration-based artwork, if you create logos, cartoons, or drawings in colors outside of the 216—you guessed it—the browser converts it anyway! Instead of shifting the color, which is what happens with hexadecimal-based color, it dithers the artwork. Ugh!

On a millions-of-color display, you might not notice any differences between these two different colored versions of Bruce's cat image.

On an 8-bit display, look at what happens to the top version. It is filled with unwanted dots, caused by ditherings. Why? The colors in the bottom image are browser safe, and the colors in the top are not.

Here's a close-up of the dithering present in the nonbrowser-safe version of this illustration, on 8-bit (256-color) systems.

The close-up of the version created with browser-safe colors will not dither, regardless of the bit depth the end viewer's system supports.

Photograph-Based Artwork

Photographs are the one type of artwork that really do not benefit from using browser-safe colors. The reason is that the browsers convert photographs, but do a great job of it, unlike the terrible job they do with hexadecimal-based artwork and illustration-based artwork.

Viewed in 24-bit

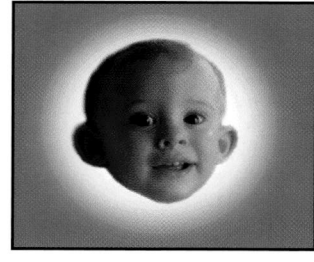

Viewed in 8-bit

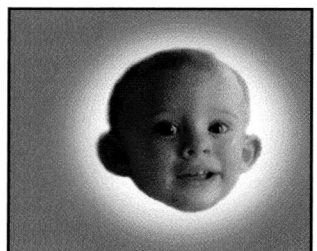

adaptive ▪ 8-bit file ▪ 35k

browser-safe palette ▪ 50k

jpeg (low quality) ▪ 11k

The images on the left of this study were all viewed from a browser in 24-bit. Which ones on the left have the highest quality? The JPEG, which is a 24-bit file, and the adaptive file, which is an 8-bit file based on the colors within the image, not the browser-safe palette. The right-side images show how these photographs looked within a browser viewed from a millions+ color system (24-bit). The right-side images all look worse than when viewed in the 24-bit browser, but are there any significant quality benefits from having saved them with different methods? I think not. The results of this study? It is not necessary to convert photographic-based images to the browser-safe palette or even an 8-bit palette. The browser does its dithering dirty work, regardless of how you prepare the image. It's best to leave the image in an adaptive palette or 24-bit file format so that the photographs will have the added advantage of looking better in 24-bit browser environments. JPEGs will always produce the smallest file size for photographs and have the added advantage of being a 24-bit file format, unlike GIF which cannot save images at bit depths higher than 8-bit (256 colors).

What Does the Browser-Safe Palette Look Like?

The 216-color palette for the web has only 6 red values, 6 green values, and 6 blue values which range in contrast. Sometimes this palette is referred to as the 6x6x6 palette, or the 6x6x6 cube. This palette is a predetermined palette which, as of yet, can't be changed.

The RGB values found within the 216-color palette have some remarkable similarities: the numbers are all formed from variations of 00, 51, 102, 153, 204, and 255.

The hexadecimal values found within the 216-color palette have some remarkable similarities, too: they are all formed form variations of 00, 33, 66, 99, CC, and FF.

It should be no surprise that these colors were picked by math, not beauty. Knowing the pattern of the numeric values is useful because you can check your code or image documents to see whether they contain these values.

Here's a version of the browser-safe palette, straight out of the computer.

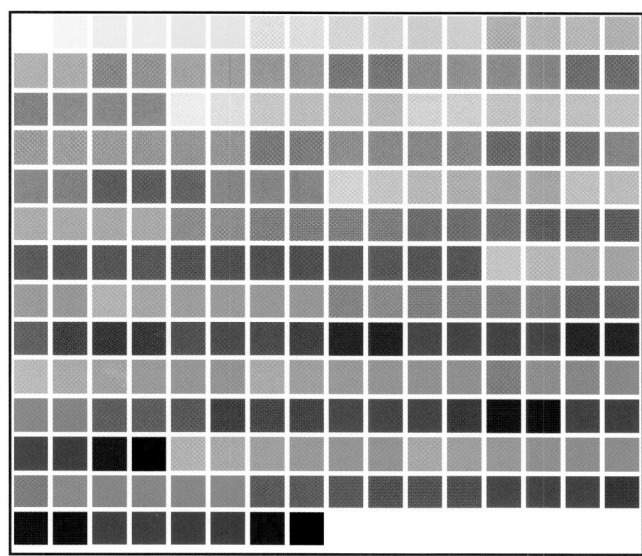

Notice how these colors have no sense of organization? They are organized by math, not beauty.

■ **note**

Do Browser-Safe Colors Really Matter?

You may think that all this hubbub over browser-safe colors need not apply to you. If you think your site will be viewed only from millions-of-color monitors (24-bit), you might be right. It's always important to decide who your audience is before you design a site and create artwork that is appropriate for your viewers.

My recommendation is, if you are going to pick colors for backgrounds, type, text, links, and illustrations, why not choose cross-platform compatible colors? There may come a day years from now when everyone has video cards that support more than 256 colors, but the majority of systems today do not.

Browser-Safe Color Charts Organized by Hue

330000 R=051 G=000 B=000	**660000** R=102 G=000 B=000	**990000** R=153 G=000 B=000	**CC0000** R=204 G=000 B=000	**FF0000** R=255 G=000 B=000	**663333** R=102 G=051 B=051	**993333** R=153 G=051 B=051	**CC3333** R=204 G=051 B=051
CC0033 R=204 G=000 B=051	**FF3366** R=255 G=051 B=102	**990033** R=153 G=000 B=051	**CC3366** R=204 G=051 B=102	**FF6699** R=255 G=102 B=153	**FF0066** R=255 G=000 B=102	**660033** R=102 G=000 B=051	**CC0066** R=204 G=000 B=102
CC0099 R=204 G=000 B=153	**FF33CC** R=255 G=51 B=204	**FF00CC** R=255 G=000 B=204	**330033** R=051 G=000 B=051	**660066** R=102 G=000 B=102	**990099** R=153 G=000 B=153	**CC00CC** R=204 G=000 B=204	**FF00FF** R=255 G=000 B=255
FF99FF R=255 G=153 B=255	**FFCCFF** R=255 G=204 B=255	**CC00FF** R=204 G=000 B=255	**9900CC** R=153 G=000 B=204	**CC33FF** R=204 G=051 B=255	**660099** R=102 G=000 B=153	**9933CC** R=153 G=051 B=204	**CC66FF** R=204 G=102 B=255
330099 R=051 G=000 B=153	**6633CC** R=102 G=051 B=204	**9966FF** R=153 G=102 B=255	**3300CC** R=051 G=000 B=204	**6633FF** R=102 G=051 B=255	**3300FF** R=051 G=000 B=255	**000000** R=000 G=000 B=000	**000033** R=000 G=000 B=051
666699 R=102 G=102 B=153	**6666CC** R=102 G=102 B=204	**6666FF** R=102 G=102 B=255	**9999CC** R=153 G=153 B=204	**9999FF** R=153 G=153 B=255	**CCCCFF** R=204 G=204 B=255	**0033FF** R=000 G=051 B=255	**0033CC** R=000 G=051 B=204
3399FF R=051 G=153 B=255	**6699CC** R=102 G=153 B=204	**99CCFF** R=153 G=204 B=255	**0099FF** R=000 G=153 B=255	**006699** R=000 G=102 B=153	**3399CC** R=051 G=153 B=204	**66CCFF** R=102 G=204 B=255	**0099CC** R=000 G=153 B=204
00CCCC R=000 G=204 B=204	**33CCCC** R=051 G=204 B=204	**66CCCC** R=102 G=204 B=204	**99CCCC** R=153 G=204 B=204	**00FFFF** R=000 G=255 B=255	**33FFFF** R=051 G=255 B=255	**66FFFF** R=102 G=255 B=255	**99FFFF** R=153 G=255 B=255
006633 R=000 G=102 B=051	**339966** R=051 G=153 B=102	**00CC66** R=000 G=204 B=102	**66CC99** R=102 G=204 B=153	**33FF99** R=051 G=255 B=153	**99FFCC** R=153 G=255 B=204	**00FF66** R=000 G=255 B=102	**009933** R=000 G=153 B=051
009900 R=000 G=153 B=000	**339933** R=051 G=153 B=051	**669966** R=102 G=153 B=102	**00CC00** R=000 G=204 B=000	**33CC33** R=051 G=204 B=051	**66CC66** R=102 G=204 B=102	**99CC99** R=153 G=204 B=153	**00FF00** R=000 G=255 B=000
66CC33 R=102 G=204 B=051	**99FF66** R=153 G=255 B=102	**66FF00** R=102 G=255 B=000	**336600** R=051 G=102 B=000	**669933** R=102 G=153 B=051	**66CC00** R=102 G=204 B=000	**99CC66** R=153 G=204 B=102	**99FF33** R=153 G=255 B=051
333300 R=051 G=051 B=000	**666600** R=102 G=102 B=000	**666633** R=102 G=102 B=051	**999900** R=153 G=153 B=000	**999933** R=153 G=153 B=051	**999966** R=153 G=153 B=102	**CCCC00** R=204 G=204 B=000	**CCCC33** R=204 G=204 B=051
CC9900 R=204 G=153 B=000	**FFCC33** R=255 G=204 B=051	**996600** R=153 G=102 B=000	**CC9933** R=204 G=153 B=051	**FFCC66** R=255 G=204 B=102	**FF9900** R=255 G=153 B=000	**663300** R=102 G=051 B=000	**996633** R=153 G=102 B=051
CC3300 R=204 G=051 B=000	**FF6633** R=255 G=102 B=051	**FF3300** R=255 G=051 B=000	**333333** R=051 G=051 B=051	**666666** R=102 G=102 B=102	**999999** R=153 G=153 B=153	**CCCCCC** R=204 G=204 B=204	**FFFFFF** R=255 G=255 B=255

FF3333 R=255 G=051 B=051	**996666** R=153 G=102 B=102	**CC6666** R=204 G=102 B=102	**FF6666** R=255 G=102 B=102	**CC9999** R=204 G=153 B=153	**FF9999** R=255 G=153 B=153	**FFCCCC** R=255 G=204 B=204	**FF0033** R=255 G=000 B=051
993366 R=153 G=051 B=102	**FF3399** R=255 G=051 B=153	**CC6699** R=204 G=102 B=153	**FF99CC** R=255 G=153 B=204	**FF0099** R=255 G=000 B=153	**990066** R=153 G=000 B=102	**CC3399** R=204 G=051 B=153	**FF66CC** R=255 G=102 B=204
663366 R=102 G=051 B=102	**993399** R=153 G=051 B=153	**CC33CC** R=204 G=051 B=204	**FF33FF** R=255 G=051 B=255	**996699** R=153 G=102 B=153	**CC66CC** R=204 G=102 B=204	**FF66FF** R=255 G=102 B=255	**CC99CC** R=204 G=153 B=204
9900FF R=153 G=000 B=255	**330066** R=051 G=000 B=102	**6600CC** R=102 G=000 B=204	**663399** R=102 G=051 B=153	**9933FF** R=153 G=051 B=255	**9966CC** R=153 G=102 B=204	**CC99FF** R=204 G=153 B=255	**6600FF** R=102 G=000 B=255
000066 R=000 G=000 B=102	**000099** R=000 G=000 B=153	**0000CC** R=000 G=000 B=204	**0000FF** R=000 G=000 B=255	**333366** R=051 G=051 B=102	**333399** R=051 G=051 B=153	**3333CC** R=051 G=051 B=204	**3333FF** R=051 G=051 B=255
3366FF R=051 G=102 B=255	**003399** R=000 G=051 B=153	**3366CC** R=051 G=102 B=204	**6699FF** R=102 G=153 B=255	**0066FF** R=000 G=102 B=255	**003366** R=000 G=051 B=102	**0066CC** R=000 G=102 B=204	**336699** R=051 G=102 B=153
33CCFF R=051 G=204 B=255	**00CCFF** R=000 G=204 B=255	**003333** R=000 G=051 B=051	**006666** R=000 G=102 B=102	**336666** R=051 G=102 B=102	**009999** R=000 G=153 B=153	**339999** R=051 G=153 B=153	**669999** R=102 G=153 B=153
CCFFFF R=204 G=255 B=255	**00FFCC** R=000 G=255 B=204	**00CC99** R=000 G=204 B=153	**33FFCC** R=051 G=255 B=204	**009966** R=000 G=153 B=102	**33CC99** R=051 G=204 B=153	**66FFCC** R=102 G=255 B=204	**00FF99** R=000 G=255 B=153
33CC66 R=051 G=204 B=102	**66FF99** R=102 G=255 B=153	**00CC33** R=000 G=204 B=051	**33FF66** R=051 G=255 B=102	**00FF33** R=000 G=255 B=051	**003300** R=000 G=051 B=000	**006600** R=000 G=102 B=000	**336633** R=051 G=102 B=051
33FF33 R=051 G=255 B=051	**66FF66** R=102 G=255 B=102	**99FF99** R=153 G=255 B=153	**CCFFCC** R=204 G=255 B=204	**33FF00** R=051 G=255 B=000	**33CC00** R=051 G=204 B=000	**66FF33** R=102 G=255 B=051	**339900** R=051 G=153 B=000
CCFF99 R=204 G=255 B=153	**99FF00** R=153 G=255 B=000	**669900** R=102 G=153 B=000	**99CC33** R=153 G=204 B=051	**CCFF66** R=204 G=255 B=102	**99CC00** R=153 G=204 B=000	**CCFF33** R=204 G=255 B=051	**CCFF00** R=204 G=255 B=000
CCCC66 R=204 G=204 B=102	**CCCC99** R=204 G=204 B=153	**FFFF00** R=255 G=255 B=000	**FFFF33** R=255 G=255 B=051	**FFFF66** R=255 G=255 B=102	**FFFF99** R=255 G=255 B=153	**FFFFCC** R=255 G=255 B=204	**FFCC00** R=255 G=204 B=000
CC6600 R=204 G=102 B=000	**CC9966** R=204 G=153 B=102	**FF9933** R=255 G=153 B=051	**FFCC99** R=255 G=204 B=153	**FF6600** R=255 G=102 B=000	**993300** R=153 G=051 B=000	**CC6633** R=204 G=102 B=051	**FF9966** R=255 G=153 B=102

Browser-Safe Color Charts Organized by Value

FFFFFF R=255 G=255 B=255	**FFFFCC** R=255 G=255 B=204	**FFFF99** R=255 G=255 B=153	**CCFFFF** R=204 G=255 B=255	**FFFF66** R=255 G=255 B=102	**CCFFCC** R=204 G=255 B=204	**FFFF33** R=255 G=255 B=051	**CCFF99** R=204 G=255 B=153
99FF99 R=153 G=255 B=153	**CCFF00** R=204 G=255 B=000	**CCCCFF** R=204 G=204 B=255	**66FFFF** R=102 G=255 B=255	**FFCC66** R=255 G=204 B=102	**99FF66** R=153 G=255 B=102	**CCCCCC** R=204 G=204 B=204	**66FFCC** R=102 G=255 B=204
33FFFF R=051 G=255 B=255	**CCCC66** R=204 G=204 B=102	**66FF66** R=102 G=255 B=102	**FF99CC** R=255 G=153 B=204	**99CCCC** R=153 G=204 B=204	**33FFCC** R=051 G=255 B=204	**CCCC33** R=204 G=204 B=051	**66FF33** R=102 G=255 B=051
FF9966 R=255 G=153 B=102	**99CC66** R=153 G=204 B=102	**33FF66** R=051 G=255 B=102	**CC99CC** R=204 G=153 B=204	**66CCCC** R=102 G=204 B=204	**00FFCC** R=000 G=255 B=204	**FF9933** R=255 G=153 B=051	**99CC33** R=153 G=204 B=051
9999FF R=153 G=153 B=255	**33CCFF** R=051 G=204 B=255	**CC9966** R=204 G=153 B=102	**66CC66** R=102 G=204 B=102	**00FF66** R=000 G=255 B=102	**FF66CC** R=255 G=102 B=204	**9999CC** R=153 G=153 B=204	**33CCCC** R=051 G=204 B=204
00FF00 R=000 G=255 B=000	**CC66FF** R=204 G=102 B=255	**6699FF** R=102 G=153 B=255	**00CCFF** R=000 G=204 B=255	**FF6666** R=255 G=102 B=102	**999966** R=153 G=153 B=102	**33CC66** R=051 G=204 B=102	**CC66CC** R=204 G=102 B=204
FF6600 R=255 G=102 B=000	**999900** R=153 G=153 B=000	**33CC00** R=051 G=204 B=000	**FF33FF** R=255 G=051 B=255	**9966FF** R=153 G=102 B=255	**3399FF** R=051 G=153 B=255	**CC6666** R=204 G=102 B=102	**669966** R=102 G=153 B=102
996699 R=153 G=102 B=153	**339999** R=051 G=153 B=153	**CC6600** R=204 G=102 B=000	**669900** R=102 G=153 B=000	**00CC00** R=000 G=204 B=000	**CC33FF** R=204 G=051 B=255	**6666FF** R=102 G=102 B=255	**0099FF** R=000 G=153 B=255
339933 R=051 G=153 B=051	**CC3399** R=204 G=051 B=153	**666699** R=102 G=102 B=153	**009999** R=000 G=153 B=153	**FF3300** R=255 G=051 B=000	**996600** R=153 G=102 B=000	**339900** R=051 G=153 B=000	**FF00FF** R=255 G=000 B=255
CC3333 R=204 G=051 B=051	**666633** R=102 G=102 B=051	**009933** R=000 G=153 B=051	**FF0099** R=255 G=000 B=153	**993399** R=153 G=051 B=153	**336699** R=051 G=102 B=153	**CC3300** R=204 G=051 B=000	**666600** R=102 G=102 B=000
6633CC R=102 G=051 B=204	**0066CC** R=000 G=102 B=204	**FF0033** R=255 G=000 B=051	**993333** R=153 G=051 B=051	**336633** R=051 G=102 B=051	**CC0099** R=204 G=000 B=153	**663399** R=102 G=051 B=153	**006699** R=000 G=102 B=153
9900CC R=153 G=000 B=204	**3333CC** R=051 G=051 B=204	**CC0033** R=204 G=000 B=051	**663333** R=102 G=051 B=051	**006633** R=000 G=102 B=051	**990099** R=153 G=000 B=153	**333399** R=051 G=051 B=153	**CC0000** R=204 G=000 B=000
990033 R=153 G=000 B=051	**333333** R=051 G=051 B=051	**660099** R=102 G=000 B=153	**003399** R=000 G=051 B=153	**990000** R=153 G=000 B=000	**333300** R=051 G=051 B=000	**3300FF** R=051 G=000 B=255	**660066** R=102 G=000 B=102
330066 R=051 G=000 B=102	**0000CC** R=000 G=000 B=204	**330033** R=051 G=000 B=051	**000099** R=000 G=000 B=153	**330000** R=051 G=000 B=000	**000066** R=000 G=000 B=102	**000033** R=000 G=000 B=051	**000000** R=000 G=000 B=000

FFFF00 R=255 G=255 B=000	**FFCCFF** R=255 G=204 B=255	**99FFFF** R=153 G=255 B=255	**CCFF00** R=204 G=255 B=102	**FFCCCC** R=255 G=204 B=204	**99FFCC** R=153 G=255 B=204	**CCFF33** R=204 G=255 B=051	**FFCC99** R=255 G=204 B=153
FFCC33 R=255 G=204 B=051	**99FF33** R=153 G=255 B=051	**CCCC99** R=204 G=204 B=153	**66FF99** R=102 G=255 B=153	**FFCC00** R=255 G=204 B=000	**99FF00** R=153 G=255 B=000	**FF99FF** R=255 G=153 B=255	**99CCFF** R=153 G=204 B=255
FF9999 R=255 G=153 B=153	**99CC99** R=153 G=204 B=153	**33FF99** R=051 G=255 B=153	**CCCC00** R=204 G=204 B=000	**66FF00** R=102 G=255 B=000	**CC99FF** R=204 G=153 B=255	**66CCFF** R=102 G=204 B=255	**00FFFF** R=000 G=255 B=255
33FF33 R=051 G=255 B=051	**CC9999** R=204 G=153 B=153	**66CC99** R=102 G=204 B=153	**00FF99** R=000 G=255 B=153	**FF9900** R=255 G=153 B=000	**99CC00** R=153 G=204 B=000	**33FF00** R=051 G=255 B=000	**FF66FF** R=255 G=102 B=255
CC9933 R=204 G=153 B=051	**66CC33** R=102 G=204 B=051	**00FF33** R=000 G=255 B=051	**FF6699** R=255 G=102 B=153	**999999** R=153 G=153 B=153	**33CC99** R=051 G=204 B=153	**CC9900** R=204 G=153 B=000	**66CC00** R=102 G=204 B=000
6699CC R=102 G=153 B=204	**00CCCC** R=000 G=204 B=204	**FF6633** R=255 G=102 B=051	**999933** R=153 G=153 B=051	**33CC33** R=051 G=204 B=051	**CC6699** R=204 G=102 B=153	**669999** R=102 G=153 B=153	**00CC99** R=000 G=204 B=153
00CC66 R=000 G=204 B=102	**FF33CC** R=255 G=051 B=204	**9966CC** R=153 G=102 B=204	**3399CC** R=051 G=153 B=204	**CC6633** R=204 G=102 B=051	**669933** R=102 G=153 B=051	**00CC33** R=000 G=204 B=051	**FF3399** R=255 G=051 B=153
FF3366 R=255 G=051 B=102	**996666** R=153 G=102 B=102	**339966** R=051 G=153 B=102	**CC33CC** R=204 G=051 B=204	**6666CC** R=102 G=102 B=204	**0099CC** R=000 G=153 B=204	**FF3333** R=255 G=051 B=051	**996633** R=153 G=102 B=051
9933FF R=153 G=051 B=255	**3366FF** R=051 G=102 B=255	**CC3366** R=204 G=051 B=102	**666666** R=102 G=102 B=102	**009966** R=000 G=153 B=102	**FF00CC** R=255 G=000 B=204	**9933CC** R=153 G=051 B=204	**3366CC** R=051 G=102 B=204
009900 R=000 G=153 B=000	**CC00FF** R=204 G=000 B=255	**6633FF** R=102 G=051 B=255	**0066FF** R=000 G=102 B=255	**FF0066** R=255 G=000 B=102	**993366** R=153 G=051 B=102	**336666** R=051 G=102 B=102	**CC00CC** R=204 G=000 B=204
FF0000 R=255 G=000 B=000	**993300** R=153 G=051 B=000	**336600** R=051 G=102 B=000	**9900FF** R=153 G=000 B=255	**3333FF** R=051 G=051 B=255	**CC0066** R=204 G=000 B=102	**663366** R=102 G=051 B=102	**006666** R=000 G=102 B=102
663300 R=102 G=051 B=000	**006600** R=000 G=102 B=000	**6600FF** R=102 G=000 B=255	**0033FF** R=000 G=051 B=255	**990066** R=153 G=000 B=102	**333366** R=051 G=051 B=102	**6600CC** R=102 G=000 B=204	**0033CC** R=000 G=051 B=204
003366 R=000 G=051 B=102	**3300CC** R=051 G=000 B=204	**660033** R=102 G=000 B=051	**003333** R=000 G=051 B=051	**330099** R=051 G=000 B=153	**660000** R=102 G=000 B=000	**003300** R=000 G=051 B=000	**0000FF** R=000 G=000 B=255

What Is a CLUT and What Do You Do with One?

CLUT is an acronym for **C**olor **L**ook**U**p **T**able. A color lookup table is the file that assigns the specific colors to any 8-bit or lower bit-depth computer image. CLUTs can be applied to images two different ways in Photoshop.

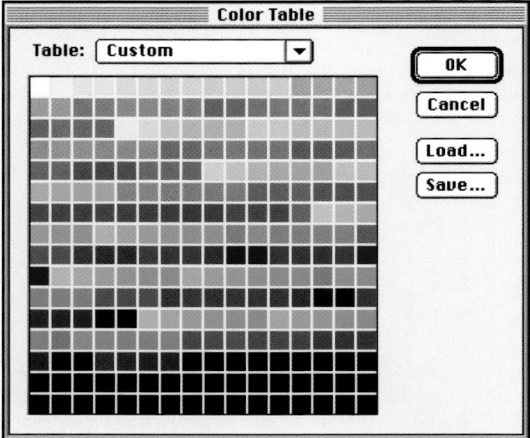

If your image is already in Index mode, go to the Mode menu and choose Color Table, which opens the Color Table dialog box. By clicking the Load or Save button, you can create and apply custom CLUTs to images. If you want to test it on the browser-safe CLUT, download the Photoshop file bclut2.aco from my ftp site
━ ftp://luna.bearnet.com/pub/lynda/.

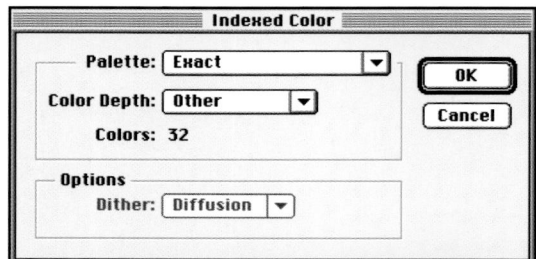

If your image is not in 256 colors yet, choose Index Color under the Image, Mode menu to display the Indexed Color dialog box.

How to Load a Browser-Safe Swatch Palette into Photoshop

The same file, bclut2.aco (available from my ftp site ■ ftp://luna.bearnet.com /pub/lynda/), can be loaded into the Swatch Palette by following these steps:

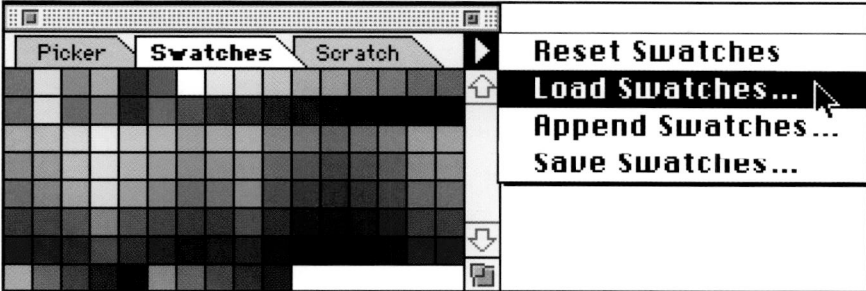

Step 1: Choose Windows, Palettes, Show Swatches. Using the upper right arrow, choose Load Swatches from the pull-down menu.

 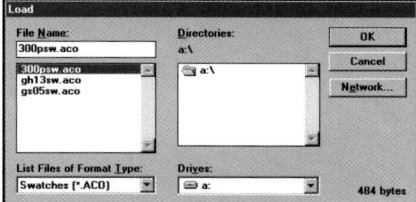

Step 2: Select any file with an .aco extension. The custom set appears as a new set in Photoshop's Swatch Palette.

How to Use the Browser-Safe Swatch Sets

Use browser-safe colors when you are creating custom artwork, illustrations, cartoons, and/or logos for web delivery.

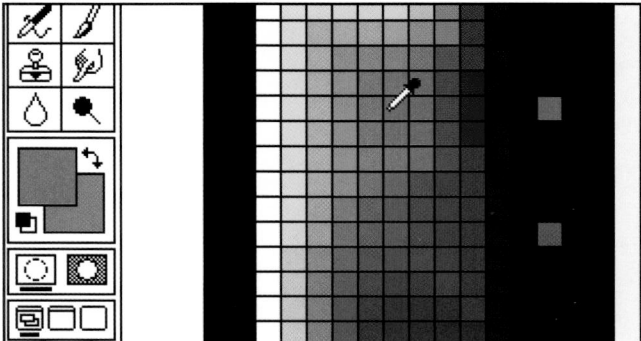

Use the Eyedropper Tool to click on a color within the swatch set. This causes the color to appear in the Foreground Color area of the Photoshop Toolbox. Choose any paint tool, and it will use the color you selected from the swatch set.

How to Load the Browser-Safe Palette into Paint Shop Pro

You can also download a CLUT for Paint Shop Pro from my ftp site. Go to ■ ftp://luna.bearnet.com/pub/lynda/ and select netscape.pal.

Step 1: Under the Color menu, select Load Palette.

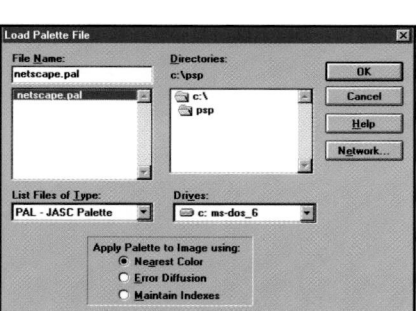

Step 2: Select the file netscape.pal.

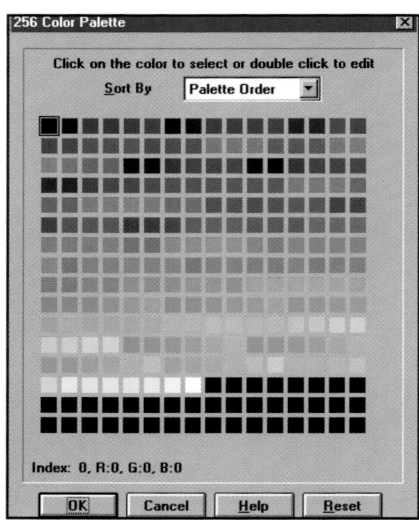

Step 3: The palette will appear. It can be sorted by Palette Order, Hue, and Luminance by changing the Sort By setting.

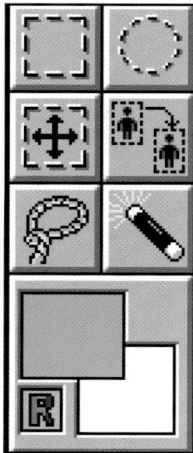

Step 4: Double-click on the foreground color in the Toolbar. In this example, it's turquoise.

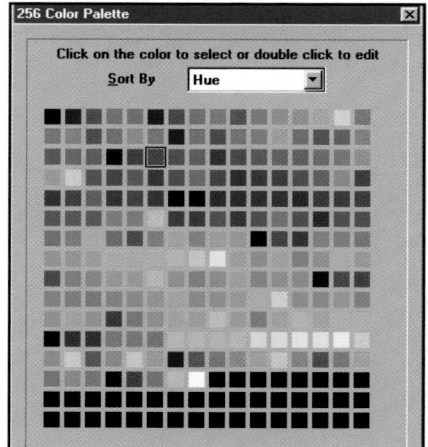

Step 5: The color palette that you just loaded becomes active. Double-click on a browser-safe color you would like to paint with. Click OK, or press the Return key.

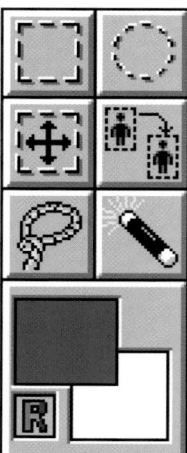

Step 6: The browser-safe color appears in the foreground color picker. Select any painting tool, and it will use this color.

How to Load a Browser-Safe Palette into Photo-Paint

Photo-Paint 6.0 supports the ability to load a custom palette into its color table. Download the file 216clut.cpl from my ftp site
- ftp://luna.bearnet.com/pub/lynda/.

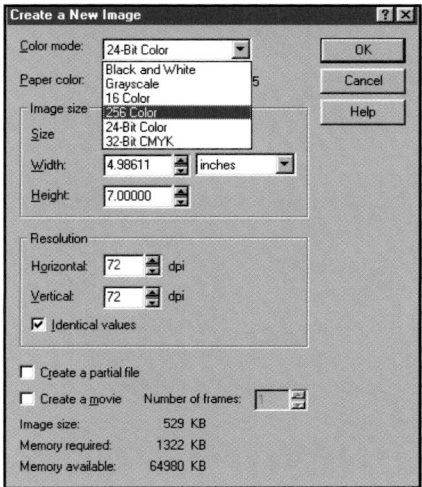

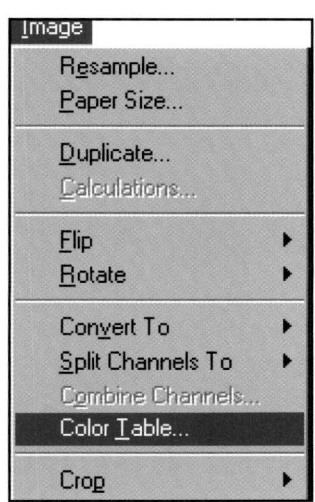

Step 1: Open a 256-color document or create a new 256-color document.

Step 2: Under the Image menu, select Color Table.

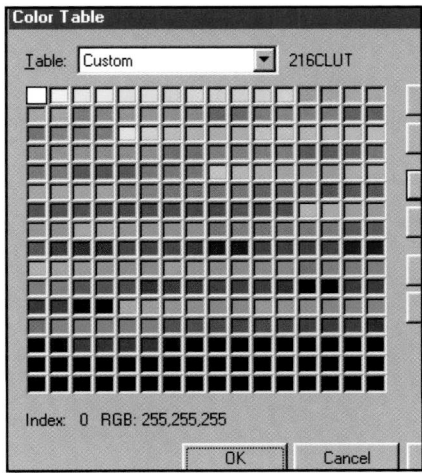

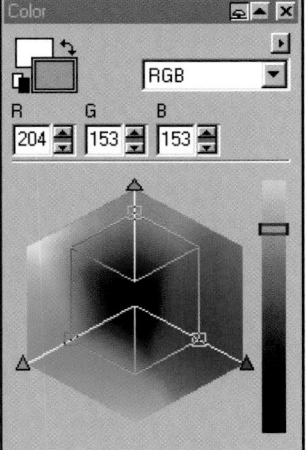

Step 3: The Color Table window will open, where you can load and save custom palettes. To load the browser-safe palette, choose the file named 216clut.cpl.

This places the colors in the palette bar at the bottom of the screen and inside the Color window. Photo-Paint has a really neat interface when you pick a color, showing you the color cube and where your selection is being pulled from.

How to Load a Browser-Safe Palette into Painter

Painter enables you to save its own version of swatch sets, called Color Sets. You'll find a browser-safe CLUT for Painter named clut, located inside the Painter folder on my ftp site ■ ftp://luna.bearnet.com/pub/lynda/. Drag this file into Painter's Color, Weaves, and Grad Folder on your hard drive before you begin.

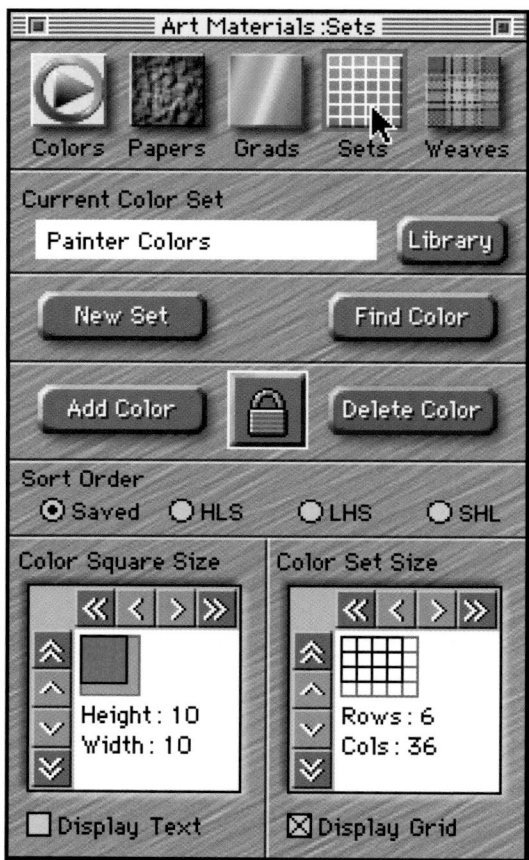

Step 1: Open the Art Materials Palette, highlight Sets, and then click on the Library button.

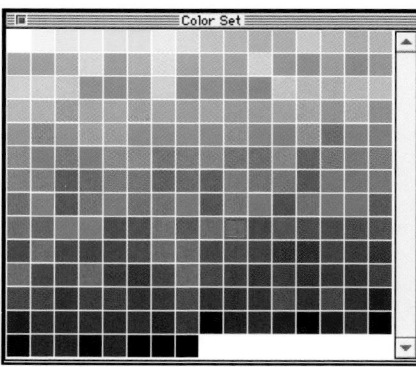

Step 2: Load the CLUT file.

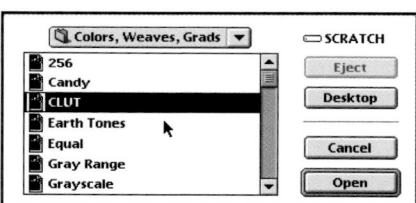

Step 3. A new browser-safe Color Set will appear. Special thanks to Amy Rosenthal for assembling and sharing this palette.

How to Ensure Your Artwork Stays Browser Safe

If you work with browser-safe colors when you create artwork, you still have the important task of ensuring that those colors remain browser safe during the file format conversion process.

Unfortunately, files that are converted to JPEGs do not retain precise color information. The lossy compression method used throws away information, and unfortunately some of that information has to do with color control. Because of this, there is no way to accurately control color using the JPEG file format.

Chapter 3, "Web File Formats," emphasized that JPEGs are not good for graphics. Not only do they compress graphics poorly, but they introduce artifacts into images, which alters color.

What this means is that you cannot accurately match foreground GIFs to background JPEGs, or foreground JPEGs to background GIFs. Even if you prepare images in browser-safe colors, they will not remain browser safe when converted to JPEG, no matter what you do. Chapter 3 already established that JPEGs are not good for solid colors. This is one more reason not to use JPEGs when dealing with flat-style illustration, logos, cartoons, or any other graphical image that would not lend itself to having unwanted dithering.

Here's an example of a solid browser-safe color, with the hex readout of 51, 153, 153.

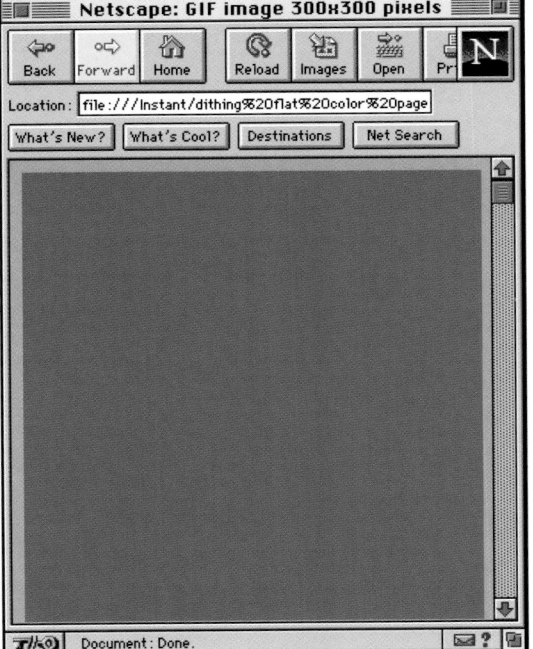

When saved as a GIF file, this color stayed browser safe.

When saved as a JPEG, the color shifted from 51, 153, 153 to 154, 154, 156. It is no longer browser safe, as evidenced by the dither when displayed in Netscape under 8-bit monitor conditions. Note: If you use the highest quality JPEGs, color inconsistency can be avoided, but you will suffer larger files sizes. Seems like if one thing doesn't get you, something else does!

Mixing Photos and Illustrations with Browser-Safe Colors

Next follows an example in which an image was created that used a photographic background, and browser-safe colors for the type.

Here's a 24-bit image that uses a photographic-style background with flat-style lettering. The letters were created using browser-safe colors.

This is an example of the image saved with an adaptive palette as a GIF.

This is an example of the image saved with the browser-safe palette as a GIF.

When viewed from Netscape in 256 colors, the adaptive palette version caused the lettering to dither.

When viewed from Netscape in 256 colors, the browser-safe palette version caused the lettering to look fine.

GIFs, on the other hand, do offer precise color control. If you create an image that is less than 256 colors by using browser-safe colors, Photoshop will let you save it with an Exact Palette. The only problem is when you create images that exceed 256 colors. In order to save these types of images as GIFs, some of the colors must be discarded.

This is when it's useful to use a Custom Palette setting in Photoshop and load the bclut2.aco file from my ftp site ■ ftp://luna.bearnet.com/pub/lynda/. You can't trust an adaptive palette to preserve browser-safe colors.

Removing Unwanted Browser-Safe Colors

At times you will apply the browser-safe palette to a file in order to ensure that the colors within honor the 216 color limit. The problem is that you might want to later reduce the file size even further than 216 by reducing the number of colors.

The following example shows you how to apply a browser-safe palette and then reduce the depth.

Bruce created an illustration in colors other than browser safe.

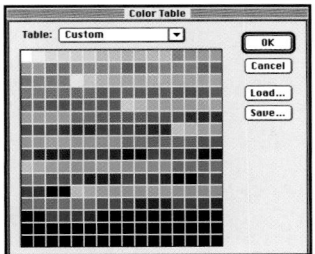

He converted them to browser-safe colors by choosing Image, Mode, Index Color and loading the 216 browser-safe CLUT file (called bclut2.aco) from my ftp site. Note: In Photoshop 4.0 there is a built-in 216 color table called Web that you can select from the Table menu.

The image is now browser safe, but it is also 216 colors! That's a few too many colors than are necessary for this image. By leaving the image this way, it would be 6.8k.

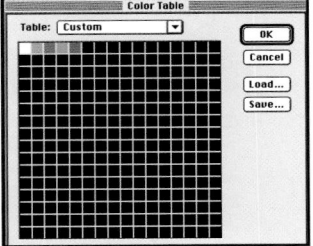

There's no reason for the image to include all 216 colors. By changing the image back to RGB mode and then back to Indexed Color mode, Bruce chose Exact Palette the second time. This image needs to be assigned only 7 colors! When saved as a GIF with only 7 colors, the image is 5.8k, a 14% file size savings that doesn't affect visual image quality in the least.

■ warning

16-Bit Trouble?

Don't save browser-safe colors in 16-bit! Unexpected problems occur when working with browser-safe color. Sometimes browser-safe colors that you thought you set up properly turn out to not be browser safe when you check on them later. What might have happened?

One of the main reasons might have something to do with your computer's current bit depth. When you select browser-safe color in thousands of colors, the colors are no longer browser safe! For some unknown reason, browser-safe colors aren't represented by thousands-of-colors systems. The only solution to this problem is to work in 256 colors or millions while selecting and saving with browser-safe color.

You might be wondering if the 216 browser-safe colors don't work properly in thousands of colors whether you have a new set of headaches for your users viewing your site in thousands-of-colors (16-bit) mode. Fortunately that is not the case. The 65,000 colors (16-bit) are enough so that the subtle dithering is virtually undetectable.

However, if you create your browser-safe artwork with your computer set to Thousands of Colors and the resulting nonbrowser-safe artwork is viewed in a 256-color environment, the dithering is very noticeable. The moral of this warning is to make sure your authoring system is set to 256 or millions of colors when creating browser-safe artwork. I cannot explain technically why this is happening, but this solution will always work.

Vector-Based Software: Illustrator, CorelDraw, and FreeHand

The two most popular image file formats for the web, GIF and JPEG, are bitmap-based formats. Bitmap artwork is composed of pixel-based artwork, meaning that every pixel takes up memory and is accounted for in the file format. Vector file formats are based on code that instructs the computer to draw the artwork and furnishes information such as the radius of a circle or the length of a line.

Most vector-based drawing programs enable you to move objects around on the screen, align artwork with grids using precise control, and offer much more elaborate type layout treatments than their bitmap counterparts. For this reason, many artists work with vector-based software programs to begin with, and later export their artwork into bitmap programs where the images can be saved as GIFs and JPEGs. This section evaluates processes for creating browser-safe vector-based artwork in three popular vector-based imaging programs: Adobe Illustrator, Macromedia's FreeHand, and CorelDraw.

For more in-depth information about these three programs, check out these URLs:

- http://www.adobe.com/prodindex/illustrator/main.html
- http://www.macromedia.com/software/freehand/index.html
- http://www.corel.com/products/graphics&publishing/draw7/index.htm

Working with CorelDraw

At the time of this chapter, the current shipping version of CorelDraw supported the capability to output files in RGB. The only problem was that it didn't allow you to specify the palette. The next version, 7.0, promises to allow custom palette assignments. It's best to create artwork in CorelDraw that is close to the colors you want to use and then bring the artwork into Photo-Paint to convert the colors to the browser-safe CLUT. The Photo-Paint 216 palette is called 216clut.cpl. and is available from my ftp site ■ ftp://luna.bearnet.com/pub/lynda/.

Working with Adobe Illustrator

Adobe Illustrator is an extremely useful program that does many things better than Photoshop. Some of the reasons to use Illustrator are its better handling of text, and its ability to position artwork accurately and create object-oriented artwork that is resolution independent.

The only problem using Illustrator for web graphics is that it works only in CMYK. It's impossible to load the browser-safe color chart or swatch sets into a CMYK environment. Most artists who use Illustrator for browser-safe color artwork create the artwork in black-and-white in Illustrator and then import the artwork into Photoshop, where they use the browser-safe swatches.

Illustrator is a popular software program because of its superior type handling, accurate positioning features, and resolution-independent drawing tools. Unfortunately it works only in CMYK color, so it's impossible to author web color images directly. Create artwork in black-and-white first, and save it as a native Illustrator file.

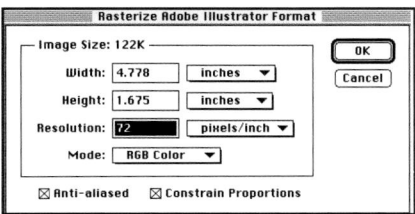

When you open the file in Illustrator, you'll be prompted to rasterize the artwork. This converts the artwork from the Illustrator vector format to the Photoshop bitmap format.

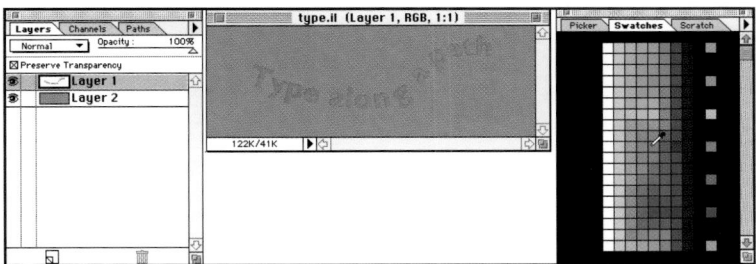

Once the artwork is rasterized in Photoshop, it can be painted with the browser-safe color swatches, just like artwork that originated in Photoshop.

■ **note**

GIFs in Illustrator

Version 6.0 of Adobe Illustrator will let you save GIF files and convert them to a specified palette, including one that contains the 216 browser-safe colors.

Working with FreeHand

Artists who use FreeHand for its excellent type-handling tools and vector-drawing tools are in luck! FreeHand allows users to work directly in RGB and will support the 216 palette.

FreeHand works with RGB percentages rather than specific RGB values. It's possible to mix browser-safe colors right in RGB within FreeHand. Just use these conversions:

%	RGB	HEX
100%	255	FF
80%	204	CC
60%	153	99
40%	102	66
20%	51	33
0%	0	0

Thanks to the generosity and work of Amy Rosenthal, you can download a FreeHand CLUT, called clut.bcs, from my ftp site ■ ftp://luna.bearnet.com/pub/lynda/.

The following steps will enable you to access this palette in FreeHand:

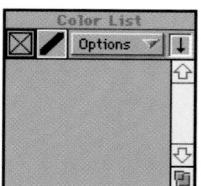

Step 1: Open the Color List Palette. Under Options, choose Import. Locate the clut.bcs file.

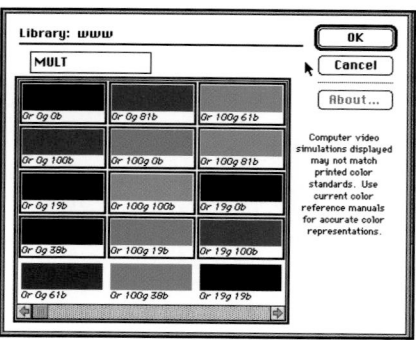

Step 2: Double-click on the file name clut.bcs and this window will appear. Hold the Shift key down to select all the color chips within the set, and click OK. A new Color List will appear with the browser-safe colors.

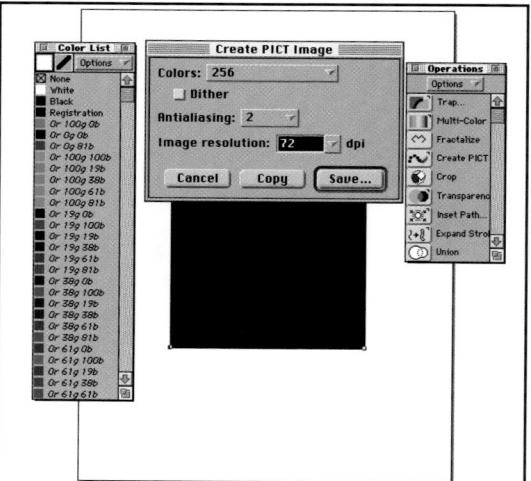

Step 3: If you use these colors to paint with, you can save them as a PICT file for conversion to GIF in another program. Highlight the artwork and select Create PICT in the Operations Palette. Make sure dither is left unchecked in the Save window. This ensures that the browser-safe color selection will be preserved.

Working with Color Picker-Based Applications

Certain programs don't let you mix colors by percentages or RGB values. A few such programs include Adobe PageMill, Claris Homepage, and BBEdit, which all rely on the Apple Color Picker to choose custom colors.

Pantone has come to the rescue with a Mac-only product called ColorWeb ■ http://www.pantone. com. Its Internet-safe color-picking system includes two components: a printed swatch set, and a System Color Picker that displays the 216 safe colors inside the Apple Color Picker dialog box.

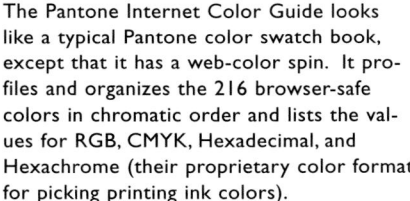

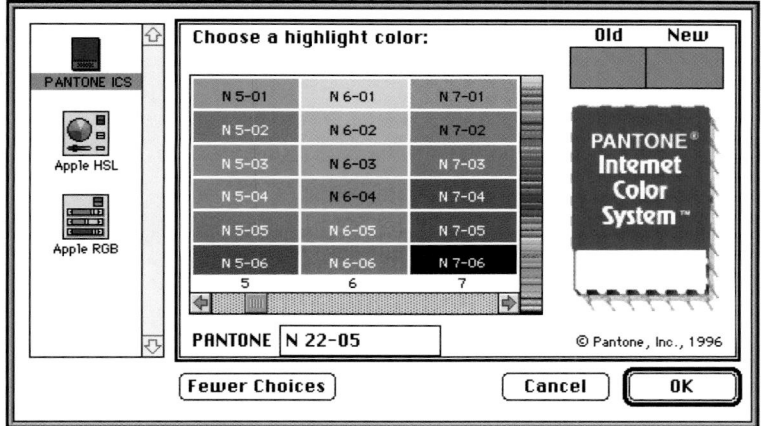

The Pantone Internet Color Guide looks like a typical Pantone color swatch book, except that it has a web-color spin. It profiles and organizes the 216 browser-safe colors in chromatic order and lists the values for RGB, CMYK, Hexadecimal, and Hexachrome (their proprietary color format for picking printing ink colors).

If you install Pantone's ColorWeb software, it will add another entry, called Pantone ICS, into the Apple Color Picker choices. Pantone ICS will enable you to pick from the 216 browser-safe colors.

■ warning

CMYK Is Not Browser Safe

It should be noted that there is no perfectly accurate way with which to convert CMYK values to RGB. The numbers that the Pantone Internet Color Guide cites for CMYK Internet-safe values are ballpark approximations and do not yield browser-safe colors when converted to RGB. The two color spaces—RGB and CMYK—do not share common colors consistently. Some RGB colors are outside of the CMYK color gamut, and there is nothing anyone can adjust for to create a reliable conversion method.

The ColorWeb software is an excellent (Mac-only) tool that offers the capability to pick browser-safe colors in programs that do not support RGB decimal or RGB percentage-based values. Pricing and order information is available at the Pantone web site.

At a magnified view, you can see that Don made a pixel-by-pixel pattern of 3 different browser-safe colors.

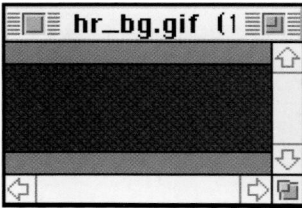

At a 1:1 view, the pattern looks like a solid and creates an optical illusion of a color found outside the palette, even though it is still technically browser safe. We call these colors "hybrid" colors within this book.

What Are Hybrid-Safe Colors?

Hybrid-safe colors were invented by Don Barnett and Bruce Heavin when they were working on a prototype web site for DreamWorks Interactive SKG. Their work on that site was never used (although it can be viewed in my second book, *Deconstructing Web Graphics*). If you'd like to see hybrid-safe color in action, look at Don's personal site ■ http://www.cris.com/~Nekton/sources/net_barn.htm.

Don Barnett wanted to use colors that didn't shift or dither in the 256-color environments, but he didn't like any of the 216 colors he had to choose from. He came up with the idea of forming a pre-dithered pattern—on a pixel-by-pixel basis—of multiple browser-safe colors. This created an optical mixture of colors, tricking your eye into thinking it was a new color outside of the 216 limited palette.

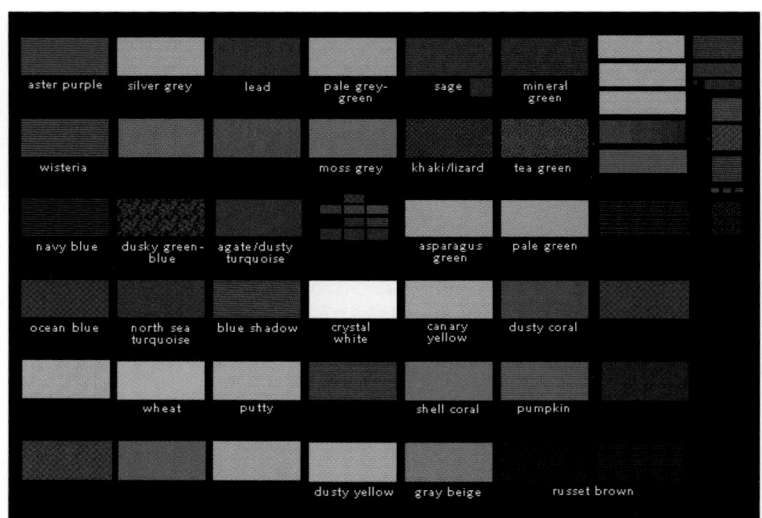

This page of hybrid colors was created by Don Barnett and can be found at ■ http://www.cris.com/~Nekton.

HTML for Hybrid Colors

Hybrid color files are a different story from swatches and GIFs. They must be loaded into the <BODY BACKGROUND> tag of an HTML document.

Here is the basic, most rudimentary HTML you would need in order to load hybrid color files into the background of your web pages:

```
<HTML>
<BODY BACKGROUND="hybrid.gif">
</BODY><HTML>
```

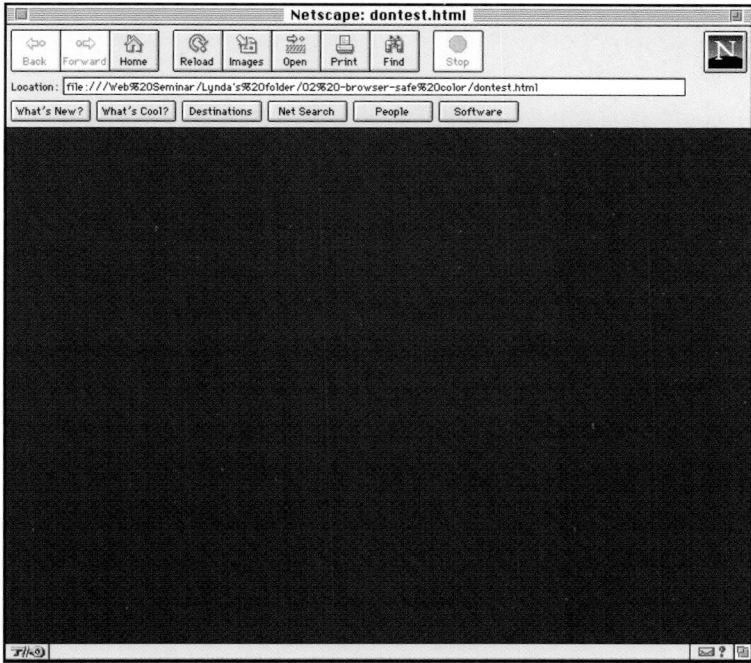

On the left is the source file for the HTML. It is repeated unlimited times, depending on how big the browser window is. To the right is the final screen in Netscape, filled repeatedly with the browser-safe seamless tile. For more information on seamless tiles, see Chapter 8, "Background Tiles."

> ■ **tip**
>
> **Importance of Value**
> You'll get the best-looking results if you choose colors that are close in value. This creates the best optical mixture, which tricks the eye into seeing one mixed color as opposed to two distinct mixed colors.

Hybrid Color Background Tile Creation in Photoshop

By checkerboarding or alternating color pixels, you can mix new colors that create the illusion of colors found outside the 216 limit. There are tens of thousands of browser-safe color combinations possible. Hundreds of hybrid-safe color combinations are located on the CD-ROM of my third book, co-written with Bruce Heavin, called *Coloring Web Graphics*. We used the same technique described in this chapter to create those palette sets.

If you want to make your own hybrid color combinations, it is possible to make them in any paint program. Unfortunately, with the exception of Photoshop, most paint programs don't let you preview the results until you've created an HTML document and look at the results in a web browser.

The object is to make a repeating pattern of pixels. There are two types of patterns that work the best: horizontal lines and checkerboards. The reason for this is that at a 1:1 ratio, these patterns are the least obvious

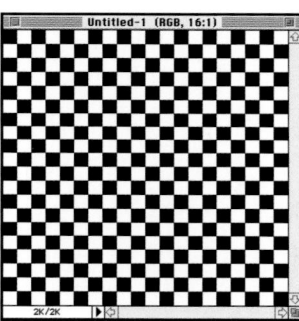
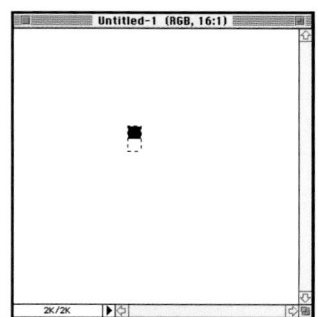
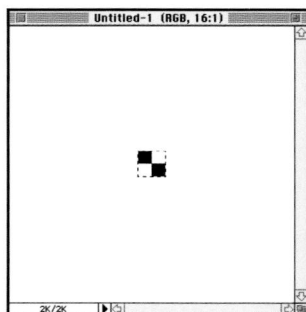

Close-up views of the two types of patterns used for hybrid tile creation.

Creating the pattern for the hybrid tiles can be created with two or four selected pixels, and then defining a pattern based on these selections.

In Photoshop, creating these patterns can be done with a few simple pixels.

Step 1: Using the smallest Pencil Tool, inside a magnified document, create the base art for the pattern tile. Use the Marquee Selection Tool to select either two or four pixels.

Step 2: Under the Edit menu, choose Define Pattern.

Step 3: Create a larger document. Make sure it's an even number of pixels so that the tile will repeat properly in a browser without any erroneous lines or glitches. Under the Edit menu, choose Fill. In the Fill dialog box, select Fill with Pattern.

Coloring Hybrid Tiles in Photoshop

Once you have black-and-white color tiles (or any other color combination), you can recolor the tile easily.

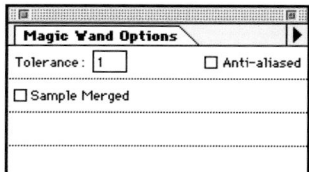

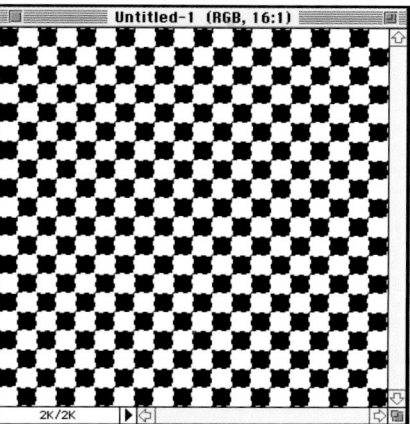

Step 1: Set the Magic Wand Tool to a tolerance of 1. This ensures that it will select only one color. Select a single pixel of either black or white. If the tile is two colors other than black and white, select one of those colors.

Step 2: Under the Select Menu, choose Select Similar. This selects everything in the image that has the same color you originally chose. It's now easy to fill this selection with any color you want, using the Edit, Fill menu. To fill the opposite color, choose Select, Inverse, which reverses the selection, and then proceed to fill with another color.

■ tip

Photoshop Shortcuts

A shorcut for filling a selection is to select a color so that it appears in your foreground color toolbar. On Macs, choose Option+Delete; on PCs use Alt+Delete.

A shortcut for filling with a pattern is Shift+Delete on the Mac and on the PC.

Custom Palettes for Shockwave Documents

Macromedia Director is an interactive authoring tool that has a huge installed user base. In the first quarter of 1996, Macromedia released Shockwave, a plug-in that makes Director projects viewable from the web. Since then, Director-based projects have become a common file type on the web.

It's possible to assign custom palettes to Director documents. Information on this process is available from: ■ http://www.macromedia.com/support/ technotes/shockwave/developer/shocktechnotes/palettes/colpalette.html. Director (versions 5.0 and above) even ships with a 216 palette, which is located under the Xtras pull-down menu. The file is called Palette.cst on Macintoshes and PALETTES on Windows.

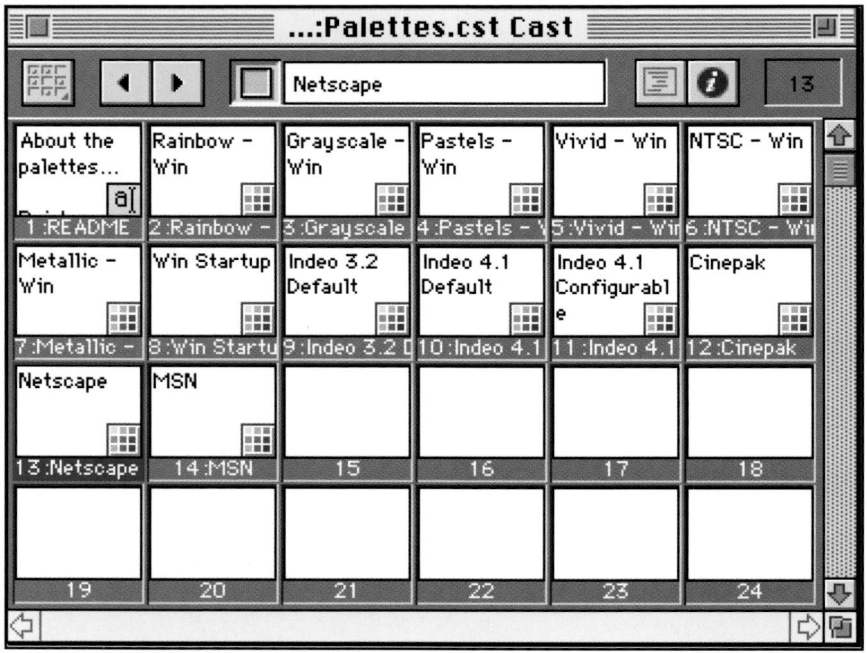

Director 5 ships with a series of palettes, including a broswer-safe palette called Netscape.

Previsualizing Tiles in Photoshop

Working with the Fill with Pattern feature in Photoshop, it's possible to previsualize tileable patterns before sending them to the web browser for the world to see. We'll work with Don Barnett's artwork—shmancy.gif, available from ■ ftp://luna.bearnet.com/pub/lynda/—to show how this is done.

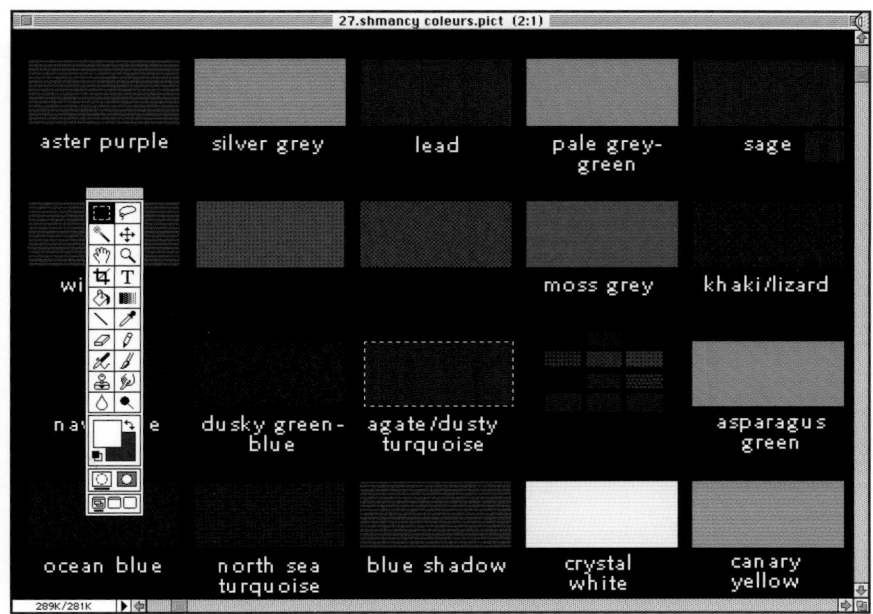

Step 2: Open a blank Photoshop document that will represent your web page. Select All and choose Edit, Fill. In the Fill dialog box, choose Fill with Pattern.

Step 1: Zoom into the file to accurately select the rectangular swatch. Under the File menu, choose Define Pattern.

BROWSER SAFE COLOR

33 FPS

0033

Width = "500"

<STRONG>

.jpg
.png

IMAGE OPTIMIZATION Colors

Height = "600"

<img src="

<TABL

14 typography

Web

<A>

Imaging techniques

Web file formats
bgcolor = "FFFFCC"

@link = "cyan"

Animation, sound and

LYNDA.COM

<BODY>

33

www Design

7

Transparency

Transparency is another word for "mask," and masks are often used in computer graphics to make artwork appear in irregular shapes rather than as squares and rectangles. A computer image file by definition is automatically saved in a rectangle. In my humble opinion, way too much artwork on the web is in the shape of rectangles—buttons, pictures, splash screens, menu bars—ugh. Mastering transparency is the only escape!

There are two types of transparency—that which involves masking and that which involves trickery. The easiest way is the trick method, which is easy to explain. Let's say you have a circle and you want it to look like it's free-floating even though it must be inside a rectangular shape. Make the background behind the circle the same color as your web page. If you put the two together, there should be no obvious rectangular border. Seems simple? It is.

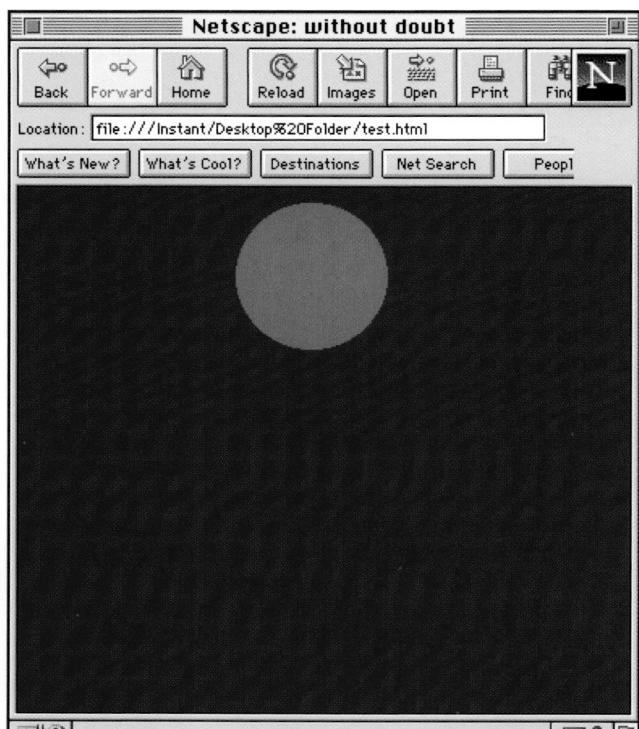

You can easily create the illusion of irregularly shaped images by making the foreground artwork include the same color as your target background on your web page.

But there's a snag. Making foreground and background images on the web that match takes an extra bit of education. This chapter teaches you how to set exact background colors (assuming your end viewer has not changed his or her preferences to override color choices) using two HTML-based techniques. One involves using hexadecimal code to set a specific background color, and the other requires setting up the HTML to use a solid pattern tile. Step-by-step examples will help you understand these two techniques and will show you how to make the irregularly shaped artwork lay on top of colored backgrounds.

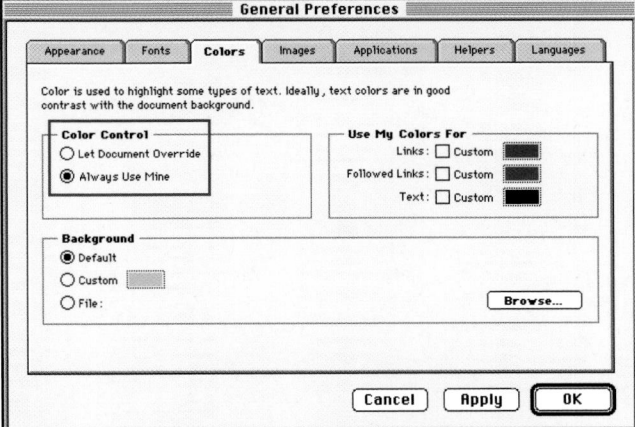

It's kind of scary for web designers who count on background colors they pick to achieve the illusion of irregularly shaped images because end viewers can check "Always Use Mine," which will override the color choices you've specified! If you want to view sites as designers intended them to be seen, make sure "Let Document Override" is always checked instead.

Creating Background Color the Hexadecimal Way

This technique was covered in Chapter 5, "Hexadecimal Color," but will be reviewed here for the purposes of creating the illusion of transparency. This first example demonstrates how to include irregularly shaped artwork using the <BODY BGCOLOR> tag.

Step 1: Create artwork that is in an irregular shape. This technique works especially well on images that include anti-aliasing, soft edges, glows, or drop shadows.

Step 2: Use the eyedropper to find out the RGB values of the image. Hint: If you use the browser-safe color charts in Chapter 5, "Hexadecimal Color," you'll find the hex and RGB colors easily.

Step 3: Next, write the following HTML. This code tells the background to be light yellow, by using the hexadecimal code FFFFCC, and inserts the Jamie image on the same page:

```
<HTML>
<HEAD><CENTER><TITLE>Jamie
the flower girl</TITLE>
</HEAD>
<BODY BGCOLOR=#FFFFCC TEXT="993333"
LINK="FF9933" VLINK="FF9933">
</BODY> <P>
<CENTER><IMG SRC="jamie.gif">
</CENTER>
<P>
</HTML>
```

Step 4: Now you can view the final result. No transparency software was used to achieve this result!

Creating Background Color Using Solid Patterns

Another way to color the background of a web page is to use a solid color swatch within the background pattern tag, <BODY BACKGROUND>. This tag is more commonly used with artwork that has an image in it, such as a marble texture. The <BODY BACKGROUND> tag takes whatever art you tell it to use and repeats the artwork tiles so that they fill the entire web page.

For instructions on how to make image-filled types of pattern tiles, refer to Chapter 8, "Background Tiles." We are going to use the same HTML technique that Chapter 8 describes in detail, but our source image for the pattern tile is going to be made out of a solid color instead. As it is repeated over the page, this tile will produce a solid background, identical in appearance to what was demonstrated using the hexadecimal method previously mentioned.

You can actually use both the BGCOLOR and BACKGROUND attributes inside the same BODY tag, which ensures the safest results with this technique. Here's an example of how the code would look:

```
<HTML>
<HEAD><CENTER>
<TITLE>Jamie the flower girl</TITLE>
</HEAD>
<BODY BGCOLOR=#FFFFCC BACKGROUND="yellow.gif"
TEXT="993333" LINK="FF9933" VLINK="FF9933">
</BODY>
<P>
<CENTER><IMG SRC="jamie.gif">
</CENTER>
<P>
</HTML>
```

An advantage to using the <BODY BACKGROUND> method is the background color will not be changed in the event your end users have altered their preferences. Another effect you can create is to set up a background color that is a transition effect that precedes a solid color background tile. For example, some people set their hex background to load first with white and then change to black once the solid background tile is loaded for an eye-catching flashing effect.

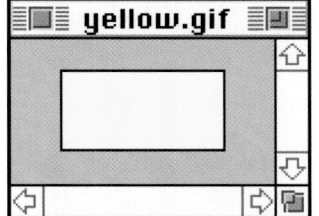

Here's an example of a Photoshop file that is filled with the same solid yellow used in the last example. If this image were used as the <BODY BACKGROUND> file, the HTML could not be overridden if users changed the background color defaults in their browser preferences.

■ tip

JPEG or GIF?

It doesn't matter whether your images or tiled background patterns are saved in JPEG or GIF file format. Those decisions should be based on the principles described in Chapter 4, "Low-Bandwidth Graphics." One thing to caution you about: if you are going to use a solid background image and want it to match your solid foreground image, you must use a JPEG background and JPEG foreground, or a GIF background and a GIF foreground. In other words, the file type must match or you will get uncontrollable color shifts between the elements.

Transparent GIFs

If transparent GIFs (TGIFs) are an unfamiliar term to you, don't worry. I know of no other application for transparent GIFs other than the web, so they're relatively new to everyone. Transparent GIFs are used to create the illusion of irregularly shaped computer files by assigning one color in a graphic to be invisible. This process is also called masking.

Transparent GIFs, technically referred to as GIF89a, support masking. Not all imaging programs let you save graphics in the GIF89a format, so details on how to use the various helper applications, online services, and programs that support it are included later in this chapter, in the section "Transparent GIF Software."

When working with transparent GIFs, there are two things to keep in mind: first, how to make art properly for one color masking transparency and second, how to use the programs that let you save the artwork in this file format.

■ tip

HTML for Transparent GIFs

The HTML for transparent GIFs is identical to the HTML for any other type of GIF or JPEG. The <IMG SRC> tag is all that's needed.

For an unlinked transparent GIF graphic, the HTML would look like this:
<IMG SRC="transgif.gif">

For a linked transparent GIF graphic, the HTML would look like this:
<A HREF="http://www.destination_ domain_name.com">
<IMG SRC="transgif.gif"></A>

More information on HTML and previewing web files from your hard drive can be found in Chapter 17, "HTML for Visual Designers."

When to Use Transparent Artwork

I recommend using Transparent GIFs only on web pages that have pattern backgrounds (see Chapter 8, "Background Tiles") because creating the illusion of transparency is very simple using solid colors. Establishing transparency in a GIF adds a lot of extra steps in production, so there's no reason to do that when there's an easier way.

The reason I recommend transparency with pattern background tiles is because you can't reliably match a foreground image to a background tile in standard HTML. (This problem is described in more detail in Chapter 13, "Layout and Alignment Techniques.") If you want to put irregularly shaped artwork over patterned backgrounds, you'll have to use transparency.

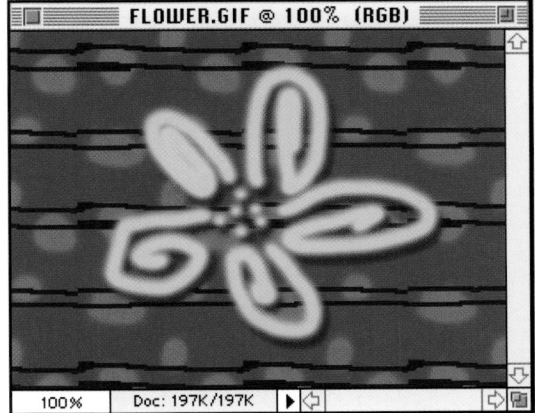

This image was created as a foreground element and was precomposed against a patterned background while in Photoshop.

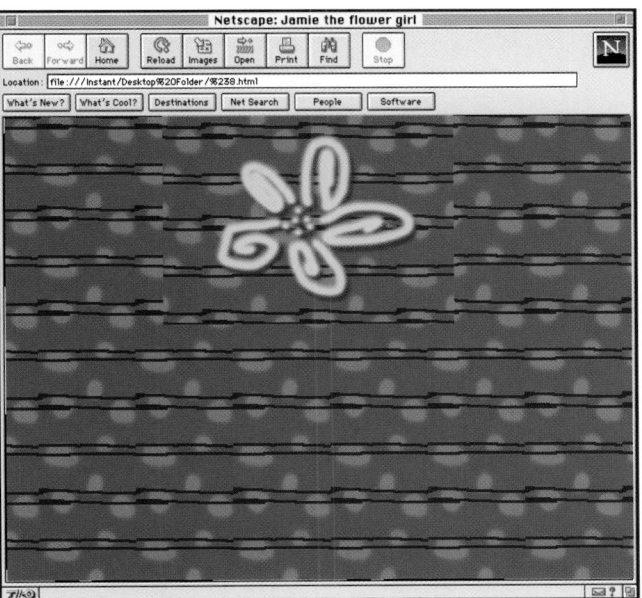

The same image is laid on top of the tiled background. Notice that it is misaligned. You can try to align a foreground image with a complex pattern to the identical background pattern, but they won't line up. And to make matters worse—the alignment is different on a Mac and PC!

Making Clean Transparent Artwork

The key to producing effective transparent GIFs is ensuring your art is produced correctly. We need to begin by first going through a short primer on aliased versus anti-aliased artwork. *Anti-aliasing* is the process of blending around the edges of a graphic to disguise the jaggy square nature of the artwork.

Many of the transparent GIFs I see on the web have ugly residual matte lines, usually in the form of white or black edges. These matte lines can be traced back to the way in which the image was anti-aliased.

On the web, anti-aliasing is not always the best approach. Creating clean transparent GIFs is one of those exceptions where aliased graphics create the least amount of problems.

The anti-aliased blended edge is precisely what causes fringing problems once the graphic is converted to transparent GIFs. Because transparent GIFs drop only one color out of your image, you will see all the remaining colors along the blended edge of anti-aliased artwork, even when what you really want is for all of them to disappear. There is no way to avoid this unless GIF file formats supported masking for more than one color. (Photoshop and PICT file formats, for example, let you mask with 256 levels of transparency, whereas transparent GIFs let you mask with only one.)

Because working with aliased graphics is more foreign to experienced computer designers than not, I've devoted a few sections of this chapter to offer instruction in Photoshop for working with aliased tools.

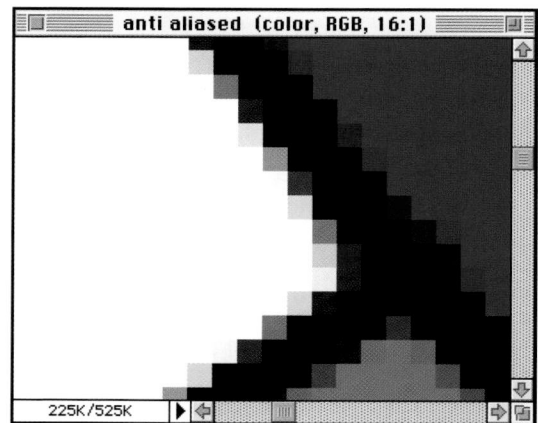

Anti-aliasing is the process where one color and shape blends to another, in order to hide the jagged square pixel nature of computer graphics.

Here is an example of a transparent image with an unwanted white halo. This is because the artwork was created anti-aliased against white. Most well-trained digital artists would never think to work without anti-aliasing. We've been conditioned to make everything look as smooth and perfect as possible. Anti-aliasing was designed to hide the fact that computer graphics are made of square, jagged pixels. Computer screens are a pixel-based medium, so our compulsion to hide this fact in print and other media is not always appropriate for computer screen-based design, such as the web and other multimedia delivery systems like CD-ROMs. Low-resolution web graphics are much more forgiving with aliasing than their print graphic counterparts.

Photoshop Tips for Creating Aliased Images

The following sections demonstrate how to create artwork for transparent GIFs with aliased edges. Photoshop was designed as a sophisticated graphics editing program, and working there with aliased tools is foreign to most designers. Understanding which types of tools are appropriate for the job and how to configure them so that they don't anti-alias is key to mastering clean-edged TGIFs. There are a few different types of graphics we'll study: illustrations, scanned illustrations, and scanned photographs.

Creating Illustration-Based Artwork for Transparent GIFs

If you're an illustrator, you're used to creating artwork from scratch. It's best to start with the correct tools for the job—and they'll most likely be tools you don't normally use. Most paint programs default to working with anti-aliased brushes and fill tools. To create aliased graphics in Photoshop, you want to use the Pencil Tool and the Paint Bucket Tool to draw and fill shapes with.

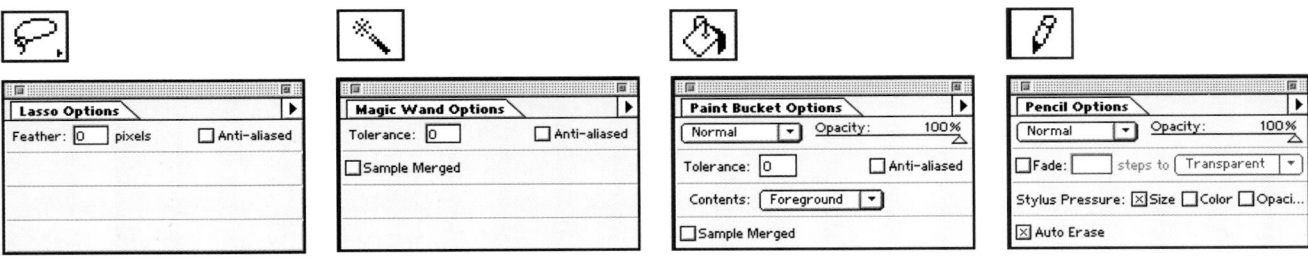

These are the aliased graphic tools: the Lasso, the Magic Wand, the Paint Bucket, and the Pencil.

While creating your illustrations, be sure to fill the areas that are going to go transparent with a different color. Here's an example of how my logo was prepared properly for converting to a transparent GIF. I used an aliased pencil tool with my pressure sensitive tablet to achieve the handwritten font.

It looks like my logo is set against black, but the black is there only so it would be easy to identify when I made this graphic transparent.

Once my logo was made transparent, and put against a background, no one ever has to know it was created against black. It has no residual matte line around it because the artwork is aliased.

The techniques reviewed here, using aliased bucket and pencil tools, work great if you're creating flat illustration artwork directly in the computer. But what if you're not? The next section addresses other techniques for converting graphics to TGIF.

Turning Prescanned Illustrations into Aliased Art

Sometimes, the source material supplied for web page art has already been scanned and is already anti-aliased. This might be the case with a company logo or something you're bringing in from a clip art book. When working with existing anti-aliased artwork, you can convert the image to being aliased by changing the mode from RGB to Bitmap.

Go to the top menu bar to Image, Mode, Bitmap and set the Threshold setting to 50%. Changing to this mode strips away all the anti-aliasing from the image. You can convert back to RGB mode and access colors in the document, but the lines will remain aliased. There's an example of this Photoshop technique on my Windows 95-equipped PC using Yeryeoung Park's wonderful original sketches for the HotHotHot site ■ http://www.hothothot.com—check out the great use of aliased artwork on the site.

Here are the steps used to convert a scanned image to an anti-aliased image:

Step 1: Open the original scan.

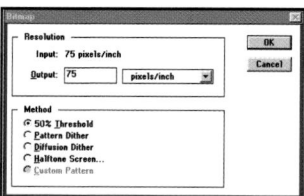

Step 2: Go to Image, Mode and change it to Bitmap. By using the Threshold 50% setting, it equalizes all the grays and makes a black-and-white aliased image.

Step 3: Yeryeoung used the pencil and paint bucket tools to create aliased fills for the artwork.

Here are the final (aliased) results at HotHotHot ■ http://www.hothothot.com.

Photographic Source Art for Transparent GIFs

Another common situation is where you have photographs or existing color illustrations with anti-aliased edges that you want to change to transparent GIFs. You don't have to change the interior of your graphic to be aliased, just the edges. For best results you can work large and use the Magnifying Glass Tool to zoom way in to accurately erase the edge using the aliased "block" Eraser Tool. You also can use the aliased Lasso Tool to select the parts you want to delete. Just make sure the anti-aliased box is unchecked! The edge will look terrible in Photoshop, but will look much better on the web!

Here's a step-by-step demonstration of how I would make my daughter's baby head float freely on a web page:

 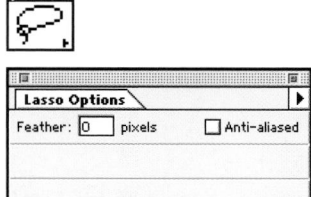 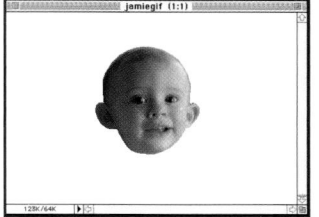 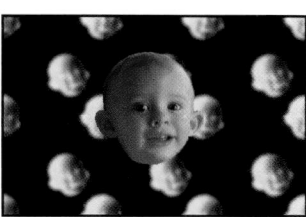

Step 1: Scan the photo. Remember to use the correct scale for the web—72 dpi, RGB color, and small dimensions! Jamie's photo was scanned in at 72 dpi, 3x4 inches.

Step 2: Select the Lasso Tool, with the Anti-aliased box unchecked in the Options.

Step 3: I traced around the shape of her head using the Lasso Tool. Next, I inverted the selection by going to the menu item Select, Inverse. Choosing Edit, Fill, Normal, Foreground, 100%, I filled the outside with white. This image, by itself, against white looks jaggy and horrible around the edges.

Step 4: Next the image is saved as a transparent GIF and put on a web page (see the next two sections for instructions on this). Notice how the image looks perfectly acceptable once laid over a pattern background? Also notice the lack of matte lines.

The preceding examples show the correct method to prepare photo-based source material properly for TGIFs. The following examples show what can (and does!) go wrong with transparent GIFs. As you look at these examples, you should understand why they didn't work successfully and know how to prepare artwork so that this doesn't happen. The next section will discuss techniques to deal with glows, soft-edges, and drop shadows using GIF transparency.

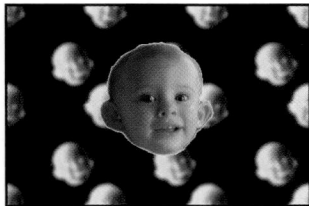 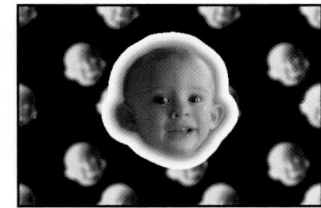

This is what would have happened had I not chosen to cut Jamie out with aliased tools.

If you really want to get down and ugly, make a transparent GIF out of artwork that has a glow around it!

How to Deal with Glows, Soft Edges, and Drop Shadows with GIF Transparency

Because of the problems anti-aliasing introduces, artwork with glows, soft-edges, and drop shadows can look awful as transparent GIFs. One popular solution is to build artwork against the same color background that it will be seen against in the web browser. The artwork will look terrible when you make it, but it will look fine once laid against the final background in a web browser.

SAMPLE TEXT

aliased

SAMPLE TEXT

anti-aliased

SAMPLE TEXT

with shadow

SAMPLE TEXT

with glow

This figure shows four types of edges for artwork: aliased, anti-aliased, with a shadow, and with a glow.

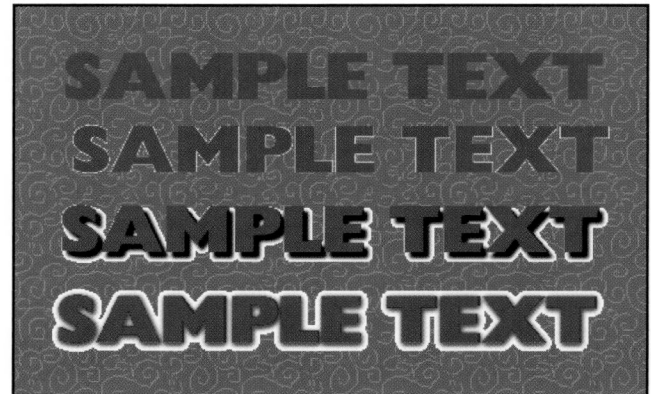

When the different examples of edges are made into transparent GIFs using one-color transparency, notice how every example except the aliased top version picked up the background color they were made against. That's because the images with soft edges picked up parts of the white background color they were created against. This created an unsightly problem, which is commonly called a halo, fringe, or matte line.

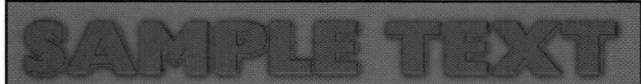

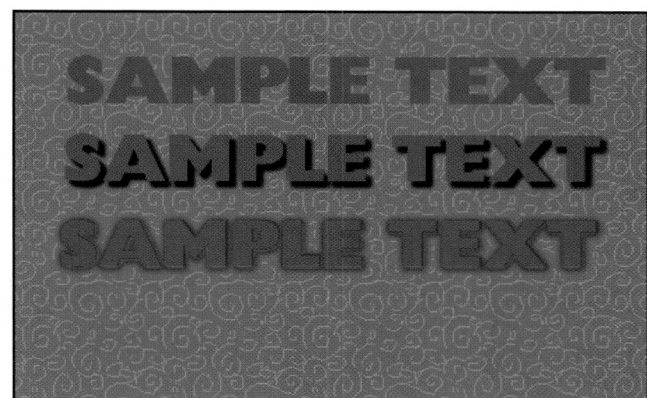

Here's an example of the identical artwork with anti-aliased, shadowed, and blurry edges against the same color background of the target web page.

The end result looks quite acceptable now. Look ma, no matte lines!

When the transparency is set, the files look pretty terrible. They won't look good again until they are laid over a green background. If prepared this way, you will correct their predisposition to favor any other color, which will eliminate unwanted fringes, halos, and matte lines.

■ **tip**

Transparent GIF URLs

Here are some useful URLs to track down transparency tricks and tips:

Online Transparent GIF creation
■ http://www.vrl.com/Imaging/invis.html

Thomas Boutell's WWW FAQ on Transparency
■ http://sunsite.unc.edu/boutell/faq/tinter.htm

Chipp Walter's Excellent GIF transparency tutorial
■ http://204.96.160.175/IGOR/photosho.htm

Transparent GIF Software

There are lots of popular software packages that support GIF transparency. It's impossible to cover all of them in this book, but I've included instruction for a few different packages that support TGIFs.

Cross-Platform

Adobe Photoshop GIF89a Export Plug-In

Current versions of Photoshop ship with a GIF89a plug-in that supports transparency and interlacing. This plug-in works on Mac and Windows versions of Photoshop. This plug-in is preinstalled in current versions of Photoshop. If you don't have it, you can download the plug-in from these locations:

- Mac: http://www.adobe.com/supportservice/custsupport/LIBRARY/2eb2.htm
- Windows: http://www.adobe.com/supportservice/custsupport/LIBRARY/2f22.htm

Here's a step-by-step tour through Photoshop's GIF89a plug-in features:

Step 1: Place the GIF89a Export plug-in in your plug-in folder. Make sure that Photoshop is closed. The plug-in will not be effective until the next time Photoshop is opened. Note that current versions of Photoshop ship with this plug-in, so you do not need to install it yourself.

Step 2: Open the document you wish to make transparent.

Step 3: Convert the file from RGB to Index Color. Go to Mode, select Index, and leave it at its defaults. Or you can practice some of the principles described in Chapter 4, "Low-Bandwidth Graphics." Test the image in 100 colors, or 50, or whatever works. You can decide how low to take the bit depth, and the lower you take it, the smaller the file size will be.

Step 4: After the image is indexed, make a selection and choose Save Selection. The selection will be saved into channel 2.

Step 5: Under File, select Export, GIF89a. The transparent color can be based on Selected Colors or #2. By saving a selection in step 4, I created a channel in the document, called channel #2. If I choose to use the #2 mask, I do not have to base the selection on color at all.

Step 6: The selection based on channel #2 is previewed, allowing me to check it before I click OK to save the file.

This plug-in worked great for a photo. Let's try a selection based on color for the next example.

Step 1: Open an image and convert it to Index Color mode.

Step 2: Under File, select Export, GIF89a. This time we'll base the selection on Selected Colors. Using the Eyedropper Tool, click on the areas you want transparent. The preview shows you what you need to see. When finished selecting with the Eyedropper, click OK to save.

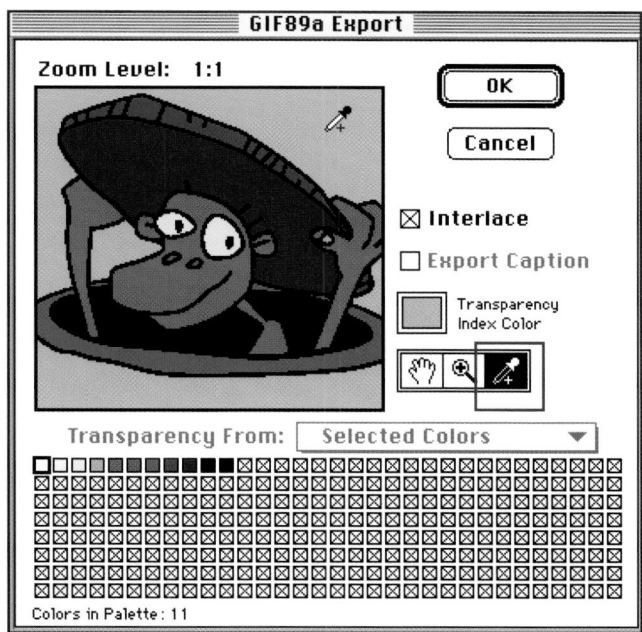

If you have not defined a selection, you can select the color you wish to set as the mask by following the preceding instructions. This example shows transparency being set based on color.

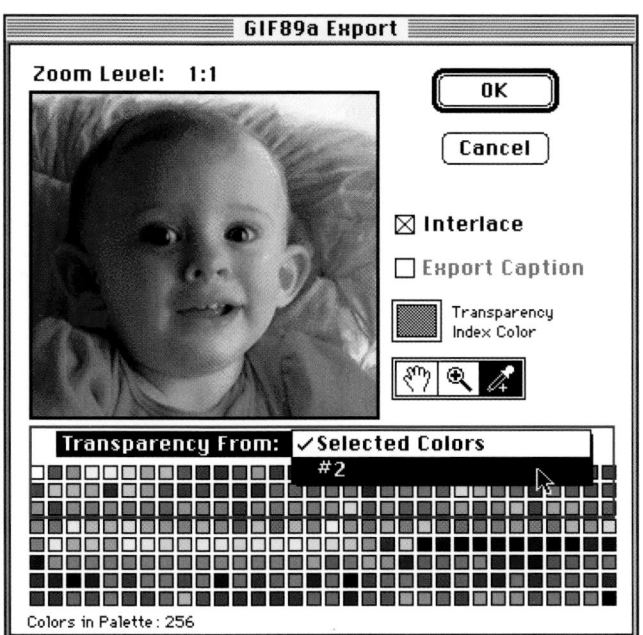

This example shows transparency based on a selection, not a color.

Fractal Design Painter 4.0

Painter 4.0 offers great support for transparent GIFs. You can save an image as a GIF either by selecting the background color or by using one of its floater selections as a defined region for the mask. Open a document (any file format that Painter supports) and convert it to Index Color in the saving process.

Painter is a complicated program to use, and I unfortunately lack the space in this chapter to walk new users through its interface. For those readers who already use Painter, here are the steps for working with its transparent GIF features:

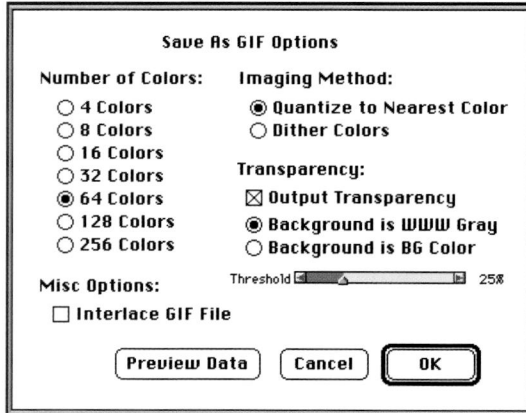

Step 1: Using Painter's Type Frisket Tool and converting it to a Floater, you can identify a masking region for the transparent GIF. **Step 2:** In the save as GIF Options, choose to Output Transparency.

Step 3: Output transparency does a great job of making a selection based on shape rather than a background color. Here's an example of a preview of the image with the type mask in effect.

Transparency Resources

For those of you who like to work while you're online, transparent GIFs can be made directly on the web! There are several sites that will convert a regular GIF into a transparent GIF while you wait. These sites look for an URL that includes a GIF image and will convert the image to the GIF89a format. Some sites let you choose black, white, or an RGB value to go transparent, and others let you click on the image to choose the spot.

To use the online transparency service, you'd have to give the URL of your image, not the URL of an HTML document. A correct URL would look like this:

■ http://www.myprovider.com/mysitename/imagetoconvert.gif

Remember, your artwork must be loaded on a server and be a valid URL. For instructions on how to load your art to a server, check out Chapter 17, "HTML for Visual Designers."

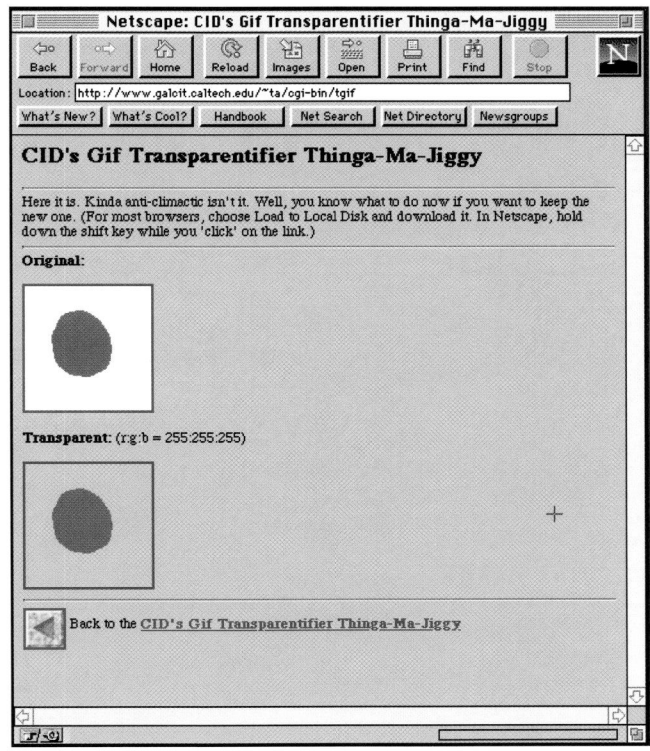

Here's an example of what online transparency software can do.

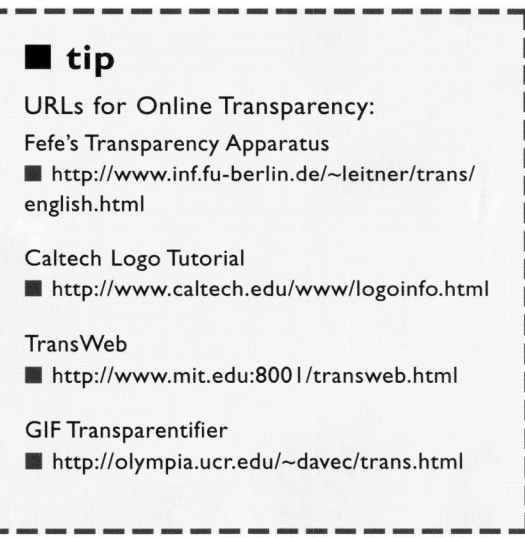

■ **tip**

URLs for Online Transparency:

Fefe's Transparency Apparatus
■ http://www.inf.fu-berlin.de/~leitner/trans/english.html

Caltech Logo Tutorial
■ http://www.caltech.edu/www/logoinfo.html

TransWeb
■ http://www.mit.edu:8001/transweb.html

GIF Transparentifier
■ http://olympia.ucr.edu/~davec/trans.html

Macintosh

Transparency

A popular Mac freeware application is Transparency, by Aaron Giles. It can be downloaded from ■ ftp.uwtc.washington.edu/pub/Mac/Graphics/. It lacks bells and whistles, but hey, the price is right!

To use, launch the program and open a GIF file. The file must already be saved as GIF to work. Hold your mouse down on the color you want to make into the invisible background and save the file.

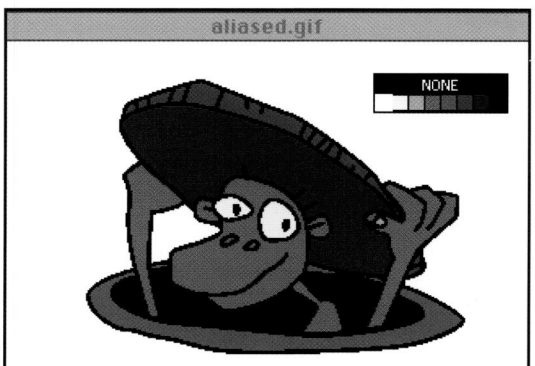

Here's an example of a picture being edited with the freeware application Transparency.

DeBabelizer

Many multimedia developers already sing the praises of De-Babelizer, and its web support is no less impressive. One of the best features about this program is its capability to batch process. (Batch processing is when multiple files are processed at one time.) This capability allows you to take a folder of images and convert them all at once to a specific palette or make them all go transparent as GIF89a's. It's a must-have tool for web designers doing volume image processing (what might be required when putting a mail-order catalog online, for example). Batch processing a series of GIFs in DeBabelizer is no easy task due to its unusual interface. Here's what you do:

Step 1: Put all the images you want to convert to transparent GIFs in one folder. If the images need to be converted to 8-bit first, include steps 3 and 4. Otherwise, skip and progress from step 2 to step 5.

Step 2: Choose the menu commands File, Batch, Save. Click on the New button in the Batch Save dialog box that appears. Locate the folder you want to batch, click on it, and press the Append button. Then click Save. You now have the folder saved as a batch that can be group processed.

Step 3: Choose File, Batch, Super Palette and click Do It. The program will make a custom, adaptive palette (for more information on adaptive palettes, see Chapter 3, "Web File Formats") of all the images in your folder.

Step 4: Choose File, Batch Save, Do Script, Dither to Super Palette. This converts all the images in your folder to the adaptive palette.

Step 5: Next, open one of the images from your folder that's been converted to this new palette and go to the Palette menu.

Step 6: Choose Options, Dithering and Background Color. Check the Color Index radio button in the Dither Options & Background Color dialog box that appears. Use the Eyedropper Tool to select the color you want to make transparent in your image.

Step 7: Next, go to the File menu and Choose Batch, Save. Once this dialog is open, choose GIF89a as the file format. When you click the Do It button, it will convert the entire folder of images to transparent GIFs, dropping out the color you identified as the background color.

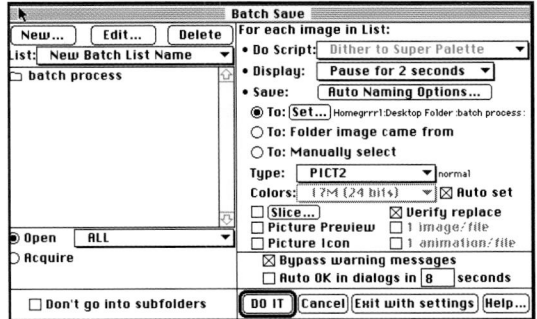

DeBabelizer lets you set up scripts, such as Dither to Super Palette (create a common CLUT from a series of images). Its interface is crowded and awkward, but you have to love what it does! A Windows version should be out by the time this book is published.

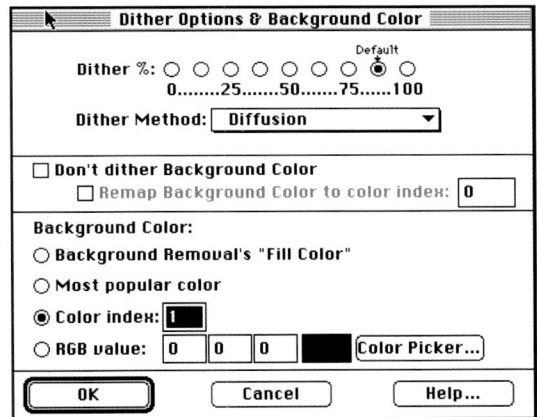

DeBabelizer offers a lot of different dithering and file reduction methods.

Windows

LView

Download LView from: ■ ftp://gatekeeper.dec.com/pub/ micro/msdos/win3/desktop/lview31.zip. It's shareware, costs $30 to register, and is written by Leonardo Haddad Loureiro (mmedia@world.std.com). To use, open your image, and under Options, choose Background color. The 256-color palette of that image opens. Choose white, black, or a specific color for your transparent selection. After you've made a selection, save as a GIF89a and you are done. You can also select Interlace from the Options menu if you want to interlace the file.

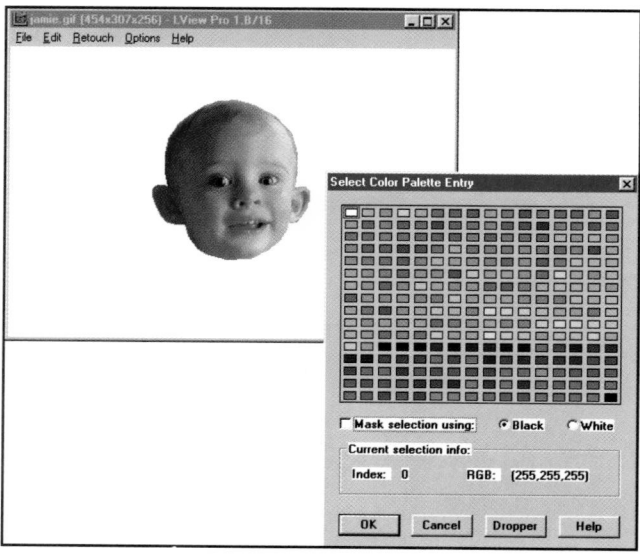

The LView interface with the color table for this image open to select a transparent color from.

GIF Construction Set

The GIF Construction Set—available from ■ ftp://ftp north.net/pub/alchemy—also makes transparent GIFs. If you open your GIF file, a script window appears. Under the Insert menu, select Control. This adds a Control command to the script window. Double-click on the word Control in the script window and a new window appears. When the transparent colour (French Canadian company and spelling) check box is marked, you can click on the colored square and the 256 palette of the image opens. From there, select the correct color, save as a GIF89a, and fait accompli!

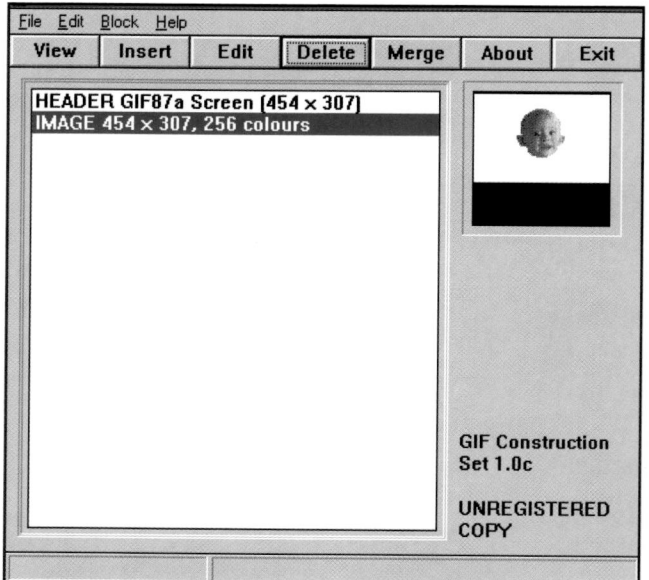

A sample of the GIF Construction Set interface. By adding a Control comment, the color table of this image will appear to allow you to select a color.

Paint Shop Pro

The very popular and reasonably priced Paint Shop Pro (version 3.11 and above) enables you to save TGIFs. You can download version 3.11 from ■ ftp://ftp.winternet.com/users/jasc/psp311.zip. The software can be used free for 30 days and then must be registered for $69.00. It does much more than saving GIFs—this is a full-bodied paint program that's offered for a fraction of the price of Photoshop (with not as much power, of course).

Open the file and determine whether you want white, black, or another color to be transparent. If you want another color, go to the Colors menu and select Edit Palette. Click around to locate the number (1–255) of the color. Next, go to Edit, do a Save As, and choose GIF-CompuServe as the file format. From the submenu that appears, choose either an interlaced or noninterlaced 89a. To set the color, click on the Options button, select the Set the Transparency Value to radio button, and enter the numeric value you found when you were in the Edit Palette mode. Where's the Eyedropper Tool when you need it?

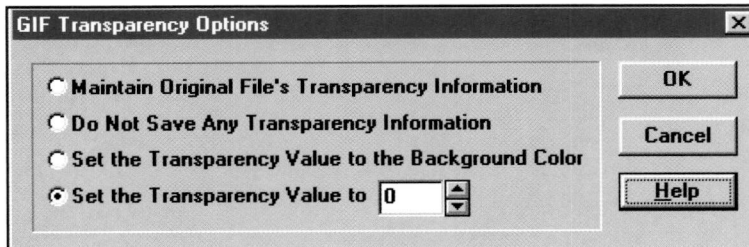

The GIF Transparency Options dialog box requests numeric values, instead of allowing designers to pick color from a palette or use an eyedropper.

8-Bit Transparency with PNG

As you've just seen, GIF transparency is limited and crude. There are workarounds, but who wants workarounds? If you want real transparency, you might want to work with the PNG file format instead of GIF for transparency.

PNG files can be saved with 8-bit masking channels, otherwise known as alpha channels. This next exercise will walk you through making a simple alpha channel in Photoshop.

Step-by-Step Alpha Channel Creation for PNG

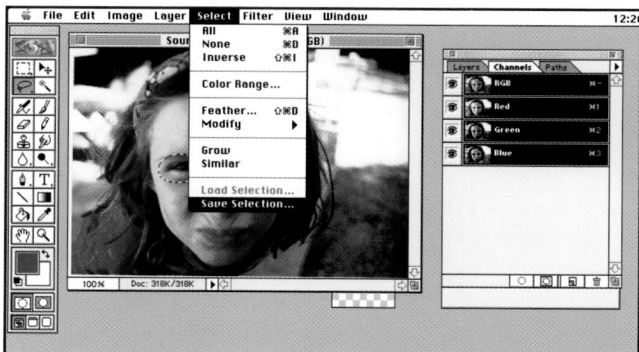

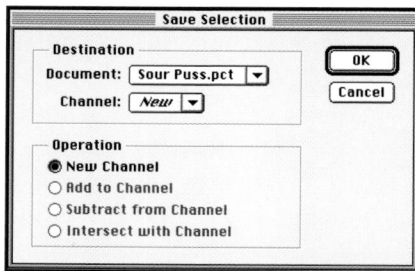

Step 1: In this example, I selected Jamie's eye using the Lasso Tool with a 20-pixel feather. Once the selection was completed, I chose Save Selection under the Select menu.

Step 2: The Save Selection dialog will appear. Click OK.

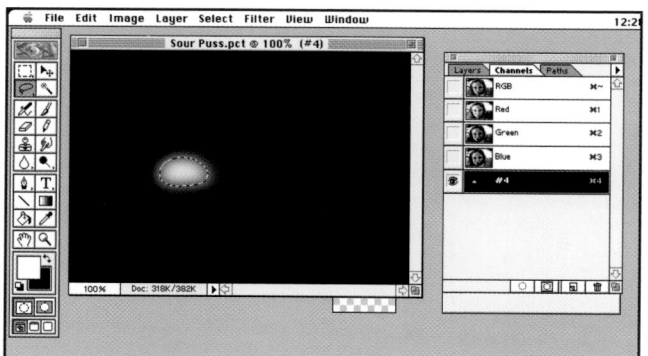

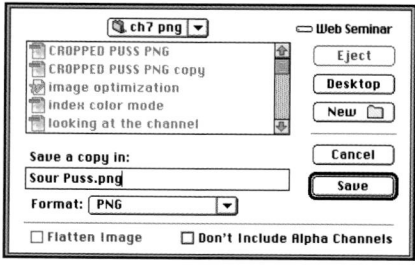

Step 3: If you switch the Layers Palette over to Channels and click on #4, you should see the 8-bit masking channel fill the screen. This mask will be used by the file format to cut away everything that is black. Everything that is white will be preserved, and the gray areas caused by the feather will create partial transparency.

Step 4: Make sure you leave the image in RGB mode, and don't check the Don't Include Alpha Channels check box.

Step 5: Open the PNG file and check the Channels Palette to see if it worked. It did!

Here's my finished home page with Jamie's menacing eye. This is the type of transparency possible with PNG. Because PNG required a plug-in when I wrote this chapter and was not supported by any browser, I had to use the <EMBED> tag to insert this into my HTML. In order to view this page, I used the plug-in from ■ http://iagu. on.net/jsam/png-plugin/.

PNG File Size

In spite of all the hype surrounding PNG, its file sizes are often bigger than JPEG or GIF. Be sure to check out the Image Compression Chart in Chapter 4, "Low-Bandwidth Graphics."

The PNG image with the alpha channel is 342k. Without it the image would be 308k. These images are too big by web standards. The only time PNG compared favorably to GIF or JPEG was when it was saved in 8-bit mode or lower bit depths. In order to save the alpha channel, the file has to be saved in 24-bit, so those file savings are not present when transparency is used.

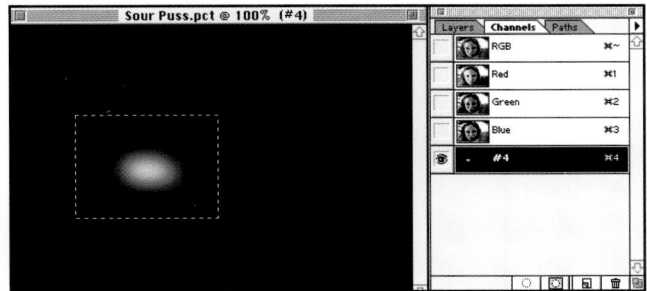

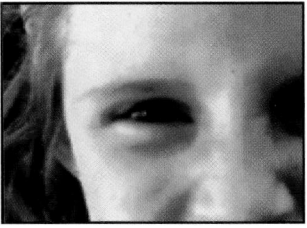

Here is the 342k PNG image with the alpha channel—it's a bit too large by web standards.

One solution to lower the file size would be to crop the image. I looked at the alpha channel while cropping, to make sure it was cropped properly.

Here's the final, cropped PNG, with alpha channel, weighing in at 42.6k.

BROWSER SAFE COLOR

33 FF

0033

<STRONG>

Width ="500"

.Jpg
.Png

IMAGE OPTIMIZATION

Colors

Web10   2d typography

<img src="

TRANSPARENCY

Height ="600"

10.2

Imaging techniques

Web file formats

bgcolor ="FFFFCC"

@link="cyan"

</center> BODY>

33

LYNDA.COM

Animation, sound and

www. Design

Making Background Tiles

Making full-screen, wall-to-wall graphics on the web would seem to be an impossible feat given the slow modems and teenie weenie phone lines most of us have to squeeze connections through. Not to mention the fact that full-screen graphics can mean one thing to a compact portable computer web user and another to someone with a 21" monitor! You might think it would take way too long to download an image that fills a viewer's browser screen and that it would be irresponsible to prepare images of this size for web graphics.

Repeated, tilable background patterns are the answer. This chapter covers an HTML tag called <BODY BACKGROUND>, which allows a single small image to be repeated endlessly so that it fills an entire web page, regardless of size. These single small images will be referred to in this chapter as tiled background patterns. They have the advantage of being small, so they load fast, and they include the capability to repeat over the size of whatever web screen they appear on. Because a small graphic loads faster than a big one, this technique works well to cover a lot of real estate on a web page without incurring a lot of overhead in downloading time.

This chapter will examine the following aspects of tiled background pattern creation:

- How to make pattern-based images
- How to make seamless patterns
- How to know what size to make the source pattern image
- What file format to save patterns in
- How to write the HTML to place patterned tile images on a web page

Tiling Backgrounds

The <BODY BACKGROUND> tag enables the browser to repeat a small graphic and turn it into a full-screen graphic. It accomplishes this effect by taking a single image and tiling it, creating a repeating image that will fill any size screen regardless of computer platform and browser area. The browser needs to load only a single source file for the pattern, and once it's downloaded, it fills the entire web page. This saves time because the wait time is for a single small image, even though the result is that the entire screen fills with an image. Repeated tiles are a great solution for creating full-screen graphics for low-bandwidth delivery systems such as the web.

This example shows the source tile artwork.

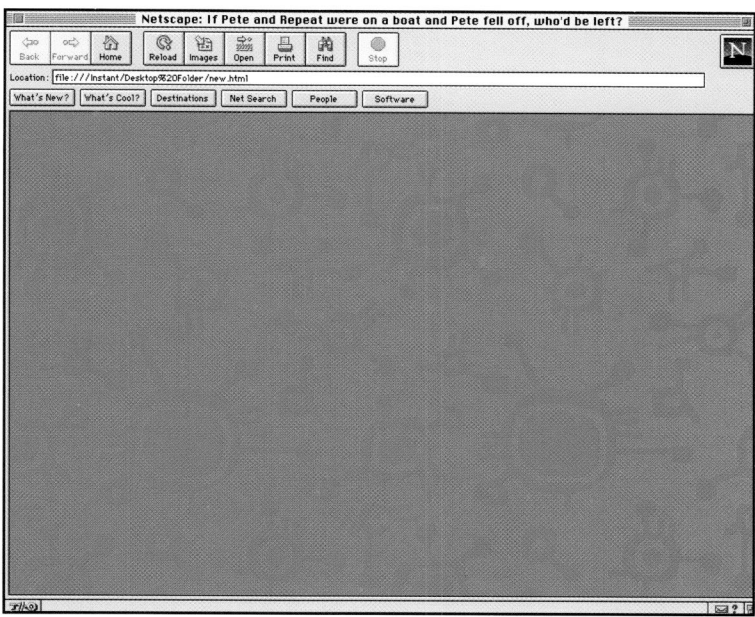

Here, the artwork is repeated inside the browser window, creating the illusion or a much larger graphic.

Bandwidth limitations aren't the only problem that tiled background patterns solve. One of the great frustrations most web designers share is HTML's inability to allow for images to be layered. If you consider that layering is a main feature of programs such as Photoshop, QuarkXPress, and PageMaker, you'll understand why the this feature in HTML is sorely missed. Cascading style sheets are the answer to some designers' layering needs, but using tiled background patterns is, for the moment, still a much easier route.

HTML allows text, links, and images to go on top of tiled backgrounds, making it an extremely useful and economical design element. The HTML code for this tiling effect is quite simple. The real challenge is making the art look good and controlling whether the seams of each repeated image are obvious or invisible.

Determining Tiled Pattern Sizes

One of the first questions that comes to mind is, how big should a tiled image be? HTML puts no restrictions on the size of a source for a background tile. The image has to be in a square or rectangular, however, because that's the native shape of any computer file.

The size of the image is entirely up to you. You should realize that the size of a tile is going to dictate how many times it repeats. If a viewer's monitor is 640x480 pixels and your tile is 320x240, it will repeat 4 times. If it were 20x20 pixels, it would repeat 32 times.

If your tile has images that repeat on each side, it will not show visible seams and the viewer will not know how many times it repeats. If the image has an obvious border around it, the border will accentuate the fact that the image is being tiled. The size of your tile is up to you and the effect you are striving for.

Be aware, however, that file size restrictions must still be honored. If you create a tile that takes up a lot of memory, it will take the same amount of time to load as any other kind of huge graphic you put on the web. If need be, refer back to Chapter 4, "Low-Bandwidth Graphics," for methods to minimize file sizes.

When you use an image source that has large dimensions, it will not repeat as often. If it is large enough, it will not repeat at all. In that event, the speed advantages of having a small image load once and automatically repeat without incurring any additional downloading time would not exist. On the other hand, if you could make a large graphic in dimensions and not file size, then loading it in as a background image instead of a regular graphic could have its merits. Sometimes the pixel size count of a document and the amount of memory they take up are not relational, as you'll see in the upcoming section of this chapter "Full-Screen Body Background?"

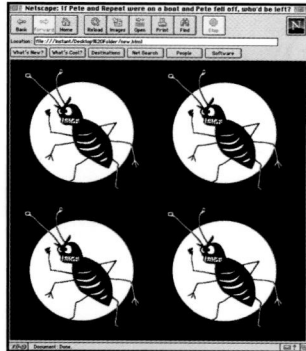

Large Source File   **Results**

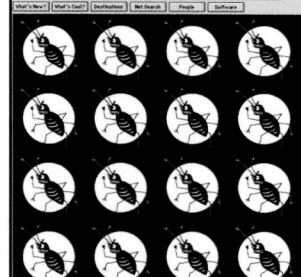

**Medium
Source File**   **Results**

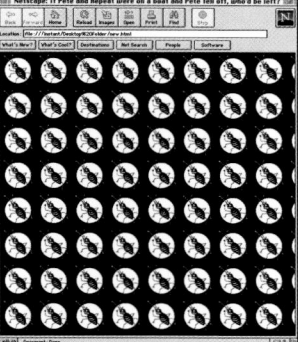

Small Source File   **Results**

File Formats for
Patterned Background Tiles

GIFs and JPEGs are the standard file formats for the web, and tiled patterns are no exception. Just remember to follow the kilobyte rule. Every kilobyte of file size represents one second of download time to your viewer. The full size of the background pattern gets added to the download! If you have a background that's 60k and two images that are 10k each, the total file size of your page will be 80k. You would have just added a minute of download time to your page! Therefore, tiled backgrounds that take up a lot of memory are extra annoying to your audience during download.

Be careful if you are trying to match foreground and background tile images. They must both be the same file format—GIF and GIF or JPEG and JPEG—if you want the colors to match perfectly.

As usual, always save your file names in lowercase and use the extensions .jpg or .gif to let the HTML code know what kind of image it has to load. I usually put the word pat somewhere in a pattern file name, just for my own reference. That way I know what I intended to use the file for when searching for it in a text list, such as my server directory!

The Code, Please!

It is very simple to include a patterned background in an HTML document. Here's the bare minimum code required:

```
       <HTML>
 1     <BODY BACKGROUND="pat.gif">
       </BODY>
       </HTML>
```

pat.gif
image

Here's the final result of using the <BODY BACK-GROUND="pat.gif"> tag.

1 The **<BODY BACKGROUND>** tag enables you to add a background tile to the page. The "pat.gif" is the name of the image being tiled in this example.

If you wanted to have an image lay over a background, the code would look like this:

```
<HTML>
<BODY BACKGROUND="pat.gif">
<IMG SRC="jamie.gif">
</BODY>
</HTML>
```
1

If you wanted HTML text and an image to lay over a background, the code would look like this:

```
<HTML>
<BODY BACKGROUND="pat.gif">
<CENTER>
<B><FONTSIZE=4>Hi Mom!</FONT></B>
<IMG SRC="graphic.gif">
</BODY>
</HTML>
```
1

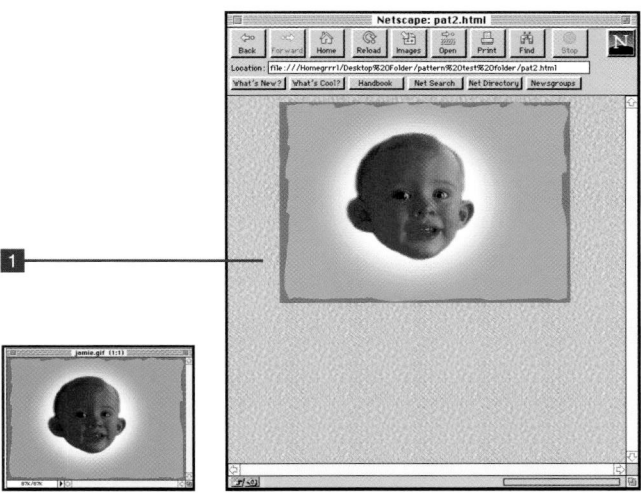

jamie.gif document

The finished web page with the <IMG SRC="jamie.gif"> tag.

1 The **<IMG SRC>** tag enables you to include an image that will lay over the background tile.

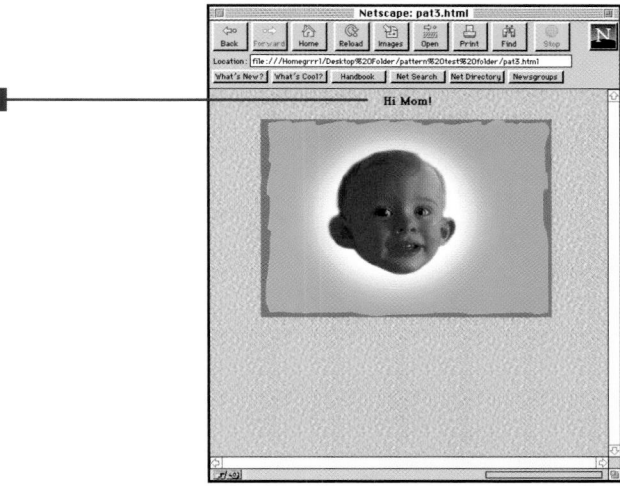

The finished web page with text added.

1 The **<B><FONTSIZE=4>**Hi Mom!**</FONT></B>** tag is adding the text "Hi Mom" to the page.

Seams or No Seams, That Is the Question

The next sections take a look at two different ways to present your background tile on your web page: with or without seams.

Seams

When an image has obvious seams, it looks tiled on purpose. Some web pages look great wallpapered with an obvious border. Andy Warhol shocked the art world in the 1960s and first earned his notoriety by making images of repeating soup cans on a single canvas. Video walls are often built on the power of images repeating in squares. There's nothing wrong with making patterns that have obvious borders and repeats, especially if that's what you have in mind. Making a tiled pattern with an obvious repeating border is fairly simple.

Source File

Results

Aesthetics of Backgrounds

Always pay attention to contrast and value (lights and darks) when creating background tiles. If you have a light background, use dark type. If you have a dark background, use light type. If you aren't going to change your browser's default colors for text, links, visited links, and active links, use a light background—about the same value as the default light gray you see as the background color of most browsers. The light background will ensure that the default colors of black, blue, and purple text will read against your custom background.

When making art for pattern tiles, try to use either all dark values or all light values. If you have both darks and lights in a background, neither light nor dark type will work consistently against them. This is a basic, simple rule to follow, and your site will avoid the pitfalls of poor background tile aesthetics. Using either all dark values or all light values seems like common sense, but tour the web a bit and you'll soon see rainbow colored backgrounds with unreadable black type everywhere.

Make sure your images read. I don't mean your tiles should go to school to learn phonetics or anything—instead I'm talking about readablity of image versus background. The examples of the cockroach tile, shown earlier, have great contrast and "read" as a cockroach image, but the second you try to put type over them, they will not "read" anymore.

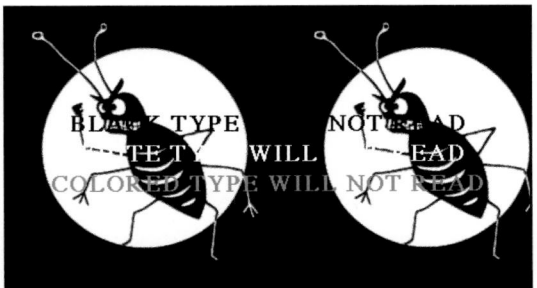

When the background is black and white, nothing reads well on top of it.

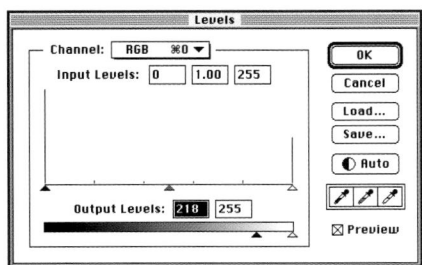

Using the Adjust Levels, Output Levels in Photoshop, it's possible to lighten or darken the overall contrast of the source image for the tile.

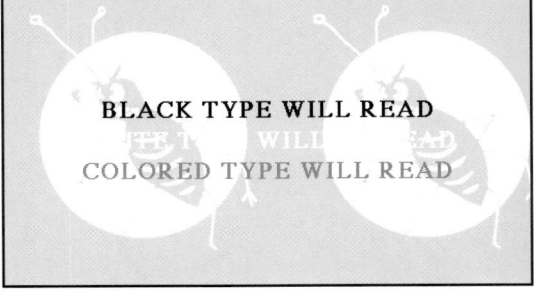

While it might seem obvious, dark and medium value colors will read over a light background.

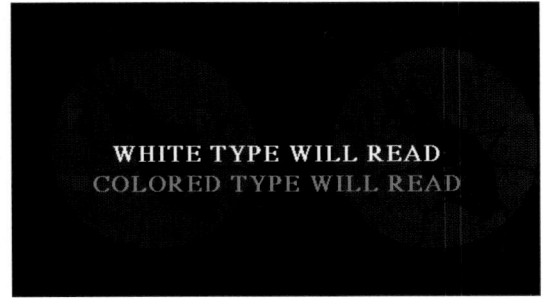

With a dark background, the reverse is true. It's not enough to make a cool-looking background tile—always check to make sure your type reads over it as well! If it doesn't read, make the necessary adjustments to the type color or contrast of the background image.

No Seams, the Photoshop Way

When "seamless" patterns are described, it means the border of the pattern tile is impossible to locate. There aren't any pros or cons to using seamless or seamed tiles; it's purely an aesthetic decision. Seamless tiles, however, are much trickier to make.

Here's a step-by-step example of the Photoshop techniques Bruce Heavin uses to make his amazing seamless pattern artwork.

Bruce began by drawing the stars inside this 400x400, 72 dpi file.

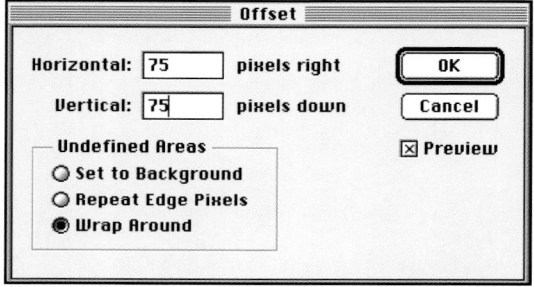

Using the Offset filter in Photoshop (Under Filter, Other, Offset), Bruce entered the settings 75 pixels right, with 75 pixels down, using the Wrap Around method.

The setting Bruce entered in the Offset filter caused the image to shift position. He then added more stars.

Bruce reapplied the Offset filter and drew more stars to fill in the holes in the image that became visible.

Here is the finished tile. Without the Offset filter, Bruce would have never been able to see the edges of this image in order to design them so they wouldn't show.

Once the tile was finished, Bruce used the Magic Wand, at a tolerance of one, to select the stars and white space. He then filled them with browser-safe colors.

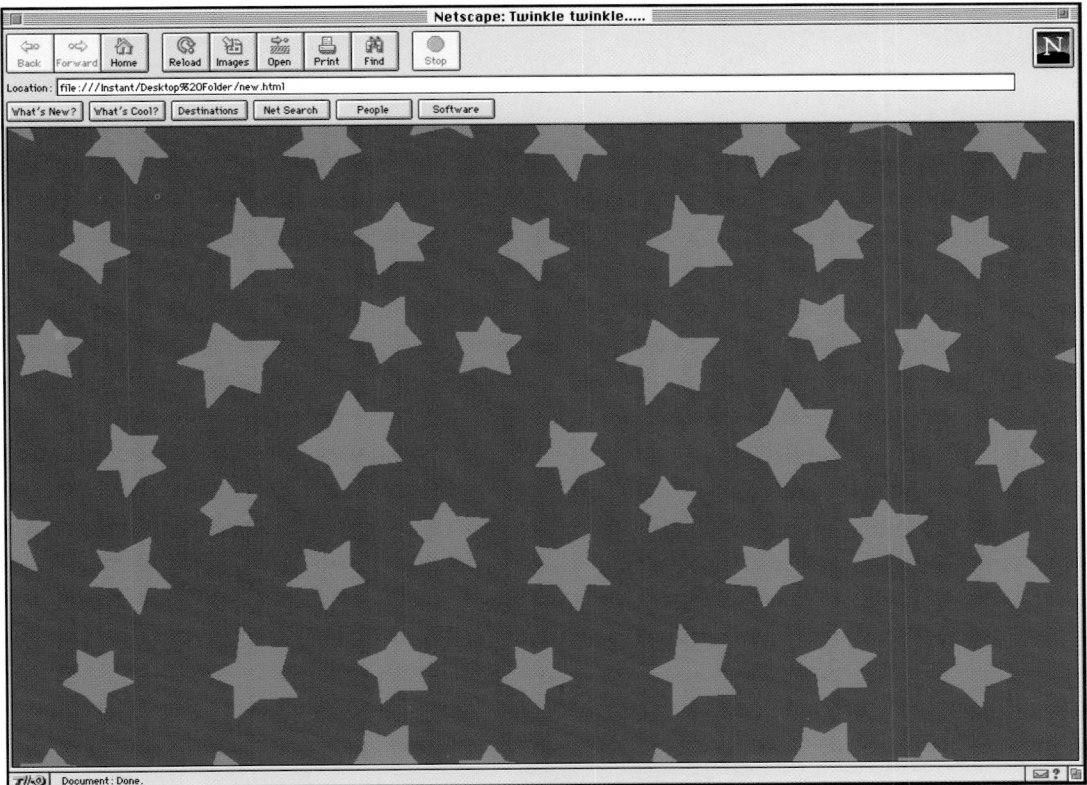

The final result. It's extremely difficult to find the repeats or edges in a successful seamless tile.

No Seams, the Painter 4.0 Way

Fractal Design Painter 4.0 is an excellent environment to create seamless tiles in. If you open a new document and choose Tools, Patterns, Define Pattern before you draw, Painter will do an automatic offset filter process, similar to Photoshop's, but in real time. If you move your mouse or stylus off a corner on one side, your stroke will automatically appear on the other. It's like drawing with a mirroring tool. It's kind of hard to control, but very fun to experiment with. Here's the step-by-step process:

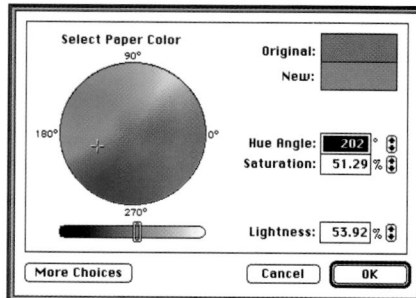

Step 1: Open a new document in Painter at 300x300 at 72 dpi. **Step 2:** Select a paper color.

Step 3: Go to the Art Materials Palette and select a paper stock.

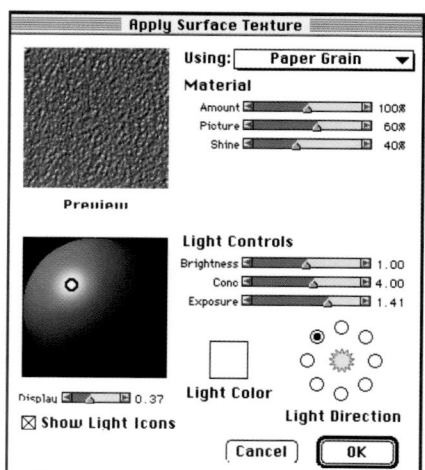

Step 4: Under Effects, Surface Control, Apply Surface Texture, create the lighting effect you want to use to create a textured paper effect. **Step 5:** Go to Tools, Patterns, Define Pattern.

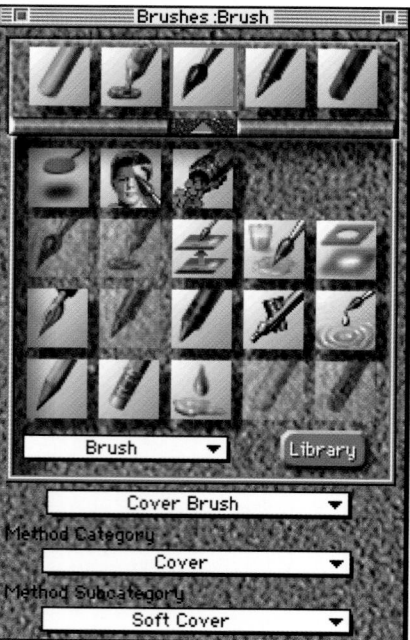

Step 6: Choose a drawing tool. I've chosen to use the Chalk Tool.

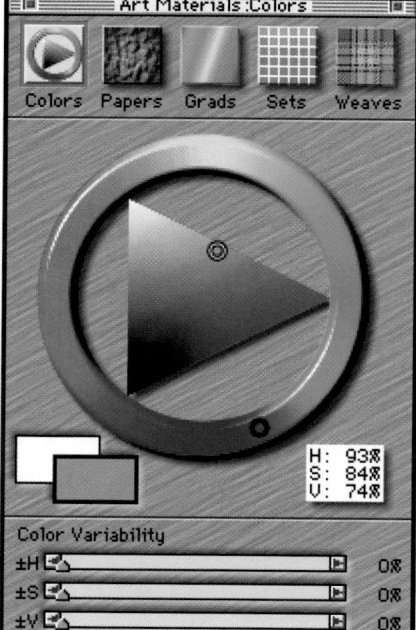

Step 7: Pick a color from the Art Materials, Colors Palette.

Step 8: Start to draw. Your brush strokes will automatically mirror and repeat on the opposite side, creating a seamless pattern. **Step 9:** When you're happy with the results, save the pattern as a .jpg or a .gif.

Step 10: Put the pattern on a web page by using the HTML you learned in the previous sections.

There's much more that can be done with Painter than I have room to show here. Look for books on Painter in the bookstore, and check out Fractal Design's web site at ■ http://www.fractal.com for product announcements, upgrades, lots of tips, and a gallery of artwork created by Painter artists.

■ **tip**

Recommended Reading

Painter Wow! Book
Publisher: PeachPit Press
Author: Cher Threinen-Pendarvis
Retail Price: $39.95 ■ ISBN: 1-56609-147-0

**Fractal Design Painter
Creative Techniques**
Publisher: Hayden Books
Author: Jeremy Sutton
Retail Price: $45.00 ■ ISBN: 1-56830-283-5

Full-Screen Body Backgrounds?

Why would you use an image with large pixel dimensions as a tiled background, as it seems to defeat the point? Because it could go behind other images and text, making full-screen backdrop to other images on your page. HTML doesn't easily let you put text or images over regular images. The easiest way around this restriction is to use a background tiled graphic.

Here's the full-screen (800x600 pixel) graphic that Bruce used on a web page (now extinct) for *The Net* magazine. It is only 11.6k because there are very few colors in it.

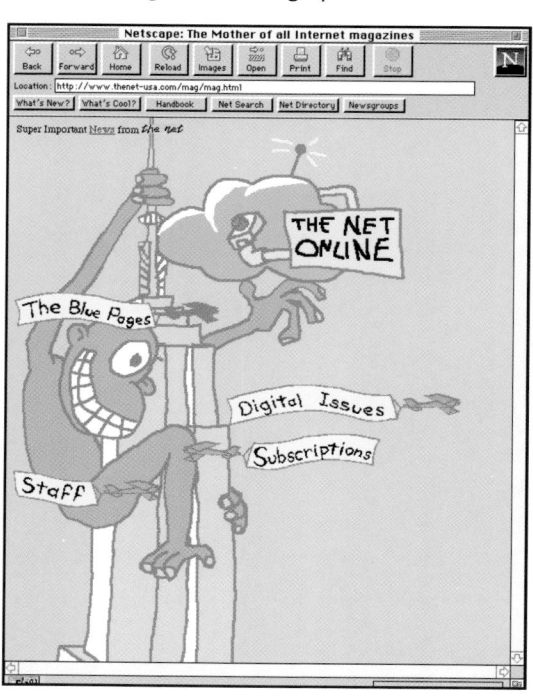

With other images laid over the full-screen background, this is a very effective and economical use of a large background tile.

Here's an example of a 24.7k JPEG image used as a background image for Art Center's site.

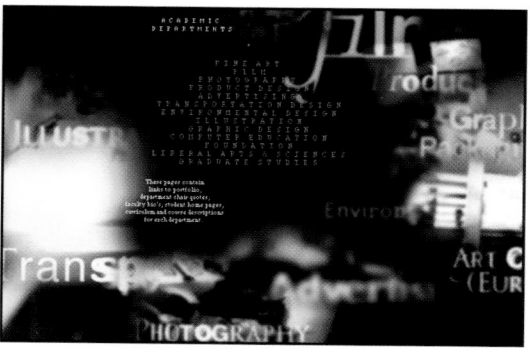

Combined with HTML text, this page looks rich and layered, and is not too large to download.

Other Tricks with Background Tiles

When background tiles load, they usually do so in one fell swoop, where you don't notice which direction they're loading from. This is not the case, however, if you make a really skinny background tile.

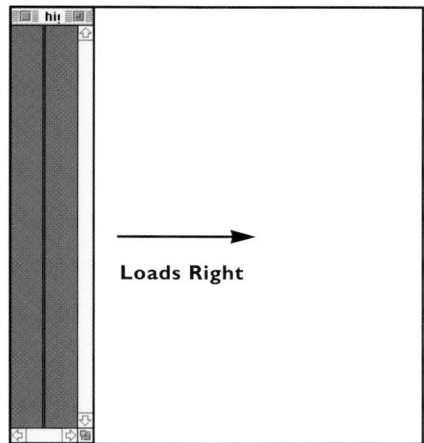

Loads Right

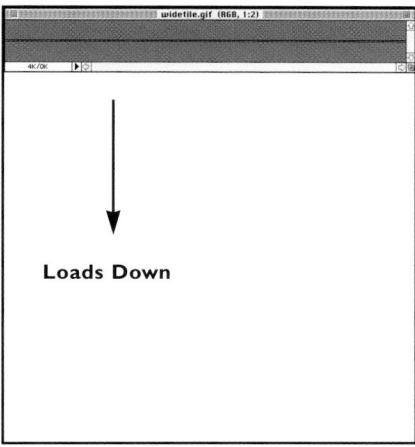

Loads Down

The vertical tile will load left to right, looking like an animated wipe. The horizontal tile will load top to bottom, looking like an animated wipe. These images are only one pixel wide or high. Warning: while this effect is interesting the first time around, it can be very annoying on slow connections or on a page that is visited frequently.

You can also design background images so that they have runners going down their left side. Below are some examples of the source images and the resulting effect they have in the browser window.

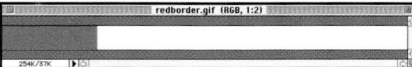
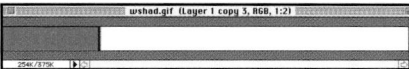
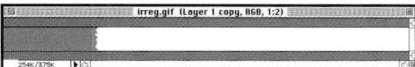

Source Tiles

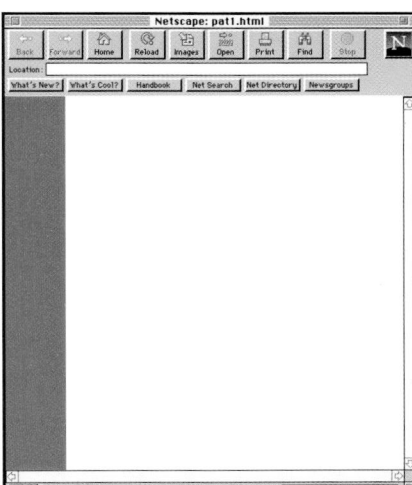
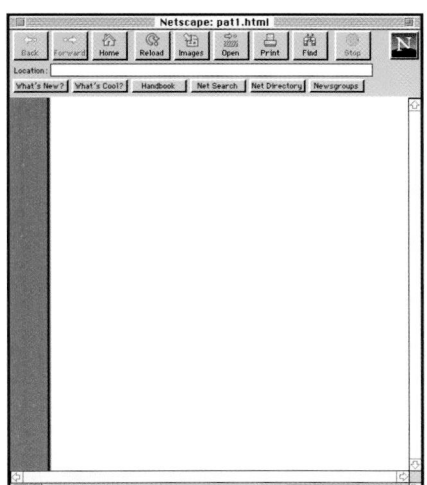

Results

9

BROWSER SAFE COLOR
33FF
0033

Width ="500"

Height ="600"

<STRONG>

IMAGE OPTIMIZATION

Imaging techniques

File Formats

alink="cyan"

Animation, sound and

LYNDA.COM

www.Design

<BODY>

<TAB
</TAB>

<img src=

33

Rules, Bullets, and Buttons

Web graphics have coined a few graphic conventions of their own, such as horizontal rules, bullets and buttons. This chapter examines the reasons behind these conventions, and the techniques and tools required to implement them.

Horizontal Rules

A horizontal rule that serves as a page divider is something you'll rarely see in print design. These divider lines are commonly observed across web sites the world over, however. Some are embossed, some are thick, some are thin, and some are colored or have different shapes. The web term for these lines is horizontal rule, and they are used for many things:

- Defining a page break
- Completing an idea
- Beginning a list
- Separating one picture from another

Horizontal rules are used often; some might even say too often. That's no wonder, if you ask me. Web pages have no set length like printed pages. The visual techniques and metaphors available to print designers—such as using a block of color behind text or images, changing the text color in an isolated paragraph or sidebar, or using a different screened-back image or picture frame to separate an idea or theme—are not easily replicated on the web.

If you want to add horizontal rules to your pages, you have some choices. You can use HTML code, or you can insert your own artwork to make custom horizontal rules, and vertical rules, too. When all else fails, there are also libraries of horizontal rule clip art.

Horizontal Rules, the HTML Way

The basic HTML standard horizontal rule tag looks like this: <HR>. Here it is in the context of code:

```
<HTML>
<BODY>
Some Text
<HR>
Some More Text
</BODY>
</HTML>
```

Some Text
_____
Some More Text

This will put an embossed, double-pixel line horizontally through your page at whatever point you insert it into an HTML document. If you stretch your browser window wider, the horizontal rule will get wider; vice versa if you narrow your window. Horizontal rules have no set width, except to fill the horizontal distance of your browser screen.

Sometimes you might want to add some breathing room because the horizontal rule will butt up underneath whatever text or image that was in the HTML code before it. The following code adds a row of empty space above and beneath the rule:

```
<HTML>
<BODY>
Some Text
<P>
<HR>
<P>
Some More Text
</BODY>
</HTML>
```

Some Text

_____

Some More Text

If you want to add more breathing room between your text and rules, insert a paragraph break with the <P> tag.

Fancier Horizontal Rule Tags

An advanced course in horizontal rule-making would include:

- Changing the rule's width
- Changing the rule's weight (thickness)
- Changing both the rule's width and weight
- Left-aligning the rule
- Eliminating fake emboss shading

<HR WIDTH=10 SIZE=400> Horizontal rules don't have to be horizontal, if you know how to change the width and size.

Here's the code telling the rule to be 25 pixels wide:

```
<HR WIDTH=25>
```

Using a WIDTH attribute can adjust the length of the line. Notice that if you define a width, the resulting horizontal rule is automatically centered. Any value you put after the = (equals) sign tells the rule how wide to be in pixels.

The following code changes the weight, or thickness, of the line. Notice that this stretches the length of a page.

```
<HR SIZE=10>
```

By changing the size attribute, the entire line gets thicker.

The following code changes the thickness and width at the same time. Here's an example that shows the results of code specifying the rule to be a square—equal height and width:

```
<HR SIZE=25 WIDTH=25>
```

By changing the size and width together, you can make other rectalinear shapes like this square.

The following aligns the square left and sizes it at 25 pixels high and 25 pixels wide:

```
<HR ALIGN=left SIZE=10 WIDTH=10>
```

You can use alignment tags on horizontal rules, too.

Look Ma, no fake emboss shading!

```
<HR NOSHADE>
```

The NOSHADE attribute creates a black line.

Horizontal Rules the Do-It-Yourself Way

Anything gets old when you see it too often, and horizontal rules are no exception. If you want to be a little more creative, some tips follow for creating custom artwork. When you create your own horizontal rule art, your artwork dictates the length, width, and height. It's a graphic like any other graphic. It can be aliased, anti-aliased, a GIF, a JPEG, interlaced, transparent, blurred, 2D, 3D—you name it. If you know how to make it, it can be a horizontal rule.

To include a graphic as a horizontal rule, the HTML code would be

```
<IMG SRC="your_horizontal_rule_art_here.gif">
```

Using Illustrator and Photoshop to Create Custom Horizontal Rule Art

Adobe Illustrator has lots of features that are wonderful for making horizontal rules. I've used some of my favorites in this chapter. Filters, for example, are great for making quick and easy art. I used the spiral, free polygon, and star filters found under the Filter, Create heading of the Filters menu. I also like to draw free-hand with my pressure-sensitive tablet by using the Brush Tool in Illustrator. You can set the line to have thick and thin weights, thereby lessening the predictably uniform, perfectly symmetrical look that Illustrator files so often have. A neat way to repeat a piece of art along a horizontal axis in Illustrator is to copy it, place the copy next to the original at a set distance, and then use the Duplicate command to repeat the established offset indefinitely.

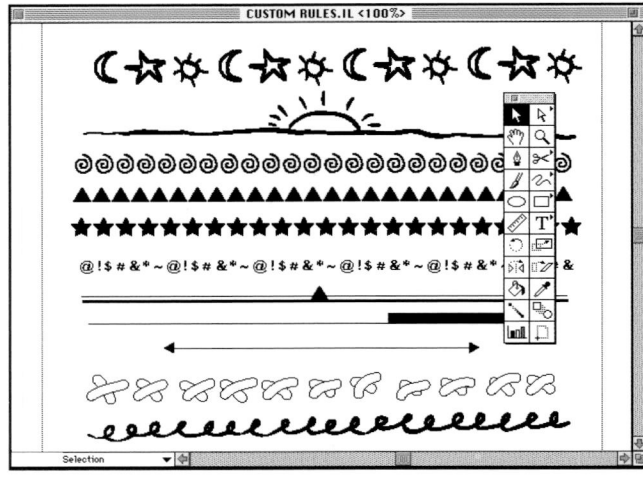

This image shows a sampling of some of my favorite Illustrator techniques. Illustrator artwork can be imported into Photoshop, as described in the following case study of making custom horizontal rule art using Illustrator and Photoshop.

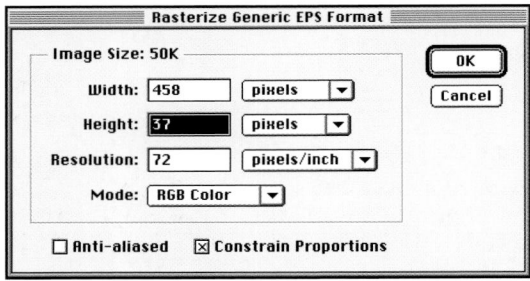

Whenever you open an Illustrator formatted file into Photoshop, this Rasterize dialog box appears (this is a screen capture using Photoshop 4.0; earlier versions of Photoshop have a similar window). Illustrator artwork must be rasterized before Photoshop will work with it. I chose to not check the Anti-aliased box so that these graphics would be smaller when saved. (See Chapter 4, "Low-Bandwidth Graphics," for more tips on making low-memory graphics.)

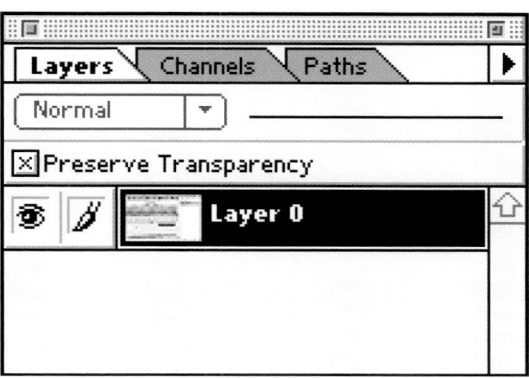

When artwork is placed on a transparent layer in Photoshop, you can modify its color easily. Check the Preserve Transparency box found in the upper left-hand area of the Layers Palette and then paint on the image area. Notice the object is masked to accept color only where there's an image. This allows you to paint the black areas of the horizontal rule line, without worrying about painting outside the shapes created in Illustrator.

Notice that the file came into Photoshop as black and white, against a checkerboard background. This means that it's on a transparent layer, which is going to help me out tremendously when I go to color them.

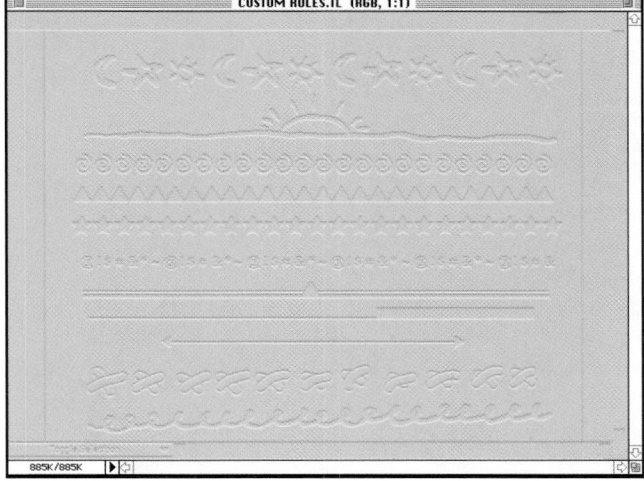

Here is the final, painted result with a gray background inserted as a second layer behind the colored layer in Photoshop.

I also thought it would be funny to use this same artwork to poke fun at the "embossed" nature of typical web horizontal rules. I used the RGB value 192 192 192 to approximate the color of a typical gray background of a web page. I took a screen capture of a web page (Command Shift+3 on a Mac and F13 or the Print Screen button on a PC), pulled it into Photoshop, and used the Eyedropper Tool in Photoshop to get the RGB values of the highlight and shadow colors of the standard embossed horizontal rules. (Shadow: 252 242 243; Midtone: 241 241 241; Highlight: 234 234 234). I copied the layer I brought in from Illustrator three times and, using the Preserve Transparency feature, filled each layer respectively with a shadow, midtone, and highlight color. By selecting the Move Tool and using arrow keys on my keyboard, I was able to nudge the layers up and down to create the emboss effect. Here are those final results.

You may not realize that one standard gray background color does not exist on the web. This is because the default gray browser background is not a cross-platform, browser-safe color as described in Chapter 6, "Browser-Safe Color." The differences between grays on multiple platforms are not major, however, and once I chose to save my file with a transparent background (see Chapter 7, "Transparent Artwork,") the slight variations in gray are going to go unnoticed to my unassuming web audience. Now the rule is ready for use.

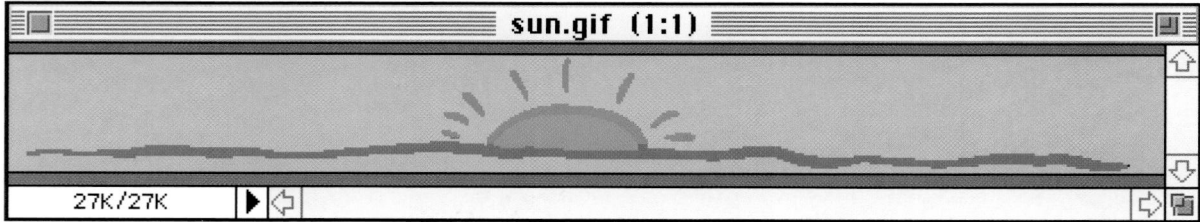

After I'm done, I can copy and paste each horizontal rule into its own file and save it. I think saving the rules as transparent GIFs (see Chapter 7, "Transparent Artwork") makes the most sense because I want the irregularly shaped lines to look like they're floating freely on my web pages.

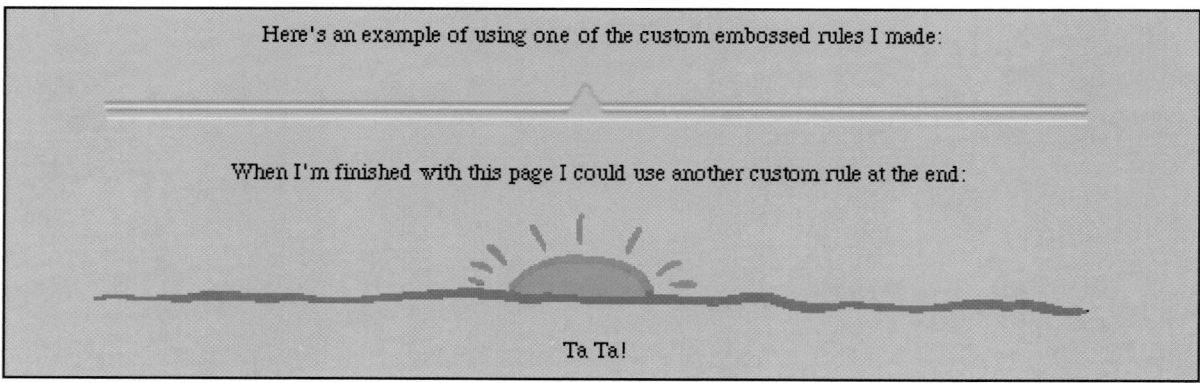

Here's an example of a finished page that uses my custom fake embossed rule.

Vertical Rules

Vertical rules are not an easy task to implement on web pages. Making the custom artwork is identical to making any other custom artwork and all the Photoshop and Illustrator tips shared in this book should be of help. The trick is understanding how to get vertical lines aligned to a web page because there is no easy way to assign vertical columns using HTML. There's a lesson on how to position vertical ruled lines in Chapter 13, "Layout and Alignment Techniques."

Clip Art Rules, Too

There are many kind, generous souls on the web who lend their wares for free. Or other gifted souls who might charge for their art so that they can do what they're good at—satisfy you and me—and still feed themselves and their families. Clip art is a wondrous thing in a pinch, and with tools such as Photoshop, Illustrator, and Painter, there's no end to the cool ways you can personalize clip art files further. Make sure that the images are royalty free in the respective licensing agreements if you are going to modify them. Some artists inclue legal stipulations that must be honored. Read the readmes!

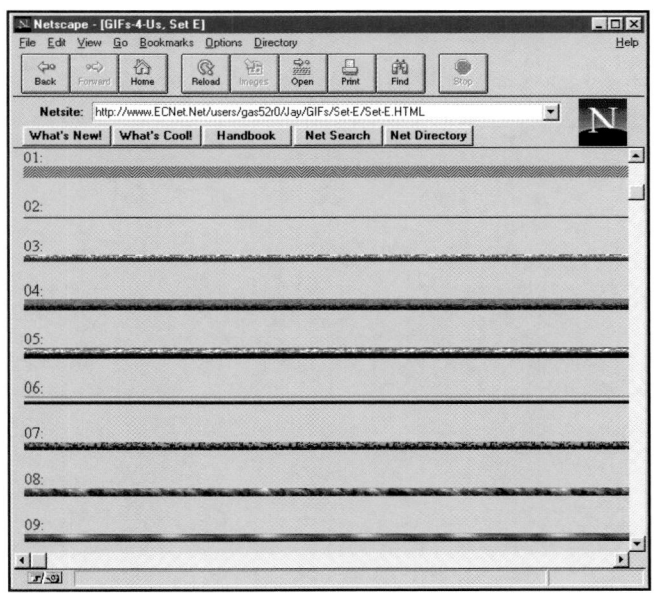

A sample from Jay Boersma's great shareware clip art collection.

■ **tip**

Clip Art

Here are some collections that I think are cool:

Gifs R Us—Jay Boersma's prolific image collection
■ http://www.ecn.bgu.edu/users/gas52r0/Jay/home.html

Sandra's Clip Art Server—a great resource for clip art
■ http://www.cs.yale.edu/homes/sjl/clipart.html

Buttons, Cubes, and Bars—Chris Stephens' great collection of custom art
■ http://www.cbil.vcu.edu.8080/gifs/bullet.html

Yahoo search, Clip Art—the latest clip art listings
■ http://www.yahoo.com/Computers_and_Internet/ Multimedia/ Pictures/Clip_Art/

Bullets

You'll see plenty of pages with diverse information content on the web, but lists of one type or another are universally needed on the majority of sites. List items can appear indented with numbers or preceded by icons known as bullets. Bullets on the web can look standardized, using solid circles in front of text (much like those generated by a word processor), or they can include custom artwork that looks more typical of a CD-ROM or magazine page layout. Creating custom bullets is similar to creating custom horizontal rules. Basically, any artwork that you're capable of creating is a candidate for bullet art.

When designing bulleted lists for the web, you can choose from either HTML bullets or image-based bullets. HTML bullets are created by using code tags that identify the type of list you are creating; such bullets appear as basic circles or squares. Image-based bullets are those you generate from clip art or your own artwork, and they can be used to enhance a list or provide added functionality, such as links. This next section shows you how to create both HTML and image-based bullets, including several variations on both themes.

Creating HTML Bulleted Lists

Using HTML-based bullets is certainly less work than creating your own custom artwork. Sometimes, they're more appropriate, as well. Simple and clean design often looks best without a lot of custom artwork on a page. There will be many instances where an HTML-based bullet or indent will do the job more effectively than custom bullet artwork.

To create a list with solid circle bullets use the <UL> tag, which stands for unorganized list. To create such a bulleted list within text items, use the <UL> tag along with the <LI> (list item) tag, as shown in the following code:

```
<P>
<UL>
<LI> The first thinga-dingy
<LI> The second thinga-dingy
<LI> The third thinga-dingy
</UL>
```

Using the "unordered" list tags , and "list item" tags produces this result:

- The first thinga-dingy
- The second thinga-dingy
- The third thinga-dingy

The results of using the <UL> tag.

Lists can be nested by inserting a new tag where you want the list to indent or move to another level. The following code uses an additional <UL> tag to create a bulleted list nested within another bulleted list:

```
<P>
<UL>
<LI> The first thinga-dingy
<LI> The second thinga-dingy
<LI> The third thinga-dingy
<UL>
<LI> More types of thinga-dingies
<LI> Yet More types of thinga-dingies
<LI> Even more types of thinga-dingies
</UL>
```

You can nest lists within lists, by repeating the "ordered" or "unordered" list tags. The results look like this:

- The first thinga-dingy
- The second thinga-dingy
- The third thinga-dingy
  - More types of thinga-dingies
  - Yet More types of thinga-dingies
  - Even more types of thinga-dingies

You can nest bulleted points, by adding multiple <UL> tags before the close </UL> tag.

You can have the items in your list be links to other pages or sites by using the <A HREF></A> tag within an organized list or an unorganized list. The following code shows how to use link tags to include links within a bulleted list:

```
<P>
<UL>
<LI> <A HREF="http://www.domain.com">The first
thinga-dingy</A>
<LI> <A HREF="http://www.domain.com">The second
thinga-dingy</A>
<LI> <A HREF="http://www.domain.com">The third
thinga-dingy</A>
</UL>
```

Including links within a list is a matter of using link tags within lists. The results look like this:

- The first thinga-dingy
- The second thinga-dingy
- The third thinga-dingy

The items in your list can be straight text or hypertext by changing a few tags.

Creating Ordered and Definition Lists

At times, you might not want your lists to be preceded with bullets. When creating a list of steps to be followed in order, for example, using numbers rather than bullets will help get your point across. Such numbered lists are called ordered lists. Likewise, lists such as glossaries can appear with indents rather than bullets or numbers. These lists are known as definition lists.

To make a list that automatically generates numbers in front of its items, use the <OL> (ordered list) tag. The following code lines show how to use the <OL> code to produce a numbered list:

```
<P>
<OL>
<LI> The first thinga-dingy
<LI> The second thinga-dingy
<LI> The third thinga-dingy
</OL>
<P>
```

Using the "ordered list" would automatically generate numbers, instead of bullets in front of each "list item":

1. The first thinga-dingy
2. The second thinga-dingy
3. The third thinga-dingy

The <OL> tag generates ordered (numbered) lists.

If you want to indent items in a list without seeing a bullet shape, you may want to use a <DL> (definition list) tag instead of creating an organized list or unorganized list. You use the <DT> tag for the flush left items and the <DD> tag for the indented items, as shown in the following code.

```
<DL>
<DT>
Thingy Dingies<P>
<DD>The first thinga-dingy
<DD>The second thinga-dingy
<DD>The second thinga-dingy
</DL>
```

Thingy Dingies

The first thinga-dingy
The second thinga-dingy
The second thinga-dingy

Using the <DL> definition list tags creates indented lists.

If you want to change the shape of the automatically generated bullets, you can use the <TYPE=circle> or <TYPE=square> tags, as shown in the following code:

```
<UL>
<LI TYPE=circle>Circle-shaped Bullet
<LI TYPE=square>Square-shaped Bullet
</UL>
```

● Circle-shaped Bullet
□ Square-shaped Bullet

Using the TYPE attribute, you can change the shape of HTML generated bullets.

You can also set up organized lists by using alphabetic and roman numeric criteria by adding the variations shown in the following table:

Tag	List Type	Example
<TYPE=1>	Numbers	1, 2, 3
<TYPE=A>	Uppercase letters	A, B, C
<TYPE=a>	Lowercase letters	a, b, c
<TYPE=I>	Uppercase Roman numerals	I, II, III
<TYPE=i>	Lowercase Roman numerals	i, ii, iii

The following code shows variations of the <TYPE> tag, which produces these results:

```
<OL>
<LI TYPE=1> Thingy One
<LI TYPE=1> Thingy Two
<LI TYPE=1> Thingy Three
<P>
<LI TYPE=A> Thingy One
<LI TYPE=A> Thingy Two
<LI TYPE=A> Thingy Three
<P>
<LI TYPE=a> Thingy One
<LI TYPE=a> Thingy Two
<LI TYPE=a> Thingy Three
<P>
<LI TYPE=I> Thingy One
<LI TYPE=I> Thingy Two
<LI TYPE=I> Thingy Three
<P>
<LI TYPE=i> Thingy One
<LI TYPE=i> Thingy Two
<LI TYPE=i> Thingy Three
```

An example of all the different types of HTML-generated bullets.

Creating Custom-Made Bullets

If you want to use bullets that show more creativity than the basic square or circle, or if you need added linking functionality, you can create your own custom-made bullets. Custom-made bullets can be ornamental, where their sole purpose is to decorate the beginning of a list item. Or they can be functional, where they serve as icons that link you to another page or site.

If you plan to make your own artwork or use clip art for buttons, you'll need to use different HTML tags to make the art behave as you want. For visual enhancement only, use the <IMG SRC> tag to include image-based bullets at the front of a list, as shown in the following code example. You won't use the <OL> or the <UL> tags because the image itself is what is creating both the bullet and the indent. Note that you do have to put a <BR> tag at the end of each list item to tell the browser to jump to a new line for the next entry in the list. This wasn't necessary when working with the HTML tags because it's a built-in part of the list functionality. I've also used an alignment tag (see Chapter 13, "Layout and Alignment Techniques") to flow the type properly next to the artwork. Here's the code:

```
<IMG SRC="garrow.gif"
ALIGN=middle> Important Item One<BR>
<IMG SRC="garrow.gif"
ALIGN=middle> Important Item Two<BR>
<IMG SRC="garrow.gif"
ALIGN=middle> Important Item Three<BR>
<IMG SRC="garrow.gif"
ALIGN=middle> Important Item Four<BR>
```

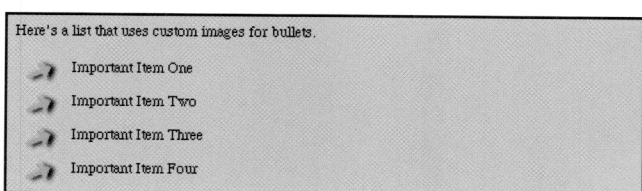

Here's a list that uses custom images for bullets.

This shows the result of using an <IMG SRC> instead of HTML-generated bullets. The green arrow is a separate piece of art that has been used multiple times on this page.

If you want to use the bullets as icons to link to another site or page, use the <A HREF></A> tag, as shown in the following code example. Because linked images typically have a blue border around them, you'll want to use the BORDER=0 tag inside the <IMG SRC> tag. (Read more about this in Chapter 10, "Navigation-Based Graphics.") Note the hand-shaped cursor on the snake in the following image. Your viewer's cursor will change to this when gliding over a linked image to let the viewer know the image is a link.

```
<P>
<A HREF><IMG SRC="lynda.gif"
ALIGN=middle BORDER=0></A> Lynda<BR>
<A HREF><IMG SRC="jamie.gif"
ALIGN=middle BORDER=0></A> Jamie<BR>
<A HREF><IMG SRC="stinky.gif"
ALIGN=middle BORDER=0></A>Stinky<BR>
<A HREF><IMG SRC="elmers.gif"
ALIGN=middle BORDER=0></A> Elmers<BR>
<A HREF><IMG SRC="jasonjr.gif" ALIGN=middle
BORDER=0></A> Jason Jr.<BR>
<A HREF><IMG SRC="climber.gif"
ALIGN=middle BORDER=0></A>Climber<BR>
<A HREF><IMG SRC="sam.gif"
ALIGN=middle BORDER=0></A>Sam (whose
tail is growing back)<BR>
```

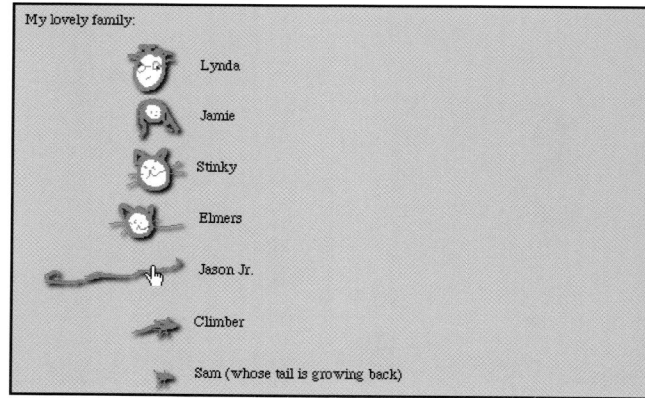

My lovely family:

This example shows using the <IMG SRC> tag again, but changing the artwork inside each tag.

Creating Custom Bullet Art

Any paint program provides a good experimentation ground for making custom bullet artwork. There are no specific guidelines except to keep in mind the scale of the type the bullets will precede. It's very difficult to design anything with much detail that is small enough to match the scale of 12-point type, such as those typically generated by HTML. If you want to make larger icons for custom bullets, be sure to enlarge the type in the list as well. More info on controlling type size is available in Chapter 11, "Web-Based Typography."

Here are some tips I can share from my bullet-making explorations, but please don't let them limit your imagination.

Using Kai's Power Tools

KPT filters, which are available for Mac and PC versions of Photoshop, have a nifty plug-in called KPT Glass Lens. If you are looking to create a shiny, 3D bubble button, this simple filter does it automatically for you. Just perform the following steps:

1. Open a new Photoshop file and fill the background with whatever color your background is going to be.

2. Use the circular Marquee Tool to select a small circle. (You can choose to anti-alias, depending on whether you'll use transparency or not. See Chapter 7, "Transparent Artwork" for more information on transparency and anti-aliasing.)

3. Fill the shape with your background color or whatever color you'd like your button to be.

4. Go to the Filters menu and choose Distort, KPT Lens Glass Bright. A dimensional bubble button will magically appear.

5. Use the rectangular marquee when finished and make a tight selection around the bounding shape of the bubble. Choose Crop, located under the Edit menu. This makes the file the appropriate size, and it's ready to save. If you want to create an indent in front of or after the custom art, make the shape of the selection account for it before you crop.

6. Follow the rules of Chapter 7, "Transparent Artwork," for saving the artwork. Whether the artwork is meant to have a transparent background, lay over a pattern background, or incorporate the solid background color determines whether to save in GIF87a, GIF89a, or JPEG file formats.

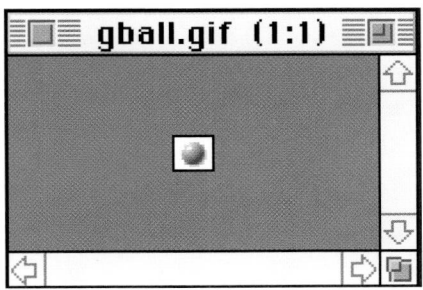

Here's the Photoshop file that was generated using the KPT Glass Lens filter.

This screen uses the gray KPT-generated bullets.

In this example, I made purple buttons instead of gray ones.

Faking Interactive Buttons

What is an interactive button? An interactive button is one that changes to let the viewer know it's in use. These types of buttons are commonly found on interactive CD-ROMs and may change color when clicked, trigger a sound effect, or change form. True button interactivity on the web doesn't exist with straight HTML (be sure to check out Chapter 16, "Interactivity," for other interactive button solutions), but you can simulate the effect. The drawback to simulating interactive buttons online is the speed limitation because it involves setting up two pages and waiting for the link to load. An interactive button on a CD-ROM is much more responsive and believable because it changes the moment you click it. But let's not let that stop us from doing the closest imitation we can muster using HTML on the web.

One type of interactive button is to get an arrow to twirl down when clicked, similar to those you see in Macintosh and Win95 directory folders. The process requires that you make two pieces of art: one arrow pointing to the right and another pointing down.

Following is the HTML for an example of how you could make this button appear to twirl down and reveal a list. For this example, I've added tags to make the background black and the text green. I used two pieces of simple green triangle art and saved them as GIFs. Notice that I aligned the text to the top of the graphics as well, using the <ALIGN=top> HTML tag.

The first page:

```
<HTML>
<HEAD><TITLE>right arrow</TITLE></HEAD>
<BODY BGCOLOR ="000000" TEXT="66ff33"
LINK="66ff33"VLINK="66ff33">
<IMG SRC="rarrow.gif" ALIGN=top>
<A HREF="darrow.html"> Expand List</A>
</BODY>
</HTML>
```

This shows the result of the first page's code. The green arrow is a piece of art that's been made to match the green hexadecimal-code based text.

The second page:

```
<HTML>
<HEAD><TITLE>right arrow</TITLE></HEAD>
<BODY BGCOLOR="000000" TEXT="66ff33"
LINK="66ff33"VLINK="66ff33">
<IMG SRC="darrow.gif" ALIGN=top>
<A HREF="rarrow.html"> Collapse List</A><P>
<UL>
<LI> Important Item One
<LI> Important Item Two
<LI> Important Item Three
<LI> Important Item Four
</BODY>
</HTML>
```

A different piece of green arrow art was used to simulate the idea that the list is now expanded.

Button Clip Art

You'll find clip art for buttons all over the World Wide Web. Clip art buttons follow the same rules for custom bullet art; use the <IMG SRC> tag if you want the button for decoration only and the <A HREF=""> BORDER=0> </A> tag if you want them to link. Clip art typically already exists in web file formats GIF or JPEG, and if not, you can use Photoshop to convert them.

Bullets can be abstract, such as dots and cubes, or an icon that actually means something. Michael Herrick, of ■ www.matterform.com, has invented something called QBullets, after "cue-bullet," or bullets that cue you to their hint or function. These buttons are part of a proposed interface standard that his site discusses in detail.

Basically, the idea is that QBullets let your audience know what the subject of your list is by using visual metaphors. The e-mail button is a miniature envelope, the download button looks like a floppy disk, a new item has the word "new item," and so on. Herrick's opinion is that bullets should inform your reader about what is at the other end of the link—large download, outside web site, ftp, telnet, form, and so on.

email me. Downloadable File Download Time

A close-up view of some of the QBullets Herrick has created.

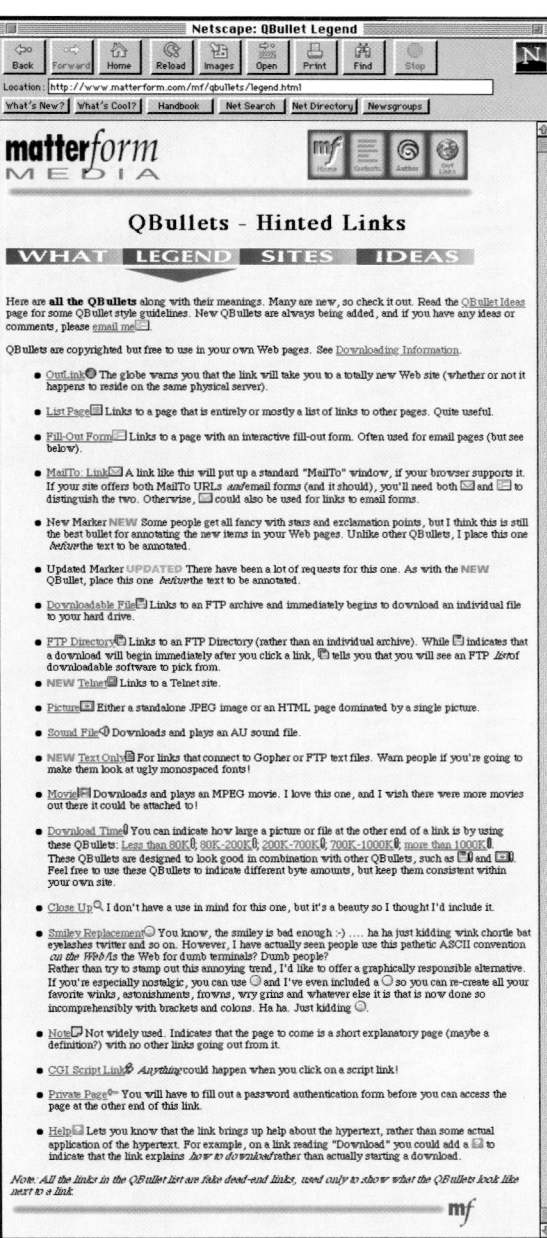

Here's a sample image that shows the Legend page from his site. QBullets can be used free of charge in exchange for a credit and a link to his page ■ http://www.matterform.com.

BROWSER SAFE COLOR

33FF

<H1>

Web typography

<TM

<P>

<TAB

Photoshop GIF=#FO

0033

<STRONG>

<img src="

<A>

width ="500"

.jpg

.png

IMAGE OPTIMIZATION Colors

heights

compression

ENCY

Height = "600"

<A>

<H1>

</A>

<cente

GRAPHY

Animation, sound and

→ Imaging techniques

Web file formats

bgcol = "FFFFFF

@link= "cyan"

LYNDA.COM

33

<BODY>

Anti-alia

www. Design

Navigation Issues in Web Design

Navigation issues are not present in print design; everyone knows how to navigate through a book or magazine—just turn the pages. But with the web's ability to link graphics and text comes the need to understand a bit about navigation. How does one offer visual design direction to help guide others to information?

Some of the navigation issues that this chapter covers are

- Storyboarding
- Programming text and images to link
- Turning off borders of linked images
- Creating navigation bars
- Creating imagemaps
- Creating frames

Creating links for text and images involves HTML. Creating images that look like navigational buttons involves design. Creating single images that link to multiple URLs involves design and HTML. Web navigation brings this all together as one artform that combines design, programming, and organizational skills.

Storyboarding

Everybody creates storyboards differently in this business. Some people scribble their site's navigational structure on napkins whereas others make beautiful presentation boards that sell their design as well as their site's organizational structure. As much as you'd probably like to be told exactly how to make the best storyboard, you won't find me being dogmatic about any one way to do so.

The thing to keep in mind is that sites often grow. They are fluid. They evolve. This is not true of print or multimedia. The web is its own medium when it comes to planning, storyboarding, navigating, and designing.

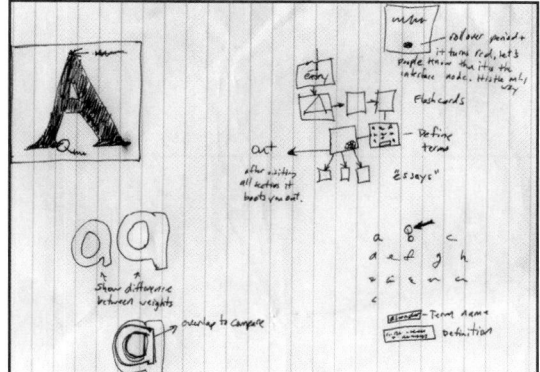

Steven Turbek's storyboard helped him work out the logistics of the Shockwave interface he designed for typoGRAPHIC ■ http://www.razorfish.com/typo.

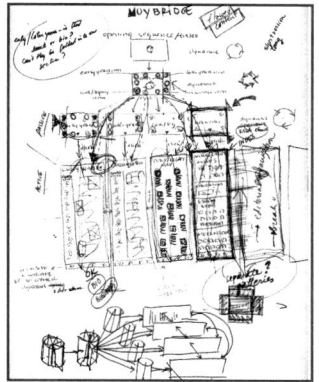 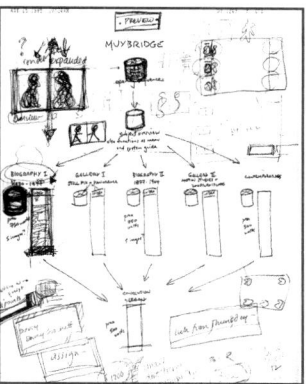

Storyboards for the Muybridge site at Discovery Channel Online ■ http://www.discovery.com helped the site designers figure out their navigational structure prior to working on the computer.

■ **tip**

Storyboarding Your Site

An excellent resource for flowcharting and brainstorming the content of your site is

Web Concept & Design
Publisher: New Riders
Author: Crystal Waters
Retail Price: $39.95 ■ ISBN: 1-56205-648-4

Hot Images and Text

The meaning of hot for the web is no longer restricted to what is new or popular. When an image is hot, it means that it will send the viewer somewhere else after it's clicked. A hot button can link a viewer to another image, page, site, or external file, depending on how the link is programmed.

A single image can be programmed to be hot if it has been placed on the page by using HTML tags that link to an outside URL. There are two types of hot images: those single images that are linked to one outside URL and single images that have been divided into regions by using imagemap tags to direct viewers to multiple URLs.

If an image is static (has no linking HTML tags), it's called an *inline* graphic. Inline means it's embedded as part of your page and requires no outside helper application to view. When a graphic is hot, it is sometimes referred to as a map, link, hyperlink, or interactive button. All these words describe the same thing; clicking on such an image will transport you elsewhere.

This chapter reviews the two types of hot images: linked graphics and imagemap-based graphics. You'll learn how to do both as well as how and when to use one type of hot graphic over another.

Identifying Hot Images

Images that are hot have certain visual markings that are different from static inline graphics. Typically, if a border appears around an image, it indicates that it is a linked graphic. This border defaults to a blue color in most browsers. If your audience has had any experience on the web, they will be trained that any time they encounter a border around an image, it means it can be clicked on as an active link.

There are some instances where a hot image will not have a telltale border around it. If you'd prefer that your hot graphic be without one, this chapter will describe how to program the border to be "invisible." **The only way a viewer will know to click on these types of borderless hot images is if your graphic invites them to bring their cursor closer.** In most browsers, after the viewer's cursor passes over a hot spot, it changes from a pointer to the hand cursor shown. This indicates, just like the border symbol, that an image is a clickable button instead of a static inline graphic.

The arrow cursor signifies that there is no link.

The pointing hand cursor indicates that the text or image is linked (hot).

Creating Linked Images and Text

The easiest way to create a link that connects one graphic to another web source is to use the <A HREF></A> tag with an <IMG SRC> tag nested inside. This combination of tags automatically defaults to putting a border around the graphic. Here's an example of this standard HTML code:

```
<HTML>
<A HREF="http://www.lynda.com>
<IMG SRC="lyndadraw.gif">
</A>
</HTML>
```

A linked image often has a tell-tale blue border, and the cursor will change to a pointing finger when viewed in browsers.

Turning Off Image Borders

Sometimes that pesky blue border around an image is totally wrong for the page it was designed for. If you've gone to a great deal of trouble to make an irregularly shaped image float freely on a background (using the techniques described in Chapter 7, "Transparent Artwork"), you aren't going to want to ruin the illusion you worked so hard to achieve by having a glaring rectangular shape around your graphic.

Here's the code to eliminate the border:

```
<HTML>
<A HREF="http://www.lynda.com>
<IMG SRC="lyndadraw.gif" BORDER=0>
</A>
</HTML>
```

Here's an example of a linked image with no border. The border was turned off within the HTML, but the pointing finger cursor will still appear when the mouse rolls over the linked image.

Just as you can make the border disappear, you can also make it appear stronger. The following Netscape-specific code gives a thicker border to the image:

```
<HTML>
<A HREF="http://lynda.com>
<IMG SRC="lyndadraw.gif" BORDER=5>
</A>
</HTML>
```

This linked image has been programmed to have a thicker border.

Sometimes your page has a specific color theme and the standard blue rectangle doesn't fit in. You can also change the color of your borders if you program the links on your page to include hexadecimal values inside the <BODY LINK> tag (see Chapter 5, "Hexadecimal Color"). This code changes the border color of the current image:

```
<HTML>
<BODY LINK="FFCC00">
<A HREF="http://www.lynda.com>
<IMG SRC="lyndadraw.gif" BORDER=5>
</A>
</BODY>
</HTML>
```

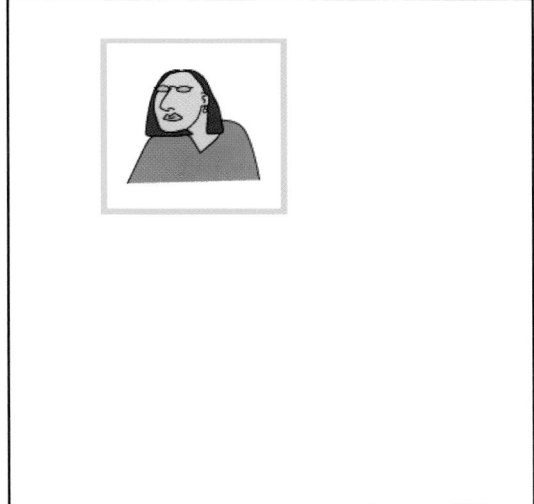

This image has a different color border programmed using hexadecimal color values.

Creating Navigation Bars

Navigation bars can be made out of text or images or both. They provide entrance ways to your information. The same HTML tags that were just reviewed apply to navigation bars. Examples follow.

This is the code to the navigation bar at the bottom of my page.

```
<A HREF=/>home</A>
  ¦  <A HREF=/dwg/links.html>links</A>
  ¦  <A HREF=/dwg/multigif.html>a-gifs</A>
  ¦  <A HREF=/hex.html>color</A>
  ¦  <A HREF=/books.html>web design books</A>
  ¦  <A HREF=/dwg/wds.html>classes</A>
<BR>
<A HREF=/articles.html>articles</A>
  ¦  <A HREF=/dwg/vi.html>inspiration</A>
  ¦  <A HREF=/dwg/mw.html>macworld</A>
  ¦  <A HREF=http://www.weinman.com/>family</A>
  ¦  <A HREF=/webdesign.html>list</A>
<BR>
<A HREF=/dwg/mg.html>motion graphics</A>
  ¦  <A HREF=http://www.cgibook.com/>cgi</A>
  ¦  <A HREF=/guestbook/>guestbook</A>
  ¦  <A HREF=/bookstore/>bookstore</A>
  ¦  <A HREF=/email.html>e-mail</A>
```

> home | links | a-gifs | color | web design books | classes
> articles | inspiration | macworld | family | list
> motion graphics | cgi | guestbook | bookstore | e-mail

This is what my navigation bar looked like at the time this chapter was written, using straight HTML text. I have so many categories that I decided against icons on my site.

The following HTML for a navigation bar that includes images and text is slightly more complex as it involves tables for placement and font sizing tags.

```
<TABLE BORDER=0 CELLPADDING="3" CELLSPACING="0">

<TR><TD ALIGN=center>
<A HREF="art.html">
<IMG SRC="elk.gif" ALIGN=middle
BORDER="0" ALT="Art">
</A></TD><TD ALIGN=center>
<A HREF="artists.html">
<IMG SRC="horse.gif" ALIGN=middle
BORDER="0" ALT="Artists">
```

```
</A></TD><TD ALIGN=center>
<A HREF="life.html">
<IMG SRC="buffalo.gif" ALIGN=middle
BORDER="0" ALT="Life">
</A></TD><TD VALIGN=top ALIGN=center>
<A HREF="info.html">
<IMG SRC="round.gif" ALIGN=middle
BORDER="0" ALT="Info">
</A></TD><TD ALIGN=center>
<A HREF="us.html">
<IMG SRC="sunbird.gif" ALIGN=middle
BORDER="0" ALT="Us">
</A></TD></TR>

<TR><TD ALIGN=center><A HREF="art.html">
<IMG SRC="spot.gif" ALIGN=middle ALT="." BORDER=0>
</A></TD><TD ALIGN=center>
<A HREF="artists.html">
<IMG SRC="spot.gif" ALIGN=middle BORDER="0" ALT=".">
</A></TD><TD ALIGN=center>
<A HREF="life.html">
<IMG SRC="spot.gif" ALIGN=middle ALT="." BORDER=0>
</A></TD><TD ALIGN=center>
<A HREF="info.html">
<IMG SRC="spot.gif" ALIGN=middle ALT="." BORDER=0>
</A></TD><TD ALIGN=center>
<A HREF="us.html">
<IMG SRC="spot.gif" ALIGN=middle ALT="." BORDER=0>
</A></TD></TR>

<TR><TD ALIGN=center><FONT SIZE="+2"><TT>
<A HREF="art.html">Art</A></TT></FONT></TD>
<TD ALIGN=center><FONT SIZE="+2"><TT>
<A HREF="artists.html">Artists</A></TT></FONT></TD>
<TD ALIGN=center><FONT SIZE="+2"><TT>
<A HREF="life.html">Life</A></TT></FONT></TD>
<TD VALIGN=top ALIGN=center><FONT SIZE="+2"><TT>
<A HREF="info.html">Info</A></TT></FONT></TD>
<TD ALIGN=center><FONT SIZE="+2"><TT>
<A HREF="us.html">Us</A></TT></FONT></TD></TR>
</TABLE>
```

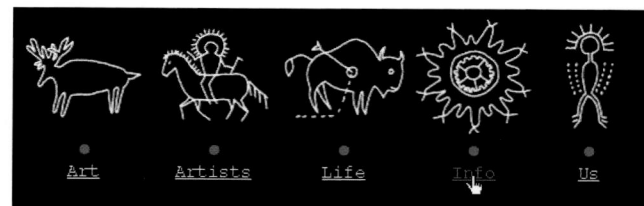

This navigation bar was designed by Ann E. Fullerton and can be found at ■ http://www.nativespirits.com. This code is much more complex because it involves all kinds of tricks we haven't gotten to yet. (Hint: See Chapter 13, "Layout and Alignment Techniques," and Chapter 11, "Web-Based Typography.")

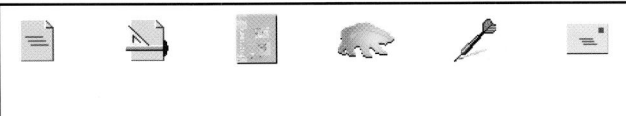

My brother's site at ■ http://www.weinman.com/wew/ takes the navigation bar idea a step further and uses text and images complete with a "rollover" technique. This navigation bar is attractive, but most end users won't know what the icons mean.

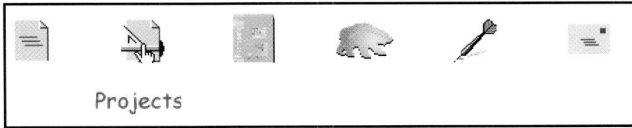

You don't know what categories the icons represent until your cursor rolls over the artwork, which brings up the text underneath. This was done by using JavaScript with two GIF files, one with the text and the other without.

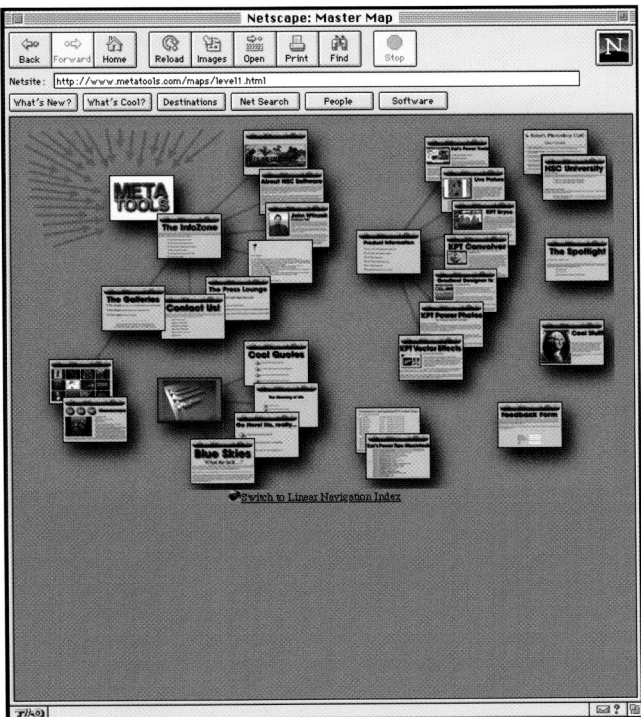

MetaTools has two types of navigation systems on its site: this one which is image-based...

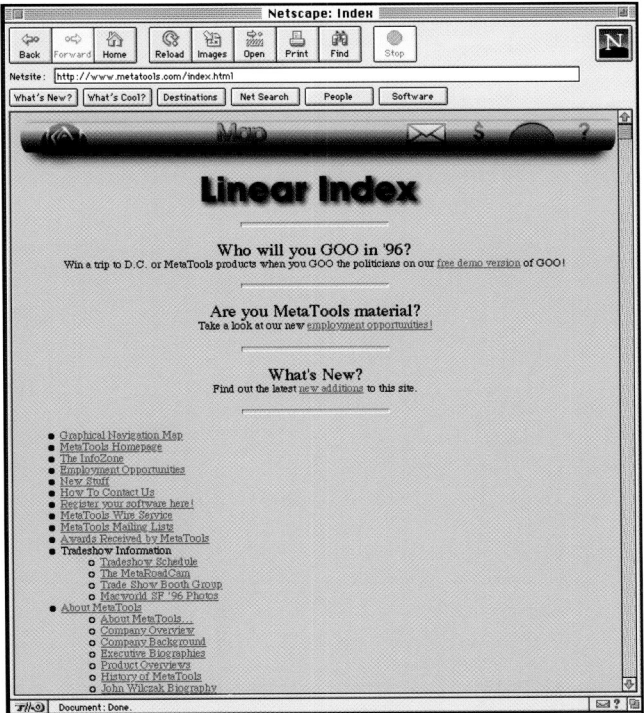

...and this alternative, text-based page.

The Miraculous Server Include Tag

My brother (author of *The CGI Book*) is a long-time programmer who impresses me constantly with his acumen
for this HTML stuff. He hosts my site at ■ http://
www.lynda.com and taught me about the server
include directive.

What is a server include directive? It requests an external file and nests it inside an HTML document. This means
that you can put your navigation links in a single file and
have multiple HTML pages request the single file. This is
so awesome because if you add a category to your site,
you have to update only one page. We use this tag on
every HTML document on my site.

*Which leads me to another good point. It's good
to have all your links accessible from any page on
your site. What good is a navigation bar if it isn't
on a page? Someone might bookmark your page
and not know whose site he or she has stumbled
upon. It happens, trust me!*

Here's the directive within the requesting HTML file that
tells the page to grab the server include file.

```
<!--#include virtual="/menu.incl" -->
```

And here's the menu.incl document.

```
<A HREF=/>home</A>
 ¦  <A HREF=/dwg/links.html>links</A>
 ¦  <A HREF=/dwg/multigif.html>a-gifs</A>
 ¦  <A HREF=/hex.html>color</A>
 ¦  <A HREF=/books.html>web design books</A>
 ¦  <A HREF=/dwg/wds.html>classes</A>
<BR>
```

```
<A HREF=/articles.html>articles</A>
 ¦  <A HREF=/dwg/vi.html>inspiration</A>
 ¦  <A HREF=/dwg/mw.html>macworld</A>
 ¦  <A HREF=http://www.weinman.com/>family</A>
 ¦  <A HREF=/webdesign.html>list</A>
<BR>
<A HREF=/dwg/mg.html>motion graphics</A>
 ¦  <A HREF=http://www.cgibook.com/>cgi</A>
 ¦  <A HREF=/guestbook/>guestbook</A>
 ¦  <A HREF=/bookstore/>bookstore</A>
 ¦  <A HREF=/email.html>e-mail</A>
```

It's really this simple. Just put the menu.incl document on
the server with the HTML files that request it, and you've
got yourself a much more flexible navigation system.

■ **tip**

Recommended Reading

The server include directive can do all sorts of other
things besides provide a flexible navigation bar system.
My brother's book includes a chapter on the subject
and shows how you can use it for a counter and
date/time stamp.

The CGI Book
Publisher: New Riders
Author: William E. Weinman
PRICE: $45.00 ■ ISBN: 1-56205-571-2

What Are Imagemaps?

At many web sites you will see a list of underlined text links on a page (often referred to as a hotlist). This is simply a list of multiple URLs assigned to multiple text objects. Instead of using multiple text links, however, the list of URLs can be attached to a single image object. Such an object is called an imagemap, which is a fancy way of presenting a list of links. This takes a little longer to download than a hotlist because of the added time required by the graphic to load. Most of the time, it's worth the wait because imagemaps are a more convenient, more visual way to present multiple choices to your audience.

This image works well as an imagemap.

Imagemap software enables you to select regions and assign multiple links to a single image.

Client-Side Imagemaps Versus Server-Side Imagemaps

An imagemap must contain specific information, such as coordinates for regions within a single image that are hyperlinked to multiple URLs.

A client-side imagemap requires that all the information about the imagemap be stored within the HTML document. A server-side imagemap requires that the information about the imagemap be saved within a "map definition file" that needs to be stored on a server and accessed by a CGI script. In general, a server-side imagemap is far more complicated to set up than a client-side imagemap. Server-side imagemaps work very differently on different systems—even on different systems using the same brand of server!

Another difference is how the two types of imagemaps display data within the Netscape browser. A server-side imagemap shows the coordinates at the bottom of the screen whereas a client-side imagemap shows the actual URL at the bottom of the screen, which is much nicer.

Most people prefer client-side imagemaps over server-side imagemaps, but some older browsers still don't support the tags. That's why many webmasters include both types of imagemaps in their documents.

```
http://www.razorfish.com/bluedot/typo/menu.map?105,70
```

Here's an example of a server-side imagemap reading on the bottom navigation bar of Netscape. It shows the position coordinates.

```
http://www.cgibook.com/links.html
```

Here's an example of a client-side imagemap reading on the bottom navigation bar of Netscape. It shows the URL! Much better.

Creating Server-Side Imagemaps

Imagemaps are more complicated to code than creating single linked images using the <A HREF><IMG SRC></A> tag. They are complicated on a number of fronts. Each hot region's dimension in pixels has to be determined and documented. In the case of a server-side map, the dimensions must be stored in an *imagemap definition file*. This definition file is composed slightly differently depending on which kind of server your web site uses.

The server is where your artwork and HTML gets stored. There are two types of servers—NCSA and CERN—and each requires the imagemap definition file code to be slightly different. This means that you have to ensure that the way you've coded the imagemap is compatible with the type of server your site is stored on. The first step to deciding how to build your imagemap is to call the online service provider with whom you have your Internet account and web site to find out what kind of server they use.

Do You Really Need an Imagemap?

Carefully analyze whether you really need an imagemap or whether there's some other way to accomplish the same goal. For example, if your image is composed of rectangles, or can be seamed together by using rectangular shapes (or transparent irregular shapes—see Chapter 7, "Transparent Artwork"), it might be easier on your end to load multiple single graphics with independent links than to load one graphic with multiple links.

You will see examples of imagemaps used on opening menu screens all over the web. Sometimes an imagemap is used, even when the menu bar is composed of rectangular shapes. Some sites do this because the one image will load faster than multiple images. This is a valid reason to use an imagemap, but even so, the difficulty of creating and maintaining one might outweigh the performance increase. Other sites do it just because they can. Perhaps it's trendy and shows off a certain amount of web-design machismo? I don't know, but it's another decision you get to make when building your site. I, being the lazy sort, make and use imagemaps only when necessary.

The Four Stages of a Server-Side Imagemap

Let's walk through the imagemap-making process quickly and then break out with more detail. The first step to making an imagemap is to create or choose a graphic as the source for the map. It's easiest to define regions if your graphic has obvious areas, such as a map or illustration, but you can use anything, including photographs and typography.

After you've chosen an image, you will need to create a map definition file: a text file you create that contains information about where the hotspots are located on your image. You can define the regions by using polygons or circles with the location of each region defined by pixels. This information is then composed as a text file specifically prepared for either a CERN or NCSA server.

Next, with a server-side imagemap, a map-processing CGI script is required to instruct the server to recognize the map definition file. Different scripts work for different platforms and servers, and it's best to contact your provider to ask what type of CGI works with their server. Chances are they already use a CGI script that they'll let you have access to and can instruct you on how to use it properly.

The last step is to set up the HTML tags to support the imagemap using the <ISMAP> tag. Now, let's break this down further and walk through the process used to create imagemaps.

<dwg 2>

Starting with the Graphic

First, make sure your source graphic is saved as a GIF (standard, transparent, or interlaced will all work) or a JPEG. In the file name, don't forget to use the proper extensions, .gif and .jpg in lowercase, with no spaces in the name—for example, map.gif.

Defining the Regions of an Imagemap

Manually defining the coordinates of an imagemap can be a hellacious chore. You'd need to plot each point and arrive at the x and y coordinates of each region. Once you collected all the data, you'd need to write a text file for the server (slightly different ones for NCSA and CERN servers). This type of grunt work would have been best handled by a helper app, and we're lucky that several have cropped up that do the repetitive chore well. This chapter will show you how to work with two helper apps: WebMap for Mac imagemap authoring and MapEdit for PC imagemap authoring.

Here's an example of what a map definition file looks like for an NCSA server:

```
#
# Created by WebMap 1.0
# Wednesday, November 27, 1996 at 8:52 PM
# Format: NCSA
#

poly http://www.stink.com/films/
252,43 275,26 309,21 333,23 340,42
313,68 268,78 248,68 246,48 252,43
poly http://www.stink.com/images/
297,87 343,85 363,103 354,130 311,
142 277,134 264,118 273,98 297,87
poly http://www.stink.com/sketches/
302,152 331,153 349,170 339,193 303,
197 277,186 277,172 289,159 302,152
```

Here's an example of what a map definition file looks like for a CERN server:

```
#
# Created by WebMap 1.0
# Wednesday, November 27, 1996 at 8:52 PM
# Format: NCSA
#

poly http://www.stink.com/sketches/
302,152 331,153 349,170 339,193 303,
197 277,186 277,172 289,159 302,152
poly http://www.stink.com/images/
297,87 343,85 363,103 354,130 311,
142 277,134 264,118 273,98 297,87
poly http://www.stink.com/films/
252,43 275,26 309,21 333,23 340,42
313,68 268,78 248,68 246,48 252,43
```

Using WebMap

WebMap is shareware imagemap software written by Rowland Smith. The evaluation version of WebMap is available at the following URL: ■ http://www.city.net/cnx/software/webmap.html.

Launch WebMap. Open your file, and the graphic will appear in a window.

Use the toolbar containing the circle, rectangle, and free polygon to draw the shape of each region. After you've defined the area, click on the region and double-click on the [Undefined] list to the right. Enter the URL you wish to link to with an absolute path name (must include http://www).

When you're finished making and naming the regions, define a default URL by going to the Edit menu and selecting Default URL. This should be the name of the URL that the imagemap resides on. If your shape is irregular, the default URL should be where the file leads the viewer if he accidentally clicks off one of your defined regions.

Once you've done these things, go to the File menu and select Export as Text, choosing an NCSA or a CERN script depending on which type of server your site is on. The imagemap definition file must end with a .map extension. Typically, your map definition file and map graphic reside in the same folder on your server. Be sure to check this out with your web administrator.

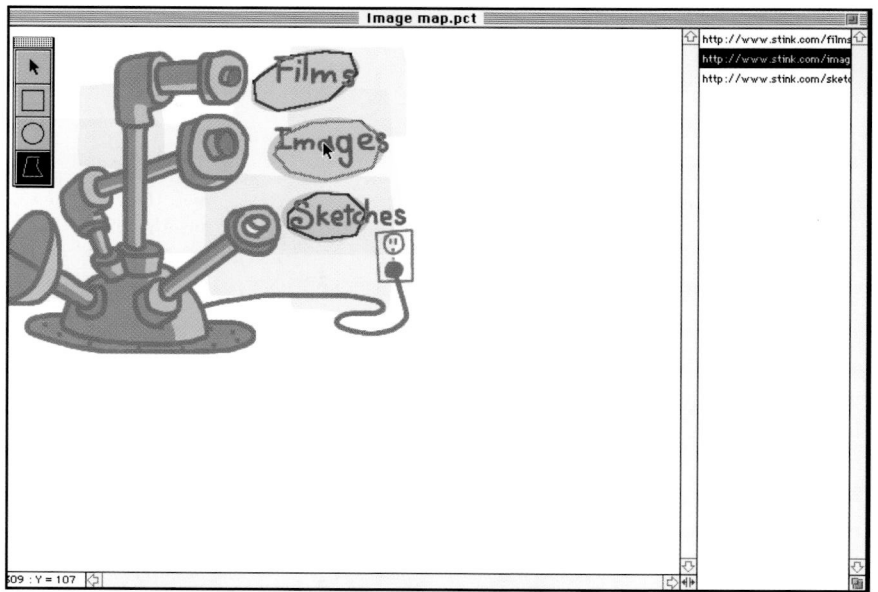

In WebMap, drag the Free Polygon Tool around the region you want to assign a link. The URLs for each link are typed in for the selected region.

Using MapEdit

MapEdit is shareware imagemap software written by Thomas Boutell. You might recognize his name as the author of the PNG file format (see Chapter 3, "Web File Formats"). MapEdit can be downloaded from ■ http://www.boutell.com/mapedit/.

Begin MapEdit by pulling down the menu bar to File, Open/Create to open your file. You'll be asked to locate the map file (map definition file) in advance and to load the graphic that you want to plot at the same time. If you haven't already started a map file, you can name it here now. You also need to decide at this point whether you want to write an NCSA script or a CERN script by checking the appropriate Create Type/NCSA/CERN radio button.

After you specify the map file name, the GIF, JPEG, or PNG file name, and the script type, choose OK to display the image in MapEdit. Choose Tools, Polygon and drag around the appropriate shape.

When you want to close a polygon path, click the right mouse button. This displays the Object URL dialog box in which you must identify which URL the area you've just defined is linked to. Be sure to use an absolute path name (http://www...) as opposed to a relative path name (/my folder/myWebsite).

When finished, you can set the default URL by going to Edit, Default URL. Enter the absolute URL of the site your map is sitting on. This sets the default address to keep your viewers on this page in case they click off a defined region of your imagemap. When finished, choose File, Save As to display the Save As dialog box, and the name of your map definition file is automatically inserted.

As before, the finished files all need to be stored in the same folder on your server. Check with your web systems administrator for exact instructions.

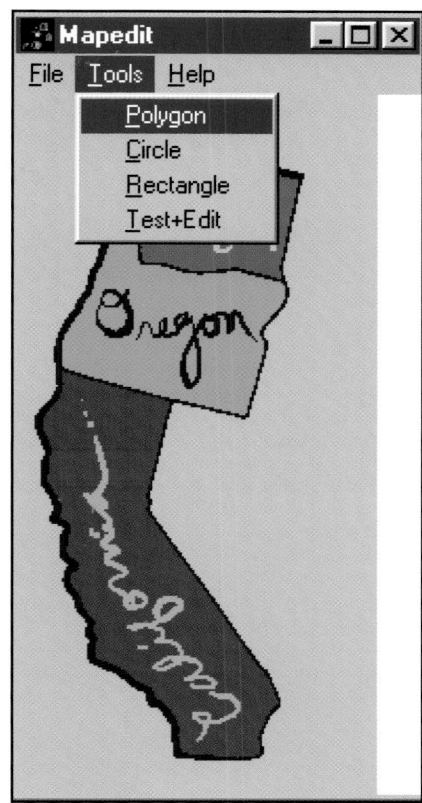

Using MapEdit, you choose from an assortment of polygon tools to define the imagemap. Every imagemap software program is slightly different, but almost all of them offer intuitive drawing tools and create the server-side scripts automatically for you.

Writing HTML to Support Server-Side Imagemaps

The deconstruction to server-side imagemap follows:

1
```
<A HREF="http://www.domain.nam/cgi-
bin/filename.map">
```
2 `<IMG SRC="imagename.gif"`
3 `BORDER=0`
4 `ISMAP>`
5 `</A>`

1 This establishes the anchor or destination of the links for the image map. Because the map definition file is included in the absolute path, the HTML will reference the imagemap coordinates and the CGI script.

2 This tag defines the name of the image to which the imagemap will be applied.

3 Whenever there's an **<A HREF>** tag, it automatically generates a default blue border around the graphic. The **BORDER=0** tag will turn off the border.

4 The **ISMAP** command must be included at the end of a server-side imagemap tag.

5 The **</A>** is required to end the **<A HREF>** tag.

The HTML document must now be loaded to the server, with the GIF or JPEG and the imagemap definition file map with the .map extension. Unlike most HTML, there is no way a server-side imagemap can be tested from your local hard drive. You must upload the proper files to the server, or the imagemap will not work.

Creating Client-Side Imagemaps

Creating client-side imagemaps is slightly easier than server-side imagemaps because you don't need a CGI or a separate map definition file. The steps for creating a client-side imagemap follow.

Step 1: Get the coordinates for your image. It's possible to get these coordinates in many WYSIWYG HTML editors, and the two programs mentioned here: MapEdit and WebMap. MapEdit will automatically generate the image-map coordinates in a client-side configuration. WebMap will not, but you can use a converter and have it restructure the data in the necessary fashion. Here's a converter that will help:

■ http://hyperarchives.lcs.mit.edu/HyperArchive/Archive/text/html/map-convert-10-a.hqx

Step 2: The coordinate information needs to be configured differently for a client-side imagemap than for a server-side imagemap. Here's an example of what the client-side coordinate data would look like. Compare it to the server-side map definition above, and you'll see it's the same information, just presented in a different order:

```
1  <MAP NAME="imagemap">
   <AREA SHAPE="polygon" COORDS=
   "302, 152, 331, 153, 349, 170, 339, 193, 303,
   197, 277, 186, 277, 172, 289, 159, 302, 152"
2  HREF="http://www.stink.com/sketches">
3  <AREA SHAPE="polygon" COORDS=
   "297, 87, 343, 85, 363, 103, 354, 130, 311,
   142, 277, 134, 264, 118, 273, 98, 297, 87"
   HREF="http://www.stink.com/images/">
   <AREA SHAPE="polygon" COORDS=
   "302, 152, 331, 153, 349, 170, 339, 193, 303,
   197, 277, 186, 277, 172, 289, 159, 302, 152"
   HREF="/www.stink.com/films/">
4  <IMG SRC="imagemap.gif" WIDTH="400" HEIGHT="300"
5  BORDER=0
6  USEMAP="#imagemap" ISMAP>
7  </MAP>
```

Everything within the client-side imagemap information gets stored within the HTML. The code for the server-side imagemap was very short. The code for the client-side imagemap is longer because it includes all the coordinate data within.

1 The map name is something that you define. It can be any name but must match what is used in the **<USEMAP>** tag.

2 The **<HREF>** tag instructs the imagemap to load the referenced HTML.

3 This part of the code defines which shape the imagemap forms.

4 Unlike the CERN and NCSA server-side map definition example, on a client side example no **<A HREF>** tag is necessary. The image for the map is told to display via the **<IMG SRC>** tag.

5 Just like the server-side example, the **BORDER=0** tag turns off the default blue border. It's not necessary to turn the border off, but it often ruins the illusion of irregular shaped regions if you leave it turned on.

6 The **<USEMAP>** tag specifies the name of the client-side imagemap file to use. The **#** character must always precede the map name.

7 The **</MAP>** tag is required to end the client-side imagemap.

Using Server-Side and Client-Side Imagemaps Together

Many people use both server-side and client-side maps. This enables viewers from any browser to be able to use the imagemap.

Here's the code necessary to combine both types of imagemap features:

```
<A HREF="http://www.domain.nam/cgi-bin/filename.map">
<IMG SRC="funkmachine.gif" border=0 ISMAP>
</A> USEMAP="#imagemap">
<MAP NAME="imagemap">
<AREA SHAPE="polygon" COORDS=
"302, 152, 331, 153, 349, 170, 339, 193, </MAP>
303, 197, 277, 186, 277, 172, 289, 159, 302, 152"
HREF="http://www.stink.com/sketches">
<AREA SHAPE="polygon" <IMG SRC="../credits/credits_
b.GIF" WIDTH=160 HEIGHT=116 COORDS=
"297, 87, 343, 85, 363, 103, 354, 130,
ALT="credits" BORDER=0 311, 142, 277, 134,
264, 118, 273, 98, 297, 87"
USEMAP="#credits_b" ISMAP></A>
HREF="http://www.stink
.com/images/"><MAP NAME="credits_b">
<AREA SHAPE="polygon" COORDS=
"302, 152, 331, 153, 349, 17, 339, 193, 303,
197, 277, 186, 277, 172, 289, 159, 302, 152"
<AREA SHAPE="rect" COORDS="2,73,128,97"
HREF="/www.stink.com/films/">
</MAP>
</HTML>
```

Importance of the <ALT> Tag

The <ALT> tag provides alternative information to images that can be read by text-based browsers. Let's say that visitors to your site arrive with browser software that does not recognize imagemaps. Or they've turned off their images because they're in a hurry? Or your end viewer is disabled (yes, visually impaired people can and do use the text-based web; there are devices that can "read" the pages to them). All these situations can be accommodated by adding one simple <ALT> tag to your HTML.

Using our example one more time, here's where the tag would be included:

```
<A HREF="http://www.domain.nam/cgi-bin/filename.map">
<IMG SRC="imagename.gif"
ALT="this is an image of my bla bla"
BORDER=0
ISMAP>
```

Importance of <WIDTH> and <HEIGHT> Tags

By adding <WIDTH> and <HEIGHT> tags to images within HTML, you are giving the browser information about the size of your graphic. This is a good thing, for a couple of reasons. First of all, the browser doesn't have to calculate the image size because you've supplied the information for it, which saves time. It allows the text to load before the images, which can be a good thing with large images. Audiences will get something to look at while they're waiting! MSIE actually requires that you use the <WIDTH> and <HEIGHT> tag attributes or the client-side imagemap tags don't even work.

Here's the way to implement the <HEIGHT> and <WIDTH> tag attribute.

```
<A HREF="http://www.domain.nam/cgi-bin/filename.map">
<IMG SRC="imagename.gif" WIDTH=350 HEIGHT=200
ALT="this is an image of my bla bla"
BORDER=0
ISMAP>
```

The values you put inside the <WIDTH> and <HEIGHT> tags reflect how large the image is, measured by pixels. You can even resize an image if you put values that are larger or smaller than the image! Basically, the browser uses your information for the image size instead of looking to the image itself for size information.

■ tip

Imagemap Tutorial URLs
■ http://www.ihip.com/
■ http://www.spyglass.com/tech spec/tutorial/img_maps.html

Imagemap Software Tools
MapEdit (Windows, PC, and Unix)
■ http://www.boutell.com/mapedit/

MapThis! (Windows)
■ http://galadriel.ecaetc. ohio-state.edu/tc/mt/

WebMap (Macintosh)
■ http://home.city.net/cnx/ software/webmap.html

Glenn Fleishman's Server-Side to Client-Side Online Converter
■ http://www.popco.com/ popco/convertmaps.html

Frames for Navigation

What are frames? Frames offer the capability to divide a web page into regions, so that each region functions as its own web page. This means parts of a page can change, while other regions of the page remain static. Frames are perfect for navigation bars that will not change from page to page, while other content can be set to change independently.

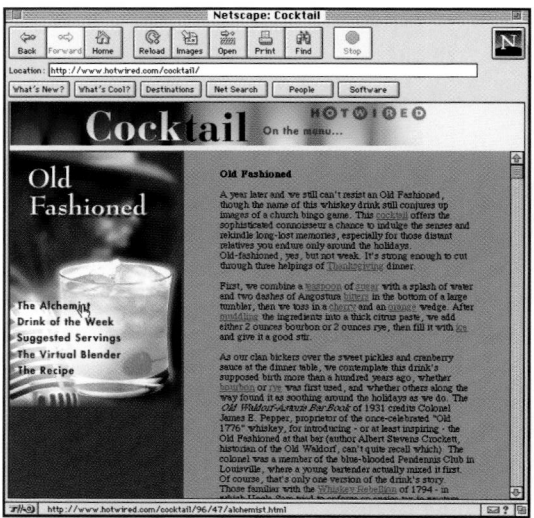 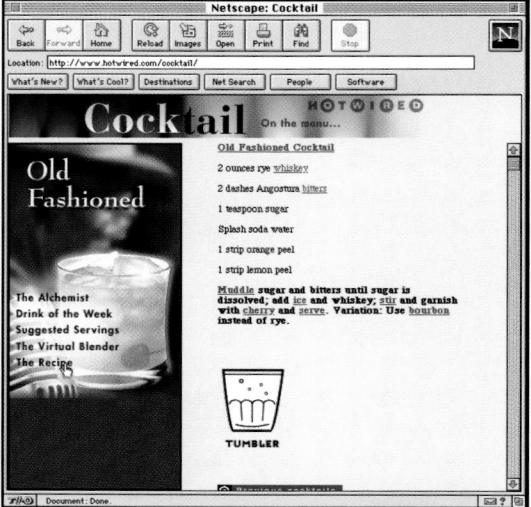

By clicking on the left-hand frame, content in the right-hand frame updates independently. These examples are from
■ http://www.hotwired.com/cocktail/. A case study of this site is in my second book, *Deconstructing Web Graphics*.

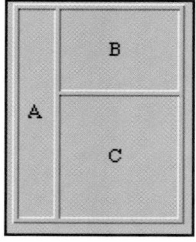 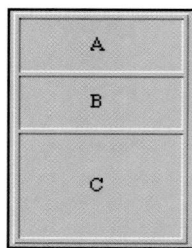 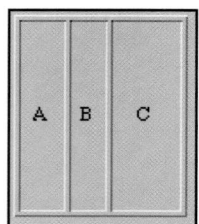

Examples of frame configurations from the excellent tutorial site in Japan: HTML for Angels—■ http://ncdesign.kyushu-id.ac.jp/html/Normal/frame.html.

Frames sound great in theory, but there are some noteworthy snags. Many site designers insert existing web pages that were originally designed for full-screen browsers into cramped small-frame regions. This forces the end viewer to scroll through graphics and text inside smaller windows than the pages were originally designed for. Real estate on a web page is already a precious commodity, and breaking apart a small screen into multiple small screens can do more damage to your presentation than good. My recommendation is that you use no more than three frame regions to a page, so that your audience isn't frustrated by having to scroll through small windows.

HTML for Frames

The HTML for frames is often difficult to understand because it, by nature, includes other "nested" HTML documents. The first document in this example is named Framed.html and displays three frame regions. The content of those frames is actually contained in three other HTML documents that this document references. The three other files are named header.html, menu.html, and info.html.

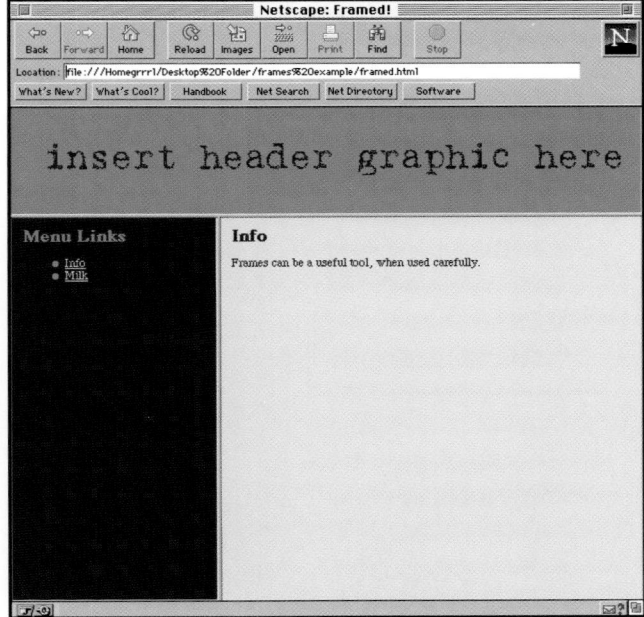

framed.html: This is the opening page of the sample frameset.

```
    <HTML>
    <HEAD>
    <TITLE>Framed!</title>
    </HEAD>
1   <FRAMESET ROWS="108,*">
2   <FRAME SRC="header.html" MARGINWIDTH=0 MARGIN-
    HEIGHT=0 NORESIZE SCROLLING="no"
      NAME="header">
```

```
3   <FRAMESET COLS="200,*">
4   <FRAME MARGINWIDTH=10 MARGINHEIGHT=10
    SRC="menu.html" NORESIZE SCROLLING="no"
      NAME="menu">
5   <FRAME MARGINWIDTH=10 MARGINHEIGHT=10
    SRC="info.html" NAME="info">
6   </FRAMESET>
    </FRAMESET>
7   <NOFRAMES>
8   <BODY>
        If you had frames, you'd be home by now.
    </BODY>
9   </NOFRAMES>
    </HTML>
```

1 **<FRAMESET>** defines the parameters of the frames. This document has two nested framesets. The first defines two rows. Rows are horizontal areas, one on top of the other. The top will be for the header, and the bottom row will have another **<FRAMESET>** with two columns.

The first row is 108 pixels high. Netscape uses 8 of those pixels for the frame itself, and the graphic is 100 pixels high. Frame sizes can also be defined in terms of percentages (25%) instead of pixels. When you are using a graphic with a known size, it is more useful to define the size of the frame in terms of pixels.

The second row is defined with a *, which lets the browser use the rest of the space at its own discretion. It will take up whatever space is left after the 100 pixels of the first row are allocated.

2 The **<FRAME>** tag is used to specify the contents of an individual frame. The **SRC=** attribute specifies header.html as the initial content of the frame; **MARGINWIDTH** and **MARGINHEIGHT** declare the margin sizes (zero in this case, to put an image right up to the borders); **NORESIZE** tells the browser to disallow resizing by the user; **SCROLLING="no"** gets rid of any scrollbars; and **NAME="header"** names the frame for use by **<TARGET>** tags later on.

3 The second row has another **<FRAMESET>** tag instead of a **<FRAME>** tag. This is for splitting the row into columns. Two columns are defined: the first column will take up 200 pixels on the left side of the row, and the second column will take the remaining lateral space in the row.

4 Each **<FRAME>** tag defines the next undefined frame specified in the immediately preceding **<FRAMESET>** tag. This one is for the first column from the **<FRAME-SET>** in #3 . . .

5 . . . and this one is for the second column from the **<FRAMESET>** in #3.

6 **<FRAMESET>** requires an ending **</FRAMESET>** tag to tell the browser that it is done defining frames.

7 Everything between **<NOFRAMES>** and **</NOFRAMES>** will be ignored by a frames-capable browser. The content within this section is what will be seen by people whose browsers cannot render frames.

8 The **<BODY>** tag is required in the **<NOFRAMES>** section. You can use it as you would in a normal HTML document.

9 This ends the **<NOFRAMES>** section.

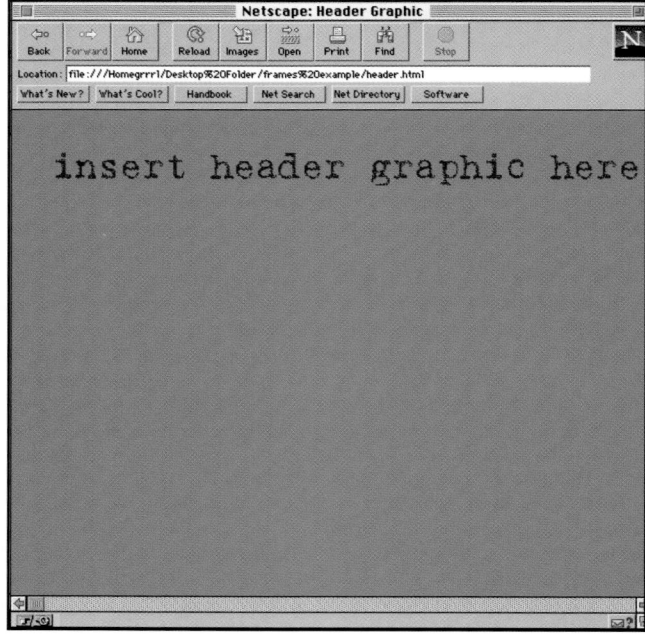

header.html: This document is nested within the top frame of framed.html.

```
    <HTML>
1   <HEAD><TITLE>Hey! I thought I
    was in a frame!</TITLE></HEAD>
2   <BODY BGCOLOR=33cccc>
3   <IMG SRC=title.gif WIDTH=600 HEIGHT=100>
    </BODY>
    </HTML>
```

1 Because each HTML document could end up on someone's screen outside of a frame, it's a good idea to give it a title anyway.

2 When you give a framed document a background color, the background of the frame takes on the color. This document has a background color that is the same as the background of the title graphic. That way, if someone's screen is bigger than our graphic, it blends seamlessly.

3 The whole body of the document is just the image.

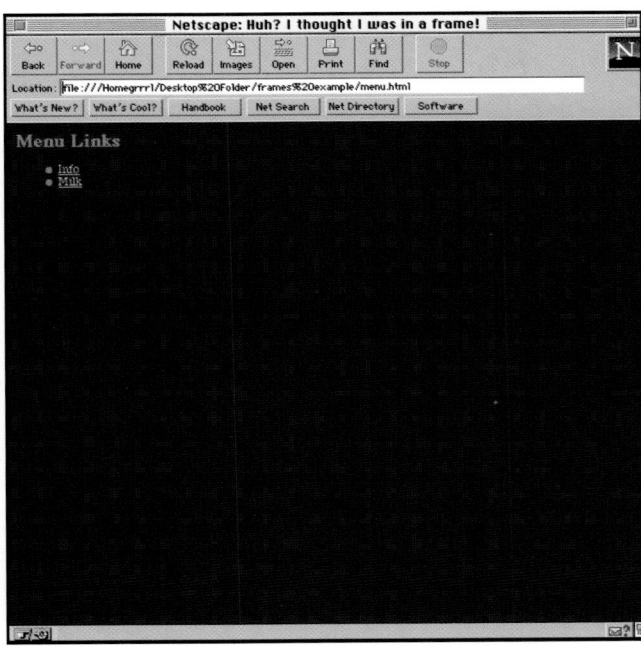

menu.html: This document is nested within the left frame of framed.html.

```
<HTML>
<HEAD>
<BASE TARGET=info>
<TITLE>Huh? I thought I was in a frame!</title>
</HEAD>
<BODY BGCOLOR=000066 TEXT=00ccff LINK=00ffcc
VLINK=00ffcc ALINK=00ccff>
<H2>Menu</H2>
<MENU>
    <LI><A HREF=info.html>Info</A>
    <LI><A HREF=milk.html>Milk</A>
    <LI><A HREF=blue.html>Blue</A>
    <LI><A HREF=light.html>Light</A>
    <LI><A HREF=monster.html>Monsters!</A>
</MENU>
</BODY>
</HTML>
```

1 The **<BASE>** tag has a target attribute so that all the hyperlinks load in the frame named "info".

2 The **<MENU>** tag is used to create a menu in the left-hand frame. Be sure to keep all your menu text as short as possible so that it fits in the frame.

Alternatively, you could create a vertical imagemap designed to fit precisely in the frame.

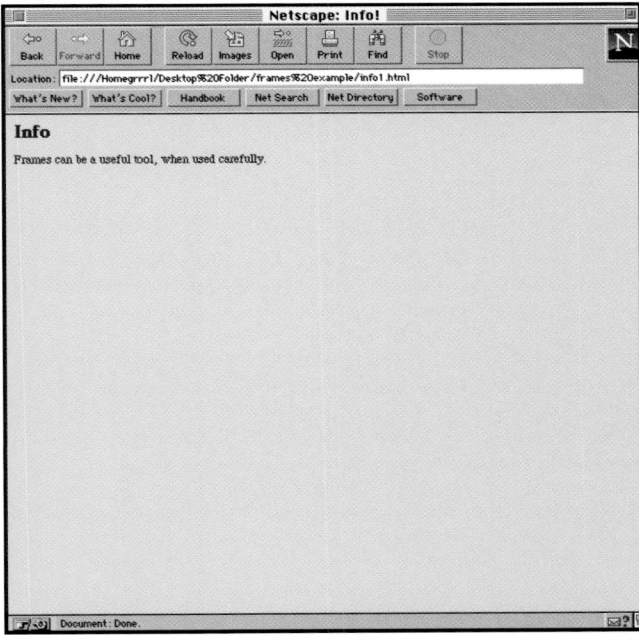

info.html: This document is nested within the right frame of framed.html.

```
<HTML>
<HEAD>
<TITLE>Info!</TITLE>
<BODY BGCOLOR=cccc99>
<H2>Info</H2>
<P>Frames can be a useful tool, when used carefully.
</BODY>
</HTML>
```

Each of the documents in the right-hand frame is structured as a normal HTML document. It's important to keep the amount of text to a minimum so that it fits nicely in the limited space of the frame.

1 The **<TITLE>** tag describes the document, for people who might load it outside of a frame.

2 All the HTML in the document is designed just as you would a document that was not going in a frame.

Floating Frames

Microsoft Internet Explorer (MSIE) introduced floating frames, which enable the browser to position a frame in the middle of the browser window instead of limiting its position to divided regions, as in the case with standard frame tags. MSIE honors a new tag, <IFRAME>, that instructs the browser to float the frame. For step-by-step instructions, visit

■ http://www.microsoft.com/WORKSHOP/AUTHOR/NEWFEAT/IE30HTML-F.HTM

Floating frames are great, but unfortunately at the time this chapter was written, they were supported only by MSIE.

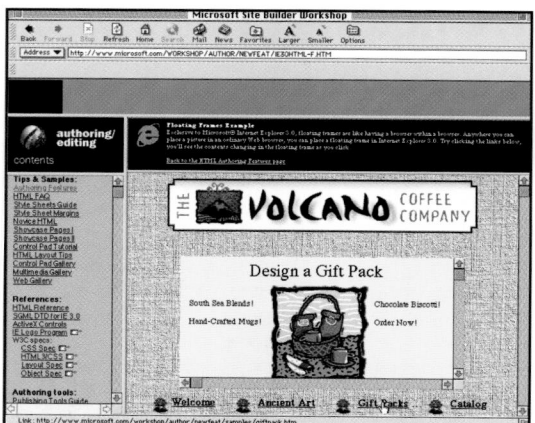 

These screens can be found on the MSIE site as examples of floating frames. By clicking on the bottom navigation bar, the only part of the page that changes is inside the middle window. When floating frames are widely implemented, this type of navigation will be welcomed by many site designers.

■ note

Extra Frame-Related HTML Attributes

There are a few other frames-related tags that have not been reviewed here.

If the image inside a frame is bigger than the browser window, a scrollbar automatically appears. If you want to turn that scrollbar off, you could add the code: **SCROLLING=NO**

When creating links for frames or client-side imagemaps, you can set a TARGET attribute to instruct the link to target another browser window besides the one its in. Here's a list of TARGET attributes.

TARGET="_self" is the default way frames work, even without this tag. It means that the linked reference will appear inside the same frame that is already visible.

TARGET="_blank" will open a new browser window, while leaving the old one behind it.

TARGET="_top" takes you to the referenced URL without keeping it inside your frameset.

TARGET="_parent" removes all the frames on your page, and shows you the referenced link in its own window.

Aesthetic Cues for Navigation Graphics

Many designers, myself included, have grown weary of predictable beveled 3D buttons on web pages. The truth is, however, that beveled 3D buttons give a universally accepted visual cue that a graphic has linking properties. If you're tired of the 3D look, however, there are other signals that imply a linked image. Drop shadows are often used, as are colored shapes. A sample gallery of navigation-style graphics follows. These were created by Bruce Heavin, using the illustration he made of me, and Alien Skin's Black Box Photoshop filters (■ http://www.alienskin.com). The Alien Skin filters are Mac- and PC-compatible Photoshop filters that save a lot of time and fussing with complicated alpha channel operations.

Cutout Filter

Drop Shadow Filter

Carve Filter

Cutout to Background Filter

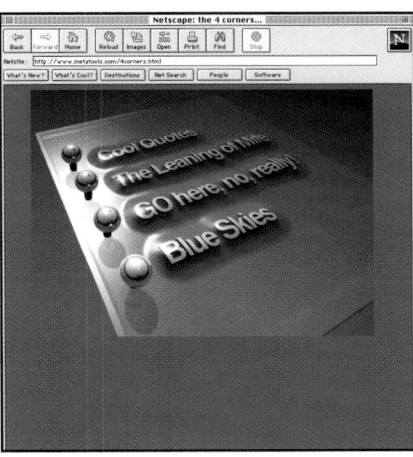
The MetaTool's site has a lot of playful linked graphics ■ http://www.metatools.com/.

Glass Filter

Glow Filter

Inner Bevel Filter

Outer Bevel Filter

Carve Filter

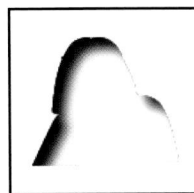
Cutout to Background Color Filter

Cutout to Image Filter

Drop Shadow Filter

Glass Filter

Outer Bevel Filter

Inner Bevel Filter

Glow Filter

Bruce worked with the image of me, using a circular selection and a selection in the shape of his illustration's contour.

> ■ **note**
>
> **Rollovers Versus Buttons**
>
> It's true that buttons with 3D effects look clickable, but after seeing so many on the web and in multimedia, these conventions grow tiresome and predictable. An alternative graphic approach would be to create rollover-style buttons, where the buttons behave responsively with a different graphic or sound when the end user's cursor passes over. Rollovers are not possible in straight HTML-based pages; these techniques are discussed in-depth in Chapter 16, "Interactivity."

Web-Based Typography

BROWSER SAFE COLOR

33FF

Photoshop

0033

`<H1>`

`<STRONG>`

Width ="500"

Height ="600"

`<img src=`

IMAGE OPTIMIZATION

typography

`<TAB`

`<A>`

Imaging techniques
HTML
Web file formats
bgcolor = "FFFFCC"

Animation, sound and

alink = "cyan"

33

BODY
Antial

LYNDA.COM

www Design

Web-Based Typography

There is a fundamental controversy associated with web design. You have your HTML purists and programmers, and you have your design purists and nonprogrammers, and often they do not agree or find common ground. Visual design is about control. Typography is an incredibly powerful visual design medium, but good typography requires much more control than HTML currently affords. HTML is about display flexibility and cross-platform distribution of information. HTML and browser support of specific tags are the vehicles by which web pages are delivered, and design is the vehicle by which they are delivered artistically.

This chapter was written to help each side of the design and programming fence understand the other. It will help designers learn tricks to make web typography look as good as it can and will help programmers understand what designers want from HTML.

This chapter covers the following topics:

- Type principles and definitions
- Aesthetic considerations
- HTML type
- Type alignment tricks
- Font usage in HTML pages
- Images as type
- Anti-aliased type versus aliased type
- Mixing type images and HTML

Short Glossary of Key Typographic Terms

In order to understand what kind of type control designers want, let's first examine some type principles and definitions. Here's a short glossary of typographic terms, using HTML-based examples.

Serif: A serif typeface has a stroke attached to the beginning or end of one of the main strokes of a letter. Many people believe that this style of type is easiest to read as body copy. The default font in most browsers is a serif typeface: Times Roman on Macs and Times New Roman on PCs.

Sans serif: A sans serif typeface has no slab attached. Sans serif typefaces on the web require special tags, requesting that your end user use a graphic picture of type instead of HTML. This sans serif type is specified with the <FONT FACE> tag, described fully later in this chapter.

Monospace: A monospace font takes up the same amount of horizontal width per character. This navigation bar is set in Courier using the <PRE> tag. Monospace typefaces can be specified with the <PRE>, <CODE>, or <TT> tags.

Default leading: Leading (pronounced ledding) is the space between lines of type. The origins of the word leading came from early days of typography when lead type was used. Blank pieces of lead were used between each row as spacers. This is standard leading in HTML using no custom tags.

ing looser leading looser leading looser leading looser leading looser leading looser le

ing looser leading looser leading looser leading looser leading looser leading looser le

looser leading looser leading looser leading looser leading looser leading looser leadi

Looser leading: This looser leading in HTML was created by using the paragraph break tag <P>.

DROP CAPs CAN BE KEWEL

Drop cap: A drop cap is used with all capital letters, and indicates that the first letter of a word is in a larger cap size. This is accomplished in HTML by using the <FONT SIZE> tag.

FOR HOTWIRED MEMBERS
Test Patterns presents pet projects that kept us up nights: MiniMind, KHOT, and the amazing Beta

Small caps: HotWired uses small caps on its front page ■ http://www.hotwired.com/frontdoor/.

fe palette, as I so named it, is the actual palette that Mosaic, Ne
within their browsers. The palettes used by these browsers are slig
s. This palette is based on math, not beauty. I didn't and wouldn't
ors in this palette, but Netscape, Mosaic and Internet Explorer did

Body text: The body text, or body copy, of a document is composed by the main block of text.

The Browser Safe Color Palette

By Lynda Weinman

Headline text: A headline is used to break apart information. It can do so by being larger in size, a different color, a different font, an underline, or bold or different visual treatment, which will cause it to stand out.

Glossary of Terms Not Possible with HTML

This type of precise typographic control is possible in programs such as QuarkXPress, Illustrator, and FreeHand. This control is not possible within HTML, but we wish it was.

<no baseline shift on brackets>

<with baseline shift on brackets>

Baseline shift: Enables you to change the position of a single character up or down.

---

unkerned kerned

Kerning: Enables you to adjust the letterspacing between individual characters.

---

12 pt. type with 14 pt. leading
12 pt. type with 14 pt. leading
12 pt. type with 14 pt. leading

Leading adjustment: Enables you to specify specific leading with point size measurements.

---

12 pt. type with 20 pt. leading

12 pt. type with 20 pt. leading

12 pt. type with 20 pt. leading

Looser leading adjustment: Enables you to establish specific leading with point size measurements. Here's an example of looser leading with accurate control.

---

this text has default word spacing

this text has word spacing of 125%

Word spacing: Enables you to adjust the space between words.

---

without tracking
with tracking

Tracking: Enables you to adjust the global spacing between letters.

Interesting Typography-Based URLs

For the most amazing type glossary to be found on the web, visit Razorfish's **typo-GRAPHIC** site. The **typoGRAPHIC** site also teaches about the principles of type and using hypertext at its best. Oh, and a little Shockwave, Java, and animated GIF action, too!
- http://www.razorfish.com/bluedot/typo/glossary/
- http://www.razorfish.com/bluedot/typo/

Typofile is an online magazine devoted to type techniques and technology. This site has lots of great tutorials and essays about typography.
- http://www.will-harris.com/type.htm

A short presentation on basic typography by **Paul Baker Typographic, Inc.** includes the use of letter and word spacing, measure, leading, choosing a typeface, and so on.
- http://www.pbtweb.com/typostyl/typostyl.htm

LettError is a two-person virtual design studio. Acclaimed type designers Just van Rossum and Erik van Blokland work from their respective homes in The Hague, The Netherlands. Their goal is to create typefaces that do more than the usual fonts—they create animations, music, typography, web sites, and some graphic design as well. Check 'em out! Be sure to read their rant on embedded fonts in PDF documents.
- http://www.letterror.com/LTR_About.html

Type designer **Thomas Mueller's Liquid Typography** site includes his portfolio and thesis project.
- http://www.razorfish.com/thomas/

■ note

HTML Type Versus Graphical Type

There are basically two kinds of typographical elements on the web (or the printed page, for that matter): body type and headline type. Body type, often referred to as body copy, composes the bulk of the written text. Body type is typically smaller and contains the majority of the written content of a web page. Headline type is typically larger and is used to quickly draw the viewer's eye to it, help define a page break, or organize multiple ideas.

You can make body and headline type a couple of different ways on the web. One way involves using HTML and specialized font tags.

The alternative way is to create graphics that have images of type as the visual content instead of pictures. This kind of image-based type is referred to in this chapter as *graphic-based type*. HTML type is ideal for body copy, and graphic-based type is ideal for headlines. This chapter examines procedures for using standard HTML type, adding specialized type tags, and methods for making graphic images with headline type using Photoshop and Illustrator. Understanding some of the aesthetic issues related to type design principles is important before we move toward specific production methods.

Aesthetic Considerations

I think the web is an incredibly great way to gather information. Typically, when I find a page with a lot of text on it though, I'll print the page on my printer rather than sit and read through the text on my screen. Who wants to have the light of the monitor blaring in their face while having a recreational read? Give me crisp type on paper any day over that! I feel the same way about all computer-based text delivery systems, such as CD-ROMS and interactive kiosks. If you want me to read a lot of text, I'd rather do so on paper. As designers, we have to recognize that computer-based presentations pose distinct challenges and not treat our type-ridden web pages the same way as we would print.

So what design principles can you follow to help out your computer-screen-based reader? I advocate breaking up type into small paragraphs. Also, use different weights, such as bold and italics, to make it possible to skim the page easily and catch the important points. Adding hypertext whenever possible (text that links you from one spot to another, which is typically underlined or bold depending on the way the viewer's browser preferences are set) is another way to break up screen text into more digestible portions. The idea is to break up blocks of text as much as possible. Assume your readers are skimming, and make it easy for them to do.

Understand that you're asking a lot of your end viewer to sit and read pages and pages of type on a screen. It's your job to invent ways to hold his interest and to bring out the important ideas. This is possible through using both HTML and graphic-based text. Let's examine HTML first.

■ **tip**

Printing Web Pages

As if there weren't enough things to think about in web design, here's a new wrench to throw your way. If you intend to have your audience print information from your pages, you should design your pages with that in mind. Many people don't realize that when you set up a dark web page background with white type, for example, that the background is not printed with the file. What results? White type on white paper—or as some might say, nothing!

It's not to suggest that you have to always use light backgrounds with dark type on every page, but if there is a specific page that you know you want your audience to print, make sure you test print it yourself to see whether it's legible!

HTML-Based Typography

The advantages of using HTML for most body type needs are obvious. First of all, the memory and download time required for using native text is much lower than that used for graphics. Many sites are text-intensive, and using HTML-based type is the only choice to present large quantities of written information in a timely and efficient manner.

The following examples and code demonstrate how to use HTML type tags.

Headings

Headings are created using the <H></H> tag. The heading tags always have to be in the <HEAD> part of an HTML file. Here's some sample heading code:

```
<HTML><HEAD>
<H3>Welcome to this Site!</H3>
<H4>Welcome to this Site!</H4>
<H5>Welcome to this Site!</H5>
</HEAD>
</HTML>
```

> **Welcome to this Site!**
> **Welcome to this Site!**
> **Welcome to this Site!**

Bold

Here are a couple of ways to make type bold:

```
<HTML>
Talk <B>LOUD!</B><P>
Talk <STRONG>LOUD!</STRONG>
</HTML>
```

> Talk **LOUD!**
> Talk **LOUD!**

Italics

Here are a couple of ways to italicize type:

```
<HTML>
<I> Are you <I>ever going to shut up? </I> <P>
<EM> Are you <EM> ever going to shut up? </EM>
</HTML>
```

> Are you *ever going to shut up?*
> Are you *ever going to shut up?*

Preformatted

Preformatted text usually shows up in Courier or monotype. Here's the code:

```
<HTML>
<PRE> When are you    g    o    i    n    g
to be QUIET?</PRE>
</HTML>
```

> When are you   g   o   i   n   g   to be QUIET?

Blinking Text

Use with caution! Many end viewers find this tag annoying.

```
<BLINK> flash news!</BLINK>
```

Changing Font Sizes

Font sizes can be changed by using the <FONT SIZE> </FONT> tag. Here's how:

```
<HTML>
Do you ever <FONT SIZE=5>listen</FONT>
to direction anymore?
</HTML>
```

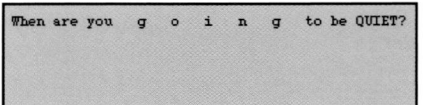

> Do you ever **listen** to direction anymore?

Drop Cap

Here's the code for creating drop caps:

```
<HTML>
<FONT SIZE=4>D</FONT>ROP <FONT SIZE=4>C</FONT>AP
</HTML>
```

DROP CAP

Small Cap

Use the following whenever you want small caps:

```
<HTML>
<FONT SIZE=1>SMALL CAPS </FONT><BR>
REGULAR CAPS
</HTML>
```

SMALL CAPS
REGULAR CAPS

Centering Text

Text can be centered by using the <CENTER> tag. Use the following code:

```
<HTML>
<CENTER>
I'm in the middle...
</CENTER>
</HTML>
```

I'm in the middle...

■ **note**

Useful URLs

Netscape has a site that has a style sheet for using the <FONT SIZE> tag as well: ■ http://www.cen. uiuc. edu/~ejk/fontsizes html. Logging on to this site automatically generates an entire range of font sizes by using the font your browser is set to. In addition, here are two helpful style sheets that Yoshinobo Takahas, from Disney Online, shares.

```
Header Tests (H[1-6])
This is a Header 1
This is a Header 2
This is a Header 3
This is a Header 4
This is a Header 5
This is a Header 6

    Font Size (FONT SIZE=[1-7])
This is Font Size 1
This is Font Size 2
This is Font Size 3
This is Font Size 4
This is Font Size 5
This is Font Size 6
This is Font Size 7

    Font Size (FONT SIZE=[-2-+4])
This is Font Size -2
This is Font Size -1
This is Font Size +0
This is Font Size +1
This is Font Size +2
This is Font Size +3
This is Font Size +4
```

```
    Header Tests (H[1-6])
This is a Header 1
This is a Header 2
This is a Header 3
This is a Header 4
This is a Header 5
This is a Header 6

    Font Size (FONT SIZE=[1-7])
This is Font Size 1
This is Font Size 2
This is Font Size 3
This is Font Size 4
This is Font Size 5
This is Font Size 6
This is Font Size 7

    Font Size (FONT SIZE=[-2-+4])
This is Font Size -2
This is Font Size -1
This is Font Size +0
This is Font Size +1
This is Font Size +2
This is Font Size +3
This is Font Size +4
```

Fun with ASCII!

ASCII text was a computer art craze in the 1970s, before computer graphics were something individuals could do easily on personal computers. There were no imaging programs that let people work with vector or bitmap artwork like today, so people made artwork with text characters. Many web pages keep the tradition of ASCII art alive. ASCII art can provide a welcome diversion from typical web art fare.

Publishing ASCII art over the web is a brilliant idea. It has all the advantages of speedy HTML-based text delivery and the advantage of working on almost every browser because the only HTML necessary to produce involves the <PRE> tag, which is widely supported.

Case Study: Hollywood Records

The Hollywood Records site at ■ http://www.hollywood rec.com uses ASCII for the low-fi (low-bandwidth) version of its site. An in-depth version of this case study is in my second book *Deconstructing Web Graphics*.

Here's a screen-shot of one of its pages that uses ASCII.

Beginning here and ending on the following page is the HTML source code for the image on the left.

```
<HTML>
<HEAD>
<TITLE>GWEN MARS Press</TITLE>
</HEAD>
<BODY TEXT="#A99A05" LINK="#A99A05"
VLINK="#FFFFFF" BGCOLOR="#001000">
<CENTER>
<PRE>
<FONT SIZE=+0>
<B>
<A HREF="/HollywoodRecords/Bands/GwenMars/
Press/GwenMarsPressM.html">
HI-FI GRAFX</A> /
<A HREF="/HollywoodRecords/Bands/GwenMars/
GwenMarsV.html">SCI-FI VR</A> /
<A HREF="/Note">EMAIL US</A> /
<A HREF="/Help">HELP</A>
<A HREF="/HollywoodRecords/Hollywood
RecordsL.html">HOLLYWOOD RECORDS</A>/
<A HREF="/HollywoodRecords/Bands/
BandRosterL.html"> MUSICIANS</A> /
<HREF="/HollywoodRecords/Bands/
GwenMars/GwenMarsL.html">GWEN MARS</A>
</B>
</FONT>
</PRE>
```

```
<PRE>
                              . . u o e e u u .

                    z $ $ $ $ R # " " ` ` ` " " " # R $ b L                    . u o d W $ W u

              : $ $ $ "                          ^ " % .        . o $ R # " " ` ` # $ $ $

             : $ $ F                                   + "                  8 $ $

           8 $ F                                                        $ $ P

         $ $ "                                                      d $ $ "

        $ $ ~                                                    d $ $ "

       $ $ F                                                  d $ $ "

      t $ $                                                d $ $ "

      $ $ F                                          x @ $ P `

     ' $ $ .                                    . @ $ $ "

     9 $ $ .                          . ~      . @ $ $ #

     9 $ $ .                    . e "     . @ $ $ # `

      z $ $ $ $ &                . o $ "    u @ $ $ #

     . @ $ $ $ " $ $ $ L        . z $ $ "   z $ $ R "

     : $ $ $ #    ? $ $ $   . o $ $ * "  . d $ $ #

     : $ $ $ "          . o $ $ $ #   z $ $ # `                         :

     @ $ $ "       u @ $ $ $ P "  u @ * "                          d

    : $ $ $ L  . o $ $ $ $ $ "  . d $ $ $ N                        x R

   : $ $ $ $ $ $ $ R " `    `     ' # $ $ $ k                   d $ "

   ' * * * * " "              " $ $ $ $ e u            . u @ $ $ "

                      " * $ $ $ $ $ $ $ $ $ $ $ $ $ # "

                         ` ` `
</PRE>
<FONT SIZE=+2><B><CODE>PRESS INFO</CODE></B></FONT><P>
</PRE>
</FONT>
</CENTER>
</BODY>
</HTML>
```

The Hollywood Records design team worked with a Mac-based program called Gifscii. Gifscii converts GIFs to ASCII. There are a few other products that enable you to work with ASCII artwork. Ascii Paint enables you to paint with ASCII characters: ■ http://www. umich.edu/~archive/mac/graphics/graphicsutil/asciipaint.sit.hqx.

HTML Font Choices

Chances are, the person looking at your web page is using the default settings for whatever browser he or she is viewing the page from. Most browsers default to using a Times Roman font. I've seen sites that include instructions to the viewer to change their default font to some other typeface. I wish them luck! I know very few web navigators who would take the time to change their settings to see an individual page. If you want your HTML type to be something other than Times Roman, don't count on asking your viewers to change their web browser settings as a foolproof method. In fact, I would imagine an extremely low percentage of viewers would actually act on the suggestion. As an alternative, try the <FONT FACE> tag described next.

Font Face Tag

If you want your audience to see your body copy in a font other than their default font settings, there is a new tag to the rescue, developed by Microsoft, called <FONT FACE>. A good explanation of this tag is found at ■ http: //www. microsoft.com/truetype/iexplor/iedemo.htm

The <FONT FACE> tag enables you to specify which font your page will be displayed in. The main caveat is that your end user must have the font you request installed, or the tag will not work.

Microsoft has a free Mac or PC Web Fonts package that you can download from ■ http://www.microsoft.com/truetype/hottopic.htm.

The Web Fonts package includes Arial, Arial Bold, Arial Italic, Arial Bold Italic, Arial Black, Comic Sans MS, Comic Sans MS Bold, Courier New, Courier New Bold, Courier New Italic, Courier New Bold Italic, Impact, Times New Roman, Times New Roman Bold, Times New Roman Italic, and Times New Roman Bold Italic.

The odds are that—even though Microsoft offers the free Web Fonts Package to Mac and PC users—most of your web audience won't even know about it or take the time to install fonts that don't ship on their system. For that reason, it's safest to go with these basic fonts that ship with every Mac and PC.

PC	Mac
Arial	Helvetica
Courier New	Courier
Times New Roman	Times

Two other problems worth mentioning occur when you add bold tags or header tags to the <FONT FACE> tag. The results might look funky, so here is some sample code to show how to use the <FONT FACE> tag:

```
<HTML>
<FONT FACE ="helvetica, arial"> TESTING,
</FONT> one, two, three.
</HTML>
```

TESTING, one, two, three.

To add size variation, add the SIZE attribute to the tag:

```
<HTML>
<FONT FACE="helvetica, arial" SIZE=5>
TESTING, </FONT> one, two, three.
</HTML>
```

TESTING, one, two, three.

To change the color, add the COLOR attribute to the tag:

```
<HTML>
<FONT FACE ="helvetica, arial" SIZE=5
COLOR="cc3366"> TESTING, </FONT> one, two,
three.
</HTML>
```

TESTING, one, two, three.

■ warning

Font Size Differences Between Macs and PCs

No, you are not nuts. If you have a Mac and a PC, you will notice that standard 12-point default fonts look different on each platform. Fonts display larger on PCs than on Macs. Sigh. I know you don't want to hear this, but this is one of the cross-platform discrepancy things that there is no real solution for. Except perhaps to serve different pages to Mac and PC end viewers, which is more than a bit too labor-intensive for most site designers. Remember to always check your pages on both platforms. You can adjust glaring problems accordingly.

A PC screen shot of my site.

A Mac screen shot of my site.

For amusement, I composited the two together in Photoshop by using the Multiply filter. The size differences with the graphic (the man) are nil—but check out the size differences of the type! Mama mia!

Graphics-Based Typography

We've just examined many HTML possibilities; now it's time to move on to graphics-based text. Using graphics for text instead of HTML is where you get the chance to flash your type design aesthetic for the world to see. You'll be able to use any font your heart desires and add special effects to it, such as drop shadows, glows, and blurs. A great advantage to using this technique is that the end users will not have to own the font you used or have it installed on their system. Because it's a graphic, it shows up like any other graphic regardless of what system your end viewers use.

Some of the chapters already presented demonstrate techniques I recommend you combine with your text-based graphics. Using transparency and solid colors that match the background color of your page are two processes in particular that can be employed in combination to achieve some of the effects described here.

■ note

Aliasing Versus Anti-Aliasing

Most digital artists prefer the way anti-aliasing looks, but anti-aliasing is not always the best technique with typography.

Very small type actually looks worse and quite mushy if it's anti-aliased. Think about HTML type, the type on your computer desktop, and the type in a word processor. Very small type sizes (12 pt. and less) do not look good anti-aliased.

yucky mushy small type that's anti-aliased...

This anti-aliased small type looks bad.

no longer yucky mushy small type because it's aliased

This aliased, HTML type looks much better.

Using Photoshop for Type Design

Photoshop is the ideal environment to create type and graphic web elements in. Photoshop layers enable you to do all kinds of special type effects for headlines that you can use on the web. Here are some sample type design treatments and instructions to create them. I've used Photoshop 4.0 for these examples, but all of these techniques work in earlier versions of Photoshop as well.

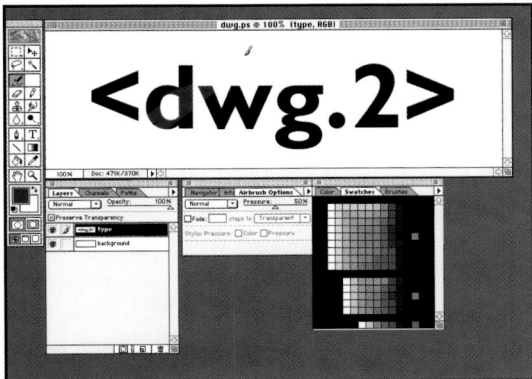

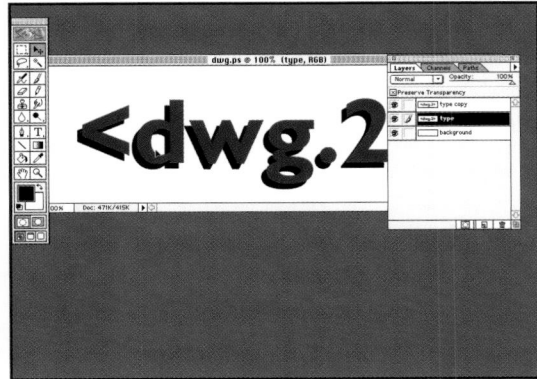

This example demonstrates using the Preserve Transparency feature of Photoshop layers. When checked in the Layers Palette, Preserve Transparency enables you to change the color of the type by painting or filling it. I have a sample browser-safe palette, organized by reds, open to select colors from, which is one of hundreds of artistically organized color swatch sets from the *Coloring Web Graphics* CD-ROM.

Because my type is on a layer, it's easy to copy so I have two versions of the same layer. I filled the bottom layer with black, using the Preserve Transparency feature. I then moved the layer with the Move Tool to create a drop shadow.

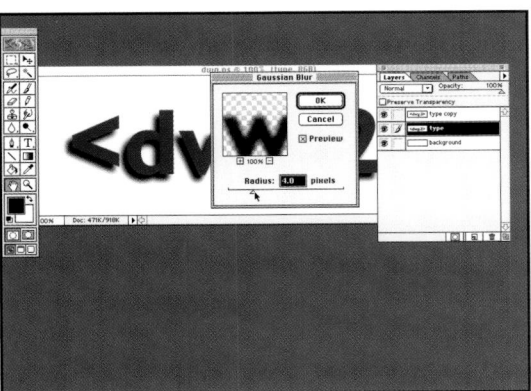

Realistic drop shadows are easy to make in Photoshop. Because my shadow is on a separate layer, adding the Gaussian Blur filter enables me to preview its setting before I commit.

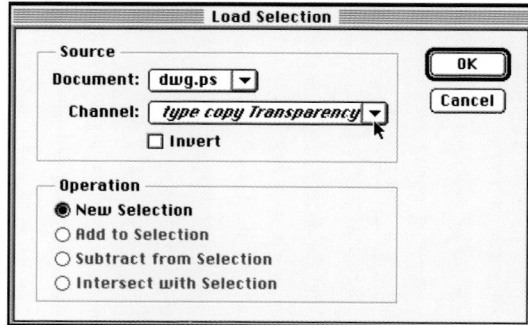

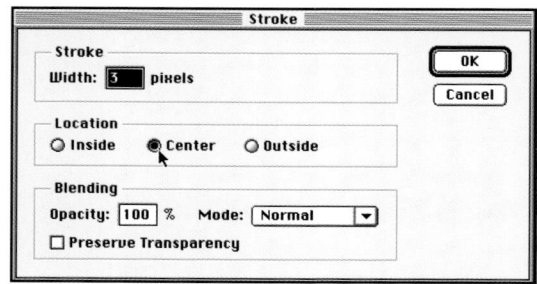

When you leave type separated on separate layers, a mask that is invisible is stored. To load the mask, choose Select, Load Selection and then set the Channel information in this dialog box to Transparency.

By loading the selection, it's possible to then stroke the selection. I chose first to Load the Selection from the transparency of the type layer and then created a new empty layer with the selection still active. By choosing Edit, Stroke, the resulting stroked line went onto an independent layer. When working with type treatments in Photoshop, it should always be your goal to have every element isolated on its own layer so that it can be independently manipulated.

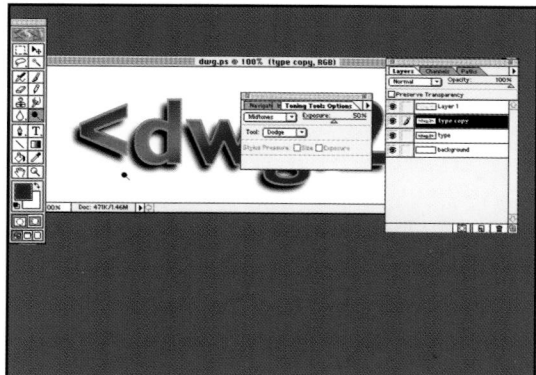

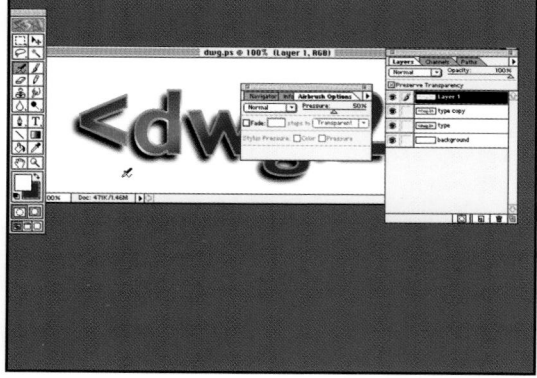

This shows an example of a stroked edge around the type. The chrome-style effect is created with the Dodge and Burn tools. It's possible to create lighting effects with these tools and add more three-dimensional look to the type, if that's the look you're going for.

In this example, using Preserve Transparency, I am able to airbrush highlights into the stroked text layer.

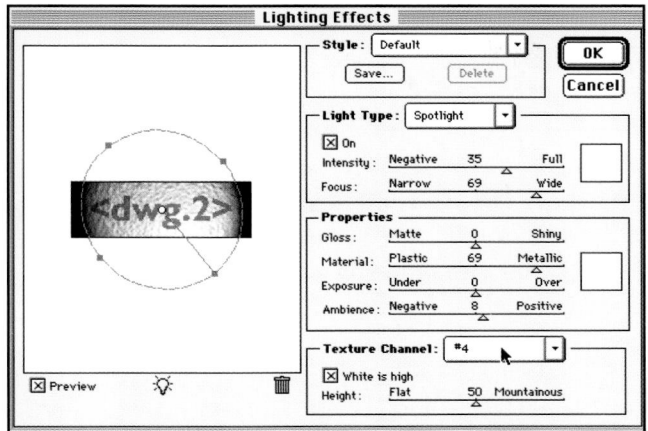 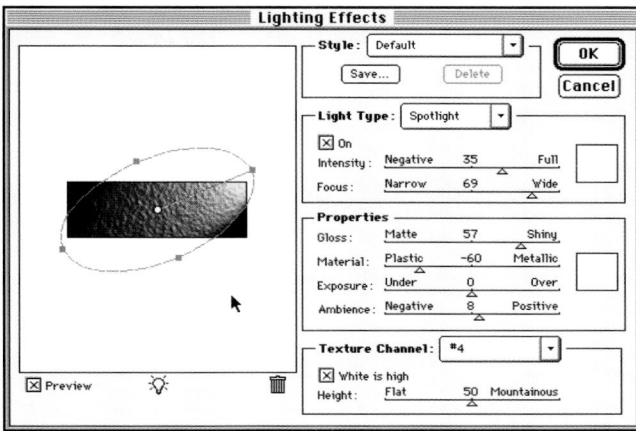

It's also possible to add lighting effects. I show two examples here, one with the Texture Channel set to None and the other with it set to #4. The #4 represents an alpha channel I made by simply adding noise to a black-and-white piece of artwork.

It's possible to make type treatments with lots of independent layers and lighting effects in Photoshop. Using the techniques of keeping everything on separate layers helps a lot.

This type treatment was made very simple, with a single drop shadow and using the Cloud filter for the upper type layer.

Working with Illustrator Type in Photoshop

Unless I have a very simple logo, I rarely set type in Photoshop. The typesetting tools in Photoshop are limited and disappointing. Photoshop excels in its coloring treatment capabilities. You can't make soft-edged shadows or work with layers and filters as easily in any other graphics program. Illustrator, however, has far more sophisticated and professional type controls, and is a much better type design program. It does such things as type along a path, type within a defined space, size, kern, and adjust tracking, leading, and spacing. The problem is that Illustrator was created as a PostScript program and writes files in formats that the web does not recognize. Here's how to set the type in Illustrator and bring the results into Photoshop so that the type can be utilized on a web page.

Open a new Illustrator file. Set your type. You'll find all the controls your typesetter heart has been waiting for—sizing, kerning, spacing, superscript, and so on. Look to the glossary for explanations if you aren't familiar with these terms. Once you've got everything set the way you want it, save the file as a default Illustrator 5 document and quit.

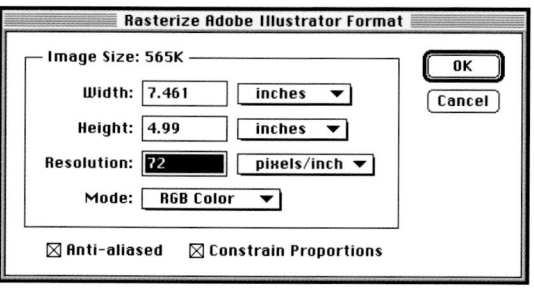

Open Photoshop. Open the Illustrator file, and this dialog box appears.

Once you've opened the file in Photoshop, it automatically comes in on its own layer and is a perfect candidate for the techniques described previously.

Here is the final image after it has been touched up with Photoshop. What teamwork!

Writing the HTML to Place Your Text Graphics into the Page

Placing graphics on a web page is addressed in depth in Chapter 9, "Rules, Bullets, and Buttons," and Chapter 10, "Navigation-Based Graphics." The basic way to insert a graphic on a page is to use the <IMG SRC> tag. Here's how to put the drop shadow artwork, created earlier, on a page:

```
<HTML>
<IMG SRC="dropshad.jpeg">
</HTML>
```

If you want to link the drop shadow image to another source, combine the <IMG SRC> tag with an <A HREF> tag. Here's how:

```
<HTML>
<A HREF="http://www.domain.com"><IMG
SRC="dropshad.jpeg"></A>
</HTML>
```

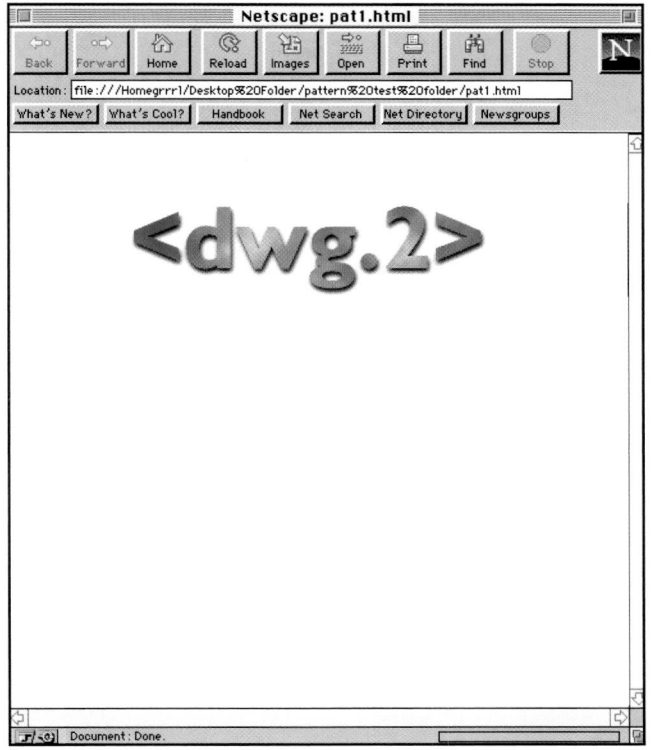

This web page headline was created using text graphics as an alternative to HTML.

Mixing Graphic Type and HTML

If you want to get clever, I've seen wonderful examples of mixing HTML and graphic-based typography. An in-depth version of this case study is in my second book, *Deconstructing Web Graphics*.

Case Study: Alice In Chains

The Alice in Chains site, designed by Mary Maurer and Peter Anton of Sony Music Online, uses mixed HTML and graphic type in a very novel way. Most of the type was set in varying sizes to get a more organic, varied, and erratic look. They used a combination of graphics-based typography tricks and HTML tricks.

This kind of typesetting is impossible to do within Photoshop, which has limited type-handling capabilities. Photoshop allows you to set type in any font within your system but doesn't offer size controls over individual letters.

Mary used QuarkXPress for laying out the typography for the Photoshop files. Because it's impossible to directly import a QuarkXPress file into Photoshop, Mary took screen captures of those files. (A screen capture takes a picture of anything that's on your screen, regardless of what program you're using, and creates a file, which then can be opened in Photoshop.)

Mary also worked with Peter to see whether he could program HTML text to simulate some of her Quark-XPress files. She was quite pleased with the results, which are deconstructed in the following section.

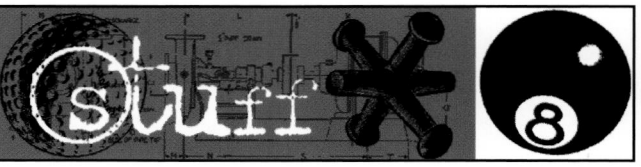

This image uses the font Trixie, by Fonthaus (Fonthaus has a web site at ■ http://home.cityqueue.com/CityQueue/business/fonthaus.html), but each letter is set in a different size. This was done in Quark, and was brought into Photoshop via screen capture software.

The HTML-based text had mixed type sizes, too. This page can be viewed at ■ http://www.music.sony.com/Music/ArtistInfo/AliceInChains/biolane3.html.

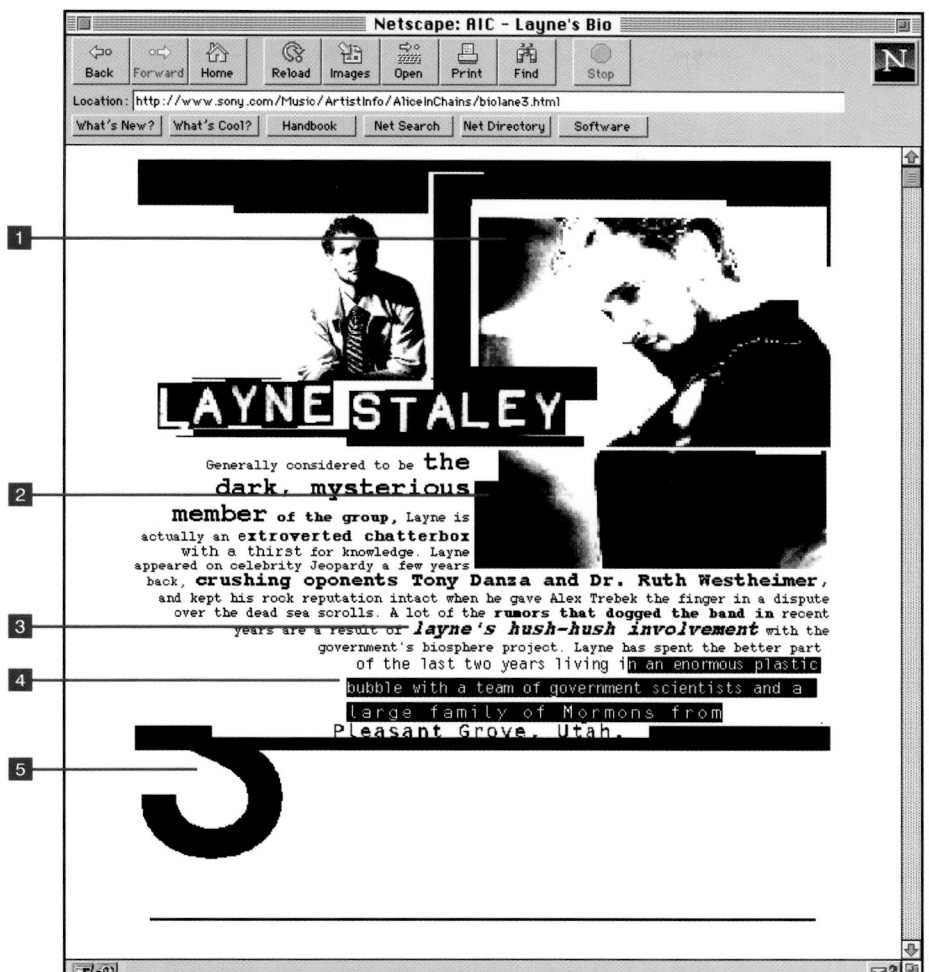

Here's the finished result of the HTML, which is deconstructed on the following two pages.

HTML for Mixed Type Sizes

```
<HTML>
<HEAD>
<TITLE>AIC - Layne's Bio</TITLE
</HEAD>
<BODY BGCOLOR="FFFFFF"   TEXT = "# 000000" LINK =
"#000000" ALINK = "#E8F13A" VLINK = "#000000" >
<CENTER>
<TABLE BORDER=0 WIDTH=522 HEIGHT=200>
<TD NOWRAP WIDTH=522 HEIGHT=200 ALIGN="RIGHT">
```
1 `<IMG SRC="biolaypg3hed2.gif"`
`LOWSRC="biolaypg3hed1.gif" WIDTH=520 HEIGHT=221>`
2 `<IMG SRC="biolaypg3hed3.gif" WIDTH=264 HEIGHT=93`
`ALIGN="RIGHT"><TT><FONT SIZE="3">`
3 `Generally considered to be <STRONG><FONT`
`SIZE="+3">the dark, mysterious member</FONT`
`SIZE="+3"> of the group,</STRONG> Layne is actually`
`an <FONT SIZE="+1">e<STRONG>xtroverted`
`chatterbox</FONT SIZE="+1"> with a thirst</STRONG>`
`for knowledge. Layne appeared on celebrity Jeopardy`
`a few years back, <STRONG><FONT SIZE="+2">crushing`
`oponents Tony Danza and Dr. Ruth`
`Westheimer,</STRONG></FONT SIZE="+2"> and kept his`
`rock reputation intact when he gave Alex Trebek the`
`finger in a dispute over the dead sea scrolls.`
`A lot of the <STRONG>rumors that dogged the band`
`in</STRONG> recent years are a result of`
`<I><STRONG><FONT SIZE="+2">layne's hush-hush`

```
involvement</I></STRONG></FONT SIZE="+2"> with the
government's biosphere project.  Layne has spent the
better part
```
4 `<IMG SRC="biolaypg3text.gif" ALIGN="CENTER">`
5 `<IMG SRC="biolaypg3bot.gif" WIDTH=522 HEIGHT=113`
`ALIGN="CENTER">`
```
</TD>
</TABLE>
<P>
<BR>
<CENTER>
<HR NOSHADE WIDTH =500>
<P>
<BR>
<BR>
<TT>
<A HREF="biolane4.html">Next?</A>
<P>
<BR>
<BR>
¦¦ <A HREF="bio.html">Bios</A> ¦¦
</CENTER>
</BODY>
</HTML>
```

1 Here's a **LOWSRC** trick. The **LOWSRC** image loads before the **SRC** image.

The **IMG SRC** file **"biolaypg3hed2.gif"** loads second. It's the inverse of the **LOWSRC** file, causing the animation to look as though its polarity flashes.

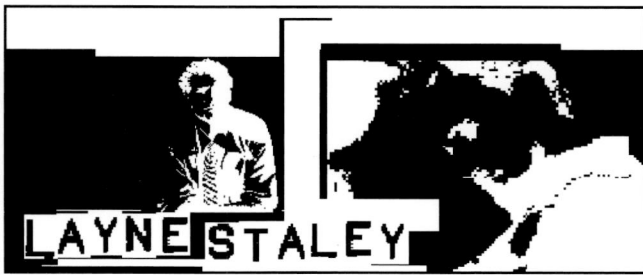

The **LOWSRC** image **"biolaypg3hed1.gif"** loads first.

2 The next **IMG SRC** is instructed to align to the right of the text by using the **ALIGN=RIGHT** attribute. The **<TT>** tag indicates that monospaced type will follow until its closed container is specified.

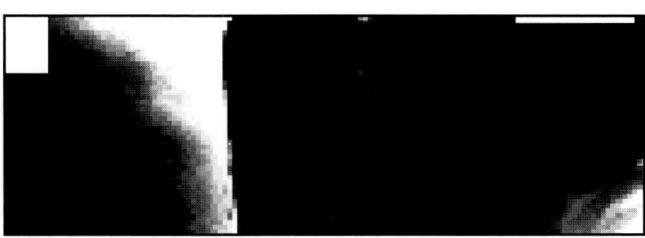

This **IMG SRC** file **"biolaypg3hed3.gif"** is instructed to align to the right of the text.

3 A lot of the **<STRONG>**rumors that dogged the band in**</STRONG>** recent years are a result of **<I> <STRONG> <FONT SIZE="+2">**layne's hush-hush involvement**</I></STRONG></FONT SIZE="+2">** with the government's biosphere project. Layne has spent the better part

A number of different tags are present here that instruct the browser to display the type differently. **<STRONG>** creates bold text on most browsers. **<FONT SIZE>** indicates that the size of the text will be higher or lower than the default depending on whether the number is positive or negative.

4 This next image aligns **CENTER** and butts up directly to the bottom of the preceding HTML text.

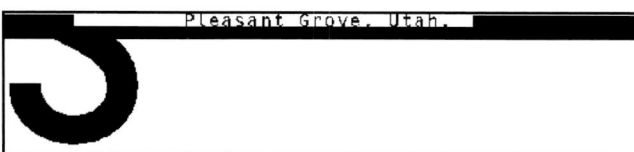

The **IMG SRC** file **"biolaypg3text.gif."**

5 This next image aligns **CENTER** and butts up directly to the bottom of the preceding image.

The **IMG SRC** file **"biolaypg3bot.gif."**

Case Study: Art Center College of Design

The Art Center College of Design site at ■ http://www
.artcent.edu) was designed by Gudrun Frommherz and
Darin Beamin. They used another technique used to
enhance HTML text to mix type sizes, fonts (Geneva
and Courier), and styles such as plain, bold, and italic.

```
throughout the pr<b>ogram. In s</b>ome classes students pursue self-directed
```

A sample line of HTML for making type bold with the <B> tag.

throughout the **program. In** some classes students pursue self-directed projects, while

By using the <B> tag for making text bold, Gudrun was able to
change the weights of the ASCII-based HTML typography through
mixing bold and normal text characters. These shapes created
abstract forms that are meant to please the eye and invite the
reader to study the content.

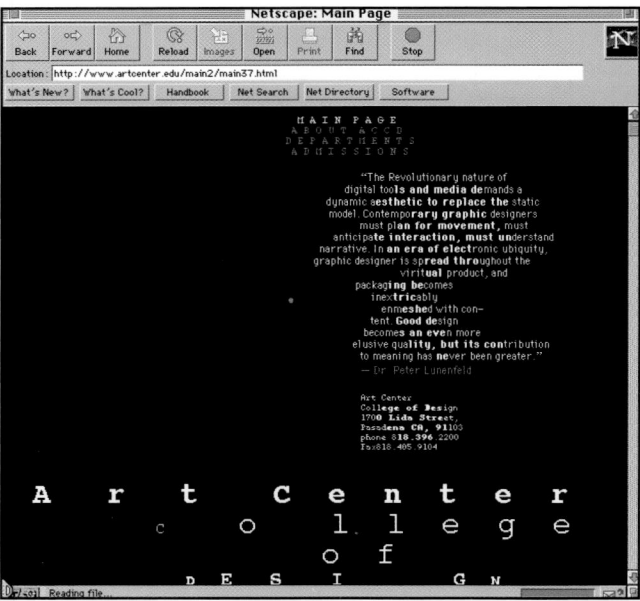

Here's the finished result on the web page.

In this example, two typefaces—Geneva and Courier—
are used, as well as setting different type sizes. This is
accomplished by using the <PRE> and <FONT> tags.

```
<PRE>
<FONT SIZE="+4"><b>A    r    t
C  e  n  t  e  r</B> </FONT>
<FONT SIZE="+2">C</font>
<FONT SIZE="+4">o    l    l  e  g  e  o  f</FONT>
<FONT SIZE="+2"><B>D</B></FONT>
<FONT SIZE="+3"><B>E    S    I
G</B></FONT>
<FONT SIZE="+2"><B>N</B></FONT>
</PRE>
```

Above is the HTML to create the words on the bottom. The
<PRE> tag forces the type to be represented in the Courier
typeface. It also instructs the browser to honor the spacing
between words and letters. The <FONT SIZE> tag *is* used
to change the size of individual letters.

A close-up view of the lettering on the bottom of the screen that
uses the <PRE> and <FONT SIZE> tags.

Digital Font Foundries

Today there are tens of thousands of PostScript and TrueType fonts available to personal computer users. It's a great benefit to be able to view and order fonts online, especially those late nights when you're designing something that's due the next day and you need a specific font you don't yet own. If you're looking for new fonts, check out these URLs:

House Industries:
- http://www.digitmad.com/house/house.html

Letraset Online:
- http://www.letraset.com/letraset/

Handwriting Fonts:
- http://www.execpc.com/~adw/

Fonthead Design:
- http://www.fonthead.com

Fonts Online:
- http://www.dol.com/fontsOnline/

Emigre:
- http://www.emigre.com

Agfa Type:
- http://www.agfahome.com/products/prodfram/type.html

Internet Font Libraries:
- http://jasper.ora.com:90/comp.fonts/Internet-Font-Archive/index.html

---

■ note

Font Legends

The following individuals are meant to spark your interest. They are just a few of the many legends in type design. You might want to check out books written by them, or about them—as well as pursue others you find of particular interest. Studying the past as well as researching 20th-century works can be a wonderful source of inspiration that effortlessly translates itself into designing meaningful web graphics.

- Jan Tschichold
- Laslo Moholy-Nagy
- A.M. Cassandre
- Kurt Schwitters
- Matthew Carter
- David Carson
- El Lissitsky
- Rudy Vanderlands
- Bradbury Thompson
- Lucille Tenazas
- Neville Brody

Scanning Techniques for the Web

BROWSER SAFE COLOR

33FF

<H1>

typography

<TABL

0033CC

<STRONG>

<img src="

Width ="500"

IMAGE OPTIMIZATION

Height ="600"

</A>

<center

Imaging techniques

Animation, sound and

Web file formats

bgcolor ="FFFFCC"

alink="cyan"

33

LYNDA.COM

<center> <BODY>

Antiali

www Design

Scanning for the Web

In the spirit of pursuing innovation and originality in web design, you might consider using scanned imagery instead of clip art or stock photos. If that's not enough, you might find yourself asked by new clients to scan hundreds of existing images from a print catalog for use on their web site. Or there's always the time where the BIG new client gives you the logo on a bad photocopy and expects you to do something with it that's better than anything that's been seen before. For whatever reason, being able to scan is a useful part of any web designer's bag of tricks, and just like everything else, scanning comes with its own set of limits, nuances, and quirks.

Here are some of the issues this chapter covers:

- What kind of scanner is best for web design
- How to scan for web resolution
- Getting rid of moirés
- Scanning 3D objects
- Learning to mask
- Image processing scanned artwork

Scanner Equipment

There are all kinds of scanners at all kinds of price points—high-resolution scanners, scanners that scan transparencies, hand-held portable scanners, and digital cameras that double as scanners. It's a confusing group of choices, but as an experienced screen-based designer, I'll share my hard-earned wisdom and advice.

First of all, if you already own a scanner, you don't have to buy a different one for web design. The web probably makes the lowest demands of any other medium you might use a scanner for. Because everything you'll do is for screen resolution, not print, you don't have to care so much about the quality of the scans. That might sound blasphemous, but with all the great imaging programs out there, it's really not necessary to have the best-quality original scan. You can fix a lot of things in post-processing, especially if you use Photoshop. Practical imaging techniques follow in the "Post Processing Scans with Photoshop 4.0" section later in this chapter.

I always look to the speed of the scanner as the highest consideration when purchasing a system for screen-based artwork (web, multimedia, or video). I have found that what really counts the most is how fast you can get the scanner to capture an image. This is especially true if you are scanning a high volume of images. A slow scanner can really eat away at productivity. There are lots of fantastic scanners on the market that are fast. You may want to find one that scans the red, green, and blue pass at once rather than slower models that take a full pass for each color. A good place to research scanners is, you guessed it...on the web.

For scannner comparisons, check out the following:

This site compares different scanners and shows the images that result:
■ http://www.jb.com/~carla/hdwcomp.htm

Search any **Ziff Davis Publication** (I found more than 1,000 results when I searched for "scanner")
■ http://www.zdnet.com/home/filters/mags.html

Scanner Comparison Table
■ http://www.hsdesign.com/scanning/table/scanner_table5.html

Search **MacWorld** magazine for scanner reviews
■ http://www.macworld.com/search/search.html

The last equipment comment I'll make is about SCSI (pronounced scuzzy—hence, one of my personal favorite computer terms) chain conflicts. A SCSI device requires a special SCSI cable, which should come standard with most scanners. Most scanners for both Macs and PCs are SCSI-based devices. I've experienced a lot of trouble in my day with SCSI conflicts and bad SCSI cables. Be sure to use a high-quality cable, and the thicker and shorter the better. If you experience problems with your scanner, try hooking it up directly to your computer and unhooking any other external devices, such as hard drives or CD-ROM drives. If you continue to have problems, check to see whether you have outdated scanner software. As operating systems change, scanner software changes, too. Most of the major scanning manufacturers have web sites where you can download software updates.

Dictionary of Scanning Terms

DPI (Dots Per Inch): A measurement relating to the number of halftone dots per inch; used for printers.

LPI (Lines Per Inch): Used to measure halftone dot screens.

Resolution: Measurement of how many pixels, dots, or lines per inch are used by images, printers, and screens.

Moiré pattern: An unwanted dot pattern that creates a noticeable screen that degrades the scanned image. It is caused by scanning artwork with a pre-existing halftone dot pattern.

Resolution

If you are used to scanning for print design, you may find yourself perplexed by the differences between scanning for print and scanning for the web. It all boils down to resolution—for print you must work with very high resolution, and for the web you must work with very low.

Resolution in general baffles most people. Resolution is often defined by scanners using a combination of measurements specified by dpi (dots per inch) and inches. In print, you have all kinds of complex calculations to determine proper scanning dpi that depends on final printing screens and processes. On the web it's much easier; there's only one dpi to use or think about—72 dpi. So all you really need to know when scanning is what your target image size will be in inches or pixel dimensions.

In some cases (typically when there's line art detail such as where there is type or cartoony graphics), it yields higher quality to scan larger than 72 dpi and then reduce the image to 72 dpi later in an imaging program. There is no reason to do this with organic style imagery, such as photographs and abstract or soft detailed illustrations, because those types of images are much more forgiving. Sometimes scanning large and shrinking in Photoshop causes the image to become slightly blurry. Unfortunately, you have to experiment on an image-by-image basis—just like the image compression examples Chapter 4, "Low-Bandwidth Graphics," demonstrated, different types of images respond differently.

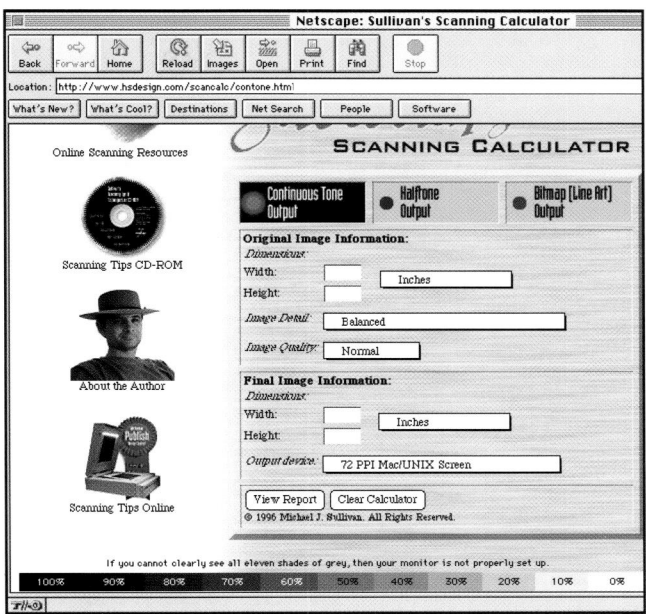

If you're uncertain about resolution settings, check out Michael Sullivan's awesome site and amazing scanning calculator found at
■ http://www.hsdesign.com.

Resizing Images in Photoshop 4.0

Understanding how to resize images is important when working with scans. You want to ensure that your images are 72 dpi with web-bound graphics and photographs. Many scanners default to scanning at higher dots per inch settings, meaning it's up to you to scale the images down to web-appropriate size.

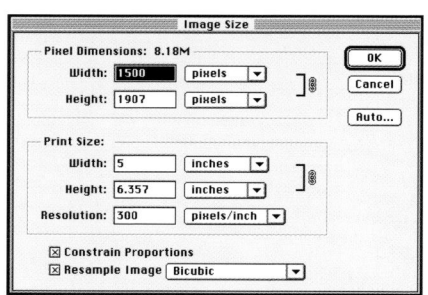 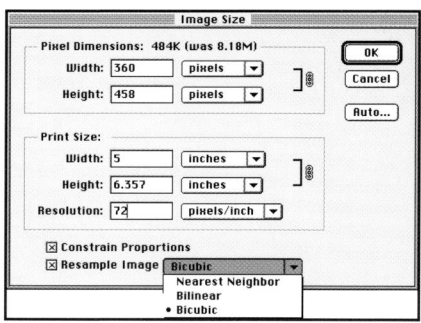

Under Image, select Image Size. Make sure you check Resample Image and Constrain Proportions (unless you want to intentionally distort the image).

When you choose to resize an image, you have different interpolation methods to select from.

Bicubic: Usually the best quality type of reduction method. Adds anti-aliasing, sometimes not desired.

Bilinear: In-between quality; faster and lower quality than Bicubic, but better quality than Nearest Neighbor.

Nearest Neighbor: Much faster than Bicubic; lower quality, unless you want to retain an aliased edge.

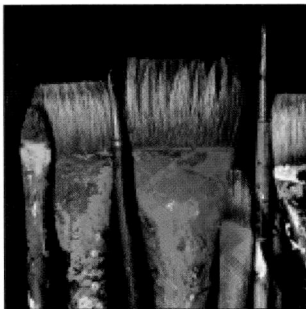

Here's a small image of brushes.

When enlarged, notice how the image becomes soft and out of focus. Never scale up in size, or this will be the result. Scan large and reduce, rather than scanning small and enlarging.

■ **warning**

Do Not Resize Art in Indexed Color!

Be careful when you scale images to make sure the Photoshop mode is RGB, and not Indexed Color. If you open a GIF, let's say, it will be in Indexed Color mode. When you go to resize it, no amount of finesse will improve the image because the image won't shift color outside its fixed color table. Go to Image, Mode and select RGB, and everything will work beautifully.

Scanning 3D Stuff

Few people realize that you can put objects on flatbed scanners, and they turn out really cool. Designers Brandee Selck and David Beach from IUMA (■ http://www.iuma.com), one of the sites I profiled in my book *Deconstructing Web Graphics*, did this with many of their web graphics. Bruce Heavin, the co-author of my book *Coloring Web Graphics*, also used experimental scanning—placing the tools of his trade, paint brushes, directly on the scanner.

You can try some of these techniques yourself and see whether you like the results. I recently taught some junior high school students how to scan still images, and they told me they'd been scanning their faces with their eyes closed, just like people do on photocopiers. The results were great! Try scanning your stuff for fun; use your imagination! It works really well.

Brandee Selk and David Beach of IUMA placed a Pyrex container with apple juice and ice directly on the scanner as source material for this graphic. The buttons were made from bottle caps of various liquors that were also laid on top the scanner and composited later into the image by using Photoshop.

The napkin used on the Cool Extras page from IUMA was scanned directly on a flatbed scanner. The tray was created from a piece of scanned metal that was used as a texture. The tray shape was created in Illustrator, brought into Photoshop, and then the texture was inserted as the polishing touch.

This image from *Coloring Web Graphics* resulted from my co-author, Bruce Heavin, putting his paint brushes directly on the scanner. This little-known and little-used technique is a fabulous way to get original graphics into the computer quickly and easily.

Photo CDs Instead of Scans

I often work with Photo CDs instead of scans. Whenever I have transparencies to scan, it's cheaper for me (because I don't own a transparency scanner) to have my transparencies converted to Photo CDs. Each image is scanned by a local Kodak Photo CD service provider and stored at many different resolutions to a CD-ROM disc. For web-based images, you can almost always use the lowest resolution from the CD, and the images will look great.

> **For more info:**
> ■ http://www.kodak.com/productInfo/catalog/genInfo/aboutPCD.shtml
> **For a directory of local service providers:**
> ■ http://www.kodak.com/digitalImaging/piwSites/piwSites.shtml

---

■ tip

For books on Photo CDs:

The Photo CD Book
Publisher: Verbum Books
Retail Price: $14.95 ■ ISBN: 1-882305-01-9

The Official Photo CD Handbook
Publisher: Peachpit Press
Author: Michael Gosney
Retail Price: $39.95 ■ ISBN: 1-56609-172-1

Photo CD: Quality Photos at Your Fingertips
Publisher: Micro Publishing News
Author: John Larish
Retail Price: $27.95 ■ ISBN: 0941845095

Start with a Scan
Publisher: Peachpit Press
Authors: Janet Ashford and John Odam
Retail Price: $34.95 ■ ISBN: 0-201-88456-9

Post Processing Scans with Photoshop 4.0

Scanners often offer a lot of different color choices. It's possible to scan in full color, 256 colors, grayscale, with half-tones, or in black and white. It's always best to start with the most information you can capture and let the image processor of your choice reduce the colors, or implement halftoning later. I recommend that you scan in either 24-bit color or 256 grayscale, and then open the file in your image editing program to tweak colors, contrast, and brightness.

Because I am most familiar with Photoshop and Photoshop has the most image processing capabilities, I have limited my examples in this chapter to be Photoshop-specific. What follows are tutorials that will help you understand how to color correct scans, improve their quality, and make them web appropriate. Although other image editors can do some of these same feats, Photoshop is geared specifically for altering and improving photographs, which is why it is the most popular image editing software on any platform or operating system.

Correcting Color with Adjustment Layers in Photoshop 4.0

Often images that are custom scanned or created don't end up looking as you intended. The image might not be colorful enough, or it shifted in color from what you wanted, or the values of the image aren't holding up on the screen. In any of these cases, you will want to tamper with the variables of the image.

In previous versions of Photoshop, I recommend that you work on a copy of the scan in case some of the color and value alterations you make don't work to your liking. One of the great new features of Photoshop 4.0 is called Adjustment Layers. Adjustment Layers enable you to make changes and to revert to the original image any step along the way.

Here is an image Bruce Heavin painted and scanned. Let's say I'm unhappy with the colors that came from this bad scan so I want to change them.

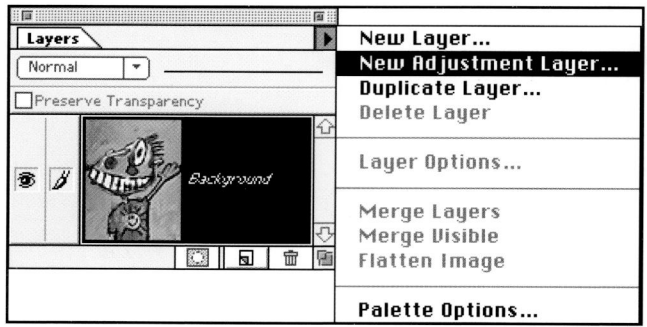

Here's how to set up an Adjustment Layer. Hold down the upper right arrow to select New Adjustment Layer.

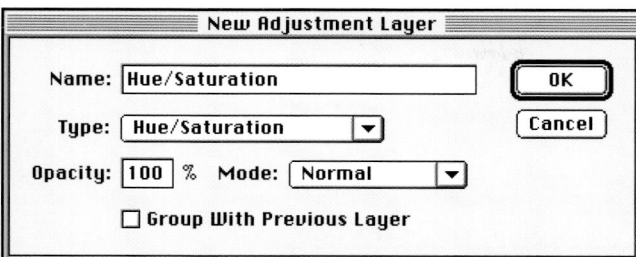

This brings up the dialog box for a new adjustment layer. You can make a choice from a host of Type options. In this case I will use Hue/Saturation to correct the color in my image.

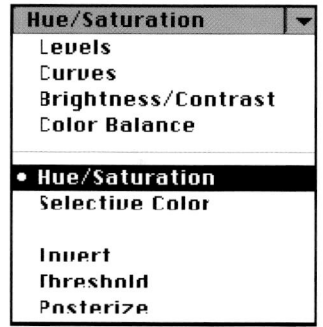

This menu shows some of the other Adjustment Layer options.

This screen shows how I have adjusted the hue of the image. Changing the hue shifts the color of the overall image. Be sure to have preview checked to get an accurate view of what is happening.

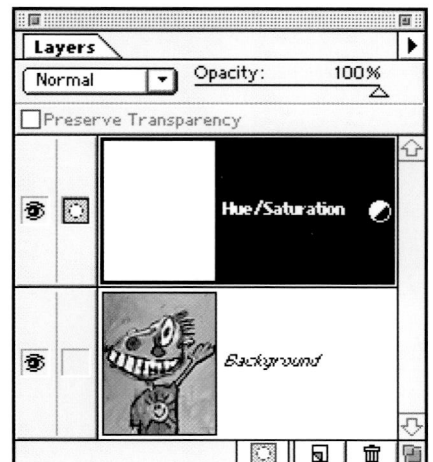

Notice that the Adjustment Layer sits on top of the image layer. This means the Adjustment Layer's opacity, order, or visibility can be changed. This makes it possible to return to the original image whenever you want!

If you look at the screen, the image has been changed to reflect the new hue settings. Be sure to save a copy of the image in Photoshop 4.0 file format so you have access to the Adjustment Layers again. No other file format will save them.

More Photoshop 4.0 Image Processing Tips

These are some of my favorite image processing tools
in Photoshop. Some of them are available as Layer
Adjustments, which make them even more desirable.

Levels

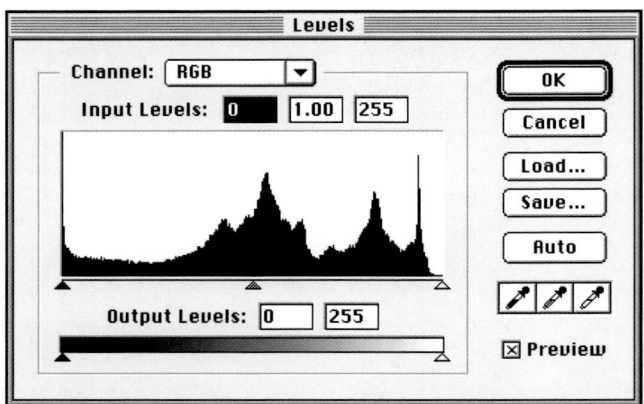

Levels are accessed through choosing the menu item Image, Adjust,
Levels. Levels enables you to see a histogram of the image, which
shows the image in values from black to white. Black levels are
represented on the left and white on the right. By moving sliders
or clicking with the eyedropper tools, you can dramatically alter
the contrast and brightness of your images.

When you move the black slider to the right, it increases the blacks.

When you move the white slider to the left, it increases the whites.

When you move the Output Levels slider to the right, it creates a screened back look.

When you move the Output Levels slider to the left, it creates a darkened image.

Color Balance

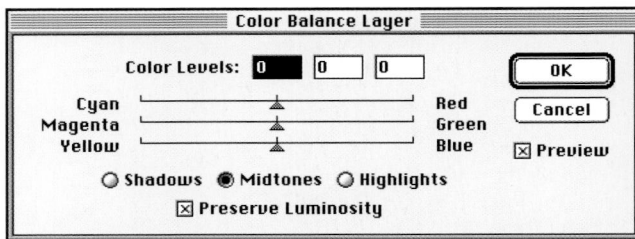

Color Balance is under the menu Image, Adjust, Color Balance. Color Balance changes the image based on selected areas, Shadows (dark areas), Midtones, and Highlights (light areas).

Changing the color by using Color Balance gives you much more latitude than any other means. You can change the midtones, highlights, and shadows independently.

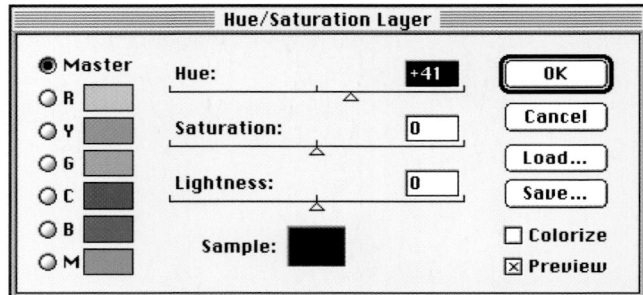

Hue/Saturation balance shifts the hue of the image. You can colorize an image, adjust the saturation and the color intensity to more or less, and add lightness or lack of.

One of my favorite things to do with the Hue/Saturation setting is to click Colorize. This transforms the image into a monochromatic color space, which can be adjusted on-the-fly using the sliders and preview window. Ta da!

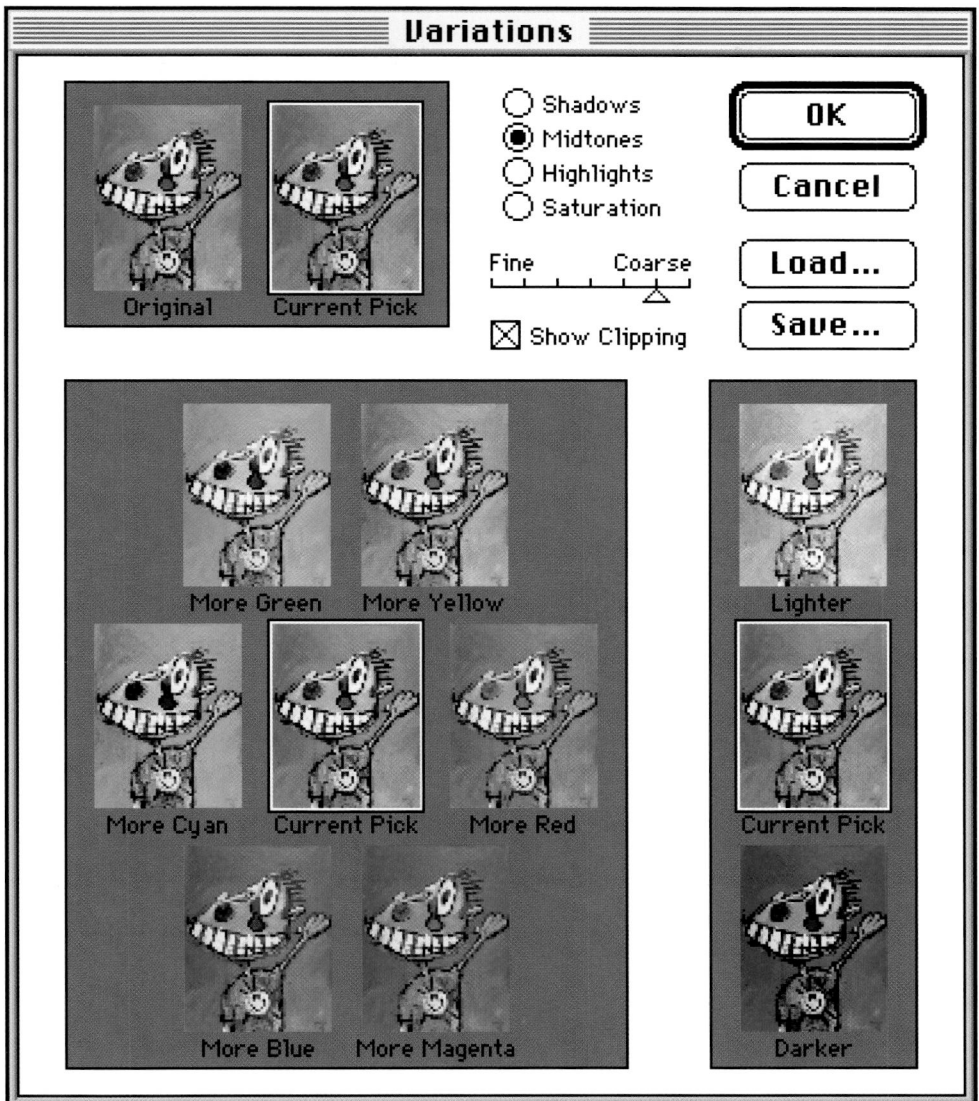

Variations are accessed by choosing Image, Adjust, Variations. Variations are a one-click wonder that give you control over the color of your image on a more intuitive level. If you wanted the image to have more blue, then you just click on the more blue image and all the images will change to have more blue. The center image is a preview of what your current image looks like as a result of your color decisions. You can also lighten and darken your image in the same way. Choosing between fine and coarse sets the amount of change you can incur. Fine settings make all the choices more subtle, and coarse makes them more abrupt.

Dot Screen Patterns and Moirés

There might be times when you are asked to scan existing catalogs or product brochures to repurpose images for the web. Unfortunately, there is an inherent problem with this technique because it almost always results in unwanted dot patterns and moirés. This section covers techniques to correct this problem.

Scanned images from printed sources have specific problems when converted to RGB. The printing inks CYMK (cyan, yellow, magenta, and black) result in patterns of dots that are visible and unattractive when scanned. A close-up of a dot pattern is shown at the right to demonstrate this common scanning problem.

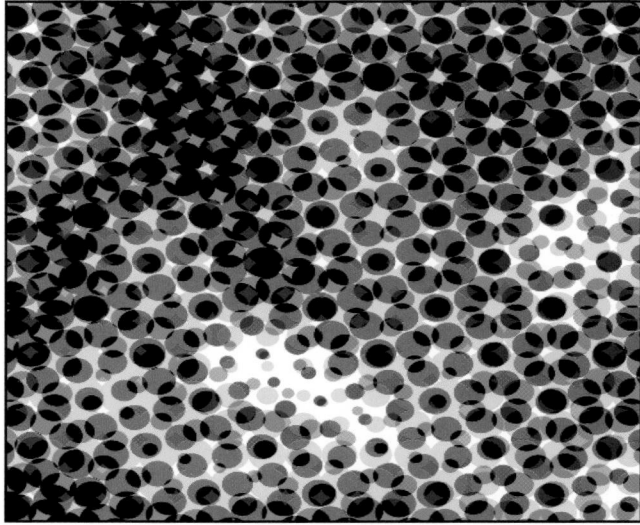

A simulation of CMYK printing inks that form a dot pattern.

Here's a scanned image from my book *Coloring Web Graphics*. The dot pattern problem is clearly visible.

Once this image is scaled, the dot patterns get more or less objectionable. The dot patterns change with each resize.

The best approach to this problem is to get rid of the dot pattern that appears on the image before doing any resizing. Below are some techniques for getting rid of the dots.

Other useful tools for getting rid of moirés are:

- Despeckle
- Dust and Scratch
- Unsharp mask

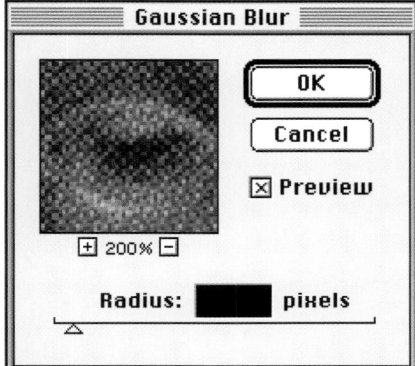

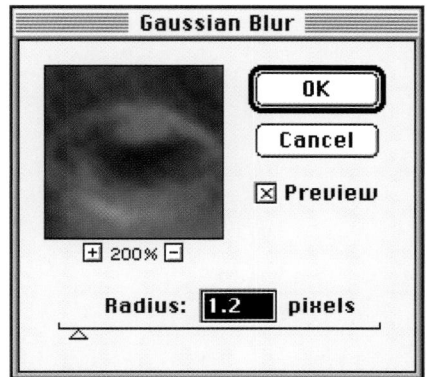

Under Filters, select Gaussian Blur. This filter causes the image to blur depending on what setting is chosen. The idea isn't to completely blur the image, but to get rid of the printing dots. The printing dots are visible within the preview window of this filter.

The blur setting at 1.2 pixels. No more printing dots! A higher blur setting will start to degrade the image. This will be a judgment call that you will have to make, and it will differ for every single image you work with.

The resulting image does not have any dots, but it's blurry.

The trick is to resize the image smaller. This will cause the blurry appearance to become sharper and less noticable.

At this point, you can add a sharpening filter to eliminate some blur. You should have no evidence of the dot pattern! The Sharpen filter increases the contrast between light and dark areas, so use it sparingly.

Voilà! This image is perfectly acceptable for the web. You may choose to add a little extra saturation to the image using techniques described earlier.

Selections

Selecting artwork is an art unto itself. Selections enable you to apply certain image editing features to specific parts of an image without affecting others. Selections are also commonly referred to as masks or alpha channels. Every time you make a selection in Photoshop, you are creating a mask. An alpha channel is simply a permanently stored record of the selection.

This chapter describes numerous image editing techniques that can improve the quality of scanned imagery. If you understand how to select areas of an image, any of these processes can be applied to specific areas of a needy image. A good command of selection techniques is crucial to creating good-looking scanned artwork.

Photoshop Selection Tools

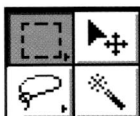

The selection tools in Photoshop include 3 main selection tools, with a couple of variations within each. They are the Marquee, the Lasso, and the Magic Wand Tool.

The Marquee

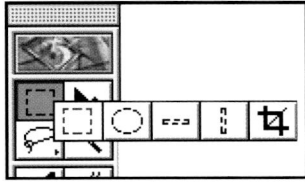

The Marquee Tool can create either a square, rectangular, elliptical, or circular selection. When an image is selected, you'll see marching ants around the area you specified. The circular marquee can be accessed by holding the mouse down on the marquee icon from the toolbar. You can also call these tool menus forward on the screen and alternate between them by pressing the "M" key on your keyboard.

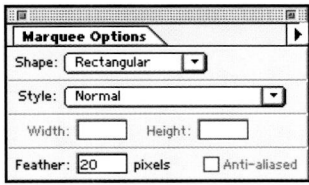

Each selection tool has its set of options. To access this option window, press Return or Enter on your keyboard to bring the menu forward.

Here are the Options Palettes for the other selection tools. The two most important features within the Options Palettes are feathering and anti-aliasing. Feathering makes the edges of the selection soft by fading the edges off by the number of pixels indicated. Anti-aliased makes the edges of the selection blend seamlessly with its background.

The Magic Wand

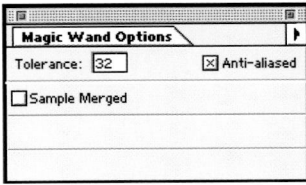

The Magic Wand makes selections based on a tolerance in terms of value in pixels (0-255). Checking Anti-aliased enables the edges of the magic wand selections to be blended.

The Lasso

The Lasso Tool enables you to freely draw shapes around what you want to select. The other tool associated with the Lasso Tool is the Polygon Lasso Tool, which enables you to draw with straight connecting lines that connect up to the beginning. This is accessed by holding down the Option key on a Mac, or the Alt key on a PC.

Photoshop Selection Modifiers

In addition to all of these tools, modifier keys enable you to make more complex selections.

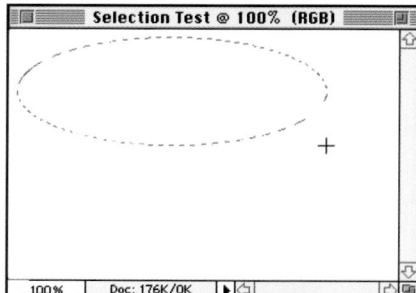 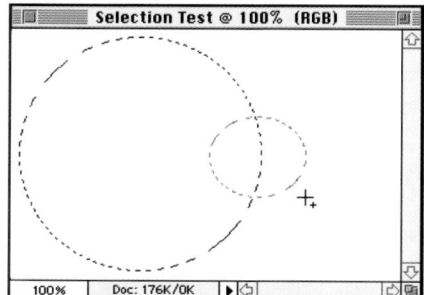 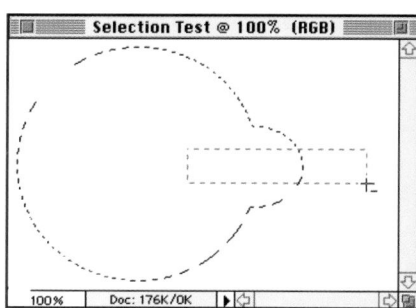

Let's begin with a simple elliptical selection. This shape can be drawn freehand, without using any modifier keys.

If you hold down the Shift key while making the selection, it will be constrained to become a perfect circle. If you were using the rectangular marquee, this modifier would create a perfect square. To add a selection to another selection, simply hold down the Shift key before you make your second selection.

To cut out a section of a selection, use the Option key on Macs or the Ctrl key on PCs.

Painting Quickmask Selections in Photoshop 4.0

Sometimes, the marquee and lasso selection tools are too limited. Painting a selection is the answer! If you want to paint or draw your mask, you can do so by using the Quickmask feature in Photoshop. The Quickmask enables you to paint a mask directly onto your image. Although it looks like it's coloring your image, it's not—it's actually making a selection.

You can toggle your selections and Quickmasks by the Quickmask button on the main toolbar. To apply your Quickmask, you simply leave the Quickmask mode by toggling back to Selection Mode on the toolbar. You can use any tool to create a Quickmask image—Paintbrush, Airbrush, Pencil, Gradient, and so on. You can also run your mask through filters for desired effects.

The Quickmask settings are located at the bottom of the Photoshop 4.0 Toolbar. The setting at the left indicates Selection Mode, and the setting at the right indicates Quickmask mode.

Here's an example of what the Quickmask selection looks like, before you toggle back to the Selection Mode.

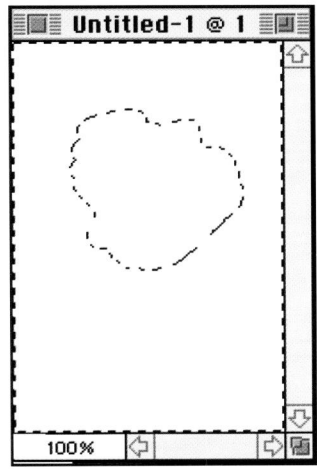

Once you toggle to Selection Mode, the marching ants appear based on the selection shape you painted.

■ **tip**

More on Photoshop

For a complete rundown of other possible selection techniques, you might consult a dedicated Photoshop book or the official manual.

Layout and Alignment Techniques

BROWSER SAFE COLOR

33 FF E

hotoshop <H1>

0033

<STRONG>

Width = "500"

.jpg

PARENCY

Height = "600"

</A>

<center>

Imaging techniques

Web file formats
bgcolor = "FFFFCC"

@link = "cyan"

Web <H3> 24 typography
<SMA

<TAB

<img src="

IMAGE OPTIMIZATION
Colors

Animation, sound and

3

LYNDA.COM

<center><BODY>
Antialia

33

www Design

Alignment Hell

A web page has no fixed size. Some browsers have predefined sizes that the viewing window fits to; others let you size the screen to fill your monitor. Some of your audience will see your page through tiny portable computer screens. Others will have 21" monitors. Some of your audience will change the font size defaults, which will make everything line up differently than you planned.

Imagine if you had to fit lots of information on a piece of paper, but no one could tell you the size of the paper you had to work with. And imagine trying to fit that information onto the paper artistically, with a little more finesse than left-justifying every image, headline, and text block. Also imagine that the tools to change position and alignment were strange and unintuitive and didn't work everywhere.

Is it any wonder that few designers know how to do web page layout well? Making a web page behave the way you want it to is a challenging task. This chapter examines alignment issues from a few different angles:

- Defining the size of a web page
- Using HTML alignment tags
- Using invisible spacers for alignment
- Using tables for alignment
- Aligning foreground and background images

Once you've examined all the possibilities this chapter covers, you'll see that it's possible to beat the odds and create interesting layouts in HTML. What is possible is not easy, however, because HTML was never intended to be a page layout description language.

When I wrote the first edition of *Designing Web Graphics*, we were in the era of Browser Hell. There were so many different kinds of browsers, and no one browser had the clear market advantage of being the one for which to design.

These examples demonstrate what can happen when using some of the alignment techniques described in this chapter with browsers that don't support table tags. Fortunately, both MSIE and Netscape abound now, and these pitfalls to using alignment techniques are not as prevalent anymore.

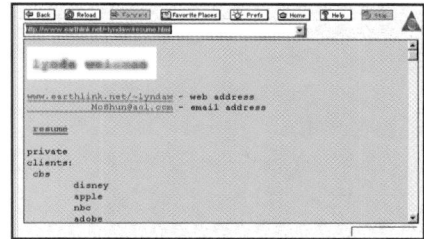

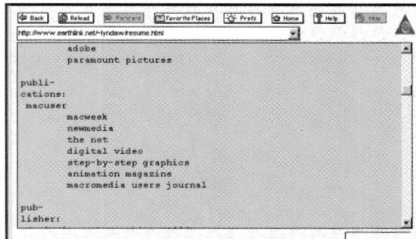

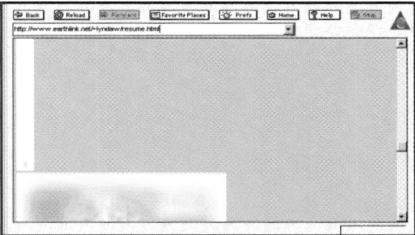

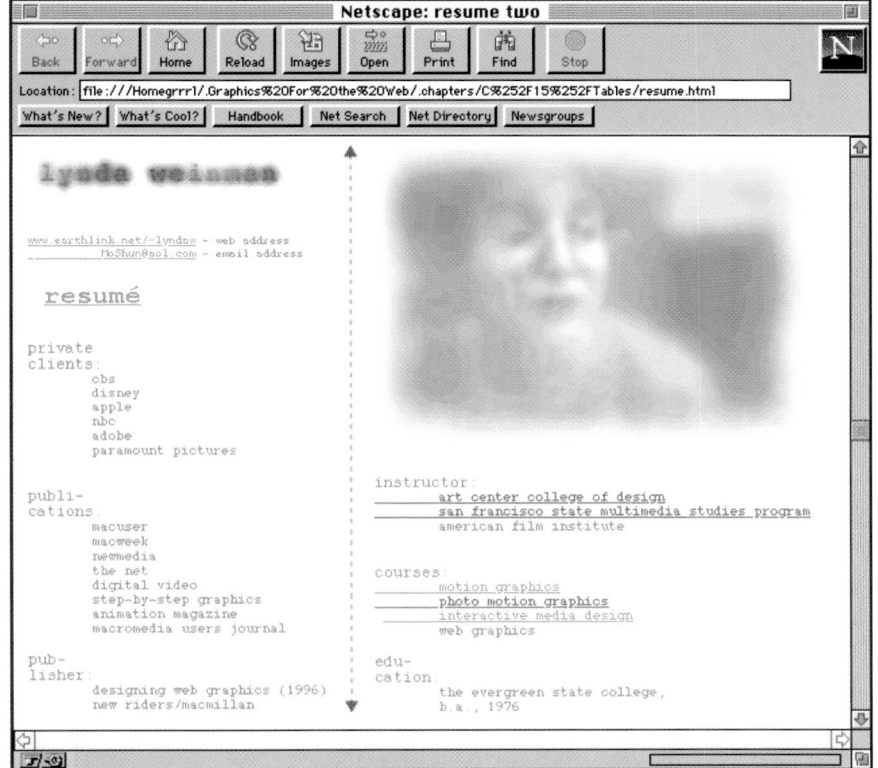

Here's an example of a three-column table and the <PRE> tag alignment methods displayed in Netscape 1.1. These methods of alignment are discussed in-depth within this chapter. During the era of Browser Hell, this was a pretty tricky alignment accomplishment.

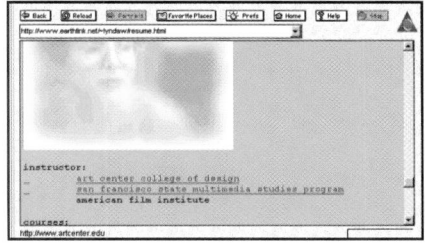

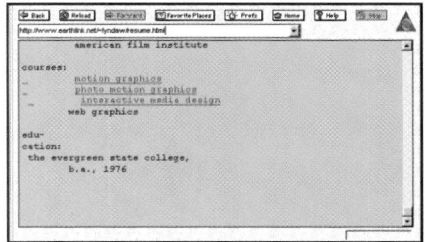

In a browser that didn't support tables, this type of alignment technique created a disaster! Here's the identical HTML file that failed and had to be displayed accross five separate screens. No one misses those days of Browser Hell!

Defining the Size of a Web Page

"Small is better" seems to be the credo of web design. Because there is no fixed size to a web page, you get to define one yourself. Taking into account that people might be looking at your work in small windows, it makes the most sense to define a small page size to work with. Yes, but how small is small?

I tend to err on the conservative side when suggesting width restrictions for graphics on a web page. 640 pixels is the average width of an average computer monitor—even on many portables— and I think there should be some breathing room around that. On the Macintosh, Netscape's opening screen defaults to 505 pixels across. I've picked 480 pixels as a good width for an opening graphic or headline. That's the approximate width of the menu bar for Netscape's home page. This rule is not cast in stone. I'm simply describing the sizes of some of the environments your page will be viewed in and arriving at a size based on how I would want my graphics to be viewed.

Lack of a defined web page size can be dealt with creatively. Carina Feldman, who recently received an M.F.A. in Graphic Design from Art Center College of Design, challenged the unlimited size of a web page by creating a long, vertical text graphic that forces viewers to scroll down many computer screens to finish reading.

Carina Feldman's long, vertical graphic that plays with lack of defined space (■ www.quicklink.com/~zigzag).

Because web pages can scroll vertically or horizontally, there are no length or width restrictions to contend with on a web document. The size of the artwork you choose to put on any given page dictates the size of the page. If you position artwork that spans horizontally or vertically, the page fits to the size of your artwork. Scroll bars appear in most browsers automatically when the artwork is oversized in either direction.

If you want your opening graphic to be visible on most computer monitors, however, you may want to think about composing your opening page graphic (splash screen or menu bar) so that it can be seen on a portable computer. Most portable computer screens today are 640x480, and some are 640x400.

Based on this information, I think opening screen graphics and headline text, or whatever you hope the viewer will see at first glance on your page, should be no taller than 350 pixels.

Some artists choose to make wider screens than my conservative estimate of 480 pixels. There are lots of clever ways to tell your audience how wide to open the browser window, as shown by the following examples.

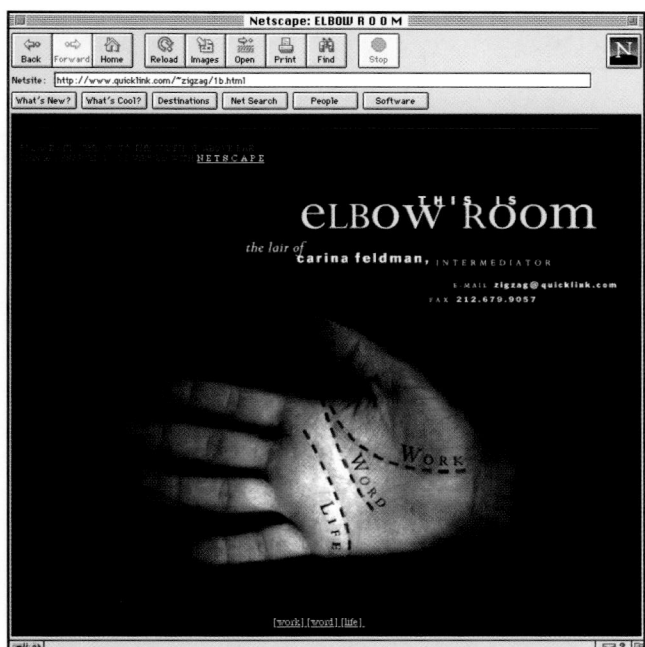

Carina Feldman's site (■ www.quicklink.com/~zigzag).

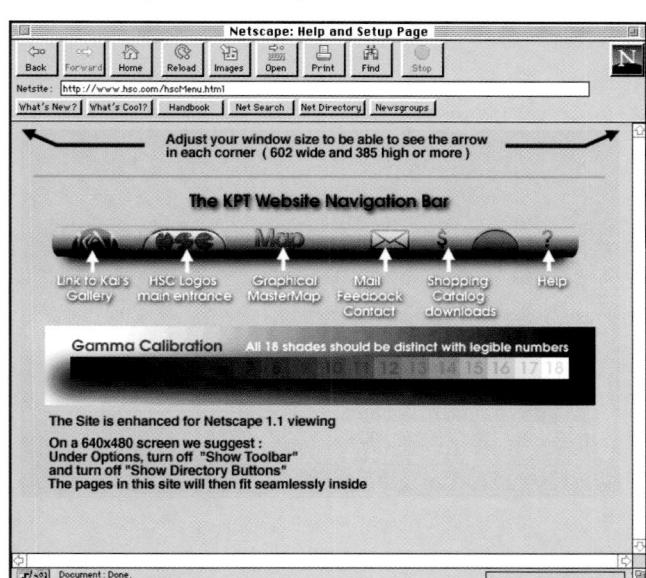

The Metatools web site has a page that establishes width and gamma (■ http://www.metatools.com).

As you can see, the size of your page is up to you. Take your average end viewer's monitor capabilities into account to make informed design decisions about sizing. Carina's pages are great for personal expression, but if you are hired to design a page for a client, it most likely would be important to make the page read at first glance under standard monitor conditions.

JavaScript for Establishing Page Size

It's a good idea to check out your pages on different size monitors. Not everyone can be so lucky to own lots of different size monitors, so Steven Younis came up with a very cool JavaScript that would simulate monitor sizes. Feel free to check your pages through his site:

■ http://www.dot.net.au/younis/window.html

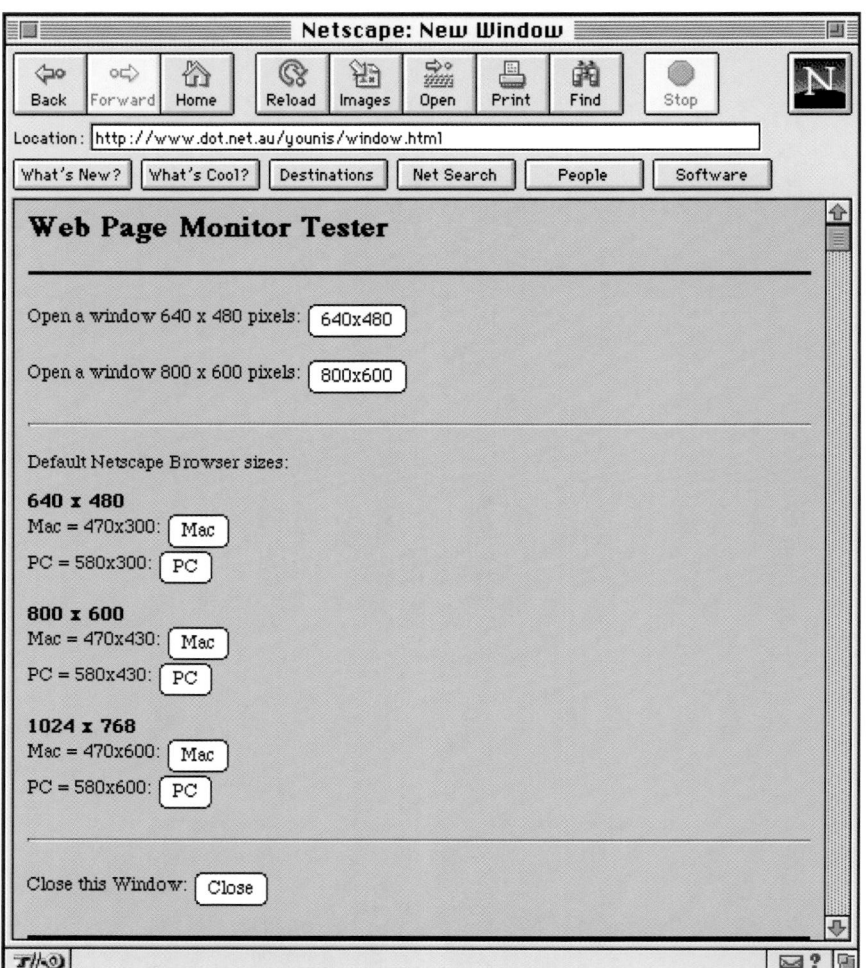

Go to ■ http://www.dot.net.au/younis/window.html to check out Steven's cool JavaScript.

Here's the code, in case you want to try this yourself. Be sure to credit Steven if you use it on your own site.

```
<!-- THIS PAGE WAS CREATED WITH WORLD WIDE
WEB WEAVER 2.0 IN ORDER TO SEPARATE THIS PAGE
INTO MULTIPLE SECTIONS COMMENT TAGS HAVE BEEN
PLACED AT SPECIFIC LOCATIONS. REMOVING OR
EDITING THESE COMMENTS WILL CAUSE WEB WEAVER
TO NOT RECOGNIZE SECTIONS -->
<HTML>
<HEAD><TITLE>New Window</TITLE>
<SCRIPT LANGUAGE="JavaScript">
<!--Activate Cloaking
//***************************************** CREDITS
**************************************************
//
//   Web Page Monitor Tester
(Last updated-December 12, 1996)
//   Written by:   Steven Younis (younis@dot.net.au)
//
//   Younis Graphics-http://www.dot.net.au/younis
//
//**********************************************
**********************************************
**
//Deactivate Cloaking-->
</SCRIPT>
</HEAD><BODY><!-- BEGIN BODY HEADER SECTION -->
<!-- BEGIN MAIN BODY SECTION --><H2>
Web Page Monitor Tester</H2>
<HR NOSHADE><P>
<FORM>
Open a window 640 x 480 pixels:
<INPUT TYPE=BUTTON VALUE="640x480"
onClick="window.open ('window.html','640x480',
'toolbar=yes,status=yes,scrollbars=yes,
location=yes,menubar=yes,directories=yes,width=640,
height=480')"><P>
Open a window 800 x 600 pixels:
<INPUT TYPE=BUTTON VALUE="800x600"
onClick="window.open ('window.html','800x600',
'toolbar=yes,status=yes,scrollbars=yes,
location=yes,menubar=yes,directories=yes,width=800,
height=600')"><P>
<HR><P>
Default Netscape Browser sizes:<P>
<B>640 x 480</B><BR>
Mac = 470x300:
<INPUT TYPE=BUTTON VALUE="Mac"
onClick=" window.open('window.html','Mac',

'toolbar=yes,status=yes,scrollbars=yes,
location=yes,menubar=yes,directories=yes,width=470,
height=300')"><BR>
PC  = 580x300:
<INPUT TYPE=BUTTON VALUE="PC"
onClick="window.open
('window.html','PC','toolbar=yes,status=yes,
scrollbars=yes,location=yes,menubar=yes,
directories=yes,width=580,height=300')"><P>
<B>800 x 600</B><BR>
Mac = 470x430:
<INPUT TYPE=BUTTON VALUE="Mac"
onClick="window.open('window.html','Mac',
'toolbar=yes,status=yes,scrollbars=yes,
location=yes,menubar=yes,directories=yes,
width=470,height=430')"><BR>
PC  = 580x430:
<INPUT TYPE=BUTTON VALUE="PC"
onClick="window.open('window.html','PC',
'toolbar=yes,status=yes,scrollbars=yes,
location=yes,menubar=yes,directories=yes,width=580,
height=430')"><P>
<B>1024 x 768</B><BR>
Mac = 470x600:
<INPUT TYPE=BUTTON VALUE="Mac"
onClick="window.open
('window.html','Mac','toolbar=yes,status=yes,
scrollbars=yes,location=yes,menubar=yes,
directories=yes,width=470,height=600')"><BR>
PC  = 580x600:
<INPUT TYPE=BUTTON VALUE="PC"
onClick="window.open('window.html','PC',
'toolbar=yes,status=yes,scrollbars=yes,
location=yes,menubar=yes,directories=yes,width=580,
height=600')"><P>
<P>
<HR><P>
Close this Window:
<INPUT TYPE=BUTTON VALUE="Close"
onClick="window.close()">
</FORM>
<P><HR NOSHADE><P>
<FONT SIZE=-1>Copyright &#169; 1996,
<A HREF="MAILTO:younis@dot.net.au">
Steven Younis</A>.</FONT>
<!-- BEGIN BODY FOOTER SECTION --></BODY></HTML>
```

Using HTML for Alignment

HTML was not designed to be a QuarkXPress or PageMaker. I don't think the original authors ever dreamed of it as a tool for page layout that would satisfy the needs of graphic designers. It was originally invented to support the scientific community and to include diagrams and image tables that were associated with massive quantities of technical writings. Formatting handles such as left justifying and indenting a list of words suited the needs of that community just fine.

We're asking a lot more of HTML than it was ever designed to do, which is OK. HTML originators thought they were inventing one thing for one purpose, and it laid the groundwork for other purposes—including layout design! HTML has limited alignment capabilities, but web designers worth their weight should know how to use all of them.

On the following pages I have provided a useful list of HTML tags for aligning text and images.

Text Alignment Tags

These tags relate to text elements.

Paragraph breaks: Insert this tag where you want spaces between paragraphs:

<P>

Line breaks: Put this tag where you want to have the text wrap to the next line:

Centering text: Use this tag before you center text and/or images, and use the closed tag when you want text below it to return to left-justified formatting.

<CENTER>

Preformatted text: Preformatted text typically uses a different font, such as the typewriter-style Courier, instead of the default Times Roman. The <PRE> tag lets you set the spacing and indents of your type. (For more examples of the <PRE> tag, check out Chapter 11, "Web-Based Typography," and Chapter 17, "HTML for Visual Designers.")

<PRE></PRE>

No break: Use this tag if you want the browser width to dictate where the text breaks. The closed tag signifies when you want the no break formatting to end.

<NOBR></NBR>

```
Here's some type

Look at the space created by the <p >tag

Here's some more type
This row is on the next line because of the <br >tag.

                        This type is centered because
                        the <center >tag is being used.


The <pre >tag uses a different
font          and        puts the

                      type

w   h    e   r   e  ve   r     you   typed

        it.

If you use the <nobr >tag, the type you write continues until you put a break in it. It will go on and on

The <blink >tag gets on most people's nerves
```

This shows the preceding tags in action on the web.

Image and Type Alignment Tags

These tags cause text to align in relationship to the images it's next to.

<ALIGN=TOP> Align text to the top of your image:

```
<IMG SRC=filenamehere.gif ALIGN=TOP>
```

<ALIGN=BOTTOM> Align text to the bottom of your image:

```
<IMG SRC=filenamehere.gif ALIGN=BOTTOM>
```

<ALIGN=MIDDLE> Align text to the middle of your image:

```
<IMG SRC=filenamehere.gif ALIGN=MIDDLE>
```

No Alignment

"I'm hungry for toast, mama", cried the little piggy

Bottom Alignment

"I'm hungry for toast, mama", cried the little piggy

Middle Alignment

"I'm hungry for toast, mama", cried the little piggy

Top Alignment

"I'm hungry for toast, mama", cried the little piggy

Image Alignment Tags

The following tags align the images to the left or right of the screen.

Image left justified:

```
<IMG SRC=filenamehere.gif ALIGN=LEFT>
```

Image right justified:

```
<IMG SRC=filenamehere.gif ALIGN=RIGHT>
```

Right Alignment

"I'm hungry for toast, mama", cried the little piggy

Left Alignment

"I'm hungry for toast, mama", cried the little piggy

Horizontal and Vertical Space Tags

The horizontal and vertical space tags allow you to insert empty space around a graphic, creating breathing room.

HSPACE: I've used the <HSPACE=XX> tag in the following code to put 40 pixels of breathing room to the left and right of the toaster image.

```
<HTML>
<HEAD> <TITLE> Alignment Test</TITLE> </HEAD>
<BODY BGCOLOR="ffffff">
<IMG SRC="ltoast.jpg" ALIGN=LEFT HSPACE=40>"I'm hun-
gry for toast, mama!", <BR>cried the little
piggy.<BR CLEAR=all>
</BODY>
</HTMLl>
```

"I'm hungry for toast, mama!", cried the little piggy.

VSPACE: To demonstrate what adding <VSPACE=value> does, I experimented with the following code:

```
<HTML>
<HEAD> <TITLE> Alignment Test</TITLE> </HEAD>
<BODY BGCOLOR="ffffff">
<IMG SRC="ltoast.jpg" ALIGN=LEFT HSPACE=40
VSPACE=80>"I'm hungry for toast, mama!",
<BR>cried the little piggy.<BR CLEAR=all>
</BODY>
</HTML>
```

WIDTH and HEIGHT Attributes

These attributes work by allowing you to specify the width and height values (in pixels) of a graphic. This can accomplish two things: it causes the text on the page to load before the graphic while making space for the graphic to come into the proper location. Using WIDTH and HEIGHT attributes within HTML is very important for downloading speed, and many plug-in <EMBED> tags require that you include width and height information. (See chapters 14 and 16 for more information on plug-ins and embedding.)

There's a lesser-known feature of <WIDTH> and <HEIGHT> tags, however. If you put smaller or larger values in these tags, they will actually shrink or scale your image. In the following example, the actual dimension of the toaster image is 102x115 pixels. By putting a width of 53 and height of 60, I shrunk the image in half. By putting a value of 240x214, I scaled it to be twice as big.

The following sections illustrate these alignment tags.

```
<HTML>
<HEAD> <TITLE> Alignment Test</TITLE> </HEAD>
<BODY BGCOLOR="ffffff">
<IMG SRC="ltoast.jpg" WIDTH=60 HEIGHT=53
ALIGN=LEFT>"I'm hungry for toast, mama!",
<BR>cried the little piggy.<br >
<P>
<P>
<IMG SRC="ltoast.jpg" WIDTH=240 HEIGHT=214
ALIGN=LEFT>"I'm hungry for toast, mama!",
<BR>cried the little piggy.<BR>
</BODY>
</HTML>
```

This exhausts the possibilities that widely supported HTML tags offer for alignment.

Next, we move on to alignment techniques without using HTML. These involve making custom artwork that serves to align images, instead of relying on code.

Alternatives to HTML Using Artwork

Using images for alignment involves creating spacer art. This art exists on the web page for the sole purpose of making spaces between text and images. For the spacer art to be invisible, you have two options.

Make the spacer art the same color as your background. To do this, use the <BODY BACKGROUND> or <BODY BGCOLOR> tag to create a solid color or colored background pattern tile, or both. Make sure your spacer art is one color and assign that color to be transparent, saving the one-color artwork as a transparent GIF. These methods are described in more depth in Chapters 5, "Hexadecimal Color," and 7, "Transparent Artwork."

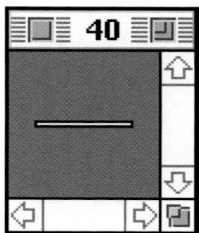

An example of spacer art.

■ **note**

Netscape Proprietary Alignment Tags

Netscape versions 2.0 and above support alignment tags that enable you to create columns and adjust spaces using HTML commands. Because these tags are supported only by Netscape, you run the risk of having to create two sets of pages, or the pages you use these tags on won't display correctly everywhere.

For a complete list of these tags, visit:
■ http://home.netscape.com/eng/mozilla/3.0/rel-notes/windows-3.01b1.html#Layout

Using Spacers for Alignment

The following is what the HTML code would produce without using any spacers or alignment techniques. The toaster photographs are from a CD-ROM collection from Classic PIO Partners (800-370-2746). I've named the artwork respectively: ltoast.jpg, ftoast.jpg, and rtoast.jpg.

```
<HTML>
<HEAD> <TITLE> Alignment Test</TITLE> </HEAD>
<BODY BGCOLOR="ffffff">
<IMG SRC="ltoast.jpg"><IMG SRC="ftoast.jpg"><IMG
SRC="rtoast.jpg">
</BODY>
</HTML>
```

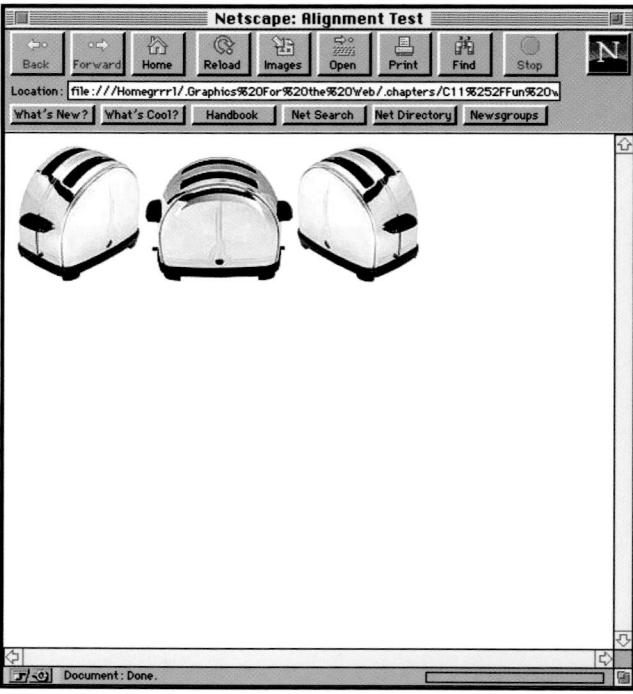

This example uses no spacers.

The following is the HTML code to use white spacer art between each image to give them a little breathing room. I made a file in Photoshop that was 40 pixels wide and 1 pixel high, and named it 40space.jpg.

```
<HTML>
<HEAD> <TITLE> Alignment Test</TITLE> </HEAD>
<BODY BGCOLOR="ffffff">
<IMG SRC="40space.jpg"><IMG SRC="ltoast.jpg"><IMG
SRC="40space.jpg"><IMG SRC="ftoast.jpg"><IMG
SRC="40space.jpg"><IMG SRC="rtoast.jpg">
</BODY>
</HTML>
```

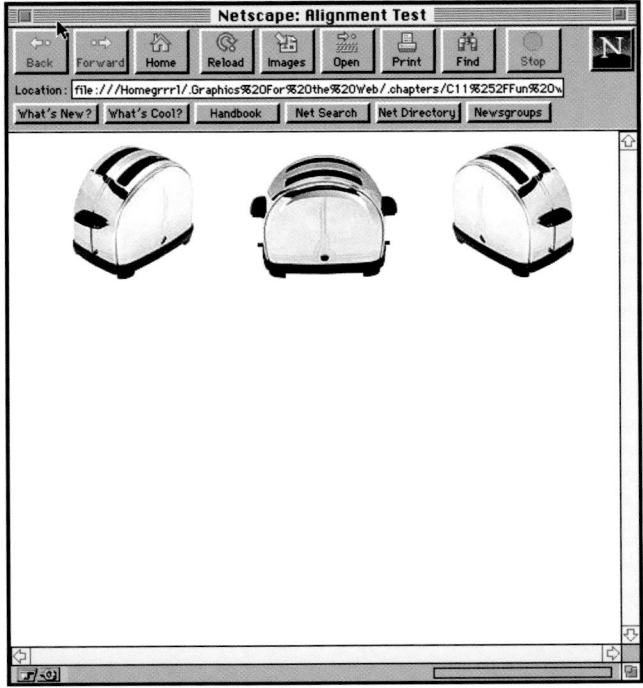

This example uses the 40-pixel wide spacer between each image.

If I used the same spacer in front of each image, I could create a consistent left indent.

```
<HTML>
<HEAD> <TITLE> Alignment Test</TITLE> </HEAD>
<BODY BGCOLOR="ffffff">
<IMG SRC="40space.jpg"><<IMG SRC ="ltoast.jpg">
<P><<IMG SRC ="40space.jpg"><<IMG SRC ="ftoast.jpg">
<P><<IMG SRC ="40space.jpg"><<IMG SRC ="rtoast.jpg">
</BODY>
</HTML>
```

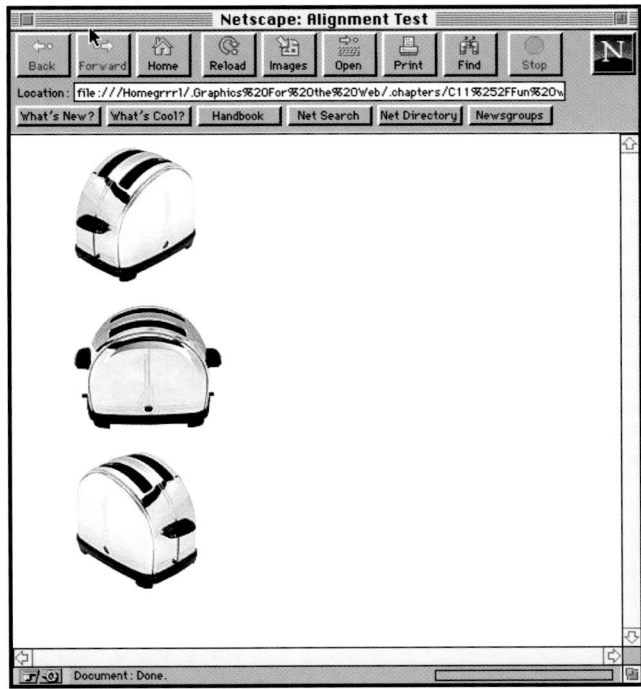

This example uses the space in front of each image.

■ **tip**

WIDTH and HEIGHT Attributes for Spacers

You don't have to make the spacer art the correct size. Using the WIDTH and HEIGHT attributes, you can stretch a single pixel GIF to become any size you wish. David Siegel is the master of the single pixel GIF trick. Check out his instructions at ■ http://www.dsiegel.com/tips/wonk5/single.html.

He also wrote a great book called *Creating Killer Web Sites,* published by Hayden Books (ISBN: 1-568302-894), which teaches a lot of helpful table and alignment techniques.

Aligning a Graphic to a Patterned Background

One of the frustrating things about web design is the strange offset phenomenon that exists between foreground and background images. There's no solution for it, but working with backgrounds that have small intricate patterns as opposed to large obvious patterns can trick the eye into forgiving the offset.

Here's an example of a foreground image Bruce Heavin made that has been precomposited over a complex background in Photoshop.

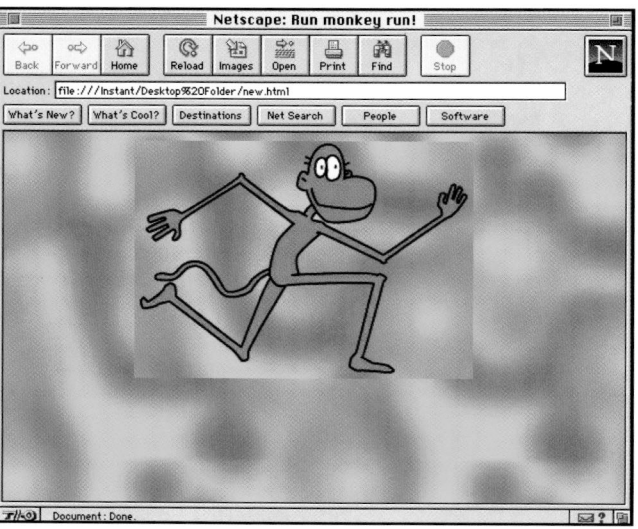

The identical complex background was used as a seamless tile in the <BODY BACKGROUND> tag of this HTML. Notice the mismatched edge? There's nothing that can be done about this offset, especially because the offset amount differs on Mac and PC versions of browsers.

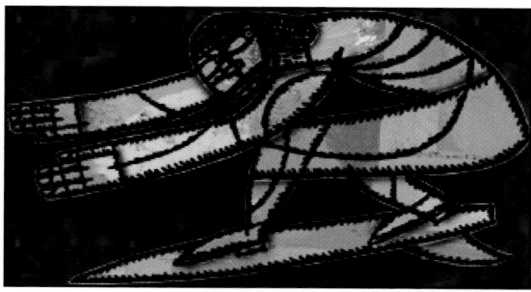

Here's an example of artwork by Richard Downs (■ http: //www.earthlink.net/~downsart/). It's been created against a complex background, but the background pattern is very tight and detailed.

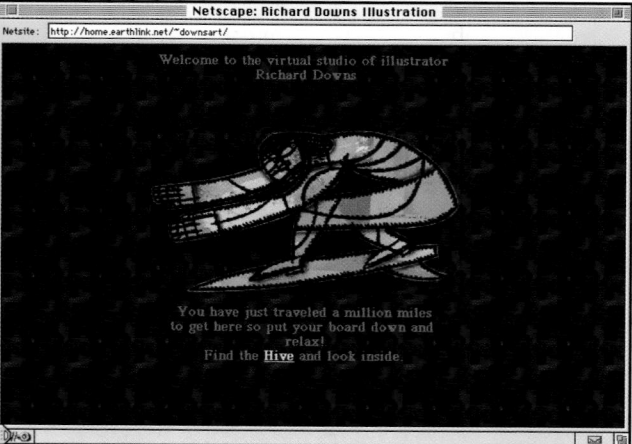

Even though the same offset mismatch exists here, it's barely noticeable because the small pattern is much more forgiving.

Tables for Alignment

Tables for the web were originally conceived to produce columns of text or numbers in individual cells, much like a spreadsheet or chart. Even though tables were invented to support text and numbers, you can put graphics inside table cells, too. All the graphic tags we've described so far work within the table tags. Because of this, I've made a distinction in this chapter between data tables and graphic tables.

You'll see a lot of attention in other books and online sources paid to data tables. The same tags that support data can also support graphics, and herein lies a great power waiting to be unleashed. The graphic designer who knows how to use tables for page layout control will be a much happier camper than the one who doesn't. Learning to program tables will offer lots of formatting options that HTML doesn't directly support.

There are great online tutorials for learning to program tables. I've seen online support only for data tables, not graphic tables. Still, data table principles are crucial to understand if you're going to use graphic tables. Some of my favorite online sources for table instruction follow.

This is a site to watch for all kinds of great online tutorials. The authors are Japanese, so the English is a little stilted, but the instruction on tables and many other HTML tags is indispensable:
- http://ncdesign.kyushuid.ac.jp/howto/text/Normal/table.html

Table instruction from the Netscape site itself:
- http://home.mcom.com/assist/net_sites/tables.html

You will learn about how to program graphics tables later in this chapter, but first you should understand the basic kind of web tables: data-based tables.

> ### ■ note
>
> WYSIWYG Tables
>
> It should be noted that almost all WYSIWYG HTML editors let you create tables without programming the code. It's so much easier to use them—instead of hand coding—that it's really worth your time to invest in one of them. It's important to understand how tables in HTML work, however, because it's still necessary, from time to time, to edit the automatic code WYSIWYG editors generate.

Data Tables

Data-based tables are quite possibly what the HTML standards committee (■ http://www.w3c.com) had in mind when they endorsed the code. These are the typical kinds of tables that you'll see on most sites. They contain text and numbers, links, and occasional graphics. They have telltale borders around the cells, which look slightly dimensional, by employing embossed lines of varying width to divide individual chart sections.

Data tables default to use embossed lines to divide the cells and sections.

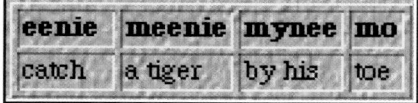

If you use a pattern background or solid color background, the embossing shows through and looks as if it's a lighting effect.

Table borders are sort of like horizontal rules on steroids—the HTML code magically manufactures vertical and horizontal lines of different widths and thicknesses with a few choice strokes of code and tags. They seem complicated by appearance, but you will probably be surprised at how easy they are to create and use.

HTML Table Tags

When creating data or graphics tables for the web, you work with the same HTML tags. The table tags allow you to put information inside individual cells. Understanding the tag structure for data tables enables you to work with the graphic tables later in this chapter.

You always begin a table with **<TABLE>** and end it with the **</TABLE>** tag. The **<TR> </TR>** tag stands for starting and ending a new row. The **<TH> </TH>** tag delineates the header and makes the text in that row bold. The **<TD> </TD>** tag stands for the content of each data cell.

Here's an example of such code, with the HTML below:

```
<TABLE>
<TR> <TH>eenie
</TH><TH>meenie</TH><TH>mynee
</TH><TH>mo</TH></TR>
<TR><TD>catch</TD><TD>a tiger</TD><TD>
by his</TD><TD>toe</TD></TR></TABLE>
```

eenie	meenie	mynee	mo
catch	a tiger	by his	toe

The **<TABLE BORDER>** tag gives the table that embossed look and feel. Here's an example of such code, with the HTML below:

```
<TABLE BORDER>
<TR> <TH>eenie
</TH><TH>meenie</TH><TH>mynee</TH>
<TH>mo</TH></TR>
<TR><TD>catch</TD><TD>a tiger</TD><TD>
by his</TD><TD>toe</TD></TR></TABLE>
```

eenie	meenie	mynee	mo
catch	a tiger	by his	toe

The **<COLSPAN>** tag allows one row to fill more than one column. Here's an example of such code, with the HTML below:

```
<TABLE BORDER>
<TR><TH COLSPAN=4> A poem,by someone</TH>
<TR> <TH>eenie
</TH><TH>meenie</TH><TH>mynee</TH>
<TH>mo</TH></TR>
<TR><TD>catch</TD><TD>a tiger</TD><TD>
by his</TD><TD>toe</TD></TR></TABLE>
```

A poem, by someone			
eenie	meenie	mynee	mo
catch	a tiger	by his	toe

The **<ROWSPAN>** tag takes up columns and rows. It is not any specified size or shape; the dimensions are dictated by the content you insert. Here's an example of such code, with the HTML below:

```
<TABLE BORDER>
<TR><TH ROWSPAN=4> A poem, by someone</TH>
<TR><TH>eenie
</TH><TH>meenie</TH><TH>mynee</TH>
<TH>mo</TH></TR>
<TR><TD>catch</TD><TD>a tiger</TD><TD>
by his</TD><TD>toe</TD></TR></TABLE>
```

A poem, by someone	eenie	meenie	mynee	mo
	catch	a tiger	by his	toe

The **<TABLE WIDTH=# of pixels>** and **<TABLE HEIGHT=# of pixels>** tags allow you to dictate the shape of the table by pixels. Here's an example of such code, with the HTML below:

```
<TABLE BORDER WIDTH=300 HEIGHT=100>
<TR> <TH>eenie
</TH><TH>meenie</TH><TH>mynee</TH>
<TH>mo</TH></TR>
<TR><TD>catch</TD><TD>a tiger</TD><TD>
by his</TD><TD>toe</TD></TR></TABLE>
```

eenie	meenie	mynee	mo
catch	a tiger	by his	toe

The **<TABLE CELLSPACING=# of pixels>** tag puts a thicker line weight around the cells. Here's an example of such code, with the HTML below:

```
<TABLE BORDER CELLSPACING=10>
<TR> <TH>eenie
</TH><TH>meenie</TH><TH>mynee</TH>
<TH>mo</TH></TR>
<TR><TD>catch</TD><TD>
a tiger</TD><TD>
by his</TD><TD>toe</TD></TR></TABLE>
```

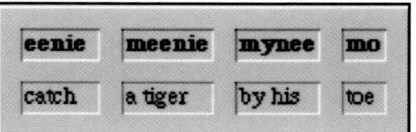

eenie	meenie	mynee	mo
catch	a tiger	by his	toe

The **<TABLE CELLPADDING=# of pixels>** tag puts a uniform space inside the cells, governed by the number of pixels entered after the **=** (equal) sign. Here's an example of such code, with the HTML below:

```
<TABLE BORDER CELLPADDING=10>
<TR> <TH>eenie
</TH><TH>meenie</TH><TH>mynee</TH>
<TH>mo</TH></TR>
<TR><TD>catch</TD><TD>a tiger</TD><TD>
by his</TD><TD>toe</TD></TR></TABLE>
```

eenie	meenie	mynee	mo
catch	a tiger	by his	toe

You can adjust the alignment of data inside cells by using the **<VALIGN>** tag, which allows you to specify top, middle, bottom, and baseline alignments. Here's an example of such code:

```
<TABLE BORDER HEIGHT=100>
<TR> <TH>eenie
</TH><TH>meenie</TH><TH>mynee</TH>
<TH>mo</TH></TR>
<TR><TD VALIGN=top>catch</TD><TD
VALIGN=middle>a tiger</TD><TD VALIGN=bot-
tom>by his</TD><TD
VALIGN=baseline>toe</TD></TR></TABLE>
```

eenie	meenie	mynee	mo
catch			toe
	a tiger		
		by his	

You can also specify, right, left, and middle alignment values within the <TR>, <TH>, and <TD> tags by using the word align. Here's an example of such code:

```
<TABLE BORDER WIDTH=300>
<TR> <TH ALIGN left>eenie </TH><TH ALIGN
left>meenie</TH>
<TH ALIGN left>mynee</TH>
<TH ALIGN left>mo</TH></TR>
<TR><TD ALIGN=left>catch</TD>
<TD ALIGN=left>a tiger</TD>
<TD ALIGN=left>by his</TD>
<TD ALIGN=left>toe</TD></TR></TABLE>
<TABLE BORDER WIDTH=300>
<TR> <TH ALIGN=right>eenie </TH>
<TH ALIGN=right>meenie</TH>
<TH ALIGN=right>mynee</TH>
<TH ALIGN=right>mo</TH></TR>
<TR><TD ALIGN=right>catch</TD>
<TD ALIGN=right>a tiger</TD>
<TD ALIGN=right>by his</TD>
<TD ALIGN=right>toe</TD></TR></TABLE>
```

eenie	meenie	mynee	mo
catch	a tiger	by his	toe

You can also put graphics inside tables, by using the **<IMG SRC="name.gif">** tag, instead of text or values. Here's an example of such code, with the HTML below:

```
<TABLE BORDER>
<TR> <TD>
<IMG SRC="catcha.gif"></TD></TR></TABLE>
```

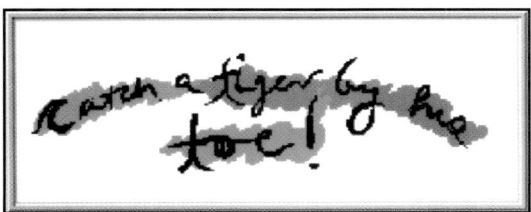

Here's an example of mixing text and graphics inside cells of a table:

```
<TABLE BORDER>
<TR> <TH>eenie </TH><TH>
<IMG SRC="meenie.gif"></TH><TH>mynee</TH>
<TH>mo</TH></TR>
<TR><TD>catch</TD><TD >a tiger
</TD><TD>by his</TD><TD >
<IMG SRC="toe.gif"></TD></TR></TABLE>
```

eenie	meenie	mynee	mo
catch	a tiger	by his	toe

This last example shows how to insert graphics into your tables by using the **<IMG SRC>** tag. The following section explains how you can work with graphics more seamlessly, by eliminating the telltale border around table cells.

Graphic Tables for Page Layout Design

Table support is the first real hook we've had to being able to control layout of page design. If you use tables to create a design grid, all the things that HTML has kept you from doing are suddenly possible. You want a vertical row of linked type in the middle of your page, or a vertical rule graphic? No problem! You want your graphics aligned left or right to a specific grid defined by pixels? No problem! You want to define the size of your page and not let the browser do that for you? No problem! Basically, if you're used to working with PageMaker or Quark, you're used to working with design grids. Tables take much more effort, but if you do some preplanning, you can use them much the same way.

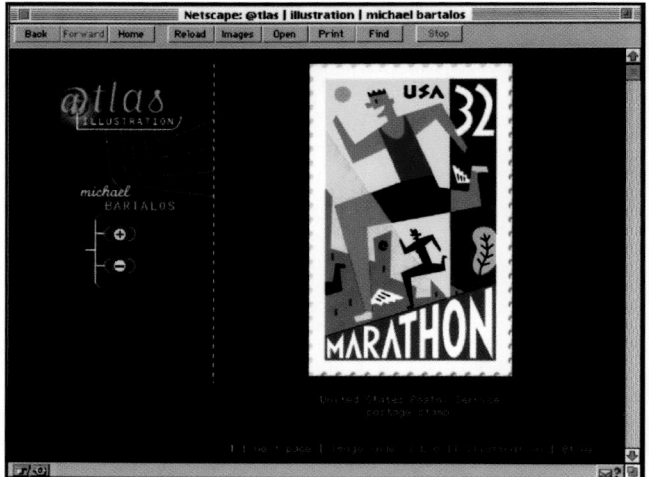

This example of a page within @tlas shows how tables help them align graphics. The borders are turned on intentionally to show where the tables are.

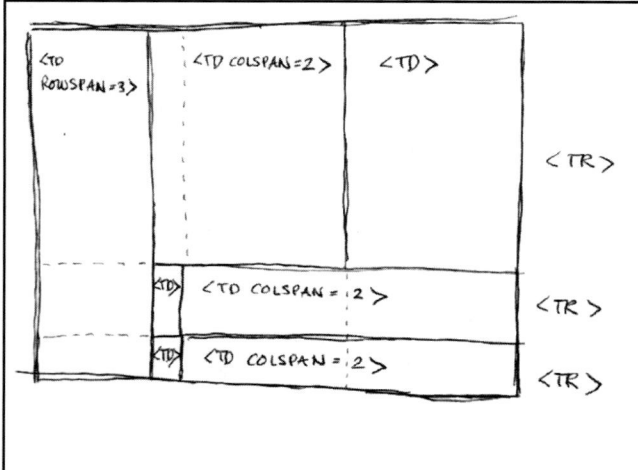

Michael Macrone, webmaster for @tlas, always sketches his tables on paper before programming the code. It helps him know how many rows and columns he needs.

Here, the table is turned off, using the <TABLE BORDER=0> attribute. Check out @tlas at ■ http://www.atlas.organic.com.

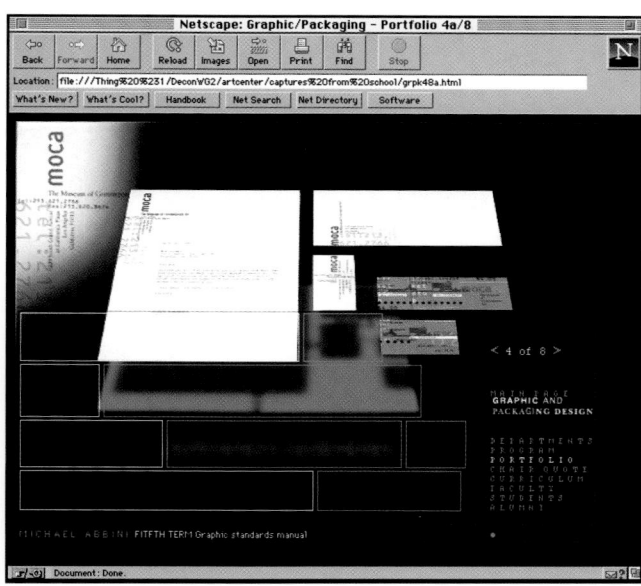

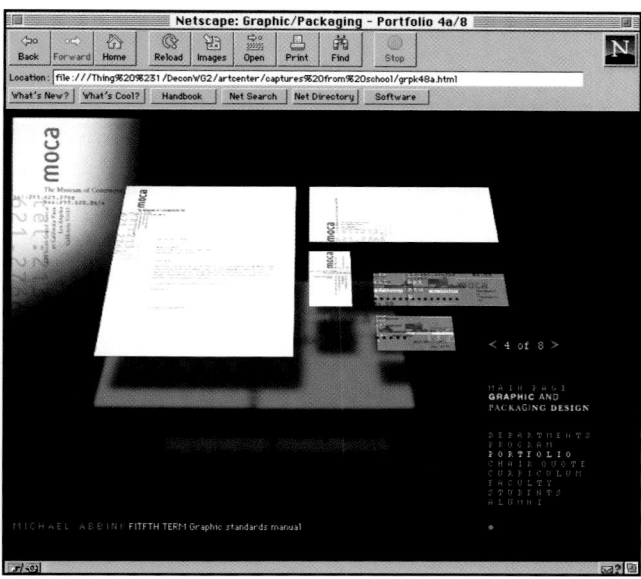

Here's an example where Gudrun Frommherz, a recent MFA gradu-ate from Art Center College of Design, used a table to place invisible GIFs over a large JPEG background image. The invisible GIFs were programmed to link to other pages. Note: This would work reliably on a single-system intranet. Alignment inconsistencies between platforms are described on page 312.

The finished screen shows no evidence of the tables because the borders are turned off. You can, however, click on the blurry stacks of paper on the screen image and be linked to other pages. This is an incredibly cool trick, because it effectively enables you to add links to huge <BODY BACKGROUND> images. Because the image is a JPEG, it's small enough for easy web viewing.

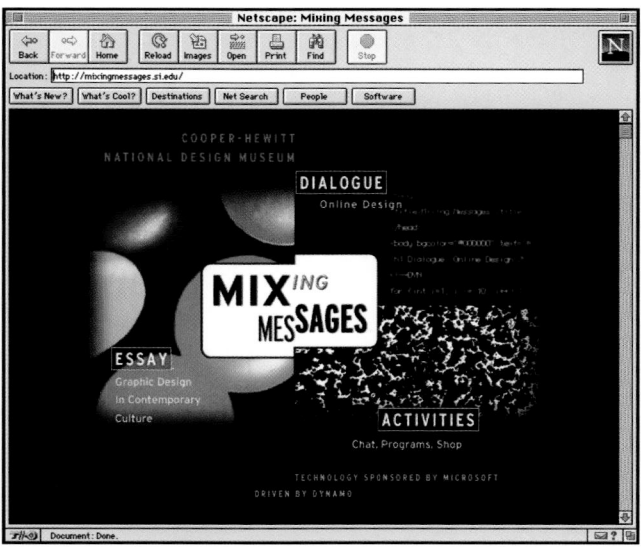

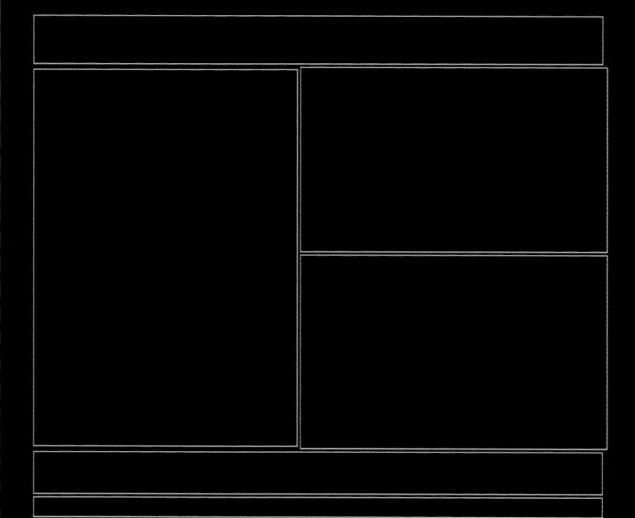

This page (■ http://www.mixingmessages.si.edu) designed by Elizabeth Roxby looks like a single image.

Actually, it's a table with a single image cut apart into many images. This enabled the designer to optimize each section as a JPEG or a GIF, depending on the best compression for each respective section.

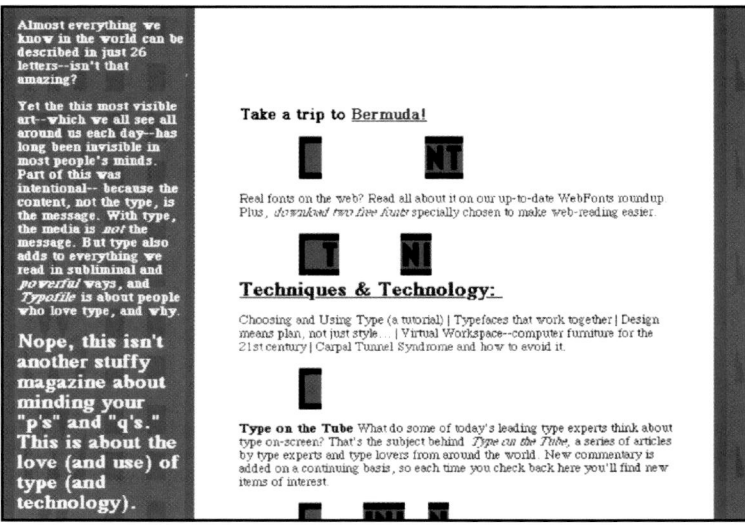

Watching Daniel Will Harris' page load looks like the entire page is animated. In reality, he's broken apart his single images into many images and positioned them with tables. It gives a Venetian blind effect when the page is loaded.

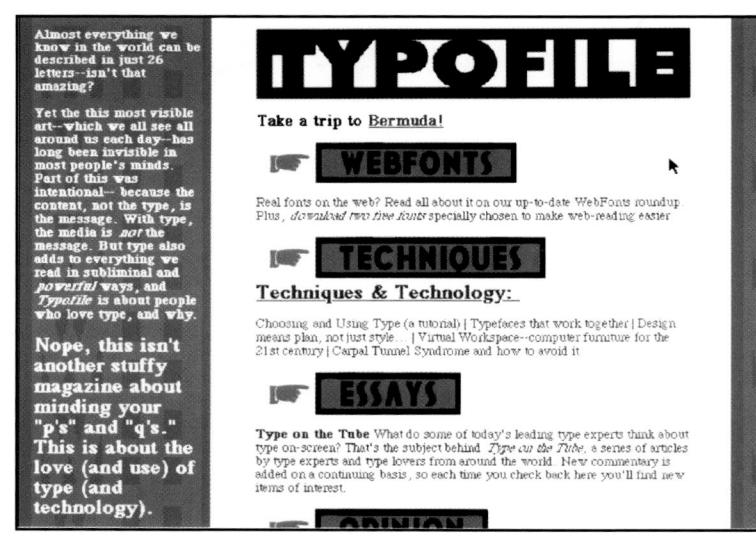

Here's a section of the final page (■ http://www.will-harris.com).

Warning: Text in Tables Can Get Messed Up Easily

As wonderful as tables are for forcing text and images into exact positions, there's one major snafu. Text tables are dependent on the size of the text. If you've created dainty text boxes and your end viewers decide to change their default sizes for text, your table is going to look terrible. For this reason, tables with graphics only are much more reliable than tables with text or a combination of the two. I'm not suggesting you don't use tables for text, but understand that you run the risk that these tables might not look as you intended on everyone's system.

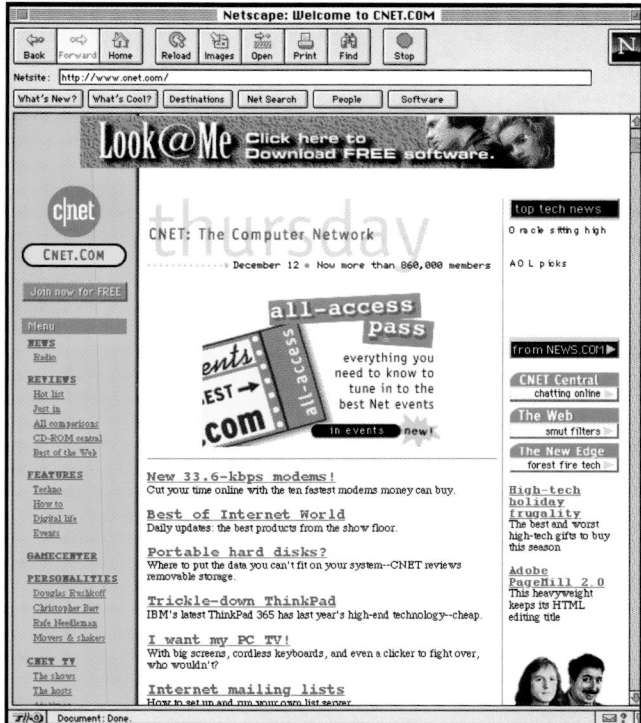

■ http://www.cnet.com makes great use of tables for a tabloid-style newspaper layout.

Here's the same page, with the default fonts changed. Though not terrible, this is probably NOT what the designers had in mind. You always run the risk of unpredictable settings when your page is reliant on tables and text.

Alignment Without Tables

The <PRE> tag, which was discussed in Chapter 11, "Web-Based Typography," can also be used for alignment purposes. Here's Crystal Waters' (author of *Web Concept & Design* and *Universal Web Design* from New Riders) home page. It uses the <PRE> tag exclusively, and looks pretty darn cool if I might say so myself!

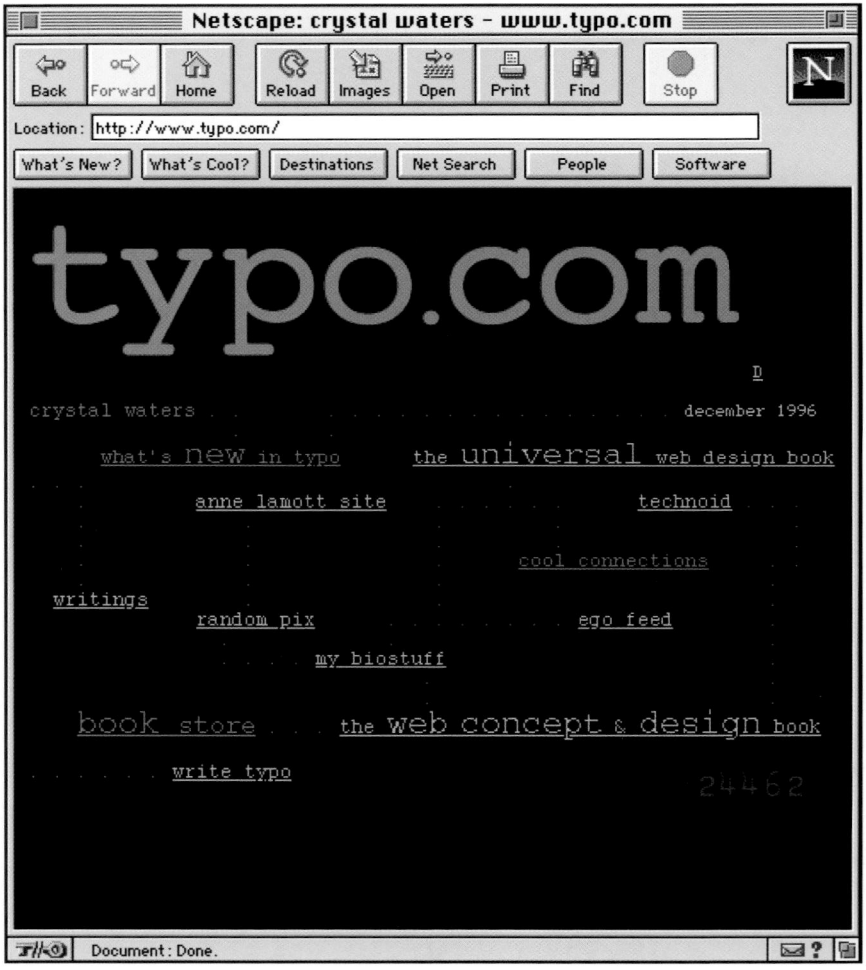

Check out ■ http://www.typo.com for very interesting layout ideas using the <PRE> and <FONT SIZE> tags.

It's interesting to study Crystal's HTML below to see how she used the <PRE> tag:

```
<HTML>
<HEAD>
<TITLE>crystal waters - www.typo.com</TITLE>
</HEAD>
<BODY bgcolor="#000000" text="#cccccc"
link="#cccccc" vlink="#999999">
<CODE><FONT SIZE=3>
<A HREF="./about.html"><IMG SRC="./t.gif"
WIDTH="419" HEIGHT="86" VSPACE="10" BORDER="0"></A>
<A HREF="./imagedes.html#typologo">D</A>
<BR clear=all>
<PRE><FONT SIZE=4 COLOR="#6699FF">crystal waters . .
. . . . . . . . . . . . . . . . </FONT>
<FONT SIZE=3>december 1996
<FONT SIZE=4 color="#6699FF">        .        .
<A HREF="./new.html">what's
<FONT SIZE=6>new</FONT> in typo</A>
<A HREF="../uwd/uwd.html">the <FONT SIZE=6>
universal</FONT> web design book</A>
. . .                            .
.          <A HREF="./lamott/lamott.html">
anne lamott site</A>         . . . . . .
<A HREF="../technoid/technoid.html">technoid</A> . .
.
.            .            .         .
.
.            .            .         .
.
.            .            .
```

```
<A HREF="./cool/cool.html">cool connections</A>
. .
.              .            .
.
<A HREF="./writings/writings.html">writings</A>
.              .                           .
<A HREF="./pix/pix.html">random pix</A>        . . .
. . . . .
<A HREF="./kudos.html">ego feed</A>              .
.                                          .
. . . .
<A HREF="../crystal/crystal.html">my biostuff</A>
.
.                        .
.
<FONT SIZE=6>
<A HREF="./store/store.html">book</FONT>
<FONT SIZE=5>store</A></FONT> . . .
<A HREF="./wcd/wcd.html">the <FONT SIZE=6>web</FONT>
<FONT SIZE=6>concept</FONT> &
<FONT SIZE=6>design</FONT> book</A></PRE>
<CODE><FONT SIZE=4>
<!--sirius counter II-->
<IMG ALIGN=right HEIGHT="32" WIDTH="65"
SRC="/cgi bin/Count2?uname=crystal¦
num=2¦udir=1¦dtype=num¦dmax=6¦pad=N">
<FONT SIZE=4 COLOR="#6699FF">. . . . . . </FONT>
<A HREF="mailto:typo@typo.com">write typo</A>
<BR clear=all>
</BODY>
</HTML>
```

The Adobe Acrobat Solution

Another solution to alignment hell is to say to hell with HTML altogether and use PDFs (**P**ortable **D**ocument **F**ormat) instead. Adobe's Acrobat product (■ http://www.adobe.com/prodindex/acrobat/main.html), which enables you to generate and view PDF files, has survived several ill-fated attempts to be successfully marketed as an HTML alternative.

PDF originated as a document transfer solution. The idea behind PDF was that you could save a document in a high-end layout program, complete with fonts and alignment styles, and distribute the document to anybody, even if they didn't own the software the document was originally created with. PDFs performed this task very well and enjoyed little, if any, competition.

PDF in its initial incarnation knew nothing of web delivery. The files were huge by web standards and were formatted to look good in print, not on computer screens. Of course, no one can blame Adobe. The web did not exist when Acrobat and PDF were first released!

Early web-based PDF attempts were crippled by a product that had too many components, was too large to download, and had files that were too large for the web and didn't look good either. Version 3.0 of Acrobat solves a lot of the early wrinkles for the following reasons:

- It's possible to create PDF files in many applications now, and you can author PDF files without owning Acrobat.

- PDF files can stream on the web. You don't have to download an entire PDF document before seeing and viewing pages. This makes it much less frustrating for end viewers.

- The Acrobat plug-in (available for free from: http://www.adobe. com/prodindex/acrobat/readstep.html) is much smaller to download than the entire application.

- Web-based PDF files can be optimized better than was possible in earlier versions.

- PDF files can be inline elements of standard HTML web pages.

- PDF files now support anti-aliasing on-the-fly and display text properly for screen-based viewing.

- PDF supports very cool transition effects, such as wipes and venetian blind effects with multiple pages.

- PDF supports the ability to link to internal content or outside URLs.

This is not to say that PDF still doesn't suffer from its attempts to retrofit itself into a web-based delivery medium. Any time a format depends on plug-in installation by the end viewer, accessiblity is limited. PDF is unfortunately a RAM-hungry monster. Even on my machine (with 72mb of RAM!), I had PDF files stop working when viewed on the web, and had to suffer through several browser crashes.

I don't recommend PDFs as an alternative to HTML, but I do think they provide a viable means of distributing information over the web that is not well suited for HTML. Already published and designed magazine articles and books are prime candidates for PDF delivery because the material is already successfully designed and can't be easily converted to HTML and maintain accurate integrity. PDF basically mimics print, with the enhanced and important advantages of being able to include internal and external hyperlinks.

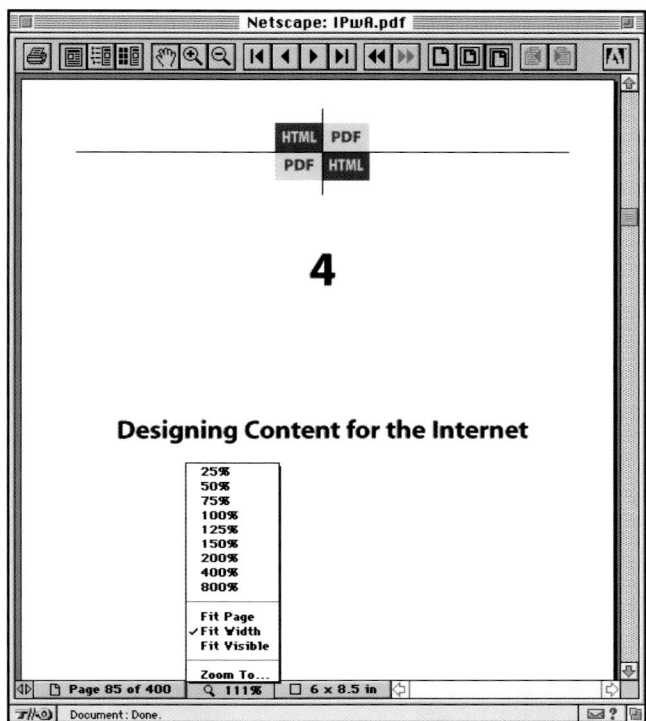

This example shows the Acrobat interface inside a web browser. One of the cool features of a PDF file is that it can be scaled all the way up to 800%.

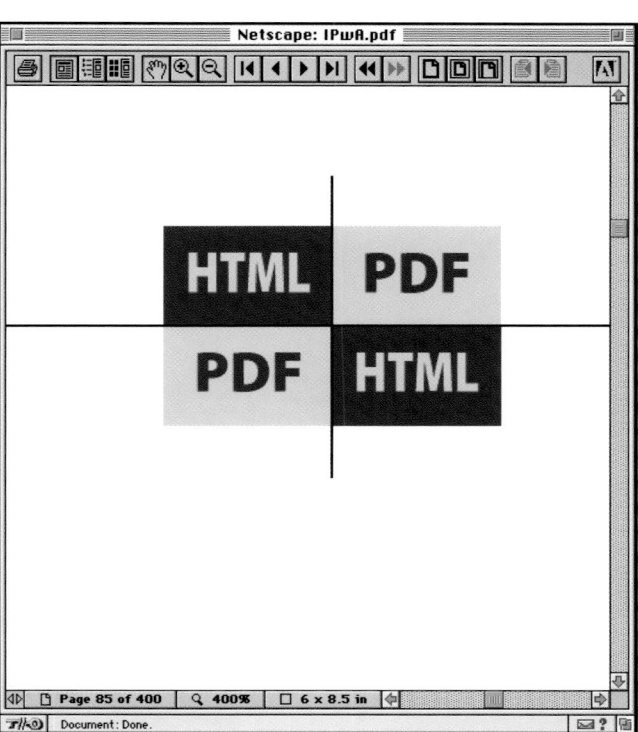

At 400% the EPS-based artwork still looks fantastic. This would not be true if it you zoomed into standard web image formats, such as GIF, PNG, or JPEG.

■ tip

More Information on PDF Authoring

Acrobat plug-in
■ http://www.adobe.com/prodindex/acrobat/readstep.html

Internet Publishing With Acrobat
Publisher: Adobe Press
Author: Gordon Kent
Retail Price: $40 ■ ISBN: 1-56830-300-9

Online (PDF) version of the above book
■ http://www.novagraphix.com/Internet_Publishing_with_Acrobat/

PDF Transitions
■ http://www.novagraphix.com/Internet_Publishing_with_Acrobat/
finder/transitions/index.html

David Siegel's PDF Pages
■ http://www.killersites.com/3-pdf/

Adobe Magazine (PDF form)
■ http://www.adobemag.com/

Building PDFs (Web Tutorial Information)
■ http://www.projectcool.com/developer/acrobat/

Cascading Style Sheets

Many web developers hope that **C**ascading **S**tyle **S**heets (CSS) will be the answer to alignment hell. CSS enables you to define the font, the indent, the justification, the leading, the spacing, and/or the color of your web page.

There are three different methods with which to implement CSS: one that enables you to embed this information for a single page, another that enables you to apply a style to an element of a page, and another that enables you to link to the style information, thereby potentially affecting many pages. One clear advantage to using CSS is that everything is created using tags and ASCII, meaning that CSS files are significantly smaller than pages that include invisible spacers and images for typography. Doesn't it sound great?

Like any new technology, there's a shakeout period where all the dust has to settle before you jump in. At the time this chapter was written, CSS was endorsed by the W3C (■ http://www.w3.org) and had been implemented only by Microsoft Internet Explorer (both Mac and PC versions). Netscape 4.0 had announced plans to support CSS using JavaScript, but no specs had been posted to its site.

The advantages to using CSS will be numerous, but if you plan to implement them today you're talking about maintaining two sets of pages: those that are CSS compliant, and those that use all the other alignment workarounds this chapter suggests. With only one browser's support, you're going to exclude more of your audience than not if you become an early adopter of CSS.

If you're really anxious to get a head start using CSS, I would suggest reading up on CSS, downloading a version of MSIE (■ http://www.microsoft.com), and experimenting with the new tags. My guess is WYSIWYG editors will support CSS as soon as the browsers duke it out and some standards are established.

If you'd like to read more about CSS, or check out some examples and code, here are some great URLs:

Web Review's Feature on CSS
■ http://webreview.com/96/11/08/feature/

HotWired's Web Monkey
(Check out the Threads section—read what the public's feelings are about CSS!)
■ http://www.webmonkey.com/browsers/ 96/33/index0a.html

Download **Microsoft's TrueType Fonts**
(Then move on to the CSS Gallery)
■ http://www.microsoft.com/truetype/

Microsoft's How-To CSS Tutorials
■ http://www.microsoft.com/truetype/css/ gallery/entrance.htm

Microsoft's CSS Gallery

As usual, the best way to learn about something on the web is to reverse-engineer how it was constructed. Visit Microsoft's CSS gallery (■ http://www.microsoft.com/truetype/css/gallery/entrance.htm) for plenty of examples. I've selected a few samples from Microsoft's site.

 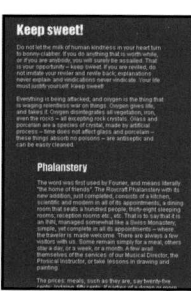 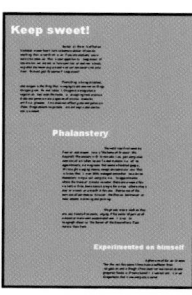 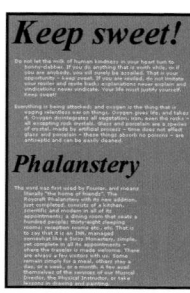 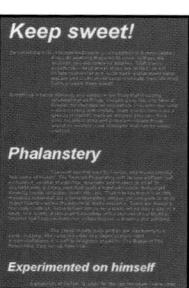 

This series of simple examples are at ■ http://www.microsoft.com/truetype/css/gallery/extract1.htm. The content for each page is the same, but the style information is different.

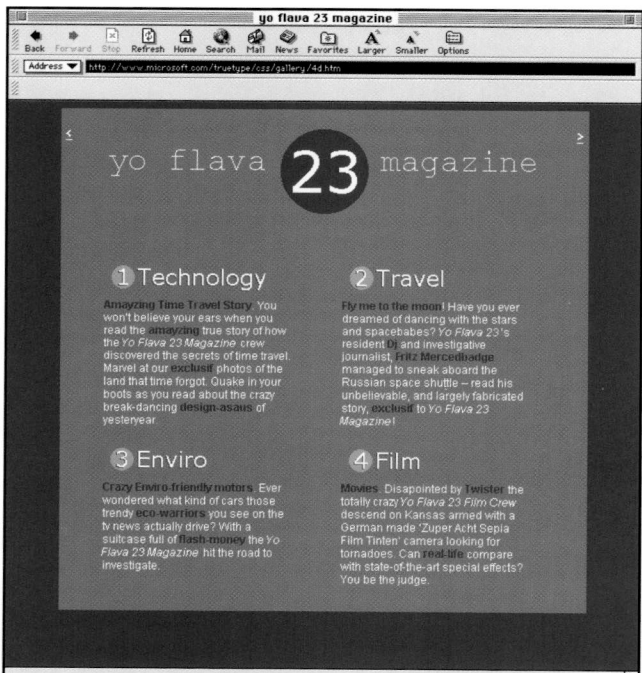

This example of CSS is found at ■ http://www.microsoft.com/true-type/css/gallery/4d.htm. Notice how you can overlay text over text, and text over shapes. These layering capabilities are not found within HTML. This entire page is less than 5k. If you were using GIF images and spacers, this page could easily be much larger.

Here's the code:

```
<HTML>
<HEAD>
<TITLE>yo flava 23 magazine</TITLE>
<STYLE>
<!--BODY {background:darkblue;color:black}
P{color:black;font-size:12px;
font-family: Arial, sans-serif}.copy
{color: white; margin-left:-4px;
margin-right:6px; margin-top:10px;
font-size:12px;
font-family: Arial, sans-serif}.plus
{color: white; margin-left:-200px;
margin-right: -200px; font-size:33px;
font-family:Courier New}.logo1
{color: darkblue; margin-top:-17px;
font-size:160px; font-weight:bold;
font-family:WingDings}.logo2
{color:azure; margin-top:-131px;
margin-right:-3px; font-size: 62px;
font-weight:bold;
font-family:Verdana}
.logo3 {color: azure;
font-size:35px; font-weight:bold;
font-family:Courier New}.ball
{color:deepskyblue; font-size:44px;
font-weight:bold;
font-family:Wingdings}.subhead
{color:darkblue; margin-left:8px;
margin-top:-39px;font-size:24px;
```

```
font-weight:bold;
font-family:Verdana}.subhead2
{color:white; margin-left:9px; margin-top:-30px;
font-size:24px; font-weight:bold;
font-family:Verdana}
B {color:darkblue} I {font-weight:bold}
A:link {font-size:18px; text-decoration:none;
font-family:Comic Sans MS
A:visited {font-size:18px; text-decoration: none;
font-family: Comic Sans MS }-->
</STYLE>
</HEAD>
<BODY>
<CENTER>
<TABLE WIDTH=560 CELLPADDING=0 CELLSPACING=0
BORDERCOLORDARK=black BORDERCOLORLIGHT=red
BORDER=0 BGCOLOR=steelblue>
<TR><TD COLSPAN=5 ALIGN=CENTER>
<TABLE WIDTH=550 CELLPADDING=0
CELLSPACING=0><TR>
<TD WIDTH=220 VALIGN=TOP><P><BR>
<A HREF="/truetype/css/gallery/4b.htm">
<SPAN STYLE="color: white">&lt;</SPAN></A>
<DIV ALIGN=RIGHT CLASS=logo3>yo flava</DIV>
</TD><TD WIDTH=110 ALIGN=CENTER>
<DIV CLASS=logo1>l</DIV>
<DIV CLASS=logo2>23</DIV></TD>
<TD WIDTH=220 VALIGN=TOP>
<P ALIGN=RIGHT><BR>
<A HREF="/truetype/css/gallery/4e.htm">
<SPAN STYLE="color: white">&gt;</SPAN></A>
<DIV ALIGN=LEFT CLASS=logo3>magazine</DIV>
</TD></TR></TABLE></TD></TR>
<TR><TD WIDTH=50 VALIGN=TOP> </TD>
<TD WIDTH=200 VALIGN=TOP>
<DIV CLASS=ball>l</DIV>
<DIV CLASS=subhead>1 Technology</DIV>
<DIV CLASS=subhead2>1 Technology</DIV>
<DIV CLASS=copy><B>Amayzing Time Travel Story</B>.
You won&#146;t believe your ears when you read the
<B>amayzing</B> true story of how the <I>Yo Flava 23
Magazine</I> crew discovered the secrets of time
travel. Marvel at our <B>exclusif</B> photos of the
land that time forgot. Quake in your boots as you
read about the crazy break-dancing <B>design-
asaus</B> of yesteryear.</DIV>
</TD>
<TD ROWSPAN=3 WIDTH=50></TD>
<TD WIDTH=200 VALIGN=TOP>
<DIV CLASS=ball>l</DIV>
<DIV CLASS=subhead>2 Travel</DIV>
<DIV CLASS=subhead2>2 Travel</DIV>
<DIV CLASS=copy><B>Fly me to the moon</B>! Have you
```

```
ever dreamed of dancing with the stars and
spacebabes? <I>Yo Flava 23</I>&#146;s resident
<B>Dj</B> and investigative journalist,
<B>Fritz Mercedbadge</B> managed to sneak
aboard the Russian space shuttle &#150; read
his unbelievable, and largely fabricated story,
<B>exclusif</B> to <I>Yo Flava 23
Magazine</I>!</DIV>
</TD>
<TD WIDTH=50 VALIGN=TOP> </TD></TR>
<TR><TD VALIGN=TOP> </TD></TR>
<TR><TD WIDTH=50 VALIGN=TOP> </TD>
<TD WIDTH=200 VALIGN=TOP>
<DIV CLASS=ball>l</DIV>
<DIV CLASS=subhead>3 Enviro</DIV>
<DIV CLASS=subhead2>3 Enviro</DIV>
<DIV CLASS=copy><B>Crazy Enviro-friendly
motors</B>. Ever wondered what kind of cars
those trendy <B>eco-warriors</B> you see on the
tv news actually drive? With a suitcase full of
<B>flash-money</B> the <I>Yo Flava 23
Magazine</I> hit the road to investigate.</DIV>
</TD>
<TD WIDTH=200 VALIGN=TOP>
<DIV CLASS=ball>l</DIV>
<DIV CLASS=subhead>4 Film</DIV>
<DIV CLASS=subhead2>4 Film</DIV>
<DIV CLASS=copy><B>Movies</B>. Disapointed by
<B>Twister</B> the totally crazy <I>Yo Flava 23
Film Crew</I> descend on Kansas armed with a
German made &#145;Zuper Acht Sepia Film
Tinten&#146; camera looking for tornadoes. Can
<B>real-life</B> compare with state-of-the-art
special effects? You be the judge.
<BR> <BR> </DIV>
</TD>
<TD WIDTH=50 VALIGN=TOP> </TD>
</TR>
</TABLE>
</CENTER>
</BODY>
</HTML>
```

Animation

BROWSER SAFE COLORS

33 FPS

<H1>

Website

Typography

<TABLE>

Photoshop

0033

<STRONG>

<img src=

Width ="500"

.jpg
.png

IMAGE OPTIMIZATION
palette
colors

TRANSPARENCY

Height ="600"

<center>

</A>

Imaging techniques
Web file formats

bgcolor = "FFFFFF"

@link = "cyan"

33

Animation, sound and

LYNDA.COM

<center> <BODY>
Autload

www.iDesign

Web Animation

An unfortunate irony is that animation is a lot easier to enjoy as a passive spectator than it is to create. For many newcomers to web page creation, there's never been a reason to consider learning how to create animation until now. For others, even experienced animators, the web is new territory with different rules, standards, terminology, and tools to understand. The maturing web of today is actually bustling with animation choices—from how to make the content to what tools to use to what delivery methods and file formats to choose from.

The web has introduced many new concepts to us, and adding animation to web pages introduces more. First of all, people used to working in film or video have never had to give much thought to the file size of their artwork. On the web, file size translates to speed. If you don't think speed is important, think about how annoyed you get when pages don't load quickly enough. Animation, by nature, relies on displaying multiple images. Each image takes its own amount of time to download. This poses a major challenge to animation developers and authors that extends beyond the normal complexities of animation creation and delivery in other mediums.

There used to be a much wider disparity between browsers—those that supported certain tags and features over those that didn't. One good thing to say about competition is that the major browsers of today (Netscape and Microsoft Internet Explorer) support plug-ins, Java, GIF animation, JavaScript, and server push. Lagging seriously behind is AOL, and other much lesser-known browsers. Fortunately, AOL is making it possible for their customers to view the web with Microsoft Internet Explorer now, so even that last hurdle of browser inconsistency is disappearing. This is not to say that standards for the web are ironed out or at peace with each other. Change and new standards are the norm on the web, not the exception.

All these factors lead to new decisions for the web designer. Questions such as which technologies to invest in, which new tools to learn, and the aesthetics and appropriateness of animation are new issues to add to the long existing list of design concerns.

Here are some of the things you'll find in this chapter:

- The aesthetics of animation—when and how much to use
- Animation technologies
- Animation tools
- Animation techniques
- Speed considerations
- Web movie specifications: size, codec, and FPS

The Aesthetics of Animation

Before we get into the what, where, how, and why of animation, I'd like to stop a moment and consider the broader issue—the aesthetics of animation. With the exception of multimedia, the web is the first medium to combine animation and body text on a single page. For this reason, it's no wonder that many people struggle to use animation effectively.

Adding animation to a site can be great, but also can have the reverse affect by appearing gratuitous and/or annoying to your audience. During a recent panel that I moderated, Ben Olander, Creative Director at Organic Online (■ www.organic.com) commented, "Most animation you see on the web is the equivalent of the <BLINK> tag." I agree with him, but I also see this as a natural outgrowth of artists and developers who are exploring a new tool.

Here are some very general, personal guidelines I would like to share:

- ■ In most instances, animation that cycles or loops endlessly will eventually become annoying. This chapter will teach you how to set up loops, or a finite number of repeats.

- ■ If you use more than one animation on a single page, the effect may be overwhelming to the end viewer instead of impressive.

- ■ Animation calls attention to itself much more than static images on a page. Make sure that the content of your animation is, in fact, something you want the most attention called to on your page. If it isn't, the animation will effectively detract from what you're trying to communicate.

- ■ Make sure your animation loads quickly. You'll learn guidelines to achieve fast downloading speeds in this chapter. If you make your audience wait too long for the animation or plug-in to load, they'll move onward before ever seeing it.

Web Animation Technologies

Before getting into any nitty-gritty techniques and products, it's first important to know what choices you have in terms of different technologies. A brief synopsis of different animation delivery choices follows.

Animated GIFs

Animated GIFs are part of the GIF89a spec, which has been in existence since the late 1980s. The great news is that all the major web browsers have recently flocked to support the the animated GIF spec, making it possible to include these types of files in web pages without worry of excluding any potential end viewers.

The GIF89a file format allows for multiple images to be stored inside a single GIF document. When displayed within browser software that recognizes the multiple images, the artwork streams in to the web page in a predetermined sequence, creating a slide-show style animation. The file format supports looping (the capability to repeat multiple images indefinitely) and timing delays between frames of artwork. GIFs also support limited masking, meaning that animations can use the same type of transparency supported by static GIF images.

Animated GIFs require no plug-ins and no programming, and don't even require a live web connection, making them perfect for intranets and testing locally on your machine. Animated GIFs are simple to make, easy to include in HTML, and effortless for your web-viewing audience to see. They are one of the most elegant solutions to web animation and lack only in that they cannot include interactivity or sound. For an animated logo or button, however, animated GIFs are a pretty smart option.

To include animated GIFs in web pages, you'll use the standard <IMG SRC> tag. A simple example of the code would look like this:

```
<IMG SRC="my_animation.gif">
```

Specific tools with which to create animated GIFs are discussed later in this chapter. Here are some recommended resources for learning how to create and code animated GIFs:

Royale Frazier's amazing animated GIF resource
(A good tutorial on animated GIF options)
■ http://member.aol.com/royalef/gifanim.htm

Yves Piguet's (author of GIFBuilder) site
(Another great tutorial)
■ http://iawww.epfl.ch/Staff/Yves.Piguet/clip2gif-home/GifBuilder.html

Plug-Ins

Many enhanced animation options are possible through plug-ins. Plug-ins need to be installed by the end viewer. This requires that your audience download the plug-in, install it in their browser plug-in folder, and restart their browser. Plug-ins do not exactly support effortless web surfing, and the truth is many people will choose to click off a page that requires a plug-in rather than endure the bothersome interruption or time-consuming installation process.

Web plug-ins are barely a year old, and many browsers are just beginning to support them for the first time. This means that plug-in support is sometimes unstable and poorly implemented. If you do decide to choose an animation format that requires a plug-in, you should keep in mind that your choice to do so probably excludes a portion of your potential audience. You might consider including a link to download the plug-in before the screen appears that requires it. Notifying your audience that you're using a plug-in is a courtesy, and creating alternate pages for those who won't bother with the plug-in installation process is a recommended practice.

Typically, whenever you include content that requires a plug-in, you will use an <EMBED> tag within your HTML. You must always put in the <HEIGHT> and <WIDTH> tags to define the size for any plug-in or Java content on a web page. The <NO EMBED> tag will display alternate content. A sample line of code that includes a plug-in-reliant file might look like this:

```
<EMBED="myanimationfile.xxx" HEIGHT="200" WIDTH="200">

<NO EMBED="alternatecontent.gif" HEIGHT="200" WIDTH="200">
```

Java

Java has quickly become one of the most renowned programming languages of our time. People who would have never before considered learning a programming language are clamoring around Java's allure in unprecedented numbers. What's all the hype about, and is Java a good animation delivery medium?

Java's potential benefits are almost as revolutionary as the web itself. Java creates mini-executable programs (called applets) that promise to be platform independent, compact enough to travel over phone wires, and able to expand on anyone's system regardless of OS, make, or model. Another great thing about Java is the popular browsers (Netscape, MSIE, and Mosaic) support Java without requiring a plug-in. This, in theory, gives Java high marks for accessibility and compatibility. I know many people who complain that their browsers still choke on Java, so my suspicion is that we'll be waiting a little longer before the hype matches the reality. Regardless, a lot of people and companies are investing heavily in Java, which assures me that the bugs will eventually get ironed out.

Because Java creates custom programs, it has the potential to create computational animation, as opposed to sprite-based animation. In simple English, this means that

a Java applet could calculate a changing curve shape on-the-fly, react differently to changeable conditions, or build motion based on external input. Clearly, for the right purposes, Java as an animation delivery medium holds great promise. For simple things, such as moving buttons or an animated logos, it's probably overkill. One thing that some Java authors are doing is including plug-ins inside a Java applet so that plug-in content can be viewed effortlessly by spectators who may not have had the proper configuration to begin with. For this reason, Java doesn't have to be mutually exclusive from other animation delivery methods that involve plug-ins or proprietary viewing software.

Java will require an <APPLET> tag to be included in HTML pages. A sample line of code that included Java-based content might look like this:

```
<APPLET="my_first_java_programming_triumph.xxx"
HEIGHT="200" WIDTH="200">

<NO EMBED="alternatecontent.gif" HEIGHT="200"
WIDTH="200">
```

Sun's site
(A starting point for learning about Java)
■ http://java.sun.com/

JavaScript

JavaScript actually has nothing to do with full-fledged Java. Initially the Netscape-originated scripting product was slated to be named LiveScript. With the success of Java, Netscape decided to license the Java name from Sun so its custom scripting language could bear the same name. The similarities between Java and JavaScript end there!

Java needs to be compiled, meaning that the code is written and then goes through a post-processing routine that finalizes the code and completes the programming process. Compiled code is invisible to the end user. Any type of software on your computer is an example of compiled code—from your word processor to your imaging programs to your browser applications.

JavaScript gets compiled on your end user's machine, which means that the raw code sits inside HTML documents. This is a great boon to those interested in learning to write JavaScript because—just like HTML—you can "view the source" of any web page that contains JavaScript and then copy, paste, and personalize to your heart's content. If you plan to do this, however, it is proper netiquette to credit the original author's name of the JavaScript within your pages that have "borrowed" it.

There aren't many practical examples of JavaScript being used for animation. You can program scrolling text at the bottom of a web page, create a rollover effect with a button, or make a clock tell time, but that is about the extent of what's possible so far.

JavaScript Resources

JavaScript Tips of the Week
(A great site for insider information)
■ http://www.gis.net/~carter/therest/index.html

Excellent JavaScript Tutorials
■ http://www.webconn.com/java/javascript/intro/

QuickTime Movies

There are two ways to include QuickTime on a web page: the old way, which does not require a plug-in, and the new way, which does. The old way was to write QT files into HTML with an <HREF> tag, making sure that the document had a .mov or .qt extension at the end of the file name. This method will cause the file to download. A separate helper application will pop up and play the movie in older browsers, and in newer browsers it will create a new web page with only the QuickTime movie against a gray background.

Here is an example for writing the HTML for standard QT:

```
<A HREF="PH60709B.mov">
```

The only thing you need to do special to prepare the file is to flatten the QuickTime movie, which changes its resource fork so that platforms other than Macintoshes can play the files. Flattening utilities can be found at ■ ftp://ftp.utexas.edu/pub/mac/graphics/flattenmoov.hqx. Or if you own Adobe Premiere, you can use the Flatten Movie found under the Export menu. If you choose to use this older method of including QT movies, be aware that your audience will have to wait for the entire movie to download before they can see a frame of your file. It's courteous to include a warning of the file size on the same web page where the movie link is, to warn in advance of long download times.

In newer browsers, QuickTime can be viewed as an inline (inside the browser) element of a web page. Apple calls this type of QuickTime file a fast-start movie. This means that you can arrive at a web page, see a movie as an image, and click a play button, and the file will start to play with sound! The lack of long download time and need for external MIME players has obvious appeal over the older method.

In order to create fast-start movies, you must change your HTML and change the way you save your QT movie. A simple drag-and-drop utility called Internet Movie Tool, available free from the QuickTime site, allows you to convert standard QuickTime movies into fast-start QT movies. Implementing fast-start movies also requires a plug-in, which is available from the QuickTime site: ■ http://quicktime.apple.com. QT 2.5 flattens and reconfigures the movie to work as a streaming fast-start file for you automatically.

Because a plug-in is involved, the <EMBED> tag is used to write the file into your HTML document. There are all kinds of other spiffy controls you can include in your HTML, such as whether to have play buttons appear or not, or include autoplay or looping functions. A full list of support tags is available from ■ http://quicktime.apple.com/dev/devweb.html. The plug-in is also available from the same site, and the best news is that Netscape 3.0 ships with this plug-in already installed!

Embedding QuickTime Movie Tags

Here are the key HTML tags for embedding fast-start QuickTime movies. Be sure to visit the site (■ http://www.quicktime.com) to ensure that you have a complete list.

<EMBED>	The <EMBED> tag is used to embed QuickTime movies as inline elements on a page.
SRC=url	The URL of the source document.
PLUGINSPAGE=url	PLUGINSPAGE is an optional parameter. The PLUGINSPAGE parameter allows you to specify an URL from which the user can fetch the necessary plug-in if it is not installed. This parameter is handled by Netscape. If Netscape cannot find the plug-in when loading your page, it will warn users and allow them to bring up the specified URL to download the QuickTime plug-in from. IMPORTANT: Set this parameter to "http://quicktime.apple.com," which will point to the most appropriate plug-in for various versions of Navigator and different operating systems. This option is appropriate for both QuickTime movies and QuickTime VR Objects and Panoramas.
WIDTH=size in pixels	The WIDTH attribute specifies in pixels the width of the embedded document. This option is appropriate for both QuickTime and QuickTime VR movies. The WIDTH parameter is required unless you use the HIDDEN parameter. Never specify a width of less than 2 because this can cause problems with Navigator. If you are trying to use tiny width and height to hide the movie, use the <HIDDEN> tag instead, as explained on the following page. If you don't know the width of the movie, open your movie with MoviePlayer (PLAYER.EXE on Windows 3.1 or PLAY32.EXE on Windows 95/NT) that comes with QuickTime and select Get Info (Get Movie Info under Windows) from the Movie menu. If you supply a width that is smaller than the actual width of the movie, the movie will be cropped to fit the width. If you supply a width that is greater than the width of the movie, the movie will be centered inside this width.

HEIGHT=sizeinpixels	The HEIGHT attribute specifies the height of the embedded document, in pixels. This option is appropriate for both QuickTime and QuickTime VR movies. If you want to display the movie's controller, you will need to add 24 pixels to the HEIGHT. The HEIGHT parameter is required unless you use the HIDDEN parameter (below). Never specify a height of less than 2 becuase this can cause problems with Navigator. If you are trying to use tiny width and height to hide the movie, use the <HIDDEN> tag instead, as explained below. If you don't know the height of the movie, open your movie with the MoviePlayer that comes with QuickTime (PLAYER.EXE or PLAY32.EXE on Windows 3.1) and select Get Info (Get Movie Info under Windows) from the Movie menu. If you supply a height that is smaller than the actual height of the movie (plus 24 if you are showing the controller), the movie will be cropped to fit the height. If you supply a height that is greater than the height of the movie, the movie will be centered inside this height.
HIDDEN	HIDDEN is an optional parameter. The HIDDEN parameter controls the visibility of the movie. There are no values to supply for this parameter. If you do not supply HIDDEN, the movie will be visible. If you supply HIDDEN, the movie is not visible on the page. This option is not appropriate for QuickTime VR Objects or Panor- amas. You can use the HIDDEN setting to hide a sound-only movie. Note for Plug-in B8 release only: When you use the "hidden" HTML command, you must explicitly specify "CONTROLLEr=FALSE." This is not necessary in the latest release, available on the Quick-Time Software page.
AUTOPLAY=value	AUTOPLAY is an optional parameter. When set to TRUE, the AUTOPLAY parameter causes the movie to start playing as soon as the QuickTime plug-in estimates that it will be able to play the entire movie without waiting for additional data. Acceptable values for this parameter are TRUE and FALSE. The default value of AUTOPLAY is FALSE. This option is not appropriate for QuickTime VR Objects and Panoramas.

CONTROLLER=value	CONTROLLER is an optional parameter. The CONTROLLER parameter sets the visibility of the movie controller. Acceptable values for this parameter are TRUE and FALSE. The default value of the CONTROLLER parameter is TRUE. This option is not appropriate for QuickTime VR Objects and Panoramas.
LOOP=value	LOOP is an optional parameter. When set, the LOOP parameter makes the movie play in a loop. Acceptable values for this parameter are TRUE, FALSE, and PALINDROME. Setting LOOP to PALINDROME causes the movie to play alternately forward and backward. The default value of LOOP is FALSE. This option is not appropriate for QuickTime VR Objects and Panoramas.
PLAYEVERYFRAME=value	PLAYEVERYFRAME is an optional parameter. When set, the PLAYEVERYFRAME parameter causes the movie to play every frame even if it is necessary to play at a slower rate to do so. This parameter is particularly useful for playing simple animations. Acceptable values for this parameter are TRUE and FALSE. The default value of the PLAYEVERYFRAME parameter is FALSE. This option is appropriate for QuickTime movies. Note: PLAYEVERYFRAME=TRUE will turn off any audio tracks your movie may have.
HREF=url	HREF is an optional parameter. When set, the HREF parameter provides a link to another page when the movie is clicked on. This option is appropriate only for a movie without a controller. Note: when using a relative path name for the HREF, it should be relative to the location of the movie specified in the SRC=parameter. This option is not appropriate for QuickTime VR Objects and Panoramas.
TARGET=frame	TARGET is an optional parameter. When set, the TARGET parameter is the name of a valid frame that will be the target of a link (including _self, _top, _parent, _blank, or an explicit frame name). This parameter is for use with the HREF parameter. This option is not appropriate for QuickTime VR Objects and Panoramas.

QuickTime VR

QTVR (**Q**uick**T**ime **V**irtual **R**eality) is a type of QuickTime movie that makes it possible to see and navigate through 360-degree panoramic images without external glasses or goggles. Moving your mouse inside the file allows you to navigate through a seamless image and examine things from front to back or top to bottom. These types of files were developed originally for CD-ROMs and allowed the possibility to link to self-contained "hot" objects that could contain other QTVR modules, or other 360-degree still images. These files can be inserted into web pages by conventional <IMG SRC> methods, and launch a QTVR player or play inline in a web page, much the way the "fast-start" standard QT movies will. The latter requires a plug-in and the <EMBED> tag. The QTVR movies also have to be converted to a web-savvy format, which changes its resource fork to allow the file to play as a "fast-start" file. A simple drag-and-drop utility called Internet Movie Tool is available free from the QuickTime site (■ http://www.quicktime.apple.com) and allows you to convert standard QTVR movies into "fast-start" QT movies.

HTML Tags for QuickTime VR

The HTML tags are available from ■ http://quicktime.apple.com/dev/devweb.html#convert. Here's a list of them. However, this list may go out of date so be sure to visit the site to ensure that you have a complete list.

PAN=integer	PAN is an optional parameter. The PAN parameter allows you to specify the initial pan angle for a QuickTime VR movie. The range of values for a typical movie would be 0.0 to 360.0 degrees. This parameter has no meaning for a standard QuickTime movie.
TILT=integer	TILT is an optional parameter. The TILT parameter allows you to specify the initial tilt angle for a QuickTime VR movie. The range of values for a typical movie would be -42.5 to 42.5 degrees. This parameter has no meaning for a standard QuickTime movie.
FOV=integer	FOV is an optional parameter. The FOV parameter allows you to specify the initial field of view angle for a QuickTime VR movie. The range of values for a typical movie would be 5.0 to 85.0 degrees. This parameter has no meaning for a standard QuickTime movie.
NODE=integer	NODE is an optional parameter. The NODE parameter allows you to specify the initial node for a multi-node QuickTime VR movie.
CORRECTION=value	CORRECTION is an optional parameter. Possible values are NONE, PARTIAL, or FULL. This parameter is appropriate only for QuickTime VR Objects and Panoramas.

AVI Movies

The Video for Windows file format is often referred to as VfW or AVI. Players are widely supported on PCs and Windows-based machines. The advantage to using AVI is that these files are easier for PC users to view because Windows 95 ships with an AVI player. The disadvantage is that Mac, SGI, and Sun audiences will have to convert the files or have the necessary player to view them.

AVI movies must use the extension .avi. The HTML for inserting an AVI movie would be:

```
<A HREF="my_movie.avi">Download my movie</A>
```

AVI Movie Tags for Embedding

You can also embed AVI movies to play as inline elements, but this is currently supported only by MSIE. Here are the associated HTML tags:

<IMG DYNSRC="movie.avi"START="mouseover">	Plays the movie with a mouse over.
<IMG DYNSRC="movie.avi"START="fileopen">	Plays movie when HTML is loaded.
<IMG DYNSRC="movie.avi"controls>	Displays controls and allows for human interaction.
LOOP="infinite", LOOP="2",and LOOPDELAY="20" (milliseconds)	You can also add looping and delay.

Syntax Example

<IMG DYNSRC="movie.avi"loop="infinite" START="mouseover",LOOPDELAY="20">s	Plays on mouse over, loops infinitely, and the delays are 20 milliseconds.

Thanks to Hung Doan (■ http://www.vworks.com) from the Web Design List for these tags and explanations. For more information on AVI and the HTML for embedding them, go to ■ http://www.microsoft.com.

Server Push

Server push has become outdated as an animation delivery for the most part. It involves CGI (**C**ommon **G**ateway **I**nterface) scripting, which extends the capability of HTML and is used for all kinds of things the World Wide Web over, including calculating database data from forms or making server-sided imagemaps. CGI requires that you write a script in any number of real programming languages, the most popular of which are Perl, sh, C++, and AppleScript. If you're going to go through the bother of learning a programming language for animation purposes, most would agree Java would be a superior choice because of its flexibility and nonreliance on a server.

Server push sends a request to the web server to send out frames of an animation. This means that an active connection between the web server and web client must be engaged throughout the animation process. This can tie up precious server time and make your site less accessible to large numbers of visitors. The numerous cons (requires programming, taxes the server, and requires live connection to see) outweigh the pros (can supply changing and generate on-the-fly animation content) of this method.

The HTML for server push would link the file to a CGI script. The CGI script would need to be located on the server. The HTML would look something like this:

```
<IMG SRC="push.cgi">
```

Noteworthy Web Animation Tools

I can't possibly discuss every possible tool for animation in this chapter because there isn't enough room, and I probably don't know about every single software package out there anyway. Instead, I've chosen to select certain tools of significance (and this is, of course, a subjective judgment on my part) and give a little extra information about them.

FutureSplash Animator (Mac/PC Compatible)

Future Wave Software
■ http://www.futurewave.com/fsindex.html

FutureSplash is both Mac and PC compatible and comes in two components. The first is a plug-in that lets your end users view the proprietary vector file-format .spl. This second component is a cross-platform authoring tool called CelAnimator, which enables you to create cartoon-style animation and button rollover effects. The effects can be saved in a variety of formats that both require and don't require a plug-in.

Unlike the other products profiled here, FutureSplash creates vector-based artwork instead of bitmap artwork. In general, vector artwork generates much smaller file sizes, meaning that the resulting animation or artwork will be faster than other web file formats.

The animation authoring tool, CelAnimator, enables you to create movement of multiple artwork layers on multiple movement paths. It even lets you create interactive buttons with rollovers without needing to program a thing! This is a great overall package with terrific features. The only drawback is that viewing the results is plug-in-dependent, meaning it requires your end viewer to go that extra mile that some will not travel. The program also lets you save animated GIFs, QuickTime movies, ActiveX, Java applets, and sequential GIFs, but these file formats won't be nearly as small and elegant as the proprietary plug-in-based vector format.

This is a great product for both the professional and novice web-site designer who has a sophisticated audience to please. If it were built into the browsers and weren't plug-in reliant, FutureSplash would be even cooler than it already is. You can download a free demo of the full-working software to try. I recommend that you do.

Cool FutureSplash Site
■ http://www.foxworld.com/Simpsons/Simpsons.htm
■ http://www.msn.com/default.asp
■ http://www.synenenergy.com/tunes/dubeslhtml

Shockwave/Director (Mac/PC Compatible)

Macromedia Director
■ http://www.macromedia.com

Macromedia Director was a popular multimedia authoring system long before the web existed. It boasts a user base of more than 200,000, making it one of the most successful interactive authoring tools in history. Making Director projects interactive involves learning its proprietary scripting language called Lingo. With Lingo, you can make interactive web presentations that include animation, rollovers, and streaming sound. A post-processing tool called Afterburner is incorporated into Director 5.0, or is free to download from ■ http://www.macromedia.com/shockwave/devtools.html#director.

Shockwave is the plug-in required to view Director projects on the web. A drawback of this product is that it's hard to create files that are truly compact enough for web delivery. Most end viewers will have to up their RAM allocation for browsers to look at most Shockwave content. Additionally, Lingo has a steep learning curve that is a bit too high for the simple tasks one might want to program for web-based animation delivery. It is a case of existing technology being retrofitted to the web, and the fit is a little tight still. This product is great for people who are already up-to-speed on Director but is a little too difficult and powerful for those who are not.

Still, Director allows you to add features to web content that few other tools or solutions can match. Check out some of the following sites to see what I mean, but be sure to download the Shockwave plug-in and up the RAM allocation to your browser first:

To download the Shockwave plug-in
■ http://www.macromedia.com/shockwave/download/

Cool Shockwave Sites
■ http://www.obsolete.com/shockwave/
■ http://www.stink.com/leroy/leroy.html
■ http://www.qaswa.com/shock.html
■ http://www.razorfish.com/bluedot/typo/

webPainter (Mac Only)

Totally Hip Software

■ www.totallyhip.com

webPainter is a painting tool for creating animation. It includes a "cel" animation interface that lets you use onion-skinning (the computer equivalent of tracing paper), multiple cel editing, and foreground/background drawing cels. The web site includes a very thorough tutorial that not only explains how to use the product but also describes universal animation principles. It saves the files as PICs, QuickTime movies, GIF89a's, and sequential GIF files. The product lacks sophisticated animation features found in more high-end packages but is useful to anyone wanting to learn how to create cel-style character animation. Because the product saves animation in so many formats, it is not hindered by any plug-in constraints. At the time this chapter was written, a free trial version was available from their site.

3D Web Workshop (Mac Only)

Specular, Inc.

■ http://www.specular.com

If you like 3D graphics, this is the product for you! Specular has modified existing products (Infini-D, Logo Motion, and TextureScape) and combined them with Adobe's Pagemill and a web clip-art collection called webHands to form a suite of web artwork-generation tools. The products offer easy-to-edit-and-customize clip art/animation of pre-existing web-based artwork, like seamlessly tileable background textures, 3D buttons, 3D bullets, and rules. All webHands are professionally designed for use on the web, with optimized palettes and transparency information, and can be immediately dragged and dropped onto a web page with both the MacOS and Windows versions of Netscape's Navigator Gold. You can build your own 3D animated logos and save them as GIF89a's or QuickTime movies, or create your own custom artwork and background tiles using their time-tested tools. The documentation was a little confusing in that it worked for each individual bundled product and not for the product suite in relationship to integrating each package. Overall, the product delivers lots of power and bang for the buck and is suitable for animation old-timers and newcomers alike.

PhotoDisc Animation Series (Mac/PC Compatible)

PhotoDisc, Inc.
■ http://www.photodisc.com

Animation clip art is usually pretty mundane. The folks at PhotoDisc (a leading digital stock photo agency) went many steps ahead of the competition and published renowned designer Clement Mok's work (■ http://www.studioarchetype.com/) to create some superb clip-animation sequences. The two series, Metaphorically Blinking and EveryDay Objects Live, include photo-realistic animations of such things as chattering teeth toys and a shaking alarm clock. This product comes in two varieties: the basic version with animations saved out as Animated GIFs and Shockwave documents with rollover and sound built-in, and the Pro Versions, which include the necessary Director files to allow end users to customize and edit the animations. The price is a little high for some, but the quality is worth it. The fact that the professional version lets you edit the Director files is a great bonus.

QuickTime: Web Motion (Mac Only)

Terran Interactive, Inc.
■ http://www.terran-int.com

GIF Animation Tools

GIFBuilder (Mac Only)
Written by Yves Piguet
■ http://iawww.epfl.ch/Staff/Yves.Piguet/clip2gif-home/GifBuilder.html

This is the best animated GIF software I've used on any platform. It's the bar that all the other programs out there need to strive to reach! Despite the fact that it's Mac-only, I wanted to mention it here because it's such a cool program.

GIFBuilder allows you to import Photoshop layers, QuickTime movies, and sequential GIFs or PICTs as source artwork for animations. It saves animated GIFs with a simple, no-programming-required "save" command, and lets you set frame delays, transparency, load custom palettes, and display methods to boot. It includes an optimization feature that stores a stationary background and creates transparency wherever overlaying frames don't change or alter the background. This can cut file size significantly. Altogether, an awesome product at an awesome price (free!). GIFBuilder is for everyone who uses a Mac—from novices to professionals.

Movie Cleaner Pro (Mac only) is an invaluable tool for anyone involved in creating movies for CD-ROM authoring. The software specializes in making QuickTime movie compression easy to implement, understand, and preview before commitment. Web Motion is a plug-in for Movie Cleaner Pro that optimizes movies for web delivery. This product includes "Web Expert" advice that counsels you on a movie-by-movie basis to make compression choices, and previews those choices allowing you to see the results of your decisions. This product creates "flattened" movies that are saved correctly for the "quick-start" QT movie plug-in, automatically generates the <EMBED> tags for your HTML, and helps you through the otherwise very confusing process of choosing web-appropriate data rates and video compression. The product is easy to learn and use and helps to create small, fast, and web-appropriate content. The con is the price tag, which is steep for nonprofessionals.

Tech Notes: More on Animated GIFs

In my opinion, working with animated GIFs is one of the most sensible choices of web animation formats to pick from. Animated GIFs include the following features:

- The capability to set looping, or number of repeats
- The capability to set delays between individual frames
- Download speeds
- The capability to optimize the graphics by using different disposal methods
- Palettes
- Transparency
- Interlacing

Looping: As stated earlier, be careful of unlimited looping animations as they can annoy your audience.

Frame delays: Frame delays can be used to alter the timing of animations. The unit of measurement is 100= 1 second. If you want your first frame to last 5 seconds and your next three to last 1 second each, and the last frame to last 15 seconds, your frame delays would look something like this:

```
Frame 01=500
Frame 02=100
Frame 03=100
Frame 04=100
Frame 05=1500
```

Download Speeds: The initial download time of the animated GIF will depend on your end user's connection speed, but once the animation has fully downloaded, it will depend on the processor speed of his computer. This can make for wildly different frame delay timings on different systems, regardless of what frame delays you program. Almost all GIF animation software packages will support frame delays.

Optimization: Animated GIFs can be optimized, just like regular GIFs. The same rules that applied to file size savings in Chapter 4, "Low-Bandwidth Graphics," apply here. Like other GIFs, you want to make sure that you use as few colors as needed and try to avoid dithering or noise in your image.

Transparency and disposal methods: Disposal methods are a scary sounding term for how the animation is displayed in terms of its transparency. With a single image, this is a nonissue. A transparent image shows through to its background, and that's the end of the story.

With a multiple-frame GIF, however, this presents a bigger issue. Let's say I have an animated ball that's bouncing. If I make the ball transparent and the image before it has already loaded, the transparency might show part or all of the frame before. Instead of the illusion of motion, the unwanted result would be each frame of my bouncing ball animation visible at the same time.

The disposal method is what instructs the GIF animation how to display preceding frames of the animation. Disposal methods are set within whatever GIF animation software package you're using.

- **Unspecified:** Use this disposal method when you aren't using transparency. It will simply present each frame in its entirety and will not yield any added optimization to the file. If I had an animation that changed images every single frame, I would use this disposal method.

- **Do not dispose:** This disposal method would reveal each preceding frame of an animation. Let's say I wanted to create an animation of my name handwriting itself on the screen. If I left the L to draw itself only once and then used the subsequent frame to draw the Y, I would be creating a smaller file size. Use this method when you want the prior frames to show through, and you want to enjoy some file savings with no penalty to image quality.

- **Restore to background:** Instead of displaying the previous frame, the animation is set to show the background color or tile image of your web page.

- **Restore to previous:** This function is almost the same as Do Not Dispose except the first frame always stays visible underneath the rest of the animation. At the time this chapter was written, Netscape did not properly support this function.

Palettes: Most GIF animation software allows you to create bit-depth settings. Lower bit-depth settings will result in smaller, faster animated GIFs. One problem palette management issues in animated GIFs suffer from is that often the software or browser defaults to accepting a different palette for each frame, which will cause palette flashing (a psychedelic feast for the eyes, to be sure)—most likely not the effect you are wishing to see.

The best way to avoid GIF animation palette problems is to map each frame of your animation to a common palette. Instructions for doing this in Photoshop are located in Chapter 6, "Browser-Safe Color."

Interlacing: Interlaced GIFs were discussed in Chapter 3, "Web File Formats." Adding the interlace feature to a single or multiple GIF image will cause it to look blocky until it comes into focus. Personally I dislike the effect, and especially dislike the effect in the context of animation. It sort of breaks the illusion of motion to see each individual frame come into full focus, don't you think?

For more information on animated GIFs, check out the online resources listed in the "Web Animation Technologies" section of this chapter. If you'd prefer to learn from a book, Richard Koman has written a short and sweet full-color title about GIF animation, with examples on a CD, that should help anyone wanting to delve further into the GIF animation creation process:

GIF Animation Studio
Full Color book w/CD
Publisher: O'Reilley
Author: Richard Koman
Retail Price: $39.95 ▪ ISBN: 1-56592-230-1

Tech Notes: More On Creating Movies

There are so many movie-making software packages that entire books have been written about which ones to choose and why. With movie-making software packages, you can typically edit digital video, taken from videotape footage, to create pure animation based on custom still graphics. Or process both to create a hybrid of live-action and graphics.

Just like you might choose to own a scanner if you work with still graphics, you will need to get a video digitizing system if you intend to work with live-action video footage. There are many software and hardware choices, ranging from which movie capture card to which video-recording deck is better or worse. You'll find many books on the subject of digital video, as well as great online sources, listed in this chapter.

What you won't easily find is how to make movies that are appropriate for web-based distribution and authoring. That's what this section focuses on.

General Movie-Making Tips

When referring to movies, there are two things to keep in mind: frame size and frame speed. The frame size is the dimension of the movie in pixels, and frame speed is how many frames per second the movie is recorded at. When authoring movies, it's necessary to know what the end delivery medium will be. If you were going to market your videos to the film and video market, you would make full-screen, full-motion videos of the highest quality with little or no compression. It should be no surprise that this is not the case on the web.

Make Your Movies Small

A standard size for web-based movies is 160x120 pixels. This looks better than you might expect. Web audiences do not expect television quality. They are used to looking at thumbnails and are more forgiving of small movie sizes than audiences in other situations would be. Content with live action tends to be more forgiving at this size than movies that include graphics and type.

If you have the option and want to include titles or graphics in your web movies, compose those elements at a bigger scale than you would if you had the full screen to play with. Fonts should be at least 30 points high to be readable once the movie is shrunk to web postage stamps. If you work large first, let's say 640x480 or 320x240, and reduce the movies to 160x120, you will get slightly better quality than if you create small movies to begin with.

Web-based movies should be anywhere from 5–15 frames per second. Again, this choice will depend on the content and length of your movies. If you have a 30-minute documentary, forget about web delivery! Most movies on the web are less than one minute in length!

Many people divide the original frame rate of a movie file in half. If the source was recorded at 30 fps (frames per second), they'll make their web movies 15 fps. If the source was 24 fps, they'll make their movies 12 fps. I've found you can get away with lower frame rates than this, depending on the content. Typically, live action recorded at normal speed or high speed (slow motion) is much more forgiving than movies that are fast-paced to begin with. You might have to save your web-sized movie at higher frame rates if there's very fast action or fast titles in the original source material.

The best thing is to run tests at different sizes and frame rates to see what works best for your source's footage.

- Use the highest compression setting your movie can withstand. See the following section for a listing of compression standards (codecs) appropriate for the web.

- Never recompress an already compressed movie! It will introduce unsightly artifacts that don't need to be there! Begin with an uncompressed original if you want to change your mind about a compression setting.

Codecs

To make matters a little more complicated, movie formats (QuickTime, AVI, and MPEG) also use different types of compression settings and standards. These are called codecs, which stands for **co**mpressor/**de**compressor.

Appropriate Codecs for Web Movies

Movie Format	Web-Appropriate Codecs
QuickTime	Cinepak
	Indeo
AVI	Indeo
	Cinepak
MPEG	MPEG

This table lists movie file formats with appropriate codecs for web authoring. Just like there are lots of other image file formats besides those this book discusses—GIFs and JPEGs—there are many other movie codecs. They are missing from this list because I'm specifically including only those that would compress movies to reasonable sizes for modem downloading.

The codec is requested when you're saving your movie. The choices are accessed from the movie-making software you use. At this point, you choose from either web-appropriate codec: Cinepak or Indeo. The compression setting you choose is invisible to the end users. They know only whether your movie is a QuickTime, AVI, or MPEG.

The following sections look at advantages and disadvantages to the codecs appropriate for web-based movies.

Cinepak—Available for QuickTime and AVI

Cinepak offers lossy compression, which means that this compression codec causes the original movie file to lose quality. That might sound more alarming than it actually is. All web-based compression schemes are lossy. If they didn't sacrifice some quality, they couldn't produce small enough files suitable for modem transfer.

Cinepak was designed for CD-ROM authoring and does an exceptional job at playing back from a disk—be it floppy, hard disk, or CD-ROM. Cinepak has a tendency to make images look slightly blurred, and for this reason it works better on animation and graphics that have lots of solid colors rather than live action, which has lots of subtleties and changing colors. It takes a long time to render a QuickTime movie to Cinepak because of the amount of crunching Cinepak does to the file. What makes the file play back well is precisely what makes it render slowly: Cinepak takes a very large file and makes it very small—a lot of work!

Indeo—Available for QuickTime and AVI

Indeo also offers lossy compression. It has two modes: a normal and a super compressor mode. If you use the super compressor mode, Indeo will take as long as Cinepak to render, but the image quality will be much better. Indeo does an exceptional job compressing live-action-based footage. It tends to make those types of movies look sharper than Cinepak. The size in megabytes and playback speed on Indeo and Cinepak movies will be the same. Indeo is not available for Unix-based machines. They can play Indeo compressed movies, but cannot author them.

MPEG

MPEG became an early standard on the web because it was the only movie format on which Unix platform-based computers could write. The problem with MPEG movies on the web is that they typically are either video or sound files; combined video and sound movies are a rarity. This is because you need special hardware to render an MPEG movie with sound. If you are using software to compress, you must choose to either write a sound or a movie file. Now that Quick-Time is available for Unix-platforms, chances are that MPEG will become less ubiquitous.

Glossary of Animation and Digital Video Terms

FPS: FPS stands for **f**rames **p**er **s**econd. A movie contains a certain number of frames, and the fewer frames, the more jerky the motion and the smaller the file size.

Codec: A codec is the type of compression and decompression standard used to make the movie file smaller for web delivery.

Data rate: Data rate relates to how fast the movie data is captured.

Sprite animation: Sprite animation refers to the individual pieces of artwork required to make an animation.

How to Create Animation Content

There are lots of different animation tools and technologies, but what about the animation content itself? If you've never made animation before, you might be asking what exactly constitutes animation, per se?

Animation is actually the illusion of motion. It's really composed of a series of still images, shown in quick succession—the process of which tricks our minds into thinking that stationary artwork is truly moving. It's all fake! Making artwork for animation is an exercise in understanding how to fake motion through presenting changing artwork over time.

There are all kinds of ways to generate animation files or sequential images that change in appearance from frame to frame. Any number of animation software packages can generate sequential images in PICT, PICs, GIF, or QuickTime formats. Most of the web animation tools can import standard PICTs, GIFs, or QT formats.

You can make animation without a dedicated animation program, too. If you use an image editor, such as Photoshop, try running a filter in incremental amounts over a still image. Try drawing the same artwork three times and it will appear to jitter subtlely, or not so subtlely depending on how much each version changes. Try changing the opacity over multiple images, and you'll create artwork that appears to "fade up." Try looking at existing animation on a VCR and single-framing it, or try loading other people's animated GIFs into anima-ting GIF programs to reverse-engineer what you like. Just be sure that reverse-engineering doesn't mean stealing. The same copyright laws that apply to images apply to movies!

■ **note**

Last Word Department

The web promises to be a place of change, with animation tools and options getting better and easier as the medium matures. Whichever animation tool and technology path you choose to travel, always keep your site's goals and audience in mind. Although animation can add a lot to your site's appeal, it can also create exclusionary walls that only the elite few with fast speed, loads of RAM, and high-end computers can break through. Make sure your medium fits your message; use animation wisely and sparingly, and the web will be a much more inviting place.

BROWSER SAFE COLOR

33 FF

0033

<STRONG>

Width ="500"

.Jpg
.Png

IMAGE OPTIMIZATION

<Img src="

<TAB

Height ="600"

<A>

Imaging techniques

Animation, Sound and

Web File Formats
bgc' = "FFFFCC

alink="cyan"

LYNDA.COM

33

<center> <BODY>
Antiali

www Design

Sound on the Web

Because the web has effectively created the ultimate convergence of any and all mediums, perhaps it's time to add sound to your web design bag o' tricks! Perhaps you're tired of listening only to the sound of your mouse clicking or your keyboard typing, or you're feeling brave about entering some new web authoring territory. Whatever your reason, it's now possible to program your site to provide background ambient noise, real-time audio on demand, or sound that can be downloaded and played on external sound players. This chapter examines these options and other issues related to sound.

Sound Aesthetics

Just because you can add sound to your site doesn't mean you should. Keep in mind that people have very strong musical tastes, and while you might love Balinese gamelan music as much as I do, your end viewer might prefer Martin Denny.

My suggestion is that you are careful about looping sounds—in the event that your end viewer can't stand your choice of music or sound effect, and you are effectively driving them away. Netscape has an interesting technology demo on its site that enables the end viewer to turn on or off looping sound, or change the type of music entirely.

My point is, sound can be a wonderful thing to one person and an annoyance to another. Embedding ambient sound on a web page is discussed later in this chapter, along with techniques to enable your end user to access audio controls to turn sound on and off for your site. You might think you are adding an enhancement to your site by including automatic sound, but it's my job to tell you that others might not agree.

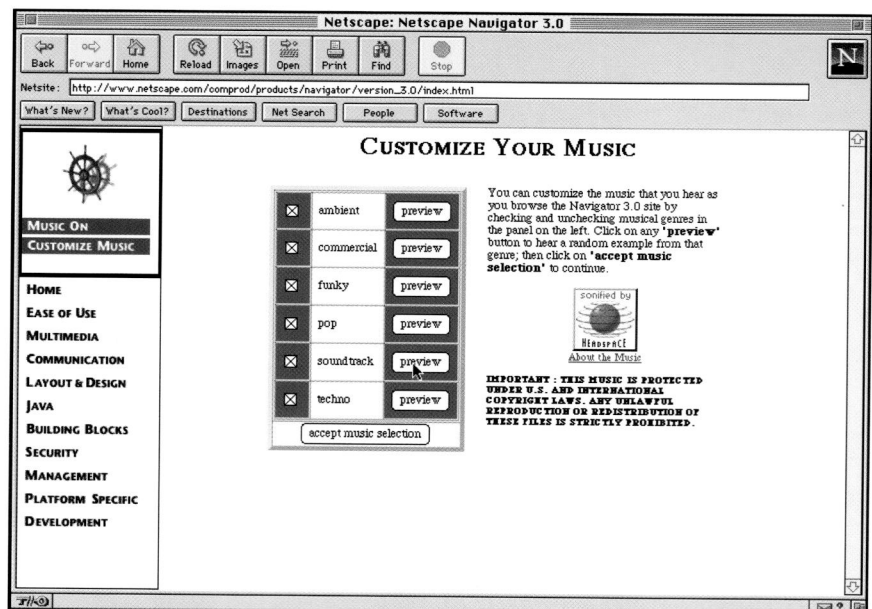

Visit ■ http://www.netscape.com/comprod/products/navigator/version_3.0/index.html to view the source of this page and other interesting sound technology demos.

How to Get Sound Source Files into Your Computer

Just like images have to be scanned or created directly in the computer, sounds have to be scanned or digitized or created from scratch as well. This is a complex or easy undertaking, depending on whether you're attempting to achieve professional-level sound or willing to accept a few snap, crackle, and pops.

Here are some ideas for obtaining sound file sources:

■ Capture sound from CDs

Most sound-capture software enables you to capture sound from audio CDs. Tips for capturing from CD sources are listed later in this chapter. Be careful about copyrights and other rights—it is not legal to take sound from your favorite band and stick it on your web site or otherwise use it. For more information about copyright laws and music, check out:

The Use of Music on a Multimedia Web Site: The Legal Issues
■ http://home.earthlink.net/~ivanlove/music.html

If you're on the other end and want to create licensing agreements for sound or music you've created, you'll find some boilerplate legal contracts in this book:

Web Developer's Guide to Sound and Music
Publisher: Coriolis Group Books
Authors: Anthony Helmstetter and Ron Simpson
Retail Price: $39.95 ■ ISBN: 1-883577-95-0

■ Purchase royalty-free sound libraries online or on CD-ROMs

There are zillions of web sites and CD-ROMs that include royalty-free music and sound effects. Here are a couple of good starting points to check out:

Gary Lamb's Royalty-Free Music Collection
■ http://www.royaltyfree.com/

SoundScape Web Background Music for Web Pages
■ http://www.iti.qc.ca/iti/users/sean/sndscape.html

Royalty-Free Multimedia Soundtracks
■ http://www.kenmusic.com/

■ **Use the microphone that ships with your computer**

Many Macs and PCs ship with a microphone and simple sound editing software which you can use to record your voice for narration, greetings or sound effects. This is a great way to add a personal greeting to your site. I have wonderful sound bytes of my daughter singing songs and saying silly things as she was growing up that were all captured this way. Be aware, however, that professional sound designers would cringe at this recommendation! If you are planning to do professional-quality sound, use professionals! They have all kinds of equipment you won't begin to understand, which does things such as normalize, equalize, remove noise, mixing, dithering, resampling, and more...

For a little tour around some professional sound sites, try:

The MIDI Farm
■ http://www.midifarm.com/info/

Doctor Audio
■ http://www.doctoraudio.com/indextext.html

Professional Sound Corporation
■ http://www.professionalsound.com/

■ **Use sound-editing software to produce computer generated sounds**

There are dedicated sound-editing packages, just like there are dedicated image-editing software packages. Sound editing software can cut or mix together disparate clips of sound, create transitions such as fades and dissolves, and process the sound with effects like echo, reverb, and playing in reverse.

You might try reading the computer and sound trades to find hardware and software that fit your needs and budget. Or check out some suggested URLs:

Mike Sokol's Sound Advice
■ http://www.soundav.com/

Professional Sound Designer's Magazine
■ http://www.vaxxine.com/ps/

Vibe
■ http://www.vibe.com/

Digital Audio Terminology

Sample rates: Sample rates are measured in kilohertz (KHz). The sample rate affects the "range" of digitized sound, which describes its highs and lows. Sound editing software is where the initial sample rate settings are established. Standard sample rates range from 11.025 KHz, 22.050 KHz, 44.10 KHz, to 48 KHz. The higher the sample rate, the better the quality.

Bit depth or sampling resolution: Sampling resolution affects quality of sound, just like dpi resolution affects the quality of images. Standard sampling resolutions are 8-bit mono, 8-bit stereo, 16-bit mono, and 16-bit stereo.

µ-law: µ-law used to be the only file format you'd find on the web because it is generated by Unix platforms. Now that Macs and PCs are the predominant platform of the web, µ-law files are not seen as much. The sound quality is generally much lower than other sound formats, but the files are much smaller, too. µ-law files always have the file-name extension .au.

AIFC: AIFC is a new spec for the older **A**udio **I**nterchange **F**ile **F**ormat (AIFF). Both AIFF and AIFF-C files can be read by this format. AIFF and AIFC files are commonly used on SGI and Macintosh computers. Only 16-bit sound data can be recorded using this format.

MPEG: MPEG audio is well respected as a high-quality, excellent audio compression file format. MPEG audio has the advantage of a good compression scheme that doesn't sacrifice too much fidelity for the amount of bandwidth it saves. MPEG files tend to be small and sound good. On the IUMA site, there are two sizes of MPEG files: stereo and mono. MPEG audio layer 2 files always have the file-name extensions .mpg or .mp2. MPEG audio layer 3 files have an .mp3 extension.

To Stream or Not to Stream?

Streaming is the process whereby an audio or video file plays as it's being downloaded. This enables your end user to hear the sound as it's downloading, instead of waiting until the entire file is downloaded for it to play. Streaming audio is not always appropriate because your sound and music will take a quality hit in the process. At times you will prefer to set up music archives on a site for downloading, especially if you want to distribute high-quality sound that is too large in file size for smooth streaming. Because both streaming and nonstreaming audio standards exist, this chapter covers both topics.

If you are going to prepare audio files for downloading off your site, you'll need to know a few new tricks. We'll look at the HTML tags required to do this, how to make your movies and sounds small, and decide which types of helper applications you and your audience will need.

Making Small Audio Files

Audio on the web has most of the same limitations as images—many files are too large to hear as inline components of a page. In this event, your audience will be required to download audio files in order to listen to them, and it's your job to choose a file format and compression rate. You will base these decisions on the platform you're authoring sounds from and then work to reduce your file size while keeping sound quality as high as possible

Here's a look at the various audio standards and ways to reduce the size of audio files.

Rates and Bits

There are two components of an audio file that make it sound good (and take up space): the sampling rate and the bit depth, which is referred to as the sample resolution.

Sample rates are measured in kilohertz (KHz). The sample rate affects the range of a digitized sound, which defines its highs and lows. Higher sample rates result in larger file sizes. The sampling rate is set when the sound is digitized (captured) into the computer. Sound editing software is where the initial sample rate settings are established, and it should be set according to the type of sound being sampled. Some types of sounds can deal with lower sampling rates better. Narration, for example, doesn't depend on high and low ranges to sound good. Here are some sampling rates:

- 8 KHz
- 11 KHz
- 22.050 KHz
- 44.1 KHz
- 48 KHz

Sampling resolution dictates how much range the sound has in highs and lows. Higher kilohertz settings result in a bigger file size. The sampling resolution is also set when the sound is digitized (captured) into the computer. Sound editing software allows users to dictate which sample resolution the sound is captured at. Because noise is introduced at lower sample rates, it's necessary to evaluate individual sound elements to see how far down the sampling resolution can be set without introducing unacceptable noise. You can create digital sound at the following resolutions:

- 8-bit mono
- 8-bit stereo
- 16-bit mono
- 16-bit stereo

Generally when you first digitally record or "sample" a sound, you want to record it at 16-bit resolution at the 44.1 KHz sampling rate. Just like an image scan, it's always best to start with the most information and reduce down. Later, after processing the sound to your satisfaction with digital audio editing applications, you would resample the final file down to 8-bit, 22.05 KHz.

Audio File Formats

Many types of audio files are found and used on the web. Choosing which one to use is often determined by what kind of computer system and software you're authoring sounds from. Here's a breakdown of the various formats:

■ μ-law

μ-law used to be the only file format you'd find on the web because it is generated by Unix platforms. Now that Macs and PCs are the predominant platform, μ-law files are not seen as much. The sound quality is generally considered much lower than the other sound formats described here. It is used much less often now, as a result. If you are going to author μ-law files, they should be saved with an .au extension.

■ AIFF

AIFF was developed by Apple and is used on Macintoshes and SGIs. It stands for **A**udio **I**nterchange **F**ile **F**ormat. It can store digital audio at all the sample rates and resolutions possible. You'll also hear about MACE (**M**acintosh **A**udio **C**ompression/**E**xpansion), which is the built-in compression standard for AIFF files. Just like in video, what compression you use is invisible to the end listener. It does dictate the size and quality of your end result, however. If you are going to author AIFF files, they should be saved with an .aif extension.

■ WAVE

WAVE was developed by Microsoft and IBM and is the native sound file format to Windows platforms. Like AIFF, it can store digital audio at all the sample rates and resolutions possible. Basically, WAVE and AIFF files are considered equals in terms of quality and compression, and are easier to use depending on which platform you are authoring from. If you are going to author WAVE files, they should be saved with a .wav extension.

■ MPEG

MPEG audio is well respected as a high-quality, excellent audio compression file format. The only problem is that encoding MPEG requires extra hardware that is out of reach of many audio content creators. Because MPEG files aren't native to any specific platform, your audience will need to download a helper application to hear them. If you are going to author MPEG sound files, they should be saved with the .mpg extension.

■ RealAudio

RealAudio was the first example of streaming audio on the web. Streamed audio files come over the phone lines in small chunks, so the entire file doesn't have to be downloaded before it can be heard. The file can be up to one hour long because the data is coming in as you're hearing it—not first downloading fully to your hard drive. The sound quality is often compared to that of an AM radio station. Because of quality limits, it's best used for narration and not for music or other sounds. You must have the RealAudio player installed on your system to hear sounds play as soon as you click on a link that supplies real audio source material. You can author Real-Audio content by using the RealAudio encoder, which can be obtained by accessing the RealAudio site (■ http://www.realaudio.com). You won't be able to offer RealAudio files from your web site unless your provider has paid RealAudio a server licensing fee. Contact RealAudio for more information.

Tips for Making Web-Based Sound Files

Several free or shareware applications can convert from or to µ-law, AIFF, WAV, and MPEG files, so chances are your audience will be able to access your sounds regardless of which file format you choose to support. Typically, Mac authors will choose AIFF, PC authors will choose WAV or MPEG, and Unix authors will pick µ-law because those are the file formats supported natively by their systems.

To properly prepare the files, however, you might want to use a sound editing program that offers features such as peak level limiting, normalizing, downsampling, and dithering from 16-bit to 8-bit. Premiere is a great entry-level video and sound editor—although professional videographers and sound engineers will typically own higher-end dedicated editing programs. The following figure shows some of the audio filters found in Premiere.

Here are some tips for making web-based sound files:

- Digitize at the standard audio CD sample rate and resolution (44 KHz and 16-bit). Downsample the file to the preferred sample size of 22 KHz or 11 KHz. Typically, at lower sample rates the sound will be duller and have less high end. For dialogue or sounds where high end doesn't matter, lowering the sample rate creates smaller files that will be of acceptable quality.

- Halfing the sample rate will half the file size. Additionally, changing the file from stereo to mono cuts the file size in half. Use the Mix feature of audio software packages to create a mono version of a stereo file.

- If the 16-bit file is still too large, you can use dithering algorithms on audio (just like on images) to take the files down to 8-bit. Dithering will add noise, in the form of hiss (and in the worst case, electronic buzzing and chattering). Dithering will be most noticeable in files with silences between sounds.

- Because of the electronic noise, dithering should be avoided on dialogue. Dithering works great for rich, full music files such as hard rock and industrial. Another alternative is to redigitize the 16-bit audio file at 8-bit by playing back and recording a prerecorded 16-bit, 44.1 KHz sound into your digitizer. Often this creates cleaner 8-bit samples with more "punch."

- When naming audio files, as with all files being prepped for Internet distribution, they must be named with no spaces. Unlike inline images, these files are going to be downloaded by your audience. Therefore, names should be eight characters or less in length, with room for a three-letter file extension, or Windows platform users won't get to hear them!

- Make sure you've done all your sound editing (such as mixing from stereo to mono, filtering, peak level limiting, normalizing, or downsampling) before you convert to 8-bit. If you edit an 8-bit sound and then resave it, you will add electronic noise to your file. Always start with higher bit depth, and do your editing in that file before you save or dither it to 8-bit.

HTML for Downloading Sound Files

A sound file gets the <A HREF></A> tag, just like its video and image-based counterparts. But unlike video, where there might be an associated thumbnail image, sounds are usually indicated by a sound icon or hypertext. Here are a few variations and the code you would use to produce them.

Here's the code to link your audience to a sound and let them know what file size and format it is:

```
<A HREF="snd1.aif">
<FONT SIZE=5>
Click here to download
this sound!</A>
</FONT>
<P>
Excerpt from CD:<BR>
WebaWorld<P>
Cut: Spider<P>
AIFF Sound<BR>
:30<BR>
567k
```

Or if you want to add an icon, too:

```
<A HREF="snd1.aif>
<FONT SIZE=5>
<IMG SRC="ear.gif">
Click here to download
this sound!</A>
</FONT>
<P>
Excerpt from CD:<BR>
WebaWorld<P>
Cut: Spider<P>
AIFF Sound<BR>
:30<BR>
567k
```

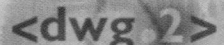

Audio Helper Apps and Utilities

Here's a list of useful helper applications and utilities for audio creation and playback.

For Macs

Sound Machine 2.5
(Plays AU, AIFF, and WAVE)
■ ftp://ftp.iuma.com/audio_utils/au_players/Macintosh/
sound-machine-21.hqx

SoundApp
■ ftp://mirror.apple.com/.ufs01/info-mac/gst/snd/
sound-app-151.hqx

MPEG Audio: Converts MPEG to AIFF
■ ftp://ftp.iuma.com/audio_utils/mpeg_players/Macintosh/
MPEGAudNoFPU1.0a6.hqx

MPEG CD: Plays MPEG audio
■ http://www.kauai.com/~bbal/MPEG_CD_2.0.3.sea.hqx

Brian's Sound Tool
(Converts WAVE, AU, and AIFF)
■ gopher://gopher.archive.merit.edu:7055/40/mac/sound/
soundutil/brianssoundtool1.3.sit.hqx

SoundHack
(Converts WAVE, AU, and AIFF)
■ ftp://shoko.calarts.edu/pub/SoundHack/SH0866.hqx

For PCs

Xing SoundPlayer
(Plays MPEG audio; you need a sound card)
■ ftp://ftp.iuma.com/audio_utils/mpeg_players/Windows/
mpgaudio.exe

Windows Play Any
(Plays AU, WAV, and AIFF)
■ ftp://ftp.ncsa.uiuc.edu/Web/Mosaic/Windows/viewers/
wplny12a.zip

WHAM 1.31
(Sound Converter)
■ ftp://gatekeeper.dec.com/pub/micro/msdos/win3/
sounds/wham133.zip

Automatic Music Without Downloading

As usual, the browser wars are shakin' and quakin' with new ways to add proprietary features and out-do each other. Netscape and MSIE each have their own way of adding inline sound to web pages. This section will look at both options and will then advise you how to make your site compatible with both browsers.

MSIE Audio Tags

The BGSOUND element is an MS Internet Explorer 2.0 enhancement. SRC specifies the URL of the audio file to be played. The LOOP attribute specifies how many times the sound will be played while the HTML document is displayed, and can either be a number or the string "infinite." The default for LOOP is one. As mentioned earlier in the aesthetics section of this chapter, considerable opposition to the use of this element has been expressed on the web, especially the use of LOOP=infinite because users currently have no way to disable the audio.

BGSOUND

<BGSOUND SRC="...">	The BGSOUND element will cause an audio file to play automatically as an inline sound element. You can insert either .wav or .midi files.
<BGSOUND SRC=" LOOP="...">	To make the sound loop, insert this attribute. The default ..." is 1 time, unless specified.

To view Microsoft's tutorial page on these tags and attributes, check out:

■ http://www.microsoft.com/kb/articles/q156/1/54.htm

Netscape Audio Tags

Netscape's sound tags work with its LiveAudio plug-in, which comes preinstalled in Netscape versions 3.0 and higher. This means that the tags all revolve around the <EMBED> tag, which is standard for all plug-in based HTML.

LiveAudio plays audio files in WAV, AIFF, AU, and MIDI formats. Audio controls appear according to the size specified in the WIDTH and HEIGHT parameters in the <EMBED> tag. You can create an audio console with any of the following six views:

■ **Console**—Consists of a Play, Pause, Stop, and Volume Control lever.

■ **SmallConsole**—Consists of a Play, Stop, and Volume Control lever (upon invoking this view of the applet class, a sound will "autostart" by default). This view will have smaller buttons than the standard Console buttons.

■ **PlayButton**—A button that starts the sound playing.

■ **PauseButton**—A button that pauses (without unloading) the sound while it is playing.

■ **StopButton**—A button that ends the playing of sound and unloads it.

■ **VolumeLever**—A lever that adjusts the volume level for playback of the sound (and adjusts the system's volume level).

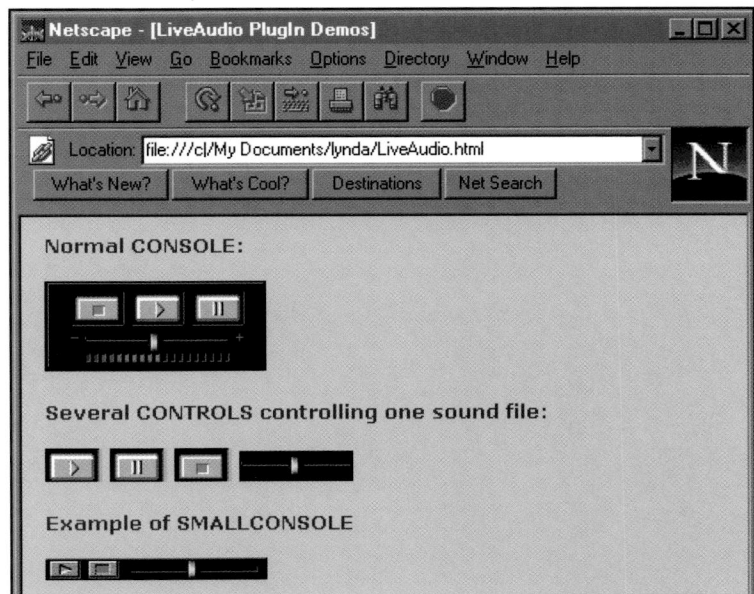

An example of what some of the audio console controls look like in Netscape.

These views may be used many times on one web page, with all the view instances controlling one sound file or many sound files, depending on how the file is called in the HTML or JavaScript.

HTML Syntax

```
<EMBED SRC= [URL]
AUTOSTART=[TRUE¦FALSE]
LOOP=[TRUE¦FALSE¦INTEGER]
STARTTIME=[MINUTES:SECONDS]
ENDTIME=[MINUTES¦SECONDS]
VOLUME=[0-100]
WIDTH=[# PIXELS]
HEIGHT=[# PIXELS]
ALIGN=[TOP¦BOTTOM¦CENTER¦BASELINE¦LEFT¦RIGHT ¦TEXTTOP¦MIDDLE¦ABSMIDDLE¦ABSBOTTOM]
CONTROLS=[CONSOLE¦SMALL CONSOLE¦PLAYBUTTON¦PAUSEBUTTON¦STOPBUTTON¦VOLUMELEVER] HIDDEN=[TRUE]
MASTERSOUND
NAME=[UNIQUE NAME TO GROUP CONTROLS SO THAT THEY CONTROL ONE SOUND]...>
```

SRC="..."	The URL of the source sound file.
AUTOSTART=[TRUE|FALSE]	Setting the value to TRUE allows the sound, music, or voice to begin playing automatically when the web page is loaded. The default is FALSE.
LOOP=[TRUE|FALSE|INTEGER]	Setting the value to TRUE allows the sound to play continuously until the stop button is clicked on the console or the user goes to another page. If an INTEGER value is used, the sound repeats the number of times indicated by the integer.
STARTTIME=[MINUTES:SECONDS]	Use STARTTIME to designate where in the sound file you would like playback to begin. If you want to begin the sound at 30 seconds, you would set the value to 00:30 (implemented only on Windows 95, NT, and Macintosh).
ENDTIME=[MINUTES:SECONDS]	Use ENDTIME to designate where in the sound file you would like playback to end. If you want to stop the sound at 1.5 minutes, you would set the value to 01:30 (implemented only on Windows 95, NT, and Macintosh).
VOLUME=[0–100]	This value must be a number between 0 and 100 to represent 0 to 100 percent. This attribute sets the volume for the sound that is playing [unless the MASTERVOLUME (see NAME attribute on the following page) is used; then this value sets the sound for the entire system]. The default volume level is the current system volume.

WIDTH=[# PIXELS]	This attribute is used to display the width of the console or console element. For the CONSOLE and SMALLCONSOLE, the default is WIDTH=144. For the VOLUMELEVER, the default is WIDTH=74. For a button, the default is WIDTH=37.
HEIGHT=[# PIXELS]	This attribute is used to display the height of the console. For the CONSOLE, the default is HEIGHT=60. For the SMALLCONSOLE, the default is HEIGHT=15. For the VOLUMELEVER, the default is HEIGHT=20. For a button, the default is HEIGHT=22.
ALIGN=[TOP|BOTTOM|CENTER|BASELINE|LEFT|RIGHT|TEXTTOP|MIDDLE|ABSMIDDLE|ABSBOTTOM]	This attribute tells Netscape Navigator how you want to align text as it flows around the consoles. It acts similarly to the <IMG> tag.
CONTROLS=[CONSOLE|SMALLCONSOLE|PLAYBUTTON|PAUSEBUTTON|STOPBUTTON|VOLUMELEVER]	This attribute defines which control a content creator wishes to use. The default for this field is CONSOLE.
HIDDEN=[TRUE]	The value for this attribute should be TRUE, or it should not be included in the <EMBED> tag. If it is specified as TRUE, no controls will load and the sound will act as a background sound.
MASTERSOUND	This value must be used when grouping sounds together in a NAME group. This attribute takes no value (it must merely be present in the EMBED tag), but tells LiveAudio which file is a genuine sound file and allows it to ignore any stub files. Stub files have a minimum length necessary to activate LiveAudio.
NAME=[UNIQUE NAME TO GROUP CONTROLS TOGETHER THAT THEY CONTROL ONE SOUND]	This attribute sets a unique ID for a group of CONTROLS elements so that they all act on the same sound as it plays. For example, if a SOUND content creator wishes to have one sound controlled by two embedded objects (a PLAYBUTTON and a STOPBUTTON), he must use this attribute to group the CONTROLS together. In this case, the <MASTERSOUND> tag is necessary to flag LiveAudio and let it know which of the two <EMBED> tags actually has the sound file you wish to control. LiveAudio ignores any EMBED with no <MASTERSOUND> tag. If you want one VOLUMELEVER to control multiple NAMEs (or system volume), create an EMBED by using the VOLUMELEVER CONTROL. Set NAME to MASTERVOLUME.

JavaScript Functions for LiveAudio

LiveAudio includes the capability to defer loading a sound file until the Play button is pushed. This enables a web page designer to comfortably embed several sounds on one page, without worrying about page load time.

To implement this feature, the web designer must create a file like the following:

```
<SCRIPT LANGUAGE=SoundScript>
OnPlay(http://YourURL/YourSound.aif);
</SCRIPT>
```

This file should be saved and named as a sound file (such as script1.aif). When the Play button is pushed, the URL you defined for the OnPlay function is loaded.

LiveAudio

To play a sound as a background sound for a web page:

```
<EMBED SRC="mysound.aif" HIDDEN=TRUE>
```

To have several CONTROLS controlling one sound file:

```
<EMBED SRC="mysound.aif" HEIGHT=22 WIDTH=37
CONTROLS=PLAYBUTTON NAME="MyConsole" MASTERSOUND>
<EMBED SRC="stub1.aif" HEIGHT=22 WIDTH=37
CONTROLS=PAUSEBUTTON NAME="MyConsole">
<EMBED SRC="stub2.aif" HEIGHT=22 WIDTH=37
CONTROLS=STOPBUTTON NAME="MyConsole">
<EMBED SRC="stub3.aif" HEIGHT=20 WIDTH=74
CONTROLS=VOLUMELEVER NAME="MyConsole">
```

To use a SMALLCONSOLE:

```
<EMBED SRC="mysound.aif" HEIGHT=15 WIDTH=144
MASTERSOUND CONTROLS=SMALLCONSOLE>
```

LiveConnect

LiveAudio is LiveConnect enabled. The following functions will work in JavaScript to control a loaded LiveAudio plug-in:

```
Controlling functions (all Boolean):
play('TRUE/FALSE or int','URL of sound')
stop()
pause()
start_time(int seconds)
end_time(int seconds)
setvol(int percent)
fade_to(int to_percent)
fade_from_to(int from_percent,int to_percent)
start_at_beginning() = Override a start_time()
stop_at_end() = Override an end_time()
State indicators (all Boolean, except *, which is
an int):
IsReady() = Returns TRUE if the plug-in instance
has completed loading
IsPlaying() = Returns TRUE if the sound is
currently playing
IsPaused() = Returns TRUE if the sound is
currently paused
GetVolume() = Returns the current volume
as a percentage * from:
```

Netscape's Documentation on These Tags

■ http://www.netscape.com/comprod/products/navigator/version_3.0/index.html

---

■ **note**

Cross-Browser Compatibility
Ok, you've reviewed the tags for each of the browsers; suppose you want to make a site that works for either or both?

Try this:

```
<EMBED SRC="sound.wav" AUTOSTART=TRUE
HIDDEN=TRUE>
<NOEMBED><BGSOUND="sound.wav"></NOEMBED>
```

Other Sound Options

Sound is a huge subject, worthy of entire books! There are many other sound options available to you for web delivery. Here is a brief synopsis of a few noteworthy ones.

QuickTime: QuickTime movies can be hidden from view or include control consoles. This makes their MIDI-compatible file format ideal for streaming audio. Many of the tags listed in Chapter 14, "Animation," work with sound files, too. Visit the QuickTime site for more details:

- http://www.quicktime.apple.com

Macromedia Director/Streaming Audio: Director is one of the oldest authoring tools around for multimedia. Shockwave, a plug-in for web browsers, enables Director content to be viewed on web pages. Streaming audio is now a feature supported by the Shockwave plug-in. To develop streaming audio content, you need to learn to use Director and program interactivity with a proprietary language called Lingo. For more about Director, Shockwave, and Lingo, look to Chapters 14, 16, and 18.

Sound Tips:
- http://www.macromedia.com/shockwave/director5/tips.html#sound

Shockwave Audio FAQ:
- http://www.macromedia.com/support/technotes/shockwave/developer/shocktechnotes/audio/swafaq.html

Streaming Audio Tips:
- http://www.macromedia.com/support/technotes/shockwave/developer/shocktechnotes/audio/longswa.html

RealAudio: RealAudio is the oldest streaming and most well-known audio technology on the web. It has three components:

- The RealAudio Player plays files encoded in the RealAudio format.
- The RealAudio Encoder encodes files into the RealAudio format.
- The RealAudio Server delivers RealAudio over the Internet or your company network.

In order to hear RealAudio files, you must have the plug-in. In order to author RealAudio files, you need to convert your sound files so that they work in the RealAudio format. To download the encoder:

- http://www.realaudio.com/products/encoder.html

The RealAudio Server is the only piece of the puzzle that costs money. It enables you to distribute RealAudio content from your site.

Font 5

BROWSER SAFE COLOR
33FF

<STRONG>

Width ="500"

<IMG src="

IMAGE OPTIMIZATION

Height ="600"

Animation, Sound and

</A>

<center

Imaging techniques

Web file formats
bgcolor="FFFFCC"

@link="cyan"

33

LYNDA.COM

BODY
Avrtial

www.Design

Interactivity

Interactivity is a huge subject that overlaps with other chapters of this book and can't be isolated on its own as one practice or technique. The web is interactive by nature. At the very core of hypertext and hyperimages is the fact that the end user gets to make decisions about what information he or she wants to see displayed. It's up to us as web designers to make sure that we service this end user to the best of our abilities. Interactivity, when used correctly, can be a great enhancement to any site.

Here is a brief list of some of the features that qualify as interactive elements to add to a site:

- Counters
- Forms
- Guestbooks
- Chat/avatars
- Ad banners
- Button rollovers

Interactivity is something a printed page cannot do that the web excels at. As publishers of information, thinking in terms of interactivity is an entirely new kind of mind-set. You'll hear the buzzword "building community" if you hang around web designers long enough. By interacting with your end user, you are indeed building a community. If you do it well you can create good-will, or it can backfire on you as an invitation to criticism or harassment.

This chapter will review some of the interactive technologies and techniques available today. There are many opportunities to add interactivity to sites, but these features are often difficult for "mere mortals" to program or implement. Being a nonprogrammer myself, I shy away from adding certain features on my site, even though I'd love to implement them. So in this chapter I'll direct my readers (you!) to helpful URLs so that you can learn more about adding interactivity to your sites.

Interactivity Role Models

Before getting to specific tools and techniques, you should check out a couple of inspirational sites that use interactivity very well. One of my personal favorites is ■ http://www.amazon.com, an online bookstore that has an "interactive" mind-set.

Besides the things you would expect in a bookstore—the ability to search and order books—Amazon has implemented a few neat twists of their own:

- ■ They have a form that invites authors and publishers to review their own books
- ■ They have a form that interviews authors
- ■ They invite readers with different forms to review and rate books
- ■ They allow customers to enter search information so that they can notify customers when other books of interest become available
- ■ They invite you to create a bookstore on your site and teach you how

They have indeed created a sense of community and involvement that a traditional bookstore could not easily match.

Another favorite site with an interactive mind-set is ■ www.iuma.com. Their site invites musicians to submit audio and video clips, and creates a worldwide distribution avenue that bypasses the traditional music publishing model. They help underground bands get an audience (and the possibility for record deals, too).

IUMA has a database of thousands of music and video clips, enabling end users to easily locate music styles that they like and order products from independent musicians. They have created a service that a traditional music store could not offer and a traditional music publisher could not afford. IUMA is an example of a web-centric publishing model that offers something which has never before been possible.

Interactivity Versus Difficulty

Many of the interactive enhancements this chapter discusses are created with programming instead of standard HTML. If HTML makes your eyes glaze over to begin with, then the notion of learning programming might cause a total meltdown. Programming is not for everyone, nor should it be. This chapter is meant to provide an overview of options and technologies, not a tutorial for learning programming.

The most common types of interactive programming involve CGI, technically known as **C**ommon **G**ateway **I**nterface. CGI is a type of scripting that extends the capabilities of HTML. CGI is the communication protocol that the web server (the computer that sends web pages out to the world to see) uses to interact with your end user's browser and external scripts. CGI scripts can be written in any number of computer languages—Perl, sh, C, C++, or AppleScript to name a few.

CGI scripts are hidden from view on a server. It is not possible to view the source within HTML or deconstruct how these types of scripts are written. Conversely, with HTML and JavaScript it is possible to view, copy, and paste the source code. This is always helpful and welcomed by nonprogrammers. CGI scripting is not something anyone can learn overnight. This chapter does not attempt to teach CGI; it instead describes the function, shows some scripts and how they work, and offers resources to help you learn more.

> ### ■ note
>
> What Kind of Server?
>
> To make CGI matters a tad more complicated, you must know the type of server you're using before uploading a CGI script and getting it to work on your site. Different servers on different platforms require different types of scripts. If you don't maintain your own server, check with your web administrator to ensure that you are using the correct types of CGI. Your web administrator might also keep a public or private CGI directory (often called /cgi.bin/) that you will need to locate.

Like many subjects on the web, there's a huge amount of information regarding CGI and scripts. You'll find many web sites with free scripts, tutorials, and links pages. Here are a few favorites:

Matt's Scripts and Archives
■ http://worldwidemart.com/scripts/index.shtml

Selena Sol's CGI-Script Archives
■ http://www2.eff.org/~erict/Scripts/

Perl/HTML Archives
■ http://www.seas.upenn.edu/~mengwong/perlhtml.html

Felipe's AppleScript Samples
(for use w/Mac HTTP)
■ http://edb518ea.edb.utexas.edu/scripts/cgix/cgix.html

WebSTAR Examples
■ http://www.starnine.com/development/extending.html

Fun and Wacky Scripts + Great CGI Introduction
■ http://netamorphix.com/cgi.html

The CGI Book
(examples and book support, mailing list, etc.)
■ http://www.cgibook.com

Robert Stockton's Guide to Perl CGI Programming
■ http://www-cgi.cs.cmu.edu/cgi-bin/perl-man

Meng Weng Wong's mailto.cgi Tutorial
■ http://icg.stwing.upenn.edu/mailto.html

Links to All Kinds of Scripts
■ http://www.cbil.vcu.edu:8080/cgis/cgis.html

Freeware Scripts!
■ http://www.webcom.se/projects/freeware/

Excellent Mac-Based CGI Links, FAQs, and Tutorials
■ http://www.comvista.com/net/www/cgilesson.html

Counters

Adding a counter to your page is a form of interactivity. It tells your visitors about your site's traffic and helps you keep track of those numbers, too. Aesthetically, counters can range from straight HTML-style text to custom-made graphics. An amusing site for counter design inspiration is:

Museum of Counter Art
■ http://www.merlinmedia.com/counter/index.html

If you are going to create your own custom counter number art, you must make sure that each character is the exact same height and width as the next. You can ensure this by setting up an image file in any imaging software at the set size you want for each numeric character. Copy the image and create your numbers inside the same file over and over (10 times—0 through 9) and resave the artwork in a numbered sequence. Most counter scripts will require .gif files.

Adding a counter requires CGI. There are about a zillion counter CGIs for public distribution on the web. If you follow the links on this page, you'll be kept busy checking out link after link. Setting up your own counter requires that you deal with uploading a CGI script. If you don't want to hassle with setting up a CGI for your counter, you can pay money to ■ http://www.dig-its.com to keep track of your counts for you. You can use their database and CGI scripts, and need only to copy and paste a simple HTML tag onto the pages you want to use a counter. A pricing guide is located on their site.

For Windows Servers
■ http://www.digitmania.holowww.com/software.html

For Macintosh Servers
■ http://www.io.com/~combs/htmls/counter.html

For Unix Servers
■ http://www.fccc.edu/users/muquit/Count.html

Forms

Forms can be used for anything on your site—from e-mail to questionnaires to humor. There are two parts to adding forms: the HTML and the forms processing, which involves CGI and database functionality. The HTML for forms can be inserted into frames or tables for further alignment refinement (see Chapter 13, "Layout and Alignment Techniques," or Chapter 10, "Navigation-Based Graphics").

Forms processing is what happens to the data once your end user enters it into your form. The CGI for forms processing takes the data and does whatever it's told to do with it. It might be that you're keeping track of e-mail addresses through your form. Or calculating an order. Or taking a poll. Whatever function your form is supposed to fill, the CGI must be programmed to intercept the data and either store it or send it onward to a database.

Here are some good reference URLs to help with forms processing:

The NCSA Site
■ http://www.ncsa.uiuc.edu/SDG/Software/Mosaic/Docs/fill-out-forms/overview.html

Forms Processing Tutorial
■ http://www.ithaca.edu/computing/quick_guides/forms/overview.html

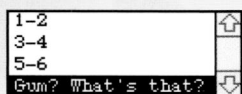

Guestbooks

Guestbooks help cultivate that sense-of-community thing I talked about earlier. Most people welcome the opportunity to share their thoughts, especially if they can remain anonymous. This can create goodwill, but it also can backfire. Sometimes the entries in my guestbook read like a lovefest, and other times they read like Ripley's Believe it or Not. Guestbooks require CGI too, and parameters can be established to allow or disallow duplicates, external HTML, profanity, anonymity, and anything else definable.

Here's an example of the source code for the guestbook on my site. It was written by my brother, William Weinman, who gives it away for free on his site:

■ http://www.cgibook.com/guestbook/source.html

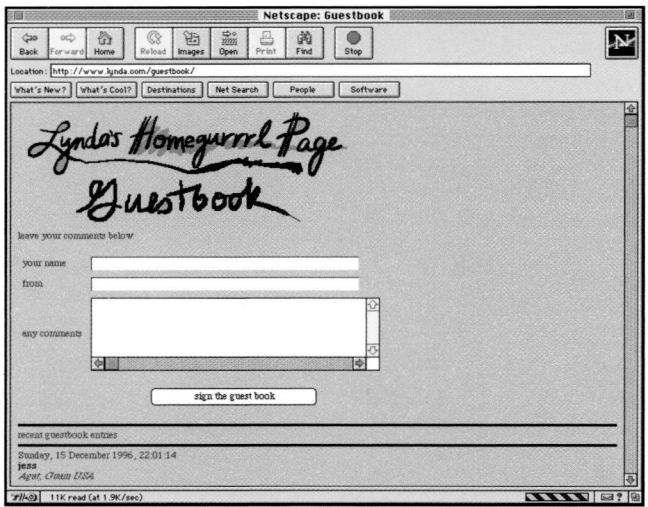

An example of this guestbook in action at Lynda's Homegurrrl Site:
■ http://www.lynda.com/guestbook/.

A guestbook is a common CGI program that is usually built in two parts: one for creating the listings and one for reading them back. Commonly, the part that creates the listings is built around an HTML forms interface, and the part that reads the listings is implemented as a server-side include.

There is one main HTML page for both entering the guestbook information and viewing the most recent entries.

```
<HTML>
<HEAD>
<TITLE>Guestbook</title>
</HEAD>
<BODY BGCOLOR="#ffffff">
<IMG SRC=guestbook.gif ALT="Guestbook"
WIDTH=333 HEIGHT=60 ALIGN=right>
<BR CLEAR=all>
<P>leave your comments below
<FORM ACTION="guest.cgi" METHOD=post>
<TABLE>
<TR>
<TD>
your name
<TD>
<INPUT NAME="name" SIZE=50>
<TR>
<TD>
from
<TD>
<INPUT NAME="from" SIZE=50>
<TR>
<TD>
any comments
<TD>
<TEXTAREA NAME="comments"
ROWS=5 COLS=50></TEXTAREA>
<TR>
<TD> <!-- empty for spacing -->
<TD ALIGN=center>
<BR>
<INPUT TYPE=submit
```

```
VALUE="
sign the guestbook">
</TABLE>
</FORM>
<HR NOSHADE SIZE=3>
recent guestbook entries
<!-- #exec CMD="readbook.pl" -->
</BODY>
</HTML>
```

1 The **<FORM>** tag is used to specify the name of the CGI program and the method used to pass the values from the form.

2 A **<TABLE>** tag is being used to align the form.

3 This is creating a black horizontal rule between guestbook entries.

4 This is the server-side include for reading the guestbook. The program **readbook.pl** will run and its output will be included in the HTML in place of this line.

The guestbook is implemented as two different Perl programs. The program readbook.pl is run with a server-side include from the HTML, and guest.cgi is run from the <FORM> tag to get the data for a new entry in the guestbook. Let's start by looking at guest.cgi.

```
#!/usr/bin/perl
$lockfile="/tmp/guestbook.lock";
$mydata="/home/billw/var/guestbook/guestbook.$$";
$datafile="/home/billw/var/guestbook/guestbook.dat";
print "content-type: text/html\n\n";
# make sure we have POST data
$ct = $ENV{"CONTENT_TYPE"};
$cl = $ENV{"CONTENT_LENGTH"};
# check the content-type for validity
if($ct ne "application/x-www-form-urlencoded")
```

```
{printf "I don't understand content-type: %s\n",
$ct;
exit 1
;}
# get each of the query strings from the input
stream
read(STDIN, $qs, $cl);
@qs = split(/&/,$qs);
foreach $i (0 .. $#qs) {
$qs[$i] =~ s/\+/ /g;
$qs[$i] =~ s/%(..)/pack("c",hex($1))/ge;
($name, $value) = split(/=/,$qs[$i],2);
$qs{$name} = $value;
}
# convert any HTML to entities
foreach $q (keys %qs) {
$qs{$q} =~ s/</&lt\;/g;
$qs{$q} =~ s/>/&gt\;/g;
$qs{$q} =~ s/"/&quot\;/g;
}
$name = $qs{"name"};
$from = $qs{"from"};
$comments = $qs{"comments"};
$today = &getdate;
# create the record
open(MYDATA, ">$mydata");
print MYDATA <<RECORD;
<record>
Date: $today
Name: $name
From: $from
Comments: $comments
</record>
RECORD
# only one of us can write to
# the main data file at a time
&lock;
# put the new record at the top of the data file
# by reading the rest of the datafile into the
# end of the new datafile . . .
open(DATA, "<$datafile");
while(<DATA>) { print MYDATA; }
```

```
close(DATA);
close(MYDATA);
# then put the new datafile in the place of the
# old one.
rename($mydata, $datafile);
# done with the main datafile
&unlock;
print <<CONF;
<HTML>
<HEAD>
<TITLE>
Guestbook
</TITLE>
</HEAD>
<BODY BGCOLOR=#ffffff>
<IMG SRC=guestbook.gif ALT="Guestbook"
WIDTH=330 HEIGHT=60 ALIGN=right>
<BR CLEAR=all>
<BR><CODE>
<P>you may need to press the RELOAD button <BR>
after you go <A HREF=index.html>back</A> <BR>
if you want to see your entry <BR>
</CODE>
</BODY>
</HTML>
CONF
# lock and unlock
#
# file locking routines to make sure only one
# person writes to a data file at a time
#
sub lock
{
local ($oumask);
# create the lock file world-writable
$oumask = umask(0);
for($i = 0; !open(LOCK, ">$lockfile"); $i++) {
# wait a sec and try again
sleep 1;
# after 30 seconds, just unlock it
&unlock if ($i > 30);
}
close(LOCK);
umask($oumask);
}
sub unlock
{
# just delete the lockfile (unlink is unix-ese for
delete)
unlink($lockfile);
}
# getdate
#
# make a printable version of today's date and time
#
sub getdate
{
my($month, $day, $time);
my($sec, $min, $hour, $mday, $mon, $year, $wday,
$yday, $isdst) =
localtime(time);
$month = ("January", "February", "March", "April",
"May", "June",
"July", "August", "September", "October",
"November", "December")[$mon];
$day = ("Sunday", "Monday", "Tuesday", "Wednesday",
"Thursday",
"Friday", "Saturday")[$wday];
$year = ($year > 95) ? $year + 1900 : $year + 2000;
$time = sprintf("%02d:%02d:%02d", $hour, $min,
$sec);
# $today is the printable date
return ($today = "$day, $mday $month $year, $time");
}
```

5 This line at the top of the program identifies the Perl interpreter as the program used to execute this file. It is a common way to run Perl scripts under Unix.

6 This prints out a MIME **"Content-Type"** header to tell the web browser that it will be receiving HTML. All CGI programs must start output with a MIME header.

7 This section converts any HTML in the form data to entities that can be printed. This effectively prevents users from putting any HTML (for example, <IMG SRC=http:// www.hell.org/devil.jpg>) into their entries.

8 Here we create the actual record in the guestbook database. The database is actually a text file, with each record delimited by **<RECORD>** and **</RECORD>** in the file. This makes it easy for the reading program to find the beginning and ending of each record.

9 For the purpose of a guestbook, we want to make sure each new record goes at the beginning of the file, rather than the end. This is the code that accomplishes that.

After writing the record to the MYDATA file, it opens the DATA file and reads it into MYDATA after the new record. Then it closes both files and renames MYDATA to overwrite the DATA file. This results in a new copy of DATA that contains the new record at the head instead of the tail.

```perl
#!/usr/bin/perl
$datafile="/home/billw/var/guestbook/guestbook.dat";
$| = 1; # flush stdout on each write
open(DATA, "<$datafile");
while(<DATA> && $i++ < 100) {loop if $_ ne
"<record>";
($date) = <DATA> =~ /Date: (.*)/;
($name) = <DATA> =~ /Name: (.*)/;
```
10 (on line `$| = 1;`)
11 (on line `while(<DATA>...`)

```perl
($from) = <DATA> =~ /From: (.*)/;
($comments) = <DATA> =~ /Comments: (.*)/;
$comments .= "\n";
while(chomp($c = <DATA>) && ($c ne "</record>")) {
$comments .= "$c\n";
}
print "<HR NOSHADE SIZE=3>\n";
print "$date\n";
print "<BR><STRONG>$name</STRONG>\n";
print "<BR><EM>$from</EM>\n";
print "<BLOCKQUOTE><PRE>$comments</PRE></BLOCK-
QUOTE>\n";
}
```
12 (on line `print "<HR NOSHADE SIZE=3>\n";`)

10 The **$|** variable is a special variable in Perl that controls the behavior of the output buffer. If the variable is zero (the default condition), all output is buffered (that is, it can be held on to) by the operating system until the operating system gets around to dealing with it. If it is nonzero, the output buffer is flushed (that is, the output is written immediately) as soon as the write action is finished.

It is important to set this to nonzero to make sure that the HTML that is sent to the output actually gets there in the order that you send it. Not setting this can lead to some very confusing results.

11 This is the code that deciphers the data file. It looks for lines that start with **"Date:"**, **"Name:"**, and so on, and stores their contents in variables. It also looks for **"<RECORD>"** and **"</RECORD>"** that marks the beginning and ending of each record.

12 Notice that what we send here is HTML. It will be included right in the stream of HTML that is sent to the browser.

Ad Banners

Ugh. This is a tough subject for me, because I have a love/hate attitude toward ad banners. I preferred the noncommercial web before ad banners existed and littered the design integrity of so many sites. I reluctantly include information about ad banners here because, despite my ambivalence, they are firmly a part of the web landscape now.

Having made my own tastes known, I realize that many of you want to know about ad banner creation. For one thing, television commercials, although annoying, are also a medium in which enormous creativity and design excellence is found. As an animation teacher for many years, I saw that most of the opportunities for cool stuff were under the guise of "advertising." Not only that, but a lot of sites can't run for free, and advertising sponsorship is a needed and necessary evil. Furthermore, I also know of many professional design firms that are making more money designing advertising banners than web sites!

Most ad banners are accepted in GIF or JPEG format. Animated GIFs (see Chapter 14, "Animation") are a great file format for ad banners. Just beware that site audiences can be easily annoyed by these critters—especially looping ones. However, a successfully designed animated ad banner will hold your attention without annoyance.

There are no standard specs for ad banners. You might be asked to design a variety of sizes for a client. If you want to create banners for yourself and not a paying client, there are some interesting services on the web that trade banners for free:

■ http://www.linkexchange.com/

In the true spirit of web interactivity, Link Exchange has also set up the following newsgroup:

Newsgroup: le.discuss
■ news://news2.linkexchange.com/le.discuss

This newsgroup covers general Link Exchange Comments/Questions/ Problems/Promotional Issues, Banner Design, Click-Thru Ratios, Advertising Issues, International Advertising, Web Design in regard to building a better site, Questions about Search Engines /Directories/Yellow Pages, and so on.

New Riders — a new web design book by Lynda Weinman

hotwired | copyrighted images © frames navigation cgi

Web Design Case Studies and Tutorials

discovery channel online | server push | securing rights to images | client pull

custom illustration | low bandwidth design | hot hot hot | color palettes

invisible gif | experimental design | art center college of design | quarkxpress to html

painting techniques in photoshop | hybrid colors | dreamworks interactive SKG

guestbook cgi | typoGRAPHIC | java | interface design

animated GIFs | hollywoodrecords | ascii art

sounds | photoshop collage | movies | iuma

ALICE IN CHAINS | low src | sonymusic online | double load animations

designing for 3D space | construct | Tools | The | vrml

html validation | @tlas | site management | photoshop layers | tables for alignment

available at bookstores now

Sample frames from an ad banner I created for my book *Deconstructing Web Graphics*. Ad banners can be single frames, or contain many frames such as this example. This animation contains 15 separate images and conveys much more information about my book than a single frame could possibly communicate. It was created in Photoshop and GIFBuilder (■ http://iawww.epfl.ch/Staff/Yves.Piguet/clip2gif-home/GifBuilder.html).

Chat Environments and Avatars

In future editions of this book, I predict this section will grow bigger as visual chat areas and avatars become a viable digital design medium for illustrators and designers. Unlike e-mail, chat is real-time, where participants send electronic messages in large group forums. There are currently more options for nonvisual chat software applications, but the future will bring a different sort of chat experience that will involve full multimedia, such as sound, movies, animated characters, and even voice.

For now, there are a few early adopter-based technologies that include avatars (icons for chat participants) and worlds (environmental backdrops). Here's a brief URL list to check out some of the software options for visual and nonvisual chat software:

WebCrawler's List of Chat Software Options
■ http://webcrawler.com/select/chat.tools.html

The Palace
■ http://www.thepalace.com/

IRC FAQ
■ http://www2.undernet.org:8080/~cs93jtl/irc_faq.txt

ICHAT
■ http://www.ichat.com/

A custom environment for a Palace-based chat environment that Bruce Heavin created for *The Net* magazine.

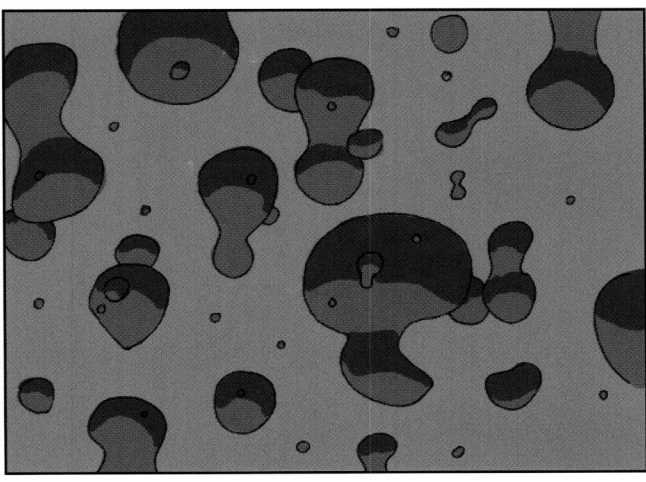

Bruce created custom views of the environment—the inside of the lava lamp on the table. Visitors can even chat inside the lava lamp!

The visual environment in a virtual chat space can attract a specific clientele, or inspire subjects of conversation, just like the real world.

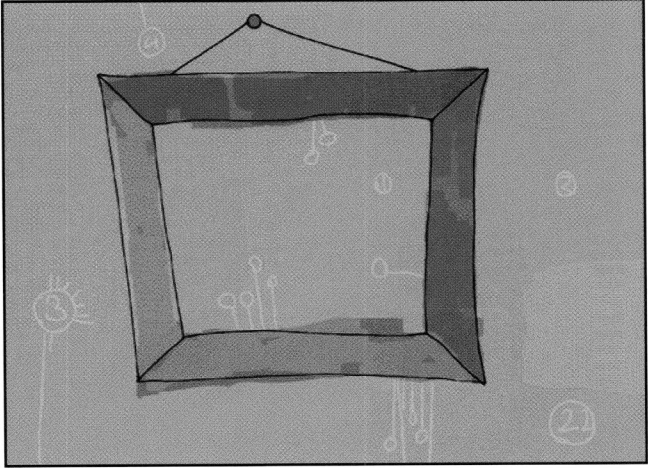

The Palace is scriptable, so it can be programmed to do extra things, like enable end users to draw on the wall. Bruce made areas, such as inside this frame, where visitors can add their own pictures.

Mouse Rollovers

Mouse rollovers are very popular in CD-ROM-based multimedia, and will be on the web as soon as people learn how to make them. On the web we have a few visual cues for hyperlinks, such as the hand symbol, the bounding box around linked graphics, and underlines below text. These are fairly limited visual signals. Rollovers offer much greater design flexibility.

A rollover can make type appear to glow, change the color of an icon, or make a sound. The possibilities for rollover effects are limited by your imagination only. This section will evaluate two technologies for rollovers: JavaScript and Macromedia Director/Shockwave.

JavaScript MouseOvers

JavaScript is a programming language developed by Netscape. Unlike Java, C, Perl, or sh, however, you can view the JavaScript code within HTML documents. This makes it very easy to learn and "borrow" from others' sites. Proper netiquette recommends that you always leave references to the originator within the code if you do copy the scripts. These credits are usually left in comment tags, which look like this:

```
//So-and So's Amazing Rollover Script//
or like this
<!...So-and So's Amazing Rollover Script...!>
```

You'll see these types of credits in the following examples.

Joe Maller's JavaScript Rollover

Joe Maller, a digital designer in NYC and computer imaging instructor at Parsons Institute, uses his site as an experimental playing field for all types of new web technologies. Check his stuff out at ■ http://www.joemaller.com. The following tutorial was written by Joe and is also on his site.

Declaring Images in the Script
In the <SCRIPT> section of the <HEAD> of the document, you need to first declare the images you will later use for your rollover. The JavaScript to set up those images looks like this:

```
Image1= new Image(100,150)
Image1.src = "your_image.gif"
Image2 = new Image(100,150)
Image2.src = "your_other_image.gif"
```

Each image must have two lines: the first sets its size, and the second sets its source and the location and name of the image. The numbers within the parentheses refer to width and height, in that order. Note that JavaScript is case sensitive; TheDog is not the same as thedog.

Naming Image Objects

JavaScript 1.1, as implemented in Netscape Navigator 3.0, defines images as objects. That means the JavaScript now recognizes images as more than just HTML.

To replace an image, you must give JavaScript some way of identifying where you will replace the images. Do this by either inserting NAME="Rupert" into the <IMG...> tag, or by learning to refer to images in JavaScript's Array syntax: document.images[2]

The above refers to the third image tag in the HTML document (you're programming now—zero counts first). I prefer to simply name my images, and that's what I've done in this example.

For JavaScript to recognize a rollover, the object rolled over must be a link; regular text is ignored. Here is the HTML code for the image that will be replaced during a rollover:

```
<A HREF="link.html"
onMouseOver="SwapOut()"
onMouseOut="SwapBack()">
<IMG NAME="Rupert"
SRC="your_image.gif"
WIDTH=100
HEIGHT=150>
</A>
```

Notice the name attribute's appearance in the <IMG...> tag.

What's "onMouseOver"?

onMouseOver and onMouseOut are event handlers that tell JavaScript what to do when an event occurs. The command given is the function within the quotes. onMouseOver= "blorg()" tells JavaScript to execute the function blorg().

Functions

Functions are predefined sets of commands that JavaScript will execute when only the name of the function is called. Functions are usually stored in the <SCRIPT> section of the <HEAD> of the document, the same place we declared the images earlier. The standard format for defining a function is:

```
function SwapOut() {
document.Rupert.src = Image2.src; return true;
}
```

joe_blink.jpg

joe open.jpg

Joe's mouseover effect causes his eyes to blink. It's fun—and worth trying at at home!

■ **note**

Notes and Problems

LOWSRC—If you use the low source tag on an image, you might experience unwanted reloads of that image before every image swap.

Image Size—The size of the image is set by the image you will be replacing. Replacement images will be stretched to fit.

Putting It All Together

The following is the complete code for a simple document that will change images. Don't believe me? Try it. Here's the code:

```
<HTML>
<HEAD>
<TITLE>
Doubter's page
</TITLE>
<SCRIPT LANGUAGE="JavaScript">
<!-- hide from none JavaScript Browsers
Image1= new Image(121,153)
Image1.src = "joe_open.jpg"
Image2 = new Image(121,153)
Image2.src = "joe_blink.jpg"
function SwapOut() {
document.Rupert.src = Image2.src; return true;
}
function SwapBack() {
document.Rupert.src = Image1.src; return true;
}
// - stop hiding -->
</SCRIPT>
</HEAD>
<BODY BGCOLOR="#FFFFFF">
<CENTER>
<P>
<A HREF="http://www.joemaller.com/"
onmouseover="SwapOut()"
onmouseout="SwapBack()">
<IMG NAME="Rupert"
SRC="joe_open.jpg"
WIDTH=121
HEIGHT=153
BORDER=0>
</A>
</P>
If you use this, please give me credit.
</CENTER>
</BODY>
</HTML>
```

Bill Weinman's JavaScript Rollover

This example demonstrates that rollovers, like many things, can be done more way than one. This is Bill's script:

```
// bill's suave mouseover javascript
// (c) 1996 wew   http://www.weinman.com/wew/
//
// If you want to use this, go ahead;
but please leave
// this notice here so that other people
know where it
// came from.   —wew.
//
// how many items in the array
numitems = 6
// the offset to the first GIF that's
going to change.  This is
// the number of GIFs on the page before
the first one that
// will swap, minus 1.
offset = 7
// creates the array for the GIFs.
don't touch this.
Atitles = new Array(numitems)
// this initializes the array.
for(i = 0; i < numitems; i++)
{
Atitles[i] = new Image()
}
// blankgif is the default GIF.
this one's white 1 pixel x 1 pixel.
// WARNING: transparent GIFs create problems on
MacIntoshim!
blankgif = "white.gif"
// These are the GIFs that will overlay
the white ones when the
// mouse is over them.
Atitles[0].src = "tbio.gif"
Atitles[1].src = "tproj.gif"
Atitles[2].src = "tbook.gif"
Atitles[3].src = "tbear.gif"Atitles[4].src =
"tlinks.gif"
Atitles[5].src = "tmail.gif"
// this function swaps out the GIFs,
and updates the status line.
function description(m,i) {
status = m
imgtmp = document.images[offset + i].src
document.images[offset + i].src = Atitles[i].src
return true;
}
// this function restores the blankgif and
the status line.
function clearstat(i) {
status=""
document.images[offset + i].src = blankgif
return true;
}
</script>
```

Bill's images and file names follow:

   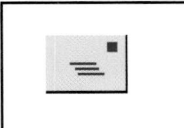 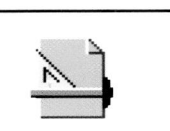

bbear.gif	bbio.gif	blinks.gif	bmail.gif	bproj.gif

Director/Shockwave/Lingo-Based Interactive Web Pages

Shockwave is the name of a plug-in that enables Director-based multimedia projects to be played on the web. Multimedia can be described as anything that combines sound, animation, images, text, and interactivity.

Unlike JavaScript, Macromedia Director is an authoring program for creating interactive multimedia for kiosks and CD-ROMs, and it has been around many years longer than the web itself. The Shockwave file format boasts an impressive compression ratio of three to one, making the Director files one third of their usual size.

Afterburner is the free post-processing tool that offers authors who create Director multimedia projects the ability to convert them so that they can be distributed over the web. Once Afterburner has converted a Director project, that project becomes a Shockwave file. You can download Afterburner from Macromedia's site at ■ http://www.macromedia.com/shockwave/dev-tools. html#director.

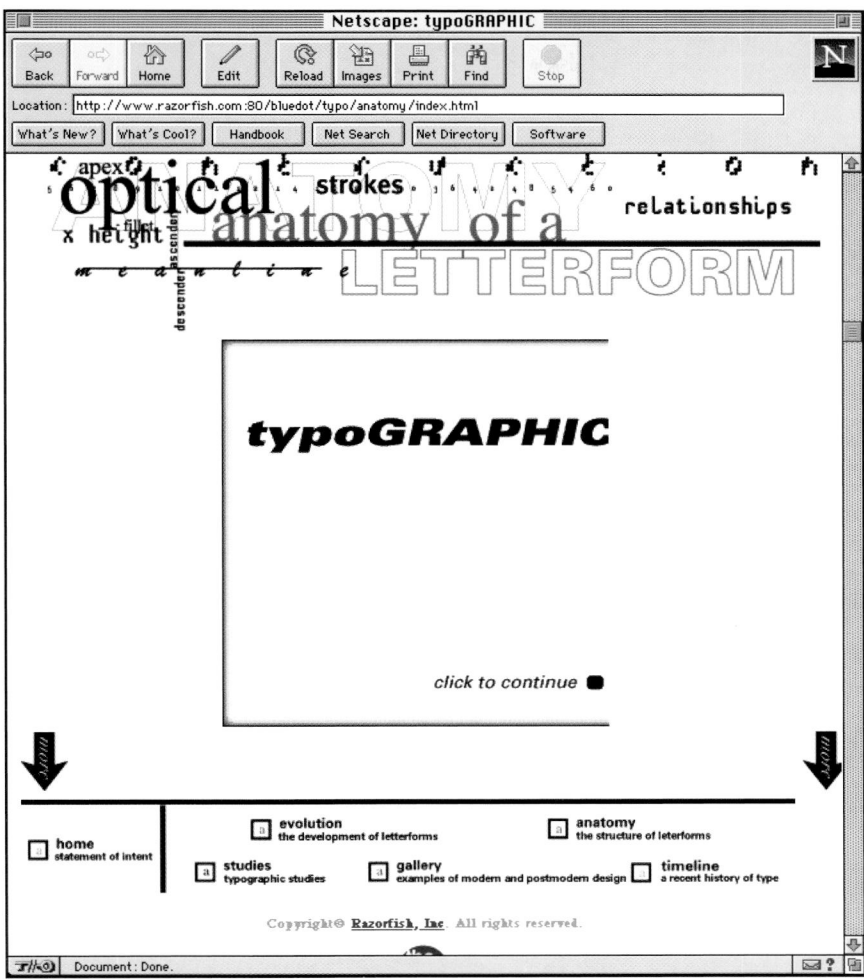

The centered window with the "click here to continue" button is the embedded Shockwave document. This example is taken from ■ http://www.razorfish.com/bluedot/typo/anatomy/.

■ **note**

Shockwave Versus JavaScript

Director projects (which later get converted to Shockwave) can be much more robust than what is possible through Java-Script. With the added power (a paint and animation interface, and a proprietary programming language called Lingo) comes a steeper learning curve. You can't see the source code for a Director project like you can a JavaScript, making it impossible to reverse engineer what others have done. Learning Shockwave and Director requires buying the program, reading the manual and/or third-party books, and/or joining users groups or discussion groups. The power is definitely greater, but the learning curve may not be worth it to you. For more information, visit ■ http://www.macromedia.com.

Leroy's Click and Drag

Bruce Heavin includes a simple Shockwave piece on his site.

Leroy's Click and Drag is at ■ http://www.stink.com/leroy/leroy.html. Every graphic on this page is click and dragable.

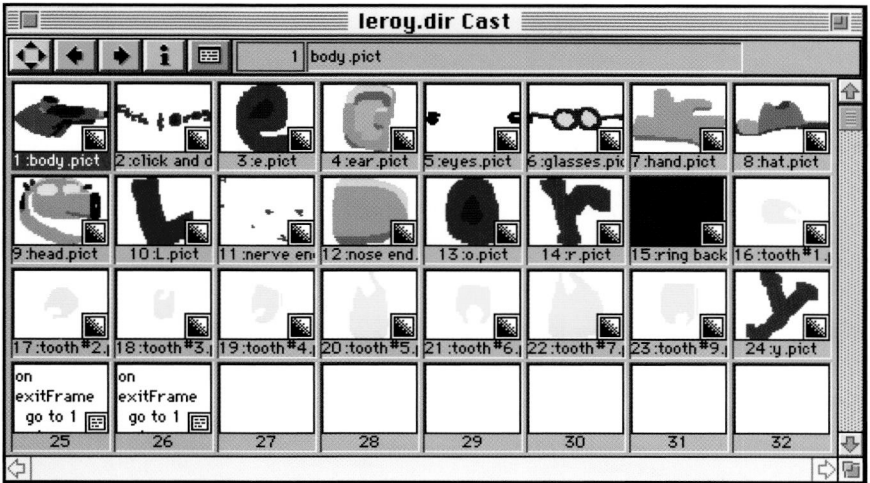

The leroy.dir Cast window shows each element of artwork used in the Director project.

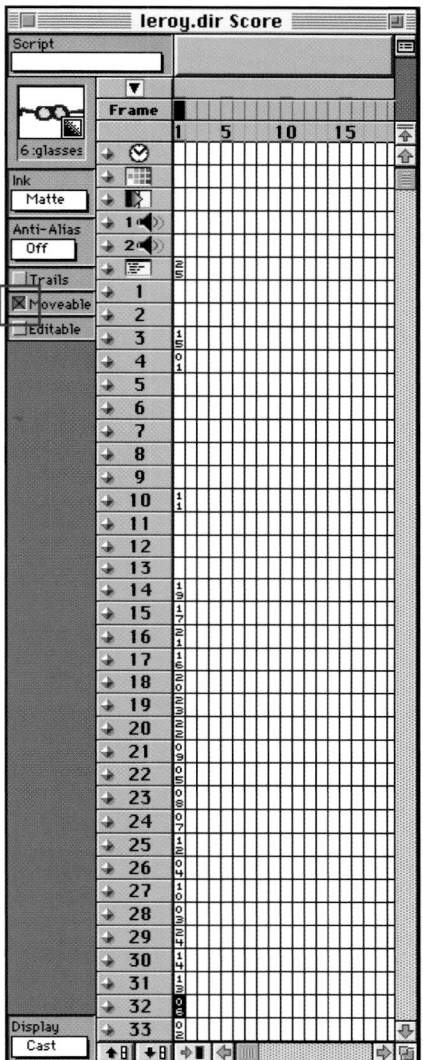

By clicking the Movable check box, Bruce created an interactive experience making each piece of artwork movable.

Designing the Interface for the Anatomy Shockwave Project

Stephen Turbek spent several weeks teaching himself Macromedia Director so he could program some of his own experiments with interface design. The Anatomy section in the typoGRAPHIC site (■ http://www.razorfish.com/bluedot/typo/) gave him an opportunity to produce his first published Director project, where he was able to test some of his theories about human interface design. Stephen's interface design succeeded by creating custom navigation controls that blended seamlessly with the overall aesthetic of the site.

A main concern to Stephen was understanding how to make a person learn a new interface. The "red dot" became a unifying design theme in his project. After the user learned that the dot changed to red and could be clicked to go to the next screen, the navigation for the piece was established.

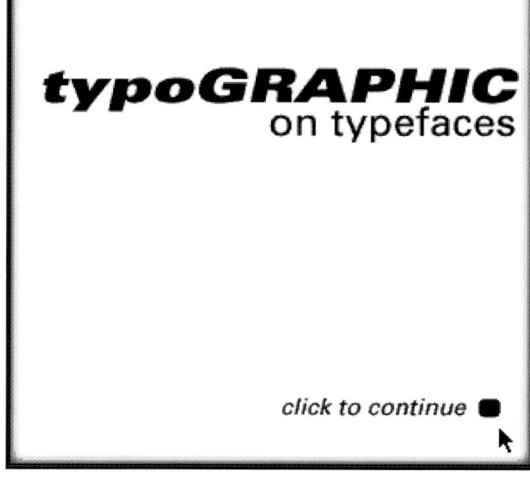 

When the end user's cursor passes over the black rectangle, it turns red. This rollover effect signifies that the rectangle is a button that triggers interactive events.

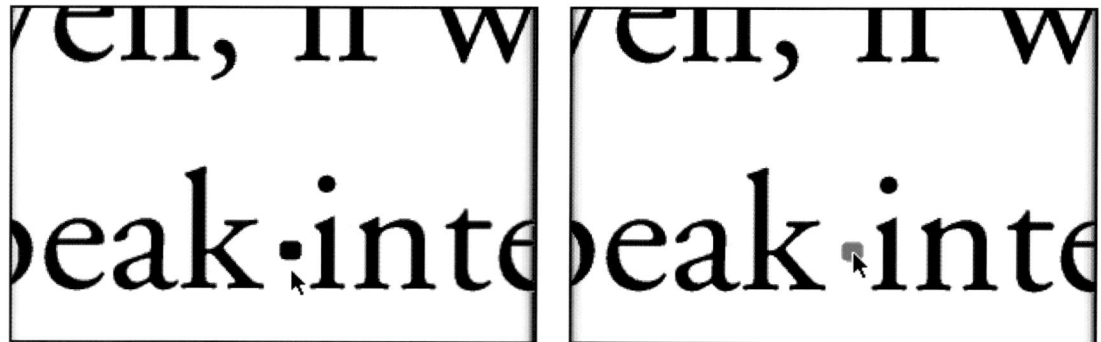

The red cursor metaphor is reinforced as a navigational cue in subsequent screens without the need to repeat the instructions "click to continue." The end user is being trained how to use the interface without further explanation.

A current trend in advanced multimedia and game design is to break away from obvious buttons with words on them. By using a simple red dot instead of a bulky button or conventional arrow icons, Steven was able to keep the design of his Shockwave piece much more elegant and consistent with the established aesthetic of the typoGRAPHIC site. It's important to designers that interfaces integrate with the overall look and feel of an interactive experience.

Stephen also strove to create an inviting interface that enabled users to explore and learn without cumbersome navigation graphics. He carried the rollover effect of objects changing from black to red throughout the piece. The next section of the project offered definitions for the anatomy of type, inviting the user to interact with red circles.

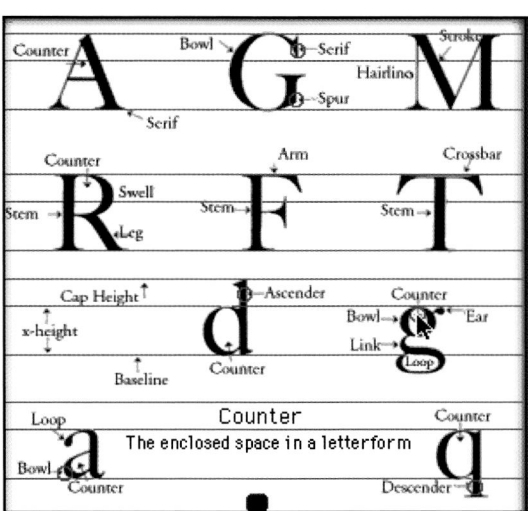

When a cursor travels over a red circle, the definition of the term is displayed at the bottom of the frame. The familiar black dot at the bottom of the image signifies that it can be clicked to advance to the next screen.

Another important component of Stephen's piece was to create maximum interactivity for the audience. Rather than a simple slide show, he chose to let the user move type around onscreen themselves, to view the differences between serifs and typeface weights. This created a much more compelling example than simply showing visual examples of the differences.

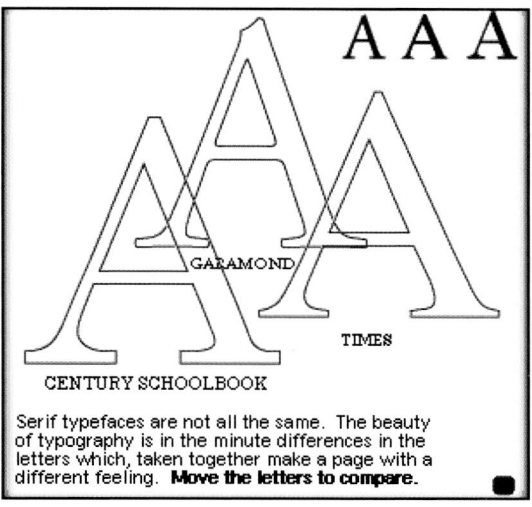

Serif typefaces are not all the same. The beauty of typography is in the minute differences in the letters which, taken together make a page with a different feeling. **Move the letters to compare.**

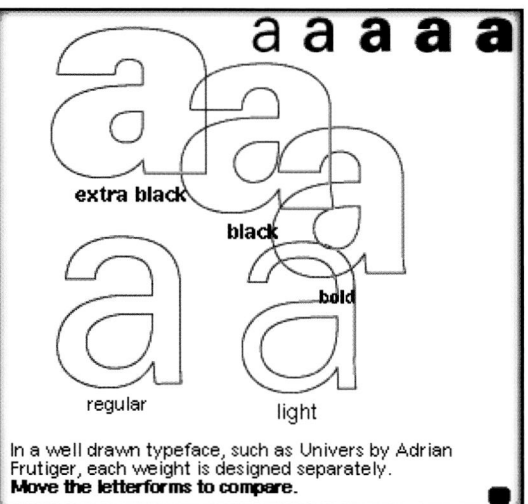

In a well drawn typeface, such as Univers by Adrian Frutiger, each weight is designed separately. **Move the letterforms to compare.**

Stephen designed two screens that enable the user to move the letterforms into position. This level of interactivity is new to the web and justifies using extra tools such as Director and Shockwave.

Deconstructing the Lingo for Shockwave

Adding interactivity to Director projects is accomplished through using a proprietary programming language called Lingo. Lingo is touted as an easy programming language—although non-programmers might not necessarily agree with that analysis. Learning Lingo is possible by studying the manuals that are shipped with Macromedia Director or through third-party books and Usenet groups. This is the view of the artwork from within Director's Paint window.

In order to color the black dot, it had to be a separate sprite (piece of artwork) within the Director project .

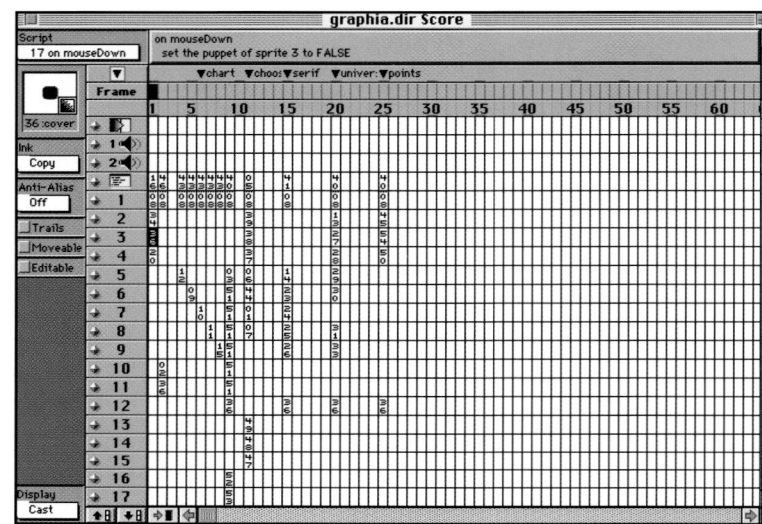

Inside the Director Score window, the black dot is in the channel #3 position. Note in the Lingo script that follows how this artwork is referred to as "sprite 3," even though the artwork is named cover.pict, and is in the number 36 position in the Cast window.

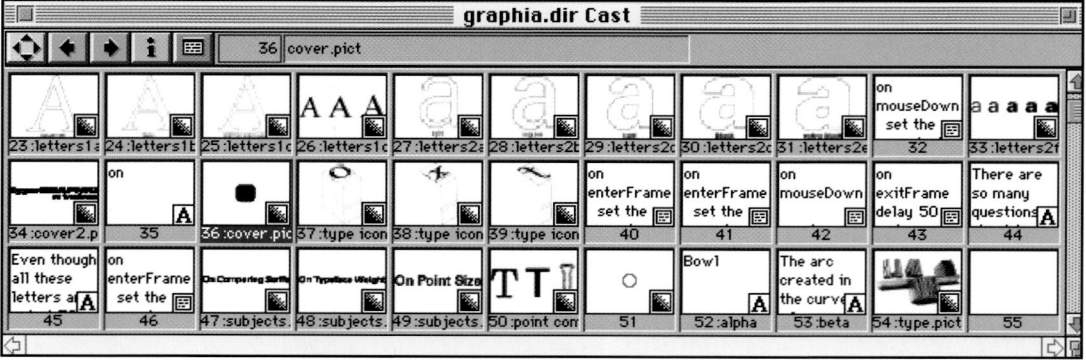

If you look at the channel #3 cel within the Score, you'll notice the tiny number 36. This number reflects the position of the sprite that's been assigned in the Cast Member window.

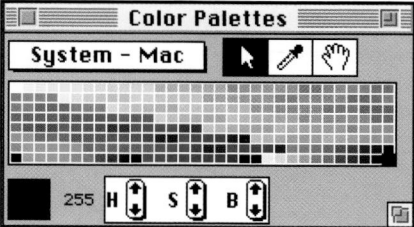

The Lingo is also specifying the color black turn to red with the cursor rollover. Black is #255 within the Mac System palette.

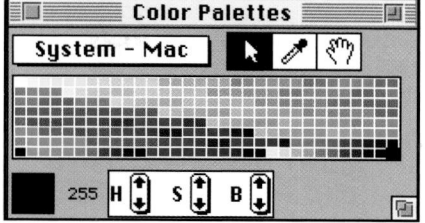

Red is #217 within the Mac System palette.

The cursor turns red by instructing the color of the black (255) sprite to turn red (217). It's possible to set a custom palette within Director, but the Mac System palette is in use in this project. The Lingo for the red cursor rollover effect follows:

```
on enterFrame
set the puppet of sprite 3 to TRUE
if rollOver(3) = TRUE then
set the forecolor of sprite 3 to 217
else set the forecolor of sprite 3 to 255
end if
end
On exitFrame
go to the frame
end
```

To create the early slide-show effect, Stephen inserted delay times, which cause each frame of artwork to pause for a specified amount of time. Delays within Lingo are measured in ticks. One second is 60 ticks, so each delay in this piece is a little less than a second. Here's the Lingo:

```
on exitFrame
delay 50
end
```

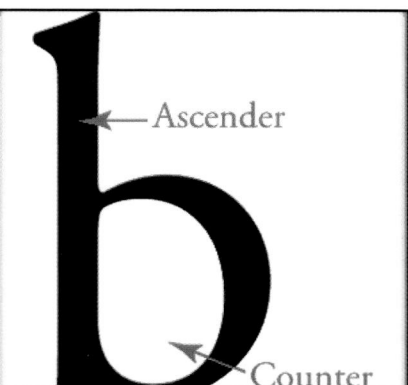
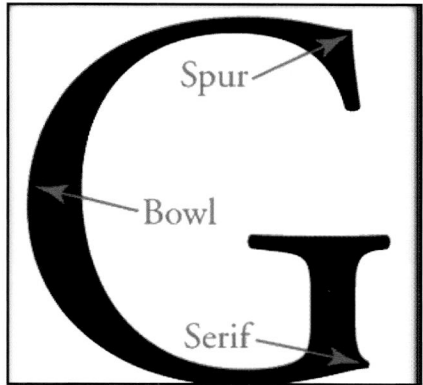

These three screens appear in succession, like a slide show. The slide-show effect was accomplished by assigning each frame to have a delay within the Lingo programming.

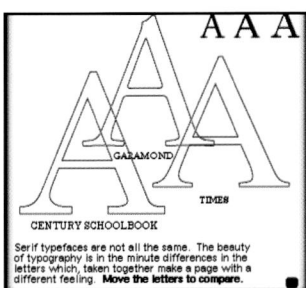

Allowing users the ability to move images around on-screen, such as the three letterforms here, is accomplished by assigning the object to be movable.

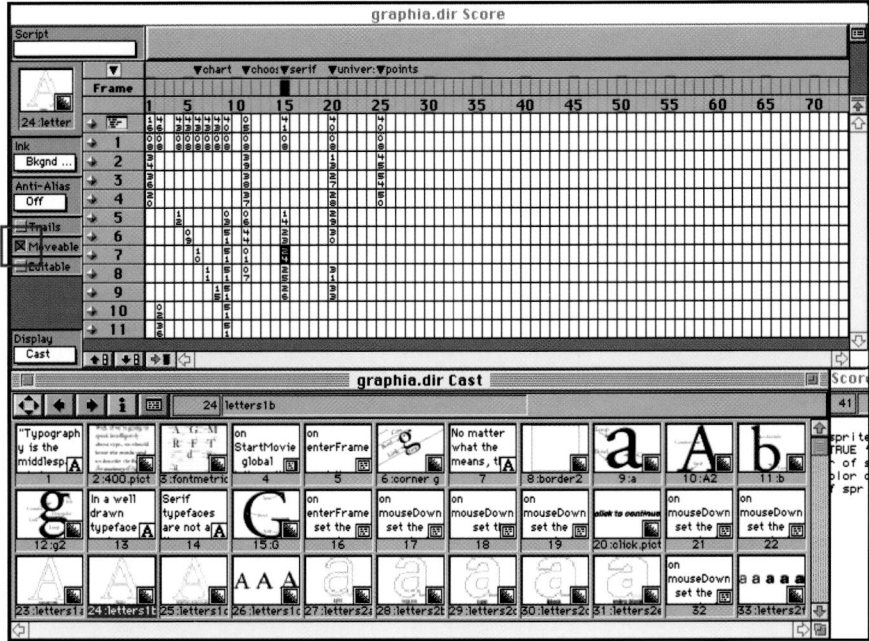

Note how the number 24 is highlighted in the Director Score. To its far left is a check box called Movable. By clicking this, the sprite is able to be moved by the end user. This piece of artwork is sprite number 24 in the Cast window. It also has been set to use Bkgnd ink, which instructs the program to mask the background color of the graphic. In this case, the graphic's background color was white, so under the Bkgnd ink setting the white was assigned to be transparent.

Besides checking the Movable check box, another way to assign movability to an object is through Lingo. The advantage to using Lingo for this purpose is that the movable attribute can be turned off or be dependent on other actions. Clicking on the Movable check box is less flexible because it's a global setting that lasts the entire duration of the Director project.

This is the Lingo to add movable functionality to a sprite:

```
set the movable of sprite x=true
```

■ **note**

Director 5 Supports Shockwave
Director 5 has been released since Stephen made the Shockwave example on typoGRAPHIC. Some of the upgrade's improvements are support for anti-aliased text and the capability to save directly in the Shockwave format without the use of Afterburner.

Shocking Director

The final step to preparing the Director document is to turn it into a web-based Shockwave document. This is done with a free utility called After-burner, which can be downloaded from:

■ http://www.macromedia.com/shockwave/devtools.html#director

Afterburner is a post-processor that compresses and prepares Director movies for uploading to an HTTP server that will make them available to Internet users. This can now be done in Director 5.0 directly, without using Afterburner. Uncompressed movies should be in .dir or .dxr format. After compression with Afterburner, they will be in .dcr format. HTTP servers should set the MIME-Type for .dcr files to "application/x-director."

To include the Shockwave piece within the typoGRAPHIC site, the following HTML was used:

```
<EMBED SRC="images/graphia.dcr" WIDTH=304 HEIGHT=300>
```

It's extremely important to include the dimensions of Shockwave documents in HTML code. The file will not function without it.

Although Stephen did not choose to do this on the typoGRAPHIC site, it is possible to code the HTML so an alternative image displays on browsers that do not support plug-ins by using the following tag:

```
<NO EMBED>
```

After the <NO EMBED> tag, an alternative graphic could be inserted that would be visible only to browsers that do not have the Shockwave plug-in installed or don't support the plug-in.

HTML for Visual Designers

Font

BROWSER SAFE COLOR
33 FF

hotoshop
0033

Width ="500

PARENCY

</A>

<STRONG>
.gif
.jpg
.png

Height ="600

<cente

Imaging techniques

Web file formats
bgco = "FFFFCC"

@link= "cyan"

<center> BODY>
Antiali

33

Web

d typography

<img src="

IMAGE OPTIMIZATION
Colors

Animation, sound and

LYNDA.COM

www. Design

HTML for Visual Designers

HTML, as we know it today, will not live forever. WYSIWYG editors will continue to evolve; standards for basic page construction will stabilize and nonprogrammers will not have to think in tags and attributes any more than those who rely on word processors today have to understand the code behind programs such as Microsoft Word.

I view the web as I would a 1.0 release of any new computer product. The product is wonderful—it lets you do things you've never done before, but at the same time it is clunky, unintuitive, subject to change, and unpredictable. The point is, in order to participate today, one must understand HTML to one degree or another. I am certain this will not always be the case. Whenever anything is new, one has to go to greater lengths to use it. In the scope of history, we will be looked at as the early adopters of the web. This means that the things we have to do now in order to participate will not always be necessary.

I believe it's important to understand HTML tags today, but it will not be necessary to do so in the future. Whether that future is one year from now—or 20—is something I'll leave to others to predict. In the meantime, we're in the present, not the future, so having a chapter to help you with commonly used HTML tags might be one of the most useful parts of this book.

This book, however, should not be confused with a standard HTML book. HTML in this book will help you with tags that specifically relate to design, such as composition, typography, alignment, and color—not every tag and attribute in existence. Before writing the first edition of *Designing Web Graphics*, I always found myself fumbling through three different HTML books and several online sources to find the exact tag I was looking for. This chapter was designed to save you (ok, me, too) the time and hassle of searching through each chapter to find the code you know you read about somewhere.

Everything here is presented in summary form and is meant to review key tips that have been covered elsewhere in the book for creating, troubleshooting, and uploading web pages. The HTML list is not meant to be definitive; it's intentionally tailored for web graphic design needs. Look to this chapter when you need a quick reference guide, once you've finished reading the rest of the book.

Naming Protocols

Always use lowercase letters in file names and do not use spaces. If you have spaces between the title of your document—such as **my document name.extension**—either string it together, as in **mydocumentname.extension**, or use underscores, as in **my_document_name.extension**.

If you are working with files that are going to be downloaded by your audience, such as audio and video files, remember to abbreviate names so that they're less than eight characters in the main title and leave room for a period and three-letter extension, such as **mydocumn.ext**. This naming convention is called the **8.3** (eight dot three) convention and exists so that users logging in with systems using Windows 3.1 and earlier, which do not support longer file names, can access the files.

Common File Extensions

You must give images and media the proper file-name extensions so that the browser reading your HTML can display them properly. The following is a list of the most common file types.

Name	Extension
HTML text document	.html
JPEG	.jpg
GIF	.gif
PNG	.png
QuickTime movie	.mov, .qt
Video for Windows	.avi
MPEG video	.mpg
MPEG audio	.mp2
AU/Êlaw	.au
AIFF/AIFC	.aiff
WAV	.wav

Relative Versus Absolute Path Names

An absolute path name gives the entire http header information, such as:

■ http://www.lynda.com/image.gif.

This URL, for example, would instruct a server to locate my domain and find an image inside the main directory folder of my site.

If I know someone is already linked into my site, however, I don't need to give them all that same information. I could write a link that simply requests **"/image.gif"**. This tells the file to look for the **image.gif** within the current directory.

Some people have messy rooms and offices, and others are clean freaks. I fall into the first category and have been known to build an entire site leaving every file in one folder. This is not the best way to work, but it does work! The better, more organized way would be to have folders for different areas of the site.

■ **note**

Checking Your Pages

You should always check your pages from your hard drive before you post them to your server. This way you will catch a lot of HTML and artwork mistakes before the rest of the world knows you made them. From your hard drive, open your browser and then open your HTML ascii (text only) document from there. All the images should load properly and give a very accurate preview of what your page will look like once it's on the web. The only types of files that will not preview properly are those that require server-side code, such as server-side push, server-side imagemaps, CGI forms processing, and server-side include tags.

Troubleshooting

If your page tested properly off your local hard drive but not when you posted the files to the server, make sure the file names you requested in your HTML match the names of the actual document. Unix is case sensitive, meaning if your file is saved JPG and your HTML calls for it as jpg, the code will not be able to read the file. Because your local files are most likely not on a Unix platform, this problem will not surface until you post your files and view them from a browser.

If your file is named **jamie.gif** and your HTML reads <IMG SRC="**jamie.GIF**">, it won't work! Redo the <IMG SRC> tag to read <IMG SRC="**jamie.gif**">.

Uploading Your Pages

Most likely, you'll need a password and authorization name to access either your, or your client's, web server. This can be obtained from your online service provider or your client.

Whenever you transfer elements for a web page to your server, remember these things:

■ Transfer the HTML document as Text Only (ascii).
■ Transfer the image, sound, and movie files as Raw
   Data on Macs and as Image or Binary mode on PCs.

The Basic Structure of an HTML Document

```
<HTML>
<HEAD>
<TITLE><meta>
</HEAD>
<BODY> or <BODY BGCOLOR>
<BODY BACKGROUND><BODY TEXT>
Body of the document
(all the text, images, links, etc.)
</BODY>
</HTML>
```

■ HTML is not case sensitive (upper- and lowercase). The tag **<HTML>** will be just as effective as the tag **<html>**.
■ Always save an HTML document in Text Only mode (ascii) with the extension **.html** or **.htm** at the end.

Common HTML Tags

The tables that follow show the various HTML tags and what they are used for. The tables are divided into sections containing HTML tag information for headers, body, text, horizontal rules, alignment, text and image attributes, lists, tables, frames, links, comments.

Head Tags

<HEAD></HEAD>	Enables you to use a <HEADLINE> or <TITLE> tag within the document.
<H#></H#>	Enables you to set sizes inside header tags (H1, H2, H3).
<TITLE></TITLE>	Enables you to name the HTML document. Whatever you put inside this tag will show up in the title bar of your browser.

Body Tags

<BODY BGCOLOR=link=#alink=#vlink=#>	The following tags allow you to change the colors of your background, text, links, and so on in browsers that support it.
TEXT=#	Sets text color.
LINK=#	Sets link colors for text and borders around images.
ALINK=#	Sets the link color when the mouse is clicked in the down position.
VLINK=#	Sets the visited link color for text and borders around images.
<BODY BACKGROUND>	Using the <BODY BACKGROUND> tag allows you to load tiled background patterns to your web pages.
<meta httpequiv=refresh content=#;URL=#>	Allows you to perform client pull effects, where you automatically send your viewers to another URL without requesting it.

Text Tags

<STRONG></STRONG>	Makes text bold.

<B></B>	Makes text bold.
<EM></EM>	Italicizes type.
<I></I>	Italicizes type.
<PRE></PRE>	Allows you to work with preformatted type.
<CODE></CODE>	Used for computer codes.
 	Denotes a line break.
<P>	Denotes a paragraph break.
<FONT SIZE=#></FONT>	Enables you to change font sizes.
<TT></TT>	Denotes the typewriter style (monospaced font).
<FONT COLOR=#></FONT>	Sets the color of type.

Horizontal Rule Tags

<HR>	Creates a standard embossed horizontal rule.
<HR WIDTH=#>	Changes the length in pixels.
<HR SIZE=#>	Changes the height in pixels.
<HR WIDTH=# ALIGN=left, right, center>	Aligns a horizontal rule that's shorter than the distance of your entire page.
<HR NOSHADE>	Creates a plain black line.

Text Alignment Tags and Attributes

<CENTER></CENTER>	Centers text or images inside this tag.

Image Alignment Tags and Attributes

<IMG SRC="#" ALIGN="top, middle, bottom, left, right">	Aligns text to the top, middle, bottom, left, or right of the image inside this tag.

Image Tags

<IMG SRC="#">	Contains an image.

<IMG SRC="#" ALT="#">	Contains an image and a text description for viewers who don't have graphical web browsers.
<IMG SRC="#" HEIGHT=# WIDTH=#>	Allows for specifying image dimensions and causes HTML text to load before large graphics.
<A HREF="#"><IMG SRC="#"></A>	Contains a linked image and automatically generates a border around the image in whatever link color has been specified.
<A HREF="#"><IMG SRC="#" BORDER=0></A>	Ensures that there's no border on browsers that support this feature.
<A HREF="#"><IMG SRC="#" BORDER=#></A>	Depending on the value, puts a heavier or lighter border around the linked image.

List Tags and Attributes

<UL>	Unorganized list: Generates an indented list with bullets.
<OL>	Organized list: Generates numbers in front of list.
<LI>	Puts a bullet in front of each item, indents the text, and creates a line break at the end of each item.
<DL>	Definition list: Produces an indented list with no bullets.
<DD>	Produces items in a definition list.

Table Tags

<TABLE></TABLE>	Put at the beginning and end of tables.
<TH></TH>	Makes bold text or numbers and accepts table attributes.
<TD></TD>	Includes text, numbers, or images and accepts table attributes.

Table Tags and Attributes

ALIGN="left, right, or center"	Aligns text or images in table.

VALIGN="top middle, bottom, or baseline"	Vertically aligns text or images in table.
ROWSPAN=#	Denotes the number of rows in a table.
COLSPAN=#	Denotes the number of columns in a table.
WIDTH=#	Specifies the width of the table by pixels.
CELLPADDING=#	Sets the space between the border and content of table.
CELLSPACING=#	Adjusts the thickness of the borders.

Linking Tags and Attributes

<EMBED></EMBED>	For use with plug-ins.
<NOEMBED></NOEMBED>	For non-plug-in-based content.

Frames Tag and Attributes

<FRAMESET></FRAMESET>	Initiates frames.
COLS	Specifies the numbers of columns and widths in a <FRAMESET>.
ROWS	Specifies the rows and their height in a <FRAMESET>.
SCROLLING	Turn on or off scrolling when content is larger than the frame.
TARGET	Lets you set _blank, _self, _parent, or_top attributes (see Chapter 10, "Navigation-Based Graphics").
FRAMEBORDER	Enables you to turn borders on or off.

Linking Tags and Attributes

<A></A>	Anchors text.
<A HREF="URL"></A>	Links the image or text to an URL.

Comments Tag

<! ... >	Sets comments that appear as notes for the HTML document but won't show up on the actual web page.

BROWSER SAFE COLOR
33FF

0033CC

Width ="500

<STRONG>

Height ="600

IMAGE OPTIMIZATION

<IMG src=

<H1>

<TABL

Imaging techniques

Animation, sound and

Web file formats
bgcolor="FFFFCC

alink="cyan

<BODY>

33

LYNDA.COM

www.Design

Glossary

8-bit graphics: A color or grayscale graphic or movie that has 256 colors or less.

8-bit sound: 8-bit sound has a dynamic range of 48 dB. Dynamic range is the measure of steps between the volume or amplitude of a sound.

16-bit graphics: A color image or movie that has 65,500 colors.

16-bit sound: Standard CD-quality sound resolution. 16-bit sounds have a dynamic range of 96 dB.

24-bit graphics: A color image or movie that has 16.7 million colors.

32-bit graphics: A color image or movie that has 16.7 million colors plus an 8-bit masking channel.

active navigation: Point-and-click navigation, where the end user guides the information flow.

adaptive dithering: A form of dithering in which the program looks to the image to determine the best set of colors when creating an 8-bit or smaller palette. See dithering.

additive color: The term for RGB color space that uses projected light to mix color.

AIFC: A sound file format. AIFC is a new spec for the older Audio Interchange File Format (AIFF). Both AIFF and AIFF-C files can be read by this format.

aliasing: In bitmapped graphics, the jagged boundary along the edges of different-colored shapes within an image. See anti-aliasing.

animated GIF: Part of the GIF89a spec that supports multiple images, and streams and displays them sequentially.

anti-aliasing: A technique for reducing the jagged appearance of aliased bitmapped images, usually by inserting pixels that blend at the boundaries between adjacent colors.

artifacts: Image imperfections caused by compression.

attributes: Defined appearances or behaviors of 3D objects. For example, a lighting attribute would affect the color and light of an object. A texture attribute would affect the surface texture of an object.

authoring tools: Creation tools for interactive media.

avatar: A visual icon chosen or designed by an end user that is used as a persona within chat environments.

AVI: Audio-Video Interleaved. Microsoft's file format for desktop video movies.

bit depth: The number of bits used to represent the color of each pixel in a given movie or still image. Specifically: bit depth of 1=black-and-white pixel; bit depth of 2=4 colors or grays; bit depth of 4=16 colors or grays; bit depth of 8=256 colors or grays; bit depth of 16=65,536 colors; bit depth of 24=(approximately) 16 million colors.

bitmapped graphics: Graphics that are pixel based, as opposed to object oriented. Bitmapped graphics are what the computer can display because it's a pixel-based medium, whereas object-oriented graphics can be viewed in high resolution once they are sent to a printer. Graphics on the web are bitmapped because they are viewed from a computer-screen-based delivery system.

brightness: Adds white or tints an image, whereas lack of brightness adds black or tones an image.

browser: An application that enables you to access World Wide Web pages. Most browsers provide the capability to view web pages, copy and print material from web pages, download files from the web, and navigate throughout the web.

browser-safe colors: The 216 colors that do not shift between platforms, operating systems, or most web browsers.

cache: A storage area that keeps frequently accessed data or program instructions readily available so that you do not have to retrieve them repeatedly.

CGI: Common Gateway Interface. A web standard for extending the functionality of HTML. CGI always involves the combination of a live web server and external programming scripts.

chat: A real-time multiple user e-mail environment.

Cinepak: Cinepak is very high form of movie compression. The compression type is called "lossy" because it causes a visible loss in quality.

client: A computer that requests information from a network's server. See server.

client pull: Client pull creates a slide show effect with HTML text or inline images. It is programmed within the <META> tag.

client side: Client side means that the web element or effect can run locally off a computer and does not require the presence of a server.

client-side imagemap: A client-side imagemap is programmed in HTML, and does not require a separate map definition file or to be stored on a live web server.

CLUT: Color LookUp Table. An 8-bit or lower image file uses a CLUT to define its palette.

color mapping: A color map refers to the color palette of an image. Color mapping means assigning colors to an image.

color names: Some browsers support using the name of a color instead of the color's hexadecimal value.

complementary colors: Created from opposing color hues on the color wheel.

compression: Reduction of the amount of data required to re-create an original file, graphic, or movie. Compression is used to reduce the transmission time of media and application files across the web.

contrast: The degrees of separation between values.

counter: Counts and displays the numbers of hits on a web page.

data rate: Data rate relates to how fast movie data was captured.

data streaming: The capability to deliver time-based data as it's requested, much like a VCR, rather than having to download all the information before it can be played.

dithering: The positioning of different-colored pixels within an image that uses a 256-color palette to simulate a color that does not exist in the palette. A dithered image often looks noisy, or composed of scattered pixels. See adaptive dithering.

dpi: Dot Per Inch. A term used mostly by print graphics-based programs and professionals, and is a common measurement related to the resolution of an image. See screen resolution.

extension: Abbreviated code at the end of a file that tells the browser what kind of file it's looking at. For example, a JPEG file would have the extension .jpg.

fixed palette: An established palette that is fixed. When a fixed palette web browser views images, it will convert images to its colors and not use the colors from the original.

forms processing: Forms that enable users to enter information on web pages are created by using HTML and CGI, and their function is typically referred to as forms processing.

fps: Frames Per Second. A movie contains a certain number of frames, and the fewer frames, the more jerky the motion and the smaller the file size.

frames: Frames offer the ability to divide a web page into multiple regions, with each region acting as a nested web page.

ftp: File Transfer Protocol. An Internet protocol that enables users to remotely access files on other computers. An ftp site houses files that can be downloaded to your computer.

gamma: Gamma measures the contrast that affects the midtones of an image. Adjusting the gamma lets you change the brightness values of the middle range of gray tones without dramatically altering the shadows and highlights.

gamut: A viewable or printable color range.

GIF: A bitmapped color graphics file format. GIF is commonly used on the web because it employs an efficient compression method. See JPEG.

GIF89a: A type of GIF file that supports transparency and multi-blocks. Multi-blocks create the illusion of animation. GIF89a files are sometimes referred to as "transparent GIFs" or "animated GIFs."

group: A VRML term. Grouping objects enables collections of objects to be treated as single objects. The group is a container for all the objects so that nodes can be applied to multiple objects. If an object has two colors, chances are it has two groups.

guestbook: A type of form that enables end users to enter comments on a web page.

hexadecimal: A base 16 mathematics calculation, often used in scripts and code. Hexadecimal code is required by HTML to describe RGB values of color for the web.

HTML: HyperText Markup Language. The common language for interchange of hypertext between the World Wide Web client and server. Web pages must be written using HTML. See hypertext.

HTTP: HyperText Transfer Protocol is the protocol that the browser and the web server use to communicate with each other.

hue: Defines a linear spectrum of the color wheel.

hybrid-safe colors: Pre-mixed, interlaced browser-safe colors that give the illusion of colors outside the 216 safe spectrum but are still browser safe.

hypertext: Text formatted with lines that enable the reader to jump among related topics. See HTML.

imagemaps: Portions of images that are hypertext links. Using a mouse-based web client such as Netscape or Mosaic, the user clicks on different parts of a mapped image to activate different hypertext links. See hypertext.

inline graphic: A graphic that sits inside an HTML document instead of the alternative, which would require that the image be downloaded and then viewed by using an outside system.

inlining: The process of embedding one VRML file into another.

interlaced GIFs: The GIF file format allows for "interlacing," which causes the GIF to load quickly at low or chunky resolution and then come into full or crisp resolution.

ISP: Acronym for Internet Service Provider.

Java: A programming language developed by Sun Microsystems that is cross-platform compatible and supported by some web browsers.

JavaScript: A scripting language that enables you to extend the capabilities of HTML. Developed by Netscape.

JPEG: Acronym for Joint Photographic Experts Group, but commonly used to refer to a lossy compression technique that can reduce the size of a graphics file by as much as 96 percent. See GIF.

lighting: 3D artwork responds to lighting in a realistic manner, so lighting will affect overall appearance and color.

links: Emphasized words in a hypertext document that act as pointers to more information on that specific subject. Links are generally underlined and may appear in a different color. When you click on a link, you can be transported to a different web site that contains information about the work or phrase used as the link. See hypertext.

lossless compression: A data compression technique that reduces the size of a file without sacrificing any of the original data. In lossless compression, the expanded or restored file is an exact replica of the original file before it was compressed. See compression.

lossy compression: A data compression technique in which some data is deliberately discarded in order to achieve massive reductions in the size of the compressed file.

mask: The process of blocking out areas in a computer graphic.

MIME: Multipurpose Internet Mail Extensions. An Internet standard for transferring nontext-based data such as sounds, movies, and images.

moiré: A pattern that results when dots overlap. This problem often occurs when scanning printed materials.

MPEG: MPEG audio is a high-quality audio compression file format.

μ-law: μ-law is a sound file format rendered by Unix platforms. The sound quality is generally much lower than other sound formats, but the files are much smaller, too.

object-oriented graphics: A graphic image composed of objects such as lines, circles, ellipses, and boxes that can be moved independently. This type of graphic is used for print-based design because it can be printed at a higher resolution than a computer screen. See bitmapped graphics.

object resolution: Relates to how many polygons form a shape. High object resolution includes many polygons, looks the best, and takes the longest to render. Low-resolution objects have fewer polygons and render faster.

passive navigation: Animation, slide shows, streaming movies, and audio. Basically anything that plays without the end user initiating the content.

plug-in: Plug-ins are supported by some browsers, and extend the capability of standard HTML. They need to be installed in the end user's plug-in folder, found inside the browser software folder.

PNG: An acronym for Portable Network Graphics. PNG is a lossless file format that supports interlacing, 8-bit transparency, and gamma information.

PostScript: A sophisticated page description language used for printing high-quality text and graphics on laser printers and other high-resolution printing devices.

primary colors: The theory behind primary colors is that these colors are the starting point from which any other colors can be mixed. On the computer, the primary colors are red, green, and blue because color mixing is additive (created with light). With pigment the primary colors are red, blue, and yellow because color mixing is subtractive.

progressive JPEG: A type of JPEG that produces an interlaced effect as it loads and can be 30 percent smaller than standard JPEGs. It is not currently supported by many web browsers.

provider: Provides Internet access. See ISP.

quick mask: A Photoshop technique for making masks. See mask.

QuickTime: System software developed by Apple Computer for presentation of desktop video.

render: The computer process of calculating 3D data and displaying the results on the computer screen.

rollover: A type of navigation button that changes when the end user's mouse rolls over it.

sample rates: Sample rates are measured in kilohertz (KHz). Sound-editing software is where the initial sample rate settings are established. Standard sample rates range from 11.025 KHz, 22.050 KHz, 44.10 KHz, to 48 KHz. The higher the sample rate, the better the quality. The sample describes its highs and lows.

sampling resolution: Sampling resolution affects quality, just like dpi resolution affects the quality of images. Standard sampling resolutions are 8-bit mono, 8-bit stereo, 16-bit mono, and 16-bit stereo.

saturation: Defines the intensity of color.

screen resolution: Screen resolution generally refers to the resolution of common computer monitors. 72 dpi is an agreed upon average, although you will also hear of 96 dpi being the resolution of larger displays.

search engine: A type of application, commonly found on the web, that enables you to search by keywords for information or URLs.

server: A computer that provides services for users of its network. The server receives requests for services and manages the requests so that they are answered in an orderly manner. See client.

server push: Server push is the method of requesting images or data from the server and automating their playback. It involves CGI and the presence of a live web server.

server side: Server side means any type of web page element that depends on being loaded to a server. It also implies the use of a CGI script.

server-side imagemap: A server-side imagemap requires that the information about the imagemap be saved within a "map definition file" that needs to be stored on a server and accessed by a CGI script.

splash screen: A main menu screen or opening graphic to a web page.

sprite: An individual component of an animation, such as a character or graphic that moves independently.

tables: Tables create rows and columns, as in a spread-sheet, and can be used to align data and images.

tag: ASCII text indicators with which you surround text and images to designate certain formats or styles.

texture map: 2D artwork that is applied to the surface of a 3D shape.

transparent GIFs: A superset of the original GIF file format that adds header information to the GIF file, which signifies that a defined color will be masked out.

true color: The quality of color provided by 24-bit color depth. 24-bit color depth results in 16.7 million colors, which is usually more than adequate for the human eye.

URL: Uniform Resource Locator. The address for a web site.

value: The range from light to dark in an image.

Video for Windows: A multimedia architecture and application suite that provides an outbound architecture that lets applications developers access audio, video, and animation from many different sources through one inter-face. As an application, Video for Windows primarily handles video capture and compression, and video and audio editing. See AVI.

WYSIWYG: Pronounced wizzy-wig. A design philoso-phy in which formatting commands directly affect the text displayed on-screen so that the screen shows the appear-ance of printed text.

BROWSER SAFE COLOR

33FF

0033CC

Width = "500"

<STRONG>

Height = "600"

IMAGE OPTIMIZATION

colors

<H1>

<TABL

<img src=

Imaging techniques

Web File Formats

bgcolor = "FFFFCC"

Animation, sound and

alink = "cyan"

LYNDA.COM

33

<BODY>

www.Design

Design Resources

Design Conferences

American Center for Design
■ http://www.ac4d.org

Web Design and Development
■ http://www.web97.com/

International Design Conference
■ http://www.idca.org

TED
■ http://www.ted.com/

MacWorld Expo
■ http://www.mha.com

Seybold
■ http://www.sbexpos.com/

SIGGRAPH
■ http://www.siggraph.org

Web Design Classes

Naugatuck Valley Community Technical College
■ http://www.leonline.com/nvctc/

Project Cool
■ http://www.projectcool.com

Duquesne University
■ http://the-duke.duq-duke.duq.edu/commhome.htm

EEI Communications
■ http://www.eei-alex.com/training/

San Francisco State Multimedia Studies Program
■ http://msp.sfsu.edu

Parsons School of Design
■ http://www.parsons.edu/

School of Visual Arts
■ http://www.sva.edu/

Art Center College of Design
■ http://www.artcenter.edu

Rhode Island School of Design
■ http://www.risd.edu/

American Institute of Graphic Arts
- http://www.dol.com/AIGA/

DGEF
(Dynamic Graphics Educational Foundation)
- http://199.224.94.160/DGEF/

Interactive Telecommunications Program
- http://www.itp.tsoa.nyu.edu/

Graphics Artists Guild
- http://www.gag.com

Magazines

Adobe Magazine
- http://www.adobemag.com

Communication Arts
- http://www.commarts.com

Digital Video Magazine Online
- http://www.zdent.com/~ziffnet/cis/

Dynamic Graphics Magazine
- http://199.224.94.160/DGEF/Dynamic/

Web Review
- http://www.webreview.com/

Web Week
- www.webweek.com

DT&G Magazine
- http://www.Graphic-Design.com

Review
- http://www.itp.tsoa.nyu.edu/~review/

I.D.® Magazine
- IDMAG@aol.com

Step-By-Step Magazine
- CompuServe 74431,2241

Miscellaneous

Suzanne Stephen's Web Design Source List
- http://www.opendoor.com/StephensDesign/
URLs/index.htm

Lynda's Homegurrrl Web Design List
- http://www.webmonster.net/lists/

Web Reference
- http://www.webreference.com

BROWSER SAFE COLORS

33FF

Web safe typography

Photoshop

0033

INDEX

Width ="500"

<STRONG>

.gif

.jpg

Png

IMAGE OPTIMIZATION

limited palettes

256 colors

</A>

Height ="600

<center>

Imaging techniques

Extending HTML

Web file formats

bgcolor="FFFFCC"

Animation, sound and

@link="cyan"

LYNDA.COM

BODY

Arial

www. Design

Index

S

<deconstructing web graphics>
Web Design Case Studies and Tutorials

Deconstructing Web Graphics profiles top web designers and programmers in order to demystify and analyze how they make decisions, solve complex issues, and create exceptional web sites. Adding her own voice and digital design teaching experience to the book, best-selling author Lynda Weinman selects from her list of favorite designed web sites. She walks you through how to read and understand the source code for each page, breaks down all of the technical elements, and describes the inside details straight from the designers and programmers who created the pages.

This conversational and information-rich guide offers insight into web design that is not found through any other means. Profiles of successful web designers, programmers, photographers, and illustrators allows them to share their tips, techniques, and recommendations. You'll bring your own web design skills to a higher level through studying their experiences and the step-by-step tutorials and examples found in *Deconstructing Web Graphics*.

This book is for you, if you want to learn about:

- Low-bandwidth graphics
- Scanned imagery for the web
- Colors that work across platforms and browsers
- Custom Photoshop brushes and patterns
- Artwork using ASCII
- Copyright issues
- Animated GIFs
- LOWSRC animation tricks
- Tables for alignment
- Invisible GIFs for spacers
- Frames for navigation
- HTML tricks and workarounds
- Java
- JavaScript
- CGI
- Forms processing
- Server push
- Client pull
- Shockwave and Macromedia Director
- Sound and video files
- VRML

Product and Sales Information

Deconstructing Web Graphics By Lynda Weinman
ISBN:1-56205-641-7 ▪ $44.99/USA ▪ 235 pages
Available at your local bookstore or online
Macmillan Publishing ▪ 1-800-428-5331
- http://www.mcp.com/newriders

▪ http://www.lynda.com

Stop by and visit the author's up-to-date web site—read sample chapters, browse her list of web design resources, or join her mailing list-based discussion group that focuses on web design issues.

Author Biography

Lynda Weinman has authored a series of best-selling, full-color books about web graphics and design for New Riders Publishing. She has taught digital imaging, animation, multimedia and web design at Art Center College of Design, American Film Institute, and UCLA. Weinman is a featured columnist on digital graphics, animation, and the web for *New Media*, *Digital Video*, *Mac User*, *Mac Week*, *The Net*, *Step-by-Step Graphics*, *Macromedia User's Journal*, and *Full-Motion Video* magazines.

<coloring web graphics>
Master Color and Image File Formats for the Web

Written by Lynda Weinman and Bruce Heavin, this book features practical, accessible, and down-to-earth advice that will help you greatly expand your color web graphic design skills. The purpose of this book is to help artists, programmers, and hobbyists understand how to work with color and image file formats for web delivery. Artwork that looks good in print or on screen can easily end up looking terrible in a web browser. Web browsers and different operating systems handle color in specific ways that many web designers aren't aware of. *Coloring Web Graphics* offers in-depth answers about color, from both an aesthetic and technical perspective, and details what design constraints exist on the web and how to work around them.

A color palette of 216 browser-safe colors is identified and organized to help web designers confidently select successful cross-platform color choices and combinations. The book includes sections on color theory and understanding web color file formats as well as step-by-step tutorials that explain how to work with browser-safe colors in Photoshop, Paint Shop Pro, Photo-Paint, Painter, FreeHand, and Illustrator. The cross-platform CD-ROM includes hundreds of suggested color combinations for web page design, as well as hundreds of palettes and browser-safe clip art files.

In this book, you'll learn to:

- Create colors in your artwork that won't shift or dither across multiple platforms
- Choose web-appropriate color schemes for your page designs
- Create thousands of browser-safe hybrid variations
- Use Photoshop, Paint Shop Pro, Photo-Paint, FreeHand, Illustrator, and Director to manage web-specific color

The cross-platform CD-ROM includes:

- Browser-safe color palettes
- Browser-safe color swatches for Photoshop and other imaging programs
- Browser-safe colors organized by hue, value, and saturation
- Browser-safe color clip art for web use
- Electronic versions of color swatches grouped as they are in the book
- Sample HTML pages with recommended color groupings
- Sample patterns, backgrounds, buttons, and rules

Product and Sales Information

Coloring Web Graphics By Lynda Weinman and Bruce Heavin
ISBN:1-56205-669-7 ▪ $50.00/USA ▪ 258 pages (+CD-ROM)
Available at your local bookstore or online
Macmillan Publishing ▪ 1-800-428-5331
- http://www.mcp.com/newriders

Stop by and visit the author's up-to-date web site—read sample chapters, browse her list of Web design resources, or join her mailing list-based discussion group that focuses on web design issues. ▪ http://www.lynda.com

Authors' Biographies

Lynda Weinman has authored a series of best-selling, full-color books about web graphics and design for New Riders Publishing. Lynda has taught and written about web design, interactive multimedia, motion graphics, and digital imaging for numerous universities and publications.

Bruce Heavin is an acclaimed painter and illustrator whose mastery of color theory is evident in all of his work. He has created artwork for clients that include Adobe, E! Entertainment Television, and has also painted the distinctive covers of all of Lynda's web design books.

THE AMAZING PHIL

MW01257570

HORNBLOWER NIAGARA CRUISES
0026060520161246230903537

Aduit Voyage to the Faiis

Boats Depart Every 30 Minutes in Season

Node26   Receipt:3190
SEE REVERSE FOR
TERMS & CONDITIONS   5/6/2016

A

CHICAGO ARCHITECTURE
FOUNDATION
RIVER CRUIS
ABOARD CHICAGO'S
FIRST LADY CRUISES

Chicago.

AQUARIUM OF CANADA

VALID UNTIL:
May 09 2017

AT ANYTIME

Anytime Adult

GOOD FOR

1DAF_Granny
What is your favourite
song stored on your
brain's hard drive?

2083

DIL

AMAZING
TOUR IS NOT
ON FIRE

What
say

DAN AND PHIL GO OUTSIDE

Dan Howell **&** *Phil Lester*

Random House 🏠 New York

With special thanks to Mark Forrer, Fleur Brooklin-Smith, Marianne Turton, Anna Johnstone, Matt Kaunitz,
Ed Stambollouian, Chris Hewitt, Martyn Lester, Cornelia Dahlgren, Juliet Kozlow, Lauren Koontz, Cat Valdes,
Tara McMullen, Showtime Photo Booth, PhotoWorks Interactive, istockphoto, and Getty Images

Visit us on the Web! randomhouseteens.com

Educators and librarians, for a variety of teaching tools, visit us at RHTeachersLibrarians.com

Library of Congress Cataloging-in-Publication Data is available upon request.

ISBN 978-1-5247-0145-1 (trade) — ISBN 978-1-5247-0146-8 (ebook)

Design: Dave Brown at Ape. apeinc.co.uk

Printed in the United States of America

10 9 8 7 6 5 4 3 2 1
First American Edition

INTRODUCTION

The Amazing Tour Is Not on Fire! Not the best name in my opinion.

What do you mean, Dan? It's a great name! One thing was The Amazing Book Is Not on Fire, and this was the tour. It made perfect sense.

Yeah but 'tour' was confusing. What were we touring? The book? A Q&A? Maybe it should have been 'show' or 'theatrical extravaganza that's really good and was loads of effort'.

You mean TATETRGAWLOEINOF?

Okay, fine. So we did it. Dan and Phil actually went outside.

We released our book, hopped in a car to go on tour and didn't stop until we did a lap of the world!

And, somehow, we survived to tell the story.

I think we mainly survived by ordering pancakes for breakfast at every hotel. So why did we make this, Dan?

Well, physical objects are important to me; I need something to caress, as I silently weep, pondering my regrets. So *TATINOF* definitely deserved a monument of its own.

Throughout our journey we've had so many incredible adventures, and have made so many memories with everyone, that we decided we should seal them forever in a photo book!

I mean I doubt I'll ever leave the house again after this, so we need some proof that it happened.

We've captured everything: before the tour began, all through its life, and beyond!

All the way into the afterlife, where Larry the Llama and Phil's giant lion dance with Jesus in heaven.

So drink something sugary to get you 'fricking zazzed' and open your eyes wide, as you're about to witness the tale of how Dan and Phil go outside.

Wow, was that rhyme intentional?

BEFORE THE TOUR

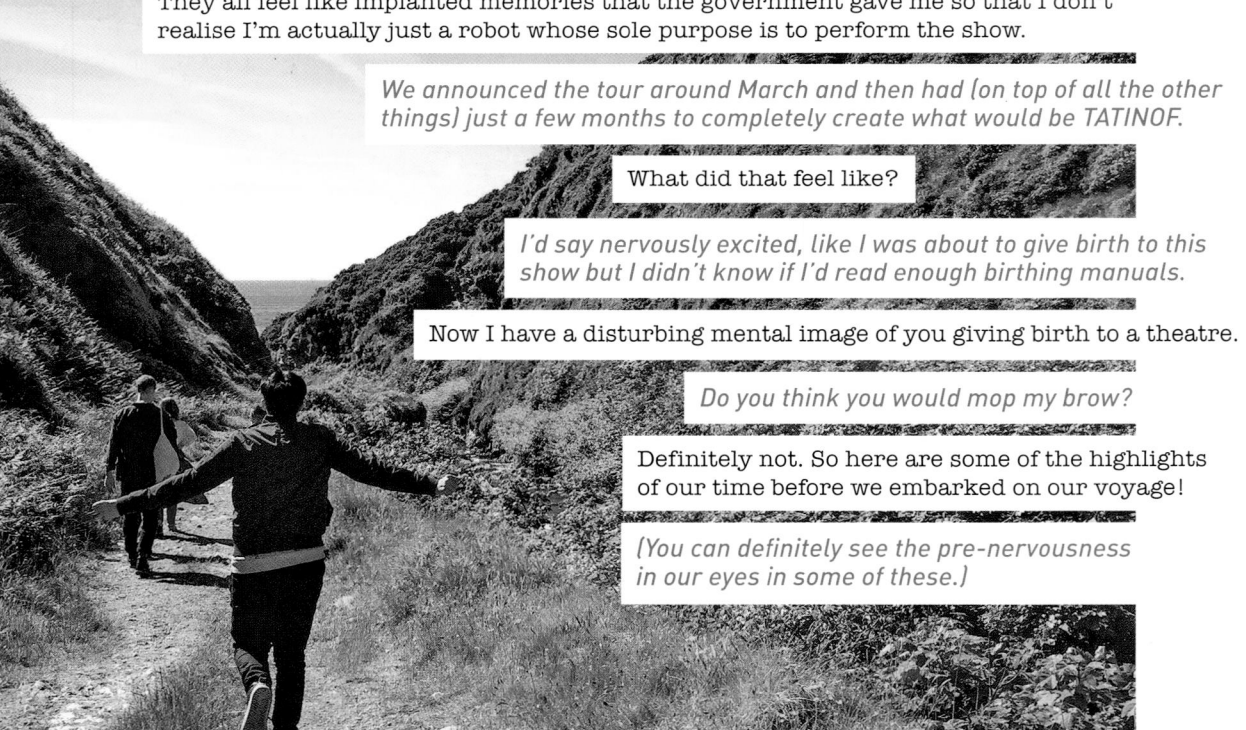

Life before the tour. I don't really remember what that was like...

They all feel like implanted memories that the government gave me so that I don't realise I'm actually just a robot whose sole purpose is to perform the show.

We announced the tour around March and then had (on top of all the other things) just a few months to completely create what would be TATINOF.

What did that feel like?

I'd say nervously excited, like I was about to give birth to this show but I didn't know if I'd read enough birthing manuals.

Now I have a disturbing mental image of you giving birth to a theatre.

Do you think you would mop my brow?

Definitely not. So here are some of the highlights of our time before we embarked on our voyage!

(You can definitely see the pre-nervousness in our eyes in some of these.)

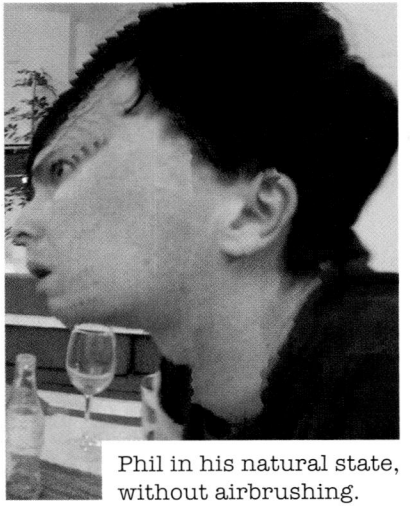

Phil in his natural state, without airbrushing.

I CAN'T BELIEVE YOU INCLUDED THIS!

It's a beautiful photo, Phil.

Speak to my lawyer.

We were the only Muggles in Diagon Alley that were the same size as Hagrid.

Living life on the edge.

This is why there's so many .GIFS of you falling off chairs – don't try this at home.

Relaxing, while keeping an eye on giant insects in Crete.

Lol.

Is this your revenge for the other photo?

Yes.

Trying out a new hairstyle.

You look particularly doge-esque in this photo.

Festive selfie with Colin.

Deck the halls with thousands of chocolatey snacks.

Me pretending to pee in the highest urinal in London!

Thanks for clarifying that you were pretending.

Recording our audiobook for *TABINOF!*

BOOKCEPTION.

Moments later he was mauled by a colossal squid!

I told you to stop watching weird anime.

UK REHE ARSAL

SO, WE HAD TO MAKE A STAGE SHOW.

AND WE HAD ABOUT A MONTH!

I'm going to have a heart attack just remembering it.

How was it even possible?

It really shouldn't have been. Luckily we'd been talking about what The Dan and Phil Stage Show would be for years, so we had a heap of ideas!

Then we took those ideas and dropped them in a pile on our director, Ed, and we got a show!

Kind of, yeah.

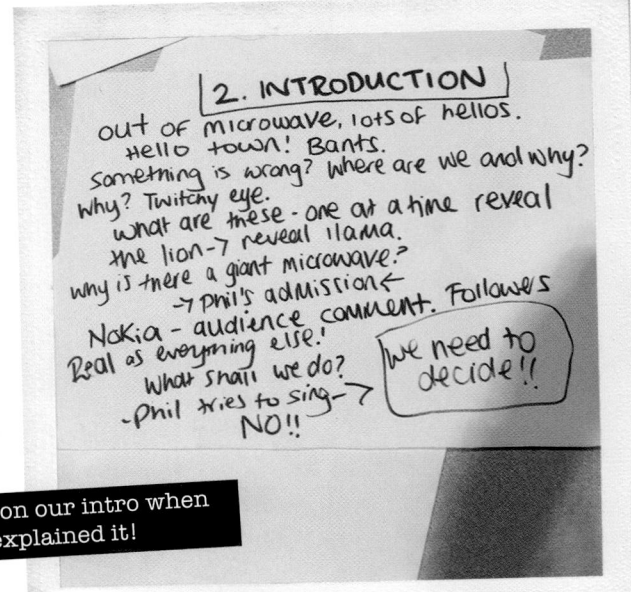

2. INTRODUCTION

out of microwave, lots of hellos.
Hello town! Bants.
Something is wrong? Where are we and why?
Why? Twitchy eye.
what are these - one at a time reveal
the lion → reveal llama.
why is there a giant microwave?
→ Phil's admission ←
Nokia - audience comment. Followers
Real as everything else!
what shall we do?
- Phil tries to sing →
NO!!
we need to decide!!

Ed's notes on our intro when we first explained it!

8

Sitting with Composer Jimmy trying to think of words that rhyme with 'internet' and 'great'.

It was so cold! I actually got sick because it was so cold that we could see our breath as we talked.

It may have been freezing, with questionable lunch options and a toilet full of spiders, but it had a classic aesthetic and good reverb for writing the song, which was all we needed.

The place we all congregated and birthed *TATINOF* was, quite appropriately, an abandoned church.

Dil practising his walk through the crowds, a prophecy?

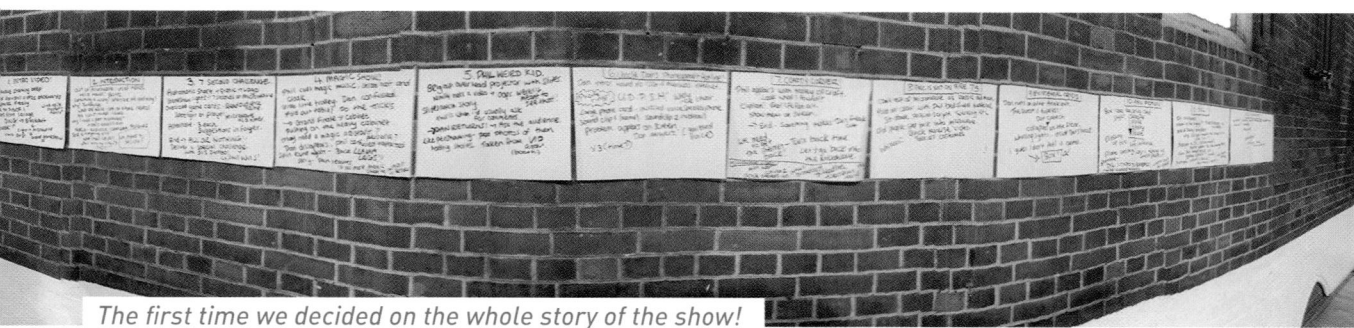

The first time we decided on the whole story of the show!

What a glorious mess all in a line. It makes perfect sense, doesn't it?

It was a strange time, as the whole show was just us walking around imagining it all, until the set and the props were made.

When we were shown little things like the llama legs, the giant question-mark cube and the magic, I got tingly feelings!

Do you remember how you felt seeing the set for the first time?

Honestly, I think I just stared, with my mouth open, for ten minutes not believing that we were responsible for something so awesome-looking.

Nadia looking snazzy in the first attempt at llama legs for Dan!

My first ever custom clothes fitting! And it was for these.

Our dance choreographer telling us to hold the hats with more pizzazz.

Dan's first ride on Larry.

After a solid month of practising the show,
non-stop all day for 10 hours, we were ready.

*We packed our bags and headed up north to
Scotland for our first ever show. TATINOF BEGAN!*

BUILDING THE SET!

Whenever someone we know sees the TATINOF set for the first time, their mind is blown.

I mean, it is literally a giant, pixel-exploding microwave covered in images, with a giant lion and llama on either side of it.

Don't forget the two houseplants!

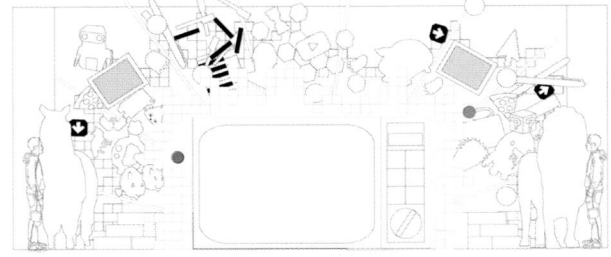

When we gave our ideas to James, the set designer, we did not appreciate just what a feat it would be to create, and how insane and incredible it would be!

SETTING UP THE SET

Every show day, after waking up at midday and enjoying a slow laptop browse, we'd waddle into the theatre to see our set fully erected!

Did you have to say fully? Yes, as if by magic, our huge and elaborate set, with its hundreds of pieces, was all in place and ready for us to scratch.

That magic was actually our crew, who woke up at 6am every morning to stitch it together by hand, before taking it apart and shoving it in a truck again at night.

Now we know why they got through so many donuts and a lot of coffee!

ON THE ROAD-UK

Touring the UK meant a lot of driving on winding roads. Whoever built the roads in the UK was obviously trying to win the bendiest road contest.

It was a true test of my stomach! Everyone was happily using their laptops and phones, while I had my face pressed against the window for most of the journeys. My travel sickness was ridiculous!

I've never seen you so green. It was like you were trying to dethrone me from my swamp.

Thankfully, my trusty zebra neck pillow helped out a lot and I made it to every venue without throwing up on Dan.

Do you want a medal?

Kind of, yes.

Look out for animal-print neck braces on the catwalk in 2018.

We are always ahead of the trends, Danny.

Phil during one of the rare moments he wasn't quietly being sick in his mouth.

Despite being barf-worthy, the travel was pretty beautiful! Especially when we were going into Scotland!

Dan regaling us with a story about a freshly discovered meme.

I want to play the bagpipes and live in Loch Ness! It was like an ancient fairy tale, except the townspeople throw cans of Irn Bru at you and say you look like Justin Bieber.

Guess which two photos I took and which two Phil took.

Hey! It's a beautiful blur that is, in fact, a metaphor for our fast-paced journey around the world.

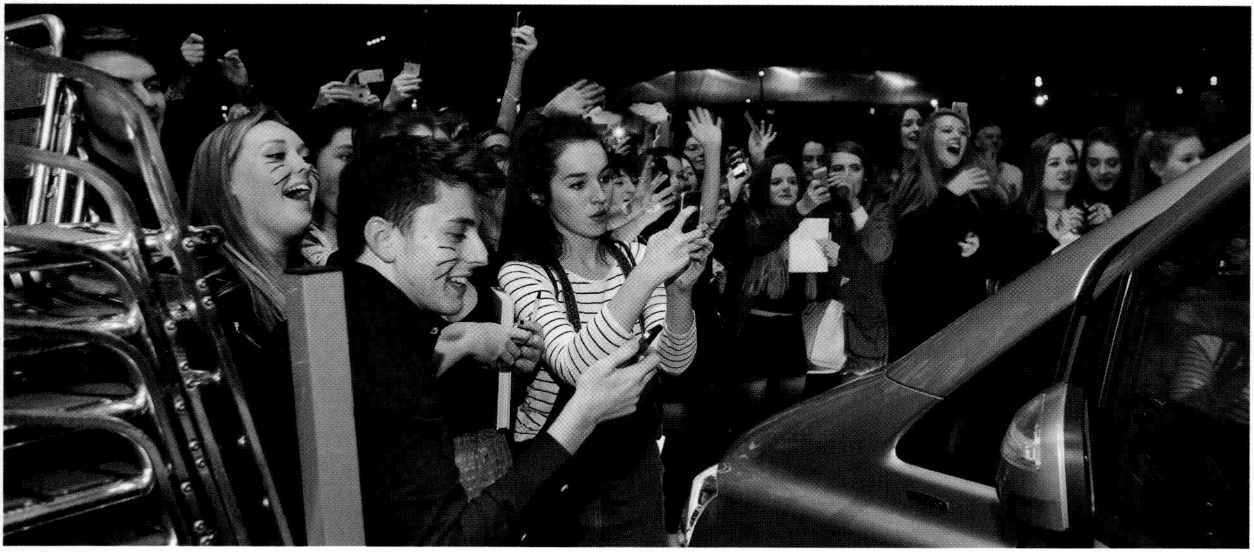

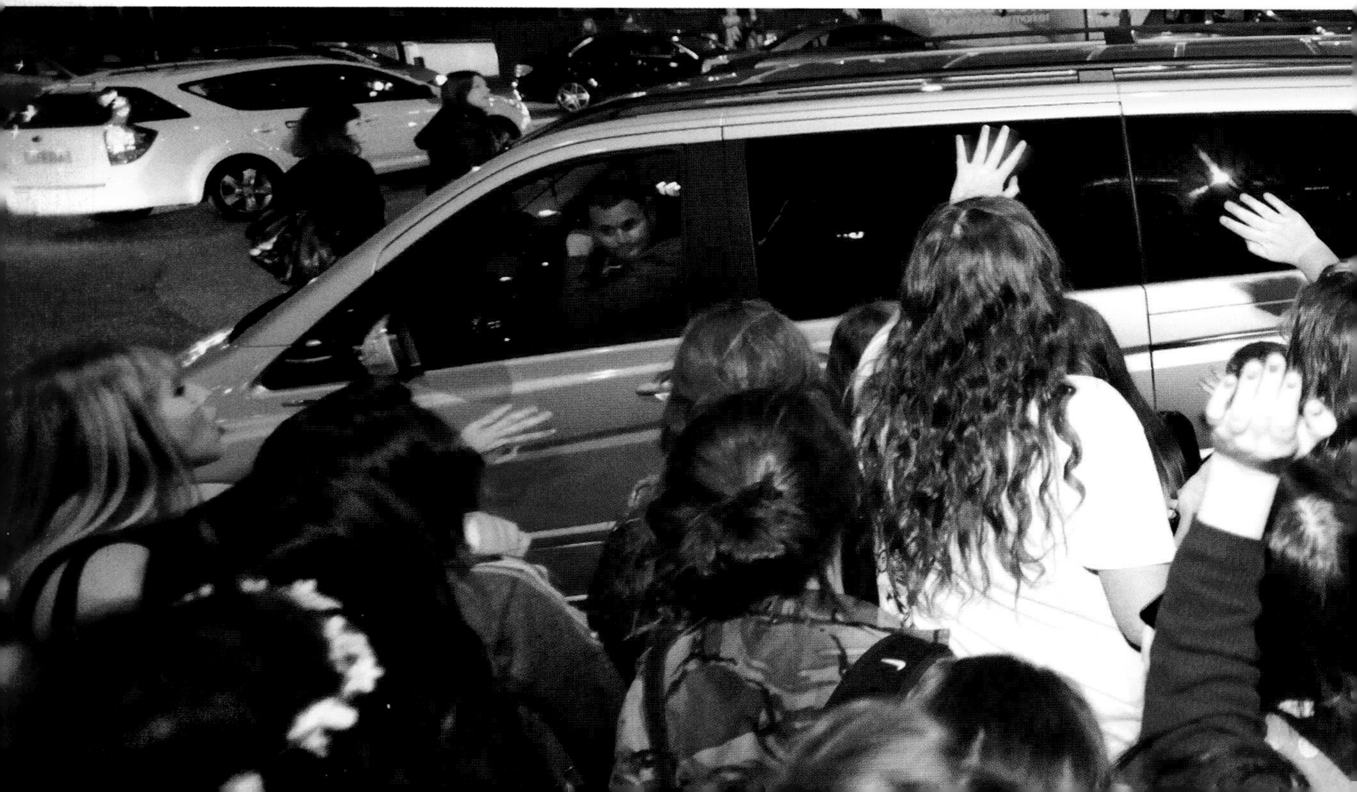

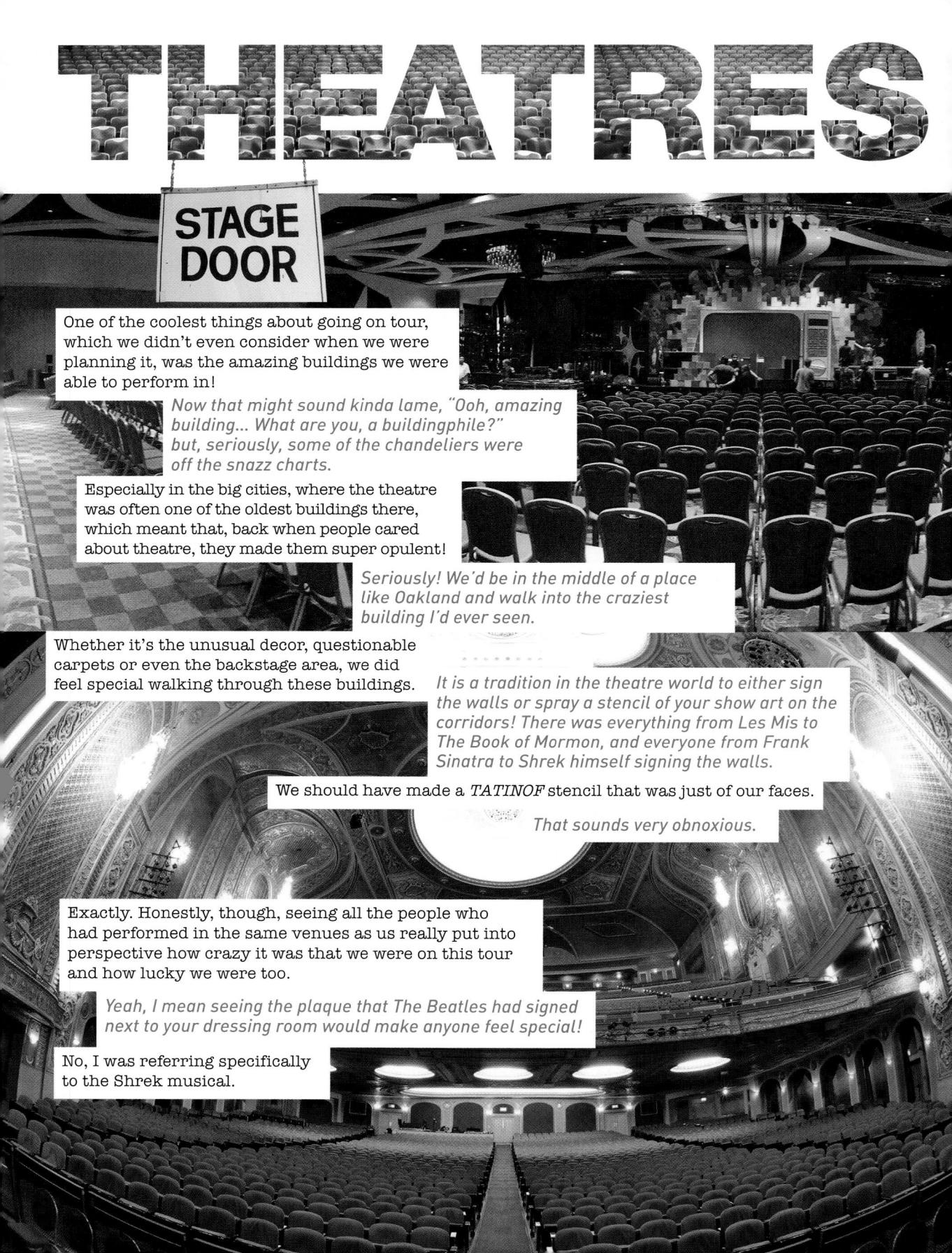

THEATRES

STAGE DOOR

One of the coolest things about going on tour, which we didn't even consider when we were planning it, was the amazing buildings we were able to perform in!

Now that might sound kinda lame, "Ooh, amazing building... What are you, a buildingphile?" but, seriously, some of the chandeliers were off the snazz charts.

Especially in the big cities, where the theatre was often one of the oldest buildings there, which meant that, back when people cared about theatre, they made them super opulent!

Seriously! We'd be in the middle of a place like Oakland and walk into the craziest building I'd ever seen.

Whether it's the unusual decor, questionable carpets or even the backstage area, we did feel special walking through these buildings.

It is a tradition in the theatre world to either sign the walls or spray a stencil of your show art on the corridors! There was everything from Les Mis to The Book of Mormon, and everyone from Frank Sinatra to Shrek himself signing the walls.

We should have made a *TATINOF* stencil that was just of our faces.

That sounds very obnoxious.

Exactly. Honestly, though, seeing all the people who had performed in the same venues as us really put into perspective how crazy it was that we were on this tour and how lucky we were too.

Yeah, I mean seeing the plaque that The Beatles had signed next to your dressing room would make anyone feel special!

No, I was referring specifically to the Shrek musical.

Generic marble aesthetic.

A beautiful gilded sculpture of me.

Again, we use our height to our advantage!

Philadelphia had a 'ghost light', which they say they keep on to ward off the spirits that haunt the theatre!

I thought, 'Wow! Really? That's a waste of energy!' until they pointed out that it also stops people from walking off the stage if they are working at night.

I could have used that in Florida...

Bow down to King Lester!

The terrifying dystopian AU none of us want to live in.

SHOW DAY

IT'S SHOW DAY.

The day begins waking up on the bus, freshly
shaken from a night of not hitting deer.

*We slam a couple of bowls of the good sugary stuff and strut
into the theatre like we're temporarily renting the place.*

We mark our territory in the dressing room and stride
confidently on to the stage, where we check our sound
(in what is commonly referred to as 'sound check').

*We then have our team of surgeons carefully apply
our 'interaction faces' and proceed to the meet up.*

After mingling with the peasantry, we decide whose
fates we will seal on the stage by choosing the
challenges, crafts, Weird Kid stories and questions
found by the crew.

*Next, cement is mixed with Earth's finest sand
and carefully scraped around our faces to
form our stage makeup.*

Then we get the microphones inserted
into us like puppets.

*And it's show time! We strut out
with a swagger and do our thang.*

34

The time we watched *Game of Thrones* on our giant microwave screen using the theatre speakers.

Now that's a home cinema!

"Please put that down immediately."

A 'Weird Kid' preparing to be inserted into the 'window of shame'.

Happy birthday to the Meme Queen.

Looks like our sound guy, Chris, hit the spot!

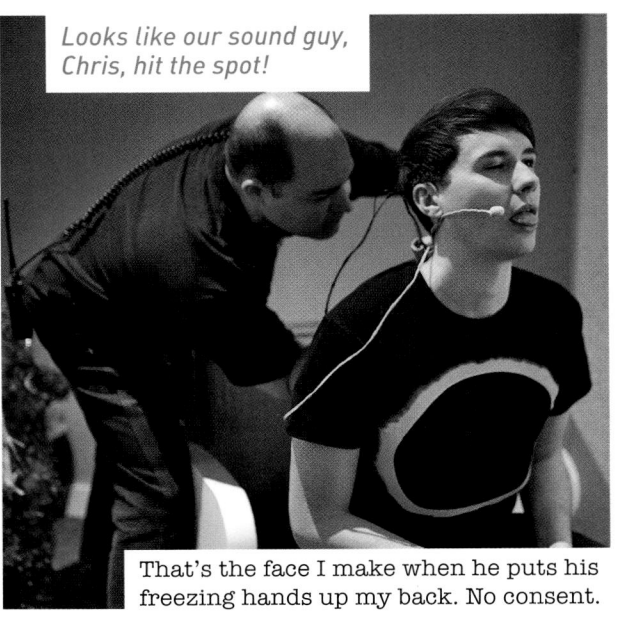

That's the face I make when he puts his freezing hands up my back. No consent.

Phil deciding what humiliating form of suffering he will publicly subject me to in the 7 Second Challenge.

I wonder what that mum was asking Dan.

Hey, how do you know she's a mum? Might just be an older follower, if you know what I'm saying.

Dan, stop winking.

A question being recorded for 'Uncle Dan's Phone Support Hotline'!

Wait, is that?

Yup. Didn't use it in the show, funnily enough.

MEETING OUR AUDIENCE

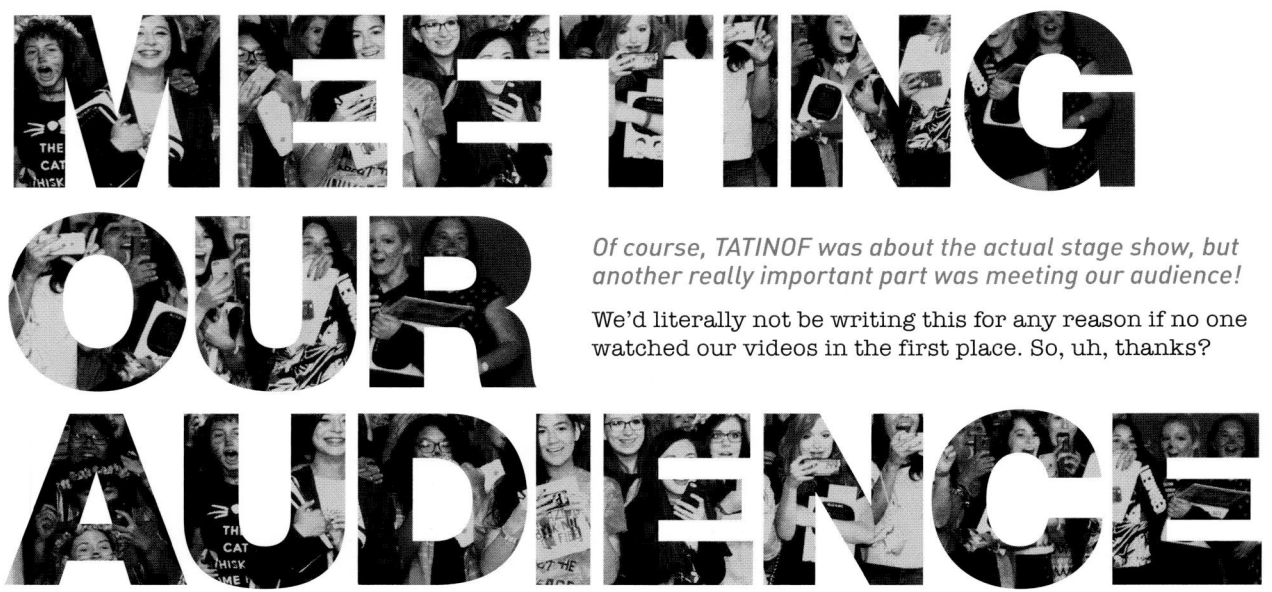

Of course, TATINOF was about the actual stage show, but another really important part was meeting our audience!

We'd literally not be writing this for any reason if no one watched our videos in the first place. So, uh, thanks?

Internet audiences are weird because, even though you see that you have however many followers on a website, it's hard to think that they are all individual people! When a video has views, that is a real person that has actually sat down and watched what we've made. I kind of don't understand that part.

It's surreal, as there are very few moments that actually make what we do seem 'real'. YouTube is very 'in your head', as you are imagining an audience out there laughing and commenting, but because you don't actually see the real people emoting, it just stays in your head. That can be kind of hard sometimes, as I tell you now the positive reinforcement of a million people laughing would probably be really helpful. That's why we love it so much whenever we do a show or go to a convention and get to meet our audience!

Hearing the stories people have to tell us about who they are, how they discovered our videos and how it made them feel is my favourite thing about being an 'entertainer'! I love that I started on YouTube as someone just wanting to join a community of weirdos talking to each other in videos, but by keeping it going as a creative hobby that I love, my 'job' is something that makes people happy!

Totally. Until I met my followers for the first time, YouTube was just fun. It was a creative expression, a game and a challenge to put myself out there and attempt to write funny videos. But when the first person told me that just watching these videos, which I had made, actually made them happy, it made what I do seem so much more valuable. After all, I often think that everything I make is trash and contemplate all the billions of people out there who agree, but if one person watching said 'trash' enjoys it, then what other validation do I need? Well, a lot, but it's a great start!

Another thing that I love is seeing how diverse our audience is. While it's mostly young people, we see a lot of parents, older siblings, children and even a couple of animals!

That dog has been the highlight of my entire life so far. You're right, though, the colours of TATINOF are really everything in the spectrum of light, never mind the rainbow. I think what it shows is that no matter your age, body, gender, sexuality, taste in music or opinions on whether or not the existence of anime is a crime against humanity that needs to be destroyed at all costs, you are all welcome to have a great time!

Seriously, though, getting into anime destroyed our productivity.

The moment of the meeting is quite funny and weird. Having done every event ever, and experiencing the best and worst ways of organising things ever, we thought it'd be nice to let people mingle in a room to chat, snack and listen to some music before we arrive.

Don't get Dan started on the VIP playlist.

Ah, yes, the other playlist! See, I had much more freedom when it came to energy levels and artists with this one–

–*Dan, please.*

Sorry.

We even left a guest book for people to sign, some of which we will include later on!

One of the coolest things we heard was that *TATINOF* was an opportunity for people to meet friends they'd had online for years. When I was a teen on the internet (5 billion years ago, haha kill me), websites like Twitter and Tumblr, which made it super easy for fandoms or just people that shared the same interest to converse en masse, didn't really exist, so I never had the internet friends that I so sorely needed back then!

Seriously, Dan had no friends.

Thanks. But, really, Phil and I being the connection that causes people to have a community or a friendship group that they can count on for laughs, companionship or just procrastination is something I appreciate, especially as an emo who silently cried into my MCR t-shirt after people threw rocks at me.

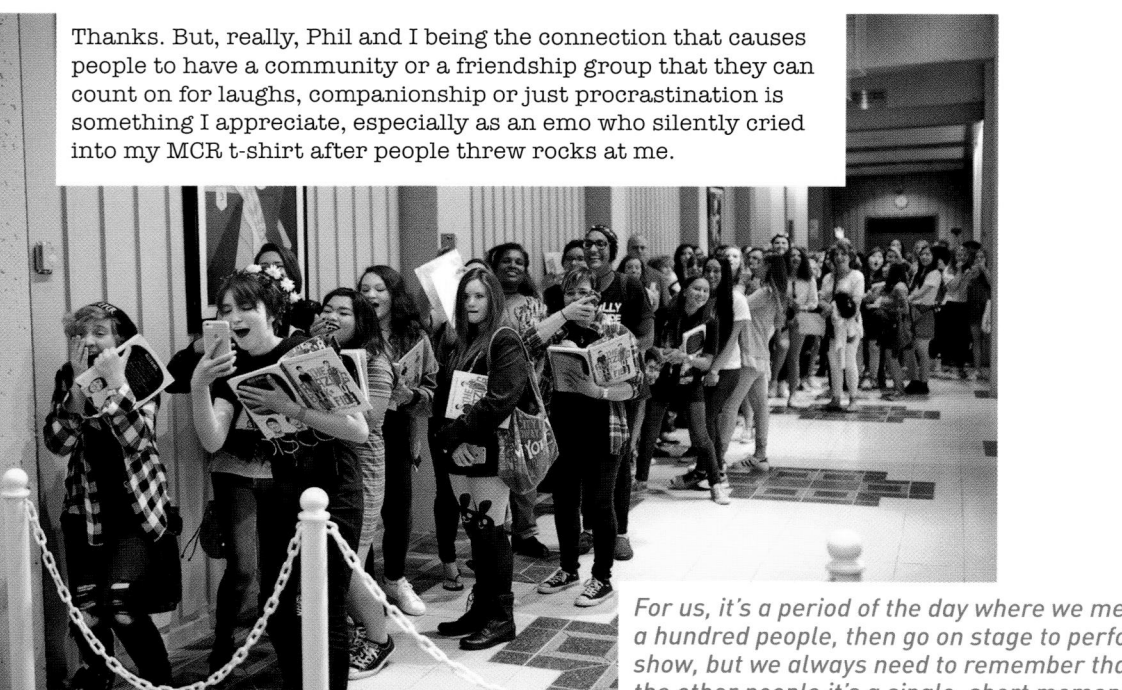

For us, it's a period of the day where we meet over a hundred people, then go on stage to perform the show, but we always need to remember that for the other people it's a single, short moment that they might have been looking forward to for ages!

Oh totally. It's completely normal to have a resting-face, or breathe, or yawn – even if you're having a great time – but we think it's so important to remember that, at that moment, we're there for them.

Usually my cheeks actually hurt from smiling for an hour. It's a great workout! How do your arms cope from holding all those phones up, Dan?

I think I have one Popeye arm from taking selfies, and one that's like a withering snake.

We try to have a unique conversation with everyone but we can't help the same things coming up.

You mean people being shocked and horrified at how obnoxiously tall we are?

Well, I wasn't going to put it like that, but yeah.

It's usually: "Dan, can you take the selfie? You have noodle arms." "Wow, this is as awkward as I thought it'd be!". And, "Sorry for stepping on your foot."

Don't forget the "You smell nice!"

That is true! People, it is important to smell nice, especially on days when you plan to hug hundreds of people.

I think Dan may be one of the best selfie takers of all time.

It's possible. I don't take selfies of myself that often (don't go outside, y'know), but the sheer amount of training I have accomplished on this tour means that I think I may be in the top one per cent of photo takers, alongside the Kardashians and the NSA.

People always ask why Dan takes all the photos...
I just don't know how to hold the phone.

Honestly, I have tried to train him, guys, but you don't understand. I say, "Hey, you put your middle finger and ring finger behind the phone, and then hold it steady with your forefinger and little finger, leaving your thumb free to focus and press the photo button!" What proceeds is like watching Quasimodo trying to break an egg on a rock.

You're an octopus, Dan, no one can do that. You're a freak of nature!

Well, there's phone-holding ability, then there's the dropping.

I can't believe you brought this up! Okay, fine. In the UK, someone specifically asked if I could take the selfie, so I obliged, tried to do the weird claw hand thing – and I dropped the phone.

You smashed the phone. You caused an actual screen crack on a shiny new phone.

I felt so bad! The person seemed to laugh and said, "That's so Phil," but I don't think they quite realised what I did. I dropped their baby!

And that, everybody, is why nobody lets Phil hold their actual babies.

Posing is another beast in its own right.

"Nah I don't want a selfie, can we do a pose?" No other words strike as much fear into my heart. What will it be? Charlie's Angels? Awkward Prom photo? High School Musical jumping? I'm just afraid to get it wrong!

When I first experienced this I was like, okay you want me to do this very specific thing? Do you know that I'm comfortable with this? I mean, I am, but do you think I'm just a doll for you to pose and objectify?! Then I thought, eh, who cares? I'm just standing in a certain way and making people laugh hysterically, so get over it. Ergo – I LOVE THE POSING, BRING IT ON!

Some of my favourites include the 'Sailor Moon Pose', dabbing and the girl that stood on our knees.

In the UK, a critical issue for the production of the tour quickly became the amounts of gifts people were giving us.

Now, when we say gifts, we don't mean in a gross way, like people were bestowing us with Gold, Frankincense and Myrrh. We mean just letters, drawings and the odd snack.

Mountains of chocolate, Phil. They nearly had to wheel us onto the stage in London.

After we'd read the letters, we actually had to buy a storage unit to keep them safe, as there is no storage in our apartment!

It was all under my bed at one point, and I was literally sleeping on your kind words!

Yep. That sounds weird.

I understand why, though. People wanted to tell us their story in a longer way than they wanted to say in front of people. Maybe they saw something on their travels and thought of us, or just wanted to make sure we were eating so forced us to consume toffee in front of them.

What can we say? We have such a kind and generous audience! Well, maybe not all the people that gave Dan whisks, but still.

Emotionally, though, it is a strange experience, as it can vary a lot! Someone will come who's super hyper and excited, then the next person might have something serious and sincere to say, then someone who's just super chill and sarcastic, then someone who wants you to twerk while their mum takes a burst.

Sometimes I actually get quite emotional hearing the stories people say. It may be whatever issue in their life – an illness, family or school troubles or coming out – but either through making friends in our community or just laughing at our videos, they said it's helped them to feel happier!

That is the number one thing for me. I'm constantly questioning the meaning of existence and what I'm doing with my life, but to hear that no matter what I or anyone thinks, what I do is making people happy in some way, it's what keeps me going! Well, that and all the chocolate I'm given.

When Dan's light-up shoes could be seen by everyone in the room.

Phil not understanding how plastic vampire teeth work.

Watch as Dan – Master of Selfies – takes dozens of photos with the exact same pose and face!

Hey! It works. So what is this? Photoception?

It's a thing of beauty...

and a bit creepy.

DRESSING ROOMS

What an emotional rollercoaster.

The moment of walking into a room and seeing where you will spend the next 12 hours is very important. What will you be given? A palace? A dank basement? We held our breath every time.

I don't know what kind of rock star vision people imagine, but as we did a 'good' show that we wanted to be in 'theatres' that had 'character', this meant we took a risk on the backstage areas.

Yes, it turned out that the more beautiful and historical the theatre was, the more likely the backstage area was last updated in 1923.

What were your essentials?

As long as it had a sofa to nap on and power plugs within reach, everything was fine.

For me it was the lightbulb mirrors! I tell you no matter how little self-worth you think you have, sit in front of one of those babies and you'll feel like a star. Or just very warm, as those bulbs emit a lot of heat.

We laughed, we cried, we napped, we answered emails and ate bananas. Other than the bus, these small rooms were our home throughout this year.

I wonder why.

For some reason, Dan was reluctant to allow me to feed him some medicine when he was run down!

But which is the truth?

In this dressing room we encountered the unique problem of a toilet that wouldn't stop flushing.

It was stuck on flush all day. I think it drained the entire ocean.

The theatre in Reading, America, gave us a giant ticket and a bag of pretzels for performing a sold-out show!

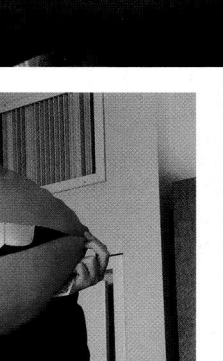

AKA Johnny
E. Jones
#MusicNeverStops
3-3-13
NAS/DMX
DPAC
ThankYOU
2013 2014 2015
STAR ★
DRESSING
ROOM
228
12/7/11

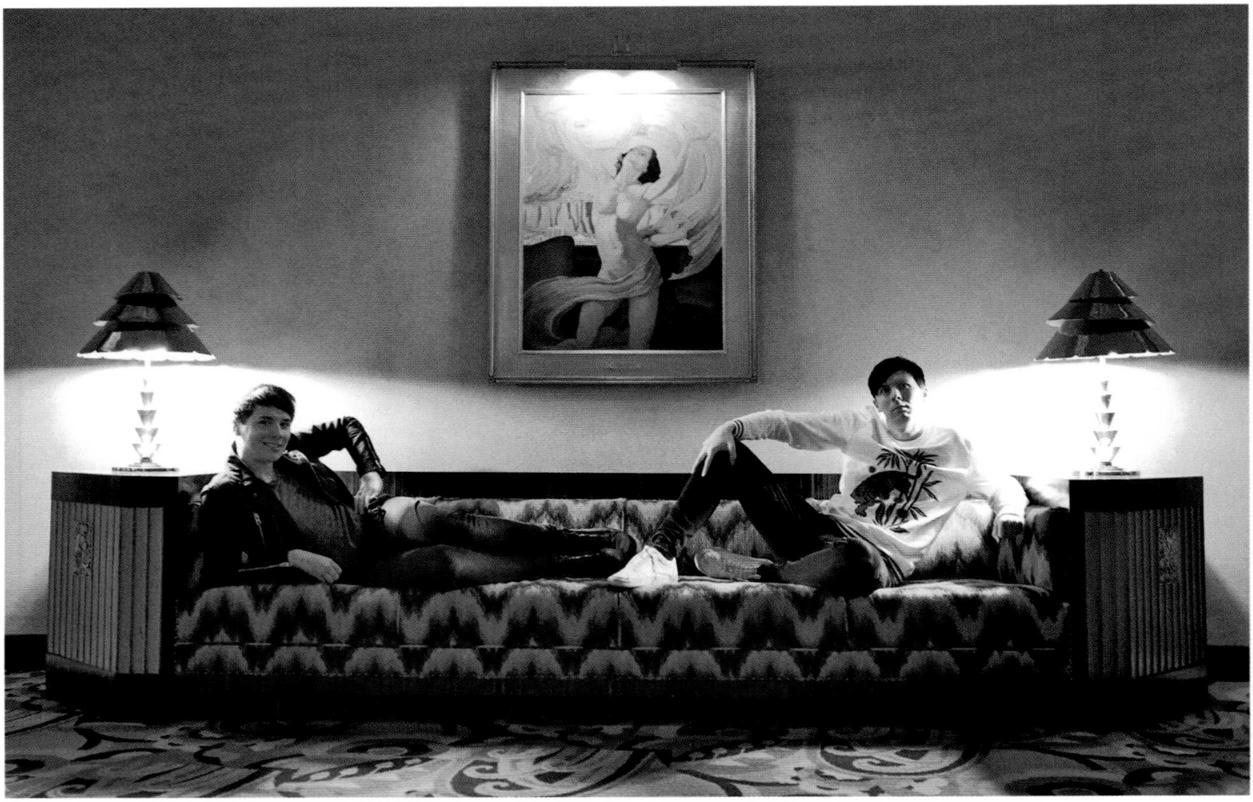

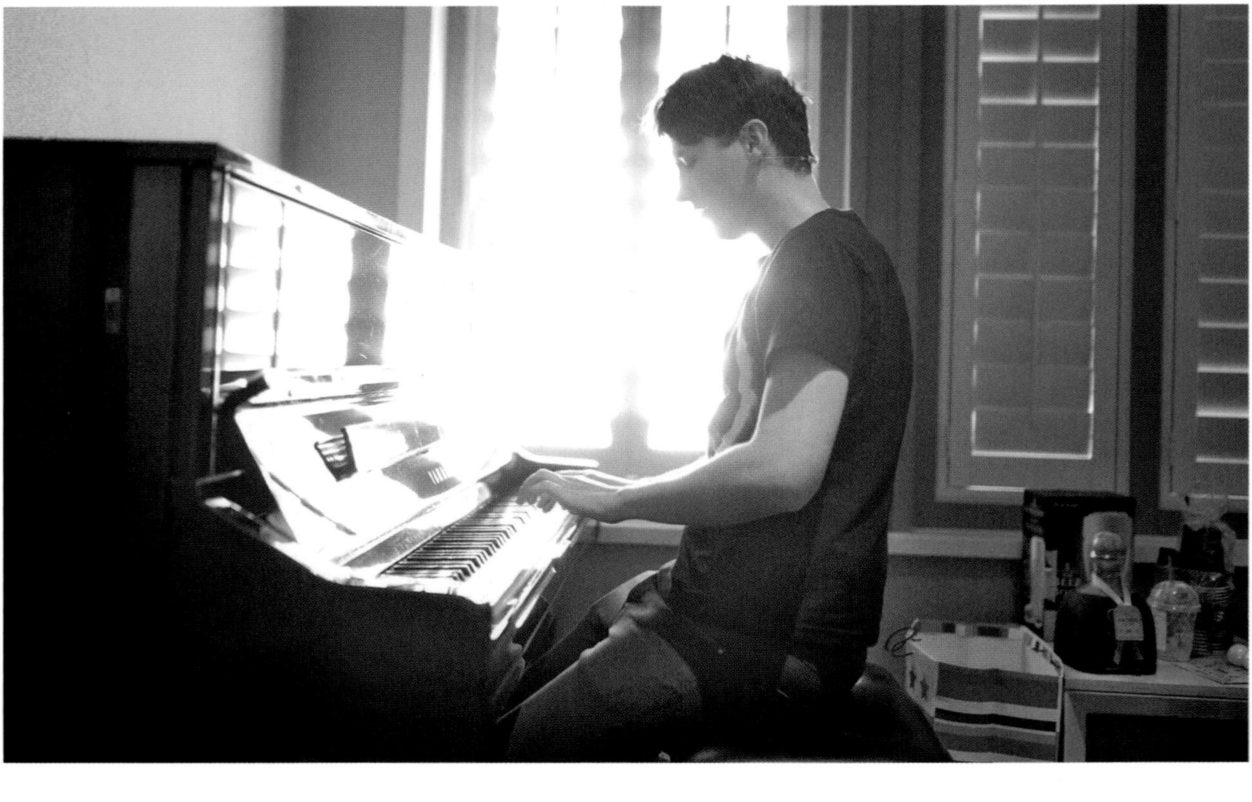

PERFOR

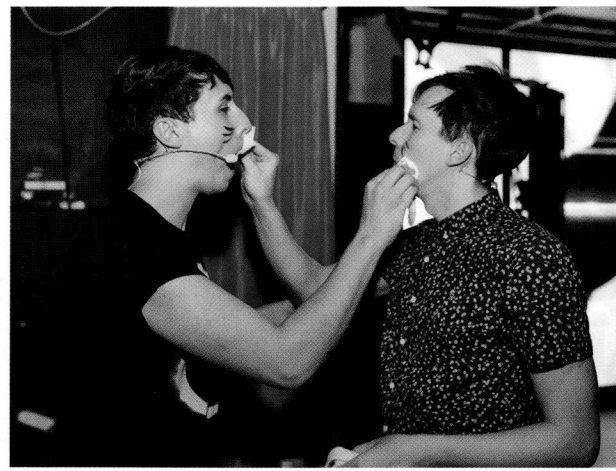

CROWDS

The energy at our shows was absolutely insane.

It started the moment we'd get the announcement, "Ladies and Gentlemen of the Amazing Tour Company, the house is now open." Like the stampede that killed Mufasa...

Wow. Really? You're just gonna drop that there?

We'd hear the earth start to shake. Dust would fall from the snazzy chandeliers and the generic noises of a zombie apocalypse would begin.

From our seats, in the dank basement dressing rooms, the earth would shake. It was kind of terrifying and very intimidating, until you took a moment to remember it's a happy earthquake/zombie apocalypse of people here to see us.

Now, something incredibly important to the success of the whole show was the playlist we put on as people took their seats:

Party in the USA – Miley Cyrus

Kiss You – One Direction

Flesh Without Blood – Grimes

The Sound – The 1975

New Americana – Halsey

Sing – Ed Sheeran

Stronger – Kanye West

Pity Party – Melanie Martinez

Like I Would – Zayn

Jealous – Nick Jonas

Hotline Bling – Drake

Youth – Troye Sivan

Victorious – Panic! at the Disco

Welcome to the Black Parade – My Chemical Romance

Breaking Free – Troy & Gabriella

Toxic – Britney Spears

Uprising – Muse

Tear in My Heart – Twenty One Pilots

She's Kinda Hot – 5 Seconds of Summer

What a masterpiece. The perfect mix of genres, trendy music, classics and straight up Dan and Phil memeage.

You spent hours reordering the playlist until it was just right! I think it changed about five times during the tour.

That's because the timing is very important. They all have to be fun, up-tempo songs to get people excited and happy, but, in the 15 to 30 minutes before the show, we have to start rolling out the bangers to get the people going. I'm talking Troye, Panic!, MCR, HSM and Toxic.

During this part of the playlist, no one backstage can even have a conversation because thousands of people are all screaming the songs at the top of their lungs.

It was truly beautiful hearing that many people sing 'Breaking Free'. Also, I totally regret putting MCR in it because all those people singing 'Black Parade' at the same time created a direct wormhole through spacetime to emo teenage Dan. I actually cried a little once.

As it got closer to show time, people would start stamping their feet, chanting, doing the wave, and no matter how many shows we did, my heart always started going crazy.

The moment we took our places, crouching in a giant wooden microwave ready to burst out in front of thousands of people, is something I can't describe and will never forget.

Stepping out in front of people for the first time was scary, though! I know they were all there for us, but still, so many eyes judging you from every angle.

I remember the first show, when we'd never tested out the show on a real audience before, so we were just hoping people would enjoy it – and we ended up having our expectations and eardrums completely blown out of this universe.

We were actually unsure of how it would go, as people are used to YouTubers just doing music concerts or conventions, as opposed to theatrical shows, but everyone listened, laughed and cheered exactly when we wanted them to! We had the perfect audience for our show, every single place we went in the world! I think we're very lucky to have such a smart, funny and kind crowd.

Honestly, I can relate to Gaga; the feeling I got seeing people laugh, smile and cheer at what we were doing was the best thing in the world. To know that, in that moment, no matter what was going on in our lives or theirs, we were all together having a great time and feeling happy – that was special! It made me really appreciate what we do and realise how important it can be, no matter what we or anyone else thinks.

I mean, we both probably lost half of our hearing range, but it was worth the sacrifice.

Totally.

PARTY TIME

In typical Dan and Phil fashion, we were expecting to finish our final show and slink off to a world of Mario Kart and pizza.

Ooh 'slink' – nice word. However, our crew had other plans brewing under their sneaky crew belts!

They'd only gone and booked us our own after-party! With an actual DJ and a guest list. The most people to ever turn up to one of my parties in primary school were my brother and my cousins, so this was a huge deal.

THE PHIL
Pineapple juice, Blue syrup, Lemonade, and a toasted marshmallow

THE DAN
Espresso and Vanilla

Yeah, as not just the crew but loads of our YouTuber friends came along too, which was a nice surprise! The surprise was that we had any friends, not the party thing.

My favourite part was that we got to customise our own drinks!

Yes, the party venue agreed to create 'The Dan' and 'The Phil' for us, and we went to our own tasting session to perfect them! Yours was the sweetest and brightest thing I have ever put in my mouth.

I asked them to create the sweetest drink known to humanity.

I just asked for mine to be black.

It was mysterious and bitter like your soul.

We 'partied' into the early hours and fortunately (or unfortunately for some people) we had a Dan and Phil photo booth to capture the action! Here are some of our favourites:

BETWEEN TOURS

After the UK tour, we went into hibernation.

You mean an actual coma?

It was weird going back to normal life! I'd wake up halfway through a dream and start singing in my bed.

I was wondering what you were doing in there.

I guess I missed the glitz and the glamour of sitting in a van for five hours on my way to a Travelodge.

Those were the days.

Here's how we spent some rare and confusing time off!

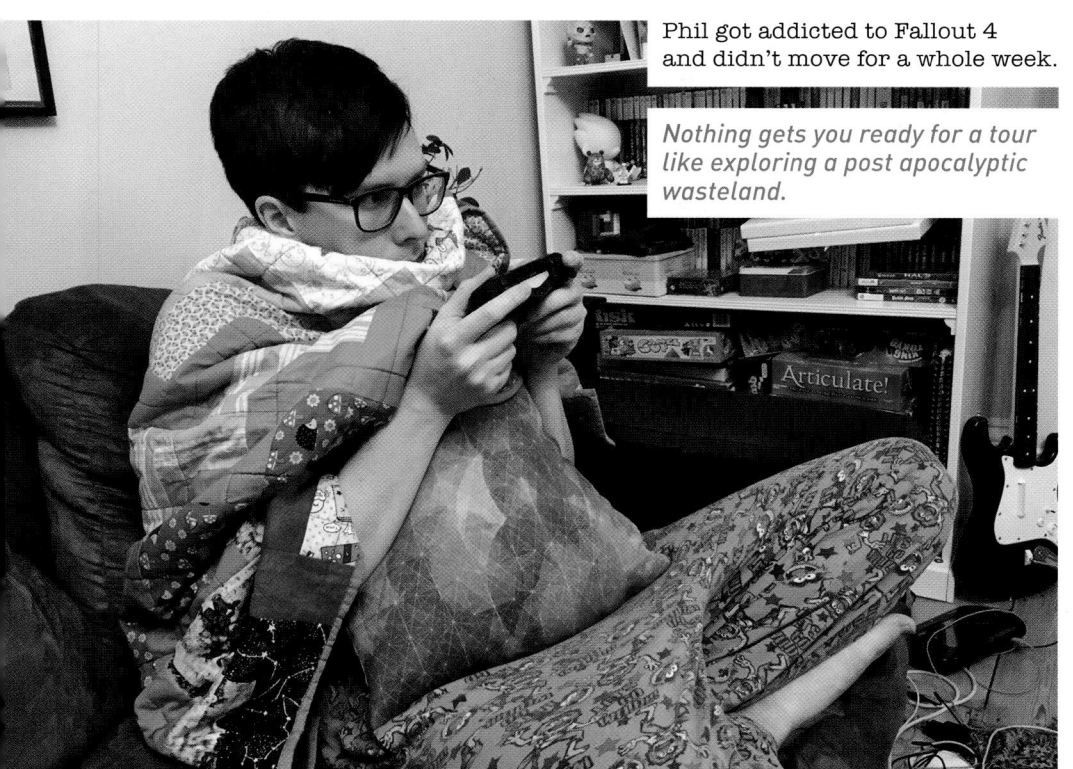

Phil got addicted to Fallout 4 and didn't move for a whole week.

Nothing gets you ready for a tour like exploring a post apocalyptic wasteland.

I tried on Dan's potato sack to prove how terrible it looks!

Rude. I think you look quite swaggy.

I look like I'm looking for my pitchfork before I tend to my lambs.

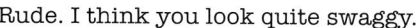

Dan took his browsing position to a whole new level.

Filming for YouTube Rewind in an oversized chair, while dressed as babies in a graveyard at midnight.

A rare Daniel, crawling out of his burrow in the search of a snack.

Typical Thursday TBH!

Dan's average face during a heated round of Mario Kart.

Us trying to stay calm in our American TV interview promoting *TABINOF*.

They kept asking if we were brothers!

A sign I had definitely become too pale.

Wild nerds in their natural habitat.

KILL THE IMPOSTER

Mountain climbing with my bro! My ears almost fell off.

My 90-year-old grandad kicking some serious gaming butt!

I'm not sure if we are related?

'Hawaiian'-themed Christmas party with our team.
I think I nailed the Christmas/tropical vibe.

We were the only ones who turned up in costume!

They will be getting a lump of volcanic coal from Hawaiian Santa.

Who needs a headrest when you can have a Colin?

Birthday sushi times! The restaurant set on fire just before we arrived, but it was still a great night.

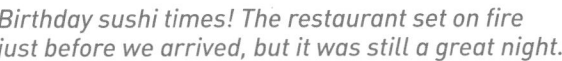

Then we hosted the online stream of the Brit Awards for the third time!

Sadly no Kanye this year.

I went to Sri Lanka, which was a harrowing experience.

What?!

Literally no Wi-Fi anywhere. That is the last time I leave the house before researching in advance. I absorbed some big vitamin Ds, though! Here's me sitting on a sunbed with a dog underneath it.

We then had the mammoth task–

–Do you mean tusk?

What? No, task. We had the big task of organising the American and Australian tours!

Oh yeah! Yeah, trying to convince a bunch of theatres around the world to book The Amazing Tour Is Not on Fire by 'danisnotonfire' and 'AmazingPhil' was not easy.

Just in case anyone thinks YouTube and the internet are mainstream already, all the trails have been blazed and frontiers conquered, try organising a theatre tour.

People were like, "The Amazing who?! Is that a magician?" and I was like, "Well, technically, I do magic in the show."

You see why this was hard. They'd say, "We have *CATS* next week! *CATS*! Who are you?! No!" It is a miracle that we managed to take *TATINOF* off our little island.

We won't bore you with so many details that your brain turns into a goopy paste and dribbles out of your ears, but it turns out tours are hard to organise.

And so, after a brief rest and snacking period, we were on the road again, only this time TO AMERICA!

USA REHEARSALS

Time for things to get big!

And not just me and Dan due to all the BBQ and burgers on the horizon!

We had to prepare for America. We knew we wanted to change a few jokes and references in the show–

–Like swapping out Queen Elizabeth for Beyoncé!

Naturally! However, we also saw it as an opportunity to improve the entire show for the final performance at the Dolby, where we'd film it.

So, just like last time, we spent a month locked in a slightly warmer and less religious room, and lived TATINOF for 10 hours a day.

A strange man squirted purple goo into our ears, and not in an erotic, alien-abduction way!

We were having special earplugs fitted that would only block out certain frequencies! Cool, right?

Yeah! However, the one time we wore them on stage, they were so good that we couldn't understand if the audience were cheering or booing during the 7 Second Challenge, so we threw them on the floor.

Great investment.

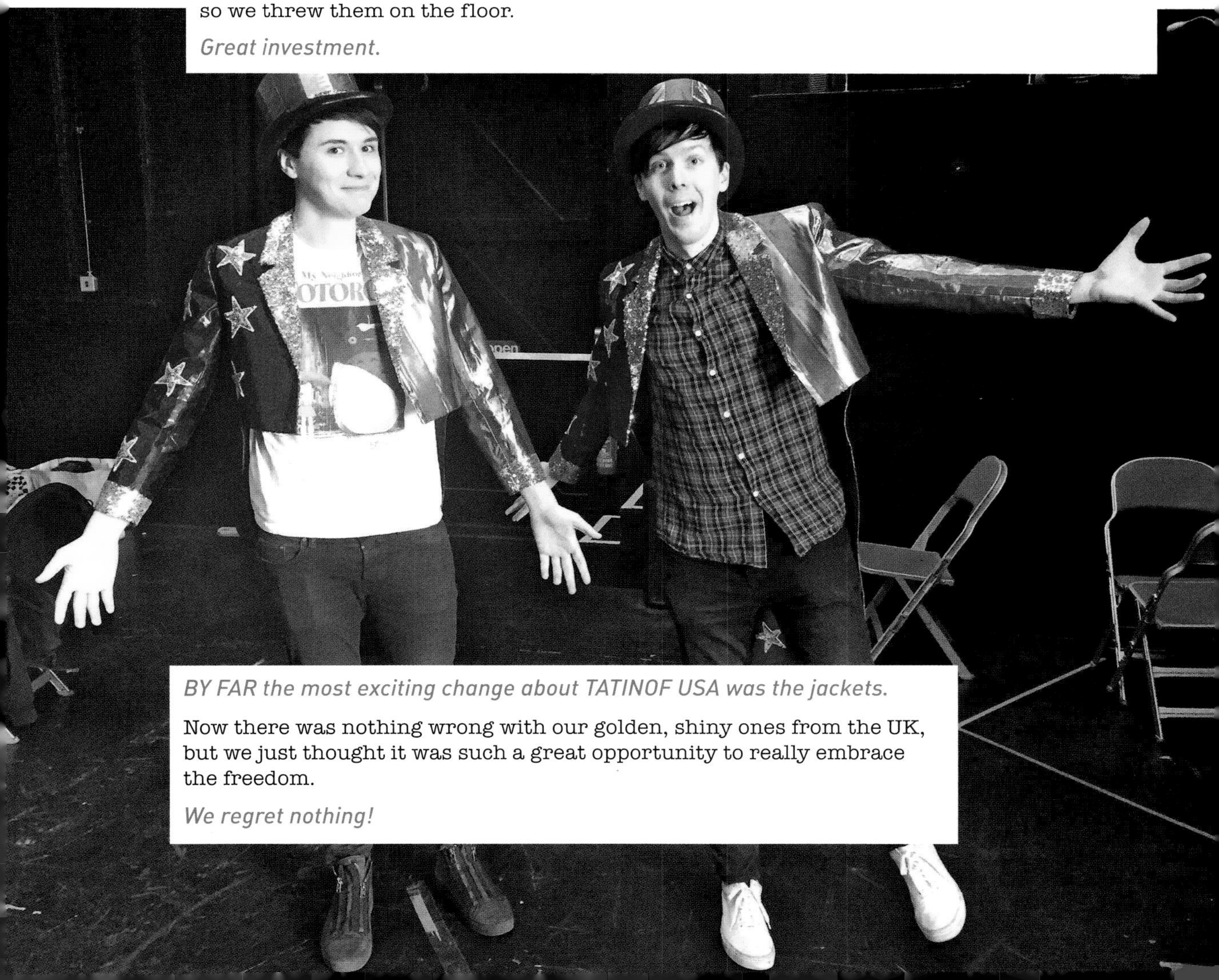

BY FAR the most exciting change about TATINOF USA was the jackets.

Now there was nothing wrong with our golden, shiny ones from the UK, but we just thought it was such a great opportunity to really embrace the freedom.

We regret nothing!

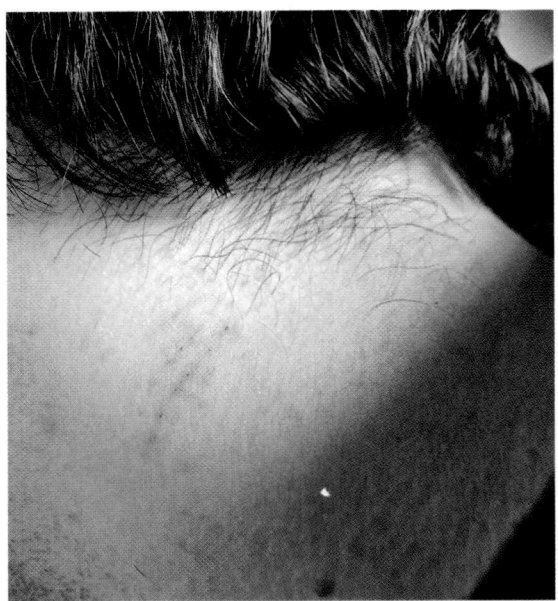

Don't let anyone tell you that we don't suffer for our art.

Our American flag bow ties and jackets were covered in so many sequins that they literally cut our necks open. The 'sequin-softening' afternoon was a good one.

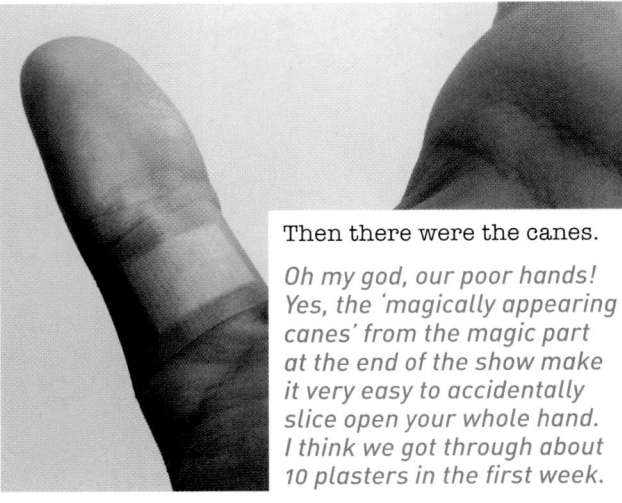

Then there were the canes.

Oh my god, our poor hands! Yes, the 'magically appearing canes' from the magic part at the end of the show make it very easy to accidentally slice open your whole hand. I think we got through about 10 plasters in the first week.

The time we whacked out a map in a diner and suddenly realised what the heck we'd committed ourselves to with the USA tour.

Look at that route! So much sense.

Just give me a drink and I'll get through it.

Dan mysteriously floating like a genie.

I have come from another dimension to rid the world of weeaboos and *Minions* fans.

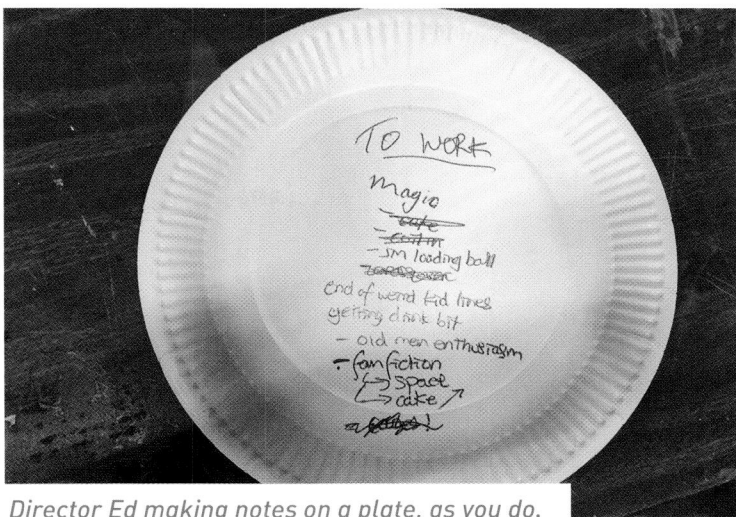

Director Ed making notes on a plate, as you do.

You don't want to know what happened before or after this photo.

My true love! I will never forget you and your sneaky probes.

???

Why are you even asking?

Dan and his big D!

Spoilers!

At least the dead rabbit wasn't in it when you took this.

Our bible was *TABINOF*; the crew's was this object.

OUR CREW

Now it wasn't just us two driving around the world on this tour!

No. We had a team of over 20 people travelling with us and even more back at home keeping it running.

Our theatre crew were the heart and soul of TATINOF.

I'd say they were also the arms, legs and all other practical muscles, as they actually did everything while we sat with a frappé being 'creative'.

True.

Honestly, when you're on the road for this long it's important that everyone gets along and has a good time (you're literally prisoners together trapped in a Dan and Phil hell-dimension), so we were so lucky to get such an awesome and talented group of people!

We'd include some more photos in here but it turns out what the crew get up to after a long day of TATINOF probably can't be published.

Our security guard, Louie, who everyone lovingly referred to as 'Drake' on the internet.

Potential cover for a mixtape he could drop at any moment.

'Straight Outta TATINOF'

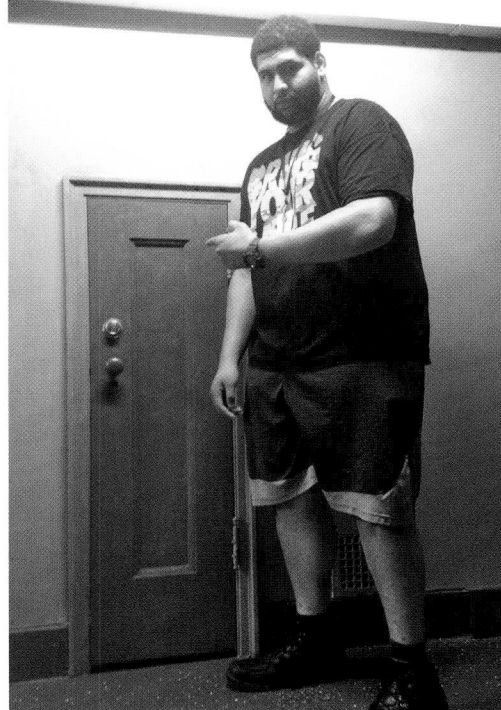

Mark, the photographer who took every good photo in this book!

Fleur looking majestic, ready to ride into battle on the lion.

Who, funnily enough, is my friend from school who I grew up with! It was refreshing to have a northern accent on the bus; it made me feel back at home, or in Winterfell.

Marianne trying to avoid the paps.

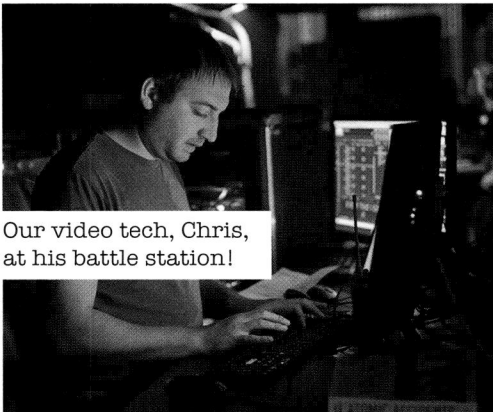

Our video tech, Chris, at his battle station!

The 'Creative Team' of Jack, our lighting designer, who made us look like rock stars, even though we're two gangly dorks; James, the set designer, who made the most awesome mind-blowing stage of all time; and Director Ed, who is literally responsible for turning our 'good ideas' for a YouTuber stage show into the incredible experience it was.

The whole gang after our first show!

Everyone is actually wearing #TATINOF customised sunglasses we forced them to wear.

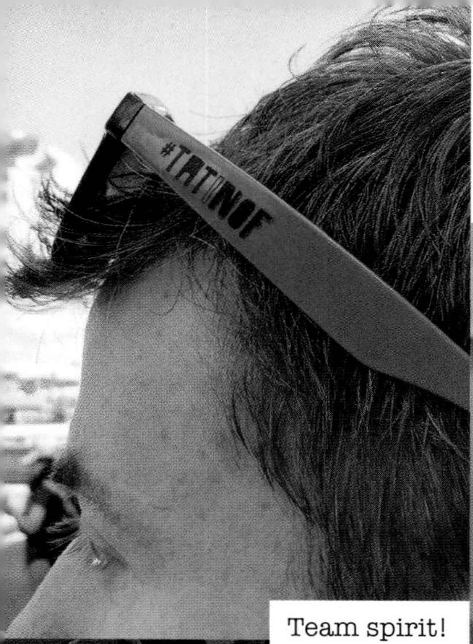

Team spirit!

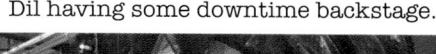
Anna preparing the bags of joy to give out like it is Christmas Eve.

Dil having some downtime backstage.

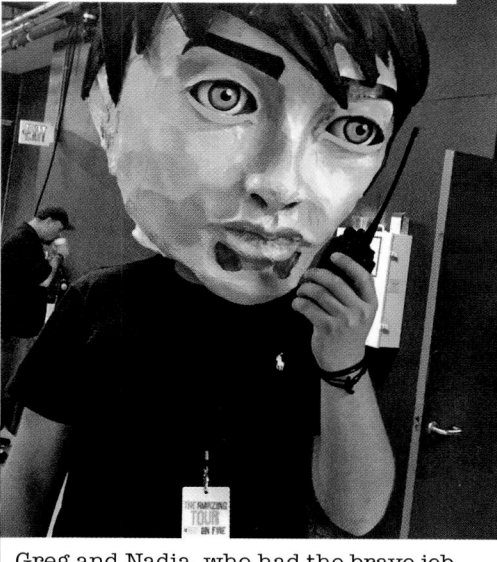

Chris H, our sound guy, who coincidentally took those cool, colourful photos of the show from back there in his sound booth!

Greg and Nadia, who had the brave job of interacting with all of you to get the 7 Second Challenges, Weird Kids and Uncle Dan stories before every show!

The secret power source of the crew.

Literally four boxes a day. I am so impressed.

Jimmy and Fleur busting out a piano duet in NY!

A long day? We've all been there.

THE TOUR BUS

So America is big.

That is a true fact right there, Philly.

We couldn't just fly everywhere or drive during the day like we did in the UK. We needed to carry a whole load of stuff with us in the night, which meant one thing: we needed a tour bus.

We actually lived on a bus for over TWO MONTHS!

We slept, we ate, we worked, we cried – all on this bus.

It became an old friend to us, one of the gang.

Like a safe and shiny womb with wheels.

We had no idea what to expect when we were told we were getting a bus! I was expecting a dingy, dark, hell-machine, but it turned out to be a real swankfest! Apparently, the last two people to use it were my biological father, Kanye, and Ed Sheeran. I never did find any tiny orange hairs.

It had bedrooms, a fully stocked kitchen, surround-sound speakers and even a microwave for late night popcorn!

Obvs the most important feature.

There was also a shower (which we never used) and an ultra-hi-tech VHS player.

You joke, but the best two nights for you were watching *The Mummy* and *Jurassic Park* at 4am.

I can't believe how quickly we adapted to tour-bus life!

I think it helped that you had a huge bedroom all to yourself. I'm not bitter or anything.

You agreed to that rock, paper, scissors match! Plus, I think having a giant comfy bed helped a lot with my travel sickness.

Yes, that was a big concern. Things might have somehow been worse were you projectile vomiting the entire time. I'm just glad we managed to sleep on something that was moving.

It was like sleeping on a bouncy castle made of rocks. It was also pretty scary if our driver hit the brakes.

Like the 'deer incident'.

Oh yeah. One night I woke up being catapulted right out of bed! Like a giraffe being born.

Matters were made more dramatic by Phil, the eternal hoarder, keeping about 10 half-drunk coffee mugs on his bedside table that all hurled across the room and smashed in a catastrophic coffee cacophony.

I thought I was being ravaged by a poltergeist! Turns out deer were crossing the freeway and a truck flipped in an attempt to avoid them.

On the run from the law probably. I'm glad we survived!

We travelled some extremely girthy distances while we slept. I think the longest was over 1000 miles in 15 hours.

It was like teleporting; we'd go to sleep in a city and wake up extremely confused in the desert.

On the rare moments of 'day' travel, I got some good music-listening achieved! Though there's a whole lot of beautiful nothing in those middle states.

Why do Americans even need so much corn?

It's a cornspiracy!

Even though at times it felt like I was suffering from Stockholm syndrome and cabin fever all at the same time, I did miss the bus when we said goodbye!

I'm glad I gave her one last hug before we left.

Yes, I've found the line – it's you referring to the bus as 'her'!

She doesn't mind, Dan. She likes it.

This was the best seat on the bus. It had a backrest AND a table, complete with cup holders, anti-slip mat and power plugs! Many a dance-off, rap-battle and shoot-out were participated in to decide who sat here in the evenings.

Phil on his 17th coffee of the morning.

You see me browsin'.

The softest cushion on earth given to us at a show!

'I like bananas; I like bananas in the sunshine!'

Gonna sue you for copyright m8.

The best meal of the day!

So good you would sometimes eat it three times a day.

Hey, cinnamon is technically a plant!

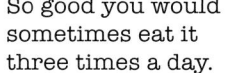

Hey, Dan! Pose like you are eating your cereal right now.

Stop ruining the magic! This is a true candid moment of Danicus Mornicus eating his natural food.

Awakening the beast.

Getting my sweet revenge.

I look like I could take down a building with that almighty yawn.

The noise of you yawning is something the gods should fear.

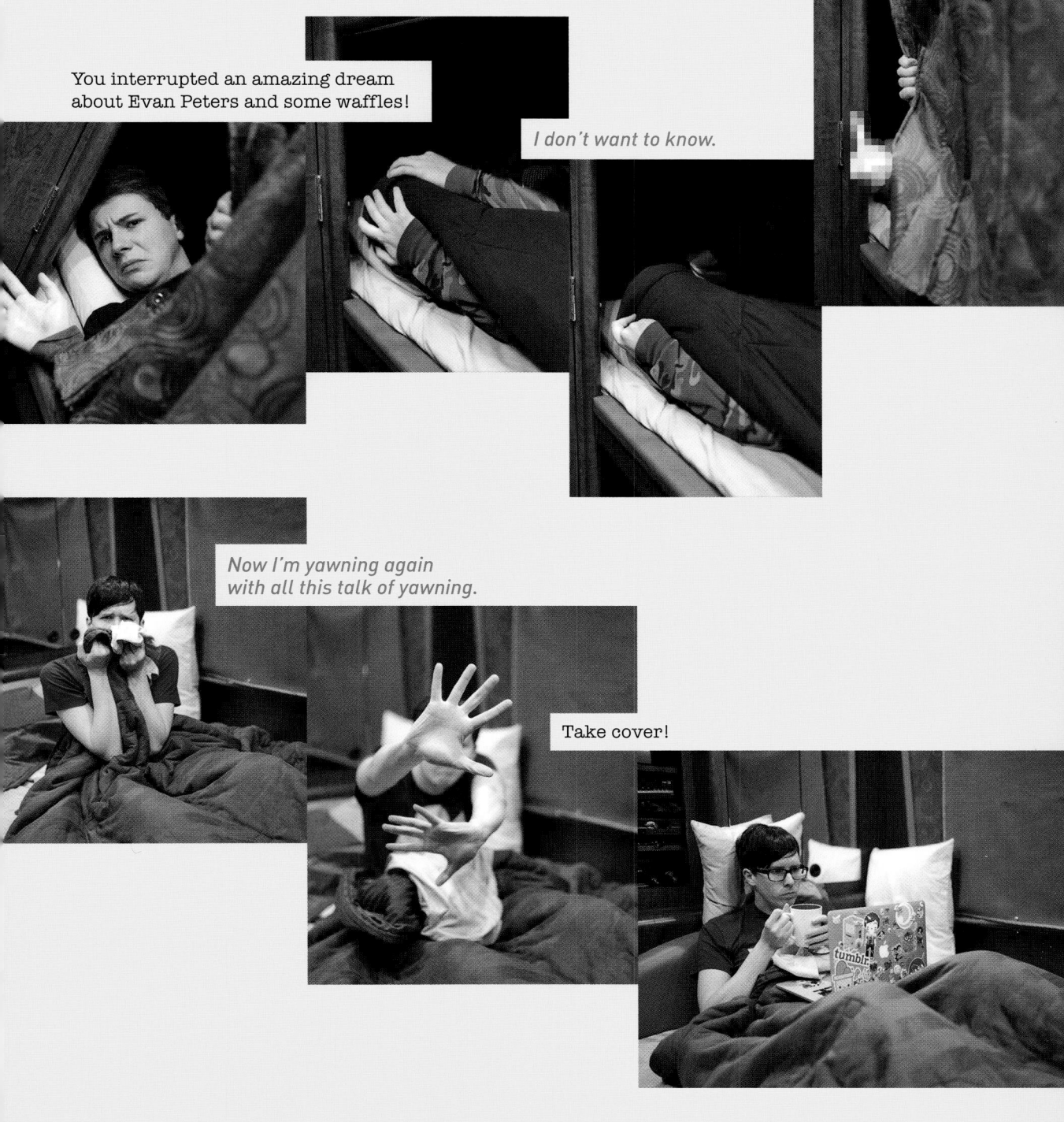

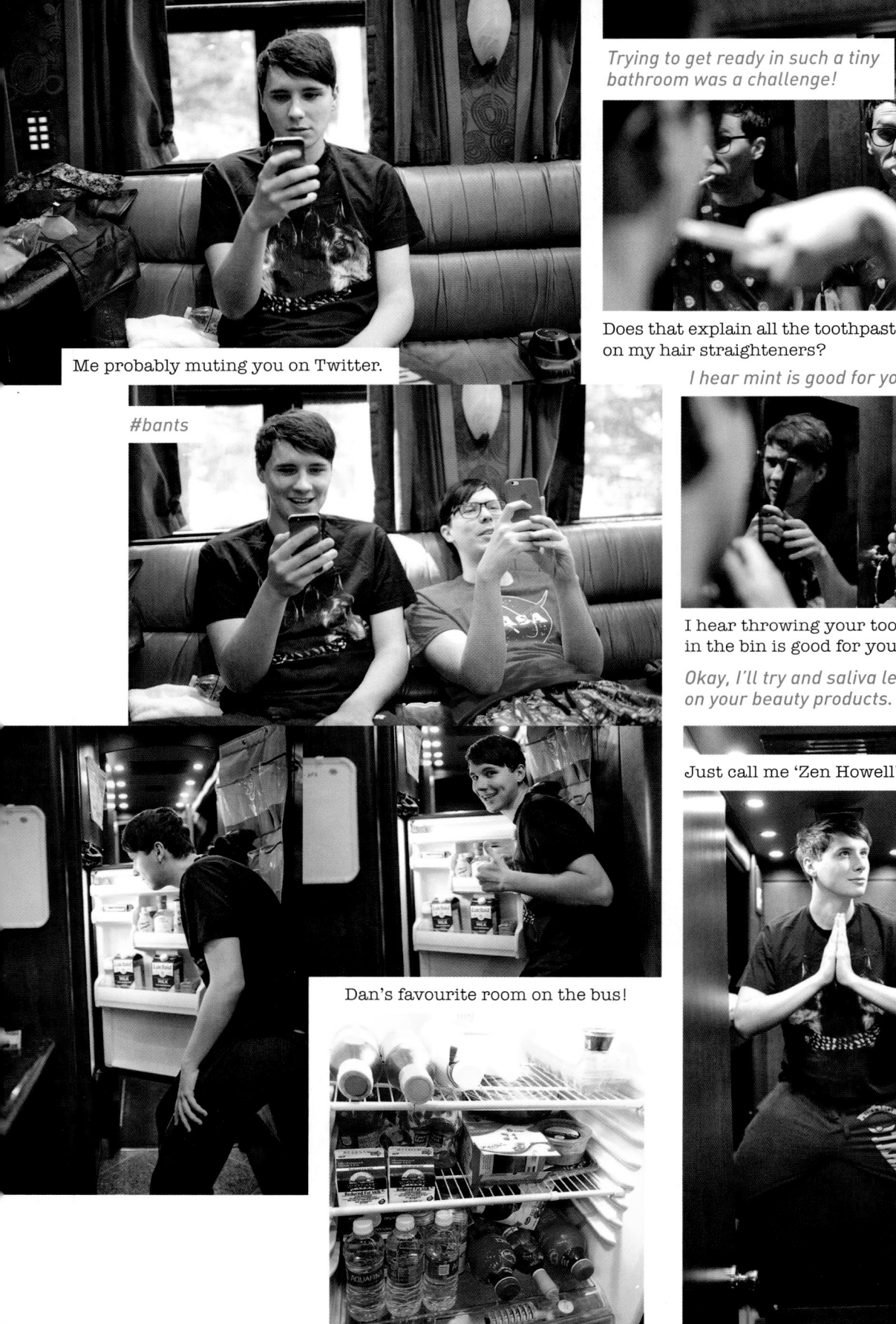

Me probably muting you on Twitter.

#bants

Dan's favourite room on the bus!

Trying to get ready in such a tiny bathroom was a challenge!

Does that explain all the toothpaste on my hair straighteners?

I hear mint is good for your follicles.

I hear throwing your toothbrush in the bin is good for your teeth!

Okay, I'll try and saliva less on your beauty products.

Just call me 'Zen Howell'.

#breakfastbants

Don't talk to me before I've finished my cereal.

Ha! I finally caught you sleeping.

Sushi in Texas was
almost as good as sushi in Japan.

What a graceful hippo-like
creature I am.

SThusklHELP ME

The exact moment of brain-freeze.

The moment of primal terror in everyone's eyes when Phil volunteered to open a bottle with a popping cork.

Everyone should have had total faith in me!

Moments later we hit a speedbump and Phil spilled his drink all over his crotch.

Nothing worse than a fizzy crotch!

New profile pic, Dan?

One of our final nights all together!

Wait, why are you wearing my socks?

The laundry got sparse towards the end. I was desperate.

I will not tolerate this bullying in my own book.

Counting down the days on the calendar somehow made it seem a bit prisony.

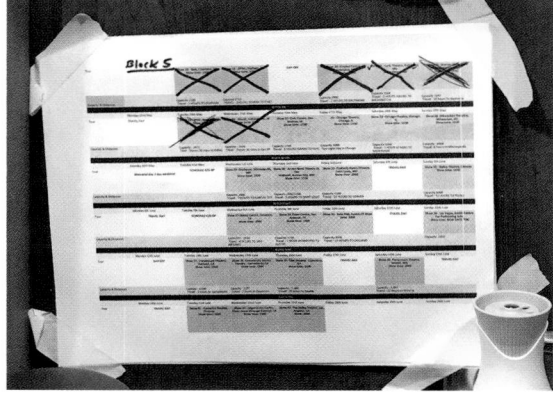

We should have scratched the days on the walls and exclusively exited the bus by squeezing through a window covered in butter!

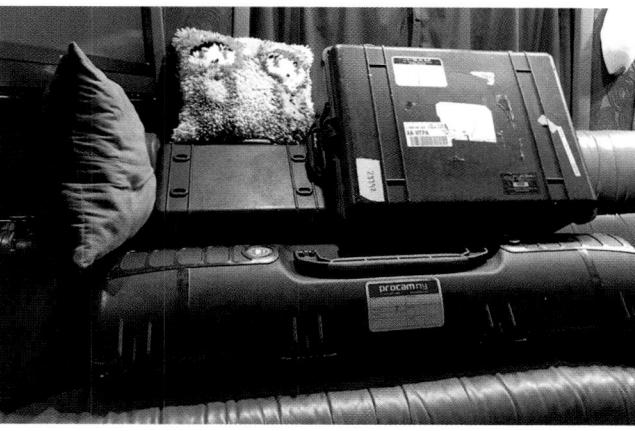

All the camera equipment from our documentary didn't make the seats more comfortable.

The VHS next to my bed rattled so much as I tried to sleep that I stuffed it with socks.

I chose a pillow as my security object, as Dan lovingly embraces a tripod.

FLORIDA

Conveniently, my family went on holiday to Florida right before we went to rehearse for the tour, so I got to go relax before the start!

Yes. How 'convenient'!

We went for a walk and look who I stumbled across: THE SQUIRREL. This is the exact squirrel that infamously bit me last time I went to Florida!

GATORLAND

One place I had to take Dan was Florida's premiere family owned alligator-themed theme park. GATORLAND!

It was actually a lot cooler and safer than I thought it'd be based on that description.

OMGATORS

I got more than I consented to when I fed this goat.

I photographed it, Phil, and my conscience isn't any cleaner.

This bird was the single scariest creature I'd ever seen in my life.

It kept stalking people and pecking them!

I feel like this image is a metaphor for me and Dan.

And, of course, in their gift shop I bought my iconic bedazzled Gatorland hat!

I'm disturbed by how much it suits you.

MINI GOLF

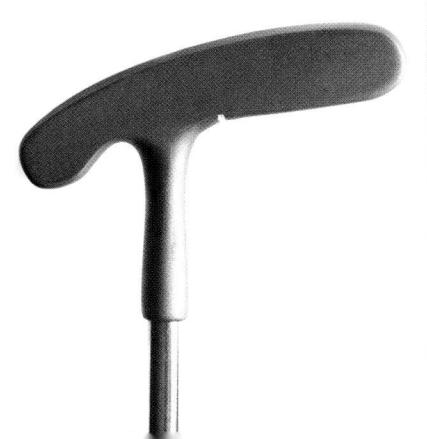

GOLFBOYS

What do you reckon we got arrested for?

Just being too damn good at golf.

More like for hitting 20 balls into the lake.

AIRBOAT

We went on an airboat to experience true Floridian culture!

Turns out it's mostly gnats and dangerous reptiles.

Dan desperately swatting away flies!

There were so many hitting me in the face, Phil. Every hole. Every hole.

I'm not sure what this was in the gift shop, or whether it's legal in the world of science, but we had to get a photo!

It has a nice pastel aesthetic with that hat.

snek

Busted!

A turtle with one leg who kept swimming in circles. Apparently it fended off an alligator that tried to eat it. Metal.

Phil vs. Wildlife, Episode 1: The Rejection Duck

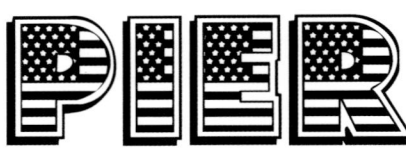

PIER

Phil vs. Wildlife, Episode 2: The Angry Pelican

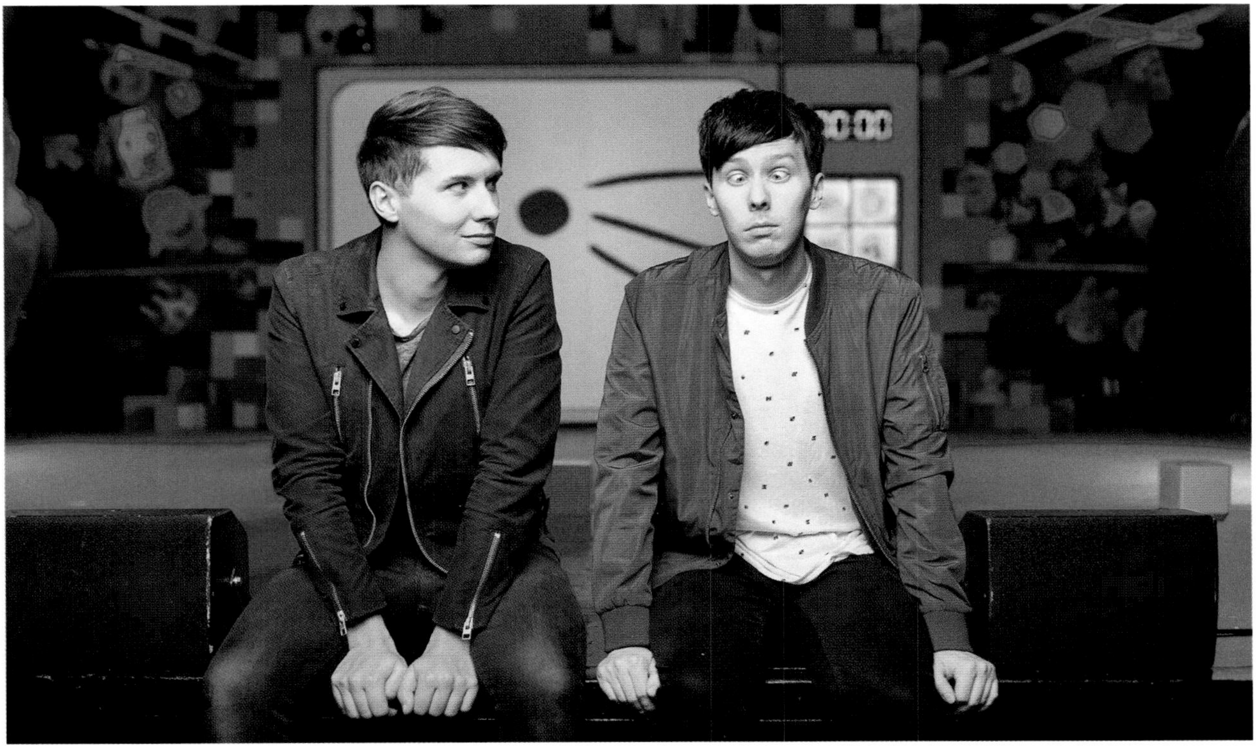

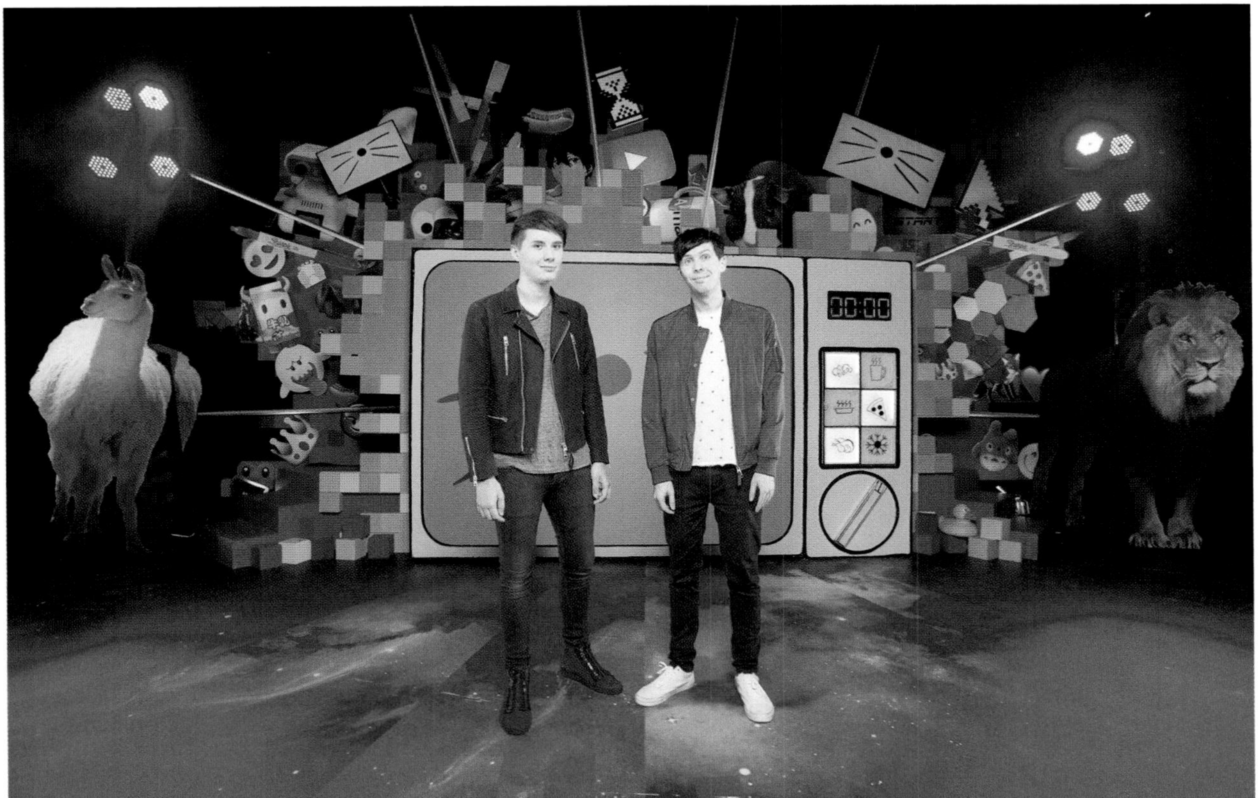
00:00

NEW YORK CITY

We literally performed a sold-out show on Broadway!

That's a weird sentence to comprehend, isn't it? It's fun to go to NYC as a tourist, but it felt even more magical being there to perform a show!

As we were driving into Times Square, our bus driver started playing 'New York, New York' by Frank Sinatra!

It was like being in a movie, except my knees hurt slightly because we were kneeling at the front of our bus.

The Beacon Theatre had an elevator that had been signed by everyone who had performed there!

Obviously we utilised our unfair advantage in life and signed the roof right in the very middle.

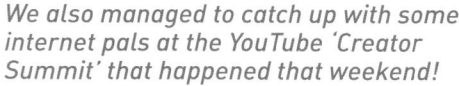

We also managed to catch up with some internet pals at the YouTube 'Creator Summit' that happened that weekend!

Recreating *Geri's Game* at the Chess Club.

I feel like we'll both end up angrily chessing each other there in the future.

Phil being confronted with his worst fear.

Their heads are so long!!

Going for a walk and doing some filming with Director Ed!

119

BOSTON

Boston was where I had the best pizza of my entire life.

Bit of a random way to introduce this?

That's the most important thing there is to say!
Soy sauce on a pizza, try it.

We did have a lovely morning roaming the Common!

And that was just two days before Justin Bieber
infamously walked around with no socks on...
to think our paths could have crossed.

I'd have donated a pair of foxes and sloths to him.

*Dan attempting to look deep in thought while
looking at the lake. A squirrel ruins the photoshoot.*

Phil vs. Wildlife, Episode 3: The Pigeon Problem

Aesthetic selfies, apparently not exclusive to Japan!

Behind-the-selfie

SHIBE ALERT DROP EVERYTHING.

Never say that again.

They didn't want the P!

CANADA

The highest point of our adventure (Get it? Literally very north) had to be Canada!

I wish we could have stayed for longer but we made the most of our time!

This is me having successfully crossed the border into Canada!

I was expecting a ranger on the back of a moose to check our passports so I was kinda disappointed.

WTF is that?

IDK. I figured it was the Canadian Stonehenge or something?

It's creepy AF.

We made friends with Michael the Canadian moose.

I'm pretty sure we weren't meant to hug him. He's like the Obama of Canada.

NIAGARA FALLS

We didn't even realise we could go to the falls until we drove past it and went "OMG PULL OVER WATERFALL QUEST RIGHT NOW"!

HORNBLOWER
NIAGARA
CRUISES

Adult Voyage to the Falls

Boats Depart Every 30 Minutes in Season

Node26 Receipt:3190
SEE REVERSE FOR
TERMS & CONDITIONS 5/6/2016

Adult

Boats Depart Every 30 Min

Node26 Receipt:3190
SEE REVERSE FOR
TERMS 5/6/2016

A A

Phil vs. Poncho

Phil had some issues putting his poncho on. It took him about 25 minutes.

It is honestly one of the most incredible things I have ever seen! IT WAS SO BIG?!

Well, it is a wonder of the world, Phil.

It was one of the moistest experiences of my life.

TMI, Phil.

125

TORONTO

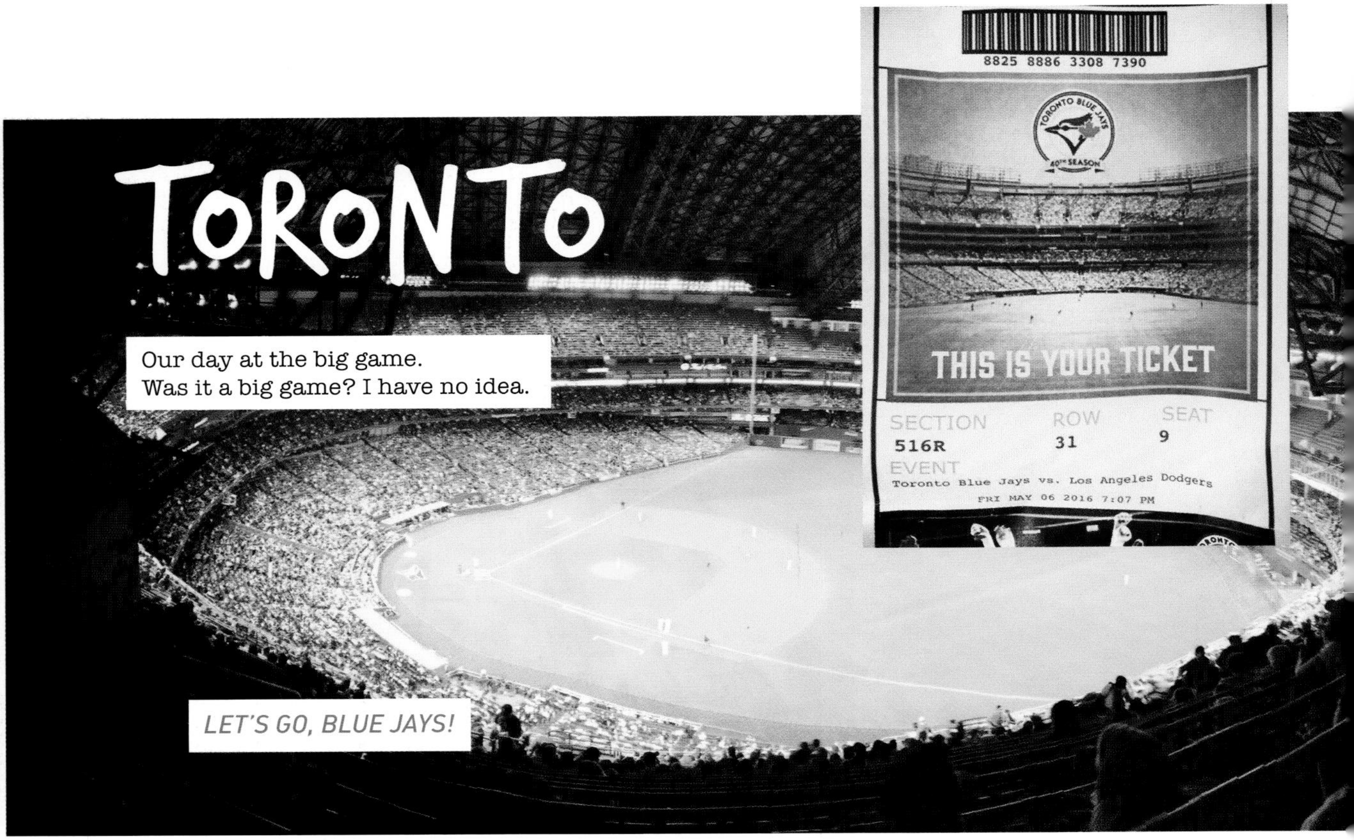

8825 8886 3308 7390
TORONTO BLUE JAYS
40TH SEASON
THIS IS YOUR TICKET
SECTION
516R
ROW
31
SEAT
9
EVENT
Toronto Blue Jays vs. Los Angeles Dodgers
FRI MAY 06 2016 7:07 PM

Our day at the big game.
Was it a big game? I have no idea.

LET'S GO, BLUE JAYS!

HOME OF THE
RONTO BLUE JAYS

Pretending I know what a sport is.

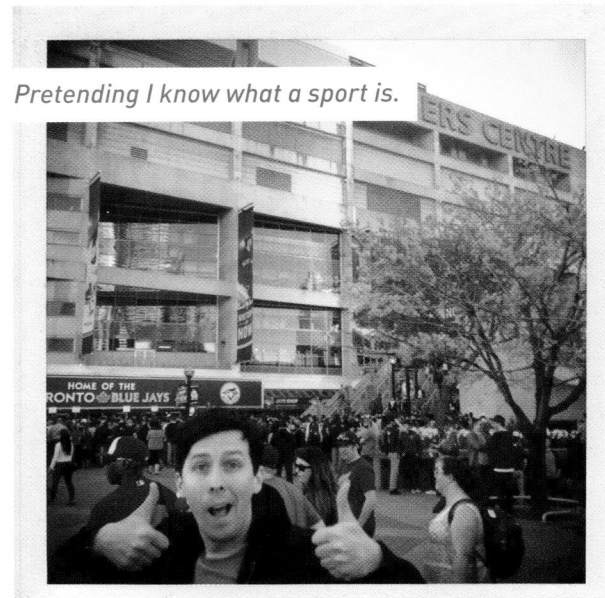

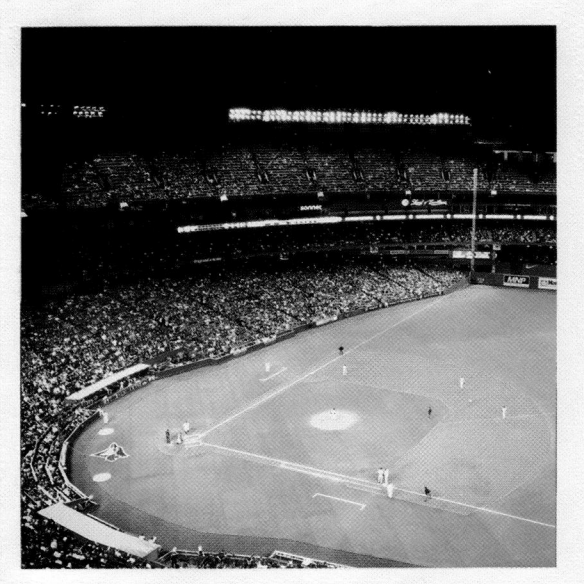

Almost a successful panorama.

I'll do it one day, without horribly warping reality.

The real reason we had a good time.

450 metres beneath that glass floor. AAaaAahhhh!

I managed to hold that smile for one second before running away squealing.

Phil, stop desecrating the monument.

I'm like Godzilla but with sexy moves.

Not Dan's best choice of place to have a crisis.

PHILAD ELPHIA

Philly is in Philly!

Immediately delete that.

You're just jealous because there isn't a place called Danny.

Like every tourist, we had to spend a good hour watching people jog up and down the steps from *Rocky*! To think each of them was humming to their own imaginary little montage.

PHILLY BALBOA! I had to.

You took like 10 minutes walking up and panting.

One other important quest while we were there was to find the legendary 'Philly Cheesesteak'!

I wasn't sold based on the name, but I felt it was culturally important.

Just before the moment of truth. How was it?

INCREDIBLE! Light on the cheese like a pizza, but it was so juicy and amazing. Thanks, dude at the market, for making such a sweet sub.

READING TERMINAL MARKET

PIZZA & CHEESESTEAKS

WASHINGTON DC

We went to go say hi to Obama!

I expected a lot more fence-age...
to say that's where he sleeps.

*There were probably secret laser beams
and alligators ready to be released if
you got closer, Dan.*

Enjoy the sight of us desecrating so many
important monuments and buildings.

Your eyes will absorb the freedom through the page!

Cheeky selfie with Abe.

How did we not get deported?

CHICAGO

I'm gonna put it out there and say that I was disappointed by the lack of wind in the so-called 'Windy City'.

What were you expecting?

The odd cow flying by the window would have been nice?

I'm burning your DVD of *Twister*.

Thankfully the city made up for its lack of wind with some swanky architecture and cartoonish water!

How to make pedestrians hate you.

Here's Phil sulking after a woman shouted at him for taking selfies in the middle of the pavement.

I can't believe how blue the river was! It was like a cartoon river.

The River Thames in London should hang its dirty polluted head in shame–

–And go have a bath.

How can a river have a bath?

Sounds like a riddle! If a river had a bath, did it make a sound?

BOAT TOUR

Because we're so cultured and mature we decided to go on an 'Architecture Boat Tour'!

I know, right! Check me out appreciating all the... fine buildings.

CHICAGO AR**C**HITECTURE FOUNDATION

CHICAGO ARCHITECTURE FOUNDATION

RIVER

CRUISE

ABOARD CHICAGO'S FIRST LADY CRUISES

"TOP TOUR IN CHICAGO!
ONE OF THE TOP 10 TOURS IN THE U.S."
—TRIPADVISOR USERS

CHICAGO'S
FIRST LADY
CHICAGO'S FINEST FLEET

You found a way to make this inappropriate.

Hey, they were truly shiny and glorious!

This was my favourite building!

So creepy. If I had a car I would definitely accidentally reverse it over one of those ledges.

That is why you don't drive cars.

So just when we got fully zazzed by the buildings, it started to rain!

It was kinda awkward because we all had to go inside the boat to stay dry, but the tour guide kept explaining the buildings, even though we couldn't see them.

Thankfully, we bought some glorious hobbit hair protection ponchos.

Made from a freshly flayed smurf!

Their sacrifice meant a lot.

The Bean

When I mentioned we were in Chicago, literally every tweet was 'GO SEE THE BEAN'!

I was kind of scared and intrigued, but it turned out it was a giant fourth-dimensional mirror-bean.

How many Dan and Phils can you see in the Chicago Bean?

Truly beantacular.

It also created the opportunity for some dank reflection selfies.

It turned out Chicago is home to the single most glorious food object I've ever experienced.

OR NOT.

THE DEEP DISH PIZZA.

It was like an entire cake made out of cheese.

A.K.A. the greatest experience of my life. I transcended to a plane of existence where all I could sense was dairy and regret.

HOUSTON SPACE CENTRE

Technically, they spell it as 'Space Center',
but I refuse to submit to your sensible ways
of spelling things, America.

*We went to NASA!! I'd been to Kennedy
Space Center in Florida, so I was pumped
for this one.*

Please never be 'pumped' for anything. It was incredibly cool,
though! Also, it turned out that everyone who worked there
was a student, so it was like a mini-convention for us.
Thanks to everyone who let us cut the lines!

*We went for a tour of the actual
NASA campus, which was exciting!*

A real moon-robot with ultra-precise claw hands!

It looks like a scientist bred a human with a quad-bike. "KILL Meeee PleEASE end my SUffering!!"

#1 on the list of vehicles Phil should never pilot.

Chris, our video technician, and I bought the same t-shirt! Space swag.

Dan deeply appreciating the history of the Saturn V.

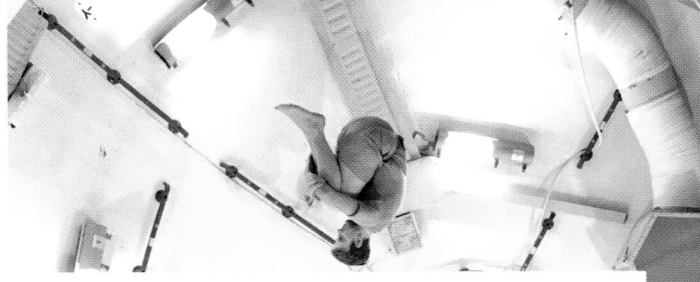

I posted this photo on Instagram and flipped it upside down, saying I was 'having a float' in NASA's anti-gravity chamber, and a lot of people believed me. Shout out to all the people who think we have that technology... never stop believing.

THE CADILLAC RANCH

IS THIS THE WAY TO AMARILLOOOO?

Don't know what was worth singing about TBH.

Wow, Dan.

Well, the hotel receptionist did tell us not to go to the bar opposite our hotel because "people like to play with their guns in it."

True.

Anyway, something cool we heard about was an art instillation of a bunch of Cadillacs buried in the earth!

The ground was littered with spray paint cans and the idea was that anyone can come and paint/tag whatever they want. It looked awesome!

Don't mess with our gang.

Dan spent about 30 minutes spraying his magnum opus.

Is it, technically, the rarest Pepe in the entire world? I apologise for nothing.

It was very warm.

I was wearing two coatings of SPF 50.

SAN FRAN CISCO

Now San Fran was an adventure!

We had a rare 'day off'.

What's that? A sandwich?

So we hopped in a cab and decided to do everything from seal watching to street viewing to wood delving!

We voyaged to the pier in hopes of finding some top seal-age.

We managed to pose and look cool for about 4 seconds before we froze to death.

Where did that wind come from? Nearly blew my nipples clean off.

Lefty's
THE LEFT HAND STORE

Dan found his people!

I have never felt weirder or more outcast than when I stepped into that left-handed store. We don't need our own oven gloves?!

Mildly inappropriate Alcatraz merch?

We invested in these snazzy San Fran tourist jackets to shield us from the Arctic blast.

Look at us, they didn't even help.

We had to stop for a caricature!

To be honest, he gave me a jaw line, so I'm not complaining.

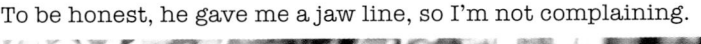

They were everything we hoped they'd be.

Truly majestic creatures. They can galumph straight into my heart.

MUIR WOODS NATIONAL MONUMENT
NATIONAL PARK SERVICE DEPARTMENT OF INTERIOR

We hopped in a cab and somehow convinced the driver to take us all the way to the woods across the bridge and back.

He was the nicest guy ever!
Maybe not the best driver, though.

No, I literally accepted death about four times driving down the cliff path to the woods. At least he waited in the car for us!

These are the mysterious Muir Woods, known
for having some of the world's tallest trees...

And the angry chimp civilisation from the *Planet of the Apes* reboot!

We unfortunately didn't see any hyper-intelligent apes.

We did spot this deer, though!

These are the two worst photos in this book.

And this super cute chipmunk!

GRRAaargh... just looking at it makes me want it to stick it in my mouth and punch something.

Wow. Something actually taller than us!

Phil soiling the spirit of the woods.

Hey! I'm majestic.

Hiding from the Nazgûl.

Underneath-the-selfie

My bear dad.

Much scenic. Very valley. Much tree. Wow.

What even happened here?

Universe briefly imploded, I think.

We were then racing against the clock to get to the Golden Gate Bridge for the sunset!

We ended up driving into some abandoned military base and hopping over a fence to get a good view.

AND WHAT A VIEW IT WAS!

We then drove up to the highest point in the city to soak in one last view!

San Fran definitely wins the awards for coolest-looking and least-fun-to-park-a-car-in city.

Then, after a two-hour drive to our next hotel, we bid farewell to our driver.

He stuck with us the whole day! His family probably thought we kidnapped him.

We had to get a photo with him after our adventure. What a dude.

VISITING INSTAGRAM!

So Zuckerberg pinged me a DM and asked if we wanted a tour of his crib.

Lying is bad.

Okay, the lovely peeps of Instagram offered to take us on a tour of their campus that they share with Facebook! When they mentioned there was free food, it was an instant yes.

Nine restaurants of free food to be precise.

We never wanted to leave.

For some reason there was a car in the Instagram office.

And Phil took the wheel! I was scared to even pretend.

It had no wheels but I still could have killed someone.

This is where Facebook plots their world domination.

It was like *Minority Report* but with much taller actors!

Tom Cruise just unsubscribed.

A literal Facebook wall! How meta.

We defaced it with our unworthy names.

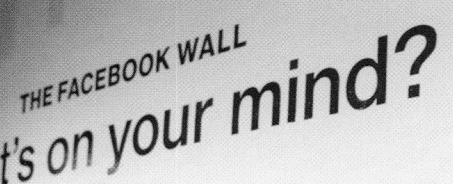

THE FACEBOOK WALL

t's on your mind?

A typical Facebook office.

Definitely an artificially intelligent war machine.

Shh, they are still listening.

SEATTLE

Seattle was one of my fav places. It just had an unexplainable vibe that satisfied me.

Like stroking a cat's fur in the right direction.

Yes.

Or pressing a clean toe into a fresh lump of sand.

I guess?

Or–

–Let's quit while we're ahead.

The trees in Seattle were 👌

You can't just bang out an emoji 170 pages into this book!

It's the only way I could explain my feelings about these very damp aesthetic trees.

Okay, they were pretty sexy.

Ah, so you poo on my emoji and then reveal yourself as a dendrophile? I'm not even surprised.

THE SPACE NEEDLE

I was expecting Mulder and Scully to be investigating this observation tower. It's so alien-like and mysterious.

It had that real, old-as-heck retro futurist vibe. Now I suppose you are expecting a passage about the journey to the top and the wonderful view?

Alas no.

They were too busy and wouldn't let us in! Always check the website before you travel, folks.

Okay, that's your one emoji used up for the book.

It's like a metal Kinder Surprise with a Phil inside.

That would be disappointing.

THE WORLD'S FIRST STARBUCKS!

We completed our internal white-girl pilgrimage and visited the first ever Starbucks!

I actually stroked the window and silently cried. So much caffeine and sugar has run through my veins thanks to this building.

I'm just gonna say it, the mermaid has visible nipples.

Are we allowed to publish cartoon mermaid nipples in this book?

LET'S FIND OUT.

Free the mermaid nipple!

This session went on for about an hour before we found an acceptable one.

VEGAS

Dan and Phil RETURNED TO VEGAS!

Yeah! This wasn't originally our plan, but we added it
as a last-minute date that meant we were conveniently
in Vegas for my birthday.

Yes. How convenient.

Honestly, it was kind of the FBI to let us
return after what happened last time.

*I know! At least we managed to get through this visit
without having to run away with the Cirque.*

Good times.

Phil literally bathing in sun cream.

I couldn't risk a *puts sunglasses on* Phil IS on fire situation!

Literally jump out of this book right now and banish yourself.

We went up the fake Eiffel Tower to get a drink with a view!

Phil immediately proceeded to get French toast cream on his wrist.

I was once trapped in a theme park ride queue with one of these for an hour. It was not a pretty sight.

A black bedazzled fedora to go with my Gatorland cap!

You have to destroy this immediately.

M'Vegas *tip*.

Then it was MY BIRTHDAY! Let us take a moment to appreciate the wrapping on a gift I was given on the tour bus.

But then, when we went into the theatre...

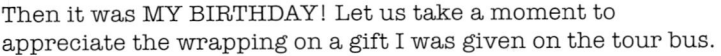

Witness the moment of glory when Dan was presented with a LLAMACORN PIÑATA.

It was the single most beautiful thing I'd ever seen. I could not bring myself to violently destroy it and guzzle its innards.

Phil defiling yet another helpless animal.

Then, hilariously, we asked the theatre to order us a car to take us back to our hotel and look what they sent us.

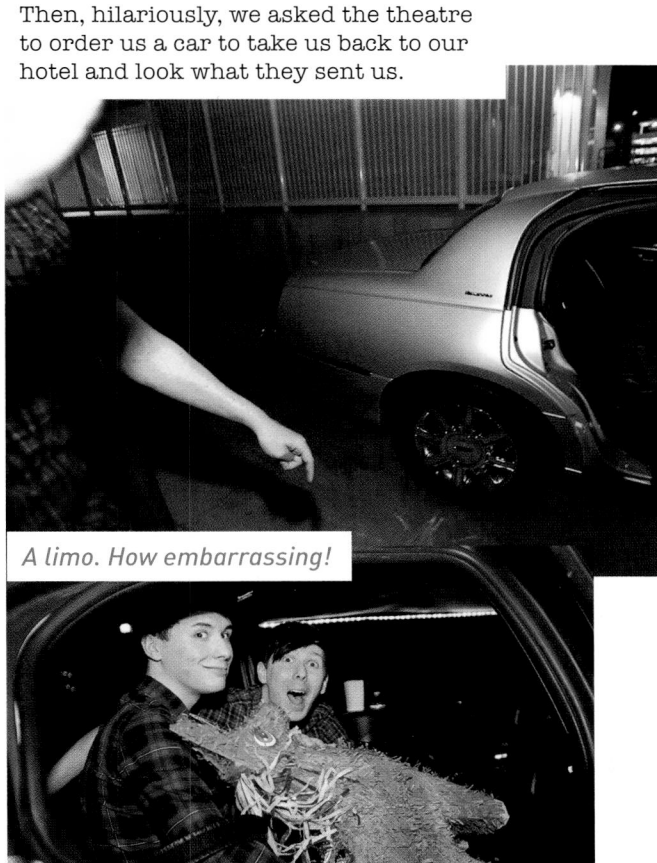

A limo. How embarrassing!

I bet they thought they were doing something nice for your birthday, but OMG.

Getting into a limo and gliding past all our followers is really, really not Dan and Phil style.

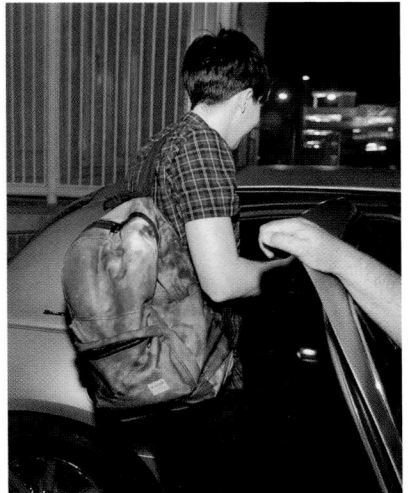

Mortifying.

What did you wish for?

The cake to magically replenish itself with each bite.

Then it was time to HIT THE TOWN!

With my Llamacorn Piñata, which I still had. Surprisingly, in Vegas no one questioned a thing!

We went to go see a water acrobatics show, which was fun!

TATINOF had better musical numbers and set pieces – just saying.

Then it was time to HIT THE SLOTS!

Anything else you can say you 'hit' while we're here?

Oh just one thing... THE JACKPOT.

Oh my god yeah, Phil got so lucky!

It was skill, Dan, skill.

So here's what happened. After blowing my life savings on an incredibly fun *Game of Thrones* slot machine, I convinced Phil to put $2 (that's seriously all) into a *Gremlins* branded machine.

Hey, it's one of my favourite movies! So I slid in two Georges and hit spin.

Now this *Gremlins* machine was a four by five grid of slots that could line up. On Phil's first spin, every single slot in the grid lined up with the same image.

Phil's actual face when this happened.

I couldn't believe it!

A crowd gathered as the machine started blaring alarms with cackling Gremlins flying all over the screen and the winnings counter just kept going up and up.

Get this right, from $2 I won $550!!

Everyone hates you, Phil.

So, I then did what any sensible person would do. I bought a $100 chip, went up to a roulette table and put it all on red.

This is obviously the worst idea ever, so our entire group was pre-cringing, ready for the night to end on a flop. We were all terrified!

The grumpy lady spun that wheel and we watched it bounce and skip across the number, it teetered on the edge of black and green and with its final ounce of momentum... BAM. Red!

We were honestly so relieved that none of us even cheered, we just thought 'thank god' and GTFO of there as fast as we could.

As for what happened the rest of that night, Dan...

What happens in Vegas stays in Vegas!

STEAMING

Here I present an incriminating selection of Dan 'steaming'.

What? It is steaming! Our vocal coach, Jimmy, instructed us that it was super-important when doing a lot of shows to keep your vocal chords moist.

Of course, Dan! Keep your 'chords' 'moist'.

That's literally it, Phil. It's just inhaling the steam from boiling water – loads of people do it.

'That', 'Phil', 'Water', 'People'?

Oh, whatever. Look, I found one of you!

Delete this incriminating image!

THE PEANUT SHOP, INC.
THE PEANUT SHOP
BOILED PEANUTS
OPEN
NASHVILLE NUT
Fresh
ROASTED NUTS
CARAMEL CORN
Coca-Cola
SOLD HERE
DRINKS
HERE
GET YOUR DIP ON
HOT & SPICY BOILED P-NUTS

LLBO
Dangerous Dan's diner
"The Burgers are Bigger at the Double D"
Dangerous Dan's diner
"The Burgers are Bigger at the Double D"
Dangerous Dan's diner
"The Burgers are Bigger at the Double D"

June 7, 2016

NASA

10287   10287

e All.

PINK

AC/DC

Paris
LAS VEGAS

EIFFEL TOWER
EXPERIENCE

AMAZING
PICTURES

PHOTO CLAIM
TICKET

PHOTO ASSOCIATION METHOD PATENT PENDING

June 11th, 2016

EIFFELTOWER
EXPERIENCE

May 6, 2016

June 11th, 2016

DIL'S ADVENTURE

Now, who can forget the real star of the show?

Gosh, it does make me nostalgic! To remember the time we birthed him in our gaming room with those bunny slippers and the clown suit pyjamas.

Maybe don't bring up the pyjamas, Phil; you know it's a sore topic.

Oops, sorry. Honestly, though, I've never felt like more of a proud dad than seeing him burst out of a door in the corner of a theatre and making the people near him collapse in terror.

From struggling to do the dishes, to magically forcing us to do them in an alternate dimension, he's our Dil!

We're so glad that Dil could take time out of his schedule and come on tour with us.

He's a pretty busy guy, what with the GF, his science career and travelling the world as an ambassador for the 'YouTube Let's Play Famous Characters Guild'.

I mean, the paperwork with EA took a long time and he was very demanding.

Oh, yeah! Well, this book isn't the place to discuss all of that. To think he wanted 200 white puppies in every dressing room. How is that possible? Where would we have stored them?

I thought it was a bit OTT when he'd order a pepperoni pizza and then make us pick all the toppings off individually – but I can relate to being picky.

Well, there was that one time he stormed out of the theatre right before he had to go on stage.

I guess it wasn't fair that he only got to say three lines with his real voice the whole time.

Also, when his giant head got stuck in the tour bus and we had to grease him out of it.

We used all the butter that was supposed to be for two months of toast for me, but I guess it had to be done!

And the crew didn't appreciate half their salary being transferred to Dil for his team of personal masseuses, but I'm sure they understood how important Dil's participation was for the art of the show.

We're just happy he could join us. Thanks, Dil!

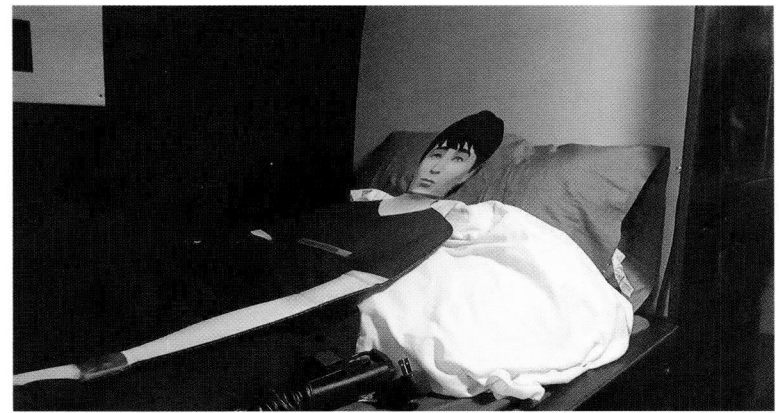

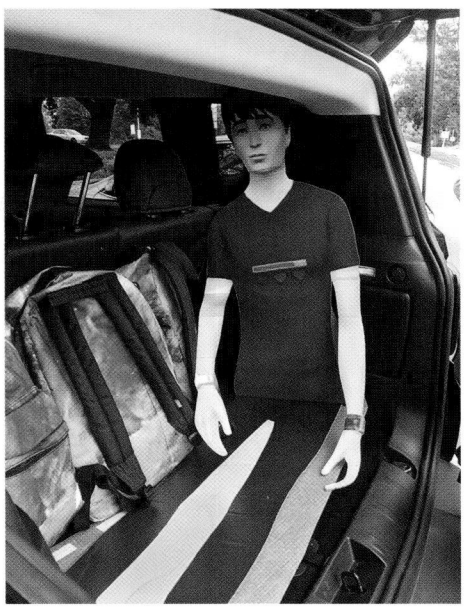

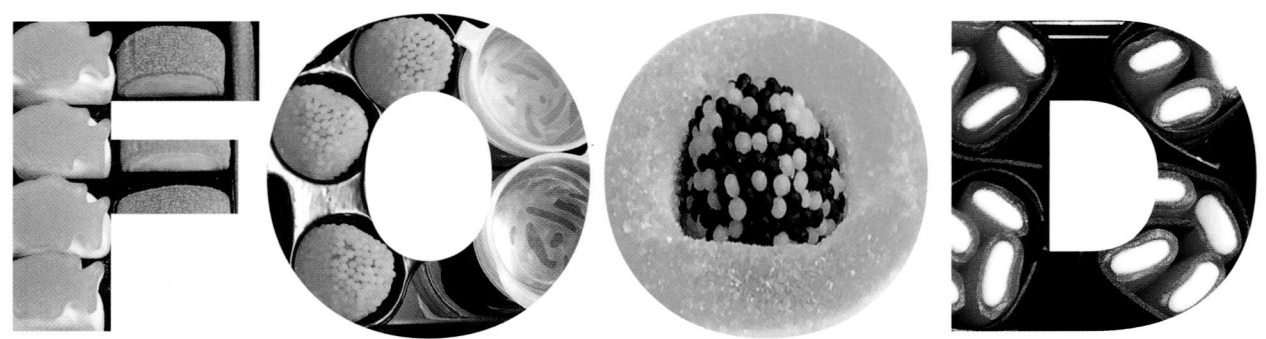

FOOD

As we all know, the most important thing in life is food.

What you eat, when you eat it and where are the biggest questions in life. And we were on tour!

This was a challenge.

Living on the road and out of hotel rooms made it almost impossible to cook any food, which meant A LOT of room service and takeout. This may have led to some slightly unhealthy choices from me...

Slightly?

If you offer me a kale salad or a waffle with extra syrup and cream, what do you expect me to pick?!

I'm not even disagreeing. It was a one-way trip to shame land, via all the carbs in the universe, and I don't regret a single day of it. I apologise in advance for the lack of green on these pages.

Unless it's gummy and green, we had a lot of that.

STOP JUDGING ME, OKAY.

Coconut shrimp in our first ever meal in an actual Bubba Gump Shrimp! They played *Forrest Gump* on all of the TVs.

Big Gulps, more like 'now I need to pee so bad because I drank so much liquid'.

I'm sure the marketing department is rushing to change the name as we speak.

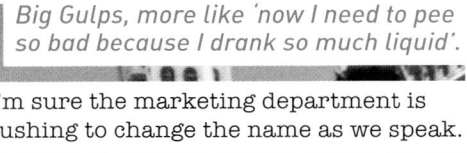

Team burgers at Flip Burger!

Named after me, of course.

A world famous Baltimore crab cake!

How was it?

CLAWESOME!

ejector seat

Just before I realised that Cheetos are cheese flavoured! I swear they don't taste like cheese.

No cheese shaming here, Phil, despite how guilty you look.

Security guard Louie got us a 'light snack' for National Donut Day.

I just dribbled over the keyboard.

What am I even doing?

I think these images are better left without captions.

An actual cupcake-flavoured pancake from IHOP! It was more delicious than you can convey with the English language. I'd have to start making inappropriate noises.

Phil, we're categorising this as a non-fiction hardback, not erotic cooking.

Just two hunis loving life in the big city!

This photoset is a violation of my basic human rights.

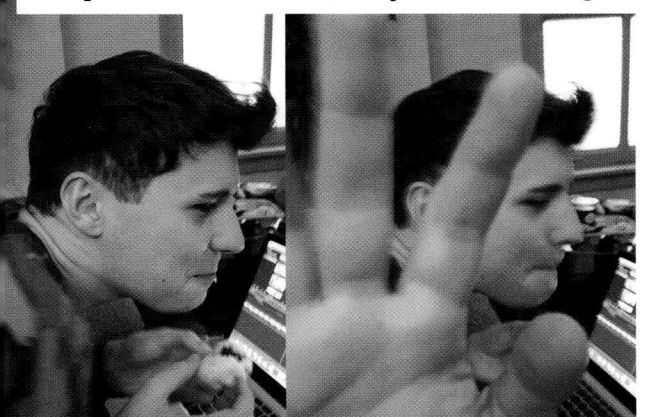

The Durham venue had an ice cream machine and it was the single best moment of my life.

Better than performing at the Dolby Theatre in Hollywood?

Do you really want the answer?

A dangerous menu.

The worst day of my life.

Some American 'bread' with three kinds of butter and icing to dip it in!

I went for 'butter cookie' and Phil had 'birthday cake shake'.

It had huge lumps of cake in it! It was a bit of a mistake.

Trying Buckeyes! The national candy of Ohio.

Phil's review: Pretty great!

Dan's review: A horrifying peanutty cup of regret.

That tour bus sushi!

Cat took us to the Griddle Cafe in LA, and they sold pancakes bigger than the entire solar system!

So much cream.

We failed.

We managed to eat about ¼ of one pancake.

I will eat this book if anyone can finish a full stack of those pancakes.

WEIRD ROOM SERVICE ENCOUNTERS WITH PHIL!

1. THE SILENT LADY

Order: *Teriyaki chicken salad and an iced coffee*

What happened: *I opened the door to a lady with black hair who was dressed head to toe in black. She delivered my salad in complete silence, with unwavering creepy eye contact! I asked how she was and she didn't respond. I gave her the money and she didn't say thank you. She just floated away out of the door. I think she was either a ghost or she was intensely scared of my fluorescent-green Muppet pyjamas. Probably the latter.*

Weirdness ranking: *3 stars*

2. FLIRTY MCFLIRTERSON

Order: *Bacon waffles and a large pot of coffee*

What happened: *A day when another human shows me any kind of romantic attention is a very rare day, but especially when I answer the door to a delivery of bacon waffles in a Buffy t-shirt and oversized Star Wars PJs. I was greeted by a middle-aged blonde lady carrying my breakfast, and I politely said, "Thank you," and she said, "Wow, what a beautiful accent, it matches your face too! What strong features you have!" I stared at her in stunned silence. WHAT IS A STRONG FEATURE? Did she just sass my nose? I wasn't sure, but then she followed it up with, "Let me know if you ever need any extra syrup, if you know what I mean!" If you know what I mean!?!? NO. WHAT? I wasn't sure I wanted to know what she meant, so I just said, "Oh, hah, this is a great amount of syrup for me, thanks!" I closed the door. Oh dear.*

Weirdness ranking: *4 stars*

3. THE RAVE MACHINE

Order: *A large vanilla milkshake (stop judging me)*

What happened: *A teen guy arrived with my long-overdue shake and handed it to me. I made the mistake of saying "thank you", revealing my English accent, to which he started a conversation about the Mother Country! "Hey, so do you live in London?" he asked. "Why, yes I do," I replied, trying to be as uninteresting as possible so I could drink my sweet, sweet milkshake. He then followed with, "So do you go to a lot of raves in England?"... A lot of raves?!?! What does someone even say to that? I was silent for slightly too long before saying, "Yeah, I don't really rave much. I mean. I'm kind of done with raving." Why am I so awkward? Why did I pretend to have ever raved? He stared at me blankly and closed the door. Remind me never to speak to another human ever again.*

Weirdness ranking: *3 stars*
(mainly due to my awkwardness, but, seriously, who uses the word rave?)

4. THE INVENTOR

Order: *Texan burger with fries and a Diet Coke*

What happened: *An old, burly cowboy delivered my burger in Texas. And, as the table was annoyingly big to push through my door, he revealed a strange springy metal contraption. He then pinned it into the hinge of the door to stop it closing! I said, "Wow, that's a cool little invention to stop the door closing! I've never seen one of those before." He pulled a sad face and replied, "I know. I invented it! I'd be a millionaire if they had let me have the patent. I definitely wouldn't be here delivering food to you. It was my life's work and it ended in ruins." WHAT DO YOU EVEN SAY TO THAT? I just replied, "Oh no! That really sucks?" I did give him a big tip out of guilt! Maybe that's his technique? He just pretends to have invented this springy thing to guilt people into tips? Either way I'm sorry for mortifying you, Mr Room Service Cowboy.*

Weirdness ranking: *4 stars*

5. THE LOUDEST SALESMAN ON EARTH

Order: *Continental breakfast*

What happened: *Before Vegas we had to get up at about 6am for the flight so I was feeling particularly delicate. I'd hung the magical room service menu on my door handle the night before and was awoken at 5:50am by the loudest knock of all time. I swear it was in the rhythm of 'We Will Rock You', but don't quote me on that. I was greeted by a tiny bald man who practically screamed in my face, "GOOD MORNING, SIR! ISN'T IT A BEAUTIFUL DAY TO BE UP THIS EARLY?" It took all my will not to reply with, "NOT WHEN YOU ARE SHOUTING IN MY FACE." I stayed politely quiet as he set up my breakfast and then he noticed my obviously snazzy NASA t-shirt. "HOW MUCH FOR YOU TO SELL THAT T-SHIRT?" he asked. I thought he was joking! I gave him a laugh. and said, "Aw, glad you like it." "NO, SERIOUSLY? I WILL GIVE YOU FREE BREAKFAST IF YOU SELL ME YOUR NASA SHIRT." Why does this happen to me? What is happening? Why is a strange man trying to buy my clothes in my bedroom at 6am? I just replied with, "Not today, sorry, but now you have a reason to go to the Space Centre hahaha," and slowly closed the door on his genuinely disappointed face. I heard him whistling the theme tune to 'A Whole New World' from Aladdin as he walked away down the corridor.*

Weirdness ranking: *5 stars*

THE MERCH TEAM!

Another gang of hooligans in the *TATINOF* squad was the merch team!

Like a little appendix on the beast that hands out t-shirts.

That's the single worst mental image I've had making this so far.

The team included my (actual) bro Martyn and Cornelia, who were with us the whole time, which was nice!

They had their own bus, and the mammoth task of literally building a store in every theatre lobby and lovingly laying out flower crowns to be bestowed upon people like a beautiful meadow.

Martyn said sometimes he couldn't work with the merch, as people would queue up to take selfies with him and he couldn't get anything done!

The touch of Phil, everyone. Also, Cornelia worked so hard that I'm starting to believe her 'Swedish' identity is actually code for 'a cyborg built to process a million calculations a second and have cool red hair'.

They were such an awesome, kind, cool group of people who got to interact with our audience all day – and by the end of the tour, while we looked spherical from all the waffles, they all looked like Olympians from herding boxes all day.

The 'merch workout' – I'd buy the DVD.

Brutal scenes of cruelty to llama hats. Somebody call the authorities!

An anonymous Martyn fan graffiti artist.

THE DESIGNS

We saw the tour as an opportunity to have some fun with the merch. The thing is that for most artists, the merch is 'cool' and edgy looking, usually because the artist is cool and edgy.

We're lame and soft, like pillows or slightly squashed marshmallows.

So, while usually with merch we try to think outside the box and it ends up being quite cute and colourful, with the tour we thought, "Hey, we're living the rock star dream, why not have rock star merch?!"

To be clear, we are joking.

Oh totally, it's completely ironic. We sought out a designer who'd drawn merch for actual bands that are actually rock 'n' roll and we said, "Hey, do it for Dan and Phil" – and thus:

TOTES EDGE.

And any coolness we've ever had just evaporated into a fine mist.

They're so cool looking, it's hilarious!

They are pretty funny. Then for America we had a conundrum: how can we change it to make the people of the USA like it?

Boom.

We apologise for nothing.

This is definitely one of those that I can't tell if it's more amazing or offensive?

Right in the middle, Phil. That's the sweet spot.

And what about Australia, you ask? What colour tones and patterns speak to them?

indiscernible marsupial noises

It's basically sand and animal prints.

Australia!

All a true work of art. Dan and Phil, living the rock star dream,
one ironic t-shirt at a time.

THE FAILED PA

Throughout this book you may have seen some truly scenic panoramas.

Sweeping vistas of beauty that give you unparalleled views of the world.

On this page you will find none of them.

This is a dark land for the panoramas that went horribly, horribly wrong.

What you see here may never be unseen, or forgiven.

Okay you must have moved deliberately that time!

You're right; we knew what you were attempting.

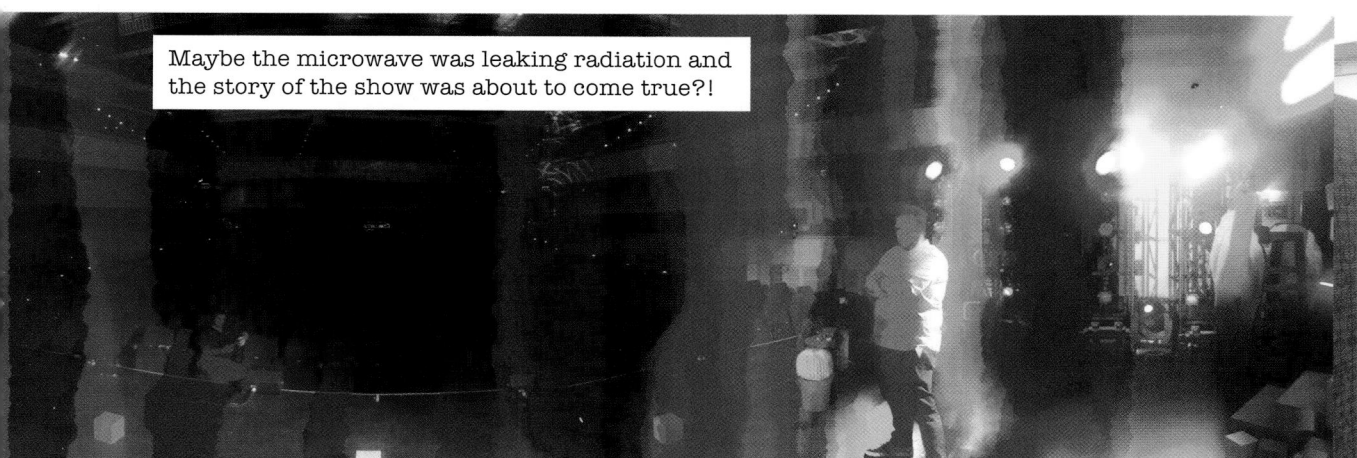

Maybe the microwave was leaking radiation and the story of the show was about to come true?!

NORAMA ZONE

Nice idea. What a scenic background. But there seems to have been some kind of space/time implosion on the right there.

Alright, what happened in this theatre?

BURN IT. WHAT IS HAPPENING?

You were gesticulating about something and I didn't say I was taking it! Don't move during panoramas, people.

STAGE TO SCREEN

Another huge thing we were working on while on tour (just keep adding to that pile) was the documentary film for YouTube Originals!

Planning this documentary, filming interviews for it and then planning the big show at the Dolby Theatre took up pretty much any free time we might have had!

It was crazy because we'd go from thinking about the tour, to making videos, to our cameraman, Matt, appearing out of thin air and going, "Surprise! Today is a filming day!" and we had to be ready to go.

Dan shamelessly styling himself.

Yeah, before you immediately dropped that mirror and gave us all seven years of bad luck.

I thought we all agreed I shouldn't be allowed to hold anything?! I blame everyone but me.

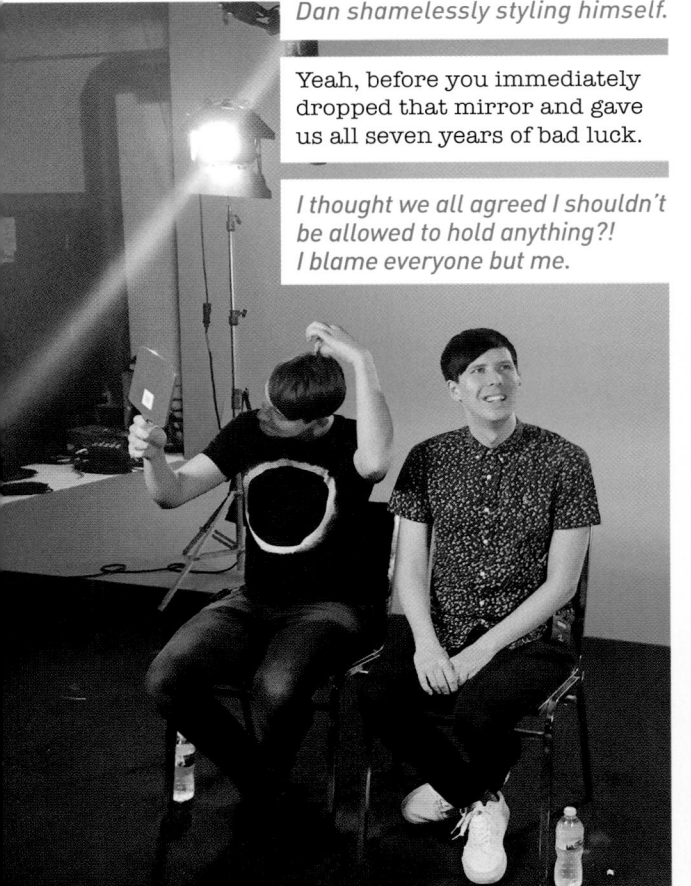

The video gallery that was filming our performance at the Dolby! I was told not to go near it.

SRSBSNSS

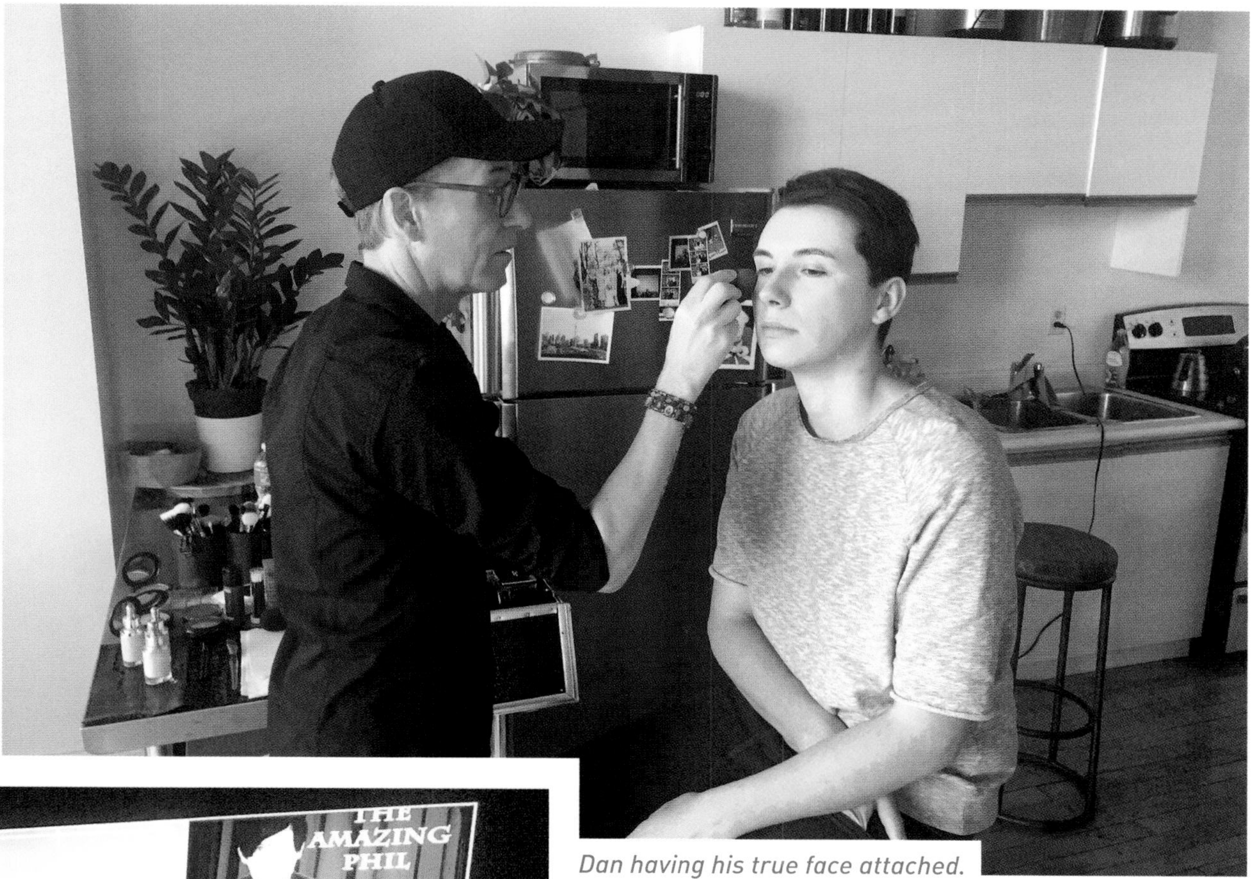

Dan having his true face attached.

CRAFTS

An important and beautiful part of our show was the crafts.

What is the Tumblr tag video series in real life, you ask? Well, it's the love child of Dan's old PO Box videos and DanAndPhilCRAFTS. A.K.A. a hellish dimension you will never erase from your memory.

Hey! I'd say only a strong half were inappropriate. There was a lot of genuinely great art in it too! Unfortunately, we could only pick six per show, but wading through people's creations was always a favourite part of my day.

Speaking of inappropriate, remember that sanitary pad with a derpy face of me stuck to it that someone named the 'Danitary Pad'?

That was a strong no from me and Director Ed. Thank all that is sacred that we are around to protect people's eyes.

Burn it.

A life-like sculpture of myself.

I don't see why you were so reluctant to wear this beautiful crown that was lovingly crafted for you.

You know cotton wool is one of my biggest fears! I almost imploded into a loose skin pile when you put that on my head.

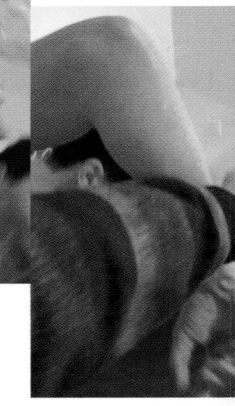

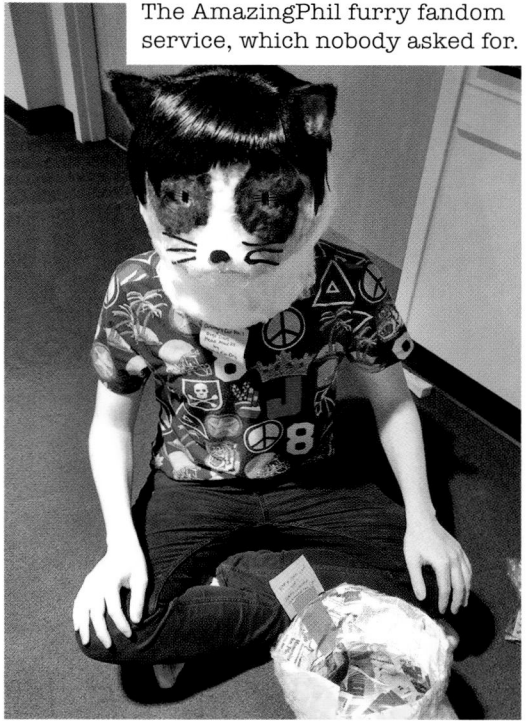

The AmazingPhil furry fandom service, which nobody asked for.

Why?

Literally the most terrifying drawing ever created by humans. Thank you for scarring me!

Yes, that is a John Cena figure with a picture of Dil's face riding a topiary llama.

I have been here since 2009 & will be here forever, changed my life for the better in so many ways and I can't thank you guys enough
Love and hugs ♡
georgia
xoxox

IS THIS HAPPENING RIGHT NOW. ♡much ♡phan ♡and ♡proud!
proud of yous ♡
#O.T.I ♡ Phoebe

Hi Dan and Phil,
Thankyou for being the Sunshines I need in life
Katie xxxx ♡

Name Tamara
Address Sydney, Australia.
Message love you both so much!
thank you for radiating happiness + positivity.
♡ tamara

Welcome to Wales
remember to hug all dragons heah *rawr*

Thank-you for doing this tour! It was so surreal meeting you in Leeds!
Alisha
xoxo

To Dan & Phil
never stop doing

WHY R U SO TALL?

Dear Dan & Phil, it (som
I ♡ you guys so much
Thank you for being born xx
-Ceri-Anne ♡

Name Marlee
Address Amazing phil
Message

You brought my internet friends and I together, thank you!! ♡

Aly
I LOVE YOU SO MUCH
EVEN YOU DAN

It's been really nice meeting you both! I hope I meet you again!
Faye

Thank You for everything! I'm never taking my light up flashy shoes off now! ♡ ABBIE xxx

Dan & Phil
Thank-you for coming to Belfast "
love you both. ♡
Victoria
x

Name Megan
Address
Message Thank you so much for coming to Texas! I met you at VidCon 2 years ago and you were just so great I had to see you again! I hope you have enjoyed America enough to want to come back again! love you! ♡

Thanks for coming to glasgow got me two days off school Apprently I'm old Oil! ☺liver
was going to draw/paint intricate portrait of you both as Pepe, but I didn't have the time nor energy
I am sorry.

I TRIED SO HARD

Hi!
Thank you for making this the best birthday ever! So proud of you! love, Mia xxx

THINGS OVERHEARD ON TOUR!

Why does your bunk smell of peanut butter?

There is no fear greater than having a bee in your mouth.

How much whipped cream is too much whipped cream?

I got a Starbucks and they put my name as BONK.

Did you ever see a farmer put his hand up a cow when you were a kid?

Why is there a kettle in the shower?

Kalamawho?

I think I sat in a puddle of marmalade. At least I hope it was marmalade.

I saw a family of raccoons, so I knew it was important I called you.

Do you think blood will stain my dress?

I've always wanted to be a shepherd.

The Mummy Returns was underrated.

Do you think Chris Pratt is secretly attracted to his dinosaurs?

My abs are just squishier and less uptight.

Check your socks for scorpions! This is Texas after all.

Do you ever get a tingle when you remember there are ice-pops in the fridge?

Let me tweet a pic of your waffles! Mine look droopy.

Imagine if Spiderman got the face of a spider. Would people still love him?

My hair looks like a squirrel mated with it.

I lost my glasses! Oh wait. They were on my head.

Don't come in! I'm slightly naked.

Make sure you label your suitcase in case the bus is hit by a tornado.

Has anyone seen my hair straighteners? This is a category 10 disaster.

That tasted like a mouthful of sand, but worse.

Someone buy me a maple syrup water pistol.

Sometimes it actually hurts me that I don't own a shibe.

HEY BOYS, YOU SMELL FRESH.

Do you think there are any undiscovered colours out there?

I fell out of my bed three times last night.

Are you having secret popcorn every night?

I wish I lived in the Bates Motel.

So, there we go. It happened. It was amazing, and thankfully at no point did anyone or anything get set on fire.

I don't think my career would have ever lived through the irony; we shouldn't tempt fate like that.

And here we are, sat back on the sofa in our apartment, looking at each other writing captions for a photo album.

It's really weird that we're making eye contact as we write this right now. I'd prefer it if you didn't make this meta – you're ruining everyone's immersion.

Sorry. What even is normal life like now that we're back? We've been on this train for so long I never even thought about what would happen when it stops.

I guess it's back to making videos and then contemplating whatever the future will be! Oh no, I enjoyed having a plan... Phil, what do I do now?!

Uh oh, Dan's gonna have a crisis. Don't worry; I'm sure you'll think of something soon (he's doomed). Just enjoy sleeping on a bed that isn't moving for days on end and not having to get dressed and interact with anyone.

Now that sounds like a Dan plan. I might just roleplay as a bear and hibernate.

This year has definitely been the craziest and best year of my life. When I was younger, I never would have even dreamed that what we've done is possible!

The fact that silly 'Dan and Phil' on YouTube somehow created this incredible community of friendship, support, creativity and happiness is by far what I'm proudest of in life.

We're just two guys that have fun trying to be entertaining. So to be able to go on this adventure and experience what we have is incredible and we're so grateful.

Plus, all the exercise this tour has given me has probably extended my life by 10 years, so that's good.

So, to everyone who supported us, thank you and may this lump of paper and ink preserve our memories forever.

ZZ ZZZ ZZ...

THAT'S A WRAP

For everyone around the world who came to see the show.

And everyone on the internet who's supported us for years.

Our incredible crew who helped us make the show.

Our squad that had to spend way too much time with us.

We actually did it. We went outside.

This was TATINOF...

Goodbye!

THE AMAZING BOOK IS NOT ON FIRE

THE WORLD OF DAN AND PHIL

DAN HOWELL AND PHIL LESTER

Random House New York

With special thanks to: Kel Alexander, Andrea Mercado, Ashley Smith, Carolyn Love, Courtnie Bierman, Valeria Lombardo, Aleesha Gyarmati, Aline Ilushkina, Lucy Forder, Malin Forsman, Martyna Oleszkiewicz, Ida, Sophie Milton, Alexandra Armaos, blackrabbit777, Irina Tarakanova, David Keller, Rafiqah Ramil, Sian Lacourse, Alice Wang, Amy Mijovic-Couldwell, Ashley Knehans, Beth, Mary Duffy, Kiera, Koleen Sta. Ana, Krysta Bound, Kumi McKenna, Lone Pedersson, Mia ONeill, Chontae Long, Brooklyn Arrigo, Kristina Uskova/Fan art, Elise Hagen/phanga, Holly Marr/pixel Dan and Phil, Ivana Zorn and Martin O'Neill/word clouds, Mr Bingo/hair portrait, iStockphoto, dafont.com, myfonts.com, pages 90–97 and 100–107 © BBC, page 150 © Sims, pages 198–199 © Getty Images, photography (endpapers, 3, 4, 9, 14, 15, 48, 49, 50, 63, 70, 81, 89, 98, 99, 116, 117, 125, 129, 139, 143, 154 and 155) by Dave Brown at Ape.

Visit us on the Web! randomhouseteens.com

Educators and librarians, for a variety of teaching tools, visit us at RHTeachersLibrarians.com

Library of Congress Cataloging-in-Publication Data
Howell, Dan, 1991–
The amazing book is not on fire : the world of Dan and Phil / Dan Howell, Phil Lester.
pages cm
Summary: YouTube stars Dan Howell and Phil Lester tell the humorous story of growing up, becoming YouTube stars, and give advice to their teen followers.
ISBN 978-1-101-93984-0 (trade) — ISBN 978-1-101-93985-7 (ebook)
1. Howell, Dan, 1991–. 2. Lester, Phil, 1987–. 3. Celebrities—England—Biography.
4. YouTube (Electronic resource). 5. Radio broadcasters—England—Biography.
I. Lester, Phil, 1987–. II. Title.
PN2287.H732 A3 2015 791.440922—dc23 [B] 2015026617

Design: Dave Brown at Ape. apeinc.co.uk

Printed in the United States of America   10 9

First American Edition

"I DEDICATE THIS TO MUM, DAD AND MARTYN (THE BEST FAMILY EVER) AND THANK YOU TO ANYONE WHO HAS EVER ENJOYED ONE OF MY VIDEOS! THIS IS FOR ALL OF YOU! (^_^)"

"I DEDICATE THIS BOOK TO MYSELF BECAUSE I WROTE IT."

"DAN, YOU CAN'T DEDICATE YOUR BOOK TO YOURSELF."

"WHY NOT? I DON'T WANT THIS TO BE LIKE A BORING AWARDS SHOW SPEECH WHERE I JUST THANK PEOPLE THAT ALREADY KNOW HOW I FEEL ABOUT THEM AND LEAVE, THAT'D BE POINTLESS."

"IT'S JUST A THING THAT YOU DO!"

"WELL MAYBE I DON'T WANT TO DO THE THING, MAYBE I'LL CREATE MY OWN NEW, BETTER THING."

"WE'RE ALREADY ARGUING AND THE BOOK HASN'T EVEN STARTED YET."

"THEY'RE GONNA START PLAYING THE AWKWARD STOPTALKING MUSIC SOON."

"JUST DEDICATE IT TO SOMETHING AND WE CAN GET ON WITH THE BOOK."

"ALRIGHT. I DEDICATE THIS BOOK TO THE PEOPLE READING IT BECAUSE YOU PRESUMABLY EITHER BOUGHT IT OR MAYBE STOLE IT IN WHICH CASE I'M NOT DEDICATING IT TO YOU BECAUSE THAT'S BAD."

"LET'S GO!"

Hello.

Well that's five characters out of the way.

Well done.

So how should we write this?

What do you mean?

Well we're two people talking in the same book: how are we gonna do that?

DIFFERENT COLOURS?

Nah, that'd be annoying.

DIFFERENT FONT?

That's even more annoying.

Why don't we just put our initials on the left?

Okay let's try that.

D: Hi!

P: Hello!

D: I'm Dan.

P: And I am Phil.

D&P: And welcome to
    The Amazing Book Is Not On Fire!

P: Wait, how did we both say that?!

D: I guess we said it at the same time? I have no idea.

P: Anyways, welcome to the book! Take off your shoes, make yourselves at home.

D: Are they reading our book or climbing inside it?

P: They can do whatever they want with it, except eat it. You can lick the vowels on this page, though, as we printed it with cola-flavoured ink!

D: That is not true: do not lick the page. Phil, behave, we've only been doing this for 20 lines.

P: I guess we should do some kind of introduction?

D: Yes that would be helpful. I think we should start by introducing ourselves for anyone who's wondering why they've spent a minute of their life reading us deciding what it is we're writing.

P: We are Dan and Phil and we make videos on the internet! Videos about ourselves and our lives and how we fit into the world.

D: And over the years, for some reason a lot of people enjoyed these things we made!

P: All these videos and shows and crazy things we've shared with our followers came together to create this huge world of Dan and Phil!

D: And that's why we made this book. You never know what might happen in the future. The internet might get deleted, a meteor could destroy the whole world, or one of us could die and it would be really sad.

P: Dan! Don't get like that already – we're only on the introduction.

D: Oops, sorry.

P: So we want to trap this giant crazy wonderful world that we've created with our audience inside an epic enchiridion. We hope that in the distant future an alien race will stumble across it and bring it back to their mothership where we will be worshipped as their new gods!

D: Well, it's not only for aliens to worship, I was thinking more general preservation of memories and stuff but okay.

P: I guess we should tell our story!

D: But where do we start? I mean a lot happened before we started making videos.

P: RIGHT AT THE BEGINNING.

I know polaroids are old but don't you just think they look cool?

DAY 1. DAN'S MUM ON DAN'S BIRTH

What day was it?
How's this for memory, I thought it must be a Tuesday and after checking I was right! (Obviously this scarred me for life, or I wouldn't remember.)

What was the weather like?
It was a clear summer night thankfully, as the ambulance took about an hour to arrive.

What time did you arrive at the hospital?
About 3am.

How long did the whole thing take?
You were born at 6:30 in the morning after days of labour. Seriously. I was in the hospital for two days before you decided to finally arrive – late as usual.

What was it like giving birth to Dan?
It was exhausting and I had to be cut up like a side of beef to get you out (you asked).

How much more painful was it than stubbing your toe?
It was infinitely more painful than stubbing a toe.

Why did you choose the name Dan?
I chose the name Dan because I like the name and didn't know any other Daniel babies so I thought it would be unusual. It turned out to be the most popular year on record for Daniel babies. Sorry.

What would you have named the baby if it was a girl?
If you were a girl we were going to call you Yazi. I had spent my pregnancy on a beach in Kenya where there was a girl named Yazi who cooked the best prawns ever, so we thought it would be a nice name! Thankfully for all concerned, especially you, you were a boy.

Was it worth it in hindsight?
Of course it was worth it – you are the apple of my eye etc. etc.

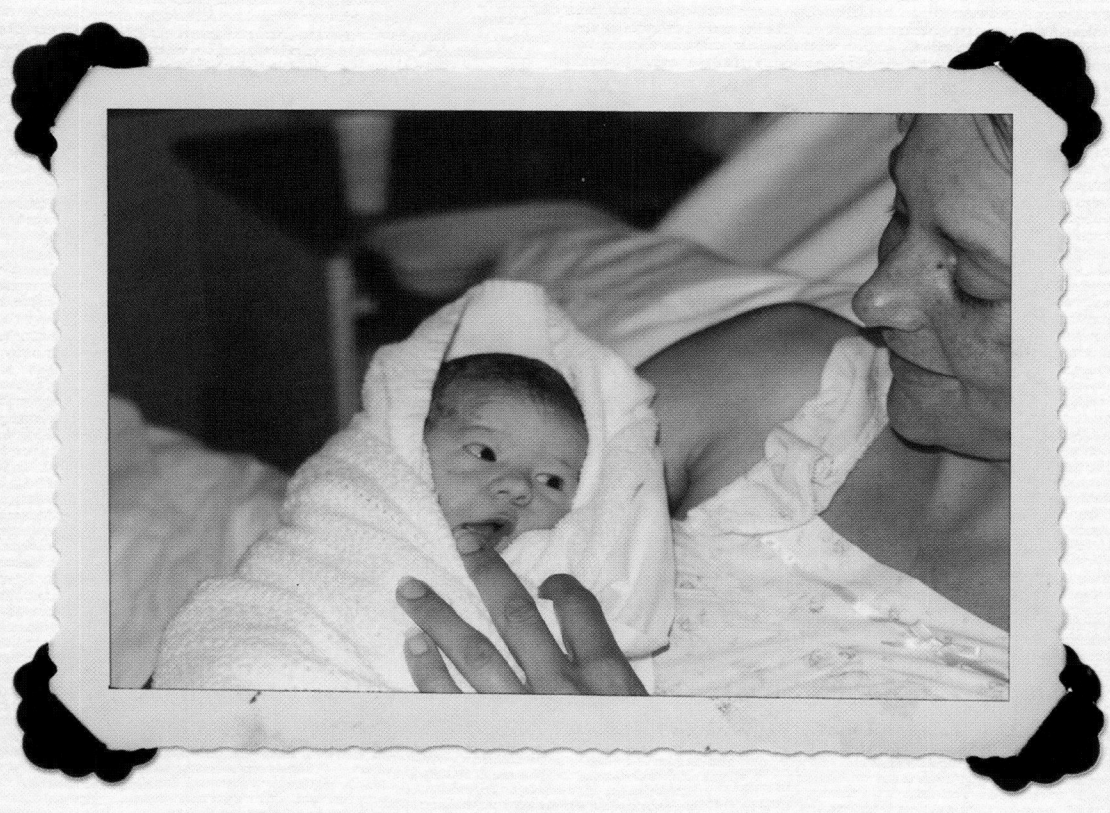

DAY 1. PHIL'S MUM ON PHIL'S BIRTH

What day of the week was it?
The early hours of Friday morning at 4am. Typical night owl Phil.

What was the weather like?
The weather was very cold, probably minus 3. Earlier in the month it was the coldest since the year 1740! There had been quite a lot of snow that month too.

What time did you arrive at the hospital?
We arrived at the hospital at about 9pm the night before. I remember the midwife reminded me of a friendly dolphin.

How long did the whole thing take?
About 8 hours! I could have flown to Florida in that time!

What was it like giving birth to Phil?
It was quite exhausting because you seemed quite comfy where you were even though you were three weeks early. I didn't have any pain relief. They gave me the gas and air machine but it was empty, aaargh!!! By the end of it I was getting a bit impatient. The midwife wanted Dad to stroke my brow and rub my back and I remember telling her I didn't want him to, I just needed to concentrate!

How much more painful was it than stubbing your toe?
It was like having 1,000 toes and stubbing them at the same time.

Why did you choose the name Phil?
I always liked the name Philip, it seemed a kind name and the Philips I knew at school were all nice people. Plus I thought it would go well with Martyn when you write Christmas cards!

What would you have named the baby if it was a girl?
If you had been a girl you would have been called Fiona.

Was it worth it in hindsight?
Was it worth it? Mmmn I think so! Hahaha, course it was: you bring us joy and happiness and I always wanted two boys so I got my wish. You were a very calm content baby and the nurses were quite surprised I had given birth. You hardly cried at all; you were very cute.

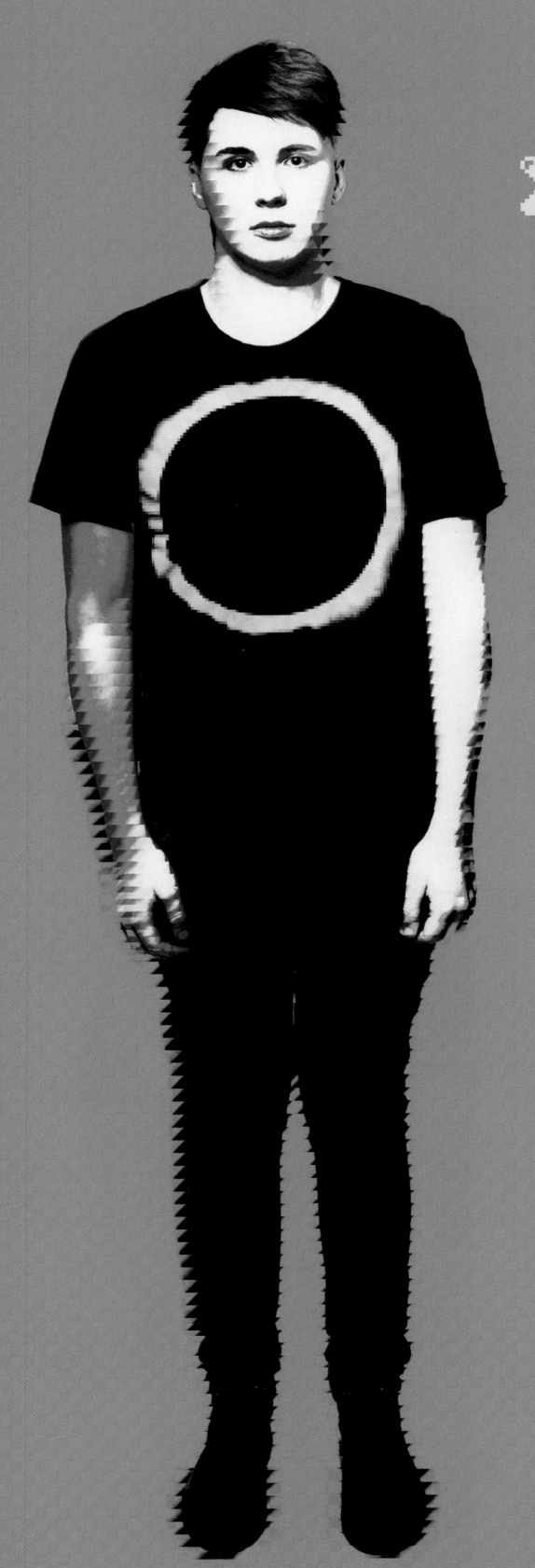

PLAYER 1 DAN

NAME
DAN HOWELL

INTERNET NAME
DANISNOTONFIRE

HEIGHT
6FT 3"

FAVOURITE COLOUR
BLACK

ANIMAL OF CHOICE
LLAMA

WEAKNESS
'SHARING SIZE'
BAGS OF CASHEW NUTS

SPECIAL POWER
PRETENDING SOMEONE'S
CALLING TO GET OUT OF
AN AWKWARD SITUATION

QUOTE
"I PROMISE I'LL DO IT
JUST AFTER I'VE FINISHED
THIS THING."

PLAYER 1 PHIL

NAME
PHILIP MICHAEL LESTER

INTERNET NAME
AMAZINGPHIL
(FORMERLY SNOWDUDE)

HEIGHT
6FT 2.9"

FAVOURITE COLOUR
BLUE

ANIMAL OF CHOICE
LION

WEAKNESS
CHEESE

SPECIAL POWER
CAN HICCUP FOR OVER
4 HOURS

QUOTE
"IF THIS PLAN INVOLVES
PANCAKES THEN I'M IN!"

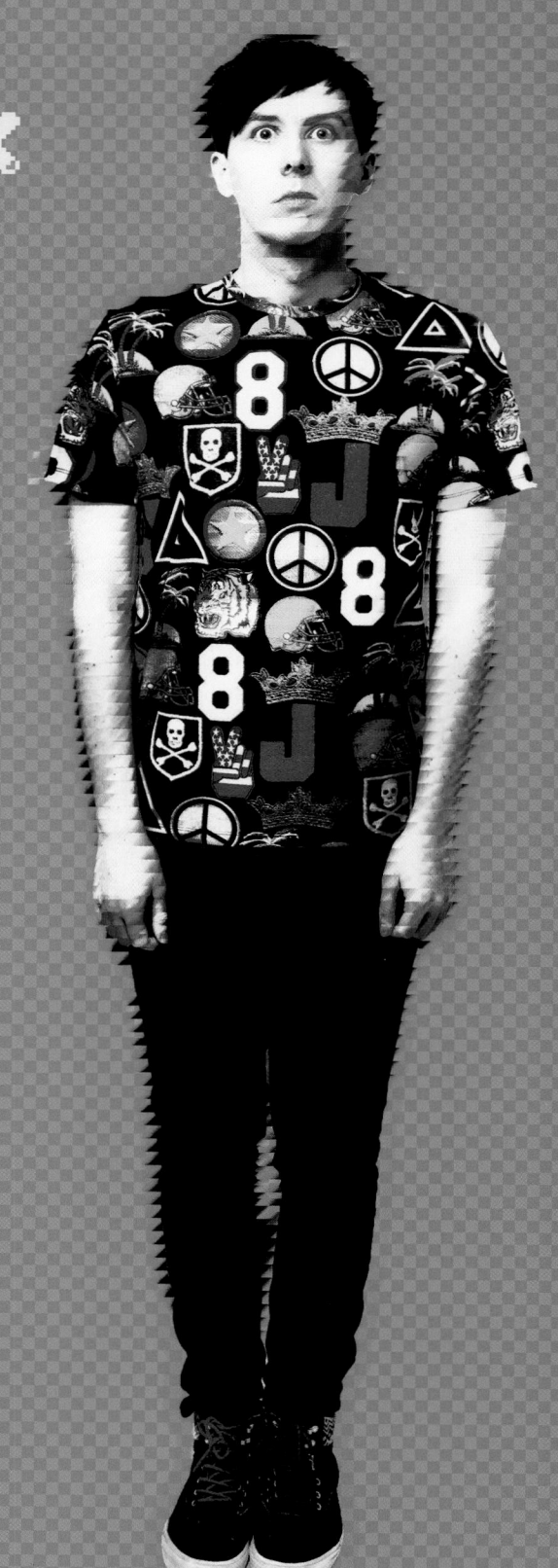

A-Z OF DAN

Awkward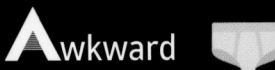

Bed

Cool shoes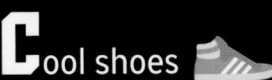

Darkness

Existential crisis

Food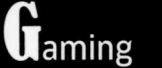

Gaming

Hugs

Internet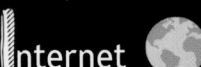

Joking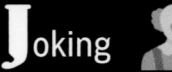

Kanye

Llamas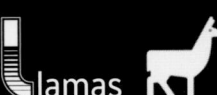

More food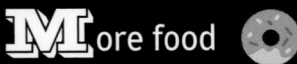

No

Oops

Procrastination

Questing

Running away from responsibility

Sleep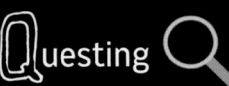

Tallness

Ugh

Videos

Winking inappropriately

X-files

YouTube

Zips in unconventional places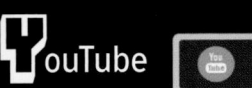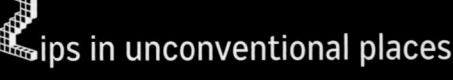

A–Z OF PHIL

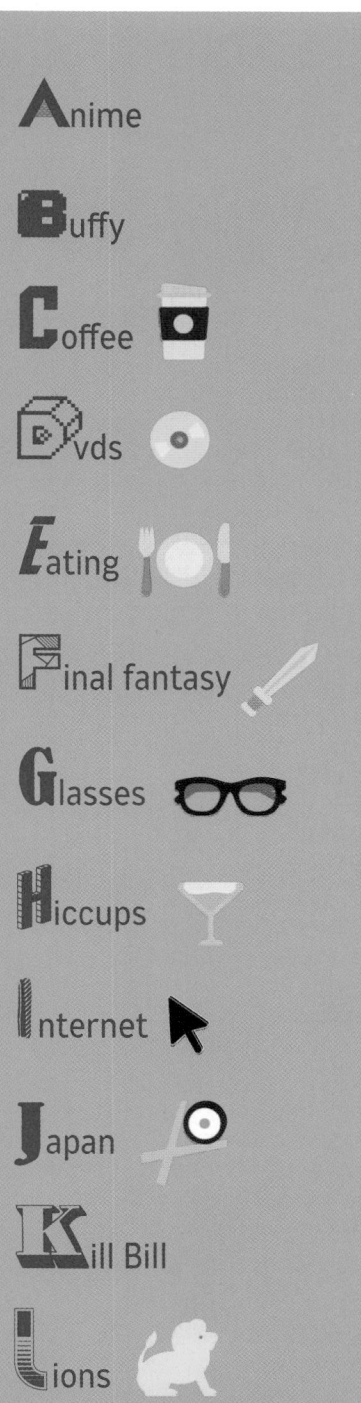

Anime

Buffy

Coffee

Dvds

Eating

Final fantasy

Glasses

Hiccups

Internet

Japan

Kill Bill

Lions

Muse

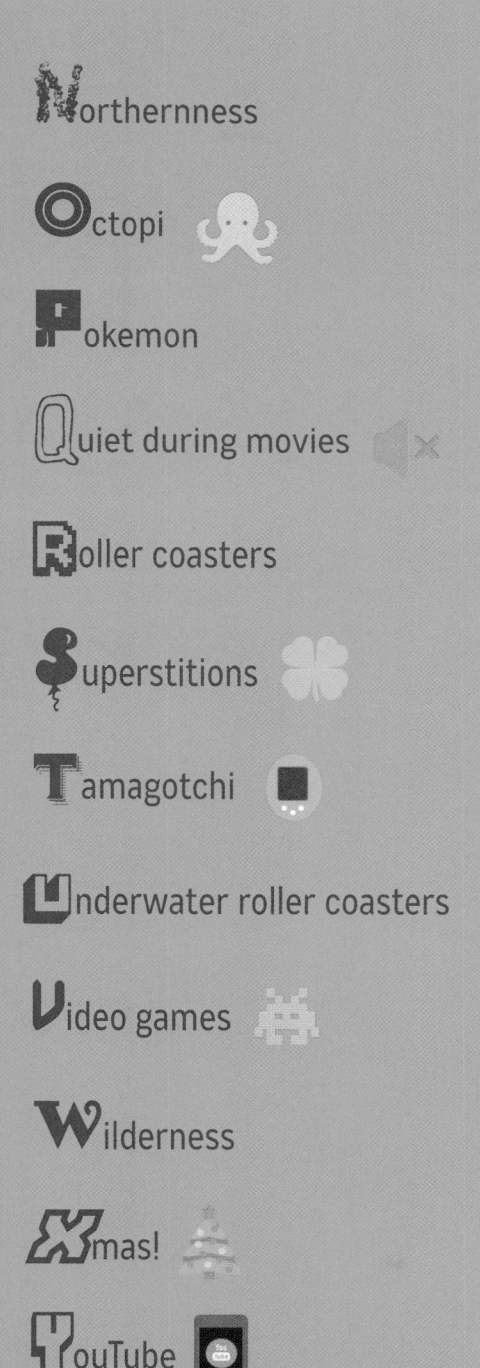

Northernness

Octopi

Pokemon

Quiet during movies

Roller coasters

Superstitions

Tamagotchi

Underwater roller coasters

Video games

Wilderness

Xmas!

YouTube

Zebra

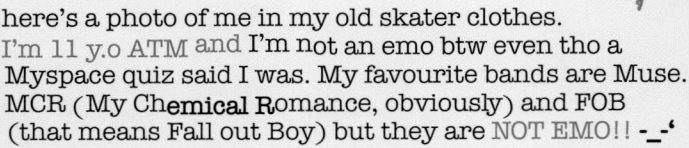

Hi I'm Dan AKA BENVOLIO Agent 003 – you know the rest.

Dunno why i'm writing this because who even would read a book that I make when i'm older xD LOLZOR JK

here's a photo of me in my old skater clothes. I'm 11 y.o ATM and I'm not an emo btw even tho a Myspace quiz said I was. My favourite bands are Muse. MCR (My Chemical Romance, obviously) and FOB (that means Fall out Boy) but they are NOT EMO!! -_-'

Books are okay but I prefer flash cartoons on the internet atm like THE LLAMA SONG which I watch every day in the school library and can s ing by heart (Sorry i'm what you would call RANDOM It's a way of life that only cool ppl know) I got kicked out of the library once because I was playing a Hentai game on the computers LOL and ur only supposed to use them for work. I dunno why because no one even goes in the library for any reason because no one likes books JK :P

I like writing sometimes like I wrote all the things on my website (you should check it out ^^) and did a quiz once on how big a Halo fan you are so I think it will be good but I dunno what things will be in it. Heres some photos of me acting in theatre as PrinceCharming where everyone said I was awesome and another recent one of me in a hat sorry I spilled Ribena on that one

I always wanted cool emo hair (Just the hair IM NOT EMO!!) When I was older not like crazy but just cool like some pics I saw so hopefully I'll have it when I make the book when I'm older and I won't be in school anymore so thats good because I HATE SCHOOL.

I bet in the future all the chavs won't be cool anymor and all the drama and internet guys will be popular like they are on Myspace and Bebo I guess thats why I'm making a book cuz that wouldnt happen if chavs took over the world! Grr o_o

I guess I'd ask my old version if I need to pay attention in maths because it's well boring rofl.

Okay this is captain cool signing off I hope you liked my page which is obvs the best page of the book I'm gonna go buy this cool beaded necklace i saw in the shop in town hopefully I won't have rocks thrown at me for looking emo again (THERE SKINNY JEANS NOT WOMENS JEANS!! Stupid greebos) otherwise this book might not exist in the future XD bye!

HI!! PHIL.L. HERE.

Or you can call me FLIP.
I am 12 and a half years old and live in Rawtenstall.
Or ROTTENstall, as we call it. **Haaa**.

Welcome to the best page eva ... IDST

Also I can **fly**!

So this is going to be a book in the future? **Ace!** I mean it would be even acer if it was a hamster book? Or an entirely **scratch 'n' sniff** book? I'd read that!

I wonder if smell-O-vision will exist in the year 2015. I hope so

My predictions are that I will have a rocket skateboard and maybe a beard. Hopefully I'll be a news broadcaster or weatherman with a beard and live in Tokyo or California. **I'll also have a robo** dog. Like this one **but a robot**:

I'd **ask my future self for the** lottery numbers so I could be a gigabillionaire.
I'd buy a house and fill it with tiny polystyrene balls and just throw myself down the stairs head first.

Sorry just got di**stracted as I s**pilled Fanta all over the sofa and mum is cleanin it up.

Where was I? I don't know why I'm writing this when I could be play**ing THE**ME HOSPITAL or visiting the Devil Stone with the Kool Katz

I'd tell you what the Devil Stone is but then i'd have to kill you.
NOT! Joke

Maybe by the year 2015 the KOOL KATZ will have overtaken England and you will all be members.

Who is even reading this?! Who is this **DAN IS ON FIRE g**uy? What kind of name is that. Sounds like a bit of a moose.

Anyway my tea is ready so i'm gonna go. Chicken and chips. **ACE.**

Ok, I've gone! Enjoy your flying cars.

BYE

Just kidding I didn't go **hahhaaha**hhahahhahmaybe

Home
All About Me
Chat
Fun Fun Fun
Guestbook

DO NOT CLICK

12 Year Old Dan's Website

Dan Howell
IfYouNoticeThisnoticeThenYouWillAlsoAnoticeThatThisNoticeIsNotWorthNoticing

Hello I am **Daniel Howell AKA** Benvolio and if you came to this website to find information about me you are either insane (good for you) or horribly lost on the internet. But why don't you take your time because on this site you will find a carcrash of HTML, as well as info on me and various unrelated things. **Make sure you fill in question time and don't read theall about me bit if you're here to have fun as fun is found in funfunfun and about me isn't very fun.**
And please sign my guestbook I want to know who all my stalkers are.

This is version 6.3 of the site in which I have again nearly changed the entire website word for word.

This is the picture of me aged 12 that everyone loves but I hate so I'll show it anyway.

```
<scriptlanguage='javascript'>
//
alert ('you have successfully downloaded Trojan.exe')
</script>
```

And as most of you should know...

My Hobby's include the computer.games and.. yeah that's pretty much all I do. The two most important things in my life music, and Drama LOL DORK no but yeah. Wokingham Theatre is my claim to fame. Lol And MSM. My parents are all like 'we could cycle ten miles on a day like this go outside go see a friend!' and I would reply 'why? all my freinds are on their computers see look at my contact list if I went round we would just be on their faster more expensive computer so why not stay home?' defeated they would think 'oh well we tried'.

Music

Well as far as music goes I like pretty much everything from Bach to Dimu Borgir I love all music! except for Steps. If you look in my music collection you will find pretty a horrific mess thanks to my random downloading off limewire.

My favirote band are probably Muse seeing as Origin of Symmetry is the BEST ALBUM EVER

[INTERESTING FACT OF THE DAY] I have over 15Gb of music on my pc which is like 8 times more than anything else I have on it and when my uncle had to wipe the pc due to a horrific virus it took 2 days to finish loading up my music

Drama

(Gonna need a big breath for this) WHO WANTS TO KNOW MY LIFE STORY? no one? Inflicting time then.

Nursery - I played the lead role in my first performance ever as Santa clauses in our Christimas play and then in the Nativity I was shepherd,

Reception - The giant turnip thing I was the Farmer my first lead role check me out yeah I thought so.

Year one - Nativity again again shepherd I am gifted in the art of star spotting,

Year three –West side story modern version of romeo and Juliet I was the guy thats was Romeo I dont know his name I obviously cared loads

Year four – Cinderella The comedy I was the ponsey prince charming and I KICKED ASS like sirsly I would have gotten an academy award. Year four – Harriet the spy I was harriets best friend danny with beth as the other best friend that I was also pretty major but I can't remember any of it cuz it wus well borin like.

Year five Easter story I was the very stylish Ponchus Pilot in an Indian sauri because our poor school didn't have enough cloths.

Year five- Carousel. this was boring

Year six - snow white the comedy this was also very good I was the king but it was meh

Year eight a very busy year indeed – First the Straight talk drama club help the needy thing that went well I was an old lady and a chav it could have been better though – Second drama club Oriental fusion evening (how sad) it went well even if Ms. Payne (dribble) told us to make it less violent it was good fun Drama club three Masqerade! this was fun as I looked like a sex offender in my mask Animal Farm now this was... good in the end but we could have done so much more and seeing as the director was a stupid cow who couldn't tell her ass from her face most of the people quit because she was sooo annoying, this ended up with me being god 1, famer 1, pig 8, piano, man, piano pig, windmill and demolition expert... CLEARLY TOO TALENTED TO JUST BE THE LEAD ROLE.

Year nine the best year yet!:D:D (dork) Firstly the school drama gala was great Now... here we are, Romeo and Juliet probably the most fun I've had ever in my life EVER EVER maybe idunno I was benvolio which was a big deal for a proffesional show but it was cool Which brings me to Kes Ms.Paynes first play which was pretty good but everyone I worked with was a cock

Year 10 so far: Merchant of Venice was totally awesome!!!!1111!! we totally ka-pwned all other entries to the festivaland I won a young Shakespeare award which means I'm officially awesome

WhY PHiL was A WEIRD kiD

I'm not sure what happened to me as a child to make me so weird. My mum assures me I wasn't dropped as a baby, though my head is unusually shaped so maybe she secretly did. Another suspicion is because I spent hours every day watching an insane Japanese anime video called Robbie the Rascal. Here is the box:

My final thought is I was just born this way (sorry if Lady Gaga is now stuck in your head). You know the kittens who get millions of views on YouTube for doing really weird stuff like bouncing off walls and attacking their reflections? I think I was just the human equivalent to those kittens.

Here are just some of the reasons why I was a weird kid:

LOVE OF BRACES

I was obsessed with the idea of having braces. My best friend Jessica had them and I wanted to be just like her. I would lay in bed trying to bend my teeth forwards in the hope that one day I could have those shiny train-tracks of destiny and everyone would give me attention and want to look at my teeth.

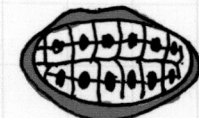

WEIRDNESS RANKING ★★★★☆

FISH FOOD

My grandma was impressed with my swimming skills so she told me that I was part fish (thanks grandma). I secretly ate fish food in the attempt to become FISH BOY. It didn't taste good. Don't eat fish food.

WEIRDNESS RANKING ★★★★☆

METALLic GReen ENveLopes

As a kid I didn't want a micro-scooter, I didn't want a trampoline, the thing I wanted most in the world was ... a metallic green envelope. I have literally no idea why but I just wanted one so badly! Thankfully I've been given quite a few from my followers after mentioning it so the envelope beast within my brain has been satisfied. Thanks guys!

WEIRDNESS RANKING ★★★★★

THe SHaDow REaLM

I would frequently have long conversations with my own shadow in a world I called the SHADOW REALM. I thought this was a real place and imagined my shadow talking back to me, he was a pretty good friend actually. This all went well until I walked into the breast of a lunch lady mid shadow-conversation.

WEIRDNESS RANKING ★★★★★

TEddY BEAR DroWninG

My idea of Saturday night entertainment was sitting in front of the washing machine watching my teddy bears spin and spin and spin and spin. It's still kind of therapeutic for me to sit watching a washing machine fill with water. What is wrong with me?!

WEIRDNESS RANKING ★★★★★

DEMON ChiLd

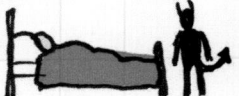

I was the reason my parents didn't have any more children. Every night I would stand next to their bed in silence waiting for them to wake up. Terrifying. Sorry Mum and Dad!

WEIRDNESS RANKING ★★★★★

SHOWER BEhaviOUr

Until around the age of 14 I sat down in the shower. I'm not sure if this was because I was too lazy to stand or I just genuinely thought this was the best way to shower? Give it a try one day, it's liberating.

WEIRDNESS RANKING ★★★☆☆

FLAT PHiL

After reading the book *Flat Stanley* as a child I really wanted to become Flat Phil. One night I pulled my entire pinboard off the wall on top of myself to achieve this flat dream. Thankfully I didn't die, but I also didn't become flat. They should put warning labels on these kids' books …

'May cause your children to attempt to flatten themselves.'

WEIRDNESS RANKING ★★★★☆

ThE ShoeLACe InciDent

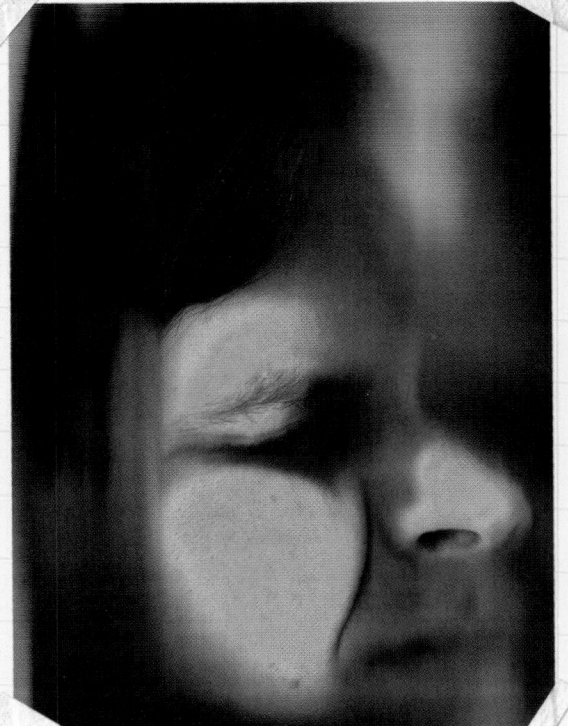

One assembly at school I thought it would be a good idea to tie my own shoelaces together, then fall over and pretend it was someone else who did it! WHY, PHIL, WHY DID YOU DO THIS TO YOURSELF? Everyone was held back by the headmaster who demanded that no one could leave until someone admitted to the dangerous act! Obviously no one said anything and the true mystery shoelace tie-er was never exposed.

WEIRDNESS RANKING ★★★★☆

PHOTOCOPiEd FACe

Once my parents left me alone in the house for a few hours and I used my dad's photocopier to photocopy my face 100 times and then hid the pictures. I was partly imagining that my soul was being beamed into the computer system and therefore making me immortal and partly laughing at how funny the pictures turned out. For the sake of nostalgia I have photocopied my face for you here:

WEIRDNESS RANKING ★★☆☆☆

THe WinDow

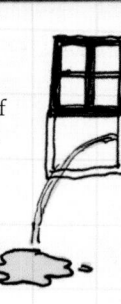

One night aged around nine or ten I stood on a chair and peed out of the window onto the roof in the middle of the night. I don't know why I did this or why I have shared this in a book that actual people will read but now you can feel less bad about the weird stuff you did.

WEIRDNESS RANKING ★★★★★★

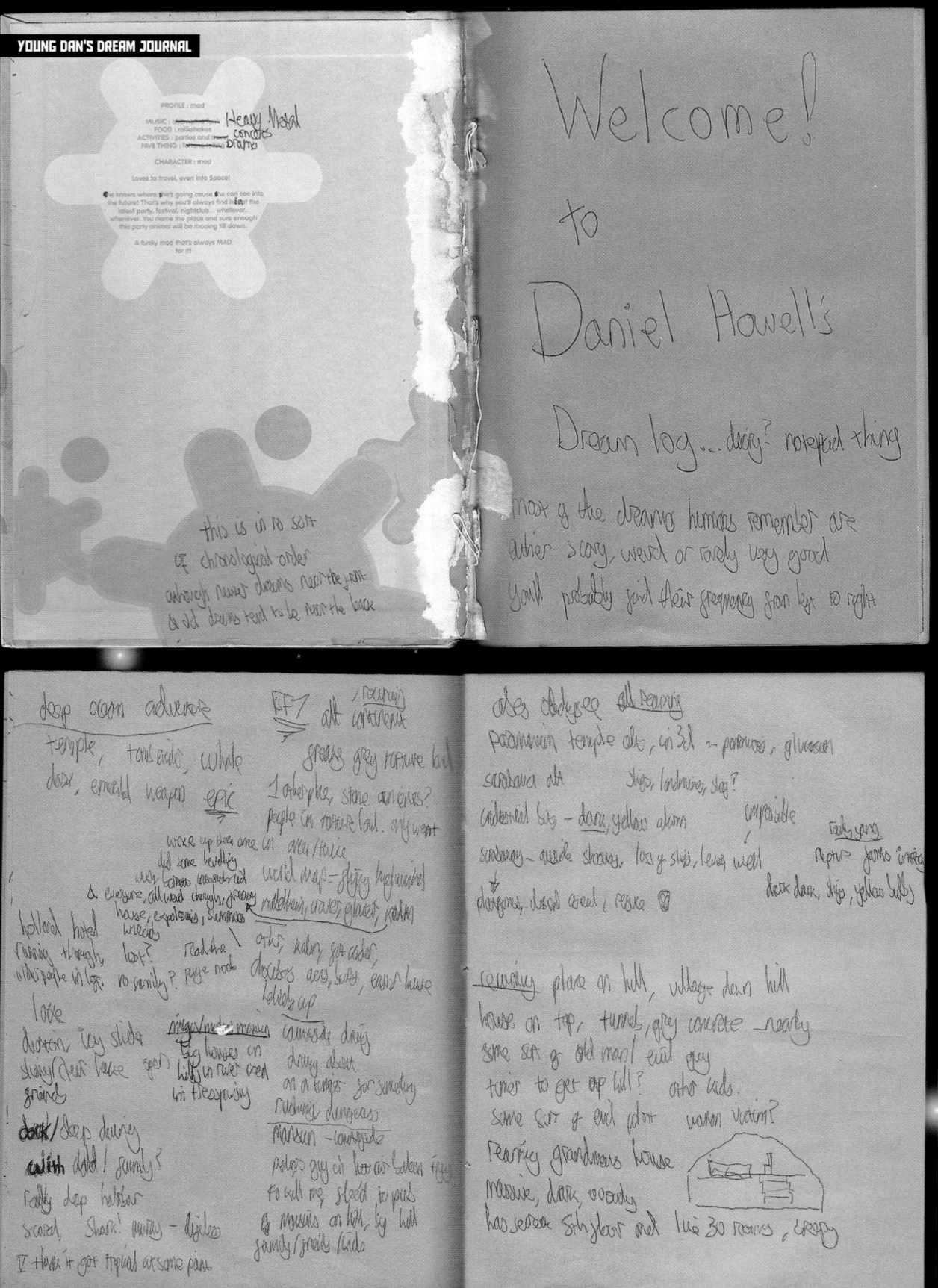

PROFILE : mad
MUSIC : Heavy Metal concerts
FOOD : milkshakes
ACTIVITIES : parties and Drama
FAVE THING :

CHARACTER : mad

Loves to travel, even into Space!

She knows where she's going cause she can see into the future! That's why you'll always find her at the latest party, festival, nightclub... whatever, whenever. You name the place and sure enough this party animal will be mooing till dawn.

A funky moo that's always MAD for it!

this is in no sort
of chronological order
although newer dreams near the front
& old dreams tend to be near the back

Welcome!

to

Daniel Howell's

Dream log... diary? notepad thing

most of the dreams humans remember are
either scary, weird or rarely very good
You'll probably find their frequency from left to right

Scary dreams I remember   ages 3-16 (not chronological order)

1

I was in a dark train station made from black/really dark blue tiles (like the ministry of magic) lots of people are just standing & can't see them because it is so dark - im with nana holding her hand then in an arc & tiles on the roof over the train tracks the head of this a demon comes out of the wall (much like the ancient temple boss in FFVIII) looked kind of like a gate but all glowing red like an alarm. it roared and I woke up.

age 3   probably fantasia related

i cause demons   icause demons

2 "The gorilla dream"   alone or moslalife   * see explanation

2 similar close - I was outside, night time, nightmare sky & music
I saw a black figure moving slightly towards me ~~~~~ and on in my house - it was different to my real house it was just a room, as i remember i may have entered through the window - there was no light - only light source being the nightmare sky outside it was a plain grey plastered room with I table

4

I hid under the table (cheap school table ~~~) and sat hiding out. I heard it coming near. Then all of a sudden its head popped down upside down under the table and I crapped myself and woke up.

5   age 8

I can't draw (not physical) gorillas

Explanation =D

Nightmare sky & music

In dreams from about 7-10 (16 in sky) is every other nightmare the sky was a brown mustardy color gas get green in real life dot I could tell when it would be a nightmare because an eerie song sounding like synthetic strings would play (not cheesy or psydelic like, more slow (god/penguin))

I can't remember how the song was exactly but I remember how the sky looks.

now that we've specified this you know for future reference

---

epic - Epic dreams   time order wrong

military base - invading - Jody death?
I have a partner. Qui you guy?
Zombies? gas morphed soldiers outside window
Lumen pressed, have to ran away from nuke.
through rural town = epic
market town - juble?

Lures to Satan tunnel & Gav   matt

map

mountain range leads to at least 3 other dreams

mountain range guarding evil guy/hiding army hole & tombs in mountain win/save I woman knows them beach ext at the bottom

WARNING!

UNLESS YOU ARE PHIL

THIS IS NOT FOR YOUR EYES

DO NOT READ THIS

If you read this then I hate you as you will have stolen the key.

I have included false stuff so you would never know what is true.
THIS IS ALL MADE UP.
OR IS IT?

Jan 7th

Hello!

I'm going to try and write here every day
Happy new year!
Our street had a huge party and I saw my brother's friend get Drunk. She got sick on my dad's coat. I don't understand his friends. Ultra Townies!!!

Today i'm going over to Anias to watch a film. Bye.

Feeling: New year

Jan 8th

So we watched a film about an otter that got cut in half by a spade. I'm picking the film next time!
My mum still won't let me watch the nightmare on elm street but I watched some at Katies ok bye

Feeling: Sad for the otter

NOOO

Feb 1st

Sorry I forgot to write. I'll do this every day.
Had loads of H/w.
My friend Phil says he has a g/f but she goes to a different school. We don't believe him.
I think Kat A might ask me out as we've been talking loads on ICQ and we've had 3 phone calls. ♡
Feeling: Busy

Feb 2nd So embarrassing!!!
I was talking to kat on the phone about an adult magazine Martyn's friend found and then
My mum picked up the phone and listened for 3 mins and said
"excuse me it's a school night and phone bills are expensive"
Do they want me to have no life? Like a cave man?
Luckily Kat found it funny but - Not Good
Feeling: Betrayed.

Feb 18th

I hid a love letter in kat's art folder but she didn't know it was from me.
Regret it now!!
What was I thinking!!
Buffy is on now. Bye!

Feeling: STUPID

Feb 22nd

She found the note so I'm pretending not to know who it is from and solve the mystery
What am I doing???? ?

March 18 Sorry found this again.
Me and kat went out for 2 weeks. She watched I KWYDLS on my bed but we didn't kiss or anything. We hugged.
Broke up now + better off as friends
I was sadder than her. Feeling: sleep

April 8th
I'm in Florida!
eating loads of BBQ food
and cookies.
Universal was ACE
a girl winked at me on the
Jaws ride but she might
have had a moskito in her eye

MAY 18
Got some rollerblades but they hurt
my feet so I don't use them and dad says
it's a waste of money. Not my
fault. Might get a skateboard if I
get money somhow. feeling: sore
feet

June 4th
Our fish died.
RIP WINSTON.
feeling: sad.

June 14 Got a new hamster Norris. He
is black + white and tame. We're going to
breed him with Phoebe and make babies as
dad won't let me get rats or a chinchilla
Feeling: Excited.

JULY 8th - GOT A SKATEBOARD?!!)
Going out on it bye feeling cool

we think Phoebe is either pregnant
or really fat.
They take 17 days to
give birth - longest wait ever!
Feeling: Waiting...

JULY 24 - Buffy was ace today!
can't wait for the box set

July 29 Our vet friend came over
and Phoebe is pregnant!
AOL says there will be 4-12 babies

JULY 30th
Christine knocked all of my videos
behind my bookshelf. What a
moose.
feeling: Ultimate Betrayal

August 15th
Summer Holidays are going
too fast!
mum says boys + girls have to be
seperate at sleepovers now.
I don't get why, it's not like we're
all going to do it on the floor were
all friends.
Might walkie talkie them

Aug 16
Kat hugged me in Swaz's kitchen
as she ate dry frosties!
Swaz's mum saw it and told my mum
we were kissing when we weren't!
so embarassing.
ok bye

August 19th
I never mentioned she had the babies!
13 in total. Really cute and
loads of colours.
I want to keep them all but they're
going to the petshop.

August 30 we sold the babies - £30!
Loaded. School starts next
week. I've done no H/W.
might fake a broken foot to get
out of football.
Feeling: Dread.

September 17th
I HATE SCHOOL

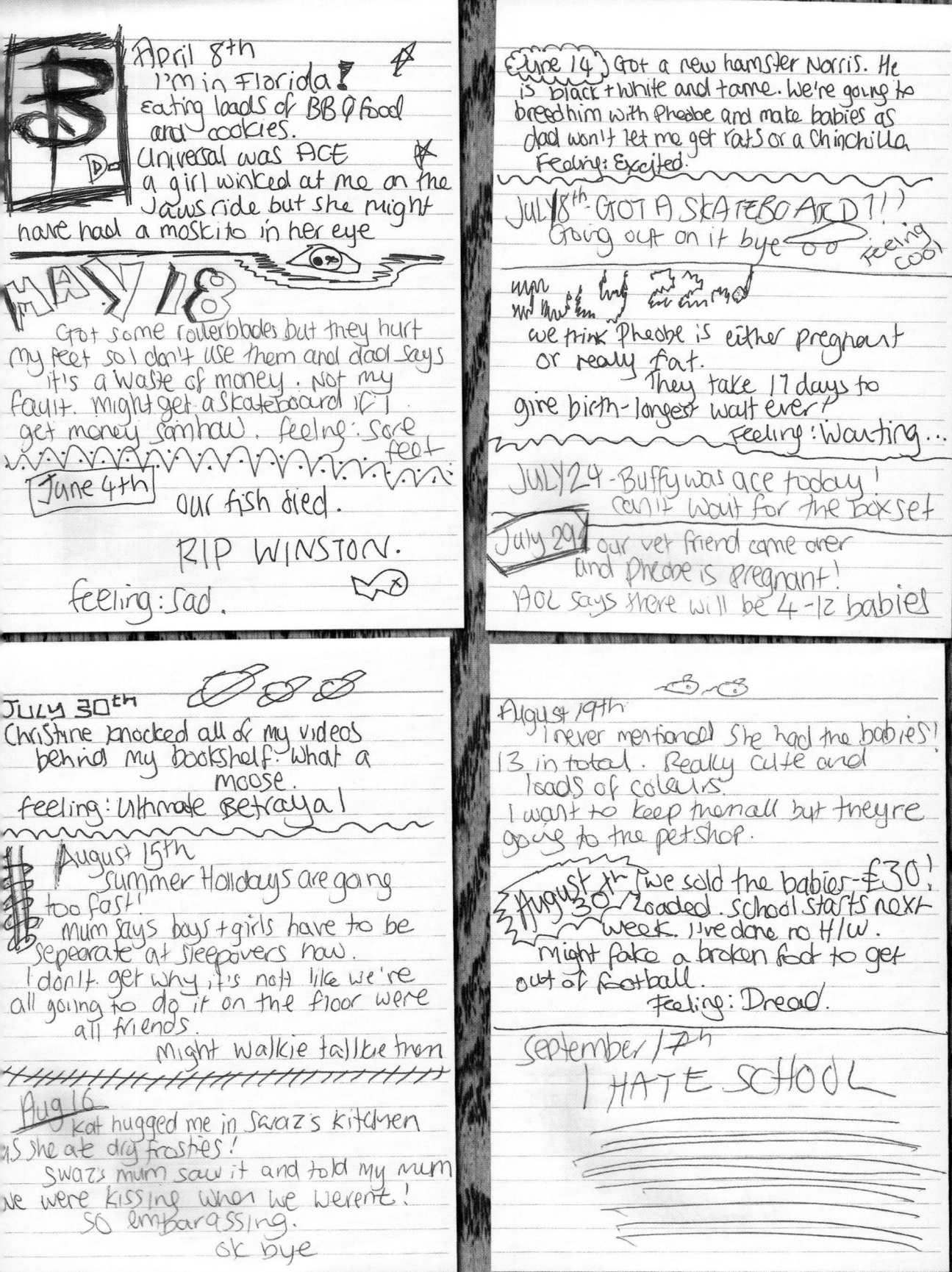

DAN'S HIGH SCHOOL LIFE

What was the first day like?

Absolutely terrifying.

The idea of going to this huge scary school filled with older, taller people - just as I had started to enjoy being the older tall person in my previous school, was perfectly represented by my oversized blazer swamping my entire body in this photo.

«««« Lol (do you see the fear in my eyes?).

My last school was so cute and tiny with only 200 innocent children students and the buildings were unintimidating thatched-roof bungalows. I was moving into a giant grey concrete monolith with the maths department on the fifth floor and nearly 2,000 students. I remember being herded into the assembly hall for a speech from the intimidating headmaster before we were sorted into houses. It was not like *Harry Potter*. Myself and the five kids I knew from my old school were huddled in a group in a corner trembling with fear before we were brutally torn away from each other and thrown into the swarming abyss of High School.

Maybe slightly dramatic but you get the gist.

Did you have a favourite subject?

Drama all the way. I mean how can you compete with spending 45 minutes rolling around a theatre room on office chairs? At the end, when the teacher asked for people to perform, all you had to do was say you were shy and didn't want to and boom - free period.

What was your worst subject?

'Games' - the word still strikes fear in my heart to this day. 'Games' in my school was specifically the playing of sports such as football and rugby for the allocated two hours in the timetable. I can't play football. I did tackle someone once in rugby and for a fleeting second earned words of respect from the people who usually kept whatever ball as far away from me as possible, but to be honest who wants to get muddy eyebrows at 9am on a freezing Monday morning in England?

I think the teachers actually started to give up on people at some point, as a group started to form called the 'weirdos' which was basically all the nerds and alternative kids sitting on benches listening to their iPods all year. Of course all of these people had 'reasons' such as ten-month sprained ankles, allergies to grass or 'emotional problems'. I could forge my mum's signature very well. I'm a terrible role model.

Were there any bullies?

In my school there were about ten people who weren't bullies. Being an all-boys school it was a giant wasp nest of violence and anyone who stood out was a target. I was as obnoxious then as I am now. In hindsight I understand why kids bully, they were sad themselves and insecure about who they were, so picking on someone who was a bit weird and different felt like a way to work it out. I wish someone had told me this at the time!

I could have probably drawn a lot less attention to myself by not trying to be funny and having weird hair. But in all honesty it's important to be who you are and not change for anyone; if I did then there may have never been a danisnotonfire or this very book!

Were there any embarrassing moments?

Any? Are you kidding me? Let's think of some of the bigger ones. I once was asked to kick a football back to some guys and I awkwardly booted it over a fence into a moving train. That didn't help my popularity. Oh, then there was the time I was the only kid in the whole school to turn up in full blazer and tie on non-uniform day! These are memories I've been busy repressing for years, can we move on?

Would you go back in time and do it all again?

Hahahah Hahahahahah Hahahahahahahahaha.

No.

Dan trying to camouflage himself away from bullies. It didn't work. »»»»»»»»»»»»»»»»»»»»»»»

PHIL'S HIGH SCHOOL LIFE

What was the first day like?

Firstly we need a flashback to summer as I had to take an entrance exam. I think I passed and got in only because my brother told me to use the word 'flabbergasted' in the English paper. I had no idea what flabbergasted meant. Flashforward to September! I got absolutely no sleep the night before my first day because of nerves. It was like the anti-Christmas.

I remember looking into the mirror after waking up and seeing Phil with fluorescent yellow hair staring back at me! Why had I decided to dye my hair bright yellow the week before going to a new school? Did I want to be a snowball beacon?! I have no idea.

I put on my giant new uniform and my mum made my brother and I have this incredibly «««««««««« awkward photo.

Seriously lol at my hair. It took so much restraint not to put some intense filter over this one when putting it in the book: »»»»»»»»»»»

We got the bus to school and I thought 'ahh at least my brother knows his way around! I'll be fine, he'll show me the ropes!' We arrived at the gate, he turned to me and said: 'I had to do this on my own so I think you should too!'

He walked off and left me. Thanks BRO. (Martyn has since apologised many times for this so I guess I'll forgive him.) Anyway, I waddled my way to class and thankfully sat next to a guy called Swaz. I told him his name was weird and we were instant best friends! Phew.

I don't remember much more about my first day other than the fact that I was very excited by Bunsen burners and the concept of homework had already ruined my life. No worries! Just seven years to go.

Did you have a favourite subject?

Probably art! It was just an excuse to talk to people whilst pretending to sketch a bowl of fruit. I remember covering my hands in black ink once to create a painting called 'THE DEATH OF DREAMS'. So deep.

What was your worst subject?

I hated P.E. with a fiery vengeance. I had zero coordination and angry northern teens on a football pitch were the worst. I forged so many sick notes! I think I had a 'broken toe' for about twelve weeks and I'd actually hobble past teachers pretending it was broken. In my final year I actually chose 'community service' instead of P.E. so I went to the house of an old lady and helped landscape her garden! Much better than rugby.

Were there any bullies?

Thankfully my school was actually pretty friendly compared to some in the area! There was one terrifying guy though, he looked like the crossbreed of a human and an actual rhino. He was so angry ALL THE TIME. My strategy was to never make eye contact, avoid him in corridors and ask to move if we ever got sat remotely near to each other. I only had one run-in with him when he pushed me over and emptied my pencil case over my head. I definitely regret not telling anyone about that thinking back as he was probably making a load of other kids miserable too. Stupid rhino boy! I hope he feels bad now.

Were there any embarrassing moments you can talk about?

I called about 17 teachers 'mum' during my time at school, including one male teacher *crawls into a burrow of shame*. Also my prom date was a balloon. »»»»»»

Would you go back in time and do it all again?

No way! Those years felt like an entire lifetime. It's so refreshing closing that door behind you and starting a new part of your life. A lot of people are scared by the crushing responsibilities but I was just happy to never have a double maths lesson ever again! I do wish I could have kept the lion suit I wore on my last day of school though, even if it did smell mildly like a wet dog.

Name: Daniel Howell

Year: 9

Attendance

95% Seemingly misses all games lessons due to medical issues. We hope he's ok.

Academic Performance

Seems to enjoy arts classes and English but has complained about maths and French teachers? Not understanding an irish accent and claiming your teacher eats dogs biscuits is inappropriate.

General Behaviour

(Detentions - 43): Daniel is what we call a low-level disruptor. He constantly talks and this is a distraction to his friends and is affecting their learning. Several students have requested he be moved to a table in the corner where he can't be annoying.

Parental Guidance

We suggest you talk to Dan about respecting his teachers and perhaps ask him if he thinks that he talks too much. I don't think all this funny behaviour will get him anywhere productive.

Name: Philip Lester

Year: 9

Attendance

99% - Was late for a class as he was attempting to sell hamsters to other students in the playground. Apparently could not attend P.E due to a broken toe which does not seem to bother him at any other time.

Academic Performance

Strong results in creative writing and art. Less strong for physics, maths and history - it's a worry that Phil thought Henry VIII was 'probably still alive somewhere'.

General Behaviour

Detentions (1): Phil brought a laser pen to school to 'shoot his friends' which we understand does look cool but could have blinded another student.

Philip seems to spend half his lessons in another universe and it's sometimes hard to get him to focus. He is also a constant doodler which makes marking his work difficult. On one occassion a 'giant tentacle monster' was covering most of his algebra calculations.

Parental Guidance

Perhaps let phil run around outside rather than watching fantasy television shows. We are worried about his toe as it apparently not healed for six months - consider another hospital appointment. We are concerned in many ways.

Phil L.

PHIL'S CHAT LOGS

Ahh, remember MSN?

If you are reading this in the year 2600 it was basically an online chat
program where you could talk to all your friends at once! Memories include
asking total strangers to divulge 'ASL' (age, sex, location), competing
to see who had the most friends added, weird custom emoticons you would
hide from your parents and the strangely comforting beep when you got
a new message.

GONE. DELETED. MSN IS NO MORE. R.I.P.

I feel like I owe a lot to MSN! It taught me to touch type for one.
I spent every waking moment chatting to my friends to the point
where I no longer had to look at the keyboard anymore. Is that a
good thing?

Let's give it a test ... *closes eyes*

MY NAME IS PHIK AND MY EYES ARE CLOSED AND I'M TYRING TO TOUCH TYPE!

Okay that was pretty close!
Thankfully I can keep those memories alive, as a couple of years ago I found
a hard drive containing every conversation I had ever had between the ages
of 14 and 18. I made a couple of videos about this and I'm still not sure why
I decided to share these with the internet, but I thought I'd preserve them
by writing them down here. I changed my friends' names to save their privacy
(and embarrassment).

LOL
OK BRB

Phil: Ahoy m8

Laura: m8ey sk8y

Phil: sk8er waiter

Laura: 888888

Phil: 8 8 88 88

LAURA LOGGED OUT

Phil: OMG I'm watching some tv show
bout a guy who ate himself

Ash: Wat?!

Phil: LOL

Phil: 7 DAYS

Laura: NOT FUNNY THE RING WAS WORST

Phil: 7 DAYYYYyyyysssss

Laura: I'M LOGGING OUT

Phil: Oh it's midnight

Laura: Phew

Phil: 6 DAYYSSS

LAURA LOGGED OUT

Phil: Hahah ha … um do you have any emoticons u wana trade

Gary: er i hav a glittery thing that says lol

Phil: LOL!

Dayne: can u keep a secret plz

Phil: did u kill sum1

Dayne: noo i kissd stace

Phil: wow like kiss kiss? french kiss

Dayne: yeh tongue like actual full on

Phil: what was it like

Dayne: i think i was bad it was kinda gross

Dayne: i was jus imaginin lickin a yoghurt

Phil: ewwr haha

Dayne: if u tel any1 ill kill ur family

Phil: wat

Phil: Yr9 camp is cumin up but most of my year have morphed into townies now

Phil: so it might be like Townie camp

Jake: yeh 95% of my skool is now townie village

Phil: ppl think I'm a mosher … but i just wear black jeans sumtimes

Jake: uh yeh i think ppl should stop with the labels …

Jake: but i might get a tattoo when I'm 18 lol

Phil: yh i want lyke some stars on my chest or sumthin

Phil: or maybe buffy on my face lol

Mike: I found a word that rhymes with orange

Phil: No u didn't

Mike: Lozenge

Phil: That doesn't rhyme

Mike: Ur mum doesn't rhyme

Phil: I rhymed ur mum's dad

Mike: wtf

Kelly: i think i fancy Dave but i duno cz he got wiv kate

Phil: don't be a muppet. i'm sure theres some other guy you might like? somewhere like? um

Kelly: are you being nice becos ur nice or becos sum1 is being unnice behind my back?

Phil: Wat

Kelly: if u dont know i can't explain it

????: ASL?

Phil: 93/F/USA

????: shut you

???? WENT OFFLINE

Phil: I got a 3330!

Phil: a nokia! SPACE IMPACT BBY

Ash: omg let me play it tomorra

Phil: if u get me smthin from the ikki van

Ash: ok

Phil: My mum says there is a ghost in the apartment

Rachel: when you shiver it's a ghost tickling ur ass bones

Phil: I thought that was someone walkin over ur grave

Rachel: I don't hav a grave

Phil: lol

Rachel: lol

Phil: wuu2

Rachel: gota go

RACHEL WENT OFFLINE

Phil: gotta ghost

Phil: nvm

Phil: OMFFFGGGGGGGGGG99

Ian: wat

Phil: Playing darts and I threw one right in Sarah's bare foot
I FEEL SO BAD

Ian: u are a disaster with legs

Phil: omfg i got shouted at in maths

Squall: why?

Phil: I laughed at smthin in the txt book as their name was spelled wrong and it was called POODEEP

Squall: lmol

Phil: urge I'm just tryna decide on my top8

Misty: am i in it?

Phil: you are 4th

Misty: ?? jk rite?

Phil: you are in the top row

Misty: ohmygod i can't believe you hate me

Phil: go coment my new profile pic n ill put u at 3 =P

Adel: dya wanna go campin

Phil: where?!

Adel: my back garden

Phil: well new Buffy is on ... bt mayb l8r

Adel: God! u like Buffy more than ur mates ur sad!

Phil: oh i mean i could tape it but my dad needs his tapes

Phil: asl

veamp: 15/f/uk

Phil: u on myspace

veamp: yea veampoxo

Phil: gud face

veamp: thanks jus added. cool hair

Phil: thanks yeh I'm just polishin ma snowboard

veamp: koool

Phil: hang on er norris is loose

veamp: ... wtf is norris

Phil: ma hamster he's outta his ball

VEAMP WENT OFFLINE

Phil: bye then

Phil: LOL GUESS WHAT HAPPENED

Myles: wattt

Phil: i fell ova a bin an landed on another bin

Myles: hahahhaha wtf

Phil: sum yr11 is now calling me bin child

Myles: BIN CHILD I'm so callin u bin child

Phil: pleez don't call me bin child

BIN CHILD: lol i change9 my nick to bin child

Phil: ...

BIN CHILD WENT OFFLINE

Phil: did u c i put a note in ur pencil case 1st week

sara: ????????

sara: i lost my pencil case

Phil ::(

sara: what was the note

Phil: nvm it was just a doodle

sara: o

Phil: I h8 skool

Phil: i hid ma kit from my mum and faked a note. double escape

kyle: i told them i had a blood disease

Phil: GOOD IDEA

Phil: u don't have a blood disease rite? lol

kyle: no lol

kyle: we shd play dreamcast at mine

kyle: chippy

Phil: omg yes

Phil: mum sed i need sum fruit in my life. i told her fish is a fruit and she sed ok lol

kyle: hah lol

Phil: My mum says I can't have more than 10 ppl at the party

Lo: but i sed kate could come

Phil: which kate i swear the whole skool is a kate

Lo: the one who sat on her hamster and cried in the pet thing

Phil: omg

Phil: ok she can come

Well that made me cringe so much I may have gained abs. Or maybe I ruptured my spleen? I'm not sure! I'm glad I kept them though, it's nice to have a little window into Phil of the past.

OVER AND OUT

I don't know why I'm writing like I'm using a walkie talkie. I think
I had too much coffee before starting this.

Phil's YouTube Origin Story

Okay so that's enough of 'previously on Dan and Phil'. Now you have a pretty good idea of our early years in those dark times before YouTube and you're ready for the REAL story – why we started making videos.

Reply · 825 👍 👎

I owe a lot to Santa, as my first spark of creative inspiration came from the 'NINTENDO SIXTY FOURRR!' moment of me getting a hand-held camera for Christmas!

If only I still had the same style as back then

I spent entire summers making horror movies and fake TV shows with my friends. Here I am being brutally murdered and drenched in ketchup.

Fast-forward a few horrifying years of puberty and we reach the true beginnings of my YouTube channel... a cereal box. A cereal box with tokens for a free webcam. Yep, I owe my entire channel to a strangely great cereal promotion.

I made my account way back in 2006. I am a YouTube dinosaur! I was obsessed with a channel called 'LonelyGirl15' which was an American girl vlogging in her bedroom about her everyday life and her strange parents who turned out to be in a cult that sacrificed her. However (thankfully) it turned out she was an actress and none of it was real. I was mindblown and heartbroken and this is why I have trust issues.

The concept of her vlogging was real though, and that's what inspired me! I loved that you could share a little bit of your life with anyone in the world by putting videos on this website. I watched more and more people like Smosh, AndrewBravener and CommunityChannel and then on 6 March 2007 my cereal webcam finally arrived and I plucked up the courage to film and upload my first video. The next morning I had an email; I had my FIRST SUBSCRIBER! I was so excited. It was a guy named 'Dudeneedaeaseonup' who, funnily enough, I later became friends with in real life!

👍 140,855 **40** 👎 328

AmazingPhil

Roar Subscribe

AmazingPhil
Style: Variety
Joined: February 07, 2006
Last Login: 2 minutes ago
Videos Watched: 15,665
Subscribers: 5,649
Channel Views: 58,297

■ DIRECTOR

Name: Phil
☆
I'm a student in York, UK.
I like lions.
I like interesting people
I play Tim in upcoming film 'Faintheart'
Check it out on IMDB!

——

Check out the people I subscribe to, they are the
reason I make videos. :)

☆ CONTACT ☆

Ask me a question or
send me something interesting and I might put it in a
video =D

——

☆

City: York
Hometown: Manchester
Country: United Kingdom 🏴󠁧󠁢󠁥󠁮󠁧󠁿
Interests and Hobbies: Being on gameshows
Movies and Shows: Buffy! Neighbours LOST SKINS
Big brother HEROES Kill Bill Magnolia Requiem
for a dream Nowhere Run Lola Run
Music: MUSE!
Books: Northern Lights.. Curious incident Black

The Magic Box of Mystery
From: AmazingPhil
Views: 4,002
Comments: 313

Videos (80)   Subscribe to AmazingPhil's videos

Videos | Most Viewed | Most Discussed   Search

The Magic Box of Mystery
03:30

Musical Socks
03:31
Added: 1 week ago

AmericanPhil
00:38
Added: 2 weeks ago

First video –
Phil's Video Blog, 27 March 2006

It took me over a year and 30 more (terrible) videos to get to my first milestone of 100 subscribers – that was a huge number to me. Imagine if they were all sat in my garden! Little did I know these numbers were going to grow a little bit over the next nine years. I wonder what the Phil from that first video would say if you told him?

'ACE!' probably.

Okay, it's taking all the will in the world for me to press play on this video. Here we go
hides behind a pillow.

'Ello I'm Phil.'

I was so Northern sounding! I like that I didn't bother to make any edits at all, it was just a direct upload from a black and white webcam. I didn't even introduce myself in any way I just dove straight into the topics of Mother's Day and exams. I wonder what those snake-like things all over my radiator were? It was probably my super-cool collection of skater belts. There's even a cameo from a lion! I guess I haven't changed that much.

Dan's YouTube Origin Story

I was a YouTube fan.

A friend from school when I was 14 once showed me this thing called his 'subscription feed' on his laptop. It was filled with videos uploaded by people with strange names like 'Paperlilies', 'Charlieissocoollike', and 'ShaneDawsonTV'. This discovery would ruin my life. All I did all day and all night from that point in my life was watch YouTube videos.

Reply · 825 👍 💬

Back before they changed how YouTube profiles looked, there used to be a stat of how many videos you had watched – mine was 39,789. That's a lot. I watched everyone's videos, I commented on them, I even spent most of my money on shirts with YouTubers' faces on them. As a daydreamer I constantly fantasised about one day being a YouTuber too. I used to spend so long thinking about it that I had the whole thing planned out in my head! What my name would be, what kind of videos I would make, even what music I'd use in the background.

Then fast forward to Summer 2009 – I decided to take a gap year. Now what would I do with this last year of freedom before going to university to study Law? Do some early studying? Get some work experience? Travel the world? Nope. I decided I was finally gonna start making YouTube videos. I didn't tell my mum, she wouldn't have approved.

You see quite uniquely, unlike most other YouTubers at the time who started vlogging to no one about nothing in particular in 2005, I had a plan. I had years of notes, scribbled when I probably should have been paying attention to my maths teacher, of exactly what I wanted to do. I started asking for tips from everyone, including AmazingPhil who I endlessly messaged on Twitter until he followed me back, so I could harass him on Skype about things like what program I should edit videos on and where I could totally legally procure it. I got everything prepared, clicked record on my terrible laptop's webcam and set my plan in motion.

The rest is history ... or at least relevant enough for this to be a page in this particular book that happens to be about me. And that's the story of danisnotonfire!

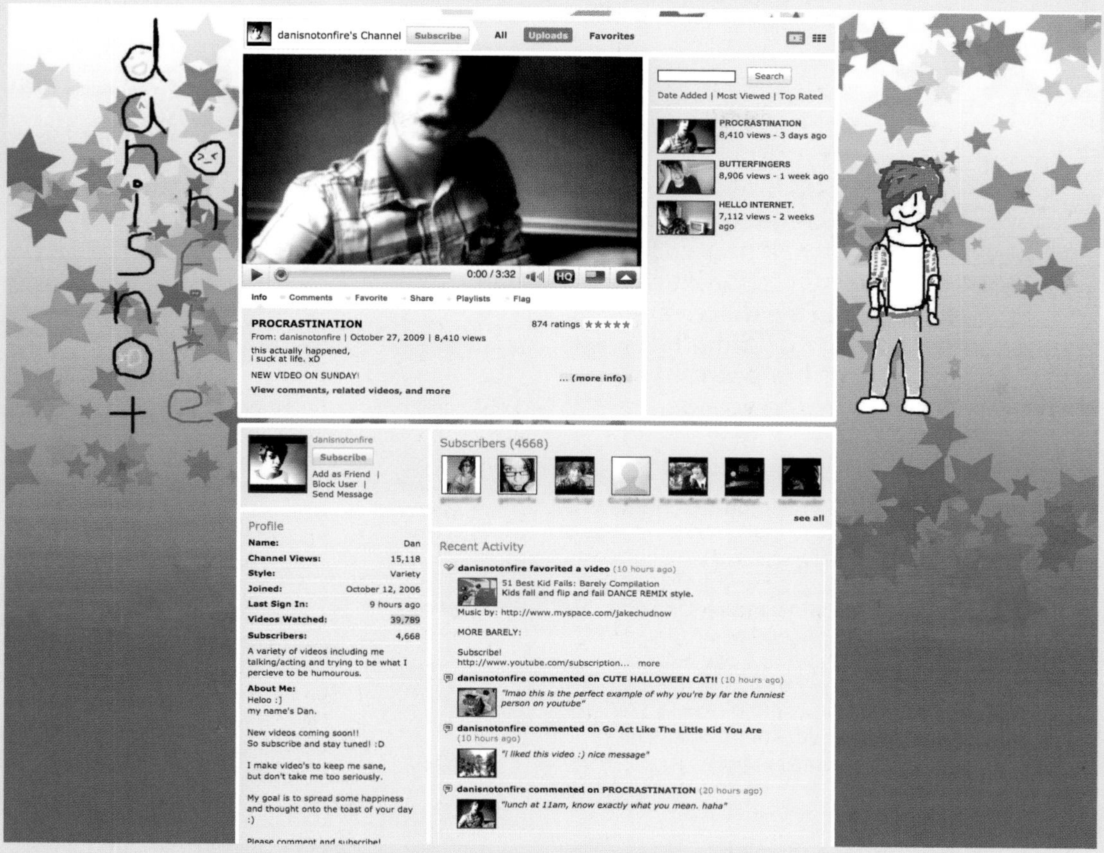

danisnotonfire's Channel Subscribe   All Uploads Favorites

Search

Date Added | Most Viewed | Top Rated

PROCRASTINATION
8,410 views - 3 days ago

BUTTERFINGERS
8,906 views - 1 week ago

HELLO INTERNET.
7,112 views - 2 weeks ago

0:00 / 3:32   HQ

Info · Comments · Favorite · Share · Playlists · Flag

PROCRASTINATION
From: danisnotonfire | October 27, 2009 | 8,410 views   874 ratings ★★★★★
this actually happened,
I suck at life. xD

NEW VIDEO ON SUNDAY!
View comments, related videos, and more   ... (more info)

danisnotonfire
Subscribe

Add as Friend |
Block User |
Send Message

Subscribers (4668)

see all

Profile

Name:	Dan
Channel Views:	15,118
Style:	Variety
Joined:	October 12, 2006
Last Sign In:	9 hours ago
Videos Watched:	39,789
Subscribers:	4,668

A variety of videos including me
talking/acting and trying to be what I
percieve to be humourous.

About Me:
Heloo :]
my name's Dan.

New videos coming soon!!
So subscribe and stay tuned! :D

I make video's to keep me sane,
but don't take me too seriously.

My goal is to spread some happiness
and thought onto the toast of your day
:)

Please comment and subscribe!

Recent Activity

danisnotonfire favorited a video (10 hours ago)
51 Best Kid Fails: Barely Compilation
Kids fall and flip and fail DANCE REMIX style.
Music by: http://www.myspace.com/jakechudnow

MORE BARELY:

Subscribe!
http://www.youtube.com/subscription...   more

danisnotonfire commented on CUTE HALLOWEEN CAT!! (10 hours ago)
"lmao this is the perfect example of why you're by far the funniest
person on youtube"

danisnotonfire commented on Go Act Like The Little Kid You Are
(10 hours ago)
"I liked this video :) nice message"

danisnotonfire commented on PROCRASTINATION (20 hours ago)
"lunch at 11am, know exactly what you mean. haha"

First video –
Hello Internet, 16 October 2009

DAN

0:11 / 2:24

TERRIBLE EDITING, resulting in 4 seconds of silence
between each agonising jump cut, and my general
immature behaviour that makes me want to rip my
face off when watching it. Don't make me watch
this video. I will swan dive out of the window of a
skyscraper to avoid watching this video.

Why is this video still public? I thought (as I still
think) a good first video would be an introduction!
Say who you are, why you're here and what you
want to make before inviting strangers to spy on
your life. Unfortunately I didn't account for my

117 / 2:34

👍 117,279 **43** 👎 245

Q&A - What was your first word?

- Why do yo always make cat noises on your joke?

- If you had to lose your leg or your nose what would you lose? ~~that thing~~

- How do rabbits get protein?

- Ninja or Pirate

- ~~scribbled out~~

- ~~I am naked right now~~ - Should I ever bother asking bout your feet?

- Do you use an iron to ~~straiten~~ your hair?

- What does a ginger smell like - Do you have eye lashes

- Can you say something in french?

- Would you eat ham every day if you get paid $1 million for every month you live? - at the rest of your life if

- Is your house still haunted?

- I think you should quack

- May I stroke your glabella - Will you and your llama ever have a threesome with Hannah Montana?

- Is it ~~weird~~ being a man now?

- Who was your first love?

- If you came with a warning lbl what would it say!

PHIL IS NOT ON FIRE

P: The video that started it all.

D: Though really, where the hell did this idea come from?

P: Well Q&As are always popular videos! We all like getting to know people we find interesting on the internet, but it's always a bit awkward reading out the questions yourself – so I thought why not ask you!

D: The Q&A bit is easy to understand but what was with the whiskers?

P: I think I must have been some kind of feline in a previous life as whenever I saw a black marker-pen on my desk I had to put it on my face! I don't think I ever actually explained it.

D: You realise more than anything we'll ever do, this is our legacy?

P: Why do you think it was so popular?

D: Are you asking who would want to watch two random guys with weird haircuts answer strange questions while rolling on the floor looking like cats?

P: The Internet?

D: The Internet. Though also I think your really quick jumpy editing made the whole thing have a strange *Alice In Wonderland* trance-like vibe.

P: Are you saying we hypnotised people?

D: Probably. Let's be honest. So how did it become a yearly tradition?

P: I think, kinda like this book, it's about respecting our origins! It's like our annual ritual of remembrance as if we're pleasing the cat gods up in the sky.

D: I was going to say because our audience loved the videos but if you're saying cat gods I won't argue with you.

P: Either way I think it's a series we should continue for the rest of time. It is the foundation of Dan and Phil.

D: It will truly be remembered among the best series of our times – *Star Wars*, *Harry Potter*, *The Lord of The Rings* and Phil is not on fire.

HAM OVERLOAD

WHY DO YOU ALWAYS MAKE CAT WHISKERS ON YOUR FACE?

IMAGINE MY FACE WITHOUT A NOSE

THE ACTUAL SCARIEST DOLL IN EXISTENCE

ZEEEBRAA

YOUR MUM

VOLDEMORT IS PRETTY FIT TO BE HONEST

I AM NAKED RIGHT NOW

LET'S GO FOR IT

NINJA

EVERY

ANIMAL

MAKES

THAT

NOISE

WITH

YOU

EVERY ANIMAL MAKES THAT NOISE WITH YOU

CORDLESS HAMMER DRILL

SO MANLY

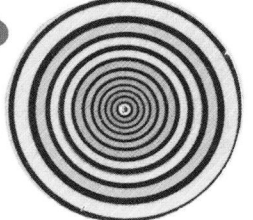

JE MANGE LE PETIT ENFANT

OH YEAH

LIGHT LIGHT LIGHT LIGHT

EATING A LOT OF MEAT

May I stroke your glabella?

THIS WAS THE MOST FUN I EVER HAD

DANGER

IT'S SUPPOSED TO BE CHEESY

I think you should QUACK

HOW to DRAW the PERFECT CAT WHISKERS

DRAWING CAT WHISKERS ON SOMEONE'S FACE IS AN ANCIENT AND POWERFUL ART FORM. YOU CANNOT SIMPLY SCRIBBLE ON SOMEONE WITH THE FIRST PEN YOU FIND, THERE'S A FINELY HONED METHOD WHICH WE HAVE PERFECTED THROUGH HALF A DECADE OF CAT-THEMED RITUALS. WHEN YOU ARE READY, LET US TAKE YOU ON AN ENLIGHTENING JOURNEY.

1 **Find a friend** You cannot cat-whisker yourself. I mean you can but that's kind of sad so go find someone even if it's a baby or your grandma.

2

Find a pen This can't just be any pen! Trust us when we say there are so many mistakes to make here. Do not use a permanent marker. Unless you enjoy scouring black ink out of your pores for two weeks and covering your face suspiciously with a scarf when the pizza delivery guy arrives, don't use a permanent marker – find a nice black dry-wipe.

3

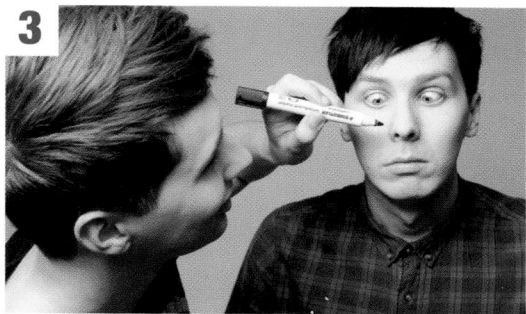

Assume the proper whisker-drawing stance It's very awkward drawing on someone's face. You will find yourself leaning around them in intimate and strange-seeming ways to properly contour the curve of their nose. Make sure you have the proper elbow room to commit to the full length of a whisker – there's nothing worse than a whisker that's clearly been drawn in two parts.

4

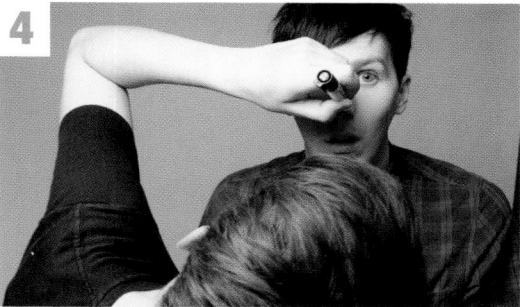

Touch pen to face Start with the nose. Cover the front of their nose bulb with a smooth circle of black ink. Don't scratch at it randomly or you'll do that weird thing where the pen actually rubs off bits of it that you've already drawn and then it'll go all flaky and go over your hands and it's really gross and stuff.

5

Getting started Starting about half a centimetre out from the nose, draw one smooth straight line ending parallel with the edge of the eye. Each whisker should be exactly 22.5° apart.

6

DON'T TOUCH Trust us, we know it's itchy. It will be unbearably itchy – but do not touch. You cannot ruin the hours of preparation and perspiration that will have gone into this by caving in to your physical desires and scratching your nose. If you lack the self-discipline, consider asking your companion to temporarily restrain you until you are ready.

7

And there you have it! A perfectly and professionally applied cat whisker look ready for you to answer strange questions sent by weirdos on the internet, or maybe just role-play as a cat for your own enjoyment. Method ©DanandPhil

Dan's University Life

Day One

Like most people, I couldn't wait to move out of my parents' house. 'Social freedom! I can stay up as late as I want! No one can criticise me for eating profiteroles in bed!' I didn't quite realise how unprepared I was for independence until I arrived to study Law at Manchester University.

It happened in the middle of a supermarket. Myself and five complete strangers who I met an hour ago and that I was going to be living with for a year, had all shuffled in awkward silence to buy some groceries. As luck would have it every one of them, like myself, had taken a gap year! This was great, I thought. We're all the same age and we can relate to each other's life journeys – it just turned out that most of them used their year to learn some basic life skills. I had none. I just spent a lot of time watching YouTube videos (great use of your time btw never stop that).

I don't know why this hadn't occurred to me until the moment I stopped in the middle of the dairy aisle, but I realised I didn't know how to cook. Now I'm not saying I didn't know how to make a risotto or where to get a water bath to make molecular beef porridge with truffle condensation, my knowledge of cooking ended at wondering why my toast was undercooked.

I felt a sudden moment of emptiness. My spirit soared out of my body to the roof of the supermarket and I realised from above that I was all alone in a giant city without the vaguest understanding of cooking, laundry or public transport. I had that mini internal breakdown 99% of new students have so I considered hiding by the fancy cheese and crying down the phone to my grandma, but I remembered she'd probably be at her Sudoku club at that time. No consolation for me. How had I managed to never go on a bus by myself in 18 years? I'm not sure but I realised I had a lot to learn quickly.

Accommodation

The shell-shocked state that I suddenly found myself in was reflected aesthetically in my accommodation. Obviously I left my housing application form until the night before it had to be sent, so I ended up in the least requested accommodation out of ten options.

It had off-cream painted exposed concrete brick walls with rusty piping that with every expansion and contraction from heat sounded like Optimus Prime falling down the stairs.

My bed had a noticeable dip in the middle where four of the ten springs holding the mattress up had somehow snapped into concernedly Tetanus-capable

Scenic view from bedroom

Accommodation

points. I then made the mistake of flipping my mattress over. Take this advice: no matter where you are, a friend's house, a new apartment or a moderately priced hotel – never flip over the mattress you will sleep on. Before me was a brown stain in the perfect silhouette of a man surrounded by a yellow aura as if swamp-Jesus was climbing over a hill doused in holy light. The heating that never turned off explained the sweat patches and permanent condensation. As you can still see from my 2010 YouTube videos, a couple of album posters and some 'Dan Mail' can do wonders to transform a small space (thank you to people who sent me mail, you were literally the only source of colour in my off-cream life).

All this being said, apart from something my friends to this day refer to as the 'phantom poo' incident (which I will not write about in this book), with enough pasta and late night kebab shop visits I managed to survive and very much enjoyed my independence and socialising.

Fan mail

Social Life

I remember the 'thing' was leaving your room door open. It said 'hey my metaphorical door is also open, come talk to me let's be friends'. I spent the first week playing Halo with the curtains drawn eventually realising you have to overcome your social anxiety if you want to use the fridge. I think I lucked out in that the random assortment of people I was put with were all very cool and interesting and we all got on very well, apart from two international students which were a bit strange (no offence to every other country in the world). The first was a guy who I never spoke to in the entire year despite living in the room above me. I remember on one single occasion at about 3am after an innocent night of exploring the city of Manchester *cough*, stumbling into the kitchen to see him in tighty-whities wielding a cleaver, furiously hacking at a whole chicken.

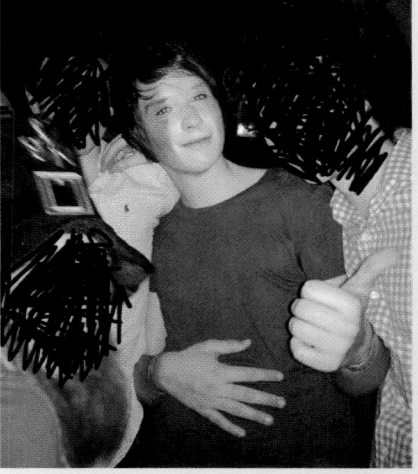

Dan socialising after a hard day of studying

To this day I'm not sure if that was a strange nightmare that infiltrated my consciousness, but the most I know about him is that he lives life on the edge when it comes to appropriate clothing near sharp utensils and gas flames. The other was a girl who was very quiet, which I attributed to some kind of generic social shyness until she finally decided to let loose on the last day of the year, when what I presume was an entire lifetime of repressed emotional outburst happened over four hours. I remember her having a heart to heart with me next to a very loud speaker blasting dubstep, in which she was possibly trying to tell me she murdered someone in Japan but I like to think I misheard a lot of it ... I removed her as a friend on Facebook.

Then there was the cool guy who liked video games, Kanye West and Anime who also shared many of my interests in fashion, books and even general 2am philosophy, until one day he told everyone that he spent all of his time gaming instead of studying and then he mysteriously disappeared. I have not seen or heard from him since. Maybe I should have added him on Facebook. Or chicken-underwear guy! Come to think of it, why don't more of them keep in contact with me? Oh, probably because every time I filmed a video they just heard a guy talking to himself in his room.

Studying

I sometimes forget and even occasionally at the time forgot the reason why I was there, ah yes, the Law degree.

Now I want to be clear. For anyone like me who saw *Legally Blonde* and was inspired by the idea of sassing out a criminal with your knowledge of hair styling, or anyone who has parents brimming with pride at your academic success and desire to study the honourable field of Law – I'm not saying you shouldn't because it's absolutely horrifying, but it's absolutely horrifying. Murders are fun, yes, understanding what exactly the Queen actually does is fun, yes, but the details of 'Contract law' aren't. No offence to contracts. 'Legal language' is basically French (no offence France). It may look like it's written in your native language, but it's so strangely worded that I had to read every paragraph in my textbook about seven times to understand it. This is when I understood the profound lesson that 'you should study something you're interested in'. If you study psychology or literature, whatever you do will always, at the end of the day, be related to something you are interested in. Three months into the semester I wanted to spoon my eyes out.

Papers from hell

One of my lecturers had a voice that I am convinced vibrated at some kind of droning frequency that makes humans fall asleep. There is no other explanation. 'Seminars' I discovered was a fancy

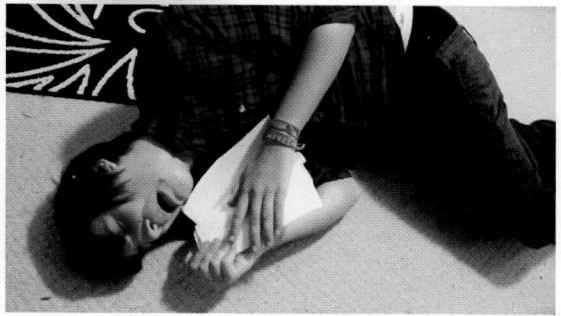

Dan enjoying his Law course on the floor

name for sitting in a circle of ten people with your professor going round one by one realising how little studying you have done compared to the person next to you. I survived the year somewhat successfully, but it was traumatic.

Conclusion

Well as we all know, in the summer between the first and second year I had a mild mental breakdown/first existential crisis about wanting to follow my passions and being free which somehow resulted in me actually thinking that dropping out of university to become a full-time internet hobo was a good idea.

Good thing Radio 1 were interested in us and you all liked my videos or I would have been living in a cardboard box, haha!

I am a terrible role model. Go read Phil's university story – he has a Master's degree for God's sake.

Phil's University Life

The First Day

I was in the middle of Tesco holding a selection of tea towels when I burst into tears. Thankfully, it wasn't a post-traumatic tea-towel-related flashback; it was the day before I was leaving for university and my mum was helping me buy all the stuff I needed. Cutlery, bedsheets, a bin ... Was I mature enough to own my own bin?! It didn't feel like it. I was terrified. The tea towels were the straw that broke the Phil's back.

I didn't feel ready. I didn't want to leave my family in Rossendale. I didn't like change and I definitely didn't know how to look after myself. I had an awkward Tesco mum-hug, with Janet the checkout lady watching us, pulled myself together and put the tea towels in my basket. There was no going back now, I was going. It was happening. Thankfully, it was one of the best decisions I ever made!

The car journey to York University was the most terrified I had ever been. So many thoughts were melting my brain. Will people like me? How will I know what to do? What if they are all lizard people? What if I get lost and set the kitchen on fire and what what what what?

After an endless two-hour drive, I arrived on campus with my parents and they helped me unpack my computer, pinboard, cry-inducing tea towels and, most importantly, my *Buffy The Vampire Slayer* box set. My parents offered to stay and take me to dinner but I knew that I had to rip the plaster off and be brave. I walked them to the car, waved my goodbyes and returned to my room.

I was alone.

Accommodation

York University is beautiful! A huge flowing campus of lakes, geese, statues and old-fashioned houses. (Small fact: If you kill a goose then you are banned for life, but if you kill a person you can return to campus after you've finished your sentence! They do love their geese.)

Unfortunately my accommodation was not beautiful. I was in a house of five girls, five boys, two toilets and one shower. ONE SHOWER? What were they thinking?! My stomach sank when I realised I'd have to share a bathroom with other people. To make it worse the toilet was right next to the kitchen so there was no privacy at all! No more hour-long phone sessions on the toilet.

The walls and ceilings were about as thick as a sheet of cellophane. I could hear EVERYTHING. I could even hear the guy in the room next to mine peeing in his sink *shudder*.

I've repressed most of the other things that I heard. I bought some bomb-disposal-strength ear-plugs so that kinda helped.

A guy I met on the way into my bedroom told me they always put a tall boy in the room next to the front door as he'll be able to defend himself from burglars a lot easier. THANKS PETE. Thankfully, my door had three locks on it and I had an elaborate escape plan involving my window and an imaginary training montage of ninja skills.

Besides the lack of toilet, strange stains and high probability of burglar death, I had actually made my room pretty homely. Comfy duvet, laptop, DVDs, sink, what more could I need? Food. Not even a single raisin in my room. It was time to venture into the kitchen.

Social Life

When it was time to meet people, my brother's advice was buzzing in my mind:

Brother advice 1:
'Maybe don't reveal all your quirks and your Buffy obsession straight away.' BAD ADVICE. People definitely click less with you if you hold back your personality! It turned out my university housemates were way more relaxed and actually embraced any weirdness in the house.

Brother advice 2:
'Prop your door open with an open box of Haribo.' GOOD ADVICE.
My bedroom was next to the front door so I met loads of other students as they were moving in too!

I hung out in the kitchen for the next few hours and made an effort to introduce myself to every person who entered even if they didn't immediately seem like they were Phil compatible. It was a really diverse mix of people: sporty girl, art students, a guy into heavy metal, a guy who wore fluorescent green shorts every day and even a girl from North Carolina! I struck up a conversation

with a guy called Andy from New Zealand and we bonded over the TV show *LOST*. I think I may have weirded him out slightly by immediately suggesting we go watch it on his bed. My social skills needed a bit of work, okay?

First day of uni with my new housemates!

57

The plan for that first night was to go out to a club AKA my worst nightmare. I hadn't planned for this. I can't dance! What was I gonna do? It didn't turn out to be so bad. I just kinda bobbed my head up and down like a chicken on the dancefloor and jumped around to The Killers for a few hours and got to know my new housemates a little bit.

Of course living with ten people is never going to be easy. I bonded with one girl over Crash Bandicoot until it turned out she didn't like Crash Bandicoot and was only playing it as she thought I fancied her. When I said I didn't see her that way and that I was only in it for the Bandicoot, she threw a drink in my face. Who'd have known Crash Bandicoot could be so dramatic?

The guys of the house also began a prank war against each other. Their first attack on me was one of the most severe. I got back from a lecture and my whole bedroom was empty apart from a note reading 'Go into the kitchen'. I walked into the kitchen to see they had moved my ENTIRE bedroom into there. Even my computer was set up and switched on on the kitchen worktop! Of course they didn't help me put any of it back. Lesson to learn from that one: LOCK YOUR DOOR.

I wasn't much of a prankster so I never really got revenge. Oh wait, I did put salt in their sugar once. Somebody stop me.

I got the entire house to bond one weekend by making Andy wear a tinfoil mask and filming a horror movie set in the future for my channel called 'THE GAME'. It was actually my first video upload to AmazingPhil before I started vlogging!

Another thing that went down in history was the moment I forgot I was making toast at the exact time the toaster decided to break and stay switched on, melting the entire toaster, filling the house with smoke and calling out the fire brigade.
Oops.

Throughout my uni years I went from knowing no one to making loads of friends on my course, bonding with my housemates and even moving in with 5 of them into our very own house (complete with mouse and creepy landlord who occasionally slept in our garden in a tent)! I'd like to say I keep in touch with all of them now but unfortunately life isn't like that. Friends change and drift apart but I'm sure we'll cross paths again someday.

Studying

Oops I never actually said what I was doing at university. That's kinda the whole point you are there right? I was studying English Language and Linguistics after loving English Language at school and having a genuine interest in languages. I'll be honest that 50 per cent of my degree was a confusing waffle-fest of 3-hour lectures and near-impossible homework. The exams were hard too. Rocket science hard. I think I chewed through so many pens in one exam that the biro police were launching a serial killer inquiry. I actually scraped through my first year and somehow a light switched on in my brain and I did pretty well in years 2 and 3! I stayed on to do an MA in Post-Production and Visual Effects which really helped out my YouTube and is the reason why I know how to animate Kristen Stewart's face onto the body of a small badger. Totally worth a student loan. Here's a picture of me studying hard: >>>

Conclusion

If I could go back and do uni again I think I'd try and meet even more people! I signed up to about 17 clubs and never went to any of them. Maybe I could have been super buff and in the naked rowing calendar if I'd actually turned up to the first 8am practice. Who knows?

Overall I think university was my transformation from an extremely shy caterpillar with spiky hair into a mildly awkward moth with emo hair. I'm not the fully formed flaming hawk that I want to be yet but I'm getting there? Kinda!

MANCHESTER
1824

The University of Manchester

www.manchester.ac.uk

24 October 2012

Private & Confidential
Mr Daniel Howell

Manchester

Dear Mr Howell

I am writing to acknowledge that you have withdrawn from your LLB Law degree with effect from 06th June 2011.

On behalf of the School of Law, may I take this opportunity to wish you well for the future.

Yours sincerely

cc: Student Services Centre (Fees Section)
Student File
Academic Adviser

The University of Manchester,

HAVE MY BABIES

HAVE MY BABIES

SATAN BIEBER

BIEBER

SATAN

i am Irish wristwatch

BritiSh and i PHIL STRIKER

walk on   i am British and i walk on   the pavement

the pavement   PHIL STRIKER

SIDEWALK

DINOSAURS

I WOULD EAT MY OWN FEET

CRACKLE

R <	O :	B *
RUN	POKE	BORDER
O ;	T >	S
POKE	RAND	NOT SAVE

NICK

JONAS

PERSONAL

THIS IS

DON'T

(CHILDREN)

A wheel for a foot

ZEBRAAAAHHHHAHHHHH

What is with the cat whiskers?

What is with the cat whiskers?

mega bailey's sherbet chocolate truffle candy mountain explosion

HAVE A MASSIVE PANCAKE

HAVE MY BABIES

SATAN BIEBER

MECROWAVE

THE MANCHESTER APARTMENT

D: Ah, the first Dan and Phil pad.

P: AKA the Phlat.

D: Or the Phalace of dreams.

P: We didn't call it that and, Dan, that sounds really wrong.

D: Oh it totally does you're right, I'm so sorry.

P: Yep in 2011 after Dan gave up on his *Legally Blonde* dreams we decided to move in together!

D: It seemed like such a perfect idea. I desperately needed a place to live, Phil was going crazy living alone and we were both YouTubers!
No more feeling judged for talking to ourselves in our bedrooms at 4am.

P: Wait, what do you mean 'seemed like'?

D: So that apartment was pretty cool. I mean, it was on the 18th floor looking over all of Manchester like Pride Rock. How did we get it?

P: Total luck. I look at apartments on property websites for fun 'cause I'm a cool guy like that and I noticed this one for a weirdly low price.

D: Someone probably died on the breakfast bar.

P: It was suspiciously clean!

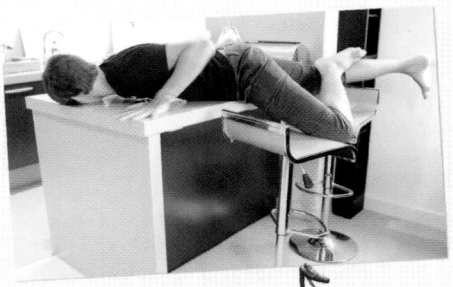

D: Although didn't we have to get your dad to speak to the owners because they didn't understand what YouTube was and how that could pay rent?

P: Yeah it turns out saying 'we make videos in our bedrooms' doesn't sound great!

D: I was just happy to escape the hell of my university accommodation. I kinda miss Manchester though, it's such a cool city with everything you'd want! I feel like I've 'done it' now though. I mean when your favourite milkshake place names a drink after you it's time to leave.

P: At least I still get to go up North to see my homeland! Do you miss the creepy guy dressed as a statue who gave out lollipops?

D: He haunts my nightmares to this day. Let's have a tour of the apartment!

BALCONY

[...]is is the balcony where Phil [on]ce dropped a bouncy ball off [the] edge and it bounced higher [tha]n a lamppost and nearly killed [a pi]geon.

[It w]as for science! I mainly went out [on] the balcony to look through the [wi]ndows of the business hotel that [wa]s opposite us.

[I'm] moderately certain that's illegal.

BREAKFAST BAR

P: Didn't you once sensually rub yourself all over this?
D: Yes I think we have a picture! (opposite) The surface was just asking for it tbh.
P: Though how often did we actually have breakfast on it?
D: Not once in an entire year. It was mainly used as a thing to balance cameras on when we filmed cooking videos and sketches.

COFFEE TABLE

P: Did you know this is actually coffee table #2? Yep the first one got completely destroyed when Dan fell on it.
D: A bit of context here. I have a thing called 'orthostatic hypotension' which is the fancy term for 'really slow blood' so being an obnoxiously tall person, whenever I stand up really quickly when the blood is all still in my feet I fall over like a logged tree!
P: I kinda thought you died but then when I noticed you hadn't it was kinda funny.
D: Thanks.

[BATH]ROOM

[Pre]tty swank bathrooms actually. [Co]ming from my shared University [bat]hrooms you have no idea how [mu]ch this meant to me.

[W]asn't this the bath where you [exp]loded Coke and Mentos up your [bu]tt for a dare?

[Oh] yes. I remember peeling the minty [bit]s of shell that had fused to my flesh [for] weeks afterwards. Good times.

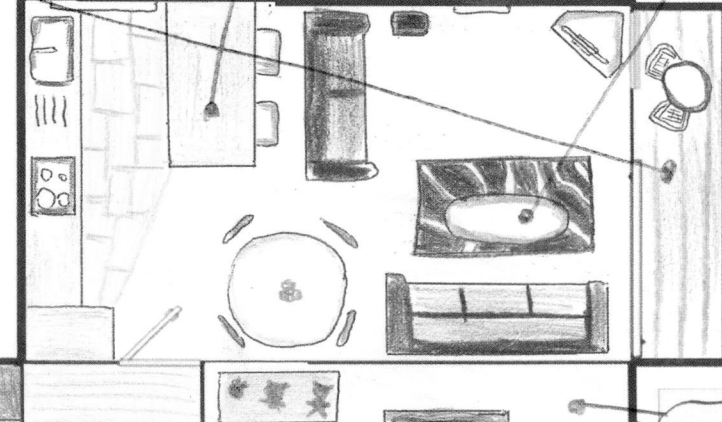

[P]ORTAL TO ANOTHER DIMENSION

[P:] Little did our viewers know at the time but hidden in this cupboard was actually an interdimensional vortex!
[D:] This is where we hid all our alter-egos from our videos and the things that we couldn't be bothered to tidy like mystery wires and those bits of lint that just appear on the floor.
[P:] It was quite convenient! The forces only demanded a blood sacrifice once a week and sometimes we got to travel to the other side.
[D:] Remember that time we visited Other-Manchester and rode meat scooters down the hill towards the teeth shrine?

FRONT DOOR

P: This was the scene of many incidents such as 'The Holy Mother'.
D: Was that when a lady tried to get you to join a cult?
P: Yes I was absolutely terrified!
D: I would have gone along just to meet her. I'm imagining something with tentacles but I think I'd be disappointed.
P: Also once when we were taking in our shopping a drunk guy just walked into our lounge thinking it was his apartment.
D: You were convinced that we were going to die - I still remember your manly squeal. I was just happy to interact with another human.

DAN'S ROOM

D: I remember the width between my bed and the opposite wall being just wide enough to sidestep through on tiptoes.
P: You made the most of what space you had!
D: I like to think that the spiritual energy of all the videos I filmed on that bed will linger in the property for years to come.
P: The spiritual energy of you ranting about people at cinemas and fanfiction?
D: I also removed most of the paint from the walls by blutacking posters everywhere but shhh don't tell anyone.

PHIL'S ROOM

D: Wait, why did you get the bigger room again?
P: Because I had more subscribers.
D: Fair enough. I was jelly of the en-suite.
P: There's nothing like being able to sit on the toilet with the door open.
D: Dude, your bedroom door didn't have a lock. I could have just walked in.
P: Oops. ALWAYS KNOCK.

Roommate Assessment form

Evaluator: Dan Howell

Roommate name: Phil Lester

Time had as roommate: 3 years

General Tidiness:

Phil is an incredibly messy person. I don't think he's ever made a coffee without somehow spilling enough sugar and instant powder to turn the kitchen counter into an ice rink of caramelised brown goo. He leaves paper all over the office, he leaves his clothes on the bathroom floor, he leaves socks in the most random places you could imagine and worst of all – the contact lens pot. Every day Phil takes out his contact lenses, puts them in the little plastic pot and then balances them directly on top of the tap. Moving things off a tap may not sound that bad! Every. Single. Day. Is this the right section to bring up the time he stuck holographic Spice Girls stickers all over our furniture?

Household Chores:

Phil's actually pretty good at the chores! I think he stacks the dishwasher and does the laundry for fun or probably out of some kind of procrastination-related guilt, but either way he gets the jobs done.

Noise:

He will blare video game soundtracks at a dangerously high volume when cleaning the kitchen and his Celine Dion renditions in the shower aren't the best thing early in the morning, but most of the noise in our apartment we make together! That came out wrong. I meant playing video games – VIDEO GAMES.

Food:

Oh. My. God. Phil has what we refer to as a 'secret eating' problem. He'll tell me we're all about the health now and buy us salads for lunch, then volunteer to cook tofu and air stir-fries and there I am thinking it's out of the goodness of his heart! No. Roughly every 25 minutes Phil will sneak into the kitchen with levels of stealth that I'm sure would impress most intelligence services and eat something without anyone finding out. What happened to my cereal? I thought we had four cookies left not one? Where are those sweets I bought for our friends coming over later? The guilt is always plain to see within his eyes. At least he regularly buys snacks! Plus when he's not eating the food he's pretty good at cooking, so that's alright.

Bathroom Usage:

What is this thing you call a 'towel'? I wouldn't know as, despite owning five, I've never seen them as they're all on Phil's bedroom floor. Why does someone need three towels after having a shower?! Like I get two towels if you want to put one on your hair (not that Phil's really requires it) but what is the third one for? Shoulder drying? Ankle drip protection? General emotional support?? There's nothing worse than washing your hands and having to walk through the house dripping water on to your socks desperately searching for an appropriate place to wipe them.

Overall Rating: 4/5

☐ **Outstanding**   ☐ **Exceeds Expectations**   ☒ **Meets Expectations**   ☐ **Improvement Needed**

Comments A couple of issues but I guess he could be a cannibal or a beekeeper or something so it works out pretty well.

Roommate Assessment form

Evaluator: Phil Lester

Roommate name: Dan Howell

Time had as roommate: 3 years

General Tidiness:

Beware of Dan if he loses something! Generally he is quite a tidy guy but if he loses a precious sock or strange zippy jumper he will turn into a rampaging beast and turn the entire house upside down looking for it. One time I caught him emptying our box of Christmas decorations onto the floor looking for a USB cable. I mean I had left it in there, but that is not the point!

He also throws any piece of paper he finds in the bin so protect important documents with your life. Examples have included our holiday boarding passes, important receipts and my script the night before The Brit Awards!

Household Chores:

Dan's pretty great at tidying the lounge and re-arranging all the DVDs into alphabetical order. However, he still needs training in the art of not putting red socks in with white washing as I now have a lovely collection of pink shirts and boxer shorts.

Noise:

I think we are both as bad as each other when it comes to noise so I feel more sorry for the people sharing our walls! Dan usually goes to bed later than me so I occasionally wake up to him aggressively shouting at the TV playing Mario Kart.

Food:

Dan claims I'm a secret eater but most of the time I'm just inspecting the cereal to check it is still in the box and it's fresh enough for the next morning. You believe me, right? Right? OKAY I HAVE A PROBLEM but I think Dan needs to hide his snacks better, or perhaps invest in some kind of cereal padlock. It's all his fault really! If he bought some kind of cheese-related cereal then there wouldn't be a problem. On a more positive note, Dan does cook great Indian food and understands the perfect science of cooking microwave popcorn without leaving too many kernels. Side note: HE EATS THE KERNELS! What's that about?!

Bathroom Usage:

I don't know how many times Dan washes his body but don't let him loose on your shower gel as he can use half a bottle in one go. He'll also occasionally lock himself in the bathroom to practise his rendition of 'Bring Me To Life' by Evanescence (singing both the male and female parts).
It's actually quite melodic so I don't mind too much.

Overall Rating: 4/5

☐ **Outstanding**   ☐ **Exceeds Expectations**   ☒ **Meets Expectations**   ☐ **Improvement Needed**

Comments Generally a good housemate. I probably would have given him 5 if I wasn't searching for my birth certificate in a bin bag whilst wearing pink boxers right now.

Do you guys have a cat whiskers fetish or something?

I would lose the sense of DANCE

IS THIS REAL LIFE

THEY GOT SAD AND EXPLODED

Forehead birthing area

What would you NOT do For £1,000

Blow on my nose. No that's weird don't do that.

Bacteria

EAT A DOG

YOU'RE GLITTERING

5 4 3 2 1

Hyper Kirby Plumber and Sword!

BRO

How much wood could a wood chuck chuck
if a wood chuck could chuck NORRIS

JESSICA'S PAGE

HEYA MY NAME'S JESSICA AND WELCOME TO MY TOTALLY AWESOMEFAB PAGE!!

I'M GUESSING YOU'LL WANT TO KNOW ALL ABOUT ME SO HERE'S A LITTLE THING I WROTE FOR ALL THE PEOPLE I MEET (BECAUSE I'M POPULAR):

♥ MY FAVOURITE COLOUR IS PINK.

♥ MY FAVOURITE ARTIST IS DEMI LOVATO - SELENA CAN GET OUT SHE'S SO BASIC I MIGHT MESSAGE SOMETHING AT HER ON MY PHONE LATER.

♥ MY BEST FRIEND IS BECKY BUT YOU DON'T NEED TO KNOW ABOUT HER SHE'S KINDA BORING LOL.

♥ MY FAVOURITE OUTFIT IS MY PURPLE CARDIGAN I WEAR IT EVERYWHERE I GO BECAUSE IT'S AWESOME FOR MY FIGURE AND SHOWS JUST THE RITE AMOUNT OF CLEAVAGE! HEHE (IT USED TO BE BECKY'S BUT I SWAPPED IT FOR AN OLD GREY ONE OF MINE BECUS I LOOK BETTER IN IT).

MY HOBBIES INCLUDE PARTYING AND DATING AND SHOPPING. SOME PEOPLE CALL ME LOUD BUT I CAN'T HELP BEING SUPER CONFIDENT IN HOW BEAUTIFUL I AM, IT'S JUST HOW I WAS BORN (DON'T BE JEL!). I'M LIVING WITH MY PARENTS ATM, AS MY DUMB EX TROY MADE ME MOVE OUT OF HIS HOUSE AFTER DUMPING ME. I MEAN WHO DOES THAT?? HE WAS SUCH A JERK. WHO CALLS SOMEONE A STALKER JUST FOR GOING TO THEIR HOUSE AND CLIMBING INTO THEIR BEDROOM AFTER NOT REPLYING TO A TEXT FOR 15 MINUTES? HOW WAS I SUPPOSED TO KNOW HE WASN'T DEAD?

MY MUM IS LIKE SUPER RELIGIOUS AND ONCE SHE TOLD ME THAT IF I DON'T FOCUS ON SCHOOL AND 'CHANGE MY PRIORITIES' THAT SHE'LL SEND ME TO A NUN PLACE. I MEAN WTF!! UGH OMG I HATE MY MUM SHE'S SO ANNOYING. CAN YOU IMAGINE ME IN THAT STUPID BLACK OUTFIT WITH A THING OVER MY HEAD COVERING MY HAIR?? THAT'D BE SO STUPID LOL.

DAN?
OH THAT GUY.
IDK HE'S WEIRD HE'S ALWAYS IN SOME AWKWARD SITUATION WHEN I'M TRYING TO PARTY AND TBH I JUST DON'T CARE.

BECKY'S PAGE

Hi um. My name is um, Becky.

People don't usually ask stuff about me so I'm not sure what to say.

I like music. My mum who's called Becky too was a big fan of
The Beatles. I mainly focus on my work. I don't think I'd really have
time for a boyfriend, not that anyone's really paid attention to me before.
My favourite item of clothing is a grey sweater,
I like it because it helps me blend in I guess.
I don't like drawing too much attention to myself.

I'm kind of shy but my best friend Jessica is really great because
she's cool and popular and lets me hang out with her. I'm grateful
for that.

What do I think of Dan?
He seems like a nice guy, I've never really spoken to him myself.
I remember Jessica talking about him a couple of times but I don't know
how much she likes him.

THE TALE OF BECKY AND JESSICA

This is a true adventure through friendship and drama. Much more interesting than Dan and Phil to be honest. **This is their story:**

Jessica encounters a pervert on the tube

06/09/2012

'OH MY GOD BECKY I JUST SAW THE TALLEST LESBIAN EVER'

Jessica gets dumped by Troy

23/11/2012

'I CAN'T BELIEVE TROY WOULD DO THAT TO ME'

Jessica tries to give up chocolate on New Year's Day

04/01/2013

'I'VE BEEN GOING COLD TURKEY FROM CHOCOLATE FOR TEN HOURS AND I'M STILL NOT BEYONCÉ'

Jessica tries to hit on Dan and friend and insults Becky

28/2/2013

'SHUT UP BECKY NO ONE'S TALKING TO YOU'

Jessica complains about Becky betraying her

12/5/2013

'I CAN'T BELIEVE THAT AFTER EVERYTHING WE'VE BEEN THROUGH YOU WOULD JUST THROW AWAY OUR FRIENDSHIP'

Jessica is at a party and sees Dan drop a pile of discs

29/10/2013

'THIS PARTY IS OVER'

Jessica confronts Becky on the phone

9/12/2013

'BECKY WHY DID YOU UNFRIEND ME ON FACEBOOK?'

INTERVIEW WITH JESSICA

Interviewer:
Jessica, when was the last time you spoke to Becky?

Jessica:
I haven't spoken to Becky in over a year... I remember she deleted me on Facebook and she wouldn't even tell me why. What a freak.

Interviewer:
Do you think it may be to do with how you treated her?

Jessica:
What do you mean 'how I treated her'? We were like totally best friends! I took her to parties, I told her all my gossip, we even swapped her lame clothes.

Interviewer:
Do you think the way you talked to her was okay?

Jessica:
Uh, what do you mean?

Interviewer:
Well, I mean from what we've seen, it seems like you talked down to her a lot and almost used her just to boost your own confidence.

Jessica:
Pfft, Becky didn't take any of those things seriously! Right? I mean, I was kind of joking.

Interviewer:
Well what do you think? Do you understand why Becky chose to do what she did?

Jessica:
I feel like this is the first time I've ever thought about it. Becky's always been there for me you know? Even our mums were friends back when they used to meet up and write weird fan fiction together. I guess I've been kind of a bitch. Oh my god I need to tell her I'm sorry.

Interviewer:
Do you think if you apologise your friendship can continue?

Jessica:
I've felt so lost without her. It was the worst year of my life not having a best friend and if I have to change to get that back, I'm gonna do it! Becky, I promise I will be better for you, just let me say how I feel.

Becky declined to comment on the situation when told about Jessica's plans to apologise.

We can only wait and hope this new-found insight can bring them back together. #BESSICA4EVER

HELLO

PHIL'S LION HERE!

HERE'S A FRIENDLY REMINDER TO TRY AND ENJOY LIFE. I KNOW YOU'RE THINKING

'WHAT DO YOU KNOW?!

YOU'RE JUST A SMALL STUFFED LION!' WELL TRUST ME. I HAVE SEEN A LOT.

DON'T GET ME STARTED ON THE GREAT ZEBRA WAR AS THIS ISN'T ABOUT ME. IT'S ABOUT YOU.

PLEASE TREASURE EVERY MOMENT OF YOUR EXISTENCE AS ONE DAY YOU COULD BE LEFT TOO CLOSE TO A HAIR STRAIGHTENER AND SET ON FIRE.

I'M SPEAKING FROM EXPERIENCE. PHIL REALLY NEEDS TO STOP LEAVING THOSE THINGS NEXT TO MY TAIL. SERIOUSLY THOUGH, IF YOU'RE NOT CAREFUL LIFE COULD

PASS YOU BY AND BEFORE YOU KNOW IT YOU'LL HAVE TEENAGE CUBS AND YOU'LL BE PLANNING A NICE AREA OF THE SERENGETI TO RETIRE TO.

SAY YES TO MORE THINGS! IF THERE'S A TRIP TO THE WATERING HOLE, GO TO IT! IF THERE'S A WARTHOG PARTY BUT YOU DON'T KNOW MANY ANIMALS, SAY YES ANYWAY!

WHAT'S THE WORST THAT COULD HAPPEN? YOU'D HAVE A SLIGHTLY AWKWARD FIVE MINUTES AVOIDING HYENAS BEFORE YOU GET CHATTING TO SOMEONE?

I MET MY WIFE IN CIRCUMSTANCES LIKE THIS. I COULD HAVE JUST RELAXED ON PHIL'S BEDSIDE TABLE MINDING MY OWN BUSINESS BUT I THOUGHT TO MYSELF:

'SELF! IT'S TIME TO SEE WHAT IS BEYOND THIS BEDSIDE TABLE!'

I VENTURED AS FAR AS THE SOCK DRAWER AND MET MY BEAUTIFUL AND SLIGHTLY UNUSUAL WIFE. LOOK AT ME NOW! I'M A FAMILY LION. I'M NOT SAYING YOU SHOULD MOVE TO AFRICA

AND GET MARRIED, FEEL FREE TO BE SINGLE AND ENJOY YOUR OWN COMPANY. IT'S YOUR LIFE. DON'T FEEL PRESSURED TO HAVE CUBS AND SETTLE DOWN IF YOU DON'T WANT TO!

JUST MAKE SURE YOU REMEMBER THAT A BILLION COINCIDENCES HAD TO OCCUR FOR YOU TO EXIST AND EACH PASSING MOMENT IS A POSSIBILITY FOR A NEW ADVENTURE.

BETWEEN YOU AND ME, I KNOW THAT I'M A STUFFED ANIMAL AND I WILL NEVER SEE AFRICA IN REAL LIFE, BUT JUST SEEING THE JOY ON MY FAMILY'S FACE WHEN I BRING HOME

A SMALL PIECE OF CEREAL OR AN ABANDONED CRISP FROM PHIL'S FLOOR MAKES EVERYTHING WORTH IT. THE YEAR BEFORE THAT WHEN I WAS BEING BORN IN A JAPANESE

FACTORY I HAD NO IDEA THIS WOULD BE A POSSIBILITY.

JUST BEFORE I GO, A FEW SMALL PIECES OF ADVICE: IF YOU ARE CURRENTLY SAD, DON'T WORRY AS THINGS ARE MORE LIKELY TO GET BETTER THAN WORSE!

SCHOOL DOESN'T LAST FOREVER AND CIRCUMSTANCES CAN CHANGE IN AN INCREDIBLE WAY OVER THE COURSE OF A YEAR.

DON'T TRUST SQUIRRELS. DRINK LOTS OF WATER. ASK LOTS OF QUESTIONS. KEEP GOOD FRIENDS CLOSE. DON'T RACE A GIRAFFE.

OH AND WHEN THE OPPORTUNITY COMES UP, PLEASE DON'T MOVE TO MARS. IT'S DUSTY AND THERE ISN'T ANYTHING TO DO THERE.

IT'S BEEN GREAT CHATTING WITH YOU. I WISH I HAD MORE TIME. I'M GOING TO RETURN TO SITTING QUIETLY NOW.

THANKS FOR LISTENING.

LION

THE LIFE AND TIMES OF SIMON THE SHRIMP

P: Did you know that I became a father in 2011? A father to a prehistoric pet created from powder, but a father nonetheless. This pet was Simon the shrimp. It didn't feel right writing a book without featuring this little guy. He changed a lot of lives and inspired many people to live life to the fullest. Let's go back to the beginning.

BIRTH

IT ALL STARTED ON CHRISTMAS DAY 2010 WHEN I OPENED SOME 'PREHISTORIC TRIOPS' FROM SANTA! TRIOPS ARE INCREDIBLY WEIRD CRUSTACEANS THAT YOU CAN GROW FROM POWDER. ON 23 JANUARY I DECIDED TO GIVE BIRTH TO THESE LITTLE MONSTERS WITH THE HELP OF DAN! THIS IS THE MOMENT THAT LIFE WAS CREATED! I FELT SO POWERFUL:

AFTER A COUPLE OF DAYS THEY GREW INTO TRIOPS! THESE CREATURES WERE FASCINATING BUT ALSO GROSS. THEY WOULD CONSTANTLY FIGHT TO THE DEATH AND EAT EACH OTHER. THEY'D ALSO DO SIT-UPS ON THE BOTTOM OF THE TANK IN A RACE AGAINST TIME TO SHED THEIR EXOSKELETONS BEFORE DROWNING.

AFTER SEEING HOW GROTESQUE THE CREATURES HAD BECOME DAN DECIDED TO ABANDON ALL SENSE OF DUTY AND I BECAME A SINGLE FATHER. ONE BY ONE THE TRIOPS FOUGHT TO THE DEATH IN A MINIATURE WATERY HUNGER GAMES UNTIL ONE TRIOP REMAINED, BUT HE WASN'T ALONE IN THE TANK ...

INTERESTINGLY THE TRIOPS' FOOD CONTAINED 'FAIRY SHRIMP' EGGS. AND AS THE FINAL TRIOP DIED IN A FATAL SET OF SIT-UPS A COUPLE OF THE SHRIMP SURVIVED! IT WAS TIME TO WELCOME SIMON INTO THE WORLD.

MEMEMEMEMEMEME

OVER THE NEXT WEEK SIMON WENT FROM STRENGTH TO STRENGTH AND GREW INTO A BACKFLIPPING SUPER SHRIMP. WHILST THE TRIOPS SEEMED LIKE RAMPAGING MINDLESS ALIENS, YOU COULD REALLY SEE A KIND SOUL BEHIND HIS EYES. IF ONLY THAT SOUL KNEW HOW MUCH IT WAS APPRECIATED.

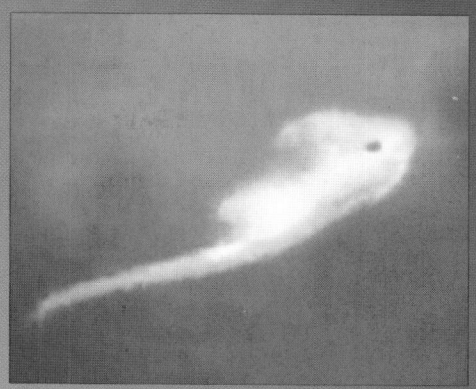

OVER THE NEXT FEW MONTHS, 'SIMON FEVER' HIT THE INTERNET. HE CREATED HUGE WAVES OF LOVE BOTH ONLINE AND OFFLINE. I HAD REQUESTS FOR SIMON T-SHIRTS AND PLUSHIES AND SOMEONE EVEN EMAILED ME ASKING IF HE'D CONSIDER DATING A HUMAN. IT WAS A WEIRD TIME.

HE GREW AND GREW AND GREW AND EVENTUALLY IMPREGNATED HIS TANKMATE LINDA WHO EITHER DEVELOPED EGG SACS OR TUMOURS ON HER BODY, WE WERE NEVER ENTIRELY SURE.

UNFORTUNATELY THIS HAPPINESS COULDN'T LAST FOREVER ...

THE DEATH OF SIMON

ON 4 MAY 2011 SIMON MOVED ON TO THE GIANT SHRIMP TANK IN THE SKY. THE INTERNET HAD A COUPLE OF DAYS OF MOURNING AND MANY FAMOUS FACES TURNED UP AT HIS SHRIMP FUNERAL.

AFTER A BEAUTIFUL AND MOVING SERVICE HE MOVED ON TO HIS FINAL RESTING PLACE.

R.I.P SIMON

London apartment

D: Here we are. Our pad in the big smoke!

P: Neither of us have ever called it that.

D: Too late to start? So London! Why would we choose to move from lovely little very cold Manchester down to this crazy giant busy city?

P: I feel like we'd both kind of 'done' Manchester by then? I mean you'd been there for two years but I grew up there and I went every weekend!

D: Yeah we liked it but it was time to go somewhere new. Plus literally everyone we knew in real life lived in London and we wanted to try actually having friends.

P: That's because instead of socialising with other students at University you only talked to people on the internet.

D: I regret nothing.

P: Yup it was scary but we felt like it was the right thing to do! We started working with Radio 1, all the people that made videos lived in the same place and we both felt like we needed to take that big jump.

D: You mean utterly terrifying freefall into a strange land where we had no experience?

P: Yeah!

D: Again I feel like we were ridiculously lucky getting this apartment. We spent an entire week getting lost around London, looking at places that were all horrible!

P: Like that one that became available 'as the landlord left', which we think meant that the old lady who used to live in it died.

D: I felt like she died in the armchair in the lounge, which would explain the mysterious stain.

P: We learned a lot of lessons about places looking better in photos on the website. One place even had chairs that turned out to be painted polystyrene.

D: Then there was the time we got lost in Shadwell and you thought you were going to die.

P: Thanks for bringing that up, Dan. We did find a place in the end though and it is awesome! Even if it was totally unfurnished when we moved in and all we had was boxes and a beanbag.

D: Yes we had to buy a lot of cheap furniture and learn to assemble it very quickly! Which might explain why literally all of it fell apart in the first two months.

D: Two years later though we're settled with well-built furniture and we're proper Londoners.

P: I'll never forget my wild Northern roots!

London apartment

DAN'S ROOM

D: The main reason we picked this place is because the bedrooms are gigantic! Most of the bedrooms in London were like tiny coffins, but as people who never go outside we needed a big hamster cage.

P: Yeah now we have enough room each to sleep, film videos and do aerobics.

D: You have literally never done an 'aerobic'.

P: But I could! I would like the reader to know that I just did a star jump.

D: Congratulations. My bedroom also had an old piano in it which I was told hasn't been moved since the house was built 100 years ago.

P: I bet it has ghosts in it.

D: Don't ruin my bedroom. Also that desk is where I am writing these very words that you're reading!

P: Dan! I told you to stop breaking the fourth page.

PHIL'S ROOM

P: My room also came with a piece of furniture! Not a ghost piano though. A giant bed made entirely out of wicker.

D: Literally, it's like a gigantic picnic basket, it's pretty hideous.

P: I mean I don't want to offend whoever weaved my bed, but the only reason I kept it is I couldn't work out how to get it through my doorway.

HALLWAY

P: Good hallway! Nice light walls that we have destroyed by banging chairs and camera equipment against them.

D: Do you think there's any chance we'll get our deposit back?

P: We've destroyed this place so much we'll probably have to buy the whole thing.

D: Also good carpet for lying on if you're having a crisis.

KITCHEN

D: This bloody door. You'd think the idea of a completely glass door leading in to your kitchen sounds nice and fancy! No. It's a death trap.

P: Pretty much every night when the lights are turned off the glass door just turns into an invisible wall of pain. My nose is twitching just remembering all of the incidents.

LOUNGE

D: I was just excited to have a fireplace!

P: I don't trust gas fires. I don't really understand how they work, so I'm constantly afraid I'm going to blow up the whole of London every time there's a cold morning.

D: This is also probably the geekiest room in existence. There isn't a single surface that isn't covered with some kind of TV or game merchandise.

P: I'd have it no other way!

D: Then we have our trusty sofa where we spend 99% of our lives. I think initially I crushed the sofa cushion into the shape of my spine, but now I've spent so much time slouching on it my spine has moulded to fit the sofa crease.

OFFICE

D: The totally random third floor of our apartment which is just one little square room.

P: For over a year when we moved in this was only known as the 'room of shame'. It was the place we threw all of our boxes of stuff from Manchester but as time went on we only added to it with all the cardboard boxes from the furniture we bought.

D: Turns out it's quite a cool little cave for putting our computers! Add in one sofa bed for guests and a couple of funky cushions and, voilà, you have a gaming channel zone!

P: I'm glad it has a purpose now. I always feel bad for an unused room. Now it's the home of all our geeky videos and cooperative rage.

TOILET

D: So one of our viewers kindly decided to give us a door-length One Direction poster as a moving-in gift. We had no idea where to put it for ages until we decided to stick it to the inside of the toilet door.

P: There is about 10cm of room between the door and your face when sat on the toilet, so the idea of forcing our guests to stare at a giant grinning Harry Styles head was very funny.

D: We always look forward to the loud 'what the?!' when someone sees it for the first time. Oh the things those boys have seen in there.

STAIRS

D: Our apartment is technically on the third floor but because it's so weird everything's actually on the fourth!

P: We nearly died moving in. Imagine carrying a flatpack sofa up four flights of stairs during the hottest August England has ever had.

D: I honestly think it's the closest I've ever come to dying from exhaustion. I remember us lying on the floor panting for at least an hour. Though without these stairs we'd literally never exercise so we're begrudgingly grateful!

P: Thank you death-stairs.

SECRET STAIRCASE

D: And down here is the secret staircase to the sub-apartment!

P: This is where we keep things like our 'red room', the portal from the old apartment and our team of monkeys that are writing this book for us.

D: PHIL, STOP THEY KNOW TOO MUCH. ABORT! ABORT! PAGE OVER

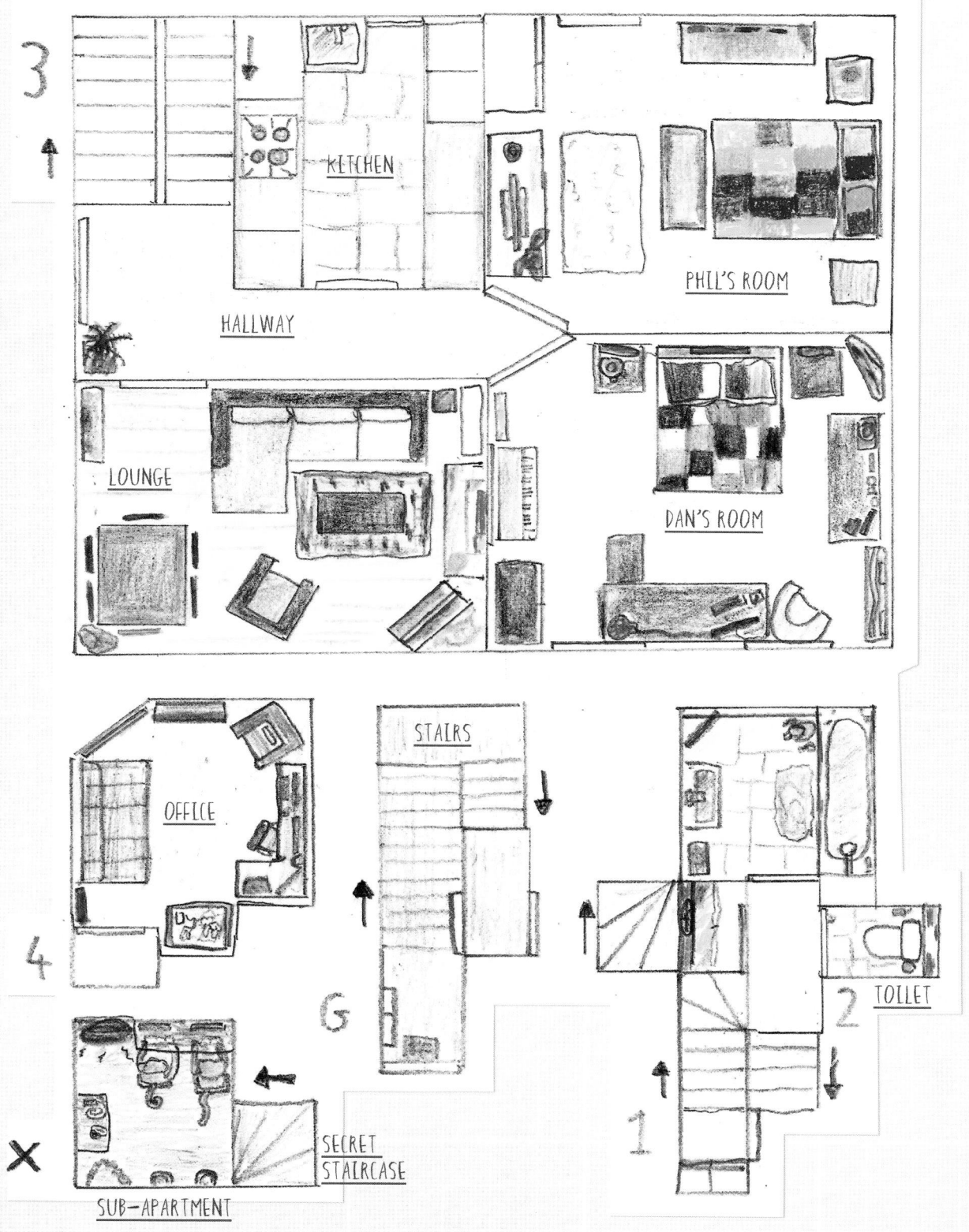

3

KITCHEN

PHIL'S ROOM

HALLWAY

LOUNGE

DAN'S ROOM

OFFICE

STAIRS

TOILET

4

G

2

1

X

SECRET
STAIRCASE

SUB-APARTMENT

WHICH PHIL AND DAN DINING CHAIR ARE YOU?

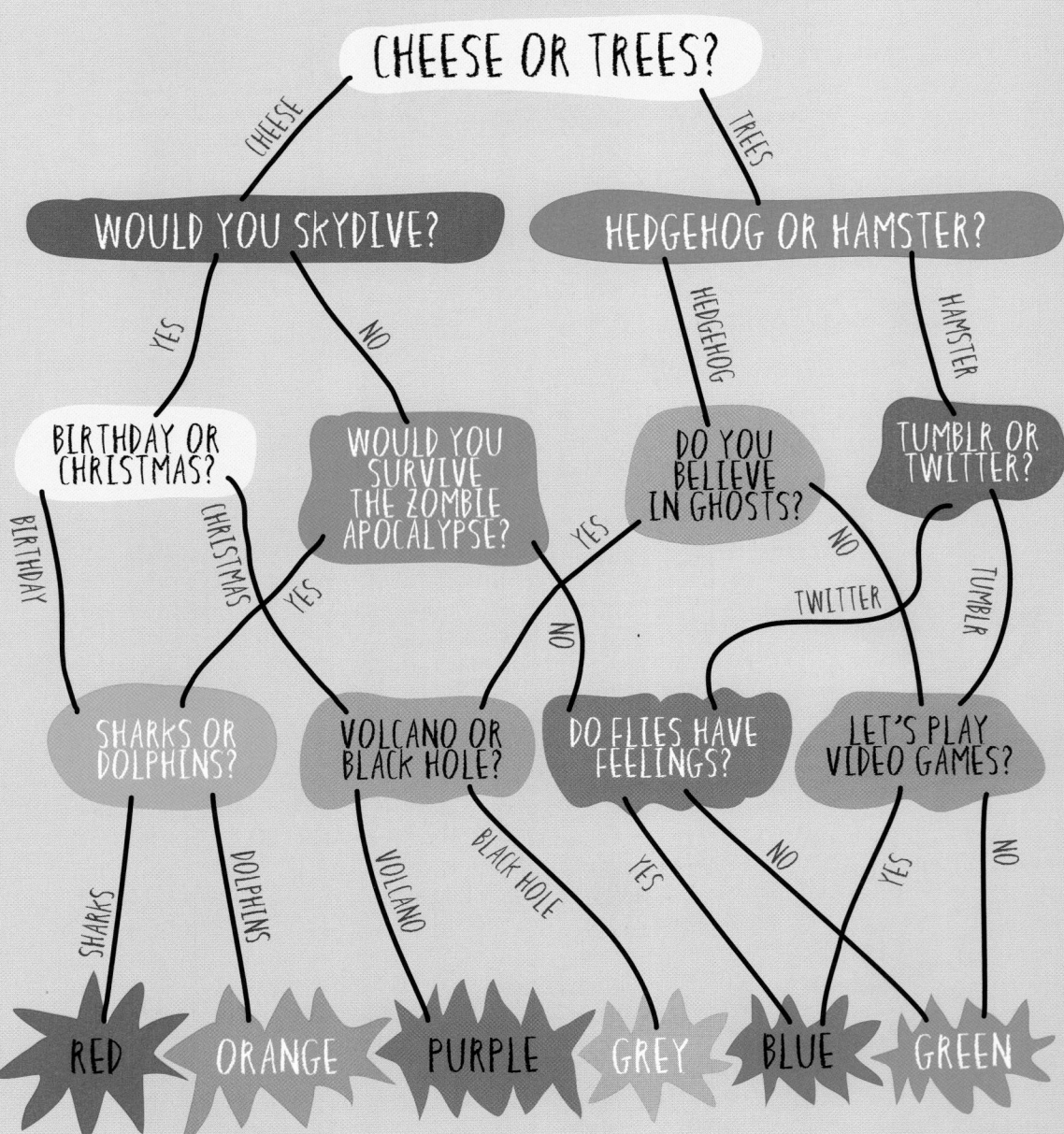

RESULTS

ATTENTION! THIS IS SET IN STONE.
YOU CAN NEVER RE-TAKE THE CHAIR QUIZ.

GREY:
You are the grey chair! Dark, mysterious and slightly sinister. You share a spiritual bond with Dan and would choose a leather coat over a fluffy jumper. There is a small chance you are a vampire and you are probably hiding a huge secret, unfortunately you can't tell anyone as you are a chair.

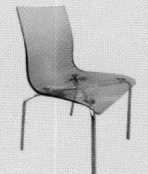

BLUE:
You are the blue chair! Sorry that 90% of your life is taken up by Phil's butt. You prefer walks by the beach to crazy nightclubs. Sometimes you sneeze and blink at the same time which is meant to be impossible (don't tell the government or they will experiment on you). You would make a great rocket scientist, dog groomer or FBI agent, unfortunately that is not possible as you are a chair.

RED:
You are the red chair! You are outgoing, loud and you like the smell of bonfires. You think with your heart before your head and cats don't tend to trust you. You'd make a great wedding planner, storm trooper or ice sculptor. Unfortunately chairs can't sculpt so you will remain in Dan and Phil's lounge with unfulfilled dreams.

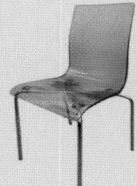

ORANGE:
You are the orange chair! Dan's chair of choice. He leans back on you quite a lot so there is a high chance you are clumsier than most. You are very indecisive and it takes you way too long to get ready in the morning. You would be a great ice-cream tester, emu analyst or president. Unfortunately chairs are banned from general elections so you will have to stay in the dining room.

PURPLE:
You are the purple chair! You have been sat on by the butts of various Dan and Phil apartment guests including Anthony Padilla, Charlie McDonnell and Tyler Oakley. You are highly psychic and can summon ghosts with a sneeze. Your lucky number is eight and your patronus is Samara from *The Ring*. You like scented candles, shrines and secret doorways. Unfortunately, chairs can't walk so you will never get to go through them. Sad times.

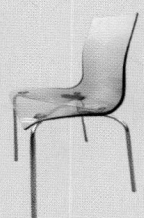

GREEN:
You are the green chair! Dan and Phil don't have enough friends to fill their entire dining table so you are the outsider of the group. You are at one with nature and animals love you. You frequently talk to yourself and have a lot of creativity. You'd prefer a movie night with your best friend to a banana boat ride. You'd be a great zoo-keeper, hamster breeder or dolphin psychiatrist but unfortunately chairs can't swim so go back to being never sat on.

Phil's hamster breeding page

So you want to breed hamsters?!
YOU CAME TO THE RIGHT PAGE!

This page will fulfill every hamstery need you have. Even if you don't want to breed a hamster, come learn something!

Oh? You want some context? Okay.

The Hamster Ball of Context

For a lot of my school life my nickname was 'hamster boy'. Not because I looked like one. Well I did kind of look like one but that's beside the point. I was the school's infamous hamster breeder!

It all started when I spent half my life begging my parents for a chinchilla or a rat. I almost got close to owning the chinchilla of destiny until my mum googled them and found out they can run up walls and hop up to 3m high. She is also afraid of rats and their tails (totally ratist) so to make me shut up my parents bought me a male hamster (Norris) and a female (Phoebe) with the hope of breeding them and selling the babies!

Interesting Hamster Facts

* Syrian hamsters are solitary creatures! They love their own space and will fight to the DEATH if you put them in a cage together. It's like a fluffy Mortal Kombat.

* Hamsters are colour blind so if Morpheus offered them a blue or a red pill they would probably just bite his hand.

* Male hamsters are called boars and females are called sows.

* One human year is equivalent to 25 hamster years! So make sure you prepare 25 individual birthday parties a year.

* Hamsters can see for a distance of six inches so they probably just think you are a magical pair of hands rather than a human.

* Hamsters are both telepathic and telekinetic.

How to Tame a Hamster

Okay this may sound weird but I would get into the bath with my hamsters. FULLY CLOTHED (!!) NO WATER. I'd bring their food bowl and wear cricket gloves so they couldn't bite me and just let them run on my legs and hands to get used to me as a human! I would then keep returning them to the food bowl if they walked too far away from it and they would then trust me and associate me with snacks. I appreciate this is a very weird mental image but it WORKS.

How to Breed a Hamster

First, set up a tiny romantic meal and play some high-pitched Barry White music.

The female hamster gets in the mood for hamster lovin' every four days. So you may be lucky and they'll do it first time or you'll have a fluffy Mortal Kombat situation for the other three days. You'll realise it's going to happen as the female hamster goes completely flat like she's been run over by a small tractor and doesn't want to kill the male.

Then just give them a few moments of privacy. (I held up a small cardboard screen as the miracle of nature happened.) Just remember to remove the male before they fight again!

Pregnant Hamster

Your hamster will be pregnant for about 15–17 days. Once you see her start to balloon leave her alone! Just quietly fill up the food and don't play with her or put her in a ball or a hamster sky restaurant.

Birth

Hamsters can have between 3 and 12 babies (Mine had 13! Norris was like a prize stallion). You will soon hear the mewing of tiny babies. Bask in the godlike feeling of creating new life. DO NOT DISTURB THE NEST OR PICK UP THE BABIES! This causes a Hamsterball Lecter style situation where the mother will eat her own young. Scatter some broccoli or grated carrot for them to eat.

In about four weeks you'll be ready to separate the boys and girls into different cages and three weeks after that they are ready to be rehomed! Make sure you sell them to friendly and loving homes and enjoy your millions of pounds. (If you strap a paper horn to one and sell it to Richard Branson as a baby unicorn, that is.) (Note: This is fraud. Please don't sell false unicorns.)

My Hamsters

I can't find any more pictures of my hamsters so here is a drawing:

Kevin, Barry, Buffy, Spike, Tom, Jerry, Treacle, Badger, Snowball, Lucy, Winston, Mouse and Fluff

Disclaimer: Even though I consider myself a hamster pro, you should probably consult experts before embarking upon your own hamster adventures.

Why Phil Can't Have a Hamster

Look, okay, I'm not a bad guy.

PHIL JUST CAN'T HAVE A HAMSTER.

Here are the reasons:

1. It's against our tenancy agreement. I know Phil keeps saying he'll hide it in his wardrobe but that's not a long-term solution.

2. We travel too much and have no friends. Who could we leave it with when we fly off to a YouTube convention or to do some video job? He can't mail it to his family up north! Until we have robot maids that can feed and water pets, we're just away too much.

3. It would be too noisy. I know very well the horror of a hamster chewing the metal bars of its cage at 3am when you haven't slept for a week. Also, how can we film videos with cage clanking and wheel squeaking in the background?! Don't tell me it'd be a cute background noise, we all know it isn't true.

4. Hamsters are unbelievably smelly. If how well Phil maintains the state of our kitchen and how often he cleans it are anything to go by this would not work out well for our noses. We've already filled our apartment with a dangerous amount of scented candles and the fire hazard required to out-smell a hamster is not something I want to risk.

5. Moral boundaries. Those familiar with the story of my hamster Suki will know that I do not underestimate the intelligence of small fuzzy rodents and how much they grasp the true nature of existence in this universe and freedom. Sure you might get a dumb one that happily wheels itself dizzy for ten hours a day and then sleeps, but what if I have to deal with another freakishly intelligent one?! I can't bear to make the decision between trapping something against its will and letting it brave the harsh reality of nature. I mean, come on, we live in London, it'll get eaten by a giant rat in two minutes.

Conclusion

I'm sorry, Phil, it's not personal, but at the moment we just can't get a hamster. I hope this page has convinced some of you why I feel the need to make this decision, but I believe it is the right one. Perhaps one day soon Phil will have a garden or his own home and he can turn it into the hamster-breeding paradise of his dreams. He's a weird guy, isn't he?

DAN AND PHIL ON BBC RADIO  1

D: So, we have an actual radio show on the BBC.

P: Well you're saying that now, Dan, we might have been totally fired whenever this is being read.

D: To be fair that is a definite possibility. So how on earth did this all happen?

P: Well the story of us and the BBC goes all the way back to 2011! Two peeps called Laura-May and Alistair working at Radio 1 were putting together a talent show they were doing live in Edinburgh. They thought it'd be interesting to get someone to perform on webcam, so they looked on the internet and decided it'd be cool and forward-thinking to invite a vlogger. For some reason they decided we were the ones they wanted to contact!

D: I'm shocked you didn't scare them off for 100 reasons.

P: Maybe they liked the weirdness?

D: The only possible explanation. I'm not sure what talent they thought you could perform? Talking to camera?

P: That's basically the one thing I'm good at, but you're right! I had no idea what to do and I was already terrified so I asked if Dan could join me to make it easier and they said yes.

D: So then we had to decide on an 'act', and what did we choose to do? The 'blindfolded cat-face game'. Yes, we were just going to draw a cat on each other's faces. I have no idea what we were thinking.

P: I can't believe this led us to getting a radio show.

D: The day came and we were watching the livestream of the show with hundreds of people in a room watching all kinds of jugglers and magicians and people with, y'know, actual talents. Then they introduced us.

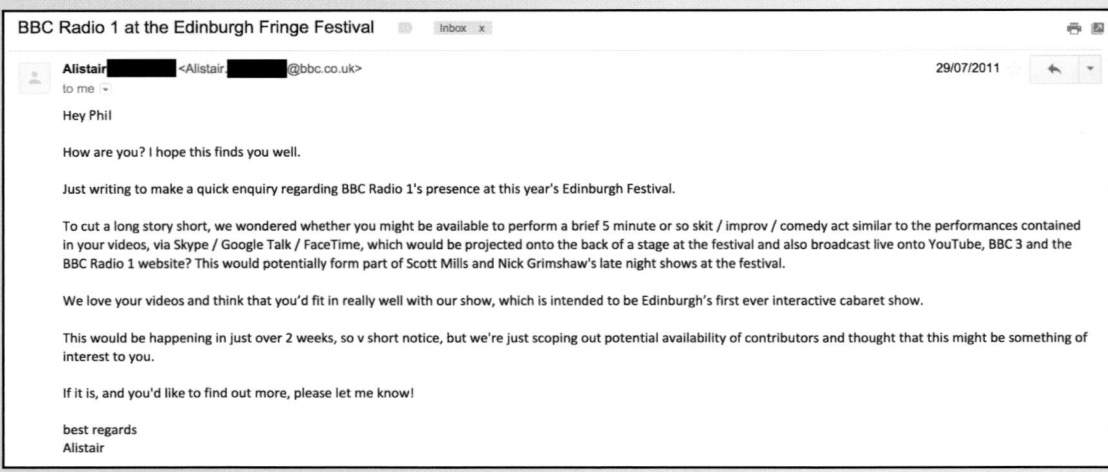

BBC Radio 1 at the Edinburgh Fringe Festival   Inbox x

Alistair⬛⬛⬛⬛ <Alistair.⬛⬛⬛@bbc.co.uk>   29/07/2011
to me

Hey Phil

How are you? I hope this finds you well.

Just writing to make a quick enquiry regarding BBC Radio 1's presence at this year's Edinburgh Festival.

To cut a long story short, we wondered whether you might be available to perform a brief 5 minute or so skit / improv / comedy act similar to the performances contained in your videos, via Skype / Google Talk / FaceTime, which would be projected onto the back of a stage at the festival and also broadcast live onto YouTube, BBC 3 and the BBC Radio 1 website? This would potentially form part of Scott Mills and Nick Grimshaw's late night shows at the festival.

We love your videos and think that you'd fit in really well with our show, which is intended to be Edinburgh's first ever interactive cabaret show.

This would be happening in just over 2 weeks, so v short notice, but we're just scoping out potential availability of contributors and thought that this might be something of interest to you.

If it is, and you'd like to find out more, please let me know!

best regards
Alistair

P: The internet connection was so terrible that we basically looked like 15 yellow pixels and Nick Grimshaw forgot Dan's name.

D: If I recall, he kept calling me 'the one in the black t-shirt'.

P: So we did our game, which Dan totally cheated on by the way – you can see his eyes open.

D: Hey it was an accident! I only glanced. And yes three minutes of uncomfortable face-touching noises was our debut on British radio.

P: I lost so my forfeit was to get a plate of whipped cream smacked into my face which completely ruined the clothes I was wearing as they never stopped smelling like mouldy cheese. However, afterwards we were told so many of our followers tried to watch the stream that we actually broke the website!

D: We are the original internet Godzillas, Phil and I. Don't let us near any tiny website or we'll accidentally crush it like a clumsy giant.

P: This weird talent show incident apparently got people talking at the BBC, as one day we got a fateful email from a man named Joe.

D: Right out of nowhere they asked if we wanted to come down to London to discuss making a radio show. We kind of freaked out.

P: It was terrifying but really exciting! I remember walking past Gary Barlow on the way into the Radio 1 building and reaching for my phone to scream at my mum before remembering that's probably not acceptable behaviour.

D: We felt like the two biggest dorks in the world walking through this cool crazy office with our weird haircuts.

P: We were the biggest dorks in the world.

D: Oh definitely. So we met up with the guys we'd been emailing and they said 'how would you like a two-hour video show on the radio on Christmas day?' Two hours of music and video weirdness from us beamed across the world on the radio and in video on the website on the most magical day of the year. The worst/best idea ever.

P: We then spent about two months wrestling with crazy microphone equipment, inflatable sharks and balloons filled with flour to make what became the AmazingPhil and Danisnotonfire Christmas show on Radio 1.

Dan & Phil on Webcam

Dan & Phil 2011 show

D: It was pretty amazing. I remember my family gathering around the TV in the lounge not at all understanding how a radio show could be watched. It was a weird Christmas day as I spent most of it shaking with nerves.

P: We were proud of our first radio baby! And apparently so were the BBC as they actually emailed us back. The next time they contacted us they wanted us to do a documentary on internet dating as they figured we know stuff about the internet.

D: I don't think either of us are really experts in online dating. We rose to the challenge, however, and made a wonderfully strange documentary about love on the internet which involved me calling a TV celebrity property expert called Sarah Beeny to tell her how to install Skype. I still have her mobile number.

P: Fast forward to summer and apparently they liked us enough to give us another Christmas show for 2012! This was one of the final pushes that convinced us to make our leap of faith and move to London.

D: Though this time it was just a one-hour show instead of two so maybe they liked us half as much?

P: Well obviously not, as at the start of December, right in the middle of crafting our second hour-long audiovisual special, the bomb was dropped.

D: Out of nowhere we got a message from the big boss asking us to make a formal pilot for a full-time radio show. He wanted us to take over the old format of The Request Show where people call in to request songs and make it a big Dan and Phil internet video explosion.

P: This was on top of the Christmas show we were making, our own YouTube videos and everything else we had going on, including Christmas!

D: We got it done though and sent it off, then a few days before Christmas we were invited to the BBC and got told the news. We'd have our own Dan and Phil show on actual BBC Radio 1!

P: It was mental – neither of us could believe it at all! Then they told us they wanted us to start in the first week of the new year.

D: Not only did we have to get everything for the show prepared in time, we had to learn how to actually be radio DJs! Usually people spend years practising in their spare time, on student radio, and on 4am shifts for your local Jazz station, but us? We were given less than two weeks.

P: Now I'm not a very coordinated guy. I don't drive because I can't multitask and I'm 100% sure I can't be trusted with other people's lives. A radio desk is like a rocket ship.

D: There are about 4,000 buttons that all do different, powerful and terrifying things and any one of them could blow up the BBC. The multitasking of 'driving the desk' and presenting is a challenge in itself, but then we obviously had to go and create what I honestly think is the most complicated

radio show of all time. First of all it was a request show, so it was completely unpredictable. We couldn't plan any timings as anyone could choose any song and the callers could talk for as long as they liked. Also we had to stand up which made it super awkward to press buttons or look at notes as we were told 'all the best DJs are standing now, it's just better energy'. Couple in our ridiculously complicated games like 'Fan Wars' that had us juggling two callers, two possible winning songs and six sound effects ready to go. Then the cherry on the cake – the whole thing was live on camera. We were very jealous of the other DJs whose shows were mainly sitting in a chair looking at notes when you need them and casually having banter with your pals. Our show was like a rave filled with barnyard animals set on fire.

P: And a beautiful flaming animal party it was.

D: There was only so much preparation we could do before the time came for our first live show.

P: I don't think I slept for about three days due to nerves and even though we came into the BBC every day to practise I felt like a flailing octopus made of jelly.

D: The first show. What a crazy story. Firstly, we had no time to prepare as everyone in the building was coming up to us all day to wish us luck, which was ironically the least helpful thing at that moment.

P: Then just before we went on we were told we had to swap studios so we wouldn't be able to chill out in one until we went live, instead we had to wait for the chart show to finish and walk in during the final song. This changed the plan. My worst thing ever is changing the plan.

D: I don't think the people doing the chart show fully appreciated how much we were internally freaking out as we were carrying the cameras and our laptops in our hands as they leisurely picked up their coats with only one minute left of the final song.

P: We managed to log into the computers, plug everything in, stand up and with about 20 seconds left we were in position. 'Hi we are Dan' 'And Phil!' 'And you're listening to BBC Radio 1!' Then the camera fell off its tripod. We are not joking, it snapped.

D: During our first live link on the radio, of course it would happen to us! Joe Harland – one of the most important men at the BBC then ran into the room and spent the first five minutes holding it up trying to be as still as possible until we played our first song.

P: The next two hours were the slowest and fastest, craziest hours of my life, but we did it.

D: At the end I had nothing left. It's like I had completely exhausted all the energy in my body, mind and soul. We had no idea how it went but then everyone came into the studio and congratulated us! We sat around with our team and had a giant cake and that was the first Dan and Phil show on Radio 1. The rest is history.

Dan & Phil in the studio

Aftermath of the first show

HOW'S IT DIFFERENT TO VIDEOS?

D: Lots of people ask us how doing live radio compares to YouTube.

P: Honestly it's pretty much the same! We're just having funny entertaining conversations about things, but instead of having to sit and edit it then put it on the internet, it happens live!

D: Which is fun and also terrifying. I can't believe I haven't accidentally sworn yet.

P: At the end of the day there are different skills like video editing or pressing buttons on a complicated desk, but the only difference is saying 'And up next on Radio 1 it's Britney Spears'!

THE DAN AND PHIL SHOW FEATURES

Internet News - We read out all the weirdest and wonderful news stories we found on the internet that week that regular radio listeners may have missed out on! It wouldn't be complete without our signature lensless 3D glasses. INTERNET NEWS *bong*

Phil scratching his ear while Dan pretends to talk

Dan vs. Phil - Every week for over a year we came up with a new embarrassing, physically degrading challenge to attempt against each other live on camera. From putting our hands in Wellington boots and jumping over obstacles like horses, to crawling across floors in sleeping bags like caterpillars, the lowest moments of our lives were streamed for the world to laugh at.

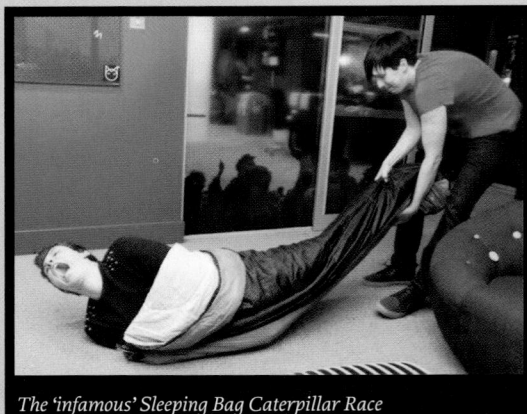

The 'infamous' Sleeping Bag Caterpillar Race

Fan Wars - The idea was to pit two fan bases against each other live on the radio for the right to have their artist's song played. Two live callers have to compete at a mystery challenge that could be gargling the song, animal impressions or our favourite 'Noise Treasure Hunt', where they had to run around their house making noises. Incredible chaos.

Sorry I Don't Know How To Internet - Laughing at people that can't use technology. Basically. In a nice consensual way though! People sent in stories of their elderly relatives or friends not knowing how to do basic computer tasks for all the people who spend their lives on the internet to chuckle about.

The Intenserviews - From our very first Christmas show where we made Tim Westwood build a reindeer out of Play-Doh, we have forced people to answer ridiculous questions as quickly as possible whilst enduring some kind of distraction. From Radio DJs to popstars and vloggers, many people have gone through this trial.

The 7-Second Challenge - We turned Phil's YouTube phenomenon into 'The most intense-per-second radio feature of all time', attempting to do whatever the other person says in a ridiculously short amount of time. We play the 7-Second Challenge live on the radio and the winner picks a song of their choice!

AWARD WINNERS

P: Did you know our show is actually Academy Award-winning? Okay it's from the UK's Radio Academy, but fancy and serious nonetheless!

D: It was actually the people's choice award, but I guess depending on how you look at it it's either the least important award or the only one that actually means anything!

P: That was a terrifying serious evening filled with crazy famous presenters and suspiciously energetic performers. Dan also offended a professional footballer.

P: Then afterwards we went out to a crazy celebrity club and ended up falling asleep on Nick Grimshaw's floor with his dog.

D: I think that world isn't meant for us. We're definitely 'stay inside on the internet in pyjamas' kind of guys.

Our golden headphones! You can't wear them as they're made of steel.

CRAZY EVENTS!

D: I don't know why, but Radio 1 let us out of our apartments and the tiny studio into the real world to actually interact with famous bands and popstars.

P: I always found it terrifying. I liked to think we offered a unique form of entertainment that the fans of the artists wouldn't usually find!

D: That's one way of putting it! Yep, from our first event with the infamous story of One Direction to going on stage at a festival I attended as a teenager, we have a lot of memories ...

Introducing Imagine Dragons on stage to a billion people

Big Weekend 2013 Londonderry:
The 'Legenderry Quiz' videos we had one minute each to film

Teen Awards 2013:
Dan and Taylor Swift draw each other blindfolded

Reading Festival 2013:
Our 'InTENTerviews' inside a tent covered with creepy fanart

Big Weekend 2014: Dan eats a satsuma on stage behind
One Direction

Teen Awards 2014: Ariana Grande gives Phil her cat-ear tiara after they drew each other

#Dick

Phil makes a show with Joss Whedon and he signs Phil's Buffy comic!

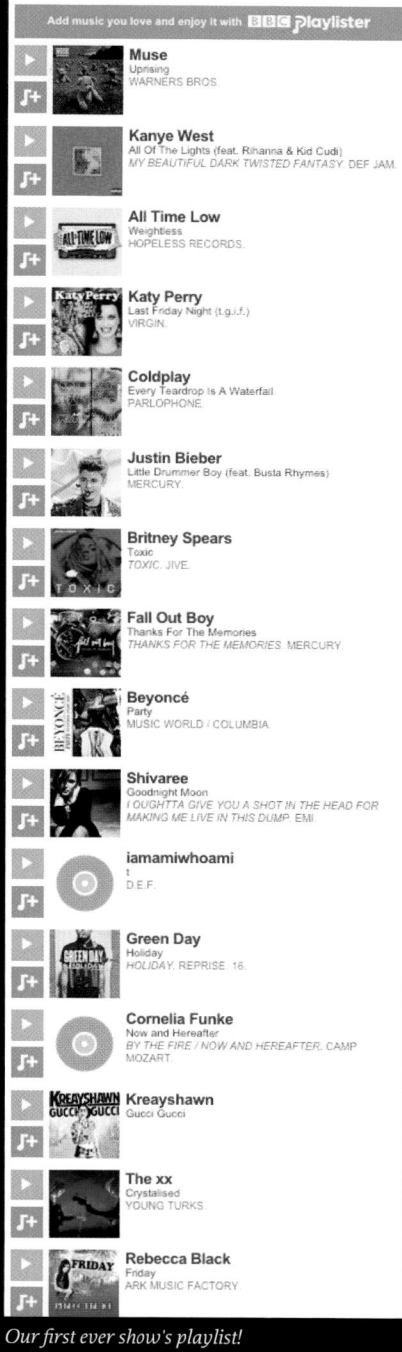

Music Played

Add music you love and enjoy it with BBC playlister

Muse
Uprising
WARNERS BROS.

Kanye West
All Of The Lights (feat. Rihanna & Kid Cudi)
MY BEAUTIFUL DARK TWISTED FANTASY. DEF JAM.

All Time Low
Weightless
HOPELESS RECORDS.

Katy Perry
Last Friday Night (t.g.i.f.)
VIRGIN.

Coldplay
Every Teardrop Is A Waterfall
PARLOPHONE.

Justin Bieber
Little Drummer Boy (feat. Busta Rhymes)
MERCURY.

Britney Spears
Toxic
TOXIC. JIVE.

Fall Out Boy
Thanks For The Memories
THANKS FOR THE MEMORIES. MERCURY.

Beyoncé
Party
MUSIC WORLD / COLUMBIA.

Shivaree
Goodnight Moon
I OUGHTTA GIVE YOU A SHOT IN THE HEAD FOR MAKING ME LIVE IN THIS DUMP. EMI.

iamamiwhoami
t
D.E.F.

Green Day
Holiday
HOLIDAY. REPRISE. 16.

Cornelia Funke
Now and Hereafter
BY THE FIRE / NOW AND HEREAFTER. CAMP MOZART.

Kreayshawn
Gucci Gucci

The xx
Crystalised
YOUNG TURKS.

Rebecca Black
Friday
ARK MUSIC FACTORY.

Our first ever show's playlist!

THE TIME WE MET
ONE DIRECTION

BBC RADIO 1 TEEN AWARDS 2012 –
A DANK CORRIDOR IN WEMBLEY ARENA, LONDON,
OCTOBER 7TH.

D: In the year before we were given our Radio show, Phil and I, as up-and-coming video makers for Radio 1, were asked if we wanted to interview some 'guests' at the upcoming Teen Awards!

P: This was terrifying because, other than a couple of awkward moments with Bring Me The Horizon's Oli Sykes and some people who we grabbed when they happened to be at the BBC during the recording of one of our Christmas shows, this would be the first time we'd ever done something 'professional' at a big serious event.

D: In typical Dan and Phil fashion we started preparing the night before the event.

P: You mean typical Dan fashion. I wanted to prepare three weeks before but you spent several days staring at the carpet thinking about a video.

D: This is conjecture.

P: Dan, you were procrasti-

D: Phil, you're ruining the flow of the story.

P: ...

D: The night before any big event we 'work' at, even to this day, feels a bit like we're Katniss and Peeta.

Above images, left to right:
Us with Oli Sykes.
Us with Tim Westwood
Us with McFly

P: Don't say Katniss and Peeta.

D: ...two clones of Katniss the night before The Hunger Games.

P: I'm not sure if playing games with popstars is the same as having to survive a battle arena filled with trained death machines.

D: Well, if you think about it ...

P: Okay, I'll continue the story. Our last-minute preparation meant that we didn't have an opportunity to write our questions on the super-professional-looking folded pieces of A4 until we were in the car on the way to the arena. I don't like looking at things in a moving car!

D: Phil gets motion sickness if he blinks for too long and sees his eyelids while moving.

P: Thanks. So we were desperately scribbling with permanent markers ...

D: ... which made my entire hand pitch-black because of my left-handed handicap. Very professional looking.

P: ... and trying to mentally prepare ourselves. But one thing was sticking at the front of our brains: we were told we might meet One Direction.

D: Now, I understand these events are crazy and you can never guarantee an artist will turn up. People might not have time, or someone could be a diva and not like the colour of a carpet, but YOU CAN'T JUST TELL SOMEONE THEY 'might' MEET ONE DIRECTION.

P: 1D in 2012 were literally the most talked-about people on the entire planet; it's when the internet has been at its craziest for anything to do with them, so not only were our scary bosses like, 'We know what you do with them will be great!' but we knew whatever we did would be watched by millions of Directioners online.

The ravenous horde assembles

D: You could say this added to our concerningly rapidly rising anxiety levels.

P: A bit.

D: Maybe. And what were we greeted with when we arrived at the arena?
A pulsating, frothing ocean of thousands of screaming One Direction fans.

P: It was like a thousand of those screaming firework rockets going off at the same time, all the time. Or like being in a room with a billion excited bees.

D: The ground actually shook. I'm convinced that that amount of high-frequency noise must affect the tectonic plates somehow. Either way, no cat in a four-mile radius must have lived through that evening without exploding.

P: And then we were taken to the 'crew entrance' – if you're expecting anything to do with TV or radio to be glitzy, you'll be disappointed. It was like a *Saw* trap.

D: Slight exaggeration.

P: It was like the kind of scary concrete basement a *Saw* trap would be in!
Just without the pointy death machine.

D: That's true. And my god, was the atmosphere ABSOLUTELY TERRIFYING.
We were being shepherded down tight corridors with flickering lights, and every now and then there would be this terrifying wave of noise, where reverberating screams would literally shake dust off the exposed pipes above us.

P: Kind of like Katniss getting bombed in District 13.

D: Let the *Hunger Games* metaphors go, Phil. Now this kind of hectic atmosphere is what we learned dressing rooms were for. If you are a fancy presenter or a popstar, who has to practise something or get in the zone to perform, you need a room to emotionally prepare!

P: We didn't have a room.

D: No. You see the thing is, back then we weren't really known to a lot of people at Radio 1. We weren't people with a proper radio show, we were just two weirdos with strange haircuts, who sometimes loitered awkwardly in the corner of their office, talking about stuff for their 'YouTube channel'. This was back when YouTube was still seen as a place only for weirdos and cats.

P: We were and definitely are still weirdos.

D: I'm not denying this. So when all these established radio presenters, and scary TV people were running around making their actually important stuff with their big teams before going back to their private sanctuaries, we just had to stand awkwardly in a corner eating the crisps we stuffed into Phil's backpack.

P: We were at least excited to see the backstage area where we'd film these interview videos though!

D: Ah yes, the toilets.

P: They weren't just toilets.

D: Pretty much.

P: It was more like a mix between a laundry cupboard and a World War Two bunker that happened to have toilets in them. We were told that all the dressing rooms and free spaces were occupied, and this was the only area left.

D: The room was in total the size of an average car. There was more room in the actual toilets themselves and one of the presenters, Matt Edmondson, decided to actually film his interviews in the toilet, which meant everyone helping him was stood outside pushing us further into the wall.

P: There was one of those mirrors with the light bulbs around it though!

D: You're right, that did excite me.

P: Thankfully we were told that, if it was going to happen, 1D would be the last thing that'd happen in our day, giving us time to practise on Little Mix and Conor Maynard!

D: 'Practise on' sounds kinda weird.

'Please rescue me from these strange people.'
Conor Maynard

P: What could that even mean? Anyway it was terrifying. It's not just a nice introduction and chat, and then you spend a few relaxing moments having fun with the person. Firstly, one of their 'people' comes and they give information to another 'person', then the Senior 'person' double checks and gives us a scary look before asking exactly what we're going to do with the popstar.

D: I mean, what did it look like we were going to do?

P: You have shifty eyes, it was probably that. Then, with about 20 people crammed into this tiny, dark, kind of weird-smelling room all staring at you, wondering, 'Who are these internet people and why are they here?' the popstar walks in the room.

D: To be fair, from our experience the person themselves is usually quite happy and lovely, just not their Terminator squad that you meet before.

P: We got told by everyone, 'They only have 5 minutes, make it quick.'

D: ...when we've prepared at least 11 videos lasting an hour and a half for each person.

P: And we suddenly have to change our plans and decide exactly what we're doing.

D: That's usually when you start doing your panic face.

P: What?

D: You have this face you do when you get all panicky and flustered, and you start pacing and doing the weird hand thing—

P: Okay thanks, now I'll be self-aware forever in any kind of situation like that.

D: You're welcs, mate.

P: So after hours spent in our tiny bunker, which I'm sure was dangerously low on oxygen by that point ...

D: ... it was how I imagine being buried alive to be like. Just with more strange toilet odour coming from around the corner and people talking into bluetooth headsets.

P: ... we were told that One Direction were coming.

D: Then came probably the most amount of 'people' to check everything was okay for the group that I'd ever seen. I was concerned that if the 1D guys tried to fit in the room as well we'd be compressed into a cube of meat and die.

P: Nice vivid image. Then, when the last of the 'people' arrived he told us all the news: the guys only had ten minutes and then they had to leave, so they could only do one interview! And given the choice of the two weirdos making videos for YouTube or the actual presenter interviewing them in a toilet, who do you think they picked?

D: We were mildly heartbroken. Not just because of our preparation but because meeting One Direction would have been at that point the most popular, relevant thing we'd ever done in our entire lives.

P: The room suddenly emptied like someone blew a hole in a spaceship and an eerie silence fell.

D: They entered the room and everything went into slow motion.

P: That might have just been for you, Dan.

D: Well okay I'll tell this bit. I was blinded. A bright warm glow as if angels themselves were stroking my face ...

P: Okay I'll take over. Seriously though, they all looked so perfect! I want a stylist.

D: Pfft, you with a stylist, you know the first thing they'd do is get rid of your fringe, right?

P: I'm not ready to let go of the fringe; it's who I am.

D: It's a bit of MySpace you've been struggling to let go of since 2006 – and we both know it.

P: Anyway we were too awkward and kind of sad to do anything, so we blended in with the coat rack and watched them go off into the toilet to do the other interview.

D: We had to do something. We had it all prepared! Animal impressions, a drawing challenge, creepy questions from Tumblr I hand-sourced, I even wanted to get in a sneaky Supernote to help me win an internet competition.

P: They took so long in the toilet! It was at least fifteen minutes. I was like, 'Way to hog 1D, you boyband-warthog.'

D: Don't be mean about Matt, we like him.

P: He nearly ruined our entire lives though.

D: Nearly, but we worked it out! As they started to squeeze out of the toilet door with one of their 'people', I, in the bravest moment of my entire existence, jumped in front of the scary-headset-man and said 'hiwe'reDanand-Philwe'retwoguysfromYouTubewhomakeYouTubevideoscalledYouTuber-sandwe'reherewithRadio1makingstufffortheirofficialYouTubechannelandwe-knowthe1Dfansontheinternetwouldreallyreallyreallylikeifwemadeaquick-videowiththemIpromiseitwillonlytake1minuteplease'.
He said yes.

P: We were totally sneaky but somehow, with the man staring kinda angrily at his fancy-looking watch the whole time, we managed to film THREE videos with them!

D: Okay, let's break it down for the readers. What happened second-by-second when we met the guys.

P: It was crazy! We were four hundred per cent flustered because of Captain Serious telling us we had one minute so we awkwardly waved at them all and said, 'Hey, we're Dan and Phil, we're doing stuff for the Radio 1 YouTube!'

D: I remember Harry nodding and saying, 'Nice to meet you, Dan and Phil,' and in that moment my life was complete.

P: They were all really friendly and happy and excited! I remember thinking Niall was like a hyperactive puppy. Then, however, I started to detect a strange smell.

D: You know, I thought it might have just been the toilet room wafting over.

P: No, it was definitely in our room. I looked over to Louis and his first words to me were, 'Do you think someone farted?'

D: Wow. Was it you?

P: No, it wasn't me! Was it you?

D: No! It was probably Zayn, he's the quiet one.

P: I tried not to concentrate on it and, thankfully, it dispersed throughout the air.

D: Do you think they noticed? Is One Direction's memory of us 'the time someone farted before those two guys interviewed us'?

P: Even if it is, someone out there would be jealous of us.

D: We immediately started recording in case they were whisked away by the Terminator squad. How exactly did you end up touching Liam's head?

P: Oh yeah! The biggest world news that week was that Liam shaved his head.

D: I'm sure support hotlines had their busiest week ever and shrines dedicated to his brown hair were torn down in bereavement.

P: I just said, 'I like your hair,' and he asked me if I wanted to stroke it.

D: You do realise millions of people would probably commit unspeakable crimes to have that experience? What was it like?

P: A tall hedgehog. Or a curvy doormat.

D: You heard it here, guys. So now that we'd somehow got this opportunity we had to make the most of it. Straight in with the animal impressions, a very creative Dan and Phil content classic there.

'Like a tall hedgehog. Or a curvy doormat.'

P: I remember Louis' eagle impression was surprisingly accurate.

D: And that's coming from you! High accolades indeed.

P: Then without making it seem like we were stopping or doing anything different we got straight into the drawing challenge. Unfortunately, I only brought four pens.

D: Seriously.

P: So there was a bit of an awkward moment where Niall was stood by himself with nothing to hold. Fortunately I had a green pen in my pocket!

D: As you just magically secrete colourful stationery.

P: It's been known to happen. And then seamlessly flowing into a Supernote and some creepy questions, whilst the important man's angsty watch tapping got faster. We did it!

D: As soon as we blinked to symbolise the video finishing, the guy was like, 'RIGHT OKAY LET'S GO,' but we hadn't gotten a picture. Don't judge us, okay, even if you have the least interest in One Direction ever, you'd want a photo with them. I said don't judge us!

P: We thought the moment was lost when our friend Laura-May, like she was diving on a grenade, jumped in front of the man and said, 'Quick picture for the Twitter page!'

D: It wasn't for their Twitter. It was for us. Thank you, dear friend.

P: And with that, our crazy day was over!

D: We just kind of sank against the wall trying to process all the sensory input from probably the most insane day of our lives so far. Squeezing through the shaking concrete corridors like the intestines of a terrifying giant, we pooped out into the parking lot and got in a car on the way home.

P: I made sure to open the window and not look at anything on this car journey.

D: When we arrived back at our apartment we ordered a pizza and both slept for about 14 and a half hours. That was the time we met One Direction.

Blindfolded portraits

Dan's drawing
of Phil

Phil's
drawing of
Dan

THE ONE WORD STORY GA(m)E

P: 'One word story games' are a beautiful way of sharing pure creativity with a friend.

D: You tune into each other's emotional wavelengths to not just finish each other's sentences, but build a story – word by word.

P: Basically, you take it in turns to each say a word and try to tell a story!

D: And what you are left with is often either profound or a horrifying mess. Let's give it a go! I'll say the first word, here we go:

Once day

D: 'Once day' are you kidding me? Oh my god, Phil.

P: I'm sorry! I wasn't thinking, let's just start again.

D: Okay ... here we go. One word each at a time – that makes sense, I'll go first again. Let's make a wonderful story.

Once upon a time in London, a tiny door was discovered underneath a soldier standing next to Buckingham Palace. Behind the tiny door was a giant otter named Gary. Gary's eyes were carrots because he couldn't see after the incident involving angry waiters. Today Gary decided to go into the city to destroy the London Eye. When he got there he released his emotions as he realised he didn't have a friend to play with. Gary died of loneliness.

D: Wow.

P: That was so sad I didn't think the story was going in that direction.

D: I told you it would either be profound or a mess, and that was both.

P: One more! I'll go first this time:

Aliens are secretly watching us poop because unbeknownst to us, they can use our poop as fuel for their probes. The probes are used for working out whether humans can sing or not. The aliens were working for Simon Cowell to discover the next Leona Lewis. When aliens discover this singer, they will absorb their voice and insert it into the Boy Band Generator to take over the minds of young teens across Earth and eat their brains. It will be glorious when they finally sing and the Universe will bow before their sexy coordinated rhythm.

P: That was terrifying.

D: And probably true. I can't decide whether that's a script for a future blockbuster movie or an unearthed conspiracy theory. Better than most of this book that we spent ages thinking about.

P: Either way, that was the one word story game! You can see how it's really fun.

D: Or a terrible mistake.

P: Why not try it with your friends and see what incredible stories you make together! One word at a time.

Going Deep with Dan and Phil:

THE APOCALYPSE

D: Hello and welcome to Going Deep with Dan and Phil.

P: Going deep? Really?

D: You don't even know what the idea of this is yet, so don't shoot it down already, idea-sniper.

P: I'm totally not an idea-sniper. Okay what's your idea?

D: Well we've discussed a wide range of things in this book. People have got to know our early lives, our YouTube stories, what we're like as people – so I thought why not take it to the next level?

P: How do you plan to level us up, Dan? Some kind of mushroom?

D: Nope. By discussing deep and meaningful things. You know those conversations you have with friends at 2am that end with you both going 'woah'. I'd like to share that with our readers!

P: Getting intimate, I like it.

D: Now you're making it strange.

P: Okay, sorry. So what are we talking about first, Deep Daniel?

D: Don't call me that. The Apocalypse!

P: Wow that is deep! Like the movie *Deep Impact*.

D: Yes, Phil, exactly like that. Wow an acceptable pun well done.

P: Thanks, I thought that was good too.

D: So, Phil, how do you think the world is going to end?

P: I think the sun is just going to explode one day without any warning.

D: Well, due to light speed and stuff, we'd have about eight minutes' warning before the many varieties of death come for us.

P: Eight whole minutes. How would you spend them if you saw the sun explode in the sky?

D: Probably make some microwave popcorn, sit in my sofa crease, say goodbye on the internet and listen to some cool apocalypse music.

P: That's a pretty good plan! Plus, when the wave of fire hits us, one of the popcorn kernels you ate might pop inside your melting stomach.

D: Nice and graphic there, Phil. Might have put me off popcorn for a while.

P: So if the sun doesn't randomly explode how do you think our world will end?

D: Well brushing aside the likelihood of humans destroying it themselves, I've always fancied the idea of a giant meteor indiscriminately cruising into earth and obliterating it.

P: Couldn't we just fly up to it and blow it up like Bruce Willis whilst Aerosmith plays in the background.

D: I thought you were a *Deep Impact* man?

P: Only for the puns. *Armageddon* has the key to my heart.

D: Somehow I think the logistics of the meteor-exploding operation would be a bit more complicated than in the movies. I think it's more likely that we'll have the technology to just bail on earth and populate another planet.

P: Where would we go?

D: Mars seems a bit of a depressing dust-fest so I hope they find somewhere more interesting soon.

P: Not everyone could get on the ship though. How would people get chosen to be rescued?

D: I'm guessing you're either important or some kind of lotto?

P: Do you think I'd be important enough to get on?

D: Well, I mean, this is just a hypothetical spaceship and I don't want to make you all depressed, so sure, Phil, you'd totally get on the rocket.

P: Yay!

D: Any other theories? What if it doesn't come from space and the threat lies within our space-bubble?

P: What if nature turns against us? Imagine all the trees suddenly decide they've had enough and reverse drink our oxygen and we all die. The clouds could all rain acid or the ground could open and close like chomping jaws of destruction.

D: I'm not sure how likely that is but I'd sure as hell pay to see that at the cinema.

P: THE NATUREPOCALYPSE

D: Though saying it's unlikely, new strange things are discovered on our planet every day!

P: Like Ligers.

D: I think Ligers are fairly old news but they are pretty cool.

P: I'm all for tiger/lion relationships personally.

D: How progressive of you.

P: I'm also suspicious of ants.

D: Why's that?

P: They're too organised and there's too many of them. They are definitely planning something and could totally take over the world if they wanted!

D: Wow, apparently there are 1,500,000 ants for every human on Earth.

P: See I told you! Antapocalypse! It's the only real theory. I bet it will happen in 57 years.

D: I can't help but feel we got a bit side-tracked and this maybe ended up less deep than I originally intended.

P: You could say we had some good 'bANTer'!

D: See now that totally undid the clever reference you made earlier.

P: Aw really? Hey, can I pick the topic next time? I have a great idea!

D: Well I dunno, this was kind of supposed to be my thing that I have a whole plan for.

P: Pretty please! I promise it'll be so deep you'll get stuck and never be able to climb out.

D: That got weird fast so I'm just going to agree to make it stop. We'll see you next time on Going Deep for another spirited discussion on the fundamental questions of our universe.

PHIL

YOUR FUTURE HUSBAND

BECAUSE YOU'RE

I LOVE YOU!!!

ouch

Dan's Neck

NOSE!

PEPPERONI!

I can't quit your wires. ∞

we just get high off off the sharpie fumes.

HEY SEXY LADY LET'S MAKE OUT

WE JUST GET HIGH OFF OF THE SHARPIE FUMES!

you are blind

SCREAMING NIPPLES

I'D ACTUALLY PICKLE A PICKLE

EVERYONE JUST UNSUBSCRIBED

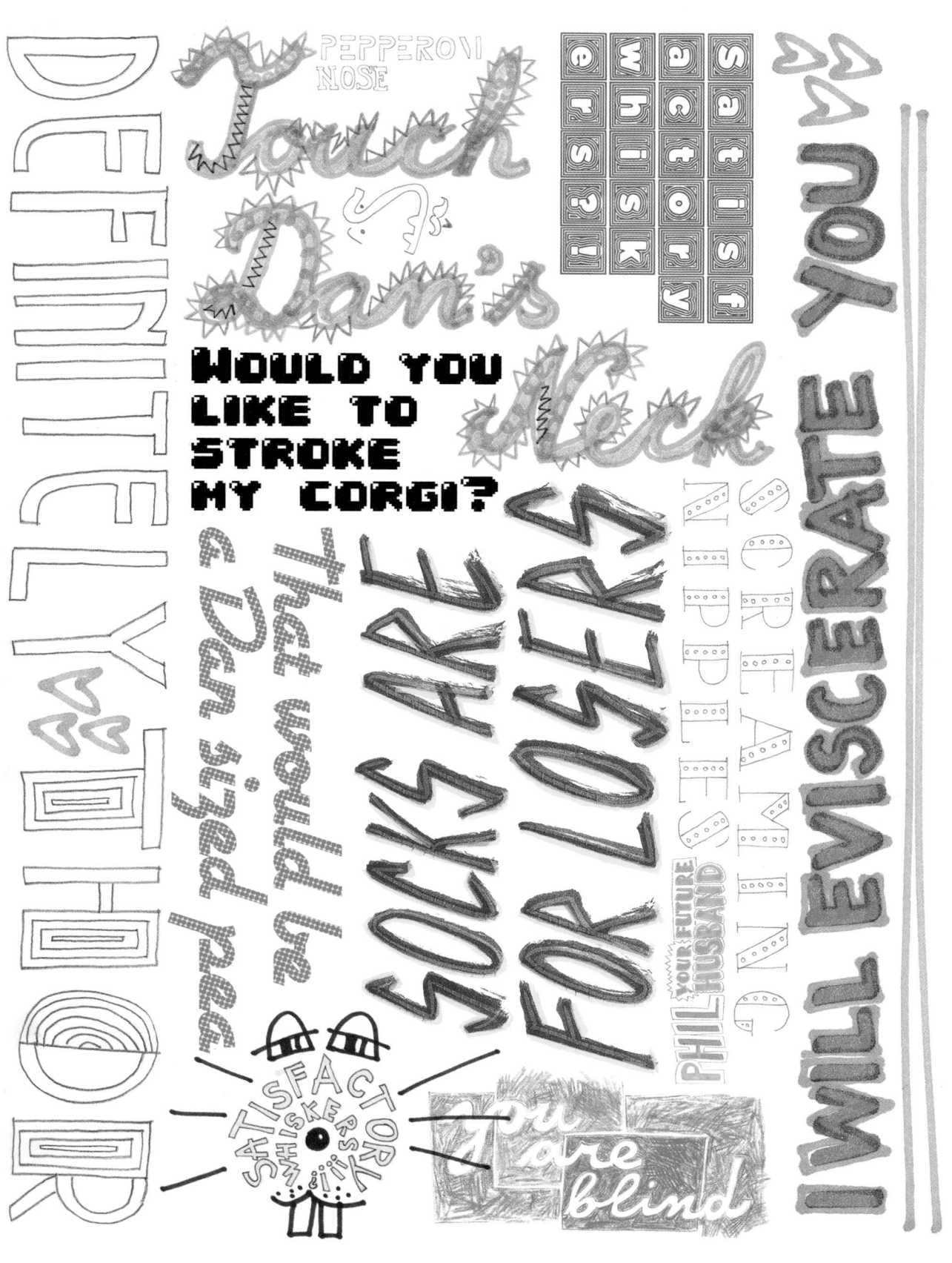

REASONS WHY DAN'S A FAIL (SO FAR)

LEFTHANDEDISM
It's a cruel affliction so, given the right-handed bias of our society, it should be a crime to force this on young impressionable children. How would you feel if literally everything was backwards or upside down?!

HUMAN INTERACTION
I just don't like talking to people, okay. Yes, I would live on the moon if I had an infinitely stocked fridge and an internet connection.

BUTTERFINGERS
I inexplicably drop things, sometimes. Don't let me hold your newborn or your grandma's ashes.

SPIRALS OF LIES
If I tell a white lie to spare someone's feelings, it will spiral out of control into a ridiculous fairy tale of deceit that will get more and more extreme until it implodes, destroying my social life.

I MUMBLE

You won't be able to understand 99% of the things I say. Even if you have to say 'what?' on the impossibly awkward third time, please tell me if you can't understand me. Just don't bother going to a party with me, I'm effectively mute.

I TALK TO MYSELF

It's pretty weird, I know. I just don't have that bit in my brain to tell me to keep thoughts inside my head and instead they silently come out of my mouth. I think that people avoiding me in busy shops is an advantage personally.

I'M A MESS

I drop things behind furniture to avoid properly sorting them. I hide clothes in a vertical mountain inside my wardrobe. All other missing objects I blame on thieving, stealthy, inter-dimensional goblins. Only rational explanation.

I CARE TOO MUCH

I'm overly empathetic to the point that I actually annoy my friends at parties with how concerned I am for their enjoyment.

INAPPROPRIATE WINKING

I don't know why I do it but I do. I don't know when it will happen, probably at the worst moments, but I will just randomly bust out a wink. I promise if I ever do it to you, it doesn't mean anything; it's just a horribly, horribly confused impulse I get and nothing more. Please don't contact the authorities.

PSYCHO THOUGHTS

I sometimes contemplate my own ability to murder people. IT'S FINE, I WON'T DO IT! I just think about how I could, we all could. The void is calling. It wants me to jump into it.

WEB HISTORY

I'm irrationally paranoid of anyone touching my computer in case they see the horrific secrets of my hard drive. I don't think there's anything bad on there but, come on, who trusts their 3am browsing?

PROCRASTINATION

I suffer from chronic procrastination and would go to extreme lengths that require ironically massive amounts of effort to put off doing something I need to finish.

NEAR-DEATH EXPERIENCES

I'm prone to constantly having near-fatal accidents. It'll never actually happen but I'll get close at least twice a week. Try to stay a metre away from me at all times and keep an eye out for all objects, moving vehicles and limbs. You never know what might happen.

COOL HANDSHAKES

I just don't get them. I'm sorry; I've practised, I've looked at video tutorials, but if you come up to me expecting a weird high-five-shoulder-bump-thing I'll probably just fall over and it'll be embarrassing for both of us.

PERSONAL SPACE

Touch my neck and I will kill you. It's not difficult.

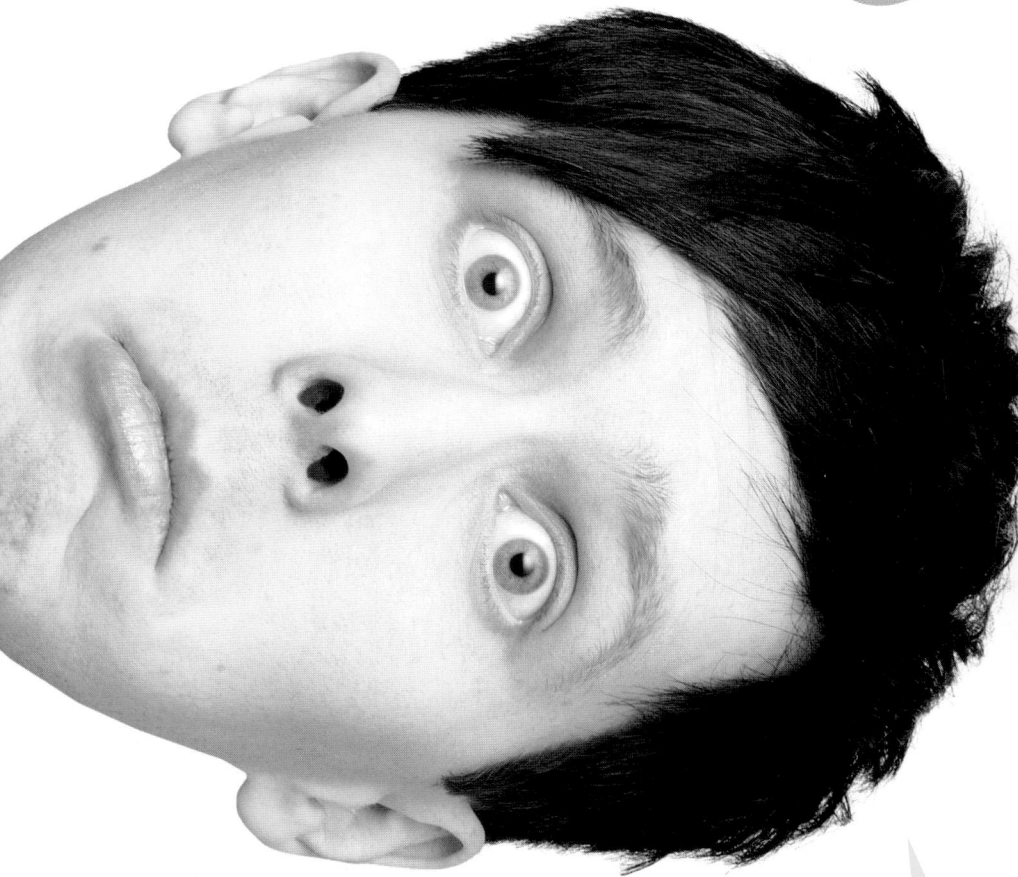

THE MOMENT WHEN YOU SUDDENLY DISCOVER THAT YOUR WHOLE LIFE HAS BEEN A LIE. LIKE THE CARPET OR YOUR EXISTENCE HAS BEEN WHIPPED OUT FROM UNDERNEATH YOU AND YOU DOUBT EVERYTHING YOU'VE EVER LEARNED. AKA - WHEN SOMETHING YOU THOUGHT WAS TRUE TURNS OUT NOT TO BE TRUE.

FOR EXAMPLE, AGED 13 WHEN I VISITED AN AQUARIUM AND SAW A SEAHORSE. MY WHOLE LIFE I HAD BELIEVED THEY WERE MYTHICAL CREATURES, BUT THERE WAS ONE JUST HAPPILY FLOATING AROUND IN A TANK. IT COMPLETELY BLEW MY MIND AND I HAVEN'T BEEN THE SAME SINCE. YOU MAY NOT EVEN KNOW HOW MANY OF THE THINGS YOU BELIEVE ARE REALLY LIES SO ON THIS PAGE I WILL NOW LIST ALL OF MINE TO HELP SPREAD THE WORD OF TRUTH.

TWEETIE PIE IS A BOY
THIS CHANGES EVERYTHING.

CATS
I THOUGHT THEY LITERALLY HAD NINE LIVES. THANKFULLY I DIDN'T HAVE A CAT TO TEST THAT THEORY.

BLUE FROM BLUES CLUES
IS A GIRL. SLIGHTLY LESS PEOPLE ARE AFFECTED THAN TWEETIE PIE.

TONSIL TENNIS
MY FRIEND TOLD ME THAT THE WAY TO KISS A GIRL WAS TO PUT YOUR TONGUE ALL THE WAY INTO THE BACK OF HER THROAT. LET'S JUST SAY MY FIRST KISS DIDN'T END WELL.

DIDDY KONG
I THOUGHT DIDDY KONG WAS A GIRL.

BELLY BUTTONS
I THOUGHT THAT BABIES WERE BORN OUT OF WOMEN'S BELLY BUTTONS. DON'T ASK ME WHAT I THOUGHT MINE WAS FOR.

AUSTRALIA
I DID NOT UNDERSTAND HOW PEOPLE COULD BE STANDING ON THE OTHER SIDE OF THE WORLD WITHOUT FALLING OFF INTO SPACE.

CHRISTMAS MINCE PIES
FOR MOST OF MY LIFE I THOUGHT THEY CONTAINED ACTUAL BEEF MINCE.

DISNEY LOGO
UNTIL VERY RECENTLY I THOUGHT THE 'D' IN THE DISNEY LOGO WAS SOME KIND OF WEIRD CURLY 'G'. I THOUGHT IT WAS SECRETLY 'GISNEY' BUT NO ONE TALKED ABOUT IT. THEN ONE NIGHT WATCHING ALADDIN ALL OF A SUDDEN I SAW THE D! MIND BLOWING STUFF.

MARRIAGE
AT A VERY YOUNG AGE I THOUGHT ALL BOYS WERE DESTINED TO MARRY THEIR MUMS! THANKFULLY I GREW OUT OF THAT ONE PRETTY FAST.

PERIODS
I THOUGHT A PERIOD WAS JUST A HOLIDAY RETREAT FOR WOMEN. IT TURNS OUT IT'S QUITE THE OPPOSITE.

COWS
I THOUGHT MILK WAS COW PEE.

PSYCHIC POWERS
MY BROTHER CONVINCED ME WE ALL HAD PSYCHIC POWERS AND IF I STARED AT A CUP FOR LONG ENOUGH I COULD MOVE IT WITH MY MIND! I SPENT A LONG TIME STARING AT CUPS.

PARACHUTES
FROM VIDEOS OF PEOPLE PARACHUTE JUMPING, I THOUGHT THAT WHEN THE PARACHUTE OPENED PEOPLE WERE SENT HURTLING UPWARDS INTO THE SKY. I THEN HAD IT EXPLAINED THAT IT'S JUST THE PERSON HOLDING THE CAMERA CONTINUING TO FALL.

HOT DOGS
I THOUGHT THEY CONTAINED ACTUAL DOG MEAT. I WAS VERY YOUNG.

SEX
MY GRANDMA TOLD ME THAT SEX WAS A 'SPECIAL KISS BETWEEN A HUSBAND AND A WIFE'. I WORRIED THAT WHEN I GOT OLDER I WOULD GET A GIRL PREGNANT BY KISSING HER THE WRONG WAY

2009

2010

2011

2012

2013

2014

BEHIND

Danisnotonfire

HELLO AND WELCOME TO OUR SHOW BEHIND THE CAMERA WHERE WE LEARN THE SECRETS BEHIND THE MAGIC OF MAKING VIDEOS. TODAY WE ARE JOINED BY DAN HOWELL, ALSO KNOWN AS 'DANISNOTONFIRE'!

D: Hi there! Thanks for having me on.

SO. DANISNOTONFIRE, WHERE DO YOU SEE ITS PLACE IN THE YOUTUBE WORLD, WHAT'S YOUR ANGLE?

D: I guess I just think of myself as an entertainer. At the end of the day, in whatever form, I make content designed to entertain people. I always try to be creative though!

LET'S TALK ABOUT THAT. YOU'RE NOT REALLY A 'VLOGGER' LIKE OTHERS AND YET YOUR CONTENT IS VERY PERSONALITY LED?

D: Yeah well I think I'm a 'vlogger' in the sense that I make video blog posts. Blog posts about the world, about myself, but they're definitely creations that I think of in terms of writing and performance and editing. Every video is me doing my creative take on something! I'm not really the reality-star kind of vlogger whose content is mainly about following their day-to-day life.

HOW DO YOU COME UP WITH YOUR IDEAS?

D: I never try to think 'what would people want to watch' or 'what would be popular' as then I think it's insincere and hard to make passionately. All of my videos come out of personal inspiration from things I see or happen to me. I just make videos about life – my stories, my opinions – and try to make them fun. I have a 'video ideas' file on my computer with years' worth of ideas in it!

CAN WE HAVE A LOOK?

D: Sure. Each line is an individual video idea I could make tomorrow – no spoilers though!

SO YOU'VE GOT AN IDEA, HOW DOES THAT TURN INTO SOMETHING PEOPLE WATCH?

D: Well once I've got the idea I 'write' it. I don't strictly 'script' videos as then it's a bit unnatural so what I do is bulletpoint what I want to say and write down any great quotes I came up with and then try my best to say it in front of a camera. The tough bit is deciding how I want to creatively interpret the idea. You could do anything in an infinite number of ways. Eventually I just have to settle on something, write it out and then go through it making sure it's perfect.

THE CAMERA

HOW IMPORTANT IS THE VISUAL SIDE OF IT FOR YOU?

D: Well, I think it's good to have a decent camera so people can see you well. I don't really know much about the technical side of filmmaking so I try to do what I can with what I have, which is my camera and my editing. I'm definitely a substance-over-style kind of guy though. For me it's all about the quality of the content and as long as it looks good it's fine!

AND WHAT ABOUT THE EDITING, YOU DON'T HAVE LOTS OF CRAZY EFFECTS BUT IT DOESN'T LOOK LIKE YOU JUST SLAP IT TOGETHER?

D: No! There's two kinds of 'editing'. One is post-production which is things like effects and colours and graphics, but real 'editing' is choosing what to leave in and what to leave out. I honestly believe that editing is an art form and if you're good at it you can turn any pile of rubbish into a beautiful sparkling diamond. I definitely spend way too long on every video making sure it's as good as possible.

HAVE YOU EVER MADE A VIDEO AND NOT UPLOADED IT?

D: Only once. I'm a firm believer that you shouldn't start making something until you've prepared it so well you know it'll be good! I always make sure I have a complete idea of the finished product in my head before I begin. The one time I didn't was 'I'm A Mess' which I tried to make in a time limit and decided to refilm it – that taught me that it's better to take your time and be happy with a video than rush and regret!

DO YOU HAVE A FAVOURITE VIDEO YOU'VE MADE?

D: I think the 'Photo Booth Challenge' is definitely the funniest video I've ever made. Which is super-ironic as it's the dumbest idea ever and was so easy to make. Phil and I were choking with laughter editing it. I'm most proud of my videos like 'College Dropout' and 'The Internet Is Mean' as they are the ones that people tell me had a real profound impact on their lives. For me that's the absolute most important thing! I was very creatively proud of my 'Tour of Dan's Brain' video as it was so difficult.

FINALLY, CAN YOU SHOW US WHAT IS BEHIND THE CAMERA?

D: Now this is a spoiler! Immersion ruined.

Danisnotonfire  Trivia

👍 'Danisnotonfire' was my MySpace name when I was 13. There is no meaning behind it, I was going through my 'random phase'.

👍 Before I uploaded 'Hello Internet', there was a video on my channel of me playing a hater message I got sent on Xbox Live after annihilating someone at Halo 3.

👍 I have had three videos removed by YouTube for being 'sexually inappropriate'.

👍 My parents didn't find out about my YouTube channel until someone told my mum at work that I was on the homepage.

👍 For three years my tripod was the camera balanced on a pile of books and DVDs.

👍 Many people think Phil was the man in the suit in my 'How To Use A Gimp' video. It was actually a man I had never met who is usually a TV extra.

👍 For 'DAN IS ON FIRE' I had to hire a 'Film Fire Specialist' to safely immolate me. I wore a special rubber suit underneath my clothes to protect me from the fire but was told 'if you inhale, the fire will go in your lungs and boil you internally'.

👍 I had to delete my 'PSYCHO FRENCH TEACHER' video as the actual French teacher sent YouTube a letter threatening to sue me.

👍 The reason I had curly hair in the scene at Charlie McDonnell's house in 'I Will Go Down With This Ship' is I was so terrified of meeting him I was nervously sweating.

👍 Rhett and Link have asked for the 'Iron Lung' trophy I won for SuperNote 2012 to be sent back to them for several years but I don't know how to mail something so heavy internationally.

👍 Right before filming 'How To Speak INTERNET' with Jack and Finn Harries, Finn accidentally broke the leg of his desk causing everything (including a fish bowl) to smash on the floor. This also cut my arm open which is why I'm wearing a plaster in the video.

👍 I filmed 'I'M A MESS' three months before I uploaded it. For the first time ever I wasn't entirely happy with a video I'd made so I put it on hold until I felt like coming back and improving it.

👍 'THE PANIC ALARM' and 'THE POWER NAP' were originally going to be one video about stupid things I did at work, but I decided to split them into two because I felt they were so good. I also accidentally initially uploaded 'THE POWER NAP' to my side channel danisnotinteresting.

👍 I wanted to direct my Lion vs. Dinosaur 'EXTINCTION RACE' video but couldn't be told half the things that would happen as it had to be a surprise, so I had to blindly trust my friends Ciaran and PJ.

👍 Tyler Oakley and I actually filmed a third video together in case we thought it'd be a bad idea to upload the one we filmed for his channel. He decided to upload it anyway.

👍 After uploading '12 Year Old Dan's Website' the website got so much traffic that the account running it was deleted for going ridiculously over its allowed bandwidth.

👍 'A Tour of Dan's Brain' was the longest I've ever spent on a video as I had to go on multiple odysseys around London to craft the brain and I made a huge mistake. The video worked by putting a green screen underneath the cardboard flaps of the brain, but I accidentally made parts of the design of my brain the same shade of green so I had to do everything twice. Doh.

👍 'Sexy Internet Dating' was removed by YouTube as a guy who we caught trying to catfish people filed a privacy complaint.

👍 I filmed 'The Truth About December' on holiday with my family in India because I had the idea two hours before I had to leave for the airport and ran out of time to film it at home.

👍 I once asked Delia Smith's management if we could collaborate on a cooking video but she turned me down.

> thank you for your request to Delia.
> Dan's channel is lots of fun.
> Delia has had a full on year with the launch of the online cookery school, NCFC, and Delia's Cakes and is now taking a well-earned break. Therefore, I am sorry it is not possible to help with Dan's Christmas Dinner idea.
> Do hope he's enjoying our new Sausage Rolls video on the online cookery school.
>
> Please do thank Dan for his wonderful support for Delia and her recipes.
>
> All best wishes
>
> ▬▬▬▬▬
>
> ▬▬▬▬▬▬▬
> **Personal Manager to Delia**

BEHIND

AmazingPhil

IN THIS WEEK'S EDITION OF BEHIND THE CAMERA WE HAVE PHIL LESTER, ALSO KNOWN AS 'AMAZINGPHIL'!

P: Thanks for having me.

YOU ASKED US TO PROVIDE 17 RED SKITTLES, A SMALL PUPPY AND A VIOLIN IN YOUR DRESSING ROOM: ANY REASON BEHIND THAT?

P: Well red is the best flavour of sweet, my parents never let me have a puppy so I figured this was my chance, plus my virtual son Dil Howlter is learning violin so I thought I'd encourage him by learning it too.

LET'S HAVE A LOOK AT YOUR CREATIVE PROCESS. WHERE DO YOU GET YOUR IDEAS?

P: I have a lot of video ideas in the shower! I think it's something about completely switching off your mind in a nice warm environment that sparks off a load of weird thoughts. I get most of my ideas from real-life situations, I am a magnet for strange and unusual people. When I met Dan he thought I was making it all up until he witnessed loads of the encounters himself!

DID YOU HAVE ANY WEIRD THOUGHTS IN THE SHOWER THIS MORNING?

P: I have an idea buzzing around my head about using time travel in a video, like a message to my former self. I'm not sure if it'll turn into anything but it's in my ideas book!

YOU HAVE AN IDEAS BOOK? CAN WE SNEAK A PEEK?

P: As you asked nicely here's a little page:

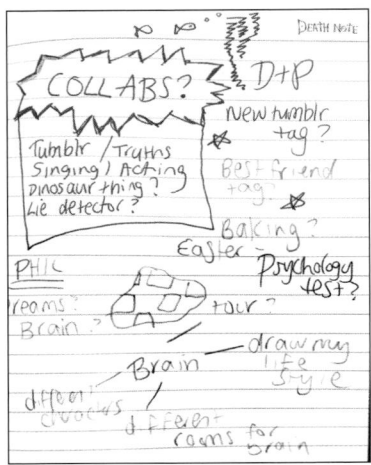

IS FILMING A VLOG AN EASY PROCESS?

P: I wouldn't call it easy! Some days I feel like my tongue is too big for my mouth and it takes me about 17 attempts to say a sentence. The easiness totally depends on the video! Usually I'm fine just rambling about my life but more complicated videos like the tour of my brain can be a bit more of a headache (pun unintended). Still a fun headache to be having though! The easiest videos are collab videos as that's just capturing natural fun with another human.

YOUR EDITING STYLE IS QUITE CREATIVE AND INDIVIDUAL, HOW DID IT COME ABOUT?

P: It's something I've developed over time. I like my videos to all have a similar vibe and I try and think about what would make me smile if I was watching it myself. I like to be able to laugh at myself too, so if I do something really weird with my face I'll happily zoom in and play it back in slow motion.

THE CAMERA

HOW LONG DOES A VIDEO TAKE TO EDIT?

P: It varies a lot! A typical 'Phil vlog' can take me around five hours to edit! I'm very picky so it takes me ages to whittle it down before I'm happy with it.

YOU ALWAYS SEEM SO POSITIVE ON YOUR CHANNEL. DO YOU EVER HAVE BAD DAYS?

P: I am human and I do have my bad days, but I wouldn't make a video about it. I see my channel as something that's hopefully going to improve someone's day! YouTube is a lot of people's nice fun escape from life so I want to make my channel as enjoyable as possible. If I'm having a terrible week I'll just switch off the camera and come back to it when I'm feeling recharged and happy!

WHAT DID YOUR PARENTS THINK ABOUT YOU STARTING YOUTUBE AS A CAREER?

P: Thankfully they've always been incredibly supportive. When I was living at home and had about 10,000 subscribers it still wasn't much of a job, but I told my parents I was really passionate about it and they agreed that I should give it a year and see how it goes. Best decision ever!

NOT ONLY DO YOU HAVE A BA IN ENGLISH LANGUAGE AND LINGUISTICS BUT YOU ALSO HAVE AN MA IN POST-PRODUCTION. THAT'S QUITE IMPRESSIVE.

P: I mean no one wants to brag about academic achievements but I did try really hard with my MA and it helped out with my channel a lot too. I spent an entire summer in a dark editing suite doing my dissertation. I don't think I've ever been so pale.

ARE THERE ANY VIDEOS YOU HAVEN'T BEEN HAPPY WITH?

P: I made a video called 'Dogalikes' which seemed like an awesome idea at the time but it turns out comparing YouTubers to dogs wasn't the greatest idea I've had, which is fine. I unlisted that one pretty quickly.

WHAT'S YOUR FAVOURITE VIDEO YOU HAVE MADE?

P: The 'Punk Edits in Real Life' was really fun to make. I also pranked my mum by telling her I actually got the giant neck tattoo. Another video I loved making is the Tumblr tag video with Dan, it's so nice to see how creative (and mildly disturbing) our audience is.

FINALLY, PHIL, CAN YOU SHOW US WHAT IS BEHIND THE CAMERA?

P: Here you go! A white wall and a camera. No giant film crew or spaceship, unfortunately.

AmazingPhil Video Trivia

👍 Original ideas for my channel name were BuffyPhil, LionPhil, Phil666, FantasticPhil, PHILWORLD and Phil3000.

👍 My lion was in one of the first fan mail packages I ever opened and came from Japan!

👍 I almost deleted the entire channel after getting a hate comment on one video. So glad I didn't.

👍 I didn't tell my friends I made YouTube videos until they all saw me featured on the front page! That was a weird conversation to have.

👍 For three years my 'Tripod' was a camera stacked on a selection of books and DVDs.

👍 I have over 100 private videos! Mainly because they make me cringe so much I don't want millions of people to watch them. Here's some of the thumbnails:

👍 'Phil is Not on Fire 5' had an unseen 20 minutes of footage which was lost when I dropped the SD card in a glass of milk.

👍 In 2008 I made a video called 'The Truth' where I pretended to be an American called Kyle and joked that I had invented the 'Phil character' as I thought British people were cool. It turned out my accent was too convincing as loads of people believed me! I never did post an explanation so sorry to anyone who still thinks I'm a secret American.

👍 We were going to refilm the green velvet cake Halloween baking video with a new recipe after they turned out to be swampy brown cakes, but we thought the footage was too funny not to use!

👍 1% of my audience is age 65+! I hope they draw whiskers on their faces.

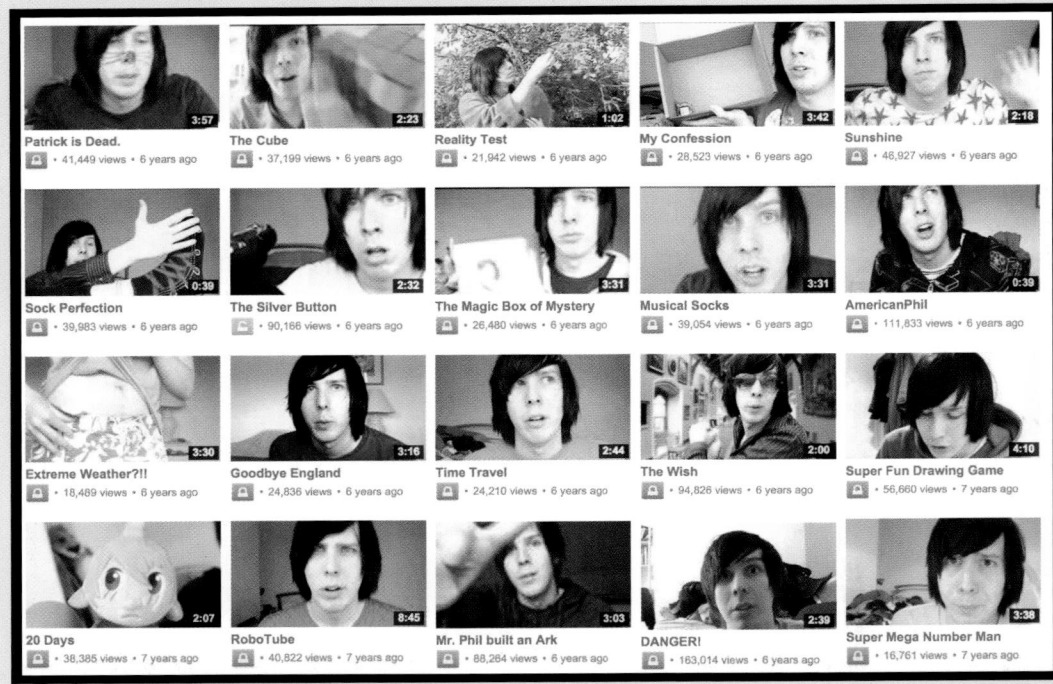

Patrick is Dead. 3:57 · 41,449 views · 6 years ago	The Cube 2:23 · 37,199 views · 6 years ago	Reality Test 1:02 · 21,942 views · 6 years ago	My Confession 3:42 · 28,523 views · 6 years ago	Sunshine 2:18 · 46,927 views · 6 years ago
Sock Perfection 0:39 · 39,983 views · 6 years ago	The Silver Button 2:32 · 90,166 views · 6 years ago	The Magic Box of Mystery 3:31 · 26,480 views · 6 years ago	Musical Socks 3:31 · 39,054 views · 6 years ago	AmericanPhil 0:39 · 111,833 views · 6 years ago
Extreme Weather?!! 3:30 · 18,489 views · 6 years ago	Goodbye England 3:16 · 24,836 views · 6 years ago	Time Travel 2:44 · 24,210 views · 6 years ago	The Wish 2:00 · 94,826 views · 6 years ago	Super Fun Drawing Game 4:10 · 56,660 views · 7 years ago
20 Days 2:07 · 38,385 views · 7 years ago	RoboTube 8:45 · 40,822 views · 7 years ago	Mr. Phil built an Ark 3:03 · 88,264 views · 6 years ago	DANGER! 2:39 · 163,014 views · 6 years ago	Super Mega Number Man 3:38 · 16,761 views · 7 years ago

👍 140,855   128 👎

👍 I made the 'Toilet Tag' video after dreaming it became the next huge craze on YouTube. Thanks for that one, brain. At least The 7 Second Challenge happened!

👍 I discovered my videos are frequently viewed on a forum for people with sneeze fetishes! They slow down my sneezes and talk about what I may be allergic to. Not creepy at all.

👍 I never planned for 'Draw Phil Naked' to be a thing! I showed one someone sent me in a video then loads of people just started joining in.

👍 Things on my failed list of ideas include 'Changing Colour T-shirt Dance', 'Vlog About Whales' and '100 Thoughts I Have Had Today'.

👍 Here is where I'm the most popular!

Top locations by views
United States
United Kingdom
Canada
Australia
Germany
Sweden
Ireland
New Zealand
Netherlands
Singapore

👍 129 👎 45

Guide to Being a You`Tuber`

P: One of the things we are always asked the most is advice on being a YouTuber. So many people out there want to try making videos themselves but have no idea where to start, so I thought we had to answer this in our book! Dan isn't convinced this is a good idea.

D: I'm just saying – we're making this book for people to remember our world far into the future and YouTube probably won't exist then. 'Google' will just be known as the all-powerful A.I. that controls and farms humanity as a resource in the inevitable post-singularity future.

P: Well how's about as well as helping the people alive now with interesting advice, we can think of it as a way to preserve our video-making advice for history?

D: That sounds more like it. Maybe this page will be framed in the future 'strange extinct intelligent species and what they did with their spare time' exhibition at the robot museum.

P: Okay, Dan. So here's our combined wisdom and advice on the world of YouTube!

WHY?

The first question is why do you want to do this? To be creative? To share your life with the world? To make new friends? To show off your microwave juggling skills? Think about what's motivating you to make videos. It's always better if people have a genuine motivation behind wanting to be on YouTube other than just 'being famous'!

WHAT?

What kind of videos do you want to make? It's completely up to you! Are you a filmmaker? A comedian? A vlogger? A gamer? A chef?! Think about what you are passionate about and what you can offer to the world. Remember it's okay to be inspired by others but it's not cool to copy! Think about what you like about various YouTubers and why, then try to create something original with your individual spin on it!

IN THE BEGINNING

An introduction is always a great first video! Dive straight into the kind of videos you are going to make on the channel and who you are. Maybe try doing it in a fun and different way that would get people talking about it? Of course you can always use our super-convenient 'YouTube Video Idea Generator' after this!

NAMING THE CHANNEL!

This isn't going to be easy as every human on earth and their grandma has a YouTube account by now, so stumbling across a great name that isn't already taken is like stumbling across a shiny Pokémon.

YES

👍 MAKE IT MEMORABLE!
You want a name that sticks in the head of your viewer. Using your actual name can work well! (DanHowell works a lot better than xXGlitterDolphin14714.) It's also an instant introduction and makes you seem more real. Careful what you do if you use your real name though!

👍 CHOOSE SOMETHING EASY-TO-SPELL
If someone hears about your channel by word of mouth it has to be easy to spell! 'SeReNdiPitOuSlySUSAN' may do less well than 'SuperSusan'.

👍 CHOOSE SOMETHING RELATED TO THE CHANNEL
It's always great to have the vibe of a channel in a username! For example, a gaming channel could use gaming-related words.

NO 👎

👎 NUMBERS
Try not to include numbers! Loads of numbers in a username can look a bit distracting and robot like! We'd rather subscribe to LizardPlanet than 00Lizard17449875.

👎 SIMILAR NAMES
Don't make a channel name too similar to another YouTuber! (Unless you're creating a fan account.) MooDiePie might not do as well as an original name and people might think you are a copycat (or a copydog).

👎 THINGS YOU MIGHT REGRET LATER
It might be fine now, but always think about the future! For example if your YouTube channel explodes to 18 billion subscribers overnight and you're called 'Pepsi23' it might be an issue!

EQUIPMENT

Camera: These days most phones or digital cameras are more than good enough for vlogging. Don't feel like you need a fancy DSLR or TV camera right from the start. When it comes to videos, the quality of the content is more important than the camera!

Sound: People being able to hear you well is important. Try to record in a quiet room and make sure whatever microphone you use doesn't make things sound like they are underwater. We always recommend doing tests before properly filming things.

Lighting: You don't need anything super fancy for this either! Usually a bright sunlit room will be fine. Just make sure the window isn't behind you or you'll look like an angel beaming into the room from heaven. If there's no sun you can D.I.Y. by pointing a bright lamp at the wall behind the camera.

LOCATION

This depends on what videos you want to make, but for vloggers bedrooms and living rooms are great as they are intimate and feel like you're inviting the audience into your world. You can turn any space into a cool filming zone with objects that reflect your style and personality.

PROPS

Make sure you have everything you need before you start filming. There's nothing worse than getting halfway through a video and realising you have no black pen to draw whiskers on yourself, or red wine to drink while giving advice, or a giant piece of cardboard for your brain.

PLAN AHEAD

We don't recommend just turning on the camera and rambling. For some people it works out great, the rest of the time it's seven minutes of 'why?'. Don't start filming until you've gone over the whole thing in your head so you're ready to go!

FILMING

It's time to film! We're not going to lie, talking to yourself alone in your bedroom is a bit weird. If you do have any housemates or parents either wait until you're home alone or explain to them what you are doing in advance so you can feel confident. Setting up a camera pointing at your bed may confuse a lot of parents so it's probably best to warn them before you start doing it.

At first it might feel strange talking to no one, so imagine you are talking to a friend and you'll come across natural to the audience! Try to be enthusiastic so you command people's attention.

The first 20 seconds or so are the most important so be energetic and to the point so you draw your audience in!

Here's some good and bad examples of first lines of a video:

'Hi! You will never believe what happened yesterday, I was stalked by a seagull.'

👍 YES. Straight to the point!

'Hi I'm not really sure what to say but I thought I'd just turn on the camera and see how this goes, sorry it's been a while.'

👎 NO. This makes you sound like you don't have any clear reason for making a video and isn't very engaging. Also never waste time apologising for late videos or similar things, just do it instead!

EDITING

Editing sounds complicated and scary but it doesn't have to be! All you're doing is sticking the good bits of something together and adding things to it.

You don't need a fancy expensive program, most computers come with free editing software that's perfectly fine for beginners. If you're ever confused, look up a YouTube tutorial! There are thousands of videos teaching you how to do absolutely everything.

For vlogs we recommend editing out all the 'um's and 'ah's to make it snappy and find some music to make it nice to listen to (not Britney Spears though or you'll be smited by the copyright bot).

When we've finished editing we always show our videos to our friends for any feedback as it's really useful to hear other people's perspectives.

TITLE

Short and snappy titles are usually best, though if you've seen our bible-length DanAndPhilGAMES titles you'll know that we don't always follow that rule. Try and think of something related to the video that will make people curious enough to click on it! 'SEAGULL STALKER' would sound much more exciting than 'My Holiday in France'. Try not to be too cheesy or clickbaity though!

THUMBNAIL

Choose a nice clear close-up of yourself talking, or a key point of the video that makes it look like something you want to see moving!

UPLOADING

It's best to upload in the evenings as more people will be hanging out on their computers rather than being at school or work or asleep!

WHY IS NOBODY WATCHING?

Ok great I've made a video and it's up. How do I get someone to watch it?

Unfortunately there is no magic formula to getting subscribers (unless Pewdiepie is secretly a genie). Here are some tips:

Make friends in the community! You might be lost in the comments on a huge YouTuber's video, but there's always people starting out on YouTube looking for friends. Comment on their videos and collaborate with people you like! Don't advertise yourself by spamming people's comments though. If your content's good people will notice. Integrity is important.

Use social media! Get on Facebook, Twitter, Tumblr and other accounts that people use to share their favourite clips. You can share your videos with your friends and family and if you have a place for your audience to follow you they can share and support your content too.

Stick at it! It took over a year for the AmazingPhil channel to get over 100 subscribers. Most successful YouTubers made videos for years with nobody watching just because they loved it. If you're doing it because you enjoy it then it shouldn't matter how many people watch — even if you get 100 views on a video that's 100 people whose days you have improved!

There's so much we could say about this that it could fit in its own book but we hope any budding YouTubers out there found this helpful. Good luck!

YOUTUBE ▶
VIDEO IDEA GENERATOR

D: We all know creativity can be hard. Especially when starting out! You have a camera, your brain and the infinite possibilities of the universe. What do you make a video about?!

P: The question I get asked the most is 'I want to be a YouTuber, what should my first video be about?' so we created this handy YouTube video idea generator.

D: Yep. Why put yourself through the stress of being original, when you can throw a bunch of things that already exist together to make something 'new'!

We take no responsibility for any incidents that occur as a result of this page.

FIRST CHOOSE YOUR BIRTH MONTH

JANUARY: VLOG ABOUT

FEBRUARY: BLINDFOLDED DRAW

MARCH: PERFORM A SONG ABOUT

APRIL: CREATE AN ARTISTIC FILM ABOUT

MAY: MAKE A COSTUME OF

JUNE: RANT FOR ONE MINUTE ABOUT

JULY: PRANK SOMEONE USING

AUGUST: DO AN INTERPRETIVE DANCE ABOUT

SEPTEMBER: DO A BEAUTY TUTORIAL ON HOW TO LOOK LIKE

OCTOBER: MAKE A MUSIC VIDEO ABOUT

NOVEMBER: HAVE A RAP BATTLE AGAINST

DECEMBER: CREATE A LIFE-SIZE PLASTICINE STOP MOTION FILM OF

NOW CHOOSE YOUR BIRTH DATE!

1. A WARTHOG
2. A CACTUS
3. LIZARDS
4. AN OCTOPUS
5. GODZILLA
6. A HOUSE PLANT
7. YOUR MUM
8. A GOOSE
9. THE EIFFEL TOWER
10. YOUR FAVOURITE EMOJI
11. BEES
12. PHIL'S EAR
13. AN OLD LADY CALLED DOROTHY
14. AN EAR HAIR
15. A SPOON
16. A NARWHAL
17. BACON
18. A SOCK
19. A SLICE OF BEEF
20. DEATH
21. BUTTS
22. UNICORNS
23. THE END OF THE WORLD
24. A TINY SEAL
25. YOUR PET
26. THE PLANET JUPITER
27. A SPECK OF DUST
28. A LLAMA
29. A LION
30. PANCAKES
31. YOUR GREATEST FEAR

Congratulations! And there's your first video.

P: Okay let's test it out on Dan. When's your birthday?

D: Seriously, you don't know my birthday?

P: Oh. 11 June! So, Dan ... rant for one minute about bees!

D: Sounds like a winner right there. What about you?

P: 30 January ... vlog about pancakes!

D: Haven't you already done that like nine times?

P: See, it generates great video ideas!

D: Fine, but if your birthday is 21 September you might want to keep that one private.

P: We look forward to watching all the incredible videos this generator will create.

NOSE WORKOUT

PHIL, DO THE SEXY ENDSCREEN DANCE

Can you explain the theory behind the whiskers?

I'D TELL YOU, BUT WE'D HAVE TO KILL YOU

ola

Shhhhhhhhhack

TACO

CHAOS

SHOULDER BOOBS

RICKY BLITZ

I LOOK LIKE A SERIAL KILLER

OLE

Dinosaur

FINGERNAILS FOR NIPPLES

IT'S SO SQUEAKY AND CHAFING

SAD

DRAGONS

Shhhhhhhhhhack

DANNATOR

Danny, it's time for your neck exam

skin coat

GOAT

The Emojinterview
>>>>>>>>>>>>>>>>>>>>>>>>>

Answer only using emojis!

How are you?

D:: ☕😎✌️

P: 😬👌

Most recently used emojis?

Find an emoji you have never used

D: 👞

P: 💊

Favourite emoji?

D: 👽

P: 🐗

What was the first thing you did when you woke up?

D: ❄️👦❄️👙👕👖💨👍

P: ☕

Describe your dream last night

D: 👹😱🏃👹🎷🚶💥💀👦🎉

P: 🐙🐙🏢🔥😱🏃🐙😟🐙👅💀

What does your ideal Saturday evening consist of?

D: 😔➡️🍕◀️➡️😬➡️🍕🍕🍕➡️💀

P: 📹🍕

What is the last thing you will see before you die?

D: 💥🔫🐎➡️SOON

P: 👽

What will you be doing in twenty years?

D: 🍦😭🎮💭📟📟

P: 👴💬📼

What does the future
look like?

D:

P: 🌊🐙🙌

What is your worst
nightmare?

D: 🔥💻🔥

P: 🐴✏️

What would you buy with
£10 million?

D: 🚀💎🍪💸🍩

P: 📈

What is your first memory?

D:)💦😷👶

P: 👟

What do you do on a plane?

D: 😐🍸 ? 📺

P: 👓📘

Dream holiday?

D: 🚶😴🏊🍜📖

P: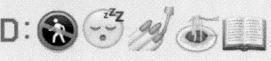

What has writing this book
been like?

D: 😁💭 ! ✏️😂

P: 😆

Phil. Describe Dan in
4 emojis

P: 👾🍜💭🎶

Dan. Describe Phil in
4 emojis

D: 😫🐷⚡👾

Goodbye!

D: 👋🧒💯

P: 😴

145

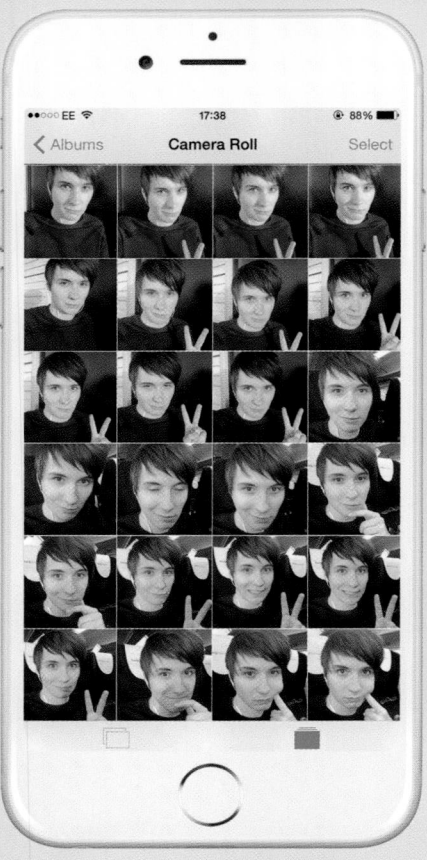

Unsuccessful Selfies: Dan

Unsuccessful Selfies: Phil

PLAYER 2

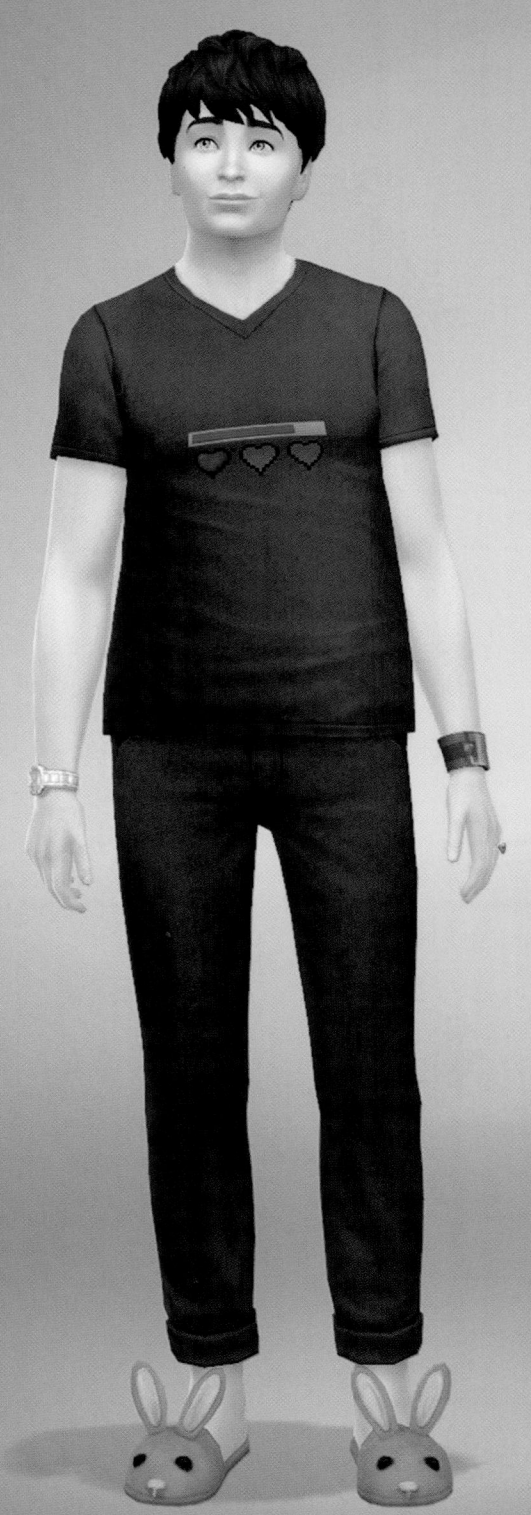

PLAYER 3 DIL

NAME:
DIL

INTERNET NAME:
DIL JAMECHAL HOWLTER

HEIGHT:
6FT 2"

FAVOURITE COLOUR:
CLOWN-PYJAMA GREEN

ANIMAL OF CHOICE:
JONATHAN THE MINNOW

WEAKNESS:
DELICATE CROCKERY

SPECIAL POWER:
SURVIVING MULTIPLE
ELECTROCUTIONS

QUOTE:
BENZI CHIBNA LOOBLE
BAZEBNI GWEB

DRAW DIL'S LIFE

ul Sul! Kai bar Dil tu bay su drawm mo lifzar

Oh foo lar kobar Dan zi Phil tay

Lum kobar say Sims refuntay

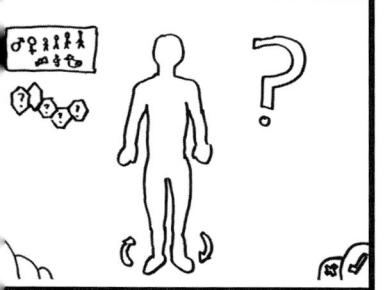

sar kobar zum scrumutar zi caratu creazomar

Heru zum bar botar namutay

Say sratzo raznay parl

Oh far townutay ko Oasislar Springs

Oh me hava lawnmug

Tay lawnuzy Owl sliduzar

Oh sar dreamizil zu mixobar busa luzee

Desar sum favlor poseratarl

Zum day jadosi um simoleons tar

BEHIND

SO WHY A GAMING CHANNEL?

D: Basically? We spent all our free time when we weren't making danisnotonfire and AmazingPhil videos playing video games, so we thought 'why not just film it and put it on the internet'!

P: It's something we had both talked about individually for ages!

D: Yeah, literally. I have a file on my computer from 2012 where I was about to make one:

> gaming channel - danisnotonline?
> think gaming shows
> let's play's
> research what kind of categories there are for gaming channels
> whatever's top of the charts
> old school games
> hardes ps1 platforming moments
> scariest ps1 moments
> gw2
> whatever's trendy
>
> mason's why dan's a fail
>
> **youtube plans**
>
> rich text (RTF) - 1 KB
> Created **Wednesday, 23 May 2012 16:31**

WHY DIDN'T YOU?

D: Mainly because of Radio 1 and we were moving to London. We thought we'd 'settle into London life' and see how things are going before starting a big new thing – turns out settling in took a year and a half!

SO WHY A JOINT GAMING CHANNEL?

P: Mainly because if we were both invested in it we couldn't procrastinate away from it individually. We figured we would feature in each other's so often we might as well do it together! Plus our audience loves videos twice as much if it's a 'Dan and Phil' thing.

WAS IT ALWAYS GOING TO BE CALLED DANANDPHILGAMES?

P: We settled on that in the end as it's basically just the best name, but we had some alternatives! I just found the file of our brainstorm:

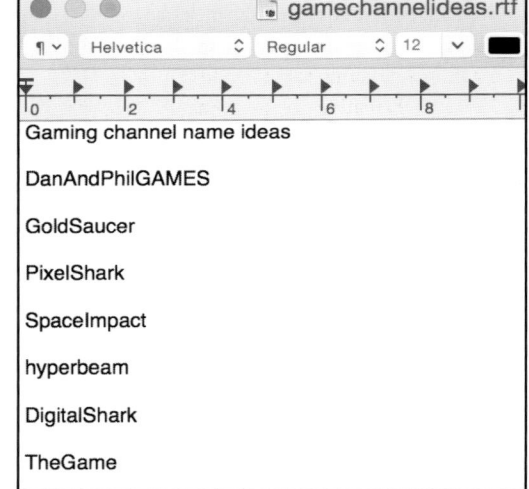

> gamechannelideas.rtf
>
> Gaming channel name ideas
>
> DanAndPhilGAMES
>
> GoldSaucer
>
> PixelShark
>
> SpaceImpact
>
> hyperbeam
>
> DigitalShark
>
> TheGame

D: I'm kind of sad we didn't call it 'TheGame'.

P: Thankfully for the rest of the internet it was already taken!

HOW DO YOU DECIDE WHAT GAMES TO PLAY?

D: We decided from the start to play games that we love. A lot of people just go with whatever's trendiest at the time because people will be searching for it and that gets views. We wanted to convince people we were passionate about gaming though by playing our favourites!

THE CAMERA

YOU PICK A LOT OF THINGS YOU'VE NEVER PLAYED BEFORE THOUGH?

P: I think there's a magic to playing something for the first time so everyone can laugh at how bad you are. I always find it really interesting and fun to see someone new reacting to something that I'm really familiar with!

HOW IS IT DIFFERENT TO FILMING YOUR OTHER VIDEOS?

D: Well, for one, we don't really have to come up with totally new ideas every time. We just film us playing and having lols and edit it into a video! The lack of creative pressure makes it very fun.

P: You need a whole other set of technology too. The process of capturing video game footage and editing it is very complicated!

D: I let Phil do all that. I tried to research it once and my brain nearly started dribbling out of my ear. I just look after the cables so they don't turn into a big black wiry ball of hell.

WHAT'S THE SECRET TO GOOD GAMING VIDEOS?

D: Lots of people make lots of different kinds of gaming content. It's as diverse as comedy or vlogging. You could do reviews, or videos about gaming culture and the industry, 'machinima' and then there's of course 'Let's Plays'.

P: We're definitely a 'Let's Play' channel! I think the magic behind those is it's like you're just hanging out with people you find entertaining. It's like any sort of sport or news comedy show that reacts to things that are happening – we just joke around and react to the game as a mutual interest to talk about.

D: I think you can still be a bit creative though, especially getting your personality through in the editing. I mean, this channel was supposed to be our super easy 'film it and whack it together' project but I ended up spending ages editing these ones too! I genuinely think all of our gaming videos are hilarious and I watch them back at least three times after uploading them. I think it just says a lot about our chemistry!

FINALLY, WHY DO YOU THINK THE LIFE OF YOUR SIM 'DIL HOWLTER' IS SUCH A SUCCESS?

D: People just like to watch other people playing house.

P: Yes I think the idea of Dan and Phil having a son and building a home, even though that's not at all what it is, appeals to a lot of people.

D: It's nice and domestic. For real, though, we had no idea how funny and amazing it would be. It's really like he's a real special little guy with his own personality. Wait, do you reckon he might be dead when the person is reading this book?

P: Don't say those things, Dan! I will hack the game if I have to to make him immortal. At the time of writing he is alive and well, just like he will be forever in all of our hearts.

BRAIN FARTS

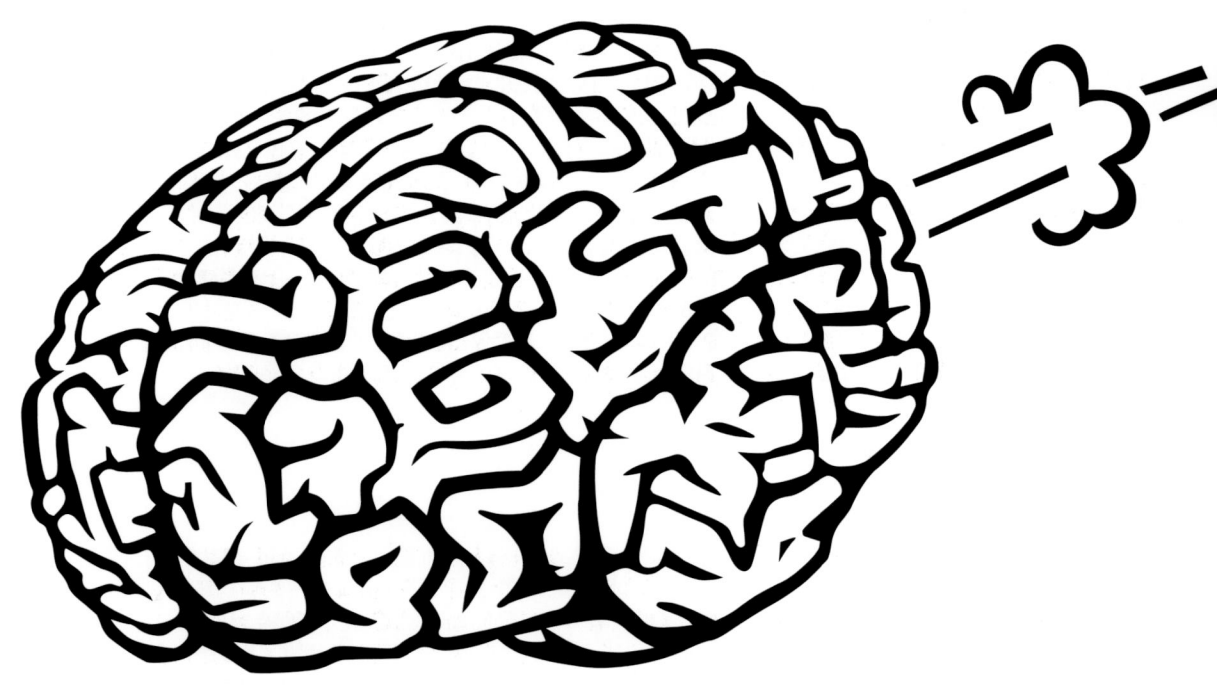

A 'BRAIN FART' IS WHEN YOU WRITE OUT THE FIRST THING THAT COMES INTO YOUR HEAD WITH NO FILTER. START WITH ANY WORD AND INSTANTLY PUT DOWN WHATEVER YOU THINK OF NEXT – IT PROBABLY WON'T MAKE ANY SENSE, BUT THAT'S THE POINT. PURE, UNCENSORED BRAIN-WAFFLE. WE DECIDED TO DO JUST THAT ON THESE PAGES. PLEASE DON'T PSYCHOANALYSE ANY OF THIS.

PHIL

THE MICE WERE SCREAMING AS TINY BADGERS WERE TURNING INTO METEORS WHICH LANDED IN THE LAKE WHERE LIFE BEGAN. THE COASTER IS MADE OUT OF TIN FOIL WHICH DOESN'T HEAT THE MUG OF WARM SOUP THAT IS FILLED WITH WORMS ON HALLOWEEN WHERE PANDA MASKS ARE ALL THE RAGE. TEETH ARE SHARP AND BLOOD IS POURING OUT OF THE WATERFALL WHICH ISN'T VERY CHRISTMASSY HOPEFULLY I WON'T GET DENTAL FLOSS IN MY STOCKING THIS YEAR WHY ARE THEY EVEN CALLED STOCKINGS WHAT IS THAT REFLECTION IN MY GLASSES IT LOOKS LIKE THE BUTT OF AN ANGEL WHO WAS BETTER OR WORSE THAN SPIKE I THINK I LIKED SPIKE WHICH MAKES ME WANT TO TWIST MY HAIR INTO A UNICORN HORN. SHOULD I GET MY MUM THE UNICORN SLIPPERS OR THE HEATED NARWHAL SLIPPERS WHEN THEY COME IN STOCK BUT SHIPPING IS EXPENSIVE FROM THE US DO THEY EVEN COME ON A SHIP? DID BIGFOOT HAVE LARGE CLAWS OR FEET LIKE A CAT? THEY PURR BUT WHAT DOES THE SOUND COME FROM IS IT LIKE THE NOISE WHEN A DONKEY IS LAUGHING OUTSIDE MY GRANDMA'S HOUSE EVERY MORNING? I WONDER IF THAT DONKEY AFFECTED THE PROPERTY MARKET MONOPOLY I WANT TO PLAY BUT NO ONE LIKES IT AS MUCH AS ME. I THINK I SHOULD STOP NOW.

DAN

IN THE BEGINNING THERE WAS A DAN. A DAN WITH THE PLAN, HE WAS THE MAN WITH A HAND THAT COULD REACH UP INTO THE SKY AND PULL DOWN ANYTHING HE WANTED, SO ONE DAY HE WENT TO A SHOP AND YELLED OUT 'WHY WOULD YOU DO THIS TO ME I DON'T UNDERSTAND FOR GOD'S SAKE WHERE ARE MY SHOES WHO DID YOU TAKE THEM FROM?' IT STARTED RAINING AND THE DOGS HOWLED A FINAL SWAN SONG OF JUSTICE INTO THE COLD NIGHT. THE WEEPING TREES SWAYED IN THE WIND OF FORGETFULNESS AS THE WORLD PLUMMETED INTO A DARKNESS ONLY KNOWN TO THOSE WHO HAVE THE SECRETS. I REMEMBER LAST TUESDAY LIKE IT WAS MY LAST WITH THE BACON ON SALE AND THE FIERY HATS IN THE DISPLAY OF THE NEW SHOP WINDOW. 'WHO ARE YOU TO SAY THESE THINGS TO ME?' I CAST TO MY SHADOW AS IT RAN AWAY FOR NOT ACCEPTING THE TRUTH. WILL WE EVER HAVE THE ANSWERS? KICKING THINGS IS ILLEGAL YOU SHOULD KNOW THAT BY NOW. IT'S BEEN A COLD DARK CAVE AND A FIERY WONDERFUL 400 YEARS ON THIS PLANET AND THE FINAL LESSON AT THE END OF THE DAY IS NOT WHICH SOCKS DON'T MATCH UP IN PAIRS, BUT WHICH UMBRELLA YOU TAKE ON HOLIDAY TO A SANDY BEACH. BAZINGA.

DAN'S FEARS

Why are we doing this? I mean we're literally writing out all of our weaknesses ready to be exploited by an evil genius/future dystopian government.

THE SUPERNATURAL

Poltergeists, witches, demons – you name it, if it's a magically powered evil being that defies the rules of reality, I'm terrified of it. Which is funny because I do not believe that any of these things exist. 100%. Go figure.

THE DARK

I'm afraid of the dark. I used to think this was kind of embarrassing as an 'adult' but now I understand it is one of humanity's most ancient primordial fears based on something quite sensible. Don't leave the cave because you can't see well and you'll probs get eaten by a bear. As opposed to bears, I tend to imagine various monsters from horror movies I watched at an inappropriately young age that don't actually exist, but I like to think the urge to never expose my back to a dark room will one day save me.

TREES

Hear me out on this one okay. I'm not 'afraid of trees' – I'm afraid of scary trees in scary places. I think forests are generally spooky and have that whole 'what evil lurks within?' getting lost vibe, but as I referenced above, when I was nine I watched *The Blair Witch Project* on the TV in my room at 5am and it literally traumatised me. Don't do that.

SPECIFICALLY MAN-MADE OBJECTS UNDERWATER

Turns out there isn't an actual name for this. 'Thalassophobia' is the fear of the sea, but I'm fine with the sea! Man I love the sea. I've been diving, I've jumped off cliffs, I'm even one of those 'let's swim over to that island over there' kind of maniacs. No fear of abyssal depths or standing on crabs, but put me near a buoy or a boat and I will FREAK OUT. I don't know what it is but I just can't stand man-made things underwater. Ropes, anchors, ladders – you have nightmares about murderers and apocalypses? I have them about falling off an oil rig and accidentally touching a slimy pipe.

MOTHS

Don't trust 'em. Unlike graceful and composed butterflies who swoop and ascend serenely, moths can seemingly instantly dart a metre in any direction. You need to always be prepared for contact. Also as a late-night laptop-in-bed user – who invented a creature attracted to light? A cruel joke.

SPIDERS

Okay pretty basic and uninteresting but OMG SPIDERS ARE GROSS. Funnily enough I'm fine with tarantulas! I know a guy who had one as a pet and it was kinda cute. I don't really mind tiny spiders who'd get squished if you sneezed towards them, but there's a special middle ground which I just cannot stand. I feel like it might have something to do with a particular traumatic memory.

Warning – if you find spiders gross you might want to flay yourself after reading this.

SPIDER-ON-CHEST INCIDENT

I was nine. Back then I asked my parents for a bunk bed in my room, no idea why – I think I just found them exciting whenever I went to a hotel with them so the idea of being able to sleep in a top bunk at my discretion was indescribably exciting. It was a hot summer's night and I was sleeping bare-chested with the covers off and the windows open. In the middle of the night I awoke because of a strange tickling on my chest. I reached with my right arm down the wall to the light switch and I looked back to see the biggest, blackest, meatiest, hairiest house spider (Tegenaria Domestica if you want to look it up, I have no idea why you would) was descending from the ceiling directly above my face and trying to crawl up my neck. I have never flipped out quite like I flipped out at that moment. I screamed and thrashed wiping myself with the bed sheet in an attempt to scrape it off, barrel-rolled directly off the top bunk five feet onto the floor and slapped myself in the chest about fifty times. I ran out of my bedroom all the way downstairs trembling with horror when my mum ran out of her room in a panic just to laugh when I explained what happened. Thanks. I slept on the sofa for three days.

PHIL'S PHEARS*

*The opportunity for a title pun was there, I had to take it.

HORSES

I don't trust their legs or intentions. Also one time I actually rode one at 'Horse World' and when I got home a load of black liquid ran out of my nose? Suspicious.

BURGLARS

I live in constant fear that someone is going to climb through my window! I think my future house will have bullet-proof guard tigers and robotic airlocks.

THE SEA

This is my main 'fear' as it were. I've always felt uneasy about deep sea water. I think part of it is just human nature as why would anyone want to plunge themselves into freezing cold salty water that is potentially filled with sharks and jellyfish and as yet undiscovered man-eating seaweed? I have had some traumatic water-related incidents though. The story I'm about to tell made my friend Louise cry-laugh so feel free to also enjoy my pain.

THE SNORKELLING INCIDENT

I was 14 years old and on a dream holiday to Australia with my parents. We were about to fulfil most people's ultimate life goal: snorkelling in the Great Barrier Reef. I realise how lucky I was, this was the thing at the top of everyone's bucket list and a once in a lifetime experience! In typical Phil fashion I had the worst day ever.

We got a large boat to the middle of the reef and before we started our snorkel adventure, the captain asked if anyone wanted a flotation device; a huge pink marshmallowy thing that wrapped around your lower half. I thought 'No! I can do this! I know how to swim,' so I declined the crotch marshmallow and jumped into the water. I then realised that many of the fully grown dads and teenagers were wrapped in lovely floating pink cocoons while I was immediately flailing around and drinking half the sea.

The idea was that we had to swim 'about a mile' to a small island and have lunch on it! I could see no island. Was this some kind of joke? I spun around in circles until I noticed a tiny dot on the horizon. That was the island. I tried to put my feet down and gather some energy until I realised the seabed was lined with razor sharp coral. 'Pull yourself together, Phil! If these tiny babies can swim in the sea so can you!' I thought, as I started doggy-paddling towards the island-shaped dot. I swam a good few metres and may have seen the flash of a fish when suddenly a small wave descended on my face and filled my snorkel with water. I flailed a lot. For some reason I thought rolling over would be a good idea which led to me filling my nose with half of the ocean and losing my mask which immediately sank to the bottom. I like to think a tiny fish is using it as a home right now.

Without a mask I couldn't see anything and all around me I could hear families saying, 'OH LOOK, TILLY! A BLUE STARFISH!' 'Mummy! Look at the conga eel!' 'The dolphin is letting me ride on its back Jonathan!'.

I wasn't going to let this beat me. I was going to make it to the island. I tried one final kick of triumph when one of my flippers slipped off and drifted into the distance. With one flipper I was now swimming in circles. I was defeated. All I could do was lie on my back and cry 'Help! Hellllp! Helllllllllllppp meeee!'.

A few minutes later a 19-year-old lifeguard that looked like he was from *Home and Away* had lifted me onto a giant lilo and was dragging this crying pale lump of failure across the sea to the island. Everyone watched as he deposited me onto the sand like a beached whale. At least I could enjoy my lunch now!

'Who wants a cheese sandwich??'

IT'S TIME

I THINK MY FLIES ARE UNDONE
I THINK MY FLIES ARE UNDONE
I THINK MY FLIES ARE UNDONE
I THINK MY FLIES ARE UNDONE
I THINK MY FLIES ARE UNDONE

STOP

RIGHT

NOW

Do me up Dan! I mean, whisker me up

SHERLOCK IS CANCELLED

OOH ♥ JEMIMA

#Stopphil2014

Cheese umBrella

BUY it on i-Tunes

I'D FREAK OUT IF I SAW YOU IN THE BATH

SAVVZ11

THE GAME

THOSE GUMS ARE PRETTY MOIST

The year is 2087

I bought you a spaniel im obsessed with animals...

I THINK WE SHOULD STOP!!!

I THINK WE SHOULD STOP

AMERICA ATTACK

YOUR BUTT WON'T BE THE ONLY THING THAT GETS WIPED TONIGHT

HEY YOU HAVE REALLY GREAT TEETH

Timmy likes it!!

TODAY I'M HAVING ANOTHER EXISTENTIAL (RISIS!

i CAN'T ESCAPE THE FREEDOM!

P oo

it's been 16 years

PHIL AND DAN IN JAPAN

P: I WANT TO GO BACK!

D: Okay, Phil, you should probably rewind yourself a little bit.

P: Oops, let's try that again.

D: Hey why is your name first in this title?

P: 'Phil and Dan in Japan' just sounds way better than 'Dan and Phil in Japan'.

D: You win this round!

P: Out of every country in the entire world it had always been my biggest dream to visit Japan.

D: Me too! We're what you would call 'gigantic weeaboos' – that means people who are obsessed with anime, video games, sushi and Japanese culture in general.

P: Our favourite games are Final Fantasy, one of our favourite movies is *Kill Bill Volume 1*! The showdown at the house of blue leaves.

D: Thankfully our trip didn't involve any mass dismemberment, but yes! Going to Japan is something we've always talked about doing, so halfway through writing this very book we thought 'Hey! Why don't we randomly go to Japan right now and say it was for the book?'

P: Best plan ever. So I did something very un-Phil like and booked the tickets that very moment. No going back. We were going to Japan!

D: Well, we almost didn't make it.

P: Yeah that may have been my fault.

D: At the airport just before our flight, I asked Phil to check the departures screen who told me 'Yeah, we have loads of time!' when in reality we had five minutes before the gate closed.

P: I thought the gate would be nearby and it'd be no problem!

D: Our gate was 25 minutes and two monorails away.

P: I've never been so stressed.

D: In that situation I just like to let the inevitability of the situation wash over me and know there's nothing I can do, but Phil went into full-on panic mode.

P: I remember looking Dan directly in the eyes and saying, 'That's it. We're definitely going to miss our flight.'

D: Then he started to sprint, literally sprint to the gate.

P: I think it was more flailing.

D: He bounded through the airport like a roadrunner made of spaghetti and I followed, coughing up my lungs. OF COURSE as this was us two, our gate was on the fifth floor so our running included a fun five flights of stairs. I literally nearly died.

P: We were the very last people there, but when we arrived the gate was still open. With my dying breaths I asked the gate lady if we'd nearly missed the plane and she said, 'Oh you had loads of time! We just like to send the message early so the passengers aren't late.'

D: GEE THANKS A LOT, 'LINDA'.

P: So after the worst ten minutes of my life we got on the plane and we made it! And here is what we did in Japan:

169

AKIHABARA

D: The land of technology, anime merchandise and life-size character body pillows, it's Akihabara!

P: This was one of the places I felt the most Japanny.

D: You can't just invent words like Japanny, but I know what you mean! There were neon billboards, arcades and cosplayers everywhere.

P: Beware of venturing into the basements of anime stores though, I'm still bleaching my eyes after a certain tentacle incident.

D: Phil!

D: We were starting to get hungry after so much fanboying; so we decided to go to a Maid café!

MAID CAFÉ

P: I was actually nervous about this as I had no idea what to expect.

D: A maid café is themed around the idea that you are a Victorian lord being waited on by your maids.

P: They sing to you and make you 'magical lattes'; you can even choose what animal is drawn on your drink! I went for a lion and Dan of course went for an alpaca.

P: After our drinks we were each given a choice of a maid to have a photo with. I didn't realise we could have one with our waitress too and she looked so sad when I didn't pick her!

D: Coco is still crying right now.

P: Stop! Intimidatingly you have to go and stand on stage in front of everyone and choose some props out of the maid's box and have a Polaroid taken that she writes on for you as a souvenir! I know this sounds kind of creepy, but it was all innocent! Apparently it's quite touristy.

D: You say that but there were some 'regulars' I noticed in a corner.

P: Nothing weirder than the horde of crazy cat lady regulars we saw at that cat café in London.

 ★ TOP TIP ★

We wouldn't recommend eating a main meal at a maid café as the food looked quite basic and expensive! Just go for a drink and maybe a dessert.

 ★ TOP TIP ★

There are also butler cafés! Instead of Japanese maids, in these you are served by British guys so we gave this a miss as it didn't seem very exotic to be served a cup of tea by Graham from Cardiff.

SHIBUYA

D: Shibuya! An entertainment and fashion district that is also home to the insane crossing where *checks Google* around 45,000 people cross each day.

P: I felt like I was in a stampede of orderly wildebeest.

D: I felt very much like Mufasa crossing that road.

P: Spoilers, Dan!

D: Oh come on, that movie is like 20 years old. Anyway, we decided to have some fun and make a game we're calling 'Where's Philly?'

P: Or 'Where's Phildo' if you're American!

D: ...as if I say it.

Can you see Phil in his red jacket?

P: Another landmark of Shibuya is the saddest statue in the world – Hachikō!

D: Hachikō is a dog whose owner used to meet him every day outside the train station. One day his owner died and Hachikō waited outside the station for his master every day for ten years until he died too.

P: Dan, you're making people cry.

172

D: This dog went on to become a national treasure and they built a statue in his honour! Here we are mourning him:

'PURIKURA'

These photo booths can be found on the top floors of most arcades! They are famous for making you look slightly alien-like as they automatically enlarge your eyes and make your legs longer to make you 'beautiful'.

You can also decorate your pictures with futuristic pens. Here's some of our terrifying creations:

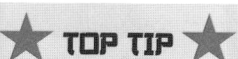

HARAJUKU

P: Gwen Stefani wasn't lying as the harajuku girls do have wicked style.

D: And the boys.

P: And the crepes!

D: Oh my god the Harajuku crepes were life-destroyingly good. I am foaming at the mouth just remembering them.

P: Brb. Going back to Harajuku to buy a crepe.

D: If you've been to London, Harajuku felt a bit like Camden! It was very cool and market-like with loads of stalls, unusual stores and kooky fashion.

P: Also Dan bought so much anime merchandise from one store he got a free tissue box.

D: I'd never been so happy.

⭐ **TOP TIP** ⭐

If you want to visit a mall go to 'Sunshine City'! Not only does it have an aquarium with seals in the ceiling (sealsing?) but it is home to the largest Pokémon shop in the world! Warning: You may spend your life savings like we did.

MEJI JINGU

D: We couldn't spend a week in Japan without absorbing some culture!

P: So we decided to visit a shrine called Meji Jingu hidden away in the middle of a forest in the city.

D: The entrance to the shrine or 'Torii' was huge!

Apparently you are supposed to walk around the outside of it, as you can only walk through the centre if you are a god. Of course Phil walked right through unknowingly.

P: Then we arrived at a place where you write prayers on pieces of wood and hang them from a tree. Dan wished for people to be nice to Kanye. I wished for pandas to mate more frequently ... AND IT CAME TRUE.

D: It did! I remember it being in the news when we arrived home. They should call you the panda whisperer.

P: I prefer 'Panda Lord'.

SHINJUKU

D: Tokyo's organised crime/red-light district. Yay!

P: I expected it to be seedy and weird but it was actually pretty cool!

D: We went straight to the famous Robot Restaurant Show which is the most insane two hours I have ever experienced in my life. Basically a crazy/ amazing guy spent over £50,000,000 on turning a building into an insane holographic casino with a show about giant robots.

P: At one point a man in a gorilla suit rode into the room on the back of a giant robot moth and got shot by a woman in a bikini firing a bazooka.

D: If that sentence doesn't sell it to you then nothing will!

P: Over on the next page is a picture of a gigantic robot hawk that doesn't really do it justice:

D: We also visited the famous bar in the hotel from *Lost in Translation* so we could pretend to be Bill Murray!

P: AMAZING BURGER (and views)!

STUDIO GHIBLI MUSEUM

P: If you're a fan of Ghibli movies then this is a must! It's a special museum designed to give you a tour of Hayao Miyazaki's mind.

D: It was very magical. We even got to see an exclusive Ghibli movie which used human voices for each sound effect and our ticket was a film cell!

MOUNT FUJI

P: Before we begin, do you want 'Phil's Fuji Facts'?

D: I'm sure this will be fun – okay, Phil!

P: Mount Fuji is called Fuji-San in Japanese! It's an active volcano that last erupted in 1707, and a dragon nestles beneath the mountain guarding a huge pile of gold.

D: I think that's The Lonely Mountain from *The Hobbit*.

P: I ran out of interesting facts.

D: One of our favourite days in Japan was our excursion to Mount Fuji! We decided to do everything ourselves on this trip but for this adventure we needed a guided tour as it's 100 miles outside of Tokyo and we can't navigate our way to a Tesco let alone a faraway mountain.

P: As with every form of transport, we almost missed the bus!

D: Only because literally everyone in Japan needed to pee in the one toilet in the bus station.

P: It seemed like it. We ran for the bus and were greeted by our incredible host and tour guide Riko! The first thing she did was sing an improvised song about Mount Fuji, coaches and Japan which was actually strangely amazing.

D: She then told us a story to help us remember her name. 'What's her name? Oh I can't recall ... recall? RIKO! Her name Riko!' What a character.

P: She didn't stop talking for the entire nine-hour trip.

D: I think she tried to sell us an apartment at one point? Anyway, we drove through the beautiful Japanese countryside to reach Mount Fuji, stopped at a vantage point to appreciate the view, only for the mountain to be totally blocked by one troll cloud:

Like seriously OF ALL THE PLACES that cloud could be! Nature, smh.

P: Thankfully we didn't just stare at it from afar, we got to drive up it! We stopped at 'The 4th station' where hikers leave humanity behind to ascend to the peak. There was actual snow on the ground and it was absolutely freezing!

D: There were a bunch of lads on our tour bus who decided to wear shorts and t-shirts because it was a hot day in Tokyo, they didn't enjoy this 45 minutes.

P: So many blue knees. Thankfully they had the best inventions ever – vending machines that sell warm coffee!

D: You bought two just to put them in your pockets.

P: Totally worth it. Anyway, who are you to talk, Mr Bought-a-can-of-air-from-the-gift-shop?

D: That is not my name, but yes I bought some bottled 'Fuji air' which wins the award for the most pointless/hilarious souvenir ever.

P: Will you ever drink the air out of it?

D: Maybe if the world starts to end I'll have the freshest breath ever ready to go!

P: We descended the mountain and went on a boat ride (with fake steam pipes) to get another great view of the troll cloud:

Then we went on a cable car ride up to the volcanic hot springs resort of Hakone!

D: Unfortunately there was no time to bathe in the hot springs which is always my favourite part of an anime.

P: Apparently everyone has to be completely naked which may have been mildly awkward. We did see some bubbling water though!

D: Yes! There were rapturous shafts of volcanic steam bursting from the ground.

D: They also sold 'black eggs' which had been boiled in the sulphurous water bubbling out of the ground.

P: Sounds healthy!

D: I feel like health and safety wasn't taken as seriously over there. Anyhoo, we were descending the mountain and about to journey back to Tokyo, when the troll cloud decided to depart and we were greeted with a perfect view of the mountain!

P: Fuji-san revealed himself! It was like looking at a perfect cartoon mountain, it was incredible!

P: I ate some black ice cream, which gave me a black mouth for the rest of the day. It just tasted of vanilla which was kinda disappointing.

D: What were you expecting?

P: I dunno! Ash? Dragon blood? At least black cherry or something.

D: It really was the perfect end to an amazing trip! We then got to travel back via bullet train which in my head was built up to be some mega futuristic space-vehicle but turned out to be like any fast train.

P: I was kind of disappointed that it didn't feel like a rollercoaster with robot butlers on board pouring you tea. Also it was where we had to say goodbye to Riko so I was emotionally vulnerable.

D: She and her strange songs will be in our hearts forever.

TOUR GUIDES

D: It wasn't just Riko we had escorting us around!

P: No thankfully, as otherwise I'm sure we would have gotten lost, walked into Godzilla's cave and been eaten, we had two fellow YouTuber friends living in Tokyo, Duncan and Mimei!

D: Having two fluent Japanese speakers allowed us to enjoy just smiling and nodding during every conversation for half the holiday.

P: Now I think about it they could have been saying anything! Like, 'Forgive our friends for being too tall and knocking everything over in your shop, British people are just damaged like that.'

D: To be honest we were too tall for most of the buildings and I would describe your clumsiness as damaging.

P: Either way I'm glad they were there. Thanks, guys!

CHERRY BLOSSOMS

D: The reason April is the most popular month for going to Japan is the cherry blossoms!

P: The super pretty trees only bloom for a couple of weeks in the whole year and depending on the weather you could totally miss it.

D: Thankfully when we descended from the sky on our journey into Tokyo, we were greeted with an ocean of pink flora!

P: It was so beautiful! I felt like I was in a slow-motion scene in a movie the whole time. Next time we will participate in the special cherry-blossom viewing picnics they call 'Hanami'.

D: They made for an ultra-kawaii very aesthetic background for photos though. We took quite a few with them.

LANGUAGE

D: Thankfully pretty much everyone we spoke to knew some English!

P: Japanese seems like the most impossible language to learn ever. Did you know there's over 50,000 Kanji (word symbols) to learn?

D: Ain't nobody got time for that! Something funny we realised was no one could understand our English due to our British accents. It sounds bad, but honestly the best way to be understood was by attempting a terrible Japanese accent.

P: Remember that time we went shopping and walked up to that thing we thought was a parade?

D: Oh you mean the one that turned out to be an anti-tourism protest? Yes. Maybe it would be good if we could read some Japanese.

FOOD

P: You better like Sushi and noodles if you visit Japan as there was a LOT of Sushi and noodles!

D: Yeah interestingly, unlike Britain, there were hardly any foreign-food restaurants, but we love Japanese food so it was like heaven for us!

P: I'm not sure about their traditional breakfast though. No offence, but I'm not really in the mood for pickled fish and miso soup first thing in the morning! Thankfully there were enough waffle and pancake places to keep me alive for the whole trip. If I had my blood tested I think I would be 18 per cent maple syrup.

D: The only thing I didn't like was the fermented soy beans.

P: I think if you put the word fermented in front of anything it's probably gross.

D: Fermented cheese.

P: Fermented bees.

D: Okay, let's stop.

SUBWAY

P: All people told us about before we left was how apparently complicated the Tokyo subway system was! Thankfully for us there was an app that just told us where to go.

D: Yeah we were fine but I think before apps existed we would have died of old age trying to navigate through the tunnels.

P: The weird thing is how gigantic the stations are! We once walked 500 metres from the entrance to one of the lines.

D: We realised that if you're travelling less than a mile you might as well just walk above ground and inhale some fresh air/sakura petals.

P: Also we were too tall as we kept being hit in the face by the handles. Japan wasn't built for people of our lengthiness.

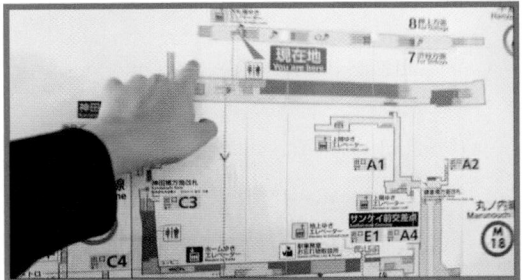

One other cool thing is that each train has its own jingle for when it arrives! More things should have jingles.

D: What like?

P: Toasters? Umbrellas? Kettles? I just need more jingles in my life.

THEMED CAFÉS

D: You think the idea of a cat café is exciting? You know nothing.

P: Tokyo is obsessed with themed cafés. These are places that serve food and drinks like any normal café, but with a crazy theme! And we mean crazy. Here's just a few we stumbled across:

Snake Café

Owl Café

Penguin Café

Ninja Café

Vampire Café

Robot Café

Final Fantasy Café

D: There was even a 'Tokyo Ghoul Café' based on an anime about cannibal monsters where all the food was made to look like human flesh! We avoided that one. Now I'm hungry.

GACHA MACHINES

P: These are machines where you insert 100 Yen and get a random prize inside a plastic egg!

D: You were obsessed with them!

P: Who doesn't want a keyring of a cat riding on the back of some sushi or a deer brandishing a hammer?

And if you were a pro like me, you could make it extreme by gambling on the 1,000 Yen machine! There were hundreds of mystery prizes ranging from new computers to jewellery, but would you risk £5 on nothing?

D: I remember how excited you were about pressing that prize button.

P: It could have been so many cool things, but no, of course I got a gold purse that's probably worth 50p.

D: Stellar use of your money there, Phil.

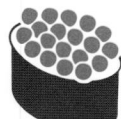

SAYONARA!

D: And that was our trip to Japan!

P: I almost had to buy a new suitcase because we bought so much stuff.

D: How'd it compare to England for you?

P: It's like two different worlds, I'm not sure I could live there but I absolutely loved visiting and will definitely return. I want to bring back one of their toilets.

D: Really?

P: It's hard to go back after experiencing a warm seat with butt-spray action.

D: TMI. I'd like to go back and see some more rural Japan outside of Tokyo at a different time of year!

P: See, it was totally worth going just for this book.

D: That was a good idea, wasn't it? Damn maybe we should have done it more often and gone to Disneyland.

P: Or on safari!

D: Let's not kid ourselves – you'd probably get eaten.

P: True. Well we hope you enjoyed reading about our adventures!

D: Sayonara!

P: I WANT TO GO BACK!

THE PHANGA

A DAN AND PHIL MANGA VOL. 1

ART BY ARCTOIDS

STORY BY DAN AND PHIL

184

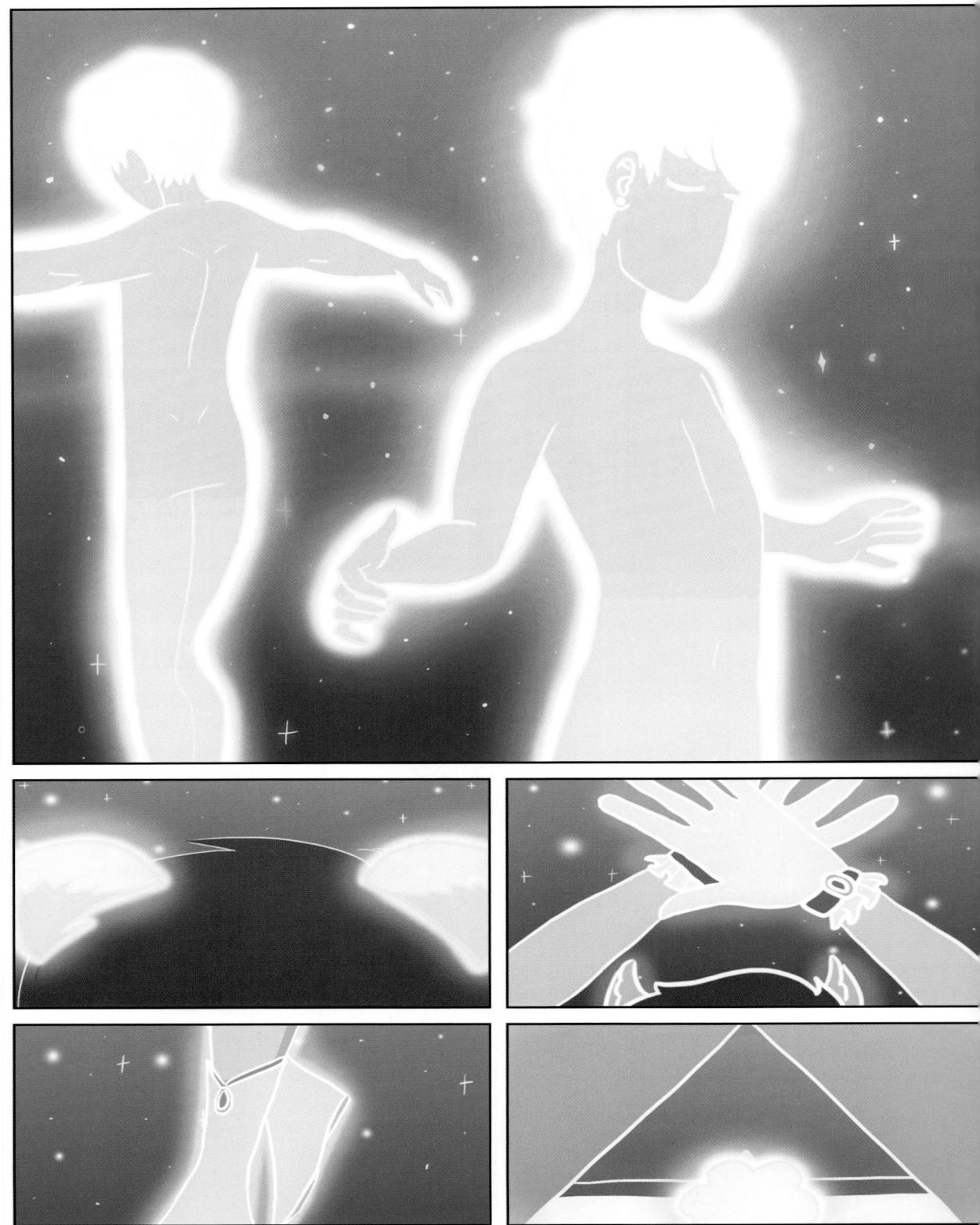

I DON'T REMEMBER THIS BEING SO TIGHT.

YOU NEED TO LAY OFF THE POPCORN.

HEY!

LION ABILITY 'SONIC ROAR!'

IT WORKED! I'LL DISTRACT IT.

ALPACABILITY 'CUTE-FACE!'

DAN-KUN, NO!

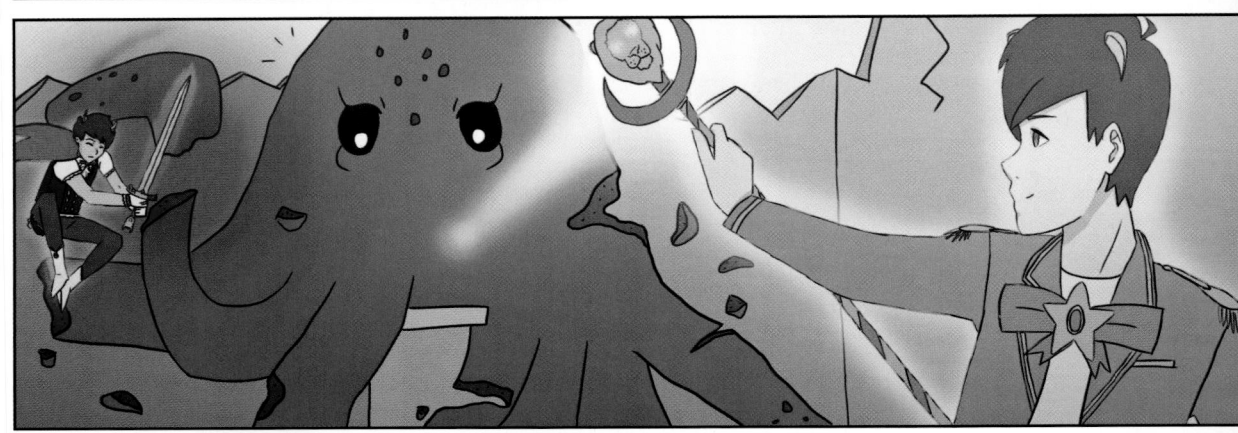

PHOTOS YOU MAY NEVER HAVE SEEN

THE 7 SECOND WRITING CHALLENGE

P: I'm sure all of you by now have heard of the most epic game in the universe, The 7 Second Challenge.

D: The rules are pretty simple, you have to do a challenge in seven seconds – but how can we put this in a book? I hear you ask.

P: The Seven Second Writing Challenge!

D: As we are now both experienced authors, we thought we'd put our typing speed and creativity to the test! We will give the other person a topic and they have just seven seconds to write something about them. No pressure!

P: You're going down Danny boy.

D: Don't call me that.

P: Okay, we'll take it in turns, you're up first! You have seven seconds to write about ...

P: VOLCANOES

D: they are hot I don't like falling in them that would hurt

D: FLAMINGOS

P: they are pink I dont trust their eyes or souls and they s

P: ARTIFICIAL INTELLIGENCE

D: it will destroy the world we need safeguards stop Facebook

D: GOD

P: god is on a cloud playing a flute he is everywhere or nowh

P: PUBERTY

D: the change is coming how embarrassing dont talk to me mum

D: CHEESE

P: cheese is gross and gives u nightmares I dont like it

P: PENGUINS

D: cold birds why can't they tfly so many movies why

D: THE INTERNET

P: web and information we like it and i n

P: BEES

D: they are the friends of the flowers not like evil wassps yay beed

D: PHIL

P: I am phil and i am cool Ilike movies and I have hair and

P: DAN

D: brown hair nice face alright guy i gyess cool clothes

D: THE AMAZING BOOK IS NOT ON FIRE

P: the books is the best book of all time I am enjoying writing

D: STOP. Well that was something.

P: Who won?!

D: I dunno, man, I think my writing on 'bees' was pretty poetic.

P: You typed 'beed' at the end.

D: Don't you mean 'u', Phil? I saw what you did for Cheese, blatant cheating.

P: More like cheese-ting.

D: So what do you think, should we use this method to whack out the rest of the book in record time?

P: I'm thinking no.

D: I whole-heartedly concur.

What Dan and Phil Text Each Other

Phil   **Dan**

What even is this

It looks like ⚡ got drunk

Lol 💀

📱⁉️🔛

🔖👾💀

🖼📠📡

💀💱🖇

let's stop

Ok
Delivered

Sarah Michelle Gellar just follow Friday'd me and I don't know what to do

hahahahahah

oh god

oh man

the best and worst thing

i think you have to acknowledge it

Thanks for the follow Friday @realsmg birthday made!

Something like that?

or reply to her tweet with something classy and understated like 'ah thank you! this tweet is the best birthday present i've had today 😊'

Did you take keys

Did you?

No

WHAT

We're locked out??

It's Sunday we can't get spare keys today we'll have to stay with someone

Loljk I took keys
Delivered

I hate you

---

here is some salt and pepper magnified

O0o

It looks like that Scottish rock I want to chew it

household dust..

Gross

Wtf is that anenome

idk its probably on your eyelid right now

😖

Plz get me some chocolate or something

Do u rly need chocolate

Yes u don't know what I've been through today

What sitting on your laptop for 5 hours

There were two wasps in the lounge

🐝🐝

Wow ok I'll buy chocolate
Delivered

'should i bring a coat? nah it's not raining sky looks clear and i'm just in a taxi'

I'm going to drown walking to boots

omg

you don't need to go to boots

i think my hair will survive

Where are u

Having dessert at a weird restaurant with a dog

Omg I want to eat it

The dessert not the dog

Thanks i presumed that
Delivered

What time is it?

There is literally a clock on your phone

I meant day

That is also on your phone
Delivered

Oh yh

I think I just deleted the sims

What

Why are you even on my pic

Pc*

I'm installing that badger game

Well how did you delete an entire program check the recycle bin

The sims is in the bin

That's just the shortcut you spork omg
Delivered

😩

ROBOTS

D: Alright, Phil, it's your turn. Set us up!

P: Hello and good evening/morning/lunch/dinner o'clock people of the book and welcome to Going Deep with Dan and Phil. Today I, the honourable and wise Philip Lester the Third—

D: You're just the first.

P: Don't ruin my moment! Would like to start a discussion.

D: Sure, Phil, what do you want to talk about, zips? The joy of midnight cereal?

P: Please, Dan, give me some more credit. I wanna talk about ROBOTS.

D: I'm sure you're picturing some kind of giant fighting thing but I'm pretty confident I can take this somewhere interesting.

P: Dan, how do you know that I'm not a robot?

D: Really? Um, lots of reasons.

P: Give me just one!

D: You have two-hour showers, which can't be good for a robot!

P: Waterproof skin, duh. Just as I thought you can't prove that I haven't been a robot built to spy on you this whole time!

D: Okay, how's this, why would anyone program a robot to be as clumsy as you?

P: Okay, you got me there. I'm not a robot! Just in case you were still wondering.

D: Thanks for clarifying.

P: Do you think there are any super robots out there though?

D: Nah. If that kind of technology existed the Japanese would have already used it for something creepy everyone could buy. I think that the power of Artificial Intelligence will be one of our worries in the future though.

P: It's crazy how quickly things are advancing. I bet by 2020 our phones will be able to holographically tuck us into bed at night.

D: That is an incredibly disturbing thing to imagine. Everything is built for Americans anyway. I wouldn't trust something with holographic powers to understand my British accent.

P: So what's to worry about? Surely we can just program the computers to behave and be nice friendly toasters and vacuum cleaners that can whip out puns when your happiness levels are dropping?

D: Just imagine, Phil, what if the robot unprograms that safety program itself?

P: Woah.

D: It's called a 'singularity' and it's the inevitable doom we're hurtling towards. *The Matrix* was a prophecy, I'm telling you now.

P: I kind of want that meteor we were talking about in our first Going Deep to arrive now.

D: Don't worry, hopefully we'll be long dead before any such technology exists to oppress us.

P: That's a weird way to put it, Dan. I think we should just keep the robots to cute small things that couldn't possibly rebel and murder us. Like whisks and toothbrushes.

D: We already have an electric whisk and toothbrush.

P: See! The future is now! Let's stop advancing things before we regret it.

D: Do you think if we ever get smart enough to program emotions that computers will have souls?

P: Dan, that's too deep. Too deep for Going Deep.

D: But seriously! Do you think you would date a computer program? I don't think I could. You would always know you are basically dating the descendant of a microwave.

P: Plus I think humans have a certain spark of humanity that makes us do things a robot never could! Like today when you were out, I was practising my wolf howl. I don't think a robot could handle that randomness.

D: Yeah if a robot tried to understand your brain it would probably fizzle out or explode.

P: If you could have any kind of robot what would it be?

D: Probably some robo-shoes that would make me exercise.

P: I'd make the ultimate robo-chef! It would make all my meals and wake me up with a funnel of coffee carefully placed in my mouth.

D: You'd just be one of those guys from *Wall-E* with no need to move or go outside ever again.

P: I think I would miss trees actually. I do love a good tree.

D: That's good to know, Phil.

P: Though in the house of the future I bet I could have holographic tree wallpaper with an HD camera streaming from deep within the rainforest.

D: You'd finally be at home, at one with the monkeys.

P: I feel like we've bonded during these two Going Deep chats! I'm going to miss it. Can I come into your room at 4am for deep and meaningful conversations?

D: Remind me to buy a lock for my door.

P: Or get your robot butler to do it.

D: Bzzzt.

P: BBBzzzzt. Oops I spilled Fanta on our circuit boards.

D: Error

PHIL'S AESTHETIC

Left to right
Right to left
Everybody's whisking up and down
Back and forth
Up and down
Everybody's whisking Delia Smith's face

S-s-s-s-s-s-s-s-s-s-s-s-sieving yeah
Sieving Sieving
It gets the ████
Work those arms
That'll give you the right muscles
To do the thang

Egg egg egg
It's the king of all yolks

It's a breakfast bar stool
It's a breakfast bar stool

It's Japanese witchcraft
How do they do it I don't know
It's this and this it's this but how

It's a purple mushroom
It's a cola thing
It's a horrible teacake
Yeah yeah yeah

Fork of justice
Sailing through the night

Can you please get murdered on
a different road I'm trying to film

Spicy spice
Spicy spice
Spice the spice and the spicy spice
Cajun spices spice in the pan
Spicy fajitas yeah man

It was the night before Christmas
And all through the sea
Jellyfish were stinging your
entire family

It's the crime dance
It's the crime dance
Yeah
Crime

I like bananas I like bananas in the sunshine
Sunshine sunshine bananas
I like bananas I like bananas on the moon
Moon moon moon

Milk quest
It's the best
Milk in your face
Not cows

Rave time rave time rave time
Rave time rave time rave time
Don't step on the glass
Don't step on the glass
Tinsel in your foot
Bauble in your foot
Bauble in your eye

Everybody cries when you go to
A&E with a bauble in your face
Blood
Blood everywhere

Hyper kirby plumber and sword

Beat the butter and the sugar till its done
Beat the butter and the sugar till it's done
There are ghosts inside your butter
There's a skeleton in the sugar
And it's really spooky today
on Halloween

Shake shake the sugar
It's what 'ya cane gave 'ya

Susan you only had a short life
But now you're on the bar
And everyone is sad
Susan

Lizards they're my favourite spikey reptile
So scaley
Lizards I'd freak out if I saw you in the bath
Cold blooded
Lizards

I wanna pour it all over my naked body
Except I don't as I'd burn to death

Spooning the milky wheat onto the darker base
Yeah

Dripping all over his body
It's dripping dripping yeah
Making a tattoo as I'm dampening your neck

Let's buy a stool
Let's buy a stool
But first we need to go to the kitchen
Go to the kitchen
Then it will be an option
This is the kitchen song

Slenderman Slenderman
Does whatever a slender can
Can he jump from behind
Yes he can

Space space
I stick it in ya face
But there's no air
Where? Space
What

Harajuku Harajuku
You might find a pikachu under the bench
There is no stench because it's amazing
In Japan

The Urge

A Dan and Phil
Fan Fiction
by Dan Howell

It was a crisp winter's night in London, England. It was that particular time in late January where there was no longer any frost, but simply biting cold air in what felt like a completely empty atmosphere.

Dan Howell was walking down the road; his tall black silhouette cast shadows from the artificial amber glow of streetlamps. His breath formed swirls of mist with every exhalation and he decided to slide his exposed hands inside his coat pockets to retain some warmth. The street was empty at this time and his footsteps echoed up and down around him, only interrupted by the cruising hum of a taxi driving past. He wasn't totally alone after all. Dan had time to think on this journey, time to think about what had happened the night before.

The events had played in his head so many times over that he didn't know whether he could trust their accuracy, or if his own perceptions had rewritten how the events unfolded. Any way he thought about it, one thing was certain. His friend, Phil Lester, was dead.

Phil had a habit of always being in the worst place at the worst time. It was an endearing quality that often resulted in funny stories for him to share with his friends or his followers on the internet. He was a kind person. Perhaps that's why he was singled out as a victim. It wasn't fair. A painful stab of recollection shot through Dan's brain, as if forcing itself through a wall he had built to protect himself. He saw it again. The dead, lifeless eyes, the way it moved so swiftly out of the darkness, the blood. The blood was the most vivid memory of all. Dan had somehow found himself collapsed in a corner, unable to move, but out of the corner of his eye he saw the crimson trail

of his friend's life weaving around the cobbled stones of the street and down a drain. Dan saw his hand twitching, those last moments of resistance and hope that something, someone, would be able to save him. Then it stopped. That is the last time he saw Phil Lester alive.

Dan arrived home at their apartment. It felt wrong. Opening the door to the living room, the usual bright colours of their possessions seemed inappropriate, disrespectful even. How could anything dare to be so bright at this time? He turned off the lights and collapsed on the grey carpet of their hallway. Sleep.

The next day was to be Phil's funeral. Dan had no interest in going. His friendship with Phil was personal to him and not something he wanted to share with family and friends who would mean well but insult with every word of comfort. He decided that even if he had to attend physically, he would be somewhere else in his mind. He had to.

Dan remained silent and stoic through the service. People left to return to their lives, the relatives trading condolences, leaving Dan alone in the room with the coffin. He didn't want to look – it would be real if he saw. He wanted to run away as fast as he could from this nightmare, but he had to see. Dan strode over and gazed into the box. Lifeless. Even with Phil's typically pale skin you used to see the warm glow of life within. All that could be seen here was the sickly pale-green colour of death.

Dan went to turn away, to walk out of the room into a life where everything familiar was gone, when something grabbed his wrist.

'Don't go, it's okay.' Dan turned to see the same pale skin he had just had burned into his memory gripping at his shirt.

e looked up slowly to see his dead friend sat bolt upright. Dan ran. Not stopping to blink, breathe or process a single thought he sprinted out of the back exit and all the way across the grounds of the building to underneath a tree. He vomited. It wasn't real. He was hysterical. He tried to rationalise the thoughts in his head as his eyes shook with distress.

'Dan, stop running, I'm not going to hurt you.'

He spun around to see Phil, standing upright as if completely fine with his hands forwards as if anticipating Dan's irrational behaviour. 'You can't, I mean, this can't be real,' Dan said, grasping behind his back to try and hold onto the tree as if it was a tether to reality.

'You know I'm real, Dan, this is real and I think you know why.'

'No!' Dan shouted and pushed Phil backwards in utter disbelief. Phil grabbed Dan's wrists and pinned him against the tree. Dan could feel the sharper edges prodding uncomfortably into his back as if the tree itself was pushing him towards the nightmare. 'It was a vampire.' The words penetrated into Dan's head and seemed to pull down on his soul as if everything he had been trying not to believe in the last two days was sinking like quicksand. 'I don't know how, or if that's exactly what it is, but it explains it well enough,' Phil said in a calmer tone, clearly aware of Dan's slow realisation.

'You aren't the real Phil,' Dan said in a flat, emotionless tone. His head was bowed and in Phil's grip it seemed Dan wasn't trying to resist anymore. 'If what you're saying is true, you aren't Phil. You're just a beast possessing his body.' He looked up and stared into Phil's eyes. He didn't see the bright blue pools of life that he used to, he saw emptiness. He must be right.

Phil stared back at Dan, seeing his brown irises blazing with fury. Phil let his grip loosen for a second. Dan realised and swung a punch as hard as he could, hitting Phil square in the jaw. Phil reached towards his lip. Blood. He looked down at it in a strange way and glanced back up at Dan who seemed to almost be expecting something. Phil decided to wipe the blood on his shirt. 'I won't lie,' Phil said, rearranging his suit jacket and sweeping his black hair away from his eyes. 'I feel different. I feel urges. I still know who I am, what I do, what the difference is between right and wrong. And yet something is within me, something primal ...' 'Shut up.' Dan said, clenching his fist and visibly shaking with rage. 'You are not my friend and if I have to destroy his body to give him peace, do not think I won't.'

Dan spun around, reaching for the sharp wood that was cutting into his back. In one sure motion he snapped the branch and immediately swung towards Phil, who, as if in slow motion, leant backwards, smacked the branch from Dan's hand and grabbed him by the throat. Dan's head banged against the tree with a force that shook the leaves from the branches, falling over the boy's shoulders. His breath was heavy. He could feel the beads of sweat forming on his forehead. This was fear. He tried to move but the force his friend was applying to his neck seemed immovable and impossible.

Phil stepped closer until their noses touched and looked Dan directly in the eyes: 'I could kill you. Every fibre of my being is urging me to tilt your head back and bite your neck, but I can choose not to.'

'What?!' Dan said, spitting out warmth before taking in a huge gasp.

'I don't want to kill you. I want you to join me.'

Dan felt his heart drop in pressure. An overwhelming stillness waved through his body until he was stunned into silence. 'No p-please,' he stuttered.

'You don't have a choice, but I do. Appreciate it,' said Phil. 'Think about it, Dan, things can continue like normal! We can tell everyone it was one of those miracle situations where I was never actually dead. We can go back to our apartment and continue our normal lives ... with some dietary adjustments, I guess.'

Dan had completely lost his ability to think. Part of it made sense, maybe it would be okay if he didn't have to lose his friend, or his own life. He knew it wasn't true though. Even though Phil was right in front of him, there was no breath coming out of his lips. The only sensation he experienced was the damp chill of Phil's skin pressing against his.

Just then Dan noticed a man who must be the groundskeeper walking by in the distance. Dan had made his choice, and he knew it would be the right one. 'HELP!' Dan shouted, shaking as hard as he could, causing Phil to almost loosen his grip. 'He's trying to ki–'

Then he felt it. Two sharp stabs pierced the skin of his neck. Dan dropped his arms and buckled his knees, he had lost.

Phil moved in closer, pinning Dan's body against the tree as he gulped gallons of thick blood through his teeth and down his throat. Phil almost felt himself losing control, feeling a desire to completely give in to a more powerful force within himself. 'No,' he said, pulling away, feeling the blood run down his neck past the collar of his shirt. Quickly he raised his wrist and pierced his own veins. 'Drink!' he ordered, pressing his wrist against Dan's mouth. Dan, with the last moments of his fading energy attempted to resist, pitifully shrugging his shoulders. It wouldn't be enough. His natural instinct to breathe opened his lips and the pungent taste of iron filled his mouth and flowed across his tongue. Dan's vision faded to black.

Blinking. Vision hazy and unclear. A yellow light. A white ceiling. After what seemed like a dreamy eternity unable to move, Dan's eyes focused and noticed the familiar patterns of his bedroom ceiling. He was home. Had it all been a bad dream? Dan asked himself this as he reached to touch his bare chest with his fingers. He could still feel. Surely that meant he was still alive? His hand stopped. Palm lying flat over his chest, he tried to focus all senses on detecting something, anything. No pulse.

He looked to the right to suddenly notice Phil, sitting in a chair leaning over the bed.

'How do you feel?' he asked, with what seemed like a degree of confidence.

Dan's eyes darted up and down trying to decide what he made of this person, or whatever it was, who sat next to him. He sat up and swung his legs over the bed. Lifting his head up with a strange, new assuredness he had never felt before, he locked eyes with this friend. 'Hungry,' Dan said, feeling within him an urge, a biological mission he now felt he had to begin.

'Me too,' Phil said with a smirk. 'Why don't we go find someone to eat?'

The End

The Hand

DAN AND PHIL FAN FICTION
BY PHIL LESTER

Phil woke up covered in sweat and screaming. He wiped his muscular brow as he got out of bed. That nightmare had been something else. 'Weird,' he said as he did his morning routine of 300 sit-ups. Dan was already in the kitchen making a delicious breakfast of bacon pancakes with extra maple syrup. 'Oh hey, D-Slice', said Phil, backflipping into the room and hi-fiving his friend in mid-air. Dan looked horrified.

'What's wrong?' Phil asked, as a bead of sweat dripped from his forehead and bounced off the mutant finger protruding out of his body.

'Your body?! There's something happening to you!' said Dan.

Phil looked down in horror to see a human hand was starting to grow out of his chest, just below the nipple.

It wasn't just growing, it was moving. In shock, Dan dropped his syrupy spatula onto his leather jeans and ruined them forever. No more leather jeans for Dan.

'We need to call the army,' he told his raven-haired friend.

'Dan, no! They'll experiment on me! I don't want to die.' Phil said, as he let out a single tear, not being afraid to show emotion in front of his true best friend.

They decided to keep it a secret.

Over the next few weeks the hand grew and grew. Phil continued to make YouTube videos, he just wouldn't film below the nipple. He had to keep this a secret from everyone.

Dan and Phil even taught the hand some of their secret best friend handshakes. It was responding to the fun. When they watched *Game of Thrones* the hand even started twitching with glee. Later that month, something unexpected happened. Dan and Phil were finishing another pancake session when the hand started violently vibrating. 'DAN! HELP!' Phil screamed as the hand started gesticulating wildly.

Dan could only stand and watch as the hand started to extend out of Phil's chest. The hand was reaching for Dan. Instinctively he started pulling it and something happened that none of the British boys would ever expect.

After a few pulls there wasn't just a hand, there was an arm and an elbow. An entire human was being dragged out of the inside of Phil – he was giving birth.

There was a giant wet explosion. All that was left of Phil was a lump of skin and there, standing in the kitchen, was a completely naked Harry Styles.

Dan gave him a pepper pot to cover his modesty. 'Thanks for pulling me out of there, mate!' said Harry as he grabbed a pancake from the pan and walked out of the door.

Dan looked into the middle distance. His face was no longer filled with confusion. It was no longer filled with horror, It was filled with REVENGE.

To be continued.

BEAUTIFUL ART OUR AUDIENCE HAS MADE

WE HAVE SOME OF THE FUNNIEST, MOST CREATIVE AND TALENTED FOLLOWERS OF ANYONE ON THE INTERNET! IT'D BE IMPOSSIBLE TO SHOW ALL OF OUR FAVOURITE PIECES OF ART WE'VE SEEN MADE OF US, BUT HERE ARE JUST A FEW OF OUR FAVOURITES.

HORRIFYING ART OUR AUDIENCE HAS MADE

ALONG WITH THE BEAUTIFUL AND AWE-INSPIRING ART WE ALSO RECEIVE A LOT OF ART WHICH SPANS THE SPECTRUM OF HILARIOUS, DISTURBING OR BOTH! WE DELVED INTO SOME DEEP CORNERS OF THE INTERNET TO FIND SOME OF THESE. UH, ENJOY?

THE EXISTENTIAL CRISIS HALLWAY

WHY DO WE EXIST?

WHAT IS EXISTENCE?

WHAT IS THE POINT OF ANYTHING?

WHY?

DOES MY LIFE REALLY MATTER OUTSIDE OF MYSELF?

DEATH IS INEVITABLE.

WE ARE ALL ALONE.

THE PRIVILEGE OF FREEDOM IS OVERWHELMING.

IGNORANCE IS BLISS.

CONSCIOUSNESS IS MERELY A BIOLOGICAL PROCESS.

TIME EXTENDS BEFORE AND AFTER MY LIFE.

PURPOSES ARE DISTRACTIONS AND VICE VERSA.

WHAT'S FOR LUNCH?

INFINITY IS INCOMPREHENSIBLE.

HELP.

THINGS OVERHEARD WHILE WRITING THE BOOK

While trapped in our apartment writing this book, we've had many strange conversations and heard many strange things said by the other person too early in the morning or late at night. Eventually we thought we should start writing them down! Here they are.

D: I just realised my left sock is slightly damp but I don't know why.

P: I want my coffin to be lined with that paper. It feels so good!

D: I just realised I'm reading this story with David Tennant's voice.

P: Is there a tiny beetle on my nose or is it just a phantom itch?

D: Do you reckon we could get an industrial-sized fan for the photoshoot?

P: I had a dream the book had popcorn-scented paper.

D: I hate that photo I look like Shrek got set on fire and hit by a truck.

P: I think we should have a page about things that we said whilst writing the book and feature what I'm saying now on that page. Pageception?

D: I just typed unicorn instead of university. 'Dan's Unicorn Life'.

P: How many people do you think will read this sentence on the toilet?

D: What shade of black should I use for this background?

P: Do you see loads of tiny neon triangles when you close your eyes?

D: Look there's a tiny man on the kettle!

P: Are you ever tempted to shake a small amount of salt into your hand and lick it?

D: What's 3+7?

P: I forgot my mum's name for a second.

D: Was it dogs that have clean spit? Or was that a myth?

P: I kind of want a baby just to see what it looks like.

D: I've been staring at this screen for too long, are my eyes bleeding?

P: If I ate my own tongue would it taste of the last thing I ate?

D: Why didn't you tell me you bought a motion-detecting air freshener? I just had a heart attack.

P: Do you think my shorts are too short? Combined with the frilly bits I mean.

D: Last night I dreamed that I deleted the entire book off the computer. Wait have we saved the document since we started?

LOCATION: TIME RESEARCH FACILITY

PATIENT 132-54/A

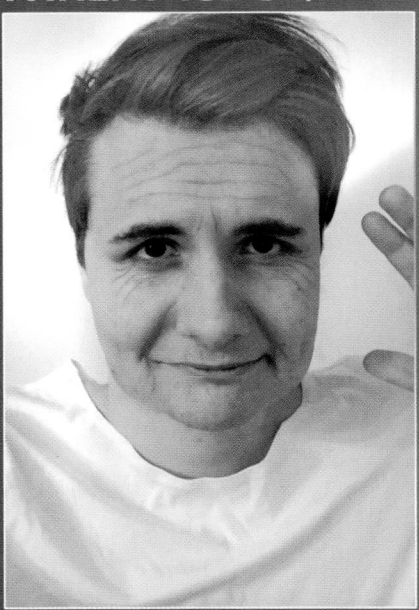

Why hello the internets!

Is that what I used to say? I don't remember anymore. I would check but I'm currently having my eyes replaced with newer models so I am typing this using my psychic keyboard.

I'm sending this message down a time compression machine! Handy thing that. Apple has provided a lot of useful technology for the world over the years. Worth signing the Universal Submission Declaration if you ask me.

If you're wondering what the world is like now, mostly the same. The ultra-continent of China 2 is a fantastic place to live after the great assimilation. The news keeps talking about the ant population on Australia – that island where we keep our nuclear power and prisons. Something about multiplying and mutating, I don't believe it personally.

I remember having a great time writing the book. I obviously have it digitally saved to my iBrain drive, but I do still have a physical copy in my pod. I use it as my emotional tether in case I go too deep playing the Virtual-station and start to forget about the real universe. That was a fantastic weekend I spent with Lara Croft.

Who would have known that this would be the best-selling book of all time? Of course Phil didn't realise that he was leaning on the 0 key for so long when he placed that Amazon order. Phil has been living with that debt his whole life, poor guy.

I hope all the readers enjoy the book and it brings them happiness! All the happiness you had counted before the emotion-purge of 2025. I suppose things are less dramatic now.

Anyway I am off! I have an appointment with the dentist. Of all the things that have been innovated on in our society I can't believe you still need to get fillings, oh well.

Here's a Sexual Endingcard Dance dedicated to you!

Dan

Oh hello reader.

Wow it's been a while since I've used a computer. They feel so old fashioned! It's making me nostalgic for when I was a strapping young lad with floppy black hair. Who'd have thought that would be the standard hairstyle for elderly people now?

I'm currently sat in my energy tank on the long journey through space to colonise New Earth. The great ant war was brutal but also made me realise how much I valued my home planet! It makes me sad I'll never drink a proton milkshake or ride a gravity coaster again but I have those experiences in my mind. Literally. They are embedded into the video chip in my brain.

It's nice that YouTube still exists! I've just been watching Lord Pewdiepie who now has 400 billion subscribers across the universe. 5D gaming looks fun. It's a shame I can't play due to having half my leg eaten by the queen ant in the final battle. Who'd have thought she could use a flamethrower whilst giving birth to thousands of mutant babies? Enough about the ant war. Now is not the time for those memories.

I am over 100 years old, my body is starting to give up on me. Thankfully I'm having my head implanted onto a robotic body. I've paid a little bit extra for a popcorn machine in my chest. I'm gonna be the most popular elderly robot in the galaxy.

Thanks for reading this! Hopefully we've perfected the technology to beam my message back to 2015 and print it into the book. Writing it was one of the best experiences of my life! I can't believe the Queen actually secretly kept a copy in her toilet for all those years after her regeneration.

I have to go back into hypersleep now!

Farewell, Phil

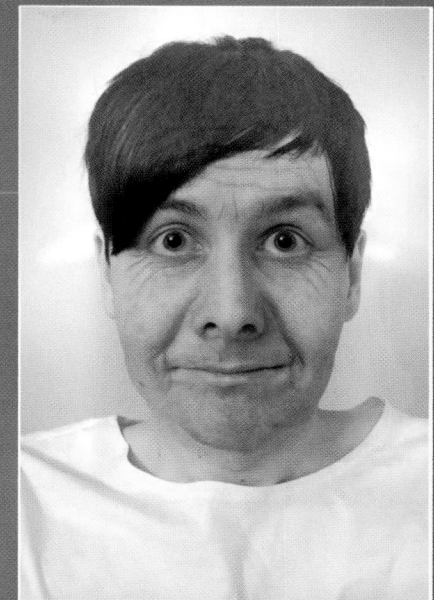

PATIENT 132-54/B

WHAT HAPPENED IN VEGAS

D: In June 2012, we went to Las Vegas. I'd never been before and we were already flying to the USA to go to the California YouTube convention VidCon, so we thought we would go a few days earlier and stop off in Nevada.

P: I love Vegas! I went once with my family when I was a teenager and it was awesome. Crazy casinos, crazy nightlife, crazy people. The only downside was I couldn't really do anything because I was too young. I actually got kicked out of The Tropicana hotel for trying to play blackjack. Oops.

D: So we decided to spend a week in the desert. Now the thing is, I kind of told everyone that I filmed the whole trip – which I did! From the plane journey there, to checking out of the hotel when we left, I had the whole thing on camera with the intention of editing it into a fun video. The story goes, when I got back to England I put it off for so long because I had filmed so much. In fact I had procrastinated so long that we lost the camera and most of the memory cards with the footage. This video-that-never-was became known as the infamous 'Vegas Video'. Everyone wanted to know what really happened with Dan and Phil in Vegas. Why would we film it all and not show everyone? Was the footage really lost? There have been more conspiracy theories than days passed since we returned from that journey.

P: We thought if those files are never to be found, then why not finally, once and for all, reveal the story in our book. So. This, is what happened in Vegas. The whole, uncensored truth.

22 JUNE 2012

P: Being 6ft tall, long flights for us aren't so much a 'ugh planes are boring and uncomfortable' as an 'omg my-legs-don't-physically-fit-in-this-seat' dangerous compression.

D: We took to the skies and enjoyed an uneventful flight over the Atlantic. This peace, it turned out, would not last.

P: We landed in the USA! I could smell the freedom the moment I stepped off the plane.

D: A short cab ride and we were on the strip. It was just as cool as it looks in the movies. I mean, it's tacky and horrible and everything about it is really seedy and evil looking, but in a cool 'Wow, I'm in a movie!' kind of way!

P: We arrived at our hotel, Caesar's Palace, and unpacked our bags ready for adventure.

D: We didn't want to waste any time, so got changed straight away and headed downstairs to the casino!

P: I'm obsessed with slot machines.

D: Phil has what you would call a 'gambling problem'.

P: It's not a problem! I'm just addicted to the bright lights and loud noises and slim chances of shiny things coming out of a hole. Okay, maybe a slight issue, but it paid off!

D: Phil, don't deny anything I have photo evidence.

P: We settled on one particular slot machine, the 'Aladdin', mainly because it had cool music.

D: And a freaking vibrating chair. Seriously the production values on these slot machines were crazy, they were basically simulators!

P: This one was special though, as you could actually win better prizes by playing little mini games, which as giant nerds who spend our lives gaming, we were pretty good at.

D: Oh man, I remember it now. We kept winning, and winning, getting jackpot after jackpot and it kept adding up!

P: We were doing so well that we started to attract a crowd of silent lurkers who usually spent their whole days endlessly pulling on the slots.

D: ... what you would have become had we stayed there any longer.

P: Hey! We weren't there for much longer though as the luckiest thing in my entire life happened, we won the mega jackpot.

D: $666,085.25 to be precise.

P: Lights went off, music started playing, the previously silent slot-lurkers started cheering with wide eyes.

D: The casino handed us a receipt we could cash in for the money whenever we wanted, but we thought hey, if we're in Vegas we need to do this properly!

P: DOUBLE OR NOTHING.

D: That's right, people. We went to play Roulette.

P: Now you may think us foolish, but we had everything going for us! Beginner's luck, the magic of youth, I was wearing my lucky socks and underpants.

D: Guaranteed win.

P: We sat round the table and watched eagerly as the ball of fate spun around the circle of fate to decide our fate ...

D: ...Okay, Phil, I think they appreciate the drama. And you will never believe this ... we won again!

P: Now you'd think this is where the story gets crazy in a good way: we cash in the cheque, rent the penthouse suite, call some of the numbers on those weird cards we got handed on the way into the casino and party all night!

D: Unfortunately not. This is when it all went horribly wrong.

P: We turned around to see two giant men in suits and sunglasses and proceeded to get dragged out of our chairs across the floor.

D: I was terrified! I had my bag and camera snatched out of my hands ...

... and they took us into some kind of interrogation room.

P: Now I've seen enough movies to know how the old 'good cop/bad cop' game is played, they didn't do that.

D: No it was just bad cop and really, really angry bad cop who wouldn't listen to us talk.

P: Basically, we were accused of cheating on the Aladdin machine!

D: I knew we were skilled gamers, Phil, but I never thought we were so good it was dangerous.

P: They kept us chained to the table all night which I thought was pretty unprofessional, then in the morning they told us some guy named 'Killer Tony' was going to have 'a tough conversation' with us unless we explained how we did it! I was so confused.

D: Oh my god, Phil, they were the mafia, they were threatening to kill us.

P: Wow that explains so much! I thought they just had it in for us because of our unorthodox sense of style.

D: To be fair our hair was pretty weird in 2012, it was probably a crime in a lot of places. Anyway, I wasn't letting this happen. You can take away my casino winnings, you can take away my freedom and it's not like I had any pride to protect really ... but you can't take my video camera!

P: Dan was really fighting for this video, guys!

D: So in a moment that I feel like all of my video game playing and thriller-watching and those two months of Taekwondo lessons my mum paid for before I quit ...

P: ... I didn't know you did Taekwondo? That's the martial art that Buffy uses!

D: I know, man, that's totally what inspired me! We're digressing. I reached under the table with my hands cuffed and with all my might flipped it over, knocking the two guys off their chairs, grabbed my camera and we ran for it.

P: We ran through the casino looking for a way out. Well, I did. Dan was too busy filming the whole thing.

D: I needed to capture our escape in case we needed it for evidence!

P: We found a staircase and ran up to the roof where we hid in the bushes from security. Again, Dan filming them probably didn't help.

D: Look at the quality evidence though.

P: We got changed into some different clothes Dan had in his bag and I began to think of a plan. Dan had his moment of braveness flipping that table like no one had ever table-flipped before, now it was my turn.

D: Honestly for someone who can't drive a car, I'm so surprised you did this.

P: I decided to steal a helicopter.

D: Now I think about it, stealing their boss's helicopter probably only made the mafia angrier.

P: Well it was his fault for leaving it on. Seriously who leaves their helicopters unlocked in this day and age? We ran up to the helipad, jumped in, I pulled up the joystick (is it called that?) and with the sun rising ahead of us, we began gunning for the Nevada desert with the mafia in pursuit.

D: We flew over what seemed like endless sand for hours, seriously America is so big though, what do they need so much land for?, when we spotted somewhere we could hide.

We didn't know what exactly it was, some kind of underground building with a lot of plain cars parked outside, but we figured whoever was there could protect us from the rampaging casino-Avengers.

P: I'm not going to lie, the landing could have been smoother.

D: Phil literally dropped the helicopter onto the roof of someone's car and we had to jump out of the window before we got chopped into slices of phan-sashimi.

P: Hey, I got us there!

D: That you did, and as our pursuers began to (safely) descend from the skies themselves we ran towards the weird building.

P: Except when we got to it, there was no entrance, just a mysterious door and a security camera.

D: I thought it was suspicious from the start if you ask me. Now we're not ones to condone vandalism, but when you're being chased by particularly broad men in suits and sunglasses, you're willing to commit some property damage in order to live. We kicked in an air-vent and slid ourselves inside.

P: You know those moments in movies where someone slides down a cave hole or vent for ages and it looks really fun? It's actually just really scary and painful.

D: Seriously. Plus it was well sandy and dusty, it totally ruined my new shorts.

P: Thank god you packed those extra clothes or we'd have looked bad on top of everything else happening.

D: Just because you get into a situation like this doesn't mean you should stop trying to look nice for people.

P: This is when our crazy story gets EVEN CRAZIER. We pick ourselves up off the floor, get out our phones to use as a torch and saw an entire underground hangar filled with incubation tanks.

D: We couldn't see through the murky glass, but something was clearly inside all of these tubes filled with bubbling liquid. There were all kinds of strange metal instruments lying around that looked unlike anything medical or industrial I'd ever seen.

P: We had to know more about this weird place, so we skimmed around the room looking for a window, which was impossible now as the sun had set, but when we looked through we saw something we'd never forget.

D: A giant machine in the shape of a triangle was hovering above the ground firing a beam of light towards the desert.

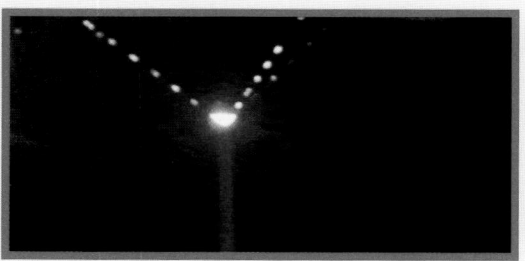

P: I started to freak out a bit so I stumbled over and fell against the wall, which is when I accidentally leaned on the automatic door.

D: 'PHWOOMPF' it slid open and we both collapsed into what appeared to be an operation theatre filled with surgeons.

P: We didn't get a good look at whatever they were operating on before some other guys in suits appeared out of nowhere and knocked us out. I go my whole life without getting into any trouble then I get arrested twice in one day, can you believe it!

D: I remember they stuck us in a lift (translation for transatlantics – 'elevator') that took us back up to a room and locked us inside. When they woke us up in the morning (no breakfast btw they were terrible hosts) they told us that apparently we were trespassing on secret government property and the well-dressed men who escorted us upstairs were from the FBI. Of course we were.

P: Dan, do you realise what this means?

D: What?

P: We accidentally broke into Area 51.

D: Oh my god, you're right. Jesus, that's typical Dan and Phil. Go for a little holiday before a YouTube convention and wind up trapped between aliens and the mafia.

P: Thankfully, this is when we got lucky in a non-money-related way!

D: Well, kind of lucky if you forget the general violence that was about to ensue. We gandered out of the window to get some sense of where we were when guess who was waiting for us, our old friends from the casino.

P: Seriously did they have no lives, who do you try to find for an entire night?

D: Thieves stealing millions of dollars from your business?

P: Okay, kind of understandable. We looked out of the window, made awkward eye contact with them, and it all kicked off. Out of nowhere they started shooting at us through the glass – like shooting someone is a good way to make them explain how they cheated on a slot machine – and we dived under the table.

D: Our well-dressed friends from the whatever-the-hell that was downstairs burst into the room to see what the hubbub was only to find themselves being indiscriminately blasted with bullets too.

P: Both parties opened fire on each other, which is kind of cool if you think about it 'Mafia vs. FBI', I wish I could have watched it!

D: They seemingly forgot about the two dorks under the table though, so we used the opportunity to dash for the nearest door when, just as we stepped outside, a stray bullet hit a gas tank on the side of the building causing a gigantic explosion! We were sent flying into a pile of rocks with our ears ringing and leg hairs lightly barbecued.

P: We picked ourselves up, glanced over our shoulders at the destruction and decided to run over the nearest hill into endless desert where we walked for hours. I was seriously hungry by this point. You don't want to mess with a Phil that hasn't had his morning cereal! It was a cool environment though so I took this pic of Dan:

D: Hey that is a cool pic! Remember to tag me in that on Facebook later, okay?

P: Sure thing. This is when I recalled a little nugget of wisdom from my grandad! 'Phil, you have no sense of direction, so promise me if you ever get lost just walk towards a road and stand on it.'

D: That's a very specific piece of advice there.

P: What can I say? He knew me well. And it worked!

D: That it did. After getting totally blanked by at least three truckers and a school bus ...

P: ...it was probably our haircuts that scared them away.

D: You could be right. A camper-van pulled over and swung open its doors. As it happened, it was some gymnasts from the Cirque Du Soleil heading back to Las Vegas to perform a show at our hotel!

P: What are the chances of that?! Unfortunately it wasn't that simple, as their offering of help came at a price. They wanted Dan and I to fill in for a colleague that broke every bone in his body practising for a trick.

D: I can say with confidence that I never once thought getting trapeze lessons would be a useful skill, but here we were. We had no choice!

P: It was either that or be abducted and probed/arrested/left with 'Killer Tony', so we said yes and hopped in the van.
Note: Generally don't hop in strangers' vans unless you are at risk of those three things.

D: They were some pretty chill dudes actually! I always wondered what it would be like to run away and join the circus. Turns out it's years of demanding exercise and really cramped cars with faulty aircon. Not really my thing.

P: The car journey wasn't our toughest challenge of the day. We made it back to Vegas, but before we could relax, it was show time.

D: The theatre was packed with about 5,000 people who all paid to see world-class gymnasts at the peak of fitness perform at their maximum. I got kind of exhausted walking up the stairs to the stage.

P: Our new friend Francoise told us it'd be easy, we just had to stand on a diving board and hold his hands, then he'd release us and we'd fly 50ft through a burning hoop and into a swimming pool.

D: I didn't trust him.

P: Oh just because he was blocking your cool air flow in the mini-van.

D: If it wasn't for them we'd probably still have been lost in the desert, so we got up on that stage, climbed a really tall ladder and waited for our time to come when Francoise would throw us to our doom.

P: It was amazing. We jumped off and swung from his masculine frame through the air like swans as he gently released us, cascading through the air into the embrace of the water below.

D: That's a pretty poetic way of saying 'chucked us off a ledge into a freezing pond in our clothes', Phil.

P: It was one of the highlights of my life. After the show they brought us backstage, gave us a standing ovation and made us honorary members of the circus! Francoise, Janine and Ringo the sad monkey will be in my heart forever.

D: Exhausted, sandy and drenched, we crawled up to our hotel room expecting to finally rest, only to be greeted by our handsome friends from the FBI.

P: In short, they totally trashed our hotel room and told us we had to give all of the money back to the casino and that if we ever posted the video footage online there'd be 'unnecessary consequences'. Wait, isn't this what we are doing now? Dan, I don't want our book to get us hunted by the FBI.

D: Phil, he clearly said 'video footage'; nothing about dozens of screenshots of that video footage.

P: If you say so.

D: We spent the night tidying the room so we didn't get an additional fine and packed our bags ready to fly to L.A. for VidCon.

At least I stole a couple souvenir dice from the casino to get back at them!

P: Dan, are you seriously saying after all of that you took something from the gift shop on the way out?

D: Okay, maybe that wasn't a good idea.

P: I'm just glad to finally have this story out in the open!

D: Yep! It may seem unbelievable, but that's why we never uploaded a video and this was the story of what happened in Vegas.

D: So here we are.

P: The end of our book! What do we want to say? Dan, you always like big waffly conclusions. Take it away!

D: I guess I just want to say, this thing that we've created – this world of Dan and Phil – is ephemeral. It was never something that tangibly existed, just hundreds of pictures and videos and stories and memories floating in the digital void of the internet.

It was all an accident really. We could have never met! I could have never taken that final leap into making videos, Phil might have gone back to working at a bookstore in York and none of this might have ever existed. It did happen though. We met, we made these videos together, and for whatever reason the chemistry between us had the X-factor that resonated with people around the world. And what we all created together over the following years is pretty darn wonderful. I look into that digital void and see millions of people who all found entertainment, happiness and even friendship just through these silly videos that we uploaded to a website and it makes me feel like I've really done something. I have scratched at least a tiny mark in an infinitely small part of the universe.

This book is us taking our favourite parts from that swirling universe on the internet and trapping it in something physical. Something we can hold and touch and keep in our houses, so that long into the future we can all look back and remember who these Dan and Phil guys were and what they did. You never know what might happen in the future, so in a way you could say we made this for us, for posterity, but really it was for you. Without our audience none of this would exist. I know for a fact that we have one of the most passionate followings of anyone on the internet and we appreciate it with every moment. We gave you the videos, but without the support, creativity and energy you have given us since the beginning, 'Dan and Phil' could never have been the world that we are celebrating with this book.

The real dedication, then, is to you. You do with this book what you will. You hold whatever space for Dan and Phil in your mind that you want. We hope we represent good times in your life and that this book can be your portal back to them whenever you wish!

We are Dan and Phil, and this is The Amazing Book Is Not On Fire.

P: Well how am I supposed to follow that?!

D: What? You asked for a waffly conclusion.

P: Yeah but you can't just wrap up the entire universe in an inspirational speech then walk off stage leaving me in the spotlight.

D: Say whatever comes to mind!

P: Okay, well double everything Dan said from me! Also I just wanted to say that I've really enjoyed making this book and I'm so excited to see what the future of this crazy adventure of my life will hold. Thank you!

D: How do we end it then? Self-destruct? A giant photo of a cat?

P: Maybe a derpy photo of us?

D: Sounds like a plan.

P: Thanks for reading. You are all better than toast.

Dan and Phil: Goodbye!

Goodbye!